SOURCES
of the
WESTERN
TRADITION

SOURCES *of the* WESTERN TRADITION

FIFTH EDITION

VOLUME II: FROM THE RENAISSANCE TO THE PRESENT

Marvin Perry

Baruch College, City University of New York

Joseph R. Peden

Baruch College, City University of New York

Theodore H. Von Laue

Clark University

George W. Bock, Editorial Associate

HOUGHTON MIFFLIN COMPANY   BOSTON   NEW YORK

Senior Sponsoring Editor: Nancy Blaine
Development Editor: Julie Dunn
Project Editor: Ylang Nguyen
Editorial Assistant: Wendy Thayer
Associate Production/Design Coordinator: Christine Gervais
Manufacturing Manager: Florence Cadran
Senior Marketing Manager: Sandra McGuire

List of Sources
Chapter 1
Section 1 P. 6: From J.H. Robinson and H.W. Rolfe, *Petrarch, the first Modern Scholar and Man of Letters* (New York: G.P. Putnam's Sons, 1909), pp. 208, 210, 213. P. 7: "Love for Greek Literature" from Henry Osborn Taylor, *Thought and Expression in the Sixteenth Century,* 2nd rev. ed. (New York: Frederick Ungar, 1930; repub. 1959), I, 36–37. **Section 2** P. 10: From Ernst Cassirer et. al (eds.), *The Renaissance Philosophy of Man,* pp. 223–225. Reprinted by permission of the publisher, The University of Chicago Press.

Credits are continued on p. 529.

Printed in the U.S.A.
ISBN: 0-618-16228-3
Library of Congress Catalog Card Number: 2001133327
56789-QF-09 08 07 06 05

Contents

PART TWO: MODERN EUROPE   97

CHAPTER 4   *The French Revolution   97*

CHAPTER 5   *The Industrial Revolution   127*

PART THREE: WESTERN
CIVILIZATION
IN CRISIS   291

CHAPTER 11   *World War I*   291

CHAPTER 12 *Era of Totalitarianism   333*

CHAPTER 13 *World War II   388*

Preface

Teachers of the Western Civilization survey have long recognized the pedagogical value of primary sources, which are the raw materials of history. The fifth edition of *Sources of the Western Tradition* contains a wide assortment of documents—some 200 in Volume I and 220 in Volume II and principally primary sources—that have been carefully selected and edited to fit the needs of the survey and to supplement standard texts.

We have based our choice of documents for the two volumes on several criteria. In order to introduce students to those ideas and values that characterize the Western tradition, *Sources of the Western Tradition* emphasizes primarily the works of the great thinkers. While focusing on the great ideas that have shaped the Western heritage, however, the reader also provides a balanced treatment of political, economic, and social history. We have tried to select documents that capture the characteristic outlook of an age and that provide a sense of the movement and development of Western history. The readings are of sufficient length to convey their essential meaning, and we have carefully extracted those passages that focus on the documents' main ideas.

An important feature of the reader is the grouping of several documents that illuminate a single theme; such a constellation of related readings reinforces understanding of important themes and invites comparison, analysis, and interpretation. In Volume I, Chapter 9, for example, Section 1, "The Humanists' Fascination with Antiquity," contains three interrelated readings: "The Father of Humanism," by Petrarch, "Study of Greek Literature and a Humanist Educational Program," by Leonardo Bruni, and "The Importance of Liberal Studies," by Petrus Paulus Vergerius. In Volume II, Chapter 8, "Politics and Society, 1845–1914," Section 2, "The Lower Classes," contains four readings:

"The Pains of Poverty," by Jeanne Bouvier, "The Yearning for Social Justice," by Nikolaus Osterroth, "In Darkest England," by William Booth, and "Working Conditions for Women in Russian Factories," by M. I. Pokrovskaia.

An overriding concern of the editors in preparing this compilation was to make the documents accessible—to enable students to comprehend and to interpret historical documents on their own. We have provided several pedagogical features to facilitate this aim. Introductions of three types explain the historical setting, the authors' intent, and the meaning and significance of the readings. First, introductions to each chapter—thirteen in Volume I and fifteen in Volume II—provide comprehensive overviews to periods. Second, introductions to each numbered section or grouping treat the historical background for the reading(s) that follow(s). Third, each reading has a brief headnote that provides specific details about that reading.

Within some readings, interlinear notes, clearly set off from the text of the document, serve as transitions and suggest the main themes of the passages that follow. Used primarily in longer extracts of the great thinkers, these interlinear notes help to guide students through the readings.

To aid students' comprehension, brief, bracketed editorial definitions or notes that explain unfamiliar or foreign terms are inserted into the running text. When terms or concepts in the documents require fuller explanations, these appear at the bottom of pages as editors' footnotes. Where helpful, we have retained the notes of authors, translators, or editors from whose works the documents were acquired. (The latter have asterisks, daggers, et cetera, to distinguish them from our numbered explanatory notes.) The review questions that appear at the ends of sections enable students to check their understanding of the documents; sometimes the questions ask for comparisons with other readings, linking or contrasting key concepts.

For ancient sources, we have generally selected recent translations that are both faithful to the text and readable. For some seventeenth- and eighteenth-century English documents, the archaic spelling has been retained, when this does not preclude comprehension, in order to show students how the English language has evolved over time.

For the fifth edition, we have reworked most chapters, dropping some documents and adding new ones. All new documents have been carefully edited: extraneous passages deleted, notes inserted to explain historical events, names identified, and technical terms defined. Wherever possible, we have extended the constellation format that groups related documents into one section. For this edition we have added a prologue discussing how historians approach primary sources.

The fifth edition of Volume I contains about thirty new sources. In Chapter 2, a new section, "Human Sinfulness," has been created. Consisting of passages from Genesis, the Book of Job, and Jeremiah, it deals with the Hebrew conception of wrongdoing and punishment. Chapter 3 contains four new selections: a passage from *The Persians* by Aeschylus, which glorifies the Greek victory over Persia and illustrates the concept of *hubris*, excessive pride; the famous lines from *Medea* by Euripides depicting a Greek woman's ordeal; Diodorus Siculus describing the cultural flowering in Greece after the Persian Wars; and Plutarch's account of cultural fusion in the era of Alexander the Great. A new section, "The Spread of Greek Philosophy to Rome," has been added to Chapter 4. It contains passages from Lucretius advocating Epicureanism and from Cicero illustrating Stoicism as well as an expression of Cato's hostility to Greek philosophy. Josephus's analysis of the Roman military and Ammianus Marcellinus's account of the battle of Adrianople are now in Chapter 5. Two selections, one from

Saint Jerome and the other from Cassian of Marseilles, both describing the solitary life of early Christian monks, are incorporated into Chapter 6. Other new readings in this chapter are Clement of Alexandria and Lactantius discussing Christian views of right and wrong and Saint John Chrysostom's venomous attack on Jews. Added to Chapter 7 is Procopius's description of the construction of Saint Sophia. In Chapter 8, William of Tyre's description of the capture of Jerusalem is added to the section "The First Crusade," and a poem revealing the foibles of a wandering scholar is added to the section "Medieval Universities." A poem showing the reverence medieval people felt for the Virgin Mary is inserted in the section "The Status of Women in Medieval Society." Two other selections inserted into this chapter are "Attack on the Worldly Power of the Church" by Marsilius of Padua and an anonymous poem, "The Vanity of This World," which illustrates medieval otherworldliness. Added to Chapter 9 is "The Importance of Liberal Studies" by Petrus Paulus Vergerius, which treats the educational ideals of Renaissance humanists. Chapter 11 contains a new section, "The Jews of Spain and Portugal: Expulsion, Forced Conversion, Inquisition." Two readings, one denouncing and the other defending slavery, are added to the section "The Atlantic Slave Trade." Bishop Bossuet's advocacy of absolutism is another new document in this chapter. Added to Chapter 13 is a selection in which Denis Diderot uses travel literature about lands beyond Europe to question European values that conflict with reason and nature and a new section, "Slavery Condemned," which contains passages from the *Encyclopedia*, Condorcet, and John Wesley, the religious reformer.

Volume II contains about fifty new selections and a new concluding chapter, "The West in an Age of Globalism" (Chapter 15). The restructuring of the readings from the end of World War I to the end of World War II has led to a new chapter arrangement: "Era of Totalitarianism" (Chapter 12) and "World War II" (Chapter 13). Added to Chapter 4 is a passage from

Gracchus Babeuf demanding economic justice for the poor during the French Revolution. A statement by Metternich has been added to the constellation "Conservatism" in Chapter 6. The new section, "Prostitution," in Chapter 8 contains descriptions of prostitution in London, Paris, and Hamburg. A new section, "The Political Potential of the Irrational," has been inserted in Chapter 10; it contains passages from Georges Sorel and Gustave Le Bon. The section on militarism in Chapter 11 has been expanded to include Friedrich von Bernhardi's glorification of war and Karl Liebknecht's denunciation of militarism. Also added to the chapter on World War I are Austria's response to the assassination of Francis Ferdinand and a report from Russian army intelligence describing the breakdown of military discipline in 1917. The restructured Chapter 12 contains Miron Dolot's distressing account of Stalin's planned famine in Ukraine in the 1930s. Kurt G. W. Ludecke's description of Hitler's oratorical ability is added to the section "The Rise of Nazism," and Ernst Huber makes the case for Hitler's unlimited power. An account of the burning of books is included in the section "The Nazification of Culture and Society." The section "Persecution of Jews" contains two accounts by German women of Jewish suffering during the early years of the Third Reich. Chapter 13 opens with "Prescient Observers of Nazi Germany," warnings by two diplomats that Hitler intended war. Also included in this chapter is Stefan Zweig's description of the glee with which Austrians welcomed the Nazi takeover and Hitler's plan to conquer Poland. The section "The Fall of France" contains General Heinz Guderian's assessment of the failure of French leadership. An official account of Omaha Beachhead on D-Day, describing the ordeal and heroism of the American soldiers, is incorporated into the chapter. The concluding section, "The End of the Third Reich," contains an inmate's description of the liberation of Dachau concentration camp, entries from Joseph Goebbels' diaries, a German woman's account of the mayhem inflicted on German citizens by Russian soldiers, and

Hitler's last words to the German people. In Chapter 14, the first section contains two descriptions of a ruined Europe. Andor Heller's account of the Hungarian Revolution is added to the section "Communist Repression." A new section, "The Twilight of Imperialism," contains three readings dealing with both the evils and benefits of imperialism. Chapter 15 contains constellations focusing on the problems of the new Russia and European ethnic minorities, including ethnic cleansing in Yugoslavia, French objections to female genital mutilation by Africans living in France, and the fears of conservatives in Britain and Austria that immigration is changing the character of their country. Ingo Hasselbach's account of his years as a neo-Nazi illustrates the lingering appeal of fascism. The concluding section, "Globalization: Patterns and Problems," includes a selection on the world-wide impact of globalization and an analysis of Islamic terrorism, which culminated in the terrible events of September 11, 2001.

To accompany the fifth edition is a revised *Instructor's Resource Manual with Test Items.* In addition to an introduction with suggestions on how to use *Sources of the Western Tradition* in class, there are chapter overviews, summaries of the sections, and, for each chapter, several questions for discussion or essay assignments and ten to twenty multiple-choice questions.

We wish to thank the following instructors for their critical reading of the manuscript and for their many valuable suggestions.

David Coleman, Eastern Kentucky University
Maribel Dietz, Louisiana State University
Jeffrey S. Gaab, SUNY–Farmingdale
Dale Hoak, College of William & Mary
David Imhoof, Susquehanna University
Amy Thompson McCandless, College of Charleston
Robert J. Mueller, Utah State University
Susan Mitchell Sommers, St. Vincent College
Mark Walker, Union College
Leigh Whaley, Acadia University

We are grateful to the staff of Houghton Mifflin Company who lent their talents to the project. We would like to thank Nancy Blaine, senior sponsoring editor, and Julie Dunn, development editor, for guiding the new edition from its inception, and Ylang Nguyen, project editor, for her careful attention to detail. Although Freda Alexander, Frances Gay, and Jean Woy did not work on this edition, their excellent editorial efforts in previous editions are still very much evident. We are particularly grateful to Holly Webber for her superb copyediting skills.

I am pleased that my friend George W. Bock continues to work closely with me in every phase of the reader's development. I thank my wife Phyllis Perry for her encouragement and computer expertise, which saved me time and aggravation. Joseph Peden, a conscientious colleague, died in 1996 and is still greatly missed. Another sad note is the recent passing of Theodore H. Von Laue, whose superb insights into European history added so much to the book's quality. I am fortunate that his wife, Angela Von Laue, brings her research and literary skills to the project.

M.P.

Prologue
Examining Primary Sources

When historians try to reconstruct and apprehend past events, they rely on primary or original sources—official documents prepared by institutions and eyewitness reports. Similarly, when they attempt to describe the essential outlook or world-view of a given era, people, or movement, historians examine other types of primary sources—the literature, art, philosophy, and religious expressions of the time. These original sources differ from secondary or derivative sources—accounts of events and times written at a later date by people who may or may not have had access to primary sources. *Sources of the Western Tradition* consists principally of primary sources, which are the raw materials of history; they provide historians with the basic facts, details, and thinking needed for an accurate reconstruction of the past.

Historians have to examine a document with a critical spirit. The first question asked is: Is the document authentic and reliable? An early illustration of critical historical awareness was demonstrated by the Renaissance thinker Lorenzo Valla (c. 1407–1457) in *Declamation Concerning the False Decretals of Constantine.* The so-called Donation of Constantine, which was used by popes to support their claim to temporal authority, stated that the fourth-century Roman emperor Constantine had given the papacy dominion over the western Empire. By showing that some of the words in the document were unknown in Constantine's time and therefore could not have been used by the emperor, Valla proved that the document was forged by church officials several hundred years after Constantine's death. A more recent example of the need for caution is shown by the discovery of the "Hitler Diaries" in the mid–1980s. Several prominent historians "authenticated" the manuscript before it was exposed as a forgery—the

paper dated from the 1950s and Hitler died in 1945. Nor can all eyewitness accounts be trusted, something Thucydides, the great Greek historian, noted 2,400 years ago.

[E]ither I was present myself at the events which I have described or else I heard of them from eye-witnesses whose reports I have checked with as much thoroughness as possible. Not that even so the truth was easy to discover: different eye-witnesses give different accounts of the same events, speaking out of partiality for one side or the other or else from imperfect memories.

An eyewitness's personal bias can render a document worthless. For example, in *The Auschwitz Lie* (1973), Thies Christophersen, a former SS guard at Auschwitz-Birkenau, denied the existence of gas chambers and mass killings in the notorious Nazi death camp, which he described as a sort of resort where prisoners, after work, could swim, listen to music in their rooms, or visit a brothel. Years later he was captured on videotape—he mistakenly thought the interviewers were fellow neo-Nazis—confessing that he had lied about the gas chambers because of loyalty to the SS and his desire to protect Germany's honor.

After examining the relevant primary sources and deciding on their usefulness, historians have to construct a consistent narrative and provide a plausible interpretation. This requires that they examine documentary evidence in a wholly neutral, detached, and objective way. But is it possible to write history without being influenced by one's own particular viewpoint and personal biases? The historian has a responsibility to be ever vigilant against using sources selectively and prejudicially, particularly when dealing with sensitive issues of religion, ethnicity, gender, and sexual orientation.

A flagrant example of writers of history misusing sources and distorting evidence in order to fortify their own prejudices is the recent case of British historian David Irving, author of numerous books on World War II, several of them well reviewed. Increasingly Irving revealed an undisguised admiration for Hitler and an antipathy toward Jews, which led him to minimize and disguise atrocities committed by the Third Reich. Addressing neo-Nazi audiences in several lands, he asserted that the Holocaust is "a major fraud. . . . There were no gas chambers. They were fakes and frauds." In *Lying about Hitler: History, Holocaust and the David Irving Trial* (2001), Richard J. Evans, a specialist in modern German history with a broad background in archival research, exposed instance after instance of how Irving, in his attempt to whitewash Hitler, misquoted sources, "misrepresented data, . . . skewed documents [and] ignored or deliberately suppressed material when it ran counter to his arguments. . . . [W]hen I followed Irving's claims and statements back to the original documents on which they purported to rest . . . Irving's work in this respect was revealed as a house of cards, a vast apparatus of deception and deceit."

The sources in this anthology can be read on several levels. First, they enhance understanding of the historical period in which they were written, shedding light on how people lived and thought and the chief concerns of the time. Several of the sources, written by some of humanity's greatest minds, have broader implications. They are founts of wisdom, providing insights of enduring value into human nature and the human condition. Finally, the documents also reveal those core ideas and values—reason, freedom, and respect for the individual—that constitute the Western heritage. The events of September 11, 2001, demonstrate that there are people who find this heritage abhorrent; it is essential that every generation comprehend, value, and reaffirm it.

Introduction
The Middle Ages and the Modern World

Historians have traditionally divided Western history into three broad periods: ancient, medieval, and modern. What is meant by modernity? What has the modern world inherited from the Middle Ages? How does the modern West differ fundamentally from the Middle Ages?[1]

Medieval civilization began to decline in the fourteenth century, but no dark age comparable to the three centuries following Rome's fall descended on Europe; its economic and political institutions and technological skills had grown too strong. Instead, the waning of the Middle Ages opened up possibilities for another stage in Western civilization: the modern age.

The modern world is linked to the Middle Ages in innumerable ways. European cities, the middle class, the state system, English common law, universities—all had their origins in the Middle Ages. During medieval times, important advances were made in business practices, including partnerships, systematic bookkeeping, and the bill of exchange. By translating and commenting on the writings of Greek and Arabic thinkers, medieval scholars preserved a priceless intellectual heritage, without which the modern mind could never have evolved. In addition, numerous strands connect the thought of the scholastics and that of early modern philosophers.

Feudal traditions lasted long after the Middle Ages. Up to the French Revolution, for instance, French aristocrats enjoyed special privileges and exercised power over local government. In England, the aristocracy controlled local government until the Industrial Revolu-

tion transformed English society in the nineteenth century. Retaining the medieval ideal of the noble warrior, aristocrats continued to dominate the officer corps of European armies through the nineteenth century and even into the twentieth. Aristocratic notions of duty, honor, loyalty, and courtly love had endured into the twentieth century.

During the Middle Ages, Europeans began to take the lead over the Muslims, the Byzantines, the Chinese, and all the other peoples in the use of technology. Medieval technology and inventiveness stemmed in part from Christianity, which taught that God had created the world specifically for human beings to subdue and exploit. Consequently, medieval people employed animal power and labor-saving machinery to relieve human drudgery. Moreover, Christianity taught that God was above nature, not within it, so the Christian had no spiritual obstacle to exploiting nature—unlike, for instance, the Hindu. In contrast to classical humanism, the Christian outlook did not consider manual work degrading; even monks combined it with study.

The Christian stress on the sacred worth of the individual and on the higher law of God has never ceased to influence Western civilization. Even though in modern times the various Christian churches have not often taken the lead in political and social reform, the ideals identified with the Judeo-Christian tradition have become part of the Western heritage. As such, they have inspired social reformers who may no longer identify with their ancestral religion.

Believing that God's law was superior to state or national decrees, medieval philosophers provided a theoretical basis for opposing tyrannical kings who violated Christian prin-

---

[1]Material for this introduction is taken from Marvin Perry, et al., *Western Civilization,* 5th ed. (Boston: Houghton Mifflin, 1996), pp. 290–295.

ciples. The idea that both the ruler and the ruled are bound by a higher law would, in a secularized form, become a principal element of modern liberal thought.

Feudalism also contributed to the history of liberty. According to feudal theory, the king, as a member of the feudal community, was duty-bound to honor agreements made with his vassals. Lords possessed personal rights, which the king was obliged to respect. Resentful of a king who ran roughshod over customary feudal rights, lords also negotiated contracts with the crown, such as the famous Magna Carta (1215), to define and guard their customary liberties. To protect themselves from the arbitrary behavior of a king, feudal lords initiated what came to be called *government by consent* and the *rule of law.*

During the Middle Ages, then, there gradually emerged the idea that law was not imposed on inferiors by an absolute monarch but required the collaboration of the king and his subjects; that the king, too, was bound by the law; and that lords had the right to resist a monarch who violated agreements. A related phenomenon was the rise of representative institutions, with which the king was expected to consult on the realm's affairs. The most notable such institution was the British Parliament; although subordinate to the king, it became a permanent part of the state. Later, in the seventeenth century, Parliament would successfully challenge royal authority. Thus, continuity exists between the feudal tradition of a king bound by law and the modern practice of limiting the authority of the head of state.

Although the elements of continuity are clear, the characteristic outlook of the Middle Ages is as different from that of the modern age as it was from the outlook of the ancient world. Religion was the integrating feature of the Middle Ages, whereas science and secularism—a preoccupation with worldly life—determine the modern outlook. The period from the Italian Renaissance of the fifteenth century through the eighteenth-century Age of Enlightenment constituted a gradual breaking away from the medieval world-view—a rejection of the medieval conception of nature, the individual, and the purpose of life. The transition from medieval to modern was neither sudden nor complete, for there are no sharp demarcation lines separating historical periods. While many distinctively medieval ways endured in the sixteenth, seventeenth, and even eighteenth centuries, these centuries saw as well the rise of new intellectual, political, and economic forms, which marked the emergence of modernity.

Medieval thought began with the existence of God and the truth of his revelation as interpreted by the church, which set the standards and defined the purposes for human endeavor. The medieval mind rejected the fundamental principle of Greek philosophy: the autonomy of reason. Without the guidance of revealed truth, reason was seen as feeble.

Scholastics engaged in genuine philosophical speculation, but they did not allow philosophy to challenge the basic premises of their faith. Unlike either ancient or modern thinkers, medieval schoolmen ultimately believed that reason alone could not provide a unified view of nature or society. A rational soul had to be guided by a divine light. For all medieval philosophers, the natural order depended on a supernatural order for its origin and purpose. To understand the natural world properly, it was necessary to know its relationship to the higher world. The discoveries of reason had to accord with Scripture as interpreted by the church. In medieval thought, says historian-philosopher Ernst Cassirer,

neither science nor morality, neither law nor state, can be erected on its own foundations. Supernatural assistance is always needed to bring them to true perfection. . . . Reason is and remains the servant of revelation; within the sphere of natural intellectual and psychological forces, reason leads toward, and prepares the ground for, revelation.[2]

In the modern view, both nature and the human intellect are self-sufficient. Nature is a mathematical system that operates without miracles or any other form of divine intervention. To comprehend nature and society, the mind needs no divine assistance; it accepts no authority above reason. The modern mentality finds it unacceptable to reject the conclusions of science on the basis of clerical authority and revelation or to ground politics, law, or economics on religious dogma. It refuses to settle public issues by appeals to religious belief.

The medieval philosopher understood both nature and society to be a hierarchical order. God was the source of moral values, and the church was responsible for teaching and upholding these ethical norms. Kings acquired their right to rule from God. The entire social structure constituted a hierarchy: the clergy guided society according to Christian standards; lords defended Christian society from its enemies; and serfs, lowest in the social order, toiled for the good of all. In the hierarchy of knowledge, a lower form of knowledge derived from the senses, and the highest type of knowledge, theology, dealt with God's revelation. To the medieval mind, this hierarchical ordering of nature, society, and knowledge had a divine sanction.

Rejecting the medieval division of the universe into higher and lower realms and superior and inferior substances, the modern view postulated the uniformity of nature and nature's laws: the cosmos knows no privilege of rank; heavenly bodies follow the same laws of nature as earthly objects. Space is geometric and homogeneous, not hierarchical, heterogeneous, and qualitative. The universe was no longer conceived as finite and closed but as infinite, and the operations of nature were explained mathematically. The modern thinker studies mathematical law and chemical composition, not grades of perfection. Spiritual meaning is not sought in an examination of the material world. Roger Bacon, for example, described seven coverings of the eye and then concluded that God had fashioned the eye in this manner in order to express the seven gifts of the Spirit. This way of thinking is alien to the modern outlook. So, too, is the medieval belief that natural disasters, such as plagues and famines, are God's punishments for people's sins.

The outlook of the modern West also broke with the rigid division of medieval society into three orders: clergy, nobles, and commoners. The intellectual justification for this arrangement, as expressed by the English prelate John of Salisbury (c. 1115–1180), has been rejected by modern Westerners: "For inferiors owe it to their superiors to provide them with service, just as the superiors in their turn owe it to their inferiors to provide them with all things needful for their protection and succor."[3] Opposing the feudal principle that an individual's obligations and rights are a function of his or her rank in society, the modern view stressed equality of opportunity and equal treatment under the law. It rejected the idea that society should be guided by clergy, who were deemed to possess a special wisdom; by nobles, who were entitled to special privileges; and by monarchs, who were thought to receive their power from God.

The modern West also rejected the personal and customary character of feudal law. As the modern state developed, law assumed an impersonal and objective character. For example, if the lord demanded more than the customary forty days of military service, the vassal might refuse to comply, because he would see the lord's request as an unpardonable violation of custom and agreement, as well as an infringement on his liberties. In the modern state, with a constitution and a representative assembly, if a new law

[2]Ernst Cassirer, *The Philosophy of the Enlightenment* (Boston: Beacon, 1955), p. 40.

[3]John of Salisbury, *Policraticus,* trans. John Dickinson (New York: Russell & Russell, 1963), pp. 243–244.

increasing the length of military service is passed, it merely replaces the old law. People do not refuse to obey it because the government has broken faith or violated custom.

In the modern world, the individual's relationship to the universe has been radically transformed. Medieval people lived in a geocentric universe that was finite in space and time. The universe was small, enclosed by a sphere of stars, beyond which were the heavens. The universe, it was believed, was some four thousand years old, and, in the not-too-distant future, Christ would return and human history would end. People in the Middle Ages knew why they were on earth and what was expected of them; they never doubted that heaven would be their reward for living a Christian life. Preparation for heaven was the ultimate aim of life. J. H. Randall, Jr., a historian of ideas, eloquently sums up the medieval view of a purposeful universe, in which the human being's position was clearly defined:

> The world was governed throughout by the omnipotent will and omniscient mind of God, whose sole interests were centered in man, his trial, his fall, his suffering and his glory. Worm of the dust as he was, man was yet the central object in the whole universe. . . . And when his destiny was completed, the heavens would be rolled up as a scroll and he would dwell with the Lord forever. Only those who rejected God's freely offered grace and with hardened hearts refused repentance would be cut off from this eternal life.[4]

This comforting medieval vision is alien to the modern outlook. Today, in a universe some 12 billion years old, in which the earth is a tiny speck floating in an endless cosmic ocean, where life evolved over tens of millions of years, many Westerners no longer believe that human beings are special children of God; that heaven is their ultimate goal; that under their feet is hell, where grotesque demons torment sinners; and that God is an active agent in human history. To many intellectuals, the universe seems unresponsive to the religious supplications of people, and life's purpose is sought within the limits of earthly existence. Science and secularism have driven Christianity and faith from their central position to the periphery of human concerns.

The modern outlook developed gradually from the Renaissance to the eighteenth-century Age of Enlightenment. Mathematics rendered the universe comprehensible. Economic and political thought broke free of the religious frame of reference. Science became the great hope of the future. The thinkers of the Enlightenment wanted to liberate humanity from supersititon, ignorance, and traditions that could not pass the test of reason. They saw themselves as emancipating culture from theological dogma and clerical authority. Rejecting the Christian idea of a person's inherent sinfulness, they held that the individual was basically good and that evil resulted from faulty institutions, poor education, and bad leadership. Thus, the concept of a rational and free society in which individuals could realize their potential slowly emerged.

---

[4]J. H. Randall, Jr., *The Making of the Modern Mind* (Boston: Houghton Mifflin, 1940), p. 34.

SOURCES
of the
WESTERN
TRADITION

CHAPTER 1

The Rise of Modernity

THE TRIUMPH OF GALETEA, Raphael, 1513. This fresco from the Palazzo della Farnesina in Rome exemplifies the Renaissance artist's elevation of the human form. The mythological subject is also humanistic in its evocation of the ancient Greek tradition. *(Giraudon/Art Resource, N.Y.)*

From the fifteenth through the seventeenth centuries, medieval attitudes and institutions broke down, and distinctly modern cultural, economic, and political forms emerged. For many historians, the Renaissance, which originated in the city-states of Italy, marks the starting point of the modern era. The Renaissance was characterized by a rebirth of interest in the humanist culture and outlook of ancient Greece and Rome. Although Renaissance individuals did not repudiate Christianity, they valued worldly activities and interests to a much greater degree than did the people of the Middle Ages, whose outlook was dominated by Christian otherworldliness. Renaissance individuals were fascinated by *this* world and by life's possibilities; they aspired to live a rich and creative life on earth and to fulfill themselves through artistic and literary activity.

Individualism was a hallmark of the Renaissance. The urban elite sought to demonstrate their unique talents, to assert their own individuality, and to gain recognition for their accomplishments. The most admired person during the Renaissance was the multitalented individual, the "universal man," who distinguished himself as a writer, artist, linguist, athlete. Disdaining Christian humility, Renaissance individuals took pride in their talents and worldly accomplishments—"I can work miracles," said the great Leonardo da Vinci.

During the High Middle Ages there had been a revival of Greek and Roman learning. Yet there were two important differences between the period called the Twelfth-Century Awakening and the Renaissance. First, many more ancient works were restored to circulation during the Renaissance than during the cultural revival of the Middle Ages. Second, medieval scholastics had tried to fit the ideas of the ancients into a Christian framework; they used Greek philosophy to explain Christian teachings. Renaissance scholars, on the other hand, valued ancient works for their own sake, believing that Greek and Roman authors could teach much about the art of living.

A distinguishing feature of the Renaissance period was the humanist movement, an educational and cultural program based on the study of ancient Greek and Latin literature. By studying the humanities—history, literature, rhetoric, moral and political philosophy—humanists aimed to revive the worldly spirit of the ancient Greeks and Romans, which they believed had been lost in the Middle Ages.

Humanists were thus fascinated by the writings of the ancients. From the works of Thucydides, Plato, Cicero, Seneca, and other ancient authors, humanists sought guidelines for living life well in this world and looked for stylistic models for their own literary efforts. To the humanists, the ancients had written brilliantly, in an incomparable literary style, on friendship, citizenship, love, bravery, statesmanship, beauty, excellence, and every other topic devoted to the enrichment of human life.

Like the humanist movement, Renaissance art also marked a break with medieval culture. The art of the Middle Ages had served a religious function; its purpose was to lift the mind to God. It depicted a spiritual universe in which the supernatural was the supreme reality. The Gothic cathedral, with its flying buttresses, soared toward heaven, rising in ascending tiers; it reflected the medieval conception of a hierarchical universe with God at its apex. Painting also expressed gradations of spiritual values. Traditionally, the left side of a painting portrayed the damned, the right side the saved; dark colors expressed evil, light colors good. Spatial proportion was relative to spirituality—the less spiritually valuable a thing was, the less form it had (or the more deformed it was). Medieval art perfectly expressed the Christian view of the universe and the individual. The Renaissance shattered the dominance of religion over art, shifting attention from heaven to the natural world and to the human being; Renaissance artists often dealt with religious themes, but they placed their subjects in a naturalistic setting. Renaissance art also developed a new concept of visual space that was defined from the standpoint of the individual observer. It was a quantitative space in which the artist, employing reason and mathematics, portrayed the essential form of the object as it appeared in three dimensions to the human eye, that is, it depicted the object in perspective.

The Renaissance began in the middle of the fourteenth century in the northern Italian city-states, which had grown prosperous from the revival of trade in the Middle Ages. Italian merchants and bankers had the wealth to acquire libraries and fine works of art and to support art, literature, and scholarship. Surrounded by reminders of ancient Rome—amphitheaters, monuments, and sculpture—the well-to-do took an interest in classical culture and thought. In the late fifteenth and the sixteenth centuries, Renaissance ideas spread to Germany, France, Spain, and England through books available in great numbers due to the invention of the printing press.

By weakening the church and dividing Europe into Catholic and Protestant, the Reformation of the sixteenth century also contributed to the rise of modernity. The reformation of the church in the sixteenth century was rooted in demands for spiritual renewal and institutional change. These pressures began as early as the late fourteenth century and came from many sources.

The papacy and orthodox Catholic theology were challenged by English theologian John Wycliffe (c. 1320–1384) and Czech theologian John Huss (c. 1369–1415). Both attacked the bishops' involvement in temporal politics and urged a return to the simple practices of the early apostolic church; and both, claiming that the Bible alone—not the church hierarchy—was the highest authority for Christians, emphasized study of the Holy Scriptures by the laity and sermons in the common language of the people. Wycliffe, though not Huss, also undermined the clergy's authority by denying the priests' power to change the bread and wine into Christ's body and blood during the Mass. Despite severe persecution by church and state, followers of Wycliffe's and Huss's beliefs continued to exist and participated in the sixteenth-century Protestant movement.

By that time there was a widespread popular yearning for a more genuine spirituality. It took many forms: the rise of new pious practices; greater interest in mystical experiences and in the study of the Bible; the development of communal ways for lay people to live and work following the apostles' example; and a heightened search for ways within secular society to imitate more perfectly the life of Christ—called the New Devotion movement.

Several secular factors contributed to this heightening of spiritual feeling. The many wars, famines, and plagues of the late fourteenth and the fifteenth centuries had traumatized Europe. The increasing educational level of the urban middle class and skilled laborers and the invention of the printing press allowed the rapid and relatively inexpensive spread of new ideas. Finally, there was the influence of the humanist movement, particularly in northern Europe and Spain. Many humanists dedicated themselves to promoting higher levels of religious education. They stimulated public interest in biblical study by publishing new editions of the Holy Scriptures and the writings of the church fathers, along with new devotional literature. Nearly all the religious reformers of the sixteenth century were deeply influenced by the ideals and methods of the Christian humanist movement.

In Germany economic and political considerations fused with the demand for reform of church and religious life. The middle class resented the flow of tax money from Germany to Rome; by supporting Martin Luther's break with the church, nobles saw a way of seizing church property in their territories and of resisting the centralizing efforts of Holy Roman Emperor Charles V, who sided with the papacy.

By dividing Europe into Catholic and Protestant regions, the Reformation ended medieval religious unity. It also accentuated the importance of the individual person, a distinctive feature of the modern outlook. It stressed individual conscience rather than clerical authority, called for a personal relationship between each man and woman and God, and called attention to the individual's inner religious capacities.

At the same time that the Renaissance and Reformation were transforming European cultural and religious life, the discovery of new trade routes to East Asia and of new lands across the Atlantic widened the imagination and ambitions of Europeans and precipitated a commercial revolution. Exploration and commercial expansion created the foundations of a global economy in which the European economy was tied to Asian spices, African slaves, and American silver. A wide variety of goods circulated all over the globe. From the West Indies and East Asia, sugar, rice, tea, cacao, and tobacco flowed into Europe. From the Americas, potatoes, corn, sweet potatoes, and manioc (from which tapioca is made) spread to the rest of the world. Europeans paid for Asian silks and spices with American silver.

The increasing demand for goods and a rise in prices produced more opportunities for the accumulation and investment of capital by private individuals, which is the essence of capitalism. State policies designed to increase national wealth and power also stimulated the growth of capitalism. Governments subsidized new industries, chartered joint-stock companies to engage in overseas trade, and struck at internal tariffs and guild regulations that hampered domestic economic growth. Improvements in banking, shipbuilding, mining, and manufacturing further stimulated economic growth.

In the sixteenth and seventeenth centuries the old medieval political order dissolved, and the modern state began to emerge. The modern state has a strong central government that issues laws that apply throughout the land and a permanent army of professional soldiers paid by the state. Trained bureaucrats, responsible to the central government, collect taxes, enforce laws, and administer justice. The modern state has a secular character; promotion of religion is not the state's concern, and churches do not determine state policy. These features of the modern state were generally not prevalent in the Middle Ages, when the nobles, church, and towns possessed powers and privileges that impeded central authority, and kings were expected to rule in accordance with Christian principles. In the sixteenth and seventeenth centuries, monarchs were exercising central authority with ever-greater effectiveness at the expense of nobles and clergy. The secularization of the state became firmly established after the Thirty Years' War (1618–1648); with their states worn out by Catholic-Protestant conflicts, kings came to act less for religious motives than for reasons of national security and power.

Historically, the modern state has been characterized by a devotion to the nation and by feelings of national pride. There is a national language that is used throughout the land, and the people have a sense of sharing a common culture and history, of being distinct from other peoples. There were some signs of growing national feeling during the sixteenth and seventeenth centuries, but this feature of the modern state did not become a major part of European political life until the nineteenth century. During the early modern period, loyalty was largely given to a town, to a province, to a noble, or to the person of the king rather than to the nation, the people as a whole.

1   The Humanists' Fascination with Antiquity

Humanists believed that a refined person must know the literature of Greece and Rome. They strove to imitate the style of the ancients, to speak and write as eloquently as the Greeks and Romans. Toward these ends, they sought to read, print, and restore to circulation every scrap of ancient literature that could still be found.

Petrarch
THE FATHER OF HUMANISM

During his lifetime, Francesco Petrarca, or Petrarch (1304–1374), had an astounding reputation as a poet and scholar. Often called the "father of humanism," he inspired other humanists through his love for classical learning; his criticism of medieval Latin as barbaric in contrast to the style of Cicero, Seneca, and other Romans; and his literary works based on classical models. Petrarch saw his own age as a restoration of classical brilliance after an interval of medieval darkness.

A distinctly modern element in Petrarch's thought is the subjective and individualistic character of his writing. In talking about himself and probing his own feelings, Petrarch demonstrates a self-consciousness characteristic of the modern outlook.

Like many other humanists, Petrarch remained devoted to Christianity: "When it comes to thinking or speaking of religion, that is, of the highest truth, of true happiness and eternal salvation," he declared, "I certainly am not a Ciceronian or a Platonist but a Christian." Petrarch was a forerunner of the Christian humanism best represented by Erasmus. Christian humanists combined an intense devotion to Christianity with a great love for classical literature, which they much preferred to the dull and turgid treatises written by scholastic philosophers and theologians. In the following passage, Petrarch criticizes his contemporaries for their ignorance of ancient writers and shows his commitment to classical learning.

. . . O inglorious age! that scorns antiquity, its mother, to whom it owes every noble art—that dares to declare itself not only equal but superior to the glorious past. I say nothing of the vulgar, the dregs of mankind, whose sayings and opinions may raise a laugh but hardly merit serious censure. . . .

. . . But what can be said in defense of men of education who ought not to be ignorant of antiquity and yet are plunged in this same darkness and delusion?

You see that I cannot speak of these matters without the greatest irritation and indignation. There has arisen of late a set of dialecticians [experts in logical argument],[1] who are

not only ignorant but demented. Like a black army of ants from some old rotten oak, they swarm forth from their hiding places and devastate the fields of sound learning. They condemn Plato and Aristotle, and laugh at Socrates and Pythagoras.[2] And, good God! under what silly and incompetent leaders these

---

[1]Throughout the text, words in brackets have been added as glosses by the editors. Brackets around glosses from the original sources have been changed to parentheses to distinguish them.

Throughout the text, the editors' notes carry numbers, whereas notes from the original sources are indicated by asterisks, daggers, et cetera.

[2]The work of Aristotle (384–322 B.C.), a leading Greek philosopher, had an enormous influence among medieval and Renaissance scholars. A student of the philosopher Socrates, Plato (c. 427–347 B.C.) was one of the greatest philosophers of ancient Greece. His work grew to be extremely influential in the West during the Renaissance period, as new texts of his writings were discovered and translated into Latin and more Westerners could read the originals in Greek. Pythagoras (c. 582–c. 507 B.C.) was a Greek philosopher whose work influenced both Socrates and Plato.

opinions are put forth. . . . What shall we say of men who scorn Marcus Tullius Cicero,[3] the bright sun of eloquence? Of those who scoff at Varro and Seneca,[4] and are scandalized at what they choose to call the crude, unfinished style of Livy and Sallust [Roman historians]? . . .

Such are the times, my friend, upon which we have fallen; such is the period in which we live and are growing old. Such are the critics of today, as I so often have occasion to lament and complain—men who are innocent of knowledge and virtue, and yet harbour the most exalted opinion of themselves. Not content with losing the words of the ancients, they must attack their genius and their ashes. They rejoice in their ignorance, as if what they did not know were not worth knowing. They give full rein to their license and conceit, and freely introduce among us new authors and outlandish teachings.

---

[3]Cicero (106–43 B.C.) was a Roman statesman and rhetorician. His Latin style was especially admired and emulated during the Renaissance.

[4]Varro (116–27 B.C.) was a Roman scholar and historian. Seneca (4 B.C.–A.D. 65) was a Roman statesman, dramatist, and Stoic philosopher whose literary style was greatly admired during the Renaissance.

Leonardo Bruni
STUDY OF GREEK LITERATURE AND A HUMANIST EDUCATIONAL PROGRAM

Leonardo Bruni (1374–1444) was a Florentine humanist who extolled both intellectual study and active involvement in public affairs, an outlook called civic humanism. In the first reading from his *History of His Own Times in Italy*, Bruni expresses the humanist's love for ancient Greek literature and language.

In a treatise, *De Studiis et Literis* (On Learning and Literature), addressed to the noble lady Baptista di Montefeltro (1383–1450), daughter of the Count of Urbino, Bruni outlines the basic course of studies that the humanists recommended as the best preparation for a life of wisdom and virtue. In addition to the study of Christian literature, Bruni encourages a wide familiarity with the best minds and stylists of ancient Greek and Latin cultures.

LOVE FOR GREEK LITERATURE

Then first came a knowledge of Greek, which had not been in use among us for seven hundred years. Chrysoloras the Byzantine,[1] a man of noble birth and well versed in Greek letters, brought Greek learning to us. When his country was invaded by the Turks, he came by sea, first to Venice. The report of him soon spread, and he was cordially invited and besought and promised a public stipend, to come to Florence and open his store of riches to the youth. I was then studying Civil Law,[2] but . . . I burned with love of academic studies, and had spent no little pains on dialectic and rhetoric. At the

---

[1]Chrysoloras (c. 1355–1415), a Byzantine writer and teacher, introduced the study of Greek literature to the Italians, helping to open a new age of Western humanistic learning.

[2]Civil Law refers to the Roman law as codified by Emperor Justinian in the early sixth century A.D. and studied in medieval law schools.

coming of Chrysoloras I was torn in mind, deeming it shameful to desert the law, and yet a crime to lose such a chance of studying Greek literature; and often with youthful impulse I would say to myself: "Thou, when it is permitted thee to gaze on Homer, Plato and Demosthenes,[3] and the other [Greek] poets, philosophers, orators, of whom such glorious things are spread abroad, and speak with them and be instructed in their admirable teaching, wilt thou desert and rob thyself? Wilt thou neglect this opportunity so divinely offered? For seven hundred years, no one in Italy has possessed Greek letters; and yet we confess that all knowledge is derived from them. How great advantage to your knowledge, enhancement of your fame, increase of your pleasure, will come from an understanding of this tongue? There are doctors of civil law everywhere; and the chance of learning will not fail thee. But if this one and only doctor of Greek letters disappears, no one can be found to teach thee." Overcome at length by these reasons, I gave myself to Chrysoloras, with such zeal to learn, that what through the wakeful day I gathered, I followed after in the night, even when asleep.

ON LEARNING AND LITERATURE

. . . The foundations of all true learning must be laid in the sound and thorough knowledge of Latin: which implies study marked by a broad spirit, accurate scholarship, and careful attention to details. Unless this solid basis be secured it is useless to attempt to rear an enduring edifice. Without it the great monuments of literature are unintelligible, and the art of composition impossible. To attain this essential knowledge we must never relax our careful attention to the grammar of the language, but perpetually confirm and extend our acquaintance with it until it is thoroughly our

own. . . . To this end we must be supremely careful in our choice of authors, lest an inartistic and debased style infect our own writing and degrade our taste; which danger is best avoided by bringing a keen, critical sense to bear upon select works, observing the sense of each passage, the structure of the sentence, the force of every word down to the least important particle. In this way our reading reacts directly upon our style. . . .

But we must not forget that true distinction is to be gained by a wide and varied range of such studies as conduce to the profitable enjoyment of life, in which, however, we must observe due proportion in the attention and time we devote to them.

First amongst such studies I place History: a subject which must not on any account be neglected by one who aspires to true cultivation. For it is our duty to understand the origins of our own history and its development; and the achievements of Peoples and of Kings.

For the careful study of the past enlarges our foresight in contemporary affairs and affords to citizens and to monarchs lessons of incitement or warning in the ordering of public policy. From History, also, we draw our store of examples of moral precepts.

In the monuments of ancient literature which have come down to us History holds a position of great distinction. We specially prize such [Roman] authors as Livy, Sallust and Curtius;[4] and, perhaps even above these, Julius Caesar; the style of whose Commentaries, so elegant and so limpid, entitles them to our warm admiration. . . .

The great Orators of antiquity must by all means be included. Nowhere do we find the virtues more warmly extolled, the vices so fiercely decried. From them we may learn, also, how to express consolation, encouragement, dis-

---

[3]Demosthenes (384–322 B.C.) was an Athenian statesman and orator whose oratorical style was much admired by Renaissance humanists.

[4]Q. Curtius Rufus, a Roman historian and rhetorician of the mid-first century A.D., composed a biography of Alexander the Great.

suasion or advice. If the principles which orators set forth are portrayed for us by philosophers, it is from the former that we learn how to employ the emotions—such as indignation, or pity—in driving home their application in individual cases. Further, from oratory we derive our store of those elegant or striking turns of expression which are used with so much effect in literary compositions. Lastly, in oratory we find that wealth of vocabulary, that clear easy-flowing style, that verve and force, which are invaluable to us both in writing and in conversation.

I come now to Poetry and the Poets. . . . For we cannot point to any great mind of the past for whom the Poets had not a powerful attraction. Aristotle, in constantly quoting Homer, Hesiod, Pindar, Euripides and other [Greek] poets, proves that he knew their works hardly less intimately than those of the philosophers. Plato, also, frequently appeals to them, and in this way covers them with his approval. If we turn to Cicero, we find him not content with quoting Ennius, Accius,[5] and others of the Latins, but rendering poems from the Greek and employing them habitually. . . . Hence my view that familiarity with the great poets of antiquity is essential to any claim to true education. For in their writings we find deep speculations upon Nature, and upon the Causes and Origins of things, which must carry

weight with us both from their antiquity and from their authorship. Besides these, many important truths upon matters of daily life are suggested or illustrated. All this is expressed with such grace and dignity as demands our admiration. . . . To sum up what I have endeavoured to set forth. That high standard of education to which I referred at the outset is only to be reached by one who has seen many things and read much. Poet, Orator, Historian, and the rest, all must be studied, each must contribute a share. Our learning thus becomes full, ready, varied and elegant, available for action or for discourse in all subjects. But to enable us to make effectual use of what we know we must add to our knowledge the power of expression. These two sides of learning, indeed, should not be separated: they afford mutual aid and distinction. Proficiency in literary form, not accompanied by broad acquaintance with facts and truths, is a barren attainment; whilst information, however vast, which lacks all grace of expression, would seem to be put under a bushel or partly thrown away. Indeed, one may fairly ask what advantage it is to possess profound and varied learning if one cannot convey it in language worthy of the subject. Where, however, this double capacity exists— breadth of learning and grace of style—we allow the highest title to distinction and to abiding fame. If we review the great names of ancient [Greek and Roman] literature, Plato, Democritus, Aristotle, Theophrastus, Varro, Cicero, Seneca, Augustine, Jerome, Lactantius, we shall find it hard to say whether we admire more their attainments or their literary power.

---

[5]Ennius (239–169 B.C.) wrote the first great Latin epic poem, which was based on the legends of Rome's founding and its early history. Accius (c. 170–c. 90 B.C.), also a Roman, authored a history of Greek and Latin literature.

REVIEW QUESTIONS

1. What do historians mean by the term "Renaissance humanism"?
2. What made Petrarch aware that a renaissance, or rebirth, of classical learning was necessary in his time?
3. Why did Leonardo Bruni abandon his earlier course of studies to pursue the study of Greek literature?
4. What subjects made up the basic course of studies advocated by Bruni?

2 Human Dignity

In his short lifetime, Giovanni Pico della Mirandola (1463–1494) mastered Greek, Latin, Hebrew, and Arabic and aspired to synthesize the Hebrew, Greek, and Christian traditions. His most renowned work, *Oration on the Dignity of Man,* has been called the humanist manifesto.

Pico della Mirandola
ORATION ON THE DIGNITY OF MAN[1]

In the opening section of the *Oration,* Pico declares that unlike other creatures, human beings have not been assigned a fixed place in the universe. Our destiny is not determined by anything outside us. Rather, God has bestowed upon us a unique distinction: the liberty to determine the form and value our lives shall acquire. The notion that people have the power to shape their own lives is a key element in the emergence of the modern outlook.

I have read in the records of the Arabians, reverend Fathers, that Abdala the Saracen,[2] when questioned as to what on this stage of the world, as it were, could be seen most worthy of wonder, replied: "There is nothing to be seen more wonderful than man." In agreement with this opinion is the saying of Hermes Trismegistus: "A great miracle, Asclepius, is man."[3] But when I weighed the reason for these maxims, the many grounds for the excellence of human nature reported by many men failed to satisfy me—that man is the intermediary between creatures, the intimate of the gods, the king of the lower beings, by the acuteness of his senses, by the discernment of his reason, and by the light of his intelligence the interpreter of nature, the interval between fixed eternity and fleeting time, and (as the Persians say) the bond, nay, rather, the marriage song of the world, on David's [biblical king] testimony but little lower than the angels. Admittedly great though these reasons be, they are not the principal grounds, that is, those which may rightfully claim for themselves the privilege of the highest admiration. For why should we not admire more the angels themselves and the blessed choirs of heaven? At last it seems to me I have come to understand why man is the most fortunate of creatures and consequently worthy of all admiration and what precisely is that rank which is his lot in the universal chain of Being—a rank to be envied not only by brutes but even by the stars and by minds beyond this world. It is a matter past faith and a wondrous one. Why should it not be? For it is on this very account that man is rightly called and judged a great miracle and a wonderful creature indeed. . . .

. . . God the Father, the supreme Architect, had already built this cosmic home we behold, the most sacred temple of His godhead, by the laws of His mysterious wisdom. The region above the heavens He had adorned with Intel-

---

[1]Throughout the text, titles original to the source appear in italics. Titles added by the editors are not italicized.

[2]Abdala the Saracen possibly refers to the eighth-century A.D. writer Abd-Allah Ibn al-Muqaffa.

[3]Ancient writings dealing with magic, alchemy, astrology, and occult philosophy were erroneously attributed to an assumed Egyptian priest, Hermes Trismegistus. Asclepius was a Greek god of healing.

ligences, the heavenly spheres He had quickened with eternal souls, and the excrementary and filthy parts of the lower world He had filled with a multitude of animals of every kind. But, when the work was finished, the Craftsman kept wishing that there were someone to ponder the plan of so great a work, to love its beauty, and to wonder at its vastness. Therefore, when everything was done (as Moses and Timaeus[4] bear witness), He finally took thought concerning the creation of man. But there was not among His archetypes that from which He could fashion a new offspring, nor was there in His treasurehouses anything which He might bestow on His new son as an inheritance, nor was there in the seats of all the world a place where the latter might sit to contemplate the universe. All was now complete; all things had been assigned to the highest, the middle, and the lowest orders. But in its final creation it was not the part of the Father's power to fail as though exhausted. It was not the part of His wisdom to waver in a needful matter through poverty of counsel. It was not the part of His kindly love that he who was to praise God's divine generosity in regard to others should be compelled to condemn it in regard to himself.

At last the best of artisans [God] ordained that that creature to whom He had been able to give nothing proper to himself should have joint possession of whatever had been peculiar to each of the different kinds of being. He therefore took man as a creature of indeterminate nature and, assigning him a place in the middle of the world, addressed him thus: "Neither a fixed abode nor a form that is thine alone nor any function peculiar to thyself have we given thee, Adam, to the end that according to thy longing and according to thy judgment thou mayest have and possess what abode, what form, and what functions thou

thyself shalt desire. The nature of all other beings is limited and constrained within the bounds of laws prescribed by Us. Thou, constrained by no limits, in accordance with thine own free will, in whose hand We have placed thee, shalt ordain for thyself the limits of thy nature. We have set thee at the world's center that thou mayest from thence more easily observe whatever is in the world. We have made thee neither of heaven nor of earth, neither mortal nor immortal, so that with freedom of choice and with honor, as though the maker and molder of thyself, thou mayest fashion thyself in whatever shape thou shalt prefer. Thou shalt have the power to degenerate into the lower forms of life, which are brutish. Thou shalt have the power, out of thy soul's judgment, to be reborn into the higher forms, which are divine."

O supreme generosity of God the Father, O highest and most marvelous felicity of man! To him it is granted to have whatever he chooses, to be whatever he wills. Beasts as soon as they are born (so says Lucilius)[5] bring with them from their mother's womb all they will ever possess. Spiritual beings [angels], either from the beginning or soon thereafter, become what they are to be for ever and ever. On man when he came into life the Father conferred the seeds of all kinds and the germs of every way of life. Whatever seeds each man cultivates will grow to maturity and bear in him their own fruit. If they be vegetative, he will be like a plant. If sensitive, he will become brutish. If rational, he will grow into a heavenly being. If intellectual, he will be an angel and the son of God. And if, happy in the lot of no created thing, he withdraws into the center of his own unity, his spirit, made one with God, in the solitary darkness of God, who is set above all things, shall surpass them all.

---

[4]Timaeus, a Greek Pythagorean philosopher, was a central character in Plato's famous dialogue *Timaeus*.

[5]Lucilius, a first-century A.D. Roman poet and Stoic philosopher, was a close friend of Seneca, the philosopher-dramatist.

REVIEW QUESTIONS

1. According to Pico della Mirandola, what quality did humans alone possess? What did its possession allow them to do?
2. How does Pico's oration on human dignity exemplify the emergence of the new psychological outlook of the Renaissance?

---

3 Break with Medieval Political Theory

Turning away from the religious orientation of the Middle Ages, Renaissance thinkers discussed the human condition in secular terms and opened up possibilities for thinking about moral and political problems in new ways. Thus, Niccolò Machiavelli (1469–1527), a Florentine statesman and political theorist, broke with medieval political theory. Medieval political thinkers held that the ruler derived power from God and had a religious obligation to rule in accordance with God's precepts. Machiavelli, though, ascribed no divine origin to kingship, nor did he attribute events to the mysterious will of God; and he explicitly rejected the principle that kings should adhere to Christian moral teachings. For Machiavelli, the state was a purely human creation. Successful kings or princes, he asserted, should be concerned only with preserving and strengthening the state's power and must ignore questions of good and evil, morality and immorality. Machiavelli did not assert that religion was supernatural in origin and rejected prevailing belief that Christian morality should guide political life. For him, religion's value derived from other factors: a ruler could utilize religion to unite his subjects and to foster obedience to law.

Niccolò Machiavelli
THE PRINCE

In contrast to medieval thinkers, Machiavelli did not seek to construct an ideal Christian community but to discover how politics was *really* conducted. He studied politics in the cold light of reason, as the following passage from *The Prince* illustrates.

It now remains to be seen what are the methods and rules for a prince as regards his subjects and friends. And as I know that many have written of this, I fear that my writing about it may be deemed presumptuous, differing as I do, especially in this matter, from the opinions of others. But my intention being to write something of use to those who understand, it appears to me more proper to go to the real truth of the matter than to its imagination; and many have imagined republics and principalities which have never been seen or known to exist in reality; for how we live is so far removed from how we ought to live, that he who abandons what is done for what ought to be done, will rather learn to bring about his own ruin than his preservation.

Machiavelli removed ethics from political thinking. A successful ruler, he contended, is indifferent to moral and religious considerations. But will not the prince be punished on the Day of Judgment for violating Christian teachings? In startling contrast to medieval theorists, Machiavelli simply ignored the question. The action of a prince, he said, should be governed solely by necessity.

A man who wishes to make a profession of goodness in everything must necessarily come to grief among so many who are not good. Therefore it is necessary for a prince, who wishes to maintain himself, to learn how not to be good, and to use this knowledge and not use it, according to the necessity of the case.

Leaving on one side, then, those things which concern only an imaginary prince, and speaking of those that are real, I state that all men, and especially princes, who are placed at a greater height, are reputed for certain qualities which bring them either praise or blame. Thus one is considered liberal, another . . . miserly; . . . one a free giver, another rapacious; one cruel, another merciful; one a breaker of his word, another trustworthy; one effeminate and pusillanimous, another fierce and high-spirited; one humane, another haughty; one lascivious, another chaste; one frank, another astute; one hard, another easy; one serious, another frivolous; one religious, another an unbeliever, and so on. I know that every one will admit that it would be highly praiseworthy in a prince to possess all the above-named qualities that are reputed good, but as they cannot all be possessed or observed, human conditions

not permitting of it, it is necessary that he should be prudent enough to avoid the scandal of those vices which would lose him the state, and guard himself if possible against those which will not lose it [for] him, but if not able to, he can indulge them with less scruple. And yet he must not mind incurring the scandal of those vices, without which it would be difficult to save the state, for if one considers well, it will be found that some things which seem virtues would, if followed, lead to one's ruin, and some others which appear vices result in one's greater security and wellbeing. . . .

. . . I say that every prince must desire to be considered merciful and not cruel. He must, however, take care not to misuse this mercifulness. Cesare Borgia was considered cruel, but his cruelty had brought order to the Romagna,[1] united it, and reduced it to peace and fealty. If this is considered well, it will be seen that he was really much more merciful than the Florentine people, who, to avoid the name of cruelty, allowed Pistoia[2] to be destroyed. A prince, therefore, must not mind incurring the charge of cruelty for the purpose of keeping his subjects united and faithful; for, with a very few examples, he will be more merciful than those who, from excess of tenderness, allow disorders to arise, from whence spring bloodshed and rapine; for these as a rule injure the whole community, while the executions carried out by the prince injure only individuals. . . .

---

[1]Cesare Borgia (c. 1476–1507) was the bastard son of Rodrigo Borgia, then a Spanish cardinal, and later Pope Alexander VI (1492–1503). With his father's aid he attempted to carve out for himself an independent duchy in north-central Italy, with Romagna as its heart. Through cruelty, violence, and treachery, he succeeded at first in his ambition, but ultimately his principality collapsed. Romagna was eventually incorporated into the Papal State under Pope Julius II (1503–1513).

[2]Pistoia, a small Italian city in Tuscany, came under the control of Florence in the fourteenth century.

Machiavelli's rigorous investigation of politics led him to view human nature from the standpoint of its limitations and imperfections. The astute prince, he said, recognizes that human beings are by nature selfish, cowardly, and dishonest, and regulates his political strategy accordingly.

From this arises the question whether it is better to be loved more than feared, or feared more than loved. The reply is, that one ought to be both feared and loved, but as it is difficult for the two to go together, it is much safer to be feared than loved, if one of the two has to be wanting. For it may be said of men in general that they are ungrateful, voluble, dissemblers, anxious to avoid danger, and covetous of gain; as long as you benefit them, they are entirely yours; they offer you their blood, their goods, their life, and their children, as I have before said, when the necessity is remote; but when it approaches, they revolt. And the prince who has relied solely on their words, without making other preparations, is ruined; for the friendship which is gained by purchase and not through grandeur and nobility of spirit is bought but not secured, and at a pinch is not to be expended in your service. And men have less scruple in offending one who makes himself loved than one who makes himself feared; for love is held by a chain of obligation which, men being selfish, is broken whenever it serves their purpose; but fear is maintained by a dread of punishment which never fails.

Still, a prince should make himself feared in such a way that if he does not gain love, he at any rate avoids hatred; for fear and the absence of hatred may well go together, and will be always attained by one who abstains from interfering with the property of his citizens and subjects or with their women. And when he is obliged to take the life of any one, let him do so when there is a proper justification and manifest reason for it; but above all he must abstain from taking the property of others, for men forget more easily the death of their father than the loss of their patrimony. Then also pretexts for seizing property are never wanting, and one who begins to live by rapine will always find some reason for taking the goods of others, whereas causes for taking life are rarer and more fleeting.

But when the prince is with his army and has a large number of soldiers under his control, then it is extremely necessary that he should not mind being thought cruel; for without this reputation he could not keep an army united or disposed to any duty. Among the noteworthy actions of Hannibal[3] is numbered this, that although he had an enormous army, composed of men of all nations and fighting in foreign countries, there never arose any dissension either among them or against the prince, either in good fortune or in bad. This could not be due to anything but his inhuman cruelty, which together with his infinite other virtues, made him always venerated and terrible in the sight of his soldiers, and without it his other virtues would not have sufficed to produce that effect. Thoughtless writers admire on the one hand his actions, and on the other blame the principal cause of them. . . .

Again in marked contrast to the teachings of Christian (and ancient) moralists, Machiavelli said that the successful prince will use any means to achieve and sustain political power. If the end is desirable, all means are justified.

How laudable it is for a prince to keep good faith and live with integrity, and not with as-

---

[3]Hannibal (247–182 B.C.) was a brilliant Carthaginian general whose military victories almost destroyed Roman power. He was finally defeated at the battle of Zama in 202 B.C. by the Roman general Scipio Africanus.

tuteness, every one knows. Still the experience of our times shows those princes to have done great things who have had little regard for good faith, and have been able by astuteness to confuse men's brains, and who have ultimately overcome those who have made loyalty their foundation.

You must know, then, that there are two methods of fighting, the one by law, the other by force: the first method is that of men, the second of beasts; but as the first method is often insufficient, one must have recourse to the second. It is therefore necessary for a prince to know well how to use both the beast and the man. . . .

A prince being thus obliged to know well how to act as a beast must imitate the fox and the lion, for the lion cannot protect himself from traps, and the fox cannot defend himself from wolves. One must therefore be a fox to recognise traps, and a lion to frighten wolves. Those that wish to be only lions do not understand this. Therefore, a prudent ruler ought not to keep faith when by so doing it would be against his interest, and when the reasons which made him bind himself no longer exist. If men were all good, this precept would not be a good one; but as they are bad, and would not observe their faith with you, so you are not bound to keep faith with them. Nor have legitimate grounds ever failed a prince who wished to show [plausible] excuse for the non-fulfilment of his promise. Of this one could furnish an infinite number of modern examples, and show how many times peace has been broken, and how many promises rendered worthless, by the faithlessness of princes, and those that have been best able to imitate the fox have succeeded best. But it is necessary to be able to disguise this character well, and to be a great feigner and dissembler; and men are so simple and so ready to obey present necessities, that one who deceives will always find those who allow themselves to be deceived. . . .

. . . Thus it is well to seem merciful, faithful, humane, sincere, religious, and also to be so; but you must have the mind so disposed that when it is needful to be otherwise you may be able to change to the opposite qualities. And it must be understood that a prince, and especially a new prince, cannot observe all those things which are considered good in men, being often obliged, in order to maintain the state, to act against faith, against charity, against humanity, and against religion. And, therefore, he must have a mind disposed to adapt itself according to the wind, and as the variations of fortune dictate, and, as I said before, not deviate from what is good, if possible, but be able to do evil if constrained.

A prince must take great care that nothing goes out of his mouth which is not full of the above-named five qualities, and, to see and hear him, he should seem to be all mercy, faith, integrity, humanity, and religion. And nothing is more necessary than to seem to have this last quality, for men in general judge more by the eyes than by the hands, for every one can see, but very few have to feel. Everybody sees what you appear to be, few feel what you are, and those few will not dare to oppose themselves to the many, who have the majesty of the state to defend them; and in the actions of men, and especially of princes, from which there is no appeal, the end justifies the means. Let a prince therefore aim at conquering and maintaining the state, and the means will always be judged honourable and praised by every one, for the vulgar is always taken by appearances and the issue of the event; and the world consists only of the vulgar, and the few who are not vulgar are isolated when the many have a rallying point in the prince. A certain prince of the present time, whom it is well not to name, never does anything but preach peace and good faith, but he is really a great enemy to both, and either of them, had he observed them, would have lost him state or repuation on many occasions.

REVIEW QUESTIONS

1. In what ways was Niccolò Machiavelli's advice to princes a break from the teachings of medieval political and moral philosophers?
2. What was Machiavelli's view of human nature? How did it influence his political thought?
3. Would Machiavelli's political advice help or hurt a politician in a modern democratic society?

---

4   The Lutheran Reformation

The reformation of the Western Christian church in the sixteenth century was precipitated by Martin Luther (1483–1546). A pious German Augustinian monk and theologian, Luther had no intention of founding a new church or over-throwing the political and ecclesiastical order of late medieval Europe. He was educated in the tradition of the New Devotion, and as a theology professor at the university in Wittenberg, Germany, he opposed rationalistic, scholastic theology. Sympathetic at first to the ideas of Christian humanists like Erasmus, Luther too sought a reform of morals and an end to abusive practices within the church. But a visit to the papal court in Rome in 1510 left him profoundly shocked at its worldliness and disillusioned with the papacy's role in the church's governance.

Martin Luther
ON PAPAL POWER, JUSTIFICATION BY FAITH, THE INTERPRETATION OF THE BIBLE, AND THE NATURE OF THE CLERGY

To finance the rebuilding of St. Peter's church in Rome, the papacy in 1515 of-fered indulgences to those who gave alms for this pious work. An indulgence was a mitigation or remission of the austere penance imposed by a priest in ab-solving a penitent who confessed a sin and indicated remorse. Indulgences were granted by papal decrees for those who agreed to perform some act of charity, almsgiving, prayer, pilgrimage, or other pious work. Some preachers of this particular papal indulgence deceived people into believing that a "purchase" of this indulgence would win them, or even the dead, a secure place in heaven.

In 1517, Luther denounced the abuses connected with the preaching of papal indulgences. The quarrel led quickly to other and more profound theological issues. His opponents defended the use of indulgences on the basis of papal authority, shifting the debate to questions about the nature of papal power within the church. Luther responded with a vigorous attack on the whole system of papal governance. The principal points of his criticism were set out in his *Address to the Christian Nobility of the German Nation Concerning the Reform of the Christian Estate,* published in August 1520. In the first excerpt that follows, Luther argued that the papacy was blocking any reform of the church and appealed to the nobility of Germany to intervene by summoning a "free council" to reform the church.

A central point of contention between Luther and Catholic critics was his theological teaching on justification (salvation) by faith and on the role of good works in the scheme of salvation. Luther had suffered anguish about his unworthiness before God. Then, during a mystical experience, Luther suddenly perceived that his salvation came not because of his good works but as a free gift from God due to Luther's faith in Jesus Christ. Thus, while never denying that a Christian was obliged to perform good works, Luther argued that such pious acts were not helpful in achieving salvation. His claim that salvation or justification was attained through faith in Jesus Christ as Lord and Savior, and through that act of faith alone, became the rallying point of the Protestant reformers.

The Catholic position, not authoritatively clarified until the Council of Trent (1545–1563), argued that justification came not only through faith, but through hope and love as well, obeying God's commandments and doing good works. In *The Freedom of a Christian,* published in 1520, Luther outlined his teaching on justification by faith and on the inefficacy of good works; the second excerpt is from this work.

Another dispute between Luther and papal theologians was the question of interpretation of the Bible. In the medieval church, the final authority in any dispute over the meaning of Scriptural texts or church doctrine was ordinarily the pope alone, speaking as supreme head of the church or in concert with the bishops in an ecumenical council. The doctrine of papal infallibility (that the pope could not err in teaching matters of faith and morals) was already well known, but belief in this doctrine had not been formally required. Luther argued that the literal text of Scripture was alone the foundation of Christian truth, not the teaching of popes or councils. Moreover, Luther denied any special ordination of the clergy to power or authority in the church. He said that all believers were priests, and the clergy did not hold any power beyond that of the laity; therefore the special privileges of the clergy were unjustified. The third excerpt contains Luther's views on the interpretation of Scripture and the nature of priestly offices.

ON PAPAL POWER

The Romanists [traditional Catholics loyal to the papacy] have very cleverly built three walls around themselves. Hitherto they have protected themselves by these walls in such a way that no one has been able to reform them. As a result, the whole of Christendom has fallen abominably.

In the first place, when pressed by the temporal power they have made decrees and declared that the temporal power had no jurisdiction over them, but that, on the contrary, the spiritual power is above the temporal. In the second place, when the attempt is made to reprove them with the Scriptures, they raise the objection that only the pope may interpret the Scriptures. In the third place, if threatened with a council, their story is that no one may summon a council but the pope.

In this way they have cunningly stolen our three rods from us, that they may go unpunished. They have [settled] themselves within the safe stronghold of these three walls so that they can practice all the knavery and wickedness which we see today. Even when they have been compelled to hold a council they have weakened its power in advance by putting the princes under oath to let them remain as they were. In addition, they have given the pope full authority over all decisions of a council, so that it is all the same whether there are many councils or no councils. They only deceive us with puppet shows and sham fights. They fear terribly for their skin in a really free council! They have so intimidated kings and princes with this technique that they believe it would be an offense against God not to be obedient to the Romanists in all their knavish and ghoulish deceits. . . .

The Romanists have no basis in Scripture for their claim that the pope alone has the right to call or confirm a council. This is just their own ruling, and it is only valid as long as it is not harmful to Christendom or contrary to the laws of God. Now when the pope deserves punishment, this ruling no longer obtains, for not to punish him by authority of a council is harmful to Christendom. . . .

Therefore, when necessity demands it, and the pope is an offense to Christendom, the first man who is able should, as a true member of the whole body, do what he can to bring about a truly free council. No one can do this so well as the temporal authorities, especially since they are also fellow-Christians, fellow-priests, fellow-members of the spiritual estate, fellow-lords over all things. Whenever it is necessary or profitable they ought to exercise the office and work which they have received from God over everyone.

JUSTIFICATION BY FAITH

You may ask, "What then is the Word of God, and how shall it be used, since there are so many words of God?" I answer: The Apostle explains this in Romans 1. The Word is the gospel of God concerning his Son, who was made flesh, suffered, rose from the dead, and was glorified through the Spirit who sanctifies. To preach Christ means to feed the soul, make it righteous, set it free, and save it, provided it believes the preaching. Faith alone is the saving and efficacious use of the Word of God, according to Rom. 10 (:9): "If you confess with your lips that Jesus is Lord and believe in your heart that God raised him from the dead, you will be saved." Furthermore, "Christ is the end of the law, that every one who has faith may be justified" (Rom. 10:4). Again, in Rom. 1 (:17), "He who through faith is righteous shall live." The Word of God cannot be received and cherished by any works whatever but only by faith. Therefore it is clear that, as the soul needs only the Word of God for its life and righteousness, so it is justified by faith alone and not any works; for if it could be justified by anything else, it would not need the Word, and consequently it would not need faith.

This faith cannot exist in connection with works—that is to say, if you at the same time claim to be justified by works, whatever their character—for that would be the same as "limping with two different opinions" (I Kings 18:21), as worshipping Baal and kissing one's own hand (Job 31:27–28), which, as Job says, is a very great iniquity. Therefore the moment you begin to have faith you learn that all things in you are altogether blameworthy, sinful, and damnable, as the Apostle says in Rom. 3 (:23), "Since all have sinned and fall short of the glory of God," and, "None is righteous, no, not one; . . . all have turned aside, together they have gone wrong" (Rom. 3:10–12). When you have learned this you will know that you need Christ, who suffered and rose again for you so that, if you believe in him, you may through this faith become a new man in so far as your sins are forgiven and you are justified by the merits of another, namely, of Christ alone.

Since, therefore, this faith can rule only in the inner man, as Rom. 10 (:10) says, "For man believes with his heart and so is justified," and since faith alone justifies, it is clear that the inner man cannot be justified, freed, or saved by any outer work or action at all, and that these works, whatever their character, have nothing to do with this inner man. On the other hand, only ungodliness and unbelief of heart, and no outer work, make him guilty and a damnable servant of sin. Wherefore it ought to be the first concern of every Christian to lay aside all confidence in works and increasingly to strengthen faith alone and through faith to grow in the knowledge, not of works, but of Christ Jesus, who suffered and rose for him, as Peter teaches in the last chapter of his first Epistle (I Pet. 5:10). No other work makes a Christian. . . .

Our faith in Christ does not free us from works but from false opinions concerning works, that is, from the foolish presumption that justification is acquired by works. Faith redeems, corrects, and preserves our consciences so that we know that righteousness does not consist in works, although works neither can nor ought to be wanting; just as we cannot be without food and drink and all the works of this mortal body, yet our righteousness is not in them, but in faith; and yet those works of the body are not to be despised or neglected on that account. In this world we are bound by the needs of our bodily life, but we are not righteous because of them. "My kingship is not of this world" (John 18:36), says Christ. He does not, however, say, "My kingship is not here, that is, in this world." And Paul says, "Though we live in the world we are not carrying on a worldly war" (II Cor. 10:3), and in Gal. 2 (:20), "The life I now live in the flesh I live by faith in the Son of God." Thus what we do, live, and are in works and ceremonies, we do because of the necessities of this life and of the effort to rule our body. Nevertheless we are righteous, not in these, but in the faith of the Son of God.

THE INTERPRETATION OF THE BIBLE AND THE NATURE OF THE CLERGY

They (the Roman Catholic Popes) want to be the only masters of Scriptures. . . . They assume sole authority for themselves and would persuade us with insolent juggling of words that the Pope, whether he be bad or good, cannot err in matters of faith. . . .

. . . They cannot produce a letter to prove that the interpretation of Scripture . . . belongs to the Pope alone. They themselves have usurped this power . . . and though they allege that this power was conferred on Peter when the keys were given to him, it is plain enough that the keys were not given to Peter alone but to the entire body of Christians (Matt. 16:19; 18:18). . . .

. . . Every baptized Christian is a priest already, not by appointment or ordination from the Pope or any other man, but because Christ Himself has begotten him as a priest . . . in baptism. . . .

The Pope has usurped the term "priest" for his anointed and tonsured hordes [clergy and monks]. By this means they have separated themselves from the ordinary Christians and have called themselves uniquely the "clergy of God," God's heritage and chosen people who must help other Christians by their sacrifice and worship. . . . Therefore the Pope argues that he alone has the right and power to ordain and do what he will. . . .

[But] the preaching office is no more than a public service which happens to be conferred on someone by the entire congregation all the members of which are priests. . . .

. . . The fact that a pope or bishop anoints, makes tonsures, ordains, consecrates [makes holy], and prescribes garb different from those of the laity . . . nevermore makes a Christian and a spiritual man. Accordingly, through baptism all of us are consecrated to the priesthood, as St. Peter says. . . . (I Peter 2:9).

To make it still clearer, if a small group of pious Christian laymen were taken captive and settled in a wilderness and had among them no priest consecrated by a bishop, if they were to agree to choose one from their midst, married or unmarried, and were to charge him with the office of baptizing, saying Mass, absolving [forgiving of sins], and preaching, such a man would be as truly a priest as he would if all bishops and popes had consecrated him.

REVIEW QUESTIONS

1. Why did Martin Luther see the papacy as the crucial block to any meaningful reform of the church?
2. How did Luther's teaching undermine the power of the clergy and traditional forms of piety?

---

5 Justification of Absolute Monarchy by Divine Right

Effectively blocking royal absolutism in the Middle Ages were the dispersion of power between kings and feudal lords, the vigorous sense of personal freedom and urban autonomy of the townspeople, and the limitations on royal power imposed by the church. However, by the late sixteenth century, monarchs were asserting their authority over competing groups with ever-greater effectiveness. In this new balance of political forces, European kings acted out their claim to absolute power as monarchs chosen by and responsible to God alone. This theory, called the divine right of kings, became the dominant political ideology of seventeenth- and eighteenth-century Europe.

James I
TRUE LAW OF FREE MONARCHIES
AND A SPEECH TO PARLIAMENT

One of the most articulate defenders of the divine right of monarchy was James VI, who was king of Scotland (1567–1625) and as James I (1603–1625) also was king of England. A scholar as well as a king, James in 1598 anonymously published a widely read book called the *True Law of Free Monarchies.* He claimed that the king alone was the true legislator. James's notions of the royal prerogative and of the role of Parliament are detailed in the following passages from the *True Law* and a speech to Parliament.

TRUE LAW
Prerogative and Parliament

According to these fundamental laws already alleged, we daily see that in the parliament (which is nothing else but the head court of the king and his vassals) the laws are but craved by his subjects, and only made by him at their [proposal] and with their advice: for albeit the king make daily statutes and ordinances, [imposing] such pains thereto as he thinks [fit], without any advice of parliament or estates, yet it lies in the power of no parliament to make any kind of law or statute, without his sceptre [that is, authority] be to it, for giving it the force of a law. . . . And as ye see it manifest that the king is over-lord of the whole land, so is he master over every person that inhabiteth the same, having power over the life and death of every one of them: for although a just prince will not take the life of any of his subjects without a clear law, yet the same laws whereby he taketh them are made by himself or his predecessors; and so the power flows always from himself. . . . Where he sees the law doubtsome or rigorous, he may interpret or mitigate the same, lest otherwise *summum jus* be *summa injuria* [the greatest right be the greatest wrong]: and therefore general laws made publicly in parliament may upon . . . [the king's] authority be mitigated and suspended upon causes only known to him.

As likewise, although I have said a good king will frame all his actions to be according to the law, yet is he not bound thereto but of his good will, and for good example-giving to his subjects. . . . So as I have already said, a good king, though he be above the law, will subject and frame his actions thereto, for example's sake to his subjects, and of his own free will, but not as subject or bound thereto. . . .

In a speech before the English Parliament in March 1610, James elaborated on his exalted theory of the monarch's absolute power.

A SPEECH TO PARLIAMENT

. . . The state of monarchy is the supremest thing upon earth: for kings are not only God's lieutenants upon earth and sit upon God's throne, but even by God himself they are called gods. There be three principal [comparisons] that illustrate the state of monarchy: one taken out of the word of God, and the two other out of the grounds of policy and philosophy. In the Scriptures kings are called gods, and so their power after a certain relation compared to the Divine power. Kings are also compared to fathers of families: for a king is truly *parens patriae* [parent of the country], the politic father of his people. And lastly, kings are compared to the head of this microcosm of the body of man. . . .

I conclude then this point touching the power of kings with this axiom of divinity, That as to dispute what God may do is blasphemy, . . . so it is sedition in subjects to dispute what a king may do in the height of his power. But just kings will ever be willing to declare what they will do, if they will not incur the curse of God. I will not be content that my power be disputed upon; but I shall ever be willing to make the reason appear of all my doings, and rule my actions according to my laws. . . .

Now the second general ground whereof I am to speak concerns the matter of grievances. . . . First then, I am not to find fault that you inform yourselves of the particular just grievances of the people; nay I must tell you, ye can neither be just nor faithful to me or to your countries that trust and employ you, if you do it not.

. . . But I would wish you to be careful to avoid [these] things in the matter of grievances.

First, that you do not meddle with the main points of government: that is my craft . . . to meddle with that, were to lesson me. I am now an old king . . .;

I must not be taught my office.

Secondly, I would not have you meddle with such ancient rights of mine as I have received from my predecessors, possessing them *more majorum* [as ancestral customs]: such things I would be sorry should be accounted for grievances. All novelties are dangerous as well in a politic as in a natural body: and therefore I would be loath to be quarrelled in my ancient rights and possessions: for that were to judge me unworthy of that which my predecessors had and left me.

REVIEW QUESTIONS

1. What was the theory of kingship by divine authority embraced by King James I of England?
2. What was the proper role of Parliament, according to James I?

---

6   A Secular Defense of Absolutism

Thomas Hobbes (1588–1679), a British philosopher and political theorist, witnessed the agonies of the English civil war, including the execution of Charles I in 1649. These developments fortified Hobbes's conviction that absolutism was the most desirable and logical form of government. Only the unlimited power of a sovereign, said Hobbes, could contain human passions that disrupt the social order and threaten civilized life; only absolute rule could provide an environment secure enough for people to pursue their individual interests.

Leviathan (1651), Hobbes's principal work of political thought, broke with medieval political theory. Medieval thinkers assigned each group of people—clergy, lords, serfs, guildsmen—a place in a fixed social order; an individual's social duties were set by ancient traditions believed to have been ordained by God. During early modern times, the great expansion of commerce and capitalism spurred the new individualism already pronounced in Renaissance culture; group ties were shattered by competition and accelerating social mobility. Hobbes gave expression to a society where people confronted each other as competing individuals.

Thomas Hobbes
LEVIATHAN

Hobbes was influenced by the new scientific thought that saw mathematical knowledge as the avenue to truth. Using geometry as a model, Hobbes began with what he believed were self-evident axioms regarding human nature, from which he deduced other truths. He aimed at constructing political philosophy on a scientific foundation and rejected the authority of tradition and religion as inconsistent with a science of politics. Thus, although Hobbes supported absolutism, he dismissed the idea advanced by other theorists of absolutism that the monarch's power derived from God. He also rejected the idea that the state should not be obeyed when it violated God's law. *Leviathan* is a rational and secular political statement. In this modern approach, rather than in Hobbes's justification of absolutism, lies the work's significance.

Hobbes had a pessimistic view of human nature. Believing that people are innately selfish and grasping, he maintained that competition and dissension, rather than cooperation, characterize human relations. Even when reason teaches that cooperation is more advantageous than competition, Hobbes observed that people are reluctant to alter their ways, because passion, not reason, governs their behavior. In the following passages from *Leviathan,* Hobbes described the causes of human conflicts.

Nature hath made men so equall, in the faculties of body, and mind; as that though there bee found one man sometimes manifestly stronger in body, or of quicker mind than another; yet when all is reckoned together, the difference between man, and man, is not so considerable, as that one man can thereupon claim to himselfe any benefit, to which another may not pretend, as well as he. For as to the strength of body, the weakest has strength enough to kill the strongest, either by secret machination, or by confederacy with others, that are in the same danger with himselfe. . . .

And so as to the faculties of the mind . . . men are . . . [more] equall than unequall. . . .

From this equality of ability, ariseth equality of hope in the attaining of our Ends. And therefore if any two men desire the same thing, which neverthelesse they cannot both enjoy, they become enemies; and in the way to their End, . . . endeavour to destroy, or subdue one another. . . . If one plant, sow, build, or possesse a convenient Seat, others may probably be expected to come prepared with forces united, to dispossesse, and deprive him, not only of the fruit of his labour, but also of his life, or liberty. . . .

So that in the nature of man, we find three principall causes of quarrell. First, Competition; Secondly, Diffidence; Thirdly, Glory.

The first, maketh men invade for Gain; the second, for Safety; and the third, for Reputation. The first use Violence, to make themselves Masters of other men's persons, wives, children, and cattell; the second, to defend them; the third, for trifles, as a word, a smile, a different opinion, and any other signe of undervalue, either direct in their Persons, or by reflexion in their Kindred, their Friends, their Nation, their Profession, or their Name.

Hereby it is manifest, that during the time men live without a common Power to keep them all in awe, they are in that condition which is called Warre; and such a warre, as is of every man, against every man. . . .

Hobbes then described a state of nature—the hypothetical condition of humanity prior to the formation of the state—as a war of all against all. For Hobbes, the state of nature is a logical abstraction, a device employed to make his point. Only a strong ruling entity—the state—will end the perpetual strife and provide security. For

Hobbes, the state is merely a useful arrangement that permits individuals to exchange goods and services in a secure environment. The ruling authority in the state, the sovereign, must have supreme power, or society will collapse and the anarchy of the state of nature will return.

Whatsoever therefore is consequent to a time of Warre, where every man is Enemy to every man; the same is consequent to the time, wherein men live without other security, than what their own strength, and their own invention shall furnish them withall. In such condition, there is no place for Industry; because the fruit thereof is uncertain: and consequently no Culture of the Earth; no Navigation, nor use of the commodities that may be imported by Sea; no commodious Building; no Instruments of moving, and removing such things as require much force; no Knowledge of the face of the Earth; no account of Time; no Arts; no Letters; no Society; and which is worst of all, continuall feare, and danger of violent death; And the life of man, solitary, poore, nasty, brutish, and short. . . .

The Passions that encline men to Peace, are Feare of Death; Desire of such things as are necessary to commodious living; and a Hope by their Industry to obtain them. And Reason suggesteth convenient Articles of Peace, upon which men may be drawn to agreement. . . .

And because the condition of Man, (as hath been declared in the precedent Chapter) is a condition of Warre of every one against every one; in which case every one is governed by his own Reason; and there is nothing he can make use of, that may not be a help unto him, in preserving his life against his enemyes; It followeth, that in such a condition, every man has a Right to every thing; even to one another's body. And therefore, as long as this naturall Right of every man to every thing endureth, there can be no security to any man, (how strong or wise soever he be,) of living out the

time, which Nature ordinarily alloweth men to live. . . .

. . . If there be no Power erected, or not great enough for our security; every man will and may lawfully rely on his own strength and art, for caution against all other men. . . .

The only way to erect . . . a Common Power, as may be able to defend them from the invasion of [foreigners] and the injuries of one another, and thereby to secure them in such sort, as that by their owne industrie, and by the fruites of the Earth, they may nourish themselves and live contentedly; is, to conferre all their power and strength upon one Man, or upon one Assembly of men, that may reduce all their Wills, by plurality of voices, unto one Will . . . and therein to submit their Wills, every one to his Will, and their Judgements, to his Judgement. This is more than Consent, or Concord; it is a reall Unitie of them all, in one and the same Person, made by Covenant of every man with every man, in such manner, as if every man should say to every man, *I Authorise and give up my Right of Governing my selfe, to this Man, or to this Assembly of men, on this condition, that thou give up thy Right to him, and Authorise all his Actions in like manner.* This done, the Multitude so united in one Person, is called a COMMON-WEALTH. . . . For by this Authoritie, given him by every particular man in the Common-wealth, he hath the use of so much Power and Strength . . . conferred on him, that by terror thereof, he is inabled to forme the wills of them all, to Peace at home, and mutuall [aid] against their enemies abroad. And in him consisteth the Essence of the Common-wealth; which (to define it), is *One Person, of whose Acts a great Multitude, by mutuall Covenants one with another, have made themselves every one the Author, to the end he may use the strength and means of them all, as he shall think expedient, for their Peace and Common Defence.*

And he that carryeth this Person, is called SOVERAIGNE, and said to have *Soveraigne Power;* and every one besides, his SUBJECT. . . .

. . . They that have already Instituted a Common-wealth, being thereby bound by Covenant . . . cannot lawfully make a new Covenant, amongst themselves, to be obedient to any other, in any thing whatsoever, without his permission. And therefore, they that are subjects to a Monarch, cannot without his leave cast off Monarchy, and return to the confusion of a disunited Multitude; nor transferre their Person from him that beareth it, to another Man, or other Assembly of men: for they . . . are bound, every man to every man, to [acknowledge] . . . that he that already is their Soveraigne, shall do, and judge fit to be done; so that [those who do not obey] break their Covenant made to that man, which is injustice: and they have also every man given the Soveraignty to him that beareth their Person; and therefore if they depose him, they take from him that which is his own, and so again it is injustice. . . . And whereas some men have pretended for their disobedience to their Soveraign, a new Covenant, made, not with men, but with God; this also is unjust: for there is no Covenant with God, but by mediation of some body that representeth God's Person; which none doth but God's Lieutenant, who hath the Soveraignty under God. But this pretence of Covenant with God, is so evident a [lie], even in the pretender's own consciences, that it is not onely an act of an unjust, but also of a vile, and unmanly disposition. . . .

. . . Consequently none of [the sovereign's] Subjects, by any pretence of forfeiture, can be freed from his Subjection.

REVIEW QUESTIONS

1. What was Thomas Hobbes's view of human nature and what conclusions did he draw from it about the best form of government?
2. What has been the political legacy of Hobbes's notion of the state?

7 The Triumph of Constitutional Monarchy in England: The Glorious Revolution

The struggle against absolute monarchy in England during the early seventeenth century reached a climax during the reign of Charles I (1625–1649). The king's failure to support the Protestant cause during the Thirty Years' War (1618–1648) on the Continent and his fervent support of the Anglican Episcopal Church earned him many enemies. Among them were the Puritans, Presbyterians, and Independents (Congregationalists), who composed an influential minority in his early Parliaments. Faced with rising costs of government, the king tried to obtain more revenues by vote of Parliament, but the parliamentarians refused to consent to new taxes unless the king followed policies they supported. After four bitter years of controversy, the king dismissed Parliament in 1629. He ruled in an increasingly absolutist manner without calling a new Parliament for the next eleven years and levied many taxes without the consent of the people's representatives.

Charles's policies collapsed in 1640 when he was compelled to summon Parliament to raise money for an army to put down a rebellion of Scottish Presbyterians. The new Parliament set forth demands for reforms of church and state, which the king refused. He claimed monarchical power and policies to be unlimited by parliamentary controls or consent.

Parliament raised its own army as civil war broke out between its supporters and those of the king. The parties were divided not only on constitutional issues but also by religious differences. Most of the Puritans, Presbyterians, and Independents supported the parliamentary cause; Anglicans and Catholics were overwhelmingly royalist. Captured by the Scottish Presbyterian rebels in 1646 and turned over to the English parliamentary army in 1647, Charles was held prisoner for two years until the Puritan parliamentary general Oliver Cromwell (1599–1658) decided to put him on trial for treason. The king was found guilty and executed in 1649.

The revolutionary parliamentary regime evolved into a military dictatorship headed by Cromwell. After Cromwell's death, Parliament restored the monarchy in 1660 and invited the late king's heir to end his exile and take the throne. Charles II (1660–1685), by discretion and skilled statesmanship, managed to avoid a major confrontation with Parliament. When his brother James II (1685–1688), a staunch Catholic, succeeded to the throne, the hostility between Parliament and monarchy mounted. Parliament feared that James II aimed to impose Catholicism and absolutism on England.

When the king's wife gave birth to a son, making the heir to the throne another Catholic, almost all factions (except the Catholics) abandoned James II and invited the Dutch Protestant Prince William of Orange and his wife Mary, James II's Protestant daughter, to come to England. James and his Catholic family and friends fled to France. Parliament declared the throne vacant and offered it to William and Mary as joint sovereigns. As a result of the bloodless "Glorious Revolution," the English monarchy became clearly limited by the will of Parliament.

THE ENGLISH DECLARATION OF RIGHTS

In depriving James II of the throne, Parliament had destroyed forever in Britain the theory of divine right as an operating principle of government and had firmly established a limited constitutional monarchy. The appointment of William and Mary was accompanied by a declaration of rights (later enacted as the Bill of Rights), which enumerated and declared illegal James II's arbitrary acts. The Declaration of Rights, excerpted below, compelled William and Mary and future monarchs to recognize the right of the people's representatives to dispose of the royal office and to set limits on its powers. These rights were subsequently formulated into laws passed by Parliament. Prior to the American Revolution, colonists protested that British actions in the American colonies violated certain rights guaranteed in the English Bill of Rights. Several of these rights were later included in the Constitution of the United States.

And whereas the said late king James the Second having abdicated the government and the throne being thereby vacant, His Highness the prince of Orange (whom it hath pleased Almighty God to make the glorious instrument of delivering this kingdom from popery and arbitrary power) did (by the advice of the lords spiritual and temporal and divers principal persons of the commons)[1] cause letters to be written to the lords spiritual and temporal, being Protestants; and other letters to the several counties, cities, universities, boroughs and Cinque ports[2] for the choosing of such persons to represent them, as were of right to be sent to parliament, to meet and sit at Westminster upon the two and twentieth day of January in this year one thousand six hundred eighty and eight,[3] in order to [guarantee] . . . that their religion, laws and liberties might not again be in danger of being subverted; upon which letters elections having been accordingly made,

And thereupon the said lords spiritual and temporal and commons pursuant to their respective letters and elections being now assembled in a full and free representative of this nation, taking into their most serious consideration the best means for attaining the ends aforesaid, do in the first place (as their ancestors in like case have usually done) for the vindicating and asserting their ancient rights and liberties, declare:

That the pretended power of suspending of laws or the execution of laws by regal authority without consent of parliament is illegal.

That the pretended power of dispensing with laws or the execution of laws by regal authority as it hath been assumed and exercised of late is illegal.

That the commission for erecting the late court of commissioners for ecclesiastical causes and all other commissions and courts of like nature are illegal and pernicious.

That the levying money for or to the use of the crown by pretence of prerogative without grant of parliament for a longer time or in other manner than the same is or shall be granted is illegal.

That it is the right of the subjects to petition the king and all commitments and prosecutions for such petitioning are illegal.

That the raising or keeping a standing army within the kingdom in time of peace unless it be with consent of parliament is against law.

That the subjects which are Protestants may have arms for their defence suitable to their conditions and as allowed by law.

That election of members of parliament ought to be free.

That the freedom of speech and debates or proceedings in parliament ought not to be impeached or questioned in any court or place out of parliament.

That excessive bail ought not to be required nor excessive fines imposed nor cruel and unusual punishments inflicted.

That jurors ought to be duly impanelled and returned and jurors which pass upon men in trials for high treason ought to be freeholders.

---

[1]The lords spiritual refers to the bishops of the Church of England who sat in the House of Lords, and the lords temporal refers to the nobility entitled to sit in the House of Lords. The commons refers to the elected representatives in the House of Commons.

[2]The Cinque ports along England's southeastern coast (originally five in number) enjoyed special privileges because of their military duties in providing for coastal defense.

[3]The year was in fact 1689 because until 1752, the English used March 25 as the beginning of the new year.

That all grants and promises of fines and forfeitures of particular persons before conviction are illegal and void.

And that for redress of all grievances and for the amending, strengthening and preserving of the laws parliaments ought to be held frequently.

And they do claim, demand and insist upon all and singular the premises as their undoubted rights and liberties and that no declarations, judgments, doings or proceedings to the prejudice of the people in any of the said premises ought in any wise to be drawn hereafter into consequence or example.

REVIEW QUESTIONS

1. How did the Declaration of Rights limit royal authority? With what result?
2. In what ways did the Glorious Revolution influence the American rebellion in the 1770s?

CHAPTER 2

The Scientific Revolution

GALILEO IN VENICE demonstrating the satellites of Jupiter through his telescope. *(Stock Montage)*

The Scientific Revolution of the sixteenth and seventeenth centuries replaced the medieval view of the universe with a new cosmology and produced a new way of investigating nature. It overthrew the medieval conception of nature as a hierarchical order ascending toward a realm of perfection. Rejecting reliance on authority, the thinkers of the Scientific Revolution affirmed the individual's ability to know the natural world through the method of mathematical reasoning, the direct observation of nature, and carefully controlled experiments.

The medieval view of the universe had blended the theories of Aristotle and Ptolemy, two ancient Greek thinkers, with Christian teachings. In that view, a stationary earth stood in the center of the universe just above hell. Revolving around the earth were seven planets: the moon, Mercury, Venus, the sun, Mars, Jupiter, and Saturn. Because people believed that earth did not move, it was not considered a planet. Each planet was attached to a transparent sphere that turned around the earth. Encompassing the universe was a sphere of fixed stars; beyond the stars lay three heavenly spheres, the outermost of which was the abode of God. An earth-centered universe accorded with the Christian idea that God had created the universe for men and women and that salvation was the aim of life.

Also agreeable to the medieval Christian view was Aristotle's division of the universe into a lower, earthly realm and a higher realm beyond the moon. Two sets of laws operated in the universe, one on earth and the other in the celestial realm. Earthly objects were composed of four elements: earth, water, fire, and air; celestial objects were composed of the divine ether—a substance too pure, too clear, too fine, too spiritual to be found on earth. Celestial objects naturally moved in perfectly circular orbits around the earth; earthly objects, composed mainly of the heavy elements of earth and water, naturally fell downward, whereas objects made of the lighter elements of air and fire naturally flew upward toward the sky.

The destruction of the medieval world picture began with the publication in 1543 of *On the Revolutions of the Heavenly Spheres,* by Nicolaus Copernicus, a Polish mathematician, astronomer, and clergyman. In Copernicus's system, the sun was in the center of the universe, and the earth was another planet that moved around the sun. Most thinkers of the time, committed to the Aristotelian-Ptolemaic system and to the biblical statements that seemed to support it, rejected Copernicus's conclusions.

The work of Galileo Galilei, an Italian mathematician, astronomer, and physicist, was decisive in the shattering of the medieval cosmos and the shaping of the modern scientific outlook. Galileo advanced the modern view that knowledge of nature derives from direct observation and from mathematics. For Galileo, the universe was a "grand book which . . . is written in the language of mathematics, and its characters are triangles, circles, and other geometric figures without which it is humanly impossible to understand a single word of it." Galileo also pioneered experimental physics, advanced the modern idea that nature is uniform throughout the universe, and attacked reliance on scholastic authority rather than on experimentation in resolving scientific controversies.

Johannes Kepler (1571–1630), a contemporary of Galileo, discovered three laws of planetary motion that greatly advanced astronomical knowledge. Kepler showed that the path of a planet was an ellipse, not a circle as Ptolemy (and Copernicus) had believed, and that planets do not move at uniform speed but accelerate as they near the sun. He devised formulas to calculate accurately both a planet's speed at each point in its orbit around the sun and a planet's location at a particular time. Kepler's laws provided further evidence that Copernicus had been right, for they made sense only in a sun-centered universe, but Kepler could not explain why planets stayed in their orbits rather than flying off into space or crashing into the sun. The resolution of that question was left to Sir Isaac Newton.

Newton's great achievement was integrating the findings of Copernicus, Galileo, and Kepler into a single theoretical system. In *Principia Mathematica* (1687), he formulated the mechanical laws of motion and attraction that govern celestial and terrestrial objects.

The creation of a new model of the universe was one great achievement of the Scientific Revolution; another accomplishment was the formulation of the scientific method. The scientific method encompasses two approaches to knowledge, which usually complement each other: the empirical (inductive) and the rational (deductive). Although all sciences use both approaches, the inductive method is generally more applicable in such descriptive sciences as biology, anatomy, and geology, which rely on the accumulation of data. In the inductive approach, general principles are derived from analyzing external experiences—observations and the results of experiments. In the deductive approach, used in mathematics and theoretical physics, truths are derived in successive steps from indubitable axioms. Whereas the inductive method builds its concepts from an analysis of sense experience, the deductive approach constructs its ideas from self-evident principles that are conceived by the mind itself without external experience. The deductive and inductive approaches to knowledge, and their interplay, have been a constantly recurring feature in Western intellectual history since the rationalism of Plato and the empiricism of Aristotle. The success of the scientific method in modern times arose from the skillful synchronization of induction and deduction by such giants as Leonardo, Copernicus, Kepler, Galileo, and Newton.

The Scientific Revolution was instrumental in shaping the modern outlook. It destroyed the medieval conception of the universe and established the scientific method as the means for investigating nature and acquiring knowledge, even in areas having little to do with the study of the physical world. By demonstrating the powers of the human mind, the Scientific Revolution gave thinkers great confidence in reason and led eventually to a rejection of traditional beliefs in magic, astrology, and witches. In the eighteenth century, this growing skepticism led thinkers to question miracles and other Christian beliefs that seemed contrary to reason.

1   The Copernican Revolution

In proclaiming that the earth was not stationary but revolved around the sun, Nicolaus Copernicus (1473–1543) revolutionized the science of astronomy. Fearing controversy and scorn, Copernicus long refused to publish his great work, *On the Revolutions of the Heavenly Spheres.* However, persuaded by friends, he finally relented and permitted publication; a copy of his book reached him on his deathbed. As Copernicus anticipated, his ideas aroused the ire of many thinkers.

Both Catholic and Protestant philosophers and theologians, including Martin Luther, attacked Copernicus for contradicting the Bible and Aristotle and Ptolemy, and they raised several specific objections. First, certain passages in the Bible imply a stationary earth and a sun that moves (for example, Psalm 93 says, "Yea, the world is established; it shall never be moved"; and in attacking Copernicus, Luther pointed out that "sacred Scripture tells us that Joshua commanded the sun to stand still, and not the earth"). Second, a body as heavy as the earth cannot move through space at such speed as Copernicus suggested. Third, if the earth spins on its axis, why does a stone dropped from a height land directly below instead of at a point behind where it was dropped? Fourth, if the earth moved, objects would fly off it. And finally, the moon cannot orbit both the earth and the sun at the same time.

Nicolaus Copernicus
ON THE REVOLUTIONS OF THE HEAVENLY SPHERES

On the Revolutions of the Heavenly Spheres was dedicated to Pope Paul III, whom Copernicus asked to protect him from vilification. In the dedication, Copernicus explains his reason for delaying publication of *Revolutions.*

To His Holiness, Pope Paul III, Nicholas Copernicus' Preface to His Books on the Revolutions

I can readily imagine, Holy Father, that as soon as some people hear that in this volume, which I have written about the revolutions of the spheres of the universe, I ascribe certain motions to the terrestrial globe, they will shout that I must be immediately repudiated together with this belief. For I am not so enamored of my own opinions that I disregard what others may think of them. I am aware that a philosopher's ideas are not subject to the judgement of ordinary persons, because it is his endeavor to seek the truth in all things, to the extent permitted to human reason by God. Yet I hold that completely erroneous views should be shunned. Those who know that the consensus of many centuries has sanctioned the conception that the earth remains at rest in the middle of the heaven as its center would, I reflected, regard it as an insane pronouncement if I made the opposite assertion that the earth moves. Therefore I debated with myself for a long time whether to publish the volume which I wrote to prove the earth's motion or rather to follow the example of the Pythagoreans[1] and certain others, who used to transmit philosophy's secrets only to kinsmen and friends, not in writing but by word of mouth. . . . And they did so, it seems to me, not, as some suppose, because they were in some way jealous about their teachings, which would be spread around; on the contrary, they wanted the very beautiful thoughts attained by great men of deep devotion not to be ridiculed by those who are reluctant to exert themselves vigorously in any literary pursuit unless it is lucrative; or if they are stimulated to the nonacquisitive study of philosophy by the exhortation and example of others, yet because of their dullness of mind they play the same part among philosophers as drones among bees. When I weighed these considerations, the scorn which I had reason to fear on account of the novelty and unconventionality of my opinion almost induced me to abandon completely the work which I had undertaken.

But while I hesitated for a long time and even resisted, my friends [encouraged me]. . . .

Foremost among them was the cardinal of Capua [a city in southern Italy], Nicholas Schönberg, renowned in every field of learning. Next to him was a man who loves me dearly, Tiedemann Giese, bishop of Chelmno [a city in northern Poland], a close student of sacred letters as well as of all good literature. For he repeatedly encouraged me and, sometimes adding reproaches, urgently requested me to publish this volume and finally permit it to appear after being buried among my papers and lying concealed not merely until the ninth year[2] but by now the fourth period of nine years. The same conduct was recommended to me by not a few other very eminent scholars. They exhorted me no longer to refuse, on account of the fear which I felt, to make my work available for the general use of students of astronomy. The crazier my doctrine of the earth's motion now appeared to most people, the argument ran, so much the more admiration and thanks would it gain after they saw the publication of my writings dispel the fog of absurdity by most luminous proofs. Influenced therefore by these persuasive men and by this hope, in the end I allowed my friends to bring out an edition of the volume, as they had long besought me to do. . . .

But you [your Holiness] are rather waiting to hear from me how it occurred to me to venture to conceive any motion of the earth, against the traditional opinion of astronomers and almost against common sense. . . . [Copernicus then describes some of the problems connected with the Ptolemaic system.]

For a long time, then, I reflected on this confusion in the astronomical traditions concerning the derivation of the motions of the universe's spheres. I began to be annoyed that the movements of the world machine, created for our sake by the best and most systematic

[1]Pythagoreans were followers of Pythagoras, a Greek mathematician and philosopher of the sixth century B.C.; they were particularly interested in cosmology.

[2]The Roman poet Horace, who lived in the first century B.C., suggested in *Ars Poetica* that writers should keep a new manuscript in a cupboard "until the ninth year" before publishing it. Only then, he argued, would they have enough objectivity to judge its value. Copernicus is referring to this famous piece of advice.

Artisan of all [God], were not understood with greater certainty by the philosophers, who otherwise examined so precisely the most insignificant trifles of this world. For this reason I undertook the task of rereading the works of all the philosophers which I could obtain to learn whether anyone had ever proposed other motions of the universe's spheres than those expounded by the teachers of astronomy in the schools. And in fact first I found in Cicero that Hicetas supposed the earth to move. Later I also discovered in Plutarch[3] that certain others were of this opinion. . . .

Therefore, having obtained the opportunity from these sources, I too began to consider the mobility of the earth. . . . I thought that I too would be readily permitted to ascertain whether explanations sounder than those of my predecessors could be found for the revolution of the celestial spheres on the assumption of some motion of the earth.

Having thus assumed the motions which I ascribe to the earth later on in the volume, by long and intense study I finally found that if the motions of the other planets are correlated with the orbiting of the earth, and are computed for the revolution of each planet, not only do their phenomena follow therefrom but also the order and size of all the planets and spheres, and heaven itself is so linked together that in no portion of it can anything be shifted without disrupting the remaining parts and the universe as a whole. Accordingly in the arrangement of the volume too I have adopted the following order. In the first book I set forth the entire distribution of the spheres together with the motions which I attribute to the earth, so that this book contains, as it were, the general structure of the universe. Then in the remaining books I correlate the motions

of the other planets and of all the spheres with the movement of the earth so that I may thereby determine to what extent the motions and appearances of the other planets and spheres can be saved if they are correlated with the earth's motions. I have no doubt that acute and learned astronomers will agree with me if, as this discipline especially requires, they are willing to examine and consider, not superficially but thoroughly, what I adduce in this volume in proof of these matters. However, in order that the educated and uneducated alike may see that I do not run away from the judgement of anybody at all, I have preferred dedicating my studies to Your Holiness rather than to anyone else. For even in this very remote corner of the earth where I live you are considered the highest authority by virtue of the loftiness of your office and your love for all literature and astronomy too. Hence by your prestige and judgement you can easily suppress calumnious attacks although, as the proverb has it, there is no remedy for a backbite.

Perhaps there will be babblers who claim to be judges of astronomy although completely ignorant of the subject and, badly distorting some passage of Scripture to their purpose, will dare to find fault with my undertaking and censure it. I disregard them even to the extent of despising their criticism as unfounded. For it is not unknown that Lactantius,[4] otherwise an illustrious writer but hardly an astronomer, speaks quite childishly about the earth's shape, when he mocks those who declared that the earth has the form of a globe. Hence scholars need not be surprised if any such persons will likewise ridicule me. Astronomy is written for astronomers. To them my work too will seem, unless I am mistaken, to make some contribution.

---

[3]Hicetas, a Pythagorean philosopher of the fourth century B.C., taught that the earth rotated on its axis while the other heavenly bodies were at rest. Cicero was a Roman statesman of the first century B.C. Plutarch (A.D. c. 50–c. 120) was a Greek moral philosopher and biographer whose works were especially popular among Renaissance humanists.

---

[4]Renaissance humanists admired Lactantius (c. 240–c. 320), a Latin rhetorician and Christian apologist, for his classical, Ciceronian literary style.

Cardinal Bellarmine
ATTACK ON THE COPERNICAN THEORY

In 1615, Cardinal Bellarmine, who in the name of the Inquisition warned Galileo (see Sections 2 and 3) not to defend the Copernican theory, expressed his displeasure with heliocentrism in a letter to Paolo Antonio Foscarini. Foscarini, head of the Carmelites, an order of mendicant friars, in Calabria and professor of theology, had tried to show that the earth's motion was not incompatible with biblical statements.

Cardinal Bellarmine to Foscarini (12 April 1615)

My Very Reverend Father,

I have read with interest the letter in Italian and the essay in Latin which Your [Reverence] sent me; I thank you for the one and for the other and confess that they are full of intelligence and erudition. You ask for my opinion, and so I shall give it to you, but very briefly, since now you have little time for reading and I for writing.

First, . . . to want to affirm that in reality the sun is at the center of the world and only turns on itself without moving from east to west, and the earth . . . revolves with great speed around the sun . . . is a very dangerous thing, likely not only to irritate all scholastic philosophers and theologians, but also to harm the Holy Faith by rendering Holy Scripture false. For your [Reverence] has well shown many ways of interpreting Holy Scripture, but has not applied them to particular cases; without a doubt you would have encountered very great difficulties if you had wanted to interpret all those passages you yourself cited.

Second, I say that, as you know, the Council [of Trent] prohibits interpreting Scripture against the common consensus of the Holy Fathers; and if Your [Reverence] wants to read not only the Holy Fathers, but also the modern commentaries on Genesis, the Psalms, Ecclesiastes, and Joshua, you will find all agreeing in the literal interpretation that the sun is in heaven and turns around the earth with great speed, and that the earth is very far from heaven and sits motionless at the center of the world. Consider now, with your sense of prudence, whether the Church can tolerate giving Scripture a meaning contrary to the Holy Fathers and to all the Greek and Latin commentators. Nor can one answer that this is not a matter of faith, since if it is not a matter of faith "as regards the topic," it is a matter of faith "as regards the speaker"; and so it would be heretical to say that Abraham did not have two children and Jacob twelve, as well as to say that Christ was not born of a virgin, because both are said by the Holy Spirit through the mouth of the prophets and the apostles.

Third, I say that if there were a true demonstration that the sun is at the center of the world and the earth in the third heaven, and that the sun does not circle the earth but the earth circles the sun, then one would have to proceed with great care in explaining the Scriptures that appear contrary, and say rather that we do not understand them than that what is demonstrated is false. But I will not believe that there is such a demonstration, until it is shown to me. . . . and in case of doubt one must not abandon the Holy Scripture as interpreted by the Holy Fathers. I add that the one who wrote, "The sun also ariseth, and the sun goeth down, and hasteth to his place where he arose," was Solomon [King of ancient Israel], who not only spoke inspired by God, but was a man above all others wise and learned in the human sciences and in the knowledge of created things; he received all this wisdom from God; therefore it is not likely that he was affirming something that was contrary to truth already demonstrated or capable of being demonstrated.

REVIEW QUESTIONS

1. What led Nicolaus Copernicus to investigate the motions of the universe's spheres?
2. Why did he fear to publish his theory about the earth's motion?
3. On what grounds did Cardinal Bellarmine reject the Copernican theory?

---

2 Expanding the New Astronomy

The brilliant Italian scientist Galileo Galilei (1564–1642) rejected the medieval division of the universe into higher and lower realms and proclaimed the modern idea of nature's uniformity. Learning that a telescope had been invented in Holland, Galileo built one for himself and used it to investigate the heavens. Through his telescope, Galileo saw craters and mountains on the moon; he concluded that celestial bodies were not pure, perfect, and immutable, as had been believed. There was no difference in quality between heavenly and earthly bodies; nature was the same throughout.

Galileo Galilei
THE STARRY MESSENGER

In the following reading from *The Starry Messenger* (1610), Galileo reported the findings observed through his telescope, which led him to proclaim the uniformity of nature, a key principle of modern science.

About ten months ago a report reached my ears that a certain Fleming [a native of Flanders]* had constructed a spyglass by means of which visible objects, though very distant from the eye of the observer, were distinctly seen as if nearby. Of this truly remarkable effect several experiences were related, to which some persons gave credence while others denied them. A few days later the report was confirmed to me in a letter from a noble Frenchman at Paris, Jacques Badovere,[†] which caused me to apply myself wholeheartedly to inquire into the means by which I might arrive at the invention of a similar instrument. This I did shortly afterwards, my basis being the theory of refraction. First I prepared a tube of lead, at the ends of which I fitted two glass lenses, both plane on one side while on the other side one was spherically convex and the other concave. Then placing my eye near the concave lens I perceived objects satisfactorily large and near, for they appeared three times closer and nine times larger than when seen with the naked eye alone. Next I constructed another one, more accurate, which represented objects as enlarged more than sixty times. Finally, sparing neither labor nor expense, I succeeded in constructing for myself so excellent an instrument that objects seen by means of it appeared nearly one thousand times larger and over thirty times closer than when regarded with our natural vision.

---

*Credit for the original invention is generally assigned to Hans Lipperhey, a lens grinder in Holland who chanced upon this property of combined lenses and applied for a patent on it in 1608.

[†]Badovere studied in Italy toward the close of the sixteenth century and is said to have been a pupil of Galileo's in about 1598. When he wrote concerning the new instrument in 1609, he was in the French diplomatic service at Paris, where he died in 1620.

It would be superfluous to enumerate the number and importance of the advantages of such an instrument at sea as well as on land. But forsaking terrestrial observations, I turned to celestial ones, and first I saw the moon from as near at hand as if it were scarcely two terrestrial radii [a measure of distance, obscure today] away. After that I observed often with wondering delight both the planets and the fixed stars, and since I saw these latter to be very crowded, I began to seek (and eventually found) a method by which I might measure their distances apart. . . .

Now let us review the observations made during the past two months, once more inviting the attention of all who are eager for true philosophy to the first steps of such important contemplations. Let us speak first of that surface of the moon which faces us. For greater clarity I distinguish two parts of this surface, a lighter and a darker; the lighter part seems to surround and to pervade the whole hemisphere, while the darker part discolors the moon's surface like a kind of cloud, and makes it appear covered with spots. Now those spots which are fairly dark and rather large are plain to everyone and have been seen throughout the ages; these I shall call the "large" or "ancient" spots, distinguishing them from others that are smaller in size but so numerous as to occur all over the lunar surface, and especially the lighter part. The latter spots had never been seen by anyone before me. From observations of these spots repeated many times I have been led to the opinion and conviction that the surface of the moon is not smooth, uniform, and precisely spherical as a great number of philosophers believe it (and the other heavenly bodies) to be, but is uneven, rough, and full of cavities and prominences, being not unlike the face of the earth, relieved by chains of mountains and deep valleys. . . .

With his telescope, Galileo discovered four moons orbiting Jupiter, an observation that overcame a principal objection to the Copernican system. Galileo showed that a celestial body could indeed move around a center other than the earth; that earth was not the common center for all celestial bodies; that a celestial body (earth's moon or Jupiter's moons) could orbit a planet at the same time that the planet revolved around another body (namely, the sun).

On the seventh day of January in this present year 1610, at the first hour of night, when I was viewing the heavenly bodies with a telescope, Jupiter presented itself to me; and because I had prepared a very excellent instrument for myself, I perceived (as I had not before, on account of the weakness of my previous instrument) that beside the planet there were three starlets, small indeed, but very bright. Though I believed them to be among the host of fixed stars, they aroused my curiosity somewhat by appearing to lie in an exact straight line parallel to the ecliptic, and by their being more splendid than others of their size. Their arrangement with respect to Jupiter and each other was the following:

East   ✳   ✳   **O**   ✳   *West*

that is, there were two stars on the eastern side and one to the west. The most easterly star and the western one appeared larger than the other. I paid no attention to the distances between them and Jupiter, for at the outset I thought them to be fixed stars, as I have said.[‡] But returning to the same investigation on January eighth—led by what, I do not know—I found a very different arrangement. The three starlets

[‡]The reader should remember that the telescope was nightly revealing to Galileo hundreds of fixed stars never previously observed. His unusual gifts for astronomical observation are illustrated by his having noticed and remembered these three merely by reason of their alignment, and recalling them so well that when by chance he happened to see them the following night he was certain that they had changed their positions.

were now all to the west of Jupiter, closer together, and at equal intervals from one another
as shown in the following sketch:

East   **O**   *   *   *   *West*

On the tenth of January, however, the stars
appeared in this position with respect to
Jupiter:

East   *   *   **O**   *West*

that is, there were but two of them, both easterly, the third (as I supposed) being hidden behind Jupiter. . . . There was no way in which
such alterations could be attributed to Jupiter's motion, yet being certain that these were
still the same stars I had observed . . . my per-
plexity was now transformed into amazement.
I was sure that the apparent changes belonged
not to Jupiter but to the observed stars, and I
resolved to pursue this investigation with
greater care and attention. . . .

I had now decided beyond all question that
there existed in the heavens three stars wandering about Jupiter as do Venus and Mercury
about the sun, and this became plainer than
daylight from observations on similar occasions which followed. Nor were there just
three such stars; four wanderers complete their
revolutions about Jupiter. . . .

Here we have a fine and elegant argument for
quieting the doubts of those who, while accepting with tranquil mind the revolutions of the
planets about the sun in the Copernican system,
are mightily disturbed to have the moon alone
revolve about the earth and accompany it in an
annual rotation about the sun. Some have believed that this structure of the universe should
be rejected as impossible. But now we have not
just one planet rotating about another while
both run through a great orbit around the sun;
our own eyes show us four stars which wander
around Jupiter as does the moon around the
earth, while all together trace out a grand revolution about the sun in the space of twelve years.

REVIEW QUESTIONS

1. What methods did Galileo Galilei use in his scientific investigations?
2. What was the implication for modern astronomy of Galileo's observation of the
   surface of the moon? Of the moons of Jupiter?

---

3 Critique of Authority

Galileo appealed to the Roman Catholic authorities asking them to halt their actions against the theories of Copernicus, but was unsuccessful. His support of
Copernicus aroused the ire of both clergy and scholastic philosophers. In 1616,
the church placed Copernicus's book on the index of forbidden books, and
Galileo was ordered to cease his defense of the Copernican theory. In 1632,
Galileo published *Dialogue Concerning the Two Chief World Systems* in which
he upheld the Copernican view. Widely distributed and acclaimed, the book
antagonized Galileo's enemies, who succeeded in halting further printing.
Summoned to Rome, the aging and infirm scientist was put on trial by the Inquisition and ordered to renounce the Copernican theory. Galileo bowed to the
Inquisition, which condemned the *Dialogue* and sentenced him to life imprisonment—largely house arrest at his own villa near Florence, where he was
treated humanely.

Galileo Galilei
LETTER TO THE GRAND DUCHESS CHRISTINA AND *DIALOGUE CONCERNING THE TWO CHIEF WORLD SYSTEMS— PTOLEMAIC AND COPERNICAN*

The first reading illustrates Galileo's active involvement in a struggle for freedom of inquiry many years before the *Dialogue* was published. In 1615, in a letter addressed to Grand Duchess Christina of Tuscany, Galileo argued that passages from the Bible had no authority in scientific disputes.

The second reading (from the *Dialogue*) reveals Galileo's views on Aristotle. Medieval scholastics regarded Aristotle as the supreme authority on questions concerning nature, an attitude that was perpetuated by early modern scholastics. Galileo insisted that such reliance on authority was a hindrance to scientific investigation, that it is through observation, experiment, and reason that one arrives at physical truth.

BIBLICAL AUTHORITY

Some years ago, as Your Serene Highness well knows, I discovered in the heavens many things that had not been seen before our own age. The novelty of these things, as well as some consequences which followed from them in contradiction to the physical notions commonly. held among academic philosophers, stirred up against me no small number of professors—as if I had placed these things in the sky with my own hands in order to upset nature and overturn the sciences. They seemed to forget that the increase of known truths stimulates the investigation, establishment, and growth of the arts; not their diminution or destruction.

Showing a greater fondness for their own opinions than for truth, they sought to deny and disprove the new things which, if they had cared to look for themselves, their own senses would have demonstrated to them. To this end they hurled various charges and published numerous writings filled with vain arguments, and they made the grave mistake of sprinkling these with passages taken from places in the Bible which they had failed to understand properly, and which were ill suited to their purposes. . . .

. . . Men who were well grounded in astronomical and physical science were persuaded as soon as they received my first message. There were others who denied them or remained in doubt only because of their novel and unexpected character, and because they had not yet had the opportunity to see for themselves. These men have by degrees come to be satisfied. But some, besides allegiance to their original error, possess I know not what fanciful interest in remaining hostile not so much toward the things in question as toward their discoverer. No longer being able to deny them, these men now take refuge in obstinate silence, but being more than ever exasperated by that which has pacified and quieted other men, they divert their thoughts to other fancies and seek new ways to damage me. . . .

. . . Possibly because they are disturbed by the known truth of other propositions of mine which differ from those commonly held, and therefore mistrusting their defense so long as they confine themselves to the field of philosophy, these men have resolved to fabricate a shield for their fallacies out of the mantle of pretended religion and the authority of the Bible. These they apply, with little judgment, to the refutation of arguments that they do not understand and have not even listened to.

First they have endeavored to spread the opinion that such propositions in general are contrary to the Bible and are consequently damnable and heretical. . . . Hence they have had no trouble in finding men who would preach the damnability and heresy of the new doctrine from their very pulpits with unwonted confidence, thus doing impious and inconsiderate injury not only to that doctrine and its followers but to all mathematics and mathematicians in general. . . .

. . . They go about invoking the Bible, which they would have minister to their deceitful purposes. Contrary to the sense of the Bible and the intention of the holy [Church] Fathers, if I am not mistaken, they would extend such authorities until even in purely physical matters—where faith is not involved—they would have us altogether abandon reason and the evidence of our senses in favor of some biblical passage, though under the surface meaning of its words this passage may contain a different sense.

I hope to show that I proceed with much greater piety than they do, when I argue not against condemning [Copernicus'] book, but against condemning it in the way they suggest—that is, without understanding it, weighing it, or so much as reading it. For Copernicus never discusses matters of religion or faith, nor does he use arguments that depend in any way upon the authority of sacred writings which he might have interpreted erroneously. He stands always upon physical conclusions pertaining to the celestial motions, and deals with them by astronomical and geometrical demonstrations, founded primarily upon sense experiences and very exact observations. He did not ignore the Bible, but he knew very well that if his doc-

trine were proved, then it could not contradict the Scriptures when they were rightly understood. . . .

The reason produced for condemning the opinion that the earth moves and the sun stands still is that in many places in the Bible one may read that the sun moves and the earth stands still. Since the Bible cannot err, it follows as a necessary consequence that anyone takes an erroneous and heretical position who maintains that the sun is inherently motionless and the earth movable.

With regard to this argument, I think in the first place that it is very pious to say and prudent to affirm that the holy Bible can never speak untruth—whenever its true meaning is understood. But I believe nobody will deny that it is often very abstruse, and may say things which are quite different from what its bare words signify. Hence in expounding the Bible if one were always to confine oneself to the unadorned grammatical meaning, one might fall into error. . . .

. . . Now the Bible, merely to condescend to popular capacity, has not hesitated to obscure some very important pronouncements, attributing to God himself some qualities extremely remote from (and even contrary to) His essence. Who, then, would positively declare that this principle has been set aside, and the Bible has confined itself rigorously to the bare and restricted sense of its words, when speaking but casually of the earth, of water, of the sun, or of any other created thing? Especially in view of the fact that these things in no way concern the primary purpose of the sacred writings, which is the service of God and the salvation of souls—matters infinitely beyond the comprehension of the common people.

This being granted, I think that in discussions of physical problems we ought to begin not from the authority of scriptural passages, but from sense-experiences and necessary demonstrations. . . . Nothing physical which sense-experience sets before our eyes, or which necessary demonstrations prove to us, ought to be called in question (much less condemned) upon the testimony of biblical passages which may have some different meaning beneath their words. . . .

. . . I do not feel obliged to believe that that same God who has endowed us with senses, reason, and intellect has intended to forgo their use and by some other means to give us knowledge which we can attain by them. He would not require us to deny sense and reason in physical matters which are set before our eyes and minds by direct experience or necessary demonstrations. . . .

It is obvious that such [anti-Copernican] authors, not having penetrated the true senses of Scripture, would impose upon others an obligation to subscribe to conclusions that are repugnant to manifest reason and sense, if they had any authority to do so. God forbid that this sort of abuse should gain countenance and authority, for then in a short time it would be necessary to proscribe all the contemplative sciences. People who are unable to understand perfectly both the Bible and the sciences far outnumber those who do understand. The former, glancing superficially through the Bible, would arrogate to themselves the authority to decree upon every question of physics on the strength of some word which they have misunderstood, and which was employed by the sacred authors for some different purpose. And the smaller number of understanding men could not dam up the furious torrent of such people, who would gain the majority of followers simply because it is much more pleasant to gain a reputation for wisdom without effort or study than to consume oneself tirelessly in the most laborious disciplines.

Galileo attacked the unquestioning acceptance of Aristotle's teachings in his Dialogue Concerning the Two Chief World Systems—Ptolemaic and Copernican. In the Dialogue, Simplicio is an Aristotelian and Salviati is a spokesman for Galileo; Sagredo, a third participant, introduces the problem of relying on the authority of Aristotle.

ARISTOTELIAN AUTHORITY

SAGREDO One day I was at the home of a very famous doctor in Venice, where many persons came on account of their studies, and others occasionally came out of curiosity to see some anatomical dissection performed by a man who was truly no less learned than he was a careful and expert anatomist. It happened on this day that he was investigating the source and origin of the nerves, about which there exists a notorious controversy between the Galenist and Peripatetic doctors.[1] The anatomist showed that the great trunk of nerves, leaving the brain and passing through the nape, extended on down the spine and then branched out through the whole body, and that only a single strand as fine as a thread arrived at the heart. Turning to a gentleman whom we knew to be a Peripatetic philosopher, and on whose account he had been exhibiting and demonstrating everything with unusual care, he asked this man whether he was at last satisfied and convinced that the nerves originated in the brain and not in the heart. The philosopher, after considering for awhile, answered: "You have made me see this matter so plainly and palpably that if Aristotle's text were not contrary to it, stating clearly that the nerves originate in the heart, I should be forced to admit it to be true." . . .

SIMPLICIO But if Aristotle is to be abandoned, whom shall we have for a guide in philosophy? Suppose you name some author.

SALVIATI We need guides in forests and in unknown lands, but on plains and in open places only the blind need guides. It is better for such people to stay at home, but anyone with eyes in his head and his wits about him could serve as a guide for them. In saying this, I do not mean that a person should not listen to Aristotle; indeed, I applaud the reading

---

[1]Galenist doctors followed the medical theories of Galen (A.D. 129–c. 199), a Greek anatomist and physician whose writings had great authority among medieval and early modern physicians. Peripatetic doctors followed Aristotle's teachings.

and careful study of his works, and I reproach only those who give themselves up as slaves to him in such a way as to subscribe blindly to everything he says and take it as an inviolable decree without looking for any other reasons. This abuse carries with it another profound disorder, that other people do not try harder to comprehend the strength of his demonstrations. And what is more revolting in a public dispute, when someone is dealing with demonstrable conclusions, than to hear him interrupted by a text (often written to some quite different purpose) thrown into his teeth by an opponent? If, indeed, you wish to continue in this method of studying, then put aside the name of philosophers and call yourselves historians, or memory experts; for it is not proper that those who never philosophize should usurp the honorable title of philosopher.

REVIEW QUESTIONS

1. What was Galileo Galilei's objection to using the Bible as a source of knowledge of physical things? According to him, how did one acquire knowledge of nature?
2. What point was Galileo making in telling the story of the anatomical dissection?
3. What was Galileo's view on the use of Aristotle's works as a basis for scientific endeavors?

4 Prophet of Modern Science

Sir Francis Bacon (1561–1626), an English statesman and philosopher, vigorously supported the advancement of science and the scientific method. He believed that increased comprehension and mastery of nature would improve living conditions for people and therefore wanted science to encompass systematic research; he urged the state to fund scientific institutions. Bacon denounced universities for merely repeating Aristotelian concepts and discussing problems—Is matter formless? Are all natural substances composed of matter?—that did not increase understanding of nature or contribute to human betterment. The webs spun by these scholastics, he said, were ingenious but valueless. Bacon wanted an educational program that stressed direct contact with nature and fostered new discoveries.

Bacon was among the first to appreciate the new science's value and to explain its method clearly. Like Leonardo da Vinci, Bacon gave supreme value to the direct observation of nature; for this reason he is one of the founders of the empirical tradition in modern philosophy. Bacon upheld the inductive approach—careful investigation of nature, accumulation of data, and experimentation—as the way to truth and useful knowledge. Because he wanted science to serve a practical function, Bacon praised artisans and technicians who improved technology.

Francis Bacon
ATTACK ON AUTHORITY AND ADVOCACY OF EXPERIMENTAL SCIENCE

Bacon was not himself a scientist; he made no discoveries and had no laboratory. Nevertheless, for his advocacy of the scientific method, Bacon is deservedly regarded as a prophet of modern science. In the first passage from *Redargutio Philosophiarum* (The Refutation of Philosophies), a treatise on the "idols of the theater"—fallacious ways of thinking based on given systems of philosophy—Bacon attacks the slavish reliance on Aristotle.

But even though Aristotle were the man he is thought to be I should still warn you against receiving as oracles the thoughts and opinions of one man. What justification can there be for this self-imposed servitude [that] . . . you are content to repeat Aristotle after two thousand [years]? . . . But if you will be guided by me you will deny, not only to this man but to any mortal now living or who shall live hereafter, the right to dictate your opinions. . . . You will never be sorry for trusting your own strength, if you but once make trial of it. You may be inferior to Aristotle on the whole, but not in everything. Finally, and this is the head and front of the whole matter, there is at least one thing in which you are far ahead of him—in precedents, in experience, in the lessons of time. Aristotle, it is said, wrote a book in which he gathered together the laws and institutions of two hundred and fifty-five cities; yet I have no doubt that the customs of Rome are worth more than all of them combined so far as military and political science are concerned. The position is the same in natural philosophy. Are you of a mind to cast aside not only your own endowments but the gifts of time? Assert yourselves before it is too late. Apply yourselves to the study of things themselves. Be not for ever the property of one man.

With these scattered excerpts from *The New Organon* (New System of Logic), in

1620 Bacon criticized contemporary methods used to inquire into nature. He expressed his ideas in the form of aphorisms—concise statements of principles or general truths.

I. Man, being the servant and interpreter of Nature, can do and understand so much and so much only as he has observed in fact or in thought of the course of nature: beyond this he neither knows anything nor can do anything.

VIII. . . . The sciences we now possess are merely systems for the nice ordering and setting forth of things already invented; not methods of invention or directions for new works.

XII. The logic now in use serves rather to fix and give stability to the errors which have their foundation in commonly received notions than to help the search after truth. So it does more harm than good.

XIX. There are and can be only two ways of searching into and discovering truth. The one flies from the senses and particulars to the most general axioms, and from these principles, the truth of which it takes for settled and immoveable, proceeds to judgment and to the discovery of middle axioms. And this way is now in fashion. The other derives axioms from the senses and particulars, rising by a gradual and unbroken ascent, so that it arrives at the most general axioms last of all. This is the true way, but as yet untried.

XXIII. There is a great difference between . . . certain empty dogmas, and the true signatures and marks set upon the works of creation as they are found in nature.

XXIV. It cannot be that axioms established by argumentation should avail for the discovery of new works; since the subtlety of nature is greater many times over than the subtlety of argument. But axioms duly and orderly formed from particulars easily discover the way to new particulars, and thus render sciences active.

XXXI. It is idle to expect any great advancement in science from the superinducing [adding] and engrafting of new things upon old. We must begin anew from the very foundations, unless we would revolve for ever in a circle with mean and contemptible progress.

CIX. There is therefore much ground for hoping that there are still laid up in the womb of nature many secrets of excellent use, having no affinity or parallelism with any thing that is now known, but lying entirely out of the beat of the imagination, which have not yet been found out. They too no doubt will some time or other, in the course and revolution of many ages, come to light of themselves, just as the others did; only by the method of which we are now treating they can be speedily and suddenly and simultaneously presented and anticipated.

Bacon describes those "idols" or false notions that hamper human understanding.

XXXVIII. The idols and false notions which are now in possession of the human understanding, and have taken deep root therein, not only so beset men's minds that truth can hardly find entrance, but even after entrance is obtained, they will again in the very instauration [renewal] of the sciences meet and trouble us, unless men being forewarned of the danger fortify themselves as far as may be against their assaults.

XXXIX. There are four classes of Idols which beset men's minds. To these for distinc-

tion's sake I have assigned names,—calling the first class *Idols of the Tribe*; the second, *Idols of the Cave*; the third, *Idols of the Market-place*; the fourth, *Idols of the Theatre*.

XLI. The Idols of the Tribe have their foundation in human nature itself, and in the tribe or race of men. For it is a false assertion that the sense of man is the measure of things. On the contrary, all perceptions as well of the sense as of the mind are according to the measure of the universe. And the human understanding is like a false mirror, which, receiving rays irregularly, distorts and discolours the nature of things by mingling its own nature with it.

XLII. The Idols of the Cave are the idols of the individual man. For every one (besides the errors common to human nature in general) has a cave or den of his own, which refracts and discolours the light of nature; owing either to his own proper and peculiar nature; or to his education and conversation with others; or to the reading of books, and the authority of those whom he esteems and admires; or to the differences of impressions, accordingly as they take place in a mind preoccupied and predisposed or in a mind indifferent and settled; or the like. . . .

XLIII. There are also Idols formed by the intercourse and association of men with each other, which I call Idols of the Market-place, on account of the commerce and consort of men there. For it is by discourse that men associate; and words are imposed according to the apprehension of the vulgar. And therefore the ill and unfit choice of words wonderfully obstructs the understanding. Nor do the definitions or explanations wherewith in some things learned men are wont to guard and defend themselves, by any means set the matter right. But words plainly force and overrule the understanding, and throw all into confusion, and lead men away into numberless empty controversies and idle fancies.

XLIV. Lastly, there are Idols which have immigrated into men's minds from the various dogmas of philosophies, and also from wrong laws of demonstration. These I call Idols of the Theatre; because in my judgment all the received systems are but so many stage-plays, representing worlds of their own creation after an unreal and scenic fashion. Nor is it only of the systems now in vogue, or only of the ancient sects and philosophies, that I speak; for many more plays of the same kind may yet be composed and in like artificial manner set forth; seeing that errors the most widely differ-ent have nevertheless causes for the most part alike. Neither again do I mean this only of entire systems, but also of many principles and axioms in science, which by tradition, credulity, and negligence have come to be received.

But of these several kinds of Idols I must speak more largely and exactly, that the understanding may be duly cautioned.

REVIEW QUESTIONS

1. What intellectual attitude did Francis Bacon believe obstructed new scientific discoveries in his time?
2. What method of scientific inquiry did Bacon advocate?
3. Explain how each one of Bacon's idols hampers human understanding.

---

5 The Autonomy of the Mind

René Descartes (1596–1650), a French mathematician and philosopher, united the new currents of thought initiated during the Renaissance and the Scientific Revolution. Descartes said that the universe was a mechanical system whose inner laws could be discovered through mathematical thinking and formulated in mathematical terms. With Descartes' assertions on the power of thought, human beings became fully aware of their capacity to comprehend the world through their mental powers. For this reason he is regarded as the founder of modern philosophy.

The deductive approach stressed by Descartes presumes that inherent in the mind are mathematical principles, logical relationships, the principle of cause and effect, concepts of size and motion, and so on—ideas that exist independently of human experience with the external world. Descartes, for example, would say that the properties of a right-angle triangle ($a^2 + b^2 = c^2$) are implicit in human consciousness prior to any experience one might have with a triangle. These innate ideas, said Descartes, permit the mind to give order and coherence to the physical world. Descartes held that the mind arrives at truth when it "intuits" or comprehends the logical necessity of its own ideas and expresses these ideas with clarity, certainty, and precision.

René Descartes
DISCOURSE ON METHOD

In the *Discourse on Method* (1637), Descartes proclaimed the mind's autonomy and importance, and its ability and right to comprehend truth. In this work he offered a method whereby one could achieve certainty and thereby produce a comprehensive understanding of nature and human culture. In the following passage from the *Discourse on Method,* he explained the purpose of his inquiry. How he did so is almost as revolutionary as the ideas he wished to express. He spoke in the first person, autobiographically, as an individual employing his own reason, and he addressed himself to other individuals, inviting them to use their reason. He brought to his narrative an unprecedented confidence in the power of his own judgment and a deep disenchantment with the learning of his times.

PART ONE

From my childhood I lived in a world of books, and since I was taught that by their help I could gain a clear and assured knowledge of everything useful in life, I was eager to learn from them. But as soon as I had finished the course of studies which usually admits one to the ranks of the learned, I changed my opinion completely. For I found myself saddled with so many doubts and errors that I seemed to have gained nothing in trying to educate myself unless it was to discover more and more fully how ignorant I was.

Nevertheless I had been in one of the most celebrated schools in Europe, where I thought there should be wise men if wise men existed anywhere on earth. I had learned there everything that others learned, and, not satisfied with merely the knowledge that was taught, I had perused as many books as I could find which contained more unusual and recondite knowledge. . . . And finally, it did not seem to me that our times were less flourishing and fertile than were any of the earlier periods. All this led me to conclude that I could judge others by myself, and to decide that there was no such wisdom in the world as I had previously hoped to find. . . .

I revered our theology, and hoped as much as anyone else to get to heaven, but having learned on great authority that the road was just as open to the most ignorant as to the most learned, and that the truths of revelation which lead thereto are beyond our understanding, I would not have dared to submit them to the weakness of my reasonings. I thought that to succeed in their examination it would be necessary to have some extraordinary assistance from heaven, and to be more than a man.

I will say nothing of philosophy except that it has been studied for many centuries by the most outstanding minds without having produced anything which is not in dispute and consequently doubtful. I did not have enough presumption to hope to succeed better than the others; and when I noticed how many different opinions learned men may hold on the same subject, despite the fact that no more than one of them can ever be right, I resolved to consider almost as false any opinion which was merely plausible. . . .

This is why I gave up my studies entirely as soon as I reached the age when I was no longer under the control of my teachers. I resolved to seek no other knowledge than that which I might find within myself, or perhaps in the great book of nature. I spent a few years of my adolescence traveling, seeing courts and armies, living with people of diverse types and stations of life, acquiring varied experience, testing myself in the episodes which fortune sent me, and, above all, thinking about the things around me so that I could derive some profit from them. For it seemed to me that I might find much more of the truth in the cogitations [reflections] which each man made on things which were important to him, and where he would be the loser if he judged badly, than in the cogitations of a man of letters in his study, concerned with speculations which produce no effect, and which have no consequences to him. . . .

. . . After spending several years in thus studying the book of nature and acquiring experience, I eventually reached the decision to study my own self, and to employ all my abilities to try to choose the right path. This produced much better results in my case, I think, than would have been produced if I had never left my books and my country. . . .

PART TWO

. . . As far as the opinions which I had been receiving since my birth were concerned, I could not do better than to reject them completely for once in my lifetime, and to resume them afterwards, or perhaps accept better ones in their place, when I had determined how they fitted into a rational scheme. And I firmly believed that by this means I would succeed in conducting my life much better than if I built only upon the old foundations and gave credence to the principles which I had acquired in my childhood without ever having examined them to see whether they were true or not. . . .

. . . Never has my intention been more than to try to reform my own ideas, and rebuild them on foundations that would be wholly mine. . . . The decision to abandon all one's preconceived notions is not an example for all to follow. . . .

As for myself, I should no doubt have . . . [never attempted it] if I had had but a single teacher or if I had not known the differences which have always existed among the most learned. I had discovered in college that one cannot imagine anything so strange and unbelievable but that it has been upheld by some philosopher; and in my travels I had found that those who held opinions contrary to ours were neither barbarians nor savages, but that many of them were at least as reasonable as ourselves. I had considered how the same man, with the same capacity for reason, becomes different as a result of being brought up among Frenchmen or Germans than he would be if he had been brought up among Chinese or cannibals; and how, in our fashions, the thing which pleased us ten years ago and perhaps will please us again ten years in the future, now seems extravagant and ridiculous; and I felt that in all these ways we are much more greatly influenced by custom and example than by any certain knowledge. Faced with this divergence of opinion, I could not accept the testimony of the majority, for I

thought it worthless as a proof of anything somewhat difficult to discover, since it is much more likely that a single man will have discovered it than a whole people. Nor, on the other hand, could I select anyone whose opinions seemed to me to be preferable to those of others, and I was thus constrained to embark on the investigation for myself.

Nevertheless, like a man who walks alone in the darkness, I resolved to go so slowly and circumspectly that if I did not get ahead very rapidly I was at least safe from falling. Also, I did not want to reject all the opinions which had slipped irrationally into my consciousness since birth, until I had first spent enough time planning how to accomplish the task which I was then undertaking, and seeking the true method of obtaining knowledge of everything which my mind was capable of understanding. . . .

Descartes' method consists of four principles that place the capacity to arrive at truth entirely within the province of the human mind. First one finds a self-evident principle, such as a geometric axiom. From this general principle, other truths are deduced through logical reasoning. This is accomplished by breaking a problem down into its elementary components and then, step by step, moving toward more complex knowledge.

. . . I thought that some other method [beside that of logic, algebra, and geometry] must be found to combine the advantages of these three and to escape their faults. Finally, just as the multitude of laws frequently furnishes an excuse for vice, and a state is much better governed with a few laws which are strictly adhered to, so I thought that instead of the great number of precepts of which logic is composed, I would have enough with the four following ones, provided that I made a firm and unalterable resolution not to violate them even in a single instance.

The first rule was never to accept anything as true unless I recognized it to be evidently such: that is, carefully to avoid precipitation and prejudgment, and to include nothing in my conclusions unless it presented itself so clearly and distinctly to my mind that there was no occasion to doubt it.

The second was to divide each of the difficulties which I encountered into as many parts as possible, and as might be required for an easier solution.

The third was to think in an orderly fashion, beginning with the things which were simplest and easiest to understand, and gradually and by degrees reaching toward more complex knowledge, even treating as though ordered materials which were not necessarily so.

The last was always to make enumerations so complete, and reviews so general, that I would be certain that nothing was omitted. . . .

What pleased me most about this method was that it enabled me to reason in all things, if not perfectly, at least as well as was in my power. In addition, I felt that in practicing it my mind was gradually becoming accustomed to conceive its objects more clearly and distinctly. . . .

Descartes was searching for an incontrovertible truth that could serve as the first principle of philosophy. His arrival at the famous dictum "I think, therefore I am" marks the beginning of modern philosophy.

PART FOUR

. . . As I desired to devote myself wholly to the search for truth, I thought that I should . . . reject as absolutely false anything of which I could have the least doubt, in order to see whether anything would be left after this procedure which could be called wholly certain. Thus, as our senses deceive us at times, I was ready to suppose that nothing was at all the way our senses represented them to be. As there are men who make mistakes in reasoning even on the simplest topics in geometry, I judged that I was as liable to error as any other, and rejected as false all the reasoning which I had previously accepted as valid demonstration. Finally, as the same precepts which we have when awake may come to us when asleep without their being true, I decided to suppose that nothing that had ever entered my mind was more real than the illusions of my dreams. But I soon noticed that while I thus wished to think everything false, it was necessarily true that I who thought so was something. Since this truth, *I think, therefore I am,* was so firm and assured that all the most extravagant suppositions of the sceptics[1] were unable to shake it, I judged that I could safely accept it as the first principle of the philosophy I was seeking.

---

[1] The skeptics belonged to the ancient Greek philosophic school that held true knowledge to be beyond human grasp and treated all knowledge as uncertain.

REVIEW QUESTIONS

1. Why was René Descartes critical of the learning of his day?
2. What are the implications of Descartes' famous words: "I think, therefore I am"?
3. Compare Descartes' method with the approach advocated by Francis Bacon.

---

6 The Mechanical Universe

By demonstrating that all bodies in the universe—earthly objects as well as moons, planets, and stars—obey the same laws of motion and gravitation, Sir Isaac Newton (1646–1723) completed the destruction of the medieval view of the universe. The idea that the same laws governed the movement of earthly and heavenly bodies was completely foreign to medieval thinkers, who drew a sharp division between a higher celestial world and a lower terrestrial one. In the *Principia Mathematica* (1687), Newton showed that the same forces that hold celestial bodies in their orbits around the sun make apples fall to the ground. For Newton, the universe was like a giant clock, all of whose parts obeyed strict mechanical principles and worked together in perfect precision. To Newton's contemporaries, it seemed as if mystery had been banished from the universe.

Isaac Newton
PRINCIPIA MATHEMATICA

In the first of the following passages from *Principia Mathematica,* Newton stated the principle of universal law and lauded the experimental method as the means of acquiring knowledge.

RULES OF REASONING IN PHILOSOPHY

Rule I.   We are to admit no more causes of natural things than such as are both true and sufficient to explain their appearances.

To this purpose the philosophers say that Nature does nothing in vain, and more is in vain when less will serve; for Nature is pleased with simplicity, and affects not the pomp of superfluous causes.

Rule II.   Therefore to the same natural effects we must, as far as possible, assign the same causes.

As to respiration in a man and in a beast; the descent of stones [meteorites] in *Europe* and in *America*; the light of our culinary fire and of the sun; the reflection of light in the earth, and in the planets.

Rule III.   The qualities of bodies, which admit neither [intensification] nor remission of degrees, and which are found to belong to all bodies within the reach of our experiments, are to be esteemed the universal qualities of all bodies whatsoever.

For since the qualities of bodies are only known to us by experiments, we are to hold for universal all such as universally agree

with experiments; and such as are not liable to diminution can never be quite taken away. We are certainly not to relinquish the evidence of experiments for the sake of dreams and vain fictions of our own devising; nor are we to recede from the analogy of Nature, which [is] . . . simple, and always consonant to itself. We no other way know the extension of bodies than by our senses, nor do these reach it in all bodies; but because we perceive extension in all that are sensible, therefore, we ascribe it universally to all others also. That abundance of bodies are hard, we learn by experience; and because the hardness of the whole arises from the hardness of the parts, we, therefore, justly infer the hardness of the undivided particles not only of the bodies we feel but of all others. That all bodies are impenetrable, we gather not from reason, but from sensation. The bodies which we handle we find impenetrable, and thence, conclude impenetrability to be an universal property of all bodies whatsoever. That all bodies are moveable, and endowed with certain powers (which we call . . . {*inertia*}) of persevering in their motion, or in their rest, we only infer from the like properties observed in the bodies which we have seen. The extension, hardness, impenetrability, mobility, . . . of the whole, result from the extension, hardness, impenetrability, mobility, . . . of the parts; and thence we conclude the least particles of all bodies to be also all extended, and hard and impenetrable, and moveable, . . . And this is the foundation of all philosophy. . . .

Lastly, if it universally appears, by experiments and astronomical observations, that all bodies about the earth gravitate towards the earth, and that in proportion to the quantity of matter which they severally contain; that the moon likewise, according to the quantity of its matter, gravitates towards the earth; that, on the other hand, our sea gravitates towards the moon; and all the planets mutually one towards another; and the comets in like manner towards the sun; we must, in consequence of this rule, universally allow that all bodies whatsoever are endowed with a principle of mutual gravitation. . . .

Rule IV.   In experimental philosophy we are to look upon propositions collected by general induction from phenomena as accurately or very nearly true, notwithstanding any contrary hypotheses that may be imagined, till such time as other phenomena occur, by which they may either be made more accurate, or liable to exceptions.

This rule we must follow, that the argument of induction may not be evaded by hypotheses.

Newton describes further his concepts of gravity and scientific methodology.

GRAVITY

Hitherto, we have explained the phenomena of the heavens and of our sea by the power of gravity, but have not yet assigned the cause of this power. This is certain, that it must proceed from a cause that penetrates to the very centres of the sun and planets, without suffering the least diminution of its force; that operates not according to the quantity of the surfaces of the particles upon which it acts (as mechanical causes used to do) but according to

the quantity of the solid matter which they contain, and propagates its virtue on all sides to immense distances, decreasing always in the duplicate portion of the distances. . . .

Hitherto I have not been able to discover the cause of those properties of gravity from the phenomena, and I frame no hypothesis; for whatever is not deduced from the phenomena is to be called an hypothesis; and hypotheses, whether metaphysical or physical, whether of occult qualities or mechanical, have no place in experimental philosophy. In this philosophy particular propositions are inferred from the phenomena, and afterward rendered general by induction. Thus it was the impenetrability, the mobility, and the impulsive forces of bodies, and the laws of motion and of gravitation were discovered. And to us it is enough that gravity does really exist, and acts according to the laws which we have explained, and abundantly serves to account for all the motions of the celestial bodies, and of our sea.

A devoted Anglican, Newton believed that God had created this superbly organized universe. The following selection is also from the *Principia.*

GOD AND THE UNIVERSE

This most beautiful system of the sun, planets, and comets could only proceed from the counsel and dominion of an intelligent and powerful Being. And if the fixed stars are the centers of other like systems, these, being formed by the like wise counsel, must be all subject to the dominion of One, especially since the light of the fixed stars is of the same nature with the light of the sun and from every system light passes into all the other systems; and lest the systems of the fixed stars should, by their gravity, fall on each other mutually, he hath placed those systems at immense distances from one another.

This Being governs all things not as the soul of the world, but as Lord over all; and on account of his dominion he is wont to be called "Lord

God" . . . or "Universal Ruler." . . . It is the dominion of a spiritual being which constitutes a God. . . . And from his true dominion it follows that the true God is a living, intelligent and powerful Being. . .(he governs all things, and knows all things that are or can be done. . . . He endures for ever, and is every where present; and by existing always and every where, he constitutes duration and space. . . .) In him are all things contained and moved; yet neither affects the other: God suffers nothing from the motion of bodies; bodies find no resistance from the omnipresence of God. . . . As a blind man has no idea of colors so we have no idea of the manner by which the all-wise God preserves and understands all things. He is utterly void of all body and bodily figure, and can therefore neither be seen, nor heard, nor touched; nor ought to be worshipped under the representation of any corporeal thing. We have ideas of his attributes, but what the real substance of any thing is we know not. . . . Much less, then, have we any idea of the substance of God. We know him only by his most wise and excellent contrivances of things. . . . [W]e reverence and adore him as his servants; and a god without dominion, providence, and final causes, is nothing else but Fate and Nature. Blind metaphysical necessity, which is certainly the same always and everywhere, could produce no variety of things. All that diversity of natural things which we find suited to different times and places could arise from nothing but the ideas and will of a Being necessarily existing. . . . And thus much concerning God; to discourse of whom from the appearances of things does certainly belong to Natural Philosophy.

REVIEW QUESTIONS

1. What did Isaac Newton mean by universal law? What examples of universal law did he provide?
2. What method for investigating nature did Newton advocate?
3. Summarize Newton's arguments for God's existence.
4. For Newton, what is God's relationship to the universe?

CHAPTER 3
The Enlightenment

THE GEOGRAPHY LESSON, Pietro Longhi, c. 1750. This scene depicting a bourgeois family's lesson in geography illustrates the widespread interest in intellectual pursuits that typified this age. *(Oil on canvas. Galleria Querini Stampalia, Venice. Scala/Art Resource, N.Y.)*

The Enlightenment of the eighteenth century culminated the movement toward modernity that started in the Renaissance era. The thinkers of the Enlightenment, called *philosophes,* attacked medieval otherworldliness, dethroned theology from its once-proud position as queen of the sciences, and based their understanding of nature and society on reason alone, unaided by revelation or priestly authority.

From the broad spectrum of Western history, several traditions flowed into the Enlightenment: the rational spirit born in classical Greece, the Stoic emphasis on natural law that applies to all human beings, and the Christian belief that all individuals are equal in God's eyes. A more immediate influence on the Enlightenment was Renaissance humanism, which focused on the individual and worldly human accomplishments and which criticized medieval theology-philosophy for its preoccupation with questions that seemed unrelated to the human condition. In many ways, the Enlightenment grew directly out of the Scientific Revolution. The philosophes praised both Newton's discovery of the mechanical laws that govern the universe and the scientific method that made this discovery possible. They wanted to transfer the scientific method—the reliance on experience and the critical use of the intellect—to the realm of society. They maintained that independent of clerical authority, human beings through reason could grasp the natural laws that govern the social world, just as Newton had uncovered the laws of nature that operate in the physical world. The philosophes said that those institutions and traditions that could not meet the test of reason, because they were based on authority, ignorance, or superstition, had to be reformed or dispensed with.

For medieval philosophers, reason had been subordinate to revelation; the Christian outlook determined the medieval concept of nature, morality, government, law, and life's purpose. During the Renaissance and Scientific Revolution, reason increasingly asserted its autonomy. For example, Machiavelli rejected the principle that politics should be based on Christian teachings; he recognized no higher world as the source of a higher truth. Galileo held that on questions regarding nature, one should trust to observation, experimentation, and mathematical reasoning and should not rely on Scripture. Descartes rejected reliance on past authority and maintained that through thought alone one could attain knowledge that has absolute certainty. Agreeing with Descartes that the mind is self-sufficient, the philosophes rejected the guidance of revelation and its priestly interpreters. They believed that through the use of reason, individuals could comprehend and reform society.

The Enlightenment philosophes articulated basic principles of the modern outlook: confidence in the self-sufficiency of the human mind, belief that individuals possess natural rights that governments should not violate, and the desire to reform society in accordance with rational principles. Their views influenced the reformers of the French Revolution and the founding fathers of the United States.

---

1 The Enlightenment Outlook

The critical use of the intellect was the central principle of the Enlightenment. The philosophes rejected beliefs and traditions that seemed to conflict with reason and attacked clerical and political authorities for interfering with the free use of the intellect.

Immanuel Kant
WHAT IS ENLIGHTENMENT?

The German philosopher Immanuel Kant (1724–1804) is a giant in the history of modern philosophy. Several twentieth-century philosophic movements have their origins in Kantian thought, and many issues raised by Kant still retain their importance. For example, in *Metaphysical Foundations of Morals* (1785), Kant set forth the categorical imperative that remains a crucial principle in moral philosophy. Kant asserted that when confronted with a moral choice, people should ask themselves: "Canst thou also will that thy maxim should be a universal law?" By this, Kant meant that people should ponder whether they would want the moral principle underlying their action to be elevated to a universal law that would govern others in similar circumstances. If they concluded that it should not, then the maxim should be rejected and the action avoided.

Kant valued the essential ideals of the Enlightenment and viewed the French Revolution, which put these ideals into law, as the triumph of liberty over despotism. In an essay entitled "What Is Enlightenment?" (1784), he contended that the Enlightenment marked a new way of thinking and eloquently affirmed the Enlightenment's confidence in and commitment to reason.

Enlightenment is man's leaving his self-caused immaturity. Immaturity is the incapacity to use one's intelligence without the guidance of another. Such immaturity is self-caused if it is not caused by lack of intelligence, but by lack of determination and courage to use one's intelligence without being guided by another. *Sapere Aude!* [Dare to know!] Have the courage to use your own intelligence! is therefore the motto of the enlightenment.

Through laziness and cowardice a large part of mankind, even after nature has freed them from alien guidance, gladly remain immature. It is because of laziness and cowardice that it is so easy for others to usurp the role of guardians. It is so comfortable to be a minor! If I have a book which provides meaning for me, a pastor who has conscience for me, a doctor who will judge my diet for me and so on, then I do not need to exert myself. I do not have any need to think; if I can pay, others will take over the tedious job for me. The guardians who have kindly undertaken the supervision will see to it that by far the largest part of mankind, including the entire "beautiful sex," should consider the step into maturity, not only as difficult but as very dangerous.

After having made their domestic animals dumb and having carefully prevented these quiet creatures from daring to take any step beyond the lead-strings to which they have fastened them, these guardians then show them the danger which threatens them, should they attempt to walk alone. Now this danger is not really so very great; for they would presumably learn to walk after some stumbling. However, an example of this kind intimidates and frightens people out of all further attempts.

It is difficult for the isolated individual to work himself out of the immaturity which has become almost natural for him. He has even become fond of it and for the time being is incapable of employing his own intelligence, because he has never been allowed to make the attempt. Statutes and formulas, these mechanical tools of a serviceable use, or rather misuse, of his natural faculties, are the ankle-chains of a continuous immaturity. Whoever threw it off would make an uncertain jump over the smallest trench because he is not accustomed to such free movement. Therefore there are only a few who have pursued a firm path and have succeeded in escaping from immaturity by their own cultivation of the mind.

But it is more nearly possible for a public to enlighten itself: this is even inescapable if only the public is given its freedom. For there will always be some people who think for themselves, even among the self-appointed guardians of the great mass who, after having

thrown off the yoke of immaturity themselves, will spread about them the spirit of a reasonable estimate of their own value and of the need for every man to think for himself. . . . [A] public can only arrive at enlightenment slowly. Through revolution, the abandonment of personal despotism may be engendered and the end of profit-seeking and domineering oppression may occur, but never a true reform of the state of mind. Instead, new prejudices, just like the old ones, will serve as the guiding reins of the great, unthinking mass. . . .

All that is required for this enlightenment is *freedom*; and particularly the least harmful of all that may be called freedom, namely, the freedom for man to make *public use* of his reason in all matters. But I hear people clamor on all sides: Don't argue! The officer says: Don't argue, drill! The tax collector: Don't argue, pay! The pastor: Don't argue, believe! . . . Here we have restrictions on freedom everywhere. Which restriction is hampering enlightenment, and which does not, or even promotes it? I answer: The *public use* of a man's reason must be free at all times, and this alone can bring enlightenment among men. . . .

I mean by the public use of one's reason, the use which a scholar makes of it before the entire reading public. . . .

The question may now be put: Do we live at present in an enlightened age? The answer is: No, but in an age of enlightenment. Much still prevents men from being placed in a position . . . to use their own minds securely and well in matters of religion. But we do have very definite indications that this field of endeavor is being opened up for men to work freely and reduce gradually the hindrances preventing a general enlightenment and an escape from self-caused immaturity.

REVIEW QUESTIONS

1. What did Immanuel Kant mean by the terms *enlightenment* and *freedom*?
2. In Kant's view, what factors delayed the progress of human enlightenment?
3. What are the political implications of Kant's views?

2 Political Liberty

John Locke (1632–1704), a British statesman, philosopher, and political theorist, was a principal source of the Enlightenment. Eighteenth-century thinkers were particularly influenced by Locke's advocacy of religious toleration, his reliance on experience as the source of knowledge, and his concern for liberty. In his first *Letter Concerning Toleration,* Locke declared that Christians who persecute others in the name of religion vitiate Christ's teachings. Locke's political philosophy as formulated in the *Two Treatises on Government* (1690) complements his theory of knowledge (see page 39); both were rational and secular attempts to understand and improve the human condition. The Lockean spirit pervades the American Declaration of Independence, the Constitution, and the Bill of Rights and is the basis of the liberal tradition that aims to protect individual liberty from despotic state authority.

Viewing human beings as brutish and selfish, Thomas Hobbes, the British philosopher and political theorist, had prescribed a state with unlimited power; only in this way, he said, could people be protected from each other and civilized life preserved. Locke, regarding people as essentially good and humane, developed a conception of the state differing fundamentally from Hobbes's. Locke held that human beings are born with natural rights of life, liberty, and property; they establish the state to protect these rights. Consequently, neither executive nor legislature, neither king nor assembly has the authority to deprive individuals of their natural rights. Whereas Hobbes justified absolute monarchy, Locke explicitly endorsed constitutional government in which the power to govern derives from the consent of the governed and the state's authority is limited by agreement.

John Locke
SECOND TREATISE ON GOVERNMENT

Locke said that originally, in establishing a government, human beings had never agreed to surrender their natural rights to any state authority. The state's founders intended the new polity to preserve these natural rights and to implement the people's will. Therefore, as the following passage from Locke's *Second Treatise on Government* illustrates, the power exercised by magistrates cannot be absolute or arbitrary.

. . . *Political power* is that power, which every man having in the state of nature, has given up into the hands of the society, and therein to the governors, whom the society hath set over itself, with this express or tacit trust, that it shall be employed for their good, and

the preservation of their property: now this *power,* which every man has *in the state of nature,* and which he parts with to the society in all such cases where the society can secure him, is to use such means, for the preserving of his own property, as he thinks good, and nature allows him; and to punish the breach of the law of nature in others, so as (according to the best of his reason) may most conduce to the preservation of himself, and the rest of mankind. So that the *end and measure of this power,* when in every man's hands in the state of nature, being the preservation of all of his society, that is, all mankind in general, it can have no other *end or measure,* when in the hands of the magistrate, but to preserve the members of that society in their lives, liberties, and possessions; and so cannot be an absolute, arbitrary power over their lives and fortunes, which are as much as possible to be preserved; but a *power to make laws,* and annex such *penalties* to them, as may tend to the preservation of the whole, by cutting off those parts, and those only, which are so corrupt, that they threaten the sound and healthy, without which no severity is lawful. And this *power has its original only from compact,* and agreement, and the mutual consent of those who make up the community. . . .

These are the *bounds,* which the trust, that is put in them by the society, and the law of God and nature, have *set to the legislative* power of every common-wealth, in all forms of government.

First, They are to govern by *promulgated established laws,* not to be varied in particular cases, but to have one rule for rich and poor, for the favourite at court, and the country man at plough.

Secondly, These *laws* also ought to be designed *for* no other end ultimately, but *the good of the people.*

Thirdly, They must *not raise taxes on the property of the people, without the consent of the people,* given by themselves, or their deputies. And this properly concerns only such governments, where the *legislative* is always in being, or at least where the people have not reserved any part of the legislative to deputies, to be from time to time chosen by themselves.

Fourthly, The *legislative* neither must *nor can transfer the power of making laws* to any body else, or place it any where, but where the people have. . . .

> If government fails to fulfill the end for which it was established—the preservation of the individual's right to life, liberty, and property—the people have a right to dissolve that government.

. . . The *legislative acts against the trust* reposed in them, when they endeavour to invade the property of the subject, and to make themselves, or any part of the community, masters, or arbitrary disposers of the lives, liberties, or fortunes of the people.

The reason why men enter into society, is the preservation of their property; and the end why they chuse and authorize a legislative, is, that there may be laws made, and rules set, as guards and fences to the properties of all the members of the society, to limit the power, and moderate the dominion of every part and member of the society: for since it can never be supposed to be the will of the society, that the legislative should have a power to destroy that which every one designs to secure, by entering into society, and for which the people submitted themselves to legislators of their own making; whenever the *legislators endeavour to take away, and destroy the property of the people,* or to reduce them to slavery under arbitrary power, they put themselves into a state of war with the people, who are thereupon absolved from any farther obedience, and are left to the common refuge, which God hath provided for all men, against force and violence. Whensoever therefore the *legislative* shall transgress this fundamental rule of society; and either by ambition, fear, folly or corruption, *endeavour to grasp* themselves, *or put into the hands of any other, an absolute power* over the lives, liberties, and estates of the people; by this breach of trust they *forfeit the power* the people had put into their hands for quite contrary ends, and it devolves to the people, who have a right to resume their original liberty, and, by the establishment of a new legislative, (such as they shall think fit) provide for their own safety and security, which is the end for which they are in society. What I have said here, concerning the legislative in general, holds true also concerning the supreme executor, who having a double trust put in him, both to have a part in the legislative, and the supreme execution of the law, acts against both, when he goes about to set up his own arbitrary will as the law of the society. He *acts* also *contrary to his trust,* when he either employs the force, treasure, and offices of the society, to corrupt the *representatives,* and gain them to his purposes; or openly pre-engages the *electors,* and prescribes to their choice, such, whom he has, by sollicitations, threats, promises, or otherwise, won to his designs; and employs them to bring in such, who have promised beforehand what to vote, and what to enact. . . .

Locke responds to the charge that his theory will produce "frequent rebellion." Indeed, says Locke, the true rebels are the magistrates who, acting contrary to the trust granted them, violate the people's rights.

. . . Such *revolutions happen* not upon every little mismanagement in public affairs. *Great mistakes* in the ruling part, many wrong and inconvenient laws, and all the *slips* of human frailty, will be *borne by the people* without mutiny or murmur. But if a long train of abuses, prevarications and artifices, all tending the same way, make the design visible to the people, and they cannot but feel what they lie under, and see whither they are going; it is not to be wondered at, that they should then rouze themselves, and endeavour to put the rule into

such hands which may secure to them the ends for which government was at first erected. . . .

. . . I answer, that *this doctrine* of a power in the people of providing for their safety a-new, by a new legislative, when their legislators have acted contrary to their trust, by invading their property, is *the best defence against rebellion,* and the probablest means to hinder it: for *rebellion* being an opposition, not to persons, but authority, which is founded only in the constitutions and laws of the government; those, whoever they be, who by force break through, and by force justify their violation of them, are truly and properly *rebels*: for when men, by entering into society and civil government, have excluded force, and introduced laws for the preservation of property, peace, and unity amongst themselves, those who set up force again in opposition to the laws, do [rebel], that is, bring back again the state of war, and are properly rebels: which they who are in power, (by the pretence they have to authority, the temptation of force they have in their hands, and the flattery of those about them) being likeliest to do; the properest way to prevent the evil, is to shew them the danger and injustice of it, who are under the greatest temptation to run into it.

The end of government is the good of mankind; and which is *best for mankind,* that the people should always be exposed to the boundless will of tyranny, or that the rulers should be sometimes liable to be opposed, when they grow exorbitant in the use of their power, and employ it for the destruction, and not the preservation of the properties of their people?

Thomas Jefferson
DECLARATION OF INDEPENDENCE

Written by Thomas Jefferson (1743–1826) to justify the American colonists' break with Britain, the Declaration of Independence enumerated principles that were quite familiar to English statesmen and intellectuals. The preamble to the Declaration, excerpted below, articulated clearly Locke's philosophy of natural rights. Locke had viewed life, liberty, and property as the individual's essential natural rights; Jefferson substituted the "pursuit of happiness" for property.

A DECLARATION BY THE REPRESENTATIVES OF THE UNITED STATES OF AMERICA, IN GENERAL CONGRESS ASSEMBLED.

When in the Course of human Events, it becomes necessary for one People to dissolve the Political Bands which have connected them with another, and to assume among the Powers of the Earth, the separate and equal Station to which the Laws of Nature and of Nature's God entitle them, a decent Respect to the Opinions of Mankind requires that they should declare the causes which impel them to the Separation.

We hold these Truths to be self-evident, that all Men are created equal, that they are endowed by their Creator with certain unalienable Rights, that among these are Life, Liberty, and the Pursuit of Happiness—That to secure these Rights, Governments are instituted among Men, deriving their just Powers from the Consent of the Governed, That whenever any Form of Government becomes destructive of these Ends, it is the Right of the People to alter or to abolish it, and to institute new Gov-ernment, laying its Foundation on such Principles, and organizing its Powers in such Form, as to them shall seem most likely to effect their Safety and Happiness. Prudence, indeed, will dictate that Governments long established should not be changed for light and transient Causes; and accordingly all Experience hath shewn, that Mankind are more disposed to suffer, while Evils are sufferable, than to right themselves by abolishing the Forms to which they are accustomed. But when a long Train of Abuses and Usurpations, pursuing invariably the same Object, evinces a Design to reduce them under absolute Despotism, it is their right, it is their duty, to throw off such Government, and to provide new Guards for their future Security. Such has been the patient Sufferance of these Colonies; and such is now the Necessity which constrains them to alter their former Systems of Government. The History of the present King of Great-Britain is a History of repeated Injuries and Usurpations, all having in direct Object the Establishment of an absolute Tyranny over these States. . . .

REVIEW QUESTIONS

1. What is Locke's view of human nature, the origin and purpose of political authority, and the right of rebellion?
2. Compare Locke's theory of natural rights with the principles stated in the American Declaration of Independence.

3 Attack on the Old Regime

François Marie Arouet (1694–1778), known to the world as Voltaire, was the recognized leader of the French Enlightenment. Few of the philosophes had a better mind, and none had a sharper wit. A relentless critic of the Old Regime (the social structure in prerevolutionary France), Voltaire attacked superstition, religious fanaticism and persecution, censorship, and other abuses of eighteenth-century French society. Spending more than two years in Great Britain, Voltaire acquired a great admiration for English liberty, toleration, commerce, and science. In *Letters Concerning the English Nation* (1733), he drew unfavorable comparisons between a progressive Britain and a reactionary France.

Voltaire's angriest words were directed against established Christianity, to which he attributed many of the ills of modern society. Voltaire regarded Christianity as "the Christ-worshiping superstition" that someday would be destroyed "by the weapons of reason." He rejected revelation and the church hierarchy and was repulsed by Christian intolerance, but he accepted Christian morality and believed in God as the prime mover who set the universe in motion.

Voltaire
A PLEA FOR TOLERANCE AND REASON

The following passages compiled from Voltaire's works—grouped according to topic—provide insight into the outlook of the philosophes. The excerpts come from sources that include his *Candide* (1759), *Treatise on Tolerance* (1763), *The Philosophical Dictionary* (1764), and *Commentary on the Book of Crime and Punishments* (1766).

TOLERANCE

It does not require any great art or studied elocution to prove that Christians ought to tolerate one another. I will go even further and say that we ought to look upon all men as our brothers. What! call a Turk, a Jew, and a Siamese, my brother? Yes, of course; for are we not all children of the same father, and the creatures of the same God?

What is tolerance? . . . We are all full of weakness and errors; let us mutually pardon our follies. This is the last law of nature. . . .

It is clear that every private individual who persecutes a man, his brother, because he is not of the same opinion, is a monster. . . .

Of all religions, the Christian ought doubtless to inspire the most tolerance, although hitherto the Christians have been the most intolerant of all men.

. . . Tolerance has never brought civil war; intolerance has covered the earth with carnage . . . .

What! Is each citizen to be permitted to believe and to think that which his reason rightly or wrongly dictates? He should indeed, provided that he does not disturb the public order; for it is not contingent on man to believe or not to believe; but it is contingent on him to respect the usages of his country; and if you say that it is a crime not to believe in the dominant religion, you accuse then yourself the first Christians, your ancestors, and you justify those whom you accuse of having martyred them.

You reply that there is a great difference, that all religions are the work of men, and that the Apostolic Roman Catholic Church is alone the work of God. But in good faith, ought our religion because it is divine reign through hate, violence, exiles, usurpation of property, prisons, tortures, murders, and thanksgivings to God for these murders? The more the Christian religion is divine, the less it pertains to man to require it; if God made it, God will sustain it without you. You know that intolerance produces only hypocrites or rebels; what distressing alternatives! In short, do you want to sustain through executioners the religion of a God whom executioners have put to death and who taught only gentleness and patience?

———

I shall never cease, my dear sir, to preach tolerance from the housetops, despite the complaints of your priests and the outcries of ours, until persecution is no more. The progress of reason is slow, the roots of prejudice lie deep. Doubtless, I shall never see the fruits of my efforts, but they are seeds which may one day germinate.

DOGMA

. . . Is Jesus the Word? If He be the Word, did He emanate from God in time or before time? If He emanated from God, is He co-eternal and consubstantial with Him, or is He of a similar substance? Is He distinct from Him, or is He not? Is He made or begotten? Can He beget in His turn? Has He paternity? or productive virtue without paternity? Is the Holy Ghost made? or begotten? or produced? or proceeding from the Father? or proceeding from the Son? or proceeding from both? Can He beget? can He produce? is His hypostasis consubstantial with the hypostasis of the Father and the Son? and how is it that, having the same nature—the same essence as the Father and the Son, He cannot do the same things done by these persons who are Himself?

Assuredly, I understand nothing of this; no one has ever understood any of it, and that is why we have slaughtered one another.

The Christians tricked, cavilled, hated, and excommunicated one another, for some of these dogmas inaccessible to human intellect.

FANATICISM

Fanaticism is to superstition what delirium is to fever, what rage is to anger. He who has ecstasies and visions, who takes dreams for realities, and his own imaginations for prophecies is an enthusiast; he who reinforces his madness by murder is a fanatic. . . .

The most detestable example of fanaticism is that exhibited on the night of St. Bartholomew,[1] when the people of Paris rushed from house to house to stab, slaughter, throw out of the window, and tear in pieces their fellow citizens who did not go to mass.

There are some cold-blooded fanatics; such as those judges who sentence men to death for no other crime than that of thinking differently from themselves. . . .

Once fanaticism has infected a brain, the disease is almost incurable. I have seen convulsionaries who, while speaking of the miracles of Saint Paris [a fourth-century Italian bishop], gradually grew heated in spite of themselves. Their eyes became inflamed, their limbs shook, fury disfigured their face, and they would have killed anyone who contradicted them.

There is no other remedy for this epidemic malady than that philosophical spirit which, extending itself from one to another, at length softens the manners of men and prevents the access of the disease. For when the disorder has made any progress, we should, without loss of time, flee from it, and wait till the air has become purified.

PERSECUTION

What is a persecutor? He whose wounded pride and furious fanaticism arouse princes and magistrates against innocent men, whose only crime is that of being of a different opinion. "Impudent man! you have worshipped God; you have preached and practiced virtue; you have served man; you have protected the orphan, have helped the poor; you have changed deserts, in which slaves dragged on a miserable existence, into fertile lands peopled by happy families; but I have discovered that you despise me, and have never read my controversial

———

[1]St. Bartholomew refers to the day of August 24, 1572, when the populace of Paris, instigated by King Charles IX at his mother's urging, began a week-long slaughter of Protestants.

work. You know that I am a rogue; that I have forged G[od]'s signature, that I have stolen. You might tell these things; I must anticipate you. I will, therefore, go to the confessor [spiritual counselor] of the prime minister, or the magistrate; I will show them, with outstretched neck and twisted mouth, that you hold an erroneous opinion in relation to the cells in which the Septuagint was studied; that you have even spoken disrespectfully ten years ago of Tobit's dog,[2] which you asserted to have been a spaniel, while I proved that it was a greyhound. I will denounce you as the enemy of God and man!" Such is the language of the persecutor; and if precisely these words do not issue from his lips, they are engraven on his heart with the pointed steel of fanaticism steeped in the bitterness of envy. . . .

O God of mercy! If any man can resemble that evil being who is described as ceaselessly employed in the destruction of your works, is it not the persecutor?

SUPERSTITION

In 1749 a woman was burned in the Bishopric of Würzburg [a city in central Germany], convicted of being a witch. This is an extraordinary phenomenon in the age in which we live. Is it possible that people who boast of their reformation and of trampling superstition under foot, who indeed supposed that they had reached the perfection of reason, could nevertheless believe in witchcraft, and this more than a hundred years after the so-called reformation of their reason?

In 1652 a peasant woman named Michelle Chaudron, living in the little territory of Geneva [a major city in Switzerland], met the devil going out of the city. The devil gave her a kiss, received her homage, and imprinted on her upper lip and right breast the mark that he customarily bestows on all whom he recognizes as his favorites. This seal of the devil is a little mark which makes the skin insensitive, as all the demonographical jurists of those times affirm.

The devil ordered Michelle Chaudron to bewitch two girls. She obeyed her master punctually. The girls' parents accused her of witchcraft before the law. The girls were questioned and confronted with the accused. They declared that they felt a continual pricking in certain parts of their bodies and that they were possessed. Doctors were called, or at least, those who passed for doctors at that time. They examined the girls. They looked for the devil's seal on Michelle's body—what the statement of the case called *satanic marks.* Into them they drove a long needle, already a painful torture. Blood flowed out, and Michelle made it known, by her cries, that satanic marks certainly do not make one insensitive. The judges, seeing no definite proof that Michelle Chaudron was a witch, proceeded to torture her, a method that infallibly produces the necessary proofs: this wretched woman, yielding to the violence of torture, at last confessed every thing they desired.

The doctors again looked for the satanic mark. They found a little black spot on one of her thighs. They drove in the needle. The torment of the torture had been so horrible that the poor creature hardly felt the needle; thus the crime was established. But as customs were becoming somewhat mild at that time, she was burned only after being hanged and strangled.

In those days every tribunal of Christian Europe resounded with similar arrests. The [twigs] were lit everywhere for witches, as for heretics. People reproached the Turks most for having neither witches nor demons among them. This absence of demons was considered an infallible proof of the falseness of a religion.

A zealous friend of public welfare, of humanity, of true religion, has stated in one of his writings on behalf of innocence, that Christian tribunals have condemned to death over a hun-

---

[2]The Septuagint, the version of the Hebrew Scriptures used by Saint Paul and other early Christians, was a Greek translation done by Hellenized Jews in Alexandria sometime in the late third or the second century B.C. *Tobit's dog* appears in the Book of Tobit, a Hebrew book contained in the Catholic version of the Bible.

dred thousand accused witches. If to these judicial murders are added the infinitely superior number of massacred heretics, that part of the world will seem to be nothing but a vast scaffold covered with torturers and victims, surrounded by judges, guards and spectators.

The following passage is from *Candide,* Voltaire's most famous work of fiction. The king of the Bulgarians goes to war with the king of the Abares, and Candide is caught in the middle of the conflict.

WAR

Nothing could be smarter, more splendid, more brilliant, better drawn up than the two armies. Trumpets, fifes, hautboys [oboes], drums, cannons, formed a harmony such as has never been heard even in hell. The cannons first of all laid flat about six thousand men on each side; then the musketry removed from the best of worlds some nine or ten thousand blackguards who infested its surface. The bayonet also was the sufficient reason for the death of some thousands of men. The whole might amount to thirty thousand souls. Candide, who trembled like a philosopher, hid himself as well as he could during this heroic butchery. At last, while the two Kings each commanded a Te Deum[3] in his camp, Candide decided to go elsewhere to reason about effects and causes. He clambered over heaps of dead and dying men and reached a neighboring village, which was in ashes; it was an Abare village which the Bulgarians had burned in accordance with international law. Here, old men dazed with blows watched the dying agonies of their murdered wives who clutched their children to their bleeding breasts; there, disemboweled girls who had been made to satisfy the natural appetites of heroes gasped their last sighs; others, half-burned, begged to be put to death. Brains were scattered on the ground among dismembered arms and legs. Candide fled to another village as fast as he could; it belonged to the Bulgarians, and Abarian heroes had treated it in the same way. Candide, stumbling over quivering limbs or across ruins, at last escaped from the theater of war. . . .

---

[3]A Te Deum is a special liturgical hymn praising and thanking God for granting some special favor, like a military victory or the end of a war.

REVIEW QUESTIONS

1. What arguments did Voltaire offer in favor of religious toleration?
2. Why did Voltaire ridicule Christian theological disputation?
3. What did Voltaire mean by the term *fanaticism?* What examples of fanaticism did he provide? How was it to be cured?
4. What did Voltaire imply about the rationality and morality of war?

4　Attack on Religion

Christianity came under severe attack during the eighteenth century. The philosophes rejected Christian doctrines that seemed contrary to reason. Deism, the dominant religious outlook of the philosophes, taught that religion should accord with reason and natural law. To deists, it seemed reasonable to believe in God, for this superbly constructed universe required a creator in the same manner that a watch required a watchmaker. But, said the deists, after God had constructed the universe, he did not interfere in its operations; the universe was governed by mechanical laws. Deists denied that the Bible was God's work, rejected clerical authority, and dismissed miracles—like Jesus walking on water—as incompatible with natural law. To them, Jesus was not divine but an inspired teacher of morality. Many deists still considered themselves Christians; the clergy, however, viewed the deists' religious views with horror.

Thomas Paine
THE AGE OF REASON

Exemplifying the deist outlook was Thomas Paine (1737–1809), an Englishman who moved to America in 1774. Paine's *Common Sense* (1776) was an eloquent appeal for American independence. Paine is also famous for *The Rights of Man* (1791–1792), in which he defended the French Revolution. In *The Age of Reason* (1794–1795), he denounced Christian mysteries, miracles, and prophecies as superstition and called for a natural religion that accorded with reason and science.

I believe in one God, and no more; and I hope for happiness beyond this life.

I believe in the equality of man; and I believe that religious duties consist in doing justice, loving mercy, and endeavoring to make our fellow-creatures happy.

But, lest it should be supposed that I believe many other things in addition to these, I shall, in the progress of this work, declare the things I do not believe, and my reasons for not believing them.

I do not believe in the creed professed by the Jewish church, by the Roman church, by the Greek church, by the Turkish church, by the Protestant church, nor by any church that I know of. My own mind is my own church. . . .

When Moses told the children of Israel that he received the two tables of the [Ten] commandments from the hands of God, they were not obliged to believe him, because they had no other authority for it than his telling them so; and I have no other authority for it than some historian telling me so. The commandments carry no internal evidence of divinity with them; they contain some good moral precepts, such as any man qualified to be a law-

giver, or a legislator, could produce himself, without having recourse to supernatural intervention. . . .

When also I am told that a woman called the Virgin Mary, said, or gave out, that she was with child without any cohabitation with a man, and that her betrothed husband, Joseph, said that an angel told him so, I have a right to believe them or not; such a circumstance required a much stronger evidence than their bare word for it; but we have not even this— for neither Joseph nor Mary wrote any such matter themselves; it is only reported by others that *they said so*—it is hearsay upon hearsay, and I do not choose to rest my belief upon such evidence.

It is, however, not difficult to account for the credit that was given to the story of Jesus Christ being the son of God. He was born when the heathen mythology had still some fashion and repute in the world, and that mythology had prepared the people for the belief of such a story. Almost all the extraordinary men that lived under the heathen mythology were reputed to be the sons of some of their gods. It was not a new thing, at that time, to believe a man to have been celestially begotten; the intercourse of gods with women was then a matter of familiar opinion. Their Jupiter [chief Roman god], according to their accounts, had cohabited with hundreds: the story, therefore, had nothing in it either new, wonderful, or obscene; it was conformable to the opinions that then prevailed among the people called Gentiles, or Mythologists, and it was those people only that believed it. The Jews who had kept strictly to the belief of one God, and no more, and who had always rejected the heathen mythology, never credited the story. . . .

Nothing that is here said can apply, even with the most distant disrespect, to the real character of Jesus Christ. He was a virtuous and an amiable man. The morality that he preached and practised was of the most benevolent kind; and though similar systems of morality had been preached by Confucius [Chinese philosopher], and by some of the Greek philosophers, many years before; by the Quakers [members of the Society of Friends] since; and by many good men in all ages, it has not been exceeded by any. . . .

. . . The resurrection and ascension [of Jesus Christ], supposing them to have taken place, admitted of public and ocular demonstration, like that of the ascension of a balloon, or the sun at noon-day, to all Jerusalem at least. A thing which everybody is required to believe, requires that the proof and evidence of it should be equal to all, and universal; and as the public visibility of this last related act was the only evidence that could give sanction to the former part, the whole of it falls to the ground, because that evidence never was given. Instead of this, a small number of persons, not more than eight or nine, are introduced as proxies for the whole world, to say they saw it, and all the rest of the world are called upon to believe it. But it appears that Thomas [one of Jesus' disciples] did not believe the resurrection, and, as they say, would not believe without having ocular and manual demonstration himself. *So neither will I,* and the reason is equally as good for me, and for every other person, as for Thomas.

It is in vain to attempt to palliate or disguise this matter. The story, so far as relates to the supernatural part, has every mark of fraud and imposition stamped upon the face of it. Who were the authors of it is as impossible for us now to know, as it is for us to be assured that the books in which the account is related were written by the persons whose names they bear; the best surviving evidence we now have respecting this affair is the Jews. They are regularly descended from the people who lived in the times this resurrection and ascension is said to have happened, and they say, *it is not true.*

Baron d'Holbach
GOOD SENSE

More extreme than the deists were the atheists, who denied God's existence altogether. The foremost exponent of atheism was Paul-Henri Thiry, Baron d'Holbach (1723–1789), a prominent contributor to the *Encyclopedia* (see Section 6). Holbach hosted many leading intellectuals, including Diderot, Rousseau, and Condorcet (all represented later in this chapter), at his country estate outside of Paris. He regarded the idea of God as a product of ignorance, fear, and superstition and said that terrified by natural phenomena—storms, fire, floods—humanity's primitive ancestors attributed these occurrences to unseen spirits, whom they tried to appease through rituals. In denouncing religion, Holbach was also affirming core Enlightenment ideals—reason and freedom— as the following passage from *Good Sense* reveals.

In a word, whoever will deign to consult common sense upon religious opinions, and will bestow on this inquiry the attention that is commonly given to any objects we presume interesting, will easily perceive that those opinions have no foundation; that Religion is a mere castle in the air. Theology is but the ignorance of natural causes reduced to a system; a long tissue of fallacies and contradictions. In every country, it presents us with romances void of probability. . . .

Savage and furious nations, perpetually at war, adore, under divers names, some God, conformable to their ideas, that is to say, cruel, carnivorous, selfish, bloodthirsty. We find, in all the religions of the earth, "a God of armies," a "jealous God," an "avenging God," a "destroying God," a "God," who is pleased with carnage, and whom his worshippers consider it as a duty to serve to his taste. Lambs, bulls, children, men, heretics, infidels, kings, whole nations, are sacrificed to him. Do not the zealous servants of this barbarous God think themselves obliged even to offer up themselves as a sacrifice to him? Madmen may every where be seen who, after meditating upon their terrible God, imagine that to please him they must do themselves all possible injury, and inflict on themselves, for this honour, the most exquisite torments. The gloomy ideas more usefully formed of the Deity, far from consoling them under the evils of life, have every where disquieted their minds, and produced follies destructive to their happiness.

How could the human mind make any considerable progress, while tormented with frightful phantoms, and guided by men, interested in perpetuating its ignorance and fears? Man has been forced to vegetate in his primitive stupidity: he has been taught nothing but stories about invisible powers upon whom his happiness was supposed to depend. Occupied solely by his fears, and by unintelligible reveries, he

has always been at the mercy of his priests, who have reserved to themselves the right of thinking for him, and directing his actions.

Thus man has remained a child without experience, a slave without courage, fearing to reason, and unable to extricate himself from the labyrinth, in which he has so long been wandering. He believes himself forced to bend under the yoke of his gods, known to him only by the fabulous accounts given by his ministers, who, after binding each unhappy mortal in the chains of his prejudice, remain his masters, or else abandon him defenceless to the absolute power of tyrants, no less terrible than the gods, of whom they are the representatives upon earth.

Oppressed by the double yoke of spiritual and temporal power, it has been impossible for the people to know and pursue their happiness. As Religion, so Politics and Morality became sacred things, which the profane were not permitted to handle. Men have had no other Morality, than what their legislators and priests brought down from the unknown regions of heaven. The human mind, confused by its theological opinions ceased to know its own powers, mistrusted experience, feared truth and disdained reason, in order to follow authority. Man has been a mere machine in the hands of tyrants and priests, who alone have had the right of directing his actions. Always treated as a slave, he has contracted the vices of a slave.

Such are the true causes of the corruption of morals, to which Religion opposes only ideal and ineffectual barriers. Ignorance and servitude are calculated to make men wicked and unhappy. Knowledge, Reason, and Liberty, can alone reform them, and make them happier. But every thing conspires to blind them and to confirm them in their errors. Priests cheat them, tyrants corrupt, the better to enslave them. Tyranny ever was, and ever will be, the true cause of man's depravity, and also of his habitual calamities. Almost always fascinated by religious fiction, poor mortals turn not their eyes to the natural and obvious causes of their misery; but attribute their vices to the imperfection of their natures, and their unhappiness to the anger of the gods. They offer up to heaven vows, sacrifices, and presents, to obtain the end of their sufferings, which in reality, are attributable only to the negligence, ignorance, and perversity of their guides, to the folly of their customs, to the unreasonableness of their laws, and above all, to the general want of knowledge. Let men's minds be filled with true ideas; let their reason be cultivated; let justice govern them; and there will be no need of opposing to the passions, such a feeble barrier, as the fear of the gods. Men will be good, when they are well instructed, well governed, and when they are punished or despised for the evil, and justly rewarded for the good, which they do to their fellow citizens.

To discover the true principles of Morality, men have no need of theology, of revelation, or of gods: They have need only of common sense. They have only to commune with themselves, to reflect upon their own nature, to consult their visible interests, to consider the objects of society, and of the individuals who compose it; and they will easily perceive, that virtue is advantageous, and vice disadvantageous to such beings as themselves. Let us persuade men to be just, beneficent, moderate, sociable; not because such conduct is demanded by the gods, but, because it is pleasure to men. Let us advise them to abstain from vice and crime; not because they will be punished in the other world, but because they will suffer for it in this.—*There are,* says a great man [Montesquieu], *means to prevent crimes, and these means are punishments; there are means to reform manners, and these means are good examples. . . .*

. . . Men are unhappy, only because they are ignorant; they are ignorant, only because every thing conspires to prevent their being enlightened; they are wicked, only because their reason is not sufficiently developed.

REVIEW QUESTIONS

1. What Christian beliefs did Thomas Paine reject? Why?
2. How did Baron d'Holbach's critique of religion affirm basic Enlightenment ideals?

---

5 Epistemology and Education

The philosophes sought a naturalistic understanding of the human condition, one that examined human nature and society without reference to God's will. Toward this end, they sought to explain how the mind acquires knowledge; and as reformers, they stressed the importance of education in shaping a better person and a better society.

John Locke
ESSAY CONCERNING HUMAN UNDERSTANDING

In his *Essay Concerning Human Understanding* (1689–1693), a work of immense significance in the history of philosophy, John Locke argued that human beings are not born with innate ideas (the idea of God and principles of good and evil, for example) divinely implanted in their minds. Rather, said Locke, the human mind at birth is a blank slate upon which are imprinted sensations derived from contact with the world. These sensations, combined with the mind's reflections on them, are the source of ideas. In effect, knowledge is derived from experience. In the tradition of Francis Bacon, Locke's epistemology (theory of knowledge) implied that people should not dwell on insoluble questions, particularly sterile theological issues, but should seek practical knowledge that promotes human happiness and enlightens human beings and gives them control over their environment.

Locke's empiricism, which aspired to useful knowledge and stimulated an interest in political and ethical questions that focused on human concerns, helped to mold the utilitarian and reformist spirit of the Enlightenment. If there are no innate ideas, said the philosophes, then human beings are not born with original sin, contrary to what Christians believed. All that individuals are derives from their particular experiences. If people are provided with a proper environment and education, they will become intelligent and productive citizens. This was how the reform-minded philosophes interpreted Locke. They preferred to believe that evil stemmed from faulty institutions and poor education, both of which could be remedied, rather than from a defective human nature. Excerpts from *Essay Concerning Human Understanding* follow.

Let us then suppose the mind to be, as we say, white paper, void of all characters, without any ideas:—How comes it to be furnished? Whence comes it by that vast store which the busy and boundless fancy of man has painted on it with an almost endless variety? Whence has it all the *materials* of reason and knowledge? To this I answer, in one word, from EXPERIENCE. In that all our knowledge is founded; and from that it ultimately derives itself. Our observation employed either, about external sensible objects or about the internal operations of our minds perceived and reflected on by ourselves, is that which supplies our understandings with all the *materials* of thinking. These two are the fountains of knowledge, from whence all the ideas we have, or can naturally have, do spring.

First, our Senses, conversant about particular sensible objects, do convey into the mind several distinct perceptions of things, according to those various ways wherein those objects do affect them. And thus we come by those *ideas* we have of *yellow, white, heat, cold, soft, hard, bitter, sweet,* and all those which we call sensible

qualities; which when I say the senses convey into the mind, I mean, they from external objects convey into the mind what produces there those perceptions. This great source of most of the ideas we have, depending wholly upon our senses, and derived by them to the understanding, I call SENSATION.

Secondly, the other fountain from which experience furnisheth the understanding with ideas is,—the perception of the operations of our own mind within us, as it is employed about the ideas it has got. . . .

And such are *perception, thinking, doubting, believing, reasoning, knowing, willing,* and all the different actings of our own minds;—which we being conscious of, and observing in ourselves, do from these receive into our understandings as distinct ideas as we do from bodies affecting our senses. This source of ideas every man has wholly in himself; and though it be not sense, as having nothing to do with external objects, yet it is very like it, and might properly enough be called *internal sense.* But as I call the other Sensation, so I call this REFLECTION, the ideas it affords being such only as the mind gets by reflecting on its own operations within itself. By reflection then, in the following part of this discourse, I would be understood to mean, that notice which the mind takes of its own operations, and the manner of them, by reason whereof there come to be ideas of these operations in the understanding. These two, I say, viz. external material things, as the objects of SENSATION, and the operations of our own minds within, as the objects of RE-FLECTION, are to me the only originals from whence all our ideas take their beginnings. . . .

The understanding seems to me not to have the least glimmering of any ideas which it doth not receive from one of these two. *External objects* furnish the mind with the ideas of sensible qualities, which are all those different perceptions they produce in us; and *the mind* furnishes the understanding with ideas of its own operations.

These, when we have taken a full survey of them, and their several modes, (combinations, and relations,) we shall find to contain all our whole stock of ideas; and that we have nothing in our minds which did not come in one of these two ways. Let any one examine his own thoughts, and thoroughly search into his understanding; and then let him tell me, whether all the original ideas he has there, are any other than of the objects of his senses, or of the operations of his mind, considered as objects of his reflection. And how great a mass of knowledge soever he imagines to be lodged there, he will, upon taking a strict view, see that he has not any idea in his mind but what one of these two have imprinted;—though perhaps, with infinite variety compounded and enlarged by the understanding, as we shall see hereafter.

He that attentively considers the state of a child, at his first coming into the world, will have little reason to think him stored with plenty of ideas, that are to be the matter of his future knowledge. It is *by degrees* he comes to be furnished with them.

John Locke
SOME THOUGHTS CONCERNING EDUCATION

In *Some Thoughts Concerning Education* (1693), excerpted below, Locke expressed a warm concern for children. Deploring rote learning and physical punishment, he maintained that parents and teachers should be mild but firm, teach sound habits by example, and utilize the child's natural disposition for play to good educational advantage.

I think I may say, that of all the Men we meet with, Nine Parts of Ten are what they are, Good or Evil, useful or not, by their Education. 'Tis that which makes the great Difference in Mankind: The little, and almost insensible Impressions on our tender Infancies, have very important and lasting Consequences: And there 'tis, as in the Fountains of some Rivers, where a gentle Application of the Hand turns the flexible Waters into Chanels, that make them take quite contrary Courses, and by this little Direction given them at first in the Source, they receive different Tendencies, and arrive at last, at very remote and distant Places. . . .

If what I have said in the beginning of this Discourse be true, as I do not doubt but it is, *viz.* That the difference to be found in the Manners and Abilities of Men, is owing more to their *Education* than to any thing else; we have reason to conclude, that great care is to be had of the forming Children's *Minds,* and giving them that seasoning early, which shall influence their Lives always after. . . .

The great Mistake I have observed in People's [rearing] their Children has been, that . . . the Mind has not been made obedient to Discipline, and pliant to Reason, when at first it was most tender, most easy to be bowed. . . .

The Difference lies not in the having or not having Appetites, but in the Power to govern, and deny our selves in them. He that is not used to submit his Will to the Reason of others, *when* he is *young,* will scarce hearken or submit to his own Reason, when he is of an Age to make use of it. And what a kind of a Man such an one is like to prove, is easie to foresee. . . .

I am very apt to think that *great Severity* of Punishment does but very little Good; nay, great Harm in Education: And I believe it will be found, that, *Cæteris paribus,* those Children, who have been most *chastised,* seldom make the best Men. All that I have hitherto contended for, is, That whatsoever *Rigour* is necessary, it is more to be used the younger Children are; and having, by a due Application, wrought its Effect, it is to be relaxed, and changed into a milder Sort of Government. . . .

[I]f the *Mind* be curbed, and *humbled* too much in Children; if their *Spirits* be abased and *broken* much, by too strict an hand over them, they lose all their Vigor and Industry, and are in a worse State than the former. For extravagant young Fellows, that have Liveliness and Spirit, come sometimes to be set right, and so make Able and Great Men: But *dejected Minds,* timorous, and tame, and *low Spirits,* are hardly ever to be raised, and very seldom attain to any thing. To avoid the danger, that is on either hand, is the great Art; and he that has found a way, how to keep a Child's Spirit, easy, active and free; and yet, at the same time, to restrain him from many things he has a Mind to, and to draw him to things that are uneasy to him; he, I say, that knows how to reconcile these seeming Contradictions, has, in my Opinion, got the true Secret of Education. . . .

Beating then, and all other Sorts of slavish and corporal Punishments, are not the Discipline fit to be used in the Education of those we would have wise, good, and ingenuous Men; and therefore very rarely to be applied, and that only in great Occasions, and Cases of Extremity. On the other side, to flatter Children by *Rewards* of things, that are pleasant to them, is as carefully to be avoided.

But, if you take away the Rod on one hand, and these little Encouragements, which they are taken with, on the other, How then (will you say) shall Children be govern'd? Remove Hope and Fear, and there is an end of all Discipline. I grant, that Good and Evil, *Reward* and *Punishment,* are the only Motives to a rational Creature; these are the Spur and Reins, whereby all Mankind are set on work, and guided, and therefore they are to be made use of to Children too. For I advise their Parents and Governors always to carry this in their Minds, that Children are to be treated as rational Creatures. . . .

Rewards, I grant, and *Punishments* must be proposed to Children, if we intend to work upon them. The Mistake, I imagine, is, that those that are generally made use of, are *ill chosen.* The Pains and Pleasures of the Body are, I think, of ill consequence, when made the Rewards and Punishments, whereby Men would prevail on their Children. . . .

The *Rewards* and *Punishments* then, whereby we should keep Children in order, *are* quite of another kind, and of that force, that when we can get them once to work, the business, I think, is done, and the difficulty is over. *Esteem* and *Disgrace* are, of all others, the most powerful incentives to the Mind, when once it is brought to relish them. If you can once get into Children a love of Credit, and an apprehension of Shame and Disgrace, you have put into them the true Principle, which will constantly work, and incline them to the right. . . .

But to return to the Businesses of Rewards and Punishments. All the Actions of Childishness, and unfashionable Carriage . . . being . . . exempt from the Discipline of the Rod, there will not be so much need of beating Children, as is generally made use of. To which if we add Learning to Read, Write, Dance, Foreign

Languages, &c. as under the same Privilege, there will be but very rarely any Occasion for Blows or Force in an ingenuous Education. The right Way to teach them those Things is, to give them a Liking and Inclination to what you propose to them to be learn'd; and that will engage their Industry and Application. This I think no hard Matter to do, if Children be handled as they should be, and the Rewards and Punishments above-mentioned be carefully applied, and with them these few Rules observed in the Method of Instructing them. . . .

It will perhaps be wondered that I mention *Reasoning* with Children: And yet I cannot but think that the true Way of Dealing with them. They understand it as early as they do Language; and, if I misobserve not, they love to be treated as Rational Creatures sooner than is imagined. 'Tis a Pride should be cherished in them, and, as much as can be, made the great Instrument to turn them by.

But when I talk of *Reasoning,* I do not intend any other, but such as is suited to the Child's Capacity and Apprehension. No Body can think a Boy of Three, or Seven Years old, should be argued with, as a grown Man. Long Discourses, and Philosophical Reasonings, at best, amaze and confound, but do not instruct Children. When I say therefore, that they must be *treated as Rational Creatures,* I mean, that you should make them sensible by the Mildness of your Carriage, and the Composure even in your Correction of them, that what you do is reasonable in you, and useful and necessary for them: And that it is not out of *Caprichio,* Passion, or Fancy, that you command or forbid them any Thing. This they are capable of understanding; and there is no Vertue they should be excited to, nor Fault they should be kept from, which I do not think they may be convinced of; but it must be by such *Reasons* as their Age and Understanding are capable of, and those proposed always *in* very *few and plain Words.* . . .

But of all the Ways whereby Children are to be instructed, and their Manners formed, the plainest, easiest and most efficacious, is to set before their Eyes the *Examples* of those Things you would have them do, or avoid. Which, when they are pointed out to them, in the Practice of Persons within their Knowledge, with some Reflection on their Beauty or Unbecomingness, are of more force to draw or deterr their Imitation, than any Discourses which can be made to them.

Claude Helvétius
ESSAYS ON THE MIND AND *A TREATISE ON MAN*

Even more than did Locke, Claude-Adrien Helvétius (1715–1777) emphasized the importance of the environment in shaping the human mind. Disparities in intelligence and talent, said Helvétius, are due entirely to environmental conditions and not to inborn qualities. Since human beings are malleable and perfectible, their moral and intellectual growth depends on proper conditioning. For this reason he called for political reforms, particularly the implementation of a program of enlightened public education.

In 1758 Helvétius published *Essays on the Mind,* which treated ethics in a purely naturalistic way. Shocked by his separation of morality from God's commands and from fear of divine punishment as well as by his attacks on the clergy, the authorities suppressed the book. His second major work, *A Treatise on Man,* was published posthumously in 1777. Apparently Helvétius wanted to avoid another controversy. The following passages from both works illustrate Helvétius' belief that "education makes us what we are."

ESSAYS ON THE MIND

The general conclusion of this discourse is, that genius is common, and the circumstances, proper to unfold it, very extraordinary. If we may compare what is profane to what is sacred, we may say in this respect, Many are called, but few are chosen.

The inequality observable among men, therefore, depends on the government under which they lie; on the greater or less happiness of the age in which they are born; on the education; on their desire of improvement, and on the importance of the ideas that are the subject of their contemplations.

The man of genius is then only produced by the circumstances in which he is placed.* Thus all the art of education consists in placing young men in such a concurrence of circumstances as are proper to unfold the buds of genius and virtue. [I am led to this conclusion by] the desire of promoting the happiness of mankind. I am convinced that a good education would diffuse light, virtue, and consequently, happiness in society; and that the

opinion, that geniuses and virtue are merely gifts of nature, is a great obstacle to the making any farther progress in the science of education, and in this respect is the great favourer of idleness and negligence. With this view, examining the effects which nature and education may have upon us, I have perceived that education makes us what we are; in consequence of which I have thought that it was the duty of a citizen to make known a truth proper to awaken the attention, with respect to the means of carrying this education to perfection.

A TREATISE ON MAN

Some maintain that, *The understanding is the effect of a certain sort of interior temperament and organization.*

Locke and I say: *The inequality in minds or understandings, is the effect of a known cause, and this cause is the difference of education.* . . .

Among the great number of questions treated of in this work, one of the most important was to determine whether genius, virtue, and talents, to which nations owe their grandeur and felicity, were the effect of the difference of. . . . the organs of the five senses [that is, differences due to birth] . . . or if the same genius, the same virtues, and the same talents were the effect of education, over which the laws and the form of government are all powerful.

If I have proved the truth of the latter assertion, it must be allowed that the happiness of nations is in their own hands, and that it entirely depends on the greater or less interest they take in improving the science of education.

---

*The opinion I advance must appear very pleasing to the vanity of the greatest part of mankind, and therefore, ought to meet with a favourable reception. According to my principles, they ought not to attribute the inferiority of their abilities to the humbling cause of a less perfect organization, but to the education they have received, as well as to the circumstances in which they have been placed. Every man of moderate abilities, in conformity with my principles, has a right to think, that if he had been more favoured by fortune, if he had been born in a certain age or country, he had himself been like the great men whose genius he is forced to admire.

Jean Jacques Rousseau
ÉMILE

In *The Social Contract* (see page 49), Jean Jacques Rousseau (1712–1778), who had only contempt for absolute monarchy, sought to provide a theoretical foundation for political liberty. In *Émile* (1762), he suggested another cure for the ills of modern society: educational reforms that would instill in children self-confidence, self-reliance, and emotional security. Rousseau understood that children should not be treated like little adults. He railed against chaining young children to desks and filling their heads with rote learning. Instead, he urged that children experience direct contact with the world to develop their ingenuity, resourcefulness, and imagination so that they might become productive and responsible citizens. Excerpts from Rousseau's influential treatise on education follow.

When I thus get rid of children's lessons, I get rid of the chief cause of their sorrows, namely their books. Reading is the curse of childhood, yet it is almost the only occupation you can find for children. Emile, at twelve years old, will hardly know what a book is. "But," you say, "he must, at least, know how to read." When reading is of use to him, I admit he must learn to read, but till then he will only find it a nuisance.

If children are not to be required to do anything as a matter of obedience, it follows that they will only learn what they perceive to be of real and present value, either for use or enjoyment; what other motive could they have for learning? . . .

People make a great fuss about discovering the best way to teach children to read. They invent "bureaux"* and cards, they turn the nursery into a printer's shop. Locke would have them taught to read by means of dice. What a fine idea! And the pity of it! There is a better way than any of those, and one which is generally overlooked—it consists in the desire to learn. Arouse this desire in your scholar and have done with your "bureaux" and your dice—any method will serve.

Present interest, that is the motive power, the only motive power that takes us far and safely. Sometimes Emile receives notes of invitation from his father or mother, his relations or friends; he is invited to a dinner, a walk, a boating expedition, to see some public entertainment. These notes are short, clear, plain, and well written. Some one must read them to him, and he cannot always find anybody when wanted; no more consideration is shown to him than he himself showed to you yesterday. Time passes, the chance is lost. The note is read to him at last, but it is too late. Oh! if only he had known how to read! He receives other notes, so short, so interesting, he would like to try to read them. Sometimes he gets help, sometimes none. He does his best, and at last he makes out half the note; it is something about going to-morrow to drink cream—Where? With whom? He cannot tell—how hard he tries to make out the rest! I do not think Emile will need a "bureau." Shall I proceed to the teaching of writing? No, I am ashamed to toy with these trifles in a treatise on education. . . .

If, in accordance with the plan I have sketched, you follow rules which are just the

---

*Translator's note—The "bureau" was a sort of case containing letters to be put together to form words. It was a favourite device for the teaching of reading and gave its name to a special method, called the bureau-method, of learning to read.

opposite of the established practice, if instead of taking your scholar far afield, instead of wandering with him in distant places, in far-off lands, in remote centuries, in the ends of the earth, and in the very heavens themselves, you try to keep him to himself, to his own concerns, you will then find him able to perceive, to remember, and even to reason; this is nature's order. . . . Give his body constant exercise, make it strong and healthy, in order to make him good and wise; let him work, let him do things, let him run and shout, let him be always on the go; make a man of him in strength, and he will soon be a man in reason.

Of course by this method you will make him stupid if you are always giving him directions, always saying come here, go there, stop, do this, don't do that. If your head always guides his hands, his own mind will become useless. . . .

It is a lamentable mistake to imagine that bodily activity hinders the working of the mind, as if these two kinds of activity ought not to advance hand in hand, and as if the one were not intended to act as guide to the other. . . .

. . . Your scholar is subject to a power which is continually giving him instruction; he acts only at the word of command; he dare not eat when he is hungry, nor laugh when he is merry, nor weep when he is sad, nor offer one hand rather than the other, nor stir a foot unless he is told to do it; before long he will not venture to breathe without orders. What would you have him think about, when you do all the thinking for him? . . .

As for my pupil, or rather Nature's pupil, he has been trained from the outset to be as self-reliant as possible, he has not formed the habit of constantly seeking help from others, still less of displaying his stores of learning. On the other hand, he exercises discrimination and forethought, he reasons about everything that concerns himself. He does not chatter, he acts. Not a word does he know of what is going on in the world at large, but he knows very thoroughly what affects himself. As he is always stirring he is compelled to notice many things, to recognise many effects; he soon acquires a good deal of experience. Nature, not man, is his schoolmaster, and he learns all the quicker because he is not aware that he has any lesson to learn. So mind and body work together. He is always carrying out his own ideas, not those of other people, and thus he unites thought and action; as he grows in health and strength he grows in wisdom and discernment.

REVIEW QUESTIONS

1. According to John Locke, knowledge originates in experience and has two sources—the senses and reflection. What does this mean, and what makes this view of knowledge so revolutionary?

2. How does Locke's view of the origin of knowledge compare to that of René Descartes (see page 17)? Which view do you favor, or can you suggest another alternative?

3. How would you characterize Locke's general theory of education? Is it compatible with his theory of knowledge?

4. What implications do Locke's theory of knowledge and educational theory have for his conception of human nature?

5. In what way may Claude Helvétius be regarded as a disciple of John Locke, and how did he expand the significance of Locke's ideas?

6. What was Rousseau's basic approach to educating a child?

7. Compare Rousseau's theory of education with Locke's. How similar or different are their views, and what implications do they have for their respective conceptions of human nature?

6 Compendium of Knowledge

A 38-volume *Encyclopedia,* whose 150 or more contributors included leading Enlightenment thinkers, was undertaken in Paris during the 1740s as a monumental effort to bring together all human knowledge and to propagate Enlightenment ideas. The *Encyclopedia*'s numerous articles on science and technology and its limited coverage of theological questions attest to the new interests of eighteenth-century intellectuals. Serving as principal editor, Denis Diderot (1713–1784) steered the project through difficult periods, including the suspension of publication by French authorities. After the first two volumes were published, the authorities denounced the work for containing "maxims that would tend to destroy royal authority, foment a spirit of independence and revolt, . . . and lay the foundations for the corruption of morals and religion." In 1759, Pope Clement XIII condemned the *Encyclopedia* for having "scandalous doctrines [and] inducing scorn for religion." It required careful diplomacy and clever ruses to finish the project and still incorporate ideas considered dangerous by religious and governmental authorities. With the project's completion in 1772, Diderot and Enlightenment opinion triumphed over clerical censors and powerful elements at the French court.

Denis Diderot
ENCYCLOPEDIA

The *Encyclopedia* was a monument to the Enlightenment, as Diderot himself recognized. "This work will surely produce in time a revolution in the minds of man, and I hope that tyrants, oppressors, fanatics, and the intolerant will not gain thereby. We shall have served humanity." Some articles from the *Encyclopedia* follow.

Encyclopedia . . . In truth, the aim of an *encyclopedia* is to collect all the knowledge scattered over the face of the earth, to present its general outlines and structure to the men with whom we live, and to transmit this to those who will come after us, so that the work of past centuries may be useful to the following centuries, that our children, by becoming more educated, may at the same time become more virtuous and happier, and that we may not die without having deserved well of the human race. . . .

. . . We have seen that our *Encyclopedia* could only have been the endeavor of a philosophical century. . . .

I have said that it could only belong to a philosophical age to attempt an *encyclopedia*; and I have said this because such a work constantly demands more intellectual daring than is commonly found in [less courageous periods]. All things must be examined, debated, investigated without exception and without regard for anyone's feelings. . . . We must ride roughshod over all these ancient puerilities, overturn the barriers that reason never erected, give back to the arts and sciences the liberty that is so precious to them.... We have for quite some time needed a reasoning age when men would no longer seek the rules in classical authors but in nature....

Fanaticism ... is blind and passionate zeal born of superstitious opinions, causing people to commit ridiculous, unjust, and cruel actions, not only without any shame or remorse, but even with a kind of joy and comfort. *Fanaticism,* therefore, is only superstition put into practice....

   Fanaticism has done much more harm to the world than impiety. What do impious people claim? To free themselves of a yoke, while *fanatics* want to extend their chains over all the earth. Infernal zealomania! ...

Government ... The good of the people must be the great purpose of the *government.* The governors are appointed to fulfill it; and the civil constitution that invests them with this power is bound therein by the laws of nature and by the law of reason, which has determined that purpose in any form of *government* as the cause of its welfare. The greatest good of the people is its liberty. Liberty is to the body of the state what health is to each individual; without health man cannot enjoy pleasure; without liberty the state of welfare is excluded from nations. A patriotic governor will therefore see that the right to defend and to maintain liberty is the most sacred of his duties....

   If it happens that those who hold the reins of *government* find some resistance when they use their power for the destruction and not the conservation of things that rightfully belong to the people, they must blame themselves, because the public good and the advantage of society are the purposes of establishing a *government.* Hence it necessarily follows that power cannot be arbitrary and that it must be exercised according to the established laws so that the people may know its duty and be secure within the shelter of laws, and so that governors at the same time should be held within just limits and not be tempted to em-

ploy the power they have in hand to do harmful things to the body politic. ...

History ... *On the usefullness of history.* The advantage consists of the comparison that a statesman or a citizen can make of foreign laws, morals, and customs with those of his country. This is what stimulates modern nations to surpass one another in the arts, in commerce, and in agriculture. The great mistakes of the past are useful in all areas. We cannot describe too often the crimes and misfortunes caused by absurd quarrels. It is certain that by refreshing our memory of these quarrels, we prevent a repetition of them. ...

Humanity ... is a benevolent feeling for all men, which hardly inflames anyone without a great and sensitive soul. This sublime and noble enthusiasm is troubled by the pains of other people and by the necessity to alleviate them. With these sentiments an individual would wish to cover the entire universe in order to abolish slavery, superstition, vice, and misfortune. ...

Intolerance ... Any method that would tend to stir up men, to arm nations, and to soak the earth with blood is impious.

   It is impious to want to impose laws upon man's conscience: this is a universal rule of conduct. People must be enlightened and not constrained. ...

   What did Christ recommend to his disciples when he sent them among the Gentiles? Was it to kill or to die? Was it to persecute or to suffer? ...

   Which is the true voice of humanity, the persecutor who strikes or the persecuted who moans?

Peace ... War is the fruit of man's depravity; it is a convulsive and violent sickness of the body politic. ...

   If reason governed men and had the influence over the heads of nations that it deserves, we would never see them inconsiderately surrender themselves to the fury of war; they would not show that ferocity that characterizes wild beasts. . . .

Political Authority   No man has received from nature the right to command others. Liberty is a gift from heaven, and each individual of the same species has the right to enjoy it as soon as he enjoys the use of reason. . . .

The prince owes to his very subjects the *authority* that he has over them; and this *authority* is limited by the laws of nature and the state. The laws of nature and the state are the conditions under which they have submitted or are supposed to have submitted to its government. . . .

Moreover the government, although hereditary in a family and placed in the hands of one person, is not private property, but public property that consequently can never be taken from the people, to whom it belongs exclusively, fundamentally, and as a freehold. Consequently it is always the people who make the

lease or the agreement: they always intervene in the contract that adjudges its exercise. It is not the state that belongs to the prince, it is the prince who belongs to the state: but it does rest with the prince to govern in the state, because the state has chosen him for that purpose: he has bound himself to the people and the administration of affairs, and they in their turn are bound to obey him according to the laws. . . .

The Press   [*press* includes newspapers, magazines, books, and so forth] . . . People ask if freedom of the *press* is advantageous or prejudicial to a state. The answer is not difficult. It is of the greatest importance to conserve this practice in all states founded on liberty. I would even say that the disadvantages of this liberty are so inconsiderable compared to its advantages that this ought to be the common right of the universe, and it is certainly advisable to authorize its practice in all governments. . . .

REVIEW QUESTIONS

1. Why was the publication of the *Encyclopedia* a vital step in the philosophes' hopes for reform?
2. To what extent were John Locke's political ideals reflected in the *Encyclopedia*?
3. Why was freedom of the press of such significance to the enlightened philosophes?

7 Rousseau: Political Reform

To the philosophes, advances in the arts were hallmarks of progress. However, Jean Jacques Rousseau argued that the accumulation of knowledge improved human understanding but corrupted the morals of human beings. In *A Discourse on the Arts and Sciences* (1750) and *A Discourse on the Origin of Inequality* (1755), Rousseau diagnosed the illnesses of modern civilization. He said that human nature, which was originally good, had been corrupted by society. As a result, he stated at the beginning of *The Social Contract* (1762), "Man is born free; and everywhere he is in chains." How can humanity be made moral and free again? In *The Social Contract,* Rousseau suggested one cure: reforming the political system. He argued that in the existing civil society the rich and powerful who controlled the state oppressed the majority. Rousseau admired the small, ancient Greek city-state (polis), where citizens participated actively and directly in public affairs. A small state modeled after the ancient Greek polis, said Rousseau, would be best able to resolve the tensions between individual freedom and the requirements of the collective community.

Jean Jacques Rousseau
THE SOCIAL CONTRACT

In the opening chapters of *The Social Contract,* Rousseau rejected the principle that one person has a natural authority over others. All legitimate authority, he said, stemmed from human traditions, not from nature. Rousseau had only contempt for absolute monarchy and in *The Social Contract* sought to provide a theoretical foundation for political liberty.

[To rulers who argued that they provided security for their subjects, Rousseau responded as follows:]

It will be said that the despot assures his subjects civil tranquillity. Granted; but what do they gain, if the wars his ambition brings down upon them, his insatiable avidity, and the vexatious conduct of his ministers press harder on them than their own dissensions would have done? What do they gain, if the very tranquillity they enjoy is one of their miseries? Tranquillity is found also in dungeons; but is that enough to make them desirable places to live in? The Greeks imprisoned in the cave of the Cyclops lived there very tranquilly, while they were awaiting their turn to be devoured. . . .

Even if each man could alienate himself, he could not alienate his children: they are born men and free; their liberty belongs to them, and no one but they has the right to dispose of it. Before they come to years of discretion, the father can, in their name, lay down conditions for their preservation and well-being, but he cannot give them irrevocably and without conditions: such a gift is contrary to the ends of nature, and exceeds the rights of paternity. It would therefore be necessary, in order to legitimize an arbitrary government, that in every generation the people should be in a position to accept or reject it; but, were this so, the government would be no longer arbitrary.

To renounce liberty is to renounce being a man, to surrender the rights of humanity and even its duties. For him who renounces everything no indemnity is possible. Such a renunciation is incompatible with man's nature; to remove all liberty from his will is to remove all morality from his acts.

Like Hobbes and Locke, Rousseau refers to an original social contract that terminates the state of nature and establishes the civil state. The clash of particular interests in the state of nature necessitates the creation of civil authority.

I suppose men to have reached the point at which the obstacles in the way of their preservation in the state of nature show their power of resistance to be greater than the resources at the disposal of each individual for his maintenance in that state. That primitive condition can then subsist no longer; and the human race would perish unless it changed its manner of existence. . . .

This sum of forces can arise only where several persons come together: but, as the force and liberty of each man are the chief instruments of his self-preservation, how can he pledge them without harming his own interests, and neglecting the care he owes to himself? This difficulty, in its bearing on my present subject, may be stated in the following terms:

"The problem is to find a form of association which will defend and protect with the whole common force the person and goods of each associate, and in which each, while uniting himself with all, may still obey himself alone, and remain as free as before." This is the fundamental problem of which the *Social Contract* provides the solution.

In entering into the social contract, the individual surrenders his rights to the community as a whole, which governs in accordance with the general will—an underlying principle that expresses what is best for the community. The general will is a plainly visible truth that is easily discerned by reason and common sense purged of self-interest and unworthy motives. For Rousseau, the general will by definition is always right and always works to the community's advantage. True freedom consists of obedience to laws that coincide with the general will. Obedience to the general will transforms an individual motivated by self-interest, appetites, and passions into a higher type of person—a citizen committed to the general good. What happens, however, if a person's private will—that is, expressions of particular, selfish interests—clashes with the general will? As private interests could ruin the body politic, says Rousseau, "whoever refuses to obey the general will shall be compelled to do so by the whole body." Thus Rousseau rejects entirely the Lockean principle that citizens possess rights independently of and against the state. Because Rousseau grants the sovereign (the people constituted as a corporate body) virtually unlimited authority over the citizenry, some critics view him as a precursor of modern dictatorship.

The clauses of this contract. . . . properly understood, may be reduced to one—the total alienation of each associate, together with all his rights, to the whole community; for, in the first place, as each gives himself absolutely, the conditions are the same for all; and, this being so, no one has any interest in making them burdensome to others.

Moreover, the alienation being without reserve, the union is as perfect as it can be, and no associate has anything more to demand: for, if the individuals retained certain rights, as

there would be no common superior to decide between them and the public, each, being on one point his own judge, would ask to be so on all; the state of nature would thus continue, and the association would necessarily become inoperative or tyrannical.

Finally, each man, in giving himself to all, gives himself to nobody; and as there is no associate over which he does not acquire the same right as he yields others over himself, he gains an equivalent for everything he loses, and an increase of force for the preservation of what he has.

If then we discard from the social compact what is not of its essence, we shall find that it reduces itself to the following terms:

"Each of us puts his person and all his power in common under the supreme direction of the general will, and, in our corporate capacity, we receive each member as an indivisible part of the whole."

At once, in place of the individual personality of each contracting party, this act of association creates a moral and collective body, composed of as many members as the assembly contains voters, and receiving from this act its unity, its common identity, its life, and its will. . . .

In order then that the social compact may not be an empty formula, it tacitly includes the undertaking, which alone can give force to the rest, that whoever refuses to obey the general will shall be compelled to do so by the whole body. This means nothing less than that he will be forced to be free; for this is the condition which, by giving each citizen to his country, secures him against all personal dependence. In this lies the key to the working of the political machine; this alone legitimizes civil undertakings, which, without it, would be absurd, tyrannical, and liable to the most frightful abuses.

The passage from the state of nature to the civil state produces a very remarkable change in man, by substituting justice for instinct in his conduct, and giving his actions the morality they had formerly lacked. Then only, when the voice of duty takes the place of physical impulses and right of appetite, does man, who so far had considered only himself, find that he is forced to act on different principles, and to consult his reason before listening to his inclinations. Although, in this state, he deprives himself of some advantages which he got from nature, he gains in return others so great, his faculties are so stimulated and developed, his ideas so extended, his feelings so ennobled, and his whole soul so uplifted, that, did not the abuses of this new condition often degrade him below that which he left, he would be bound to bless continually the happy moment which took him from it for ever, and, instead of a stupid and unimaginative animal, made him an intelligent being and a man.

Let us draw up the whole account in terms easily commensurable. What man loses by the social contract is his natural liberty and an unlimited right to everything he tries to get and succeeds in getting; what he gains is civil liberty and the proprietorship of all he possesses. If we are to avoid mistake in weighing one against the other, we must clearly distinguish natural liberty, which is bounded only by the strength of the individual, from civil liberty, which is limited by the general will; and possession, which is merely the effect of force or the right of the first occupier, from property, which can be founded only on a positive title.

We might, over and above all this, add, to what man acquires in the civil state, moral liberty, which alone makes him truly master of himself; for the mere impulse of appetite is slavery, while obedience to a law which we prescribe to ourselves is liberty. . . .

The first and most important deduction from the principles we have so far laid down is that the general will alone can direct the State according to the object for which it was instituted, i.e. the common good: for if the clashing of particular interests made the establishment of societies necessary, the agreement of these very interests made it possible. The common element in these different interests is what forms the social tie; and, were there no point of agreement between them all, no society could exist. It is solely on the basis of this common

interest that every society should be governed. . . .

It follows from what has gone before that the general will is always right and tends to the public advantage; but it does not follow that the deliberations of the people are always equally correct. Our will is always for our own good, but we do not always see what that is; the people is never corrupted, but it is often deceived, and on such occasions only does it seem to will what is bad.

There is often a great deal of difference between the will of all and the general will; the latter considers only the common interest, while the former takes private interest into account, and is no more than a sum of particular wills: but take away from these same wills the pluses and minuses that cancel one another, and the general will remains as the sum of the differences.

If, when the people, being furnished with adequate information, held its deliberations, the citizens had no communication one with another, the grand total of the small differences would always give the general will, and the decision would always be good. But when factions arise, and partial associations are formed at the expense of the great association, the will of each of these associations becomes general in relation to its members, while it remains particular in relation to the State: it may then be said that there are no longer as many votes as there are men, but only as many as there are associations. The differences become less numerous and give a less general result. Lastly, when one of these associations is so great as to prevail over all the rest, the result is no longer a sum of small differences, but a single difference; in this case there is no longer a general will, and the opinion which prevails is purely particular.

It is therefore essential, if the general will is to be able to express itself, that there should be no partial society [factions] within the State, and that each citizen should think only his own thoughts. . . . But if there are partial societies, it is best to have as many as possible and to prevent them from being unequal. . . .

These precautions are the only ones that can guarantee that the general will shall be always enlightened, and that the people shall in no way deceive itself.

REVIEW QUESTIONS

1. What did Jean Jacques Rousseau mean by the "general will"? What function did it serve in his political theory?
2. Why do some thinkers view Rousseau as a champion of democracy, whereas others see him as a spiritual precursor of totalitarianism?

8 Judicial and Penal Reform

A humanitarian spirit pervaded the philosophes' outlook. Showing a warm concern for humanity, they attacked militarism, slavery, religious persecution, torture, and other violations of human dignity, as seen in passages from the *Encyclopedia* and Voltaire's works earlier in this chapter. Through reasoned arguments they sought to make humankind recognize and renounce its own barbarity. In the following selections, other eighteenth-century reformers denounce judicial torture and the abuse of prisoners.

Caesare Beccaria
ON CRIMES AND PUNISHMENTS

In *On Crimes and Punishments* (1764), Caesare Beccaria (1738–1794), an Italian economist and criminologist, condemned torture, commonly used to obtain confessions in many European countries, as irrational and inhuman.

The true relations between sovereigns and their subjects, and between nations, have been discovered. Commerce has been reanimated by the common knowledge of philosophical truths diffused by the art of printing, and there has sprung up among nations a tacit rivalry of industriousness that is most humane and truly worthy of rational beings. Such good things we owe to the productive enlightenment of this age. But very few persons have studied and fought against the cruelty of punishments and the irregularities of criminal procedures, a part of legislation that is as fundamental as it is widely neglected in almost all of Europe. Very few persons have undertaken to demolish the accumulated errors of centuries by rising to general principles, curbing, at least, with the sole force that acknowledged truths possess, the unbounded course of ill-directed power which has continually produced a long and authorized example of the most cold-blooded barbarity. And yet the groans of the weak, sacrificed to cruel ignorance and to opulent indolence; the barbarous torments, multiplied with lavish and useless severity, for crimes either not proved or wholly imaginary; the filth and horrors of a prison, intensified by that cruellest tormentor of the miserable, uncertainty—all

On Crimes and Punishments by Beccaria, translated by H. Paolucci, © 1963. Reprinted by permission of Prentice-Hall, Inc., Upper Saddle River, NJ.

these ought to have roused that breed of magistrates who direct the opinions of men. . . .

But what are to be the proper punishments for such crimes?

Is the death-penalty really *useful* and *necessary* for the security and good order of society? Are torture and torments *just,* and do they attain the *end* for which laws are instituted? What is the best way to prevent crimes? Are the same punishments equally effective for all times? What influence have they on customary behavior? These problems deserve to be analyzed with that geometric precision which the mist of sophisms, seductive eloquence, and timorous doubt cannot withstand. If I could boast only of having been the first to present to Italy, with a little more clarity, what other nations have boldly written and are beginning to practice, I would account myself fortunate. But if, by defending the rights of man and of unconquerable truth, I should help to save from the spasm and agonies of death some wretched victim of tyranny or of no less fatal ignorance, the thanks and tears of one innocent mortal in his transports of joy would console me for the contempt of all mankind. . . .

A cruelty consecrated by the practice of most nations is torture of the accused during his trial, either to make him confess the crime or to clear up contradictory statements, or to discover accomplices, or to purge him of infamy in some metaphysical and incomprehensible way, or, finally, to discover other crimes of which he might be guilty but of which he is not accused.

No man can be called *guilty* before a judge has sentenced him, nor can society deprive him of public protection before it has been decided that he has in fact violated the conditions under which such protection was accorded him. What right is it, then, if not simply that of might, which empowers a judge to inflict punishment on a citizen while doubt still remains as to his guilt or innocence? Here is the dilemma, which is nothing new: the fact of the crime is either certain or uncertain; if certain, all that is due is the punishment established by the laws, and tor-

tures are useless because the criminal's confession is useless; if uncertain, then one must not torture the innocent, for such, according to the laws, is a man whose crimes are not yet proved. . . .

. . . The impression of pain may become so great that, filling the entire sensory capacity of the tortured person, it leaves him free only to choose what for the moment is the shortest way of escape from pain. The response of the accused is then as inevitable as the impressions of fire and water. The sensitive innocent man will then confess himself guilty when he believes that, by so doing, he can put an end to his torment. Every difference between guilt and innocence disappears by virtue of the very means one pretends to be using to discover it. (Torture) is an infallible means indeed—for absolving robust scoundrels and for condemning innocent persons who happen to be weak. Such are the fatal defects of this so-called criterion of truth, a criterion fit for a cannibal. . . .

Of two men, equally innocent or equally guilty, the strong and courageous will be acquitted, the weak and timid condemned, by virtue of this rigorous rational argument: "I, the judge, was supposed to find you guilty of such and such a crime; you, the strong, have been able to resist the pain, and I therefore absolve you; you, the weak, have yielded, and I therefore condemn you. I am aware that a confession wrenched forth by torments ought to be of no weight whatsoever, but I'll torment you again if you don't confirm what you have confessed."

A strange consequence that necessarily follows from the use of torture is that the innocent person is placed in a condition worse than that of the guilty, for if both are tortured, the circumstances are all against the former. Either he confesses the crime and is condemned, or he is declared innocent and has suffered a punishment he did not deserve. The guilty man, on the contrary, finds himself in a favorable situation; that is, if, as a consequence of having firmly resisted the torture, he is absolved as innocent, he will have escaped a greater punishment by enduring a lesser one. Thus the innocent cannot but lose, whereas the guilty may gain. . . .

It would be superfluous to [cite] . . . the innumerable examples of innocent persons who have confessed themselves criminals because of the agonies of torture; there is no nation, there is no age that does not have its own to cite.

John Howard
PRISONS IN ENGLAND AND WALES

The efforts of John Howard (1726–1790), a British philanthropist, led Parliament in 1774 to enact prison reform. In 1777 Howard published *State of the Prisons in England and Wales,* excerpts from which follow.

There are prisons, into which whoever looks will, at first sight of the people confined there, be convinced, that there is some great error in the management of them: the sallow meagre countenances declare, without words, that they are very miserable: many who went in healthy, are in a few months changed to emaciated dejected objects. Some are seen pining under diseases, *"sick and in prison;"* expiring on the floors, in loathsome cells, of pestilential fevers, and . . . small-pox: victims, I must not say to the cruelty, but I will say to the inattention, of sheriffs, and gentlemen in the commission of the peace.

The cause of this distress is, that many prisons are scantily supplied, and some almost totally unprovided with the necessaries of life.

There are several Bridewells [prisons for those convicted of lesser crimes such as vagrancy and disorderly conduct] (to begin with them) in which prisoners have no allowance of FOOD at all. In some, the keeper farms what little is allowed them: and where he engages to supply each prisoner with one or two pennyworth of bread a day, I have known this shrunk to half, sometimes less than half the quantity, cut or broken from his own loaf.

It will perhaps be asked, does not their work maintain them? for every one knows that those offenders are committed to *hard labour.* The answer to that question, though true, will hardly be believed. There are very few Bridewells in which any work is done, or can be done. The prisoners have neither tools, nor materials of any kind; but spend their time in sloth, profaneness and debauchery, to a degree which, in some of those houses that I have seen, is extremely shocking. . . .

I have asked some keepers, since the late act for preserving the health of prisoners, why no care is taken of their sick: and have been answered, that the magistrates tell them *the act does not extend to Bridewells.*

In consequence of this, at the quarter sessions you see prisoners, covered (hardly covered) with rags; almost famished; and sick of diseases, which the discharged spread wherever they go, and with which those who are sent to the County-Gaols infect these prisons. . . .

Felons have in some Gaols two pennyworth of bread a day; in some three halfpennyworth; in some a pennyworth; in some a shilling a week. . . . I often weighed the bread in different prisons, and found the penny loaf 7½ to 8½ ounces, the other loaves in proportion. It is probable that when this allowance was fixed by its value, near double the quantity that the money will now purchase, might be bought for it: yet the allowance continues unaltered. . . .

This allowance being so far short of the cravings of nature, and in some prisons lessened by farming to the gaoler, many criminals are half starved: such of them as at their commitment were in health, come out almost famished, scarce able to move, and for weeks incapable of any labour.

Many prisons have NO WATER. This defect is frequent in Bridewells, and Town-Gaols. In the felons courts of some County-Gaols there is no water: in some places where there is water, prisoners are always locked up within doors, and have no more than the keeper or his servants think fit to bring them: in one place they are limited to three pints a day each—a scanty provision for drink and cleanliness! . . .

From hence any one may judge of the probability there is against the health and life of prisoners, crowded in close rooms, cells, and subterraneous dungeons, for fourteen or sixteen hours out of the four and twenty. In some of those caverns the floor is very damp: in others there is sometimes an inch or two of water; and the straw, or bedding is laid on such floors, seldom on barrack bedsteads. . . . Some Gaols have no SEWERS; and in those that have, if they be not properly attended to, they are, even to a visitant, offensive beyond expression: how noxious then to people constantly confined in those prisons!

In many Gaols, and in most Bridewells, there is no allowance of STRAW for prisoners to sleep on; and if by any means they get a little, it is not changed for months together, so that it is almost worn to dust. Some lie upon rags, others upon the bare floors. When I have complained of this to the keepers, their justification has been, "The county allows no straw; the prisoners have none but at my cost."

The evils mentioned hitherto affect the *health* and *life* of prisoners: I have now to complain of what is pernicious to their MORALS; and that is, the confining all sorts of prisoners together: debtors and felons; men and women; the young beginner and the old offender: and with all these, in some counties, such as are guilty of misdemeanors only. . . .

In some Gaols you see (and who can see it without pain?) boys of twelve or fourteen eagerly listening to the stories told by practised and experienced criminals, of their adventures, successes, stratagems, and escapes.

I must here add, that in some few Gaols are confined idiots and lunatics. . . . The insane, where they are not kept separate, disturb and terrify other prisoners. No care is taken of them, although it is probable that by medicines, and proper regimen, some of them might be restored to their senses, and to usefulness in life. . . .

A cruel custom obtains in most of our Gaols, which is that of the prisoners demanding of a new comer GARNISH, FOOTING, or (as it is called in some London Gaols) CHUMMAGE. "Pay or strip," are the fatal words. I say *fatal,* for they are so to some; who having no money, are obliged to give up part of their scanty apparel; and if they have no bedding or straw to sleep on, contract diseases, which I have known to prove mortal.

Loading prisoners with HEAVY IRONS, which make their walking, and even lying down to sleep, difficult and painful, is another custom which I cannot but condemn. In some County-Gaols the *women* do not escape this severity.

REVIEW QUESTIONS

1. What were Caesare Beccaria's arguments against the use of torture in judicial proceedings?
2. What ideals of the Enlightenment philosophes are reflected in Beccaria's arguments?
3. List the abuses in British jails that John Howard disclosed.

9 Questioning European Values

Enlightenment thinkers often used examples from the non-European world in order to attack European values that seemed contrary to nature and reason. Denis Diderot reviewed Louis Antoine de Bouganville's *Voyage Around the World* (1771) and later wrote *Supplement to the Voyage of Bouganville*. In this work, Diderot explored some ideas, particularly the sex habits of Tahitians, treated by the French explorer. Diderot also denounced European imperialism and the exploitation of non-Europeans, and questioned traditional Christian sexual standards.

Denis Diderot
SUPPLEMENT TO THE VOYAGE OF BOUGANVILLE

In *Supplement,* Diderot constructed a dialogue between a Tahitian (Orou), who possesses the wisdom of a French philosophe, and a chaplain, whose defense of Christian sexual mores reveals Diderot's critique of the Christian view of human nature. Diderot thus used a representative of an alien culture to attack those European customs and beliefs that the philosophes detested. In the opening passage, before Orou's dialogue, a Tahitian elder rebukes Bouganville and his companions for bringing the evils of European civilization to his island.

"We [Tahitians] are free—but see where you [Europeans] have driven into our earth the symbol of our future servitude. You are neither a god nor a devil—by what right, then, do you enslave people? Orou! You who understand the speech of these men, tell every one of us, as you have told me, what they have written on that strip of metal—'This land belongs to us.' This land belongs to you! And why? Because you set foot in it? If some day a Tahitian should land on your shores, and if he should engrave on one of your stones or on the bark of one of your trees: 'This land belongs to the people of Tahiti,' what would you think? You are stronger than we are! And what does that signify? When one of our lads carried off some of the miserable trinkets with which your ship is loaded, what an uproar you made, and what revenge you took! And at that very moment you were plotting, in the depths of your hearts, to steal a whole country! You are not slaves; you would suffer death rather than be enslaved, yet you want to make slaves of us! Do you believe, then, that the Tahitian does not know how to die in defense of his liberty? This Tahitian, whom you want to treat as a chattel, as a dumb animal—this Tahitian is your brother. You are both children of Nature—what right do you have over him that he does not have over you?

"You came; did we attack you? Did we plunder your vessel? Did we seize you and expose you to the arrows of our enemies? Did we force you to work in the fields alongside our beasts of burden? We respected our own image in you. Leave us our own customs, which are wiser and more decent than yours. We have no wish to barter what you call our ignorance for your useless knowledge. We possess already all that is good or necessary for our existence. Do we merit your scorn because we have not been able to create superfluous wants for ourselves? When we are hungry, we have something to eat; when we are cold, we have clothing to put on. You have been in our huts—what is lacking there, in your opinion? You are welcome to drive yourselves as hard as you please in pursuit of what you call the comforts of life, but allow sensible people to stop when they see they have nothing to gain but imaginary benefits from the continuation of their painful labors. If you persuade us to go beyond the bounds of strict necessity, when shall we come to the end of our labor? When shall we have time for enjoyment? We have reduced our daily and yearly labors to the least possible amount, because to us nothing seemed more desirable than leisure. Go and bestir yourselves in your own country; there you may torment yourselves as much as you like; but leave us in peace, and do not fill our heads with a hankering after your false needs and imaginary virtues. Look at these men—see how healthy, straight and strong they are. See these women—how straight, healthy, fresh and lovely they are. Take this bow in your hands—it is my own—and call one, two, three, four of your comrades to help you try to bend it. I can bend it myself. I work the soil, I climb mountains, I make my way through the dense forest, and I can run four leagues [about 12 miles] on the plain in less than an hour. Your young comrades have been hard put to it to keep up with me, and yet I have passed my ninetieth year. . . .

"Woe to this island! Woe to all the Tahitians now living, and to all those yet to be born, woe from the day of your arrival! We used to know but one disease—the one to which all men, all animals and all plants are subject—old age. But you have brought us a new one [venereal disease]: you have infected our blood. We shall perhaps be compelled to exterminate with our own hands some of our young girls, some of our women, some of our children, those who have lain with your women, those who have lain with your men. Our fields will be spattered with the foul blood that has passed from

your veins into ours. Or else our children, condemned to die, will nourish and perpetuate the evil disease that you have given their fathers and mothers, transmitting it forever to their descendants. . . .

Before the arrival of Christian Europeans, lovemaking was natural and enjoyable. Europeans introduced an alien element, guilt.

But a while ago, the young Tahitian girl blissfully abandoned herself to the embraces of a Tahitian youth and awaited impatiently the day when her mother, authorized to do so by her having reached the age of puberty, would remove her veil and uncover her breasts. She was proud of her ability to excite men's desires, to attract the amorous looks of strangers, of her own relatives, of her own brothers. In our presence, without shame, in the center of a throng of innocent Tahitians who danced and played the flute, she accepted the caresses of the young man whom her young heart and the secret promptings of her senses had marked out for her. The notion of crime and the fear of disease have come among us only with your coming. Now our enjoyments, formerly so sweet, are attended with guilt and terror. That man in black [a priest], who stands near to you and listens to me, has spoken to our young men, and I know not what he has said to our young girls, but our youths are hesitant and our girls blush. Creep away into the dark forest, if you wish, with the perverse companion of your pleasures, but allow the good, simple Tahitians to reproduce themselves without shame under the open sky and in broad daylight.

In the following conversation between Orou and the chaplain, Christian sexual mores and the concept of God are questioned. Orou addresses the chaplain.

[OROU] "You are young and healthy and you have just had a good supper. He who sleeps alone, sleeps badly; at night a man needs a woman at his side. Here is my wife and here are my daughters. Choose whichever one pleases you most, but if you would like to do me a favor, you will give your preference to my youngest girl, who has not yet had any children."

The mother said: "Poor girl! I don't hold it against her. It's no fault of hers."

The chaplain replied that his religion, his holy orders, his moral standards and his sense of decency all prevented him from accepting Orou's invitation.

Orou answered: "I don't know what this thing is that you call 'religion,' but I can only have a low opinion of it because it forbids you to partake of an innocent pleasure to which Nature, the sovereign mistress of us all, invites everybody. It seems to prevent you from bringing one of your fellow creatures into the world, from doing a favor asked of you by a father, a mother and their children, from repaying the kindness of a host, and from enriching a nation by giving it an additional citizen. I don't know what it is that you call 'holy orders,' but your chief duty is to be a man and to show gratitude. . . . I hope that you will not persist in disappointing us. Look at the distress you have caused to appear on the faces of these four women—they are afraid you have noticed some defect in them that arouses your distaste. But even if that were so, would it not be possible for you to do a good deed and have the pleasure of honoring one of my daughters in the sight of her sisters and friends? Come, be generous!"

THE CHAPLAIN You don't understand—it's not that. They are all four of them equally beautiful. But there is my religion! My holy orders! . . .

. . . [God] spoke to our ancestors and gave them laws; he prescribed to them the way in which he wishes to be honored; he ordained that certain actions are good and others he forbade them to do as being evil.

OROU I see. And one of these evils actions which he has forbidden is that of a man who goes to bed with a woman or girl. But in that case, why did he make two sexes?

THE CHAPLAIN In order that they might come together—but only when certain condi-

tions are satisfied and only after certain initial ceremonies have been performed. By virtue of these ceremonies one man belongs to one woman and only to her; one woman belongs to one man and only to him.

OROU For their whole lives?

THE CHAPLAIN For their whole lives.

OROU So that if it should happen that a woman should go to bed with some man who was not her husband, or some man should go to bed with a woman that was not his wife . . . but that could never happen because the workman [God] would know what was going on, and since he doesn't like that sort of thing, he wouldn't let it occur.

THE CHAPLAIN No. He lets them do as they will, and they sin against the law of God (for that is the name by which we call the great workman) and against the law of the country; they commit a crime.

OROU I should be sorry to give offense by anything I might say, but if you don't mind, I'll tell you what I think.

THE CHAPLAIN Go ahead.

OROU I find these strange precepts contrary to nature, and contrary to reason. . . . Furthermore, your laws seem to me to be contrary to the general order of things. For in truth is there anything so senseless as a precept that forbids us to heed the changing impulses that are inherent in our being, or commands that require a degree of constancy which is not possible, that violate the liberty of both male and female by chaining them perpetually to one another? Is there anything more unreasonable than this perfect fidelity that would restrict us, for the enjoyment of pleasures so capricious, to a single partner—than an oath of immutability taken by two individuals made of flesh and blood under a sky that is not the same for a moment, in a cavern that threatens to collapse upon them, at the foot of a cliff that is crumbling into dust, under a tree that is withering, on a bench of stone that is being worn away? Take my word for it, you have reduced human beings to a worse condition than that of the animals. I don't know what your great workman is, but I am very happy that he never spoke to our forefathers, and I hope that he never speaks to our children, for if he does, he may tell them the same foolishness, and they may be foolish enough to believe it. . . .

OROU Are monks faithful to their vows of sterility?

THE CHAPLAIN No.

OROU I was sure of it. Do you also have female monks?

THE CHAPLAIN Yes.

OROU As well behaved as the male monks?

THE CHAPLAIN They are kept more strictly in seclusion, they dry up from unhappiness and die of boredom.

OROU So nature is avenged for the injury done to her! Ugh! What a country! If everything is managed the way you say, you are more barbarous than we are.

REVIEW QUESTIONS

1. According to Denis Diderot, why did European imperialism violate natural law?
2. How did Europeans influence the health and sexual mores of the Tahitians?
3. How did Diderot attempt to use the Tahitians to criticize the sexual morals of Europeans?
4. How did Diderot use the concept of the law of nature to undermine Christian sexual morality?

---

10 Slavery Condemned

Montesquieu, Voltaire, Hume, Benjamin Franklin, Thomas Paine, and several other philosophes condemned slavery and the slave trade. In Book 15 of *The Spirit of the Laws,* Montesquieu scornfully refuted all justifications for slavery. Ultimately, he said, slavery, which violates the fundamental principle of justice underlying the universe, derived from base human desires to dominate and exploit other human beings. In 1780, Paine helped draft the act abolishing slavery in Pennsylvania. Five years earlier, he wrote:

> Our Traders in Men . . . must know the wickedness of that SLAVE-TRADE, if they attend to reasoning, or the dictates of their own hearts, and {those who} shun and stifle all these willfully sacrifice Conscience, and the character of integrity to that Golden Idol. . . . Most shocking of all is alleging the sacred Scriptures to favour this wicked practice.

Denis Diderot
ENCYCLOPEDIA
"MEN AND THEIR LIBERTY ARE NOT OBJECTS OF COMMERCE. . . ."

The *Encyclopedia* denounced slavery as a violation of the individual's natural rights.

[This trade] is the buying of unfortunate Negroes by Europeans on the coast of Africa to use as slaves in their colonies. This buying of Negroes, to reduce them to slavery, is one business that violates religion, morality, natural laws, and all the rights of human nature.

Negroes, says a modern Englishman full of enlightenment and humanity, have not become slaves by the right of war; neither do they deliver themselves voluntarily into bondage, and consequently their children are not born slaves. Nobody is unaware that they are bought from their own princes, who claim to have the right to dispose of their liberty, and that traders have them transported in the same way as their other goods, either in their colonies or in America, where they are displayed for sale.

If commerce of this kind can be justified by a moral principle, there is no crime, however atrocious it may be, that cannot be made legitimate. Kings, princes, and magistrates are not the proprietors of their subjects: they do not, therefore, have the right to dispose of their liberty and to sell them as slaves.

On the other hand, no man has the right to buy them or to make himself their master.

Men and their liberty are not objects of commerce; they can be neither sold nor bought nor paid for at any price. We must conclude from this that a man whose slave has run away should only blame himself, since he had acquired for money illicit goods whose acquisition is prohibited by all the laws of humanity and equity.

There is not, therefore, a single one of these unfortunate people regarded only as slaves who does not have the right to be declared free, since he has never lost his freedom, which he could not lose and which his prince, his father, and any person whatsoever in the world had not the power to dispose of. Consequently the sale that has been completed is invalid in itself. This Negro does not divest himself and can never divest himself of his natural right; he carries it everywhere with him, and he can demand everywhere that he be allowed to enjoy it. It is, therefore, patent inhumanity on the part of judges in free countries where he is transported, not to emancipate him immediately by declaring him free, since he is their fellow man, having a soul like them.

Marquis de Condorcet
THE EVILS OF SLAVERY

Marie Jean Antoine Nicolas Caritat, Marquis de Condorcet (1743–1794), was a French mathematician and historian of science. He contributed to the *Encyclopedia* and campaigned actively for religious toleration and the abolition of slavery. In 1788, Condorcet helped found The Society of the Friends of Blacks, which attacked slavery. Seven years earlier he had published a pamphlet denouncing slavery as a violation of human rights. Following are excerpts from this pamphlet.

"Dedicatory Epistle to the Negro Slaves"

My Friends,
Although I am not the same color as you, I have always regarded you as my brothers. Nature formed you with the same spirit, the same

reason, the same virtues as whites. . . . Your tyrants will reproach me with uttering only commonplaces and having nothing but chimerical [unrealistic] ideas: indeed, nothing is more common than the maxims of humanity and justice; nothing is more chimerical than to propose to men that they base their conduct on them.

Reducing a man to slavery, buying him, selling him, keeping him in servitude: these are truly crimes, and crimes worse than theft. In effect, they take from the slave, not only all forms of property but also the ability to acquire it, the control over his time, his strength, of everything that nature has given him to maintain his life and his needs. To this wrong they add that of taking from the slave the right to dispose of his own person. . . .

It follows from our principles that the inflexible justice to which kings and nations are subject like their citizens require the destruction of slavery. We have shown that this destruction will harm neither commerce nor the wealth of a nation because it would not result in any decrease in cultivation. We have shown that the master had no right over his slave; that the act of keeping him in servitude is not the enjoyment of a property right but a crime; that in freeing the slave the law does not attack property but rather ceases to tolerate an action which it should have punished with the death penalty. The sovereign therefore owes no compensation to the master of slaves just as he owes none to a thief whom a court judgment has deprived of the possession of a stolen good. The public tolerance of a crime may make punishment impossible but it cannot grant a real right to the profit from the crime.

> Defenders of slavery, says Condorcet, will blame the philosophes for stirring up trouble in the same way opponents of reform attack the philosophes for supporting other progressive causes.

If writers protest against the slavery of Negroes, it is the *philosophes,* their opponents say, thinking they have won their case. . . . If some people have been saved by inoculation from the dangers of smallpox, it's by the advice of the *philosophes.* . . . If the custom of breaking the bones of the accused between boards to make them tell the truth has been recently suppressed, it's because the *philosophes* inveighed against the practice; and it is in spite of the *philosophes* that France has been lucky enough to save a remnant of the old laws and conserve the precious practice of applying torture to condemned criminals. . . . Who is it who dares to complain in France about the barbarism of the criminal laws, about the cruelty with which the French Protestants have been deprived of the rights of man and citizen, about the harshness and injustice of the laws against smuggling and on hunting? Who had the culpable boldness to pretend that it would be useful to the people and in accord with justice to insure liberty of commerce and industry? . . . We can see clearly that it was surely the *philosophes.*

John Wesley
THOUGHTS UPON SLAVERY

John Wesley (1703–1791) was, with his brother Charles, the founder of the evangelical Methodist movement in England. Inspired by the Great Awakening in the American colonies, he launched a successful revival of Christianity in England in 1739. The rest of his long life was devoted to leadership of the Methodist movement.

Wesley's eyes were opened to the evils of slavery by reading an indictment of the slave trade by the French Quaker, Anthony Benezet. In 1774 he published the tract *Thoughts upon Slavery,* from which the extracts below are taken. Wesley drew heavily on Benezet's writings for his facts, but in warning participants in the slave trade against divine retribution he spoke in the cadences of the inspired evangelical preacher.

Wesley became one of the leaders in the movement against slavery and his pioneering work, in which he was supported by the Methodist movement, helped bring about the abolition of slavery in England in 1807.

I would inquire whether [the abuses of slavery] can be defended on the principles of even heathen honesty, whether they can be reconciled (setting the Bible out of question) with any degree of either justice or mercy.

The grand plea is, "They are authorized by law." But can law, human law, change the nature of things? Can it turn darkness into light or evil into good? By no means. Notwithstanding ten thousand laws, right is right, and wrong is wrong still. There must still remain an essential [difference] between justice and injustice, cruelty and mercy. So that I still ask, who can reconcile this treatment of the Negroes first and last, with either mercy or justice? . . . Yea, where is the justice of taking away the lives of innocent, inoffensive men, murdering thousands of them in their own land, by the hands of their own countrymen, many thousands year after year on shipboard, and then casting them like dung into the sea and tens of thousands in that cruel slavery to which they are so unjustly reduced? . . .

But if this manner of procuring and treating Negroes is not consistent either with mercy or justice, yet there is a plea for it which every man of business will acknowledge to be quite sufficient. . . . "D—n justice, it is necessity. . . . It is necessary that we should procure slaves, and when we have procured them, it is necessary to use them with severity, considering their stupidity, stubbornness and wickedness."

I answer you stumble at the threshold. I deny that villainy is ever necessary. It is impossible that it should ever be necessary for any reasonable creature to violate all the laws of justice, mercy, and truth. No circumstances can make it necessary for a man to burst in sunder all the ties of humanity. It can never be necessary for a rational being to sink himself below a brute. A man can be under no necessity of degrading himself into a wolf. The absurdity of the supposition is so glaring that one would wonder anyone can help seeing it. . . .

"But the furnishing us with slaves is necessary for the trade, and wealth, and glory of our nation." Here are several mistakes. For first wealth is not necessary to the glory of any nation, but wisdom, virtue, justice, mercy, generosity, public spirit, love of our country. These are necessary to the real glory of a nation, but abundance of wealth is not.

. . . But, secondly, it is not clear that we should have either less money or trade (only less of that detestable trade of man—stealing), if there was not a Negro in all our islands or in all English America. It is demonstrable, white men inured to it by degrees can work as well as they, and they would do it, were Negroes out of the way, and proper encouragement given them. However, thirdly, I come back to the same point: Better no trade than trade procured by villainy. It is far better to have no wealth than to gain wealth at the expense of virtue. Better is honest poverty than all the riches bought by the tears, and sweat, and blood of our fellow creatures.

"However this be, it is necessary, when we have slaves, to use them with severity." What, to whip them for every petty offence, till they are all in gore blood? To take that opportunity of rubbing pepper and salt into their raw flesh? To drop burning wax upon their skin? To castrate them? To cut off half their foot with an axe? To hang them on gibbets, that they may die by inches with heat, and hunger, and thirst? To pin them down to the ground, and then burn them by degrees from the feet to the head? To roast them alive? When did a Turk or heathen find it necessary to use a fellow-creature thus?

I pray, to what end is this usage necessary? "Why to prevent their running away, and to keep them constantly to their labour, that they may not idle away their time. So miserably stupid is this race of men, yea, so stupid and so wicked." Allowing them to be as stupid as you say, to whom is that stupidity owing? Without question it lies at the door of their inhuman masters who give them no means, no opportunity of improving their understanding. . . . Consequently it is not their fault but yours: you must answer for it before God and man. . . .

And what pains have you taken, what method have you used, to reclaim them from their wickedness? Have you carefully taught them, "That there is a God, a wise, powerful, merciful being, the creator and governor of heaven and earth? That he has appointed a day wherein he will judge the world, will take account of all our thoughts, words and actions? That in that day he will reward every child of man according to his works: that 'Then the righteous shall inherit the kingdom prepared for them from the foundation of the world: and the wicked shall be cast into everlasting fire, prepared for the devil and his angels.'" If you have not done this, if you have taken no pains or thought about the matter, can you wonder at their wickedness? What wonder if they should cut your throat? And if they did, whom could you thank for it but yourself? You first acted the villain in making them slaves (whether you stole them or bought them). You kept them stupid and wicked by cutting them off from all opportunities of improving either in knowledge or virtue. And now you assign their want of wisdom and goodness as the reason for using them worse than brute beasts. . . .

It remains only to make a little application of the preceding observations. . . I therefore add a few words to those who are more imme-

diately concerned, . . . and first to the captains employed in this trade. . . .

Is there a God? You know there is. Is he a just God? Then there must be a state of retribution; a state wherein the just God will reward every man according to his works. Then what reward will he render to you? O think betimes! Before you drop into eternity! Think now: he shall have judgment without mercy, that showed no mercy.

Are you a man? . . . Have you no sympathy? No sense of human woe? No pity for the miserable? . . . When you squeezed the agonizing creatures down in the ship, or when you threw their poor mangled remains into the sea, had you no relenting? Did not one tear drop from your eye, one sigh escape from your breast? Do you feel no relenting now? If you do not, you must go on till the measure of your iniquities is full. Then will the great God deal with *you,* as you have dealt with *them,* and require all their blood at your hands. . . .

Today resolve, God being your helper, to escape for your life. Regard not money! All that a man hath will he give for his life! Whatever you lose, lose not your soul; nothing can countervail that loss. Immediately quit the horrid trade. At all events, be an honest man.

This equally concerns every merchant who is engaged in the slave-trade. It is you that induce the African villain, to sell his countrymen, and in order thereto, to steal, rob, murder men, women and children without number. By enabling the English villain to pay him for so doing, whom you overpay for his execrable labour. It is your money that is the spring of all, that impowers him to go on. . . . And is your conscience quite reconciled to this? Does it never reproach you at all? Has gold entirely blinded your eyes, and stupefied your heart? . . . Have no more part in this detestable business. Be you a man! Not a wolf, a devourer of the human species. Be merciful that you may obtain mercy.

And this equally concerns every gentleman that has an estate in our African plantations. Yea, all slave-holders of whatever rank and degree, seeing men-buyers are exactly at a level with men-sellers. Indeed you say, "I pay honestly for my goods, and am not concerned to know how they are come by." Nay, but . . . you know they are not honestly come by. . . .

If therefore you have any regard to justice (to say nothing of mercy, nor of the revealed law of God) render unto all their due. Give liberty to whom liberty is due, that is, to every child of man, to every partaker of human nature. Let none serve you but by his own act and deed, by his own voluntary choice. Away with all whips, all chains, all compulsion. Be gentle toward all men. And see that you invariably do unto every one, as you would he should do unto you.

O thou God of love, thou who art loving to every man, and whose mercy is over all thy works: Thou who art the father of the spirits of all flesh, and who art rich in mercy unto all: Thou who hast mingled in one blood all the nations upon earth: have compassion upon these outcasts of men, who are trodden down as dung upon the earth. Arise and help these who have no helper, whose blood is spilt upon the ground like water! Are not these also the work of thine own hands, the purchase of thy Son's blood? Stir them up to cry unto thee in the land of their captivity; and let their complaint come up before thee; let it enter into thine ears! Make even those that lead them away captive to pity them. . . . O burst thou all their chains in sunder; more especially the chains of their sins: Thou, Saviour of all, make them free, that they may be free indeed!

REVIEW QUESTIONS

1. In what way did slavery destroy individual freedom, according to the *Encyclopedia?*
2. How did Condorcet show that slaves' rights are destroyed?
3. To whom did Wesley address his arguments against the slave trade?
4. What were the commercial justifications for slavery that Wesley disputed?

---

11 On the Progress of Humanity

During the French Revolution, the Marquis de Condorcet attracted the enmity of the dominant Jacobin party, and in 1793 he was forced to go into hiding. Secluded in Paris, he wrote *Sketch for a Historical Picture of the Progress of the Human Mind.* Arrested in 1794, Condorcet died during his first night in prison from either exhaustion or self-inflicted poison.

Marquis de Condorcet
PROGRESS OF THE HUMAN MIND

Sharing the philosophes' confidence in human goodness and in reason, Condorcet was optimistic about humanity's future progress. Superstition, prejudice, intolerance, and tyranny—all barriers to progress in the past—would gradually be eliminated, and humanity would enter a golden age. The following excerpts are from Condorcet's *Sketch.*

... The aim of the work that I have undertaken, and its result will be to show by appeal to reason and fact that nature has set no term to the perfection of human faculties; that the perfectibility of man is truly indefinite; and that the progress of this perfectibility, from now onwards independent of any power that might wish to halt it, has no other limit than the duration of the globe upon which nature has cast us. This progress will doubtless vary in speed, but it will never be reversed as long as the earth occupies its present place in the system of the universe, and as long as the general laws of this system produce neither a general cataclysm nor such changes as will deprive the human race of its present faculties and its present resources. . . .

... It will be necessary to indicate by what stages what must appear to us today a fantastic hope ought in time to become possible, and even likely; to show why, in spite of the transitory successes of prejudice and the support that it receives from the corruption of governments or peoples, truth alone will obtain a lasting victory; we shall demonstrate how nature has joined together indissolubly the progress of knowledge and that of liberty, virtue and respect for the natural rights of man. . . .

After long periods of error, after being led astray by vague or incomplete theories, publicists have at last discovered the true rights of man and how they can all be deduced from the single truth, that *man is a sentient being, capable of reasoning and of acquiring moral ideas.* . . .

At last man could proclaim aloud his right, which for so long had been ignored, to submit all opinions to his own reason and to use in the search for truth the only instrument for its recognition that he has been given. Every man learnt with a sort of pride that nature had not forever condemned him to base his beliefs on the opinions of others; the superstitions of antiquity and the abasement of reason before the [rapture] of supernatural religion disappeared from society as from philosophy.

Thus an understanding of the natural rights of man, the belief that these rights are inalien-

able and [cannot be forfeited], a strongly expressed desire for liberty of thought and letters, of trade and industry, and for the alleviation of the people's suffering, for the [elimination] of all penal laws against religious dissenters and the abolition of torture and barbarous punishments, the desire for a milder system of criminal legislation and jurisprudence which should give complete security to the innocent, and for a simpler civil code, more in conformance with reason and nature, indifference in all matters of religion which now were relegated to the status of superstitions and political [deception], a hatred of hypocrisy and fanaticism, a contempt for prejudice, zeal for the propagation of enlightenment: all these principles, gradually filtering down from philosophical works to every class of society whose education went beyond the catechism and the alphabet, became the common faith . . . [of enlightened people]. In some countries these principles formed a public opinion sufficiently widespread for even the mass of the people to show a willingness to be guided by it and to obey it. . . .

Force or persuasion on the part of governments, priestly intolerance, and even national prejudices, had all lost their deadly power to smother the voice of truth, and nothing could now protect the enemies of reason or the oppressors of freedom from a sentence to which the whole of Europe would soon subscribe. . . .

Our hopes for the future condition of the human race can be subsumed under three important heads: the abolition of inequality between nations, the progress of equality within each nation, and the true perfection of mankind. Will all nations one day attain that state of civilization which the most enlightened, the freest and the least burdened by prejudices, such as the French and the Anglo-Americans [by virtue of their revolutions], have attained already? Will the vast gulf that separates these peoples from the slavery of nations under the rule of monarchs, from the barbarism of African tribes, from the ignorance of savages, little by little disappear? . . .

Is the human race to better itself, either by discoveries in the sciences and the arts, and so in the means to individual welfare and general prosperity; or by progress in the principles of conduct or practical morality; or by a true perfection of the intellectual, moral, or physical faculties of man, an improvement which may result from a perfection either of the instruments used to heighten the intensity of these faculties and to direct their use or of the natural constitution of man?

In answering these three questions we shall find in the experience of the past, in the observation of the progress that the sciences and civilization have already made, in the analysis of the progress of the human mind and of the development of its faculties, the strongest reasons for believing that nature has set no limit to the realization of our hopes. . . .

The time will therefore come when the sun will shine only on free men who know no other master but their reason; when tyrants and slaves, priests and their stupid or hypocritical instruments will exist only in works of history and on the stage; and when we shall think of them only to pity their victims and their dupes; to maintain ourselves in a state of vigilance by thinking on their excesses; and to learn how to recognize and so to destroy, by force of reason, the first seeds of tyranny and superstition, should they ever dare to reappear amongst us.

REVIEW QUESTIONS

1. According to Condorcet, what economic, political, and cultural policies were sought by the philosophes?
2. Was the Enlightenment philosophy an alternative moral code to that of Christianity? Or was it an internal reformation of the traditional Christian moral order?
3. What image of human nature underlies Condorcet's theory of human progress?

CHAPTER 4

The French Revolution

WOMEN'S MARCH TO VERSAILLES. High prices and food shortages led thousands of women (and men) to march on Versailles in protest in October 1789. The king was compelled to return to Paris, a sign of his weakening power, and many aristocrats fled the country. *(Bibliothéque Nationale, Paris)*

In 1789, many participants and observers viewed the revolutionary developments in France as the fulfillment of the Enlightenment's promise—the triumph of reason over tradition and ignorance, of liberty over despotism. It seemed that the French reformers were eliminating the abuses of an unjust system and creating a new society founded on the ideals of the philosophes.

Eighteenth-century French society, the Old Regime, was divided into three orders, or estates. The First Estate (the clergy) and the Second Estate (the nobility) enjoyed special privileges sanctioned by law and custom. The church collected tithes (taxes on the land), censored books regarded as a threat to religion and morality, and paid no taxes to the state (although the church did make a "free gift" to the royal treasury). Nobles were exempt from most taxes, collected manorial dues from peasants (even from free peasants), and held the highest positions in the church, the army, and the government. Peasants, urban workers, and members of the bourgeoisie belonged to the Third Estate, which comprised about 96 percent of the population.

The bourgeoisie—which included merchants, bankers, professionals, and government officials below the top ranks—provided the leadership and ideology for the French Revolution. In 1789 the bourgeoisie possessed wealth and talent but had no political power; it was denied equality with the aristocracy, for whom the highest positions in the land were reserved on the basis of birth. By 1789 the bourgeoisie wanted to abolish the special privileges of the nobility and to open prestigious positions to men of talent regardless of their birth; it wanted to give France a constitution that limited the monarch's power, established a parliament, and protected the rights of the individual.

The immediate cause of the French Revolution was a financial crisis. The wars of Louis XIV and subsequent foreign adventures, including French aid to the American colonists during their revolution, had emptied the royal treasury. The refusal of the clergy and the nobles to surrender their tax exemptions compelled Louis XVI to call a meeting of the Estates General—a medieval assembly that had last met in 1614—to deal with impending bankruptcy. The nobility intended to use the Estates General to weaken the French throne and regain powers lost a century earlier under the absolute rule of Louis XIV. But the nobility's plans were unrealized; their revolt against the crown paved the way for the Third Estate's eventual destruction of the Old Regime.

Between June and November 1789 the bourgeoisie, aided by uprisings of the common people of Paris and the peasants in the countryside, gained control over the state and instituted reforms. During this opening and moderate phase of the Revolution (1789–1791), the bourgeoisie abolished the special privileges of the aristocracy and clergy, formulated a declaration of human rights, subordinated the church to the state, reformed the country's administrative and judicial systems, and drew up a constitution creating a parliament and limiting the king's power.

Between 1792 and 1794 came a radical stage. Three principal factors propelled the Revolution in a radical direction: pressure from the urban poor, the *sans-culottes,* who wanted the government to do something about their poverty; a counterrevolution led by clergy and aristocrats who wanted to undo the reforms of the Revolution; and war with the European powers that sought to check French expansion and to stifle the revolutionary ideals of liberty and equality.

The dethronement of Louis XVI, the establishment of a republic in September 1792, and the king's execution in January 1793 were all signs of growing radicalism. As the new Republic tottered under the twin blows of internal insurrection and foreign invasion, the revolutionary leadership grew more extreme. In June 1793 the Jacobins took power. Tightly organized, disciplined, and fiercely devoted to the Republic, the Jacobins mobilized the nation's material and human resources to defend it against the invading foreign armies. To deal with counterrevolutionaries, the Jacobins unleashed the Reign of Terror, which took the lives of some 20,000 to 40,000 people—more if the thousands summarily executed in the civil war that raged in the provinces are included—many of them innocent of any crime against the state. Although the Jacobins succeeded in saving the Revolution, their extreme measures aroused opposition. In the last part of 1794, power again passed into the hands of the moderate bourgeoisie, who wanted no part of Jacobin radicalism.

In 1799, Napoleon Bonaparte, a popular general with an inexhaustible yearning for power, overthrew the government and pushed the Revolution in still another direction, toward military dictatorship. Although Napoleon subverted the revolutionary ideal of liberty, he preserved the social gains of the Revolution—the abolition of the special privileges of the nobility and the clergy.

The era of French Revolution was a decisive period in the shaping of the modern West. By destroying aristocratic privileges and opening careers to talent, it advanced the cause of equality under the law. By weakening the power of the clergy, it promoted the secularization of society. By abolishing the divine right of monarchy, drafting a constitution, and establishing a parliament, it accelerated the growth of the liberal-democratic state. By eliminating serfdom and the sale of government offices and by reforming the tax system, it fostered a rational approach to administration. In the nineteenth century, the ideals and reforms of the French Revolution spread in shock waves across Europe; in country after country, the old order was challenged by the ideals of liberty and equality.

1   Abuses of the Old Regime

The roots of the French Revolution lay in the aristocratic structure of French society. The Third Estate resented the special privileges of the aristocracy, a legacy of the Middle Ages, and the inefficient and corrupt methods of government. To many French people influenced by the ideas of the philosophes, French society seemed an affront to reason. By 1789, reformers sought a new social order based on rationality and equality.

Arthur Young
PLIGHT OF THE FRENCH PEASANTS

French peasants in the late eighteenth century were better off than the peasants of eastern and central Europe, where serfdom predominated. The great majority of France's 21 million peasants were free; many owned their own land, and some were prosperous. Yet the countryside was burdened with severe problems, which sparked a spontaneous revolution in 1789.

A rising birthrate led to the continual subdivision of French farms among peasant sons; on the resulting small holdings, peasants struggled to squeeze out a living. Many landless peasants, who were forced to work as day laborers, were also hurt by the soaring population. An oversupply of rural day laborers reduced many of the landless to beggary. An unjust and corrupt tax system also contributed to the peasants' poverty. Peasants paid excessive taxes to the state, church, and lords; taxes and obligations due the lords were particularly onerous medieval vestiges, as most peasants were no longer serfs. A poor harvest in 1788–1789 and inflation worsened conditions.

Arthur Young (1741–1820), an English agricultural expert with a keen eye for detail, traveled through France just prior to the Revolution. In *Travels During the Years 1787, 1788, and 1789,* he reported on conditions in the countryside.

. . . The abuses attending the levy of taxes were heavy and universal. The kingdom was parceled into generalities [administrative units], with an intendant at the head of each, into whose hands the whole power of the crown was delegated for everything except the military authority; but particularly for all affairs of finance. The generalities were subdivided into elections, at the head of which was a *sub-delegue* appointed by the intendant. The rolls of the *taille,* capitation, *vingtièmes,*[1] and other taxes, were distributed among districts, parishes, and individuals, at the pleasure of the intendant, who could exempt, change, add, or diminish at

---

[1]A *taille* was a tax levied on the value of a peasant's land or wealth. A capitation was a head or poll tax paid for each person. A *vingtième* was a tax on income and was paid chiefly by peasants.

pleasure. Such an enormous power, constantly acting, and from which no man was free, must, in the nature of things, degenerate in many cases into absolute tyranny. It must be obvious that the friends, acquaintances, and dependents of the intendant, and of all his *sub-delegues,* and the friends of these friends, to a long chain of dependence, might be favoured in taxation at the expense of their miserable neighbours; and that noblemen in favour at court, to whose protection the intendant himself would naturally look up, could find little difficulty in throwing much of the weight of their taxes on others, without a similar support. Instances, and even gross ones, have been reported to me in many parts of the kingdom, that made me shudder at the oppression to which [people have been subjected] by the undue favours granted to such crooked influence. But, without recurring to such cases, what must have been the state of the poor people paying heavy taxes, from which the nobility and clergy were exempted? A cruel aggravation of their misery, to see those who could best afford to pay, exempted because able! . . . The *corvées* [taxes paid in labor, often road building], or police of the roads, were annually the ruin of many hundreds of farmers; more than 300 were reduced to beggary in filling up one vale in Lorraine: all these oppressions fell on the *tiers etat* [Third Estate] only; the nobility and clergy having been equally exempted from *tailles,* militia and *corvées.* The penal code of finance makes one shudder at the horrors of punishment inadequate to the crime. . . .

1. Smugglers of salt, armed and assembled to the number of five, in Provence, a fine of 500 liv. [*livres,* French coins] and nine years galleys [sentenced to backbreaking labor—rowing sea vessels], in all the rest of the kingdom, death.

2. Smugglers, armed, assembled, but in number under five, a fine of 300 liv. and three years galleys. Second offense, death. . . .

10. Buying smuggled salt, to resell it, the same punishments as for smuggling. . . .

The *Capitaineries* [lords' exclusive hunting rights] were a dreadful scourge on all the occupiers of land. By this term is to be understood the paramountship of certain districts, granted by the king to princes of the blood, by which they were put in possession of the property of all game, even on lands not belonging to them. . . . In speaking of the preservation of the game in these *capitaineries,* it must be observed that by game must be understood whole droves of wild boars, and herds of deer not confined by any wall or pale, but wandering at pleasure over the whole country, to the destruction of crops; and to the peopling of the galleys by the wretched peasants, who presumed to kill them in order to save that food which was to support their helpless children. . . . Now an English reader will scarcely understand it without being told, that there were numerous edicts for preserving the game which prohibited weeding and hoeing, lest the young partridges should be disturbed; . . . manuring with night soil, lest the flavour of the partridges should be injured by feeding on the corn so produced; . . . and taking away the stubble, which would deprive the birds of shelter. The tyranny exercised in these *capitaineries,* which extended over 400 leagues[2] of country, was so great that many *cahiers* [lists of the Third Estate's grievances] demanded the utter suppression of them. Such were the exertions of arbitrary power which the lower orders felt directly from the royal authority; but, heavy as they were, it is a question whether the [abuses], suffered [indirectly] through the nobility and the clergy, were not yet more oppressive. Nothing can exceed the complaints made in the *cahiers* under this head. They speak of the dispensation of justice in the manorial courts, as comprising

---

[2]Various units of distance were called leagues, and their length was from about 2.4 to 4.6 miles.

every species of despotism; the districts indeterminate—appeals endless—irreconcilable to liberty and prosperity—and irrevocably [condemned] in the opinion of the public—augmenting litigations—favouring every [form of trickery]—ruining the parties—not only by enormous expenses on the most petty objects, but by a dreadful loss of time. The judges, commonly ignorant pretenders, who hold their courts in *cabarets* [taverns]. . . are absolutely dependent on the seigneurs [lords]. Nothing can exceed the force of expression used in painting the oppressions of the seigneurs, in consequence of their feudal powers. . . . The countryman is tyrannically enslaved by it. . . . In passing through many of the French provinces, I was struck with the various and heavy complaints of the farmers and little proprietors of the feudal grievances, with the weight of which their industry was [burdened]; but I could not then conceive the multiplicity of the shackles which kept them poor and depressed. I understood it better afterwards.

GRIEVANCES OF THE THIRD ESTATE

At the same time that elections were held for the Estates General, the three estates drafted *cahiers de doléances,* the lists of grievances that deputies would take with them when the Estates General convened. The cahiers from all three estates expressed loyalty to the monarchy and the church and called for a written constitution and an elected assembly. The cahiers of the clergy and the nobility insisted on the preservation of traditional rights and privileges. The Cahier of the Third Estate of Dourdan, in the *généralité* of Orléans (one of the thirty-four administrative units into which prerevolutionary France was divided), expressed the reformist hopes of the Third Estate. Some of the grievances in the cahier follow.

29 March, 1789

The order of the third estate of the City, *Bailliage* [judicial district], and County of Dourdan, imbued with gratitude prompted by the paternal kindness of the King, who deigns to restore its former rights and its former constitution, forgets at this moment its misfortunes and impotence, to harken only to its foremost sentiment and its foremost duty, that of sacrificing everything to the glory of the *Patrie* [nation] and the service of His Majesty. It supplicates him to accept the grievances, complaints, and remonstrances which it is permitted to bring to the foot of the throne, and to see therein only the expression of its zeal and the homage of its obedience.

It wishes:

1. That his subjects of the third estate, equal by such status to all other citizens, present themselves before the common father without other distinction which might degrade them.

2. That all the orders [the three estates], already united by duty and a common desire to contribute equally to the needs of the State, also deliberate in common concerning its needs.

3. That no citizen lose his liberty except according to law; that, consequently, no one be arrested by virtue of special orders, or, if imperative circumstances necessitate such orders, that the prisoner be handed over to the regular courts of justice within forty-eight hours at the latest.

A Documentary Survey of the French Revolution by Stewart, © 1951. Adapted by permission of Prentice-Hall, Inc., Upper Saddle River, NJ.

4. That no letters or writings intercepted in the post [mails] be the cause of the detention of any citizen, or be produced in court against him, except in case of conspiracy or undertaking against the State.

5. That the property of all citizens be inviolable, and that no one be required to make sacrifice thereof for the public welfare, except upon assurance of indemnification based upon the statement of freely selected appraisers. . . .

15. That every personal tax be abolished; that thus the *capitation* and the *taille* and its accessories be merged with the *vingtièmes*[1] in a tax on land and real or nominal property.

16. That such tax be borne equally, without distinction, by all classes of citizens and by all kinds of property, even feudal and contingent rights.

17. That the tax substituted for the *corvée* [taxes paid in labor] be borne by all classes of citizens equally and without distinction. That said tax, at present beyond the capacity of those who pay it and the needs to which it is destined, be reduced by at least one-half. . . .

JUSTICE

1. That the administration of justice be reformed, either by restoring strict execution of ordinances, or by reforming the sections thereof that are contrary to the dispatch and welfare of justice. . . .

7. That venality [sale] of offices be suppressed. . . .

8. That the excessive number of offices in the necessary courts be reduced in just measure, and that no one be given an office of magistracy if he is not at least twenty-five years of age, and until after a substantial public examination has verified his morality, integrity, and ability. . . .

10. That the study of law be reformed; that it be directed in a manner analogous to our legislation, and that candidates for degrees be subjected to rigorous tests which may not be

evaded; that no dispensation of age or time be granted.

11. That a body of general customary law be drafted of all articles common to all the customs of the several provinces and *bailliages*. . . .

12. That deliberations of courts . . . which tend to prevent entry of the third estate thereto be rescinded and annulled as injurious to the citizens of that order, in contempt of the authority of the King, whose choice they limit, and contrary to the welfare of justice, the administration of which would become the patrimony of those of noble birth instead of being entrusted to merit, enlightenment, and virtue.

13. That military ordinances which restrict entrance to the service to those possessing nobility be reformed.

That naval ordinances establishing a degrading distinction between officers born into the order of nobility and those born into that of the third estate be revoked, as thoroughly injurious to an order of citizens and destructive of the competition so necessary to the glory and prosperity of the State.

FINANCES

1. That if the Estates General considers it necessary to preserve the fees of *aides* [tax on commodities], such fees be made uniform throughout the entire kingdom and reduced to a single denomination. . . .

2. That the tax of the *gabelle* [tax on salt] be eliminated if possible, or that it be regulated among the several provinces of the kingdom. . . .

3. That the taxes on hides, which have totally destroyed that branch of commerce and caused it to go abroad, be suppressed forever.

4. That . . . all useless offices, either in police or in the administration of justice, be abolished and suppressed.

AGRICULTURE

4. That the right to hunt may never affect the property of the citizen; that, accordingly,

---

[1]For an explanation of taxes, see footnote 1 on page 72.

he may at all times travel over his lands, have injurious herbs uprooted, and cut *luzernes* [alfalfa], *sainfoins* [fodder], and other produce whenever it suits him; and that stubble may be freely raked immediately after the harvest. . . .[2]

11. . . . That individuals as well as communities be permitted to free themselves from the

_____
[2]See the discussion of nobles' hunting rights and the peasants' hatred of this practice in the preceding reading by Arthur Young.

rights of *banalité* [peasants were required to use the lord's mill, winepress, and oven], and *corvée*, by payments in money or in kind, at a rate likewise established by His Majesty on the basis of the deliberations of the Estates General. . . .

15. That the militia, which devastates the country, takes workers away from husbandry, produces premature and ill-matched marriages, and imposes secret and arbitrary taxes upon those who are subject thereto, be suppressed and replaced by voluntary enlistment at the expense of the provinces.

Emmanuel Sieyès
BOURGEOIS DISDAIN FOR SPECIAL PRIVILEGES OF THE ARISTOCRACY

In a series of pamphlets, including *The Essay on Privileges* (1788) and *What Is the Third Estate?* (1789), Abbé Emmanuel Sieyès (1748–1836) expressed the bourgeoisie's disdain for the nobility. Although educated at Jesuit schools to become a priest, Sieyès had come under the influence of Enlightenment ideas. In *What Is the Third Estate?* he denounced the special privileges of the nobility, asserted that the people are the source of political authority, and maintained that national unity stands above estate or local interests. The ideals of the Revolution—liberty, equality, and fraternity—are found in Sieyès's pamphlet, excerpts of which follow.

The plan of this book is fairly simple. We must ask ourselves three questions.

1. What is the Third Estate? *Everything.*
2. What has it been until now in the political order? *Nothing.*
3. What does it want to be? *Something.* . . .

. . . Only the well-paid and honorific posts are filled by members of the privileged order [nobles]. Are we to give them credit for this? We could do so only if the Third Estate was unable or unwilling to fill these posts. We know the answer. Nevertheless, the privileged have dared to preclude the Third Estate. "No matter how useful you are," they said, "no

matter how able you are, you can go so far and no further. Honors are not for the like of you." . . .

. . . Has nobody observed that as soon as the government becomes the property of a separate class, it starts to grow out of all proportion and that posts are created not to meet the needs of the governed but of those who govern them? . . .

It suffices to have made the point that the so-called usefulness of a privileged order to the public service is a fallacy; that, without help from this order, all the arduous tasks in the service are performed by the Third Estate; that without this order the higher posts could be infinitely better filled; that they ought to be the natural prize and reward of recognised ability and service; and that if the privileged have succeeded in usurping all well-paid and honorific posts, this is both a hateful iniquity towards the generality of citizens and an act of treason to the commonwealth.

Who is bold enough to maintain that the Third Estate does not contain within itself everything needful to constitute a complete nation? It is like a strong and robust man with one arm still in chains. If the privileged order were removed, the nation would not be something less but something more. What then is the Third Estate? All; but an "all" that is fettered and oppressed. What would it be without the privileged order? It would be all; but free and flourishing. Nothing will go well without the Third Estate; everything

would go considerably better without the two others. . . .

. . . The privileged, far from being useful to the nation, can only weaken and injure it; . . . the nobility may be a *burden* for the nation. . . .

The nobility, however, is . . . a foreigner in our midst because of its *civil and political* prerogatives.

What is a nation? A body of associates living under *common* laws and represented by the same *legislative assembly,* etc.

Is it not obvious that the nobility possesses privileges and exemptions which it brazenly calls its rights and which stand distinct from the rights of the great body of citizens? Because of these special rights, the nobility does not belong to the common order, nor is it subjected to the common laws. Thus its private rights make it a people apart in the great nation.

REVIEW QUESTIONS

1. What abuses did Arthur Young see in the French systems of taxation and justice?
2. Why did Young consider the *capitaineries* (nobles' hunting rights) to be a particularly "dreadful scourge" on the peasants?
3. The principle of equality pervaded the cahiers of the Third Estate. Discuss this statement.
4. How did the Cahier of the Third Estate of Dourdan try to correct some of the abuses discussed by Arthur Young?
5. How important did Emmanuel Sieyès say the nobility (the privileged order) was to the life of the nation?
6. What importance did Sieyès attach to the contribution of the Third Estate (the bourgeoisie) to the life of the nation?

2 Liberty, Equality, Fraternity

In August 1789 the newly created National Assembly adopted the Declaration of the Rights of Man and of Citizens, which expressed the liberal and universal ideals of the Enlightenment. The Declaration proclaimed that sovereignty derives from the people, that is, that the people are the source of political power; that men are born free and equal in rights; and that it is the purpose of government to protect the natural rights of the individual. Because these ideals contrasted markedly with the outlook of an absolute monarchy, a privileged aristocracy, and an intolerant clergy, some historians view the Declaration of

Rights as the death knell of the Old Regime. Its affirmation of liberty, reason, and natural rights inspired liberal reformers in other lands.

DECLARATION OF THE RIGHTS OF MAN AND OF CITIZENS

Together with John Locke's *Second Treatise on Government,* the American Declaration of Independence, and the Constitution of the United States, the Declaration of the Rights of Man and of Citizens, which follows, is a pivotal document in the development of modern liberalism.

The Representatives of the people of FRANCE, formed into a NATIONAL ASSEMBLY, considering that ignorance, neglect, or contempt of human rights, are the sole causes of public misfortunes and corruptions of Government, have resolved to set forth in a solemn declaration, these natural, imprescriptible, and unalienable rights: that this declaration, being constantly present to the minds of the members of the body social, they may be ever kept attentive to their rights and their duties: that the acts of the legislative and executive powers of Government, being capable of being every moment compared with the end of political institutions, may be more respected: and also, that the future claims of the citizens, being directed by simple and incontestible principles, may always tend to the maintenance of the Constitution, and the general happiness.

For these reasons the NATIONAL ASSEMBLY doth recognize and declare, in the presence of the Supreme Being, and with the hope of his blessing and favor, the following *sacred* rights of men and of citizens:

I. *Men are born, and always continue, free, and equal in respect of their rights. Civil distinctions, therefore, can be founded only on public utility.*

II. *The end of all political associations, is, the preservation of the natural and imprescriptible rights of man; and these rights are liberty, property, security, and resistance of oppression.*

III. *The nation is essentially the source of all sovereignty; nor can any* INDIVIDUAL *or any* BODY OF MEN, *be entitled to any authority which is not expressly derived from it.*

IV. Political Liberty consists in the power of doing whatever does not injure another. The exercise of the natural rights of every man, has no other limits than those which are necessary to secure to every *other* man the free exercise of the same rights; and these limits are determinable only by the law.

V. The law ought to prohibit only actions hurtful to society. What is not prohibited by the law, should not be hindered; nor should any one be compelled to that which the law does not require.

VI. The law is an expression of the will of the community. All citizens have a right to concur, either personally, or by their representatives, in its formation. It should be the same to all, whether it protects or punishes; and *all being equal in its sight, are equally eligible to all honors, places, and employments, according to their different abilities, without any other distinction than that created by their virtues and talents.*

VII. No man should be accused, arrested, or held in confinement, except in cases determined by the law, and according to the forms which it has prescribed. All who promote, solicit, execute, or cause to be executed, arbitrary orders, ought to be punished; and every citizen called upon or apprehended by virtue of the law, ought immediately to obey, and renders himself culpable by resistance.

VIII. The law ought to impose no other penalties but such as are absolutely and evidently necessary; and no one ought to be punished, but in virtue of a law promulgated before the offence, and legally applied.

IX. Every man being presumed innocent till he has been convicted, whenever his detention becomes indispensible, all rigor [harshness] to him, more than is necessary to secure his person, ought to be provided against by the law.

X. No man ought to be molested on account of his opinions, not even on account of his *religious* opinions, provided his avowal of them does not disturb the public order established by the law.

XI. The unrestrained communication of thoughts and opinions being one of the most precious rights of man, every citizen may speak, write, and publish freely, provided he is responsible for the abuse of this liberty in cases determined by the law.

XII. A public force being necessary to give security to the rights of men and of citizens, that force is instituted for the benefit of the community, and not for the particu-lar benefit of the persons with whom it is entrusted.

XIII. A common contribution being necessary for the support of the public force, and for defraying the other expenses of government, it ought to be divided equally among the members of the community, according to their abilities.

XIV. Every citizen has a right, either by himself or his representative, to a free voice in determining the necessity of public contributions, the appropriation of them, and their amount, mode of assessment and duration.

XV. Every community has a right to demand of all its agents, an account of their conduct.

XVI. Every community in which a separation of powers and a security of rights is not provided for, wants a constitution.

XVII. The rights to property being inviolable and sacred, no one ought to be deprived of it, except in cases of evident public necessity, legally ascertained, and on condition of a previous just indemnity.

REVIEW QUESTIONS

1. What does the Declaration say about the nature of political liberty? What are its limits, and how are they determined?
2. How does the Declaration show the influence of John Locke (see page 28).
3. The ideals of the Declaration have become deeply embedded in the Western outlook. Discuss this statement.

3 Expansion of Human Rights

The abolition of the special privileges of the aristocracy and the ideals proclaimed by the Declaration of the Rights of Man and of Citizens aroused the hopes of reformers in several areas: in what was considered radicalism, even by the framers of the Declaration of the Rights of Man, some women began to press for equal rights; humanitarians called for the abolition of the slave trade; and Jews, who for centuries had suffered disabilities and degradation, petitioned for full citizenship.

Mary Wollstonecraft
VINDICATION OF THE RIGHTS OF WOMAN

When in 1789 the French revolutionaries issued their "Declaration of the Rights of Man," it was only a matter of time before a woman published a "Declaration of the Rights of Woman." That feat was accomplished in the same year in France by Olympe de Gouges. In England, Mary Wollstonecraft (1759–1797), strongly influenced by her, published her own statement *Vindication of the Rights of Woman* in 1792. Her protest against the prevailing submissiveness of women was reinforced by the philosophy of the Enlightenment and the ideals of the French Revolution, which she observed firsthand from 1792 to 1794. A career woman, she made her living as a prolific writer closely associated with the radicals of her time, one of whom, William Godwin, she married shortly before her death. Wollstonecraft became famous for her vigorous protests against the subjection of women. Children, husbands, and society generally, she pleaded in *Vindication of the Rights of Woman,* were best served by well-educated, self-reliant, and strong women capable of holding their own in the world.

. . . I have turned over various books written on the subject of education, and patiently observed the conduct of parents and the management of schools; but what has been the result?—a profound conviction that the neglected education of my fellow creatures is the grand source of the misery I deplore, and that women, in particular, are rendered weak and wretched. . . . The conduct and manners of women, in fact, evidently prove that their minds are not in a healthy state. . . . One cause of this . . . I attribute to a false system of education, gathered from the books written on this subject by men who, considering females rather as women than human creatures, have been more anxious to make them alluring mistresses than affectionate wives and rational mothers. . . .

. . . A degree of physical superiority of men cannot . . . be denied, and it is a noble prerogative! But not content with this natural pre-eminence, men endeavour to sink us still lower, merely to render us alluring objects for a moment. . . .

My own sex, I hope, will excuse me, if I treat them like rational creatures, instead of flattering their *fascinating* graces, and viewing them as if they were in a state of perpetual childhood, unable to stand alone. I earnestly wish to point out in what true dignity and human happiness consists. I wish to persuade women to endeavour to acquire strength, both of mind and body. . . .

Dismissing, then, those pretty feminine phrases, which the men condescendingly use to soften our slavish dependence, and despising that weak elegancy of mind, exquisite sensibility, and sweet docility of manners, supposed to be the sexual characteristics of the weaker vessel, I wish to show that elegance is inferior to virtue, that the first object of laudable ambition is to obtain a character as a human being, regardless of the distinction of sex. . . .

The education of women has of late been more attended to than formerly; yet they are still reckoned a frivolous sex, and ridiculed or pitied by the writers who endeavour by satire or instruction to improve them. It is acknowledged that they spend many of the first years of their lives in acquiring a smattering of accomplishments; meanwhile strength of body and mind are sacrificed to libertine notions of beauty, to the desire of establishing themselves—the only way women can rise in the world—by marriage. And this desire making mere animals of them, when they marry they act as such children may be expected to act,— they dress, they paint, and nickname God's creatures. Surely these weak beings are only fit for a seraglio [harem]! Can they be expected to govern a family with judgment, or take care of the poor babes whom they bring into the world? . . .

Contending for the rights of woman, my main argument is built on this simple principle, that if she be not prepared by education to become the companion of man, she will stop the progress of knowledge and virtue; for truth must be common to all, or it will be inefficacious with respect to its influence on general practice. And how can woman be expected to co-operate unless she knows why she ought to be virtuous? unless freedom strengthens her reason till she comprehends her duty, and see in what manner it is connected with her real good. If children are to be educated to understand the true principle of patriotism, their mother must be a patriot; and the love of mankind, from which an orderly train of virtues spring, can only be produced by considering the moral and civil interest of mankind; but the education and situation of woman at present shuts her out from such investigations. . . .

Consider—I address you as a legislator— whether, when men contend for their freedom, and to be allowed to judge for themselves respecting their own happiness, it be not inconsistent and unjust to subjugate women, even though you firmly believe that you are acting in the manner best calculated to promote their happiness? Who made man the exclusive judge, if woman partake with him of the gift of reason?

In this style argue tyrants of every denomination, from the weak king to the weak father of a family; they are all eager to crush reason, yet always assert that they usurp its throne only to be useful. Do you not act a similar part when you *force* all women, by denying them civil and political rights, to remain immured [imprisoned] in their families groping in the dark? for surely, sir, you will not assert that a duty can be binding which is not founded on reason? If, indeed, this be their destination, arguments may be drawn from reason; and thus augustly supported, the more understanding women acquire, the more they will be attached to their duty—comprehending it—for unless they comprehend it, unless their morals be fixed on the same immutable principle as those of man, no authority can make them discharge it in a virtuous manner. They may be convenient slaves, but slavery will have its constant effect, degrading the master and the abject dependent.

But if women are to be excluded, without having a voice, from a participation of the natural rights of mankind, prove first, to ward off the charge of injustice and inconsistency, that they [lack] reason, else this flaw in your NEW CONSTITUTION will ever show that man must, in some shape, act like a tyrant, and tyranny, in whatever part of society it rears its brazen front, will ever undermine morality. . . .

In what does man's pre-eminence over the brute creation consist? The answer is as clear as that a half is less than the whole, in Reason. . . . Yet . . . deeply rooted processes have clouded reason. . . . Men, in general, seem to employ their reason to justify prejudices, which they have imbibed, they can scarcely trace how, rather than to root them out.

The power of generalising ideas, of drawing comprehensive conclusions from individual observations . . . has not only been denied to women; but writers have insisted that it is inconsistent, with a few exceptions, with their sexual character. Let men prove this, and I shall grant that woman only exists for man. I must, however, previously remark, that the power of generalising ideas, to any great extent, is not very common amongst men or women. But this exercise is the true cultivation of the understanding; and everything conspires to render the cultivation of the understanding more difficult in the female than the male world. . . .

I shall not go back to the remote annals of antiquity to trace the history of woman; it is sufficient to allow that she has always been either a slave or a despot, and to remark that each of these situations equally retards the progress of reason. The grand source of female folly and vice has ever appeared to me to arise from narrowness of mind; and the very constitution of civil governments has put almost insuperable obstacles in the way to prevent the cultivation of the female understanding; yet virtue can be built on no other foundation. . . .

When do we hear of women who, starting out of obscurity, boldly claim respect on account of their great abilities or daring virtues? Where are they to be found? . . .

With respect to women, when they receive a careful education, they are either made fine ladies, brimful of sensibility, and teeming with capricious fancies, or mere notable women. The latter are often friendly, honest creatures, and have a shrewd kind of good sense, joined with worldly prudence, that often render them more useful members of society than the fine sentimental lady, though they possess neither greatness of mind nor taste. The intellectual world is shut against them. Take them out of their family or neighbourhood, and they stand still; the mind finding no employment, for literature affords a fund of amusement which they have never sought to relish, but frequently to despise. The sentiments and taste of more cultivated minds appear ridiculous, even in those whom chance and family connections have led them to love; but in mere acquaintance they think it all affectation.

A man of sense can only love such a woman on account of her sex, and respect her because she is a trusty servant. He lets her, to preserve his own peace, scold the servants, and go to church in clothes made of the very best materials. . . . [W]omen, whose minds are not enlarged by cultivation, or . . . by reflection, are very unfit to manage a family, for, by an undue stretch of power, they are always tyrannising to

support a superiority that only rests on the arbitrary distinction of fortune.

Women have seldom sufficient serious employment to silence their feelings; a round of little cares, or vain pursuits frittering away all strength of mind and organs, they become naturally only objects of sense. In short, the whole tenor of female education (the education of society) tends to render the best disposed romantic and inconstant; and the remainder vain and [contemptible]. In the present state of society this evil can scarcely be remedied, I am afraid, in the slightest degree; should a more laudable ambition ever gain ground they may be brought nearer to nature and reason, and become more virtuous and useful as they grow more respectable. . . .

Women . . . all want to be ladies. Which is simply to have nothing to do, but listlessly to go they scarcely care where, for they cannot tell what.

But what have women to do in society? I may be asked, but to loiter with easy grace. . . . Women might certainly study the art of healing, and be physicians as well as nurses. . . . They might also study politics . . . for the reading of history will scarcely be more useful than the study of romances. . . . Business of various kinds, they might likewise pursue, if they were educated in a more orderly manner, which might save many from common and legal prostitution. . . . The few employments open to a woman, so far from being liberal, are menial. . . .

Some of these women might be restrained from marrying by a proper spirit of delicacy, and others may not have had it in their power to escape in this pitiful way from servitude; is not that Government then very defective, and very unmindful of the happiness of one-half of its members, that does not provide for honest, independent women, by encouraging them to fill respectable stations? . . .

It is a melancholy truth; yet such is the blessed effect of civilisation! the most respectable women are the most oppressed; and, unless they have understandings far superior to the common run of understandings, taking in both sexes, they must, from being treated like contemptible beings, become contemptible. How many women thus waste life away the prey of discontent, who might have practised as physicians, regulated a farm, managed a shop, and stood erect, supported by their own industry, instead of hanging their heads. . . .

Would men but generously snap our chains, and be content with rational fellowship instead of slavish obedience, they would find us more observant daughters, more affectionate sisters, more faithful wives, more reasonable mothers—in a word, better citizens. We should then love them with true affection, because we should learn to respect ourselves; and the peace of mind of a worthy man would not be inter-rupted by the idle vanity of his wife, nor the babes sent to nestle in a strange bosom, having never found a home in their mother's. . . .

. . . The sexual distinction which men have so warmly insisted upon, is arbitrary. . . . As-serting the rights which women in common with men ought to contend for, I have not at-tempted to [make light of] their faults; but to prove them to be the natural consequence of their education and station in society. If so, it is reasonable to suppose that they will change their character, and correct their vices and fol-lies, when they are allowed to be free in a phys-ical, moral, and civil sense.

Let woman share the rights, and she will emulate the virtues of man; for she must grow more perfect when emancipated. . . .

Society of the Friends of Blacks
ADDRESS TO THE NATIONAL ASSEMBLY IN FAVOR OF THE ABOLITION OF THE SLAVE TRADE

Planters in the French West Indies and shipbuilding and sugar refining interests opposed any attempts to eliminate slavery or the slave trade since they profited handsomely from these institutions. On February 5, 1790, the Society of the Friends of Blacks, using the language of the Declaration of the Rights of Man, called for the abolition of the slave trade. Recognizing the power of proslavery forces, the society made it clear that it was not proposing the abolition of slavery itself. In 1791, the slaves of Saint Domingue revolted, and in 1794, the Jacobins in the National Convention abolished slavery in the French colonies. The island's white planters resisted the decree, and in 1801 Napoleon sent twenty thousand troops to Saint Domingue in an unsuccessful attempt to restore slavery. In 1804, the black revolutionaries established the independent state of Haiti.

Following are excerpts from the Society of the Friends of Blacks' address to the National Assembly.

The humanity, justice, and magnanimity that have guided you in the reform of the most pro-foundly rooted abuses gives hope to the Society of the Friends of Blacks that you will receive with benevolence its demand in favor of that numerous portion of humankind, so cruelly oppressed for two centuries.

This Society, slandered in such cowardly and unjust fashion, only derives its mission from the humanity that induced it to defend the blacks even under the past despotism. Oh! Can there be a more respectable title in the eyes of this august Assembly which has so often avenged the rights of man in its decrees?

You have declared them, these rights; you have engraved on an immortal monument that all men are born and remain free and equal in rights; you have restored to the French people these rights that despotism had for so long despoiled; . . . you have broken the chains of feudalism that still degraded a good number of our fellow citizens; you have announced the destruction of all the stigmatizing distinctions that religious or political prejudices introduced into the great family of humankind. . . .

We are not asking you to restore to French blacks those political rights which alone, nevertheless, attest to and maintain the dignity of man; we are not even asking for their liberty. No; slander, bought no doubt with the greed of the shipowners, ascribes that scheme to us and spreads it everywhere; they want to stir up everyone against us, provoke the planters and their numerous creditors, who take alarm even at gradual emancipation. They want to alarm all the French, to whom they depict the prosperity of the colonies as inseparable from the slave trade and the perpetuity of slavery.

No, never has such an idea entered into our minds; we have said it, printed it since the beginning of our Society, and we repeat it in order to reduce to nothing this grounds of argument, blindly adopted by all the coastal cities, the grounds on which rest almost all their addresses [to the National Assembly]. The immediate emancipation of the blacks would not only be a fatal operation for the colonies; it would even be a deadly gift for the blacks, in the state of abjection and incompetence to which cupidity has reduced them. It would be to abandon to themselves and without assistance children in the cradle or mutilated and impotent beings.

It is therefore not yet time to demand that liberty; we ask only that one cease butchering thousands of blacks regularly every year in order to take hundreds of captives; we ask that one henceforth cease the prostitution, the profaning of the French name, used to authorize these thefts, these atrocious murders; we demand in a word the abolition of the slave trade. . . .

In regard to the colonists, we will demonstrate to you that if they need to recruit blacks in Africa to sustain the population of the colonies at the same level, it is because they wear out the blacks with work, whippings, and starvation; that, if they treated them with kindness and as good fathers of families, these blacks would multiply and that this population, always growing, would increase cultivation and prosperity. . . .

Have no doubt, the time when this commerce will be abolished, even in England, is not far off. It is condemned there in public opinion, even in the opinion of the ministers. . . .

If some motive might on the contrary push them [the blacks] to insurrection, might it not be the indifference of the National Assembly about their lot? Might it not be the insistence on weighing them down with chains, when one consecrates everywhere this eternal axiom: *that all men are born free and equal in rights.* So then therefore there would only be fetters and gallows for the blacks while good fortune glimmers only for the whites? Have no doubt, our happy revolution must re-electrify the blacks whom vengeance and resentment have electrified for so long, and it is not with punishments that the effect of this upheaval will be repressed. From one insurrection badly pacified will twenty others be born, of which one alone can ruin the colonists forever.

It is worthy of the first free Assembly of France to consecrate the principle of philanthropy which makes of humankind only one single family, to declare that it is horrified by this annual carnage which takes place on the coasts of Africa, that it has the intention of abolishing it one day, of mitigating the slavery that is the result, of looking for and preparing, from this moment, the means.

PETITION OF THE JEWS OF PARIS, ALSACE, AND LORRAINE TO THE NATIONAL ASSEMBLY, JANUARY 28, 1790

After several heated debates, the National Assembly granted full citizenship to the Jews on September 27, 1791. Influenced by the French example, almost all European states in the nineteenth century would also emancipate the Jews dwelling within their borders. In the following *Petition of the Jews of Paris, Alsace, and Lorraine to the National Assembly, January 28, 1790,* the Jews pointed to historic wrongs and invoked the ideals of the Revolution as they called for equal rights.

A great question is pending before the supreme tribunal of France. *Will the Jews be citizens or not?*

Already, this question has been debated in the National Assembly; and the orators, whose intentions were equally patriotic, did not agree at all on the result of their discussion. Some wanted Jews admitted to civil status. Others found this admission dangerous. A third opinion consisted of preparing the complete improvement of the lot of the Jews by gradual reforms.

In the midst of all these debates, the national assembly believed that it ought to adjourn the question. . . .

It was also said that the adjournment was based on the necessity of knowing with assurance what were the true desires of the Jews; given, it was added, the disadvantages of according to this class of men rights more extensive than those they want.

But it is impossible that such a motive could have determined the decree of the national assembly.

First, the wish of the Jews is perfectly well-known, and cannot be equivocal. They have presented it clearly in their addresses of 26 and 31 August, 1789. The Jews of Paris repeated it in a *new address* of 24 December. They ask that all the degrading distinctions that they have

suffered to this day be abolished and that they be declared CITIZENS. . . .

Their desires, moreover, as we have just said, are well known; and we will repeat them here. They ask to be CITIZENS. . . .

In truth, [the Jews] are of a religion that is condemned by the one that predominates in France. But the time has passed when one could say that it was only the dominant religion that could grant access to advantages, to prerogatives, to the lucrative and honorable posts in society. For a long time they confronted the Protestants with this maxim, worthy of the Inquisition, and the Protestants had no civil standing in France. Today, they have just been reestablished in the possession of this status; they are assimilated to the Catholics in everything; the intolerant maxim that we have just recalled can no longer be used against them. Why would they continue to use it as an argument against the Jews?

In general, civil rights are entirely independent from religious principles. And all men of whatever religion, whatever sect they belong to, whatever creed they practice, provided that their creed, their sect, their religion does not offend the principles of a pure and severe morality, all these men, we say, equally able to serve the fatherland, defend its interests, contribute to its splendor, should all equally have the title and the rights of citizen. . . .

[The Jews] are reproached at the same time for the vices that make them unworthy of civil status and the principles which render them at once unworthy and incompetent. A rapid glance at the bizarre as well as cruel destiny of these unfortunate individuals will perhaps remove the disfavor with which some seek to cover them. . . .

Always persecuted since the destruction of Jerusalem, pursued at times by fanaticism and at others by superstition, by turn chased from the kingdoms that gave them an asylum and then called back to these same kingdoms, excluded from all the professions and arts and crafts, deprived even of the right to be heard as witnesses against a Christian, relegated to separate districts like another species of man with whom one fears having communication, pushed out of certain cities which have the privilege of not receiving them, obligated in others to pay for the air that they breathe as in Augsburg where they pay a *florin* an hour or in Bremen a *ducat* a day, subject in several places to shameful tolls. Here is the list of a part of the harassment still practiced today against the Jews.

And [critics of the Jews] would dare to complain of the state of degradation into which some of them can be plunged! They would dare to complain of their ignorance and their vices! Oh! Do not accuse the Jews, for that would only precipitate onto the Christians themselves all the weight of these accusations. . . .

Let us now enter into more details. The Jews have been accused of the crime of usury. But first of all, all of them are not usurers; and it would be as unjust to punish them all for the offense of some as to punish all the Christians for the usury committed by some of them and the speculation of many. . . .

Reflect, then, on the condition of the Jews. Excluded from all the professions, ineligible for all the positions, deprived even of the capacity to acquire property, not daring and not being able to sell openly the merchandise of their commerce, to what extremity are you reducing them? You do not want them to die, and yet you refuse them the means to live: you refuse them the means, and you crush them with taxes. You leave them therefore really no other resource than usury. . . .

Everything that one would not have dared to undertake, moreover, or what one would only have dared to undertake with an infinity of precautions a long time ago, can now be done and one must dare to undertake it in this moment of universal regeneration, when all ideas and all sentiments take a new direction; and we must hasten to do so. Could one still fear the influence of a prejudice against which reason has appealed for such a long time, when all the former abuses are destroyed and all the former prejudices overturned? Will not the numerous changes effected in the political machine uproot from the people's minds most of the ideas that dominated them? Everything is changing; the lot of the Jews must change at the same time; and the people will not be more surprised by this particular change than by all those which they see around them everyday. This is therefore the moment, the true moment to make justice triumph: attach the improvement of the lot of the Jews to the revolution; amalgamate, so to speak, this partial revolution to the general revolution. Your efforts will be crowned with success, and the people will not protest, and time will consolidate your work and render it unshakable.

REVIEW QUESTIONS

1. According to Mary Wollstonecraft, what benefits would society derive from giving equal rights to women?
2. Why did Wollstonecraft object to the traditional attitudes of men toward women?
3. How, in Wollstonecraft's opinion, should women change?

4. In proposing the abolition of the slave trade, what did the Society of the Friends of Blacks petition the National Assembly to do? Was it feasible? Do you feel it was adequate? Explain.
5. On what grounds did the Jews of Paris, Alsace, and Lorraine petition the National Assembly to grant the Jews citizenship? What historic wrongs did they decry? What views of religion and politics did they uphold?
6. What did the demands of Mary Wollstonecraft, the Society of the Friends of Blacks, and the Jews of Paris, Alsace, and Lorraine have to do with the French Revolution and the ideas of the Enlightenment, and how did they exemplify the expansion of human rights?

---

4 The Jacobin Regime

In the summer of 1793 the French Republic was threatened with internal insurrection and foreign invasion. During this period of acute crisis, the Jacobins provided strong leadership. They organized a large national army of citizen soldiers who, imbued with love for the nation, routed the invaders on the northern frontier. To deal with internal enemies, the Jacobins instituted the Reign of Terror, in which Maximilien Robespierre (1758–1794) played a pivotal role.

It was not because they were bloodthirsty or power mad that many Jacobins, including Robespierre, supported the use of terror. Rather, they were idealists who believed that terror was necessary to rescue the Republic and the Revolution from destruction. Deeply committed to republican democracy, Robespierre saw himself as the bearer of a higher faith, molding a new society founded on reason, good citizenship, patriotism, and virtue. Robespierre viewed those who prevented the implementation of this new society as traitors and sinners who had to be killed for the good of humanity.

THE LEVY IN MASS

To fight the war against foreign invaders, the Jacobins, in an act that anticipated modern conscription, drafted unmarried men between eighteen and twenty-five years of age. They mobilized the nation's material and human resources, infused the people with a nationalistic spirit, and in a remarkable demonstration of administrative skill, equipped an army of more than 800,000 men. In calling the whole nation to arms, the Jacobins heralded the emergence of modern warfare. Following is the famous levy in mass decreed on August 16, 1793.

1. Henceforth, until the enemies have been driven from the territory of the Republic, the French people are in permanent requisition for army service.

The young men shall go to battle; the married men shall forge arms and transport provisions; the women shall make tents and clothes, and shall serve in the hospitals; the children shall turn old linen into lint [for dressing wounds]; the old men shall repair to the public places, to stimulate the courage of the warriors and preach the unity of the Republic and hatred of kings.

2. National buildings shall be converted into barracks; public places into armament workshops; the soil of cellars shall be washed in lye to extract saltpeter therefrom.

3. Arms of caliber shall be turned over exclusively to those who march against the enemy; the service of the interior shall be carried on with fowling pieces and sabers.[1]

4. Saddle horses are called for to complete the cavalry corps; draught horses, other than those employed in agriculture, shall haul artillery and provisions.

5. The Committee of Public Safety is charged with taking all measures necessary for establishing, without delay, a special manufacture of arms of all kinds, in harmony with the *élan* and the energy of the French people. Accordingly, it is authorized to constitute all establishments, manufactories, workshops, and factories deemed necessary for the execution of such works, as well as to requisition for such purpose, throughout the entire extent of the Republic, the [artisans] and workmen who may contribute to their success. . . .

---

[1]*Fowling pieces* were light shotguns, so called because they were sometimes used for shooting wild fowl. *Saber* here refers to a type of bayonet, a rifle with a blade attached.

6. The representatives of the people dispatched for the execution of the present law shall have similar authority in their respective [sections] acting in concert with the Committee of Public Safety; they are invested with the unlimited powers attributed to the representatives of the people with the armies.

7. No one may obtain a substitute in the service to which he is summoned. The public functionaries shall remain at their posts.

8. The levy shall be general. Unmarried citizens or childless widowers, from eighteen to twenty-five years, shall go first; they shall meet, without delay, at the chief town of their districts, where they shall practice manual exercise daily, while awaiting the hour of departure.

9. The representatives of the people shall regulate the musters and marches so as to have armed citizens arrive at the points of assembling only in so far as supplies, munitions, and all that constitutes the material part of the army exist in sufficient proportion. . . .

11. The battalion organized in each district shall be united under a banner bearing the inscription: *The French people risen against tyrants.* . . .

14. Owners, farmers, and others possessing grain shall be required to pay, in kind, arrears of taxes. . . .

17. The Minister of War is responsible for taking all measures necessary for the prompt execution of the present decree. . . .

18. The present decree shall be conveyed to the departments by special messengers.

Maximilien Robespierre
REPUBLIC OF VIRTUE

In his speech of February 5, 1794, Robespierre provided a comprehensive statement of his political theory, in which he equated democracy with virtue and justified the use of terror in defending democracy.

What is the objective toward which we are reaching? The peaceful enjoyment of liberty and equality; the reign of that eternal justice whose laws are engraved not on marble or stone but in the hearts of all men, even in the heart of the slave who has forgotten them or of the tyrant who disowns them.

We wish an order of things where all the low and cruel passions will be curbed, all the beneficent and generous passions awakened by the laws, where ambition will be a desire to deserve glory and serve the *patrie* [nation]; where distinctions grow only out of the very system of equality; where the citizen will be subject to the authority of the magistrate, the magistrate to that of the people, and the people to that of justice; where the *patrie* assures the well-being of each individual, and where each individual shares with pride the prosperity and glory of the *patrie*; where every soul expands by the continual communication of republican sentiments, and by the need to merit the esteem of a great people; where the arts will embellish the liberty that ennobles them, and commerce will be the source of public wealth and not merely of the monstrous riches of a few families.

We wish to substitute in our country . . . all the virtues and miracles of the republic for all the vices and absurdities of the monarchy.

We wish, in a word, to fulfill the intentions of nature and the destiny of humanity, realize the promises of philosophy, and acquit providence of the long reign of crime and tyranny. We wish that France, once illustrious among enslaved nations, may, while eclipsing the glory of all the free peoples that ever existed, become a model to nations, a terror to oppressors, a consolation to the oppressed, an ornament of the universe; and that, by sealing our work with our blood, we may witness at least the dawn of universal happiness—this is our ambition, this is our aim.

What kind of government can realize these prodigies [great deeds]? A democratic or republican government only. . . .

A democracy is a state where the sovereign people, guided by laws of their own making, do for themselves everything that they can do well, and by means of delegates everything that they cannot do for themselves.

It is therefore in the principles of democratic government that you must seek the rules of your political conduct.

But in order to found democracy and consolidate it among us, in order to attain the peaceful reign of constitutional laws, we must complete the war of liberty against tyranny; . . . [S]uch is the aim of the revolutionary government that you have organized. . . .

But the French are the first people in the world who have established true democracy by calling all men to equality and to full enjoyment of the rights of citizenship; and that is, in my opinion, the true reason why all the tyrants leagued against the republic will be vanquished.

There are from this moment great conclusions to be drawn from the principles that we have just laid down.

Since virtue [good citizenship] and equality are the soul of the republic, and your aim is to found and to consolidate the republic, it follows that the first rule of your political conduct must be to relate all of your measures to the maintenance of equality and to the development of virtue; for the first care of the legislator must be to strengthen the principles on which the government rests. Hence all that tends to excite a love of country, to purify moral standards, to exalt souls, to direct the passions of the human heart toward the public good must be adopted or established by you. All that tends to concentrate and debase them into selfish egotism, to awaken an infatuation for trivial things, and scorn for great ones, must be rejected or repressed by you. In the system of the French revolution, that which is immoral is impolitic, and that which tends to corrupt is counterrevolutionary. Weakness, vices, and prejudices are the road to monarchy. . . .

. . . Externally all the despots surround you; internally all the friends of tyranny conspire. . . . It is necessary to annihilate both the internal and external enemies of the republic or perish with its fall. Now, in this situation your first political maxim should be that one guides the people by reason, and the enemies of the people by terror.

If the driving force of popular government in peacetime is virtue, that of popular government during a revolution is both *virtue and terror:* virtue, without which terror is destructive; terror, without which virtue is impotent. Terror is only justice that is prompt, severe, and inflexible; it is thus an emanation of virtue; it is less a distinct principle than a consequence of the general principle of democracy applied to the most pressing needs of the *patrie.*

In a series of notes written in the summer of 1793, Robespierre expressed his policy toward counterrevolutionaries.

DESPOTISM IN DEFENSE OF LIBERTY

What is our goal? The enforcement of the constitution for the benefit of the people.

Who will our enemies be? The vicious and the rich.

What means will they employ? Slander and hypocrisy.

What things may be favorable for the employment of these? The ignorance of the *sans-culottes.*[1]

The people must therefore be enlightened. But what are the obstacles to the enlightenment of the people? Mercenary writers who daily mislead them with impudent falsehoods.

What conclusions may be drawn from this? 1. These writers must be proscribed as the most dangerous enemies of the people. 2. Right-minded literature must be scattered about in profusion.

What are the other obstacles to the establishment of liberty? Foreign war and civil war.

How can foreign war be ended? By putting republican generals in command of our armies and punishing those who have betrayed us.

How can civil war be ended? By punishing traitors and conspirators, particularly if they are deputies or administrators; by sending loyal troops under patriotic leaders to subdue the aristocrats of Lyon, Marseille, Toulon, the Vendée, the Jura, and all other regions in which the standards of rebellion and royalism have been raised; and by making frightful examples of all scoundrels who have outraged liberty and spilled the blood of patriots.

1. Proscription [condemnation] of perfidious and counter-revolutionary writers and propagation of proper literature.
2. Punishment of traitors and conspirators, particularly deputies and administrators.
3. Appointment of patriotic generals; dismissal and punishment of others.
4. Sustenance and laws for the people.

---

[1]*Sans-culottes* literally means without the fancy breeches worn by the aristocracy. The term refers generally to a poor city dweller (who wore simple trousers). Champions of equality, the sans-culottes hated the aristocracy and the rich bourgeoisie.

REVIEW QUESTIONS

1. In what way does the levy in mass herald a new kind of warfare?
2. Compare and contrast Maximilien Robespierre's vision of the Republic of Virtue with the ideals of the Declaration of the Rights of Man and of Citizens in Section 2. What did Robespierre mean by virtue?
3. On what grounds did Robespierre justify terror?
4. Like medieval inquisitors, Robespierre regarded people with different views not as opponents but as sinners. Discuss this statement.

5 Demands for Economic Justice

The reformers who came to power in 1789 sought to fashion a constitutional government that limited the monarch's power, protected individual rights, created a more rational system of administration and justice, and ended the special privileges of the aristocracy and the clergy. Alleviating the hardships of the poor was not among their concerns.

As the Revolution proceeded, the *sans-culottes*—small shopkeepers, artisans, and wage earners—demanded that the government address their calamitous poverty by increasing wages, setting price controls on foodstuffs, and punishing food speculators and profiteers. To prevent extremes of wealth and poverty, they insisted that the government should raise taxes for the wealthy and redistribute land. The various revolutionary governments rejected most of these demands, which they regarded as a radical interference with private property.

Gracchus Babeuf
CONSPIRACY OF THE EQUALS

The moderate bourgeoisie consolidated their control of the French government in 1795 under a new constitution, which established a five-member Directory with executive power, but the discontent of the poor was not answered. In 1796, the Directory crushed a conspiracy to overthrow the government headed by François-Noel (better known as Gracchus[1]) Babeuf (1760–1797). As editor of the journal *Tribun du peuple,* which commenced publication in 1794, Babeuf had argued for a new social order in which private property would be abolished. Only such a radical measure, he declared, would end the tyranny of the rich over the poor. In 1796, Babeuf and his colleagues were arrested for conspiring to reestablish the Constitution of 1793, which mandated universal male suffrage, and freedom of thought, and to overthrow the Directory; they regarded these measures as the first step in the creation of a social order based on economic equality. Babeuf conducted his own defense, using the trial as a forum to convey his political philosophy. Babeuf and one other defendant were sentenced to death; the others were either acquitted or deported.

Babeuf's Conspiracy of the Equals is important for two reasons. First, Babeuf's passionate attack on mistreatment of the poor and his call for the abolition of private property presage nineteenth-century socialist movements. Second, the organization of a secret society conspiring to overthrow the government heralds revolutionary movements in the nineteenth and twentieth centuries.

Following are excerpts from Babeuf's defense at his trial.

---

[1]In 1795 he took the name Gracchus after the ancient Roman social reformer.

The aim of the Revolution, furthermore, is to realize the happiness of the majority. If, therefore, this aim is not fulfilled, if the people do not succeed in attaining the better life which was the object of their struggle, then the Revolution is not over. There may be those whose only concern is to substitute their own rule for that of monarchy, but it makes no difference what such people say or want. If the Revolution is brought to an end in mid-passage, it will be judged by history as little more than a catalogue of bloody crimes.

With this in mind I strove to make known the nature of the common welfare, which is the purpose of social existence, or the happiness of the greatest number, which is the purpose of the Revolution. I pondered how it could be that at a given time the majority were worse off than they ought to be; and the conclusions that I reached I ventured to set forth in one of the first issues of the *Tribune*. . . .

There are, I wrote, *historical periods during which the final result of oppressive law is the appropriation of the bulk of social wealth by a minority. Social peace, natural when men are happy, then gives way to class war. The masses can no longer find a way to go on living; they see that they possess nothing and that they suffer under the harsh and flinty oppression of a greedy ruling class. The hour strikes for great and memorable revolutionary events, already foreseen in the writings of the times, when a general overthrow of the system of private property is inevitable, when the revolt of the poor against the rich becomes a necessity that can no longer be postponed.*

I had also observed that the main actors on the revolutionary scene had realized before I did that the goal of the Revolution ought to be to redress the evil wrought by archaic and rotten social institutions, and to promote the happiness of the people. . . .

The prosecution has reproduced a document entitled "Outline of Babeuf's Doctrine." This piece has been the subject of much debate in some of the correspondence connected with this trial; and it has been viewed as the most

radical of all subversive doctrines. Let us examine it further.

Nature, we read there, *has endowed every man with an equal right to the use of nature's gifts. The function of society is to defend this equality of right from the unending attacks of those who, in the state of nature, are wicked and strong; and to enhance, by collective action, collective happiness.*

Nature has placed everyone under an obligation to work. None may exempt himself from work without committing an antisocial action. Work and its fruits should be common to all. Oppression exists when one man is ground down by toil and lacks the barest necessaries of life, while another revels in luxury and idleness. It is impossible for anyone, without committing a crime, to appropriate for his own exclusive use the fruits of the earth or of manufacture.

In a truly just social order there are neither rich nor poor. The rich, who refuse to give up their superfluous wealth for the benefit of the poor, are enemies of the people.

None may be permitted to monopolize the cultural resources of society and hence to deprive others of the education essential for their wellbeing. Education is a universal human right.

The purpose of the Revolution is to abolish inequality and to restore the common welfare. The Revolution is not yet at an end, since the wealthy have diverted its fruits, including political power, to their own exclusive use, while the poor in their toil and misery lead a life of actual slavery and count for nothing in the State.

I have pointed out, under cross-examination, that this document did not come from my pen, but that, since it was indeed a statement of the doctrines I had espoused, I gave it my approval and agreed to its being printed and published. This document was, in effect, a faithful summary of the ideas that I had set forth in the various issues of the *Tribune*. . . .

. . . As I shall try to show you, the desire to be of service to mankind has animated all my thinking. This you may see from the frank confession of my political faith, which I consider it my duty to lay before you precisely as I have propagated it. In the *Tribune of the People* I wrote:

> *. . . If the earth belongs to none and its fruits to all; if private ownership of public wealth is only the result of certain institutions that violate fundamental human rights; then it follows that this private ownership is a usurpation; and it further follows that all that a man takes of the land and its fruits beyond what is necessary for sustenance is theft from society. . . .*
>
> *All that a citizen lacks for the satisfaction of his various daily needs, he lacks because he has been deprived of a natural property right by the engrossers of the public domain. All that a citizen enjoys beyond what is necessary for the satisfaction of his daily needs he enjoys as a result of a theft from the other members of society. In this way a more or less numerous group of people is deprived of its rightful share in the public domain. . . .*
>
> *The plea of superior ability and industry is an empty rationalization to mask the machinations of those who conspire against human equality and happiness. It is ridiculous and unfair to lay claim to a higher wage for the man whose work requires more concentrated thought and more mental effort. Such effort in no way expands the capacity of the stomach. No wage can be defended over and above what is necessary for the satisfaction of a person's needs.*
>
> *The worth of intelligence is only a matter of opinion, and it still remains to be determined if natural, physical strength is not of equal worth. Clever people have set a high value upon the creations of their minds; if the toilers had also had a hand in the ordering of things, they would doubtless have insisted that brawn is entitled to equal consideration with brain and that physical fatigue is no less real than mental fatigue.*
>
> *If wages are not equalized, the clever and persevering are given a licence to rob and despoil with impunity those less fortunately endowed with natural gifts. In this way the economic equilibrium of society is upset, for nothing has been more conclusively proven than the maxim:* a man only succeeds in becoming rich through the spoliation of others.
>
> *All our civic institutions, our social relationships, are nothing else but the expression of legalized barbarism and piracy, in which every man cheats and robs his neighbor. In its festering swamp our swindling society generates vice, crime, and misery of every kind. A handful of well-intentioned people band together and wage war on these evils, but their efforts are futile. They can make no headway because they do not tackle the problem at its roots, but apply palliatives based upon the distorted thinking of a sick society.*
>
> *It is clear from the foregoing that whatever a man possesses over and above his rightful share of the social product has been stolen. It is therefore right and proper to take this wealth back again from those who have wrongfully appropriated it. . . .*
>
> *. . . Society must be made to operate in such a way that it eradicates once and for all the desire of a man to become richer, or wiser, or more powerful than others.*
>
> *Putting this more exactly, we must try to* bring our fate under control, *try to make the lot of every member of society independent of accidental circumstances, happy or unhappy. We must try to guarantee to each man and his posterity, however numerous, a sufficiency of the means of existence, and nothing more. We must try and close all possible avenues by which a man may acquire more than his fair share of the fruits of toil and the gifts of nature.*
>
> *The only way to do this is to organize a communal regime which will suppress private property, set each to work at the skill or job he understands, require each to deposit the fruits of his labor in kind at the common store, and establish an agency for the distribution of basic necessities. This agency will maintain a complete list of people and of supplies, will distribute the latter with scrupulous fairness, and will deliver them to the home of each worker.*
>
> *A system such as this has been proven practicable by actual experience, for it is used by our twelve armies with their 1,200,000 men. And what is possible on a small scale can also be done on a large one. A regime of this type alone can ensure the general welfare, or, in other words, the permanent happiness of the people—the true and proper object of organized society.*
>
> *Such a regime, I continued, will sweep away iron bars, dungeon walls, and bolted doors, trials and disputations, murders, thefts and crimes of every*

kind; it will sweep away the judges and the judged, the jails and the gibbets—all the torments of body and agony of soul that the injustice of life engenders; it will sweep away enviousness and gnawing greed, pride and deceit, the very catalogue of sins that Man is heir to; it will remove—and how important is this!—the brooding, omnipresent fear that gnaws always and in each of us concerning our fate tomorrow, next month, next year, and in our old age; concerning the fate of our children and of our children's children.

Such, gentlemen of the jury, was the body of truth that I concerned myself with and that I thought to have divined from my study of the ageless book of nature. These were truths that I did no more than discover and make known. I loved humanity; and I was convinced that a social system such as I had conceived alone would ensure the happiness of man. I was eager, therefore, to gain the attention of my fellows, to win them to my way of thinking.

REVIEW QUESTIONS

1. What was Babeuf's conception of a just social order?
2. How did Babeuf extend the ideals of the Enlightenment and the French Revolution?

---

6 Napoleon: Destroyer and Preserver of the Revolution

In 1799, a group of conspirators that included Napoleon Bonaparte (1769–1821), an ambitious and popular general, staged a successful coup d'état. Within a short time, Napoleon became a one-man ruler, and in 1804 he crowned himself emperor of the French. Under Napoleon's military dictatorship, political freedom (a principal goal of the French Revolution) was suppressed. Nevertheless, Napoleon preserved, strengthened, and spread to other lands many of the Revolution's reforms. He supported religious tolerance, secular education, and access to positions according to ability; he would not restore the privileges of the aristocracy and church.

Napoleon Bonaparte
LEADER, GENERAL, TYRANT, REFORMER

Napoleon was a brilliant military commander who carefully planned each campaign, using speed, deception, and surprise to confuse and demoralize his opponents. By rapid marches, Napoleon would concentrate a superior force against a segment of the enemy's strung-out forces. Recognizing the importance of good morale, he sought to inspire his troops by appealing to their honor, their vanity, and their love of France.

In 1796, Napoleon, then a young officer, was given command of the French army in Italy. In the Italian campaign, he demonstrated a genius for propaganda and psychological warfare, as the following proclamations to his troops indicate.

LEADER AND GENERAL

March 27, 1796

Soldiers, you are naked, ill fed! The Government owes you much; it can give you nothing. Your patience, the courage you display in the midst of these rocks, are admirable; but they procure you no glory, no fame is reflected upon you. I seek to lead you into the most fertile plains in the world. Rich provinces, great cities will be in your power. There you will find honor, glory, and riches. Soldiers of Italy, would you be lacking in courage or constancy?

April 26, 1796

Soldiers:

In a fortnight you have won six victories, taken twenty-one standards, fifty-five pieces of artillery, several strong positions, and conquered the richest part of Piedmont [a region in northern Italy]; you have captured 15,000 prisoners and killed or wounded more than 10,000 men. . . .

. . . You have won battles without cannon, crossed rivers without bridges, made forced marches without shoes, camped without brandy and often without bread. Soldiers of liberty, only republican phalanxes [infantry troops] could have endured what you have endured. Soldiers, you have our thanks! The grateful *Patrie* [nation] will owe its prosperity to you. . . .

The two armies which but recently attacked you with audacity are fleeing before you in terror; the wicked men who laughed at your misery and rejoiced at the thought of the triumphs of your enemies are confounded and trembling.

But, soldiers, as yet you have done nothing compared with what remains to be done. . . .

. . . Undoubtedly the greatest obstacles have been overcome; but you still have battles to fight, cities to capture, rivers to cross. Is there one among you whose courage is abating? . . . No. . . . All of you are consumed with a desire to extend the glory of the French people; all of you long to humiliate those arrogant kings who dare to contemplate placing us in fetters; all of

you desire to dictate a glorious peace, one which will indemnify the *Patrie* for the immense sacrifices it has made; all of you wish to be able to say with pride as you return to your villages, "I was with the victorious army of Italy!"

Friends, I promise you this conquest; but there is one condition you must swear to fulfill—to respect the people whom you liberate, to repress the horrible pillaging committed by scoundrels incited by our enemies. Otherwise you would not be the liberators of the people; you would be their scourge. . . . Plunderers will be shot without mercy; already, several have been. . . .

Peoples of Italy, the French army comes to break your chains; the French people is the friend of all peoples; approach it with confidence; your property, your religion, and your customs will be respected.

We are waging war as generous enemies, and we wish only to crush the tyrants who enslave you.

The following passages from Napoleon's diary shed light on his generalship, ambition, and leadership qualities.

1800

What a thing is imagination! Here are men who don't know me, who have never seen me, but who only knew of me, and they are moved by my presence, they would do anything for me! And this same incident arises in all centuries and in all countries! Such is fanaticism! Yes, imagination rules the world. The defect of our modern institutions is that they do not speak to the imagination. By that alone can man be governed; without it he is but a brute.

1800

The impact of an army, like the total of mechanical coefficients, is equal to the mass multiplied by the velocity.

A battle is a dramatic action which has its beginning, its middle, and its conclusion. The result of a battle depends on the instantaneous flash of an idea. When you are about to give battle concentrate all your strength, neglect nothing; a battalion often decides the day.

In warfare every opportunity must be seized; for fortune is a woman: if you miss her to-day, you need not expect to find her to-morrow.

There is nothing in the military profession I cannot do for myself. If there is no one to make gunpowder, I know how to make it; gun carriages, I know how to construct them; if it is founding a cannon, I know that; or if the details of tactics must be taught, I can teach them.

The presence of a general is necessary: he is the head, he is the all in all of an army. It was not the Roman army conquered Gaul, but Cæsar; it was not the Carthaginians made the armies of the Republic tremble at the very gates of Rome, but Hannibal; it was not the Macedonian army marched to the Indus [River], but Alexander; . . . it was not the Prussian army that defended Prussia during seven years against the three strongest Powers of Europe, but Frederick the Great.

Concentration of forces, activity, activity with the firm resolve to die gloriously: these are the three great principles of the military art that have always made fortune favourable in all my operations. Death is nothing; but to live defeated and ingloriously, is to die every day.

I am a soldier, because that is the special faculty I was born with; that is my life, my habit. I have commanded wherever I have been. I commanded, when twenty-three years old, at the siege of Toulon; . . . I carried the soldiers of the army of Italy with me as soon as I appeared among them; I was born that way. . . .

It was by becoming a Catholic that I pacified the Vendée [region in western France], and a [Muslim] that I established myself in Egypt; it was by becoming ultramontane[1] that I won over public opinion in Italy. If I ruled a people of Jews, I would rebuild the temple of Solomon! Paradise is a central spot whither the souls of men proceed along different roads; every sect has a road of its own. . . .

1802

My power proceeds from my reputation, and my reputation from the victories I have won. My power would fall if I were not to support it with more glory and more victories. Conquest has made me what I am; only conquest can maintain me. . . .

1804

My mistress is power; I have done too much to conquer her to let her be snatched away from me. Although it may be said that power came to me of its own accord, yet I know what labour, what sleepless nights, what scheming, it has involved. . . .

1809

Again I repeat that in war morale and opinion are half the battle. The art of the great captain has always been to make his troops appear very numerous to the enemy, and the enemy's very few to his own. So that to-day, in spite of the long time we have spent in Germany, the enemy do not know my real strength. We are constantly striving to magnify our numbers. Far from confessing that I had only 100,000 men at Wagram [French victory over Austria in 1809] I am constantly suggesting that I had 220,000. In my Italian campaigns, in which I had only a handful of troops, I always exaggerated my numbers. It served my purpose, and has not lessened my glory. My generals and practised soldiers could always perceive, after the event, all the skilfulness of my operations, even that of having exaggerated the numbers of my troops.

In several ways, Napoleon anticipated the strategies of twentieth-century dictators. He concentrated power in his own hands, suppressed opposition, and sought to mold public opinion by controlling the press and education. The following Imperial Catechism of 1806, which schoolchildren were required to memorize and recite, is a pointed example of Napoleonic indoctrination.

---

[1]Favoring the pope over competing authorities.

TYRANT

*Lesson VII. Continuation of
the Fourth Commandment.*

Q. What are the duties of Christians with respect to the princes who govern them, and what in particular are our duties towards Napoleon I, our Emperor?

A. Christians owe to the princes who govern them, and we owe in particular to Napoleon I, our Emperor, *love, respect, obedience, fidelity, military service* and the tributes laid for the preservation and defence of the Empire and of his throne; we also owe to him fervent prayers for his safety and the spiritual and temporal prosperity of the state.

Q. Why are we bound to all these duties towards our Emperor?

A. First of all, because God, who creates empires and distributes them according to His will, in loading our Emperor with gifts, both in peace and in war, has established him as our sovereign and has made him the minister of His power and His image upon the earth. *To honor and to serve our Emperor is then to honor and to serve God himself.* Secondly, because our Lord Jesus Christ by His doctrine as well as by His example, has Himself taught us what we owe to our sovereign: He was born the subject of Caesar Augustus;[2] He paid the prescribed impost; and just as He ordered to render to God that which belongs to God, so He ordered to render to Caesar that which belongs to Caesar.

Q. Are there not particular reasons which ought to attach us more strongly to Napoleon I, our Emperor?

A. Yes; for it is he whom God has raised up under difficult circumstances to re-establish the public worship of the holy religion of our fathers and to be the protector of it. He has restored and preserved public order by his profound and active wisdom; he defends the state by his powerful arm; he has become the anointed of the Lord through the consecration which he received from the sovereign pontiff, head of the universal church.

Q. What ought to be thought of those who may be lacking in their duty towards our Emperor?

A. According to the apostle Saint Paul, they would be resisting the order established by God himself and would render themselves *worthy of eternal damnation.*

Q. Will the duties which are required of us towards our Emperor be equally binding with respect to his lawful successors in the order established by the constitutions of the Empire?

A. Yes, without doubt; for we read in the holy scriptures, that God, Lord of heaven and earth, by an order of His supreme will and through His providence, gives empires not only to one person in particular, but also to his family.

In the following letter (April 22, 1805) to Joseph Fouché, minister of police, Napoleon reveals his intention to regulate public opinion.

Repress the journals a little; make them produce wholesome articles. I want you to write to the editors of the . . . newspapers that are most widely read in order to let them know that the time is not far away when, seeing that they are no longer of service to me, I shall suppress them along with all the others. . . . Tell them that the . . . Revolution is over, and that there is now only one party in France; that I shall never allow the newspapers to say anything contrary to my interests; that they may publish a few little articles with just a bit of poison in them, but that one fine day somebody will shut their mouths.

With varying degrees of success, Napoleon's administrators in conquered lands provided positions based on talent, equalized taxes, and abolished serfdom and the courts of the nobility. They promoted freedom of religion, fought clerical interference with secular authority, and promoted secu-

---

[2]Caesar Augustus (27 B.C.–A.D. 14) was the Roman emperor at the time that Jesus was born.

lar education. By undermining the power of European clergy and aristocrats, Napoleon weakened the Old Regime irreparably in much of Europe. A letter from Napoleon to his brother Jérôme, King of Westphalia, illustrates Napoleon's desire for enlightened rule.

REFORMER

Fontainebleau, November 15, 1807
To Jérôme Napoléon, King of Westphalia

I enclose the Constitution for your Kingdom. It embodies the conditions on which I renounce all my rights of conquest, and all the claims I have acquired over your state. You must faithfully observe it. I am concerned for the happiness of your subjects, not only as it affects your reputation, and my own, but also for its influence on the whole European situation. Don't listen to those who say that your subjects are so accustomed to slavery that they will feel no gratitude for the benefits you give them. There is more intelligence in the Kingdom of Westphalia than they would have you believe; and your throne will never be firmly established except upon the trust and affection of the common people. What German opinion impatiently demands is that men of no rank, but of marked ability, shall have an equal claim upon your favour and your employment, and that every trace of serfdom, or of a feudal hierarchy between the sovereign and the lowest class of his subjects, shall be done away. The benefits of the Code Napoléon [legal code introduced by Napoleon], public trial, and the introduction of juries, will be the leading features of your government. And to tell you the truth, I count more upon their effects, for the extension and consolidation of your rule, than upon the most resounding victories. I want your subjects to enjoy a degree of liberty, equality, and prosperity hitherto unknown to the German people. I want this liberal regime to produce, one way or another, changes which will be of the utmost benefit to the system of the Confederation, and to the strength of your monarchy. Such a method of government will be a stronger barrier between you and Prussia than the Elbe [River], the fortresses, and the protection of France. What people will want to return under the arbitrary Prussian rule, once it has tasted the benefits of a wise and liberal administration? In Germany, as in France, Italy, and Spain, people long for equality and liberalism. I have been managing the affairs of Europe long enough now to know that the burden of the privileged classes was resented everywhere. Rule constitutionally. Even if reason, and the enlightenment of the age, were not sufficient cause, it would be good policy for one in your position; and you will find that the backing of public opinion gives you a great natural advantage over the absolute Kings who are your neighbours.

REVIEW QUESTIONS

1. In his proclamations how did Napoleon Bonaparte try to raise the morale of his troops?
2. How did Napoleon use propaganda to achieve his goals?
3. For what purpose was religious authority cited in the catechism of 1806? What would Machiavelli have thought of this device?
4. How seriously did Napoleon adhere to the ideals of the Enlightenment and French Revolution? Show how Napoleon spread the reforms of the Enlightenment.

CHAPTER 5
The Industrial Revolution

LAMBETH GASWORKS. Gustave Doré, 1872. This engraving shows the harsh conditions within industry during the latter half of the nineteenth century. At the time of this scene, most of the lighting in major cities like London was provided by gas. *(Engraving from Gustave Doré and Blanchard Jerold, London, A Pilgrimage [London, 1872]. Stock Montage.)*

In the last part of the eighteenth century, as a revolution for liberty and equality swept across France and sent shock waves across Europe, a different kind of revolution, a revolution in industry, was transforming life in Great Britain. In the nineteenth century the Industrial Revolution spread to the United States and to the European continent. Today, it encompasses virtually the entire world; everywhere the drive to substitute machines for human labor continues at a rapid pace.

After 1760, dramatic changes occurred in Britain in the way goods were produced and labor organized. New forms of power, particularly steam, replaced animal strength and human muscle. Better ways of obtaining and using raw materials were discovered, and a new form of organizing production and workers—the factory—came into common use. In the nineteenth century, technology moved from triumph to triumph with a momentum unprecedented in human history. The resulting explosion in economic production and productivity transformed society with breathtaking speed.

Rapid industrialization caused hardships for the new class of industrial workers, many of them recent arrivals from the countryside. Arduous and monotonous, factory labor was geared to the strict discipline of the clock, the machine, and the production schedule. Employment was never secure. Sick workers received no pay and were often fired; aged workers suffered pay cuts or lost their jobs. During business slumps, employers lowered wages with impunity, and laid-off workers had nowhere to turn for assistance. Because factory owners did not consider safety an important concern, accidents were frequent. Yet the Industrial Revolution was also a great force for human betterment. Ultimately it raised the standard of living, even for the lowest classes, lengthened life expectancy, and provided more leisure time and more possibilities for people to fulfill their potential.

The Industrial Revolution dramatically altered political and social life at all levels, but especially for the middle class, whose engagement in capitalist ventures brought greater political power and social recognition. During the course of the nineteenth century, the bourgeoisie came to hold many of the highest offices in western European states, completing a trend that had begun with the French Revolution.

Cities grew in size, number, and importance. Municipal authorities were unable to cope with the rapid pace of urbanization, and without adequate housing, sanitation, or recreational facilities, the exploding urban centers were another source of working-class misery. In preindustrial Britain, most people had lived in small villages. They knew where their roots were; relatives, friends, and the village church gave them a sense of belonging. The industrial centers separated people from nature and from their places of origin, shattering traditional ways of life that had given men and women a sense of security.

The plight of the working class created a demand for reform, but the British government, committed to laissez-faire economic principles that militated against state involvement, was slow to act. In the last part of the nineteenth century, however, the development of labor unions, the rising political voice of the working class, and the growing recognition that the problems created by industrialization required government intervention speeded up the pace of reform. Rejecting the road of reform, Karl Marx called for a working-class revolution that would destroy the capitalist system.

1 Early Industrialization

Several factors help to explain why the Industrial Revolution began in Great Britain. That country had an abundant labor supply, large deposits of coal and iron ore, and capital available for investing in new industries. A large domestic middle class and overseas colonies provided markets for manufactured goods. Colonies were also a source for raw materials, particularly cotton for the textile industry. The Scientific Revolution and an enthusiasm for engineering fostered a spirit of curiosity and inventiveness. Britain had enterprising and daring entrepreneurs who organized new businesses and discovered new methods of production.

Edward Baines
BRITAIN'S INDUSTRIAL ADVANTAGES AND THE FACTORY SYSTEM

In 1835, Edward Baines (1800–1890), an early student of industrialization, wrote *The History of the Cotton Manufacture in Great Britain*—about one of the leading industries in the early days of the Industrial Revolution. In the passages that follow, Baines discusses the reasons for Britain's industrial transformation and the advantages of the factory system.

Three things may be regarded as of primary importance for the successful prosecution of manufactures, namely, water-power, fuel, and iron. Wherever these exist in combination, and where they are abundant and cheap, machinery may be manufactured and put in motion at small cost; and most of the processes of making and finishing cloth, whether chemical or mechanical, depending, as they do, mainly on the two great agents of water and heat, may likewise be performed with advantage.

. . . A great number of streams . . . furnish water-power adequate to turn many hundred mills: they afford the element of water, indispensable for scouring, bleaching, printing, dyeing, and other processes of manufacture: and when collected in their larger channels, or employed to feed canals, they supply a superior inland navigation, so important for the transit of raw materials and merchandise.

Not less important for manufactures than the copious supply of good water, is the great abundance of coal. . . . This mineral fuel animates the thousand arms of the steam-engine, and furnishes the most powerful agent in all chemical and mechanical operations.

In mentioning the advantages which Lancashire [the major cotton manufacturing area] possesses as a seat of manufactures, we must not omit its ready communication with the sea by means of its well-situated port, Liverpool, through the medium of which it receives, from Ireland, a large proportion of the food that supports its population, and whose commerce brings from distant shores the raw materials of its manufactures, and again distributes them, converted into useful and elegant clothing, amongst all the nations of the earth. Through the same means a plentiful supply of timber is obtained, so needful for building purposes.

To the above natural advantages, we must add, the acquired advantage of a canal communication, which ramifies itself through all the populous parts of this country, and connects it with the inland counties, the seats of other flourishing manufactures, and the sources whence iron, lime, salt, stone, and other articles in which Lancashire is deficient, are obtained. By this means Lancashire, being already possessed of the primary requisites for manufactures, is enabled, at a very small expense, to command things of secondary importance, and to appropriate to its use the natural advantages of the whole kingdom. The canals, having been accomplished by individual enterprise, not by national funds, were constructed to supply a want already existing: they were not, therefore, original sources of the manufactures, but have extended together with them, and are to be considered as having essentially aided and accelerated that prosperity from

whose beginnings they themselves arose. The recent introduction of railways will have a great effect in making the operations of trade more intensely active, and perfecting the division of labour, already carried to so high a point. By the railway and the locomotive engine, the extremities of the land will, for every beneficial purpose, be united.

In comparing the advantages of England for manufactures with those of other countries, we can by no means overlook the excellent commercial position of the country—intermediate between the north and south of Europe; and its insular situation, which, combined with the command of the seas, secures our territory from invasion or annoyance. The German ocean, the Baltic, and the Mediterranean are the regular highways for our ships; and our western ports command an unobstructed passage to the Atlantic, and to every quarter of the world.

A temperate climate, and a hardy race of men, have also greatly contributed to promote the manufacturing industry of England.

The political and moral advantages of this country, as a seat of manufactures, are not less remarkable than its physical advantages. The arts are the daughters of peace and liberty. In no country have these blessings been enjoyed in so high a degree, or for so long a continuance, as in England. Under the reign of just laws, personal liberty and property have been secure; mercantile enterprise has been allowed to reap its reward; capital has accumulated in safety; the workman has "gone forth to his work and to his labour until the evening;" and, thus protected and favoured, the manufacturing prosperity of the country has struck its roots deep, and spread forth its branches to the ends of the earth.

England has also gained by the calamities of other countries, and the intolerance of other governments. At different periods, the Flemish and French protestants, expelled from their native lands, have taken refuge in England, and have repaid the protection given them by practising and teaching branches of industry, in which the English were then less expert than their neighbours. The wars which have at different times desolated the rest of Europe, and especially those which followed the French revolution, (when mechanical invention was producing the most wonderful effects in England,) checked the progress of manufacturing improvement on the continent, and left England for many years without a competitor. At the same time, the English navy held the sovereignty of the ocean, and under its protection the commerce of this country extended beyond all former bounds, and established a firm connexion between the manufacturers of Lancashire and their customers in the most distant lands.

When the natural, political, and adventitious causes, thus enumerated, are viewed together, it cannnot be [a] matter of surprise that England has obtained a preeminence over the rest of the world in manufactures.

A crucial feature of the Industrial Revolution was a new production system—the making of goods in factories. By bringing all the operations of manufacturing under one roof, industrialists made the process of production more efficient. Baines describes the factory system's advantages over former methods.

. . . Hitherto the cotton manufacture had been carried on almost entirely in the houses of the workmen: the hand or stock cards,[1] the spinning wheel, and the loom, required no larger apartment than that of a cottage. A spinning jenny[2] of small size might also be used in a cottage, and in many instances was so used: when the number of spindles was considerably increased, adjacent work-shops were used. But the water-frame, the carding engine, and the

other machines which [Richard] Arkwright brought out in a finished state, required both more space than could be found in a cottage, and more power than could be applied by the human arm. Their weight also rendered it necessary to place them in strongly-built mills, and they could not be advantageously turned by any power then known but that of water.

The use of machinery was accompanied by a greater division of labour than existed in the primitive state of the manufacture; the material went through many more processes; and of course the loss of time and the risk of waste would have been much increased, if its removal from house to house at every stage of the manufacture had been necessary. It became obvious that there were several important advantages in carrying on the numerous operations of an extensive manufacture in the same building. Where water power was required, it was economy to build one mill, and put up one water-wheel, rather than several. This arrangement also enabled the master spinner himself to superintend every stage of the manufacture: it gave him a greater security against the wasteful or fraudulent consumption of the material: it saved time in the transference of the work from hand to hand: and it prevented the extreme inconvenience which would have resulted from the failure of one class of workmen to perform their part, when several other classes of workmen were dependent upon them. Another circumstance which made it advantageous to have a large number of machines in one manufactory was, that mechanics must be employed on the spot, to construct and repair the machinery, and that their time could not be fully occupied with only a few machines.

All these considerations drove the cotton spinners to that important change in the economy of English manufactures, the introduction of the factory system; and when that system had once been adopted, such were its pecuniary advantages, that mercantile competition would have rendered it impossible, even had it been desirable, to abandon it.

---

[1] Prior to spinning, raw fibers had to be carded with a brushlike tool that cleaned and separated them.

[2] The spinning jenny, which was hand-powered, was the first machine that spun fiber onto multiple spindles at the same time; that is, it produced more thread or yarn in less time than the single-thread spinning wheel.

Adam Smith
THE DIVISION OF LABOR

Baines's emphasis on the division of labor in the expanding use of machinery can be traced to Adam Smith, who in the eighteenth century pioneered the study of economics. Adam Smith (1723–1790) was a bright and thoughtful academic who had attended Glasgow University in his native Scotland and then Oxford University in England before being appointed professor of logic at Glasgow at age twenty-eight and professor of moral philosophy a year later. After some years of travel on the Continent, Smith wrote over a span of years his masterpiece; *An Inquiry into the Nature and Causes of the Wealth of Nations* (see also page 113), published in 1776, made him instantly famous. He began *The Wealth of Nations* by analyzing the benefits of the division of labor—the system in which each worker performs a single set task or a single step in the manufacturing process.

The greatest improvement in the productive powers of Labour, and the greater skill, dexterity, and judgment with which it is anywhere directed, or applied, seem to have been the effects of the division of labour. . . .

This great increase of the quantity of work, which, in consequence of the division of labour, the same number of people are capable of performing, is owing to three different circumstances; first, to the increase of dexterity in every particular workman; secondly, to the saving of the time which is commonly lost in passing from one species of work to another; and lastly, to the invention of a great number of machines which facilitate and abridge labour, and enable one man to do the work of many. . . .

To take an example, therefore, from a very trifling manufacture; but one in which the division of labour has been very often taken notice of, the trade of the pin-maker; a workman not educated to this business (which the division of labour has rendered a distinct trade), nor acquainted with the use of the machinery employed in it (to the invention of which the same division of labour has probably given occasion), could scarce, perhaps, with his utmost industry, make one pin in a day, and certainly could not make twenty. But in the way in which this business is now carried on, not only

the whole work is a peculiar trade, but it is divided into a number of branches, of which the greater part are likewise peculiar trades. One man draws out the wire, another straightens it, a third cuts it, a fourth points it, a fifth grinds it at the top for receiving the head: to make the head requires two or three distinct operations; to put it on is a peculiar business; to whiten the pins is another; it is even a trade by itself to put them into the paper; and the important business of making a pin is, in this manner, divided into about eighteen distinct operations, which, in some manufactories, are all performed by distinct hands, though in others the same man will sometimes perform two or three of them. I have seen a small manufactory of this kind where ten men only were employed, and where some of them consequently performed two or three distinct operations. But though they were very poor [craftsmen], and therefore but indifferently accommodated with the necessary machinery, they could, when they exerted themselves, make among them about twelve pounds of pins in a day. There are in a pound upwards of four thousand pins of a middling size. Those ten persons, therefore, could make among them upwards of forty-eight thousand pins in a day. Each person, therefore, making a tenth part of forty-eight thousand pins, might be considered as making four thousand eight hundred pins in a day. But if they had all wrought separately and independently, and without any of them having been educated to this peculiar business, they certainly could not each of them have made twenty, perhaps not one pin in a day; that is, certainly, not the two hundred and fortieth, perhaps not the four thousand eight hundredth part of what they are at present capable of performing, in consequence of a proper division and combination of their different operations. . . .

REVIEW QUESTIONS

1. Apart from its natural resources, what other assets for industrial development did England possess?
2. What were the factory system's advantages over the domestic system of production?
3. How, according to Adam Smith, did the division of labor lead to increased productivity?

---

2 The Capitalist Ethic

The remarkable advance in industry and material prosperity in the nineteenth century has been hailed as the triumph of the middle class, or bourgeoisie, which included bankers, merchants, factory owners, professionals, and government officials. Unlike the upper classes, which lived on inherited wealth, middle-class people supported themselves by diligent, assiduous activity—what has been called "the capitalist (or bourgeois) ethic." A vigorous spirit of enterprise and the opportunity for men of ability to rise from common origins to riches and fame help explain the growth of industrialism in England. These industrial capitalists adopted the attitude of medieval monks that "idleness is the enemy of the soul," to which they added "time is money."

The ideal of dedicated and responsible hard work directed by an internal rather than an external discipline was seen as the ultimate source of human merit and was widely publicized in the nineteenth century. It encouraged upward mobility among the lower classes and sustained the morale of ambitious middle-class people immersed in the keen competition of private enterprise. By shaping highly motivated private citizens, the capitalist ethic also provided a vital source of national strength.

Samuel Smiles
SELF-HELP AND *THRIFT*

Samuel Smiles (1812–1904) was the most famous messenger of the capitalist ethic at its best. His father, a Scottish papermaker and general merchant, died early, leaving his eleven children to fend for themselves. Samuel was apprenticed to a medical office, in due time becoming a physician in general practice. Turned journalist, he edited the local newspaper in the English city of Leeds, hoping to cure the ills of society by promoting the social and intellectual development of the working classes. Leaving his editorial office, he stepped into railroad management as a friend of George Stephenson, the inventor of the locomotive and promoter of railroads, whose biography Smiles wrote in 1857. Two years later he published *Self-Help,* which had grown out of a lecture to a small mutual-improvement society in which people sought each other's help in bettering their condition. The book was an instant success and was translated into many languages, including Japanese. Having retired after twenty-one years as a railway administrator and prolific author, Smiles suffered a stroke caused by overwork. Recovered, he traveled widely, writing more books about deserving but often unknown achievers. All along, he practiced in his personal life the virtues that he preached. The following selections reveal not only Samuel Smiles's philosophy of life but also the values inspiring the achievements of capitalism.

SELF-HELP

"Heaven helps those who help themselves" is a well-tried maxim, embodying in a small compass the results of vast human experience. The spirit of self-help is the root of all genuine growth in the individual; and, exhibited in the lives of many, it constitutes the true source of national vigour and strength. Help from without is often enfeebling in its effects, but help from within invariably invigorates. Whatever is done *for* men or classes, to a certain extent takes away the stimulus and necessity of doing for themselves; and where men are subjected to over-guidance and over-government, the inevitable tendency is to render them comparatively helpless.

Even the best institutions can give a man no active help. Perhaps the most they can do is, to leave him free to develop himself and improve his individual condition. But in all times men have been prone to believe that their happiness and well-being were to be secured by means of institutions rather than by their own conduct. Hence the value of legislation as an agent in human advancement has usually been much over-estimated. . . . [N]o laws, however stringent, can make the idle industrious, the thriftless provident, or the drunken sober. Such reforms can only be effected by means of individual action, economy, and self-denial; by better habits, rather than by greater rights. . . .

National progress is the sum of individual industry, energy, and uprightness, as national decay is of individual idleness, selfishness, and vice. What we are accustomed to decry as great social evils, will, for the most part, be found to be but the outgrowth of man's own perverted life; and though we may endeavour to cut them down and extirpate them by means of Law, they will only spring up again with fresh luxuriance in some other form, unless the conditions of personal life and character are radically improved. If this view be correct, then it follows that the highest patriotism and philanthropy consist, not so much in altering laws and modifying institutions, as in helping and stimulating men to elevate and improve themselves by their own free and independent individual action.

It may be of comparatively little consequence how a man is governed from without, whilst everything depends upon how he governs himself from within. The greatest slave is not he who is ruled by a despot, great though that evil be, but he who is the thrall of his own moral ignorance, selfishness, and vice. . . .

Smiles's book *Thrift,* published in 1875, restates and expands on the themes stressed in *Self-Help.*

THRIFT

Every man is bound to do what he can to elevate his social state, and to secure his independence. For this purpose he must spare from his means in order to be independent in his condition. Industry enables men to earn their living; it should also enable them to learn to live. Independence can only be established by the exercise of forethought, prudence, frugality, and self-denial. To be just as well as generous, men must deny themselves. The essence of generosity is self-sacrifice.

The object of this book is to induce men to employ their means for worthy purposes, and not to waste them upon selfish indulgences. Many enemies have to be encountered in accomplishing this object. There are idleness, thoughtlessness, vanity, vice, intemperance. The last is the worst enemy of all. Numerous cases are cited in the course of the following book, which show that one of the best methods of abating the curse of Drink is to induce old and young to practice the virtue of Thrift. . . .

It is the savings of individuals which compose the wealth—in other words, the well-being—of every nation. On the other hand, it is the wastefulness of individuals which occasions the impoverishment of states. So that every thrifty person may be regarded as a public benefactor, and every thriftless person as a public enemy. . . .

. . . All that is great in man comes of labor—greatness in art, in literature, in science. Knowledge—"the wing wherewith we fly to heaven"—is only acquired through labor. Genius is but a capability of laboring intensely: it is the power of making great and sustained efforts. Labor may be a chastisement, but it is indeed a glorious one. It is worship, duty, praise, and immortality—for those who labor with the highest aims and for the purest purposes. . . .

. . . Of all wretched men, surely the idle are the most so—those whose life is barren of utility, who have nothing to do except to gratify their senses. Are not such men the most querulous, miserable, and dissatisfied of all, constantly in a state of *ennui* [boredom], alike useless to themselves and to others—mere cumberers [troublesome occupiers] of the earth, who, when removed, are missed by none, and whom none regret? Most wretched and ignoble lot, indeed, is the lot of the idlers.

Who have helped the world onward so much as the workers; men who have had to work from necessity or from choice? All that we call progress—civilization, well-being, and prosperity—depends upon industry, diligently applied—from the culture of a barley-stalk to the construction of a steamship; from the stitching of a collar to the sculpturing of "the statue that enchants the world."

All useful and beautiful thoughts, in like manner, are the issue of labor, of study, of observation, of research, of diligent elaboration. . . .

By the working-man we do not mean merely the man who labors with his muscles and sinews. A horse can do this. But *he* is preeminently the working-man who works with his brain also, and whose whole physical system is under the influence of his higher faculties. The man who paints a picture, who writes a book, who makes a law, who creates a poem, is a working-man of the highest order; not so necessary to the physical sustainment of the community as the plowman or the shepherd, but not less important as providing for society its highest intellectual nourishment. . . .

But a large proportion of men do not provide for the future. They do not remember the past. They think only of the present. They preserve nothing. They spend all that they earn. They do not provide for themselves; they do not provide for their families. They may make high wages, but eat and drink the whole of what they earn. Such people are constantly poor, and hanging on the verge of destitution. . . .

REVIEW QUESTIONS

1. What, according to Samuel Smiles, were the key values that should guide the individual?
2. How did Smiles define success in life?

3. What, in his opinion, were the enemies of individual and national achievement?
4. Do Smiles's writings offer good advice to the poor in the United States today? Explain why or why not.

---

3 Factory Discipline

For the new industries to succeed, workers needed to adopt the rigorous discipline exercised by the new industrial capitalists themselves. But adapting to labor with machines in factories proved traumatic for the poor, uneducated, and often unruly folk, who previously had toiled on farms and in village workshops and were used to a less demanding pace.

FACTORY RULES

The problem of adapting a preindustrial labor force to the discipline needed for coordinating large numbers of workers in the factory was common to all industrializing countries. The Foundry and Engineering Works of the Royal Overseas Trading Company, in the Moabit section of Berlin, issued the following rules in 1844. The rules aimed at instilling obedience and honesty as well as "good order and harmony" among the factory's workers. The rules not only stressed timekeeping (with appropriate fines for latecomers), but also proper conduct in all aspects of life and work in the factory.

In every large works, and in the co-ordination of any large number of workmen, good order and harmony must be looked upon as the fundamentals of success, and therefore the following rules shall be strictly observed.

Every man employed in the concern . . . shall receive a copy of these rules, so that no one can plead ignorance. Its acceptance shall be deemed to mean consent to submit to its regulations.

(1) The normal working day begins at all seasons at 6 A.M. precisely and ends, after the usual break of half an hour for breakfast, an hour for dinner and half an hour for tea, at 7 P.M., and it shall be strictly observed.

Five minutes before the beginning of the stated hours of work until their actual commencement, a bell shall ring and indicate that every worker employed in the concern has to proceed to his place of work, in order to start as soon as the bell stops.

The doorkeeper shall lock the door punctually at 6 A.M., 8:30 A.M., 1 P.M. and 4:30 P.M.

Workers arriving 2 minutes late shall lose half an hour's wages; whoever is more than 2 minutes late may not start work until after the next break, or at least shall lose his wages until then. Any disputes about the correct time shall be settled by the clock mounted above the gatekeeper's lodge.

These rules are valid both for time- and for piece-workers, and in cases of breaches of these rules, workmen shall be fined in proportion to their earnings. The deductions from the wage shall be entered in the wage-book of the gatekeeper whose duty they are; they shall be unconditionally accepted as it will not be possible to enter into any discussions about them.

(2) When the bell is rung to denote the end of the working day, every workman, both

on piece- and on day-wage, shall leave his workshop and the yard, but is not allowed to make preparations for his departure before the bell rings. Every breach of this rule shall lead to a fine of five silver groschen [pennies] to the sick fund. Only those who have obtained special permission by the overseer may stay on in the workshop in order to work.—If a workman has worked beyond the closing bell, he must give his name to the gatekeeper on leaving, on pain of losing his payment for the overtime.

(3) No workman, whether employed by time or piece, may leave before the end of the working day, without having first received permission from the overseer and having given his name to the gatekeeper. Omission of these two actions shall lead to a fine of ten silver groschen payable to the sick fund.

(4) Repeated irregular arrival at work shall lead to dismissal. This shall also apply to those who are found idling by an official or overseer, and refuse to obey their order to resume work.

(5) Entry to the firm's property by any but the designated gateway, and exit by any prohibited route, e.g. by climbing fences or walls, or by crossing the Spree [River], shall be punished by a fine of fifteen silver groschen to the sick fund for the first offences, and dismissal for the second.

(6) No worker may leave his place of work otherwise than for reasons connected with his work.

(7) All conversation with fellow-workers is prohibited; if any worker requires information about his work, he must turn to the overseer, or to the particular fellow-worker designated for the purpose.

(8) Smoking in the workshops or in the yard is prohibited during working hours; anyone caught smoking shall be fined five silver groschen for the sick fund for every such offence.

(9) Every worker is responsible for cleaning up his space in the workshop, and if in doubt, he is to turn to his overseer.—All tools must always be kept in good condition, and must be cleaned after use. This applies particularly to the turner, regarding his lathe.

(10) Natural functions must be performed at the appropriate places, and whoever is found soiling walls, fences, squares, etc., and similarly, whoever is found washing his face and hands in the workshop and not in the places assigned for the purpose, shall be fined five silver groschen for the sick fund.

(11) On completion of his piece of work, every workman must hand it over at once to his foreman or superior, in order to receive a fresh piece of work. Pattern makers must on no account hand over their patterns to the foundry without express order of their supervisors. No workman may take over work from his fellow-workman without instruction to that effect by the foreman.

(12) It goes without saying that all overseers and officials of the firm shall be obeyed without question, and shall be treated with due deference. Disobedience will be punished by dismissal.

(13) Immediate dismissal shall also be the fate of anyone found drunk in any of the workshops.

(14) Untrue allegations against superiors or officials of the concern shall lead to stern reprimand, and may lead to dismissal. The same punishment shall be meted out to those who knowingly allow errors to slip through when supervising or stocktaking.

(15) Every workman is obliged to report to his superiors any acts of dishonesty or embezzlement on the part of his fellow workmen. If he omits to do so, and it is shown after subsequent discovery of a misdemeanour that he knew about it at the time, he shall be liable to be taken to court as an accessory after the fact and the wage due to him shall be retained as punishment. Conversely, anyone denouncing a theft in such a way as to allow conviction of the thief shall receive a reward of two Thaler [dollar equivalent], and, if necessary, his name shall be kept confidential.—Further, the gatekeeper and the watchman, as well as every official, are entitled to search the baskets, parcels, aprons etc. of the women and children who are taking the dinners into the works, on their departure, as well as search any worker suspected of stealing any article whatever. . . .

(18) Advances shall be granted only to the older workers, and even to them only in exceptional circumstances. As long as he is working by the piece, the workman is entitled merely to his fixed weekly wage as subsistence pay; the extra earnings shall be paid out only on completion of the whole piece contract. If a workman leaves before his piece contract is completed, either of his own free will, or on being dismissed as punishment, or because of illness, the partly completed work shall be valued by the general manager with the help of two overseers, and he will be paid accordingly. There is no appeal against the decision of these experts.

(19) A free copy of these rules is handed to every workman, but whoever loses it and requires a new one, or cannot produce it on leaving, shall be fined 2½ silver groschen, payable to the sick fund.

REVIEW QUESTIONS

1. Judging by the Berlin factory rules, what were the differences between preindustrial and industrial work routines?
2. How might these rules have affected the lives of families?

---

4 The Dark Side of Industrialization

Among the numerous problems caused by rapid industrialization, none aroused greater concern among humanitarians than child labor in factories and mines. In preindustrial times, children had always been part of the labor force, indoors and out, a practice that was continued during the early days of the Industrial Revolution. In the cotton industry, for instance, the proportion of children and adolescents under eighteen was around 40–45 percent of the labor force; in some large firms the proportion was even greater. Employers discovered early that youngsters adapted more easily to machines and factory discipline than did adults, who were used to traditional handicraft routines. Child labor took children away from their parents, undermined family life, and deprived children of schooling. Factory routines dulled their minds, and the long hours spent in often unsanitary environments endangered their health.

Sadler Commission
REPORT ON CHILD LABOR

Due to concern about child labor, in 1832 a parliamentary committee chaired by Michael Thomas Sadler investigated the situation of children employed in British factories. The following testimony is drawn from the records of the Sadler Commission.

May 18, 1832

Michael Thomas Sadler, Esquire, in the chair.
Mr. *Matthew Crabtree,* called in; and Examined.

What age are you?—Twenty-two.[1]

What is your occupation?—A blanket manufacturer.

Have you ever been employed in a factory?—Yes.

At what age did you first go to work in one?—Eight.

How long did you continue in that occupation?—Four years.

Will you state the hours of labour at the period when you first went to the factory, in ordinary times?—From 6 in the morning to 8 at night.

Fourteen hours?—Yes.

With what intervals for refreshment and rest?—An hour at noon.

Then you had no resting time allowed in which to take your breakfast, or what is in Yorkshire called your "drinking"?—No.

When trade was brisk what were your hours?—From 5 in the morning to 9 in the evening.

Sixteen hours?—Yes.

With what intervals at dinner?—An hour.

How far did you live from the mill?—About two miles.

Was there any time allowed for you to get your breakfast in the mill?—No.

Did you take it before you left home?—Generally.

During those long hours of labour could you be punctual, how did you awake?—I seldom did awake spontaneously. I was most generally awoke or lifted out of bed, sometimes asleep, by my parents.

Were you always in time?—No.

What was the consequence if you had been too late?—I was most commonly beaten.

Severely?—Very severely, I thought.

In whose factory was this?—Messrs. Hague & Cook's, of Dewsbury.

Will you state the effect that those long hours had upon the state of your health and feelings?—I was, when working those long hours, commonly very much fatigued at night, when I left my work, so much so that I sometimes should have slept as I walked if I had not stumbled and started awake again, and so sick often that I could not eat, and what I did eat I vomited.

Did this labour destroy your appetite?—It did.

In what situation were you in that mill?—I was a piecener [see below].

Will you state to the Committee whether piecening is a very laborious employment for children, or not?—It is a very laborious employment. Pieceners are continually running to and fro, and on their feet the whole day.

The duty of the piecener is to take the cardings[2] from one part of the machinery, and to place them on another?—Yes.

So that the labour is not only continual, but it is unabated to the last?—It is unabated to the last.

Do you not think, from your own experience, that the speed of the machinery is so calculated as to demand the utmost exertions of a child, supposing the hours were moderate?—It is as much as they could do at the best; they are always upon the stretch, and it is commonly very difficult to keep up with their work.

State the condition of the children towards the latter part of the day, who have thus to keep up with the machinery?—It is as much as they can do when they are not very much fatigued to keep up with their work, and towards the close of the day, when they come to be more fatigued, they cannot keep up with it very well, and the consequence is that they are beaten to spur them on.

---

[1]In the original source, each paragraph was numbered; this reading includes paragraphs 2481–2519 and 2597–2604.

[2]*Cardings* were woolen fibers that had been combed in preparation for spinning and weaving.

Were you beaten under those circumstances?—Yes.

Frequently?—Very frequently.

And principally at the latter end of the day?—Yes.

And is it your belief that if you had not been so beaten, you should not have got through the work?—I should not if I had not been kept up to it by some means.

Does beating then principally occur at the latter end of the day, when the children are exceedingly fatigued?—It does at the latter end of the day, and in the morning sometimes, when they are very drowsy, and have not got rid of the fatigue of the day before.

What were you beaten with principally?—A strap.

Any thing else?—Yes, a stick sometimes; and there is a kind of roller which runs on the top of the machine called a billy, perhaps two or three yards in length, and perhaps an inch and a half, or more, in diameter; the circumference would be four or five inches, I cannot speak exactly.

Were you beaten with that instrument?—Yes.

Have you yourself been beaten, and have you seen other children struck severely with that roller?—I have been struck very severely with it myself, so much so as to knock me down, and I have seen other children have their heads broken with it.

You think that it is a general practice to beat the children with the roller?—It is.

You do not think then that you were worse treated than other children in the mill?—No, I was not, perhaps not so bad as some were. . . .

Can you speak as to the effect of this labour in the mills and factories on the morals of the children, as far as you have observed?—As far as I have observed with regard to morals in the mills, there is every thing about them that is disgusting to every one conscious of correct morality.

Do you find that the children, the females especially, are very early demoralized in them?—They are.

Is their language indecent?—Very indecent; and both sexes take great familiarities with each other in the mills, without at all being ashamed of their conduct.

Do you connect their immorality of language and conduct with their excessive labour?—It may be somewhat connected with it, for it is to be observed that most of that goes on towards night, when they begin to be drowsy; it is a kind of stimulus which they use to keep them awake; they say some pert thing or other to keep themselves from drowsiness, and it generally happens to be some obscene language.

Have not a considerable number of the females employed in mills illegitimate children very early in life?—I believe there are; I have known some of them have illegitimate children when they were between 16 and 17 years of age.

How many grown up females had you in the mill?—I cannot speak to the exact number that were grown up; perhaps there might be thirty-four or so that worked in the mill at that time.

How many of those had illegitimate children?—A great many of them, eighteen or nineteen of them, I think.

Did they generally marry the men by whom they had the children?—No, it sometimes happens that young women have children by married men, and I have known an instance, a few weeks since, where one of the young women had a child by a married man.

REVIEW QUESTIONS

1. According to the testimony given the Sadler Commission, how young were the children employed in the factory? How many hours and at what times of day did they work?

2. What do you think were the reasons for the employment of children from the employers' point of view? From the parents' point of view?
3. What measures did factory supervisors use to keep children alert at their tasks?

---

5 The New Science of Political Economy

The new spirit of scientific inquiry manifest in the seventeenth and eighteenth centuries extended also into the economic field, creating the new science of political economy. Its pioneer was Adam Smith, author of the classic book *The Wealth of Nations* (1776; see also page 104). Smith was an optimist, in favor of leaving individuals' economic activities to their own devices. For that reason he condemned government interference in the economy—so common in his day under the protectionist government's mercantilism policy, which sought to increase the nation's wealth by expanding exports while minimizing imports. The "invisible hand," which according to Smith turned individual gain into social advantage, also favored free trade among nations based on an international division of labor.

Adam Smith's optimistic assumptions were soon called into question by Thomas Robert Malthus (1766–1834). A Church of England clergyman and professor of history and political economy at a small college run by the East India Company, Malthus gave the study of political economy not only a moral but also a pessimistic twist; he was more concerned with the immutable poverty of nations. He contributed two books to the science of political economy. The first, *An Essay on the Principle of Population, as It Affects the Future Improvement of Society,* was published in 1798. It was followed in 1803 by a second and enlarged edition entitled *An Essay on the Principle of Population, or, a View of Its Past and Present Effects on Human Happiness.* In these works Malthus argued that population growth was the true reason for the poverty of the poor.

ADAM SMITH
THE WEALTH OF NATIONS

The Wealth of Nations carries the important message of *laissez faire,* which means that the government should intervene as little as possible in economic affairs and leave the market to its own devices. It advocates the liberation of economic production from all limiting regulation in order to benefit "the people and the sovereign," not only in Great Britain but in the community of countries. Admittedly, in his advocacy of free trade Smith made allowance for the national interest, justifying "certain public works and certain public institutions," including the government and the state. He defended, for instance, the Navigation Acts, which stipulated that goods brought from its overseas colonies into England be carried in British ships. Neither did he want to ruin established industries by introducing free trade too suddenly. Adam Smith was an eighteenth-century cosmopolitan who viewed political economy as an international system. His preference was clearly for economic cooperation among nations as a source of peace. In the passage that follows, Smith argues that economic activity unrestricted by government best serves the individual and society.

Every individual is continually exerting himself to find out the most advantageous employment for whatever capital he can command. It is his own advantage, indeed, and not that of the society, which he has in view. But the study of his own advantage, naturally, or rather necessarily, leads him to prefer that employment which is most advantageous to the society. . . .

. . . As every individual, therefore, endeavours as much as he can both to employ his capital in the support of domestic industry, and so to direct that industry that its produce may be of the greatest value, every individual necessarily labours to render the annual revenue of the society as great as he can. He generally, indeed, neither intends to promote the public interest, nor knows how much he is promoting it. By preferring the support of domestic to that of foreign industry, he intends only his own security; and by directing that industry in such a manner as its produce may be of the greatest value, he intends only his own gain, and he is in this, as in many other cases, led by an invisible hand to promote an end which was no part of his intention. Nor is it always the worse for the society that it was no part of it. By pursuing his own interest he frequently promotes that of the society more effectually than when he really intends to promote it. I have never known much good done by those who affected to trade for the public good. . . .

. . . The statesman who should attempt to direct private people in what manner they ought to employ their capitals, would not only load himself with a most unnecessary attention, but assume an authority which could safely be trusted, not only to no single person, but to no council or senate whatever,

and which would nowhere be so dangerous as in the hands of a man who had folly and presumption enough to fancy himself fit to exercise it. . . .

It is thus that every system which endeavours, either by extraordinary encouragements to draw towards a particular species of industry a greater share of the capital of the society than would naturally go to it, or, by extraordinary restraints, force from a particular species of industry some share of the capital which would otherwise be employed in it, is in reality subversive to the great purpose which it means to promote. It retards, instead of accelerating, the progress of the society towards real wealth and greatness; and diminishes, instead of increasing, the real value of the annual produce of its land and labour.

All systems either of preference or of restraint, therefore, being thus completely taken away, the obvious and simple system of natural liberty establishes itself of its own accord. Every man, as long as he does not violate the laws of justice, is left perfectly free to pursue his own interest his own way, and to bring both his industry and capital into competition with those of any other man, or order of men. The sovereign is completely discharged from a duty, in the attempting to perform which he must always be exposed to innumerable delusions, and for the proper performance of which no human wisdom or knowledge could ever be sufficient; the duty of superintending the industry of private people, and of directing it towards the employments most suitable to the interest of the society. According to the system of natural liberty, the sovereign has only three duties to attend to; three duties of great importance, indeed, but plain and intelligible to common understandings: first, the duty of protecting the society from the violence and invasion of other independent societies: secondly, the duty of protecting, as far as possible, every member of the society from the injustice or oppression of every other member of it, or the duty of establishing an exact administration of justice; and, thirdly, the duty of erecting and

maintaining certain public works and certain public institutions which it can never be for the interest of any individual, or small number of individuals, to erect and maintain; because the profit could never repay the expense to any individual or small number of individuals, though it may frequently do much more than repay it to a great society.

Thomas R. Malthus
ON THE PRINCIPLE OF POPULATION

Malthus assumed that population tended forever to outgrow the resources needed to sustain it. The balance between population and its life-sustaining resources was elementally maintained, he gloomily argued, by famine, war, and other fatal calamities. As a clergyman, he believed in sexual abstinence as the means of limiting population growth. He also saw little need to better the condition of the poor, whom he considered the most licentious part of the population, because he believed that they would then breed faster and, by upsetting the population/resource balance, bring misery to all. This view that poverty was an iron law of nature buttressed supporters of strict laissez faire who opposed government action to aid the poor.

POPULATION'S EFFECTS ON SOCIETY

I have read some of the speculations on the perfectibility of man and of society with great pleasure. I have been warmed and delighted with the enchanting picture which they hold forth. I ardently wish for such happy improvements. But I see great and, to my understanding, unconquerable difficulties in the way to them. These difficulties it is my present purpose to state, declaring, at the same time, that so far from exulting in them, as a cause of triumphing over the friends of innovation, nothing would give me greater pleasure than to see them completely removed. . . .

[These difficulties are]

First, That food is necessary to the existence of man.

Secondly, That the passion between the sexes is necessary and will remain nearly in its present state.

These two laws, ever since we have had any knowledge of mankind, appear to have been fixed laws of our nature; and as we have not hitherto seen any alteration in them, we have no right to conclude that they will ever cease to be what they are now, without an immediate act of power in that Being who first arranged the system of the universe, and for the advantage of His creatures, still executes, according to fixed laws, all its various operations. . . .

Assuming, then, my postulata as granted, I say that the power of population is indefinitely greater than the power in the earth to produce subsistence for man.

Population, when unchecked, increases in a geometrical ratio. Subsistence only increases in an arithmetical ratio. A slight acquaintance with numbers will show the immensity of the first power in comparison of the second.

By that law of our nature which makes food necessary to the life of man, the effects of these two unequal powers must be kept equal.

This implies a strong and constantly operating check on population from the difficulty of subsistence. This difficulty must fall somewhere and must necessarily be severely felt by a large portion of mankind. . . .

This natural inequality of the two powers of population and of production in the earth, and that great law of our nature which must constantly keep their efforts equal, form the great difficulty that to me appears insurmountable in the way to perfectibility of society. . . .

Consequently, if the premises are just, the argument is conclusive against the perfectibility of the mass of mankind.

POPULATION'S EFFECTS ON HUMAN HAPPINESS

The ultimate check to population appears then to be a want of food, arising necessarily from the different ratios according to which population and food increase. But this ultimate check is never the immediate check, except in cases of actual famine.

The immediate check may be stated to consist in all those customs, and all those diseases, which seem to be generated by a scarcity of the means of subsistence; and all those causes, independent of this scarcity, which tend prematurely to weaken and destroy the human frame.

These checks to population, which are constantly operating with more or less force in every society, and keep down the number to the level of the means of subsistence, may be classed under two general heads—the preventive and the positive checks.

The preventive check, as far as it is voluntary, is peculiar to man, and arises from that distinctive superiority in his reasoning faculties which enables him to calculate distant consequences. Man cannot look around him

and see the distress which frequently presses upon those who have large families; he cannot contemplate his present possessions or earnings which he now nearly consumes himself, and calculate the amount of each share, when with a little addition they must be divided, perhaps, among seven or eight, without feeling a doubt whether, if he follow the bent of his inclinations, he may be able to support the offspring which he will probably bring into the world. . . .

The conditions are calculated to prevent, and certainly do prevent, a great number of persons in all civilized nations from pursuing the dictate of nature in an early attachment to one woman. . . .

The positive checks to population are extremely various, and include every cause, whether arising from vice or misery, which in any degree contributes to shorten the natural duration of human life. Under this head, therefore, may be enumerated all unwholesome occupations, severe labor and exposure to the seasons, extreme poverty, bad nursing of children, great towns, excesses of all kinds, the whole train of common diseases and epidemics, wars, plague, and famine. . . .

POPULATION AND POVERTY

Almost everything that has been hitherto done for the poor, has tended, as if with solicitous care, to throw a veil of obscurity over this subject and to hide from them the true cause of their poverty. When the wages of labour are hardly sufficient to maintain two children, a man marries and has five or six. He of course finds himself miserably distressed. . . . He accuses his parish. . . . He accuses the avarice of the rich. . . . He accuses the partial and unjust institutions of society. . . . In searching for objects of accusation, he never [alludes] to the quarter from which all his misfortunes originate. The last person that he would think of accusing is himself. . . .

We cannot justly accuse them (the common people) of improvidence [thriftlessness] and want of industry, till . . . after it has been brought home to their comprehensions, that they are themselves the cause of their own poverty; that the means of redress are in their own hands, and in the hands of no other persons whatever; that the society in which they live and the government which presides over it, are totally without power in this respect; and however ardently they [government] may desire to relieve them, and whatever attempts they may make to do so, they are really and truly unable to execute what they benevolently wish, but unjustly promise.

REVIEW QUESTIONS

1. What did Adam Smith say were the results of a laissez-faire policy?
2. What, according to Smith, were the duties of the sovereign under the system of natural liberty? Do you think there are other duties that should be added?
3. What are the "fixed laws" of human nature according to Thomas Malthus? For Malthus, how did the power of population growth compare with that of the means to increase food?
4. What distinction did Malthus draw between preventive and positive checks to population growth?
5. Why is Malthus considered to have been a pessimist?
6. Do any of Malthus's arguments apply to our world today?

CHAPTER 6

Romanticism, Reaction, Revolution

LIBERTY LEADING THE PEOPLE, 1830, by Eugene Delacroix (1798–1863). Combining Romantic style with political beliefs in this painting, Delacroix commemorates the French Revolution of 1830, when the reactionary Charles X was replaced by Louis Philippe. *(Musée du Louvre, Paris.)*

In 1815 the European scene had changed. Napoleon was exiled to the island of St. Helena, and a Bourbon king, in the person of Louis XVIII, again reigned in France. The Great Powers of Europe, meeting at Vienna, had drawn up a peace settlement that awarded territory to the states that had fought Napoleon and restored to power some rulers dethroned by the French emperor. The Congress of Vienna also organized the Concert of Europe to guard against a resurgence of the revolutionary spirit that had kept Europe in turmoil for some twenty-five years. The conservative leaders of Europe wanted no more Robespierres who resorted to terror and no more Napoleons who sought to dominate the continent.

However, reactionary rulers' efforts to turn the clock back to the Old Regime could not contain the forces unleashed by the French Revolution. Between 1820 and 1848 a series of revolts rocked Europe. The principal causes were liberalism (which demanded constitutional government and the protection of the freedom and rights of the individual citizen) and nationalism (which called for the reawakening and unification of the nation and its liberation from foreign domination).

In the 1820s, the Concert of Europe crushed a quasi-liberal revolution in Spain and liberal uprisings in Italy, and Tsar Nicholas I subdued liberal officers who challenged tsarist autocracy. The Greeks, however, successfully fought for independence from the Ottoman Turks.

Between 1830 and 1832, another wave of revolutions swept over Europe. Italian liberals and nationalists failed to free Italy from foreign rule or to wrest reforms from autocratic princes, and the tsar's troops crushed a Polish bid for independence from Russian rule. But in France, rebels overthrew the reactionary Bourbon Charles X in 1830 and replaced him with a more moderate ruler, Louis Philippe; a little later Belgium gained its independence from Holland.

The year 1848 was decisive in the struggle for liberty and nationhood. In France, democrats overthrew Louis Philippe and established a republic that gave all men the right to vote. However, in Italy and Germany, revolutions attempting to unify each land failed, as did a bid in Hungary for independence from the Hapsburg Empire. After enjoying initial successes, the revolutionaries were crushed by superior might, and their liberal and nationalist objectives remained largely unfulfilled. By 1870, however, many nationalist aspirations had been realized. The Hapsburg Empire granted Hungary autonomy in 1867, and by 1870–1871, the period of the Franco-Prussian War, Germany and Italy became unified states. That authoritarian and militaristic Prussia unified Germany, rather than liberals like those who had fought in the revolutions of 1848, affected the future of Europe.

In the early nineteenth century a new cultural orientation, romanticism, emphasized the liberation of human emotions and the free expression of personality in artistic creations. The romantics' attack on the rationalism of the Enlightenment and their veneration of the past influenced conservative thought, and their concern for a people's history and traditions contributed to the development of nationalism. By encouraging innovation in art, music, and literature, the romantics greatly enriched European cultural life.

1   Romanticism

Romantics attacked the outlook of the Enlightenment, protesting that the philosophes' excessive intellectualizing and their mechanistic view of the physical world and human nature distorted and fettered the human spirit and thwarted cultural creativity. The rationalism of the philosophes, said the romantics, had reduced human beings to soulless thinking machines, and vibrant nature to lifeless wheels, cogs, and pulleys. In contrast to the philosophes' scientific and analytic approach, the romantics asserted the intrinsic value of emotions and imagination and extolled the spontaneity, richness, and uniqueness of the human spirit. To the philosophes, the emotions obstructed clear thinking.

For romantics, feelings and imagination were the human essence, the source of cultural creativity, and the avenue to true understanding. Their beliefs led the romantics to rebel against strict standards of esthetics that governed artistic creations. They held that artists, musicians, and writers must trust their own sensibilities and inventiveness and must not be bound by textbook rules; the romantics focused on the creative capacities inherent in the emotions and urged individuality and freedom of expression in the arts. In the Age of Romanticism, the artist and poet succeeded the scientist as the arbiters of Western civilization.

William Wordsworth
TABLES TURNED

The works of the great English poet William Wordsworth (1770–1850) exemplify many tendencies of the Romantic Movement. In the interval during which he tried to come to grips with his disenchantment with the French Revolution, Wordsworth's creativity reached its height. In the preface to *Lyrical Ballads* (1798), Wordsworth produced what has become known as the manifesto of romanticism. He wanted poetry to express powerful feelings and also contended that because it is a vehicle for the imagination, poetry is the source of truth. Wordsworth thus represented a shift in perspective comparable to the shift begun by Descartes in philosophy, but for Wordsworth imagination and feeling, not mathematics and logic, yielded highest truth.

The philosophes had regarded nature as a giant machine, all of whose parts worked in perfect precision and whose laws could be uncovered through the scientific method. The romantics rejected this mechanical model. To them, nature was a living organism filled with beautiful forms whose inner meaning was grasped through the human imagination; they sought from nature a higher truth than mechanical law. In "Tables Turned," Wordsworth exalts nature as humanity's teacher.

Up! up! my Friend, and quit your books;
Or surely you'll grow double:
Up! up! my Friend, and clear your looks;
Why all this toil and trouble?

The sun, above the mountain's head,
A freshening lustre mellow
Through all the long green fields has spread,
His first sweet evening yellow.

Books! 'tis a dull and endless strife:
Come, hear the woodland linnet [Old World finch],
How sweet his music! on my life,
There's more of wisdom in it.

And hark! how blithe the throstle [thrush] sings!
He, too, is no mean preacher:
Come forth into the light of things,
Let Nature be your Teacher.

She has a world of ready wealth,
Our minds and hearts to bless —
Spontaneous wisdom breathed by health,
Truth breathed by cheerfulness.

One impulse from a vernal wood
May teach you more of man,
Of moral evil and of good,
Than all the sages can.

Sweet is the lore which Nature brings;
Our meddling intellect
Mis-shapes the beauteous forms of things:—
We murder to dissect.

Enough of Science and of Art;
Close up those barren leaves [book pages];
Come forth, and bring with you a heart
That watches and receives.

William Blake
MILTON

William Blake (1757–1827) was a British engraver, poet, and religious mystic. He also affirmed the creative potential of the imagination and expressed distaste for the rationalist-scientific outlook of the Enlightenment, as is clear from these lines in his poem "Milton."

. . . the Reasoning Power in Man:
This is a false Body; an Incrustation [scab] over my Immortal
Spirit; a Selfhood, which must be put off & annihilated alway[s]
To cleanse the Face of my Spirit by Self-examination,
To bathe in the Waters of Life, to wash off the Not Human,
I come in Self-annihilation & the grandeur of Inspiration,

To cast off Rational Demonstration by Faith in the Saviour,
To cast off the rotten rags of Memory by Inspiration,
To cast off Bacon, Locke & Newton from Albion's covering,[1]

---

[1]Bacon, Locke, and Newton were British thinkers who valued reason and science, and Albion is an ancient name for England.

To take off his filthy garments & clothe him
　　with Imagination,
To cast aside from Poetry all that is not
　　Inspiration,
That it no longer shall dare to mock with the
　　aspersion of Madness

. . .

To cast off the idiot Questioner who is always
　　questioning
But never capable of answering, who sits with a
　　sly grin
Silent plotting when to question, like a thief
　　in a cave,
Who publishes doubt & calls it knowledge,
　　whose Science is Despair,

Whose pretence to knowledge is Envy, whose
　　whole Science is
To destroy the wisdom of ages to gratify
　　ravenous Envy
That rages round him like a Wolf day & night
　　without rest:
He smiles with condescension, he talks of
　　Benevolence & Virtue,
And those who act with Benevolence & Virtue
　　they murder time on time.
These are the destroyers of Jerusalem, these are
　　the murderers
Of Jesus, who deny the Faith & mock at Eternal
　　Life. . . .

REVIEW QUESTIONS

1. According to Wordsworth, how could the human being achieve goodness?
2. In "Tables Turned," what connection did Wordsworth see between nature and the
   human mind? How did his idea of nature differ from that of the scientist?
   According to Wordsworth, what effect did nature have on the imagination?
3. Why did William Blake attack reason?
4. The Romantic Movement was a reaction against the dominant ideas of the
   Enlightenment. Discuss this statement.

2 Conservatism

In the period after 1815, conservatism was the principal ideology of those who
repudiated the Enlightenment and the French Revolution. Conservatives valued tradition over reason, aristocratic and clerical authority over equality, and
the community over the individual. Edmund Burke (1729–1797), a leading
Anglo-Irish statesman and political thinker, was instrumental in shaping the
conservative outlook. His *Reflections on the Revolution in France* (1790) attacked
the violence and fundamental principles of the Revolution. Another leading
conservative was Joseph de Maistre (1753–1821), who fled his native Sardinia
in 1792 (and again in 1793) after it was invaded by the armies of the new French
Republic. De Maistre denounced the Enlightenment for spawning the French
Revolution, defended the church as a civilizing agent that made individuals
aware of their social obligations, and affirmed tradition as a model more valuable than instant reforms embodied in "paper constitutions."

　　The symbol of conservatism in the first half of the nineteenth century was Prince
Klemens von Metternich (1773–1859) of Austria. A bitter opponent of Jacobinism
and Napoleon, he became the pivotal figure at the Congress of Vienna (1814–1815),

where European powers met to redraw the map of Europe after their victory over France. Metternich said that the Jacobins had subverted the pillars of civilization and that Napoleon, by harnessing the forces of the Revolution, had destroyed the traditional European state system. No peace was possible with Napoleon, who championed revolutionary doctrines and dethroned kings, and whose rule rested not on legitimacy but on conquest and charisma. No balance of power could endure an adventurer who obliterated states and sought European domination.

Edmund Burke
REFLECTIONS ON THE REVOLUTION IN FRANCE

Burke regarded the revolutionaries as wild-eyed fanatics who had uprooted all established authority, tradition, and institutions, thereby plunging France into anarchy. Not sharing the faith of the philosophes in human goodness, Burke held that without the restraints of established authority, people revert to savagery. For Burke, monarchy, aristocracy, and Christianity represented civilizing forces that tamed the beast in human nature. By undermining venerable institutions, he said, the French revolutionaries had opened the door to anarchy and terror. Burke's *Reflections,* excerpts of which follow, was instrumental in the shaping of conservative thought.

. . . You [revolutionaries] chose to act as if you had never been moulded into civil society, and had every thing to begin anew. You began ill, because you began by despising every thing that belonged to you. . . . If the last generations of your country appeared without much lustre in your eyes, you might have passed them by, and derived your claims from a more early race of ancestors. Under a pious predilection for those ancestors, your imaginations would have realized in them a standard of virtue and wisdom, beyond the vulgar practice of the hour: and you would have risen with the example to whose imitation you aspired. Respecting your forefathers, you would have been taught to respect yourselves. You would not have chosen to consider the French as a people of yesterday, as a nation of low-born servile wretches, until the emancipating year of 1789. . . . By following wise examples you would have given new examples of wisdom to the world. You would have rendered the cause

of liberty venerable in the eyes of every worthy mind in every nation. . . . You would have had a free constitution; a potent monarchy; a disciplined army; a reformed and venerated clergy; a mitigated but spirited nobility, to lead your virtue. . . .

Compute your gains: see what is got by those extravagant and presumptuous speculations which have taught your leaders to despise all their predecessors, and all their contemporaries, and even to despise themselves, until the moment in which they became truly despicable. By following those false lights, France has bought undisguised calamities at a higher price than any nation has purchased the most unequivocal blessings! . . . France, when she let loose the reins of regal authority, doubled the licence, of a ferocious dissoluteness in manners, and of an insolent irreligion in opinions and practices; and has extended through all ranks of life. . . . all the unhappy corruptions that usually were the disease of wealth and power. This is one of the new principles of equality in France. . . .

. . . The science of government being therefore so practical in itself, and intended for such practical purposes, a matter which requires experience, and even more experience than any person can gain in his whole life, however sagacious and observing he may be, it is with infinite caution that any man ought to venture upon pulling down an edifice which has answered in any tolerable degree for ages the common purposes of society, or on building it up again, without having models and patterns of approved utility before his eyes. . . .

. . . The nature of man is intricate; the objects of society are of the greatest possible complexity; and therefore no simple disposition or direction of power can be suitable either to man's nature, or to the quality of his affairs.

When ancient opinions of life are taken away, the loss cannot possibly be estimated. From that moment we have no compass to govern us; nor can we know distinctly to what port we steer. . . .

. . . Nothing is more certain than that our manners, our civilization, and all the good things which are connected with manners and with civilization have, in this European world of ours, depended for ages upon two principles and were, indeed, the result of both combined: I mean the spirit of a gentleman and the spirit of religion. . . .

Burke next compares the English people with the French revolutionaries.

. . . Thanks to our sullen resistance to innovation, thanks to the cold sluggishness of our national character, we still bear the stamp of our forefathers. . . . We are not the converts of Rousseau; we are not the disciples of Voltaire; Helvetius has made no progress amongst us.[1] Atheists are not our preachers; madmen are not our lawgivers. We know that *we* have made no discoveries, and we think that no discoveries are to be made, in morality, nor many in the great principles of government. . . . We fear God; we look up with awe to kings, with affection to parliaments, with duty to magistrates, with reverence to priests, and with respect to nobility. . . .

. . . We are afraid to put men to live and trade each on his own private stock of reason, because we suspect that this stock in each man is small, and that the individuals would do better to avail themselves of the general bank and capital of nations and of ages.

---

[1]Rousseau, Voltaire, and Helvétius were French philosophes of the eighteenth century noted, respectively, for advocating democracy, attacking the abuses of the Old Regime, and applying a scientific reason to moral principles (see Chapter 2).

Klemens von Metternich
THE ODIOUS IDEAS OF THE PHILOSOPHES

Two decades of revolutionary warfare had shaped Metternich's political thinking. After the fall of Napoleon, Metternich worked to restore the European balance and to suppress revolutionary movements. In the following memorandum to Tsar Alexander I, dated December 15, 1820, Metternich denounces the French philosophes for their "false systems" and "fatal errors" that weakened the social fabric and gave rise to the French Revolution. In their presumption, the philosophes forsook the experience and wisdom of the past, trusting only their own thoughts and inclinations.

The progress of the human mind has been extremely rapid in the course of the last three centuries. This progress having been accelerated more rapidly than the growth of wisdom (the only counterpoise to passions and to error); a revolution prepared by the false systems . . . has at last broken out. . . .

. . . There were . . . some men [the philosophes], unhappily endowed with great talents, who felt their own strength, and . . . who had the art to prepare and conduct men's minds to the triumph of their detestable enterprise—an enterprise all the more odious as it was pursued without regard to results, simply abandoning themselves to the one feeling of hatred of God and of His immutable moral laws.

France had the misfortune to produce the greatest number of these men. It is in her midst that religion and all that she holds sacred, that morality and authority, and all connected with them, have been attacked with a steady and systematic animosity, and it is there that the weapon of ridicule has been used with the most ease and success.

Drag through the mud the name of God and the powers instituted by His divine decrees, and the revolution will be prepared! Speak of a social contract,[1] and the revolution is accomplished! The revolution was already completed in the palaces of Kings, in the drawing-rooms and boudoirs of certain cities, while among the great mass of the people it was still only in a state of preparation. . . .

. . . The French Revolution broke out, and has gone through a complete revolutionary cycle in a very short period, which could only have appeared long to its victims and to its contemporaries. . . .

. . . The revolutionary seed had penetrated into every country. . . . It was greatly developed under the *régime* of the military despotism of Bonaparte. His conquests displaced a number of laws, institutions, and customs; broke through bonds sacred among all nations, strong enough to resist time itself; which is more than can be said of certain benefits conferred by these innovators.

---

[1]The social contract theory consisted essentially of the following principles: (1) people voluntarily enter into an agreement to establish a political community; (2) government rests on the consent of the governed: (3) people possess natural freedom and equality, which they do not surrender to the state. These principles were used to challenge the divine right of kings and absolute monarchy.

Joseph de Maistre
ESSAY ON THE GENERATIVE PRINCIPLE OF POLITICAL CONSTITUTIONS

The following critique of the philosophes, the French Revolution, and manufactured constitutions is taken from Joseph de Maistre's *Essay on the Generative Principle of Political Constitutions* (1808–1809).

One of the greatest errors of a century which professed them all was to believe that a political constitution could be created and written *a priori*, whereas reason and experience unite in proving that a constitution is a divine work and that precisely the most fundamental and essentially constitutional of a nation's laws could not possibly be written. . . .

. . . Was it not a common belief everywhere that a constitution was the work of the intellect, like an ode or a tragedy? Had not Thomas Paine declared, with a profundity that charmed the universities, that a constitution does not exist as long as one cannot put it in his pocket? The unsuspecting, overweening self-confidence of the eighteenth century balked at nothing, and I do not believe that it produced a single stripling of any talent who did not make three things when he left school: an educational system, a constitution, and a world. . . .

. . . I do not believe that the slightest doubt remains as to the unquestionable truth of the following propositions:

The fundamental principles of political constitutions exist prior to all written law.

Constitutional law *(loi)* is and can only be the development or sanction of a pre-existing and unwritten law *(droit)*. . . .

. . . [H]e who believes himself able by writing alone to establish a clear and lasting doctrine IS A GREAT FOOL. If he really possessed the seeds of truth, he could never believe that a little black liquid and a pen could germinate them in the world, protect them from harsh weather, and make them sufficiently effective. As for whoever undertakes writing *laws or civil constitutions* in the belief that he can give them adequate conviction and stability because he has written them, he disgraces himself, whether or no other people say so. He shows an equal ignorance of the nature of inspiration and delirium, right and wrong, good and evil. This ignorance is shameful, even when approved by the whole body of the common people.

. . . [N]o real and great institution can be based on written law, since men themselves, instruments, in turn, of the established institution, do not know what it is to become and since imperceptible growth is the true promise of durability in all things. . . .

Everything brings us back to the general rule. *Man cannot create a constitution, and no legitimate constitution can be written.* The collection of fundamental laws which necessarily constitute a civil or religious society never has been or will be written *a priori.*

De Maistre assails the philosophes for attacking religion. Without Christianity, he says, people become brutalized, and civilization degenerates into anarchy.

Religion alone civilizes nations. No other known force can influence the savage. . . . [W]hat shall we think of a generation which has thrown everything to the winds, including the very foundations of the structure of society, by making education exclusively scientific? It was impossible to err more frightfully. For every educational system which does not have religion as its basis will collapse in an instant, or else diffuse only poisons throughout the State . . . if the guidance of education is not returned to the priests, and if science is not uniformly relegated to a subordinate rank, incalculable evils await us. We shall become brutalized by science, and that is the worst sort of brutality. . . .

Not until the first half of the eighteenth century did impiety really become a force. We see it at first spreading in every direction with amazing energy. From palaces to hovels, it insinuates itself everywhere, infesting everything. . . .

REVIEW QUESTIONS

1. Why was Edmund Burke opposed to the French Revolution?
2. What was Klemens von Metternich's opinion of "the progress of the human mind . . . in the . . . last three centuries" and its effect upon the society of his time?
3. What did Metternich mean by, "Drag through the mud the name of God and the powers instituted by His divine decrees, and the revolution will be prepared!"?

4. Why did Joseph de Maistre believe that man cannot create a constitution and no legitimate constitution can be written?
5. What views of late eighteenth- and early nineteenth-century conservatives are valued by American conservatives today?

---

3 Liberalism

Conservatism was the ideology of the old order that was hostile to the Enlightenment and the French Revolution; in contrast, liberalism aspired to carry out the promise of the philosophes and the Revolution. Liberals called for a constitution that protected individual liberty and denounced censorship, arbitrary arrest, and other forms of repression. They believed that through reason and education, social evils could be remedied. Liberals rejected an essential feature of the Old Regime—the special privileges of the aristocracy and the clergy—and held that the individual should be judged on the basis of achievement, not birth. At the core of the liberal outlook lay the conviction that the individual would develop into a good and productive human being and citizen if not coerced by governments and churches.

John Stuart Mill
ON LIBERTY

Freedom of thought and expression were principal concerns of nineteenth-century liberals. The classic defense of intellectual freedom is *On Liberty* (1859), written by John Stuart Mill (1806–1873), a prominent British philosopher. Mill argued that no individual or government has a monopoly on truth, for all human beings are fallible. Therefore, the government and the majority have no legitimate authority to suppress views, however unpopular; they have no right to interfere with a person's liberty so long as that person's actions do no injury to others. Nothing is more absolute, contended Mill, than the inviolable right of all adults to think and live as they please so long as they respect the rights of others. For Mill, toleration of opposing and unpopular viewpoints is a necessary trait in order for a person to become rational, moral, and civilized.

The object of this essay is to assert one very simple principle, as entitled to govern absolutely the dealings of society with the individual. . . . That principle is that the sole end for which mankind are warranted, individually or collectively, in interfering with the liberty of action of any of their number is self-protection. That the only purpose for which power can be rightfully exercised over any member of a civilized community, against his will, is to prevent harm to others. His own good, either physical or moral, is not a sufficient warrant. He cannot rightfully be compelled to do or forbear because it will be better for him to do so, because it will make him happier, because, in the opinions of others, to do so would be wise or even right. These are good reasons for remonstrating with him, or reasoning with him, or persuading him, or entreating him, but not for compelling him or visiting him with any evil in case he do otherwise. To justify that, the conduct from which it is desired to deter him must be calculated to produce evil to someone else. The only part of the conduct of anyone for which he is amenable to society is that which concerns others. In the part which merely concerns himself, his independence is, of right, absolute. Over himself, over his own body and mind, the individual is sovereign. . . .

. . . This, then, is the appropriate region of human liberty. It comprises, first, the inward domain of consciousness, demanding liberty of conscience in the most comprehensive sense, liberty of thought and feeling, absolute freedom of opinion and sentiment on all subjects, practical or speculative, scientific, moral, or theological. The liberty of expressing and publishing opinions may seem to fall under a different principle, since it belongs to that part of the conduct of an individual which concerns other people, but, being almost of as much importance as the liberty of thought itself and resting in great part on the same reasons, is practically inseparable from it. Secondly, the principle requires liberty of tastes and pursuits, of framing the plan of our life to suit our own character, of doing as we like, subject to such consequences as may follow, without impediment from our fellow creatures, so long as what we do does not harm them, even though they should think our conduct foolish, perverse, or wrong. Thirdly, from this liberty of each individual follows the liberty, within the same limits, of combination among individuals; freedom to unite for any purpose not involving harm to others: the persons combining being supposed to be of full age and not forced or deceived.

No society in which these liberties are not, on the whole, respected is free, whatever may be its form of government; and none is completely free in which they do not exist absolute and unqualified. The only freedom which deserves the name is that of pursuing our own good in our own way, so long as we do not attempt to deprive others of theirs or impede their efforts to obtain it. Each is the proper guardian of his own health, whether bodily *or* mental and spiritual. Mankind are greater gainers by suffering each other to live as seems good to themselves than by compelling each to live as seems good to the rest. . . .

. . . Let us suppose, therefore, that the government is entirely at one with the people, and never thinks of exerting any power of coercion unless in agreement with what it conceives to be their voice. But I deny the right of the people to exercise such coercion, either by themselves or by their government. The power itself is illegitimate. The best government has no more title to it than the worst. It is as noxious, or more noxious, when exerted in accordance with public opinion than when in opposition to it. If all mankind minus one were of one opinion, mankind would be no more justified in silencing that one person than he, if he had the power, would be justified in silencing mankind. Were an opinion a personal possession of no value except to the owner, if to be obstructed in the enjoyment of it were simply a private injury, it would make some difference whether the injury was inflicted only on a few persons or on many. But the peculiar evil of silencing the expression of an opinion is that it is robbing the human race, posterity as well as the existing generation—those who dissent from the opinion, still more than those who hold it. If the opinion is right, they are deprived of the opportunity of exchanging error for truth; if wrong, they lose, what is almost as great a benefit, the clearer perception and livelier impression of truth produced by its collision with error.

1. What was the purpose of John Stuart Mill's essay?
2. For Mill, what is the "peculiar evil of silencing the expression of an opinion," however unpopular?
3. On what grounds would Mill permit society to restrict individual liberty? Do you think it is ever legitimate for the state to restrain an individual from harming himself?

---

4 Nationalism and Repression in Germany

Nationalism espoused the individual's allegiance to the national community and sought to unify divided nations and to liberate subject peoples. In the early nineteenth century, most nationalists were liberals who viewed the struggle for unification and freedom from foreign oppression as an extension of the struggle for individual rights. Few liberals recognized that nationalism was a potentially dangerous force that could threaten liberal ideals of freedom and equality.

By glorifying a nation's language and ancient traditions and folkways, romanticism contributed to the evolution of modern nationalism, particularly in Germany. German romantics longed to create a true folk community in which the individual's soul would be immersed in the nation's soul. Through the national community, individuals could find the meaning in life for which they yearned. The romantic veneration of the past produced a mythical way of thinking about politics and history, one that subordinated reason to powerful emotions. In particular, some German romantics attacked the liberal-rational tradition of the Enlightenment and the French Revolution as hostile to the true German spirit.

Ernst Moritz Arndt
THE WAR OF LIBERATION

The Napoleonic wars kindled nationalist sentiments in the German states. Hatred of the French occupier evoked a feeling of outrage and a desire for national unity among some Germans, who before the occupation had thought not of a German fatherland but of their own states and princes. These Germans called for a war of liberation against Napoleon. Attracting mostly intellectuals, the idea of political unification had limited impact on the rest of the people, who remained loyal to local princes and local territories. Nevertheless, the embryo of nationalism was conceived in the German uprising against Napoleon in 1813. The writings of Ernst Moritz Arndt (1769–1860) vividly express the emerging nationalism. The following excerpts describe

Arndt's view of the War of Liberation and present his appeal for German unity.

Fired with enthusiasm, the people rose, "with God for King and Fatherland." Among the Prussians there was only one voice, one feeling, one anger and one love, to save the Fatherland and to free Germany. The Prussians wanted war; war and death they wanted; peace they feared because they could hope for no honorable peace from Napoleon. War, war, sounded the cry from the Carpathians [mountains] to the Baltic [Sea], from the Niemen to the Elbe [rivers]. War! cried the nobleman and landed proprietor who had become impoverished. War! the peasant who was driving his last horse to death. . . . War! the citizen who was growing exhausted from quartering soldiers and paying taxes. War! the widow who was sending her only son to the front. War! the young girl who, with tears of pride and pain, was leaving her betrothed. Youths who were hardly able to bear arms, men with gray hair, officers who on account of wounds and mutilations had long ago been honorably discharged, rich landed proprietors and officials, fathers of large families and managers of extensive businesses—all were unwilling to remain behind. Even young women, under all sorts of disguises, rushed to arms; all wanted to drill, arm themselves and fight and die for the Fatherland. . . .

The most beautiful thing about all this holy zeal and happy confusion was that all differences of position, class, and age were forgotten . . . that the one great feeling for the Fatherland, its freedom and honor, swallowed all other feelings, caused all other considerations and relationships to be forgotten.

In another passage, Arndt appealed for German unity.

German man, feel again God, hear and fear the eternal, and you hear and fear also your *Volk* [folk, people, nation]; you feel again in God the honor and dignity of your fathers, their glorious history rejuvenates itself again in you, their firm and gallant virtue reblossoms in you, the whole German Fatherland stands again before you in the august halo of past centuries! Then, when you feel and fear and honor all this, then you cry, then you lament, then you wrathfully reproach yourself that you have become so miserable and evil: then starts your new life and your new history. . . . From the North Sea to the Carpathians, from the Baltic to the Alps, from the Vistula to the Schelde [rivers], one faith, one love, one courage, and one enthusiasm must gather again the whole German folk in brotherly community; they must learn to feel how great, mighty, and happy their fathers were in obedience to one German emperor and one Reich, at a time when the many discords had not yet turned one against the other, when the many cowards and knaves had not yet betrayed them; . . . above the ruins and ashes of their destroyed Fatherland they must weepingly join hands and pray and swear all to stand like one man and to fight until the sacred land will be free. . . . Feel the infinite and sublime which slumbers hidden in the lap of the days, those light and mighty spirits which now glimmer in isolated meteors but which soon will shine in all suns and stars; feel the new birth of times, the higher, cleaner breath of spiritual life and do not longer be fooled and confused by the insignificant and small. No longer Catholics and Protestants, no longer Prussians and Austrians, Saxons and Bavarians, Silesians and Hanoverians, no longer of different faith, different mentality, and different will—be Germans, be one, will to be one by love and loyalty, and no devil will vanquish you.

Heinrich von Gagern
THE CALL FOR GERMAN UNITY

Heinrich von Gagern (1799–1880) was a liberal who helped to organize the Burschenschaften, *German student fraternities dedicated to national unity. In the passage that follows, von Gagern explained the nationalist purpose of the German student movement.*

It is very hard to explain the spirit of the student movement to you, but I shall try, even though I can only give you a few characteristics. . . .

. . . Those who share in this spirit have [a]. . . tendency in their student life, Love of Fatherland is their guiding principle. Their purpose is to make a better future for the Fatherland, each as best he can, to spread national consciousness, or to use the much ridiculed and maligned Germanic expression, more folkishness, and to work for better constitutions. . . .

. . . We want more sense of community among the several states of Germany, greater unity in their policies and in their principles of government; no separate policy for each state, but the nearest possible relations with one another; above all, we want Germany to be considered *one* land and the German people *one* people. In the forms of our student comradeship we show how we want to approach this as nearly as possible in the real world. Regional fraternities are forbidden, and we live in a German comradeship, one people in spirit, as we want it for all Germany in reality. We give ourselves the freest of constitutions, just as we should like Germany to have the freest possible one, insofar as that is suitable for the German people. We want a constitution for the people that fits in with the spirit of the times and with the people's own level of enlightenment, rather than what each prince gives his people according to what he likes and what serves his private interest. Above all, we want the princes to understand and to follow the principle that they exist for the country and not the country for them. In fact, the prevailing view is that the constitution should not come from the individual states at all. The main principles of the German constitution should apply to all states in common, and should be expressed by the German federal assembly. This constitution should deal not only with the absolute necessities, like fiscal administration and justice, general administration and church and military affairs and so on; this constitution ought to be extended to the education of the young, at least at the upper age levels, and to many other such things.

KARLSBAD DECREES

In 1819, Metternich and representatives from other German states meeting at Karlsbad drew up several decrees designed to stifle liberalism and nationalism.

The Karlsbad Decrees called for the dissolution of the *Burschenschaften,* the censoring of books and newspapers, and the dismissal of professors who spread liberal doctrines.

Provisional Decree relative to the Measures to be taken concerning the Universities.

Sect. 1. The Sovereign shall make choice for each university of an extraordinary commissioner, furnished with suitable instructions and powers, residing in the place where the university is established. . . .

The duty of this commissioner shall be to . . . observe carefully the spirit with which the professors and tutors are guided in their public and private lectures; . . . and to devote a constant attention to every thing which may tend to the maintenance of morality, good order and decency among the youths.

Sect. 2. The governments of the states, members of the confederation, reciprocally engage to remove from their universities and other establishments of instruction, the professors and other public teachers, against whom it may be proved, that in departing from their duty, in overstepping the bounds of their duty, in abusing their legitimate influence over the minds of youth, by the propagation of pernicious dogmas, hostile to order and public tranquility, or in sapping the foundation of existing establishments, they have shown themselves incapable of executing the important functions entrusted to them. . . .

A professor or tutor thus excluded, cannot be admitted in any other state of the confederation to any other establishment of public instruction.

Sect. 3. The laws long since made against secret or unauthorized associations at the universities, shall be maintained in all their force and rigour, and shall be particularly extended with so much the more severity against the well-known society formed some years ago under the name of the General Burschenschaft, as it has for its basis an idea, absolutely inadmissible, of community and continued correspondence between the different universities.

The governments shall mutually engage to admit to no public employment any individuals who may continue or enter into any of those associations after the publication of the present decree.

Decree relative to the Measures for preventing the Abuses of the Press.

Sect. 1. . . . No writing appearing in the form of a daily paper or periodical pamphlet . . . shall be issued from the press without the previous consent of the public authority. . . .

Sect. 7. The editor of a journal, or other periodical publication, that may be suppressed by command of the Diet, shall not be allowed, during the space of five years, to conduct any similar publication in any states of the confederation. . . .

Decree relative to the formation of a Central Commission, for the purpose of Ulterior Inquiry respecting Revolutionary Plots, discovered in some of the States of the Confederation.

Art. 1. In 15 days from the date of this decree, an extraordinary commission of inquiry, appointed by the Diet and composed of 7 members, including the President, shall assemble in the city of Mentz, a fortress of the confederation.

2. The object of this commission is, to make careful and detailed inquiries respecting the facts, the origin and the multiplied ramifications of the secret revolutionary and demagogic associations, directed against the political constitution and internal repose, as well of the confederation in general, as of the individual members thereof.

REVIEW QUESTIONS

1. Ernst Moritz Arndt's writings show the interconnection between Romanticism and nationalism. Discuss this statement.
2. What was the guiding principle behind Heinrich von Gagern's characterization of the German student movement? What were its political implications?
3. By what methods did the Karlsbad Decrees propose to preserve political stability, and on what grounds was this proposal made?
4. The Karlsbad Decrees seem to have assumed that unregulated ideas were powerful factors in disrupting civilization. If this is so, do you feel that the methods proposed to restrain ideas indicated a genuine understanding of their force and were equal to the task of repressing them? Discuss.

---

5 The Spread of Liberal Ideals to Russia

The French Revolution sharpened the already profound cultural differences between Russia and western Europe. French ideas of constitutional government and individual liberty threatened the survival of the Russian Empire, which lacked a sense of national unity and was held together by force. In 1814, two years after the disastrous retreat of Napoleon's army from Moscow, the Russian army reached Paris. Russian officers brought home with them not only the ideas of the French Revolution but also a taste of the good life in western Europe. They now looked at their own country—at the miserable serfs, corrupt officials, tyrannical landlords—with westernized eyes and found it wanting. These officers aspired to create a Russia that could hold its own in comparison with western Europe.

Tsar Alexander I (1801–1825) raised the officers' hopes by making vague promises of reform and by granting a constitution of sorts to those parts of Poland that had been annexed by the Russian Empire. At the opening of the Polish national assembly, the Diet, Alexander held out hope for a Russian constitution and an end to serfdom. But by 1820, following the lead of the reactionary monarchs of central Europe, he strengthened autocratic rule.

THE REVOLT AGAINST TSARIST AUTOCRACY

Alexander's tightening of autocracy drove the westernized officers to form secret societies and to engage in conspiracy. In December 1824, shortly after Alexander's death, the officers led their soldiers in open rebellion just as the new tsar, Nicholas I (1825–1855), ascended the throne. Although the Decembrist uprising failed miserably, it marked the beginning of a western-oriented revolutionary movement in Russia born from the ever-widening cultural gap between western Europe and tsarist autocracy.

Arrested Decembrist conspirators testified before an official Commission of Inquiry. What follows is a letter written by a member of the revolutionary circle.

EXTRACT FROM A LETTER OF KAKHOVSKY TO GENERAL LEVASHEV

Your Excellency,
Dear Sir!

The uprising of December 14 is a result of causes related above. I see, Your Excellency, that the Committee established by His Majesty is making a great effort to discover all the members of the secret Society. But the government will not derive any notable benefit from that. We were not trained within the Society but were already ready to work when we joined it. The origin and the root of the Society one must seek in the spirit of the time and in our state of mind. I know a few belonging to the secret Society but am inclined to think the membership is not very large. Among my many acquaintances who do not adhere to secret societies very few are opposed to my opinions. Frankly I state that among thousands of young men there are hardly a hundred who do not passionately long for freedom. These youths, striving with pure and strong love for the welfare of their Fatherland, toward true enlightenment, are growing mature.

The people have conceived a sacred truth—that they do not exist for governments, but that governments must be organized for them. This is the cause of struggle in all countries; peoples, after tasting the sweetness of enlightenment and freedom, strive toward them; and governments, surrounded by millions of bayonets, make efforts to repel these peoples back into the darkness of ignorance. But all these efforts will prove in vain; impressions once received can never be erased. Liberty, that torch of intellect and warmth of life, was always and everywhere the attribute of peoples emerged from primitive ignorance. We are unable to live like our ancestors, like barbarians or slaves.

REVIEW QUESTION

1. To what did Kakhovsky attribute the rise of revolutionary ideas?

---

6 The Call for Italian Unity

In 1815, Italy was a fragmented nation. Hapsburg Austria ruled Lombardy and Venetia in the north and a Bourbon king sat on the throne of the Kingdom of the Two Sicilies in the south. The duchies of Tuscany, Parma, and Modena were ruled by Hapsburg princes subservient to Austria. The papal states in central Italy were ruled by the pope. The House of Savoy, an Italian dynasty, ruled the Kingdom of Piedmont, which became the cornerstone of Italian unification. Inspired by past Italian glories—the Roman Empire and the Renaissance—Italian nationalists demanded an end to foreign occupation and the unification of the Italian peninsula. As in other lands, national revival and unification appealed principally to intellectuals and the middle class.

Giuseppe Mazzini
YOUNG ITALY

A leading figure in the *Risorgimento*—the struggle for Italian nationhood—was Giuseppe Mazzini (1805–1872). Often called the "soul of the Risorgimento," Mazzini devoted his life to the creation of a unified and republican Italy; he believed that a free and democratic Italy would serve as a model to the other nations of Europe. In 1831, he founded Young Italy, a society dedicated to the cause of Italian unity. The following reading includes the oath taken by members of Young Italy.

Young Italy is a brotherhood of Italians who believe in a law of Progress and Duty, and are convinced that Italy is destined to become one nation,—convinced also that she possesses sufficient strength within herself to become one, and that the ill success of her former efforts is to be attributed not to the weakness, but to the misdirection of the revolutionary elements within her,—that the secret of force lies in constancy and unity of effort. They join this association in the firm intent of consecrating both thought and action to the great aim of reconstituting Italy as one independent sovereign nation of free men and equals. . . .

Young Italy is Republican. . . . Republican,—Because theoretically every nation is destined, by the law of God and humanity, to form a free and equal community of brothers; and the republican is the only form of government that insures this future. . . .

The means by which Young Italy proposes to reach its aim are—education and insurrection, to be adopted simultaneously, and made to harmonize with each other. Education must ever be directed to teach by example, word, and pen the necessity of insurrection. Insurrection, whenever it can be realized, must be so conducted as to render it a means of national education. . . .

Insurrection—by means of guerrilla bands—is the true method of warfare for all nations desirous of emancipating themselves from a foreign yoke. This method of warfare supplies the want—inevitable at the commencement of the insurrection—of a regular army; it calls the greatest number of elements into the field, and yet may be sustained by the smallest number. It forms the military education of the people, and consecrates every foot of the native soil by the memory of some warlike deed. . . .

Each member will, upon his initiation into the association of Young Italy, pronounce the following form of oath, in the presence of the initiator:

In the name of God and of Italy;

In the name of all the martyrs of the holy Italian cause who have fallen beneath foreign and domestic tyranny;

By the duties which bind me to the land wherein God has placed me, and to the brothers whom God has given me;

By the love—innate in all men—I bear to the country that gave my mother birth, and will be the home of my children;

By the hatred—innate in all men—I bear to evil, injustice, usurpation and arbitrary rule;

By the blush that rises to my brow when I stand before the citizens of other lands, to know that I have no rights of citizenship, no country, and no national flag;

By the aspiration that thrills my soul towards that liberty for which it was created, and is impotent to exert; towards the good it was created to strive after, and is impotent to achieve in the silence and isolation of slavery;

By the memory of our former greatness, and the sense of our present degradation;

By the tears of Italian mothers for their sons dead on the scaffold, in prison, or in exile;

By the sufferings of the millions, —

I, . . . believing in the mission intrusted by God to Italy, and the duty of every Italian to strive to attempt its fulfillment; convinced that where God has ordained that a nation shall be, He has given the requisite power to create it; that the people are the depositaries of that power, and that in its right direction for the people, and by the people, lies the secret of victory; convinced that virtue consists in action and sacrifice, and strength in union and constancy of purpose: I give my name to Young Italy, an association of men holding the same faith, and swear:

To dedicate myself wholly and forever to the endeavor with them to constitute Italy one free, independent, republican nation; to promote by every means in my power—whether by written or spoken word, or by action—the education of my Italian brothers towards the aim of Young Italy; towards association, the sole means of its accomplishment, and to virtue, which alone can render the conquest lasting; to abstain from enrolling myself in any other association from this time forth; to obey all the instructions, in conformity with the spirit of Young Italy, given me by those who represent with me the union of my Italian brothers; and to keep the secret of these instructions, even at the cost of my life; to assist my brothers of the association both by action and counsel —

NOW AND FOREVER.

This do I swear, invoking upon my head the wrath of God, the abhorrence of man, and the infamy of the perjurer, if I ever betray the whole or a part of this my oath.

REVIEW QUESTIONS

1. Why do you suppose many students were attracted to Young Italy?
2. Giuseppe Mazzini was a democrat, a nationalist, and a romantic. Discuss this statement.

---

7 1848: The Year of Revolutions

In 1848, revolutions for political liberty and nationhood broke out in many parts of Europe. An uprising in Paris set this revolutionary tidal wave in motion. In February 1848, democrats seeking to create a French republic and to institute universal manhood suffrage precipitated a crisis; the pursuant uprising in Paris forced King Louis Philippe to abdicate. The leaders of the new French Republic championed political democracy but, with some notable exceptions like Louis Blanc (1811–1882), had little concern for the plight of the laboring poor.

The publication of the *Organization of Labor* (1839) had established Blanc as a leading French social reformer. Blanc urged the government to finance national workshops—industrial corporations, in which the directors would be elected by the workers—to provide employment for the urban poor. The government responded to Blanc's insistence that all workers have the "right to work" by indeed establishing national workshops, but these provided jobs for only a fraction of the unemployed, and many workers were given wages for doing nothing. Property owners regarded the workshops as a waste of government funds and as nests of working-class radicalism. When the government closed the workshops in June 1848, Parisian workers revolted.

Alexis de Tocqueville
THE JUNE DAYS

To the French workers the June 1848 revolt was against poverty and for a fairer distribution of property. Viewing this uprising as a threat to property and indeed to civilization, the rest of France rallied against the workers, who were crushed after several days of bitter street fighting. In his *Recollections,* Alexis de Tocqueville (1805–1859), a leading statesman and political theorist, included a speech he made on January 29, 1848, before the French Chamber of Deputies, in which he warned the officials about the mood of the laboring poor.

. . . I am told that there is no danger because there are no riots; I am told that, because there is no visible disorder on the surface of society, there is no revolution at hand.

Gentlemen, permit me to say that I believe you are deceived. True, there is no actual disorder; but it has entered deeply into men's minds. See what is passing in the breasts of the working classes, who, I grant, are at present quiet. No doubt they are not disturbed by political passion, properly so-called, to the same extent that they have been; but can you not see that their passions, instead of political, have become social? Do you not see that there are gradually forming in their breasts opinions and ideas which are destined not only to upset this or that law, ministry, or even form of government, but society itself, until it totters upon the foundations on which it rests today? Do you not listen to what they say to themselves each day? Do you not hear them repeating unceasingly that all that is above them is incapable and unworthy of governing them; that the present distribution of goods throughout the world is unjust; that property rests on a foundation which is not an equitable foundation? And do you not realize that when such opinions take root, when they spread in an almost universal manner, when they sink deeply into the masses, they are bound to bring with them sooner or later, I know not when nor how, a most formidable revolution?

This, gentlemen, is my profound conviction: I believe that we are at this moment sleeping on a volcano. I am profoundly convinced of it. . . .

Later in his *Recollections,* de Tocqueville describes the second uprising in 1848, called the June Days.

I come at last to the insurrection of June, the most extensive and the most singular that has occurred in our history, and perhaps in any other: the most extensive, because, during four days, more than a hundred thousand men were engaged in it; the most singular, because the insurgents fought without a war-cry, without leaders, without flags, and yet with a marvellous harmony and an amount of military experience that astonished the oldest officers.

What distinguished it also, among all the events of this kind which have succeeded one another in France for sixty years, is that it did not aim at changing the form of government, but at altering the order of society. It was not, strictly speaking, a political struggle, in the sense which until then we had given to the word, but a combat of class against class, a sort of Servile War [slave uprising in ancient Rome]. It represented the facts of the Revolution of February in the same manner as the theories of Socialism represented its ideas; or rather it issued naturally from these ideas, as a son does from his mother. We behold in it nothing more than a blind and rude, but powerful, effort on the part of the workmen to escape from the necessities of their condition, which had been depicted to them as one of unlawful oppression, and to open up by main force a road towards that imaginary comfort with which they had been deluded. It was this mixture of greed and false theory which first gave birth to the insurrection and then made it so formidable. These poor people had been told that the wealth of the rich was in some way the produce of a theft practised upon themselves. They had been assured that the inequality of fortunes was as opposed to morality and the welfare of society as it was to nature. Prompted by their needs and their passions, many had believed this obscure and erroneous notion of right, which, mingled with brute force, imparted to the latter an energy, a tenacity and a power which it would never have possessed unaided.

It must also be observed that this formidable insurrection was not the enterprise of a certain number of conspirators, but the revolt of one whole section of the population against another. Women took part in it as well as men. While the latter fought, the former prepared and carried ammunition; and when at last the time had come to surrender, the women were the last to yield. These women went to battle with, as it were, a housewifely ardour: they looked to victory for the comfort of their husbands and the education of their children. . . .

As we know, it was the closing of the national workshops that occasioned the rising. Dreading to disband this formidable soldiery at one stroke, the Government had tried to disperse it by send-

ing part of the workmen into the country. They refused to leave. On the 22nd of June, they marched through Paris in troops, singing in cadence, in a monotonous chant, "We won't be sent away, we won't be sent away. . . ."

. . . The spirit of insurrection circulated from one to the other of this immense class, and in each of its parts, as the blood does in the body; it filled the quarters where there was no fighting, as well as those which served as the scene of battle; it had penetrated into our houses, around, above, below us. The very places in which we thought ourselves the masters swarmed with domestic enemies; one might say that an atmosphere of civil war enveloped the whole of Paris, amid which, to whatever part we withdrew, we had to live. . . .

. . . It was easy to perceive through the multitude of contradictory reports that we had to do with the most universal, the best armed, and the most furious insurrection ever known in Paris. The national workshops and various revolutionary bands that had just been disbanded supplied it with trained and disciplined soldiers and with leaders. It was extending every moment, and it was difficult to believe that it would not end by being victorious, . . . all the great insurrections of the last sixty years had triumphed. . . .

Nevertheless, we succeeded in triumphing over this so formidable insurrection; nay more, it was just that which rendered it so terrible which saved us. . . . Had the revolt borne a less radical character and a less ferocious aspect, it is probable that the greater part of the middle class would have stayed at home; France would not have come to our aid; the National Assembly itself would perhaps have yielded, or at least a minority of its members would have advised it; and the energy of the whole body would have been greatly unnerved. But the insurrection was of such a nature that any understanding with it became at once impossible, and from the first it left us no alternative but to defeat it or to be destroyed ourselves.

Carl Schurz
REVOLUTION SPREADS TO THE GERMAN STATES

The February Revolution in Paris was eagerly received by German liberals and nationalists who yearned for a Germany governed by national parliament and a constitution that guaranteed basic liberties. In the following excerpt from his *Reminiscences,* Carl Schurz (1829–1906), then a student at the University of Bonn, recalled the expectations of German liberal-nationalists. After the revolution failed, Schurz fled to Switzerland and eventually went to the United States, where he had a distinguished career as a senator, cabinet member, and journalist.

One morning, toward the end of February, 1848, I sat quietly in my attic-chamber, working hard at my tragedy of "Ulrich von Hutten," when suddenly a friend rushed breathlessly into the room, exclaiming: "What, you sitting here! Do you not know what has happened?"

"No; what?"

"The French have driven away Louis Philippe and proclaimed the republic."

I threw down my pen—and that was the end of "Ulrich von Hutten." I never touched the manuscript again. We tore down the stairs, into the street, to the market-square, the accustomed meeting-place for all the student societies after their midday dinner. Although it was still forenoon, the market was already crowded with young men talking excitedly. There was no shouting, no noise, only agitated conversation. What did we want there? This probably no one knew. But since the French had driven away Louis Philippe and proclaimed the republic, something of course must happen here, too. Some of the students had brought their rapiers along, as if it were necessary at once to make an attack or to defend ourselves. We were dominated by a vague feeling as if a great outbreak of elemental forces had begun, as if an earthquake was impending of which we had felt the first shock, and we instinctively crowded together. Thus we wandered about in numerous

bands . . . [and] fell into conversation with all manner of strangers, to find in them the same confused, astonished and expectant state of mind; then back to the market-square, to see what might be going on there; then again somewhere else, and so on, without aim and end, until finally late in the night fatigue compelled us to find the way home.

The next morning there were the usual lectures to be attended. But how profitless! The voice of the professor sounded like a monotonous drone coming from far away. What he had to say did not seem to concern us. The pen that should have taken notes remained idle. At last we closed with a sigh the notebook and went away, impelled by a feeling that now we had something more important to do—to devote ourselves to the affairs of the fatherland. And this we did by seeking as quickly as possible again the company of our friends, in order to discuss what had happened and what was to come. In these conversations, excited as they were, certain ideas and catchwords worked themselves to the surface, which expressed more or less the feelings of the people. Now had arrived in Germany the day for the establishment of "German Unity," and the founding of a great, powerful national German Empire. In the first line the convocation of a national parliament. Then the demands for civil rights and liberties, free speech, free press, the right of free assembly, equality before the law, a freely elected representation of the people with legislative power, responsibility of ministers, self-government of the communes, the right of the people to carry arms, the formation of a civic guard with elective officers, and so on— in short, that which was called a "constitutional form of government on a broad democratic basis." Republican ideas were at first only sparingly expressed. But the word democracy was soon on all tongues, and many, too, thought it a matter of course that if the princes should try to withhold from the people the rights and liberties demanded, force would take the place of mere petition. Of course the regeneration of the fatherland must, if possible, be accomplished by peaceable means. A few days after the outbreak of this commotion I reached my nineteenth birthday. I remember to have been so entirely absorbed by what was happening that I could hardly turn my thoughts to anything else. Like many of my friends, I was dominated by the feeling that at last the great opportunity had arrived for giving to the German people the liberty which was their birthright and to the German fatherland its unity and greatness, and that it was now the first duty of every German to do and to sacrifice everything for this sacred object. We were profoundly, solemnly in earnest. . . .

Exciting news came from all sides. In Cologne a threatening ferment prevailed. In the taverns and on the streets resounded the "Marseillaise" [French national anthem, symbol of the Revolution], which at that time still passed in all Europe as the "hymn of liberty." On the public places great meetings were held to consult about the demands to be made by the people. A large deputation, headed by the late lieutenant of artillery, August von Willich, forced its way into the hall of the city council, vehemently insisting that the municipality present as its own the demands of the people of Cologne to the king. The streets resounded with the military drumbeat; the soldiery marched upon the popular gatherings, and Willich, as well as another ex-artillery officer, Fritz Anneke, were arrested; whereupon increasing excitement. . . .

. . . In Coblenz, Düsseldorf, Aachen, Crefeld, Cleves and other cities on the Rhine similar demonstrations took place. In South Germany—in Baden, Hessen-on-the-Rhine, Nassau, Würtemberg, Bavaria—the same revolutionary spirit burst forth like a prairie-fire. In Baden the Grand Duke acceded almost at once to what was asked of him, and so did the rulers of Würtemberg, Nassau, and Hessen-Darmstadt. . . .

Great news came from Vienna. There the students of the university were the first to assail the Emperor of Austria with the cry for liberty and citizens' rights. Blood flowed in the streets, and the downfall of Prince Metternich was the result. The students organized themselves as the armed guard of liberty. In the great cities of Prussia there was a mighty commotion. Not only Cologne, Coblenz and Trier, but also Breslau, Königsberg and Frankfurt-on-the-Oder, sent deputations to Berlin to entreat the king. In the Prussian capital the masses surged upon the streets, and everybody looked for events of great import.

While such tidings rushed in upon us from all sides like a roaring hurricane, we in the little university town of Bonn were also busy preparing addresses to the sovereign, to circulate them for signature and to send them to Berlin. On the 18th of March we too had our mass demonstration. A great multitude gathered for a solemn procession through the streets of the town. The most respectable citizens, not a few professors and a great number of students and people of all grades marched in close ranks. At the head of the procession Professor Kinkel bore the tricolor, black, red and gold, which so long had been prohibited as the revolutionary flag. Arrived on the market-square he mounted the steps of the city hall and spoke to the assembled throng. He spoke with wonderful eloquence, his voice ringing out in its most powerful tones as he depicted a resurrection of German unity and greatness and of the liberties and rights of the

German people, which now must be conceded by the princes or won by force by the people. And when at last he waved the black, red and gold banner, and predicted to a free German nation a magnificent future, enthusiasm without bounds broke forth. People clapped their hands, they shouted, they embraced one another, they shed tears. In a moment the city was covered with black, red and gold flags, and not only the Burschenschaft, but almost everybody wore a black-red-gold cockade on his hat. While on that 18th of March we were parading through the streets suddenly sinister rumors flew from mouth to mouth. It had been reported that the king of Prussia, after long hesitation, had finally concluded, like the other German princes, to concede the demands that were pouring upon him from all sides. But now a whispered report flew around that the soldiery had suddenly fired upon the people and that a bloody struggle was raging in the streets of Berlin.

REVIEW QUESTIONS

1. According to Alexis de Tocqueville, why did Parisian workers revolt in 1848?
2. How did the goals of Parisian workers who revolted in 1848 differ from those of members of Giuseppe Mazzini's Young Italy?
3. De Tocqueville observed that what distinguished this revolt was that it aimed to change the order of society, not the form of government. Explain.
4. What effect did the news of Louis Philippe's overthrow and the founding of the French Republic have on Carl Schurz and the young students of his day? How did they behave?
5. What were the goals of Schurz and many of his colleagues? How did they seek to reconcile nationalism and liberalism?
6. Why have university students often been attracted to revolutions? Provide examples from the twentieth century.

CHAPTER 7
Thought and Culture in an Age of Science and Industry

RHEA DARWINII, John Gould, 1834. Naturalist Darwin catalogued animal and plant life on his trips to the Southern Hemisphere. (From The Zoology of the Voyage of the H.M.S. Beagle, under the Command of Captain Fitzroy, R.N., during 1832–1836. Edited and Superintended by Charles Darwin, Part 3, "Birds." *Reprinted with permission of Cambridge University Press by permission of the British Library.*)

Romanticism dominated European art, literature, and music in the early nineteenth century. Stressing the feelings and the free expression of personality, the Romantic Movement was a reaction against the rationalism of the Enlightenment. In the middle decades of the century, realism and its close auxiliary naturalism supplanted romanticism as the chief norm of cultural expression. Rejecting religious, metaphysical, and romantic interpretations of reality, realists aspired to an exact and accurate portrayal of the external world and daily life. Realist and naturalist writers like Émile Zola used the empirical approach: the careful collection, ordering, and interpretation of facts employed in science, which was advancing steadily in the nineteenth century. Among the most important scientific theories formulated was Charles Darwin's theory of evolution, which revolutionized conceptions of time and the origins of the human species.

The principal currents of political thought, Marxism and liberalism, also reacted against romantic, religious, and metaphysical interpretations of nature and society, focused on the empirical world, and strove for scientific accuracy. This emphasis on objective reality helped to stimulate a growing criticism of social ills, for despite unprecedented material progress, reality was often sordid, somber, and dehumanizing. In the last part of the century, reformers, motivated by an expansive liberalism, revolutionary or evolutionary socialism, or a socially committed Christianity, pressed for the alleviation of social injustice.

1 Realism and Naturalism

The middle decades of the nineteenth century were characterized by the growing importance of science and industrialization in European life. A movement known as positivism sought to apply the scientific method to the study of society. Rejecting theological and metaphysical theories as unscientific, positivists sought to arrive at the general laws that underlie society by carefully assembling and classifying data.

This stress on a rigorous observation of reality also characterized realism and naturalism, the dominant movements in art and literature. In several ways, realism differed from romanticism, the dominant cultural movement in the first half of the century. Romantics were concerned with the inner life—with feelings, intuition, and imagination. They sought escape from the city into natural beauty, and they venerated the past, particularly the Middle Ages, which they viewed as noble, idyllic, and good in contrast to the spiritually impoverished present. Realists, on the other hand, shifted attention away from individual human feelings to the external world, which they investigated with the meticulous care of the scientist. Preoccupied with reality as it actually is, realist writers and artists depicted ordinary people, including the poor and humble, in ordinary circumstances. With a careful eye for detail and in a matter-of-fact way devoid of romantic exuberance and exaggeration, realists described peasants, factory workers, laundresses, beggars, criminals, and prostitutes.

Realism quickly evolved into naturalism. Naturalist writers held that human behavior was determined by the social environment. They argued that certain social and economic conditions produced predictable traits in men and women and that cause and effect operated in society as well as in physical nature.

Vissarion Belinsky
THE POETRY OF REALITY

Vissarion Grigorevich Belinsky (1811–1848), a self-taught Russian intellectual concerned with moral and social issues, provided an early definition of realism.

Thus we have here another aspect of poetry, *realistic* poetry, the poetry of life, the poetry of reality, at last the true and genuine poetry of our time. Its distinct character consists in the fact that it is true to reality; it does not create life anew, but reproduces it, and, like a convex glass, mirrors in itself, from one point of view, life's diverse phenomena, extracting from them those that are necessary to create a full, vivid, and organically unified picture. The size and the limits of the contents of this picture are decisive in judging the greatness of the poetic work. In order to complete the characterization of that which I call *realistic* poetry, I add that its eternal hero, the unchanging object of poetic inspiration, is a human being, an individual, independent, acting freely, a symbol of the world—its final manifestation, the attempts to understand the curious riddle of himself, the final question of his own mind, the ultimate enigma of his own curious aspirations. The key to this riddle, the answer to this question, the resolution of this problem must be full *consciousness,* which is the mystery, the aim and the reason for his existence!

Is it surprising, after this, that this realistic trend in poetry, this close union of art with life has developed primarily in our time? Is it surprising that the distinct characteristic of the newest works of literature in general is a merciless frankness, that life appears in them as if in order to be put to shame, in all nakedness, in all its tremendous ugliness and in all its solemn beauty, as if it were dissected with an anatomist's knife? We demand not the ideal of life, but life as it is. Be it good or bad, we do not wish to adorn it, for we think that in poetic presentation it is equally beautiful in both cases precisely because it is true, and that where there is truth, there is poetry. . . .

[Realistic poetry] is the poetry of our time par excellence, more understandable and accessible to all, more in agreement with the spirit and needs of our time.

Émile Zola
THE EXPERIMENTAL NOVEL

Émile Zola (1840–1902) was one of France's great novelists. Coming from the provinces to Paris, the young Zola, after failing to get a law degree, worked as an ill-paid clerk. When he lost his job and was unemployed for two years, he learned firsthand how the poor suffered. His life improved when he was hired by the sales department of a publishing house. He became a columnist and art critic, intensely studying life among all classes of the population but with special concern for the poor. His description of the Paris slums made him famous as both a social critic and a literary innovator. In his writing style, he combined realistic attention to detail, almost in the manner of a social scientist, with a compassionate symbolism and a poetic imagination. Living up to his ideals of hard work and social justice, he published many works and spoke out on public issues. In 1898, he wrote a famous letter in defense of Captain Alfred Dreyfus, a victim of anti-Semitism; threatened with arrest, he fled to England where he lived in exile for a time. In the following reading from *The Experimental Novel,* Zola asserted that literature too can be a science.

. . . Some day the physiologist[1] will explain to us the mechanism of the thoughts and the passions; we shall know how the individual machinery of each man works; how he thinks, how he loves, how he goes from reason to passion and folly; but these phenomena, resulting as they do from the mechanism of the organs, acting under the influence of an interior condition, are not produced in isolation or in the bare void. Man is not alone; he lives in society, in a social condition; and consequently, for us novelists, this social condition unceasingly modifies the phenomena. Indeed our great study is just there, in the reciprocal effect of society on the individual and the individual on society. For the physiologist, the exterior and interior conditions are purely chemical and physical, and this aids him in finding the laws which govern them easily. We are not yet able to prove that the social condition is also physical and chemical. It is that certainly, or rather it is the variable product of a group of living beings, who themselves are absolutely submissive to the physical and chemical laws which govern alike living beings and inanimate. From this we shall see that we can act upon the social conditions, in acting upon the phenomena of which we have made ourselves master in man. And this is what constitutes the

experimental novel: to possess a knowledge of the mechanism of the phenomena inherent in man, to show the machinery of his intellectual and sensory manifestations, under the influences of heredity and environment, such as physiology shall give them to us, and then finally to exhibit man living in social conditions produced by himself, which he modifies daily, and in the heart of which he himself experiences a continual transformation. Thus, then, we lean on physiology; we take man from the hands of the physiologist solely, in order to continue the solution of the problem, and to solve scientifically the question of how men behave when they are in society. . . .

I have reached this point: the experimental novel is a consequence of the scientific evolution of the century; it continues and completes physiology, which itself leans for support on chemistry and medicine; it substitutes for the study of the abstract and the metaphysical[2] man the study of the natural man, governed by physical and chemical laws, and modified by the influences of his surroundings; it is in one word the literature of our scientific age. . . .

. . . The metaphysical man is dead; our whole territory is transformed by the advent of the physiological man. No doubt "Achilles' Anger,"

---

[1]Physiology is the study of the functions of living organisms.

[2]Metaphysics is a branch of philosophy concerned with the first principle of things, with the ultimate reality beyond the physical appearance of things.

"Dido's Love,"[3] will last forever on account of their beauty; but today we feel the necessity of analyzing anger and love, of discovering exactly

how such passions work in the human being. This view of the matter is a new one; we have become experimentalists instead of philosophers. In short, everything is summed up in this great fact: the experimental method in letters, as in the sciences, is on the way to explain the natural phenomena, both individual and social, of which metaphysics, until now, has given only irrational and supernatural explanations.

---

[3]"Achilles' anger" is a reference to Homer's *Iliad;* Achilles, the great Greek warrior, is infuriated when King Agamemnon deprives him of his prize, the captive girl Briseis. "Dido's love" is a reference to Virgil's *Aeneid;* Dido, the queen of Carthage, has a great love for Aeneas, the Trojan prince.

Charles Dickens
HARD TIMES

British novelist Charles Dickens (1812–1870) depicted in detail the squalor of English industrial cities, the drudgery of factory labor, and the hypocrisy of society. His novel *Hard Times* (1854) was his harshest indictment of the industrial system, and it offers a good example of the realist genre in literature.

It was a town of red brick, or of brick that would have been red if the smoke and ashes had allowed it; but as matters stood it was a town of unnatural red and black like the painted face of a savage. It was a town of machinery and tall chimneys, out of which interminable serpents of smoke trailed themselves for ever and ever, and never got uncoiled. It had a black canal in it, and a river that ran purple with ill-smelling dye, and vast piles of building full of windows where there was a rattling and a trembling all day long, and where the piston of the steam-engine worked monotonously up and down like the head of an elephant in a state of melancholy madness. It contained several large streets all very like one another, and many small streets still more like one another, inhabited by people equally like one another, who all went in and out at the same hours, with the same sound upon the same pavements, to do the same work, and to whom every day was the same as yesterday and tomorrow, and every year the counterpart of the last and the next. . . .

In the hardest working part of Coketown; in the innermost fortifications of that ugly

citadel, where Nature was as strongly bricked out as killing airs and gases were bricked in; at the heart of the labyrinth of narrow courts upon courts, and close streets upon streets, which had come into existence piecemeal, every piece in a violent hurry for some one man's purpose, and the whole an unnatural family, shouldering, and trampling, and pressing one another to death; in the last close nook of this great exhausted receiver, where the chimneys, for want of air to make a draught, were built in an immense variety of stunted and crooked shapes, as though every house put out a sign of the kind of people who might be expected to be born in it; among the multitude of Coketown, generically called 'the Hands,'— a race who would have found more favour with some people, if Providence had seen fit to make them only hands, or, like the lower creatures of the seashore, only hands and stomachs—lived a certain Stephen Blackpool, forty years of age. . . .

As Coketown cast ashes not only on its own head but on the neighbourhood's too—after the manner of those pious persons who do penance for their own sins by putting other people into sackcloth—it was customary for those who now and then thirsted for a draught of pure air, which is not absolutely the most wicked among the vanities of life, to get a few miles away by the railroad, and then begin their walk, or their lounge in the fields. . . .

Though the green landscape was blotted here and there with heaps of coal, it was green elsewhere, and there were trees to see, and there were larks singing (though it was Sunday), and there were pleasant scents in the air, and all was over-arched by a bright blue sky. In the distance one way, Coketown showed as a black mist; in another distance hills began to rise; in a third, there was a faint change in the light of the horizon where it shone upon the far-off sea. Under their feet, the grass was fresh; beautiful shadows of branches flickered upon it, and speckled it; hedgerows were luxuriant; everything was at peace. Engines at pits' mouths, and lean old horses that had worn the circle of their daily labour into the ground, were alike quiet; wheels had ceased for a short space to turn; and the great wheel of earth seemed to revolve without the shocks and noises of another time.

REVIEW QUESTIONS

1. What did Vissarion Belinsky mean when he declared that "where there is truth there is poetry"? How would Wordsworth have interpreted this statement (see page 120)?
2. What relationship did Émile Zola draw between the experimental novel and the scientific age?
3. What view of the individual and society did Zola's conception of the experimental novel present? To what extent, in his view, could individuals control social conditions, and how?
4. Select one sentence that in your opinion best exemplifies Dickens's talent for realism. Explain why.

2 Theory of Evolution

In a century of outstanding scientific discoveries, none was more significant than the theory of evolution formulated by the English naturalist Charles Darwin (1809–1882). From December 1831 to 1836, Darwin had served as naturalist at sea on the *H.M.S. Beagle,* which surveyed parts of South America and some Pacific islands. He collected and classified many specimens of animal and plant life and from his investigations eventually drew several conclusions that startled the scientific community and enraged many clergy.

Before Darwin's theory of evolution, most people adhered to the biblical account of creation found in Genesis, which said that God had created the universe, the various species of animal and plant life, and human beings, all in six days. The creation account also said that God had given each species of animal and plant a form that distinguished it from every other species. It was commonly held that the creation of the universe and of the first human beings had occurred some five or six thousand years earlier.

Based on his study, Darwin maintained that all life on earth had descended from earlier living forms; that human beings had evolved from lower, nonhuman species; and that the process had taken millions of years. Adopting the Malthusian idea that population reproduces faster than the food supply increases, Darwin held that within nature there is a continual struggle for existence. He said that the advantage lies with those living things that are stronger, faster, better camouflaged from their enemies, or better fitted in some way for survival than are other members of their species; those more fit to survive pass along the advantageous trait to offspring. This principle of *natural selection* explains why some members of a species survive and reproduce and why those less fit perish.

Charles Darwin
NATURAL SELECTION

According to Darwin, members of a species inherit variations that distinguish them from others in the species, and over many generations these variations become more pronounced. In time, a new variety of life evolves that can no longer breed with the species from which it descended. In this way, new species emerge and older ones die out. Human beings were also a product of natural selection, evolving from earlier, lower, nonhuman forms of life. In this first passage, from his autobiography, Darwin described his empirical method and his discovery of a general theory that coordinated and illuminated the data he found. Succeeding excerpts are from his *The Origin of Species* (1859) and *The Descent of Man* (1871).

DARWIN'S DESCRIPTION OF HIS METHOD AND DISCOVERY

From September 1854 I devoted my whole time to arranging my huge pile of notes, to observing, and to experimenting in relation to the transmutation of species. During the voyage of the *Beagle* I had been deeply impressed by discovering in the Pampean formation[1] great fossil animals covered with armour like that on the existing armadillos; secondly, by the manner in which closely allied animals replace one another in proceeding southwards over the Continent; and thirdly, by the South American character of most of the productions of the Galapagos archipelago,[2] and more especially by the manner in which they differ

slightly on each island of the group; none of the islands appearing to be very ancient in a geological sense.

It was evident that such facts as these, as well as many others, could only be explained on the supposition that species gradually become modified; and the subject haunted me. But it was equally evident that neither the action of the surrounding conditions, nor the will of the organisms (especially in the case of plants) could account for the innumerable cases in which organisms of every kind are beautifully adapted to their habits of life— for instance, a woodpecker or a tree-frog to climb trees, or a seed for dispersal by hooks or plumes. I had always been much struck by such adaptations, and until these could be

---

[1]The Pampean formation refers to the vast plain that stretches across Argentina, from the Atlantic Ocean to the foothills of the Andes Mountains.

[2]The Galapagos Islands, a Pacific archipelago 650 miles west of Ecuador, are noted for their unusual wildlife, which Darwin observed.

explained it seemed to me almost useless to endeavour to prove by indirect evidence that species have been modified.

After my return to England it appeared to me that by following the example of Lyell[3] in Geology, and by collecting all facts which bore in any way on the variation of animals and plants under domestication and nature, some light might perhaps be thrown on the whole subject. My first note-book was opened in July 1837. I worked on true Baconian principles,[4] and without any theory collected facts on a wholesale scale, more especially with respect to domesticated productions, by printed enquiries, by conversation with skilful breeders and gardeners, and by extensive reading. When I see the list of books of all kinds which I read and abstracted, including whole series of Journals and Transactions, I am surprised at my industry. I soon perceived that selection was the keystone of man's success in making useful races of animals and plants. But how selection could be applied to organisms living in a state of nature remained for some time a mystery to me.

In October 1838, that is, fifteen months after I had begun my systematic enquiry, I happened to read for amusement Malthus[5] on *Population,* and being well prepared to appreciate the struggle for existence which everywhere goes on from long-continued observation of the habits of animals and plants, it at once struck me that under these circumstances favourable variations would tend to be preserved and unfavourable ones to be destroyed. The result of this would be the formation of new species. Here, then, I had at last got a theory by which to work. . . .

It has sometimes been said that the success of *The Origin {of Species}* proved "that the subject was in the air," or "that men's minds were prepared for it." I do not think that this is strictly true, for I occasionally sounded not a few naturalists, and never happened to come across a single one who seemed to doubt about the permanence of species. Even Lyell and Hooker,[6] though they would listen with interest to me, never seemed to agree. I tried once or twice to explain to able men what I meant by Natural Selection, but signally failed. What I believe was strictly true is that innumerable well-observed facts were stored in the minds of naturalists ready to take their proper places as soon as any theory which would receive them was sufficiently explained. . . .

My Descent of Man was published in February 1871. As soon as I had become, in the year of 1837 or 1838, convinced that species were mutable productions, I could not avoid the belief that man must come under the same law.

In the following excerpt from *The Origin of Species* (1859), Darwin explained the struggle for existence and the principle of natural selection.

THE ORIGIN OF SPECIES

. . . Owing to this struggle [for existence], variations, however slight . . . , if they be in any degree profitable to the individuals of a species, in their infinitely complex relations to other organic beings and to their physical conditions of life, will tend to the preservation of such individuals, and will generally be inherited by the offspring. The offspring, also, will thus have a better chance of surviving, for, of the many individuals of any species which are periodically born, but a small number can

[3]Sir Charles Lyell (1797–1875) was a Scottish geologist whose work showed that the planet had evolved slowly over many ages. Like Lyell, Darwin sought to interpret natural history by observing processes still going on.
[4]"Baconian principles" refers to Sir Francis Bacon (1561–1626), one of the first to insist that new knowledge should be acquired through experimentation and the accumulation of data.
[5]Thomas Malthus (1766–1834) was an English economist who maintained that population increases geometrically (2, 4, 8, 16, and so on) but the food supply increases arithmetically (1, 2, 3, 4, and so on). (See page 115.)

[6]Sir Joseph Dalton Hooker (1817–1911) was an English botanist who supported Darwin's ideas.

survive. I have called this principle, by which each slight variation, if useful, is preserved, by the term Natural Selection, in order to mark its relation to man's power of selection. But the expression often used by Mr. Herbert Spencer[7] of the Survival of the Fittest is more accurate, and is sometimes equally convenient. . . .

A struggle for existence inevitably follows from the high rate at which all organic beings tend to increase. Every being, which during its natural lifetime produces several eggs or seeds, must suffer destruction during some period of its life, and during some season or occasional year, otherwise, on the principle of geometrical increase, its numbers would quickly become so inordinately great that no country could support the product. Hence, as more individuals are produced than can possibly survive, there must in every case be a struggle for existence, either one individual with another of the same species, or with the individuals of distinct species, or with the physical conditions of life. It is the doctrine of Malthus applied with manifold force to the whole animal and vegetable kingdoms; for in this case there can be no artificial increase of food, and no prudential restraint from marriage. Although some species may be now increasing, more or less rapidly, in numbers, all cannot do so, for the world would not hold them.

There is no exception to the rule that every organic being naturally increases at so high a rate, that, if not destroyed, the earth would soon be covered by the progeny of a single pair. Even slow-breeding man has doubled in twenty-five years, and at this rate, in less than a thousand years, there would literally not be standing-room for his progeny. . . . The elephant is reckoned the slowest breeder of all known animals, and I have taken some pains to estimate its probable minimum rate of natural increase; it will be safest to assume that it begins breeding when thirty years old, and goes

on breeding till ninety years old, bringing forth six young in the interval, and surviving till one hundred years old; if this be so, after a period of from 740 to 750 years there would be nearly nineteen million elephants alive, descended from the first pair. . . .

. . . Can we doubt (remembering that many more individuals are born than can possibly survive) that individuals having any advantage, however slight, over others, would have the best chance of surviving and of procreating their kind? On the other hand, we may feel sure that any variation in the least degree injurious would be rigidly destroyed. This preservation of favourable individual differences and variations, and the destruction of those which are injurious, I have called Natural Selection, or the Survival of the Fittest. . . .

. . . Natural Selection acts solely through the preservation of variations in some way advantageous, which consequently endure. Owing to the high geometrical rate of increase of all organic beings, each area is already fully stocked with inhabitants; and it follows from this, that as the favoured forms increase in number, so, generally, will the less favoured decrease and become rare. . . .

From these several considerations I think it inevitably follows, that as new species in the course of time are formed through natural selection, others will become rarer and rarer, and finally extinct. The forms which stand in closest competition with those undergoing modification and improvement will naturally suffer most. And we have seen in the chapter on the Struggle for Existence that it is the most closely-allied forms—varieties of the same species, and species of the same genus or of related genera—which, from having nearly the same structure, constitution, and habits, generally come into the severest competition with each other; consequently, each new variety or species, during the progress of its formation, will generally press hardest on its nearest kindred, and tend to exterminate them. We see the same process of extermination amongst our

---

[7]The British philosopher Herbert Spencer (1820–1903) coined the term *survival of the fittest*. (See page 163.)

domesticated productions, through the selection of improved forms by man.

In *The Descent of Man* (1871), Darwin argued that human beings have evolved from lower forms of life.

THE DESCENT OF MAN

The main conclusion here arrived at, and now held by many naturalists who are well competent to form a sound judgment, is that man is descended from some less highly organised form. The grounds upon which this conclusion rests will never be shaken, for the close similarity between man and the lower animals in embryonic development, as well as in innumerable points of structure and constitution, both of high and of the most trifling importance,— the rudiments which he retains, and the abnormal reversions to which he is occasionally liable,—are facts which cannot be disputed. They have long been known, but until recently they told us nothing with respect to the origin of man. Now when viewed by the light of our knowledge of the whole organic world, their meaning is unmistakable. The great principle of evolution stands up clear and firm, when these groups of facts are considered in connection with others, such as the mutual affinities of the members of the same group, their geographical distribution in past and present times, and their geological succession. It is incredible that all these facts should speak falsely. He who is not content to look, like a savage, at the phenomena of nature as disconnected, cannot any longer believe that man is the work of a separate act of creation. He will be forced to admit that the close resemblance of the embryo of man to that, for instance, of a dog—the construction of his skull, limbs and whole frame on the same plan with that of other mammals, independently of the uses to which the parts may be put—the occasional reappearance of various structures, for instance of several muscles, which man does not normally possess, but which are common to the Quadrumana[8]—and a crowd of analogous facts—all point in the plainest manner to the conclusion that man is the co-descendant with other mammals of a common progenitor.

We have seen that man incessantly presents individual differences in all parts of his body and in his mental faculties. These differences or variations seem to be induced by the same general causes, and to obey the same laws as with the lower animals. In both cases similar laws of inheritance prevail. Man tends to increase at a greater rate than his means of subsistence; consequently he is occasionally subjected to a severe struggle for existence, and natural selection will have effected whatever lies within its scope. A succession of strongly-marked variations of a similar nature is by no means requisite; slight fluctuating differences in the individual suffice for the work of natural selection. . . .

Man may be excused for feeling some pride at having risen, though not through his own exertions, to the very summit of the organic scale; and the fact of his having thus risen, instead of having been aboriginally placed there, may give him hope for a still higher destiny in the distant future. But we are not here concerned with hopes or fears, only with the truth as far as our reason permits us to discover it; and I have given the evidence to the best of my ability. We must, however, acknowledge, as it seems to me, that man with all his noble qualities, with sympathy which feels for the most debased, with benevolence which extends not only to other men but to the humblest living creature, with his god-like intellect which has penetrated into the movements and constitution of the solar system—with all these exalted powers—Man still bears in his bodily frame the indelible stamp of his lowly origin.

---

[8]An order of mammals, Quadrumana includes all primates (monkeys, apes, and baboons) except human beings; the primates' hind and forefeet can be used as hands as they have opposable first digits.

REVIEW QUESTIONS

1. How did Charles Darwin make use of Thomas Malthus's theory of population growth?
2. How did Darwin account for the extinction of old species and the emergence of new ones?
3. What did Darwin mean when he said that man "with his god-like intellect . . . still bears in his bodily frame the indelible stamp of his lowly origins"?

---

3 Darwinism and Religion

Many clergymen regarded the theory of evolution as a threat to the infallibility of the Bible. Darwinism attacked the traditional belief that some five thousand years ago God had created all animal and plant species and had given each one a permanent form; evolution seemed to relegate Adam and Eve to the realm of myth. The conflict between fundamentalists—those who believed in a literal interpretation of the Bible—and advocates of the new biology was marked by great bitterness. In time, however, many Christians reconciled the theory of evolution and the biblical account of creation. They maintained that God directed the evolutionary process and that the timespan of six days for creation given in Genesis is not meant to be taken literally.

In the early seventeenth century, Galileo (see Chapter 1) had insisted that on questions concerning nature, scientists should not turn to the Bible as an authority but should rely on the evidence of observation and experiments. The controversy over evolution reaffirmed this conviction for the scientific community, which more than ever saw the scientific method as the incontestable authority for interpreting nature. The theory of evolution also contributed to a growing secularism. The central doctrine of Christianity—that human beings were created by God and that salvation was the ultimate aim of life—rested more than ever on faith rather than on reason.

Andrew D. White
A HISTORY OF THE WARFARE OF SCIENCE WITH THEOLOGY

In the following passage, Andrew D. White (1832–1918), scholar, diplomat, and president of Cornell University in Ithaca, New York, described the controversy that raged over the publication of *The Origin of Species* and *The Descent of Man.* A founder of Cornell, White himself came under attack by clergy who feared that the new institution of higher learning would teach "atheism" and "infidelity." The passage is taken from *A History of the Warfare of Science with Theology in Christendom* (1894).

Darwin's *Origin of Species* had come into the theological world like a plough into an anthill. Everywhere those thus rudely awakened from their old comfort and repose had swarmed forth angry and confused. Reviews, sermons, books light and heavy, came flying at the new thinker from all sides.

The keynote was struck at once in the *Quarterly Review* by Wilberforce, Bishop of Oxford. He declared that Darwin was guilty of "a tendency to limit God's glory in creation"; that "the principle of natural selection is absolutely incompatible with the word of God"; that it "contradicts the revealed relations of creation to its Creator"; that it is "inconsistent with the fullness of his glory"; that it is "a dishonouring view of Nature"; and that there is "a simpler explanation of the presence of these strange forms among the works of God": that explanation being—"the fall of Adam." Nor did the bishop's efforts end here; at the meeting of the British Association for the Advancement of Science he again disported himself in the tide of popular applause. Referring to the ideas of Darwin, who was absent on account of illness, he congratulated himself in a public speech that he was not descended from a monkey. The reply came from Huxley,[1] who said in substance: "If I had to choose, I would prefer to be a descendant of a humble monkey rather than of a man who employs his knowledge and eloquence in misrepresenting those who are wearing out their lives in the search for truth."

This shot reverberated through England, and indeed through other countries.

The utterances of this the most brilliant prelate of the Anglican Church received a sort of antiphonal response from the leaders of the English Catholics. . . . Cardinal Manning declared his abhorrence of the new view of Nature, and described it as "a brutal philosophy—to wit, there is no God, and the ape is our Adam."

These attacks from such eminent sources set the clerical fashion for several years. . . . Another distinguished clergyman, vice-president of a Protestant institute to combat "dangerous" science, declared Darwinism "an attempt to dethrone God." . . . Another spoke of Darwin's views as suggesting that "God is dead," and declared that Darwin's work "does open violence to everything which the Creator himself has told us in the Scriptures of the methods and results of his work." Still another theological authority asserted: "If the Darwinian theory is true, Genesis is a lie, the whole framework of the book of life falls to pieces, and the revelation of God to man, as we Christians know it, is a delusion and a snare." Another, who had shown excellent qualities as an observing naturalist, declared the Darwinian view "a huge imposture from the beginning."

Echoes came from America. One review . . . denounced Darwin's views as "infidelity"; another, representing the American branch of the Anglican Church. . . . plunged into an exceedingly dangerous line of argument in the following words: "If this hypothesis be true, then is the Bible an unbearable fiction; . . . then have Christians for nearly two thousand years been duped by a monstrous lie. . . . Darwin requires us to disbelieve the authoritative word of the Creator.". . .

Nor was the older branch of the Church to be left behind in this chorus. Bayma, in the *Catholic World,* declared, "Mr. Darwin is, we have reason to believe, the mouthpiece or chief trumpeter of that infidel clique whose well-known object is to do away with all idea of a God."

Worthy of especial note as showing the determination of the theological side at that period was the foundation of sacro-scientific organizations to combat the new ideas. First to be noted is the "Academia," planned by Cardinal Wiseman. In a circular letter the cardinal, usually so moderate and just, sounded an alarm and summed up by saying, "Now it is for the Church, which alone possesses divine certainty

---

[1]Thomas Henry Huxley (1825–1895) was an English biologist and a staunch defender of Darwin.

and divine discernment, to place itself at once in the front of a movement which threatens even the fragmentary remains of Christian belief in England." The necessary permission was obtained from Rome, the Academia was founded. . . . A similar effort was seen in Protestant quarters; the "Victoria Institute" was created, and perhaps the most noted utterance which ever came from it was the declaration of its vice-president, the Rev. Walter Mitchell, that "Darwinism endeavours to dethrone God."

In France the attack was even more violent. Fabre d'Envieu brought out the heavy artillery of theology, and in a long series of elaborate propositions demonstrated that any other doctrine than that of the fixity and persistence of species is absolutely contrary to Scripture. . . .

In Germany . . . Catholic theologians vied with Protestants in bitterness. Prof. Michelis declared Darwin's theory "a caricature of creation." Dr. Hagermann asserted that it "turned the Creator out of doors." Dr. Schund insisted that "every idea of the Holy Scriptures, from the first to the last page, stands in diametrical opposition to the Darwinian theory"; and, "if Darwin be right in his view of the development of man out of a brutal condition, then the Bible teaching in regard to man is utterly annihilated." Rougemont in Switzerland called for a crusade against the obnoxious doctrine. Luthardt, Professor of Theology at Leipsic, declared: "The idea of creation belongs to religion and not to natural science; the whole superstructure of personal religion is built upon the doctrine of creation"; and he showed the evolution theory to be in direct contradiction to Holy Writ. . . .

In 1871 was published Darwin's *Descent of Man.* Its doctrine had been anticipated by critics of his previous books, but it made, none the less, a great stir; again the opposing army trooped forth, though evidently with much less heart than before. A few were very violent. The *Dublin University Magazine,* . . . charged Mr. Darwin with . . . being "resolved to hunt God out of the world."

From America there came new echoes. . . . The Rev. Dr. Hodge, of Princeton . . . denounced it as thoroughly "atheistic"; he insisted that Christians "have a right to protest against the arraying of probabilities against the clear evidence of the Scriptures"; . . . and declared that the Darwinian theory of natural selection is "utterly inconsistent with the Scriptures," and that "an absent God, who does nothing, is to us no God"; that "to ignore design as manifested in God's creation is to dethrone God"; that "a denial of design in Nature is virtually a denial of God.". . .

Fortunately at about the time when Darwin's *Descent of Man* was published, there had come into Princeton University a Dr. James McCosh. Called to the presidency, he at once took his stand against teachings so dangerous to Christianity as those of Drs. Hodge, Duffield, and their associates. . . . He saw that the most dangerous thing which could be done to Christianity at Princeton was to reiterate in the university pulpit, week after week, solemn declarations that if evolution by natural selection, or indeed evolution at all, be true, the Scriptures are false. He tells us that he saw that this was the certain way to make the students unbelievers; he therefore not only checked this dangerous preaching but preached an opposite doctrine. With him began the inevitable compromise, and, in spite of mutterings against him as a Darwinian, he carried the day. Whatever may be thought of his general system of philosophy, no one can deny his great service in neutralizing the teachings of his predecessors and colleagues—so dangerous to all that is essential in Christianity.

Other divines of strong sense in other parts of the country began to take similar ground— namely, that men could be Christians and at the same time Darwinians. . . .

In view of the proofs accumulating in favour of the new evolutionary hypothesis, the change in the tone of controlling theologians was now rapid. From all sides came evidences of desire to compromise with the theory. . . .

Whatever additional factors may be added to natural selection—and Darwin himself fully admitted that there might be others—the theory of an evolution process in the formation of the universe and of animated nature is established, and the old theory of direct creation is gone forever. In place of it science has given us conceptions far more noble, and opened the way to an argument for design infinitely more beautiful than any ever developed by theology.

REVIEW QUESTIONS

1. For what reasons did the clergy denounce Charles Darwin's theories?
2. Darwin and the clergy who attacked his theories perceived truth differently. Discuss this statement.

---

4 The Socialist Revolution

After completing a doctorate at the University of Jena in 1841, Karl Marx (1818–1883) edited a newspaper that was suppressed by the Prussian authorities for its radicalism and atheism. He left his native Rhineland for Paris, where he became friendly with Friedrich Engels. Expelled from France at the request of Prussia, Marx went to Brussels. In 1848, Marx and Engels produced for the Communist League the *Communist Manifesto,* advocating the violent overthrow of capitalism and the creation of a socialist society. Marx returned to Prussia and participated in a minor way in the Revolutions of 1848 in Germany. Expelled from Prussia in 1849, he went to England. He spent the rest of his life there, writing and agitating for the cause of socialism.

The *Communist Manifesto* presented a philosophy of history and a theory of society that Marx expanded upon in his later works, particularly *Capital* (1867). In the tradition of the Enlightenment, he maintained that history, like the operations of nature, was governed by scientific law. To understand the past and the present and to predict the essential outlines of the future, said Marx, one must concentrate on economic forces, on how goods are produced and how wealth is distributed. Marx's call for a working-class revolution against capitalism and for the making of a classless society established the ideology of twentieth-century communist revolutionaries.

Karl Marx and Friedrich Engels
COMMUNIST MANIFESTO

In the opening section of the *Manifesto,* the basic premise of the Marxian philosophy of history is advanced: class conflict—the idea that the social order is divided into classes based on conflicting economic interests.

BOURGEOIS AND PROLETARIANS

The history of all hitherto existing society is the history of class struggles.

Freeman and slave, patrician and plebeian [aristocrat and commoner, in the ancient world], lord and serf, guild-master [master craftsman] and journeyman [who worked for a guild-master], in a word, oppressor and oppressed, stood in constant opposition to one another, carried on an uninterrupted, now hidden, now open fight, that each time ended, either in a revolutionary reconstitution of society at large, or in the common ruin of the contending classes.

In the earlier epochs of history we find almost everywhere a complicated arrangement of society into various orders, a manifold gradation of social rank. In ancient Rome we have patricians, knights, plebeians, slaves; in the Middle Ages, feudal lords, vassals [landowners pledged to lords], guild-masters, journeymen, apprentices, serfs; in almost all of these classes, again, subordinate gradations.

The modern bourgeois society that has sprouted from the ruins of feudal society, has not done away with class antagonisms. It has but established new forms of struggle in place of the old ones.

Our epoch, the epoch of the bourgeoisie [capitalist class], possesses, however, this distinctive feature; it has simplified the class antagonisms. Society as a whole is more and more splitting up into two great hostile camps, into two great classes directly facing each other: Bourgeoisie and Proletariat [industrial workers].

From the serfs of the middle ages sprang the chartered burghers of the earliest towns. From these burgesses the first elements of the bourgeoisie were developed.

The discovery of America, the rounding of the Cape, opened up fresh ground for the rising bourgeoisie. The East-Indian and Chinese markets, the colonization of America, trade with the colonies, the increase in the means of exchange and in commodities generally, gave to commerce, to navigation, to industry, an impulse never before known, and thereby, to the revolutionary element in the tottering feudal society, a rapid development.

The feudal system of industry, under which industrial production was monopolized by closed guilds, now no longer sufficed for the growing wants of the new market. The manufacturing system took its place. The guild-masters were pushed on one side by the manufacturing middle class; division of labor between the different corporate guilds vanished in the face of division of labor in each single workshop.

Meantime the markets kept ever growing, the demand ever rising. . . . Thereupon steam and machinery revolutionized industrial production. The place of manufacture was taken by the giant, Modern Industry, the place of the industrial middle class, by industrial millionaires, the leaders of whole industrial armies, the modern bourgeois.

Modern Industry has established the world's market, for which the discovery of America paved the way. This market has given an immense development to commerce, to navigation, to communication by land. This development has, in its turn, reacted on the extension of industry; and in proportion, as industry, commerce, navigation, railways extended, in the same proportion, the bourgeoisie developed, increased its capital, and pushed into the background every class handed down from the Middle Ages.

We see, therefore, how the modern bourgeoisie is itself the product of a long course of development, of a series of revolutions in the modes of production and of exchange.

Each step in the development of the bourgeoisie was accompanied by a corresponding political advance of that class. An oppressed class under the sway of the feudal nobility, an armed and self-governing association in the mediaeval commune [town], . . . the bourgeoisie has at last, since the establishment of Modern Industry and of the world's market, conquered for itself, in the modern representative State, exclusive political sway. The executive of the modern State is but a committee for managing the common affairs of the whole bourgeoisie.

The bourgeoisie, historically, has played a most revolutionary part.

The bourgeoisie, wherever it has got the upper hand, has put an end to all feudal, patriarchal, idyllic relations. It has pitilessly torn asunder the motley feudal ties that bound man to his "natural superiors," and has left remaining no other nexus [link] between man and man than naked self-interest, than callous "cash payment." It has drowned the most heavenly ecstasies of religious fervor, of chivalrous enthusiasm, . . . in the icy water of egotistical calculation. It has resolved personal worth into exchange value, and in place of the numberless indefeasible chartered freedoms, has set up that single, unconscionable freedom—Free Trade. In one word, for exploitation, veiled by religious and political illusions, it has substituted naked, shameless, direct, brutal exploitation. . . .

The bourgeoisie, states the *Manifesto,* has subjected nature's forces to human control to an unprecedented degree and has replaced feudal organization of agriculture (serfdom) and manufacturing (guild system) with capitalist free competition. But the capitalists cannot control these "gigantic means of production and exchange." Periodically, capitalist society is burdened by severe economic crises; capitalism is afflicted with overproduction—more goods are produced than the market will absorb. In all earlier epochs, which were afflicted with scarcity, the *Manifesto* declares, such a condition "would have seemed an absurdity." To deal with the crisis, the capitalists curtail production, thereby intensifying the poverty of the proletariat, who are without work. In capitalist society, the exploited worker suffers from physical poverty—a result of low wages—and spiritual poverty—a result of the monotony, regimentation, and impersonal character of the capitalist factory system. For the proletariat, work is not the satisfaction of a need but a repulsive

means for survival. The products they help make bring them no satisfaction; they are alienated from their labor.

In proportion as the bourgeoisie, *i.e.,* capital, is developed, in the same proportion is the proletariat, the modern working class, developed—a class of laborers, who live only so long as they find work, and who find work only so long as their labor increases capital. These laborers, who must sell themselves piecemeal, are a commodity, like every other article of commerce, and are consequently exposed to all the vicissitudes of competition, to all the fluctuations of the market.

Owing to the extensive use of machinery and to division of labor, the work of the proletarians has lost all individual character, and, consequently, all charm for the workman. He becomes an appendage of the machine, and it is only the most simple, most monotonous, and most easily acquired knack, that is required of him. Hence, the cost of production of a workman is restricted, almost entirely, to the means of subsistence that he requires for his maintenance, and for the propagation of his race. But the price of a commodity, and therefore also of labor, is equal to its cost of production. In proportion, therefore, as the repulsiveness of the work increases, the wage decreases. Nay more, in proportion as the use of machinery and division of labor increases, in the same proportion the burden of toil also increases, whether by prolongation of the working hours, by increase of the work exacted in a given time, or by increased speed of the machinery, etc.

Modern industry has converted the little workshop of the patriarchal master into the great factory of the industrial capitalist. Masses of laborers, crowded into the factory, are organized like soldiers. As privates of the industrial army they are placed under the command of a perfect hierarchy of officers and sergeants. Not only are they slaves of the bourgeois class, and of the bourgeois state; they are daily and hourly enslaved by the machine, by the overlooker, and, above all, by the individual bourgeois manufacturer himself. The more openly this despotism proclaims gain to be its end and aim, the more petty, the more hateful and the more embittering it is.

The less the skill and exertion of strength implied in manual labor, in other words, the more modern industry develops, the more is the labor of men superseded by that of women. Differences of age and sex have no longer any distinctive social validity for the working class. All are instruments of labor, more or less expensive to use, according to their age and sex.

No sooner has the laborer received his wages in cash, for the moment escaping exploitation by the manufacturer, than he is set upon by the other portions of the bourgeoisie, the landlord, the shop-keeper, the pawnbroker, etc. . . .

The exploited workers organize to defend their interests against the capitalist oppressors.

But with the development of industry the proletariat not only increases in number; it becomes concentrated in greater masses, its strength grows, and it feels that strength more. The various interests and conditions of life within the ranks of the proletariat are more and more equalized, in proportion as machinery obliterates all distinctions of labor and nearly everywhere reduces wages to the same low level. The growing competition among the bourgeois, and the resulting commercial crises, make the wages of the workers ever more fluctuating. The unceasing improvement of machinery, ever more rapidly developing, makes their livelihood more and more precarious: the collisions between individual workmen and individual bourgeois take more and more the character of collisions between two classes. Thereupon the workers begin to form combinations (trade unions) against the bourgeoisie; they club together in order to keep up

the rate of wages; they found permanent associations in order to make provision beforehand for these occasional revolts. Here and there the contest breaks out into riots.

Now and then the workers are victorious, but only for a time. The real fruit of their battles lies, not in the immediate results, but in [their ever-expanding unity]. . . .

This organization of the proletarians into a class, and consequently into a political party, is continually being upset again by the competition between the workers themselves. But it ever rises up again, stronger, firmer, mightier. It compels legislative recognition of particular interests of the workers, by taking advantage of the divisions among the bourgeoisie itself. Thus the ten-hour bill[1] in England was carried. . . .

Increasingly, the proletariat, no longer feeling part of the old society, seeks to destroy it.

In the conditions of the proletariat, those of the old society at large are already virtually swamped. The proletarian is without property; his relation to his wife and children has no longer anything in common with the bourgeois family relations; modern industrial labor, modern subjection to capital, the same in England as in France, in America as in Germany, has stripped him of every trace of national character. Law, morality, religion, are to him so many bourgeois prejudices, behind which lurk in ambush just as many bourgeois interests.

All the preceding classes that got the upper hand sought to fortify their already acquired status by subjecting society at large to their conditions of appropriation. The proletarians cannot become masters of the productive forces of society, except by abolishing their own pre-

---

[1]The Ten Hours Act (1847) provided a ten and a half hour day from 6 A.M. to 6 P.M., with an hour and a half for meals for women and children.

vious mode of appropriation, and thereby also every other previous mode of appropriation. They have nothing of their own to secure and to fortify; their mission is to destroy all previous securities for, and insurances of, individual property.

All previous historical movements were movements of minorities, or in the interest of minorities. The proletarian movement is the self-conscious, independent movement of the immense majority, in the interest of the immense majority. The proletariat, the lowest stratum of our present society, cannot stir, cannot raise itself up, without the whole superincumbent [overlying] strata of official society being sprung into the air.

Though not in substance, yet in form, the struggle of the proletariat with the bourgeoisie is at first a national struggle. The proletariat of each country must, of course, first of all settle matters with its own bourgeoisie.

In depicting the most general phases of the development of the proletariat, we traced the more or less veiled civil war, raging within existing society, up to the point where that war breaks out into open revolution, and where the violent overthrow of the bourgeoisie lays the foundation for the sway of the proletariat. . . .

The modern laborer . . . instead of rising with the progress of industry, sinks deeper and deeper below the conditions of existence of his own class. He becomes a pauper, and pauperism develops more rapidly than population and wealth. And here it becomes evident that the bourgeoisie is unfit any longer to be the ruling class in society and to impose its conditions of existence upon society as an overriding law. It is unfit to rule because it is incompetent to assure an existence to its slave within his slavery, because it cannot help letting him sink into such a state that it has to feed him instead of being fed by him. Society can no longer live under this bourgeoisie, in other words its existence is no longer compatible with society.

The essential condition for the existence and for the sway of the bourgeois class, is the formation and augmentation of capital; the con-

dition for capital is wage-labor. Wage-labor rests exclusively on competition between the laborers. The advance of industry, whose involuntary promoter is the bourgeoisie, replaces the isolation of the laborers, due to competition, by their revolutionary combination, due to association. The development of modern industry, therefore, cuts from under its feet the very foundation on which the bourgeoisie produces and appropriates products. What the bourgeoisie therefore produces above all, are its own gravediggers. Its fall and the victory of the proletariat are equally inevitable. . . .

Communists, says the *Manifesto,* are the most advanced and determined members of working-class parties. Among the aims of the communists are organization of the working class into a revolutionary party; overthrow of bourgeois power and the assumption of political power by the proletariat; and an end to exploitation of one individual by another and the creation of a classless society. These aims will be achieved by the abolition of bourgeois private property (private ownership of the means of production) and the abolition of the bourgeoisie as a class.

The Communists, therefore, are on the one hand, practically, the most advanced and resolute section of the working class parties of every country, that section which pushes forward all others; on the other hand, theoretically, they have over the great mass of the proletariat the advantage of clearly understanding the line of march, the conditions, and the ultimate general results of the proletarian movement.

The immediate aim of the Communists is the same as that of all the other proletarian parties: formation of the proletariat into a class, overthrow of the bourgeois supremacy, conquest of political power by the proletariat. . . .

The distinguishing feature of Communism is not the abolition of property generally, but the abolition of bourgeois property. But modern bourgeois private property is the final and most complete expression of the system of producing and appropriating products, that is based on class antagonisms, on the exploitation of the many by the few.

In this sense the theory of the Communists may be summed up in the single sentence: Abolition of private property. . . .

One argument leveled against communists by bourgeois critics, says the *Manifesto,* is that the destruction of the bourgeoisie would lead to the disappearance of bourgeois culture, which is "identical with the disappearance of all culture," and the loss of all moral and religious truths. Marx insists that these ethical and religious ideals lauded by the bourgeoisie are not universal truths at all but are common expressions of the ruling class at a particular stage in history.

That culture, the loss of which he [the bourgeois] laments, is for the enormous majority, a mere training to act as a machine.

But don't wrangle with us so long as you [the bourgeoisie] apply to our [the communists'] intended abolition of bourgeois property, the standard of your bourgeois notions of freedom, culture, law, etc. Your very ideas are but the outgrowth of the conditions of your bourgeois production and bourgeois property, just as your jurisprudence is but the will of your class made into a law for all, a will, whose essential character and direction are determined by the economical conditions of existence of your class.

The selfish misconception that induces you to transform into eternal laws of nature and of reason, the social forms springing from your present mode of production and form of property—historical relations that rise and disappear in the progress of production—this misconception you share with every ruling class that has preceded you. What you see clearly in the case of ancient property, what you admit in the case of feudal property, you

are of course forbidden to admit in the case of your own bourgeois form of property. . . .

The charges against Communism made from a religious, a philosophical, and, generally, from an ideological standpoint, are not deserving of serious examination.

Does it require deep intuition to comprehend that man's ideas, views, and conceptions, in one word, man's consciousness changes with every change in the conditions of his material existence, in his social relations and in his social life?

What else does the history of ideas prove than that intellectual production changes its character in proportion as material production is changed? The ruling ideas of each age have ever been the ideas of its ruling class. . . .

. . . The ideas of religious liberty and freedom of conscience merely gave expression to the sway of free competition within the domain of knowledge.

"Undoubtedly," it will be said, "religious, moral, philosophical, and juridical ideas have been modified in the course of historic development. But religion, morality, philosophy, political science, and law, constantly survived this change.

"There are besides, eternal truths, such as Freedom, Justice, etc., that are common to all states of society. But Communism abolishes eternal truths, it abolishes all religion and all morality, instead of constituting them on a new basis; it therefore acts as a contradiction to all past historical experience."

What does this accusation reduce itself to? The history of all past society has consisted in the development of class antagonisms, antagonisms that assumed different forms at different epochs.

But whatever form they may have taken, one fact is common to all past ages, *viz.,* the exploitation of one part of society by the other. No wonder, then, that the social consciousness of past ages, despite all the multiplicity and variety it displays, moves within certain common forms, or general ideas, which cannot completely vanish except with the total disappearance of class antagonisms.

The Communist revolution is the most radical rupture with traditional property relations; no wonder that its development involves the most radical rupture with traditional ideas.

Aroused and united by communist intellectuals, says the *Manifesto,* the proletariat will wrest power from the bourgeoisie and overthrow the capitalist system that has oppressed them. In the new society, people will be fully free.

But let us have done with the bourgeois objections to Communism.

We have seen above that the first step in the revolution by the working class is to raise the proletariat to the position of the ruling class, to win the battle of democracy.

The proletariat will use its political supremacy to wrest, by degrees, all capital from the bourgeoisie; to centralize all instruments of production in the hands of the State, *i.e.,* of the proletariat organized as the ruling class; and to increase the total of productive forces as rapidly as possible. . . .

When, in the course of development, class distinctions have disappeared and all production has been concentrated in the hands of a vast association of the whole nation, the public power will lose its political character. Political power, properly so called, is merely the organized power of one class for oppressing another. If the proletariat during its contest with the bourgeoisie is compelled, by the force of circumstances, to organize itself as a class, if, by means of a revolution, it makes itself the ruling class, and, as such, sweeps away by force the old conditions of production, then it will, along with these conditions, have swept away the conditions for the existence of class antagonism, and of classes generally, and will thereby have abolished its own supremacy as a class.

In place of the old bourgeois society with its classes and class antagonisms we shall have an association in which the free development of each is the condition for the free development of all. . . .

The Communists disdain to conceal their views and aims. They openly declare that their ends can be attained only by the forcible overthrow of all existing social conditions. Let the ruling classes tremble at a communistic revolution. The proletarians have nothing to lose but their chains. They have a world to win.

Working men of all countries, unite!

REVIEW QUESTIONS

1. What do Karl Marx and Friedrich Engels mean by the term *class conflict?* What historical examples of class conflict are provided?
2. According to the *Manifesto,* what role has the state played in the class conflict?
3. How does the *Manifesto* describe the condition of the working class under capitalism?
4. According to the *Manifesto,* why is capitalism doomed? What conditions will bring about the end of capitalism?
5. "The ruling ideas of each age have ever been the ideas of its ruling class." What is meant by this statement? Do you agree or disagree? Explain.
6. Have Marx's predictions proven accurate? Explain your answer.

5   The Evolution of Liberalism

The principal concern of early-nineteenth-century liberalism was protecting the rights of the individual against the demands of the state. For this reason, liberals advocated a constitution that limited the state's authority and a bill of rights that stipulated the citizen's basic freedoms. Believing that state interference in the economy endangered individual liberty and private property, liberals were strong advocates of laissez faire—leaving the market to its own devices. And convinced that the unpropertied and uneducated masses were not deeply committed to individual freedom, liberals approved property requirements for voting and office holding.

In the last part of the nineteenth century, however, liberalism changed substantially as many liberals came to support government reforms to deal with the problems created by unregulated industrialization. By the early twentieth century, liberalism—not without reservation and opposition on the part of some liberals—had evolved into social democracy, which maintains that government has an obligation to assist the needy.

L. T. Hobhouse
JUSTIFICATION FOR STATE INTERVENTION

Arguing that laissez faire enabled the powerful to exploit the weak, Thomas Hill Green (1836–1882), a British political theorist, urged legislation to promote better conditions of labor, education, and health. In a truly liberal society, said Green, individuals have the opportunity to develop their moral and intellectual abilities. But poor education, inadequate housing, and unhealthy living and working environments deprive people of the opportunity for self-enhancement. For these people, freedom is an empty word. Green insisted that the liberal state must concern itself not just with individual rights but with the common good. L. T. Hobhouse (1864–1929), an academic who also wrote for the *Manchester Guardian,* concurred with Green's views in *Liberalism* (1911).

[It was conceived by an earlier liberalism] that, however deplorable the condition of the working classes might be, the right way of raising them was to trust to individual enterprise and possibly, according to some thinkers, to voluntary combination. By these means the efficiency of labour might be enhanced and its regular remuneration raised. By sternly withholding all external supports we should teach the working classes to stand alone, and if there were pain in the disciplinary process there was yet hope in the future. They would come by degrees to a position of economic independence in which they would be able to face the risks of life, not in reliance upon the State, but by the force of their own brains and the strength of their own right arms.

These views no longer command the same measure of assent. On all sides we find the State making active provision for the poorer classes and not by any means for the destitute alone. We find it educating the children, providing medical inspection, authorizing the feeding of the necessitous at the expense of the rate-payers, helping them to obtain employment through free Labour Exchanges, seeking to organize the labour market with a view to the mitigation of unemployment, and providing old age pensions for all whose incomes fall below thirteen shillings a week, without exacting any contribution. Now, in all this, we may well ask, is the State going forward blindly on the paths of broad and generous but unconsidered charity? Is it and can it remain indifferent to the effect on individual initiative and personal or parental responsibility? Or may we suppose that the wiser heads are well aware of what they are about, have looked at the matter on all sides, and are guided by a reasonable conception of the duty of the State and the responsibilities of the individual? Are we, in fact—for this is really the question—seeking charity or justice?

We said above that it was the function of the State to secure the conditions upon which mind and character may develop themselves. Similarly we may say now that the function of the State is to secure conditions upon which its citizens are able to win by their own efforts all that is necessary to a full civic efficiency. It is

not for the State to feed, house, or clothe them. It is for the State to take care that the economic conditions are such that the normal man who is not defective in mind or body or will can by useful labour feed, house, and clothe himself and his family. The "right to work" and the right to a "living wage" are just as valid as the rights of person or property. That is to say, they are integral conditions of a good social order. A society in which a single honest man of normal capacity is definitely unable to find the means of maintaining himself by useful work is to that extent suffering from malorganization. There is somewhere a defect in the social system, a hitch in the economic machine. Now, the individual workman cannot put the machine straight. He is the last person to have any say in the control of the market. It is not his fault if there is over-production in his industry, or if a new and cheaper process has been introduced which makes his particular skill, perhaps the product of years of application, a drug in the market [that is, obsolete]. He does not direct or regulate industry. He is not responsible for its ups and downs, but he has to pay for them. That is why it is not charity but justice for which he is asking. . . .

If this view of the duty of the State and the right of the workman is coming to prevail, it is owing partly to an enhanced sense of common responsibility, and partly to the teaching of experience. . . .

Herbert Spencer
THE MAN VERSUS THE STATE

Committed to a traditional laissez-faire policy, however, some liberals attacked state intervention as a threat to personal freedom and a betrayal of central liberal principles. In *The Man versus the State* (1884), British philosopher Herbert Spencer (1820–1903) warned that increased government regulation would lead to socialism and slavery.

The extension of this policy . . . [of government legislation] fosters everywhere the tacit assumption that Government should step in whenever anything is not going right. "Surely you would not have this misery continue!" exclaims some one, if you hint . . . [an objection] to much that is now being said and done. Observe what is implied by this exclamation. It takes for granted. . . . that every evil can be removed: the truth being that with the existing defects of human nature, many evils can only be thrust out of one place or form into another place or form—often being increased by the change. The exclamation also implies the unhesitating belief, here especially concerning us, that evils of all kinds should be dealt with by the State. . . . Obviously, the more numerous governmental interventions become, the more confirmed does this habit of thought grow, and the more loud and perpetual the demands for intervention.

Every extension of the regulative policy involves an addition to the regulative agents— a further growth of officialism and an increasing power of the organization formed of officials. . . .

. . . Moreover, every additional State-interference strengthens the tacit assumption that it is the duty of the State to deal with all evils and secure all benefits. Increasing power of a growing administrative organization is accompanied by decreasing power of the rest of the society to resist its further growth and control. . . .

"But why is this change described as 'the coming-slavery'?" is a question which many will still ask. The reply is simple. All socialism involves slavery. . . .

Evidently then, the changes made, the changes in progress, and the changes urged, will carry us not only towards State-ownership of land and dwellings and means of communication, all to be administered and worked by State-agents, but towards State-usurpation of all industries: the private forms of which, disadvantaged more and more in competition with the State, which can arrange everything for its own convenience, will more and more die away, just as many voluntary schools have, in presence of Board-schools. And so will be brought about the desired ideal of the socialists. . . .

. . . It is a matter of common remark, often made when a marriage is impending, that those possessed by strong hopes habitually dwell on the promised pleasures and think nothing of the accompanying pains. A further exemplification of this truth is supplied by these political enthusiasts and fanatical revolutionists. Impressed with the miseries existing under our present social arrangements, and not regarding these miseries as caused by the ill-working of a human nature but partially adapted to the social state, they imagine them to be forthwith curable by this or that re-arrangement. Yet, even did their plans succeed it could only be by substituting one kind of evil for another. A little deliberate thought would show that under their proposed arrangements, their liberties must be surrendered in proportion as their material welfares were cared for.

For no form of co-operation, small or great, can be carried on without regulation, and an implied submission to the regulating agencies. . . .

. . . So that each [individual] would stand toward the governing agency in the relation of slave to master.

"But the governing agency would be a master which he and others made and kept constantly in check; and one which therefore would not control him or others more than was needful for the benefit of each and all."

To which reply the first rejoinder is that, even if so, each member of the community as an individual would be a slave to the community as a whole. Such a relation has habitually existed in militant communities, even under quasi-popular forms of government. In ancient Greece the accepted principle was that the citizen belonged neither to himself nor to his family, but belonged to his city—the city being with the Greek equivalent to the community. And this doctrine, proper to a state of constant warfare, is a doctrine which socialism unawares re-introduces into a state intended to be purely industrial. The services of each will belong to the aggregate of all; and for these services, such returns will be given as the authorities think proper. So that even if the administration is of the beneficent kind intended to be secured, slavery, however mild, must be the outcome of the arrangement. . . .

The function of Liberalism in the past was that of putting a limit to the powers of kings. The function of true Liberalism in the future will be that of putting a limit to the powers of Parliaments.

REVIEW QUESTIONS

1. Why did L. T. Hobhouse believe that state intervention was needed to create "a good social order"?
2. What was Herbert Spencer's answer to the argument that government legislation is necessary to relieve human misery? Has history proven him correct?
3. What did Spencer mean by the dictum, "All socialism involves slavery"?
4. According to Spencer, what was true liberalism? Compare his conception of liberalism with that of Hobhouse.

CHAPTER 8
Politics and Society, 1845–1914

HOMELESS CHILDREN, 1875, new arrivals at the London orphanage of Dr. Barnardo. This orphanage represents the nineteenth-century spirit of reform, which tried to address the evils and injustices of the industrial age that often affected children of the poor. *(Barnardo's Photographic & Film)*

In the last half of the nineteenth century, the people of Europe, more numerous than ever and concentrated in ever-growing cities, interacted with each other in a busy exchange of goods, ideas, and services, which led to remarkable creativity in industry, science, and the arts. The physical sciences flourished; medical science advanced; the psychoanalytic method developed under Sigmund Freud. New technologies speeded communication and transportation, which intensified human contact and competition. Industrialization, promoted by capitalist enterprise, spread throughout Europe and the United States, raising the standard of living and advancing expectations among the poor for a better life. The new mobility and social interdependence provided greater opportunity for individual gain, but they also increased social tensions.

One source of tension arose from the growing demands among the lower classes for social justice and a share of political power; the misery of the poor and disenfranchised masses became a hot political issue. At the same time the agitation for women's rights mounted; women wanted to have rights equal to men in education and politics. Although women faced strenuous resistance with regard to suffrage, they continued to fight toward that goal. A third troublesome factor in European politics and society was anti-Semitism. Of long standing in European history, it became an active political force toward the end of the nineteenth century.

No country was more threatened by sociopolitical unrest than the Russian Empire. Contact with western Europe convinced the tsarist government of the need to modernize their backward country and catch up with "the West," as Russians called the richer lands of Europe—a challenge beyond the resources of the tsarist regime. Increasing discontent among workers led to a revolution in 1905.

Despite the impressive achievements of European civilization and the domination of the globe by European states, the continent was becoming more and more deeply divided by the early 1900s. The competition for wealth and power heightened international rivalries. Nationalist ambitions, backed in most countries by popular support, and an arms race further worsened international relations. Although few people at the time recognized it, Europe's period of peace and security was ending. World War I, which broke out in 1914, was on the horizon.

The chapter opens with a tragedy—the great famine that ravaged Ireland from 1845 to 1849. Such a disaster seemed more appropriate to medieval Europe or to Asia than to the advanced European society of the nineteenth century. But in many ways modernization had not reached Ireland. During the one hundred and fiftieth anniversary of the famine in 1997, British prime minister Tony Blair admitted that the British government had precipitated the disaster, "by standing by while a crop failure turned into a massive human tragedy. That one million people died in what was then part of the richest and most powerful nation in the world is something that still causes pain."

1   The Irish Potato Famine

The Act of Union that joined Ireland to England in 1801 was designed to subjugate the rebellious Irish, and was based on mutual distrust. The English regarded the Irish with contempt; to them the Irish were feckless, untrustworthy, Catholic, and prolific. The Irish, in turn, resented English domination.

Landowners in the predominantly rural country were English; the majority of them lived in England on the considerable rents from their lands. They leased their land to tenant farmers and rented out very small plots to landless laborers. A peasant family of six could feed itself all winter on the produce of one-and-a-half acres planted solely with potatoes. In the summer they went hungry.

In 1845 potato blight destroyed a large part of the potato crop. Despite agitated reports from Ireland of impending famine, the British government was slow to provide food and employment on public works to cope with the disaster. The potato crop had failed before, but never more than two years running; between 1845 and 1848 it failed three times.

Charles Trevelyan, in charge of the British government relief effort, turned a deaf ear to constant appeals for extra food. He indeed stopped the food relief scheme "to prevent people from being habitually dependent on the government." When reports of mob violence and deaths from starvation could no longer be denied, the government opened soup kitchens, which distributed a watery soup to the starving millions. Reassured by a sound but small potato crop in 1847, the government assumed the crisis was over and closed the soup kitchens, leaving private organizations to feed the still starving people.

From the beginning, Trevelyan was determined that Ireland should pay for its own relief work by levying local rates—property taxes paid by landlords and tenants. Landlords were to pay all the rates for their poorest tenants and half for the more prosperous ones. Ironically this measure, intended to protect tenants, persuaded landlords to avoid payment by evicting their tenants. Some of the homeless wandered the roads in search of food or begged in the cities, others starved to death; the more fortunate emigrated to an uncertain future.

All along, aid came from private relief organizations in England, Ireland, and the United States. They acted swiftly and efficiently to raise money and provide clothing; the Quakers operated soup kitchens where need was greatest. Yet it was only a matter of time before fever broke out; this occurred in the middle of the winter of 1846–47. Medical resources were limited. The overcrowded, underfunded workhouses took some patients; others were treated in new fever hospitals, and "fever sheds" and army tents housed the overflow.

An attempted rebellion against England by Irish patriots in the summer of 1848 stifled any remaining compassion for Ireland. In the fall of 1848 the potato crop failed again, and there was no help from the government. Farms were abandoned, and emigration to England, Canada, and America increased. The English landlords, ruined by rates, their rental income depleted, sold bankrupt estates. Cholera devastated the masses of the poor. The depopulated, neglected countryside continued to decay.

The decennial census of 1851 reported a population decrease from 8.1 to 6.5 million, in a period when the population should have risen to nine million. The number of deaths from famine and disease is usually estimated at around one million. The remainder of the decline was due to emigration. The economic distress of Ireland continued for years to come.

Poulett Scrope
EVICTIONS

The British government could hardly claim that it was ignorant of the treatment of tenants by landlords in Ireland. Evictions of tenants whose leases had expired, or who were unable to pay their rent, had long been a way for landlords to clear their land and turn it over to cattle or grain. Unlike England, Ireland had no growing industrial towns to absorb surplus labor. Eviction, especially in winter, was frequently a death sentence.

During the potato famine, the ruined crops and the consequent inability of tenants to pay their rent led to further evictions. Poulett Scrope (1797–1876), a member of Parliament, had for years prior to the famine advocated the recognition of tenant rights in Ireland. In the speech below, delivered in the House of Commons in 1846, he clearly described what was happening in the Irish countryside.

"Remember, life is destroyed in Ireland in other ways than by the bullet of the assassin. Life is taken in Ireland by the slow agonies of want, and disease engendered by want, where human beings are deprived (however legally) of the only means of living, and no resource afforded them in its place. When a landlord clears his estate by driving from their homes hundreds of poor tenants, who have no other possible source of refuge, does he not as effectually destroy their lives (at least, many of them) as if he shot them at once? It would be a mercy to do so in comparison. Do you deny that the lives of the peasantry are unprotected by law—that they are obliged to protect themselves by these criminal outrages? I ask you if, since these very discussions began, we have not had proofs—multiplied proofs—of the mode in which the landlords of Ireland are decimating the people of Ireland? Ay, in the midst of fever and famine, was not a whole village razed by Mr. Gerrard—400 souls turned out upon

the highway—not allowed even to rest in the roadside ditches? Was not another village razed by the Marquis of Waterford? Another, I believe, by Mr. Clark, of Nenagh, who was murdered; another by Mr. Pierce Carrick, who was murdered for the same intention. All these, and numerous other facts of the same kind, are going on at this moment. Even in this morning's papers I see a fresh announcement of a clearance of 180 individuals. . . . [L]andlords consider themselves justified in consolidating their estates, and ejecting the numerous families of tenantry who have occupied under the old leases. Now, I ask, what becomes of these ejected wretches, whose houses are pulled down, who are driven forth from the land where they were born and bred, hunted even out of the roadside ditches, when they take shelter there, as was literally the case in the Gerrard clearances? Where are they to go? How are they to live? . . . If they squat on another landlord's estate they are driven off again as nuisances, pests—as people, in one word, who have no right to exist. . . . I ask, what becomes of them? Why, we know on the best authority they wander to the big towns and try to live by beggary. . . . Is not an ejectment of this kind tantamount to a sentence of death on a small farmer or cottier, whose only chance of living and maintaining his family is the occupation of a bit of land? Can you wonder at his retaliating on him whom he feels to be his oppressor? Or can you wonder that thousands, who know themselves to be exposed to this fate, every day contrive to save themselves from it by a system of outrage and intimidation?"

Nicholas Cummins
THE FAMINE IN SKIBBEREEN

The south and west of Ireland suffered worst from famine. With poor soil fit for little more than potatoes, the area was in desperate straits by the fall of 1846.

Skibereen, in the remote southwest of Ireland, lacked suitable people to form a relief committee, without which it was not eligible for government relief. Public works were the only employment and did not pay enough to feed a family. In December, when hundreds had died of hunger, two Protestant clergymen from the town confronted Trevelyan in London and pleaded for food. But Trevelyan was determined to adhere to government policy and no food was sent.

Two weeks later Nicholas Cummins, a magistrate from Cork, visited the area and was horrified. He reported to the authorities without success and then wrote a letter to the Duke of Wellington, an Irishman, with a copy to *The Times,* the most influential newspaper in London. The letter was published on Christmas Eve, 1846, and Skibbereen became a symbol of the famine disaster.

His letter received a wider circulation when meetings were held all over the United States in 1847 to raise money for famine relief in Ireland. Speakers on several occasions read his letter as an eyewitness account of the famine.

My Lord Duke,

Without apology or preface, I presume so far to trespass on your Grace as to state to you, and by the use of your illustrious name, to present to the British public the following statement of what I have myself seen within the last three days. Having for many years been intimately connected with the western portion of the County of Cork, and possessing some small property there, I thought it right personally to investigate the truth of several lamentable accounts which had reached me, of the appalling state of misery to which that part of the country was reduced. I accordingly went on the 15th instant to Skibbereen, and to give the instance of one townland which I visited, as an example of the state of the entire coast district, I shall state simply what I there saw . . . Being aware that I should have to witness scenes of frightful hunger, I provided myself with as much bread as five men could carry, and on reaching the spot I was surprised to find the wretched hamlet apparently deserted. I entered some of the hovels to ascertain the cause, and the scenes which presented themselves were such as no tongue or pen can convey the slightest idea of. In the first, six famished and ghastly skeletons, to all appearances dead, were huddled in a corner on some filthy straw, their sole covering what seemed a ragged horsecloth, their wretched legs hanging about, naked above the knees. I approached with horror, and found by a low moaning they were alive—they were in fever, four children, a woman and what had once been a man. It is impossible to go through the detail. Suffice it to say, that in a few minutes I was surrounded by at least 200 such phantoms, such frightful spectres as no words can describe, either from famine or from fever. Their demoniac yells are still ringing in my ears, and their horrible images are fixed upon my brain. My heart sickens at the recital, but I must go on.

In another case, decency would forbid what follows, but it must be told. My clothes were nearly torn off in my endeavor to escape from the throng of pestilence around, when my neckcloth was seized from behind by a grip which compelled me to turn, I found myself grasped by a woman with an infant just born in her arms and the remains of a filthy sack across her loins—the sole covering of herself and baby. The same morning the police opened a house on the adjoining lands, which was observed shut for many days, and two frozen corpses were found, lying upon the mud floor, half devoured by rats.

A mother, herself in a fever, was seen the same day to drag out the corpse of her child, a girl about twelve, perfectly naked, and leave it half covered with stones. In another house, within 500 yards of the cavalry station at Skibbereen, the dispensary doctor found seven wretches lying unable to move, under the same cloak. One had been dead many hours, but the others were unable to move either themselves or the corpse.

REVIEW QUESTIONS

1. The British government has been accused of inflicting genocide on the Irish people at the time of the potato famine. Is this accusation justified or not?
2. Apart from the British government, who else should bear responsibility for the lack of adequate relief?

---

2 The Lower Classes

The members of the upper and middle classes in European society looked down on "the lower classes"—industrial workers, domestic help, and peasants; and still further down, the street people, the mentally disturbed, the homeless, the unemployed, and vagrants; and at the bottom, the criminal underworld. These "lower classes" were most vulnerable to the vicissitudes of the business cycle and dependent on small and uncertain incomes; commonly they worked long hours under dehumanizing strain and were housed in urban slums under unsanitary conditions; they were hungry, illiterate, often reduced to outright destitution, and desperate to earn some money. In the slums of London's East End, one could see ragged men collect dog excrement for use in tanning leather; prostitution thrived.

In the economic progress of the nineteenth century, the overall material conditions of society improved remarkably, sharpening the social contrasts. Concerned people spoke of "two nations," the rich and the poor. The poor, however, were not entirely passive; workers began to rally, trying to improve their condition by political action, thereby scaring the upper classes into social awareness. At the same time, humanitarian concerns, often rising from religious inspiration, stirred some of the well-to-do. Toward the end of the nineteenth century, the misery of the poor caused lively public debate and heated political agitation.

Jeanne Bouvier
THE PAINS OF POVERTY

Jeanne Bouvier (1865–1964) grew up in the French countryside and went to a Catholic boarding school. When her father's trade slumped (he was a cooper— a maker of barrels and casks), her family was financially ruined, and they had to sell their house, land, and possessions. Jeanne became a worker, alternating between factory labor and domestic service, in demeaning, exhausting, and ill-paid jobs.

Eventually she succeeded in becoming a skilled seamstress, and then in middle age a militant trade unionist and feminist. Later in life she wrote several books, including her memoirs, from which the following passages on living and working conditions in the 1870s and 1880s are taken, beginning with her account of her first job. Despite the privations of her early life, she lived until the age of ninety-nine.

The first thing my mother did after we arrived at our new home was to go to the silk-throwing factory to ask if they wanted to hire me.* The foreman said yes, and I became a working girl. I was eleven years old. The working day began at five in the morning and did not end until eight at night. There were two hours of rest at mealtimes, from eight to nine in the morning to eat our breakfast, and from noon to one o'clock for lunch.

Before sending me off on my first day of work, my mother gave me a thousand bits of advice: "Pay close attention to what they show you, be very well behaved," and so forth. I was so afraid of being late that I was at the factory door early! The five o'clock bell finally rang, and the doors opened. The workers swept into the shop. I followed them, my heart beating with emotion. I was upset by all these changes, coming one after another: yesterday still living in the house where I had spent my childhood, then the departure from our little village, and now the arrival in this one, so full of unknowns for me. I was in a new world. There I was in a workshop with some fifty other working women.

As I entered, my eyes were drawn to everything that surrounded me: the noise of the machines and the sound of the *tavelles* (reels on which the skeins of silk were wound). The forewoman placed me under the supervision of a woman worker who was to show me the different operations involved in reeling silk. I listened to her very attentively. From time to time, I would turn around to see what was going on behind me. When eight o'clock finally rang, the women hurried out of the workshop, and I followed them.

As soon as I got outside, I set off on the double for my mother's house. She was anxious to know what impression I was going to bring back of my first shift in that factory. As soon as she saw me, she said, "So how did it go this morning?"

"It went well."

"Is it difficult, what they had you do?"

"Oh, it's as easy as pie. You just go like this to find the end, then when you have it, you have to add it to what's been rolled onto the *roquet,* the large reel. You have to make a knot like this. . . . (I was showing her with gestures.) Then you have to carefully even out the spooled raw silk with more strands, so the skein can be unreeled without breaking the thread."

---

*Silk throwing is the doubling and twisting of raw silk into thread. In the period of which Bouvier writes, this process was performed by power-driven machines.

That first morning's impression was favorable. I went running off as soon as I had eaten my breakfast and once again arrived well before the doors opened. That is how my life as a working girl began. I did not complain. I knew that poverty had entered our lives and that my thirteen-hour day at the workshop would earn me fifty centimes.

A law had been passed in 1840 making it illegal to have children under the age of twelve work more than eight hours, but it was never enforced. That is why I was working thirteen hours, or five too many.

When the first two weeks had passed, I received my first six francs in pay. I squeezed it in my hand for fear of losing it. I was proud to bring my mother the fruits of my labor.

The terrible part was winter, when I had to leave the house at quarter to five. It was so dark going out in the streets in the cold, the rain, and the snow! How I suffered, and oh how afraid I was of the dark!

Our household was desperately poor. My father was often out of work. Money was scarce in our home. My father could not pay his rent. Landlords are everywhere alike: they are hard on the poor. Ours simply had what was left of our furniture attached. When the sheriff's officer came for our belongings, I felt I was forever disgraced. It seemed to me that the local residents would all be pointing me out with their fingers. I was deeply upset, as if we were criminals, though we had committed no crime. We were simply poor, very poor.

I told my mother: "I'd never dare return to the factory. I'm too ashamed. I'd rather go drown myself than always be so miserable. And what's more, everyone will know we've had our property attached!" I was wearing an apron that was none too clean. I wanted my mother to give me another so that, when they fished me out of the river, they could not say that I was wearing a dirty apron. I had firmly resolved to end it all. I could not reconcile myself to living in such anguish. I was then twelve and a half years old. My mother refused to give me a clean apron. It is to this refusal that I owe not having done away with myself. . . .

The family is forced to rent an old hovel.

Once we were settled into this hovel, poverty did not loosen its grip. I was forced to work outside the factory once my thirteen-hour day was over. I did crochet work and often stayed up all night. I worked night after night so there would be bread in the house. Despite these sleepless nights, often there was no bread.

I remember one such time when I went nearly two days without eating. That evening, when I came home from the factory, I started to work. My mother spent the night with me, shaking me whenever, in spite of myself, I began to fall asleep. She would tell me, "Don't fall asleep. You know very well that you mustn't sleep. Tomorrow we won't have any bread." I made superhuman efforts to stay awake. It was very cold. Snow was falling against the window panes. Despite all these tortures, I continued to work until four-thirty in the morning, at which time I got ready to return to the factory.

When I left the house, it was terribly cold. There was snow up to my knees. I had to cross the whole village in this snow and the dark of night. I was shivering from cold, from fright, and because I was so hungry and so tired! My eyelids burned like hot coals. These were the circumstances in which I began my thirteen-hour workday.

At eight o'clock, the factory let out for breakfast. I rushed home to finish my work. There were a few details to finish up before quickly going to deliver it and get the pay that would permit the whole household to eat. My brother accompanied me to the lady's house. He waited at the door. The lady paid me seven francs, just as she had promised. Because it was very cold, she offered me a cup of coffee with milk to warm me up. The coffee was served in a beautiful white cup and saucer. This cup had a gilt garland—what a pretty cup!—and the coffee was delicious and hot. I did not really like coffee and milk, but I certainly liked it that time, served in such a beautiful cup! I left this lady's house in raptures.

I handed my brother the seven francs I held in my hand. I kept five centimes to buy myself a roll. The cup of coffee had not satisfied my hunger. I had not eaten for nearly forty-eight hours. My brother brought the seven francs to my mother, who made a good soup to satisfy everyone.

I lived through many other bad days. I was a good worker at the factory, but I almost never got a raise. My mother, who was always short of money, would get angry to the point of beating me. She thought that I was not working hard enough and she would call me lazy. I could not stand this insult, but though I told her how hard I worked, she would not believe me. One payday, when I had received no raise and, as usual, the foreman told me that he would give me one in two weeks, I set to thinking about how my mother would take the news. Tired of always being beaten and never getting a raise, I resolved to go look for a job in another factory. I showed up and was hired with a raise of six francs every two weeks.

I got home a little late. As soon as I arrived, my mother asked if I had gotten a raise. I told her no. She immediately began to shout, and I was about to get hit when I explained to her that I was going to work in another factory where they would give me six francs more than in the one I was leaving. This happy news calmed her down, and she did not beat me.

The following Monday, my absence was noticed by the foreman, and he was told that I had left the factory because he never gave me a raise. He sent someone to find me and tell me that he would give a raise of six francs every two weeks. The explanation behind all this was the following: the foreman would ask the owner for raises. The owner would grant them, but the foreman would keep them for himself as a way of getting rich. While poor little unfortunates like myself endured poverty and received beatings, he kept the money.

Nikolaus Osterroth
THE YEARNING FOR SOCIAL JUSTICE

Nikolaus Osterroth (1875–1933), the son of a butcher, was a clay miner from the Palatinate, a region in western Germany. His and his fellow miners' resentment at the deterioration of their working conditions undermined their traditional loyalty to their Catholic faith and prepared them for the appeal of the Social Democratic party, which, under the guidance of Marxist intellectuals, represented the interests of the German working class. Osterroth became a union and party organizer before World War I; after the war he played a part in the politics of the Weimar Republic.

This selection, taken from his autobiography published in 1920, describes in telling detail his transition from a docile clay miner to a Social Democratic agitator and organizer.

The hardest work is the rough cutting with the ax and cutting away the clumps from the seam. You can't take it for more than three hours because your hands get completely exhausted. So the shift is divided into four two-hour sections separated by breakfast, lunch, and the afternoon break. In his youth a miner's arms twitch from exhaustion even when he sleeps. . . .

. . . When there are a great number of people employed in a mine, then two tunnels on opposite sides of the shaft are worked, and one man works steadily at piling up the clumps.

He also has to load the clumps onto wagons at the top of the shaft. The poor devil has to transport 800–1,000 wet, slippery clumps, each of which weighs 100 pounds. After years of this, his back gets all crooked and his arms get long like an ape's, so that he can scratch his knees without bending over.

For several hours every day the clumps are lifted up the shaft with a winch. In earlier days this work was usually done by women or girls. It was a really murderous job and frequently resulted in premature births or great damage to the child-bearing organs of the women workers. After protracted pressure from the miners, the Bavarian Mining Law finally put an end to this disgraceful women's work. . . .

The clay-mining industry in Bavaria suffered hard times in the 1890s. The mine owners sought to reduce production costs at the expense of the workers, causing great friction.

MY FIRST ACQUAINTANCE WITH THE SOCIAL DEMOCRATS

. . . The attempt to introduce these work rules created bad blood among the miners and stirred them to resistance, which at first found an outlet only in tavern debates.

When the mine owners stood by their plan . . . the miners turned to the priest, so that he might help them fight against this obvious injustice. But instead of standing by them, the priest preached that the employer was an authority appointed by God whom one had to obey. Humble obedience was the greatest virtue of subordinates. There had always been master and servant, and God had given the master the right to command his servant.

The workers could see what the priest was driving at, and they streamed from the church over to the tavern. There they reviled the priest in most unchristian language as one who, in exchange for the gift of a new church window

from a mine owner, would preach patience to the workers instead of instilling humanity and righteousness in the mine owners. . . .

. . . [W]hen I heard with my own ears how the priest unambiguously sided against the workers instead of speaking to the conscience of the mine owners, I was angry and saw the priest above all as a Center party[1] man . . . groveling to the upper classes and ready for any betrayal of the people; leading the people by the nose with religion; and always representing the "heretics" as the only danger. . . .

. . . And how did the priest use his influence? Instead of defending the rights of the oppressed, whose leadership he regarded as his monopoly, he preached submission and patience to the workers. He sat at the table of the rich and accepted the gifts that they had wrung from the poor, instead of reminding them that their actions were hardhearted and unchristian. Instead of saying to the mine owners, "Thou shalt love thy neighbor as thyself," he said to the exploited and raped workers, "You are servants, and servants you must remain; God wills it for your salvation."

A terrible storm raged through me. I doubted everything that up until then I had held as noble and good. . . .

On the last Sunday in April a leaflet was thrown through the open window while we were eating lunch. For a while it went unnoticed. After lunch I picked up the sheet of paper and glanced at the front and back sides, without reading the text. It was labeled, "To the Voters for the Reichstag!" and on the bottom of the back side it said, "The Social Democratic Reichstag Members." Now some life came into me. That was what I was looking for: a program, an authentic pronouncement of Social Democracy!

I began to read. Sentence by sentence there was an indictment against the government and the bourgeois parties, against armaments ex-

---

[1]The Center party, representing the interests of the Catholic Church in Germany, generally followed a socially conservative course.

penditures that had been driven to unbearable heights, against the insanely increasing debt burden of the Empire, against the excess of the new naval appropriations that oppressed the people, and against the plundering of the masses by tariffs and indirect taxes. And there was more: The stagnation of social welfare; the misery and lack of rights of the working class; the prison terms that the Emperor threatened, which would destroy the workers' right to organize! All that made an enormous, totally new impression on me.

Suddenly I saw the world from the other side, from a side that up to now had been dark for me. . . . I was seized by a feeling of wild fury about the obvious injustice of a tax system that spared the ones who could best pay and plundered those who already despaired of life in their bitter misery.

But then I found something new that really gripped me: The Social Democratic leaflet not only criticized, it not only put its finger on the festering wounds and showed that the class character of society was the cause of the wrongs—no, it also produced a series of highly illuminating suggestions for the abolition of these wrongs. Numerous demands for the betterment of the condition of the people were made to the state. And then the leaflet turned to the voters, with a flaming appeal to them to make use of the universal suffrage, the greatest right of a citizen, in order to retaliate in the name of the people against a hostile government and treacherous parties.

He finds the people who had distributed the leaflet.

The leaflet affected me like a revelation. . . .
. . . [T]hey sat down again and for a whole hour they told me about the aspirations of Social Democracy and the growth of the young union movement. How heartily they laughed at the hopes I'd placed in the priest, and how convincingly and plainly they described how above all we workers lacked union organization. A union would bring together the weak uninfluential workers in order to counter the employers with the power of united action.

God, how clear and simple it all was! This new world of thought that gave the worker the weapons of self-awareness and self-consciousness was very different from the old world of priestly and economic authority where the worker was merely an object of domination and exploitation!

Once I'd gotten hold of these bringers of enlightenment I wouldn't let them go; I didn't have to be invited twice to help distribute leaflets in the remaining two villages of the county. With the winged zeal of the newly converted, I leaped from house to house, taking three steps at a time and feeling lighter and happier than ever before in my life. My new friends liked my zeal. When we parted late in the evening, they gave me an "Erfurt Program"[2] and some newspapers, and promised that they would soon send me a package of pamphlets and newspapers. I spent almost the whole night studying the program, and I had the feeling that all these thoughts were etched into my brain with flamed writing.

The next day was the first of May. After a short, feverish sleep I awoke—for the first time as a Social Democrat. This was the day that the new work rules were to go into effect. . . .

On May Day—a holiday recently proclaimed by socialists to demonstrate workers' solidarity and their defiance of capitalism—Osterroth, inciting the workers to skip work, gives a speech.

At first I stammered and got confused when I saw the many curious people hanging on my every word. But soon the joyous shouts of agreement made me overcome all obstacles. I

---

[2]Adopted in 1891, this was the official, Marxist-oriented program for the Social Democratic party.

was amazed at myself, at how fast the new ideas from the article and the leaflet popped, one after another, into my mouth. And they were as new to my audience as to me. I discussed the purpose of our festival; I spoke of how our helplessness and powerlessness had emboldened our enemies, the mine owners, to impose the oppressive measures, the wage cuts, and the work rules, and to curtail our rights. I showed my comrades how impressive our unity was, and how it would help us further if we recognized the misery of our situation and got to know and value the means of improvement. I described how the workers were politically and economically exploited, deprived of their rights, duped, and deceived, and how deliverance from economic and political misery had to come from the working class itself. I described

how the workers had to be unified and could not be allowed to fight among themselves for religious or political reasons. There were only two opposing sides that affected the workers very deeply and they were not "here the Catholics, there the non-Catholics"; rather, they were "here capital, there labor"—"here masters, there slaves"! If we wanted to prevent the deterioration of our working conditions and fight for improvements, then we needed an organization that included all of us; and if we wanted to protest against political injustice and strive for healthier political conditions, then we had to vote for the Social Democratic candidate in the upcoming Reichstag election. Only the Social Democratic party dealt fairly with the workers, for it was the only workers' party that the upper classes fought against.

William Booth
IN DARKEST ENGLAND

The poor were not without compassionate friends. One of them was William Booth (1829–1912), the founder of the Salvation Army. Growing up poor himself, he was apprenticed to a pawnbroker while still a boy. At fifteen, under Methodist influence, he experienced a religious conversion, which eventually turned him into a Methodist minister; his wife and helpmate was one of the first Methodist woman preachers. Settled in London, he combined work at a pawnshop with ministering to the poor in the slums of London's East End. Booth and his wife devoted themselves to rescuing and rehabilitating the homeless, the unemployed, and the sinners of the urban underworld. In 1879 the organization that they had evolved officially became the Salvation Army. William Booth was its general; ordained ministers were its officers; the soldiers were men and women dedicated to saving others from the misery from which they themselves had escaped. All wore the Salvation Army's special uniform. The Salvation Army grew rapidly, spreading over the world. It now serves in seventy-seven countries, with over 300,000 soldiers in the United States.

In 1890 General Booth published *In Darkest England and the Way Out,* describing the misery of the poor and outlining his methods of achieving spiritual salvation through social service. In the opening two chapters, Booth outlined the extent of poverty in England at the height of its imperial glory. He begins by comparing England with journalist-explorer Henry Stanley's description of the brutality, slavery, and disease in "Darkest Africa."

WHY "DARKEST ENGLAND"?

This summer the attention of the civilised world has been arrested by the story which Mr. Stanley has told of "Darkest Africa" and his journeyings across the heart of the Lost Continent. . . .

It is a terrible picture, and one that has engraved itself deep on the heart of civilisation. But while brooding over the awful presentation of life as it exists in the vast African forest, it seemed to me only too vivid a picture of many parts of our own land. As there is a darkest Africa is there not also a darkest England? Civilisation, which can breed its own barbarians, does it not also breed its own pygmies? May we not find a parallel at our own doors, and discover within a stone's throw of our cathedrals and palaces similar horrors to those which Stanley has found existing in the great Equatorial forest?

The more the mind dwells upon the subject, the closer the analogy appears. The [Arab] ivory raiders who brutally traffic in the unfortunate denizens of the forest glades, what are they but the [exploiters] who flourish on the weakness of our poor? . . . As in Africa, it is all trees, trees, trees with no other world conceivable; so is it here—it is all vice and poverty and crime. To many the world is all slum, with the Workhouse as an intermediate purgatory before the grave. . . . Who can battle against the ten thousand million trees? Who can hope to make headway against the innumerable adverse conditions which doom the dweller in Darkest England to eternal and immutable misery?

. . . Talk about Danté's Hell, and all the horrors and cruelties of the torture-chamber of the lost! The man who walks with open eyes and with bleeding heart through the shambles of our civilisation needs no such fantastic images of the poet to teach him horror. Often and often, when I have seen the young and the poor and the helpless go down before my eyes into the morass, trampled underfoot by beasts of prey in human shape that haunt these regions, it seemed as if God were no longer in His world, but that in His stead reigned a fiend, merciless as Hell, ruthless as the grave. Hard it is, no doubt, to read in Stanley's pages of the slave-traders coldly arranging for the surprise of a village, the capture of the inhabitants, the massacre of those who resist, and the violation of all the women; but the stony streets of London, if they could but speak, would tell of tragedies as awful, of ruin as complete, of ravishments as horrible, as if we were in Central Africa; only the ghastly devastation is covered, corpse-like, with the artificialities and hypocrisies of modern civilisation.

The lot of a negress in the Equatorial Forest is not, perhaps, a very happy one, but is it so very much worse than that of many a pretty orphan girl in our Christian capital? . . . A young penniless girl, if she be pretty, is often hunted from pillar to post by her employers, confronted always by the alternative—Starve or Sin. And when once the poor girl has consented to buy the right to earn her living by the sacrifice of her virtue, then she is treated as a slave and an outcast by the very men who have ruined her. . . . [A]nd she is swept downward. . . .

The blood boils with impotent rage at the sight of these enormities, callously inflicted, and silently borne by these miserable victims. Nor is it only women who are the victims, although their fate is the most tragic. Those firms which reduce sweating [hard labor at low wages] to a fine art, who systematically and deliberately defraud the workman of his pay, who grind the faces of the poor, and who rob the widow and the orphan, and who for a pretence make great professions of public-spirit and philanthropy, those men nowadays are sent to Parliament to make laws for the people. The old prophets sent them to Hell—but we have changed all that. They send their victims to Hell, and are rewarded by all that wealth can do to make their lives comfortable. Read the House of Lords' Report on the Sweating System, and ask if any African slave system, making due allowance for the superior civilisation, and therefore sensitiveness, of the victims, reveals more misery.

Darkest England, like Darkest Africa, reeks with malaria. The foul and fetid breath of our slums is almost as poisonous as that of the African swamp. Fever is almost as chronic there as on the Equator. Every year thousands of children are killed off by what is called defects of our sanitary system. They are in reality starved and poisoned, and all that can be said is that, in many cases, it is better for them that they were taken away from the trouble to come.

Just as in Darkest Africa it is only a part of the evil and misery that comes from the superior race who invade the forest to enslave and massacre its miserable inhabitants, so with us, much of the misery of those whose lot we are considering arises from their own habits. Drunkenness and all manner of uncleanness, moral and physical, abound. Have you ever watched by the bedside of a man in delirium tremens [trembling and delusions brought on by alcohol abuse]? Multiply the sufferings of that one drunkard by the hundred thousand, and you have some idea of what scenes are being witnessed in all our great cities at this moment. . . . A population sodden with drink, steeped in vice, eaten up by every social and physical malady, these are the denizens of Darkest England amidst whom my life has been spent, and to whose rescue I would now summon all that is best in the manhood and womanhood of our land. . . .

. . . [T]he grimmest social problems of our time should be sternly faced, not with a view to the generation of profitless emotion, but with a view to its solution. . . .

Relying on the statistics of Charles Booth (no relation), William Booth concluded that three million people, one-tenth of the population, were pauperized and degraded.

THE SUBMERGED TENTH

What, then, is Darkest England? For whom do we claim that "urgency" which gives their case priority over that of all other sections of their countrymen and countrywomen?. . .

. . . The [people] in Darkest England, for whom I appeal, are (1) those who, having no capital or income of their own, would in a month be dead from sheer starvation were they exclusively dependent upon the money earned by their own work; and (2) those who by their utmost exertions are unable to attain the regulation allowance of food which the law prescribes as indispensable even for the worst criminals in our gaols.

I sorrowfully admit that it would be Utopian in our present social arrangements to dream of attaining for every honest Englishman a gaol standard of all the necessaries of life. Some time, perhaps, we may venture to hope that every honest worker on English soil will always be as warmly clad, as healthily housed, and as regularly fed as our criminal convicts—but that is not yet.

Neither is it possible to hope for many years to come that human beings generally will be as well cared for as horses. Mr. Carlyle long ago remarked that the four-footed worker has already got all that this two-handed one is clamouring for. . . .

What, then, is the standard towards which we may venture to aim with some prospect of realisation in our time? It is a very humble one, but if realised it would solve the worst problems of modern Society.

It is the standard of the London Cab Horse. . . .

The first question, then, which confronts us is, what are the dimensions of the Evil? How many of our fellow-men dwell in this Darkest England? How can we take the census of those who have fallen below the Cab Horse standard to which it is our aim to elevate the most wretched of our countrymen?. . .

M. I. Pokrovskaia
WORKING CONDITIONS FOR WOMEN IN RUSSIAN FACTORIES

This report describing how women were treated in Russian factories was written by a Russian woman doctor and published in an English suffragist magazine in 1914.

The matter of fines which are exacted from factory workers by their employers is a very serious one. Fines are imposed for: late arrival, work which is not found to be up to standard, for laughter, even for indisposition. At a certain well-known calendar factory in St. Petersburg the women workers receive 0.45 rbls. [rubles] a day, and the fines have been known to amount to 0.50 rbls. a day. At a weaving factory, also in St. Petersburg, women operatives may earn as much as 1.25 rbls. a day, but owing to deductions for various fines the earnings often sink to as low as 0.25 rbls. a day. If a worker is feeling unwell and sits down, a fine is incurred. . . . If an article is dropped, the fine is [levied and] . . . if the worker fails to "stand to attention" at the entrance of employer or foreman and until he leaves the room, she is fined. . . . At a well-known chocolate factory in Moscow the fine for laughing is 0.75 rbls. and if a worker is 15 minutes late she is dismissed for one week. At another old established and famous chocolate factory in case of sudden illness a woman employee is instantly discharged. In a certain cartridge factory the workers are searched before leaving, and those who persist in having pockets are fined. . . .

In the majority of factories where women are employed the working day is from 10 to 11½ hours, after deducting the dinner and breakfast intervals. On Saturday, in many factories . . . the work sometimes lasts 16 and 18 hours per day. The workers are forced to work overtime on pain of instant dismissal or of transference to inferior employment, and in the case of children actual physical force is used to make them continue in their places. Dining and lunch rooms are rarely provided, and in many places no definite time is allowed for meals. In one well-known factory one hour is allowed for meals, but there is no place where the workers can eat their food except in the work-rooms or in the lavatories.

The position of women workers on the tobacco plantations is the worst. According to a report published by the Sevastopol branch of the Women's Protective Union, young girls are sometimes kept at work during 22 hours in the day. Owing to the difficulties of carrying on the process of breaking the tobacco leaves in the daytime, the girl-workers are driven into the plantations at 4 A.M. where they work until 9 A.M. After that they are engaged in the processes of weighing and tying the packets of tobacco, which work is continued through practically the whole day, with the exception of short intervals for meals. At the same time the women workers are continually exposed to brutal and degrading treatment and assault. Not infrequently their earnings are not paid to them. . . .

It happens sometimes, as on April 25th, 1913, at a cotton spinning factory in St. Petersburg, that the workers strike as a protest against the dismissal of old workers and their replacement by girls between 14 and 16 years of age. The result of the strike was a wholesale dismissal of all the women, whose places were filled by young girls. Not infrequently the women strike on account of the rude treatment which they receive from the foreman, actual bodily ill-treatment not being unknown. Such strikes rarely accomplish anything.

The worst aspect of woman's factory labour is, however, the moral danger to which women are exposed from those in power over them.

Immoral proposals from foremen and from their assistants are of general occurrence, and women who resist are persecuted in every possible way, and sometimes actually violated.

In a large tobacco factory in St. Petersburg the women workers who were asking for raised pay were cynically informed that they could augment their income by prostitution.

All these hard conditions in connection with factory life have the result of driving a certain number of women workers into tolerated houses of prostitution or into the streets. This is directly encouraged by the management of some factories.

REVIEW QUESTIONS

1. Which of Jeanne Bouvier's early experiences would be likely to influence her later work for the rights of workers, especially female workers?
2. Describe the role of the Catholic priest in the discontent of Nikolaus Osterroth and the miners.
3. Describe how the ideas expressed in the Social Democrat pamphlet were seized by Osterroth and transformed his life.
4. What, according to William Booth, were the essential aspects of life in "Darkest England"? Why did he draw the comparison to darkest Africa?
5. Do any of Booth's scathing criticisms apply to contemporary America?
6. What did the working conditions and treatment of women workers indicate about the position of women in Russian working-class society?

3 Prostitution

European countries had traditionally tolerated prostitution, regarding it as an inevitable moral problem. In the mid-nineteenth century it acquired further notoriety as a public health threat, contributing to the spread of venereal disease. Because of the low social status of women, prostitutes, rather than their customers, were blamed for spreading the disease. As a result, existing regulations and medical examinations were strictly enforced as authorities attempted to control what they could not abolish.

In French cities, prostitutes were licensed by the police and had to submit to regular, if superficial, medical examination. In Germany brothels and the prostitutes working in them were licensed by the police or city authorities. Solicitation on the streets was illegal in some areas, but widespread generally.

England ignored the large numbers of prostitutes in its growing industrial cities until the increasing danger of venereal disease forced the passage of the Contagious Diseases Acts in the 1860s. These acts permitted the police to arrest women on suspicion of prostitution; the burden was on the women to prove their innocence. Enforcement was so harsh and unjust that a public campaign succeeded in abolishing the acts late in the century.

In the second half of the nineteenth century, following several path-breaking studies of prostitution, a more sympathetic attitude became apparent. The plight of prostitutes inspired novelists and social reformers alike. It was recognized that the poverty of lower-class women, rather than loose morals, was the chief incentive for women to turn to prostitution.

Henry Mayhew
PROSTITUTION IN VICTORIAN LONDON

The destitute poor often turned to crime and prostitution for survival. In *London Labour and the London Poor,* published in 1862, Henry Mayhew (1812–1887), who had cultivated friendly contacts with London street people, including criminals and prostitutes, reported his findings with compassionate detachment. Practicing sociology with a human face, Mayhew pioneered oral history in hundreds of case studies. He hoped "to give the rich a more intimate knowledge of the sufferings and frequent heroism under those sufferings, of the poor—that it may . . . cause those who are in 'high places' and those of whom much is expected, to bestir themselves to improve the condition of a class of people whose misery, ignorance, and vice, amidst all the immense wealth and great knowledge of 'the first city in the world' is . . . a national disgrace. . . ." Below Mayhew records a young London prostitute's account of her squalid life.

STATEMENT OF A PROSTITUTE

The narrative which follows—that of a prostitute, sleeping in the low-lodging houses, where boys and girls are all huddled promiscuously together, discloses a system of depravity, atrocity, and enormity, which certainly cannot be paralleled in any nation, however barbarous, nor in any age, however "dark." The facts detailed, it will be seen, are gross enough to make us all blush for the land in which such scenes can be daily perpetrated. The circumstances, which it is impossible to publish, are of the most loathsome and revolting nature.

A good-looking girl of sixteen gave me the following awful statement:—

"I am an orphan. When I was ten I was sent to service as maid of all-work, in a small tradesman's family. It was a hard place, and my mistress used me very cruelly, beating me often. When I had been in place three weeks, my mother died; my father having died . . . years before. I stood my mistress's ill-treatment for about six months. She beat me with sticks as well as with her hands. I was black and blue, and at last I ran away. I got to Mrs. ———, a low lodging-house. I didn't know before that there was such a place. I heard of it from some girls at the Glasshouse (baths and washhouses), where I went for shelter. I went with them to

have a halfpenny worth of coffee, and they took me to the lodging-house. I then had three shillings, and stayed about a month, and did nothing wrong, living on the three shillings and what I pawned my clothes for, as I got some pretty good things away with me. In the lodging-house I saw nothing but what was bad, and heard nothing but what was bad. I was laughed at, and was told to swear. They said, 'Look at her for a d——— modest fool'—sometimes worse than that, until by degrees I got to be as bad as they were. During this time I used to see boys and girls from ten and twelve years old sleeping together, but understood nothing wrong. I had never heard of such places before I ran away. I can neither read nor write. My mother was a good woman, and I wish I'd had her to run away to. I saw things between almost children that I can't describe to you—very often I saw them, and that shocked me. At the month's end, when I was beat out, I met with a young man of fifteen—I myself was going on to twelve years old—and he persuaded me to take up with him. I stayed with him three months in the same lodging-house, living with him as his wife, though we were mere children, and being true to him. At the three months' end he was taken up for picking pockets, and got six months. I was sorry, for he was kind to me; though I was made ill through him; so I broke some windows in St. Paul's-churchyard to get into prison to get cured. I had a month in the Compter [debtors' prison], and came out well. I was scolded very much in the Compter, on account of the state I was in, being so young. I had 2s. 6d. [two shillings and sixpence] given to me when I came out, and was forced to go into the streets for a living. I continued walking the streets for three years, sometimes making a good deal of money, sometimes none, feasting one day and starving the next. The bigger girls could persuade me to do anything they liked with my money. I was never happy all the time, but I could get no character and could not get out of the life. I lodged all this time at a lodging-house in Kent-street. They were all thieves and bad girls. I have known between three and four dozen boys and girls sleep in one room. The beds were horrid filthy and full of vermin. There was very wicked carryings on. The boys, if any difference, was the worst. We lay packed on a full night, a dozen boys and girls squeedged into one bed. That was very often the case—some at the foot and some at the top—boys and girls all mixed. I can't go into all the particulars, but whatever could take place in words or acts between boys and girls did take place, and in the midst of the others. I am sorry to say I took part in these bad ways myself, but I wasn't so bad as some of the others. There was only a candle burning all night, but in summer it was light great part of the night. Some boys and girls slept without any clothes, and would dance about the room that way. I have seen them, and, wicked as I was, felt ashamed. I have seen two dozen capering about the room that way; some mere children, the boys generally the youngest. . . .

There were no men or women present. There were often fights. The deputy never interfered. This is carried on just the same as ever to this day, and is the same every night. I have heard young girls shout out to one another how often they had been obliged to go to the hospital, or the infirmary, or the workhouse. There was a great deal of boasting about what the boys and girls had stolen during the day. I have known boys and girls change their 'partners,' just for a night. At three years' end I stole a piece of beef from a butcher. I did it to get into prison. I was sick of the life I was leading, and didn't know how to get out of it. I had a month for stealing. When I got out I passed two days and a night in the streets doing nothing wrong, and then went and threatened to break Messrs. ———— windows again. I did that to get into prison again; for when I lay quiet of a night in prison I thought things over, and considered what a shocking life I was leading, and how my health might be ruined completely, and I thought I would stick to prison rather than go back to such a life. I got six months for threatening. When I got out I broke a lamp next morning for the same purpose, and had a fortnight. That was the last time I was in prison. I have since been leading the same life as I told you of for the three years, and lodging at the same houses, and seeing the same goings on. I hate such a life now more than ever. I am willing to do any work that I can in washing and cleaning. I can do a little at my needle. I could do hard work, for I have good health. I used to wash and clean in prison, and always behaved myself there. At the house where I am it is 3d. a night; but at Mrs. ————'s it is 1d. and 2d. a night, and just the same goings on. Many a girl—nearly all of them—goes out into the streets from this penny and twopenny house, to get money for their favourite boys by prostitution. If the girl cannot get money she must steal something, or will be beaten by her 'chap' when she comes home. I have seen them beaten, often kicked and beaten until they were blind from bloodshot, and their teeth knocked out with kicks from boots as the girl lays on the ground. The boys, in their turn, are out thieving all day, and the lodging-house keeper will buy any stolen provisions of them, and sell them to the lodgers. I never saw the police in the house. If a boy comes to the house on a night without money or sawney [stolen cheese or bacon], or something to sell to the lodgers, a handkerchief or something of that kind, he is not admitted, but told very plainly, 'Go thieve it, then,' Girls are treated just the same. Any body may call in the daytime at this house and have a halfpenny worth of coffee and sit any length of time until evening. I have seen three dozen sitting there that way, all thieves and bad girls. There are no chairs, and only one form [bench] in front of the fire, on which a dozen can sit. The others sit on the floor all about the room, as near the fire as they can. Bad language goes on during the day, as I have told you it did during the night, and indecencies too, but nothing like so bad as at night. They talk about where there is good places to go and thieve. The missioners call sometimes, but they're laughed at often when they're talking, and always before the door's closed on them. If a decent girl goes there to get a ha'porth of coffee, seeing the board over the door, she is always shocked. Many a poor girl has been ruined in this house since I was, and boys have boasted about it. I never knew boy or girl do good, once get used there. Get used there, indeed, and you are life-ruined. I was an only child, and haven't a friend in the world. I have heard several girls say how they would like to get out of the life, and out of the place. From those I know, I think the cruel parents and mistresses cause many to be driven there. One lodging-house keeper, Mrs. ———, goes out dressed respectable, and pawns any stolen property, or sells it at public-houses."

Guy de Maupassant
THE ODYSSEY OF A PROSTITUTE

French social studies in the nineteenth century have no equivalent to Mayhew's investigations. The voices of French prostitutes are not heard, nor are there personal accounts written by the women themselves. For this reason, one has to turn to literature. The following extract is from a short story by Guy de Maupassant (1850–1893), written during the 1880s. It could be a composite portrait of several young girls who had related to de Maupassant the tales of their inevitable descent into misery.

. . . It was after midnight. I was going from the Vaudeville to the Rue Drouot, hurrying along the boulevard through a crowd of hurrying umbrellas. A fine rain was hovering in the air rather than falling, veiling the gas jets, spreading a gloom over the street. The gleaming pavement was sticky rather than damp. Anxious to get home, the passers-by looked neither to right nor left.

The prostitutes, with skirts held up showing their legs, and revealing a white stocking to the wan gleams of evening light, were waiting in the shadow of doorways, speaking to the passers-by or hurrying brazenly past them, thrusting a stupid incomprehensible phrase at them as they passed. They followed a man for a few seconds, jostling against him, breathing their putrid breath in his face; then, seeing the futility of their appeals, they abandoned him with a sudden angry movement and took up their promenade again, jerking their hips as they walked.

I went on my way, spoken to by them all, seized by the arm, irritated, revolted and disgusted. Suddenly I saw three of them running as if they were terrified, flinging a quick phrase to the others as they ran. And the others began to run too, an open flight, bunching their clothes together so that they could run the faster. They were making a round-up of prostitutes that night.

Suddenly I felt an arm under mine, while a terrified voice murmured in my ear: "Save me, sir, save me, don't leave me."

I looked at the girl. She was not yet twenty, although already fading. "Stay with me," I said to her. "Oh, thank you," she murmured.

We reached the line of police. It opened to let me pass. . . .

I felt a sudden interest in this abandoned creature.

"Won't you tell me about yourself?" I asked her.

She told me.

"I was sixteen years old, I was in service at Yvetot, with M. Lerable, a seedsman. My parents were dead. I had no one; I knew quite well that my master looked at me strangely and tickled my cheeks; but I didn't think about it much. I knew a few things, of course. You get pretty shrewd in the country; but M. Lerable was a pious old thing who went to Mass every Sunday. I would never have believed him capable of it.

"Then one day he wanted to make up to me in my kitchen. I resisted him. He went off.

"There was a grocer opposite us, M. Dutan, who had a very agreeable assistant; so agreeable that I let him get round me. That happens to everybody, doesn't it? So I used to leave the door open in the evenings, and he used to come and see me.

"And then one night M. Lerable heard a noise. He came upstairs and found Antoine and tried to kill him. They fought with chairs and the water jug and everything. I had seized my bit of clothes and I rushed into the street. Off I went.

"I was frightened, scared stiff. I got dressed under a doorway. Then I began to walk straight on. I was sure there had been someone killed and that the police were looking for me already. I reached the high road to Rouen. I thought to myself that at Rouen I could hide myself quite safely.

"It was too dark to see the ditches and I heard dogs barking in the farms. You don't know what you hear at night. Birds screaming like a man who's having this throat cut, beasts that yelp and beasts that wheeze, and all sorts of things that you don't understand. I went all over goose-flesh. I crossed myself at every sound. You've no idea what it is that's scaring you so. When it grew light, I thought of the police again and began to run. Then I calmed down.

"I felt hungry too, in spite of my anxiety; but I hadn't anything, not a ha'penny. I'd forgotten my money, everything belonging to me in the world, eighteen francs.

"So I had to walk with a complaining stomach. It was warm. The sun scorched me. Noon passed. I went on walking.

"Suddenly I heard horses behind me. I turned round. The police! My blood ran cold; I thought I should fall; but I kept myself up. They caught up to me. They looked at me. One of them, the older, said:

"'Good afternoon, miss.'

"'Good afternoon, sir.'

"'Where are you off like this?'

"'I'm going to Rouen, to service in a situation I've been offered.'

"'Like this, on your two feet?'

"'Yes, like this.'

"My heart was beating so that I could hardly speak. I was saying to myself: 'They'll take me.' And my legs itched to run. But they would have caught me up in a minute, you see.

"The old one began again:

"'We'll jog along together as far as Barantin, miss, since we're all going the same way.'

"'Gladly, sir.'

"So we fell to talking. I made myself as agreeable as I knew how, you may be sure, so agreeable that they thought things that weren't true. And then, as I was walking through a wood, the old one said:

"'What do you say if we go and lie down a bit on the moss?'

"I answered without stopping to think:

"'Yes, if you like.'

"Then he dismounted, gave his horse to the other, and off we both went into the wood.

"There was no chance of saying no. What would you have done in my place? He took what he wanted; then he said: 'We mustn't forget the other fellow.' And he went back to hold the horses, while the other one rejoined me. I was so ashamed of it that I could have cried. But I daren't resist, you see.

"So we went on again. I had nothing more to say. I was too sad at heart. And then I was so hungry I couldn't walk any further. All the same, they offered me a glass of wine in a village, and that heartened me up for a while. And then they set off at a trot, so as not to go through Barantin in my company. Then I sat down in the ditch and cried till I couldn't cry any more.

"I was three hours longer walking to Rouen. It was seven o'clock in the evening when I arrived. At first I was dazzled by all the lights. And then I didn't know where to sit down. On the roads there's ditches and grass where you can even lie down to sleep. But in towns there's nothing.

"My legs were giving way under me, and I had such fits of giddiness I thought I was going to fall. And then it began to rain, small fine rain, like this evening, that soaks through you without your noticing it. I have no luck on rainy days. Well, I began to walk in the streets. I stared at all the houses, and said to myself: 'All those beds and all that bread in those houses, and I couldn't find even a crust and a mattress.' I went along the streets, where there were women speaking to passing men. In times like those you do what you can. I started to speak to everyone, as they were doing. But no one answered me. I wished I was dead. I went on like that till midnight. I didn't even know what I was doing now. At last, a man listens to me. 'Where do you live?' he asks. Necessity makes you sharp. I answered: 'I can't take you home, because I live with mamma. But aren't there houses where we can go?'

"'It's not often I spend a franc on a room,' he answered.

"Then he reflected and added: 'Come on. I know a quiet spot where we shan't be interrupted.'

"He took me over a bridge and then he led me to the end of the town, in a meadow near the river. I couldn't follow him any farther.

"He made me sit down, and then he began to busy himself with what we'd come for. But he was so long about his business that I was overcome with weariness and fell asleep.

"He went away without giving me anything. I didn't hardly notice it. It was raining, as I told you. Ever since that day I've had pains I can't get rid of, because I slept in the mud all the night.

"I was wakened by two cops, who took me to the police station and then, from there, to prison, where I stayed a week while they tried to find out what I could be or where I came from. I wouldn't say anything for fear of consequences.

"They found out, however, and they let me go, after pronouncing me not guilty.

"I had to begin looking for work again. I tried to get a place, but I couldn't, because of coming out of prison.

"Then I remembered an old judge who had rolled his eyes at me when he was trying me, just like old Lerable at Yvetot did. And I went to see him. I wasn't mistaken. He gave me five francs when I came away, and said: 'You shall have the same every time, but don't come oftener than twice a week.'

"I understood that all right, seeing his age. But that gave me an idea. I said to myself: 'Young men are all right for a bit of fun, and they're jolly and all that, but there's no fat living to be got there, while with old men it's another thing.' . . .

"But there. One's not left in peace long. Ill luck had it that I got to know a wealthy old devil in society. A former president, who was at least seventy-five years old.

"One evening he took me to dine in a restaurant in the suburbs. And then, you see, he hadn't the sense to go carefully. He died during the dessert.

"I got three months in prison, because I wasn't registered.

"It was then I came to Paris.

"Oh, it's a hard life here, sir. You don't eat every day. There's too many of us. Ah, well, so much the worse, everyone has their own troubles, haven't they?"

She was silent. I was walking beside her, sick at heart. Suddenly she began to talk familiarly again.

"So you're not coming home with me, dearie?"

"No. I told you so before."

"Well, good-bye, thanks all the same, and no offence taken. But I'm sure you're making a mistake."

And she went off, losing herself in the fine rain. I saw her passing under a gas jet, and then disappear in the shadows. Poor wretch!

William W. Sanger
PROSTITUTION IN HAMBURG

In the 1850s William Sanger carried out a worldwide investigation into prostitution at the request of the New York Board of Alms-Houses Governors. The resulting influential study was published in 1858.

Sanger found that the control of prostitutes varied from city to city. In Hamburg, a large port city in northern Germany, prostitution had been subject to legal oversight since the thirteenth century, but systematic control had been enforced only in 1807, following an influx of French immigrants after the French Revolution. In some parts of the city, prostitution was confined to brothels registered with the police. Sanger refers to the prostitutes in brothels as "public women," and to the other prostitutes operating, sometimes illegally, on the streets as "private women."

The selection starts with arguments made by a local writer in favor of legalized brothels, and then gives an account of the prostitutes' lives.

[Because] legislation on prostitution in Hamburg [is] based upon the principle that "prostitution is a necessary evil, and, as such, must be endured under strict supervision of the authorities," it seems an appropriate place to copy the following remarks of an eminent local writer:

That brothels are an evil no one can deny; still, the arguments against the sufferance of brothels are, except as to that incontestable truth, no answer to the 'necessity,' which is the very *gist* of the thing, and which necessity is based on the uncontrollable nature of sexual intercourse, and on the circumstances of our social condition.

The sufferance of brothels is necessary,

1. For the repression of profligacy, of private prostitution as well as of its kindred crimes, adultery, rape, abortion, infanticide, and all kinds of illicit gratification of sexual passion. The latter cases occur very rarely with us. Of Paederasty or Sodomy we find but few instances; and of that unnatural intercourse of

women with each other . . . common among the Parisian girls, we find no trace.

The sufferance of brothels operates to the suppression of private prostitution, in so far as brothel-keepers and the 'inscribed' [registered] women are, for their own interest, opposed to it, and are serviceable to the police in its detection. Unquestionably, private prostitution is an incalculably greater evil than public vice.

2. On grounds of public policy in regard to health. It is quite erroneous to suppose that these legalized brothels contribute to the spread of syphilitic maladies. This should rather be imputed to the private prostitution which would ensue on the breaking up of the brothels, and from which that medical police supervision that now limits the spread of infection would, of course, be withdrawn. The experience of all time proves that, by means of secret prostitution, the intensity and virulence of venereal disorders have been aggravated, to the multiplication of those appalling examples

familiar to every medical reader, and which cause one to shudder with horror; while numerically, disease and its consequences have been carried into every class of society. It is precisely our knowledge of these very facts which has induced the sufferance, or, rather, the regulation of these brothels.

3. *Suppression is* ABSOLUTELY IMPRACTICABLE, inasmuch as the evil is rooted in an unconquerable physical requirement. It would seem as if the zeal against public brothels implied that by their extinction a limitation of sexual intercourse, except in marriage, would be effected. This is erroneous, for reliable details prove that for every hundred brothel women there would be two hundred private prostitutes, and no human power could prevent this. In a great city and frequented sea-port like Hamburg, the hope of amending this would be purely chimerical.

Thus much for Hamburg legislation, and the sound arguments in its favor. We will now give some facts illustrative of the vice as it exists at the present time, using a pamphlet by Dr. Lippert, entitled *Prostitution in Hamburg, 1848.* . . .

The public women are under the special control and supervision of a police authority charged with this duty. Without his express cognizance and permission they can not be registered, or "written in," nor can they have liberty to change their residence, or to be "written out." This officer is the collector of the impost [tax] upon them and upon the brothel-keeper, which is paid over to the fund. We can not give the detailed application of this money, but, in general terms, it does not swell the revenues of the city, and, to avoid public scandal, is applied exclusively to the police and medical services required by the class. . . .

. . . In most cases of the registered women residing in brothels, the keeper supplies the clothes, and very often charges extravagant prices for them. Extortionate demands in this respect are a fruitful source of complaints to the police, who moderate the bills with no very tender sympathy for the creditor. . . .

The food of the house-women is good and plentiful, varying according to the rate of the brothel in which they live. . . . Drunkenness is comparatively rare among the better class, partly owing to the care of the keeper, but more from dread of the police supervision and consequent punishment.

In their intellectual capacity there is nothing to distinguish the prostitutes in Hamburg. Few can read, and fewer still can write. Those who can read seek their amusement in the old romances of the circulating libraries. . . .

Their ordinary routine of life is one of useless idleness. They rise about ten and take breakfast, of which coffee is the staple. The morning is loitered away in dressing, reading novels, playing cards or dominoes, and kindred occupations. In some of the lower-class houses they dispel their *ennui* by assisting in domestic work, but this is a matter of favor which they are careful shall not become an obligation. By the middle of the day they are ready for dinner. In the afternoon they add the finishing touches to their dress, and wait the arrival of visitors. Some resort to the public lounges or dancing saloons to form or cultivate acquaintances, but the aristocracy of the order hold it more becoming to their dignity to stay at home and wait for their "friends."

In that fine and peculiar quality of modesty, which adds the crowning grace to woman's charms, even the prostitute is not wholly deficient. Some trace of the angel attribute is visible, but mostly in the private women, where a regard for the decent proprieties of life yet lingers amid the wreck of character, and to such it frequently forms the chief attraction.

Religion has an influence over some, strangely at variance with its dictates as are their lives, but a large majority are entirely destitute of any such sentiment. Occasionally, Biblical pictures may be seen in the rooms of brothels, but merely as ornaments, for they are neutralized by the contiguity of others more consonant with the place.

In their relations to the male sex there are differences between women residing in public brothels and those living privately, whether registered or unregistered. Partly from inclination, but mainly from policy on the part of the keeper, the former seldom own allegiance to any particular lover. It is true that any one who is able and willing to pay liberally can come and go as he pleases, provided he does not interfere with the girl's "business" [with other clients]. Not so with the private women, who frequently have particular "lovers" [pimps] to whom they show much kindness, although from them they often receive but little sympathy or protection, many of these men not scrupling to exist entirely upon the earnings of a woman whom they would publicly insult if they met her away from home.

. . . Among those who live alone warm friendships are not uncommon; much timely assistance is afforded in times of sickness or want; good offices are reciprocated; and it sometimes happens, in the delicate matter of their visitors, that a man who has been in the habit of favoring one woman will not find his attentions welcomed by others.

Their crimes and offenses include the ordinary category, but it is asserted that theft is less common in Hamburg than elsewhere, and, when it does take place, it is more frequently committed by the irregular members of the body than by the duly registered women. It will be perceived that the system of registration offers too many facilities for detection, a fact to which the unusual honesty must doubtless be ascribed. Personal quarrels and assaults, or drunkenness among the older members, consign them to the House of Detention or House of Correction. . . .

The licensed brothels are supplied with inmates by females whose services are recognized by the authorities. In case of any emergency, the keeper applies to one of the procuresses, and if the girl she offers suits him, the candidate is first subjected to a medical examination. Passed safely through this ordeal, she is taken to the police office and "written in" to her new keeper, who is bound to discharge certain of her debts, as the amount due his predecessor, for instance. If the medical officers report her sick, she is sent to the infirmary if she belong to Hamburg, but if a foreigner is dispatched out of the city forthwith. In cases where a woman thus applying to the authorities has not previously lived as a prostitute, she is usually exhorted by the magistrate to abandon her intention and return to the paths of virtue, a routine piece of benevolence which is usually fruitless. The ordinary police fee for registration is two marks, the physician's fee is one mark, and the agent's usual remuneration four marks.

The registered women are thus kept strictly under the eye of the police, and, whenever they are disposed to quit their wretched life, have the special protection of that body. The keepers naturally throw all possible obstacles in the way of such a determination, especially if a girl is much in debt; but, by some means, whenever a woman is under any restraint, and is consequently unable to apply personally to the police, an anonymous note finds its way to the office, and speedily effects the desired object. The authorities do not sympathize in any way with the brothel-keepers, but use all their energies to serve the women whenever any occasion offers.

REVIEW QUESTIONS

1. How does the London prostitute's account of her life confirm the view that poverty was the underlying cause of prostitution? What circumstances prevented her from leaving the profession?
2. How might Mayhew's interviews with lower-class Londoners have helped to bring about social reform?
3. What experiences did the servant girl in de Maupassant's story have with authority figures such as police officers and judges?
4. What arguments were advanced in defense of legalized prostitution in Hamburg? Do you think that legalizing prostitution can actually limit its evils? What are the arguments against it?

4 Feminism and Antifeminism

Inspired by the ideals of equality voiced in the Enlightenment and the French Revolution, women in nineteenth-century Europe and the United States began to demand equal rights, foremost the right to vote. In the United States, the women's suffrage movement held its first convention in 1848 in Seneca Falls, New York. The women adopted a Declaration of Principles that said in part: "We hold these truths to be self-evident: that all men and women are created equal." The struggle for equal rights and voting privileges continued, and by the end of the century, women were voting in a few state elections. Finally, in 1920, the Nineteenth Amendment gave women voting privileges throughout the United States.

In England, having failed to persuade Parliament in the mid-1860s to give them the vote, women organized reform societies, drew up petitions, and protested unfair treatment. The Women's Social and Political Union (WSPU), organized by Emmeline Pankhurst, employed militant tactics, which increased the hostility of their opponents.

During World War I, women worked in offices, factories, and service industries at jobs formerly held by men. Their wartime service made it clear that women played an essential role in the economic life of nations, and many political leaders argued for the extension of the vote to them. In 1918, British women over the age of thirty gained the vote, and in 1928, Parliament lowered the voting age for British women to twenty-one, the same as for men.

The first countries to permit women to vote were New Zealand in 1893 and Australia in 1902. In Europe, women were granted voting rights by stages, first for municipal elections, later for national ones. Finland extended voting rights to women in 1906; the other Scandinavian countries followed suit, but the majority of European countries did not allow women to vote until after World War I.

In their struggle for equal rights, women faced strong opposition. Opponents argued that feminist demands would threaten society by undermining marriage and the family. Thus in 1870, a member of the British House of Commons wondered "what would become, not merely of women's influence, but of her duties at home, her care of the household, her supervision of all those duties and surroundings which make a happy home . . . if we are to see women coming forward and taking part in the government of the country." This concern for the family was combined with a traditional biased view of woman's nature, as one writer for the *Saturday Review,* an English periodical, revealed:

> The power of reasoning is so small in women that they need adventitious help, and if they have not the guidance and check of a religious conscience, it is useless to expect from them self-control on abstract principles. They do not calculate consequences, and they are reckless when they once give way, hence they are to be kept straight only through their affections, the religious sentiment and a well educated moral sense.

John Stuart Mill
THE SUBJECTION OF WOMEN

John Stuart Mill (see page 127), a British philosopher and a liberal, championed women's rights. His interest in the subject was awakened by Harriet Taylor, a long-time friend and an ardent feminist, whom he married in 1851. Mill and Taylor had an intense intellectual companionship both before and after their marriage, and Taylor helped shape his ideas on the position of women in society and the urgent need for reform. In 1867, Mill, as a member of Parliament, proposed that the suffrage be extended to women (the proposal was rejected by a vote of 194 to 74). In *The Subjection of Women* (1869), Mill argued that male dominance of women constituted a flagrant abuse of power. He maintained that female inequality, "a single relic of an old world of thought and practice exploded in everything else," violated the principle of individual rights and hindered the progress of humanity. Excerpts from Mill's classic in the history of feminism follow.

The object of this Essay is to explain, as clearly as I am able, the grounds of an opinion which I have held from the very earliest period when I had formed any opinions at all on social or political matters, and which, instead of being weakened or modified, has been constantly growing stronger by the progress of reflection and the experience of life: That the principle which regulates the existing social relations between the two sexes—the legal subordination of one sex to the other—is wrong in itself, and now one of the chief hindrances to human improvement; and that it ought to be replaced by a principle of perfect equality, admitting no power or privilege on the one side, nor disability on the other. . . .

. . . The adoption of this system of inequality never was the result of deliberation, or forethought, or any social ideas, or any notion whatever of what conduced to the benefit of humanity or the good order of society. It arose simply from the fact that from the very earliest twilight of human society, every woman (owing to the value attached to her by men, combined with her inferiority in muscular strength) was found in a state of bondage to some man. . . .

But, it will be said, the rule of men over women differs from all these others in not be-ing a rule of force: it is accepted voluntarily; women make no complaint, and are consenting parties to it. In the first place, a great number of women do not accept it. Ever since there have been women able to make their sentiments known by their writings (the only mode of publicity which society permits to them), an increasing number of them have recorded protests against their present social condition: and recently many thousands of them, headed by the most eminent women known to the public, have petitioned Parliament for their admission to the parliamentary suffrage. The claim of women to be educated as solidly, and in the same branches of knowledge, as men, is urged with growing intensity, and with a great prospect of success; while the demand for their admission into professions and occupations hitherto closed against them becomes every year more urgent. Though there are not in this country, as there are in the United States, periodical Conventions and an organized party to agitate for the Rights of Women, there is a numerous and active Society organized and managed by women, for the more limited object of obtaining the political franchise. Nor is it only in our own country and in America that women are beginning to protest, more or less collectively, against the disabilities under which they labour. France, and Italy, and Switzerland, and Russia now afford examples of the same thing. How many more women there are who silently cherish similar aspirations, no one can possibly know; but there are abundant tokens how many *would* cherish them, were they not so strenuously taught to repress them as contrary to the proprieties of their sex. . . .

Men do not want solely the obedience of women, they want their sentiments. All men, except the most brutish, desire to have, in the woman most nearly connected with them, not a forced slave but a willing one; not a slave merely, but a favourite. They have therefore put everything in practice to enslave their minds. The masters of all other slaves rely, for maintaining obedience, on fear; either fear of themselves, or religious fears. The masters of women wanted more than simple obedience, and they turned the whole force of education to effect their purpose. All women are brought up from the very earliest years in the belief that their ideal of character is the very opposite to that of men; not self-will, and government by self-control, but submission, and yielding to the control of others. All the moralities tell them that it is the duty of women, and all the current sentimentalities that it is their nature, to live for others; to make complete abnegation of themselves, and to have no life but in their affections. And by their affections are meant the only ones they are allowed to have—those to the men with whom they are connected, or to the children who constitute an additional and indefeasible tie between them and a man. When we put together three things—first, the natural attraction between opposite sexes; secondly, the wife's entire dependence on the husband, every privilege or pleasure she has being either his gift, or depending entirely on his will; and lastly, that the principal object of human pursuit, consideration, and all objects of social ambition, can in general be sought or obtained by her only through him—it would be a miracle if the object of being attractive to

men had not become the polar star of feminine education and formation of character. And, this great means of influence over the minds of women having been acquired, an instinct of selfishness made men avail themselves of it to the utmost as a means of holding women in subjection, by representing to them meekness, submissiveness, and resignation of all individual will into the hands of a man, as an essential part of sexual attractiveness. Can it be doubted that any of the other yokes which mankind have succeeded in breaking would have subsisted till now if the same means had existed, and had been as sedulously [diligently] used to bow down their minds to it?

Mill argues that women should be able to participate in political life and should not be barred from entering the professions.

On the other point which is involved in the just equality of women, their admissibility to all the functions and occupations hitherto retained as the monopoly of the stronger sex. . . . I believe that their disabilities [in occupation and civil life] elsewhere are only clung to in order to maintain their subordination in domestic life; because the generality of the male sex cannot yet tolerate the idea of living with an equal. Were it not for that, I think that almost every one, in the existing state of opinion in politics and political economy, would admit the injustice of excluding half the human race from the greater number of lucrative occupations, and from almost all high social functions; ordaining from their birth either that they are not, and cannot by any possibility become, fit for employments which are legally open to the stupidest and basest of the other sex, or else that however fit they may be, those employments shall be interdicted to them, in order to be preserved for the exclusive benefit of males. . . .

It will perhaps be sufficient if I confine myself, in the details of my argument, to functions of a public nature: since, if I am successful as to those, it probably will be readily granted that women should be admissible to all other occupations. . . . And here let me begin . . . [with] the suffrage, both parliamentary and municipal. . . .

. . . To have a voice in choosing those by whom one is to be governed, is a means of self-protection due to every one, though he were to remain for ever excluded from the function of governing. . . . Under whatever conditions, and within whatever limits, men are admitted to the suffrage, there is not a shadow of justification for not admitting women under the same. The majority of the women of any class are not likely to differ in political opinion from the majority of the men of the same class, unless the question be one in which the interests of women, as such, are in some way involved; and if they are so, women require the suffrage, as their guarantee of just and equal consideration. . . .

With regard to the fitness of women, not only to participate in elections, but themselves to hold offices or practise professions involving important public responsibilities; I have already observed that this consideration is not essential to the practical question in dispute: since any woman, who succeeds in an open profession, proves by that very fact that she is qualified for it. And in the case of public offices, if the political system of the country is such as to exclude unfit men, it will equally exclude unfit women: while if it is not, there is no additional evil in the fact that the unfit persons whom it admits may be either women or men. . . .

. . . There is no country of Europe in which the ablest men have not frequently experienced, and keenly appreciated, the value of the advice and help of clever and experienced women of the world, in the attainment both of private and of public objects; and there are important matters of public administration to which few men are equally competent with such women; among others, the detailed control of expenditure. But what we are now discussing is not the need which society has of the services of women in public business, but the dull and hopeless life to which it so often condemns them, by forbidding them to exercise the practical abilities which many of them are conscious of, in any wider field than one which to some of them never was, and to others is no longer, open. If there is anything vitally important to the happiness of human beings, it is that they should relish their habitual pursuit [that is, they should be happy in their work]. This requisite of an enjoyable life is very imperfectly granted, or altogether denied, to a large part of mankind; and by its absence many a life is a failure, which is provided, in appearance, with every requisite of success.

Emmeline Pankhurst
WHY WE ARE MILITANT

Agitation in Great Britain for woman suffrage reached a peak during the turbulent years of parliamentary reform, 1909–1911. Under the leadership of Emmeline Pankhurst (1858–1928) and her daughter Christabel, women engaged in demonstrations, disrupted political meetings, and when dragged off to jail, resorted to passive resistance and hunger strikes. Some hunger strikers were subjected to the cruelty of force feeding. In 1913 Emmeline Pankhurst carried her appeal to the United States, where she delivered the speech printed below.

I know that in your minds there are questions like these; you are saying, "Woman Suffrage is sure to come; the emancipation of humanity is an evolutionary process, and how is it that some women, instead of trusting to that evolution, instead of educating the masses of people of their country, instead of educating their own sex to prepare them for citizenship, how is it that these militant women are using violence and upsetting the business arrangements of the country in their undue impatience to attain their end?"

Let me try to explain to you the situation. . . .

The extensions of the franchise to the men of my country have been preceded by very great violence, by something like a revolution, by something like civil war. In 1832, you know we were on the edge of a civil war and on the edge of revolution, and it was at the point of the sword—no, not at the point of the sword—it was after the practice of arson on so large a scale that half the city of Bristol was burned down in a single night, it was because more and greater violence and arson were feared that the Reform Bill of 1832 [which gave the vote to the middle class] was allowed to pass into law. In 1867, . . . rioting went on all over the country, and as the result of that rioting, as the result of that unrest, . . . as a result of the fear of more rioting and violence the Reform Act of 1867 [which gave workers the vote] was put upon the statute books.

In 1884 . . . rioting was threatened and feared, and so the agricultural labourers got the vote.

Meanwhile, during the '80's, women, like men, were asking for the franchise. Appeals, larger and more numerous than for any other reform, were presented in support of Woman's Suffrage. Meetings of the great corporations [group of principal officials in a town or city government], great town councils, and city councils, passed resolutions asking that women should have the vote. More meetings were held, and larger, for Woman Suffrage than were held for votes for men, and yet the women did not get it. Men got the vote because they were and would

be violent. The women did not get it because they were constitutional and law-abiding. . . .

I believed, as many women still in England believe, that women could get their way in some mysterious manner, by purely peaceful methods. We have been so accustomed, we women, to accept one standard for men and another standard for women, that we have even applied that variation of standard to the injury of our political welfare.

Having had better opportunities of education, and having had some training in politics, having in political life come so near to the "superior" being as to see that he was not altogether such a fount of wisdom as they had supposed, that he had his human weaknesses as we had, the twentieth century women began to say to themselves, "Is it not time, since our methods have failed and the men's have succeeded, that we should take a leaf out of their political book?". . .

Well, we in Great Britain, on the eve of the General Election of 1905, a mere handful of us—why, you could almost count us on the fingers of both hands—set out on the wonderful adventure of forcing the strongest Government of modern times to give the women the vote. . . .

The Suffrage movement was almost dead. The women had lost heart. You could not get a Suffrage meeting that was attended by members of the general public. . . .

Two women changed that in a twinkling of an eye at a great Liberal demonstration in Manchester, where a Liberal leader, Sir Edward Grey, was explaining the programme to be carried out during the Liberals' next turn of office. The two women put the fateful question, "When are you going to give votes to women?" and refused to sit down until they had been answered. These two women were sent to gaol, and from that day to this the women's movement, both militant and constitutional, has never looked back. We had little more than one moribund society for Woman Suffrage in those days. Now we have nearly 50 societies for Woman Suffrage, and they are large in membership, they are rich in money, and their ranks are swelling every day that passes. That is how militancy has put back the clock of Woman Suffrage in Great Britain. . . .

I want to say here and now that the only justification for violence, the only justification for damage to property, the only justification for risk to the comfort of other human beings is the fact that you have tried all other available means and have failed to secure justice, and as a law-abiding person—and I am by nature a law-abiding person, as one hating violence, hating disorder—I want to say that from the moment we began our militant agitation to this day I have felt absolutely guiltless in this matter.

I tell you that in Great Britain there is no other way. . . .

Well, I say the time is long past when it became necessary for women to revolt in order to maintain their self respect in Great Britain. The women who are waging this war are women who would fight, if it were only for the idea of liberty—if it were only that they might be free citizens of a free country—I myself would fight for that idea alone. But we have, in addition to this love of freedom, intolerable grievances to redress. . . .

Those grievances are so pressing that, so far from it being a duty to be patient and to wait for evolution, in thinking of those grievances the idea of patience is intolerable. We feel that patience is something akin to crime when our patience involves continued suffering on the part of the oppressed.

We are fighting to get the power to alter bad laws; but some people say to us, "Go to the representatives in the House of Commons, point out to them that these laws are bad, and you will find them quite ready to alter them."

Ladies and gentlemen, there are women in my country who have spent long and useful lives trying to get reforms, and because of their voteless condition, they are unable even to get the ear of Members of Parliament, much less are they able to secure those reforms.

Our marriage and divorce laws are a disgrace to civilisation. I sometimes wonder, looking back from the serenity of past middle age, at the courage of women. I wonder that women have the courage to take upon themselves the responsibilities of marriage and motherhood when I see how little protection the law of my country affords them. I wonder that a woman will face the ordeal of childbirth with the knowledge that after she has risked her life to bring a child into the world she has absolutely no parental rights over the future of that child. Think what trust women have in men when a woman will marry a man, knowing, if she has knowledge of the law, that if that man is not all she in her love for him thinks him, he may even bring a strange woman into the house, bring his mistress into the house to live with her, and she cannot get legal relief from such a marriage as that. . . .

. . . [W]e realise how political power, how political influence, which would enable us to get better laws, would make it possible for thousands upon thousands of unhappy women to live happier lives. . . .

Take the industrial side of the question: have men's wages for a hard day's work ever been so low and inadequate as are women's wages today? Have men ever had to suffer from the laws, more injustice than women suffer? Is there a single reason which men have had for demanding liberty that does not also apply to women?

Why, if you were talking to the *men* of any other nation you would not hesitate to reply in the affirmative. There is not a man in this meeting who has not felt sympathy with the uprising of the men of other lands when suffering from intolerable tyranny, when deprived of all representative rights. You are full of sympathy with men in Russia. You are full of sympathy with nations that rise against the domination of the Turk. You are full of sympathy with all struggling people striving for independence. How is it, then, that some of you have nothing but ridicule and contempt and [condemnation] for women who are fighting for exactly the same thing?

All my life I have tried to understand why it is that men who value their citizenship as their dearest possession seem to think citizenship ridiculous when it is to be applied to the women of their race. And I find an explanation, and it is the only one I can think of. It came to me when I was in a prison cell, remembering how I had seen men laugh at the idea of women going to prison. Why they would confess they could not bear a cell door to be shut upon themselves for a single hour without asking to be let out. A thought came to me in my prison cell, and it was this: that to men women are not human beings like themselves. Some men think we are superhuman; they put us on pedestals; they revere us; they think we are too fine and too delicate to come down into the hurly-burly of life. Other men think us sub-human; they think we are a strange species unfortunately having to exist for the perpetuation of the race. They think that we are fit for drudgery, but that in some strange way our minds are not like theirs, our love for great things is not like theirs, and so we are a sort of sub-human species.

We are neither superhuman nor are we sub-human. We are just human beings like yourselves.

Our hearts burn within us when we read the great mottoes which celebrate the liberty of your country; when we go to France and we read the words, liberty, fraternity and equality, don't you think that we appreciate the meaning of those words? And then when we wake to the knowledge that these things are not for us, they are only for our brothers, then there comes a sense of bitterness into the hearts of some women, and they say to themselves, "Will men never understand?" But so far as we in England are concerned, we have come to the conclusion that we are not going to leave men any illusions upon the question.

When we were patient, when we believed in argument and persuasion, they said, "You don't really want it because, if you did, you would do something unmistakable to show you were determined to have it." And then when we did something unmistakable they said, "You are behaving so badly that you show you are not fit for it."

Now, gentlemen, in your heart of hearts you do not believe that. You know perfectly well that there never was a thing worth having that was not worth fighting for. You know perfectly well that if the situation were reversed, if you had no constitutional rights and we had all of them, if you had the duty of paying and obeying and trying to look as pleasant, and we were the proud citizens who could decide our fate and yours, because we knew what was good for you better than you knew yourselves, you know perfectly well that you wouldn't stand it for a single day, and you would be perfectly justified in rebelling against such intolerable conditions.

The Goncourt Brothers
ON FEMALE INFERIORITY

The brothers Edmund (1822–1896) and Jules (1830–1870) Goncourt were French writers who produced in partnership novels, plays, and art and literary criticism. Starting in December 1851, they kept a journal in which they recorded, often insightfully, the doings of Parisian cultural and social life. In the following entries the Goncourts reveal an extreme bias against women. Even if these sentiments were not shared by all intellectuals, they do show the traditional prejudices confronting French feminists.

A conversation about woman, after a couple of tankards of beer at Binding's. Woman is an evil, stupid animal unless she is educated and civilized to a high degree. She is incapable of dreaming, thinking, or loving. Poetry in a woman is never natural but always a product of education. Only the woman of the world is a woman; the rest are females.

Inferiority of the feminine mind to the masculine mind. All the physical beauty, all the strength, and all the development of a woman is concentrated in and as it were directed towards the central and lower parts of the body: the pelvis, the buttocks, the thighs; the beauty of a man is to be found in the upper, nobler parts, the pectoral muscles, the broad shoulders, the high forehead. Venus has a narrow forehead. Dürer's *Three Graces* have flat heads at the back and little shoulders; only their hips are big and beautiful. As regards the inferiority of the feminine mind, consider the self-assurance of a woman, even when she is only a girl, which allows her to be extremely witty with nothing but a little vivacity and a touch of spontaneity. Only man is endowed with the modesty and timidity which woman lacks and which she uses only as weapons.

Woman: the most beautiful and most admirable of laying machines.

Men like ourselves need a woman of little breeding and education who is nothing but gaiety and natural wit, because a woman of that sort can charm and please us like an agreeable animal to which we may become quite attached. But if a mistress has acquired a veneer of breeding, art, or literature, and tries to talk to us on an equal footing about our thoughts and our feeling for beauty; if she wants to be a companion and partner in the cultivation of our tastes or the writing of our books, then she becomes for us as unbearable as a piano out of tune—and very soon an object of dislike.

Almroth E. Wright
THE UNEXPURGATED CASE AGAINST WOMAN SUFFRAGE

Sir Almroth Wright (1861–1947) was an eminent physician and one of the founders of modern immunology. He was also a thinker who attempted to construct "a system of Logic which searches for Truth," as he put it.

Wright's opposition to giving women the vote was expressed in letters to *The Times* of London and in a slender book, *The Unexpurgated Case Against Woman Suffrage* (1913). In the extracts below, he described the disabilities of women which make female suffrage impossible, at one point dismissing the suffrage movement as the product of "sex-hostility" caused by the excess population of women without hope of marrying. All told, he found that women's suffrage would be a recipe for social disaster, resulting in unacceptable demands for economic and intellectual equality.

The primordial argument against giving woman the vote is that that vote would not represent physical force.

Now it is by physical force alone and by prestige—which represents physical force in the background—that a nation protects itself against foreign interference, upholds its rule over subject populations, and enforces its own laws. And nothing could in the end more certainly lead to war and revolt than the decline of the military spirit and loss of prestige which would inevitably follow if man admitted woman into political co-partnership. . . .

[A] virile and imperial race will not brook any attempt at forcible control by women. Again, no military foreign nation or native race would ever believe in the stamina and firmness of purpose of any nation that submitted even to the semblance of such control. . . .

The woman voter would be pernicious to the State not only because she could not back her vote by physical force, but also by reason of her intellectual defects.

Woman's mind . . . arrives at conclusions on incomplete evidence; has a very imperfect sense of proportion; accepts the congenial as true, and rejects the uncongenial as false; takes the imaginary which is desired for reality, and treats the undesired reality which is out of sight as nonexistent—building up for itself in this way, when biased by predilections and aversions, a very unreal picture of the external world.

The explanation of this is to be found in all the physiological attachments of woman's mind: in the fact that mental images are in her over-intimately linked up with emotional reflex responses; that yielding to such reflex responses gives gratification; that intellectual analysis and suspense of judgment involve an inhibition of reflex responses which is felt as neural distress; that precipitate judgment brings relief from this physiological strain; and that woman looks upon her mind not as an implement for the pursuit of truth, but as an instrument for providing her with creature comforts in the form of agreeable mental images. . . .

In further illustration of what has been said above, it may be pointed out that woman, even intelligent woman, nurses all sorts of misconceptions about herself. She, for instance, is constantly picturing to herself that she can as a worker lay claim to the same all-round efficiency as a man—forgetting that woman is notoriously unadapted to tasks in which severe physical hardships have to be confronted; and that hardly any one would, if other alternative offered, employ a woman in any work which imposed upon her a combined physical and mental strain, or in any work where emergencies might have to be faced. . . .

Yet a third point has to come into consideration in connexion with the woman voter. This is, that she would be pernicious to the State also by virtue of her defective moral equipment. . . .

It is only a very exceptional woman who would, when put to her election between the claims of a narrow and domestic and a wider or public morality, subordinate the former to the latter.

In ordinary life, at any rate, one finds her following in such a case the suggestions of domestic—I had almost called it animal—morality.

It would be difficult to find any one who would trust a woman to be just to the rights of others in the case where the material interests of her children, or of a devoted husband, were involved. And even to consider the question of being in such a case intellectually just to any one who came into competition with personal belongings like husband and child would, of course, lie quite beyond the moral horizon of ordinary woman. . . . In this matter one would not be very far from the truth if one alleged that there are no good women, but only women who have lived under the influence of good men. . . .

In countries, such as England, where an excess female population [of three million] has made economic difficulties for woman, and where the severe sexual restrictions, which here obtain, have bred in her sex-hostility, the suffrage movement has as its avowed ulterior object the abrogation of all distinctions which depend upon sex; and the achievement of the economic independence of woman.

To secure this economic independence every post, occupation, and Government service is to be thrown open to woman; she is to receive everywhere the same wages as man; male and female are to work side by side; and they are indiscriminately to be put in command the one over the other. Furthermore, legal rights are to be secured to the wife over her husband's property and earnings. The programme is, in fact, to give to woman an economic independence out of the earnings and taxes of man.

Nor does feminist ambition stop short here. It demands that women shall be included in every advisory committee, every governing board, every jury, every judicial bench, every electorate, every parliament, and every ministerial cabinet; further, that every masculine foundation, university, school of learning, academy, trade union, professional corporation, and scientific society shall be converted into an epicene institution [including both male and female]—until we shall have everywhere one vast cock-and-hen show.

The proposal to bring man and woman together everywhere into extremely intimate relationships raises very grave questions. It brings up, first, the question of sexual complications; secondly, the question as to whether the tradition of modesty and reticence between the sexes is to be definitely sacrificed; and, most important of all, the question as to whether [bringing men and women together] would place obstacles in the way of intellectual work. . . .

The matter cannot so lightly be disposed of. It will be necessary for us to find out whether really intimate association with woman on the purely intellectual plane is realisable. And if it is, in fact, unrealisable, it will be necessary to consider whether it is the exclusion of women from masculine corporations; or the perpetual attempt of women to force their way into these, which would deserve to be characterised as *selfish*. . . .

What we have to ask is whether—even if we leave out of regard the whole system of attractions or, as the case may be, repulsions which comes into operation when the sexes are thrown together—purely intellectual intercourse between man and the typical unselected woman is not barred by the intellectual immoralities and limitations which appear to be secondary sexual characters of woman. . . .

Wherever we look we find aversion to compulsory intellectual co-operation with woman. We see it in the sullen attitude which the ordinary male student takes up towards the presence of women students in his classes. We see it in the fact that the older English universities, which have conceded everything else to women, have made a strong stand against making them actual members of the university; for this would impose them on men as intellectual associates. Again we see the aversion in the opposition to the admission of women to the bar.

But we need not look so far afield. Practically every man feels that there is in woman—patent, or hidden away—an element of unreason which, when you come upon it, summarily puts an end to purely intellectual intercourse. One may reflect, for example, upon the way the woman's suffrage controversy has been conducted.

But the feminist will want to argue. She will—taking it as always for granted that woman has a right to all that men's hands or brains have fashioned—argue that it is very important for the intellectual development of woman that she should have exactly the same opportunities as man. And she will, scouting the idea of any differences between the intelligences of man and woman, discourse to you of their intimate affinity. . . .

From these general questions, which affect only the woman with intellectual aspirations, we pass to consider what would be the effect of feminism upon the rank and file of women if it made of these co-partners with man in work. They would suffer, not only because woman's physiological disabilities and the restrictions which arise out of her sex place her at a great disadvantage when she has to enter into competition with man, but also because under feminism man would be less and less disposed to take off woman's shoulders a part of her burden.

And there can be no dispute that the most valuable financial asset of the ordinary woman is the possibility that a man may be willing—and may, if only woman is disposed to fulfil her part of the bargain, be not only willing but anxious—to support her, and to secure for her, if he can, a measure of that freedom which comes from the possession of money.

In view of this every one who has a real fellow-feeling for woman, and who is concerned for her material welfare, as a father is concerned for his daughter's, will above everything else desire to nurture and encourage in man the sentiment of chivalry, and in woman that disposition of mind that makes chivalry possible.

And the woman workers who have to fight the battle of life for themselves would indi-rectly profit from this fostering of chivalry; for those women who are supported by men do not compete in the limited labour market which is open to the woman worker.

From every point of view, therefore, except perhaps that of the exceptional woman who would be able to hold her own against mas-culine competition—and men always issue in-formal letters of [admission] to such an excep-tional woman—the woman suffrage which leads up to feminism would be a social disaster.

REVIEW QUESTIONS

1. In John Stuart Mill's view, what was the ultimate origin of the subjection of women?
2. According to Mill, what character qualities did men seek to instill in women? Why, according to Mill's argument, should women have the right to participate in politics and public affairs on equal terms with men?
3. Why did Emmeline Pankhurst think that violence was justified in fighting for women's rights?
4. Why, according to her, did men, who valued their citizenship as their dearest possession, feel it was ridiculous to grant it to women?
5. In what ways did the Goncourt brothers consider women inferior?
6. Why did Sir Almroth Wright think that women voters would be pernicious to the state?
7. In Wright's view, how were feminist reforms disadvantageous to women?

---

5   Anti-Semitism: Regression to the Irrational

Anti-Semitism, a European phenomenon of long standing, rose to new promi-nence in the late nineteenth century. Formerly segregated by law into ghettoes, Jews, under the aegis of the Enlightenment and the French Revolution, had gained legal equality in most European lands. In the nineteenth century, Jews participated in the economic and cultural progress of the times and often achieved distinction in business, the professions, and the arts and sciences. However, driven by irrational fears and mythical conceptions that had survived from the Middle Ages, many people regarded Jews as a dangerous race of inter-national conspirators and foreign intruders who threatened their nations.

Throughout the nineteenth century, anti-Semitic outrages occurred in many European lands. Russian anti-Semitism assumed a particularly violent form in the infamous pogroms—murderous mob attacks on Jews—occasionally abetted by government officials. Even in highly civilized France, anti-Semitism proved a powerful force. At the time of the Dreyfus affair (see page 204), Catholic and na-tionalist zealots demanded that Jews be deprived of their civil rights. In Germany, anti-Semitism became associated with the ideological defense of a distinctive Ger-man culture, the volkish thought popular in the last part of the nineteenth cen-tury. After the foundation of the German Empire in 1871, the pace of economic and cultural change quickened, and with it the cultural disorientation that fanned anti-Semitism. Volkish thinkers, who valued traditional Germany—the landscape, the peasant, and the village—associated Jews with the changes brought about by rapid industrialization and modernization. Compounding the problem was the influx into Germany of Jewish immigrants from the Russian Empire, who were searching for a better life and brought with them their own distinctive culture and religion, which many Germans found offensive. Nationalists and conservatives used anti-Semitism in an effort to gain a mass following.

Racial-nationalist considerations were the decisive force behind modern anti-Semitism. Racists said that the Jews were a wicked race of Asiatics, condemned by their genes; they differed physically, intellectually, and spiritually from Europeans who were descendants of ancient Aryans. (The Aryans emerged some 4,000 years ago, probably between the Caspian Sea and the Hindu Kush Mountains. Intermingling with others, the Aryans lost whatever identity as a people they might have had.) After discovering similarities between core European languages (Greek, Latin, German) and ancient Persian and ancient Sanskrit (the language of the conquerors of India), nineteenth-century scholars believed that these languages all stemmed from a common tongue spoken by the Aryans. From there, some leaped to the conclusion that the Aryans constituted a distinct race endowed with superior racial qualities.

German racists in particular embraced the ideas of Stewart Houston Chamberlain (1855–1927), an Englishman whose boundless admiration for Germandom led him to adopt German citizenship. In *Foundations of the Nineteenth Century* (1899), Chamberlain argued that the Germans, blond, blue-eyed, long-skulled, and distinguished by an inner spiritual depth, possessed the strongest strain of Aryan blood; they were the true shapers and guardians of high civilization.

Chamberlain pitted Aryans and Jews against each other in a struggle of world historical importance. As agents of a spiritually empty capitalism and divisive liberalism, the Jews, said Chamberlain, were the opposite of the idealistic, heroic, and faithful Germans. Chamberlain denied that Jesus was a Jew, hinting that he was of Aryan stock, and held that the goal of the Jew was "to put his foot upon the neck of all the nations of the world and be lord and possessor of the whole earth." Racial anti-Semitism became a powerful force in European intellectual life, especially in Germany. It was the seedbed of Hitler's movement.

Hermann Ahlwardt
THE SEMITIC VERSUS
THE TEUTONIC RACE

In the following reading, Hermann Ahlwardt (1846–1914), an anti-Semitic member of the Reichstag and author of *The Desperate Struggle Between Aryan and Jew,* addresses the chamber on March 6, 1895, with a plea to close Germany's borders to Jewish immigrants. His speech reflects the anti-Semitic rhetoric popular among German conservatives before World War I. The material in parentheses is by Paul W. Massing, translator and editor.

It is certainly true that there are Jews in our country of whom nothing adverse can be said. Nevertheless, the Jews as a whole must be considered harmful, for the racial traits of this people are of a kind that in the long run do not agree with the racial traits of the Teutons.[1] Every Jew who at this very moment has not as yet transgressed is likely to do so at some future time under given circumstances because his racial characteristics drive him on in that direction. . . .

My political friends do not hold the view that we fight the Jews because of their religion. . . . We would not dream of waging a political struggle against anyone because of his religion. . . . We hold the view that the Jews are a different race, a different people with entirely different character traits.

Experience in all fields of nature shows that innate racial characteristics which have been acquired by the race in the course of many thousands of years are the strongest and most enduring factors that exist, and that therefore we can rid ourselves of the characteristics of our race no more than can the Jews. One need not fight the Jew individually, and we are not doing that, by the way. But, when countless specimens prove the existence of certain racial characteristics and when these characteristics are such as to make impossible a common life, well, then I believe that we who are natives here, who have tilled the soil and defended it against all enemies—that we have a duty to take a stand against the Jews who are of a quite different nature.

We Teutons are rooted in the cultural soil of labor. . . . The Jews do not believe in the culture of labor, they do not want to create values themselves, but want to appropriate, without working, the values which others have created; that is the cardinal difference that guides us in all our considerations. . . .

Herr Deputy Rickert[2] here has just expounded how few Jews we have altogether and

that their number is steadily declining. Well, gentlemen, why don't you go to the main business centers and see for yourselves whether the percentages indicated by Herr Rickert prevail there too. Why don't you walk along the Leipzigerstrasse (in Berlin) or the Zeil in Frankfurt and have a look at the shops? Wherever there are opportunities to make money, the Jews have established themselves, but not in order to work—no, they let others work for them and take what the others have produced by their labor.

Deputy Hasse . . . has committed the grave mistake of putting the Jews and other peoples on the same level, and that is the worst mistake that we could possibly make.

The Jews have an attitude toward us which differs totally from that of other peoples. It is one thing when a Pole, a Russian, a Frenchman, a Dane immigrates to our country, and quite another thing when a Jew settles here. . . . Once our (Polish, etc.) guests have lived here for ten, twenty years, they come to resemble us. For they have stood with us on the same cultural soil of labor. . . . After thirty, forty years they have become Germans and their grandchildren would be indistinguishable from us except for the strange-sounding names they still bear. The Jews have lived here for 700, 800 years, but have they become Germans? Have they placed themselves on the cultural soil of labor? They never even dreamed of such a thing; as soon as they arrived, they started to cheat and they have been doing that ever since they have been in Germany. . . .

The Jews should not be admitted, whether or not there is overpopulation, for they do not belong to a productive race, they are exploiters, parasites. . . .

(Answering Rickert's arguments that . . . it would be a shame if fifty million Germans were afraid of a few Jews, Ahlwardt continued:) . . .

Herr Rickert, who is just as tall as I am, is afraid of one single cholera bacillus—well,

---

[1]Teutons refers to the quintessential Germans. The name comes from a German tribe that once defeated a Roman army.
[2]Heinrich Rickert, a leader of the Progressives and an outspoken opponent of anti-Semitism, had pointed out that

the Jews constituted only 1.29 percent of the population of Prussia. What enraged the German Right was that the Jews accounted for 9.58 percent of the university students in Prussia.

gentlemen, the Jews are just that, cholera bacilli!

Gentlemen, the crux of the matter is Jewry's capacity for contagion and exploitation.... How many thousands of Germans have perished as a result of this Jewish exploitation, how many may have hanged themselves, shot themselves, drowned themselves, how many may have ended by the wayside as tramps in America or drawn their last breath in the gutter, all of them people who had worked industriously on the soil their fathers had acquired, perhaps in hundreds of years of hard work.... Don't you feel any pity for those countless Germans? Are they to perish unsung? Ah, why were they foolish enough to let themselves be cheated? But the Germans are by no means so foolish, they are far more intelligent than the Jews. All inventions, all great ideas come from the Germans and not from the Jews. No, I shall tell you the national difference: The German is fundamentally trusting, his heart is full of loyalty and confidence. The Jew gains this confidence, only to betray it at the proper moment, ruining and pauperizing the German. This abuse of confidence on the part of the Jews is their main weapon. And these Jewish scoundrels are to be defended here! Is there no one to think of all those hundreds of thousands, nor of those millions of workers whose wages grow smaller and smaller because Jewish competition brings the prices down? One always hears: you must be humane toward the Jews. The humanitarianism of our century ... is our curse. Why aren't you for once humane toward the oppressed? You'd better exterminate those beasts of prey and you'd better start by not letting any more of them into our country. ...

(Taking issue with the liberals' argument of Jewish achievements in the arts, Ahlwardt declared:)

Art in my opinion is the capacity for expressing one's innermost feelings in such a way as to arouse the same feelings in the other person. Now the Jewish world of emotions (*Gefühlswelt*) and the Teutonic world of emotions are two quite different things. German art can express only German feelings; Jewish art only Jewish feelings. Because Jewry has been thrusting itself forward everywhere, it has also thrust itself forward in the field of art and therefore the art that is now in the foreground is Jewish art. Nowadays the head of a family must be very careful when he decides to take his family to the theater lest his Teutonic feelings be outraged by the infamous Jewish art that has spread everywhere.

The Jew is no German. If you say, the Jew was born in Germany, he was nursed by a German wetnurse, he abides by German laws, he has to serve as a soldier—and what kind of a soldier at that! let's not talk about it—he fulfills all his obligations, he pays his taxes—then I say that all this is not the crucial factor with regard to his nationality; the crucial factor is the race from which he stems. Permit me to make a rather trite comparison which I have already used elsewhere in my speeches: a horse that is born in a cowshed is far from being a cow.

A Jew who was born in Germany does not thereby become a German; he is still a Jew. Therefore it is imperative that we realize that Jewish racial characteristics differ so greatly from ours that a common life of Jews and Germans under the same laws is quite impossible because the Germans will perish. ...

... I beg you from the bottom of my heart not to take this matter* lightly but as a very serious thing. It is a question of life and death for our people. ...

We wouldn't think of going as far as have the Austrian anti-Semites in the Federal Council (*Reichsrat*) and to move that a bounty be paid for every Jew shot or to decree that he who kills a Jew shall inherit his property. We have no such intention. We shall not go as far as that. What we want is a clear and reasonable separation of the Jews from the Germans. An immediate prerequisite is that we slam the door and see to it that no more of them get in.[†]

---

*Prohibition of Jewish immigration.
[†]At the end of the debate a vote was taken, with 218 representatives present. Of these, 51 voted for, 167 against the motion.

Édouard Drumont
JEWISH FRANCE

Édouard Drumont (1842–1917), a journalist and rabid conservative, became in the 1880s the mouthpiece of French anti-Semitism. Drumont glorified attachment to the soil, obedience to authority, and the moral discipline of an authoritarian Catholic church, addressing himself to peasants and petty bourgeois folk—to those layers of the population that preferred the simplicity of the past to the fast-moving, urban complexity of the late nineteenth century. He especially deplored the new materialism with its self-indulgence and moral laxity.

To him the chief source of the contemporary degeneracy was the Jews. In 1886 he published the book that made him famous, called *La France Juive* (Jewish France). Advertised as an essay on contemporary history, it ascribed to Jews repulsive moral attributes, repeated the medieval myth that Jews murdered Christian children for ritual purposes, and propagated the bizarre theory that Jews were in a conspiracy to dominate France and the rest of Europe. The Jews, said Drumont, caused the ruin of Europe. Reprinted many times—his book sold over a million copies—it shaped public opinion for the conviction in 1894 of Captain Alfred Dreyfus, the first Jewish officer to be appointed to the General Staff of the French army, on faked evidence of high treason. In the following passage from *La France Juive,* Drumont contrasts the Semitic Jews with the Aryan French.

Let us examine now the essential traits which differentiate Jews from other people, beginning with ethnographic, physiological, and psychological comparisons of the Semite with the Aryan. These are two distinct races irremediably hostile to each other, whose antagonism has troubled the past and will cause still more trouble in the future.

The generic name Aryan derives from a Sanskrit word signifying "noble," "illustrious," "generous," standing for the superior family of the Indo-European family. . . . All the nations of Europe are descended by a straight line from the Aryan race, from which all great civilizations have sprung. . . . The Aryan or Indo-European race alone possesses the notion of justice, the sentiment of freedom, and the concept of the Beautiful. . . .

From the earliest moment of history we find the Aryan at war with the Semite. The dream of the Semite, indeed its obsession, has always been to reduce the Aryan into servants, to throw them into subjection. . . . Today Semitism feels sure of victory. It has replaced violence by wily tricks. The noisy invasion has been replaced by silent, progressive, slow penetration. Armed hordes no longer announce their arrival by shouts, but separate individuals, gathering in small groups, opportunistically infiltrate the state, taking possession of all important positions, all the functions in the country from the lowest to the highest. Spreading out from the area of Vilna [in Russia] they have occupied Germany, leaped over the Vosges mountains, and conquered France.

There was nothing brutal in this advance; it was a soft takeover accomplished in an insinuating manner of chasing the indigenous people from their homes, their source of income, in a velvety way depriving them of their goods, their tradition, their morals, and eventually their religion. . . . By their qualities as well as their faults, the two races [Jews and Aryans] are condemned to hurt each other.

The Semite is mercantile, greedy, scheming, subtle, crafty. The Aryan is enthusiastic, heroic, chivalrous, disinterested, straight-forward, trusting to the point of naiveté. The Semite is earthbound, seeing nothing beyond the present life. The Aryan is the child of heaven, relentlessly preoccupied with superior aspirations. One lives among realities, the other among ideals.

The Semite operates by instinct; he has the vocation of a trader, a genius for exchange, for every occasion to take advantage of his fellow man. The Aryan is devoted to life on the land, a poet, a monk and above all a soldier. War is his true element; he exposes himself joyfully to danger; he braves death. The Semite lacks any creative faculty. By contrast the Aryan is an inventor. The Jew has not made the least invention. He rather exploits, organizes, and utilizes the inventions of creative Aryans, guarding them as though they were his own. . . . The Aryan organizes voyages of adventure and discovers America. The Semite. . . . attends to all that has been explored and developed in order to enrich himself at the expense of others.

THE KISHINEV POGROM, 1903

Between 1881 and 1921 there were three large-scale waves of pogroms (mob attacks against Jews) in Russia. The civil and military authorities generally made no attempt to stop the murderous rampages and, at times, provided support. The worst of the pogroms occurred during the Civil War that followed the Bolshevik Revolution of 1917; some 60,000 Jews were slaughtered, particularly in the Ukraine, long a hotbed of anti-Semitism.

None of the numerous anti-Semitic outbreaks against Russian Jews in the years before World War I had a greater impact than that of the Kishinev pogrom, in southwestern Russia, in 1903. Its exceptional brutalities left a deep mark on Jewish consciousness. In 1903 almost half of Kishinev's population was Jewish; having achieved success in commerce and petty industry, Jews were the mainstay of the city's prosperity. This condition aroused the anti-Semitic feelings of their neighbors, already predisposed to hatred of Jews by a deeply embedded Christian bias.

After the assassination of Tsar Alexander II in 1881, the anti-Semitism of the Russian government gained ground. With influential support, a journalist named Pavolski Krushevan founded a newspaper in 1897 called *The Bessarabian,* which stirred up anti-Semitic sentiment. He accused the Jews of exploiting the Christian population, and worse, of ritual murder. In the course of five years, Krushevan stepped up his agitation, printing lurid stories designed to incite popular violence against Jews. He and his like-minded associates brought public indignation to the boiling point in the spring of 1903. Calling for "a bloody reckoning with the Jews," he prepared the attack for April 6. It was Easter Sunday for the Christians and part of the Passover week for the Jews. The details of what happened in Kishinev on April 6 and 7 are taken from a report entitled *Die Judenpogrome in Russland* (The Jewish Pogroms in Russia), prepared by a Zionist organization in London and published in Germany in 1910.

Sunday morning the weather cleared. The Jews were celebrating the last two days of Passover. Not anticipating trouble, they put on their holiday clothes and went to the synagogue. . . .

. . . Suddenly at about 3 P.M. a crowd of men appeared on the square Novyi Bazar, all dressed in red shirts. The men howled like madmen, incessantly shouting: "Death to the Jews. Beat the Jews." In front of the Moscow Tavern the crowd of some hundred split into 24 groups of 10–15 men each. There and then the systematic destruction, pillaging, and robbing of Jewish houses and shops began. At first they threw stones in great quantity and force, breaking windows and shutters. Then they tore open doors and windows, breaking into the Jewish houses and living quarters, smashing whatever furniture and equipment they found. The Jews had to hand over to the robbers their jewelry, money, and whatever other valuables they possessed. If they offered the slightest resistance, they were beaten over the head with pieces of their broken furniture. The storerooms were ransacked with special fury. The goods were either carried away or thrown on the street and destroyed. A large crowd of Christians followed the rioters, members of the intelligentsia, officials, students in the theological school, and others. . . .

At 5 P.M. the first Jew was murdered. The robbers stormed a trolley car with a Jewish passenger on board, shouting "Throw out the Jew." The Jew was pushed out and from all sides beaten on his head until his skull cracked and his brains spilled out. At first the sight of a dead Jew seemed to momentarily scare the bandits, but when they saw that the police did not care, they dispersed in all directions, shouting "Kill the Jews!"

On those streets where the pillaging took place Jews had to give up all attempts at self-defense. . . . But on the square Novyi Bazar the Jewish butchers gathered to defend themselves and their families. They bravely fought back and chased away the attackers, who were as cowardly as they were wild. Then the police came and arrested the Jews.

That was the final signal for the organizers of the mob. Until 10 P.M. the unleashed passions were vented in plunder, robbery, and destruction. Seven other murders took place. . . .

The Jews spent the night from Sunday to Monday in indescribable fear, yet hoping that the terror might be over.

During that night the leaders of the pogrom prepared further attacks, as in war. First the gangs which during the previous evening had arrived from the countryside were equipped with weapons. All weapons were of the same kind: axes, iron bars, and clubs, all strong enough to break doors and shutters, and even metal cabinets and safes. All men wore the same outfit: the red workshirts were worn by all members of the rabble, by peasants, workers, petty bourgeois, even seminary students and police. The second systematic action was the marking of all Jewish houses by the committee organizing the pogrom. During the night all Jewish houses and shops were painted with white chalk. Next came the organization of a permanent information and communication network among the various gangs. Several bicyclists were engaged, who subsequently played an important role. The bicyclists were high school students, theological students, and officials. The organization covered more than the city of Kishinev. Messengers were sent out to the nearest villages inviting the peasants: "Come to the city and help plunder the Jews. Bring big bags." Around 3 A.M. the preparations were finished. The signal for the attack was given.

The terror that now followed can hardly be described—orgies of loathsome savagery, blood-thirsty brutishness, and devilish lechery claimed their victims. Forty-nine Jews were murdered in Kishinev. When one hears about the excess of horror, one recognizes that only a few victims were lucky enough to die a simple death. Most of them had to suffer a variety of unbelievable abuse and repulsive torture unusual even among barbarians.

From 3 A.M. to 8 P.M. on Monday the gangs raged through the ruins and rubble which they themselves had piled up. They plundered, robbed, destroyed Jewish property, stole it, burned it, devastated it. They chased, slew, raped, and martyred the Jews. Representatives of all layers of the population took part in this witches' sabbath: soldiers, policemen, officials, and priests; children and women; peasants, workers, and vagabonds.

Major streets resounded with the terrifying roar of murdering gangs and the heartrending cries of the unfortunate victims. . . . The storerooms and shops were robbed, as on the previous day, down to the last item. . . . In the Jewish houses, the gangs burst into the living quarters with murderous howls, demanding all money and valuables. . . . If, however, the Jews could offer nothing or did not respond quickly enough, or if the gangsters were in a murderous mood, the men were knocked down, badly wounded, or killed. The women were raped one after the other in front of their men and children. They tore the arms and legs off the children, or broke them; some children were carried to the top floor and thrown out of the window. . . .

Early Monday morning a Jewish deputation hurried to the Governor of the province to plead for protection. He answered that he could do nothing, since he had no orders from St. Petersburg [the capital]. At the same time he refused to accept private telegrams from St. Petersburg.

The vain appeal of the Jews to the governor was followed by a catastrophic worsening of their fate. The gangs henceforth could count on the patronage of the highest authority. . . .

In ever-rising fury the robbery, murder, and desecration continued. Jews had their heads hacked off. Towels were soaked in their blood and then waved like red flags. The murderers wrote with Jewish blood on white flags in large letters: "Death to the Jews!" They slit open the bodies of men and women, ripped out their guts and filled the hollows with feathers.

They jumped on the corpses and danced, roaring, and drunk with vodka—men and women of "the best society." Officials and policemen laughed at the spectacle and joined in the fun. They beat pregnant women on their stomachs until they bled to death. . . .

They cut off the breasts of women after raping them. . . . Nails were driven into Chaja Sarah Phonarji's nostrils until they penetrated her skull. They hacked off the upper jaw of David Chariton, with all his teeth and his upper lip. Another man, Jechiel Selzer, had his ears pulled off before being beaten on the head until he became insane. . . .

These are some of the inhumanities committed during the pogrom. They are certified as true by eyewitnesses and the testimony of Christian physicians and Russian newspapers, which had passed through the most anti-Semitic and despotic censorship.

The synagogues were stormed and plundered with special spite. In one synagogue the gabai [sexton] braved death in front of the holy ark holding the Torah. Dressed in the *tales* [prayer shawl] and with the *tephalin* [phylacteries] on his forehead, he prepared for the onslaught of the murderers in order to protect the sacred scroll. He was cut down in the foulest manner. Then they tore, here and elsewhere, the Torah from the holy ark and cut the parchment into small scraps (Christian children later sold them on the streets for a few kopeks as mementos of Kishinev). After that the mobsters demolished, here as elsewhere, the synagogue's interior.

The barbarism of these scenes was so shattering that no less than 13 Jews went out of their minds. . . .

It would be unjust and ungrateful not to mention those Christians who in those days of mad brutality proved themselves true human beings and illustrious exceptions. They deserve to be remembered with special esteem because they were so few. . . .

Theodor Herzl
THE JEWISH STATE

Theodor Herzl (1860–1904) was raised in a comfortable, Jewish, middle-class home. Moving from Budapest, where he was born, to Vienna, the capital of the Austro-Hungarian Empire, he started to practice law, but soon turned to journalism, writing from Paris for the leading Vienna newspaper. A keen observer of the contemporary scene, he vigorously agitated for the ideal of an independent Jewish state. It was not a new idea but one whose time had come. Nationalist ferment was rising everywhere, often combined with virulent anti-Semitism. Under the circumstances, Herzl argued, security for Jews could be guaranteed only by a separate national state for Jews, preferably in Palestine.

In 1896 he published his program in a book, *Der Judenstaat* (The Jewish State), in which he envisaged a glorious future for an independent Jewish state harmoniously cooperating with the local population. In the following year he presided over the first Congress of Zionist Organizations held in Basel (Switzerland), attended mostly by Jews from central and eastern Europe. In its program the congress called for "a publicly guaranteed homeland for the Jewish people in the land of Israel." Subsequently, Herzl negotiated with the German emperor, the British government, and the sultan of the Ottoman Empire (of which Palestine was a part) for diplomatic support. In 1901 the Jewish National Fund was created to help settlers purchase land in Palestine. At his death, Herzl firmly expected a Jewish state to arise sometime in the future. The following excerpts from his book express the main points in his plea for a Jewish state.

We are a people—one people.

We have honestly endeavored everywhere to merge ourselves in the social life of surrounding communities and to preserve the faith of our fathers. We are not permitted to do so. In vain are we loyal patriots, our loyalty in some places running to extremes; in vain do we make the same sacrifices of life and property as our fellow-citizens; in vain do we strive to increase the fame of our native land in science and art, or her wealth by trade and commerce. In countries where we have lived for centuries we are still cried down as strangers, and often by those whose ancestors were not yet domiciled in the land where Jews had already had experience of suffering. . . . I think we shall not be left in peace.

Oppression and persecution cannot exterminate us. No nation on earth has survived such struggles and sufferings as we have gone through. Jew-baiting has merely stripped off our weaklings; the strong among us were invariably true to their race when persecution broke out against them. . . .

. . . [O]ld prejudices against us still lie deep in the hearts of the people. He who would have proofs of this need only listen to the people where they speak with frankness and simplicity: proverb and fairy-tale are both Anti-Semitic. . . .

No one can deny the gravity of the situation of the Jews. Wherever they live in perceptible numbers, they are more or less persecuted. Their equality before the law, granted by statute, has become practically a dead letter. They are debarred from filling even moderately high positions, either in the army, or in any public or private capacity. And attempts are made to thrust them out of business also: "Don't buy from Jews!"

Attacks in Parliaments, in assemblies, in the press, in the pulpit, in the street, on journeys—for example, their exclusion from certain hotels—even in places of recreation, become daily more numerous. The forms of persecutions varying according to the countries and social circles in which they occur. In Russia, imposts are levied on Jewish villages; in Rumania, a few persons are put to death; in Germany, they get a good beating occasionally; in Austria, Anti-Semites exercise terrorism over all public life; in Algeria, there are travelling agitators; in Paris, the Jews are shut out of the so-called best social circles and excluded from clubs. Shades of anti-Jewish feeling are innumerable. But this is not to be an attempt to make out a doleful category of Jewish hardships.

I do not intend to arouse sympathetic emotions on our behalf. That would be a foolish, futile, and undignified proceeding. I shall content myself with putting the following questions to the Jews: Is it not true that, in countries where we live in perceptible numbers, the position of Jewish lawyers, doctors, technicians, teachers, and employees of all descriptions becomes daily more intolerable? Is it not true, that the Jewish middle classes are seriously threatened? Is it not true, that the passions of the mob are incited against our wealthy people? Is it not true, that our poor endure greater sufferings than any other proletariat? I think that this external pressure makes itself felt everywhere. In our economically upper classes it causes discomfort, in our middle classes continual and grave anxieties, in our lower classes absolute despair.

Everything tends, in fact, to one and the same conclusion, which is clearly enunciated in that classic Berlin phrase: *"Juden Raus!"* (Out with the Jews!)

I shall now put the Question in the briefest possible form: Are we to "get out" now and where to?

Or, may we yet remain? And, how long?

Let us first settle the point of staying where we are. Can we hope for better days, can we possess our souls in patience, can we wait in pious resignation till the princes and peoples of this earth are more mercifully disposed towards us? I say that we cannot hope for a change in the current of feeling. . . . The nations in whose midst Jews live are all either covertly or openly Anti-Semitic. . . .

. . . We might perhaps be able to merge ourselves entirely into surrounding races, if these were to leave us in peace for a period of two generations. But they will not leave us in peace. For a little period they manage to tolerate us, and then their hostility breaks out again and again. . . .

Thus, whether we like it or not, we are now, and shall henceforth remain, a historic group with unmistakable characteristics common to us all.

We are one people—our enemies have made us one without our consent, as repeatedly happens in history. Distress binds us together, and, thus united, we suddenly discover our strength. Yes, we are strong enough to form a State, and, indeed, a model State. We possess all human and material resources necessary for the purpose. . . .

Let the sovereignty be granted us over a portion of the globe large enough to satisfy the rightful requirements of a nation; the rest we shall manage for ourselves.

The creation of a new State is neither ridiculous nor impossible. We have in our day witnessed the process in connection with nations which were not largely members of the middle class, but poorer, less educated, and consequently weaker than ourselves. . . .

Palestine is our ever-memorable historic home. The very name of Palestine would attract our people with a force of marvellous potency. If His Majesty the Sultan were to give us Palestine, we could in return undertake to regulate the whole finances of Turkey. We should there form a portion of a rampart of Europe against Asia, an outpost of civilization as opposed to barbarism. We should as a neutral State remain in contact with all Europe, which would have to guarantee our existence. The sanctuaries of Christendom would be safeguarded by assigning to them an extra-territorial status such as is well-known to the law of nations. We should form a guard of honor about these sanctuaries, answering for the fulfillment of this duty with our existence. This guard of honor would be the great symbol of the solution of the Jewish Question after eighteen centuries of Jewish suffering.

REVIEW QUESTIONS

1. What, according to Hermann Ahlwardt, were the racial characteristics of Jews? What, in contrast, were the racial characteristics of Germans?
2. What, said Ahlwardt, would be the ultimate result if Jewish immigration into Germany was not stopped?
3. How did Ahlwardt's anti-Semitism differ from traditional Christian anti-Semitism?
4. What kind of human needs did anti-Semitism seem to satisfy? What types of people are often attracted to anti-Semitic thinking? How may anti-Semitism be regarded as a regression to mythical modes of thinking?
5. What qualities, according to Édouard Drumont, separate Jews from the Aryans?
6. What social groups in Kishinev took part in the attack upon the Jews? What does the pogrom reveal about human nature? What role did government officials play?
7. Why did Theodor Herzl believe that the creation of a Jewish state was the only solution to the Jewish question?

CHAPTER 9

European Imperialism

PREMPAH, chief of the Ashanti tribe, disregarded treaties he signed with the British and faced military defeat. Here, he and his mother submit to the authority of the British governor of the Gold Coast (now Ghana) in 1896. *(From* The Graphic, *February 29, 1896. Corbis-Bettmann)*

Overseas territorial expansion has been part of European history since the fifteenth century. Portuguese and Spaniards explored maritime routes around Africa to India and East Asia; they crossed the Atlantic to the western hemisphere, soon followed by the English, Dutch, and French. All began to establish overseas colonies as bases for their ships and traders. Acquisition of colonies became part of the European power struggle. It was based on Europe's rapid progress in science, technology, economic skills, and political organization, enriched by ready assimilation of useful achievements from around the world. No people could match western Europe's power resources.

The Europeans established a hold in India, East Asia, and coastal Africa; they populated North America with their immigrants and gained control over South America. In the late eighteenth century the English extended their seapower into the Pacific Ocean, claiming Australia and New Zealand. After achieving independence the United States too felt the expansionist urge, ultimately stretching from the Atlantic to the Pacific. In the nineteenth century the Spanish and Portuguese in South America set up their own independent states; the western hemisphere became an extension of the European state system.

In the late nineteenth century, industrial growth and worldwide trade created among Europeans a new global competition for empire. The search for vital raw materials, markets, and investments intensified economic outreach, leading to ruthless exploitation and domination. The expenses of imperialism, usually greater than its economic benefits, were justified by rising nationalism, which fueled the quest for overseas possessions. What counted by the end of the century, as the traditional European rivalries expanded around the world, was global power; overseas possessions enhanced national prestige. Britain, thanks to its seapower, emerged as the colonial giant, claiming India as the core of the British Empire and provoking imitation by other ambitious European countries. Envious of the British Empire, other states did not want to be left behind.

Thus started a frantic race to occupy the last unclaimed parts of the world. The European powers began a "scramble for Africa." The Russians pressed into the Near East and Central Asia. Anti-foreign Japan, pried open to Western influence by the U.S. Admiral Perry in 1854, quickly westernized itself without impairing its cultural continuity, a unique case in history; catching the imperialist fever, Japan looked toward neighboring China for possible conquests. In 1898 the United States moved across the Pacific, occupying Hawaii and the Philippines. In 1900, responding to the Boxer Rebellion, a massive outburst in China of anti-foreign violence, the major European powers plus the United States and Japan expanded their rule in that country, greatly limiting the power of its government and inflicting a ruinous blow to its age-old pride. In the age of imperialism the world had essentially fallen under European—or now more generally "Western"—domination.

Obviously, the imperialist impact varied, depending on local conditions. Because of its geographical obstacles (dense tropical rainforests, savannahs, and deserts) sub-Saharan Africa was penetrated by the Europeans only late in the nineteenth century, carved up by England, France, Germany, and Belgium, each imposing its own boundaries regardless of local loyalties. Once established, the imperialists began to dominate their helpless subjects; all resistance was ruthlessly suppressed with the aid of indigenous soldiers. Convinced of their superiority, the imperialists often viewed Africans with disdain, dismissing their culture as barbaric. Indigenous ways, uncomprehended and generally repulsive to Europeans, provided a profound challenge to Western attitudes. Their reactions ranged from Social Darwinist racism to a patronizing conviction that they were obliged to civilize their subjects according to their own values. In Africa especially, the Christian missionaries played an important role in this effort, at considerable personal risk; because of tropical diseases and lack of medical care their death rate was painfully high. Only gradually, and sometimes with the missionaries' help, did the imperialist masters begin to open their minds to the cultural creativity of their subjects, even then never questioning their own superiority. Extending the benefits of imperial rule over "primitive" people was a source of deep patriotic pride.

The European masters never appreciated the devastating effects of their domination upon indigenous life and traditions in African and Asian lands. All peoples were now subject to profound cultural disorientation. Their customary ways were discredited as inferior, while the Western ways remained alien and perplexing. The cultural gap between indigenous and Western life became a source of much misery and violence. In Africa the Europeans encountered the sharpest cultural contrasts with their own ways, while in India the British confronted a high civilization that lacked political power. Here too the British imperialists faced a difficult task in elevating their subjects to their own standards. Everywhere the clash between indigenous and Western ways continues to the present day.

The imperialists generally imposed their Western culture upon all other cultures, thereby also disseminating their own ideals of freedom and self-determination. After World War I these ideals began to impress the educated minority, as in India. After World War II all colonial countries struggled toward independence. Thus imperialism gave rise to the present unprecedented age of intense global interaction, in which all peoples, despite their differences, have to adjust to each other largely on Western, now simply called "modern," terms.

1 The Spirit of British Imperialism

In 1872 the British statesman Benjamin Disraeli (1804–1881) delivered a famous speech at the Crystal Palace in London that posed a crucial choice for his country: it was either insignificance in world affairs or imperial power with prosperity and global prestige. His speech was soon followed by an outburst of speeches, lectures, and books in which imperialists made claims for British worldwide superiority buttressed by arguments drawn from racist and Darwinian convictions popular at the time. These ideas, illustrated in the first three readings, found a receptive audience, yet public opinion was divided. As the concluding selection shows, anti-imperialists also spoke out.

Cecil Rhodes
CONFESSION OF FAITH

One ardent supporter of British expansion was Cecil Rhodes (1853–1902). Raised in a parsonage north of London, Rhodes went to southern Africa at the age of seventeen for his health and to join his brother. Within two years he had established himself in the diamond industry. In the 1870s, he divided his time between Africa and studying at Oxford University. While at Oxford he was inspired by Disraeli's Crystal Palace speech and the views of the prominent Oxford professor John Ruskin (1819–1900), who urged England "to found colonies as fast and as far as she is able, formed of the most energetic and worthiest of men." In this spirit Rhodes wrote, for his own satisfaction, a "Confession of Faith." Composed in 1877, when he was twenty-four years old, it offered a vision of racist expansionism popular before the First World War. It was not published in his lifetime.

His faith propelled him into political and financial prominence in South Africa. In 1889 he became head of the British South African Company, whose territory, twice as large as England, was named Rhodesia six years later (it was renamed Zimbabwe in 1980). He controlled 90 percent of the world's diamond production and a large share of South Africa's gold fields. Never regarding wealth as an end in itself—he endowed the Rhodes Scholarships at Oxford—he sought to extend British influence in East Africa and around the world.

In 1890 he was named prime minister of the British Cape Colony, where government forces were heavily involved in conflict with the original Dutch settlers, the Boers. Driven north by the British, the Boers had set up their own state. Rhodes died during the Boer War (1899–1902), which put the Boers under British rule.

Excerpts follow from the "Confession of Faith" of 1877, included in the appendix of John E. Flint's biography of Cecil Rhodes. Flint reproduced the document "in its original form without any editing of spelling or punctuation."

It often strikes a man to inquire what is the chief good in life; to one the thought comes that it is a happy marriage, to another great wealth, and as each seizes on his idea, for that he more or less works for the rest of his existence. To myself thinking over the same question the wish came to render myself useful to my country. I then asked myself how could I and after reviewing the various methods I have felt that at the present day we are actually limiting our children and perhaps bringing into the world half the human beings we might owing to the lack of country for them to inhabit that if we had retained America there would at this moment be millions more of English living. I contend that we are the finest race in the world and that the more of the world we inhabit the better it is for the human race. Just fancy those parts that are at present inhabited by the most despicable specimens of human beings what an alteration there would be if they were brought under Anglo-Saxon influence, look again at the extra employment a new country added to our dominions gives. I contend that every acre added to our territory means in the future birth to some more of the English race who otherwise would not be brought into existence. Added to this the absorption of the greater portion of the world under our rule simply means the end of all wars. . . .

The idea gleaming and dancing before ones eyes like a will-of-the-wisp at last frames itself into a plan. Why should we not form a secret society with but one object the furtherance of the British Empire and the bringing of the whole uncivilised world under British rule for the recovery of the United States for the making the Anglo-Saxon race but one Empire. What a dream, but yet it is probable, it is possible. I once heard it argued by a fellow in my own college, I am sorry to own it by an Englishman, that it was a good thing for us that we have lost the United States. There are some subjects on which there can be no arguments, and to an Englishman this is one of them, but even from an American's point of view just picture what they have lost, look at their government, are not the frauds that yearly come before the public view a disgrace to any country and especially their's which is the finest in the world. Would they have occurred had they remained under English rule great as they have become how infinitely greater they would have been with the softening and elevating influences of English rule, think of those countless 000's [thousands] of Englishmen that during the last 100 years would have crossed the Atlantic and settled and populated the United States. Would they have not made without any prejudice a finer country of it than the low class Irish and German emigrants? All this we have lost and that country loses owing to whom? Owing to two or three ignorant pig-headed statesmen of the last century, at their door lies the blame. Do you ever feel mad? do you ever feel murderous. I think I do with those men. I bring facts to prove my assertion. Does an English father when his sons wish to emigrate ever think of suggesting emigration to a country under another flag, never—it would seem a disgrace to suggest such a thing I think that we all think that poverty is better under our own flag than wealth under a foreign one.

Put your mind into another train of thought. Fancy Australia discovered and colonised under the French flag. . . . We learn from having lost to cling to what we possess. We know the size of the world we know the total extent. Africa is still lying ready for us it is our duty to take it. It is our duty to seize every opportunity of acquiring more territory and we should keep this one idea steadily before our eyes that more territory simply means more of the Anglo-Saxon race more of the best the most human, most honourable race the world possesses.

To forward such a scheme what a splendid help a secret society would be a society not openly acknowledged but who would work in secret for such an object.

I contend that there are at the present moment numbers of the ablest men in the world who would devote their whole lives to it. . . .

What has been the main cause of the success of the Romish Church? The fact that every enthusiast, call it if you like every madman finds employment in it. Let us form the same kind of society a Church for the extension of the British Empire. A society which should have its members in every part of the British Empire working with one object and one idea. . . .

(In every Colonial legislature the Society should attempt to have its members prepared at all times to vote or speak and advocate the closer union of England and the colonies, to crush all disloyalty and every movement for the severance of our Empire. The Society should inspire and even own portions of the press for the press rules the mind of the people. The Society should always be searching for members who might by their position in the world by their energies or character forward the object but the ballot and test for admittance should be severe). . . .[1]

For fear that death might cut me off before the time for attempting its development I leave all my worldly goods in trust to S. G. Shippard and the Secretary for the Colonies at the time of my death to try to form such a Society with such an object.

---

[1]It is not clear why Rhodes placed this paragraph in parentheses.

Joseph Chamberlain
THE BRITISH EMPIRE: COLONIAL COMMERCE AND "THE WHITE MAN'S BURDEN"

British imperialists like Joseph Chamberlain (1836–1914) argued that the welfare of Britain depended upon the preservation and extension of the empire, for colonies fostered trade and served as a source of raw materials. In addition, Chamberlain asserted that the British Empire had a sacred duty to carry civilization, Christianity, and British law to the "backward" peoples of Africa and Asia. As a leading statesman, Chamberlain made many speeches, both in Parliament and before local political groups, that endorsed imperialist ventures. Excerpts from these speeches, later collected and published under the title *Foreign and Colonial Speeches,* follow.

June 10, 1896

. . . The Empire, to parody a celebrated expression, is commerce. It was created by commerce, it is founded on commerce, and it could not exist a day without commerce. (Cheers). . . . The fact is history teaches us that no nation has ever achieved real greatness without the aid of commerce, and the greatness of no nation has survived the decay of its trade. Well, then, gentlemen, we have reason to be proud of our commerce and to be resolved to guard it from attack. (Cheers.). . . .

March 31, 1897

. . . We have suffered much in this country from depression of trade. We know how many of our fellow-subjects are at this moment unemployed. Is there any man in his senses who believes that the crowded population of these islands could exist for a single day if we were to cut adrift from us the great dependencies which now look to us for protection and assistance, and which are the natural markets for our trade? (Cheers.) The area of the United Kingdom is only 120,000 miles; the area of the British Empire is over 9,000,000 square miles, of which nearly 500,000 are to be found in the portion of Africa with which we have been dealing. If tomorrow it were possible, as some people apparently desire, to reduce by a stroke of the pen the British Empire to the dimensions of the United Kingdom, half at least of our population would be starved (cheers). . . .

January 22, 1894

We must look this matter in the face, and must recognise that in order that we may have more employment to give we must create more demand. (Hear, hear.) Give me the demand for more goods and then I will undertake to give plenty of employment in making the goods; and the only thing, in my opinion, that the Government can do in order to meet this great difficulty that we are considering, is so to arrange its policy that every inducement shall be given to the demand; that new markets shall be created, and that old markets shall be effectually developed. (Cheers.) . . . I am convinced that it is a necessity as well as a duty for us to uphold the dominion and empire which we now possess. (Loud cheers.) . . . I would never lose the hold which we now have over our great Indian dependency—(hear, hear)—by far the greatest and most valuable of all the customers we have or ever shall have in this country. For the same reasons I approve of the continued occupation of Egypt; and for the same reasons I have urged upon this Government, and upon previous Governments, the necessity for using every legitimate opportunity to extend our influence and control in that great African continent which is now being opened up to civilisation and to commerce; and, lastly, it is for the same reasons that I hold that our navy should be strengthened—(loud

cheers)—until its supremacy is so assured that we cannot be shaken in any of the possessions which we hold or may hold hereafter.

Believe me, if in any one of the places to which I have referred any change took place which deprived us of that control and influence of which I have been speaking, the first to suffer would be the working-men of this country. Then, indeed, we should see a distress which would not be temporary, but which would be chronic, and we should find that England was entirely unable to support the enormous population which is now maintained by the aid of her foreign trade. If the working-men of this country understand, as I believe they do—I am one of those who have had good reason through my life to rely upon their intelligence and shrewdness—if they understand their own interests, they will never lend any countenance to the doctrines of those politicians who never lose an opportunity of pouring contempt and abuse upon the brave Englishmen, who, even at this moment, in all parts of the world are carving out new dominions for Britain, and are opening up fresh markets for British commerce, and laying out fresh fields for British labour. (Applause.) . . .

March 31, 1897

. . . We feel now that our rule over these territories can only be justified if we can show that it adds to the happiness and prosperity of the people—(cheers)—and I maintain that our rule does, and has, brought security and peace and comparative prosperity to countries that never knew these blessings before. (Cheers.)

In carrying out this work of civilisation we are fulfilling what I believe to be our national mission, and we are finding scope for the exercise of those faculties and qualities which have made of us a great governing race. (Cheers.) I do not say that our success has been perfect in every case, I do not say that all our methods have been beyond reproach; but I do say that in almost every instance in which the rule of the Queen has been established and the great *Pax*

Britannica[1] has been enforced, there has come with it greater security to life and property, and a material improvement in the condition of the bulk of the population. (Cheers.) No doubt, in the first instance, when these conquests have been made, there has been bloodshed, there has been loss of life among the native populations, loss of still more precious lives among those who have been sent out to bring these countries into some kind of disciplined order, but it must be remembered that this is the condition of the mission we have to fulfil. . . .

. . . You cannot have omelettes without breaking eggs; you cannot destroy the practices of barbarism, of slavery, of superstition, which for centuries have desolated the interior of Africa, without the use of force; but if you will fairly contrast the gain to humanity with

the price which we are bound to pay for it, I think you may well rejoice in the result of such expeditions as those which have recently been conducted with such signal success— (cheers)—in Nyassaland, Ashanti, Benin, and Nupé [regions in Africa]—expeditions which may have, and indeed have, cost valuable lives, but as to which we may rest assured that for one life lost a hundred will be gained, and the cause of civilisation and the prosperity of the people will in the long run be eminently advanced. (Cheers.) But no doubt such a state of things, such a mission as I have described, involve heavy responsibility. . . . and it is a gigantic task that we have undertaken when we have determined to wield the sceptre of empire. Great is the task, great is the responsibility, but great is the honour—(cheers); and I am convinced that the conscience and the spirit of the country will rise to the height of its obligations, and that we shall have the strength to fulfil the mission which our history and our national character have imposed upon us. (Cheers.)

------

[1]*Pax Britannica* means "British Peace" in the tradition of the *Pax Romana*—the peace, stability, and prosperity that characterized the Roman Empire at its height in the first two centuries A.D.

Karl Pearson
SOCIAL DARWINISM: IMPERIALISM JUSTIFIED BY NATURE

In the last part of the nineteenth century, the spirit of expansionism was buttressed by application of Darwin's theory of evolution to human society. Theorists called Social Darwinists argued that nations and races, like the species of animals, were locked in a struggle for existence in which only the fittest survived and deserved to survive. British and American imperialists employed the language of Social Darwinism to promote and justify Anglo-Saxon expansion and domination of other peoples. Social Darwinist ideas spread to Germany, which was inspired by the examples of British and American expansion. In a lecture given in 1900 and titled "National Life from the Standpoint of Science," Karl Pearson (1857–1936), a British professor of mathematics, expressed the beliefs of Social Darwinists.

What I have said about bad stock seems to me to hold for the lower races of man. How many centuries, how many thousands of years, have

the Kaffir [a tribe in southern Africa] or the negro held large districts in Africa undisturbed by the white man? Yet their intertribal struggles have not yet produced a civilization in the least comparable with the Aryan[1] [western European]. Educate and nurture them as you will, I do not believe that you will succeed in modifying the stock. History shows me one way, and one way only, in which a high state of civilization has been produced, namely, the struggle of race with race, and the survival of the physically and mentally fitter race. . . .

. . . Let us suppose we could prevent the white man, if we liked, from going to lands of which the agricultural and mineral resources are not worked to the full; then I should say a thousand times better for him that he should not go than that he should settle down and live alongside the inferior race. The only healthy alternative is that he should go and completely drive out the inferior race. That is practically what the white man has done in North America. . . . But I venture to say that no man calmly judging will wish either that the whites had never gone to America, or would desire that whites and Red Indians were to-day living alongside each other as negro and white in the Southern States, as Kaffir and European in South Africa, still less that they had mixed their blood as Spaniard and Indian in South America. . . . I venture to assert, then, that the struggle for existence between white and red man, painful and even terrible as it was in its details, has given us a good far outbalancing its immediate evil. In place of the red man, contributing practically nothing to the work and thought of the world, we have a great nation, mistress of many arts, and able, with its youthful imagination and fresh, untrammelled impulses, to contribute much to the common stock of civilized man. . . .

But America is but one case in which we have to mark a masterful human progress following an inter-racial struggle. The Australian nation is another case of great civilization supplanting a lower race unable to work to the full the land and its resources. . . . The struggle means suffering, intense suffering, while it is in progress; but that struggle and that suffering have been the stages by which the white man has reached his present stage of development, and they account for the fact that he no longer lives in caves and feeds on roots and nuts. This dependence of progress on the survival of the fitter race, terribly black as it may seem to some of you, gives the struggle for existence its redeeming features; it is the fiery crucible out of which comes the finer metal. You may hope for a time when the sword shall be turned into the ploughshare, when American and German and English traders shall no longer compete in the markets of the world for their raw material and for their food supply, when the white man and the dark shall share the soil between them, and each till it as he lists [pleases]. But, believe me, when that day comes mankind will no longer progress; there will be nothing to check the fertility of inferior stock; the relentless law of heredity will not be controlled and guided by natural selection. Man will stagnate. . . .

The . . . great function of science in national life . . . is to show us what national life means, and how the nation is a vast organism subject . . . to the great forces of evolution. . . . There is a struggle of race against race and of nation against nation. In the early days of that struggle it was a blind, unconscious struggle of barbaric tribes. At the present day, in the case of the civilized white man, it has become more and more the conscious, carefully directed attempt of the nation to fit itself to a continuously changing environment. The nation has to foresee how and where the struggle will be carried on; the maintenance of national position is becoming more and more a conscious preparation for changing conditions, an insight into the needs of coming environments. . . .

. . . If a nation is to maintain its position in this struggle, it must be fully provided with trained brains in every department of national activity, from the government to the factory,

---

[1]Most European languages derive from the Aryan language spoken by people who lived thousands of years ago in the region from the Caspian Sea to the Hindu Kush Mountains. Around 2000 B.C., some Aryan-speaking people migrated to Europe and India. Nineteenth-century racialist thinkers held that Europeans, descendants of the ancient Aryans, were racially superior to other peoples.

and have, if possible, a *reserve of brain and physique* to fall back upon in times of national crisis. . . .

You will see that my view—and I think it may be called the scientific view of a nation—is that of an organized whole, kept up to a high pitch of internal efficiency by insuring that its numbers are substantially recruited from the better stocks, and kept up to a high pitch of external efficiency by contest, chiefly by way of war with inferior races, and with equal races by the struggle for trade-routes and for the sources of raw material and of food supply. This is the natural history view of mankind, and I do not think you can in its main features subvert it. . . .

. . . Is it not a fact that the daily bread of our millions of workers depends on their having somebody to work for? that if we give up the contest for trade-routes and for free markets and for waste lands, we indirectly give up our food-supply? Is it not a fact that our strength depends on these and upon our colonies, and that our colonies have been won by the ejection of inferior races, and are maintained against equal races only by respect for the present power of our empire? . . .

. . . We find that the law of the survival of the fitter is true of mankind, but that the struggle is that of the gregarious animal. A community not knit together by strong social instincts, by sympathy between man and man, and class and class, cannot face the external contest, the competition with other nations, by peace or by war, for the raw material of production and for its food supply. This struggle of tribe with tribe, and nation with nation, may have its mournful side; but we see as a result of it the gradual progress of mankind to higher intellectual and physical efficiency. It is idle to condemn it; we can only see that it exists and recognise what we have gained by it—civilization and social sympathy. But while the statesman has to watch this external struggle, . . . he must be very cautious that the nation is not silently rotting at its core. He must insure that the fertility of the inferior stocks is checked, and that of the superior stocks encouraged; he must regard with suspicion anything that tempts the physically and mentally fitter men and women to remain childless. . . .

. . . The path of progress is strewn with the wrecks of nations; traces are everywhere to be seen of the hecatombs {slaughtered remains} of inferior races, and of victims who found not the narrow way to perfection. Yet these dead people are, in very truth, the stepping stones on which mankind has arisen to the higher intellectual and deeper emotional life of today.

John Atkinson Hobson
AN EARLY CRITIQUE OF IMPERIALISM

One of the early English critics of imperialism was the social reformer and economist John Atkinson Hobson (1858–1940). Hobson's primary interest was social reform, and he turned to economics to try to solve the problem of poverty. Like Rhodes, he was influenced by Ruskin's ideas, but his interpretation of them led him to a diametrically opposed view of colonialism. As an economist, he argued that the unequal distribution of income made capitalism unproductive and unstable. It could not maintain itself except through investing in less-developed countries on an increasing scale, thus fostering colonial expansion. Lenin, leader of the Russian Revolution, later adopted this thesis.

Hobson's stress upon the economic causes of imperialism has been disputed by some historians who see the desire for national power and glory as a far more important cause. Hobson attacked imperialism in the following passages from his book *Imperialism* (1902).

. . . The decades of Imperialism have been prolific in wars; most of these wars have been directly motivated by aggression of white races upon "lower races," and have issued in the forcible seizure of territory. Every one of the steps of expansion in Africa, Asia, and the Pacific has been accompanied by bloodshed; each imperialist Power keeps an increasing army available for foreign service; rectification of frontiers, punitive expeditions, and other euphemisms for war are in incessant progress. The *pax Britannica,* always an impudent falsehood, has become of recent years a grotesque monster of hypocrisy; along our Indian frontiers, in West Africa, in the Soudan, in Uganda, in Rhodesia fighting has been wellnigh incessant. Although the great imperialist Powers have kept their hands off one another, save where the rising empire of the United States has found its opportunity in the falling empire of Spain, the self-restraint has been costly and precarious. Peace as a national policy is antagonised not merely by war, but by militarism, an even graver injury. Apart from the enmity of France and Germany, the main cause of the vast armaments which are draining the resources of most European countries is their conflicting interests in territorial and commercial expansion. Where thirty years ago there existed one sensitive spot in our relations with France, or Germany, or Russia, there are a dozen now; diplomatic strains are of almost monthly occurrence between Powers with African or Chinese interests, and the chiefly business nature of the national antagonisms renders them more dangerous, inasmuch as the policy of Governments passes more under the influence of distinctively financial juntos [cliques]. . . .

Our economic analysis has disclosed the fact that it is only the interests of competing cliques of business men—investors, contractors, export manufacturers, and certain professional classes—that are antagonistic; that these cliques, usurping the authority and voice of the people, use the public resources to push their private businesses, and spend the blood and money of the people in this vast and disastrous military game, feigning national antagonisms which have no basis in reality. It is not to the interest of the British people, either as producers of wealth or as tax-payers, to risk a war with Russia and France in order to join Japan in preventing Russia from seizing [K]orea; but it may serve the interests of a group of commercial politicians to promote this dangerous policy. The South African war [the Boer War, 1899–1902], openly fomented by gold speculators for their private purposes, will rank in history as a leading case of this usurpation of nationalism. . . .

. . . So long as this competitive expansion for territory and foreign markets is permitted to misrepresent itself as "national policy" the antagonism of interests seems real, and the peoples must sweat and bleed and toil to keep up an ever more expensive machinery of war. . . .

. . . The industrial and financial forces of Imperialism, operating through the party, the press, the church, the school, mould public opinion and public policy by the false idealisation of those primitive lusts of struggle, domination, and acquisitiveness which have survived throughout the eras of peaceful industrial order and whose stimulation is needed once again for the work of imperial aggression, expansion, and the forceful exploitation of lower races. For these business politicians biology and sociology weave thin convenient theories of a race struggle for the subjugation of the inferior peoples, in order that we, the

Anglo-Saxon, may take their lands and live upon their labours; while economics buttresses the argument by representing our work in conquering and ruling them as our share in the division of labour among nations, and history devises reasons why the lessons of past empire do not apply to ours, while social ethics paints the motive of "Imperialism" as the desire to bear the "burden" of educating and elevating races of "children." Thus are the "cultured" or semi-cultured classes indoctrinated with the intellectual and moral grandeur of Imperialism. For the masses there is a cruder appeal to hero-worship and sensational glory, adventure and the sporting spirit: current history falsified in coarse flaring colours, for the direct stimulation of the combative instincts. But while various methods are employed, some delicate and indirect, others coarse and flamboyant, the operation everywhere resolves itself into an incitation and direction of the brute lusts of human domination which are everywhere latent in civilised humanity, for the pursuance of a policy fraught with material gain to a minority of co-operative vested interests which usurp the title of the commonwealth. . . .

. . . The presence of a scattering of white officials, missionaries, traders, mining or plantation overseers, a dominant male caste with little knowledge of or sympathy for the institutions of the people, is ill-calculated to give to these lower races even such gains as Western civilisation might be capable of giving.

The condition of the white rulers of these lower races is distinctively parasitic; they live upon these natives, their chief work being that of organising native labour for their support.

The normal state of such a country is one in which the most fertile lands and the mineral resources are owned by white aliens and worked by natives under their direction, primarily for their gain: they do not identify themselves with the interests of the nation or its people, but remain an alien body of sojourners, a "parasite" upon the carcass of its "host," destined to extract wealth from the country and retire to consume it at home. All the hard manual or other severe routine work is done by natives. . . .

Nowhere under such conditions is the theory of white government as a trust for civilisation made valid; nowhere is there any provision to secure the predominance of the interests, either of the world at large or of the governed people, over those of the encroaching nation, or more commonly a section of that nation. The relations subsisting between the superior and the inferior nations, commonly established by pure force, and resting on that basis, are such as preclude the genuine sympathy essential to the operation of the best civilising influences, and usually resolve themselves into the maintenance of external good order so as to forward the profitable development of certain natural resources of the land, under "forced" native labour, primarily for the benefit of white traders and investors, and secondarily for the benefit of the world of white Western consumers.

This failure to justify by results the forcible rule over alien peoples is attributable to no special defect of the British or other modern European nations. It is inherent in the nature of such domination. . . .

REVIEW QUESTIONS

1. What nationalistic views were expressed in Cecil Rhodes's "Confession of Faith"?
2. What role did the concept of race—the English or Anglo-Saxon—play in the arguments of Rhodes? Compare his views with those advanced by Hermann Ahlwardt on page 201.
3. How did Chamberlain define the national mission of the "great governing race"? What were the economic benefits of that mission?
4. How did Karl Pearson define the difference between inferior and superior races?

5. What measures did Pearson advocate for keeping a nation such as Britain at its highest potential?
6. Why, in J. A. Hobson's opinion, was the *pax Britannica* an "impudent falsehood"?
7. One ideal of imperialism was to spread civilizing influences among native populations. How did Hobson interpret this sense of mission?

---

2 Seeking a Place in the Sun

In the late nineteenth century, alert patriots in the leading continental countries began to look around the world, their self-esteem and national pride diminished by their countries' secondary role in world affairs. After Bismarck established the German Empire in 1871, German ambitions rose, incited by the success of British imperialism. Was Germany being reduced to insignificance compared with the British Empire, or could it claim, as the German emperor asserted in 1901, "a place in the sun" of imperial power and global prestige? An early advocate of German colonial expansion was Friedrich Fabri; his target was Africa.

At the same time, French nationalists sought to restore their country's prestige after its defeat in the Franco-Prussian War (1870–1871). Led by Paul Leroy-Beaulieu, they urged the acquisition of colonies in Africa and East Asia. Thus envious comparison with the British Empire enrolled the two leading continental countries in the imperialist crusade.

Germany's imperial role, however, was short-lived. Under the Treaty of Versailles after World War I, Germany lost all its overseas possessions to the victors.

Friedrich Fabri
DOES GERMANY NEED COLONIES?

Coming from an intellectual family, Friedrich Fabri (1824–1891) started his career as a teacher of religion in a school concerned with agriculture and crafts; he later served as a minister at a church and was eventually appointed a professor of theology. His wide-ranging interests included church-state relations, the dangers of materialism, and also the missionary outreach into South Africa. Following the trend of the times, he became aware of the growing agitation in western Europe for colonial expansion. Stimulated by the example of the British Empire, he answered the question raised in the title of his book with a resounding YES, pioneering in newly united Germany the campaign for colonial acquisitions. Fabri mixed patriotism with an evangelical zeal for spreading German culture around the world. "German culture," according to Fabri, represented the unique German soul, the German depth of patriotic feeling which demanded "of the German Reich the acceptance of an insightful and energetic colonial policy." Excerpts from Fabri's work follow.

Above all we need to regain ample, rewarding, and reliable sources of employment; we need new and reliable export markets; in short we need a well-designed and firmly implemented commercial and labor policy. Any far-reaching and perceptive attempt to execute such a policy will necessarily lead to the irrefutable conclusion that the German State needs colonial possessions. . . .

For us, the colonial question is not at all a question of political power. Whoever is guided by the desire for expanding German power has a poor understanding of it. It is rather a question of culture. Economic needs linked to broad national perspectives point to practical action. In looking for colonial possessions Germany is not prompted by the desire for expanding its power; it wants only to fulfill a national, we may even say a moral duty. . . .

In looking for commercial colonies the question is WHERE? German participation seems most important in the colonial exploitation of newly-opened Central Africa. . . . In the 20 years since Livingstone's epoch-making discovery, Central Africa has been opened by various explorers and travellers with admirable energy; it has been a brilliant success. The significance of Central Africa is much greater in every respect than has been assumed since antiquity. Should not Germany in its need for colonies participate energetically in the competition for this massive territory? . . .

Germany has no need to strengthen its political power in the Orient. The oriental question is in no way a political one, but rather a cultural one. And for the final solution of the oriental question we claim even now the prominent participation of Germany. . . .

A German colonial policy naturally can take shape only gradually. . . . In any case, we would do well, to follow the English model in regard to colonial administration.

What matters above all is to raise our understanding about the significance and necessity of colonial possessions and thereby forcefully arouse the will of the nation in that direction. When we have overcome all opposition and

turn to effective action, our first attempts with their inevitable troubles and difficulties will justify our effort. The German nation has long experience on the oceans, is skilled in industry and commerce, more capable than others in agricultural colonization, and furnished with ample manpower like no other modern highly-cultured nation. Should it not also enter successfully upon this new venture? The more we are convinced that the colonial question has become now a question of life and death for Germany, the fewer doubts we have. Well-planned and powerfully handled, it will have the most beneficial consequences for our economic situation, and for our entire national development. The very fact that we face a new challenge, whose complex consequences are truly virgin territory for the German people, may in many ways prove a benefit. There is much bitterness, much poisonous partisanship in our newly united Germany; to open a promising new course of national development might have a liberating effect, and move the national spirit in a new direction.

Even more important is the consideration that a people at the height of their political power can successfully maintain their historic position only as long as they recognize and prove themselves as the bearers of a cultural mission. That is the only way which guarantees the stability and growth of national prosperity, which is the necessary basis for an enduring source of power. In past years Germany has contributed only its intellectual and literary work to this century; now we have turned to politics and become powerful. But if the goal of political power becomes an end in itself, it leads to hardness, even to barbarism, unless that nation is willing to undertake the inspirational, moral, and economic leadership of the times. The French economist Leroy-Beaulieu concludes his book on colonization with these words: "that nation is the greatest in the world which leads in colonization. If it does not do so today, it will do so tomorrow." Nobody can deny that in this respect England is far superior to all other states. Admittedly, during the past century we have often been told, especially in Germany, about "the declining might of England.". . . But that kind of talk is petty-bourgeois nonsense, as we look around the globe and assess the ever-increasing colonial possessions of Great Britain, the strength which it draws from them, the skills of its administration, and the dominant position which the Anglo-Saxon stock occupies in all overseas countries. England maintains its worldwide possessions and its maritime ascendancy with barely a quarter of the armed forces supporting our continental states; they are not only an economic asset but also the most convincing proof of its solid power and its cultural energy.

It would be well if we Germans began to learn from the colonial destiny of our Anglo-Saxon cousins and emulate them in peaceful competition. When, centuries ago, the German empire stood at the head of the European states, it was the foremost commercial and maritime power. If the new Germany wants to restore and preserve its traditional powerful position in future, it will conceive of it as a cultural mission and no longer hesitate to practice its colonizing vocation.

Paul Leroy-Beaulieu
COLONIZATION AMONG MODERN PEOPLE

Through his family and marriage, Paul Leroy-Beaulieu (1843–1916) was deeply involved in French political life. After his country's defeat in the Franco-Prussian War and the rise of Bismarck's united Germany, Leroy-Beaulieu advanced the message that made him famous: colonial expansion was a question of life and death for France. At first he had little success. As he complained in 1873: "How we would wish that France would participate a little more in this movement of exploration, of occupation, and of civilization of the globe."

Subsequently he made a brilliant career as a journalist, editor of influential journals, professor, and member of the Academy of Moral and Political Sciences, pleading his cause. In 1885 he published *Colonization Among Modern People,* a potent and learned plea for colonial expansion. Accepting England's leading role, he observed German and Russian colonial ambitions, while upholding France's claims to Algiers and Tunis and arguing in favor of France's mission in central Africa. He also applauded French expansion in Indo-China (now Vietnam and Cambodia).

Leroy-Beaulieu's arguments in favor of colonization cover a wide range of factors, including emigration, finance, and international relations. But the main thrust was the appeal to the national ego: colonization is the civilizing worldwide mission for France, its highest destiny. The selection printed below offers essential insights into the motives promoting imperialist expansion at the end of the nineteenth century, applicable also to Germany.

Every passing day convinces me more and more of the importance of colonial expansion in general and, above all, of its importance for France. We should therefore seize every occasion available to make our country understand its great colonizing mission, by word of mouth, by articles, books, public speeches; we should employ all means to remind France that she has been a great colonial power, which can and should be revived. In the last two centuries

French politics has lost its sense of direction. After having secured our European boundaries at the end of the 17th century, the task which faced us was to develop the immense territories which we occupied in two continents: Canada, the banks of the Mississippi, Louisiana in North America, and India in Asia.

Unfortunately our Europe-centered politics prevailed for two hundred years and left our country with diminished prestige and territory; our colonies were the ransom for our European losses. We have abandoned our colonies with casual wastefulness. What could have been more frivolous than Voltaire's comment about "the loss of some acres of snow in Canada"?[1] The Louisiana territories were sold for a few millions;[2] Santo Domingo, the pearl of the Antilles, was left to return to semi-barbarousness;[3] our immense Indian empire was reduced to five tiny dots on the map.[4] Those were catastrophes which the majority of our historians scarcely mention; it seems that for them these are negligible facts.

Today, however, the national conscience appears to be more enlightened; we begin to appreciate the importance of colonies. For the immense colonial domain we have lost in the 18th century, the 19th century can substitute a new one, no doubt smaller, less diverse, yet still considerable. Unexpected events allowed us to enter Algeria, and despite singularly inappropriate hesitation we just acquired Tunisia. In Asia Indochina may become the nucleus of an empire which, though it cannot attain the importance of India, will be one of the most beautiful dependencies which a European power

possesses on the old Asian continent. In the South Pacific, New Caledonia is more than a small island, and its empty archipelagos may still be added, if we hurry, to that distant possession of ours. Should we exploit and develop this colonial domain now at our disposal? Or are we condemned to an incurable colonizing incapacity? Should we repeat in the 19th and 20th century the mistakes we made in the 18th century?

We believe in the civilizing mission of France and our capacity for colonial development. Recent years have proved that France does not lack the spirit of enterprise. The greatest works in these times outside Europe are accomplished by Frenchmen. We have, notably in Indochina, explorers as hardened as La Salle.[5] Our country sends out adventurers as original and daring as any in this century.

France, it is said, does not have an oversupply of population, which is considered an insurmountable obstacle to colonization. This objection is not decisive. The birthrate in our country presents an annual surplus of about 100,000 people. We need much less for founding empires. We don't find 100,000 Englishmen in India; no more than 35,000 Dutchmen are in Indonesia. There are three kinds of colonies: colonies for exploitation like India or Indochina, colonies for settlement like Australia, and mixed colonies like Algeria. Only the second kind requires considerable immigration. Colonies of exploitation don't need it, and the mixed colonies can be content with a moderate influx of Europeans. If France dispatches 15–20,000 colonizers to Africa every year, this is sufficient for serving the European immigrants as well as the large indigenous population. A regular arrival in Africa of 15–20,000 Frenchmen every year will create in about a century on the other side of the Mediterranean a society of 10 to 12 million people speaking French and imbued with the French spirit.

---

[1]Voltaire was referring to the Treaty of Paris in 1763, when France ceded Canada to the British.

[2]The Louisiana Territory, conquered from Spain in 1793, was sold by Napoleon to the United States in 1803.

[3]The Spanish colony of Santo Domingo, which shared the Caribbean island of Hispaniola with Haiti, was ceded to France in 1795. After a turbulent period it was returned to Spanish rule in 1809. It achieved independence as the Dominican Republic in 1865.

[4]Its armies in India defeated by the British, France, under the Treaty of Paris in 1763, retained only a few scattered outposts, including Pondichéry and Chandernago.

[5]La Salle was a French explorer in North America. He claimed Louisiana (named after Louis XIV, the king of France) for his country in 1682.

The true nerve of colonization, however, is capital rather than emigrants. France possesses plenty of capital; it willingly and confidently disseminates it to all four corners of the universe. It is already pouring 20 to 25 billion francs into the world; every year that figure grows by at least one billion more. If a third or a half of that sum, or even a quarter, be sent to Algeria, Tunis, Senegal, or the Sudan, where I hope we will do well to assure our predominance, what splendid results we will see in 25 or 30 years!

What is lacking is a supporting spirit for our colonial politics. Colonization has been relegated to the second place in our national conscience. Today it should be placed first. Our European policy, threatening to produce only disappointments, should in the future be merely defensive. It is outside Europe that we will be able to satisfy our legitimate instincts for expansion. We should work for setting up a great African empire and a lesser one in Asia.

That is the grand enterprise which destiny holds out for us. At the beginning of the 20th century Russia will have 120 million prolific people, occupying an enormous space. Almost 60 million Germans, supporting 30 million Austrians, dominate central Europe. One hundred and twenty million Anglo-Saxons occupy the most beautiful regions of the world and impose upon almost the whole civilized world their language, which extends already today over territories inhabited by more than three hundred million people. Add to these great people the Chinese empire, which undoubtedly will start a new life! Compared with these giants, where will France be? The grand role which it played in the past, the decisive influence which gave direction to all civilized peoples: what will restore it? It is a memory fading from day to day.

Our country has a means of escaping that incurable misfortune: it must colonize. If we don't colonize, we will fall in two or three centuries below the Spaniards and Portuguese, who had the uncommon happiness of implanting their race and language in the immense spaces of South America, destined to nourish a population of hundreds of millions. Colonization is for France a question of life and death. Will France be a great African power, or will it become a second-rate European power counting, in one or two centuries, as little in the world as Greece or Romania count in Europe. We envision for our country the highest destiny: France, having become an established colonial nation, will again have open before it high hopes and big perspectives.

REVIEW QUESTIONS

1. Why, according to Fabri, did Germany need colonies? What capacities did it possess for acquiring colonies?
2. Was Fabri being truthful when he asserted that the search for colonial possessions did not mean expanding German power but rather fulfilling a national or moral duty?
3. What prerequisites for colonial expansion, according to Leroy-Beaulieu, did France possess? What was missing?
4. What was the worldwide context, past, present, and future, in which Leroy-Beaulieu placed France's "legitimate instincts for expansion"?
5. Comparing Fabri and Leroy-Beaulieu's statements, what similarities and what differences do you detect?

3 European Rule in Africa

Africa, the world's second-largest continent after Asia, posed a special challenge to European imperialists who penetrated its tropical depths. While its territories north of the Sahara desert had long been integrated into Mediterranean and Mideastern life, in sub-Saharan Africa the Europeans encountered harrowing conditions as nowhere else in the world. They were repelled by the debilitating climate, impenetrable rainforests, deadly diseases, the great variety of black-skinned peoples and their strange customs. Seen through European eyes, Africans were illiterate heathen barbarians, still trading in helpless slaves among themselves and with Arabs, decades after Western countries had banned slave trading in Africa.

Cultural differences conditioned by African geography and climate constituted an immense divide between Europeans and Africans. The profound inequality in military and political power provided the sharpest contrast. Africans lived mostly in small communities divided by over one thousand languages; a few large states like Mali and Songai had grown up under Muslim influence but had collapsed by the sixteenth century. Cut off from developments in the Far East and western Europe that had long stimulated science, technology, and political power, sub-Saharan Africans, divided among themselves, helplessly faced the Europeans, who were equipped with superior weapons and backed up by powerful states. Inevitably, they fell victim to European imperialism. By the late nineteenth century Europeans had acquired sufficient resources, including medicines against tropical diseases, to explore the interior and establish their rule. Sub-Saharan Africa now became the focus of rivalry among England, France, and Germany; even the king of Belgium claimed a share in the much publicized "scramble for Africa."

At times the European conquerors proceeded with unrestrained brutality, proclaiming that the "inferior" races of Africa had to be sacrificed to "progress," expressed in the language of Social Darwinism.

Cecil Rhodes and Lo Bengula
IMPERIALISM IN PRACTICE

A good example of how colonial expansion in Africa proceeded is furnished by Cecil Rhodes's dealings with Lo Bengula, king of Matabeleland, Mashonaland, and adjacent territories (now Zimbabwe). In his "Confession of Faith" of 1877 Rhodes had included hope for poor Africans: "just fancy those parts [of the world] that are at present inhabited by the most despicable specimens of human beings, what an alternative there would be if they were brought under Anglo-Saxon influence." Eleven years later, eager to expand his business, he arranged through three of his agents a contract with Lo Bengula, giving his agents "the complete and inclusive charge" of all the metals and minerals in the king's lands. In return, he pledged a financial subsidy and delivery of weapons. The illiterate Lo Bengula put his mark to the contract reproduced below.

Know all men by these presents, that whereas Charles Dunell Rudd, of Kimberley; Rochfort Maguire, of London; and Francis Robert Thompson, of Kimberley, have covenanted and agreed . . . to pay me . . . the sum of one hundred pounds sterling, British currency, on the first day of every lunar month: and further, to deliver at my royal kraal one thousand Martini-Henry breech-loading rifles, together with one hundred thousand rounds of suitable ball cartridges . . . and further to deliver on the Zambesi River a steamboat with guns suitable for defensive purposes, or in lieu of the said steamboat, should I [so] elect, to pay to me the sum of five hundred pounds sterling, British currency. On the execution of these presents, I, Lo Bengula, King of Matabeleland, Mashonaland, and other adjoining territories . . . do hereby grant and assign unto the said grantees . . . the complete and exclusive charge over all metals and minerals situated and contained in my kingdoms . . . together with full power to do all things that they may deem necessary to win and procure the same, and to hold, collect, and enjoy the profits and revenues, if any, derivable from the said metals and minerals, subject to the aforesaid payment; and whereas I have been much molested of late by divers persons seeking and desiring to obtain grants and concessions of land and mining rights in my territories, I do hereby authorize the said grantees . . . to exclude from my kingdom . . . all persons seeking land, metals, minerals, or mining rights therein, and I do hereby undertake to render them all such needful assistance as they may from time to time require for the exclusion of such persons, and to grant no concessions of land or mining rights . . . without their consent and concurrence. . . . This given under my hand this thirtieth day of October, in the year of our Lord 1888, at my royal kraal.

Lo Bengula X his mark
C. D. Rudd
Rochfort Maguire
F. R. Thompson

When the terms of the contract became known among Lo Bengula's subjects, they protested that their ruler had been tricked. After having his fears confirmed by friendly British missionaries, Lo Bengula executed his Head Counsellor and sent a mission to Queen Victoria. After an unsatisfactory response, he sent a formal protest on April 23, 1889. This pathetic appeal from the untutored African ruler had no effect on the course of events. He was told by the Queen's Advisor that it was "impossible for him to exclude white men." The Advisor said that the Queen had made enquiries as to the persons concerned and was satisfied that they "may be trusted to carry out the working for gold in the chief's country without molesting his people, or in any way interfering with their kraals [villages], gardens [cultivated fields], or cattle." Thus Rhodes made Lo Bengula's territories his personal domain and part of the British Empire.

Following is Lo Bengula's futile appeal to Queen Victoria.

Some time ago a party of men came to my country, the principal one appearing to be a man called Rudd. They asked me for a place to dig for gold, and said they would give me certain things for the right to do so. I told them to bring what they could give and I would show them what I would give. A document was written and presented to me for signature. I asked what it contained, and was told that in it were my words and the words of those men. I put my hand to it. About three months afterwards I heard from other sources that I had given by that document the right to all the minerals of my country. I called a meeting of my *Indunas* [counsellors], and also of the white men and demanded a copy of the document. It was proved to me that I had signed away the mineral rights of my whole country to Rudd and his friends. I have since had a meeting of my *Indunas* and they will not recognise the paper, as it contains neither my words nor the words of those who got it. . . . I write to you that you may know the truth about this thing.

Edmund Morel
THE BLACK MAN'S BURDEN

E.D. Morel (1873–1924) was an English author and journalist with a keen sense of moral responsibility, who was especially concerned with the colonial exploitation of Africa. The most extreme abuses of the nineteenth century took place in the Congo Free State established in 1885 under the personal rule of King Leopold II of Belgium. By 1904 the king's ruthless methods of enriching himself while destroying the native population had become a scandal widely publicized in England and the United States. Morel took a leading part in denouncing the selfish exploiters of the Congo System. As a result, in 1908 Leopold II was forced to turn over his colonial domain to the Belgian government, which initiated more humane policies.

After World War I, Morel, moved by "the desolation and misery into which Europe was plunged," foresaw a new era heralding the birth of "an international conscience in regard to Africa." In 1920 he published his book, *The Black Man's Burden: The White Man in Africa from the Fifteenth Century to World War I.* While recognizing the accomplishments of Europeans in Africa, "many of them worthy of admiration," he was foremost concerned with the immense suffering Europe had inflicted upon the peoples of that continent, pleading that "Africa is really helpless against the material goods of the white man, as embodied in the trinity of imperialism, capitalistic-exploitation, and militarism." He wanted to make the public aware of the evils that were still perpetrated in many African regions. As a left-wing intellectual and a member of Parliament for the Labour Party, he thus helped to set off an anti-colonial tide of compassion for the African people. The following passages are selected from Morel's description of the Congo System.

The Congo Free State—known since August, 1908, as the Belgian Congo—is roughly one million square miles in extent. When Stanley discovered the course of the Congo and observed its densely-populated river banks, he formed the, doubtless very much exaggerated, estimate that the total population amounted to forty millions. In the years that followed, when the country had been explored in every direction by travellers of divers nationalities, estimates varied between twenty and thirty millions. No estimate fell below twenty millions. In 1911 an official census was taken. It was not published in Belgium, but was reported in one of the British Consular dispatches. *It revealed that only eight and a half million people were left.* The Congo system lasted for the best part of twenty years. The loss of life can never be known with even approximate exactitude. But data, extending over successive periods, are procurable in respect of a number of regions, and a careful study of these suggests that a figure of ten million victims would be a very conservative estimate.

. . . It is very difficult for anyone who has not experienced in his person the sensations of the tropical African forest to realise the tremendous handicaps which man has to contend against whose lot is cast beneath its sombre shades; the extent to which nature, there seen in her most titanic and ruthless moods, presses upon man; the intellectual disabilities against which man must needs constantly struggle not to sink to the level of the brute; the incessant combat to preserve life and secure nourishment. Communities living in this environment who prove themselves capable of systematic agriculture and of industry; who are found to be possessed of keen commercial instincts; who are quick at learning, deft at working iron and copper, able to weave cloths of real artistic design; these are communities full of promise in which the divine spark burns brightly. To destroy these activities; to reduce all the varied, and picturesque, and stimulating episodes in savage life to a dull routine of endless toil for uncomprehended ends; to dislocate social ties and disrupt social institutions; to stifle nascent desires and crush mental development; to graft upon primitive passions the annihilating evils of scientific slavery, and the bestial imaginings of civilised man, unrestrained by convention or law; in fine, to kill the soul in a people—this is a crime which transcends physical murder. And this crime it was, which, for twenty dreadful years, white men perpetrated upon the Congo natives. . . .

From 1891 until 1912, the paramount object of European rule in the Congo was the pillaging of its natural wealth to enrich private interests in Belgium. To achieve this end a specific, well-defined System was thought out in Brussels and applied on the Congo. . . .

The Policy was quite simple. Native rights in land were deemed to be confined to the actual sites of the town or village, and the areas under food cultivation around them. Beyond those areas no such rights would be admitted. The land was "vacant," *i.e.,* without owners. Consequently the "State" was owner. The "State" was Leopold II., not in his capacity of constitutional Monarch of Belgium, but as Sovereign of the "Congo Free State." Native rights in nine-tenths of the Congo territory be-

ing thus declared non-existent, it followed that the native population had no proprietary right in the plants and trees growing upon that territory, and which yielded rubber, resins, oils, dyes, etc.: no right, in short, to anything animal, vegetable, or mineral which the land contained. In making use of the produce of the land, either for internal or external trade or internal industry and social requirements, the native population would thus obviously be making use of that which did not belong to it, but which belonged to the "State," *i.e.,* Leopold II. It followed logically that any third person—European or other—acquiring, or attempting to acquire, such produce from the native population by purchase, in exchange for corresponding goods or services, would be guilty of robbery, or attempted robbery, of "State property." A "State" required revenue. Revenue implied taxation. The only articles in the Congo territory capable of producing revenue were the ivory, the rubber, the resinous gums and oils; which had become the property of the "State." The only medium through which these articles could be gathered, prepared and exported to Europe—where they would be sold and converted into revenue—was native labour. Native labour would be called upon to furnish those articles in the name of "taxation."

. . . Regulations were issued forbidding the natives to sell rubber or ivory to European merchants, and threatening the latter with prosecution if they bought these articles from the natives. In the second place, every official in the country had to be made a partner in the business of getting rubber and ivory out of the natives in the guise of "taxation." Circulars, which remained secret for many years, were sent out, to the effect that the paramount duty of Officials was to make their districts yield the greatest possible quantity of these articles; promotion would be reckoned on that basis. As a further stimulus to "energetic action" a system of sliding-scale bonuses was elaborated, whereby the less the native was "paid" for his *labour* in producing these articles of "taxation," *i.e.,* the lower the outlay in obtaining them, the higher was the Official's commission. . . . "Concessionaire" Companies were created to which the King farmed out a large proportion of the total territory, retaining half the shares in each venture. These privileges were granted to business men, bankers, and others with whom the King thought it necessary to compound. They floated their companies on the stock exchange. The shares rose rapidly. . . .

These various measures at the European end were comparatively easy. The problem of dealing with the natives themselves was more complex. A native army was the pre-requisite. The five years . . . [from 1886 to 1891] were employed in raising the nucleus of a force of 5,000. It was successively increased to nearly 20,000 apart from the many thousands of "irregulars" employed by the Concessionaire Companies. This force was amply sufficient for the purpose, for a single native soldier armed with a rifle and with a plentiful supply of ball cartridge can terrorise a whole village. The same system of promotion and reward would apply to the native soldier as to the Official— the more rubber from the village, the greater the prospect of having a completely free hand to loot and rape. A systematic warfare upon the women and children would prove an excellent means of pressure. They would be converted into "hostages" for the good behaviour, in rubber collecting, of the men. "Hostage houses" would become an institution in the Congo. But in certain parts of the Congo the rubber-vine did not grow. This peculiarity of nature was, in one way, all to the good. For the army of Officials and native soldiers, with their wives, and concubines, and camp-followers generally, required feeding. The non-rubber producing districts should feed them. Fishing tribes would be "taxed" in fish; agricultural tribes in foodstuffs. In this case, too, the women and children would answer for the men. Frequent military expeditions would probably be an unfortunate necessity. Such expeditions would demand in every case hundreds of carriers for the transport of loads, ammunition, and general impedimenta. Here, again, was an excellent school in which this idle people could learn the dignity of labour. The whole territory would thus become a busy hive of human activities, continuously and usefully engaged for the benefit of the "owners" of the soil thousands of miles away, and their crowned Head, whose intention, proclaimed on repeated occasions to an admiring world, was the "moral and material regeneration" of the natives of the Congo.

Such was the Leopoldian "System," briefly epitomised. It was conceived by a master brain.

Richard Meinertzhagen
AN EMBATTLED COLONIAL OFFICER IN EAST AFRICA

Richard Meinertzhagen (1878–1967) was stationed as a young soldier in Kenya from 1902 to 1906, serving on the raw frontier of British imperialism. Living under great hardships in the African wilderness, exposed to poisoned arrows, his sensibilities outraged by the practices of people the colonial conquerors called "niggers" and "savages," he participated in imposing British rule on the rebellious Nandi tribe. In his spare time he enjoyed shooting wild animals, while also appreciating as an ornithologist the exotic birds he observed. The entries in his diary reprinted below provide insight into the harrowing experiences and the anguish of an isolated young Englishman facing the strains of colonial service, where Western and indigenous ways clashed more sharply than anywhere else in the world.

August 20, 1902

News came in this evening that a policeman had been murdered by a village only a mile or so from the station, as a protest against the white men. . . . At midnight I sent a reliable native to the offending village to ascertain what was happening. He returned at 3 a.m. this morning, saying all the neighbouring villages had joined forces with the offending village and were at the moment conducting an orgy round the dead policeman's body, which had been badly mutilated. A council of war had been held by the natives and they had decided to march on Fort Hall at dawn. So we marched out of the station at 3.30 a.m., crossed the Mathyoia and reached our destination half an hour before dawn. The village had bonfires burning and the Wakikuyu were dancing round them in all their war-paint. It was really rather a weird sight. The alarm was given by a native who tried to break through our rather thin cordon. He refused to stop when challenged and was shot down. There was then a rush from the village into the surrounding bush, and we killed about 17 niggers. Two policemen and one of my men were killed. I narrowly escaped a spear which whizzed past my head. Then the fun began. We at once burned the village and captured the sheep and goats. After that we systematically cleared the valley in which the village was situated, burned all the huts, and killed a few more niggers, who finally gave up the fight and cleared off, but not till 3 more of our men had been killed.

At 3 p.m. we returned to Fort Hall and told the chiefs who had assembled to meet us that they were to go out to the village at once, get into touch with the local chief, bring him in, and generally spread the news that our anger was by no means appeased. They returned just before dark with a deputation from the village, saying their chief was killed and they begged for mercy. McClean [a fellow official] fined them 50 head of cattle, at the same time intimating that half would be remitted if the murderers of the policeman were produced. This they promised to do tomorrow. We have told them that we are quite prepared to continue tomorrow what we began today, and I think they are impressed. Such nonsense as attacking the station is completely driven from their stupid heads. So order once more reigns in Kenya District.

September 8, 1902

I have performed a most unpleasant duty today. I made a night march to the village at the edge of forest where the white settler had been so brutally murdered the day before yesterday. Though the war drums were sounding throughout the night we reached the village without incident and surrounded it. By the light of fires we could see savages dancing in the village, and our guides assured me that they were dancing round the mutilated body of the white man.

I gave orders that every living thing except children should be killed without mercy. I hated the work and was anxious to get through with it. So soon as we could see to shoot we closed in. Several of the men tried to break out but were immediately shot. I then assaulted the place before any defence could be prepared. Every soul was either shot or bayoneted, and I am happy to say that no children were in the village. They, with the younger women, had already been removed by the villagers to the forest. We burned all the huts and razed the banana plantations to the ground.

In the open space in the centre of the village was a sight which horrified me—a naked white man pegged out on his back, mutilated and disembowelled, his body used as a latrine by all and sundry who passed by. We washed his corpse in a stream and buried him just outside the village. The whole of this affair took so short a time that the sun was barely up before we beat a retreat to our main camp.

My drastic action on this occasion haunted me for many years, and even now I am not sure whether I was right. My reason for killing all adults, including women, was that the latter had been the main instigators of not only the murder but the method of death, and it was the women who had befouled the corpse after death.

November 23, 1902

Meanwhile a Land Office under my friend Barton Wright has been started with a view to parcelling out land to settlers. Eliot thinks there is a great future for East Africa, transforming it into a huge white farming and stock area. Perhaps that is correct, but sooner or later it must lead to a clash between black and white. I cannot see millions of educated Africans—as there will be in a hundred years' time—submitting tamely to white domination. After all, it is an African country, and they will demand domination. Then blood will be spilled, and I have little doubt about the eventual outcome.

January 12, 1904

The authorities give no help. The administrative officers, with few exceptions, seem to dislike their country being mapped by soldiers. In fact the soldier is not in favour in British East Africa. This is largely due to the low class of man who is appointed to administrative appointments. Few of them have had any education, and many of them do not pretend to be members of the educated class. One can neither read nor write. This is not surprising when one realises that no examination is required to enter the local Civil Service. Sir Clement Hill, who recently visited the colony on behalf of the Foreign Office, remarked that "so long as Civil Servants were enlisted from the gutter" we could not expect a high standard of administration. When such men are given unlimited power over uneducated and simple-minded natives it is not extraordinary that they should abuse their powers, suffer from megalomania and regard themselves as little tin gods.

February 19, 1904

Before this expedition started I issued an order to my company and to the Masai Levies [African soldiers in the pay of the British authorities] that if any man was guilty of killing women or children he would be shot. My men are mere savages in the laws and customs of war, and the Masai are bloodthirsty villains to whom the killing of women and children means nothing.

Today we had occasion to rush a small village in which some of the enemy were concealed and from which they were firing arrows at the column. I quickly formed up 10 of my men and 30 Masai and rushed the place. The enemy ran, and we killed 4 of them. I formed up this party some 150 yards on the other side of the village before moving on, and then heard a woman shriek from the village, which I had presumed empty. I ran back to the village, where I saw two of my men and three Masai in the act of dragging a woman from a hut, and the body of a small boy on the ground, one of the Levies being in the act of withdrawing his spear from the little body. Another levy was leading a small girl by the hand and was about to knock her on the head with his knobkerrie [a short club with a knob at the end]. I yelled to him to stay his hand, but I suppose his blood was up, for he paid no attention to me and killed the child. Meanwhile one of my own men bayoneted the woman within 30 yards of me. Putting up my rifle I shot the man dead and then his companion, who I think contemplated having a pot shot at me. The Levies bolted, but I bagged them all three before they were clear of the village.

July 27, 1904

On reading through the first part of this record I am shocked by the account of taking human life and the constant slaughter of big game. I do not pretend to excuse it, but perhaps I may explain it. I have no belief in the sanctity of human life or in the dignity of the human race. Human life has never been sacred; nor has man, except in a few exceptional cases, been dignified. Moreover, in Kenya fifty years ago, when stationed with 100 soldiers amid an African population of some 300,000, in cases of emergency where local government was threatened we had to act, and act quickly. To do nothing in an emergency is to do something definitely wrong, and talking comes under the category of "nothing." There was no telegraph or telephone, no motor cars or wireless, and action was imperative for safety. Thank God there was no time or opportunity for talks, conferences and discussions.

I also regarded discipline in my company as paramount, more important when dealing with coloured troops than with one's own country-men. What may appear to have been outrageous and cruel conduct on my part was an insistence on strict discipline—the obedience of orders. I have seen so many coloured troops rendered useless by inefficient discipline.

September 15, 1905

Living isolated in a savage country, rarely speaking my own language, and surrounded by a population whose civilisation is on a much lower plane than my own are conditions to which I have indeed grown accustomed, but which do not improve on acquaintance unless one lowers one's own plane to that of the savage, when perhaps one might be contented. Isolation from my family, whose formative effect has been considerable on my character, is dreary and might of itself account for unwholesome ideas and gloomy thoughts. I seem to have received a heavy sowing of unhappiness and depression, which seems to thrive in the isolated conditions which I now experience. . . .

Normally I am healthy-minded, but the worries and conditions of the past few months have been too much for me. All men are not affected in the same way. Others with greater strength of character than myself might suffer little from moral and intellectual starvation. To others, natural history or some object of unceasing pursuit is an effective barrier against complete isolation. But my experience shows me that it is but a small percentage of white men whose characters do not in one way or another undergo a subtle process of deterioration when they are compelled to live for any length of time among savage races and under such conditions as exist in tropical climates. It is hard to resist the savagery of Africa when one falls under its spell. One soon reverts to one's ancestral character, both mind and temperament becoming brutalised. I have seen so much of it out here and I have myself felt the magnetic power of the African climate drawing me lower and lower to the level of a savage. This is a condition which is accentuated by worry or mental depression, and which has to be combated with all the force in one's power. My love of home and my family, the dread of being eventually overcome by savage Africa, the horror of losing one's veneer of western civilisation and cutting adrift from all one holds good—these are the forces which help me to fight the temptation to drift down to the temporary luxury of the civilisation of the savage.

March 17, 1906

My 5 years are up this year, and I must decide whether or not to revert to my regiment. I think I had better go back, for if I were to remain out here much longer I should get less and less anxious ever to go back to my British regiment, and that I know I would in the end regret. But I admit I am a bit tired of this sort of life. It is too solitary for any length of time. Niggers are rather getting on my nerves, the climate is making me feel depressed, and altogether I feel I want a change. I want to be more with my own folk than with these savages. . . .

March 20, 1906

Natives are queer creatures and hold still queerer ideas. No European can fully understand the working of the black mind. Their morals, ideals and principles are all based on quite different models from ours, and it frequently happens that some trivial and unnoticed incident gives them an impression which the European would never discern.

It is hard to put oneself in their place, as I try to do. A white man is so essentially different in every respect, and unless one is master of their language, manners and customs, only attainable after many years' residence in their country, it is a risky boast to imagine that one understands them. By doing so one arrives at wrong conclusions, which is worse than having an empty mind on the subject.

Albert Schweitzer
A CONCERNED DOCTOR IN TROPICAL AFRICA

The son of a Protestant minister living in Alsace, at the border between French and German cultures, Albert Schweitzer (1875–1965) early proved himself a keen student of theology, philosophy, history, and music, with an exceptional talent for playing Bach on the organ. He also turned into a prolific writer, refining his intellectual interests in the study of civilizations around the world. At the age of thirty he decided to dedicate his life to medical service in tropical Africa. While pursuing his earlier interests he completed his medical studies in 1913 and established a hospital at Lambaréné amidst the forests of Ogowe in the French colony of Equatorial Africa. With interruptions in Europe for lecturing, writing, and being celebrated as a cultural hero, he spent his life at Lambaréné, where he died at the age of 90.

The first selection below is taken from his book *On the Edge of the Primeval Forest* (1922), in which he reported his experiences when first wrestling with the relations between European civilization and the African "child of nature." His work as a physician required an un-African authority over his patients; yet his ethical convictions insisted not only upon a basic human equality but also upon a sense of guilt over the miseries inflicted by the imperialists. The second selection, from his autobiography written a decade later, takes a somewhat broader view of the clash between civilization and colonialism, casting light on African developments to the present. Both selections show the insights of an unusually perceptive and morally committed European into the bewildering relations between African and European cultures.

A word . . . about the relations between the whites and the blacks. What must be the general character of the intercourse between them? Am I to treat the black man as my equal or as my inferior? I must show him that I can re-

spect the dignity of human personality in every one, and this attitude in me he must be able to see for himself; but the essential thing is that there shall be a real feeling of brotherliness. How far this is to find complete expression in the sayings and doings of daily life must be settled by circumstances. The negro is a child, and with children nothing can be done without the use of authority. We must, therefore, so arrange the circumstances of daily life that my natural authority can find expression. With regard to the negroes, then, I have coined the formula: "I am your brother, it is true, but your elder brother. . . ."

When, before coming to Africa, I heard missionaries and traders say again and again that one must be very careful out here to maintain this authoritative position of the white man, it seemed to me to be a hard and unnatural position to take up, as it does to every one in Europe who reads or hears the same. Now I have come to see that the deepest sympathy and kindness can be combined with this insistence on certain external forms, and indeed are only possible by means of them. . . . A white man can only have real authority if the native respects him. No one must imagine that the child of nature looks up to us merely because we know more, or can do more, than he can, . . . because [the white man] possesses railways and steamer, can fly in the air, or travel under water. . . . [B]ut on one point he has an unerring intuition, and that is on the question whether any particular white man is a real, moral personality or not. If the native feels that he is this, moral authority is possible; if not, it is simply impossible to create it. The child of nature, not having been artificialised and spoilt as we have been, has only elementary standards of judgment, and he measures us by the most elementary of them all, the moral standard. Where he finds goodness, justice, and genuineness of character, real worth and dignity, that is, behind the external dignity given by social circumstances, he bows and acknowledges his master; where he does not find them he remains really defiant in spite of all appearance of submission, and says to himself: "This white is no more of a man than I am, for he is not a better one than I am."

Let me say that the child of nature thinks a great deal more than is generally supposed.

Even though he can neither read nor write, he has ideas on many more subjects than we imagine. Conversations I have had in the hospital with old natives about the ultimate things of life have deeply impressed me. The distinction between white and coloured, educated and uneducated, disappears when one gets talking with the forest dweller about our relations to each other, to mankind, to the universe, and to the infinite. "The negroes are deeper than we are," a white man once said to me, "because they don't read newspapers," and the paradox has some truth in it. . . . On the whole I feel that the primitive man is much more good natured than we Europeans are; with Christianity added to his good qualities wonderfully noble characters can result. I expect I am not the only white man who feels himself put to shame by the natives. . . .

Ever since the world's far-off lands were discovered, what has been the conduct of the white peoples to the coloured ones? What is the meaning of the simple fact that this and that people has died out, that others are dying out, and that the condition of others is getting worse and worse as a result of their discovery by men who professed to be followers of Jesus? Who can describe the injustice and the cruelties that in the course of centuries they have suffered at the hands of Europeans? Who can measure the misery produced among them by the fiery drinks and the hideous diseases that we have taken to them? If a record could be compiled of all that has happened between the white and the coloured races, it would make a book containing numbers of pages, referring to recent as well as to early times, which the reader would have to turn over unread, because their contents would be too horrible.

We and our civilisation are burdened, really, with a great debt. We are not free to confer benefits on these men, or not, as we please; it is our duty. Anything we give them is not benevolence but atonement. For every one who scattered injury someone ought to go out to take help, and when we have done all that is in our power, we shall not have atoned for the thousandth part of our guilt. That is the foundation from which all deliberations about "works of mercy" out there must begin.

It goes without saying that Governments must help with the atonement, but they cannot do so till there already exists in society a conviction on the subject. The Government alone can never discharge the duties of humanitarianism; from the nature of the case that rests with society and individuals.

In his autobiography, *Out of My Life and Thought* (1933), published eleven years after *On the Edge of the Primeval Forest,* Schweitzer added some reflections about the undesirable consequences of ending colonial rule.

Have we white people the right to impose our rule on primitive and semi-primitive peoples—my experience has been gathered among such only? No, if we only want to rule over them and draw material advantage from their country. Yes, if we seriously desire to educate them and help them to attain to a condition of well-being. If there were any sort of possibility that these peoples could live really by and for themselves, we could leave them to themselves. But as things are, the world trade which has reached them is a fact against which both we and they are powerless. They have already through it lost their freedom. Their economic and social relations are shaken by it. An inevitable development brought it about that the chiefs, with the weapons and money which commerce placed at their disposal, reduced the mass of the natives to servitude and turned them into slaves who had to work for the export trade to make a few select people rich. It sometimes happened too that, as in the days of the slave trade, the people themselves became merchandise, and were exchanged for money, lead, gunpowder, tobacco, and brandy. In view of the state of things produced by world trade

there can be no question with these peoples of real independence, but only whether it is better for them to be delivered over to the mercies, tender or otherwise, of rapacious native tyrants or to be governed by officials of European states.

That of those who were commissioned to carry out in our name the seizure of our colonial territories many were guilty of injustice, violence, and cruelty as bad as those of the native chiefs, and so brought on our heads a load of guilt, is only too true. Nor of the sins committed against the natives to-day must anything be suppressed or whitewashed. But willingness to give these primitive and semi-primitive people of our colonies an independence which would inevitably end in enslavement to their fellows, is no way of making up for our failure to treat them properly. Our only possible course is to exercise for the benefit of the natives the power we actually possess, and thus provide a moral justification for it. Even the hitherto prevailing 'imperialism' can plead that it has some qualities of ethical value. It has put an end to the slave trade; it has stopped the perpetual wars which the primitive peoples used to wage with one another, and has thus given a lasting peace to large portions of the world; it endeavours in many ways to produce in the colonies conditions which shall render more difficult the exploitation of the population by world trade. I dare not picture what the lot of the native lumbermen in the forests of the Ogowe district would be if the Government authorities which at the present time preserve their rights for them in opposition to the merchants, both white and black, should be withdrawn.

What so-called self-government means for primitive and semi-primitive peoples can be gathered from the fact that in the Black Republic of Liberia, domestic slavery and what is far worse, the compulsory shipment of labourers to other countries, have continued down to our own day. They were both abolished on October 1st, 1930—on paper.

REVIEW QUESTIONS

1. How did Cecil Rhodes gain control over the riches in Lo Bengula's land? Did his method match the good intentions expressed in his "Confession of Faith" (see page 214)?
2. What were the effects of King Leopold's rule over the Congo peoples? How did he establish the "Leopoldian System"?
3. Describe Richard Meinertzhagen's attitude toward the Africans he encountered.
4. What was Meinertzhagen's attitude toward colonial service in East Africa? Did he change his attitude during his four years there?
5. What were the essential points in Schweitzer's assessment of the personal relations between Europeans like himself and the African "child of nature"?
6. How did Schweitzer assess the moral and political aspects of colonial rule?

---

4 British Rule in India

The Indian subcontinent represented a high level of culture, but it was also deeply divided by language, ethnicity, local rule, and religion. The bitter competition between Hindus and Muslims was a constant source of tension. Europeans could not help noticing the widespread poverty and human misery. Politically weak, India had attracted European conquerors since the sixteenth century—first the Portuguese, then Dutch, French, and English. The English, acting through the East India Company, ousted their European rivals in the eighteenth century. India certainly could not match the superior military power of the Europeans.

British rule aimed at exploitation; exporting Indian cotton to Britain as a raw material, it ruined the Indian textile trade in favor of the Lancashire industrialized mills. Indian cloth could no longer be sold in Britain, but all India was a market for British textiles. Exploitation led to the Indian uprising in 1857–58, after which the British government took over direct rule from the East India Company, soon incorporating India into the British Empire; Queen Victoria became empress of India in 1877. Although it was the pride of British colonialism, "the jewel in the crown," fractious India proved difficult to govern.

The British rulers also felt a moral obligation to raise the peoples of India to their own level. Lord Lytton in 1878 suggested a profound cultural revolution for that purpose, and the British made positive changes. They introduced Western accomplishments, advancing railway construction, irrigation, public education, and religious toleration; indirectly they even promoted Indian patriotism. By 1930 independence was under discussion. Yet inevitably British rule also stirred up among British-educated Indian intellectuals a new Indian self-consciousness, radically in the case of Mohandas Gandhi's passive resistance, and more moderately expressed by Jawaharlal Nehru (see page 438) in 1944.

In 1947 India achieved independence, while Muslim Pakistan was granted separate statehood. In 1971 East Pakistan broke away from Pakistan and renamed itself Bangladesh. But independence disproved Nehru's (and Gandhi's) charge that British rule was responsible for India's poverty. Standards of living in the Indian subcontinent are still among the lowest in the world, while political tensions continue to run high.

Lord Lytton
SPEECH TO THE CALCUTTA LEGISLATURE, 1878

Lord Lytton (1831–1891) came from an aristocratic family. He gained recognition as a poet, while also serving in diplomatic posts at European capitals. In 1876, surprisingly, he was appointed viceroy of India, facing war on the Afghan frontier and trouble with Russia, as well as a major famine. He organized famine relief, promoted internal free trade in India, and decentralized the British administration, hoping to benefit the Indian masses. In 1877 he designed a triumphal pageant to celebrate the proclamation of Queen Victoria as empress of India.

Lord Lytton felt warmly about the Indians, and he tried to practice tolerance toward the native people while protecting the supremacy of British rule. His artistic temperament and lack of experience made him an ineffective administrator, and his rule was unpopular. Yet he was a man of unusual sensibility, and in a speech delivered in 1878, Lytton provided great insight into the revolutionary impact of British imperialism upon India. Excerpts from this speech follow.

We have endeavoured to base our rule in India on justice, uprightness, progressive enlightenment, and good government, as these are understood in England; and it is at least a plausible postulate, which at first sight appears to be a sound one, that, so long as these are the characteristics of our rule, we need fear no disaffection on the part of the masses.

It must, however, be remembered that the problem undertaken by the British rulers of India (a political problem more perplexing in its conditions and, as regards the results of its solution, more far-reaching than any which, since the dissolution of the Pax Romana,[1] has been undertaken by a conquering race) is the application of the most refined principles of European government, and some of the most

artificial institutions of European society, to a vast Oriental population, in whose history, habits and traditions they have had no previous existence. Such phrases as "Religious toleration," "Liberty of the press," "Personal freedom of the subject," "Social supremacy of the Law," and others, which in England have long been the mere catchwords of ideas common to the whole race, and deeply impressed upon its character by all the events of its history, and all the most cherished recollections of its earlier life, are here in India, to the vast mass of our native subjects, the mysterious formulas of a foreign, and more or less uncongenial, system of administration, which is scarcely, if at all, intelligible to the greater number of those for whose benefit it is maintained. It is a fact which, when I first came to India, was strongly impressed on my attention by one of India's wisest and most thoughtful administrators; it

---

[1]Covering the period 27 B.C. to A.D. 180, the Pax Romana (the Roman Peace) was the high point of Roman rule.

is a fact which there is no disguising; and it is also one which cannot be too constantly or too anxiously recognised, that by enforcing these principles, and establishing these institutions, we have placed, and must permanently maintain ourselves at the head of a gradual but gigantic revolution—the greatest and most momentous social, moral, and religious, as well as political, revolution which, perhaps, the world has ever witnessed.

Mohandas K. Gandhi
PASSIVE RESISTANCE

While Lord Lytton and his successors envisaged India's future in terms of British ideals, a powerful contrary trend surfaced, derived from Indian spirituality. It was led by Mohandas Gandhi, the key figure in the Indian drive for independence.

Gandhi (1869–1948) was born into a prosperous lower-caste Hindu family and studied law in London. As a lawyer he moved to British South Africa, where he, a dark-skinned Indian, was at once subjected to racist humiliation. He bravely resisted the organized discrimination against the Indian immigrant community. As their chief defender, he developed political skills drawing creatively on his Hindu heritage and significantly reducing discrimination against Indians. By 1908 Gandhi had formulated his life's conviction, which guided his political leadership: passive resistance or "soul-force." Dedicated to poverty and utter simplicity of life and a convinced vegetarian, he turned into a monkish ascetic.

In 1914 Gandhi returned to his native India, determined to practice passive resistance in the struggle for peace and unity among its divided peoples and above all for liberation from British rule. From the start he was concerned with India's poor peasants, urging them to increase their earnings by making their own cloth. He himself set a symbolic example, squatting bare-chested, all skin and bones, in front of a crude spinning wheel. More dramatically, in 1930 he organized a huge mass of peasants for a 200-mile march to the ocean in order to make salt out of seawater, in defiance of the British monopoly on salt production. Another of his major concerns was discrimination against the untouchables, the lowest Hindu caste, reduced by tradition to the most menial jobs and regarded as pariahs. Gandhi called them "children of God," and in 1932, while jailed for political agitation, conducted a "fast to death" on their behalf, thereby gaining a measure of recognition for them. His fasts became a powerful political force, watched in India and around the world.

Gandhi's main commitment, however, was to nonviolent protest against British rule. After World War I he took a leading role in the anti-British agitation that led in 1919 to the infamous slaughter of unarmed Indians by British troops at Amritsar. After spending two years in jail he rose to be an outstanding political leader, widely worshipped as *Mahatma,* a model of high-mindedness and spiritual power.

Mahatma Gandhi became a public force, recognized even in England; while there in 1931, he formally demanded India's independence. The British, however, cracked down on the resulting nonviolent protests; Gandhi and his new ally, Jawaharlal Nehru, were jailed. Subsequently Gandhi, recognizing its high cost, suspended civil disobedience. In World War II Gandhi and his disciples followed a course of quiet opposition until 1942, when Indian nationalists rejected the British offer of postwar autonomy and demanded complete independence; Gandhi was jailed again. After fasting almost to death he was released in 1944, to face the agonies that resulted from the separation of Muslim Pakistan from Hindu India, which accompanied full independence, granted at last in 1947. India now was torn by bloody riots between Muslims and Hindus, while Gandhi urged peace by demonstratively fasting, to no effect. His even-handedness toward Muslims aroused bitter hostility among high-caste Indians, one of whom assassinated him early in 1948.

India had achieved independence, but Gandhi's message of passive resistance, dramatized by his murder, remained but a hopeful vision in a forever violent world. It later inspired Martin Luther King Jr.'s nonviolent civil-rights protests in the United States. In the selection below, Gandhi describes the essence of passive resistance.

Passive resistance is a method of securing rights by personal suffering; it is the reverse of resistance by arms. When I refuse to do a thing that is repugnant to my conscience, I use soul-force. For instance, the Government of the day has passed a law which is applicable to me. I do not like it. If by using violence I force the Government to repeal the law, I am employing what may be termed body-force. If I do not obey the law and accept the penalty for its breach, I use soul-force. It involves sacrifice of self.

Everybody admits that sacrifice of self is infinitely superior to sacrifice of others. Moreover, if this kind of force is used in a cause that is unjust, only the person using it suffers. He does not make others suffer for his mistakes. Men have before now done many things which were subsequently found to have been wrong. No man can claim that he is absolutely in the right or that a particular thing is wrong because he thinks so, but it is wrong for him so long as that is his deliberate judgement. It is therefore meet that he should not do that which he knows to be wrong, and suffer the consequence whatever it may be. This is the key to the use of soul-force. . . .

When we do not like certain laws, we do not break the heads of law-givers but we suffer and do not submit to the laws. That we should obey laws whether good or bad is a new-fangled notion. There was no such thing in former days. The people disregarded those laws they did not like and suffered the penalties for their breach. It is contrary to our manhood if we obey laws repugnant to our conscience. Such teaching is opposed to religion and means slavery. If the Government were to ask us to go about without any clothing, should we do so? If I were a passive resister, I would say to them that I would have nothing to do with their law. But we have so forgotten ourselves and become so compliant that we do not mind any degrading law.

A man who has realized his manhood, who fears only God, will fear no one else. Man-made laws are not necessarily binding on him. Even the Government does not expect any such thing from us. They do not say: "You must do such and such a thing," but they say "If you do not do it, we will punish you." We are sunk so low that we fancy that it is our duty and our religion to do what the law lays down. If man will only realize that it is unmanly to obey laws that are unjust, no man's tyranny will enslave him. This is the key to self-rule or home-rule.

It is a superstition and ungodly thing to believe that an act of a majority binds a minority. Many examples can be given in which acts of majorities will be found to have been wrong and those of minorities to have been right. All reforms owe their origin to the initiation of minorities in opposition to majorities. If among a band of robbers a knowledge of robbing is obligatory, is a pious man to accept the obligation? So long as the superstition that men should obey unjust laws exists, so long will their slavery exist. And a passive resister alone can remove such a superstition.

To use brute-force, to use gunpowder, is contrary to passive resistance, for it means that we want our opponent to do by force that which we desire but he does not. And if such a use of force is justifiable, surely he is entitled to do likewise by us. And so we should never come to an agreement. We may simply fancy, like the blind horse moving in a circle round a mill, that we are making progress. Those who believe that they are not bound to obey laws which are repugnant to their conscience have only the remedy of passive resistance open to them. Any other must lead to disaster. . . .

Extremists are considered to be advocates of brute force. Why do they, then, talk about obeying laws? I do not blame them. They can say nothing else. When they succeed in driving out the English and they themselves become governors, they will want you and me to obey their laws. And that is a fitting thing for their constitution. But a passive resister will say he will not obey a law that is against his conscience, even though he may be blown to pieces at the mouth of a cannon.

What do you think? Wherein is courage required—in blowing others to pieces from behind a cannon, or with a smiling face to approach a cannon and be blown to pieces? Who is the true warrior—he who keeps death always as a bosom-friend, or he who controls the death of others? Believe me that a man devoid of courage and manhood can never be a passive resister.

This however, I will admit: that even a man weak in body is capable of suffering this resistance. One man can offer it just as well as millions. Both men and women can indulge in it. It does not require the training of an army; it needs no jiu-jitsu. Control over the mind is alone necessary, and when that is attained, man is free like the king of the forest and his very glance withers the enemy.

REVIEW QUESTIONS

1. Why did Lord Lytton consider the British impact on India "the greatest and most momentous social, moral, and religious, as well as political, revolution which, perhaps, the world has ever witnessed"?
2. How did Gandhi apply his sense of "soul-force" to the conduct of politics?
3. Considering Gandhi's worldwide fame, how would you assess the impact of his philosophy?

CHAPTER 10
Modern Consciousness

SIGMUND FREUD, the eminent and influential twentieth-century Austrian-Jewish psychiatrist, photographed in 1914 in Vienna by one of his sons. Beside Freud is a reproduction of Michelangelo's *Dying Slave*. (*Mary Evans Picture Library/Sigmund Freud Copyrights*)

The closing decades of the nineteenth century and the opening of the twentieth witnessed a crisis in Western thought. Rejecting the Enlightenment belief in the essential rationality of human beings, thinkers such as Friedrich Nietzsche and Sigmund Freud stressed the immense power of the nonrational in individual and social life. They held that subconscious drives, impulses, and instincts lay at the core of human nature, that people were moved more by religious-mythic images and symbols than by logical thought, that feelings determine human conduct more than reason does. This new image of the individual led to unsettling conclusions. If human beings are not fundamentally rational, then what are the prospects of resolving the immense problems of modern industrial civilization? Although most thinkers shared the Enlightenment's visions of humanity's future progress, doubters were also heard.

The crisis of thought also found expression in art and literature. Artists like Pablo Picasso and writers like James Joyce and Franz Kafka exhibited a growing fascination with the nonrational—with dreams, fantasies, sexual conflicts, and guilt, with tortured, fragmented, and dislocated inner lives. In the process, they rejected traditional esthetic standards established during the Renaissance and the Enlightenment and experimented with new forms of artistic and literary representation.

These developments in thought and culture produced insights into human nature and society and opened up new possibilities in art and literature. But such changes also contributed to the disorientation and insecurity that characterized the twentieth century.

1   The Overman and the Will to Power

Few modern thinkers have aroused more controversy than the German philosopher Friedrich Nietzsche (1844–1900). Although scholars pay tribute to Nietzsche's originality and genius, they are often in sharp disagreement over the meaning and influence of his work. Nietzsche was a relentless critic of modern society. He attacked democracy, universal suffrage, equality, and socialism for suppressing a higher type of human existence. Nietzsche was also critical of the Western rational tradition. The theoretical outlook, the excessive intellectualizing of philosophers, he said, smothers the will, thereby stifling creativity and nobility; reason also falsifies life through the claim that it allows apprehension of universal truth. Nietzsche was not opposed to the critical use of the intellect, but like the romantics, he focused on the immense vitality of the emotions. He also held that life is a senseless flux devoid of any overarching purpose. There are no moral values revealed by God. Indeed, Nietzsche proclaimed that God is dead. Nor are values and certainties woven into the fabric of nature that can be apprehended by reason—the "natural rights of man," for example. All the values taught by Christian and bourgeois thinkers are without foundation, said Nietzsche. There is only naked man living in a godless and absurd world.

Nietzsche called for the emergence of the *overman* or *superman,* a higher type of man who asserts his will, gives order to chaotic passions, makes great demands on himself, and lives life with a fierce joy. The overman aspires to self-perfection. Without fear or guilt, he creates his own values and defines his own life. In this way, he overcomes nihilism—the belief that there is nothing of ultimate value. It is such rare individuals, the highest specimens of humanity, that concern Nietzsche, not the herdlike masses.

The superman grasps the central reality of human existence—that people instinctively, uncompromisingly, ceaselessly, strive for power. The will to exert power is the determining factor in domestic politics, personal relations, and international affairs. Life is a contest in which the enhancement of power is the ultimate purpose of our actions; it brings supreme enjoyment: "the love of power is the demon of men. Let them have everything—health, food, a place to live, entertainment—they are and remain unhappy and low-spirited: for the demon waits and waits and will be satisfied. Take everything from them and satisfy this and they are almost happy—as happy as men and demons can be."

Friedrich Nietzsche
THE WILL TO POWER
AND *THE ANTICHRIST*

Two of Nietzsche's works—*The Will to Power* and *The Antichrist*—are represented in the following readings. First published in 1901, one year after Nietzsche's death, *The Will to Power* consists of the author's notes written in the years 1883 to 1888. The following passages from this work show Nietzsche's contempt for democracy and socialism and proclaim the will to power.

THE WILL TO POWER
720 (1886–1887)

The most fearful and fundamental desire in man, his drive for power—this drive is called "freedom"—must be held in check the longest. This is why ethics . . . has hitherto aimed at holding the desire for power in check: it disparages the tyrannical individual and with its glorification of social welfare and patriotism emphasizes the power-instinct of the herd.

728 (March–June 1888)

. . . A society that definitely and *instinctively* gives up war and conquest is in decline: it is ripe for democracy and the rule of shopkeepers—In most cases, to be sure, assurances of peace are merely narcotics.

751 (March–June 1888)

"The will to power" is so hated in democratic ages that their entire psychology seems directed toward belittling and defaming it. . . .

752 (1884)

. . . Democracy represents the disbelief in great human beings and an elite society: "Everyone is equal to everyone else." "At bottom we are one and all self-seeking cattle and mob."

753 (1885)

I am opposed to 1. socialism, because it dreams quite naively of "the good, true, and beautiful" and of "equal rights" (— anarchism also desires the same ideal, but in a more brutal fashion); 2. parliamentary government and the press, because these are the means by which the herd animal becomes master.

762 (1885)

European democracy represents a release of forces only to a very small degree. It is above all a release of laziness, of weariness, of *weakness*.

765 (Jan.–Fall 1888)

. . . Another Christian concept, no less crazy, has passed even more deeply into the tissue of modernity: the concept of the "equality of souls before God." This concept furnishes the prototype of all theories of equal rights: mankind was first taught to stammer the proposition of equality in a religious context, and only later was it made into morality: no wonder that man ended by taking it seriously, taking it practically!—that is to say, politically, democratically, socialistically, in the spirit of the pessimism of indignation.

854 (1884)

In the age of *suffrage universel,* i.e., when everyone may sit in judgment on everyone and everything, I feel impelled to reestablish *order of rank.*

855 (Spring–Fall 1887)

What determines rank, sets off rank, is only quanta of power, and nothing else.

857 (Jan.–Fall 1888)

I distinguish between a type of ascending life and another type of decay, disintegration, weakness. Is it credible that the question of the relative rank of these two types still needs to be posed?

858 (Nov. 1887–March 1888)

What determines your rank is the quantum of power you are: the rest is cowardice.

861 (1884)

A declaration of war on the masses by *higher men* is needed! Everywhere the mediocre are combining in order to make themselves master! Everything that makes soft and effeminate, that serves the ends of the "people" or the "feminine," works in favor of *suffrage universel,* i.e., the dominion of *inferior* men. But we should take reprisal and bring this whole affair (which in Europe commenced with Christianity) to light and to the bar of judgment.

862 (1884)

A doctrine is needed powerful enough to work as a breeding agent: strengthening the strong, paralyzing and destructive for the world-weary.

The annihilation of the decaying races. Decay of Europe.—The annihilation of slavish evaluations.—Dominion over the earth as a means of producing a higher type.—The annihilation of the tartuffery [hypocrisy] called "morality." . . . The annihilation of *suffrage universel;* i.e., the system through which the lowest natures prescribe themselves as laws for the higher.—The annihilation of mediocrity and its acceptance. (The onesided, individuals—peoples; to strive for fullness of nature through the pairing of opposites: race mixture to this end).—The new courage—no *a priori* [innate and universal] truths (such truths were sought by those accustomed to faith!), but a *free* subordination to a ruling idea that has its time: e.g., time as a property of space, etc.

870 (1884)

The root of all evil: that the slavish morality of meekness, chastity, selflessness, absolute obedience, has triumphed—ruling natures were thus condemned (1) to hypocrisy, (2) to torments of conscience—creative natures felt like rebels against God, uncertain and inhibited by eternal values. . . .

In summa: the best things have been slandered because the weak or the immoderate swine have cast a bad light on them—and the best men have remained hidden—and have often misunderstood themselves.

874 (1884)

The degeneration of the rulers and the ruling classes has been the cause of the greatest mischief in history! Without the Roman Caesars and Roman society, the insanity of Christianity would never have come to power.

When lesser men begin to doubt whether higher men exist, then the danger is great! And one ends by discovering that there is *virtue* also among the lowly and subjugated, the poor in spirit, and that *before God* men are equal—which has so far been the . . . [height] of nonsense on earth! For ultimately, the higher men measured themselves according to the standard of virtue of slaves—found they were "proud," etc., found all their higher qualities reprehensible.

997 (1884)

I teach: that there are higher and lower men, and that a single individual can under certain circumstances justify the existence of whole millennia—that is, a full, rich, great, whole human being in relation to countless incomplete fragmentary men.

998 (1884)

The highest men live beyond the rulers, freed from all bonds; and in the rulers they have their instruments.

999 (1884)

Order of rank: He who *determines* values and directs the will of millennia by giving direction to the highest natures is the *highest* man.

1001 (1884)

Not "mankind" but *overman* is the goal!

1067 (1885)

. . . This world is the will to power—and nothing besides! And you yourselves are also this will to power—and nothing besides!

Nietzsche regarded Christianity as a life-denying religion that appeals to the masses. Fearful and resentful of their betters, he said, the masses espouse a faith that preaches equality and compassion. He maintained that Christianity has "waged a war to the death against (the) higher type of man." The following passages are from *The Antichrist*, written in 1888.

THE ANTICHRIST

2. What is good?—All that heightens the feeling of power, the will to power, power itself in man.

What is bad?—All that proceeds from weakness.

What is happiness?—The feeling that power *increases*—that a resistance is overcome.

Not contentment, but more power; *not* peace at all, but war; *not* virtue, but proficiency (virtue in the Renaissance style, *virtù*, virtue free of moralic acid).

The weak and ill-constituted shall perish: first principle of *our* philanthropy. And one shall help them to do so.

What is more harmful than any vice?—Active sympathy for the ill-constituted and weak—Christianity. . . .

3. The problem I raise here is not what ought to succeed mankind in the sequence of species (—the human being is an *end*—): but what type of human being one ought to *breed,*

ought to *will,* as more valuable, more worthy of life, more certain of the future.

This more valuable type has existed often enough already: but as a lucky accident, as an exception, never as *willed.* He has rather been the most feared, he has hitherto been virtually *the* thing to be feared—and out of fear the reverse type has been willed, bred, *achieved:* the domestic animal, the herd animal, the sick animal man—the Christian. . . .

5. One should not embellish or dress up Christianity: it has waged *a war to the death* against this *higher* type of man, it has excommunicated all the fundamental instincts of this type, it has distilled evil, the *Evil One,* out of these instincts—the strong human being as the type of reprehensibility, as the "outcast." Christianity has taken the side of everything weak, base, ill-constituted, it has made an ideal out of *opposition* to the preservative instincts of strong life; it has depraved the reason even of the intellectually strongest natures by teaching men to feel the supreme values of intellectuality as sinful, as misleading, as *temptations.* The most deplorable example: the depraving of Pascal,[1] who believed his reason had been depraved by original sin while it had only been depraved by his Christianity!. . .

7. Christianity is called the religion of *pity.*—Pity stands in antithesis to the tonic emotions which enhance the energy of the feeling of life: it has a depressive effect. One loses force when one pities. . . .

15. In Christianity neither morality nor religion come into contact with reality at any point. Nothing but imaginary *causes* ("God," "soul," "ego," "spirit," "free will"—or "unfree will"): nothing but imaginary *effects* ("sin," "redemption," "grace," "punishment," "forgiveness of sins"). . . .

18. The Christian conception of God—God as God of the sick, God as spider, God as spirit—is one of the most corrupt conceptions of God arrived at on earth: perhaps it even represents the low-water mark in the descending development of the God type. God degenerated to the *contradiction of life,* instead of being its transfiguration and eternal *Yes!* In God a declaration of hostility towards life, nature, the will to life! God the formula for every calumny of "this world," for every lie about 'the next world'! In God, nothingness deified, the will to nothingness sanctified! . . .

21. In Christianity the instincts of the subjugated and oppressed come into the foreground: it is the lowest classes which seek their salvation in it. . . .

43. The poison of the doctrine *"equal* rights for all"—this has been more thoroughly sowed by Christianity than by anything else; from the most secret recesses of base instincts, Christianity has waged a war to the death against every feeling of reverence and distance between man and man, against, that is, the *precondition* of every elevation, every increase in culture—it has forged out of the [resentment] of the masses its *chief weapon* against *us,* against everything noble, joyful, high-spirited on earth, against our happiness on earth. . . . "Immortality" granted to every Peter and Paul has been the greatest and most malicious outrage on *noble* mankind ever committed.—*And* let us not underestimate the fatality that has crept out of Christianity even into politics! No one any longer possesses today the courage to claim special privileges or the right to rule, the courage to feel a sense of reverence towards himself and towards his equals—the courage for a *pathos of distance.* . . . Our politics is *morbid* from this lack of courage!—The aristocratic outlook has been undermined most deeply by the lie of equality of souls; and if the belief in the "prerogative of the majority" makes revolutions and *will continue to make them*—it is Christianity, let there be no doubt about it, *Christian* value judgement which translates every revolution into mere blood and crime! Christianity is a revolt of everything that crawls along the ground directed against that which is *elevated:* the Gospel of the "lowly" *makes* low. . . .

---

[1]Blaise Pascal (1623–1662) was a French mathematician, philosopher, and eloquent defender of the Christian faith.

REVIEW QUESTIONS

1. Do you agree with Friedrich Nietzsche about a human being's most elemental desire?
2. Why did Nietzsche attack democracy and socialism? How do you respond to his attack?
3. What were Nietzsche's criticisms of Christianity? How do you respond to this attack?
4. How does Nietzsche's philosophy stand in relation to the Enlightenment?

---

2 The Unconscious

After graduating from medical school in Vienna, Sigmund Freud (1856–1939), the founder of psychoanalysis, specialized in the treatment of nervous disorders. By encouraging his patients to speak to him about their troubles, Freud was able to probe deeper into their minds. These investigations led him to conclude that childhood fears and experiences, often sexual in nature, accounted for neuroses—hysteria, anxiety, depression, obsessions, and so on. So threatening and painful were these childhood emotions and experiences that his patients banished them from conscious memory to the realm of the unconscious. To understand and treat neurotic behavior, Freud said it is necessary to look behind overt symptoms and bring to the surface emotionally charged experiences and fears—childhood traumas—that lie buried in the unconscious. Freud probed the unconscious by urging his patients to say whatever came to their minds. This procedure, called free association, rests on the premise that spontaneous and uninhibited talk reveals a person's underlying preoccupations, his or her inner world. A second avenue to the unconscious is the analysis of dreams; an individual's dreams, said Freud, reveal his or her secret wishes.

Sigmund Freud
THE UNCONSCIOUS, PSYCHOANALYSIS, AND *CIVILIZATION AND ITS DISCONTENTS*

Readings from three works of Freud are included: *A Note on the Unconscious in Psychoanalysis, Five Lectures on Psychoanalysis,* and *Civilization and Its Discontents.* Freud's scientific investigation of psychic development led him to conclude that powerful mental processes hidden from consciousness govern human behavior more than reason does. His exploration of the unconscious produced a new image of the human being that has had a profound impact on twentieth-century thought. In the following excerpt from *A Note on the Unconscious in Psychoanalysis* (1912), Freud defined the term *unconscious*.

A NOTE ON THE UNCONSCIOUS IN PSYCHOANALYSIS

I wish to expound in a few words and as plainly as possible what the term 'unconscious' has come to mean in psychoanalysis and in psychoanalysis alone. . . .

. . . The well-known experiment, . . . of the 'post-hypnotic suggestion' teaches us to insist upon the importance of the distinction between *conscious* and *unconscious* and seems to increase its value.

In this experiment, as performed by Bernheim,[1] a person is put into a hypnotic state and is subsequently aroused. While he was in the hypnotic state, under the influence of the physician, he was ordered to execute a certain action at a certain fixed moment after his awakening, say half an hour later. He awakes, and seems fully conscious and in his ordinary condition; he has no recollection of his hypnotic state, and yet at the prearranged moment there rushes into his mind the impulse to do such and such a thing, and he does it consciously, though not knowing why. It seems impossible to give any other description of the phenomenon than to say that the order has been present in the mind of the person in a condition of latency, or had been present unconsciously, until the given moment came, and then had become conscious. But not the whole of it emerged into consciousness: only the conception of the act to be executed. All the other ideas associated with this conception—the order, the influence of the physician, the recollection of the hypnotic state, remained unconscious even then. . . .

[1] Hippolyte Bernheim (1840–1919), a French physician, used hypnosis in the treatment of his patients and published a successful book on the subject.

The mind of the hysterical patient is full of active yet unconscious ideas; all her symptoms proceed from such ideas. It is in fact the most striking character of the hysterical mind to be ruled by them. If the hysterical woman vomits, she may do so from the idea of being pregnant. She has, however, no knowledge of this idea, although it can easily be detected in her mind, and made conscious to her, by one of the technical procedures of psychoanalysis. If she is executing the jerks and movements constituting her 'fit,' she does not even consciously represent to herself the intended actions, and she may perceive those actions with the detached feelings of an onlooker. Nevertheless analysis will show that she was acting her part in the dramatic reproduction of some incident in her life, the memory of which was unconsciously active during the attack. The same preponderance of active unconscious ideas is revealed by analysis as the essential fact in the psychology of all other forms of neurosis. . . .

. . . The term *unconscious* . . . designates . . . ideas with a certain dynamic character, ideas keeping apart from consciousness in spite of their intensity and activity.

This passage from a lecture given in 1909 describes Freud's attempt to penetrate the world of the unconscious.

FIVE LECTURES ON PSYCHOANALYSIS

. . . At first, I must confess, this seemed a senseless and hopeless undertaking. I was set the task of learning from the patient something that I did not know and that he did not know himself. How could one hope to elicit it?

But there came to my help a recollection of a most remarkable and instructive experiment which I had witnessed when I was with Bernheim at Nancy [in 1889]. Bernheim showed us that people whom he had put into a state of hypnotic somnambulism [a hypnotically induced condition of sleep in which acts are performed], and who had had all kinds of experiences while they were in that state, only *appeared* to have lost the memory of what they had experienced during somnambulism; it was possible to revive these memories in their normal state. It is true that, when he questioned them about their somnambulistic experiences, they began by maintaining that they knew nothing about them; but if he refused to give way, and insisted, and assured them that they *did* know about them, the forgotten experiences always reappeared.

So I did the same thing with my patients. When I reached a point with them at which they maintained that they knew nothing more, I assured them that they *did* know it all the same, and that they had only to say it; and I ventured to declare that the right memory would occur to them at the moment at which I laid my hand on their forehead. In that way I succeeded, without using hypnosis, in obtaining from the patients whatever was required for establishing the connection between the pathogenic [capable of causing disease] scenes they had forgotten and the symptoms left over from those scenes. But it was a laborious procedure, and in the long run an exhausting one; and it was unsuited to serve as a permanent technique.

I did not abandon it, however, before the observations I made during my use of it afforded me decisive evidence. I found confirmation of the fact that the forgotten memories were not lost. They were in the patient's possession and were ready to emerge in association to what was still known by him; but there was some force that prevented them from becoming conscious and compelled them to remain unconscious. The existence of this force could be assumed with certainty, since one became aware of an effort corresponding to it if, in opposition to it, one tried to introduce the unconscious memories into the patient's consciousness. The force which was maintaining the pathological condition became apparent in the form of *resistance* on the part of the patient.

It was on this idea of resistance, then, that I based my view of the course of psychical events in hysteria. In order to effect a recovery, it had proved necessary to remove these resistances. Starting out from the mechanism of cure, it now became possible to construct quite definite ideas of the origin of the illness. The same forces which, in the form of resistance, were now offering opposition to the forgotten material's being made conscious, must formerly have brought about the forgetting and must have pushed the pathogenic experiences in question out of consciousness. I gave the name of *"repression"* to this hypothetical process, and I considered that it was proved by the undeniable existence of resistance.

The further question could then be raised as to what these forces were and what the determinants were of the repression in which we now recognized the pathogenic mechanism of hysteria. A comparative study of the pathogenic situations which we had come to know through the cathartic procedure made it possible to answer this question. All these experiences had involved the emergence of a wishful impulse which was in sharp contrast to the subject's other wishes and which proved incompatible with the ethical and aesthetic standards of his personality. There had been a short conflict, and the end of this internal struggle was that the idea which had appeared before consciousness as the vehicle of this irreconcilable wish fell a victim to repression, was pushed out of consciousness with all its attached memories, and was forgotten. Thus the incompatibility of the wish in question with the patient's ego was the motive for the repression; the subject's ethical and other standards were the repressing forces. An acceptance of the incompatible wishful impulse or a prolongation of the conflict would have produced a high degree of unpleasure; this unpleasure was avoided by means of repression, which was thus revealed as one of the devices serving to protect the mental personality.

To take the place of a number of instances, I will relate a single one of my cases, in which the determinants and advantages of repression are sufficiently evident. For my present purpose I shall have once again to abridge the case history and omit some important underlying material. The patient was a girl, who had lost her beloved father after she had taken a share in nursing him—a situation analogous to that of Breuer's[2] patient. Soon afterwards her elder sister married, and her new brother-in-law aroused in her a peculiar feeling of sympathy which was easily masked under a disguise of family affection. Not long afterwards her sister fell ill and died, in the absence of the patient and her mother. They were summoned in all haste without being given any definite information of the tragic event. When the girl reached the bedside of her dead sister, there came to her for a brief moment an idea that might be expressed in these words: "Now he is free and can marry me." We may assume with certainty that this idea, which betrayed to her consciousness the intense love for her brother-in-law of which she had not herself been conscious, was surrendered to repression a moment later, owing to the revolt of her feelings. The girl fell ill with severe hysterical symptoms; and while she was under my treatment it turned out that she had completely forgotten the scene by her sister's bedside and the odious egoistic impulse that had emerged in her. She remembered it during the treatment and reproduced the pathogenic moment with signs of the most violent emotion, and, as a result of the treatment, she became healthy once more.

In the tradition of the Enlightenment philosophes, Freud valued reason and science, but he did not share the philosophes' confidence in human goodness and humanity's capacity for future progress. In *Civilization*

---

[2]Joseph Breuer (1842–1925) was an Austrian physician and Freud's early collaborator.

and Its Discontents (1930), Freud posited the frightening theory that human beings are driven by an inherent aggressiveness that threatens civilized life—that civilization is fighting a losing battle with our aggressive instincts. Although Freud's pessimism was no doubt influenced by the tragedy of World War I, many ideas expressed in *Civilization and Its Discontents* derived from views that he had formulated decades earlier.

CIVILIZATION AND ITS DISCONTENTS

The element of truth behind all this, which people are so ready to disavow, is that men are not gentle creatures who want to be loved, and who at most can defend themselves if they are attacked; they are, on the contrary, creatures among whose instinctual endowments is to be reckoned a powerful share of aggressiveness. As a result, their neighbour is for them not only a potential helper or sexual object, but also someone who tempts them to satisfy their aggressiveness on him, to exploit his capacity for work without compensation, to use him sexually without his consent, to seize his possessions, to humiliate him, to cause him pain, to torture and to kill him. *Homo homini lupus.* [Man is wolf to man.] Who, in the face of all his experience of life and of history, will have the courage to dispute this assertion? As a rule this cruel aggressiveness waits for some provocation or puts itself at the service of some other purpose, whose goal might also have been reached by milder measures. In circumstances that are favourable to it, when the mental counter-forces which ordinarily inhibit it are out of action, it also manifests itself spontaneously and reveals man as a savage beast to whom consideration towards his own kind is something alien. Anyone who calls to mind the atrocities committed during the racial migrations or the invasions of the Huns, or by the people known as Mongols under Jenghiz Khan and Tamerlane, or at the capture of Jerusalem by the pious Crusaders, or even, indeed, the horrors of the recent

World War—anyone who calls these things to mind will have to bow humbly before the truth of this view.

The existence of this inclination to aggression, which we can detect in ourselves and justly assume to be present in others, is the factor which disturbs our relations with our neighbour and which forces civilization into such a high expenditure [of energy]. In consequence of this primary mutual hostility of human beings, civilized society is perpetually threatened with disintegration. The interest of work in common would not hold it together; instinctual passions are stronger than reasonable interests. Civilization has to use its utmost efforts in order to set limits to man's aggressive instincts and to hold the manifestations of them in check by psychical reaction-formations. Hence, therefore, the use of methods intended to incite people into identifications and aim-inhibited relationships of love, hence the restriction upon sexual life, and hence too the ideal's commandment to love one's neighbour as oneself—a commandment which is really justified by the fact that nothing else runs so strongly counter to the original nature of man. In spite of every effort, these endeavours of civilization have not so far achieved very much. It hopes to prevent the crudest excesses of brutal violence by itself assuming the right to use violence against criminals, but the law is not able to lay hold of the more cautious and refined manifestations of human aggressiveness. The time comes when each one of us has to give up as illusions the expectations which, in his youth, he pinned upon his fellowmen, and when he may learn how much difficulty and pain has been added to his life by their ill-will. At the same time, it would be unfair to reproach civilization with trying to eliminate strife and competition from human activity. These things are undoubtedly indispensable. But opposition is not necessarily enmity; it is merely misused and made an *occasion* for enmity.

The communists believe that they have found the path to deliverance from our evils.

According to them, man is wholly good and is well-disposed to his neighbour; but the institution of private property has corrupted his nature. The ownership of private wealth gives the individual power, and with it the temptation to ill-treat his neighbour; while the man who is excluded from possession is bound to rebel in hostility against his oppressor. If private property were abolished, all wealth held in common, and everyone allowed to share in the enjoyment of it, ill-will and hostility would disappear among men. Since everyone's needs would be satisfied, no one would have any reason to regard another as his enemy; all would willingly undertake the work that was necessary. I have no concern with any economic criticisms of the communist system. . . . But I am able to recognize that the psychological premises on which the system is based are an untenable illusion. In abolishing private property we deprive the human love of aggression of one of its instruments, certainly a strong one, though certainly not the strongest; but we have in no way altered the differences in power and influence which are misused by aggressiveness, nor have we altered anything in its nature. Aggressiveness was not created by property. It reigned almost without limit in primitive times, when property was still very scanty, and it already shows itself in the nursery almost before property has given up its primal, anal form; it forms the basis of every relation of affection and love among people (with the single exception, perhaps, of the mother's relation to her male child). If we do away with personal rights over material wealth, there still remains prerogative in the field of sexual relationships, which is bound to become the source of the strongest dislike and the most violent hostility among men who in other respects are on an equal footing. If we were to remove this factor, too, by allowing complete freedom of sexual life and thus abolishing the family, the germ-cell of civilization, we cannot, it is true, easily foresee what new paths the development of civilization could take; but one thing we can expect, and that is that this indestructible feature of human nature will follow it there.

It is clearly not easy for men to give up the satisfaction of this inclination to aggression. They do not feel comfortable without it. . . .

If civilization imposes such great sacrifices not only on man's sexuality but on his aggressivity, we can understand better why it is hard for him to be happy in that civilization. . . .

In all that follows I adopt the standpoint, therefore, that the inclination to aggression is an original, self-subsisting instinctual disposition in man, and I return to my view that it constitutes the greatest impediment to civilization.

REVIEW QUESTIONS

1. What was Sigmund Freud's definition of the *unconscious?* What examples of the power of the unconscious did he provide?
2. What did Freud mean by *repression?* What examples of repression did he provide?
3. Compare and contrast the approaches of Freud and Nietzsche to the nonrational.
4. What did Freud consider the "greatest impediment to civilization"? Why?
5. How did Freud react to the Marxist view that private property is the source of evil?
6. Compare Freud's view of human nature and reason to that of Enlightenment philosophes.

3 The Political Potential of the Irrational

The new insights into the irrational side of human nature and the growing assault on reason had immense implications for political life. In succeeding decades, these currents of irrationalism would be ideologized and politicized by unscrupulous demagogues, who sought to mobilize and manipulate the masses. The popularity after World War I of fascist movements, which openly denigrated reason and exalted race, blood, action, and will, demonstrated the naiveté of nineteenth-century liberals, who believed that reason had triumphed in human affairs.

Among the late nineteenth- and early twentieth-century social theorists who focused on the implications of the nonrational for political life were Georges Sorel and Gustave Le Bon. Twentieth-century dictators would employ these social theorists' insights into groups and mass psychology for the purpose of gaining and maintaining power.

Georges Sorel
REFLECTIONS ON VIOLENCE

Nietzsche and Freud proclaimed that irrational forces constitute the essence of human nature. French social theorist Georges Sorel (1847–1922) recognized the political potential of the nonrational. Like Nietzsche, Sorel was disillusioned with contemporary bourgeois society, which he considered decadent, unheroic, and life-denying. He placed his hopes in the proletariat, whose position made them courageous and virile. Sorel wanted workers to destroy the existing bourgeois-liberal-capitalist order and rejuvenate society by infusing it with dynamic and creative energy and a sense of moral purpose. The overthrow of decadent bourgeois society would be accomplished through a general strike: a universal work stoppage that would bring down governments and give power to the workers.

Sorel saw the general strike as having the appeal of a great myth. What was important was not that the general strike actually take place, but that its image stir all the antibourgeois resentment of the workers and inspire them to carry out their revolutionary responsibilities. Sorel understood the extraordinary potency of myth. It structures and intensifies feelings, unifies people, elicits total commitment, and incites heroic action. Because they appeal to the imagination and the emotions, myths are an effective way of organizing the masses, buoying up their spirits, and moving them to acts of revolutionary heroism. By believing in the myth of the general strike, workers would soar above the moral decadence of bourgeois society and bear the immense sacrifices that their struggle calls for. The myth serves a religious function: it unites the faithful into a collectivity with one will and induces a heroic state of mind.

Sorel applauded violence, for it intensified the revolutionaries' dedication to the cause and spurred them to acts of revolutionary heroism. Violence also accorded with his general conception that life is an unremitting battle and that history is a perpetual conflict between decay and vitality, between passivity and action. In his view, struggle purified, invigorated, and promoted creative change.

Sorel's pseudoreligious exaltation of violence and mass action—action for its own sake—his condemnation of liberal democracy and rationalism, his recognition of the power and political utility of irrational and fabricated myths, and his vision of a heroic morality emerging on the ruins of a dying shabby bourgeois world found concrete expression in the fascist movements that emerged after World War I.

In the following selection from *Reflections on Violence* (1908), Sorel explains the function of the myth of the general strike and necessity of violence if the workers are to fulfill their historical role.

Renan* asked what was it that moved the heroes of great wars. "The soldier of Napoleon was well aware that he would always be a poor man, but he felt that the epic in which he was taking part would be eternal, that he would live in the glory of France." The Greeks had fought for glory: the Russians and the Turks seek death because they expect a chimerical paradise. "A soldier is not made by promises of temporal rewards. He must have immortality. In default of paradise, there is glory, which is itself a kind of immortality."

Economic progress goes far beyond the individual life, and profits future generations more than those who create it: but does it give glory? Is there an economic epic capable of stimulating the enthusiasm of the workers? The inspiration of immortality which Renan considered so powerful is obviously without efficacy here, because artists have never produced

*Ernest Renan (1823–1892). French scholar and critic.

masterpieces under the influence of the idea that their work would procure them a place in paradise (as Turks seek death that they may enjoy the happiness promised by Mahomet). The workmen are not entirely wrong when they look on religion as a middle-class luxury, since, as a matter of fact, the emotions it calls up are not those which inspire workmen with the desire to perfect machinery, or which create methods of accelerating labour.

The question must be stated otherwise than Renan put it; do there exist among the workmen forces capable of producing enthusiasm equivalent to those of which Renan speaks, forces which could combine with the ethics of good work, so that in our days, which seem to many people to presage the darkest future, this ethic may acquire all the authority necessary to lead society along the path of economic progress?

We must be careful that the keen sentiment which we have of the necessity of such a morality, and our ardent desire to see it realised does not induce us to mistake phantoms for forces capable of moving the world. The abundant "idyllic" literature of the professors of rhetoric is evidently mere chatter. Equally vain are the attempts made by so many scholars to find institutions in the past, an imitation of which might serve as a means of disciplining their contemporaries; imitation has never produced much good and often bred much sorrow; how absurd the idea is then of borrowing from some dead and gone social structure, a suitable means of controlling a system of production, whose principal characteristic is that every day it must become more and more opposed to all preceding economic systems. Is there then nothing to hope for?

Morality is not doomed to perish because the motive forces behind it will change; it is not destined to become a mere collection of precepts as long as it can still vivify itself by an alliance with an enthusiasm capable of conquering all the obstacles, prejudices, and the need of immediate enjoyment, which oppose its progress. But it is certain that this sovereign force will not be found along the paths which contemporary philosophers, the experts of social science, and the inventors of *far-reaching reforms* would make us go. There is only one force which can produce to-day that enthusiasm without whose co-operation no morality is possible, and that is the force resulting from the propaganda in favour of a general strike. The preceding explanations have shown that the idea of the general strike (constantly rejuvenated by the feelings roused by proletarian violence) produces an entirely epic state of mind, and at the same time bends all the energies of the mind to that condition necessary to the realisation of a workshop carried on by free men, eagerly seeking the betterment of the industry; we have thus recognised that there are great resemblances between the sentiments aroused by the idea of the general strike and those which are necessary to bring about a continued progress in methods of production. We have then the right to maintain that the modern world possesses that prime mover which is necessary to the creation of the ethics of the producers.

I stop here, because it seems to me that I have accomplished the task which I imposed upon myself; I have, in fact, established that proletarian violence has an entirely different significance from that attributed to it by superficial scholars and by politicians. In the total ruin of institutions and of morals there remains something which is powerful, new, and intact, and it is that which constitutes, properly speaking, the soul of the revolutionary proletariat. Nor will this be swept away in the general decadence of moral values, if the workers have enough energy to bar the road to the middle-class corrupters, answering their advances with the plainest brutality.

I believe that I have brought an important contribution to discussions on Socialism; these discussions must henceforth deal exclusively with the conditions which allow the development of specifically proletarian forces, that is to say, *with violence enlightened by the idea of the general strike.* All the old abstract dissertations on the Socialist *régime* of the future become useless; we pass to the domain of real history, to the interpretation of facts—to the ethical evaluations of the revolutionary movement.

The bond which I pointed out in the beginning of this inquiry between Socialism and proletarian violence appears to us now in all its strength. It is to violence that Socialism owes those high ethical values by means of which it brings *salvation* to the modern world.

Gustave Le Bon
MASS PSYCHOLOGY

Gustave Le Bon (1841–1931), a French social psychologist with strong conservative leanings, examined mass psychology as demonstrated in crowd behavior, a phenomenon of considerable importance in an age of accelerating industrialization and democratization. "The substitution of the unconscious action of crowds for the conscious activity of individuals is one of the principal characteristics of the present age," Le Bon declared in the preface to *The Crowd* (1895), excerpts from which follow.

Thousands of isolated individuals may acquire at certain moments, and under the influence of certain violent emotions—such, for example, as a great national event—the characteristics of a psychological crowd. . . .

The most striking peculiarity presented by a psychological crowd is the following: Whoever be the individuals that compose it, however like or unlike be their mode of life, their occupations, their character, or their intelligence, the fact that they have been transformed into a crowd puts them in possession of a sort of collective mind which makes them feel, think, and act in a manner quite different from that in which each individual of them would feel, think, and act were he in a state of isolation. . . .

To obtain [an understanding of crowds] it is necessary in the first place to call to mind the truth established by modern psychology, that unconscious phenomena play an altogether preponderating part not only in organic life, but also in the operations of the intelligence. The conscious life of the mind is of small importance in comparison with its unconscious life. . . . Behind the avowed causes of our acts there undoubtedly lie secret causes that we do not avow, but behind these secret causes there are many others more secret still which we ourselves ignore. The greater part of our daily actions are the result of hidden motives which escape our observation. . . .

. . . In the collective mind the intellectual aptitudes of the individuals, and in consequence their individuality, are weakened . . . and the unconscious qualities obtain the upper hand. . . .

. . . In a crowd every sentiment and act is contagious, and contagious to such a degree that an individual readily sacrifices his personal interest to the collective interest. This is an aptitude very contrary to his nature, and of which a man is scarcely capable, except when he makes part of a crowd. . . .

. . . [An] individual immerged for some length of time in a crowd in action soon finds himself . . . in a special state, which much resembles the state of fascination in which the hypnotised individual finds himself in the hands of the hypnotiser. The activity of the brain being paralysed in the case of the hypnotised subject, the latter becomes the slave of all the unconscious activities of his spinal cord, which the hypnotiser directs at will. The conscious personality has entirely vanished; will and discernment are lost. All feelings and thoughts are bent in the direction determined by the hypnotiser.

Such also is approximately the state of the individual forming part of a psychological crowd. He is no longer conscious of his acts. In his case, as in the case of the hypnotised subject, at the same time that certain faculties are destroyed, others may be brought to a high degree of exaltation. Under the influence of a suggestion, he will undertake the accomplishment of certain acts with irresistible impetuosity. . . . He is no longer himself, but has become an automaton who has ceased to be guided by his will.

Moreover, by the mere fact that he forms part of an organised crowd, a man descends several rungs in the ladder of civilisation. Isolated, he may be a cultivated individual; in a crowd, he is a barbarian—that is, a creature acting by instinct. He possesses the spontaneity, the violence, the ferocity, and also the enthusiasm and heroism of primitive beings, whom he further tends to resemble by the facility with which he allows himself to be impressed by words and images—which would be entirely without action on each of the isolated individuals composing the crowd—and to be induced to commit acts contrary to his most obvious interests and his best-known habits. . . .

In consequence, a crowd perpetually hovering on the borderland of unconsciousness, readily yielding to all suggestions, having all the violence of feeling peculiar to beings who cannot appeal to the influence of reason, deprived of all critical faculty, cannot be otherwise than excessively credulous. The improbable does not exist for a crowd, and it is necessary to bear this circumstance well in mind to understand the facility with which are created and propagated the most improbable legends and stories. . . . A crowd thinks in images, and the image itself immediately calls up a series of other images, having no logical connection with the first. . . . Our reason shows us the incoherence there is in these images, but a crowd is almost blind to this truth, and confuses with the real event what the deforming action of its imagination has superimposed thereon. A crowd scarcely distinguishes between the subjective and the objective. It accepts as real the images evoked in its mind. . . .

Whatever be the ideas suggested to crowds they can only exercise effective influence on condition that they assume a very absolute, uncompromising, and simple shape. They present themselves then in the guise of images, and are only accessible to the masses under this form. These imagelike ideas are not connected by any logical bond of analogy or succession. . . .

. . . A chain of logical argumentation is totally incomprehensible to crowds, and for this reason it is permissible to say that they do not reason or that they reason falsely and are not to be influenced by reasoning. . . . An orator in intimate communication with a crowd can evoke images by which it will be seduced. . . .

. . . [The] powerlessness of crowds to reason aright prevents them displaying any trace of the critical spirit, prevents them, that is, from being capable of discerning truth from error, or of forming a precise judgment on any matter. Judgments accepted by crowds are merely judgments forced upon them and never judgments adopted after discussion. . . .

. . . Crowds are to some extent in the position of the sleeper whose reason, suspended for the time being, allows the arousing in his mind of images of extreme intensity which would quickly be dissipated could they be submitted to the action of reflection. Crowds, being incapable both of reflection and of reasoning, are devoid of the notion of improbability; and it is to be noted that in a general way it is the most improbable things that are the most striking.

This is why it happens that it is always the marvellous and legendary side of events that more specially strike crowds. . . .

Crowds being only capable of thinking in images are only to be impressed by images. It is only images that terrify or attract them and become motives of action. . . .

How is the imagination of crowds to be impressed?. . . [The] feat is never to be achieved by attempting to work upon the intelligence or reasoning faculty, that is to say, by way of demonstration. . . .

Whatever strikes the imagination of crowds presents itself under the shape of a startling and very clear image, freed from all accessory explanation . . . examples in point are a great victory, a great miracle, a great crime, or a great hope. Things must be laid before the crowd as a whole, and their genesis must never be indicated. A hundred petty crimes or petty accidents will not strike the imagination of crowds in the least, whereas a single great crime or a single great accident will profoundly impress them. . . .

When, [the convictions of crowds] are closely examined, whether at epochs marked by fervent religious faith, or by great political upheavals such as those of the last century, it is apparent that they always assume a peculiar form which I cannot better define than by giving it the name of a religious sentiment. . . .

A person is not religious solely when he worships a divinity, but when he puts all the resources of his mind, the complete submission of his will, and the whole-souled ardour of fanaticism at the service of a cause or an individual who becomes the goal and guide of his thoughts and actions.

Intolerance and fanaticism are the necessary accompaniments of the religious sentiment. . . .

All founders of religious or political creeds have established them solely because they were successful in inspiring crowds with those fanatical sentiments which have as result that men find their happiness in worship and obedience and are ready to lay down their lives for their idol. This has been the case at all epochs. . . .

We have already shown that crowds are not to be influenced by reasoning, and can only comprehend rough-and-ready associations of ideas. The orators who know how to make an impression upon them always appeal in consequence to their sentiments and never to their reason. The laws of logic have no action on crowds. To bring home conviction to crowds it is necessary first of all to thoroughly comprehend the sentiments by which they are animated, to pretend to share these sentiments. . . .

As soon as a certain number of living beings are gathered together, whether they be animals or men, they place themselves instinctively under the authority of a chief.

In the case of human crowds the chief is often nothing more than a ringleader or agitator, but as such he plays a considerable part. His will is the nucleus around which the opinions of the crowd are grouped and attain to identity. . . . A crowd is a servile flock that is incapable of ever doing without a master.

The leader has most often started as one of the led. He has himself been hypnotised by the idea, whose apostle he has since become. It has taken possession of him to such a degree that everything outside it vanishes, and that every contrary opinion appears to him an error or a superstition. An example in point is Robespierre, hypnotised by the philosophical ideas of Rousseau, and employing the methods of the Inquisition to propagate them.

The leaders we speak of are more frequently men of action than thinkers. . . . The multitude is always ready to listen to the strong-willed man, who knows how to impose himself upon it. Men gathered in a crowd lose all force of will, and turn instinctively to the person who possesses the quality they lack. . . .

When . . . it is proposed to imbue the mind of a crowd with ideas and beliefs . . . the leaders have recourse to different expedients. The principal of them are three in number and clearly defined—affirmation, repetition, and contagion. . . .

Affirmation pure and simple, kept free of all reasoning and all proof, is one of the surest means of making an idea enter the mind of crowds. The conciser an affirmation is, the more destitute of every appearance of proof and demonstration, the more weight it carries. . . .

Affirmation, however, has no real influence unless it be constantly repeated, and so far as possible in the same terms. It was Napoleon, I believe, who said that there is only one figure in rhetoric of serious importance, namely, repetition. The thing affirmed comes by repetition to fix itself in the mind in such a way that it is accepted in the end as a demonstrated truth.

The influence of repetition on crowds is comprehensible when the power is seen which it exercises on the most enlightened minds.

This power is due to the fact that the repeated statement is embedded in the long run in those profound regions of our unconscious selves in which the motives of our actions are forged. At the end of a certain time we have forgotten who is the author of the repeated assertion, and we finish by believing it.

When an affirmation has been sufficiently repeated and there is unanimity in this repetition . . . what is called a current of opinion is formed and the powerful mechanism of contagion intervenes. Ideas, sentiments, emotions, and beliefs possess in crowds a contagious power as intense as that of microbes.

REVIEW QUESTIONS

1. What relationship did Georges Sorel trace between proletarian violence and the idea of a general strike?
2. According to Gustave Le Bon, how are individuals transformed once they become part of a crowd? How does the leader sway the crowd?
3. Point out instances in recent and contemporary history that support Le Bon's insights.

CHAPTER 11

World War I

WORLD WAR I SOLDIERS charge from trenches in France. *(©Corbis)*

To many Europeans, the opening years of the twentieth century seemed full of promise. Advances in science and technology, the rising standard of living, the expansion of education, and the absence of wars between the Great Powers since the Franco-Prussian War (1870–1871) all contributed to a general feeling of optimism. Yet these accomplishments hid disruptive forces that were propelling Europe toward a cataclysm. On June 28, 1914, Archduke Francis Ferdinand, heir to the throne of Austria-Hungary, was assassinated by Gavrilo Princip, a young Serbian nationalist (and Austrian subject), at Sarajevo in the Austrian province of Bosnia, inhabited largely by South Slavs. The assassination triggered those explosive forces that lay below the surface of European life, and six weeks later, Europe was engulfed in a general war that altered the course of Western civilization.

Belligerent, irrational, and extreme nationalism was a principal cause of World War I. Placing their country above everything, nationalists in various countries fomented hatred of other nationalities and called for the expansion of their nation's borders—attitudes that fostered belligerence in foreign relations. Wedded to nationalism was a militaristic view that regarded war as heroic and as the highest expression of individual and national life.

Yet Europe might have avoided the world war had the nations not been divided into hostile alliance systems. By 1907, the Triple Alliance of Germany, Austria-Hungary, and Italy confronted the loosely organized Triple Entente of France, Russia, and Great Britain. What German chancellor Otto von Bismarck said in 1879 was just as true in 1914: "The great powers of our time are like travellers, unknown to one another, whom chance has brought together in a carriage. They watch each other, and when one of them puts his hand into his pocket, his neighbor gets ready his own revolver in order to be able to fire the first shot."

A danger inherent in an alliance is that a country, knowing that it has the support of allies, may pursue an aggressive foreign policy and may be less likely to compromise during a crisis; also, a war between two states may well draw in the other allied powers. These dangers materialized in 1914.

In the diplomatic furor of July and early August 1914, following the assassination of Francis Ferdinand, several patterns emerged. Austria-Hungary, a multinational empire dominated by Germans and Hungarians, feared the nationalist aspirations of its Slavic minorities. The nationalist yearnings of neighboring Serbia aggravated Austria-Hungary's problems, for the Serbs, a South Slav people, wanted to create a Greater Serbia by uniting with South Slavs of Austria-Hungary. If Slavic nationalism gained in intensity, the Austro-Hungarian (or Hapsburg) Empire would be broken into states based on nationality. Austria-Hungary decided to use the assassination as justification for crushing Serbia.

The system of alliances escalated the tensions between Austria-Hungary and Serbia into a general European war. Germany saw itself threatened by the Triple Entente (a conviction based more on paranoia than on objective fact) and regarded Austria-Hungary as its only reliable ally. Holding that at all costs its ally must be kept strong, German officials supported Austria-Hungary's decision to crush Serbia. Fearing that Germany and Austria-Hungary aimed to extend their power into southeastern Europe, Russia would not permit the destruction of Serbia. With the support of France, Russia began to mobilize, and when it moved to full mobilization, Germany declared war. As German battle plans, drawn up years before, called for a war with both France and Russia, France was drawn into the conflict; Germany's invasion of neutral Belgium brought Great Britain into the war.

Most European statesmen and military men believed the war would be over in a few months. Virtually no one anticipated that it would last more than four years and that the casualties would number in the millions.

World War I was a turning point in Western history. In Russia, it led to the downfall of the tsarist autocracy and the rise of the Soviet state. The war created unsettling conditions that led to the emergence of fascist movements in Italy and Germany, and it shattered, perhaps forever, the Enlightenment belief in the inevitable and perpetual progress of Western civilization.

---

1 Militarism and Anti-Militarism

Historians regard a surging militarism as an underlying cause of World War I. One sign of militarism was the rapid increase in expenditures for armaments in the years prior to 1914. Between 1910 and 1914, both Austria-Hungary and Germany, for example, doubled their military budgets. The arms race intensified suspicion among the Great Powers. A second danger was the increased power of the military in policy making, particularly in Austria-Hungary and Germany. In the crisis following the assassination, generals tended to press for a military solution. The few dissenting voices raised against militarism were all but drowned out in this martial atmosphere.

Heinrich von Treitschke
THE GREATNESS OF WAR

Coupled with the military's influence on state decisions was a romantic glorification of the nation and war, an attitude shared by both the elite and the masses. Although militarism generally pervaded Europe, it was particularly strong in Germany. In the following reading from *Politics,* the influential German historian Heinrich von Treitschke (1834–1896) glorified warfare.

. . . One must say with the greatest determination: War is for an afflicted people the only remedy. When the State exclaims: My very existence is at stake! then social self-seeking must disappear and all party hatred be silent. The individual must forget his own *ego* and feel himself a member of the whole, he must recognize how negligible is his life compared with the good of the whole. Therein lies the greatness of war that the little man completely vanishes before the great thought of the State. The sacrifice of nationalities for one another is nowhere invested with such beauty as in war. At such a time the corn is separated from the chaff. All who lived through 1870 will understand the saying of Niebuhr[1] with regard to the year 1813, that he then experienced the "bliss of sharing with all his fellow citizens, with the scholar and the ignorant, the one common feeling—no man who enjoyed this experience will to his dying day forget how loving, friendly and strong he felt."

It is indeed political idealism which fosters war, whereas materialism rejects it. What a perversion of morality to want to banish heroism from human life. The heroes of a people are the personalities who fill the youthful souls with delight and enthusiasm, and amongst authors we as boys and youths admire most those whose words sound like a flourish of trumpets. He who cannot take pleasure therein, is too cowardly to take up arms himself for his fatherland. All appeal to Christianity in this matter is perverted. The Bible states expressly that the man in authority shall wield the sword; it states likewise that: "Greater love hath no man than this that he giveth his life for his friend." Those who preach the nonsense about everlasting peace do not understand the life of the Aryan race, the Aryans are before all brave. They have always been men enough to protect by the sword what they had won by the intellect. . . .

To the historian who lives in the realms of the Will, it is quite clear that the furtherance of an everlasting peace is fundamentally reactionary. He sees that to banish war from history would be to banish all progress and becoming. It is only the periods of exhaustion, weariness and mental stagnation that have dallied with the dream of everlasting peace. . . . The living God will see to it that war returns again and again as a terrible medicine for humanity.

---

[1]Barthold G. Niebuhr (1776–1831) was a Prussian historian. The passage refers to the German War of Liberation against Napoleon, which German patriots regarded as a glorious episode in their national history.

Friedrich von Bernhardi
GERMANY AND THE NEXT WAR

Friedrich von Bernhardi (1849–1930), a German general and influential military writer, considered war "a biological necessity of the first importance." The following excerpt comes from his work *Germany and the Next War.* Published in 1911, it had already gone into a sixth edition by 1913.

. . . War is a biological necessity of the first importance, a regulative element in the life of mankind which cannot be dispensed with, since without it an unhealthy development will follow, which excludes every advancement of the race, and therefore all real civilization. "War is the father of all things." The sages of antiquity long before Darwin recognized this.

The struggle for existence is, in the life of Nature, the basis of all healthy development. . . . The law of the stronger holds good everywhere. Those forms survive which are able to procure themselves the most favourable conditions of life, and to assert themselves in the universal economy of Nature. The weaker succumb. . . .

Struggle is, therefore, a universal law of Nature, and the instinct of self-preservation which leads to struggle is acknowledged to be a natural condition of existence.

Strong, healthy, and flourishing nations increase in numbers. From a given moment they require a continual expansion of their frontiers, they require new territory for the accommodation of their surplus population. Since almost every part of the globe is inhabited, new territory must, as a rule, be obtained at the cost of its possessors—that is to say, by conquest, which thus becomes a law of necessity.

The right of conquest is universally acknowledged.

. . . Vast territories inhabited by uncivilized masses are occupied by more highly civilized States, and made subject to their rule. Higher civilization and the correspondingly greater power are the foundations of the right to annexation. . . .

Lastly, in all times the right of conquest by war has been admitted. It may be that a growing people cannot win colonies from uncivilized races, and yet the State wishes to retain the surplus population which the mother-country can no longer feed. Then the only course left is to acquire the necessary territory by war. Thus the instinct of self-preservation leads inevitably to war, and the conquest of foreign soil. It is not the possessor, but the victor, who then has the right. . . .

In such cases might gives the right to occupy or to conquer. Might is at once the supreme right, and the dispute as to what is right is decided by the arbitrament of war. War gives a biologically just decision, since its decisions rest on the very nature of things. . . .

The knowledge, therefore, that war depends on biological laws leads to the conclusion that every attempt to exclude it from international relations must be demonstrably untenable.

Karl Liebknecht
"MILITARISM . . . IMPEDES . . . PROGRESS IN CIVILIZATION"

Militarism had long been opposed by pacifist organizations in Europe, whose membership was predominantly middle class and politically left wing. They caught the public interest, but were of limited political influence.

In Germany, the Social Democratic Party under Marxist leadership established an anti-militaristic movement in the 1890s. Marxists sharply differentiated themselves from pacifists in their appeal to the working class and their belief in the necessity of the overthrow of the capitalist class by force. But they were in agreement with pacifists in deploring the effects of militarism on society.

The Social Democratic spokesman for anti-militarism was Karl Liebknecht (1871–1919). In 1907, German authorities confiscated copies of his book *Militarism and Anti-Militarism,* and he was convicted of high treason for injuring the morale of the army and advocating its abolition. He served eighteen months in prison. World War I increased Liebknecht's radicalism, and he met a violent death in the turmoil of postwar Germany as a leader of the communist revolutionary uprising known as the Spartacist Revolt.

The working-class . . . welcome the immense economic developments of our days. But they also know that this economic development could be carried on peacefully without the mailed fist, without militarism and navalism, without the trident being in our hand and without the barbarities of our colonial system, if only sensibly managed communities were to carry it on according to international understandings and in conformity with the duties and interests of civilization. They [know] that our world policy largely explains itself as an attempt to fight down and confuse forcibly and clumsily the social and political home problems confronting the ruling classes. . . . They know that the advantages of the economic development. . . , especially all the advantages of our colonial policies, flow into the ample pockets of the exploiting class, of capitalism, the arch-enemy of the proletariat. They know that the wars the ruling classes engage in for their own purposes demand of the working-class the most terrible sacrifice of blood and treasure, for which they are recompensed, after the work has been done, by miserable pensions, beggarly grants to war invalids, street organs and kicks. . . .They know that after every war a veritable mud-volcano of Hunnic brutality and baseness sends its floods over the nations participating in it, rebarbarizing all civilization for years. The worker knows that the fatherland for which he is to fight is not his fatherland; that there is only one real enemy for the proletariat of every country—the capitalist class who oppresses and exploits the proletariat; that the proletariat of every country is by its most vital interests closely bound to the proletariat of every other country; that all na-

tional interests recede before the common interests of the international proletariat; and that the international coalition of exploiters and oppressors must be opposed by the international coalition of the exploited and oppressed. He knows that the proletarians, if they were to be employed in a war, would be led to fight against their own brethren and the members of their own class, and thus against their own interests. The class-conscious proletarian therefore not only frowns upon that international purpose of the army and the entire capitalist policy of expansion, he is fighting them earnestly and with understanding. . . .

Militarism does not only serve for defence and attack against the foreign enemy; it has a second task, one which is being brought out ever more clearly with the growing accentuation of class antagonism, defining ever more clearly the form and nature of militarism, viz., that of protecting the existing state of society, that of being a pillar of capitalism and all reactionary forces in the war of liberation engaged in by the working-class. . . . This is modern militarism, . . . which arms the people against the people itself. . . .

Hence militarism dangerously impedes, and often makes impossible even such progess in civilization as in itself would advance the interest of the existing social order. Education, art and science, public sanitation, the communication system: all are treated in a [stingy] fashion since there is nothing left for works of civilization after gluttonous Moloch[1] has been

---

[1]In the Old Testament, Moloch was the god of the Ammonites and the Phoenicians to whom children were sacrificed.

fed. . . . Germany should be rich enough to fulfil all her tasks of civilization, and the more completely these tasks should be performed the easier it would be to bear their costs. But the barrier of militarism obstructs the road. . . .

But militarism also disturbs the *national peace,* not only by the brutalizing effect it has upon the people, the heavy economic burdens it imposes upon the people and the pressure of taxes and tariff thus brought about, . . . but above all by being a powerful obstacle in the way of every kind of progress, by being an ingenious and highly efficient instrument for closing by force the valve of the social steam-boiler. He who believes that the progress of humanity is inevitable must see in the existence of militarism the most important obstacle in the way of a peaceful and continuous evolution. . . .

REVIEW QUESTIONS

1. Why did Heinrich von Treitschke regard war as a far more desirable condition than peace?
2. According to Treitschke, what is the individual's highest responsibility?
3. According to Treitschke, what function does the hero serve in national life?
4. What conclusions did Friedrich von Bernhardi draw from his premise that war was "a biological necessity"?
5. According to Karl Liebknecht, how did war impede progress in civilization and promote the interests of capitalists?

2 Pan-Serbism: Nationalism and Terrorism

The conspiracy to assassinate Archduke Francis Ferdinand was organized by a secret Serbian society called Union or Death, more popularly known as the Black Hand. Founded in 1911, the Black Hand aspired to create a Greater Serbia by uniting with their kinsmen, the South Slavs dwelling in Austria-Hungary. Thus, Austrian officials regarded the aspirations of Pan-Serbs as a significant threat to the Hapsburg Empire.

THE BLACK HAND

In 1914, the Black Hand had some 2,500 members, most of them army officers. The society indoctrinated members with a fanatic nationalism and trained them in terrorist methods. The initiation ceremony, designed to strengthen a new member's commitment to the cause and to foster obedience to the society's leaders, had the appearance of a sacred rite. The candidate entered a dark room in which a table stood covered with a black cloth; resting on the table were a dagger, a revolver, and a crucifix. When the candidate declared his readiness to take the oath of allegiance, a masked member of the society's elite entered the room and stood in silence. After the initiate pronounced the oath, the masked man shook his hand and departed without uttering a word. Excerpts of the Black Hand's by-laws, including the oath of allegiance, follow.

BY-LAWS OF THE ORGANIZATION UNION OR DEATH

Article 1. This organization is created for the purpose of realizing the national ideal: the union of all Serbs. Membership is open to every Serb, without distinction of sex, religion, or place of birth, and to all those who are sincerely devoted to this cause.

Article 2. This organization prefers terrorist action to intellectual propaganda, and for this reason it must remain absolutely secret.

Article 3. The organization bears the name *Ujedinjenje ili Smirt* (Union or Death).

Article 4. To fulfill its purpose, the organization will do the following:

1. Exercise influence on government circles, on the various social classes, and on the entire social life of the kingdom of Serbia, which is considered the Piedmont[1] of the Serbian nation;
2. Organize revolutionary action in all territories inhabited by Serbs;
3. Beyond the frontiers of Serbia, fight with all means the enemies of the Serbian national idea;
4. Maintain amicable relations with all states, peoples, organizations, and individuals who support Serbia and the Serbian element;
5. Assist those nations and organizations that are fighting for their own national liberation and unification. . . .

Article 24. Every member has a duty to recruit new members, but the member shall guarantee with his life those whom he introduces into the organization.

Article 25. Members of the organization are forbidden to know each other personally. Only members of the central committee are known to each other.

Article 26. In the organization itself, the members are designated by numbers. Only the central committee in Belgrade knows their names.

Article 27. Members of the organization must obey absolutely the commands given to them by their superiors.

Article 28. Each member has a duty to communicate to the central committee at Belgrade all information that may be of interest to the organization.

Article 29. The interests of the organization stand above all other interests.

Article 30. On entering the organization, each member must know that he loses his own personality, that he can expect neither personal glory nor personal profit, material or moral. Consequently, any member who endeavors to exploit the organization for personal, social, or party motives, will be punished. If by his acts he harms the organization itself, his punishment will be death.

Article 31. Those who enter the organization may never leave it, and no one has the authority to accept a member's resignation.

Article 32. Each member must aid the organization, with weekly contributions. If need be, the organization may procure funds through coercion. . . .

Article 33. When the central committee of Belgrade pronounces a death sentence the only thing that matters is that the execution is carried out unfailingly. The method of execution is of little importance.

Article 34. The organization's seal is composed as follows. On the center of the seal a powerful arm holds in its hand an unfurled flag. On the flag, as a coat of arms, are a skull and crossed bones; by the side of the flag are a knife, a bomb and poison. Around, in a circle, are inscribed the following words reading from left to right: "Unification or Death," and at the base "The Supreme Central Directorate."

Article 35. On joining the organization, the recruit takes the following oath:

---

[1]The Piedmont was the Italian state that served as the nucleus for the unification of Italy.

"I (name), in becoming a member of the organization, 'Unification or Death,' do swear by the sun that shines on me, by the earth that nourishes me, by God, by the blood of my ancestors, on my honor and my life that from this moment until my death, I shall be faithful to the regulations of the organization and that I will be prepared to make any sacrifice for it. I swear before God, on my honor and on my life, that I shall carry with me to the grave the organization's secrets. May God condemn me and my comrades judge me if I violate or do not respect, consciously or not, my oath."

Article 36. These regulations come into force immediately.

Article 37. These regulations must not be changed.

Belgrade, 9 May 1911.

Baron von Giesl
AUSTRIAN RESPONSE TO THE ASSASSINATION

Austrian officials who wanted to use the assassination as a pretext to crush Serbia feared that Pan-Serbism would lead to revolts among Slavs living in the Hapsburg Empire. This attitude was expressed in a memorandum written on July 21, 1914, three weeks after the assassination, by Baron von Giesl, the Austrian ambassador to Serbia, to foreign minister Count Leopold von Berchtold.

Belgrade, July 21, 1914.
After the lamentable crime of June 28th, I have now been back at my post for some time, and I am able to give some judgment as to the tone which prevails here.

After the annexation crisis[1] the relations between the Monarchy and Servia [Serbia] were poisoned on the Servian side by national chauvinism, animosity and an effective propaganda of Great-Servian aspirations carried on in that part of our territory where there is a Servian population; since the last two Balkan Wars [in 1912 and 1913], the success of Servia has increased this chauvinism to a paroxysm, the expression of which in some cases bears the mark of insanity.

I may be excused from bringing proof and evidence of this; they can be had easily everywhere among all parties, in political circles as well as among the lower classes. I put it forward as a well-known axiom that the policy of Servia is built up on the separation of the territories inhabited by Southern Slavs, and as a corollary to this on the abolition of the [Hapsburg] Monarchy as a Great Power; this is its only object.

No one who has taken the trouble to move and take part in political circles here for a week can be blind to this truth. . . .

The crime at Serajevo [the assassination of Ferdinand] has aroused among the Servians an expectation that in the immediate future the Hapsburg States will fall to pieces; it was this on which they had set their hopes even before;

---

[1]Since 1878, Austria-Hungary had administered the provinces of Bosnia and Herzegovina, which were officially a part of the Ottoman Empire. The population of these lands consisted mainly of South Slavs, ethnic cousins of the Serbs. When Austria-Hungary annexed Bosnia and Herzegovina in 1908, Serbia was enraged.

there has been dangled before their eyes the cession of those territories in the Monarchy which are inhabited by the Southern Slavs, a revolution in Bosnia and Herzegovina and the unreliability of the Slav regiments—this is regarded as ascertained fact and had brought system and apparent justification into their nationalist madness.

Austria-Hungary, hated as she is, now appears to the Servians as powerless, and as scarcely worthy of waging war with; contempt is mingled with hatred; she is ripe for destruction, and she is to fall without trouble into the lap of the Great-Servian Empire, which is to be realised in the immediate future.

Newspapers, not among the most extreme, discuss the powerlessness and decrepitude of the neighbouring Monarchy in daily articles, and insult its officials without reserve and without fear of reprimand. They do not even stop short of the exalted person of our ruler. Even the official organ refers to the internal condition of Austria-Hungary as the true cause of this wicked crime. There is no longer any fear of being called to account. For decades the people of Servia has been educated by the press, and the policy at any given time is dependent on the party press; the Great-Servian propaganda and its monstrous offspring the crime of June 28th, are a fruit of this education. . . .

. . . The electoral campaign has united all parties on a platform of hostility against Austria-Hungary. None of the parties which aspire to office will incur the suspicion of being held capable of weak compliance towards the Monarchy. The campaign, therefore, is conducted under the catchword of hostility towards Austria-Hungary.

For both internal and external reasons the Monarchy is held to be powerless and incapable of any energetic action, and it is believed that the serious words which were spoken by leading men among us are only "bluff.". . .

I have allowed myself to trespass too long on the patience of Your Excellency, not because I thought that in what I have said I could tell you anything new, but because I considered this picture led up to the conclusion which forces itself upon me that a reckoning with Servia, a war for the position of the Monarchy as a Great Power, even for its existence as such, cannot be permanently avoided.

If we delay in clearing up our relations with Servia, we shall share the responsibility for the difficulties and the unfavourable situation in any future war which must, however, sooner or later be carried through.

For any observer on the spot, and for the representative of Austro-Hungarian interests in Servia, the question takes the form that we cannot any longer put up with any further injury to our prestige. . . .

Half measures, the presentation of demands, followed by long discussions and ending only in an unsound compromise, would be the hardest blow which could be directed against Austria-Hungary's reputation in Servia and her position in Europe.

REVIEW QUESTIONS

1. How did Union or Death seek to accomplish its goal of uniting all Serbs?
2. What type of people do you think were attracted to the objectives and methods of the Black Hand?
3. According to Baron von Giesl, how did Serbia view the Hapsburg monarchy? What policy toward Serbia did he advocate?

3 War as Celebration: The Mood in European Capitals

An outpouring of patriotism greeted the proclamation of war. Huge crowds thronged the avenues and squares of capital cities to express their devotion to their nations and their willingness to bear arms. Many Europeans regarded war as a sacred moment that held the promise of adventure and an escape from a hum-drum and purposeless daily existence. Going to war seemed to satisfy a yearning to surrender oneself to a noble cause: the greatness of the nation. The image of the nation united in a spirit of fraternity and self-sacrifice was immensely appealing.

Roland Doregelès
PARIS: "THAT FABULOUS DAY"

In "After Fifty Years," Roland Doregelès (1886–1973), a distinguished French writer, recalled the mood in Paris at the outbreak of the war.

"It's come!* It's posted at the district mayor's office," a passerby shouted to me as he ran.

I reached the Rue Drouot in one leap and shouldered through the mob that already filled the courtyard to approach the fascinating white sheet pasted to the door. I read the message at a glance, then reread it slowly, word for word, to convince myself that it was true:

> THE FIRST DAY OF
> MOBILIZATION WILL BE
> SUNDAY, AUGUST 2

Only three lines, written hastily by a hand that trembled. It was an announcement to a million and a half Frenchmen.

The people who had read it moved away, stunned, while others crowded in, but this silent numbness did not last. Suddenly a heroic wind lifted their heads. What? War, was it? Well, then, let's go! Without any signal, the "Marseillaise" poured from thousands of

throats, sheafs of flags appeared at windows, and howling processions rolled out on the boulevards. Each column brandished a placard: AL-SACE VOLUNTEERS, JEWISH VOLUNTEERS, POLISH VOLUNTEERS. They hailed one another above the bravos of the crowd, and this human torrent, swelling at every corner, moved on to circle around the Place de la Concorde, before the statue of Strasbourg banked with flowers, then flowed toward the Place de la République, where mobs from Belleville and the Faubourg St. Antoine yelled themselves hoarse on the refrain from the great days, *"Aux armes, citoyens!"* (To arms, citizens!) But this time it was better than a song.

To gather the news for my paper, I ran around the city in every direction. At the Cours la Reine I saw the fabled cuirassiers [cavalry] in their horsetail plumes march by, and at the Rue La Fayette footsoldiers in battle garb with women throwing flowers and kisses to them. In a marshaling yard I saw guns being loaded, their long, thin barrels twined around with branches and laurel leaves, while troops in red breeches piled gaily into delivery vans

---

*Translated from the French by Sally Abeles.

they were scrawling with challenges and caricatures. Young and old, civilians and military men burned with the same excitement. It was like a Brotherhood Day.

Dead tired but still exhilarated, I got back to *L'Homme libre* and burst into the office of Georges Clemenceau, our chief.[†]

"What is Paris saying?" he asked me.

"It's singing, sir!"

"Then everything will be all right. . . ."

His old patriot's heart was not wrong; no cloud marred that fabulous day. . . .

Less than twenty-four hours later, seeing their old dreams of peace crumble [socialist workers] would stream out into the boulevards . . . [but] they would break into the "Marseillaise," not the "Internationale"; they would cry, "To Berlin!," not "Down with war!"

What did they have to defend, these black-nailed patriots? Not even a shack, an acre to till, indeed hardly a patch of ground reserved at the Pantin Cemetery; yet they would depart, like their rivals of yesterday, a heroic song on their lips and a flower in their guns. No more poor or rich, proletarians or bourgeois, right-wingers or militant leftists; there were only Frenchmen.

[†]*L'Homme libre* (The Free Man) was but one of several periodicals Clemenceau founded and directed during his long political career.—Tr.

Beginning the next day, thousands of men eager to fight would jostle one another outside recruiting offices, waiting to join up. Men who could have stayed home, with their wives and children or an imploring mama. But no. The word "duty" had a meaning for them, and the word "country" had regained its splendor.

I close my eyes, and they appear to me, those volunteers on the great day; then I see them again in the old kepi [military cap] or blue helmet, shouting, "Here!" when somebody called for men for a raid, or hurling themselves into an attack with fixed bayonets, and I wonder, and I question their bloody [ghosts].

Tell me, comrades in eternal silence, would you have besieged the enlistment offices with the same enthusiasm, would you have fought such a courageous fight had you known that fifty years later those men in gray knit caps or steel helmets you were ordered to kill would no longer be enemies and that we would have to open our arms to them? Wouldn't the heroic "Let's go!" you shouted as you cleared the parapets have stuck in your throats? Deep in the grave where you dwell, don't you regret your sacrifice? "Why did we fight? Why did we let ourselves get killed?" This is the murmur of a million and a half voices rising from the bowels of the earth, and we, the survivors, do not know what to answer.

Stefan Zweig
VIENNA: "THE RUSHING FEELING OF FRATERNITY"

Some intellectuals viewed the war as a way of regenerating the nation; nobility and fraternity would triumph over life's petty concerns. In the following reading, Stefan Zweig (1881–1942), a prominent Austrian literary figure, recalled the scene in Vienna, the capital of the Austro-Hungarian Empire, at the outbreak of World War I. This passage comes from Zweig's autobiography written in 1941.

The next morning I was in Austria. In every station placards had been put up announcing general mobilization. The trains were filled with fresh recruits, banners were flying, music sounded, and in Vienna I found the entire city in a tumult. The first shock at the news of war—the war that no one, people or government, had wanted—the war which had slipped, much against their will, out of the clumsy hands of the diplomats who had been bluffing and toying with it, had suddenly been transformed into enthusiasm. There were parades in the street, flags, ribbons, and music burst forth everywhere, young recruits were marching triumphantly, their faces lighting up at the cheering—they, the John Does and Richard Roes who usually go unnoticed and uncelebrated.

And to be truthful, I must acknowledge that there was a majestic, rapturous, and even seductive something in this first outbreak of the people from which one could escape only with difficulty. And in spite of all my hatred and aversion for war, I should not like to have missed the memory of those first days. As never before, thousands and hundreds of thousands felt what they should have felt in peace time, that they belonged together. A city of two million, a country of nearly fifty million, in that hour felt that they were participating in world history, in a moment which would never recur, and that each one was called upon to cast his infinitesimal self into the glowing mass, there to be purified of all selfishness. All differences of class, rank, and language were flooded over at that moment by the rushing feeling of fraternity. Strangers spoke to one another in the streets, people who had avoided each other for years shook hands, everywhere one saw excited faces. Each individual experienced an exaltation of his ego, he was no longer the isolated person of former times, he had been incorporated into the mass, he was part of the people, and his person, his hitherto unnoticed person, had been given meaning. The petty mail clerk, who ordinarily sorted letters early and late, who sorted constantly, who sorted from Monday until Saturday without interruption; the clerk, the cobbler, had suddenly achieved a romantic possibility in life: he could become a hero, and everyone who wore a uniform was already being cheered by the women, and greeted beforehand with this romantic appellation by those who had to remain behind. They acknowledged the unknown power which had lifted them out of their everyday existence. Even mothers with their grief, and women with their fears, were ashamed to manifest their quite natural emotions in the face of this first transformation. But it is quite possible that a deeper, more secret power was at work in this frenzy. So deeply, so quickly did the tide break over humanity that, foaming over the surface, it churned up the depths, the subconscious primitive instincts of the human animal—that which Freud so meaningfully calls "the revulsion from culture," the desire to break out of the conventional bourgeois world of codes and statutes, and to permit the primitive instincts of the blood to rage at will. It is also possible that these powers of darkness had their share in the wild frenzy into which everything was thrown—self-sacrifice and alcohol, the spirit of adventure and the spirit of pure faith, the old magic of flags and patriotic slogans, that mysterious frenzy of the millions which can hardly be described in words, but which, for the moment, gave a wild and almost rapturous impetus to the greatest crime of our time. . . .

. . . What did the great mass know of war in 1914, after nearly half a century of peace? They did not know war, they had hardly given it a thought. It had become legendary, and distance had made it seem romantic and heroic. They still saw it in the perspective of their school readers and of paintings in museums; brilliant cavalry attacks in glittering uniforms, the fatal shot always straight through the heart, the entire campaign a resounding march of victory— "We'll be home at Christmas," the recruits shouted laughingly to their mothers in August of 1914. Who in the villages and the cities of Austria remembered "real" war? A few ancients at best, who in 1866 had fought against Prussia, which was now their ally. But what a quick, bloodless far-off war that had been, a campaign that had ended in three weeks with few victims and before it had well started! A rapid excursion into the romantic, a wild, manly adventure—that is how the war of 1914 was painted in the imagination of the simple man, and the young people were honestly afraid that they might miss this most wonderful and exciting experience of their lives; that is why they hurried and thronged to the colors, and that is why they shouted and sang in the trains that carried them to the slaughter; wildly and feverishly the red wave of blood coursed through the veins of the entire nation.

Philipp Scheidemann
BERLIN: "THE HOUR WE YEARNED FOR"

Philipp Scheidemann (1865–1939), one of the founding fathers of the Weimar Republic, described Berlin's martial mood in his memoirs, published in 1929.

At express speed I had returned to Berlin. Everywhere a word could be heard the conversation was of war and rumours of war. There was only one topic of conversation—war. The supporters of war seemed to be in a great majority. Were these pugnacious fellows, young and old, bereft of their senses? Were they so ignorant of the horrors of war? . . . Vast crowds of demonstrators paraded. . . . Schoolboys and students were there in their thousands; their bearded seniors, with their Iron Crosses of 1870–71 on their breasts, were there too in huge numbers.

Treitschke and Bernhardi[1] (to say nothing of the National Liberal beer-swilling heroes) seemed to have multiplied a thousandfold. Patriotic demonstrations had an intoxicating effect and excited the war-mongers to excess. "A call like the voice of thunder." Cheers! "In triumph we will smite France to the ground." "All hail to thee in victor's crown." Cheers! Hurrah!

The counter-demonstrations immediately organized by the Berlin Social Democrats were imposing, and certainly more disciplined than the Jingo [extremely nationalistic] processions, but could not outdo the shouts of the fire-eaters. "Good luck to him who cares for truth and right. Stand firmly round the flag." "Long live peace!" "Socialists, close up your ranks." The Socialist International cheer. The patriots were sometimes silenced by the Proletarians; then they came out on top again. This choral contest . . . went on for days.

"It is the hour we yearned for—our friends know that," so the Pan-German[2] papers shouted, that had for years been shouting for war. The *Post*, conducted by von Stumm, the Independent Conservative leader and big Industrial, had thus moaned in all its columns in 1900, at the fortieth celebration of the Franco-German War: "Another forty years of peace

---

[1]Both Heinrich von Treitschke and General von Bernhardi glorified war (see pages 265–266).

[2]The Pan-German Association, whose membership included professors, schoolteachers, journalists, lawyers, and aristocrats, spread nationalist and racial theories and glorified war as an expression of national vitality.

would be a national misfortune for Germany." Now these firebrands saw the seeds they had planted ripening. Perhaps in the heads of many who had been called upon to make every effort to keep the peace Bernhardi's words, that "the preservation of peace can and never shall be the aim of politics," had done mischief. These words are infernally like the secret instruc-

tions given by Baron von Holstein to the German delegates to the first Peace Conference at The Hague:

"For the State there is no higher aim than the preservation of its own interests; among the Great Powers these will not necessarily coincide with the maintenance of peace, but rather with the hostile policy of enemies and rivals."

Bertrand Russell
LONDON: "AVERAGE MEN AND WOMEN WERE DELIGHTED AT THE PROSPECT OF WAR"

Bertrand Russell (1872–1970), the distinguished mathematician and philosopher, was dismayed by the war fever that gripped English men and women. During the war Russell was fined and imprisoned for his pacifistic activities. The following account is from his autobiography published in 1951 and 1956.

During the hot days at the end of July, I was at Cambridge, discussing the situation with all and sundry. I found it impossible to believe that Europe would be so mad as to plunge into war, but I was persuaded that, if there was war, England would be involved. I felt strongly that England ought to remain neutral, and I collected the signatures of a large number of professors and Fellows to a statement which appeared in the *Manchester Guardian* to that effect. The day war was declared, almost all of them changed their minds. . . . I spent the evening walking round the streets, especially in the neighbourhood of Trafalgar Square, noticing cheering crowds, and making myself sensitive to the emotions of passers-by. During this and the following days I discovered to my amazement that average men and women were delighted at the prospect of war. I had fondly imagined what most pacifists contended, that

wars were forced upon a reluctant population by despotic and Machiavellian governments. . . .

The first days of the war were to me utterly amazing. My best friends, such as the Whiteheads, were savagely warlike. Men like J. L. Hammond, who had been writing for years against participation in a European war, were swept off their feet by Belgium.

Meanwhile, I was living at the highest possible emotional tension. Although I did not foresee anything like the full disaster of the war, I foresaw a great deal more than most people did. The prospect filled me with horror, but what filled me with even more horror was the fact that the anticipation of carnage was delightful to something like ninety per cent of the population. I had to revise my views on human nature. At that time I was wholly ignorant of psychoanalysis, but I arrived for myself at a view of human passions not unlike that of the psycho-analysts. I arrived at this view in an endeavour to understand popular feeling about the War. I had supposed until that time that it was quite common for parents to love their children, but the War persuaded me that it is a rare exception. I had supposed that most people liked money better than almost anything else, but I discovered that they like destruction even better. I had supposed that intellectuals frequently loved truth, but I found here again that not ten per cent of them prefer truth to popularity. . . .

. . . As a lover of truth, the national propaganda of all the belligerent nations sickened me. As a lover of civilization, the return to barbarism appalled me. As a man of thwarted parental feeling, the massacre of the young wrung my heart. I hardly supposed that much good would come of opposing the War, but I felt that for the honour of human nature those who were not swept off their feet should show that they stood firm.

On August 15, 1914, the London *Nation* published a letter written by Russell, part of which follows.

. . . Those who saw the London crowds, during the nights leading up to the Declaration of War saw a whole population, hitherto peaceable and humane, precipitated in a few days down the steep slope to primitive barbarism, letting loose, in a moment, the instincts of hatred and blood lust against which the whole fabric of society has been raised. "Patriots" in all countries acclaim this brutal orgy as a noble determination to vindicate the right; reason and mercy are swept away in one great flood of hatred; dim abstractions of unimaginable wickedness—Germany to us and the French, Russia to the Germans—conceal the simple fact that the enemy are men, like ourselves, neither better nor worse—men who love their homes and the sunshine, and all the simple pleasures of common lives.

REVIEW QUESTIONS

1. Why was war welcomed as a positive event by so many different peoples?
2. Do you think human beings are aggressive by nature? Explain your answer.
3. Why did the events of July and August 1914 cause Bertrand Russell to revise his views of human nature? Do you agree with his assessment?

4   Trench Warfare

In 1914 the young men of European nations marched off to war believing that they were embarking on a glorious and chivalrous adventure. They were eager to serve their countries, to demonstrate personal valor, and to experience life at its most intense moments. But in the trenches, where unseen enemies fired machine guns and artillery that killed indiscriminately and relentlessly, this romantic illusion about combat disintegrated.

Erich Maria Remarque
ALL QUIET ON THE WESTERN FRONT

The following reading is taken from Erich Maria Remarque's novel *All Quiet on the Western Front* (1929), the most famous literary work to emerge from World War I. A veteran of the trenches himself, Remarque (1898–1970) graphically described the slaughter that robbed Europe of its young men. His narrator is a young German soldier.

We wake up in the middle of the night. The earth booms. Heavy fire is falling on us. We crouch into corners. We distinguish shells of every calibre.

Each man lays hold of his things and looks again every minute to reassure himself that they are still there. The dug-out heaves, the night roars and flashes. We look at each other in the momentary flashes of light, and with pale faces and pressed lips shake our heads.

Every man is aware of the heavy shells tearing down the parapet, rooting up the embankment and demolishing the upper layers of concrete. When a shell lands in the trench we note how the hollow, furious blast is like a blow from the paw of a raging beast of prey. Already by morning a few of the recruits are green and vomiting. They are too inexperienced. . . .

The bombardment does not diminish. It is falling in the rear too. As far as one can see spout fountains of mud and iron. A wide belt is being raked.

The attack does not come, but the bombardment continues. We are gradually benumbed. Hardly a man speaks. We cannot make ourselves understood.

Our trench is almost gone. At many places it is only eighteen inches high, it is broken by holes, and craters, and mountains of earth. A shell lands square in front of our post. At once it is dark. We are buried and must dig ourselves out. . . .

Towards morning, while it is still dark, there is some excitement. Through the entrance rushes in a swarm of fleeing rats that try to storm the walls. Torches light up the confusion. Everyone yells and curses and slaughters.

The madness and despair of many hours unloads itself in this outburst. Faces are distorted, arms strike out, the beasts scream; we just stop in time to avoid attacking one another. . . .

Suddenly it howls and flashes terrifically, the dug-out cracks in all its joints under a direct hit, fortunately only a light one that the concrete blocks are able to withstand. It rings metallically, the walls reel, rifles, helmets, earth, mud, and dust fly everywhere. Sulphur fumes pour in.

If we were in one of those light dug-outs that they have been building lately instead of this deeper one, none of us would be alive.

But the effect is bad enough even so. The recruit starts to rave again and two others follow suit. One jumps up and rushes out, we have trouble with the other two. I start after the one who escapes and wonder whether to shoot him in the leg—then it shrieks again, I fling myself down and when I stand up the wall of the trench is plastered with smoking splinters, lumps of flesh, and bits of uniform. I scramble back.

The first recruit seems actually to have gone insane. He butts his head against the wall like a goat. We must try to-night to take him to the rear. Meanwhile we bind him, but in such a way that in case of attack he can be released at once. . . .

Suddenly the nearer explosions cease. The shelling continues but it has lifted and falls behind us, our trench is free. We seize the hand-grenades, pitch them out in front of the dug-out and jump after them. The bombardment has stopped and a heavy barrage now falls behind us. The attack has come.

No one would believe that in this howling waste there could still be men; but steel helmets now appear on all sides out of the trench, and fifty yards from us a machine-gun is already in position and barking.

The wire entanglements are torn to pieces. Yet they offer some obstacle. We see the storm-troops coming. Our artillery opens fire. Machine-guns rattle, rifles crack. The charge works its way across. Haie and Kropp begin with the hand-grenades. They throw as fast as they can, others pass them, the handles with the strings already pulled. Haie throws seventy-five yards, Kropp sixty, it has been measured, the distance is important. The enemy as they run cannot do much before they are within forty yards.

We recognize the smooth distorted faces, the helmets: they are French. They have already suffered heavily when they reach the remnants of the barbed wire entanglements. A whole line has gone down before our machine-guns; then we have a lot of stoppages and they come nearer.

I see one of them, his face upturned, fall into a wire cradle. His body collapses, his hands remain suspended as though he were praying. Then his body drops clean away and only his hands with the stumps of his arms, shot off, now hang in the wire.

The moment we are about to retreat three faces rise up from the ground in front of us. Under one of the helmets a dark pointed beard and two eyes that are fastened on me. I raise my hand, but I cannot throw into those strange eyes; for one mad moment the whole slaughter whirls like a circus round me, and these two eyes alone are motionless; then the head rises up, a hand, a movement, and my hand-grenade flies through the air and into him.

We make for the rear, pull wire cradles into the trench and leave bombs behind us with the strings pulled, which ensures us a fiery retreat. The machine-guns are already firing from the next position.

We have become wild beasts. We do not fight, we defend ourselves against annihila-

tion. It is not against men that we fling our bombs, what do we know of men in this moment when Death is hunting us down—now, for the first time in three days we can see his face, now for the first time in three days we can oppose him; we feel a mad anger. No longer do we lie helpless, waiting on the scaffold, we can destroy and kill, to save ourselves, to save ourselves and to be revenged.

We crouch behind every corner, behind every barrier of barbed wire, and hurl heaps of explosives at the feet of the advancing enemy before we run. The blast of the hand-grenades impinges powerfully on our arms and legs; crouching like cats we run on, overwhelmed by this wave that bears us along, that fills us with ferocity, turns us into thugs, into murderers, into God only knows what devils; this wave that multiplies our strength with fear and madness and greed of life, seeking and fighting for nothing but our deliverance. If your own father came over with them you would not hesitate to fling a bomb at him.

The forward trenches have been abandoned. Are they still trenches? They are blown to pieces, annihilated—there are only broken bits of trenches, holes linked by cracks, nests of craters, that is all. But the enemy's casualties increase. They did not count on so much resistance.

———

It is nearly noon. The sun blazes hotly, the sweat stings in our eyes, we wipe it off on our sleeves and often blood with it. At last we reach a trench that is in a somewhat better condition. It is manned and ready for the counterattack, it receives us. Our guns open in full blast and cut off the enemy attack.

The lines behind us stop. They can advance no farther. The attack is crushed by our artillery. We watch. The fire lifts a hundred yards and we break forward. Beside me a lance-corporal has his head torn off. He runs a few steps more while the blood spouts from his neck like a fountain.

It does not come quite to hand-to-hand fighting; they are driven back. We arrive once again at our shattered trench and pass on beyond it. . . .

We have lost all feeling for one another. We can hardly control ourselves when our glance lights on the form of some other man. We are insensible, dead men, who through some trick, some dreadful magic, are still able to run and to kill.

A young Frenchman lags behind, he is overtaken, he puts up his hands, in one he still holds his revolver—does he mean to shoot or to give himself up!—a blow from a spade cleaves through his face. A second sees it and tries to run farther; a bayonet jabs into his back. He leaps in the air, his arms thrown wide, his mouth wide open, yelling; he staggers, in his back the bayonet quivers. A third throws away his rifle, cowers down with his hands before his eyes. He is left behind with a few other prisoners to carry off the wounded.

Suddenly in the pursuit we reach the enemy line.

We are so close on the heels of our retreating enemies that we reach it almost at the same time as they. In this way we suffer few casualties. A machine-gun barks, but is silenced with a bomb. Nevertheless, the couple of seconds has sufficed to give us five stomach wounds. With the butt of his rifle Kat smashes to pulp the face of one of the unwounded machine-gunners. We bayonet the others before they have time to get out their bombs. Then thirstily we drink the water they have for cooling the gun.

Everywhere wire-cutters are snapping, planks are thrown across the entanglements, we jump through the narrow entrances into the trenches. Haie strikes his spade into the neck of a gigantic Frenchman and throws the first hand-grenade; we duck behind a breastwork for a few seconds, then the straight bit of trench ahead of us is empty. The next throw whizzes obliquely over the corner and clears a passage; as we run past we toss handfuls down into the dug-outs, the earth shudders, it crashes, smokes and groans, we stumble over slippery lumps of flesh, over yielding bodies; I fall into an open belly on which lies a clean, new officer's cap.

The fight ceases. We lose touch with the enemy. We cannot stay here long but must retire under cover of our artillery to our own position. No sooner do we know this than we dive into the nearest dug-outs, and with the utmost haste seize on whatever provisions we can see, especially the tins of corned beef and butter, before we clear out.

We get back pretty well. There is no further attack by the enemy. We lie for an hour panting and resting before anyone speaks. We are so completely played out that in spite of our great hunger we do not think of the provisions. Then gradually we become something like men again.

Siegfried Sassoon
BASE DETAILS

Front-line soldiers often looked with contempt on generals who, from a safe distance, ordered massive assaults against enemy lines protected by barbed wire and machine guns. Such attacks could cost the lives of tens of thousands of soldiers in just a few days. Siegfried Sassoon (1886–1967), a British poet who served at the front for much of the war and earned a Military Cross for bravery, showed his disdain for coldhearted officers in the following poem.

If I were fierce, and bald, and short of breath,
   I'd live with scarlet Majors at the Base,
And speed glum heroes up the line to death.
   You'd see me with my puffy petulant face,
Guzzling and gulping in the best hotel,
   Reading the Roll of Honour. 'Poor young
     chap,'

I'd say—'I used to know his father well;
   Yes, we've lost heavily in this last
     scrap.'
And when the war is done and youth stone
     dead,
I'd toddle safely home and die—in bed.

Wilfred Owen
DISABLED

Wilfred Owen (1893–1918), another British poet, volunteered for duty in 1915. At the Battle of the Somme he sustained shell shock, and he was sent to a hospital in Britain. In 1918 he returned to the front and was awarded the Military Cross; he died one week before the Armistice. In the following poem, "Disabled," Owen portrays the enduring misery of war.

He sat in a wheeled chair, waiting for dark,
And shivered in his ghastly suit of gray,
Legless, sewn short at elbow. Through the
   park
Voices of boys rang saddening like a hymn,
Voices of play and pleasure after day,
Till gathering sleep mothered them from him.

About this time Town used to swing so gay
When glow-lamps budded in the light blue
   trees,
And girls glanced lovelier as the air grew
   dim,—
In the old times, before he threw away his
   knees. . . .

He asked to join. He didn't have to beg;
Smiling they wrote his lie: aged nineteen
   years.
Germans he scarcely thought of; all their guilt,

And Austria's, did not move him. And no fears
Of Fear came yet. He thought of jeweled hilts
For daggers in plaid socks; of smart salutes;
And care of arms; and leave; and pay arrears;
*Esprit de corps,** and hints for young recruits.
And soon, he was drafted out with drums and
   cheers. . . .

Now, he will spend a few sick years in
   Institutes,
And do what things the rules consider wise,
And take whatever pity they may dole.
Tonight he noticed how the women's eyes
Passed from him to the strong men that were
   whole.
How cold and late it is! Why don't they come
And put him into bed? Why don't they come?

Esprit de corps: group spirit.

REVIEW QUESTIONS

1. In Erich Maria Remarque's account, how did the soldiers in the trenches react to artillery bombardment?
2. What ordeal did the attacking soldiers encounter as they neared the enemy trenches?
3. What were the feelings of the soldiers as they engaged the attackers?
4. Which line(s) in either poem do you consider the most powerful?

5   Women at War

In order to release men for military service, women in England, France, and Germany responded to their countries' wartime needs and replaced men in all branches of civilian life. They took jobs in munitions factories, worked on farms, were trained for commercial work and in the nursing service. They drove ambulances, mail trucks, and buses. They worked as laboratory assistants, plumbers' helpers, and bank clerks. By performing effectively in jobs formerly occupied by men, women demonstrated that they had an essential role to play in their countries' economic life. By the end of the war, little opposition remained to granting women political rights.

Naomi Loughnan
GENTEEL WOMEN IN THE FACTORIES

Naomi Loughnan was one of millions of women who replaced men in all branches of civilian life, in allied and enemy countries alike, during World War I. She was a young, upper-middle-class woman who lived with her family in London and had never had to work for her living. In her job in a munitions plant, she had to adjust to close association with women from the London slums, to hostel life, and to twelve-hour shifts doing heavy and sometimes dangerous work. The chief motivation for British women of her class was their desire to aid the war effort, not the opportunity to earn substantial wages.

We little thought when we first put on our overalls and caps and enlisted in the Munition Army how much more inspiring our life was to be than we had dared to hope. Though we munition workers sacrifice our ease we gain a life worth living. Our long days are filled with interest, and with the zest of doing work for our country in the grand cause of Freedom. As we handle the weapons of war we are learning great lessons of life. In the busy, noisy workshops we come face to face with every kind of class, and each one of these classes has something to learn from the others. Our muscles may be aching, and the brightness fading a little from our eyes, but our minds are expanding, our very souls are growing stronger. And excellent, too, is the discipline for our bodies, though we do not always recognize this. . . .

The day is long, the atmosphere is breathed and rebreathed, and the oil smells. Our hands are black with warm, thick oozings from the machines, which coat the work and, incidentally, the workers. We regard our horrible, begrimed members [limbs] with disgust and secret pride. . . .

. . . The genteel among us wear gloves. We vie with each other in finding the most up-to-date grease-removers, just as we used to vie about hats. Our hands are not alone in suffering from dirt. . . . [D]ust-clouds, filled with unwelcome life, find a resting-place in our lungs and noses.

The work is hard. It may be, perhaps, from sheer lifting and carrying and weighing, or merely because of those long dragging hours that keep us sitting on little stools in front of whirring, clattering machines that are all too easy to work. We wish sometimes they were not quite so "fool-proof," for monotony is painful. Or life may appear hard to us by reason of those same creeping hours spent on our feet, up and down, to and fro, and up and down again, hour after hour, until something altogether queer takes place in the muscles of our legs. But we go on. . . . It is amazing what we can do when there is no way of escape but desertion. . . .

. . . The first thing that strikes the newcomer, as the shop door opens, is the great wall of noise that seems to rise and confront one like a tangible substance. The crashing, tearing, rattling whirr of machinery is deafening. And yet, though this may seem almost impossible, the workers get so accustomed to it after a little time that they do not notice it until it stops. . . .

The twelve-hour shift at night, though taking greater toll of nerve and energy, has distinct charms of its own. . . . The first hours seem to go more quickly than the corresponding ones on day work, until at last two o'clock is reached. Then begins a hand-to-hand struggle with Morpheus [Greek god of dreams]. . . . A stern sense of duty, growing feebler as the moments pass, is our only weapon of defence, whereas the crafty god has a veritable armoury of leaden eyelids, weakening pulses, sleep-weighted heads, and slackening wills. He even leads the foremen away to their offices and softens the hearts of languid overlookers. Some of us succumb, but there are those among us who will not give in. An unbecoming greyness alters our faces, however young and fresh by day, a strange wilting process that steals all youth and beauty from us—until the morning. . . .

Engineering mankind is possessed of the unshakable opinion that no woman can have the mechanical sense. If one of us asks humbly why such and such an alteration is not made to prevent this or that drawback to a machine, she is told, with a superior smile, that a man has worked her machine before her for years, and that therefore if there were any improvement possible it would have been made. As long as we do exactly what we are told and do not attempt to use our brains, we give entire satisfaction, and are treated as nice, good children. Any swerving from the easy path prepared for us by our males arouses the most scathing contempt in their manly bosoms. The exceptions are as delightful to meet as they are rare. Women have, however, proved that their entry into the munition world has increased the output. Employers who forget things personal in their patriotic desire for large results are enthusiastic over the success of women in the shops. But their workmen have to be handled with the utmost tenderness and caution lest they should actually imagine it was being suggested that women could do their work equally well, given equal conditions of training—at least where muscle is not the driving force. This undercurrent of jealousy rises to the surface rather often, but as a general rule the men behave with much kindness, and are ready to help with muscle and advice whenever called upon. If eyes are very bright and hair inclined to curl, the muscle and advice do not even wait for a call.

The coming of the mixed classes of women into the factory is slowly but surely having an educative effect upon the men. "Language" is almost unconsciously becoming subdued. There are fiery exceptions who make our hair stand up on end under our close-fitting caps, but a sharp rebuke or a look of horror will often [straighten out] the most truculent. He will at the moment, perhaps, sneer at the "blooming milksop fools of women," but he will be more careful next time. It is grievous to hear the girls also swearing and using disgusting language. Shoulder to shoulder with the children of the slums, the upper classes are having their eyes prised open at last to the awful conditions among which their sisters have dwelt. Foul language, immorality, and many other evils are but the natural outcome of overcrowding and bitter poverty. If some of us, still blind and ignorant of our responsibilities, shrink horrified and repelled from the rougher set, the compliment is returned with open derision and ribald laughter. There is something, too, about the prim prudery of the "genteel" that tickles the East-Ender's [a lower-class person] sharp wit. On the other hand, attempts at friendliness from the more understanding are treated with the utmost suspicion, though once that suspicion is overcome and friendship is established, it is unshakable. Our working hours are highly flavoured by our neighbours' treatment of ourselves and of each other. Laughter, anger, acute confusion, and laughter again, are constantly changing our immediate outlook on life. Sometimes disgust will overcome us, but we are learning with painful clarity that the fault is not theirs whose actions disgust us, but must be placed to the discredit of those other classes who have allowed the continued existence of conditions which generate the things from which we shrink appalled. . . .

Whatever sacrifice we make of wearied bodies, brains dulled by interminable night-shifts, of roughened hands, and faces robbed of their soft curves, it is, after all, so small a thing. We live in safety, we have shelter, and food whenever necessary, and we are even earning quite a lot of money. What is ours beside the great sacrifice? Men in their prime, on the verge of ambition realized, surrounded by the benefits won by their earlier struggles, are offering up their very lives. And those boys with Life, all glorious and untried, spread before them at their feet, are turning a smiling face to Death.

Magda Trott
OPPOSITION TO FEMALE EMPLOYMENT

In the second year of the war a German woman described the hostility faced by women in the work force.

With the outbreak of war men were drawn away from the management of numerous organizations and, gradually, the lack of experienced personnel made itself felt. Women working in offices were therefore urged not to waste the opportunities offered them by the war, and to continue their education so that they would be prepared to take on the position once held by a male colleague, should the occasion arise.

Such occasions have indeed arisen much sooner than anticipated. The demand for educated women has risen phenomenally during the six months since the war began. Women have been employed in banks, in large commercial businesses, in urban offices—everywhere, in fact, where up till now only men had been employed. They are to be tested in order to see whether they can perform with equal success.

All those who were certain that women would be completely successful substitutes for men were painfully disappointed to discover that many women who had worked for years in a firm and were invited to step up to a higher level, now that the men were absent, suddenly handed in their resignations. An enquiry revealed that, especially in recent days, these notices were coming with great frequency and, strange as it may seem, applied mostly to women who had been working in the same company from four to seven years and had now been offered a better and even better-paid job. They said "no" and since there was no possibility for them to remain in their old jobs, they resigned.

The enemies of women's employment were delighted. Here was their proof that women are incapable of holding down responsible positions. Female workers were quite successful as clerks, stenographers, and typists, in fact, in all those positions that require no independent activity—but as soon as more serious duties were demanded of them, they failed.

Naturally, we enquired of these women why they had given up so quickly, and then the truth of the matter became plain. All women were quite ready, if with some trepidation, to accept the new positions, particularly since the boss made it clear that one of the gentlemen would carefully explain the new assignments to them. Certainly the work was almost entirely new to the young ladies since till now they had only been concerned with their stenography, their books, and so forth. However, they entered their new duties with enthusiasm.

But even on the first day it was noticeable that not everything would proceed as had been supposed. Male colleagues looked askance at the "intruder" who dared to usurp the position and bread of a colleague now fighting for the Fatherland, and who would, it was fervently hoped, return in good health. Moreover, the lady who came as a substitute received exactly half of the salary of the gentleman colleague who had previously occupied the same position. A dangerous implication, since if the lady made good, the boss might continue to draw on female personnel; the saving on salaries would clearly be substantial. It became essential to use all means to show the boss that female help was no substitute for men's work, and a united male front was organized.

It was hardly surprising that all the lady's questions were answered quite vaguely. If she asked again or even a third time, irritated remarks were passed concerning her inadequacy in comprehension, and very soon the male teacher lost patience. Naturally, most of his colleagues supported him and the lady found it difficult, if not impossible, to receive any instruction and was finally forced to resign.

This is what happened in most known cases. We must, however, also admit that occasionally the fault does lie with the lady, who simply did not have sufficient preparation to fill a difficult position. There may be male colleagues who would gladly share information with women; however, these women are unable to understand, because they have too little business experience. In order to prevent this sort of thing, we would counsel all women who are seeking a position in which they hope to advance, to educate themselves as much as possible. All those women who were forced to leave their jobs of long standing might not have been obliged to do so, had they been more concerned in previous years with understanding the overall nature of the business in which they were employed. Their colleagues would surely and generously have answered their questions and given them valuable advice, which would have offered them an overview and thereby avoided the total ignorance with which they entered these advanced positions when they were offered. At least they would have had an inkling and saved themselves the questions that betrayed their great ignorance to their colleagues. They might even have found their way through all the confusion and succeeded in the new position.

Therefore, once again: all you women who want to advance yourselves and create an independent existence, use this time of war as a learning experience and keep your eyes open.

REVIEW QUESTIONS

1. How was Naomi Loughnan's life transformed by her job as a munitions worker?
2. What insights into gender and class distinctions at the time of World War I does Loughnan provide?
3. Why, according to Magda Trott, did German women have difficulty gaining acceptance in the work force?

6 The Paris Peace Conference

The most terrible war the world had experienced ended in November 1918; in January 1919, representatives of the victorious powers assembled in Paris to draw up a peace settlement. The principal figures at the Paris Peace Conference were Woodrow Wilson (1856–1924), president of the United States; David Lloyd George (1863–1945), prime minister of Great Britain; Georges Clemenceau (1841–1929), premier of France; and Vittorio Orlando (1860–1952), premier of Italy. Disillusioned intellectuals and the war-weary masses turned to Wilson as the prince of peace who would fashion a new and better world.

Woodrow Wilson
THE IDEALISTIC VIEW

Wilson sought a peace of justice and reconciliation, one based on democratic and Christian ideals, as the following excerpts from his speeches illustrate.

(May 26, 1917)

We are fighting for the liberty, the self-government, and the undictated development of all peoples, and every feature of the settlement that concludes this war must be conceived and executed for that purpose. Wrongs must first be righted and then adequate safeguards must be created to prevent their being committed again. . . .

. . . No people must be forced under sovereignty under which it does not wish to live. No territory must change hands except for the purpose of securing those who inhabit it a fair chance of life and liberty. No indemnities must be insisted on except those that constitute payment for manifest wrongs done. No readjustments of power must be made except such as will tend to secure the future peace of the world and the future welfare and happiness of its peoples.

And then the free peoples of the world must draw together in some common covenant, some genuine and practical co-öperation that will in effect combine their force to secure peace and justice in the dealings of nations with one another.

The following are excerpts from the Fourteen Points, the plan for peace that Wilson announced on January 8, 1918.

IV. Adequate guarantees given and taken that national armaments will be reduced to the lowest point consistent with domestic safety.

V. A free, open-minded, and absolutely impartial adjustment of all colonial claims, based upon a strict observance of the principle that in determining all such questions of sovereignty the interests of the populations concerned must have equal weight with the equitable claims of the government whose title is to be determined. . . .

VIII. All French territory should be freed and the invaded portions restored, and the wrong done to France by Prussia in 1871 in the matter of Alsace-Lorraine, which has unsettled the peace of the world for nearly fifty years, should be righted, in order that peace may once more be made secure in the interest of all.

IX. A readjustment of the frontiers of Italy should be effected along clearly recognizable lines of nationality.

X. The peoples of Austria-Hungary, whose place among the nations we wish to see safeguarded and assured, should be accorded the freest opportunity of autonomous development. . . .

XII. The Turkish portions of the present Ottoman Empire should be assured a secure sovereignty, but the other nationalities which are now under Turkish rule should be assured an undoubted security of life and an absolutely unmolested opportunity of autonomous development, and the Dardanelles should be permanently opened as a free passage to the ships and commerce of all nations under international guarantees.

XIII. An independent Polish state should be erected which should include the territories inhabited by indisputably Polish populations, which should be assured a free and secure access to the sea, and whose political and economic independence and territorial integrity should be guaranteed by international covenant.

XIV. A general association of nations must be formed under specific covenants for the purpose of affording mutual guarantees of political independence and territorial integrity to great and small states alike.

———

(February 11, 1918)

. . . The principles to be applied [in the peace settlement] are these:

First, that each part of the final settlement must be based upon the essential justice of that particular case and upon such adjustments as are most likely to bring a peace that will be permanent;

Second, that peoples and provinces are not to be bartered about from sovereignty to sovereignty as if they were mere chattels and pawns in a game, even the great game, now forever discredited, of the balance of power; but that

Third, every territorial settlement involved in this war must be made in the interest and for the benefit of the populations concerned, and not as a part of any mere adjustment or compromise of claims amongst rival states; and

Fourth, that all well-defined national aspiration shall be accorded the utmost satisfaction that can be accorded them without introducing new or perpetuating old elements of discord and antagonism that would be likely in time to break the peace of Europe and consequently of the world.

———

(April 6, 1918)

. . . We are ready, whenever the final reckoning is made, to be just to the German people, deal fairly with the German power, as with all others. There can be no difference between peoples in the final judgment, if it is indeed to be a righteous judgment. To propose anything but justice, even-handed and dispassionate justice, to Germany at any time, whatever the outcome of the war, would be to renounce and dishonor our own cause. For we ask nothing that we are not willing to accord.

———

(December 16, 1918)

. . . The war through which we have just passed has illustrated in a way which never can be forgotten the extraordinary wrongs which can be perpetrated by arbitrary and irresponsible power.

It is not possible to secure the happiness and prosperity of the world, to establish an enduring peace, unless the repetition of such wrongs is rendered impossible. This has indeed been a people's war. It has been waged against absolutism and militarism, and these enemies of liberty must from this time forth be shut out from the possibility of working their cruel will upon mankind.

———

(January 3, 1919)

. . . Our task at Paris is to organize the friendship of the world, to see to it that all the moral forces that make for right and justice and liberty are united and are given a vital organization to which the peoples of the world will readily and gladly respond. In other words, our task is no less colossal than this, to set up a new international psychology, to have a new atmosphere.

————

(January 25, 1919)

. . . We are . . . here to see that every people in the world shall choose its own masters and govern its own destinies, not as we wish, but as it wishes. We are here to see, in short, that the very foundations of this war are swept away.

Those foundations were the private choice of small coteries of civil rulers and military staffs. Those foundations were the aggression of great powers upon the small. Those foundations were the holding together of empires of unwilling subjects by the duress of arms. Those foundations were the power of small bodies of men to work their will upon mankind and use them as pawns in a game. And nothing less than the emancipation of the world from these things will accomplish peace.

Georges Clemenceau
FRENCH DEMANDS FOR SECURITY AND REVENGE

Wilson's promised new world clashed with French demands for security and revenge. Almost all the fighting on the war's western front had taken place in France; its industries and farmlands lay in ruins, and many of its young men had perished. France had been invaded by Germany in 1870 as well as in 1914, so the French believed that only by crippling Germany could they gain security. Premier Clemenceau, who was called "the Tiger," dismissed Wilson's vision of a new world as mere noble sentiment divorced from reality, and he fought tenaciously to gain security for France. Clemenceau's profound hatred and mistrust of Germany are revealed in his book *Grandeur and Misery of Victory* (1930), written a decade after the Paris Peace Conference.

For the catastrophe of 1914 the Germans are responsible. Only a professional liar would deny this. . . .

What after all is this war, prepared, undertaken, and waged by the German people, who flung aside every scruple of conscience to let it loose, hoping for a peace of enslavement under the yoke of a militarism destructive of all human dignity? It is simply the continuance, the recrudescence, of those never-ending acts of violence by which the first savage tribes carried out their depredations with all the resources of barbarism. The means improve with the ages. The ends remain the same. . . .

Germany, in this matter, was unfortunate enough to allow herself (in spite of her skill at dissimulation) to be betrayed into an excess of candour by her characteristic tendency to go to extremes. *Deutschland über alles. Germany above everything!* That, and nothing less, is what she asks, and when once her demand is satisfied she will let you enjoy a peace under the yoke. Not only does she make no secret of her aim, but the intolerable arrogance of the German aristocracy, the servile good nature of the intellectual and the scholar, the gross vanity of the most competent leaders in industry, and the wide-spread influence of a violent popular poetry conspire to shatter throughout the world all the time-honoured traditions of individual, as well as international, dignity. . . .

On November 11, 1918, the fighting ceased.

It is not I who will dispute the German soldier's qualities of endurance. But he had been promised a *fresh and frolicsome war,* and for four years he had been pinned down between the anvil and the hammer. . . . Our defeat would have resulted in a relapse of human civilization into violence and bloodshed. . . .

Outrages against human civilization are in the long run defeated by their own excess, and thus I discern in the peculiar mentality of the German soldier, with his *"Deutschland über alles,"* the cause of the premature exhaustion that brought him to beg for an armistice before the French soldier, who was fighting for his independence. . . .

And what is this "Germanic civilization," this monstrous explosion of the will to power, which threatens openly to do away entirely with the diversities established by many evolutions, to set in their place the implacable mastery of a race whose lordly part would be to substitute itself, by force of arms, for all national developments? We need only read [General Friedrich von] Bernhardi's famous pamphlet *Our Future,* in which it is alleged that Germany sums up within herself, as the historian Treitschke asserts, the greatest manifestation of human supremacy, and finds herself condemned, by her very greatness, either to absorb all nations in herself or to return to nothingness. . . . Ought we not all to feel menaced in our very vitals by this mad doctrine of universal Germanic supremacy over England, France, America, and every other country?. . .

What document more suitable to reveal the direction of "German culture" than the famous manifesto of the ninety-three super-intellectuals of Germany,[1] issued to justify the bloodiest and the least excusable of military aggressions against the great centres of civilization? At the moment . . . violated Belgium lay beneath the heel of the malefactor (October 1914) . . . [and German troops were] razing . . . great historical buildings to the ground [and] burning down . . . libraries. It would need a whole book to tell of the infamous treatment inflicted upon noncombatants, to reckon up those who were shot down, or put to death, or deported, or condemned to forced labour. . . .

Well, this was the hour chosen by German intellectuals to make themselves heard. Let all the nations give ear!. . .

. . . Their learning made of them merely Germans better than all others qualified to formulate, on their own account, the extravagances of Germanic arrogance. The only difference is that they speak louder than the common people, those docile automatons. The fact is that they really believe themselves to be the representatives of a privileged *"culture"* that sets them above the errors of the human race, and confers on them the prerogative of a superior power. . . .

The whole document is nothing but denials without the support of a single proof. *"It is not true* that Germany wanted the War." [Kaiser] William II had for years been *"mocked at by his adversaries of today on account of his unshakable love of peace."* They neglect to tell us whence they got this lie. They forget that from 1871 till 1914 we received from Germany a series of war threats in the course of which Queen Victoria and also the Czar had to intervene with the *Kaiser* direct for the maintenance of peace.

I have already recalled how our German intellectuals account for the violation of the Belgian frontier:

> *It is not true that we criminally violated Belgian neutrality. It can be proved that France and England had made up their minds to violate it. It can be proved that Belgium was willing. It would have been suicide not to forestall them. . . .*

. . . And when a great chemist such as Ostwald tells us, with his colleagues, that our struggle *"against the so-called German militarism"* is really directed *"against German cul-*

---

[1]Shortly after the outbreak of war, ninety-three leading German scholars and scientists addressed a letter to the world, defending Germany's actions.

ture," we must remember that *this same savant published a history of chemistry* IN WHICH THE NAME OF [eighteenth-century French chemist Antoine] LAVOISIER WAS NOT MENTIONED.

The "intellectuals" take their place in public opinion as the most ardent propagandists of the thesis which makes Germany the very model of the *"chosen people."* The same Professor Ostwald had already written, *"Germany has reached a higher stage of civilization than the other peoples, and the result of the War will be an organization of Europe under German leadership."* Professor Haeckel had demanded *the conquest of London, the division of Belgium between Germany and Holland, the annexation of North-east France, of Poland, the Baltic Provinces, the Congo, and a great part of the English colonies.* Professor Lasson went further still:

> *We are morally and intellectually superior to all men. We are peerless.* So too are our organizations and our institutions. *Germany is the most perfect creation known in history,* and the Imperial Chancellor, Herr von Bethmann-Hollweg, is *the most eminent of living men.*

Ordinary laymen who talked in this strain would be taken off to some safe asylum. Coming from duly hallmarked professors, such statements explain all German warfare by alleging that Germany's destiny is universal domination, and that for this very reason she is bound either to disappear altogether or to exercise violence on all nations with a view to their own betterment. . . .

May I further recall, since we have to emphasize the point, that on September 17, 1914, Erzberger, the well-known German statesman,

an eminent member of the Catholic Party, wrote to the Minister of War, General von Falkenhayn, *"We must not worry about committing an offence against the rights of nations nor about violating the laws of humanity. Such feelings today are of secondary importance"*? A month later, on October 21, 1914, he wrote in *Der Tag,* "*If a way was found of entirely wiping out the whole of London it would be more humane to employ it* than to allow the blood of A SINGLE GERMAN SOLDIER to be shed on the battlefield!". . .

. . . General von Bernhardi himself, the best pupil, as I have already said, of the historian Treitschke, whose ideas are law in Germany, has just preached the doctrine of "World power or Downfall" at us. So there is nothing left for other nations, as a way of salvation, but to be conquered by Germany. . . .

I have sometimes penetrated into the sacred cave of the Germanic cult, which is, as every one knows, the *Bierhaus* [beer hall]. A great aisle of massive humanity where there accumulate, amid the fumes of tobacco and beer, the popular rumblings of a nationalism upheld by the sonorous brasses blaring to the heavens the supreme voice of Germany, *"Deutschland über alles!"* Men, women, and children, all petrified in reverence before the divine stoneware pot, brows furrowed with irrepressible power, eyes lost in a dream of infinity, mouths twisted by the intensity of will-power, drink in long draughts the celestial hope of vague expectations. These only remain to be realized presently when the chief marked out by Destiny shall have given the word. There you have the ultimate framework of an old but childish race.

German Delegation to the Paris Peace Conference
A PEACE OF MIGHT

A debate raged over the Versailles Treaty, the peace settlement imposed on Germany by the Paris Peace Conference. The treaty's defenders argued that if

Germany had won the war, it would have forced far more ruthless terms on France and other losing countries. These defenders pointed to the Treaty of Brest-Litovsk, which Germany compelled the new and weak revolutionary Russian government to sign in 1918, as an example of German peacemaking. Through this treaty, Germany seized 34 percent of Russia's population, 32 percent of its farmland, 54 percent of its industrial enterprise, and 89 percent of its coal mines.

The Germans denounced the Versailles Treaty, which they regarded both as a violation of Wilson's principles as enunciated in the Fourteen Points and other statements and as an Anglo-French plot to keep Germany economically and militarily weak. Leaders of the new German Weimar Republic, formed after a revolution had forced the emperor to abdicate, protested that in punishing and humiliating the new republic for the sins of the monarchy and the military, the peacemakers weakened the foundations of democracy in Germany, kept alive old hatreds, and planted the seeds of future conflicts. Enraged nationalists swore to erase this blot on German honor.

In the excerpts that follow, the German delegation to the Paris Peace Conference voiced its criticism of the Versailles Treaty.

The peace to be concluded with Germany was to be a peace of right, not a peace of might.

In his address to the Mexican journalists on the 9th of June, 1918, President Wilson promised to maintain the principle that the interests of the weakest and of the strongest should be equally sacred.... And in his speech before Congress on the 11th of February 1918, the President described the aim of peace as follows: "What we are striving for is a new international order based upon broad and universal principles of right and justice—no mere peace of shreds and patches.". . .

To begin with the territorial questions:

In the West, a purely German territory on the Saar [river that runs through France and Germany] with a population of at least 650,000 inhabitants is to be separated from the German Empire for at least fifteen years merely for the reason that claims are asserted to the coal abounding there.

The other cessions in the West, German-Austria and German-Bohemia will be mentioned in connection with the right of self-determination.

In Schleswig, the line of demarcation for voting has been traced through purely German districts and goes farther than Denmark herself wishes.

In the East, Upper Silesia is to be separated from Germany and given to Poland, although it has had no political connexion with Poland for the last 750 years. Contrary to this, the provinces of Posen and almost the whole of West Prussia are to be separated from the German Empire in consideration of the former extent of the old Polish state, although millions of Germans are living there. Again, the district of Memel is separated from Germany quite regardless of its historical past, in the obvious attempt to separate Germany from Russia for economic reasons. For the purpose of securing to Poland free access to the sea, East Prussia is to be completely cut off from the rest of the Empire and thereby condemned to economic and national decay. The purely German city of Danzig is to become a Free State under the suzerainty of Poland. Such terms are not founded on any principle of justice. Quite arbitrarily, here the idea of an imprescribable historical right, there the idea of ethnographical possession, there the standpoint of economic interest shall prevail, in every case the decision being unfavourable to Germany.

The settlement of the colonial question is equally contradictory to a peace of justice. For the essence of activity in colonial work does not consist in capitalistic exploitation of a less developed human race, but in raising backward peoples to a higher civilization. This gives the Powers which are advanced in culture a natural claim to take part in colonial work. Germany, whose colonial accomplishments cannot be denied, has also this natural claim, which is not recognized by a treaty of peace that deprives Germany of all of her colonies.

Not only the settlement of the territorial questions but each and every provision of the treaty of peace is governed by the ill-renowned phrase: "Might above Right!"—Here are a few illustrations:. . .

Although President Wilson . . . has acknowledged that "no single fact caused the war, but that in the last analysis the whole European system is in a deeper sense responsible for the war, with its combination of alliances and understandings, a complicated texture of intrigues and espionage that unfailingly caught the whole family of nations in its meshes," . . . Germany is to acknowledge that Germany and her allies are responsible for all damages which the enemy Governments or their subjects have incurred by her and her allies' aggression. . . . Apart from the consideration that there is no incontestable legal foundation for the obligation for reparation imposed upon Germany, the amount of such compensation is to be determined by a commission nominated solely by Germany's enemies, Germany taking no part in the findings of the commission. The commission is plainly to have power to administer Germany like the estate of a bankrupt. . . .

. . . Germany must promise to pay an indemnity, the amount of which at present is not even stated. . . .

These few instances show that that is not the just peace we were promised, not the peace "the very principle of which," according to a word of President Wilson, "is equality and the common participation in a common benefit.

The equality of nations upon which peace must be founded if it is to last must be an equality of rights.". . .

In this war, a new fundamental law has arisen which the statesmen of all belligerent peoples have again and again acknowledged to be their aim: the right of self-determination. To make it possible for all nations to put this privilege into practice was intended to be one achievement of the war. . . . On February 11, 1918, President Wilson said in Congress: "Peoples and provinces are not to be bartered about from sovereignty to sovereignty as if they were mere chattels and pawns in a game.". . .

Neither the treatment described above of the inhabitants of the Saar region . . . of consulting the population in the districts of Eupen, Malmédy, and Prussian Moresnet—which, moreover, shall not take place before they have been put under Belgian sovereignty—comply in the least with such a solemn recognition of the right of self-determination.

The same is also true with regard to Alsace-Lorraine.[1] If Germany has pledged herself "to right the wrong of 1871," this does not mean any renunciation of the right of self-determination of the inhabitants of Alsace-Lorraine. A cession of the country without consulting the population would be a new wrong, if for no other reason, because it would be inconsistent with a recognized principle of peace.

On the other hand, it is incompatible with the idea of national self-determination for two and one-half million Germans to be torn away from their native land against their own will. By the proposed demarcation of the boundary, unmistakably German territories are disposed of in favor of their Polish neighbours. Thus, from the Central Silesian districts of Guhrau and Militsch certain portions are to be wrenched away, in which, besides 44,900 Ger-

---

[1]Alsace-Lorraine is a region of mixed French and German speakers, which Germany had taken from France in the Franco-Prussian War (1870–1871); it was restored to France by the Versailles Treaty.

mans, reside at the utmost 3,700 Poles. The same may be said with reference to the towns of Schneidemühl and Bromberg of which the latter has, at the utmost, eighteen per cent Polish inhabitants, whereas in the rural district of Bromberg the Poles do not form even forty per cent of the population. . . . This disrespect of the right of self-determination is shown most grossly in the fact that Danzig is to be separated from the German Empire and made a free state. Neither historical rights nor the present ethnographical conditions of ownership of the Polish people can have any weight as compared with the German past and the German character of that city. Free access to the sea, satisfying the economic wants of Poland, can be secured by guarantees founded on international law, by the creating of free ports. Likewise the cession of the commercial town of Memel, which is to be exacted from Germany, is in no way consistent with the right of self-determination. The same may be said with reference to the fact that millions of Germans in German-Austria are to be denied the union with Germany which they desire and that, further, millions of Germans dwelling along our frontiers are to be forced to remain part of the newly created Czecho-Slovakian State.

REVIEW QUESTIONS

1. What principles did Woodrow Wilson want to serve as the basis of the peace settlement?
2. According to Wilson, what were the principal reasons for the outbreak of war in 1914?
3. What accusations did Georges Clemenceau make against the German national character? What contrasts did he draw between the Germans and the French?
4. How did Clemenceau respond to the manifesto of the German intellectuals?
5. Why, more than a decade after the war, did Clemenceau believe that Germany should still be feared?
6. According to the German delegation, how did the Treaty of Versailles violate the principle of self-determination championed by Woodrow Wilson?
7. In addition to the loss of territory, what other features of the Treaty of Versailles angered the Germans?

7 The Bolshevik Revolution

In March 1917, in the middle of World War I, Russians were demoralized. The army, poorly trained, inadequately equipped, and incompetently led, had suffered staggering losses; everywhere soldiers were deserting. Food shortages and low wages drove workers to desperation; the loss of fathers and sons at the front embittered peasants. Discontent was keenest in Petrograd, where on March 9, 200,000 striking workers shouting "Down with autocracy!" packed the streets. After some bloodshed, government troops refused to fire on the workers. Faced with a broad and debilitating crisis—violence and anarchy in the capital, breakdown of transport, uncertain food and fuel supplies, and general disorder—Tsar Nicholas II was forced to turn over authority to a provisional government, thereby ending three centuries of tsarist rule under the Romanov dynasty.

The Provisional Government, after July 1917 guided by Aleksandr Kerensky (1881–1970), sought to transform Russia into a Western-style liberal state, but the government failed to comprehend the urgency with which the Russian peasants wanted the landlords' land, and soldiers and the masses wanted peace. Resentment spiraled. Kerensky's increasing unpopularity and the magnitude of popular unrest seemed to the Bolsheviks' leader, Vladimir Ilyich Lenin (1870–1924), then in hiding, to offer the long-expected opportunity for the Bolsheviks to seize power and bring about a socialist revolution.

Army Intelligence Report
THE BREAKDOWN OF MILITARY DISCIPLINE

By the summer of 1917 demoralized Russian soldiers were deserting in large numbers. The following excerpts, drawn from an army intelligence report of October 1917, reveal the breakdown in military discipline.

Northern front.—The situation in the army has not changed and may be described as a complete lack of confidence in the officers and the higher commanding personnel. The belief is growing among the soldiers that they cannot be punished for what they do. . . .The influence of Bolshevik ideas is spreading very rapidly. To this must be added a general weariness, an irritability, and a desire for peace at any price.

Any attempt on the part of the officers to regulate the life of the army . . . is looked upon by the soldiers as counter-revolution. . . .

. . . Considerable numbers of soldiers . . . feigning sickness are leaving the front for the hospital. . . .

12th Army.—. . .The press of the political parties is no longer influencing the soldier masses. Again and again one hears the orders of the Provisional Government severely criticized. The committee of the 95th Regiment . . . declared Kerensky a traitor. . . .

Apart from the Bolshevik not a single [political] movement has any popularity. Those who read moderate newspapers are looked upon as [followers of the] "bourgeoisie" and "counter-revolutionists." An intensive agitation is being conducted in favor of an immediate cessation of military operations on all fronts. Whenever a whole regiment or battalion refuses to carry out a military order, the fact is immediately made known to other parts of the army through special agitators. . . .

Western front.— . . . Because of general war weariness, bad nourishment, mistrust of officers, etc., there has developed an intense defeatist agitation accompanied by refusals to carry out orders, threats to the commanding personnel, and attempts to fraternize with Germans. Everywhere one hears voices calling for immediate peace, because, they say, no one will stay in the trenches during the winter. . . .There is a deep-rooted conviction among the rank and file that fraternization with the enemy is a sure way of attaining peace. . . .

[Bolshevik] newspapers . . . openly advocate the immediate cessation of war, the transfer of political and military power to the proletariat, the immediate socialization of land, and a merciless struggle against capitalists and the bourgeoisie. Their method of argument is quite simple and comprehensible to the masses. It runs as follows: All the ministers of the Provisional Government are subservient to the bourgeoisie and are counter-revolutionists;

they continue to wage war to please the Allied and the Russian capitalists; the government introduced the death penalty with the view of exterminating the soldiers, workers, and peasants. . . .

Among the phenomena indicative of tendencies in the life in the rear of the Western front are the recent disturbances at the replacement depot in Gomel. On October 1 over eight thousand soldiers who were to be transferred to the front demanded to be sent home instead. . . . Incited by agitators they stormed the armory, took some fifteen hundred suits of winter equipment, and assaulted the Assistant Commissar and a member of the front committee. Similar events . . . have taken place in Smolensk. . . .

Southwestern front.— . . . Defeatist agitation is increasing and the disintegration of the army is in full swing. The Bolshevik wave is growing steadily, owing to general disintegration in the rear, the absence of strong power, and the lack of supplies and equipment. The dominant theme of conversation is peace at any price and under any condition. Every order, no matter what its source, is met with hostility. . . .

The guard-cavalry corps of the 2d Army passed a resolution of no confidence in the majority of officers. The soldiers are engaging in organized armed invasions of the surrounding country estates, plundering provisions . . . of which there is a scarcity in the army. Not a thing can be done to counteract this restlessness . . . as there is no force which could be relied upon in any attempt to enforce order. The activity of the courts is paralyzed because of the hostile attitude of the soldiers. . . .

The following general conclusions may be drawn from the reports of the commissars: The approaching winter campaign has accelerated the disintegration of the army and increased the longing for peace. It is necessary to leave nothing undone which might supply the soldiers with food, shoes, and winter clothing; to see that the army is reduced in numbers; to improve the discipline in the reserve regiments. Otherwise the ranks will be filled with such material as will lead to the complete demoralization and destruction of the army. . . .

[The rest of the report deals with the Rumanian and Caucasian fronts, describing similar conditions.]

N. N. Sukhanov
TROTSKY AROUSES THE PEOPLE

Playing a crucial role in the Bolshevik seizure of power on November 7, 1917, was Leon Trotsky (1879–1940). Born Lev Davidovich Bronstein, the son of a prosperous Jewish farmer in Ukraine, Trotsky was attracted early to the ranks of the revolutionaries, and he shared their fate. Exiled to Siberia in 1902, he escaped to Switzerland with a faked passport in the name of Leon Trotsky. Back in Russia for the Revolution of 1905, he was again exiled and again escaped. After a period abroad, he returned to Russia after the overthrow of the tsar in March 1917 and soon assumed a leading role among the Bolsheviks. In September 1917, as the moderate regime of Kerensky began to totter, Trotsky was elected chairman of the Petrograd soviet; soon afterward he masterminded the Military-Revolutionary Committee, the Bolshevik strike force.

On the evening of November 4, Trotsky delivered a rousing speech at the Peoples' House, a popular theater much used for working-class meetings. His speech is described by an eyewitness, the Menshevik (a Social Democratic moderate) leader N. N. Sukhanov, in his 1917 book, *The Russian Revolution.*

The mood of the people, more than 3,000, who filled the hall was definitely tense; they were all silently waiting for something. The audience was of course primarily workers and soldiers, but more than a few typically lower-middle-class men's and women's figures were visible.

Trotsky's ovation seemed to be cut short prematurely, out of curiosity and impatience: what was he going to say? Trotsky at once began to heat up the atmosphere, with his skill and brilliance. I remember that at length and with extraordinary power he drew a picture of the suffering of the trenches. Thoughts flashed through my mind of the inevitable incongruity of the parts in this oratorical whole. But Trotsky knew what he was doing. The whole point lay in the mood. The political conclusions had long been familiar. They could be condensed, as long as there were enough highlights.

Trotsky did this—with enough highlights. The Soviet regime was not only called upon to put an end to the suffering of the trenches. It would give land and heal the internal disorder. Once again the recipes against hunger were repeated: a soldier, a sailor, and a working girl, who would requisition bread from those who had it and distribute it gratis to the cities and front. But Trotsky went even further on this decisive "Day of the Petersburg Soviet."

"The Soviet Government will give everything the country contains to the poor and the men in the trenches. You, bourgeois, have got two fur caps!—give one of them to the soldier, who's freezing in the trenches. Have you got warm boots? Stay at home. The worker needs your boots. . . ."

These were very good and just ideas. They could not but excite the enthusiasm of a crowd who had been reared on the Tsarist whip. In any case, I certify as a direct witness that this was what was said on this last day.

All round me was a mood bordering on ecstasy. It seemed as though the crowd, spontaneously and of its own accord, would break into some religious hymn. Trotsky formulated a brief and general resolution, or pronounced some general formula like "we will defend the worker-peasant cause to the last drop of our blood."

Who was—for? The crowd of thousands, as one man, raised their hands. I saw the raised hands and burning eyes of men, women, youths, soldiers, peasants, and typically lower-middle-class faces. Were they in spiritual transport? Did they see, through the raised curtain, a corner of the "righteous land" of their longing? Or were they penetrated by a consciousness of the *political occasion,* under the influence of the political agitation of a *Socialist?* Ask no questions! Accept it as it was. . . .

Trotsky went on speaking. The innumerable crowd went on holding their hands up. Trotsky rapped out the words: "Let this vote of yours be your vow—with all your strength and at any sacrifice to support the Soviet that has taken on itself the glorious burden of bringing to a conclusion the victory of the revolution and of giving land, bread, and peace!"

The vast crowd was holding up its hands. It agreed. It vowed. Once again, accept this as it was. With an unusual feeling of oppression I looked on at this really magnificent scene.

Trotsky finished. Someone else went out on to the stage. But there was no point in waiting and looking any more.

Throughout Petersburg more or less the same thing was going on. Everywhere there were final reviews and final vows. Thousands, tens of thousands and hundreds of thousands of people . . . This, actually, was already an insurrection. Things had started. . . .

V. I. Lenin
THE CALL TO POWER

On November 6 (October 24 by the old-style calendar then in use in Russia), Lenin urged immediate action, as the following document reveals.

. . . The situation is critical in the extreme. In fact it is now absolutely clear that to delay the uprising would be fatal.

With all my might I urge comrades to realise that everything now hangs by a thread; that we are confronted by problems which are not to be solved by conferences or congresses (even congresses of Soviets), but exclusively by peoples, by the masses, by the struggle of the armed people.

The bourgeois onslaught of the Kornilovites [followers of General Kornilov, who tried to establish a military dictatorship] show that we must not wait. We must at all costs, this very evening, this very night, arrest the government, having first disarmed the officer cadets (defeating them, if they resist), and so on.

We must not wait! We may lose everything!

Who must take power?

That is not important at present. Let the Revolutionary Military Committee [Bolshevik organization working within the army and navy] do it, or "some other institution" which will declare that it will relinquish power only to the true representatives of the interests of the people, the interests of the army (the immediate proposal of peace), the interests of the peasants (the land to be taken immediately and private property abolished), the interests of the starving.

All districts, all regiments, all forces must be mobilised at once and must immediately send their delegations to the Revolutionary Military Committee and to the Central Committee of the Bolsheviks [governing organization of the Bolshevik party] with the insistent demand that under no circumstances should power be left in the hands of Kerensky and Co. . . . not under any circumstances; the matter must be decided without fail this very evening, or this very night.

History will not forgive revolutionaries for procrastinating when they could be victorious today (and they certainly will be victorious today), while they risk losing much tomorrow, in fact, they risk losing everything.

If we seize power today, we seize it not in opposition to the Soviets but on their behalf.

The seizure of power is the business of the uprising; its political purpose will become clear after the seizure. . . .

. . . It would be an infinite crime on the part of the revolutionaries were they to let the chance slip, knowing that the *salvation of the revolution,* the offer of peace, the salvation of Petrograd, salvation from famine, the transfer of the land to the peasants depend upon them.

The government is tottering. It must be *given the death-blow* at all costs.

To delay action is fatal.

REVIEW QUESTIONS

1. What caused the breakdown of military discipline in the Russian ranks in 1917?
2. With what issues and what promises did Leon Trotsky arouse the masses in support of the Bolshevik seizure of power?
3. What promises did V. I. Lenin hold out to his supporters should the revolution succeed?
4. How would you define, from the evidence here offered, a revolutionary situation? What factors create it?

8 The War and European Consciousness

World War I caused many intellectuals to have grave doubts about the Enlightenment tradition and the future of Western civilization. More than ever the belief in human goodness, reason, and the progress of humanity seemed an illusion. Despite its many accomplishments, intellectuals contended that Western civilization was flawed and perishable.

Paul Valéry
DISILLUSIONMENT

Shortly after World War I, Paul Valéry (1871–1945), a prominent French writer, expressed the mood of disillusionment that gripped many intellectuals. The following reading was written in 1919; the second reading is from a 1922 speech. Both were published in *Variety,* a collection of some of Valéry's works.

We modern civilizations have learned to recognize that we are mortal like the others.

We had heard tell of whole worlds vanished, of empires foundered with all their men and all their engines, sunk to the inexplorable depths of the centuries with their gods and laws, their academies and their pure and applied sciences, their grammars, dictionaries, classics, romantics, symbolists, their critics and the critics of their critics. We knew that all the apparent earth is made of ashes, and that ashes have a meaning. We perceived, through the misty bulk of history, the phantoms of huge vessels once laden with riches and learning. We could not count them. But these wrecks, after all, were no concern of ours.

Elam, Nineveh, Babylon were vague and splendid names; the total ruin of these worlds, for us, meant as little as did their existence. But *France, England, Russia* . . . these names, too, are splendid. . . . And now we see that the abyss of history is deep enough to bury all the world. We feel that a civilization is fragile as a life. The circumstances which will send the works of [John] Keats [English poet] and the works of [Charles] Baudelaire [French poet] to join those of Menander[1] are not at all inconceivable; they are found in the daily papers.

The following passage is from an address that Valéry delivered at the University of Zurich on November 15, 1922.

The storm has died away, and still we are restless, uneasy, as if the storm were about to break. Almost all the affairs of men remain in a terrible uncertainty. We think of what has disappeared, we are almost destroyed by what has been destroyed; we do not know what will be born, and we fear the future, not without reason. We hope vaguely, we dread precisely; our fears are infinitely more precise than our hopes; we confess that the charm of life is behind us, abundance is behind us, but doubt and disorder are in us and with us. There is no thinking man, however shrewd or learned he may be,

---

[1]Menander was an ancient Greek poet whose works were lost until fragments were found in Egypt at the end of the nineteenth century.

who can hope to dominate this anxiety, to escape from this impression of darkness, to measure the probable duration of this period when the vital relations of humanity are disturbed profoundly.

We are a very unfortunate generation, whose lot has been to see the moment of our passage through life coincide with the arrival of great and terrifying events, the echo of which will resound through all our lives.

One can say that all the fundamentals of the world have been affected by the war, or more exactly, by the circumstances of the war; something deeper has been worn away than the renewable parts of the machine. You know how greatly the general economic situation has been disturbed, and the polity of states, and the very life of the individual; you are familiar with the universal discomfort, hesitation, apprehension. *But among all these injured things is the Mind.* The Mind has indeed been cruelly wounded; its complaint is heard in the hearts of intellectual man; it passes a mournful judgment on itself. It doubts itself profoundly.

Erich Maria Remarque
THE LOST GENERATION

In Erich Maria Remarque's *All Quiet on the Western Front,* a wounded German soldier reflects on the war and his future. He sees himself as part of a lost generation. (See also page 279.)

Gradually a few of us are allowed to get up. And I am given crutches to hobble around on. But I do not make much use of them; I cannot bear Albert's gaze as I move about the room. His eyes always follow me with such a strange look. So I sometimes escape to the corridor;— there I can move about more freely.

On the next floor below are the abdominal and spine cases, head wounds and double amputations. On the right side of the wing are the jaw wounds, gas cases, nose, ear, and neck wounds. On the left the blind and the lung wounds, pelvis wounds, wounds in the joints, wounds in the kidneys, wounds in the testicles, wounds in the intestines. Here a man realizes for the first time in how many places a man can get hit.

Two fellows die of tetanus. Their skin turns pale, their limbs stiffen, at last only their eyes live—stubbornly. Many of the wounded have their shattered limbs hanging free in the air from a gallows; underneath the wound a basin is placed into which drips the pus. Every two or three hours the vessel is emptied. Other men lie in stretching bandages with heavy weights hanging from the end of the bed. I see intestine wounds that are constantly full of excreta. The surgeon's clerk shows me X-ray photographs of completely smashed hip-bones, knees, and shoulders.

A man cannot realize that above such shattered bodies there are still human faces in which life goes its daily round. And this is only one hospital, one single station; there are hundreds of thousands in Germany, hundreds of thousands in France, hundreds of thousands in Russia. How senseless is everything that can ever be written, done, or thought, when such things are possible. It must be all lies and of no account when the culture of a thousand years could not prevent this stream of blood being poured out, these torture-chambers in their hundreds of thousands. A hospital alone shows what war is.

I am young, I am twenty years old; yet I know nothing of life but despair, death, fear, and fatuous superficiality cast over an abyss of sorrow. I see how peoples are set against one another, and in silence, unknowingly, foolishly, obediently, innocently slay one another. I see that the keenest brains of the world invent weapons and words to make it yet more refined and enduring. And all men of my age, here and over there, throughout the whole world see these things; all my generation is experiencing these things with me. What would our fathers do if we suddenly stood up and came before them and proffered our account? What do they expect of us if a time ever comes when the war is over? Through the years our business has been killing;—it was our first calling in life. Our knowledge of life is limited to death. What will happen afterwards? And what shall come out of us?

Ernst von Salomon
BRUTALIZATION OF THE INDIVIDUAL

The war also produced a fascination with violence that persisted after peace had been declared. Many returned veterans, their whole being enveloped by the war, continued to yearn for the excitement of battle and the fellowship of the trenches. Brutalized by the war, these men became ideal recruits for fascist parties that relished violence and sought the destruction of the liberal state.

Immediately after the war ended, thousands of soldiers and adventurers joined the Free Corps—volunteer brigades that defended Germany's eastern borders against encroachments by the new states of Poland, Latvia, and Estonia, and fought communist revolutionaries. Many of these freebooters later became members of Hitler's movement. Ernst von Salomon, a leading spokesman of the Free Corps movement, was a sixteen-year-old student in Berlin when the defeated German army marched home. In the passage that follows, he described the soldiers who "will always carry the trenches in their blood."

The soldiers walked quickly, pressed closely to each other. Suddenly the first four came into sight, looking lifeless. They had stony, rigid faces. . . .

Then came the others. Their eyes lay deep in dark, gray, sharp-edged hollows under the shadow of their helmets. They looked neither right nor left, but straight ahead, as if under the power of a terrifying target in front of them; as if they peered from a mud hole or a trench over torn-up earth. In front of them lay emptiness. They spoke not a word. . . .

O God, how these men looked, as they came nearer—those utterly exhausted, immobile faces under their steel helmets, those bony limbs, those ragged dusty uniforms! And around them an infinite void. It was as if they had drawn a magic circle around themselves, in which dangerous forces, invisible to outsiders, worked their secret spell. Did they still carry in their minds the madness of a thousand battles compressed into whirling visions, as they carried in their uniforms the dirt and the dust of shell-torn fields? The sight was unbearable. They marched like envoys of death, of dread, of the most deadly and solitary coldness. And here was their homeland, warmth, and happiness. Why were they so silent? Why did they not smile?

. . . When I saw these deadly determined faces, these faces as hard as if hacked out of wood, these eyes that glanced past the onlookers, unresponsive, hostile—yes, hostile indeed—then I knew—it suddenly came over me in a fright—that everything had been utterly different from what we had thought, all of us who stood here watching. . . . What did we know about these men? About the war in the trenches? About our soldiers? Oh God, it was terrible: What we had been told was all untrue. We had been told lies. These were not our beloved heroes, the protectors of our homes—these were men who did not belong to us, gathered here to meet them. They did not want to belong to us; they came from other worlds with other laws and other friendships. And all of a sudden everything that I had hoped and wished for, that had inspired me, turned shallow and empty. . . . What an abysmal error it had been to believe for four years that these men belonged to us. Now that misunderstanding vanished. . . .

Then I suddenly understood. These were not workers, peasants, students; no, these were not mechanics, white-collar employees, businessmen, officials—these were soldiers. . . . These were men who had responded to the secret call of blood, of spirit, volunteers one way or the other, men who had experienced exacting comradeship and the things behind things—who had found a home in war, a fatherland, a community, and a nation. . . .

The homeland belonged to them; the nation belonged to them. What we had blabbered like marketwomen, they had actually lived. . . . The trenches were their home, their fatherland, their nation. And they had never used these words; they never believed in them; they believed in themselves. The war held them in its grip and dominated them; the war will never discharge them; they will never return home; they will always carry the trenches in their blood, the closeness of death, the dread, the intoxication, the iron. And suddenly they were to become peaceful citizens, set again in solid every-day routines? Never! That would mean a counterfeit that was bound to fail. The war is over; the warriors are still marching, . . . dissatisfied when they are demobilized, explosive when they stay together. The war had not given them answers; it had achieved no decision. The soldiers continue to march. . . .

Appeals were posted on the street corners for volunteer units to defend Germany's eastern borders. The day after the troops marched into our town, I volunteered. I was accepted and outfitted. Now I too was a soldier.

Sigmund Freud
A LEGACY OF EMBITTERMENT

In his 1915 essay, "Thoughts for the Times on War and Death," Sigmund Freud (see page 250) said that World War I's fury would shatter the bonds of a common European civilization and engulf Europeans in hatred for years to come. He reflects in the following passage on the singular destructiveness of World War I and its uniqueness in world history to date.

We cannot but feel that no event has ever destroyed so much that is precious in the common possessions of humanity, confused so many of the clearest intelligences, or so thoroughly debased what is highest. Science herself has lost her passionless impartiality; her deeply embittered servants seek for weapons from her with which to contribute towards the struggle with the enemy. Anthropologists feel driven to declare him [the enemy] inferior and degenerate, psychiatrists issue a diagnosis of his disease of mind or spirit. . . .

We had expected the great world-dominating nations of white race upon whom the leadership of the human species has fallen, who were known to have world-wide interests as their concern, to whose creative powers were due not only our technical advances towards the control of nature but the artistic and scientific standards of civilization—we had expected these peoples to succeed in discovering another way of settling misunderstandings and conflicts of interest. Within each of these nations high norms of moral conduct were laid down for the individual, to which his manner of life was bound to conform if he desired to take part in a civilized community. . . .

Relying on this unity among the civilized peoples, countless men and women have exchanged their native home for a foreign one, and made their existence dependent on the intercommunications between friendly nations. Moreover anyone who was not by stress of circumstance confined to one spot could create for himself out of all the advantages and attractions of these civilized countries a new and wider fatherland, in which he could move about without hindrance or suspicion. In this way he enjoyed the blue sea and the grey; the beauty of snow-covered mountains and of green meadow lands; the magic of northern forests and the splendour of southern vegetation; the mood evoked by landscapes that recall great historical events, and the silence of untouched nature. This new fatherland was a museum for him, too, filled with all the treasures which the artists of civilized humanity had in the successive centuries created and left behind. As he wandered from one gallery to another in this museum, he could recognize with impartial appreciation what varied types of perfection a mixture of blood, the course of history, and the special quality of their mother-earth had produced among his compatriots in this wider sense. Here he would find cool, inflexible energy developed to the highest point; there, the graceful art of beautifying existence; elsewhere the feeling for orderliness and law, or

others among the qualities which have made mankind the lords of the earth.

Nor must we forget that each of these citizens of the civilized world had created for himself a "Parnassus" and a "School of Athens" [that is, a center of high culture and learning] of his own. From among the great thinkers, writers and artists of all nations he had chosen those to whom he considered he owed the best of what he had been able to achieve in enjoyment and understanding of life, and he had venerated them along with the immortal ancients as well as with the familiar masters of his own tongue. None of these great men had seemed to him foreign because they spoke another language—neither the incomparable explorer of human passions, nor the intoxicated worshipper of beauty, nor the powerful and menacing prophet, nor the subtle satirist; and he never reproached himself on that account for being a renegade towards his own nation and his beloved mother-tongue.

The enjoyment of this common civilization was disturbed from time to time by warning voices, which declared that old traditional differences made wars inevitable, even among the members of a community such as this. We refused to believe it; but if such a war were to happen, how did we picture it? . . . [W]e pictured it as a chivalrous passage of arms, which would limit itself to establishing the superiority of one side in the struggle, while as far as possible avoiding acute suffering that could contribute nothing to the decision, and granting complete immunity for the wounded who had to withdraw from the contest, as well as for the doctors and nurses who devoted themselves to their recovery. There would, of course, be the utmost consideration for the non-combatant classes of the population—for women who take no part in war-work, and for the children who, when they are grown up, should become on both sides one another's friends and helpers. And again, all the international undertakings and institutions in which the common civilization of peace-time had been embodied would be maintained.

Even a war like this would have produced enough horror and suffering; but it would not have interrupted the development of ethical relations between the collective individuals of mankind—the peoples and states.

Then the war in which we had refused to believe broke out, and it brought—disillusionment. Not only is it more bloody and more destructive than any war of other days, because of the enormously increased perfection of weapons of attack and defence; it is at least as cruel, as embittered, as implacable as any that has preceded it. It disregards all the restrictions known as International Law, which in peace-time the states had bound themselves to observe; it ignores the prerogatives of the wounded and the medical service, the distinction between civil and military sections of the population, the claims of private property. It tramples in blind fury on all that comes in its way, as though there were to be no future and no peace among men after it is over. It cuts all the common bonds between the contending peoples, and threatens to leave a legacy of embitterment that will make any renewal of those bonds impossible for a long time to come.

REVIEW QUESTIONS

1. What did Paul Valéry mean in saying that the mind of Europe doubted itself profoundly?
2. Why do you think many veterans felt that they were part of a lost generation?
3. What reasons can you think of why many Germans were attracted to paramilitary organizations immediately after the war?
4. How did Sigmund Freud describe the prevailing mood in Europe just prior to the war? How did the war alter this mood and create a "legacy of embitterment"?

CHAPTER 12
Era of Totalitarianism

ADOLF HITLER before his Labor Service at Nuremberg, September, 1938. German Nazis designed their mass rallies, replete with pageantry and marching battalions, to arouse the emotions of the public and thereby open them to manipulation. *(UPI/Corbis-Bettmann)*

F ollowing World War I, fascist movements arose in Italy, Germany, and many other European countries. Although these movements differed—each a product of separate national histories and the outlook of its leader—they shared a hatred of liberalism, democracy, and communism; a commitment to aggressive nationalism; and a glorification of the party leader. Fascist leaders cleverly utilized myths, rituals, and pageantry to mobilize and manipulate the masses.

Several conditions fostered the rise of fascism. One factor was the fear of communism among the middle and upper classes. Inspired by the success of the Bolsheviks in Russia, communists in other lands were calling for the establishment of Soviet-style republics. Increasingly afraid of a communist takeover, industrialists, landowners, government officials, army leaders, professionals, and shopkeepers were attracted to fascist movements that promised to protect their nations from this threat. A second factor contributing to the growth of fascism was the disillusionment of World War I veterans and the mood of violence bred by the war. The thousands of veterans facing unemployment and poverty made ideal recruits for fascist parties that glorified combat and organized private armies. A third contributing factor was the inability of democratic parliamentary governments to cope with the problems that burdened postwar Europe. Having lost confidence in the procedures and values of democracy, many people joined fascist movements that promised strong leadership, an end to party conflicts, and a unified national will.

Fascism's appeal to nationalist feelings also drew people into the movement. In a sense, fascism expressed the aggressive racial nationalism that had emerged in the late nineteenth century. Fascists saw themselves as dedicated idealists engaged in a heroic struggle to rescue their nations from domestic and foreign enemies; they aspired to regain lands lost by their countries in World War I or to acquire lands denied them by the Paris Peace Conference.

Fascists glorified instinct, will, and blood as the true forces of life; they openly attacked the ideals of reason, liberty, and equality—the legacies of the Enlightenment and the French Revolution. At the center of German fascism (National Socialism or Nazism) was a bizarre racial mythology that preached the superiority of the German race and the inferiority of others, particularly Jews and Slavs.

Benito Mussolini, founder of the Italian Fascist party, came to power in 1922. Although he established a one-party state, he was less successful than Adolf Hitler, the leader of the German National Socialists, in controlling the state and the minds of the people. After gaining power as chancellor of the German government in 1933, Hitler moved to establish a totalitarian state.

In the 1930s, the term *totalitarianism* was used to describe the Fascist regime in Italy, the National Socialist regime in Germany, and the communist regime in the Soviet Union. To a degree that far exceeds the ancient tyrannies and early modern autocratic states, these dictatorships aspired to and, with varying degrees of success, attained control over the individual's consciousness and behavior and all phases of political, social, and cultural life. To many people it seemed that a crises-riddled democracy was dying and that the future belonged to these dynamic totalitarian movements.

Totalitarianism was a twentieth-century phenomenon, for such all-embracing control over the individual and society could only have been achieved in an age of modern ideology, technology, and bureaucracy. The ideological aims and social and economic policies of Hitler and Stalin differed fundamentally. However, both Soviet Russia and Nazi Germany shared the totalitarian goal of monolithic unity and total domination, and both employed similar methods to achieve it. Mussolini's Italy is more accurately called authoritarian, for the party-state either did not intend to control all phases of life or lacked the means to do so. Moreover, Mussolini hesitated to use the ruthless methods that Hitler and Stalin employed so readily.

Striving for total unity, control, and obedience, the totalitarian dictatorship is the antithesis of liberal democracy. It abolishes all competing political parties, suppresses individual liberty, eliminates or regulates private institutions, and utilizes the modern state's bureaucracy and technology to impose its ideology and enforce its commands. The party-state determines what people should believe—what values they should hold. There is no room for individual thinking, private moral judgment, or individual conscience. The individual possesses no natural rights that the state must respect.

Unlike previous dictatorial regimes, the dictatorships of both the left and the right sought to legitimatize their rule by gaining the masses' approval. They claimed that their governments were higher and truer expressions of the people's will. The Soviet and Nazi dictatorships established their rule in the name of the people—the German Volk or the Soviet proletariat.

A distinctive feature of totalitarianism is the overriding importance of the leader, who is seen as infallible and invincible. The masses' slavish adulation of the leader and their uncritical acceptance of the dogma that the leader or the party is always right promote loyalty, dedication, and obedience and distort rational thinking.

Totalitarian leaders want more than power for its own sake; in the last analysis, they seek to transform the world according to an all-embracing ideology, a set of convictions and beliefs, which, says Hannah Arendt, "pretend[s] to know the mysteries of the whole historical process—the secrets of the past, the intricacies of the present, the uncertainties of the future." The ideology constitutes a higher and exclusive truth, based on a law of history, and it contains a dazzling vision of the future—a secular New Jerusalem—that strengthens the will of the faithful and attracts converts.

Like a religion, the totalitarian ideology provides its adherents with beliefs that make society and history intelligible, that explain all of existence in an emotionally gratifying way. Again like a religion, it creates true believers, who feel that they are participating in a great cause—a heroic fight against evil—that gives meaning to their lives.

Not only did the totalitarian religion-ideology supply followers with a cause that claimed absolute goodness; it also provided a Devil. For the Soviets, the source of evil and the cause of all the people's hardships were the degenerate capitalists, the traitorous Trotskyites, or the saboteurs and foreign agents, who impeded the realization of the socialist society. For the Nazis, the Devil was the conspirator Jew. These "evil" ones must be eliminated in order to realize the totalitarian movement's vision of the future. Thus, totalitarian regimes liquidate large segments of the population designated as "enemies of the people." Historical necessity or a higher purpose demands and justifies their liquidation. The appeal to historical necessity has all the power of a great myth. Presented as a world-historical struggle between the forces of good and the forces of evil, the myth incites fanaticism and numbs the conscience. Seemingly decent people engage in terrible acts of brutality with no remorse, convinced that they are waging a righteous war.

Unlike earlier autocratic regimes, the totalitarian dictatorship is not satisfied with its subjects' outward obedience; it demands the masses' unconditional loyalty and enthusiastic support. It strives to control the inner person: to shape thoughts, feelings, and attitudes in accordance with the party ideology, which becomes an official creed. It seeks to create a "new man," one who dedicates himself body and soul to the party and its ideology. Such unquestioning, faithful subjects can be manipulated by the party.

The totalitarian dictatorship deliberately politicizes all areas of human activity. Ideology pervades works of literature, history, philosophy, art, and even science. It dominates the school curriculum and influences everyday speech and social relations. The state is concerned with everything its citizens do: there is no distinction between public and private life, and every institution comes under the party-state's authority. If voluntary support for the regime cannot be generated by indoctrination, then the state unhesitatingly resorts to terror and violence to compel obedience.

---

1   Modernize or Perish

Joseph Stalin (1879–1953) was the Communist leader who made the Soviet Union into a superpower. He was born Iosif Vissarionovich Dzhugashvili in Trans-Caucasus Georgia. A rebel from childhood, he was one of Lenin's favored professional revolutionaries, trained in the tough schools of underground agitation, tsarist prisons, and Siberian exile. Unscrupulous, energetic, and endowed with a keen nose for the realities of power within the party and the country as a whole, Stalin surpassed his political rivals in strength of will and organizational astuteness. After he was appointed secretary-general of the Communist party (then considered a minor post) in 1922, he concentrated on building, amid the disorganization caused by war, revolution, and civil war, an effective party organization adapted to the temper of the Russian people. With this structure's help, he established himself as Lenin's successor. Stalin, more powerful and more ruthless than Lenin, was determined to force his country to overcome the economic and political weakness that had led to defeat and ruin in 1917. After Lenin's death, Stalin preached the "Leninist style of work," which combined "Russian revolutionary sweep" with "American efficiency."

Joseph Stalin
THE HARD LINE

Firmly entrenched in power by 1929, Stalin started a second revolution (called the Stalin revolution), mobilizing at top speed the potential of the country, however limited the human and material resources available, whatever the obstacles, and whatever the human price. The alternative, he was sure, was foreign domination that would totally destroy his country's independence. In this spirit, he addressed a gathering of industrial managers in 1931, talking to them not in Marxist-Leninist jargon, but in terms of hard-line Russian nationalism.

It is sometimes asked whether it is not possible to slow down the tempo a bit, to put a check on the movement. No, comrades, it is not possible! The tempo must not be reduced! On the contrary, we must increase it as much as is within our powers and possibilities. This is dictated to us by our obligations to the workers and peasants of the U.S.S.R. This is dictated to us by our obligations to the working class of the whole world.

To slacken the tempo would mean falling behind. And those who fall behind get beaten. But we do not want to be beaten. No, we refuse to be beaten! One feature of the history of old Russia was the continual beatings she suffered for falling behind, for her backwardness. She was beaten by the Mongol Khans. She was beaten by the Turkish beys. She was beaten by the Swedish feudal lords. She was beaten by the Polish and Lithuanian gentry. She was beaten by the British and French capitalists. She was beaten by the Japanese barons. All beat her—for her backwardness: for military

backwardness, for cultural backwardness, for political backwardness, for industrial backwardness, for agricultural backwardness. She was beaten because to do so was profitable and could be done with impunity. Do you remember the words of the pre-revolutionary poet [Nikolai Nekrassov]: "You are poor and abundant, mighty and impotent, Mother Russia." These words of the old poet were well learned by those gentlemen. They beat her, saying: "You are abundant," so one can enrich oneself at your expense. They beat her, saying: "You are poor and impotent," so you can be beaten and plundered with impunity. Such is the law of the exploiters—to beat the backward and the weak. It is the jungle law of capitalism. You are backward, you are weak—therefore you are wrong; hence, you can be beaten and enslaved. You are mighty—therefore you are right; hence, we must be wary of you.

That is why we must no longer lag behind.

In the past we had no fatherland, nor could we have one. But now that we have overthrown capitalism and power is in the hands of the working class, we have a fatherland, and we will defend its independence. Do you want our socialist fatherland to be beaten and to lose its independence? If you do not want this you must put an end to its backwardness in the shortest possible time and develop genuine Bolshevik tempo in building up its socialist system of economy. There is no other way. That is why Lenin said during the October Revolution: "Either perish, or overtake and outstrip the advanced capitalist countries."

We are fifty or a hundred years behind the advanced countries. We must make good this distance in ten years. Either we do it, or they crush us.

This is what our obligations to the workers and peasants of the U.S.S.R. dictate to us.

REVIEW QUESTIONS

1. Why did Joseph Stalin argue that the tempo of industrialization could not be slowed down?
2. How important is the idea of "fatherland" to Stalin?

---

2   Forced Collectivization

The forced collectivization of agriculture from 1929 to 1933 was an integral part of the Stalin revolution. His argument in favor of it was simple: an economy divided against itself cannot stand—planned industrial mobilization was incompatible with small-scale private agriculture in the traditional manner. Collectivization meant combining many small peasant holdings into a single large unit run in theory by the peasants (now called collective farmers), but in practice by the collective farm chairman guided by the government's Five-Year Plan.

Joseph Stalin
LIQUIDATION OF THE KULAKS

Collectivization, not surprisingly, met with fierce resistance, especially from the more successful peasants called kulaks, who were averse to surrendering their private plots and their freedom in running their households. Their resistance therefore had to be broken, and the Communist party fomented a rural class-struggle, seeking help from the poorer peasants. Sometimes, however, even the poorest peasants sided with the local kulaks. Under these conditions, Stalin did not shrink from unleashing violence in the countryside aimed at the "liquidation of the kulaks as a class." For Stalin the collectivization drive meant an all-out war on what was for him the citadel of backwardness: the peasant tradition and rebelliousness so prominent under the tsars. The following reading—Stalin's address to the Conference of Marxist Students of the Agrarian Question, December 1929—conveys his intentions. It is a good example of Stalin's rhetoric; he drives home his point by continually restating his argument.

The characteristic feature of our work during the past year is: (a) that we, the party and the Soviet government, have developed an offensive on the whole front against the capitalist elements in the countryside; and (b) that this offensive, as you know, has brought about and is bringing about very palpable, *positive* results.

What does this mean? It means that we have passed from the policy of *restricting* the exploiting proclivities of the kulaks to the policy of *eliminating* the kulaks as a class. This means that we have made, and are still making, one of the most decisive turns in our whole policy.

. . . Could we have undertaken such an offensive against the kulaks five years or three years ago? Could we then have counted on success in such an offensive? No, we could not. That would have been the most dangerous adventurism! That would have been playing a very dangerous game at offensive. We would certainly have come to grief and, once we had come to grief, we would have strengthened the position of the kulaks. Why? Because we did not yet have strongholds in the rural districts in the shape of a wide network of state farms and collective farms upon which to rely in a determined offensive against the kulaks. Because at that time we were not yet able to *substitute* for the capitalist production of the kulaks socialist production in the shape of the collective farms and state farms. . . .

But today? What is the position? Today, we have an adequate material base which enables us to strike at the kulaks, to break their resistance, to eliminate them as a class, and to *substitute* for their output the output of the collective farms and state farms. . . .

Now, as you see, we have the material base which enables us to *substitute* for kulak output the output of the collective farms and state farms. That is why our offensive against the kulaks is now meeting with undeniable success. That is how the offensive against the kulaks must be carried on, if we mean a real offensive and not futile declamations against the kulaks.

That is why we have recently passed from the policy of *restricting* the exploiting *proclivities* of the kulaks to the policy of *eliminating the kulaks as a class*. . . . Now we are able to carry on a determined offensive against the kulaks, to break their resistance, to eliminate them as a class and substitute for their output the output of the collective farms and state farms. Now, the kulaks are being expropriated by the masses of poor and middle peasants themselves, by the masses who are putting solid collectivization into practice. Now the expropriation of the kulaks in the regions of solid collectivization is no longer just an administrative measure. Now, the expropriation of the kulaks is an integral part of the formation and development of the collective farms. . . .

. . . [Should] the kulak . . . be permitted to join the collective farms[?] Of course not, for he is a sworn enemy of the collective farm movement. Clear, one would think.

Lev Kopelev
TERROR IN THE COUNTRYSIDE

The liquidation of the kulaks began in late 1929, extending through the length and breadth of the country during the winter. The confiscation of kulak property, the deportations, and the killing rose to a brutal climax in the following spring and continued for another two years, by which time the bulk of the private farms had been eliminated. By some estimates, almost five million people were liquidated. Some were driven from their huts, deprived of all possessions, and left destitute in the dead of winter; the men were sent to forced labor and their families left abandoned. Others killed themselves or were killed outright, sometimes in pitched battles involving a whole village—men, women, and children.

The upheaval destroyed agricultural production in these years; farm animals died or were killed in huge numbers; fields lay barren. In 1932 and 1933, famine stalked the south and southeast, killing additional millions. The vast tragedy caused by collectivization did not deter Stalin from pursuing his goals: the establishment of state farms run like factories and the subordination of the rebellious and willful peasantry to state authority.

Here a militant participant in the collectivization drive, Lev Kopelev, recalls some of his experiences. Kopelev (1912–1997), raised in a Ukrainian middle-class Jewish family, evolved from a youthful Stalinist into a tolerant, gentle person in later years. After trying to keep Russian soldiers from raping and pillaging in German territory in 1945, he was given a ten-year sentence for anti-state crimes. Subsequently out of favor because of his literary protests against the inhumanities of the Soviet system, he was exiled from the Soviet Union to West Germany in 1980.

The grain front! Stalin said the struggle for grain was the struggle for socialism. I was convinced that we were warriors on an invisible front, fighting against kulak sabotage for the grain which was needed by the country, by the five-year plan. Above all, for the grain, but also for the souls of these peasants who were mired in unconscientiousness, in ignorance, who succumbed to enemy agitation, who did not understand the great truth of communism. . . .

The highest measure of coercion on the hard-core holdouts was "undisputed confiscation."

A team consisting of several young kolkhozniks [collective farmers] and members of the village soviet . . . would search the hut, barn, yard, and take away all the stores of seed, lead away the cow, the horse, the pigs.

In some cases they would be merciful and leave some potatoes, peas, corn for feeding the family. But the stricter ones would make a clean sweep. They would take not only the food and livestock, but also "all valuables and surpluses of clothing," including icons in their frames, samovars, painted carpets and even metal kitchen utensils which might be silver.

And any money they found stashed away. Special instructions ordered the removal of gold, silver and currency. . . .

Several times Volodya and I were present at such plundering raids. We even took part: we were entrusted to draw up inventories of the confiscated goods. . . . The women howled hysterically, clinging to the bags.

"Oy, that's the last thing we have! That was for the children's kasha [cereal]! Honest to God, the children will starve!"

They wailed, falling on their trunks:

"Oy, that's a keepsake from my dead mama! People, come to my aid, this is my trousseau, never e'en put on!"

I heard the children echoing them with screams, choking, coughing with screams. And I saw the looks of the men: frightened, pleading, hateful, dully impassive, extinguished with despair or flaring up with half-mad, daring ferocity.

"Take it. Take it away. Take everything away. There's still a pot of borscht on the stove. It's plain, got no meat. But still it's got beets, taters 'n' cabbage. And it's salted! Better take it, comrade citizens! Here, hang on, I'll take off my shoes. They're patched and re-patched, but maybe they'll have some use for the proletariat, for our dear Soviet power."

It was excruciating to see and hear all this. And even worse to take part in it. . . . And I persuaded myself, explained to myself. I mustn't give in to debilitating pity. We were realizing historical necessity. We were performing our revolutionary duty. We were obtaining grain for the socialist fatherland. For the five-year plan. . . .

I have always remembered the winter of the last grain collections, the weeks of the great famine. And I have always told about it. But I did not begin to write it down until many years later. . . .

How could all this have happened?

Who was guilty of the famine which destroyed millions of lives?

How could I have participated in it?. . .

We were raised as the fanatical [believers] of a new creed, the only true *religion* of scientific socialism. The party became our church militant, bequeathing to all mankind eternal salvation, eternal peace and the bliss of an earthly paradise. It victoriously surmounted all other churches, schisms and heresies. The works of Marx, Engels and Lenin were accepted as holy writ, and Stalin was the infallible high priest.

. . . Stalin was the most perspicacious, the most wise (at that time they hadn't yet started calling him "great" and "brilliant"). He said: "The struggle for grain is the struggle for socialism." And we believed him unconditionally. And later we believed that unconditional collectivization was unavoidable if we were to overcome the capriciousness and uncertainty of the market and the backwardness of individual farming, to guarantee a steady supply of grain, milk and meat to the cities. And also if we were to reeducate millions of peasants, those petty landowners and hence potential bourgeoisie, potential kulaks, to transform them into laborers with a social conscience, to liberate them from "the idiocy of country life," from ignorance and prejudice, and to accustom them to culture, to all the boons of socialism. . . .

In the following passage Kopelev reflects, even more searchingly, on his own motivation and state of mind as a participant in Stalin's collectivization drive.

With the rest of my generation I firmly believed that the ends justified the means. Our great goal was the universal triumph of Communism, and for the sake of that goal everything was permissible—to lie, to steal, to destroy hundreds of thousands and even millions of people, all those who were hindering our work or could hinder it, everyone who stood in the way. And to hesitate or doubt about all this was to give in to "intellectual squeamishness" and "stupid liberalism," the attributes of people who "could not see the forest for the trees."

That was how I had reasoned, and everyone like me, even when I did have my doubts, when I saw what "total collectivization" meant—how . . . mercilessly they stripped the peasants in the winter of 1932–33. I took part in this myself, scouring the countryside, searching for hidden grain, testing the earth with an iron rod for loose spots that might lead to buried grain. With the others, I emptied out the old folks' storage chests, stopping my ears to the children's crying and the women's wails. For I was convinced that I was accomplishing the great and necessary transformation of the countryside; that in the days to come the people who lived there would be better off for it; that their distress and suffering were a result of their own ignorance or the machinations of the class enemy; that those who sent me—and I myself—knew better than the peasants how they should live, what they should sow and when they should plow.

In the terrible spring of 1933 I saw people dying from hunger. I saw women and children with distended bellies, turning blue, still breathing but with vacant, lifeless eyes. And corpses—corpses in ragged sheepskin coats and cheap felt boots; corpses in peasant huts, in the melting snow of old Vologda, under the bridges of Kharkov. . . . I saw all this and did not go out of my mind or commit suicide. Nor did I curse those who had sent me to take away the peasants' grain in the winter, and in the spring to persuade the barely walking, skeleton-thin or sickly-swollen people to go into the fields in order to "fulfill the Bolshevik sowing plan in shock-worker style."

Nor did I lose my faith. As before, I believed because I wanted to believe. Thus from time immemorial men have believed when possessed by a desire to serve powers and values above and beyond humanity: gods, emperors, states; ideals of virtue, freedom, nation, race, class, party. . . .

Any single-minded attempt to realize these ideals exacts its toll of human sacrifice. In the name of the noblest visions promising eternal happiness to their descendants, such men bring merciless ruin on their contemporaries. Bestowing paradise on the dead, they maim and destroy the living. They become unprincipled liars and unrelenting executioners, all the while seeing themselves as virtuous and honorable militants—convinced that if they are forced into villainy, it is for the sake of future good, and that if they have to lie, it is in the name of eternal truths.

. . . That was how we thought and acted—we, the fanatical disciples of the all-saving ideals of Communism. When we saw the base and cruel acts that were committed in the name of our exalted notions of good, and when we ourselves took part in those actions, what we feared most was to lose our heads, fall into doubt or heresy and forfeit our unbounded faith. . . . The concepts of conscience, honor, humaneness we dismissed as idealistic prejudices, "intellectual" or "bourgeois," and hence, perverse.

REVIEW QUESTIONS

1. Why were the kulaks selected as special targets in the drive for collectivization?
2. How would you characterize the motivation of the young Lev Kopelev and his associates in carrying out the collectivization of agriculture?
3. How, in retrospect, did Kopelev explain his role in the collectivization drive?

3 Famine in Ukraine

The suffering caused by Stalin's collectivization drive was most cruel in Ukraine, where famine killed approximately seven million people, many of whom had already endured extreme abuse and persecution. In order to buy industrial equipment abroad so that industrialization could proceed on target, the Soviet Union had to export food, as much of it as possible and for prices disastrously lowered by the Great Depression. Let the peasants in the Ukrainian breadbasket perish so that the country could grow strong! Moreover, Stalin relished the opportunity to punish the Ukrainians for opposing the Bolsheviks during the civil war and resisting collectivization. Through rigid social control, he hoped to crush nationalist sentiments among the Ukrainians.

Miron Dolot
EXECUTION BY HUNGER

Miron Dolot witnessed the horrors of state-induced famine in Ukraine and later emigrated to the West. In *Execution by Hunger: The Hidden Holocaust* (1985), excerpted below, Dolot recounted his experiences.

The year 1932 witnessed the last battle of collectivization: the battle for bread, or to be more specific, for the crop of 1932. On the one side was the Communist government; on the other, the starving farmers. The government forces resorted to any means in getting as many agricultural products from the countryside as possible, without regard to the consequences. The farmers, already on the verge of starvation, desperately tried to keep what food they had left, and, in spite of government efforts to the contrary, tried to stay alive. . . .

The long and cold winter of 1931–1932 was slowly giving way to spring. . . .

Around this time the plight of the villagers became desperate. This was the memorable spring of 1932 when the famine broke out, and the first deaths from hunger began to occur. I remember the endless procession of beggars on roads and paths, going from house to house. They were in different stages of starvation, dirty and ragged. With outstretched hands, they begged for food, any food: a potato, a beet, or at least a kernel of corn. Those were the first victims of starvation: destitute men and women; poor widows and orphaned children who had no chance of surviving the terrible ordeal.

Some starving farmers still tried to earn their food by doing chores in or outside the village. One could see these sullen, emaciated men walking from house to house with an ax, or a shovel, in search of work. Perhaps someone might hire them to dig up the garden, or chop some firewood. They would do it for a couple of potatoes. But not many of us had a couple of potatoes to spare.

Crowds of starving wretches could be seen scattered all over the potato fields. They were looking for potatoes left over from last year's harvest. No matter what shape the potatoes were in, whether frozen or rotten, they were still edible. Others were roaming the forest in search of food; the riverbanks were crowded too; there was much new greenery around: young shoots of reed or other river plants. One might catch something, anything, in the water to eat.

But the majority of those who looked for help would go to the cities as they used to do before. It was always easier to find some work there, either gardening, cleaning backyards, or sweeping streets. But now, times had changed. It was illegal to hire farmers for any work. The purpose of the prohibition was twofold: it was done not only to stop the flow of labor from the collective farms, but also, and primarily, to prevent the farmers from receiving food rations in the cities. . . .

By this time our village was in economic ruin. Poverty was universal. We had never been rich, it is true, but economically, we had always been completely self-sufficient and had never gone hungry for so long. Now starving, we were facing the spring of 1932 with great anxiety for there was no hope of relief from the outside. Deaths from starvation became daily occurrences. There was always some burial in the village cemetery. One could see strange funeral processions: children pulling homemade hand-wagons with the bodies of their dead parents in them or the parents carting the bodies of their children. There were no coffins; no burial ceremonies performed by priests. The bodies of the starved were just deposited in a large common grave, one upon the other; that was all there was to it. . . .

Looking back to those events now, it seems to me that I lived in some kind of a wicked fantasy world. All the events which I witnessed and experienced then and which I am now describing, seem unreal to me because of their cruelty and unspeakable horror. It is simply too difficult to associate all those happenings with real life in a normal human society. . . .

The battle for the Ukrainian wheat crop of 1932 started almost two months before the harvest.

At the end of May, some strangers appeared in our village, and little by little, we began finding out who they were. The Party had mobilized 112,000 of its most active and reliable members in order to organize a speedy harvest of the new crop, and to secure its swift and smooth requisitioning and final delivery to the State. Soon these members became known to us as the Hundred Thousanders, or just Thousanders. There were nine of them in our village. . . . In no time at all, these new Thousanders took over our entire village like tyrants, imposing their wills and their demands upon us. . . .

Comrade Thousander's announcement that in 1932 we had to deliver the same quota of grain as in 1931 was a hard blow to us. We simply could not fulfill his demands. The 1932 grain quota was not based on the actual amount of grain sown, cultivated, and harvested; it was based upon an unrealistic government plan. . . .

Faced with starvation, the villagers tried everything possible to save themselves and their families. Some of them started eating dogs and cats. Others went hunting for birds: crows, magpies, swallows, sparrows, storks, and even nightingales. One could see starving villagers searching in the bushes along the river for birds' nests or looking for crabs and other small crustaceans in the water. Even their hard shells, though not edible, were cooked and the broth consumed as nourishment. One could see crowds of famished villagers combing the woods in search of roots or mushrooms and berries. Some tried to catch small forest animals.

Driven by hunger, people ate everything and anything: even food that had already rotted—potatoes, beets, and other root vegetables that pigs normally refused to eat. They even ate weeds, the leaves and bark of trees, insects, frogs, and snails. Nor did they shy away from eating the meat of diseased horses and cattle. Often that meat was already decaying and those who ate it died of food poisoning. . . .

One morning in late January 1933, while it was still dark, Mother and I set out along the main street through the center of the village for the county town. We followed the street to the main road which led straight into the town. . . .

Soon, however, as we slowly made our way through the snow toward the village center, graphic evidence of starvation became visible. We noticed a black object which, from afar, looked like a snow-covered tree stump. As we came near, however, we saw that it was the body of a dead man. Frozen limbs protruding from under the snow gave the body the appearance of some grotesque creature. I bent down and cleared the snow off the face. It was Ulas, our elderly neighbor whom we had last seen about a month ago.

A few steps further, we saw another frozen body. It was the corpse of a woman. As I brushed away the snow, horror made my blood turn cold: under her ragged coat, clutched tightly to her bosom with her stiff hands, was the frozen little body of her baby.

We finally left our village behind and stepped onto the open road which led to the county seat. However, another ghostly panorama now opened in front of us. Everywhere we looked dead and frozen bodies lay by the sides of the road. To our right were bodies of those villagers who apparently had tried to reach the town in search of work and food. Weakened by starvation, they were unable to make it and ended up lying or falling down by the roadside, never to rise again. The gentle snow mercifully covered their bodies with its white blanket.

One could easily imagine the fate of those people whose bodies were lying to our left.

They most probably were returning from the county town, without having accomplished anything. They had tramped many kilometers in vain, only to be refused a job and a chance to stay alive. They were returning home empty-handed. Death caught up with them as they trudged homeward, resigned to dying in their village.

The wide open kolhosp[1] fields, stretching for kilometers on both sides of the main road, looked like a battlefield after a great war. Littering the fields were the bodies of the starving farmers who had been combing the potato fields over and over again in the hope of finding at least a fragment of a potato that might have been overlooked or left over from the last harvest. They died where they collapsed in their endless search for food. Some of those frozen corpses must have been lying out there for months. Nobody seemed to be in a hurry to cart them away and bury them. . . .

. . . Dmytro had never returned home after he had been taken to the county center.[2] His young wife Solomia was left alone with their daughter. She had gone to work in the collective farm, taking her little child with her. As the wife of a banished man, she too was considered an "enemy of the people," and her child was refused admission to the nursery. Later, Solomia was expelled from the collective farm, and thus forced to seek a job in the city. That was impossible, however, because she could not show a certificate of release from the collective farm. She found herself trapped in the circle of the Communist death ring. She had to return to her village.

When winter came, Solomia went from house to house, willing to work for just a piece of bread. She was too proud to beg. People were sympathetic and helped her as much as they could. However, as the famine worsened, and the villagers were no longer able to help her, she was not seen on her rounds any more.

We found the front door of Solomia's house open, but the entrance was blocked with snowdrifts, and it was hard to get inside. When we finally reached the living room, we saw a pitiful sight: Solomia was hanging from the ceiling in the middle of the room. She was dressed in her Ukrainian national costume, and at her breast hung a large cross. It was obvious that she had made preparations before committing suicide. Her hair was combed neatly in two braids hanging over her shoulders.

Frightened, we ran to fetch Mother. We helped her take down Solomia's frozen body, and laid it on a bench, and covered it with a handmade blanket. It was only after we finished doing this that we noticed the dead body of her little daughter. The child was lying in a wooden tub in the corner under the icons, clean and dressed in her best clothes. Her little hands were folded across her chest.

On the table was a note:

Dear Neighbors:

Please bury our bodies properly. I have to leave you, dear neighbors. I can bear this life no longer. There is no food in the house, and there is no sense in living without my little daughter who starved to death, or my husband. If you ever see Dmytro, tell him about us. He will understand our plight, and he will forgive me. Please tell him that I died peacefully, thinking about him and our dear daughter.

I love you, my dear neighbors, and I wish with all my heart that you somehow recover from this disaster. Forgive me for troubling you. Thank you for everything you have done for me.

Solomia.

After reading the note, we stood there for a while, motionless and forlorn. Our mother tried to suppress the sound of her weeping, pressing the corner of her head scarf to her lips. Mykola gazed at the corpses in disbelief.

In my imagination I was recreating the agony of their dying: the child's hunger cries,

---

[1]The Ukrainian term for collective farm.
[2]Dmytro, a neighbor and distant relative of the author, had been jailed after punching a collective farm official who accused him of sabotage.

and then the death convulsions of its exhausted little body.

How great must have been the sufferings of the mother. She had to listen helplessly to the pleas of her child for food, while she herself was near starvation. She must have felt great relief, I thought, when she saw her little daughter breathing for the last time. Then, in my imagination, I saw the mother attending to her lifeless child: dressing her in the best and cleanest clothing she had, praying on her knees near the body, and finally kissing her for the last time before her own suicide. . . .

Toward the end of March, the famine struck us with full force. Life in the village had sunk to its lowest level, an almost animallike struggle for survival of the fittest.

The village ceased to exist as a coherent community. The inhabitants who still managed to stay alive shut themselves within the walls of their houses. People became too weak even to step outside their doors. Each house became an entity in itself. Visits became a rarity. All doors were bolted and barred against any possible intruders. Even between immediate neighbors, there was little, it any, communication, and people ceased caring about one another. In fact, they avoided each other. Friends and even relatives became strangers. Mothers abandoned their children, and brother turned away from brother. . . .

One must consider the inexorable pressure of hunger under which a person can completely become bereft of his or her senses and sink to an absolute animallike level. That happened to many of our villagers. The more resistant ones who kept on living with minimal or no food at all for some time, felt no more of the initial hunger pangs. They either lapsed into comas, or existed in a semicomatose, lethargic stupor. But some reacted differently. They became like madmen. They lost all traces of compassion, honor, and morality. They suffered from hallucinations of food, of something to bite into and chew, to satisfy the gnawing pains of their empty stomachs. Intolerable cravings assailed them; they were ready to sink their teeth into anything, even into their own hands and arms, or into the flesh of others.

The first rumors of actual cannibalism were related to the mysterious and sudden disappearances of people in the village. . . .

As the cases of missing persons grew in number, an arrest was made which shook us to our souls. A woman was taken into custody, charged with killing her two children.

Another women was found dead, her neck contorted in a crudely made noose. The neighbors who discovered the tragedy also found the reason for it. The flesh of the woman's three-year old daughter was found in the oven.

REVIEW QUESTION

1. Describe the different ways people in Ukraine responded to the famine.

---

4 Soviet Indoctrination

Pressed by the necessity to transform their country into a modern state, the communist leaders used every opportunity to force the population to adopt the attitudes and motivation necessary to effect such a transformation. Education, from nursery school to university, provided special opportunities to mold attitudes. The Soviet regime made impressive gains in promoting education among its diverse people; it also used education to foster dedication to hard work, discipline in social cooperation, and pride in the nation. For a backward country that, as Lenin had said, must "either perish or overtake and outstrip the advanced capitalist countries," such changes were considered essential, even though they were contrary to traditional Russian attitudes, and compulsory enforcement of the changes was incompatible with Western values.

During the Stalin era, artists and writers were compelled to promote the ideals of the Stalin revolution. In the style of "socialist realism," their heroes were factory workers and farmers who labored tirelessly and enthusiastically to build a new society. Even romance served a political purpose. Novelists wrote love stories following limited, prosaic themes. For example, a young girl might lose her heart to a co-worker who is a leader in the communist youth organization and who outproduces his comrades at his job; as the newly married couple is needed at the factory, they choose to forgo a honeymoon.

A. O. Avdienko
THE CULT OF STALIN

Among a people so deeply divided by ethnicity and petty localism and limited by a pervasive narrowness of perspective, building countrywide unity and consensus was a crucial challenge for the government. In the Russian past the worship of saints and the veneration of the tsar had served that purpose. The political mobilization of the masses during the revolution required an intensification of that tradition. It led to the "cult of personality," the deliberate fixation of individual dedication and loyalty on the all-powerful leader, whose personality exemplified the challenge of extraordinary times. The following selection illustrates by what emotional bonds the individual was tied to Stalin, and through Stalin to the prodigious transformation of Russian state and society that he was attempting.

Thank you, Stalin. Thank you because I am joyful. Thank you because I am well. No matter how old I become, I shall never forget how we received Stalin two days ago. Centuries will pass, and the generations still to come will regard us as the happiest of mortals, as the most fortunate of men, because we lived in the century of centuries, because we were privileged to see Stalin, our inspired leader. Yes, and we regard ourselves as the happiest of mortals because we are the contemporaries of a man who never had an equal in world history.

The men of all ages will call on thy name, which is strong, beautiful, wise and marvellous. Thy name is engraven on every factory,

every machine, every place on the earth, and in the hearts of all men.

Every time I have found myself in his presence I have been subjugated by his strength, his charm, his grandeur. I have experienced a great desire to sing, to cry out, to shout with joy and happiness. And now see me—me!—on the same platform where the Great Stalin stood a year ago. In what country, in what part of the world could such a thing happen.

I write books. I am an author. All thanks to thee, O great educator, Stalin. I love a young woman with a renewed love and shall perpetuate myself in my children—all thanks to thee, great educator, Stalin. I shall be eternally happy and joyous, all thanks to thee, great educator, Stalin. Everything belongs to thee, chief of our great country. And when the woman I love presents me with a child the first word it shall utter will be: Stalin.

O great Stalin, O leader of the peoples,
Thou who broughtest man to birth.

Thou who fructifiest the earth,
Thou who restorest the centuries,
Thou who makest bloom the spring,
Thou who makest vibrate the musical
   chords. . .
Thou, splendour of my spring, O Thou,
Sun reflected by millions of hearts. . .

Yevgeny Yevtushenko
LITERATURE AS PROPAGANDA

After Stalin's death in 1953, Soviet intellectuals breathed more freely, and they protested against the rigid Stalinist controls. In the following extract from his *Precocious Autobiography,* Russian poet Yevgeny Yevtushenko (b. 1933) looks back to the raw days of intellectual repression under Stalin.

Blankly smiling workers and collective farmers looked out from the covers of books. Almost every novel and short story had a happy ending. Painters more and more often took as their subject state banquets, weddings, solemn public meetings, and parades.

The apotheosis of this trend was a movie which in its grand finale showed thousands of collective farmers having a gargantuan feast against the background of a new power station.

Recently I had a talk with its producer, a gifted and intelligent man.

"How could you produce such a film?" I asked. "It is true that I also once wrote verses in that vein, but I was still wet behind the ears, whereas you were adult and mature."

The producer smiled a sad smile. "You know, the strangest thing to me is that I was absolutely sincere. I thought all this was a necessary part of building communism. And then I believed Stalin."

So when we talk about "the cult of personality," we should not be too hasty in accusing all those who, one way or another, were involved in it, debasing themselves with their flattery.

There were of course sycophants [servile flatterers] who used the situation for their own ends. But that many people connected with the arts sang Stalin's praises was often not vice but tragedy.

How was it possible for even gifted and intelligent people to be deceived?

To begin with, Stalin was a strong and vivid personality. When he wanted to, Stalin knew how to charm people. He charmed Gorky and Barbusse. In 1937, the cruelest year of the purges, he managed to charm that tough and experienced observer, Lion Feuchtwanger.[1]

In the second place, in the minds of the Soviet people, Stalin's name was indissolubly linked with Lenin's. Stalin knew how popular Lenin was and saw to it that history was rewritten in such a way as to make his own relations with Lenin seem much more friendly than they had been in fact. The rewriting was so thorough that perhaps Stalin himself believed his own version in the end.

---

[1]Gorky was a prominent Russian writer; Barbusse and Feuchtwanger were well-known western European writers.

There can be no doubt of Stalin's love for Lenin. His speech on Lenin's death, beginning with the words, "In leaving us, Comrade Lenin has bequeathed . . ." reads like a poem in prose. He wanted to stand as Lenin's heir not only in other people's eyes, but in his own eyes too. He deceived himself as well as the others. Even [Boris] Pasternak put the two names side by side:

> Laughter in the village,
> Voice behind the plow,
> Lenin and Stalin,
> And these verses now . . .

In reality, however, Stalin distorted Lenin's ideas, because to Lenin—and this was the whole meaning of his work—communism was to serve man, whereas under Stalin it appeared that man served communism.

Stalin's theory that people were the little cogwheels of communism was put into practice and with horrifying results. . . . Russian poets, who had produced some fine works during the war, turned dull again. If a good poem did appear now and then, it was likely to be about the war—this was simpler to write about.

Poets visited factories and construction sites but wrote more about machines than about the men who made them work. If machines could read, they might have found such poems interesting. Human beings did not.

The size of a printing was not determined by demand but by the poet's official standing. As a result bookstores were cluttered up with books of poetry which no one wanted. . . . A simple, touching poem by the young poet Vanshenkin, about a boy's first love, caused almost a sensation against this background of industrial-agricultural verse. Vinokurov's first poems, handsomely disheveled among the general sleekness, were avidly seized upon—they had human warmth. But the general situation was unchanged. Poetry remained unpopular. The older poets were silent, and when they did break their silence, it was even worse. The generation of poets that had been spawned by the war and that had raised so many hopes had petered out. Life in peacetime turned out to be more complicated than life at the front. Two of the greatest Russian poets, Zabolotsky and Smelyakov, were in concentration camps. The young poet Mandel (Korzhavin) had been deported. I don't know if Mandel's name will be remembered in the history of Russian poets but it will certainly be remembered in the history of Russian social thought.

He was the only poet who openly wrote and recited verses against Stalin while Stalin was alive. That he recited them seems to be what saved his life, for the authorities evidently thought him insane. In one poem he wrote of Stalin:

> There in Moscow, in whirling darkness,
> Wrapped in his military coat,
> Not understanding Pasternak,
> A hard and cruel man stared at the snow.

. . . Now that ten years have gone by, I realize that Stalin's greatest crime was not the arrests and the shootings he ordered. His greatest crime was the corruption of the human spirit.

REVIEW QUESTIONS

1. In light of the A. O. Avdienko reading, how would you say Communists were supposed to feel about Stalin?
2. What were Yevgeny Yevtushenko's reasons for denouncing Stalin?
3. What do you think Yevtushenko meant by the "corruption of the human spirit" under Stalin?

5 Stalin's Terror

The victims of Stalin's terror number in the many millions. Stalin had no qualms about sacrificing multitudes of people to build up the Soviet Union's strength and to make it a powerful factor in world politics. In addition, he felt entitled to settle his own private scores as well as national ones against secessionist Ukrainians. The Soviet government's first acknowledgment of Stalin's terror was made by Khrushchev.

Nikita Khrushchev
KHRUSHCHEV'S SECRET SPEECH

Nikita Khrushchev (1894–1971), first secretary of the Communist party (1953–1964) and premier of the Soviet Union (1958–1964), delivered a famous speech to an unofficial, closed session of the twentieth Party Congress on February 25, 1956. Although the speech was considered confidential, it was soon leaked to outsiders. While safeguarding the moral authority of Lenin, Khrushchev attacked Stalin, who had died three years earlier, revealing some of the crimes committed by him and his closest associates in the 1930s. The following passages from the speech draw on evidence collected by a special commission of inquiry.

We have to consider seriously and analyze correctly this matter [the crimes of the Stalin era] in order that we may preclude any possibility of a repetition in any form whatever of what took place during the life of Stalin, who absolutely did not tolerate collegiality in leadership and in work, and who practiced brutal violence, not only toward everything which opposed him, but also toward that which seemed to his capricious and despotic character, contrary to his concepts.

Stalin acted not through persuasion, explanation, and patient co-operation with people, but by imposing his concepts and demanding absolute submission to his opinion. Whoever opposed this concept or tried to prove his viewpoint, and the correctness of his position, was doomed to removal from the leading collective and to subsequent moral and physical annihilation. This was especially true during the period following the XVIIth Party Congress [1934], when many prominent Party leaders and rank-and-file Party workers, hon-

est and dedicated to the cause of Communism, fell victim to Stalin's despotism. . . .

Stalin originated the concept "enemy of the people." This term automatically rendered it unnecessary that the ideological errors of a man or men engaged in a controversy be proven; this term made possible the usage of the most cruel repression, violating all norms of revolutionary legality, against anyone who in any way disagreed with Stalin, against those who were only suspected of hostile intent, against those who had bad reputations. This concept, "enemy of the people," actually eliminated the possibility of any kind of ideological fight or the making of one's views known on this or that issue, even those of a practical character. In the main, and in actuality, the only proof of guilt used, against all norms of current legal science, was the "confession" of the accused himself; and, as subsequent probing proved, "confessions" were acquired through physical pressures against the accused.

This led to glaring violations of revolutionary legality, and to the fact that many entirely innocent persons, who in the past had defended the Party line, became victims. . . .

The Commission [of Inquiry] has become acquainted with a large quantity of materials in the NKVD [secret police, forerunner to the KGB] archives and with other documents and has established many facts pertaining to the fabrication of cases against Communists, to false accusations, to glaring abuses of socialist legality—which resulted in the death of innocent people. It became apparent that many Party, Soviet and economic activists who were branded in 1937–1938 as "enemies" were actually never enemies, spies, wreckers, etc., but were always honest Communists; they were only so stigmatized, and often, no longer able to bear barbaric tortures, they charged themselves (at the order of the investigative judges—falsifiers) with all kinds of grave and unlikely crimes. . . .

Lenin used severe methods only in the most necessary cases, when the exploiting classes were still in existence and were vigorously opposing the revolution, when the struggle for survival was decidedly assuming the sharpest forms, even including a civil war.

Stalin, on the other hand, used extreme methods and mass repressions at a time when the revolution was already victorious, when the Soviet state was strengthened, when the exploiting classes were already liquidated and Socialist relations were rooted solidly in all phases of national economy, when our Party was politically consolidated and had strengthened itself both numerically and ideologically. It is clear that here Stalin showed in a whole series of cases his intolerance, his brutality and his abuse of power. Instead of proving his political correctness and mobilizing the masses, he often chose the path of repression and physical annihilation, not only against actual enemies, but also against individuals who had not committed any crimes against the Party and the Soviet government. . . .

An example of vile provocation, of odious falsification and of criminal violation of revolutionary legality is the case of the former candidate for the Central Committee Political Bureau, one of the most eminent workers of the Party and of the Soviet government, Comrade Eikhe, who was a Party member since 1905. *(Commotion in the hall.)*

Comrade Eikhe was arrested on April 29, 1938, on the basis of slanderous materials, without the sanction of the Prosecutor of the USSR, which was finally received 15 months after the arrest.

Investigation of Eikhe's case was made in a manner which most brutally violated Soviet legality and was accompanied by willfulness and falsification.

Eikhe was forced under torture to sign ahead of time a protocol of his confession prepared by the investigative judges, in which he and several other eminent Party workers were accused of anti-Soviet activity.

On October 1, 1939, Eikhe sent his declaration to Stalin in which he categorically denied his guilt and asked for an examination of his case. In the declaration he wrote: "There is no more bitter misery than to sit in the jail of a government for which I have always fought."

A second declaration of Eikhe has been preserved which he sent to Stalin on October 27, 1939; in it he cited facts very convincingly and countered the slanderous accusations made against him, arguing that his provocatory accusation was on the one hand the work of real Trotskyites whose arrests he had sanctioned as First Secretary of the West Siberian Krai [local] Party Committee and who conspired in order to take revenge on him, and, on the other hand, the result of the base falsification of materials by the investigative judges. . . .

It would appear that such an important declaration was worth an examination by the Central Committee. This, however, was not done and the declaration was transmitted to Beria [head of the NKVD] while the terrible maltreatment of the Political Bureau candidate, Comrade Eikhe, continued.

On February 2, 1940, Eikhe was brought before the court. Here he did not confess any guilt and said as follows:

In all the so-called confessions of mine there is not one letter written by me with the exception of my signatures under the protocols which were forced from me. I have made my confession under pressure from the investigative judge who from the time of my arrest tormented me. After that I began to write all this nonsense. . . . The most important thing for me is to tell the court, the Party and Stalin that I am not guilty. I have never been guilty of any conspiracy. I will die believing in the truth of Party policy as I have believed in it during my whole life.

On February 4 Eikhe was shot. *(Indignation in the hall.)*

Lev Razgon
TRUE STORIES

"Corrective labor" was part of Stalin's efforts to terrorize the peoples of the Soviet Union into compliance with his plan to modernize the country's economy and society. All those accused of disloyalty to the party and not killed outright ended up in one of the *gulags. Gulag* is the Russian term for the Soviet forced-labor camps, scattered, like islands in an archipelago, over the entire Soviet Union. The inhabitants of that archipelago were the *zeks,* as the political prisoners were called. Their labor served a double purpose. It was designed as punishment for their alleged crimes and as a means of obtaining vital raw materials—including lumber and minerals—from areas too inhospitable for, or outright hostile to, regular labor. Forced labor also built the canal linking the Leningrad area with the White Sea in the far north.

In 1988, Lev Razgon, a survivor of Stalin's camps, published an account of his experiences, which appeared in English under the title *True Stories* in 1997. Razgon was a journalist who married the daughter of a high-ranking member of the Soviet secret police. Gaining access to the Soviet elite, in 1934 he attended the Seventeenth Party Congress. In 1937, his father-in-law was arrested for "counter-revolutionary" activities, along with many family friends; the following year the police came for Razgon and his wife. She perished in a transit prison en route to a northern camp, and Razgon spent the next seven years in a labor camp. Released in 1945, he was confined to various provincial towns, but in 1949 was rearrested and returned to the camps. Finally, he was released again in 1956 after Stalin's death.

Over the years Razgon began to write down his prison experiences for his desk drawer, with the specific intent of preserving the memory of fellow prisoners who did not survive. As the Soviet Union began to crumble, Razgon was able to publish his stories. The following extracts from *True Stories* reveal the brutality and irrationality of the Soviet prison system under Stalin. In the first selection, Razgon reproduces a discussion he had with a former prison guard, whom he met by chance in a hospital ward in 1977. The guard described to Razgon his role as an executioner of political prisoners.

THE ROUTINE OF EXECUTION

"It was like this. In the morning we'd hand everything over to the new shift and go into the guardhouse. We'd collect our weapons, and then and there they'd give us each a shot glass of vodka. After that we'd take the list and go round with the senior warder to pick them up from the cells and take them out to the truck."

"What kind of truck?"

"A closed van. Six of them and four of us in each one."

"How many trucks would leave at the same time?"

"Three or four."

"Did they know where they were going? Did someone read them their death sentence before, or what?"

"No, no sentences were announced. No one even spoke, just, 'Come out, then straight ahead, into the van—fast!'"

"Were they in handcuffs?"

"No, we didn't have any."

"How did they behave, once they were in the van?"

"The men, well, they kept quiet. But the women would start crying, they'd say: 'What are you doing, we're not guilty of anything, comrades, what are you doing?' and things like that."

"They used to take men and women together?"

"No, always separately."

"Were the women young? Were there a lot of them?"

"Not so many, about two vanloads a week. No very young ones but there were some about twenty-five or thirty. Most were older, and some even elderly."

"Did you drive them far?"

"Twelve kilometers or so, to the hill. The Distant Hill, it was called. There were hills all around and that's where we unloaded them."

"So you would unload them, and then tell them their sentence?"

"What was there to tell them?! No, we yelled, 'Out! Stand still!' They scrambled down and there was already a trench dug in front of them. They clambered down, clung together and right away we got to work. . ."

"They didn't make any noise?"

"Some didn't, others began shouting, 'We're Communists, we are being wrongly executed,' that type of thing. But the women would only cry and cling to each other. So we just got on with it. . ."

"Did you have a doctor with you?"

"What for? We would shoot them, and those still wriggling got another bullet and then we were off back to the van. The work team from the Dalag camps was already nearby, waiting."

"What work team was that?"

"There was a team of criminal inmates from Dalag who lived in a separate compound. They were the trusties[1] at Bikin and they also had to dig and fill in the pits. As soon as we left they would fill in that pit and dig a new one for the next day. When they finished their work, they went back to the compound. They got time off their sentence for it and were well fed. It was easy work, not like felling timber."

"And what about you?"

"We would arrive back at the camp, hand in our weapons at the guardhouse and then we could have as much to drink as we wanted. The others used to lap it up—it didn't cost them a kopeck. I always had my shot, went off to the canteen for a hot meal, and then back to sleep in the barracks."

"And did you sleep well? Didn't you feel bad or anything?"

"Why should I?"

"Well, that you had just killed other people. Didn't you feel sorry for them?"

"No, not at all. I didn't give it a thought. No, I slept well and then I'd go for a walk outside the camp. There's some beautiful places around there. Boring, though, with no women."

"Were any of you married?"

---

[1]Trusties were convicts regarded as trustworthy, who were given special duties and privileges.

"No, they didn't take married men. Of course, the bosses made out all right. There were some real lookers on the Dalag work team! Your head would spin! Cooks, dishwashers, floor cleaners—the bosses had them all. We went without. It was better not to even think about it . . ."

"Grigory Ivanovich, did you know that the people you were shooting were not guilty at all, that they hadn't done anything wrong?"

"Well, we didn't think about that then. Later, yes. We were summoned to the procurators [officials] and they asked us questions. They explained that those had been innocent people. There had been mistakes, they said, and—what was the word?—excesses. But they told us that it was nothing to do with us, we were not guilty of anything."

"Well, I understand, then you were under orders and you shot people. But when you learned that you had been killing men and women who were not guilty at all, didn't your conscience begin to bother you?"

"Conscience? No, Naum'ich, it didn't bother me. I never think about all that now, and when I do remember something . . . no, nothing at all, as if nothing had happened. You know, I've become so soft-hearted that one look at an old man suffering today and I feel so much pity that I even cry sometimes. But those ones, no, I'm not sorry for them. Not at all, it's just like they never existed . . ."

The "special operation" at Bikin existed for almost three years. Well, two and a half, to be more exact. It also probably had its holidays and weekends—perhaps no one was shot on Sundays, May Day, Revolution Day and the Day of the Soviet Constitution. Even so, that means that it functioned for a total of 770 days. Every morning on each of those days four trucks set out from Bikin compound for the Distant Hill. Six people in each truck, a total of 24. It took 25–30 minutes for them to reach the waiting pit. The "special operation" thus disposed of 15,000 to 18,000 people during its existence. Yet it was of a standard design, just like any transit camp. The well-tried, well-planned machinery operated without interrup-

tion, functioning regularly and efficiently, filling the ready-made pits with bodies—in the hills of the Far East, in the Siberian forests, and in the glades of the Tambov woods or the Meshchera nature reserve. They existed everywhere, yet nothing remains of them now. There are no terrible museums as there are today at Auschwitz, or at Mauthausen in Austria. There are no solemn and funereal memorials like those that testify to the Nazi atrocities at Khatyn* . . . or Lidice.[2] Thousands of unnamed graves, in which there lie mingled the bones of hundreds of thousands of victims, have now been overgrown by bushes, thick luxuriant grass and young new forest. Not exactly the same as the Germans, it must be admitted. The men and women were buried separately here. Our regime made sure that even at that point no moral laxity might occur.

And the murderers? They are still alive.

. . . There were a great many, of course, who took part in these shootings. There were yet more, however, who never made the regular journey to the Distant Hill or the other killing grounds. Only in bourgeois society are the procurator and others obliged to attend an execution. Under our regime, thank God, that was not necessary. There were many, many more involved in these murders than those who simply pulled the trigger. For them a university degree, often in the "humanities," was more common than the rudimentary education of the Niyazovs [the former guard Razgon questioned]. They drafted the instructions and decisions; they signed beneath the words "agreed," "confirmed," "to be sentenced to . . ." Today they are all retired and most of them re-

---

*In 1942 German forces massacred all the inhabitants of the Belorussian village of Khatyn. (Not to be confused with Katyn . . . where in 1940 23,500 Polish officers were murdered by the [Soviet] NKVD.)

[2]After Czech resistance fighters assassinated Richard Heydrich, Chief of the Security Police, the Germans took savage revenge on the little Czech village of Lidice. They massacred all the men and deported the women and children to concentration camps (some children with suitable "Aryan features" were sent to live with German families and to be reared as Germans). The Nazis then burned, dynamited, and levelled the village.

ceive large individual pensions. They sit in the squares and enjoy watching the children play. They go to concerts and are moved by the music. We meet them when we attend a meeting, visit friends, or find ourselves sitting at the same table, celebrating with our common acquaintances. They are alive, and there are many of them.

COLLECTIVE GUILT

In the most general terms, paragraph 17 [of the Soviet criminal code] said that each member of a criminal group (and membership in that group was expressed by knowledge of its existence and failure to report it) was responsible not only for his own individual criminal deeds but also for the deeds of the criminal group as a whole and for each of its individual members, taken separately. It did not matter that the individual in question might not know the other members of the group, might be unaware what they were up to, and might not have any idea at all what the group he belonged to was doing. The purpose of the "doctrine of complicity" was to alleviate the exhausting labors of the interrogators. Undoubtedly, however, it also lightened the burden of those under investigation. The techniques of cross-examination became far simpler. Several dozen people were linked together in a group and then one of them, the weakest, was beaten almost to death in order to obtain confessions of espionage, sabotage, subversion and, of course, attempts on the life of "one of the leaders of the Party and the government." The others could be more gently treated, only requiring beating until they admitted they knew the individual who had given a "complete and full confession." Then the same crimes, in accordance with paragraph 17, were automatically attributed to them as well. What this sounded like during a court hearing I can describe from the words of a man I came to know in the camps.

Yefim Shatalov was a very high-ranking manager and for years he headed the State Cement Administration. Why they needed to send him to prison, God only knows! He had no political interests or involvements and did not wish to have any, since he was always prepared to serve his immediate superior faithfully and truthfully, and was unquestionably loyal to his ultimate chief, Comrade Stalin. Furthermore, he was incredibly circumspect and every step he took was protected by an entire system of safety measures. When he was baldly accused of sabotage he conducted himself so aggressively in court that the judge, in panic, deferred the hearing of his case. Some time after, Shatalov was presented with a new charge sheet and within an hour he was summoned to appear before a new sitting of the Military Tribunal. The chairman now was Ulrich himself. For the defendant Vasya Ulrich was an old, dear and kind acquaintance. For many years they had always sat at the same table at the Party elite's sanatorium, The Pines; they went for walks together, shared a drink or two, and exchanged men's jokes. Evidently the chairman was observing the old principles that justice must be rapid, fair and clement in his conduct of this hearing. What follows includes almost everything that was said, as recalled by Yefim Shatalov.

ULRICH (in a business-like, quiet, and jaded voice): Defendant! you have read the charge sheet? Do you recognize your guilt?

SHATALOV (with all the force of his love and loyalty to the judge): No! I am not guilty in any respect!

ULRICH: Did you know that there was a counter-revolutionary Right-Trotskyist organization in the People's Commissariat of Heavy Industry?

SHATALOV (throwing up his arms): I had no idea whatsoever. I had no suspicion there was such a hostile gang of saboteurs and terrorists there.

ULRICH (gazing with affectionate attention at his former drinking companion): You were not in prison during the last trial of the Right-Trotskyist center, were you?

SHATALOV: No, I was not.

ULRICH: You were reading the newspapers then?

SHATALOV (slowly, trying to grasp the purpose of such a strange question): I did . . .

ULRICH: So you read Pyatakov's testimony that there was a counter-revolutionary organization in the People's Commissariat of Heavy Industry?

SHATALOV (uncertainly): Of course, of course.

ULRICH (triumphantly): Well, there we are! So you knew there was a counter-revolutionary organization in the People's Commissariat of Heavy Industry. (Turning to the secretary of the court.) Write down: the defendant acknowledges that he knew about the existence of Pyatakov's organization . . .

SHATALOV (shouts passionately, stuttering from horror): But it was from the newspapers, the newspapers, that I learnt there was an organization there!

ULRICH (calm and satisfied): But to the court it is not important where you found out. You knew! (Hurriedly, like a priest at a poorly-paid funeral.) Any questions? No. You want to say a last word? No need for repetition, we've heard it already! (Nodding right and left at his assessors.) I pronounce sentence. Mmmh . . . 15 years . . .

I shall not insist that this trial strictly met the requirement for fairness. Yet compared to others it was clement, leaving Shatalov among the living. And it was indisputably rapid. Evidently the speed was typical. In the late 1950s I attended a memorial evening at the Museum of the Revolution for Kosarev, the 1930s Komsomol leader executed by Stalin. The head of the Central Committee administrative department told me that Khrushchev had entrusted him to re-examine Kosarev's case: "The hearing began at 11.00 a.m.," read the record of the trial, "and ended at 11.10 a.m."

THE HEARTLESS BUREAUCRACY

Auntie Pasha, a kindly middle-aged woman, washed the floors in the camp office. She pitied the office workers because they were so helpless and impractical: and she darned and sewed patches on the trousers and quilt jackets of the "trusties" who were not yet privileged to wear first-hand clothing. The story of her life was simple. Auntie Pasha came from Zlatoust in the Urals. Her husband, a furnace man, died during an accident at work and she was left with two teenage sons. Their life was predictably hard. Someone taught Auntie Pasha to go to Chelyabinsk to buy stockings and then sell them (naturally, at a suitably higher price) in Zlatoust where they were not to be found. The rest was recorded in the charge sheet and the sentence passed by the court. "For the purposes of speculation" she had "obtained 72 pairs of knitted stockings in Chelyabinsk which she then tried to resell at the market in Zlatoust." Auntie Pasha was reported, arrested, tried and sentenced to seven years imprisonment with confiscation of all her property. The children were taken in by acquaintances and, besides, they were almost old enough to take up any profession at the trade school. Five years passed, the war began, and Auntie Pasha's boys had reached the age when they could defend the Motherland. So off they went to fight. First Auntie Pasha was informed that her younger son had been killed. Staying behind in the office at night to wash the floors, she moaned and beat her head against the table.

Then one evening she came up to me with a glassy-eyed expression and handed over a thick package which she had been given in Records and Distribution. This contained several medical reports and the decisions of various commissions. To these was added a letter to Auntie Pasha from the hospital administrator. It concerned her elder son. He had been severely wounded and was in the hospital. The doctors had done all within their power and he was, as they put it in his medical history, "fit, to all intents and purposes"—apart, that is, from having lost both arms and one leg. He could be discharged from the hospital if there was some close relation to look after him. Evidently the son had explained where she was because the administrator advised the mother of this wounded soldier to send an appeal to the USSR Procurator General's Office, including the enclosed documents, after which they would release her and she could come and fetch him.

"'Manuilich, dear heart," Auntie Pasha said, starting to cry, "You write for me."

So I wrote, and very persuasively. I attached all the documents and handed in the letter. Two or three months passed, and each day I reassured Auntie Pasha: they received a great many such appeals, I told her, and it would take time to process her release. I described in detail the lengthy procedures as her application passed from one level to another. Auntie Pasha wept, but believed me and each day I gave her paper on which to write her son a letter.

One day I went into Records and Distribution myself. A great pile of mail lay on the table, already sorted out to be handed over, or its contents communicated, to the prisoners. Auntie Pasha's surname caught my eye. I picked up the flimsy sheet of headed paper from the USSR Procurator General's Office and read it through. A public procurator of a certain rank or class informed Auntie Pasha that her application had been examined and her request for early release turned down because there were "no grounds." I carefully placed the single sheet on the table and went out onto the verandah, terrified that I might suddenly meet Auntie Pasha . . . Everywhere, in the barracks and in the office, there were people I did not want to see. I ran to the latrines and there, clinging to the stinking walls, started to shake uncontrollably. Only two times in my prison life did this happen. Why was I crying? Then I understood: I felt ashamed, terribly ashamed, before Auntie Pasha.

She had already served five years for 72 pairs of stockings. She had given the state her two sons. Now, there it was, there were "no grounds" . . .

REVIEW QUESTIONS

1. Why was Nikita Khrushchev careful to distinguish Stalin from Lenin?
2. What charges against Stalin did Khrushchev highlight in his speech?
3. What image of Stalin did Khrushchev draw?
4. From a reading of these passages from Lev Razgon's book, what do you think motivated the behavior of Stalin's bureaucrats who committed these terrible crimes?

6 The Rise of Italian Fascism

Benito Mussolini (1883–1945) started his political life as a socialist and in 1912 was appointed editor of *Avanti,* the leading socialist newspaper. During World War I, Mussolini was expelled from the Socialist party for advocating Italy's entry into the conflict. Immediately after the war, he organized the Fascist party. Exploiting labor unrest, fear of communism, and thwarted nationalist hopes, Mussolini gained followers among veterans and the middle class. Powerful industrialists and landowners, viewing the Fascists as a bulwark against communism, helped to finance the young movement. An opportunist, Mussolini organized a march on Rome in 1922 to bring down the government. King Victor Emmanuel, fearful of civil war, appointed the Fascist leader prime minister.

Had Italian liberals and the king taken a firm stand, the government could have crushed the 20,000 lightly armed marchers.

Benito Mussolini
FASCIST DOCTRINES

Ten years after he seized power, Mussolini, assisted by philosopher Giovanni Gentile (1875–1944), contributed an article to the *Italian Encyclopedia* in which he discussed fascist political and social doctrines. In this piece, Mussolini lauded violence as a positive experience; attacked Marxism for denying idealism by subjecting human beings to economic laws and for dividing the nation into warring classes; and denounced liberal democracy for promoting individual selfishness at the expense of the national community and for being unable to solve the nation's problems. The fascist state, he said, required unity and power, not individual freedom. The following excerpts are from Mussolini's article.

. . . Above all, Fascism, the more it considers and observes the future and the development of humanity quite apart from political considerations of the moment, believes neither in the possibility nor the utility of perpetual peace. It thus repudiates the doctrine of Pacifism—born of a renunciation of the struggle and an act of cowardice in the face of sacrifice. War alone brings up to its highest tension all human energy and puts the stamp of nobility upon the peoples who have the courage to meet it. All other trials are substitutes, which never really put men into the position where they have to make the great decision—the alternative of life or death. Thus a doctrine which is founded upon this harmful postulate of peace is hostile to Fascism. And thus hostile to the spirit of Fascism, though accepted for what use they can be in dealing with particular political situations, are all the international leagues and societies which, as history will show, can be scattered to the winds when once strong national feeling is aroused by any motive—sentimental, ideal, or practical. This anti-pacifist spirit is carried by Fascism even into the life of the individual; the proud motto of the *Squadrista,* "Me ne frego" [It doesn't matter], written on the bandage of the wound, is an act of philosophy not only stoic, the summary of a

doctrine not only political—it is the education to combat, the acceptation of the risks which combat implies, and a new way of life for Italy. Thus the Fascist accepts life and loves it, knowing nothing of and despising suicide: he rather conceives of life as duty and struggle and conquest, life which should be high and full, lived for oneself, but above all for others—those who are at hand and those who are far distant, contemporaries, and those who will come after. . . .

. . . Fascism [is] the complete opposite of . . . Marxian Socialism, the materialist conception of history; according to which the history of human civilization can be explained simply through the conflict of interests among the various social groups and by the change and development in the means and instruments of production. That the changes in the economic field—new discoveries of raw materials, new methods of working them, and the inventions of science—have their importance no one can deny; but that these factors are sufficient to explain the history of humanity excluding all others is an absurd delusion. Fascism, now and always, believes in holiness and in heroism; that is to say, in actions influenced by no economic motive, direct or indirect. And if the economic conception of history be denied, according to which theory men are no more than puppets, carried to and fro by the waves of chance, while the real directing forces are quite out of their control, it follows that the existence of an unchangeable and unchanging class-war is also denied—the natural progeny of the economic conception of history. And above all Fascism denies that class-war can be the preponderant force in the transformation of society. . . .

After Socialism, Fascism combats the whole complex system of democratic ideology, and repudiates it, whether in its theoretical premises or in its practical application. Fascism denies that the majority, by the simple fact that it is a majority, can direct human society; it denies that numbers alone can govern by means of a periodical consultation, and it affirms the immutable, beneficial, and fruitful inequality of mankind, which can never be permanently leveled through the mere operation of a mechanical process such as universal suffrage. . . .

. . . Fascism denies, in democracy, the absurd conventional untruth of political equality dressed out in the garb of collective irresponsibility, and the myth of "happiness" and indefinite progress. . . .

. . . Given that the nineteenth century was the century of Socialism, of Liberalism, and of Democracy, it does not necessarily follow that the twentieth century must also be a century of Socialism, Liberalism, and Democracy: political doctrines pass, but humanity remains; and it may rather be expected that this will be a century of authority, . . . a century of Fascism. For if the nineteenth century was a century of individualism (Liberalism always signifying individualism) it may be expected that this will be the century of collectivism, and hence the century of the State. . . .

The foundation of Fascism is the conception of the State, its character, its duty, and its aim. Fascism conceives of the State as an absolute, in comparison with which all individuals or groups are relative, only to be conceived of in their relation to the State. The conception of the Liberal State is not that of a directing force, guiding the play and development, both material and spiritual, of a collective body, but merely a force limited to the function of recording results: on the other hand, the Fascist State is itself conscious and has itself a will and a personality—thus it may be called the "ethic" State. . . .

. . . The Fascist State organizes the nation, but leaves a sufficient margin of liberty to the individual; the latter is deprived of all useless and possibly harmful freedom, but retains what is essential; the deciding power in this question cannot be the individual, but the State alone. . . .

. . . For Fascism, the growth of empire, that is to say the expansion of the nation, is an essential manifestation of vitality, and its opposite a sign of decadence. Peoples which are rising, or rising again after a period of decadence, are always imperialist; any renunciation is a sign of decay and of death. Fascism is the doctrine best adapted to represent the tendencies and the aspirations of a people, like the people of Italy, who are rising again after many centuries of abasement and foreign servitude. But empire demands discipline, the coordination of all forces and a deeply felt sense of duty and sacrifice: this fact explains many aspects of the practical working of the régime, the character of many forces in the State, and the necessarily severe measures which must be taken against those who would oppose this spontaneous and inevitable movement of Italy in the twentieth century, and would oppose it by recalling the outworn ideology of the nineteenth century—repudiated wheresoever there has been the courage to undertake great experiments of social and political transformation; for never before has the nation stood more in need of authority, of direction, and of order. If every age has its own characteristic doctrine, there are a thousand signs which point to Fascism as the characteristic doctrine of our time. For if a doctrine must be a living thing, this is proved by the fact that Fascism has created a living faith; and that this faith is very powerful in the minds of men is demonstrated by those who have suffered and died for it.

REVIEW QUESTIONS

1. Why did Benito Mussolini consider pacifism to be the enemy of fascism?
2. Why did Mussolini attack Marxism?
3. How did Mussolini view majority rule and equality?
4. What relationship did Mussolini see between the individual and the state?

---

7   The Rise of Nazism

Many extreme racist-nationalist and paramilitary organizations sprang up in postwar Germany. Adolf Hitler (1889–1945), a veteran of World War I, joined one of these organizations, which became known as the National Socialist German Worker's Party (commonly called the Nazi Party). Hitler's uncanny insight into the state of mind of postwar Germans and his extraordinary oratorical gifts enabled him to gain control of the party.

Adolf Hitler
MEIN KAMPF

In the "Beer Hall Putsch" of November 1923, Hitler attempted to overthrow the state government in Bavaria as the first step in bringing down the Weimar Republic. But the Nazis quickly scattered when the Bavarian police opened fire. Hitler was arrested and sentenced to five years' imprisonment—he served only nine months. While in prison, Hitler wrote *Mein Kampf (My Struggle),* in which he presented his views. The book came to be regarded as an authoritative expression of the Nazi world-view and served as a kind of sacred writing for the Nazi movement.

Hitler's thought—a patchwork of nineteenth-century anti-Semitic, Volkish, Social Darwinist, and anti-Marxist ideas—contrasted sharply with the core values of both the Judeo-Christian and the Enlightenment traditions. Central to Hitler's world-view was racial mythology: a heroic Germanic race that was descended from the ancient Aryans, who once swept across Europe, and was battling for survival against racial inferiors. In the following passages excerpted from *Mein Kampf,* Hitler presents his views of race, of propaganda, and of the National Socialist territorial goals.

THE PRIMACY OF RACE

Nature does not want a pairing of weaker individuals with stronger ones; it wants even less a mating of a higher race with a weaker one. Otherwise its routine labors of promoting a higher breed lasting perhaps over hundreds of thousands of years would be wiped out.

History offers much evidence for this process. It proves with terrifying clarity that any genetic mixture of Aryan blood with people of a lower quality undermines the culturally superior people. The population of North America consists to a large extent of Germanic elements, which have mixed very little with inferior people of color. Central and South America shows a different humanity and culture; here Latin immigrants mixed with the aborigines, sometimes on a large scale. This example alone allows a clear recognition of the effects of racial mixtures. Remaining racially pure the Germans of North America rose to be masters of their continent; they will remain masters as long as they do not defile their blood.

The result of mixing races in short is: a) lowering the cultural level of the higher race; b) physical and spiritual retrogression and thus the beginning of a slow but progressive decline.

To promote such a development means no less than committing sin against the will of the eternal creator. . . .

Everything that we admire on earth—science, technology, invention—is the creative product of only a few people, and perhaps originally of only *one* race; our whole culture depends upon them. If they perish, the beauties of the earth will be buried. . . .

All great cultures of the past perished because the original creative race was destroyed by the poisoning of its blood.

Such collapse always happened because people forgot that all cultures depend on human beings. In order to preserve a given culture it is necessary to preserve the human beings who created it. Cultural preservation in this world is tied to the iron law of necessity and the right to victory of the stronger and better. . . .

If we divide humanity into three categories: into founders of culture, bearers of culture, and destroyers of culture, the Aryan would undoubtedly rate first. He established the foundations and walls of all human progress. . . .

The mixing of blood and the resulting lowering of racial cohesion is the sole reason why cultures perish. People do not perish by defeat in war, but by losing the power of resistance inherent in pure blood.

All that is not pure race in this world is chaff. . . .

A state which in the age of racial poisoning dedicates itself to the cultivation of its best racial elements will one day become master of the world.

Modern anti-Semitism was a powerful legacy of the Middle Ages and the unsettling changes brought about by rapid industrialization; it was linked to racist doctrines that asserted the Jews were inherently wicked and bore dangerous racial qualities. Hitler grasped the political potential of anti-Semitism: by concentrating all evil in one enemy, he could provide non-Jews with an emotionally satisfying explanation for all their misfortunes and thus manipulate and unify the German people.

ANTI-SEMITISM

The Jew offers the most powerful contrast to the Aryan. . . . Despite all their seemingly intellectual qualities the Jewish people are without true culture, and especially without a culture of their own. What Jews seem to possess as culture is the property of others, for the most part corrupted in their hands.

In judging the Jewish position in regard to human culture, we have to keep in mind their essential characteristics. There never was—and still is no—Jewish art. The Jewish people made no original contribution to the two queen goddesses of all arts: architecture and music. What they have contributed is bowdlerization or spiritual theft. Which proves that Jews lack the very qualities distinguishing creative and culturally blessed races. . . .

The first and biggest lie of Jews is that Jewishness is not a matter of race but of religion, from which inevitably follow even more lies. One of them refers to the language of Jews. It is not a means of expressing their thoughts, but of hiding them. While speaking French a Jew thinks Jewish, and while he cobbles together some German verse, he merely expresses the mentality of his people.

As long as the Jew is not master of other peoples, he must for better or worse speak their languages. Yet as soon as the others have become his servants, then all should learn a universal language (Esperanto for instance), so that by these means the Jews can rule more easily. . . .

For hours the blackhaired Jewish boy lies in wait, with satanic joy on his face, for the unsuspecting girl whom he disgraces with his blood and thereby robs her from her people. He tries by all means possible to destroy the racial foundations of the people he wants to subjugate.

But a people of pure race conscious of its blood can never be enslaved by the Jew; he remains forever a ruler of bastards.

Thus he systematically attempts to lower racial purity by racially poisoning individuals.

In politics he begins to replace the idea of democracy with the idea of the dictatorship of the proletariat.

He found his weapon in the organized Marxist masses, which avoid democracy and instead help him to subjugate and govern people dictatorially with his brutal fists.

Systematically he works toward a double revolution, in economics and politics.

With the help of his international contacts he enmeshes people who effectively resist his attacks from within in a net of external enemies whom he incites to war, and, if necessary, goes on to unfurling the red flag of revolution over the battlefield.

He batters the national economies until the ruined state enterprises are privatized and subject to his financial control.

In politics he refuses to give the state the means for its self-preservation, destroys the bases of any national self-determination and defense, wipes out the faith in leadership, denigrates the historic past, and pulls everything truly great into the gutter.

In cultural affairs he pollutes art, literature, theatre, befuddles national sentiment, subverts all concepts of beauty and grandeur, of nobleness and goodness, and reduces people to their lowest nature.

Religion is made ridiculous, custom and morals are declared outdated, until the last props of national character in the battle for survival have collapsed. . . .

Thus the Jew is the big rabble-rouser for the complete destruction of Germany. Wherever in the world we read about attacks on Germany, Jews are the source, just as in peace and during the war the newspapers of both the Jewish stock market and the Marxists systematically incited hatred against Germany. Country after country gave up its neutrality and joined the world war coalition in disregard of the true interest of the people.

Jewish thinking in all this is clear. The Bolshevization of Germany, i.e., the destruction of the German national people-oriented intelligentsia and thereby the exploitation of German labor under the yoke of Jewish global finance are but the prelude for the expansion of the Jewish tendency to conquer the world. As so often in history, Germany is the turning point in this mighty struggle. If our people and our state become the victims of bloodthirsty and money-thirsty Jewish tyrants, the whole world will be enmeshed in the tentacles of this octopus. If, however, Germany liberates itself from this yoke, we can be sure that the greatest threat to all humanity has been broken. . . .

Hitler was a master propagandist and advanced his ideas on propaganda techniques in *Mein Kampf*. He mocked the learned and book-oriented German liberals and socialists who he felt were entirely unsuited for modern mass politics. The successful leader, he said, must win over the masses through the use of simple ideas and images, constantly repeated, to control the mind by evoking primitive feelings. Hitler contended that mass meetings were the most effective means of winning followers. What counted most at these demonstrations, he said, was will power, strength, and unflagging determination radiating from the speaker to every single individual in the crowd.

PROPAGANDA AND MASS RALLIES

The task of propaganda does not lie in the scientific training of individuals, but in directing the masses toward certain facts, events, necessities, etc., whose significance is to be brought to their attention.

The essential skill consists in doing this so well that you convince people about the reality of a fact, about the necessity of an event, about the correctness of something necessary, etc. . . . You always have to appeal to the emotions and far less to the so-called intellect. . . .

The art of propaganda lies in sensing the emotional temper of the broad masses, so that you, in psychologically effective form, can catch their attention and move their hearts. . . .

The attention span of the masses is very short, their understanding limited; they easily forget. For that reason all effective propaganda has to concentrate on very few points and drive them home through simple slogans, until even the simplest can grasp what you have in mind. As soon as you give up this principle and become too complex, you will lose your effectiveness, because the masses cannot digest and retain what you have offered. You thereby weaken your case and in the end lose it altogether.

The larger the scope of your case, the more psychologically correct must be the method of your presentation. . . .

The task of propaganda lies not in weighing right and wrong, but in driving home your own point of view. You cannot objectively explore the facts that favor others and present them in doctrinaire sincerity to the masses. You have to push relentlessly your own case. . . .

Even the most brilliant propaganda will not produce the desired results unless it follows this fundamental rule: You must stick to limiting yourself to essentials and repeat them endlessly. Persistence on this point, as in so many other cases in the world, is the first and most important precondition for success. . . .

Propaganda does not exist to furnish interesting diversions to blasé young dandies, but to convince above all the masses. In their clumsiness they always require a long lead before they are ready to take notice. Only by thousandfold repetition will the simplest concepts stick in their memories.

No variation of your presentation should change the content of your propaganda; you always have to come to the same conclusion. You may want to highlight your slogans from various sides, but at the end you always have to reaffirm it. Only consistent and uniform propaganda will succeed. . . .

Every advertisement, whether in business or politics, derives its success from its persistence and uniformity. . . .

The mass meeting is . . . necessary because an incipient supporter of a new political movement will feel lonely and anxiously isolated. He needs at the start a sense of a larger community which among most people produces vitality and courage. The same man as member of a military company or battalion and surrounded by his comrades will more lightheartedly join an attack than if he were all by himself. In a crowd he feels more sheltered, even if reality were a thousandfold against him.

The sense of community in a mass demonstration not only empowers the individual, but also promotes an esprit de corps. The person who in his business or workshop is the first to represent a new political creed is likely to be exposed to heavy discrimination. He needs the reassurance that comes from the conviction of being a member and a fighter in a large comprehensive organization. The sense of this organization comes first to him in a mass demonstration. When he for the first time goes from a petty workshop or from a large factory, where he feels insignificant, to a mass demonstration surrounded by thousands and thousands of like-minded fellows—when he as a seeker is gripped by the intoxicating surge of enthusiasm among three or four thousand others—when the visible success and the consensus of thousands of others prove the correctness of his new political creed and for the first time arouse doubts about his previous political convictions—then he submits to the miraculous influence of what we call "mass suggestion." The will, the yearning, and also the power of thousands of fellow citizens now fill every individual. The man who full of doubts and uncertain enters such a gathering, leaves it inwardly strengthened; he has become a member of a community. . . .

Hitler was an extreme nationalist who wanted a reawakened, racially united Germany to expand eastward at the expense of the Slavs, whom he viewed as racially inferior.

LEBENSRAUM

A people gains its freedom of existence only by occupying a sufficiently large space on earth. . . .

If the National Socialist movement really wants to achieve a hallowed mission in history for our people, it must, in painful awareness of its position in the world, boldly and methodically fight against the aimlessness and incapacity which have hitherto guided the foreign policy of the German people. It must then, without respect for "tradition" and prejudice, find the courage to rally the German people to a forceful advance on the road which leads from their present cramped living space to new territories. In this manner they will be liberated from the danger of perishing or being enslaved in service to others.

The National Socialist movement must try to end the disproportion between our numerous population and its limited living space, the source of our food as well as the base of our power—between our historic past and the hopelessness of our present impotence. . . .

The demand for restoring the boundaries of 1914 is a political nonsense with consequences so huge as to make it appear a crime—quite apart from the fact that our pre-war boundaries were anything but logical. They neither united all people of German nationality nor served strategic-political necessity. . . .

In the light of this fact we National Socialists must resolutely stick to our foreign policy goals, namely *to secure for the German people the territorial base to which they are entitled.* This is the only goal which before God and our German posterity justifies shedding our blood. . . .

Just as our forebears did not receive the soil on which we live as a gift from heaven—they had to risk their lives for it—so in future we will not secure the living space for our people by divine grace, but by the might of the victorious sword.

However much all of us recognize the necessity of a reckoning with France, it would remain ineffectual if we thereby limited the scope of our foreign policy. It makes sense only if we consider it as a rear-guard action for expanding our living space elsewhere in Europe. . . .

If we speak today about gaining territory in Europe, we think primarily of Russia and its border states. . . .

Kurt G. W. Ludecke
THE DEMAGOGIC ORATOR

Nazi popularity grew partly due to Hitler's power as an orator to play on the dissatisfactions of postwar Germans with the Weimar Republic. In the following selection, Kurt G. W. Ludecke, an early supporter of Hitler who later broke with the Nazis, describes Hitler's ability to mesmerize his audience.

. . . [W]hen the Nazis marched into the Koenigsplatz with banners flying, their bands playing stirring German marches, they were greeted with tremendous cheers. An excited, expectant crowd was now filling the beautiful square to the last inch and overflowing into surrounding streets. They were well over a hundred thousand. . . . I was close enough to see Hitler's face, watch every change in his expression, hear every word he said.

When the man stepped forward on the platform, there was almost no applause. He stood silent for a moment. Then he began to speak, quietly and ingratiatingly at first. Before long his voice had risen to a hoarse shriek that gave an extraordinary effect of an intensity of feeling. There were many high-pitched, rasping notes. . . .

Critically I studied this slight, pale man, his brown hair parted on one side and falling again and again over his sweating brow. Threatening and beseeching, with small, pleading hands and flaming, steel-blue eyes, he had the look of a fanatic.

Presently my critical faculty was swept away. Leaning from the tribune as if he were trying to impel his inner self into the consciousness of all these thousands, he was holding the masses, and me with them, under a hypnotic spell by the sheer force of his conviction.

He urged the revival of German honor and manhood with a blast of words that seemed to cleanse. "Bavaria is now the most German land in Germany!" he shouted, to roaring applause. Then, plunging into sarcasm, he indicted the leaders in Berlin as "November Criminals," daring to put into words thoughts that Germans were now almost afraid to think and certainly to voice.

It was clear that Hitler was feeling the exaltation of the emotional response now surging up toward him from his thousands of hearers.

His voice rising to passionate climaxes, he finished his speech with an anthem of hate against the "Novemberlings" and a pledge of undying love for the Fatherland. "Germany must be free!" was his final defiant slogan. Then two last words that were like the sting of a lash:

"Deutschland Erwache!"

Awake, Germany! There was thunderous applause. Then the masses took a solemn oath "to save Germany in Bavaria from Bolshevism."

I do not know how to describe the emotions that swept over me as I heard this man. His words were like a scourge. When he spoke of the disgrace of Germany, I felt ready to spring on any enemy. His appeal to German manhood was like a call to arms, the gospel he preached a sacred truth. He seemed another Luther. I forgot everything but the man; then, glancing round, I saw that his magnetism was holding these thousands as one.

Of course I was ripe for this experience. I was a man of thirty-two, weary of disgust and disillusionment, a wanderer seeking a cause; a patriot without a channel for his patriotism, a yearner after the heroic without a hero. The intense will of the man, the passion of his sincerity seemed to flow from him into me. I experienced an exaltation that could be likened only to religious conversion.

I felt sure that no one who had heard Hitler that afternoon could doubt that he was the man of destiny, the vitalizing force in the future of Germany. The masses who had streamed into the Koenigsplatz with a stern sense of national humiliation seemed to be going forth renewed.

The bands struck up, the thousands began to move away. I knew my search was ended. I had found myself, my leader, and my cause.

Thomas Mann
AN APPEAL TO REASON

In 1931, two years before Hitler took power, the internationally prominent German author Thomas Mann (1875–1955) wrote an article entitled "An Appeal to Reason," in which he discussed the crisis in the European soul that gave rise to fascism. He saw National Socialism and the extreme nationalism it espoused as a rejection of the Western rational tradition and as a regression to primitive and barbaric modes of behavior. Some excerpts from Mann's article follow.

. . . The economic decline of the middle classes was accompanied—or even preceded—by a feeling which amounted to an intellectual prophecy and critique of the age: the sense that here was a crisis which heralded the end of the bourgeois epoch that came in with the French revolution and the notions appertaining to it. There was proclaimed a new mental attitude for all mankind, which should have nothing to do with bourgeois principles such as freedom, justice, culture, optimism, faith in progress. As art, it gave vent to expressionistic soul-shrieks; as philosophy it repudiated . . . reason, and the . . . ideological conceptions of bygone decades; it expressed itself as an irrationalistic throwback, placing the conception *life* at the centre of thought, and raised on its standard the powers of the unconscious, the dynamic, the darkly creative, which alone were life-giving. Mind, quite simply the intellectual, it put under a taboo as destructive of life, while it set up for homage as the true inwardness of life . . . the darkness of the soul, the holy procreative underworld. Much of this nature-religion, by its very essence inclining to the orgiastic and to . . . [frenzied] excess, has gone into the nationalism of our day, making of it something quite different from the nationalism of the nineteenth century, with its bourgeois, strongly cosmopolitan and humanitarian cast. It is distinguished in its character as a nature-cult, precisely by its absolute unrestraint, its orgiastic, radically anti-humane, frenziedly dynamic character. . . .

. . . And there is even more: there are other intellectual elements come to strengthen this national-social political movement—a certain ideology, a Nordic creed, a Germanistic romanticism, from philological, academic, professorial spheres. It addresses the Germany of

1930 in a highflown wishy-washy jargon full of mystical good feeling, with hyphenated prefixes like race- and folk- and fellowship-, and lends to the movement a . . . fanatical cult-barbarism, . . . dangerous and estranging, with . . . power to clog and stultify the brain. . . .

Fed, then, by such intellectual and pseudo-intellectual currents as these, the movement which we sum up under the name of national-socialism and which has displayed such a power of enlisting recruits to its banner, mingles with the mighty wave—a wave of anomalous barbarism, of primitive popular vulgarity—that sweeps over the world to-day, assailing the nerves of mankind with wild, bewildering, stimulating, intoxicating sensations. . . . Humanity seems to have run like boys let out of school away from the humanitarian, idealistic nineteenth century, from whose morality—if we can speak at all of morality in this connection—our time represents a wide and wild reaction. Everything is possible, everything permitted as a weapon against human decency; if we have got rid of the idea of freedom as a relic of the bourgeois state of mind, as though an idea so bound up with all European feeling, upon which Europe has been founded, for which she has made such sacrifices, could ever be utterly lost—it comes back again, this cast-off conception, in a guise suited to the time: as demoralization, as a mockery of all human authority, as a free rein to instincts, as the emancipation of brutality, the dictatorship of force. . . . In all this violence demonstrates itself, and demonstrates nothing but violence, and even that is unnecessary, for all other considerations are fallen away, man does not any longer believe in them, and so the road is free to vulgarity without restraint.

This fantastic state of mind, of a humanity that has outrun its ideas, is matched by a political scene in the grotesque style, with Salvation Army methods, hallelujahs and bell-ringing and dervishlike repetition of monotonous catchwords, until everybody foams at the mouth. Fanaticism turns into a means of salvation, enthusiasm into epileptic ecstasy, politics becomes an opiate for the masses, . . . and reason veils her face.

REVIEW QUESTIONS

1. How did Adolf Hitler account for cultural greatness? Cultural decline?
2. What comparisons did Hitler draw between Aryans and Jews?
3. What kind of evidence did Hitler offer for his anti-Semitic arguments?
4. Theodor Mommsen, a nineteenth-century German historian, said that anti-Semites do not listen to "logic and ethical arguments. . . . They listen only to their own envy and hatred, to the meanest instincts." Discuss this statement.
5. What insights did Hitler have into mass psychology and propaganda?
6. What foreign policy goals did Hitler have for Germany? How did he expect them to be achieved?
7. How did Hitler mesmerize his audience?
8. According to Thomas Mann, what new mental attitude emerged that heralded the end of the bourgeois age?
9. How did Mann view extreme nationalism and National Socialism?
10. What did Mann mean by "politics becomes an opiate for the masses"?

8 The Leader-State

Adolf Hitler came to power by legal means, appointed chancellor by President Paul von Hindenburg on January 30, 1933, according to the constitution of the Weimar Republic. Thereafter, however, he proceeded to dismantle the legal structure of the Weimar system and replace it with an inflexible dictatorship that revolved around his person. Quickly reacting to the popular confusion caused by the suspicious Reichstag Fire, Hitler issued a decree on February 28 that suspended all guarantees of civil and individual freedom. In March, the Reichstag adopted the Enabling Act, which vested all legislative powers in his hands. Then Hitler proceeded to destroy the autonomy of the federal states, dissolve the trade unions, outlaw other political parties, and end freedom of the press. By the time he eliminated party rivals in a blood purge on June 30, 1934, the consolidation of power was complete. Meanwhile, much of Germany's public and institutional life fell under Nazi Party control in a process known as the *Gleichschaltung,* or coordination. The Third Reich was organized as a leader-state, in which Hitler the *Führer* (leader) embodied and expressed the real will of the German people, commanded the supreme loyalty of the nation, and had unlimited authority.

Ernst Huber
"THE AUTHORITY OF THE FÜHRER IS . . . ALL-INCLUSIVE AND UNLIMITED"

In *Verfassungsrecht des grossdeutschen Reiches* (Constitutional Law of the Greater German Reich), legal scholar Ernst Rudolf Huber (b. 1903–1990) offered a classic explication of the basic principles of National Socialism. The following excerpts from that work describe the nature of Hitler's political authority.

The Führer-Reich of the [German] people is founded on the recognition that the true will of the people cannot be disclosed through parliamentary votes and plebiscites but that the will of the people in its pure and uncorrupted form can only be expressed through the Führer. Thus a distinction must be drawn between the supposed will of the people in a parliamentary democracy, which merely reflects the conflict of the various social interests, and the true will of the people in the Führer-state, in which the collective will of the real political unit is manifested. . . .

It would be impossible for a law to be introduced and acted upon in the Reichstag which had not originated with the Führer or, at least, received his approval. The procedure is similar to that of the plebiscite: The lawgiving power does not rest in the Reichstag; it merely proclaims through its decision its agreement with the will of the Führer, who is the lawgiver of the German people.

The Führer unites in himself all the sovereign authority of the Reich; all public authority in the state as well as in the movement is derived from the authority of the Führer. We must speak not of the state's authority but of the Führer's authority if we wish to designate the character of the political authority within the Reich correctly. The state does not hold political authority as an impersonal unit but receives it from the Führer as the executor of the national will. The authority of the Führer is complete and all-embracing; it unites in itself all the means of political direction; it extends into all fields of national life; it embraces the entire people, which is bound to the Führer in loyalty and obedience. The authority of the Führer is not limited by checks and controls, by special autonomous bodies or individual rights, but it is free and independent, all-inclusive and unlimited. It is not, however, self-seeking or arbitrary and its ties are within itself. It is derived from the people; that is, it is entrusted to the Führer by the people. It exists for the people and has its justification in the people; it is free of all outward ties because it is in its innermost nature firmly bound up with the fate, the welfare, the mission, and the honor of the people.

Führung [leadership] is not, like government, the highest organ of the state, which has grown out of the order of the state, but it receives its legitimation, its call, and its mission from the people. . . .

The people cannot as a rule announce its will by means of majority vote but only through its embodiment in one man, or in a few men. The principle of the *identity* of the ruler and those who are ruled, of the government and those who are governed has been very forcibly represented as the principle of democracy. But this identity . . . becomes mechanistic and superficial if one seeks to establish it in the theory that the people are at once the governors and the governed. . . . A true organic identity is only possible when the great mass of the people recognizes its embodiment in one man and feels itself to be one nature with him.

9 The Nazification of Culture and Society

The Nazis aspired to more than political power; they also wanted to have the German people view the world in accordance with National Socialist ideology. Toward this end, the Nazis strictly regulated cultural life. Believing that the struggle of racial forces occupied the center of world history, Nazi ideologists tried to strengthen the racial consciousness of the German people. Numerous courses in "race science" introduced in schools and universities emphasized the superiority of the Nordic soul as well as the worthlessness of Jews and their threat to the nation.

Alice Hamilton
THE YOUTH WHO ARE HITLER'S STRENGTH

Young people numbered among the most ardent supporters of Nazism, in which they saw a cause worthy of their devotion. Influenced by Nazi propaganda and led astray by their youthful idealism, they equated a total commitment to the Nazi movement with a selfless dedication to the nation.

Dr. Alice Hamilton (1869–1970) wrote the following article in 1933 after her second post–World War I trip to Germany. An international authority on industrial diseases who was known for her social consciousness, she was the first woman on the faculty of the Medical School of Harvard University. Her familiarity with Germany had begun in the late nineteenth century when she pursued postgraduate studies there. Her article, which appeared in the *New York Times Magazine* eight months after Hitler gained power, shows how the Nazis exploited patriotism, idealism, and a deep-seated desire of youth for fellowship.

Hitler's movement is called a youth movement and during the first months of the Nazi rule, while I was in Germany, this certainly seemed to be true. The streets of every city swarmed with brown shirts [trademark Nazi uniform], echoed to the sound of marching men and Hitler songs; there were parades, monster mass meetings, celebrations of all kinds, day in and day out. The swastika flag flapped from every building. In Frankfurt-on-Main where I had spent, years ago, delightful student days, I went to the beautiful Römer Platz, only to find it unrecognizable, its lovely buildings hidden under fifty-three Nazi banners. Rathenau Square had been changed to Horst Wessel Square, for Wessel, the young organizer of storm detachments in the slums of Berlin, who died at the hands of Communists, is the new hero of Germany. . . .

To understand Hitler's enormous success with the young we must understand what life has meant to the post-war generation in Germany, not only the children of the poor but of the middle class as well. They were children during the years of the war when the food blockade kept them half starved, when fathers were away at the front and mothers distracted with the effort to keep their families fed. They came to manhood in a country which seemed to have no use for them. Even compulsory military training was no more and there was nothing to take its place. . . .

. . . A settlement worker told me that she knew families in which the children had come to manhood without ever realizing the connection between work and food. They had never had work, and food had come scantily and grudgingly from some governmental agency.

To these idle, hopeless youths two stirring calls to action came—one from the Communists, the other from Hitler; and to both of them German youth responded. Both appealed to hatred, both held out an ideal of a changed Germany, but Hitler's propaganda was cleverer than the Communists', because his program is narrower, more concrete. The Communist is internationally minded, his brothers are all over the world, his ideal State embraces all lands. Hitler repudiates internationalism; he is against all who are not German; his ideal State is a self-contained Germany, an object of fear to all her neighbors. The Communist is taught to hate a class, the capitalistic, the Hitlerite to hate each individual Jew. Many young Communists were brought under the banner of Hitler by appeals to national pride and race antagonism, but also by the ideal of a united Germany without class hatred.

Hitler made each insignificant, poverty-stricken, jobless youth of the slums feel himself one of the great of the earth, since the youth was a German, a Nordic, far superior to the successful Jew who was to be driven out of office and counting house to make place for the youth and his like. Hitler told the young men that the fate of Germany was in their hands, that if they joined his army they would battle with the Communists for the streets, they would see Jewish blood flow in streams, they would capture the government, deliver Germany from the Versailles treaty and then sweep triumphantly over the borders to reconquer Germany's lost land. He put them into uniforms, he taught them to march and sing together, he aroused that sense of comradeship and esprit de corps so precious to the young, and gave them what is even more precious—an

object for hero worship. Life suddenly took on meaning and importance, with the call to danger, sacrifice, even death.

Among the hundreds of thousands who make up the audiences at Hitler's or Goebbels's [Joseph Goebbels, minister of propaganda] meetings, and who seem to an outsider to be carried away by a kind of mass hysteria, there are many who are actuated by real idealism, who long to give themselves unreservedly to the great vision of a resurgent Germany. Being young they are of course contemptuous of the slow and moderate methods of the republic; they are for action, quick, arrogant, ruthless.

But their program calls for a changed Germany, one purged of all selfishness and materialism. They repudiate liberalism, for that means to them capitalism, it means the profit-making system, it means class distinctions, inequalities. The Germany the young are planning will have no division between the classes and will substitute the common good for individual profit. They really believe that Hitler will bring about a genuine socialism without class warfare and this part of their program is highly idealistic and fine, but, as is to be expected, it is mixed with the intolerance of youth, it calls for the forcible repression of opposition within the country and a battling front to be presented to the outside world. This is the outpouring of a student writing in the official organ of the Nazi students' league:

A people organically united and filled with the spirit of sacrifice for the common good, strong and eager for battle. A people fused into an unconquerable fighting unit against a hostile world. This is what we must achieve in these incomparably important days. The millions who stand aside from our movement must be made to believe in it. He is a traitor who now holds back. Our revolution marches on, over saboteurs and counter-revolutionaries, whoever they be.

The students . . . dream of reform in the courts of justice which is to be brought about by requiring each candidate for the bar to serve for eight weeks in a labor camp, working shoulder to shoulder with men from all walks of life. In every way the barriers between workers and students must be abolished. "We must strive against intellectualism and liberalism which are Jewish. We wish to be red-blooded men. Students, show the peasant and worker that you are not intellectuals.". . .

And here is one of the songs which the boys and girls sing as they march through the streets.

Seest thou the morning red in the East, a promise of sun and of freedom? We hold together for life or for death, no matter what may threaten. Many a year were we slaves to traitor Jews, but now has arisen a son of the people—he gives to Germany new hope and faith. Brothers, to arms! Young and old flock to the hooked cross banner, peasants and workers with sword and hammer. For Hitler, for freedom, for work and for bread. Germany, awaken! Death to the Jew! Brothers, to arms! . . .

In spite of the strict censorship of the press, we heard many a bloody tale of the Storm Troopers, but we heard even more about their high-handed methods in business houses and in the universities. While we were in Berlin the struggle was going on between the Nazi students and the rector of the university. It was on the issue of academic freedom. The students had nailed up twelve theses in the entrance hall of the main building and refused to take them down at the command of the rector. These were the theses that called for the expulsion of all "non-German teachers," that demanded that Jews should write only in Hebrew and that repudiated "Jewish intellectualism.". . .

It was only too clear that whatever group had put up the theses ruled the university, and there were proofs aplenty that this was true. The rector threatened to resign if the proclamation was not removed. He did resign and his

successor declared himself to be unreservedly behind the Nazi student movement. The new "Cultus-minister" soon afterward dissolved all student organizations and announced that there would be in the future one only, the Nazi students' league. He went on to praise the part played by the students in the revolution and to warn the faculties that they must no longer lag behind when youth led the way.

No wonder the students took things into their own hands, howled down the few Jewish professors who had received exceptional treatment because of war service, raided libraries, denounced suspected liberals right and left! The students of Kiel University demanded the discharge of twenty-eight professors. In Hamburg, when the university formally opened after the Spring holidays, a student arose and addressed the rector and faculty, telling them that any young Nazi was worth more to the Fatherland than the whole lot of them. His speech was received in silence. . . .

All this seemed simply stupid and ugly and primitive to an American, an incomprehensible swing-back to a day when physical force was the only thing respected and men of thought shut themselves in monasteries and were not always safe there. But this is an aspect which the students with whom I talked could not see. They were passionately behind the new movement, the revolt against intellectualism, against scientific objectivity, against all that the German universities had stood for. The burning of the books was their work and they were proud of it.

This revolt of youth against modern education is a part of Hitler's program, for Hitler has long preached the necessity for a new pedagogy, one that is directed first toward physical prowess, then character training, while purely intellectual subjects are to be left for specialists. Herr Frick, Minister of the Interior, said while I was there: "The mistake of the past was for the school to train the child as an individual. This led, especially after the war, to the destruction of nation and State. We will supplant it by a training which will sink into the blood and flesh and cannot be uprooted for generations, a training which will fuse the German into his nation and bind him by the closest ties to his history and the destiny of his people."

The most important subject in the new curriculum is history, with the emphasis laid on German heroes, German inventors, German rulers, poets, artists. The German child must be taught that his nation is superior to every other in every field. Next to this comes politics and then everything that has to do with agriculture. Such subjects as mathematics and the physical sciences take a secondary place. Physical training and mental training find their culminating point in the last year, which is the year of compulsory service in labor camps. The training in these camps is military, for "defense warfare." For girls, education ends in a year of domestic service, with training for wifehood and motherhood.

In his autobiography and in his voluminous speeches Hitler reveals himself as a man with the ambitions, the ideals, the crudities and the virtues of the adolescent. His physical courage and daring are those of the perfect soldier: he cares nothing for ease and comfort; he adores display, applause; he worships force and despises persuasion and mutual concession; he is intolerant of dissent, convinced of his own absolute rightness, and ready to commit any cruelty to carry out his own will.

It is this violent, fanatical, youthful despot, backed by some millions of like-minded youths, who now rules Germany. Truly it is a new thing in the world—a great modern country submitting itself to the will of its young men.

Johannes Stark
"JEWISH SCIENCE" VERSUS "GERMAN SCIENCE"

Several prominent German scientists endorsed the new regime and tried to make science conform to Nazi ideology. In 1934, Johannes Stark (1874–1957), who had won a Nobel Prize for his work in electromagnetism, requested fellow German Nobel Prize winners to sign a declaration supporting "Adolf Hitler . . . the savior and leader of the German people." In the following passage, Stark made the peculiar assertion that "German science" was based on an objective analysis of nature, whereas "Jewish science" (German Jews had distinguished themselves in science and medicine) sacrificed objectivity to self-interest and a subjective viewpoint.

But aside from this fundamental National Socialist demand, the slogan of the international character of science is based on an untruth, insofar as it asserts that the type and the success of scientific activity are independent of membership in a national group. Nobody can seriously assert that art is international. It is similar with science. Insofar as scientific work is not merely imitation but actual creation, like any other creative activity it is conditioned by the spiritual and characterological endowments of its practitioners. Since the individual members of a people have a common endowment, the creative activity of the scientists of a nation, as much as that of its artists and poets, thus assumes the stamp of a distinctive Volkish type. No, science is not international; it is just as national as art. This can be shown by the example of Germans and Jews in the natural sciences.

Science is the knowledge of the uniform interconnection of facts; the purpose of natural science in particular is the investigation of bodies and processes outside of the human mind, through observation and, insofar as possible, through the setting up of planned experiments. The spirit of the German enables him to observe things outside himself exactly as they are, without the interpolation of his own ideas and wishes, and his body does not shrink from the effort which the investigation of nature demands of him. The German's love of nature and his aptitude for natural science are based on this endowment. Thus it is understandable that natural science is overwhelmingly a creation of the Nordic-Germanic blood component of the Aryan peoples. Anyone who, in Lenard's classic work *Grosse Naturforscher (Great Investigators of Nature),* compares the faces of the outstanding natural scientists will find this common Nordic-Germanic feature in almost all of them. The ability to observe and respect facts, in complete disregard of the "I," is the most characteristic feature of the scientific activity of Germanic types. In addition, there is the joy and satisfaction the German derives from the acquisition of scientific knowledge, since it is principally this with which he is concerned. It is only under pressure that he decides to make his findings public, and the propaganda for them and their commercial exploitation appear to him as degradations of his scientific work.

The Jewish spirit is wholly different in its orientation: above everything else it is focused upon its own ego, its own conception, and its self-interest—and behind its egocentric conception stands its strong will to win recognition for itself and its interests. In accordance with this natural orientation the Jewish spirit strives to heed facts only to the extent that they do not hamper its opinions and purposes, and to bring them in such a connection with each other as is expedient for effecting its opinions and purposes. The Jew, therefore, is the born advocate who, unencumbered by regard for truth, mixes facts and imputations topsy-turvy in the endeavor to secure the court decision he desires. On the other hand, because of these characteristics, the Jewish spirit has little aptitude for creative activity in the sciences because it takes the individual's thinking and will as the measure of things, whereas science demands observation and respect for the facts.

It is true, however, that the Jewish spirit, thanks to the flexibility of its intellect, is capable, through imitation of Germanic examples, of producing noteworthy accomplishments, but it is not able to rise to authentic creative work, to great discoveries in the natural sciences. In recent times the Jews have frequently invoked the name of Heinrich Hertz as a counter-argument to this thesis. True, Heinrich Hertz made the great discovery of electromagnetic waves, but he was not a full-blooded Jew. He had a German mother, from whose side his spiritual endowment may well have been conditioned. When the Jew in natural science abandons the Germanic example and engages in scientific work according to his own spiritual particularity, he turns to theory. His main object is not the observation of facts and their true-to-reality presentation, but the view which he forms about them and the formal exposition to which he subjects them. In the interest of his theory he will suppress facts that are not in keeping with it and likewise, still in the interest of his theory, he will engage in propaganda on its behalf.

Jakob Graf
HEREDITY AND RACIAL BIOLOGY FOR STUDENTS

The following assignments from a textbook entitled *Hereditary and Racial Biology for Students* (1935) show how young people were indoctrinated with racist teachings.

HOW WE CAN LEARN TO RECOGNIZE A PERSON'S RACE
Assignments

1. Summarize the spiritual characteristics of the individual races.

2. Collect from stories, essays, and poems examples of ethnological illustrations. Underline those terms which describe the type and mode of the expression of the soul.

3. What are the expressions, gestures, and movements which allow us to make conclusions as to the attitude of the racial soul?

4. Determine also the physical features which go hand in hand with the specific racial soul characteristics of the individual figures.

5. Try to discover the intrinsic nature of the racial soul through the characters in stories and poetical works in terms of their inner attitude. Apply this mode of observation to persons in your own environment.

6. Collect propaganda posters and caricatures for your race book and arrange them according to a racial scheme. What image of beauty is emphasized by the artist (a) in posters publicizing sports and travel? (b) in publicity for cosmetics? How are hunters, mountain climbers, and shepherds drawn?

7. Collect from illustrated magazines, newspapers, etc., pictures of great scholars, statesmen, artists, and others who distinguish themselves by their special accomplishments (for example, in economic life, politics, sports). Determine the preponderant race and admixture, according to physical characteristics. Repeat this exercise with the pictures of great men of all nations and times.

8. When viewing monuments, busts, etc., be sure to pay attention to the race of the person portrayed with respect to figure, bearing, and physical characteristics. Try to harmonize these determinations with the features of the racial soul.

9. Observe people whose special racial features have drawn your attention, also with respect to their bearing when moving or when speaking. Observe their expressions and gestures.

10. Observe the Jew: his way of walking, his bearing, gestures, and movements when talking.

11. What strikes you about the way a Jew talks and sings?

Louis P. Lochner
BOOK BURNING

The anti-intellectualism of the Nazis was demonstrated on May 10, 1933, when the principal German student body organized students for a book-burning festival. In university towns, students consigned to the flames books that were considered a threat to the Germanic spirit. Louis P. Lochner (1887–1975), head of the Associated Press Bureau in Berlin, gave an eyewitness account of the scene in the German capital in *The Goebbels Diaries 1942–43.*

The whole civilized world was shocked when on the evening of May 10, 1933, the books of authors displeasing to the Nazis, including even those of our own Helen Keller, were solemnly burned on the immense Franz Joseph Platz between the University of Berlin and the State Opera on Unter den Linden. I was a witness to the scene.

All afternoon Nazi raiding parties had gone into public and private libraries, throwing onto the streets such books as Dr. [Joseph] Goebbels [Nazi Progaganda Minister] in his supreme wisdom had decided were unfit for Nazi Germany. From the streets Nazi columns of beerhall fighters had picked up these discarded volumes and taken them to the square above referred to.

Here the heap grew higher and higher, and every few minutes another howling mob arrived, adding more books to the impressive pyre. Then, as night fell, students from the university, mobilized by the little doctor, performed veritable Indian dances and incantations as the flames began to soar skyward.

When the orgy was at its height, a cavalcade of cars drove into sight. It was the Propaganda Minister himself, accompanied by his bodyguard and a number of fellow torch bearers of the new Nazi *Kultur*.

"Fellow students, German men and women!" he said as he stepped before a microphone for all Germany to hear him. "The age of extreme Jewish intellectualism has now ended, and the success of the German revolution has again given the right of way to the German spirit. . . .

"You are doing the right thing in committing the evil spirit of the past to the flames at this late hour of the night. It is a strong, great, and symbolic act—an act that is to bear witness before all the world to the fact that the spiritual foundation of the November Republic has disappeared. From the ashes there will rise the phoenix of a new spirit. . . .

"The past is lying in flames. The future will rise from the flames within our own hearts. . . . Brightened by these flames our vow shall be: The Reich and the Nation and our Fuehrer Adolf Hitler: *Heil! Heil! Heil!*"

The few foreign correspondents who had taken the trouble to view this "symbolic act" were stunned. What had happened to the "Land of Thinkers and Poets?" they wondered.

REVIEW QUESTIONS

1. How did Alice Hamilton interpret repression and coercion in the universities?
2. What educational theory did the Nazis espouse?
3. The idealism of youth has often been praised. What dangers did Hamilton see in this idealism?
4. What, in Johannes Stark's view, made the Nordic, Aryan people especially fitted for scientific creativity? What disqualified the non-Nordic, especially the Jewish, people from achievement in science?
5. What was Jakob Graf's purpose in teaching students how to recognize a person's race? What would your reaction be if you were given such an assignment today?
6. Why do you think the Nazis made the burning of books a public event? Why does book burning have such potent symbolism?

10 Persecution of the Jews

The Nazis deprived Jews of their German citizenship and instituted many anti-Jewish measures designed to make them outcasts. Thousands of Jewish doctors, lawyers, musicians, artists, and professors were barred from practicing their professions, and Jewish members of the civil service were dismissed. A series of laws tightened the screws of humiliation and persecution. Marriages or sexual encounters between Germans and Jews were forbidden. Universities, schools, restaurants, pharmacies. hospitals, theaters, museums, and athletic fields were gradually closed to Jews.

In November 1938, using, as a pretext, the assassination of a German official in Paris by a seventeen-year-old Jewish youth whose family had been mistreated by the Nazis, the Nazis organized an extensive pogrom. Nazis gangs murdered scores of Jews and burned and looted thousands of Jewish businesses, homes, and synagogues all over Germany—an event that became known as Night of the Broken Glass *(Kristallnacht)*. Twenty thousand Jews were thrown into concentration camps. The Reich then imposed on the Jewish community a fine of 1 billion marks. By the outbreak of the war in September 1939, approximately one-half of Germany's 600,000 Jews had fled the country. Those who stayed behind would fall victim to the last stage of the Nazi anti-Jewish campaign—the Final Solution.

Hertha Nathorff
A GERMAN JEWISH DOCTOR'S DIARY

Hertha Nathorff, niece of Albert Einstein, practiced medicine in Berlin. In her diary, she recorded the constant abuse and humiliation inflicted on Jews as a result of Nazi anti-Semitic policies. Dr. Nathorff managed to leave Germany in 1939 before the outbreak of war. Following are excerpts from her diary.

1 April 1933

Jewish Boycott.

This day is engraved in my heart in flames. To think that such things are still possible in the twentieth century. In front of all Jewish shops, lawyers' offices, doctors' surgeries and flats there are young boys with signs saying, 'Don't buy from Jews', 'Don't go to Jewish doctors', 'Anybody who buys from Jews is a traitor', 'Jews are the incarnation of lies and deceit.' Doctors' signs on the walls of houses are soiled, and sometimes damaged, and people have looked on, gawping in silence. They must have forgotten to stick anything over my sign. I think I would have reacted violently. It was afternoon before one of these boys visited me at home and asked: 'Is this a Jewish business?' 'This isn't a business at all; it's a doctor's surgery', I said. 'Are you sick?' After these ironic words the youth disappeared without posting anybody in front of my door. Of course some patients who had appointments did not turn up. One woman rang to say that of course she couldn't come today, and I said that it would be better if she didn't come any more at

all. For my own part, I shopped deliberately in places where such pickets were posted. One of them wanted to stop me going into a little soap shop, but I pushed him to one side, saying, 'I'll spend my money where I want.' Why doesn't everybody do that? That would soon settle the boycott. But people are a cowardly lot, as I know only too well.

In the evening we were with friends at the Hohenzollerndamm, three couples, all doctors. They were all quite depressed. One of the company, Emil, the optimist, tried to convince us: 'It'll all be over in a few days.' They don't understand my anger when I say, 'They should strike us dead instead. It would be more humane than the psychological death they have in mind. . . .' But my instincts have always proved right.

25 April 1933

A letter from Charlottenburg municipal authorities: 'You are requested to cease your activity as senior doctor at the women's advice centre!' Full stop.

Thrown out then—full stop. My poor women, whose hands will they fall into now? I've run that place for five years, expanded it and made it well known, and now? It's all over. I have to repeat it again and again, in order to be able to grasp it.

30 August 1933

Back from holidays in southern Germany. How tense the atmosphere is there. The situation is completely changed in my home town, where everyone knows everyone else.

My family have lived in that small town for two hundred years, looked up to, respected and now. . . . My old father said to me in passing that he no longer goes to his local [pub]. Mother got rather worked up because nobody knows how to greet her properly any more.

A friend of my sister's, a lawyer's wife, comes to visit only in the evenings after dark, until my sister suggests she doesn't bother coming at all. The Catholics are beside themselves with fear and dread. Where will it all end?

2 October 1934

I have just come from the H. mental asylum. They rang to ask if I would come. A patient had arrived during the night who was calling for me. She had been picked up on the street, in front of a hospital. They thought she was drunk, the way she was behaving, talking, crying in the street, and giving away her possessions to passers-by. Then she was brought to the asylum. Did I know her? A young colleague who is not allowed to practise. Her licence has been taken away. A love affair with an Aryan colleague suddenly came to an end. Then she tried to work as a nurse, and it proved too much for her soul, for her intellect. As a result she had gone mad.

30 November 1934

I have been to southern Germany. My dear father was seriously ill. The things I had to do to get the doctor treating him—it would be unprofessional to comment on his medical ability—to agree to send him for a consultation with the capable specialist in Ulm! 'One can't consult a Jewish doctor!' He would rather treat the patient wrongly and badly! He should be grateful that he can get an Aryan doctor to come at all. There is no Jewish doctor left in the small town, and the other Nazi doctor does not treat Jews. It's almost like the camps where they have imprisoned innocent people. 'If one happens to be a Jew, one is either healthy or dead!'

One of the Catholic nurses looking after Father told me: 'Frau Doktor, we needn't fear hell any more. The devil is already abroad in the world.'

30 December 1934

Three more suicides by people who could no longer stand the continuing defamation and spite.

The boy is afraid to go on the ice rink. Yesterday Jewish children were chased away and beaten up.

9 October 1935

I met my former secretary today. She fixed me sharply with her short-sighted eyes, and then turned away. I was so nauseated I spat into my handkerchief. She was once a patient of mine. Later I met her in the street. Her boyfriend had left her and she was out of work and without money. I took her on, trained her for years and employed her in my clinic until the last day. Now she has changed so much that she can no longer greet me; me, who rescued her from the gutter!

I never go anywhere any more. I am so well known through my profession and my position; why should I make trouble for myself and for others? I'm happy to be at home in peace.

4 December 1935

Miss G. in the surgery, completely broken. She knows nothing of Jews and Jewry. Suddenly they've dug up her Jewish grandmother! She is no longer allowed to work as an artist, and she must give up her boyfriend, a senior officer. She wants something 'to end it all.' She can only groan pitifully, 'I can't go on living.' What can I do? I can no longer help my patients, it's a living death for me.

5 August 1938

There was a telephone call as we were sitting at the table with guests. I went to the telephone myself. A colleague, S., who asks: 'Have you been listening to the radio?' 'No', I say, 'what's happened now?' The colleague, usually so calm, says with a trembling, angry voice: 'What you always said would happen. They're taking away our licenses, we are no longer allowed to practise—it's just been on the radio.' 'On the radio.' This is how we learn that they are taking away from us what we earned through years of study, what we were taught by eminent professors, famous universities. . . . All I could think at that moment was: 'And now I have to tell my husband.' How I went calmly back to the dining table, drew the meal to a close, and told my guests, 'It's nothing much', I don't know; I know only that I sat at the desk, my hands clenched and said to my husband: 'It's over—over—over.' He went to get a paper, and it had already been reported. This is how we Jewish doctors learnt of our death sentence. In the clinic they are all in a state of complete despair.

Marta Appel
MEMOIRS OF A GERMAN JEWISH WOMAN

Marta Appel and her husband, Dr. Ernst Appel, a rabbi in the city of Dortmund, fled Germany in 1937. In 1940–1941, while in the United States, she wrote her memoirs, which described conditions in Dortmund after the Nazis took power.

The children had been advised not to come to school on April 1, 1933, the day of the boycott. Even the principal of the school thought Jewish children's lives were no longer safe. One night they placed big signs on every store or house owned by Jewish people. In front of our temple, on every square and corner, billboards were scoffing at us. Everywhere, and on all occasions, we read and heard that we were vermin and had caused the ruin of the German people. No Jewish store was closed on that day, none was willing to show fear in the face of the boycott. The only building which did not open its door as usual, since it was Saturday, was the temple. We did not want this holy place desecrated by any trouble.

I even went downtown that day to see what was going on in the city. There was no cheering crowd as the Nazis had expected, no running and smashing of Jewish businesses. I heard only words of anger and disapproval. People were massed before the Jewish stores to watch the Nazi guards who were posted there to prevent anyone from entering to buy. And there were many courageous enough to enter, although they were called rude names by the Nazi guards, and their pictures were taken to show them as enemies of the German people in the daily papers. . . .

Our gentile friends and neighbors, even people whom we had scarcely known before, came to assure us of their friendship and to tell us that these horrors could not last very long. But after some months of a regime of terror, fidelity and friendship had lost their meaning, and fear and treachery had replaced them. For the sake of our gentile friends, we turned our heads so as not to greet them in the streets, for we did not want to bring upon them the danger of imprisonment for being considered a friend of Jews.

With each day of the Nazi regime, the abyss between us and our fellow citizens grew larger. Friends whom we had loved for years did not know us anymore. They suddenly saw that we were different from themselves. Of course we were different, since we were bearing the stigma of Nazi hatred, since we were hunted like deer. Through the prominent position of my husband we were in constant danger. Often we were warned to stay away from home. We were no longer safe, wherever we went.

How much our life changed in those days! Often it seemed to me I could not bear it any longer, but thinking of my children, I knew we had to be strong to make it easier for them. From then on I hated to go out, since on every corner I saw signs that the Jews were the misfortune of the people. . . .

In the evenings we sat at home at the radio listening fearfully to all the new and outrageous restrictions and laws which almost daily brought further suffering to Jewish people. . . .

Since I had lived in Dortmund, I had met every four weeks with a group of women, all of whom were born in Metz, my beloved home city. We all had been pupils or teachers in the same high school. After the Nazis came, I was afraid to go to the meetings. I did not want the presence of a Jewess to bring any trouble, since we always met publicly in a café. One day on the street, I met one of my old teachers, and with tears in her eyes she begged me: "Come again to us; we miss you; we feel ashamed that you must think we do not want you anymore. Not one of us has changed in her feeling toward you." She tried to convince me that they were still my friends, and tried to take away my doubts. I de-cided to go to the next meeting. It was a hard decision, and I had not slept the night before. I was afraid for my gentile friends. For nothing in the world did I wish to bring them trouble by my attendance, and I was also afraid for myself. I knew I would watch them, noticing the slightest expression of embarrassment in their eyes when I came. I knew they could not deceive me; I would be aware of every change in their voices. Would they be afraid to talk to me?

It was not necessary for me to read their eyes or listen to the change in their voices. The empty table in the little alcove which always had been reserved for us spoke the clearest language. It was even unnecessary for the waiter to come and say that a lady phoned that morning not to reserve the table thereafter. I could not blame them. Why should they risk losing a position only to prove to me that we still had friends in Germany?

I, personally, did not mind all those disappointments, but when my children had to face them, and were not spared being offended everywhere, my heart was filled with anguish. It required a great deal of inner strength, of love and harmony among the Jewish families, to make our children strong enough to bear all that persecution and hatred. . . . My heart was broken when I saw tears in my younger child's eyes when she had been sent home from school while all the others had been taken to a show or some other pleasure. It was not because she was denied going to the show that my little girl was weeping—she knew her Mommy always could take her—but because she had to stay apart, as if she were not good enough to associate with her comrades any longer. It was this that made it hard and bitter for her. I think that even the Nazi teacher sometimes felt ashamed when she looked into the sad eyes of my little girl, since several times, when the class was going out for pleasure, she phoned not to send her to school. Maybe it was not right to hate this teacher so much, since everything she did had been upon orders, but it was she who brought so much bitterness to my child, and never can I forget it.

Almost every lesson began to be a torture for Jewish children. There was not one subject anymore which was not used to bring up the Jewish question. And in the presence of Jewish children the teachers denounced all the Jews, without exception, as scoundrels and as the most destructive force in every country where they were living. My children were not permitted to leave the room during such a talk; they were compelled to stay and to listen; they had to feel all the other children's eyes looking and staring at them, the examples of an outcast race.

Every day they had to face another degrading and offensive incident. As Mother's Day came near, the children were practicing songs at school to celebrate that day. Every year on that occasion the whole school gathered in a joint festival. It was the day before when my girls were ordered to see the music teacher. "You have to be present for the festival," the teacher told them, "but since you are Jewish, you are not allowed to join in the songs." "Why can't we sing?" my children protested with tears in their eyes. "We have a mother too, and we wish to sing for her." But it seemed the teacher did not want to understand the children's feelings. Curtly she rebuked their protest. "I know you have a mother," she said haughtily, "but she is only a Jewish mother." At that the girls had no reply; there was no use to speak any longer to the teacher, but seldom had they been so much disturbed as when they came from school that day, when someone had tried to condemn their mother. . . .

One day, for the first time in a long while, I saw my children coming back from school with shining eyes, laughing and giggling together. Most of the classes had been gathered that morning in the big hall, since an official of the new *Rasseamt,* the office of races, had come to give a talk about the differences of races. "I asked the teacher if I could go home," my daughter was saying, "but she told me she had orders not to dismiss anyone. You may imagine it was an awful talk. He said that there are two groups of races, a high group and a low one. The high and upper race that was destined to rule the world was the Teutonic, the German race, while one of the lowest races was the Jewish race. And then, Mommy, he looked around and asked one of the girls to come to him." The children again began to giggle about their experience. "First we did not know," my girl continued, "what he intended, and we were very afraid when he picked out Eva. Then he began, and he was pointing at Eva, 'Look here, the small head of this girl, her long forehead, her very blue eyes, and blond hair,' and he was lifting one of her long blond braids. 'And look,' he said, 'at her tall and slender figure. These are the unequivocal marks of a pure and unmixed Teutonic race.' Mommy, you should have heard how at this moment all the girls burst into laughter. Even Eva could not help laughing. Then from all sides of the hall there was shouting, 'She is a Jewess!' You should have seen the officer's face! I guess he was lucky that the principal got up so quickly and, with a sign to the pupils, stopped the laughing and shouting and dismissed the man, thanking him for his interesting and very enlightening talk. At that we began again to laugh, but he stopped us immediately. Oh, I was so glad that the teacher had not dismissed me and I was there to hear it."

When my husband came home, they told him and enjoyed it again and again. And we were thankful to know that they still had not completely forgotten how to laugh and to act like happy children.

"If only I could take my children out of here!" That thought was occupying my mind more and more. I no longer hoped for any change as did my husband. Besides, even a changed Germany could not make me forget that all our friends, the whole nation, had abandoned us in our need. It was no longer the same country for me. Everything had changed, not people alone—the city, the forest, the river—the whole country looked different in my eyes.

11 The Anguish of the Intellectuals

A somber mood gripped European intellectuals in the postwar period. The memory of World War I and the hypernationalism behind it, the rise of totalitarianism, and the Great Depression caused intellectuals to have grave doubts about the nature and destiny of Western civilization. To many European liberals, it seemed that the sun was setting on the Enlightenment tradition, that the ideals of reason and freedom, already gravely weakened by World War I, could not endure the threats posed by resurgent chauvinism, economic collapse, and totalitarian ideologies.

José Ortega y Gasset
THE REVOLT OF THE MASSES

One of the thinkers who feared for the ideals of reason and freedom was the Spanish philosopher José Ortega y Gasset (1883–1955). In *The Revolt of the Masses* (1930), Ortega held that European civilization was degenerating into barbarism because of the growing power of the intellectually undisciplined and culturally unrefined masses. Ortega did not equate the masses with the working class and the elite with the nobility. For him, what distinguished the "mass-man" was an attitude that renounced rational dialogue in favor of violence and compulsion and demanded uniformity of thought. These threats to Western civilization, he said, were exemplified in both communism and fascism. Excerpts from *The Revolt of the Masses* follow.

There is one fact which, whether for good or ill, is of utmost importance in the public life of Europe at the present moment. This fact is the accession of the masses to complete social power. As the masses, by definition, neither should nor can direct their own personal existence, and still less rule society in general, this fact means that actually Europe is suffering from the greatest crisis that can afflict peoples, nations, and civilisation. . . .

Strictly speaking, the mass, as a psychological fact, can be defined without waiting for individuals to appear in mass formation. In the presence of one individual we can decide whether he is "mass" or not. The mass is all that which sets no value on itself—good or ill—based on specific grounds, but which feels itself "just like everybody," and nevertheless is not concerned about it; is, in fact, quite happy to feel itself as one with everybody else. . . .

. . . The mass believes that it has the right to impose and to give force of law to notions born in the café. I doubt whether there have been other periods of history in which the multitude has come to govern more directly than in our own. . . .

. . . *The characteristic of the hour is that the commonplace mind, knowing itself to be commonplace, has the assurance to proclaim the rights of the commonplace and to impose them wherever it will.* As they say in the United States: "to be different is to be indecent." The mass crushes beneath it everything that is different, everything that is excellent, individual, qualified and select. Anybody who is not like everybody, who does not think like everybody, runs the risk of being eliminated. . . .

. . . It is illusory to imagine that the massman of to-day . . . will be able to control, by himself, the process of civilisation. I say process, and not progress. The simple process of preserving our present civilisation is supremely complex, and demands incalculably subtle powers. Ill-fitted to direct it is this average man who has learned to use much of the machinery of civilisation, but who is characterised by root-ignorance of the very principles of that civilisation. . . .

The command over public life exercised to-day by the intellectually vulgar is perhaps the factor of the present situation which is most novel, least assimilable to anything in the past. At least in European history up to the present, the vulgar had never believed itself to have "ideas" on things. It had beliefs, traditions, experiences, proverbs, mental habits, but it never imagined itself in possession of theoretical opinions on what things are or ought to be. . . . To-day, on the other hand, the average man has the most mathematical "ideas" on all that happens or ought to happen in the universe. Hence he has lost the use of his hearing. Why should he listen if he has within him all that is necessary? There is no reason now for listening, but rather for judging, pronouncing, deciding. There is no question concerning public life, in which he does not intervene, blind and deaf as he is, imposing his "opinions."

But, is that not an advantage? Is it not a sign of immense progress that the masses should have "ideas," that is to say, should be cultured? By no means. The "ideas" of the average man are not genuine ideas, nor is their possession culture. . . . Whoever wishes to have ideas must first prepare himself to desire truth and to accept the rules of the game imposed by it. It is no use speaking of ideas when there is no acceptance of a higher authority to regulate them, a series of standards to which it is possible to appeal in a discussion. These standards are the principles on which culture rests. I am not concerned with the form they take. What I

affirm is that there is no culture where there are no standards to which our fellow-men can have recourse. There is no culture where there are no principles of legality to which to appeal. There is no culture where there is no acceptance of certain final intellectual positions to which a dispute may be referred. There is no culture where economic relations are not subject to a regulating principle to protect interests involved. There is no culture where aesthetic controversy does not recognise the necessity of justifying the work of art.

When all these things are lacking there is no culture; there is in the strictest sense of the word, barbarism. And let us not deceive ourselves, this is what is beginning to appear in Europe under the progressive rebellion of the masses. The traveller who arrives in a barbarous country knows that in that territory there are no ruling principles to which it is possible to appeal. Properly speaking, there are no barbarian standards. Barbarism is the absence of standards to which appeal can be made. . . .

. . . Under . . . Fascism there appears for the first time in Europe a type of man who does not want to give reasons or to be right, but simply shows himself resolved to impose his opinions. This is the new thing: the right not to be reasonable, the "reason of unreason." Here I see the most palpable manifestation of the new mentality of the masses, due to their having decided to rule society without the capacity for doing so. In their political conduct the structure of the new mentality is revealed in the rawest, most convincing manner. . . . The average man finds himself with "ideas" in his head, but he lacks the faculty of ideation. He has no conception even of the rare atmosphere in which ideas live. He wishes to have opinions, but is unwilling to accept the conditions and presuppositions that underlie all opinion. Hence his ideas are in effect nothing more than appetites in words. . . .

To have an idea means believing one is in possession of the reasons for having it, and consequently means believing that there is such a thing as reason, a world of intelligible truths. To have ideas, to form opinions, is identical with appealing to such an authority, submitting oneself to it, accepting its code and its decisions, and therefore believing that the highest form of intercommunion is the dialogue in which the reasons for our ideas are discussed. But the mass-man would feel himself lost if he accepted discussion, and instinctively repudiates the obligation of accepting that supreme authority lying outside himself. Hence the "new thing" in Europe is "to have done with discussions," and detestation is expressed for all forms of intercommunion which imply acceptance of objective standards, ranging from conversation to Parliament, and taking in science. This means that there is a renunciation of the common life based on culture, which is subject to standards, and a return to the common life of barbarism. All the normal processes are suppressed in order to arrive directly at the imposition of what is desired. The hermetism [closing off] of the soul which, as we have seen before, urges the mass to intervene in the whole of public life.

Arthur Koestler
"I WAS RIPE TO BE CONVERTED"

The economic misery of the Depression and the rise of fascist barbarism led many intellectuals to find a new hope, even a secular faith, in communism. They praised the Soviet Union for supplanting capitalist greed with socialist cooperation, for recognizing the dignity of work, for replacing a haphazard economic system marred by repeated depressions with one based on planned production, and for providing employment for everyone when joblessness was endemic in capitalist lands. Seduced by Soviet propaganda and desperate for an alternative to crisis-ridden liberal society, these intellectuals saw the Soviet Union as a champion of peace and social justice. To these intellectuals, it seemed that in the Soviet Union a vigorous and healthy civilization was emerging and that only communism could stem the tide of fascism. For many, however, the attraction was short-lived. Sickened by Stalin's purges and terror, the denial of individual freedom, and suppression of truth, they came to view the Soviet Union as another totalitarian state and communism as another "god that failed."

One such intellectual was Arthur Koestler. Born in Budapest of Jewish ancestry and educated in Vienna, Koestler worked as a correspondent for a leading Berlin newspaper chain. He joined the Communist Party at the very end of 1931 because he "lived in a disintegrating society thirsting for faith," was sensitized by the Depression, and saw communism as the "only force capable of resisting the inrush of the primitive [Nazi] horde." In 1938, he broke with the Party in response to Stalin's liquidations. In the following passage, written in 1949, Koestler recalled the attraction communism had held for him.

A faith is not acquired by reasoning. One does not fall in love with a woman, or enter the womb of a church, as a result of logical persuasion. Reason may defend an act of faith— but only after the act has been committed, and the man committed to the act. Persuasion may play a part in a man's conversion; but only the part of bringing to its full and conscious climax a process which has been maturing in regions where no persuasion can penetrate. A faith is not acquired; it grows like a tree. Its crown points to the sky; its roots grow downward into the past and are nourished by the dark sap of the ancestral humus. . . .

I became converted because I was ripe for it and lived in a disintegrating society thirsting for faith. But the day when I was given my Party card was merely the climax of a development which had started long before I had read about the drowned pigs or heard the names of Marx and Lenin. Its roots reach back into childhood; and though each of us, comrades of the Pink Decade, had individual roots with different twists in them, we are products of, by and large, the same generation and cultural climate. It is this unity underlying diversity which makes me hope that my story is worth telling.

I was born in 1905 in Budapest; we lived there till 1919, when we moved to Vienna. Until the First World War we were comfortably off, a typical Continental middle-middle-class family: my father was the Hungarian representative of some old-established British and German textile manufacturers. In September, 1914, this form of existence, like so many others, came to an abrupt end; my father never found his feet again. He embarked on a number of ventures which became the more fantastic the more he lost self-confidence in a changed world. He opened a factory for radioactive soap; he backed several crank-inventions (everlasting electric bulbs, self-heating bed bricks and the like); and finally lost the remains of his capital in the Austrian inflation of the early 'twenties. I left home at twenty-one, and from that day became the only financial support of my parents.

At the age of nine, when our middle-class idyl collapsed, I had suddenly become conscious of the economic Facts of Life. As an only child, I continued to be pampered by my parents; but, well aware of the family crisis, and torn by pity for my father, who was of a generous and somewhat childlike disposition, I suffered a pang of guilt whenever they bought me books or toys. This continued later on, when every suit I bought for myself meant so much less to send home. Simultaneously, I developed a strong dislike of the obviously rich; not because they could afford to buy things (envy plays a much smaller part in social conflict than is generally assumed) but because they

were able to do so without a guilty conscience. Thus I projected a personal predicament onto the structure of society at large.

It was certainly a tortuous way of acquiring a social conscience. But precisely because of the intimate nature of the conflict, the faith which grew out of it became an equally intimate part of my self. It did not, for some years, crystallize into a political creed; at first it took the form of a mawkishly sentimental attitude. Every contact with people poorer than myself was unbearable—the boy at school who had no gloves and red chilblains [inflamed swellings produced by exposure to cold] on his fingers, the former traveling salesman of my father's reduced to [begging] occasional meals—all of them were additions to the load of guilt on my back. The analyst would have no difficulty in showing that the roots of this guilt-complex go deeper than the crisis in our household budget; but if he were to dig even deeper, piercing through the individual layers of the case, he would strike the archetypal pattern which has produced millions of particular variations on the same theme— "Woe, for they chant to the sound of harps and anoint themselves, but are not grieved for the affliction of the people."

Thus sensitized by a personal conflict, I was ripe for the shock of learning that wheat was burned, fruit artificially spoiled and pigs were drowned in the depression years to keep prices up and enable fat capitalists to chant to the sound of harps, while Europe trembled under the torn boots of hunger-marchers and my father hid his frayed cuffs under the table. The frayed cuffs and drowned pigs blended into one emotional explosion, as the fuse of the archetype was touched off. We sang the "Internationale" [the communists' anthem], but the words might as well have been the older ones: "Woe to the shepherds who feed themselves, but feed not their flocks."

In other respects, too, the story is more typical than it seems. A considerable proportion of the middle classes in central Europe was, like ourselves, ruined by the inflation of the 'twenties. It was the beginning of Europe's decline. This disintegration of the middle strata of society started the fatal process of polarization which continues to this day. The pauperized bourgeois became rebels of the Right or Left; Schickelgrüber [Hitler] and Djugashwili [Stalin] shared about equally the benefits of the social migration. Those who refused to admit that they had become déclassé, who clung to the empty shell of gentility, joined the Nazis and found comfort in blaming their fate on Versailles and the Jews. Many did not even have that consolation; they lived on pointlessly, like a great black swarm of tired winterflies crawling over the dim windows of Europe, members of a class displaced by history.

The other half turned Left, thus confirming the prophecy of the "Communist Manifesto":

> Entire sections of the ruling classes are . . . precipitated into the proletariat, or are at least threatened in their conditions of existence. They . . . supply the proletariat with fresh elements of enlightenment and progress. . . .

I was ripe to be converted, as a result of my personal case-history; thousands of other members of the intelligentsia and the middle classes of my generation were ripe for it, by virtue of other personal case-histories; but, however much these differed from case to case, they had a common denominator: the rapid disintegration of moral values, of the pre-1914 pattern of life in postwar Europe, and the simultaneous lure of the new revelation which had come from the East.

I joined the Party (which to this day remains "the" Party for all of us who once belonged to it) in 1931. . . .

I lived at that time in Berlin. For the last five years, I had been working for the Ullstein chain of newspapers—first as a foreign correspondent in Palestine and the Middle East, then in Paris. Finally, in 1930, I joined the editorial staff in the Berlin "House.". . .

. . . With one-third of its wage-earners unemployed, Germany lived in a state of latent civil war, and if one wasn't prepared to be swept along as a passive victim by the approaching hurricane it became imperative to take sides. . . . The Communists, with the mighty Soviet Union behind them, seemed the only force capable of resisting the onrush of the primitive horde with its swastika totem. I began for the first time to read Marx, Engels and Lenin in earnest. By the time I had finished with *Feuerbach* and *State and Revolution,* something had clicked in my brain which shook me like a mental explosion. To say that one had "seen the light" is a poor description of the mental rapture which only the convert knows (regardless of what faith he has been converted to). The new light seems to pour from all directions across the skull; the whole universe falls into pattern like the stray pieces of a jigsaw puzzle assembled by magic at one stroke. There is now an answer to every question, doubts and conflicts are a matter of the tortured past—a past already remote, when one had lived in dismal ignorance in the tasteless, colorless world of those who *don't know.* Nothing henceforth can disturb the convert's inner peace and serenity—except the occasional fear of losing faith again, losing thereby what alone makes life worth living, and falling back into the outer darkness, where there is wailing and gnashing of teeth.

Nicolas Berdyaev
MODERN IDEOLOGIES AT VARIANCE WITH CHRISTIANITY

To Nicolas Berdyaev, a Russian Christian philosopher who fled the Soviet Union, communism and Nazism were modern forms of idolatry in opposition to the core values of Christianity. Nationalism, he said, "dehumanizes ethics" and provokes hatred among peoples; Nazi racism, which demonizes Jews because of their genes, is "unworthy of a Christian." Only by a return to Christian piety, maintained Berdyaev, can we overcome the "collective demoniac possession" that is destroying European civilization. By Christian piety, he meant an active struggle for human dignity and social justice. Berdyaev expressed these views in *The Fate of Man in the Modern World* (1935), which is excerpted below.

We are witnessing the process of dehumanization in all phases of culture and of social life. Above all, moral consciousness is being dehumanized. Man has ceased to be the supreme value: he has ceased to have any value at all. The youth of the whole world, communist, fascist, national-socialist or those simply carried away by technics . . . this youth is not only anti-humanistic in its attitudes, but often anti-human. . . .

. . . A bestial cruelty toward man is characteristic of our age, and this is more astonishing since it is displayed at the very peak of human refinement, where modern conceptions of sympathy, it would seem, have made impossible the old, barbaric forms of cruelty. Bestialism is something quite different from the old, natural, healthy barbarism; it is barbarism within a refined civilization. Here the atavistic, barbaric instincts are filtered through the prism of civilization, and hence they have a pathological character. . . . The bestialism of our time is a continuation of the war, it has poisoned mankind with the blood of war. The morals of war-time have become those of "peaceful" life, which is actually the continuation of war, a war of all against all. According to this morality, everything is permissible: man may be used in any way desired for the attainment of inhuman or anti-human aims. Bestialism is a denial of the value of the human person, of every human personality; it is a denial of all sympathy with the fate of any man. The new humanism is closing: this is inescapable.

We are entering an inhuman world, a world of inhumanness, inhuman not merely in fact, but in principle as well. Inhumanity has begun to be presented as something noble, surrounded with an aureole of heroism. Over against man there rises a class or a race, a deified collective or state. Modern nationalism bears marks of bestial inhumanity. No longer is every man held to be a man, a value, the image and likeness of God. For often even Christianity is interpreted inhumanly. The "Aryan paragraph" offered to German Christians is the project for a new form of inhumanity in Christianity. . . .

. . . The new world which is taking form is moved by other values than the value of man or of human personality, or the value of truth: it is moved by such values as power, technics, race-purity, nationality, the state, the class, the collective. The will to justice is overcome by the will to power. . . .

. . . National passion is tearing the world and threatening the destruction of European culture. This is one more proof of the strength of atavism in human society, of how much stronger than the conscious is the subconscious, of how superficial has been the humanizing process of past centuries. . . . [M]odern Nationalism means the dehumanization and bestialization of human societies. It is a reversion from the category of culture and history to that of zoology. . . .

. . . The results of the Christian-humanistic process of unifying humanity seem to be disappearing. We are witnessing the paganization of Christian society. Nationalism is polytheism: it is incompatible with monotheism.

This process of paganization takes shocking forms in Germany, which wishes no longer to be a Christian nation, has exchanged the swastika for the cross and demands of Christians that they should renounce the very fundamentals of the Christian revelation and the Christian faith, and cast aside the moral teaching of the Gospels. . . .

Nationalism turns nationality into a supreme and absolute value to which all life is subordinated. This is idolatry. The nation replaces God. Thus Nationalism cannot but come into conflict with Christian universalism, with the Christian revelation that there is neither Greek nor Jew, and that every man has absolute value. Nationalism uses everything as its own instrument, as an instrument of national power and prosperity. . . .

. . . Nationalism has no Christian roots and it is always in conflict with Christianity. . . .

. . . Nationalism involves not only love of one's own, but hatred of other nations, and hatred is usually a stronger motive than love. Nationalism preaches either seclusion, isolation, blindness to other nations and culture, self-satisfaction and particularism, or else expansion at the expense of others, conquest, subjection, imperialism. And in both cases it denies Christian conscience, contraverts the principle and the habits of the brotherhood of man. Nationalism is in complete contradiction to a personal ethic; it denies the supreme value of human personality. Modern Nationalism dehumanizes ethics, it demands of man that he renounce humanity. It is all one and the same process, in Communism as in Nationalism. Man's inner world is completely at the mercy of collectivism, national or social. . . .

[R]acialism . . . has no basis at all in Christianity. The mere consideration of the "Aryan paragraph" is unworthy of a Christian, although it is now demanded of Christians in Germany. Racialist anti-Semitism inevitably leads to anti-Christianity, as we see in Germany to-day. That Germano-Aryan Christianity now being promoted is a denial of the Gospels and of Christ Himself. The ancient religious conflict between Christianity and Judaism, a real conflict by the way, has taken such a turn in our difficult and uncertain times, that militant anti-Judaism turns out to be anti-Christianity. Truly Christian anti-Judaism is directed, not against the Bible or the Old Testament, but against the Talmudic-rabbinic Judaism which developed after the Jews' refusal to accept Christ. But when religious anti-Judaism becomes racialist anti-Semitism, it inevitably turns into anti-Christianity, for the human origins of Christianity are Hebrew. . . . [I]t is impossible, it is forbidden, for a true Christian to be a racialist and to hate the Jews. . . .

. . . According to the race theory there is no hope of salvation, whatever: if you were born a Jew or a negro, no change of consciousness or belief or conviction can save you, you are doomed. A Jew may become a Christian: that does him no good. Even if he becomes a national-socialist, he cannot be saved.

REVIEW QUESTIONS

1. According to José Ortega y Gasset, how does the domination of society by the masses lead to barbarism?
2. Why, in Ortega's view, does fascism rely on "the reason of unreason"?
3. In Arthur Koestler's account of his childhood, what social and political upheavals laid the foundation for his later attraction to communism?
4. How does a political awakening such as Koestler's mirror the experience of religious conversion? What are the benefits and dangers of such experiences?
5. According to Nicolas Berdyaev, how is nationalism contradictory to Christian values?

CHAPTER 13

World War II

"GRIEF." Photographed in the Kerch Peninsula, January 1942. (© *Dmitry Battermants/Sovfoto/Eastfoto*)

From the early days of his political career, Hitler dreamed of forging a vast German empire in central and eastern Europe. He believed that only by waging a war of conquest against Russia could the German nation gain the living space and security it required and, as a superior race, deserved. War was an essential component of National Socialist ideology; it also accorded with Hitler's temperament. For the former corporal from the trenches, the Great War had never ended. Hitler aspired to political power because he wanted to mobilize the material and human resources of the German nation for war and conquest. Whereas historians may debate the question of responsibility for World War I, few would disagree with French historian Pierre Renouvin that World War II was Hitler's war:

> It appears to be an almost incontrovertible fact that the Second World War was brought on by the actions of the Hitler government, that these actions were the expression of a policy laid down well in advance in *Mein Kampf,* and that this war could have been averted up until the last moment if the German government had so wished.

Western statesmen had sufficient warning that Hitler was a threat to peace and the essential values of Western civilization, but they failed to rally their people and take a stand until Germany had greatly increased its capacity to wage aggressive war.

World War II was the most destructive war in history. Estimates of the number of dead range as high as 50 million, including 25 million Russians, who sacrificed more than the other participants in both population and material resources. The consciousness of Europe, already profoundly damaged by World War I, was again grievously wounded. Nazi racial theories showed that even in an age of sophisticated science the mind remains attracted to irrational beliefs and mythical imagery. Nazi atrocities proved that people will torture and kill with religious zeal and machinelike indifference. The Nazi assault on reason and freedom demonstrated anew the precariousness of Western civilization. This assault would forever cast doubt on the Enlightenment conception of human goodness, secular rationality, and the progress of civilization through advances in science and technology.

1 Prescient Observers of Nazi Germany

After Hitler took power in January 1933, many Western officials hoped that his radicalism would be tamed by the responsibilities of leadership. Moreover, these officials either never read *Mein Kampf* or did not take it seriously. But there were also astute observers who, within months after Hitler became chancellor, warned that Nazi Germany constituted a threat to the European peace. They maintained that Hitler, who believed that a Darwinian struggle for existence governed relations between nations and races, would eventually launch a war in order to realize the territorial aims of Nazi ideology.

Horace Rumbold
"PACIFISM IS THE DEADLIEST OF SINS"

On April 26, 1933, Horace Rumbold (1869–1941), Britain's ambassador to Germany, sent the following dispatch to London. It is clear that Rumbold had read and correctly assessed the meaning of *Mein Kampf.*

Herr Hitler has now been Chancellor for nearly three months. . . . The Chancellor has been busy gathering all the strings of power into his hands, and he may now be said to be in a position of unchallenged supremacy. The parliamentary regime has been replaced by a regime of brute force, and the political parties have, with the exception of the Nazis and Nationalists, disappeared from the arena. For that matter Parliament has ceased to have any *raison d'être.* The Nazi leader has only to express a wish to have it fulfilled by his followers. . . .

. . . The plans of the Government are far-reaching. They will take several years to mature and they realise that it would be idle to embark on them if there were any danger of premature disturbance either abroad or at home. They may, therefore, be expected to repeat their protestations of peaceful intent from time to time and to have recourse to other measures, including propaganda, to lull the outer world into a sense of security. To ensure stability at home is an easier task. The new regime is confident that it has come to stay. At the same time it realises that the economic crisis which delivered Germany into its hands is also capable of reversing the process. It is, therefore, determined to leave no stone unturned in the effort to entrench itself in power for all time. To this end it has embarked on a programme of political propaganda on a scale for which there is no analogy in history. Hitler himself is, with good reason, a profound be-

liever in human, and particularly German, credulity. He has unlimited faith in propaganda. In his autobiography he describes with envy and admiration the successes of the Allied Governments, achieved by the aid of war propaganda. He displays a cynical and at the same time very clear understanding of the psychology of the German masses. He knows what he has achieved with oratory and cheap sentiment during the last fourteen years by his own unaided efforts. Now that he has the resources of the State at his disposal, he has good reason to believe that he can mould public opinion to his views to an unprecedented extent. After all, his recent victory is the best proof that the methods which he proposes to adopt are sound. There may, of course, be a saturation point, a point at which the masses grow sick of propaganda, but it does not seem to have been even approached as yet. The experiment which Dr. Goebbels is now conducting at the Ministry for Propaganda is one of the most interesting in political history and will in due course provide the answer. Dr. Goebbels is singularly well fitted to conduct the new Ministry. His pioneer work during the last five years has been wholly admirable, and he appears to be a man of infinite resource and invention.

Dr. Goebbels is engaged on a two-fold task, to uproot every political creed in Germany except Hitlerism and to prepare the soil for the revival of militarism. The press has been delivered into his hands, and he has declared that it is his intention to play upon it as on a piano. Next to the press he ranks wireless as a medium for propaganda. The cinema, the theatre, and, of course, public speeches delivered to mass audiences, and relayed by wireless to the nine German broadcasting stations and so to millions of listeners, are to play an important role. For long distance propaganda the elementary schools, high schools, and universities are being harnessed to the needs of the State, and the latter may be confidently expected to hand over future generations of voters to the party machine as finished products of the Nazi educational system.

The outlook for Europe is far from peaceful if the speeches of Nazi leaders, especially of the Chancellor, are borne in mind. The Chancellor's account of his political career in *Mein Kampf* contains not only the principles which have guided him during the last fourteen years, but explains how he arrived at these fundamental principles. Stripped of the verbiage in which he has clothed it, Hitler's thesis is extremely simple. He starts with the assertions that man is a fighting animal, therefore the nation is, he concludes, a fighting unit, being a community of fighters. Any living organism which ceases to fight for its existence is, he asserts, doomed to extinction. A country or a race which ceases to fight is equally doomed. The fighting capacity of a race depends on its purity. Hence the necessity for ridding it of foreign impurities. The Jewish race, owing to its universality, is of necessity pacifist and internationalist. Pacifism is the deadliest sin, for pacifism means the surrender of the race in the fight for existence. The first duty of every country is, therefore, to nationalise the masses; intelligence is of secondary importance in the case of the individual; will and determination are of higher importance. The individual who is born to command is more valuable than countless thousands of subordinate natures. Only brute force can ensure the survival of the race. Hence the necessity for military forms. The race must fight; a race that rests must rust and perish. The German race, had it been united in time, would now be mas-

ter of the globe today. The new Reich must gather within its fold all the scattered German elements in Europe. A race which has suffered defeat can be rescued by restoring its self-confidence. Above all things, the army must be taught to believe in its own invincibility. To restore the German nation again, it is only necessary to convince the people that the recovery of freedom by force of arms is a possibility.

Hitler describes at great length in his turgid style the task which the new Germany must therefore set itself. Intellectualism is undesirable. The ultimate aim of education is to produce a German who can be converted with the minimum of training into a soldier. The idea that there is something reprehensible in chauvinism is entirely mistaken. Indeed, the greatest upheavals in history would have been unthinkable had it not been for the driving force of fanatical and hysterical passions. Nothing could have been effected by the *bourgeois* virtues of peace and order. The world is now moving towards such an upheaval, and the new (German) State must see to it that the race is ready for the last and greatest decisions on this earth (p. 475, 17th edition of *Mein Kampf*). Again and again he proclaims that fanatical conviction and uncompromising resolution are indispensable qualities in a leader.

The climax of education is military service (p. 476). A man may be a living lexicon, but unless he is a soldier he will fail in the great crises of life. . . . An army is indispensable to ensure the maintenance and expansion of the race. The recovery of lost provinces has never been effected by protest and without the use of force. To forge the necessary weapons is the task of the internal political leaders of the people.

. . . Germany's lost provinces cannot be gained by solemn appeals to Heaven or by pious hopes in the League of Nations, but only by force of arms (p. 708). Germany must not repeat the mistake of fighting all her enemies at once. She must single out the most dangerous in turn and attack him with all her forces. . . . It is the business of the Government to implant in the people feelings of manly courage and passionate hatred. The world will only cease to be anti-German when Germany recovers equality of rights and resumes her place in the sun. . . .

Still more disquieting is the fact that though Germany remains nominally a member of the League of Nations the official policy of the country so far as it has been translated into action or expounded by members of the Government is fundamentally hostile to the principles on which the League is founded. Not only is it a crime to preach pacifism or condemn militarism but it is equally objectionable to preach international understanding, and while politicians and writers who have been guilty of the one have actually been arrested and incarcerated, those guilty of the other have at any rate been removed from public life and of course from official employment. . . .

[Germany has] to rearm on land, and, as Herr Hitler explains in his memoirs, they have

to lull their adversaries into such a state of coma that they will allow themselves to be engaged one by one. It may seem astonishing that the Chancellor should express himself so frankly, but it must be noted that his book was written in 1925, when his prospects of reaching power were so remote that he could afford to be candid. He would probably be glad to suppress every copy extant today. Since he assumed office, Herr Hitler has been as cautious and discreet as he was formerly blunt and frank. He declares that he is anxious that peace should be maintained for a ten-year period. What he probably means can be more accurately expressed by the [following] formula: Germany needs peace until she has recovered such strength that no country can challenge her without serious and irksome preparations. I fear that it would be misleading to base any hopes on a return to sanity or a serious modification of the views of the Chancellor and his entourage.

George S. Messersmith
"THE NAZIS WERE AFTER . . . UNLIMITED TERRITORIAL EXPANSION"

Two months after Rumbold's dispatch, George S. Messersmith, American consul general at Berlin, also reported on the "dangerous situation" developing in Germany. Appointed Minister to Austria in 1934, he continued to warn that the Nazis were serious about expanding Germany's territory.

CONSUL GENERAL MESSERSMITH'S REPORT FROM BERLIN

The United States Consul General at Berlin, George S. Messersmith, who had been at that post since 1930, reported frequently to the Department of State during this period on the menace inherent in the Nazi regime. Mr. Messersmith expressed the view, in a letter of

June 26, 1933 to Under Secretary of State Phillips, that the United States must be exceedingly careful in its dealings with Germany as long as the existing Government was in power, as that Government had no spokesmen who could really be depended upon and those who held the highest positions were "capable of actions which really outlaw them from ordinary intercourse". He reported that some of the men who were running the German Government were "psychopathic cases"; that others were in a state of exaltation and in a frame of mind that knew no reason; and that those men in the party and in responsible positions who were really worthwhile were powerless because they had to follow the orders of superiors who were suffering from the "abnormal psychology" prevailing in Germany. "There is a real revolution here and a dangerous situation", he said.

Consul General Messersmith reported further that a martial spirit was being developed in Germany; that everywhere people were seen drilling, including children from the age of five or six to persons well into middle age; that a psychology was being developed that the whole world was against Germany, which was defenseless before the world; that people were being trained against gas and airplane attacks; and that the idea of war from neighboring countries was constantly harped upon. He emphasized that Germany was headed in directions which could only carry ruin to it and create a situation "dangerous to world peace". He said we must recognize that while Germany at that time wanted peace, it was by no means a peaceful country or one looking forward to a long period of peace; that the German Government and its adherents desired peace ardently for the time being because they needed peace to carry through the changes in Germany which they wanted to bring about. What they wanted to do was to make Germany "the most capable instrument of war that there has ever existed".

Consul General Messersmith reported from Berlin five months later, in a letter of November 23, 1933 to Under Secretary Phillips, that the military spirit in Germany was constantly growing and that innumerable measures were being taken to develop the German people into a hardy, sturdy race which would "be able to meet all comers". He said that the leaders of Germany had no desire for peace unless it was a peace in complete compliance with German ambitions; that Hitler and his associates really wanted peace for the moment, but only to have a chance to prepare for the use of force if it were found essential; and that they were preparing their way so carefully that the German people would be with them when they wanted to use force and when they felt that they had the "necessary means to carry through their objects". . . .

Mr. Messersmith, who had been appointed Minister to Austria in 1934, continued to send to the Department of State reports on the situation in Germany. In February 1935 he reported that the Nazis had their eyes on Memel, Alsace-Lorraine, and the eastern frontier; that they nourished just as strongly the hope to get the Ukraine for the surplus German population; that Austria was a definite objective; and that absorption or hegemony over the whole of southeastern Europe was a definite policy. A few weeks later he reported a conversation with William E. Dodd, United States Ambassador to Germany, in which they had agreed that no faith whatsoever could be placed in the Nazi regime and its promises, that what the Nazis were after was "unlimited territorial expansion", and that there was probably in existence a German-Japanese understanding, if not an alliance.

REVIEW QUESTIONS

1. According to Rumbold, what was the basic thesis underlying Hitler's political philosophy?
2. Why according to Rumbold, did Hitler want to maintain peace for a ten-year period? How did the events of the 1930s prove Rumbold's assertions correct?
3. What indications did George Messersmith see that Germany was preparing for war?

2 The Anschluss, March 1938

One of Hitler's aims was the incorporation of Austria into the Third Reich. The Treaty of Versailles had expressly prohibited the union of the two countries, but in *Mein Kampf,* Hitler had insisted that an Anschluss was necessary for German *Lebensraum* (living space). In February 1938, under intense pressure from Hitler, Austrian Chancellor Kurt von Schuschnigg promised to accept Austrian Nazis in his cabinet and agreed to closer relations with Germany. Austrian independence was slipping away, and increasingly, Austrian Nazis undermined Schuschnigg's authority. Seeking to gain his people's support, Schuschnigg made plans for a plesbiscite on the issue of preserving Austrian independence. An enraged Hitler ordered his generals to draw up plans for an invasion of Austria. Hitler then demanded Schuschnigg's resignation and the formation of a new government headed by Arthur Seyss-Inquart, an Austrian Nazi.

Believing that Austria was not worth a war, Britain and France informed the embattled chancellor that they would not help in the event of a German invasion. Schuschnigg then resigned, and Austrian Nazis began to take control of the government. Under the pretext of preventing violence, Hitler ordered his troops to cross into Austria, and on March 13, 1938, Austrian leaders declared that Austria was a province of the German Reich.

The Anschluss was supported by many Austrians: Nazis and their sympathizers, average people who hoped it would bring improved material conditions, and opportunists who had their eyes set on social and economic advancement. Even many opponents of the Nazis felt that Austrian unity with Germany was fated to be accomplished, even as they lamented that it meant incorporation into Hitler's regime.

In the first days after the Anschluss, anti-Nazis, particularly Social Democrats, were incarcerated; a wave of dissidents, politicians, and intellectuals fled the country; and Jews were subjected to torment and humiliation. Austrian Nazis, often with the approval of their fellow citizens, plundered Jewish shops, pulled elderly Orthodox Jews around by their beards, and made Jews scour pro-Schuschnigg slogans off the streets with toothbrushes or their bare hands. One eyewitness recalled years later: "I saw in the crowd a well-dressed woman . . . holding up a little girl, a blond lovely little girl with these curls, so that the girl could see better how a . . . Nazi Storm Trooper kicked an old Jew who fell down because he wasn't allowed to kneel. He had to scrub and just bend down sort of, and he fell and he kicked him. And they all laughed and she laughed as well—it was wonderful entertainment—and that shook me."

Stefan Zweig
THE WORLD OF YESTERDAY

One of modern German-speaking Europe's most important authors, Stefan Zweig (see page 274) was born into a well-to-do Viennese Jewish household, came of age during the waning years of the monarchy, and witnessed both the devastation of World War I and the chaos of the interwar years. A passionate European and a convinced Austrian patriot, Zweig was disgusted by national chauvinisms, particularly the virulent German nationalism clearly discernible in Austria after the collapse of the Habsburg monarchy. His *World of Yesterday* both laments the loss of European cosmopolitianism and offers biting criticism of the inability, or unwillingness, of many Austrians to come to terms with the violent intolerance in their own society and the spreading danger of Nazism. Zweig's despair was all-consuming; he took his own life in South American exile, unable to reconcile himself to the changes in his beloved Europe and his Austrian homeland.

In the following selection from his autobiography, Zweig describes the orgy of hate that engulfed Vienna immediately after the Anschluss.

I thought that I had foreboded all the terror that would come to pass when Hitler's dream of hate would come true and he would triumphantly occupy Vienna, the city which had turned him off, poor and a failure, in his youth. But how timid, how petty, how lamentable my imagination, all human imagination, in the light of the inhumanity which discharged itself on that March 13, 1938, that day when Austria and Europe with it fell prey to sheer violence! The mask was off. The other States having plainly shown their fear, there was no further need to check moral inhibitions or to employ hypocritical pretexts about "Marxists" having to be politically liquidated. Who cared for England, France, for the whole world! Now there was no longer mere robbery and theft, but every private lust for revenge was given free rein. University professors were obliged to scrub the streets with their naked hands, pious white-bearded Jews were dragged into the synagogue by hooting youths and forced to do knee-exercises and to shout "Heil Hitler" in chorus. Innocent people in the streets were trapped like rabbits and herded off to clean the latrines in the S. A. barracks. All the sickly, unclean fantasies of hate that had been conceived in many orgiastic nights found raging expression in bright daylight. Breaking into homes and tearing earrings from trembling women may well have happened in the looting of cities, hundreds of years ago during medieval wars; what was new, however, was the shameless delight in public tortures, in spiritual martyrization, in the refinements of humiliation. All this has been recorded not by one but by thousands who suffered it; and a more peaceful day—not one already morally fatigued as ours is—will shudder to read what a single hate-crazed man perpetrated in that city of culture in the twentieth century. For amidst his military and political victories Hitler's most diabolic triumph was that he succeeded through progressive excesses in blunting every sense of law and order. Before this "New Order," the murder of a single man without legal process and without apparent reason would have shocked the world; torture was considered unthinkable in the twentieth century, expropriations were known by the old names, theft and robbery. But now after successive [murderous] nights the daily mortal tortures in the S. A. prisons and behind barbed wire, what did a single injustice or earthly suffering signify? In 1938, after Austria, our universe had become accustomed to inhumanity, to lawlessness, and brutality as never in centuries before. In a former day the occurrences in unhappy Vienna alone would have been sufficient to cause international proscription, but in 1938 the world conscience was silent or merely muttered surlily before it forgot and forgave.

Those days, marked by daily cries for help from the homeland when one knew close friends to be kidnapped and humiliated and one trembled helplessly for every loved one, were among the most terrible of my life. These times have so perverted our hearts that I am not ashamed to say that I was not shocked and did not mourn upon learning of the death of my mother in Vienna; on the contrary, I even felt something like composure in the knowledge that she was now safe from suffering and danger. Eighty-four years old, almost completely deaf, she occupied rooms in our old home and thus could not, even under the new "Aryan" code, be evicted for the time being and we had hoped somehow to get her abroad after a while. One of the first Viennese ordinances had hit her hard. At her advanced age she was a little shaky on her legs and was accustomed, when on her daily laborious walk, to rest on a bench in the Ringstrasse or in the park, every five or ten minutes. Hitler had not been master of the city for a week when the bestial order forbidding Jews to sit on public benches was issued—one of those orders obviously thought up only for the sadistic purpose of malicious torture. There was logic and reason in robbing Jews for with the booty from factories, the home furnishings, the villas, and the jobs compulsorily vacated they could feather their followers' nests, reward their satellites; after all, Goering's picture-gallery owes its splendor mainly to this generously exercised practice. But to deny an aged woman or an exhausted old man a few minutes on a park bench to catch his breath—this remained reserved to the twentieth century and to the man whom millions worshipped as the greatest in our day.

Fortunately, my mother was spared suffering such brutality and humiliation for long. She died a few months after the occupation of Vienna and I cannot forbear to write about an episode in connection with her passing; it seems important to me to record just such details for a time in which such things will again seem impossible.

One morning the eighty-four-year-old woman suddenly lost consciousness. The doctor who was called declared that she could hardly live through the night and engaged a nurse, a woman of about forty, to attend her deathbed. Neither my brother nor I, her only children, was there nor could we have come back, because a return to the deathbed of a mother would have been counted a misdeed by the representatives of German culture. A cousin of ours undertook to spend the night in the apartment so that at least one of the family might be present at her death. He was then a man of sixty, and in poor health; in fact he too died about a year later. As he was uncovering his bed in an adjoining room the nurse appeared and declared her regret that because of the new National-Socialist laws it was impossible for her to stay overnight with the dying woman. To her credit be it said that she was rather shamefaced about it. My cousin being a Jew and she a woman under fifty, she was not permitted to spend a night under the same roof with him, even at a deathbed, because according to the [vile Nazi] mentality, it must be a Jew's first thought to practice race defilement upon her. Of course the regulation was extremely embarrassing, but she would have to obey the law. So my sixty-year-old cousin had to leave the house in the evening so that the nurse could stay with my dying mother; it will be intelligible, then, why I considered her almost lucky not to have to live on among such people.

REVIEW QUESTIONS

1. What was the underlying purpose of the various anti-Jewish ordinances in Vienna that Stefan Zweig refers to? How might they have paved the way for even harsher actions?
2. Zweig accurately predicted that people in "a more peaceful day" would later "shudder to read what a single hate-crazed man perpetrated in that city of culture in the twentieth century." Why do you think so many of Zweig's contemporaries failed to feel the same dismay and horror as these events unfolded?

---

3   The Munich Agreement

Hitler sought power to build a great German empire in Europe, a goal that he revealed in *Mein Kampf.* In 1935, Hitler declared that Germany was no longer bound by the Versailles Treaty and would restore military conscription. Germany remilitarized the Rhineland in 1936 and incorporated Austria into the Third Reich in 1938. Although these actions violated the Versailles Treaty, Britain and France offered no resistance.

In 1938, Hitler also threatened war if Czechoslovakia did not cede to Germany the Sudetenland with its large German population—of the 3.5 million people living in the Czech Sudetenland, some 2.8 million were Germans. In September 1938, Hitler met with other European leaders at Munich. Prime Minister Neville Chamberlain (1869–1940) of Great Britain and Prime Minister Édouard Daladier (1884–1970) of France agreed to Hitler's demands, despite France's mutual assistance pact with Czechoslovakia and the Czechs' expressed determination to resist the dismemberment of their country. Both Chamberlain and Daladier were praised by their compatriots for ensuring, as Chamberlain said, "peace in our time."

Neville Chamberlain
IN DEFENSE OF APPEASEMENT

Britain and France pursued a policy of appeasement—giving in to Germany in the hope that a satisfied Hitler would not drag Europe into another war. Appeasement expressed the widespread British desire to heal the wounds of World War I and to correct what many British officials regarded as the injustices of the Versailles Treaty. Some officials, lauding Hitler's anticommunism, regarded a powerful Germany as a bulwark against the Soviet Union. Britain's lack of military preparedness was another compelling reason for not resisting Hitler. On September 27, 1938, when negotiations between Hitler and Chamberlain reached a tense moment, the British prime minister addressed his nation. Excerpts of this speech and of another before the House of Commons, which appeared in his *In Search of Peace* (1939), follow.

First of all I must say something to those who have written to my wife or myself in these last weeks to tell us of their gratitude for my efforts and to assure us of their prayers for my success. Most of these letters have come from women— mothers or sisters of our own countrymen. But there are countless others besides—from France, from Belgium, from Italy, even from Germany, and it has been heartbreaking to read of the growing anxiety they reveal and their intense relief when they thought, too soon, that the danger of war was past.

If I felt my responsibility heavy before, to read such letters has made it seem almost over- whelming. How horrible, fantastic, incredible it is we should be digging trenches and trying on gas masks here because of a quarrel in a far-away country between people of whom we know nothing. It seems still more impossi- ble that a quarrel which has already been set- tled in principle should be the subject of war.

I can well understand the reasons why the Czech Government have felt unable to accept the terms which have been put before them in the German memorandum. Yet I believe after my talks with Herr Hitler that, if only time were allowed, it ought to be possible for the arrangements for transferring the territory that the Czech Government has agreed to give to Germany to be settled by agreement under conditions which would assure fair treatment to the population concerned. . . .

However much we may sympathise with a small nation confronted by a big and powerful neighbour, we cannot in all circumstances un- dertake to involve the whole British Empire in war simply on her account. If we have to fight it must be on larger issues than that. I am my- self a man of peace to the depths of my soul. Armed conflict between nations is a nightmare to me; but if I were convinced that any nation had made up its mind to dominate the world by fear of its force, I should feel that it must be resisted. Under such a domination life for people who believe in liberty would not be worth living; but war is a fearful thing, and we must be very clear, before we embark on it,

that it is really the great issues that are at stake, and that the call to risk everything in their defence, when all the consequences are weighed, is irresistible.

For the present I ask you to await as calmly as you can the events of the next few days. As long as war has not begun, there is always hope that it may be prevented, and you know that I am going to work for peace to the last mo- ment. Good night. . . .

On October 6, 1938, in a speech to Britain's House of Commons, Chamberlain defended the Munich agreement signed on September 30.

Since I first went to Berchtesgaden [to con- fer with Hitler in Germany] more than 20,000 letters and telegrams have come to No. 10, Downing Street [British prime minister's resi- dence]. Of course, I have only been able to look at a tiny fraction of them, but I have seen enough to know that the people who wrote did not feel that they had such a cause for which to fight, if they were asked to go to war in order that the Sudeten Germans might not join the Reich. That is how they are feeling. That is my answer to those who say that we should have told Germany weeks ago that, if her army crossed the border of Czechoslovakia, we should be at war with her. We had no treaty obliga- tions and no legal obligations to Czechoslo- vakia and if we had said that, we feel that we should have received no support from the peo- ple of this country. . . .

. . . When we were convinced, as we became convinced, that nothing any longer would keep the Sudetenland within the Czechoslo- vakian State, we urged the Czech Government as strongly as we could to agree to the cession of territory, and to agree promptly. The Czech Government, through the wisdom and courage of President Benes, accepted the advice of the French Government and ourselves. It was a hard decision for anyone who loved his country to take, but to accuse us of having by that advice betrayed the Czechoslovakian State is simply preposterous. What we did was to save her from annihilation and give her a chance of new life as a new State, which involves the loss of territory and fortifications, but may perhaps enable her to enjoy in the future and develop a national existence under a neutrality and security comparable to that which we see in Switzerland to-day. Therefore, I think the Government deserve the approval of this House for their conduct of affairs in this recent crisis which has saved Czechoslovakia from destruction and Europe from Armageddon.

Does the experience of the Great War and of the years that followed it give us reasonable hope that, if some new war started, that would end war any more than the last one did? . . .

One good thing, at any rate, has come out of this emergency through which we have passed. It has thrown a vivid light upon our preparations for defence, on their strength and on their weakness. I should not think we were doing our duty if we had not already ordered that a prompt and thorough inquiry should be made to cover the whole of our preparations, military and civil, in order to see, in the light of what has happened during these hectic days, what further steps may be necessary to make good our deficiencies in the shortest possible time.

Winston Churchill
"A DISASTER OF THE FIRST MAGNITUDE"

On October 5, 1938, Britain's elder statesman Winston Churchill (1874–1965) delivered a speech in the House of Commons attacking the Munich agreement and British policy toward Nazi Germany.

. . . I will begin by saying what everybody would like to ignore or forget but which must nevertheless be stated, namely, that we have sustained a total and unmitigated defeat, and that France has suffered even more than we have. . . .

. . . And I will say this, that I believe the Czechs, left to themselves and told they were going to get no help from the Western Powers, would have been able to make better terms than they have got—they could hardly have worse—after all this tremendous perturbation. . . .

. . . I have always held the view that the maintenance of peace depends upon the accumulation of deterrents against the aggressor, coupled with a sincere effort to redress grievances. . . . After [Hitler's] seizure of Austria in March . . . I ventured to appeal to the Government . . . to give a pledge that in conjunction with France and other Powers they would guarantee the security of Czechoslovakia while the Sudeten-Deutsch question was being examined either by a League of Nations Commission or some other impartial body, and I still believe that if that course had been followed events would not have fallen into this disastrous state. . . .

France and Great Britain together, especially if they had maintained a close contact with Russia, which certainly was not done, would have been able in those days in the summer, when they had the prestige, to influence many of the smaller States of Europe, and I believe they could have determined the attitude of Poland. Such a combination, prepared at a time when the German dictator was not deeply and irrevocably committed to his new adventure, would, I believe, have given strength to all those forces in Germany which resisted this departure, this new design. They were varying forces, those of a military character which declared that Germany was not ready to undertake a world war, and all that mass of moderate opinion and popular opinion which dreaded war, and some elements of which still have some influence upon the German Government. Such action would have given strength to all that intense desire for peace which the helpless German masses share with their British and French fellow men. . . .

. . . I do not think it is fair to charge those who wished to see this course followed, and followed consistently and resolutely, with having wished for an immediate war. Between submission and immediate war there was this third alternative, which gave a hope not only of peace but of justice. It is quite true that such a policy in order to succeed demanded that Britain should declare straight out and a long time beforehand that she would, with others, join to defend Czechoslovakia against an unprovoked aggression. His Majesty's Government refused to give that guarantee when it would have saved the situation. . . .

All is over. Silent, mournful, abandoned, broken, Czechoslovakia recedes into the darkness. She has suffered in every respect by her association with the Western democracies and with the League of Nations, of which she has always been an obedient servant. She has suffered in particular from her association with France, under whose guidance and policy she has been actuated for so long. . . .

We in this country, as in other Liberal and democratic countries, have a perfect right to exalt the principle of self-determination, but it comes ill out of the mouths of those in totalitarian States who deny even the smallest element of toleration to every section and creed within their bounds. . . .

What is the remaining position of Czechoslovakia? Not only are they politically mutilated, but, economically and financially, they are in complete confusion. Their banking, their railway arrangements, are severed and broken, their industries are curtailed, and the movement of their population is most cruel. The Sudeten miners, who are all Czechs and whose families have lived in that area for centuries, must now flee into an area where there are hardly any mines left for them to work. It is a tragedy which has occurred. . . .

I venture to think that in future the Czechoslovak State cannot be maintained as an independent entity. You will find that in a period of time which may be measured by years, but may be measured only by months, Czechoslovakia will be engulfed in the Nazi régime. Perhaps they may join it in despair or in revenge. At any rate, that story is over and told. But we cannot consider the abandonment and ruin of Czechoslovakia in the light only of what happened only last month. It is the most grievous consequence which we have yet experienced of what we have done and of what we have left undone in the last five years—five years of futile good intention, five years of eager search for the line of least resistance, five years of uninterrupted retreat of British power, five years of neglect of our air defences. Those are the features which I stand here to declare and which marked an improvident stewardship for which Great Britain and France have dearly to pay. We have been reduced in those five years from a position of security so overwhelming and so unchallengeable that we never cared to think about it. We have been reduced from a position where the very word "war" was considered one which would be used only by persons qualifying for a lunatic asylum. We have been reduced from a position of safety and power—power to do good, power to be generous to a beaten foe, power to make terms with Germany, power to give her proper redress for her grievances, power to stop her arming if we chose, power to take any step in strength or mercy or justice which we thought right—reduced in five years from a position safe and unchallenged to where we stand now.

When I think of the fair hopes of a long peace which still lay before Europe at the beginning of 1933 when Herr Hitler first obtained power, and of all the opportunities of arresting the growth of the Nazi power which have been thrown away, when I think of the immense combinations and resources which have been neglected or squandered, I cannot believe that a parallel exists in the whole course of history. So far as this country is concerned the responsibility must rest with those who have the undisputed control of our political affairs. They neither prevented Germany from rearming, nor did they rearm ourselves in time. . . . They neglected to make alliances and combinations which might have repaired previous errors, and thus they left us in the hour of trial without adequate national defence or effective international security. . . .

We are in the presence of a disaster of the first magnitude which has befallen Great Britain and France. Do not let us blind ourselves to that. It must now be accepted that all the countries of Central and Eastern Europe will make the best terms they can with the triumphant Nazi Power. The system of alliances in Central Europe upon which France has relied for her safety has been swept away, and I can see no means by which it can be reconstituted. . . .

. . . If the Nazi dictator should choose to look westward, as he may, bitterly will France and England regret the loss of that fine army of ancient Bohemia [Czechoslovakia] which was estimated last week to require not fewer than 30 German divisions for its destruction. . . .

. . . Many people, no doubt, honestly believe that they are only giving away the interests of Czechoslovakia, whereas I fear we shall find that we have deeply compromised, and perhaps fatally endangered, the safety and even the independence of Great Britain and France. . . . [T]here can never be friendship between the British democracy and the Nazi Power, that Power which spurns Christian ethics, which cheers its onward course by a barbarous paganism, which vaunts the spirit of aggression and conquest, which derives strength and perverted pleasure from persecution, and uses, as we have seen, with pitiless brutality the threat of murderous force. That Power cannot ever be the trusted friend of the British democracy. . . .

. . . [O]ur loyal, brave people . . . should know the truth. They should know that there has been gross neglect and deficiency in our defences; they should know that we have sustained a defeat without a war, the consequences of which will travel far with us along our road; they should know that we have passed an awful milestone in our history, when the whole equilibrium of Europe has been deranged, and that the terrible words have for the time being been pronounced against the Western democracies:

Thou art weighed in the balance and found wanting.

And do not suppose that this is the end. This is only the beginning of the reckoning. This is only the first sip, the first foretaste of a bitter cup which will be proffered to us year by year unless by a supreme recovery of moral health and martial vigour, we arise again and take our stand for freedom as in the olden time.

REVIEW QUESTIONS

1. In Neville Chamberlain's view, how did the British people regard a war with Germany over the Sudetenland?
2. How did Chamberlain respond to the accusation that Britain and France had betrayed Czechoslovakia?
3. What did Chamberlain consider to be the "one good thing" to come out of the Sudetenland crisis?
4. Why did Winston Churchill believe that "there [could] never be friendship between the British democracy and the Nazi Power"?
5. Why did Churchill believe that the Munich agreement was "a disaster of the first magnitude" for Britain and France?
6. What policy toward Nazi Germany did Churchill advocate?

4   World War II Begins

After Czechoslovakia, Hitler turned to Poland. In the middle of June 1939, the army presented him with a battle plan for an invasion of Poland, and on August 22, Hitler informed his leading generals that war with Poland was necessary. The following day, Nazi Germany signed a nonaggression pact with Communist Russia, which blocked Britain and France from duplicating their World War I alliance against Germany. The Nazi-Soviet pact was the green light for an attack on Poland. At dawn on September 1, German forces, striking with coordinated speed and power, invaded Poland, starting World War II.

Adolf Hitler
"POLAND WILL BE DEPOPULATED AND SETTLED WITH GERMANS"

An American journalist was given a copy of Hitler's speech to his generals at the August 22 conference. Probably the supplier was an official close to Admiral Canaris, an opponent of Hitler who had attended the conference. The journalist then gave it to the British ambassador. The speech is reproduced below.

Decision to attack Poland was arrived at in spring. Originally there was fear that because of the political constellation we would have to strike at the same time against England, France, Russia and Poland. This risk too we should have had to take. Göring had demonstrated to us that his Four-Year Plan is a failure and that we are at the end of our strength, if we do not achieve victory in a coming war.

Since the autumn of 1938 and since I have realised that Japan will not go with us unconditionally and that Mussolini is endangered by that nitwit of a King and the treacherous scoundrel of a Crown Prince, I decided to go with Stalin. After all there are only three great statesmen in the world, Stalin, I and Mussolini. Mussolini is the weakest, for he has been able to break the power neither of the crown nor of the Church. Stalin and I are the only ones who visualise the future. So in a few weeks hence I shall stretch out my hand to Stalin at the common German-Russian frontier and with him undertake to re-distribute the world.

Our strength lies in our quickness and in our brutality; Genghis Khan has sent millions of women and children into death knowingly and with a light heart. History sees in him only the great founder of States. As to what the weak Western European civilisation asserts about me, that is of no account. I have given the command and I shall shoot everyone who utters one word of criticism, for the goal to be obtained in the war is not that of reaching certain lines but of physically demolishing the opponent. And so for the present only in the East I have put my death-head formations[1] in place with the command relentlessly and without compassion to send into death many women and children of Polish origin and language. Only thus we can gain the living space that we need. Who after all is today speaking about the destruction of the Armenians?

---

[1]The S.S. Death's Head formations were principally employed in peace-time in guarding concentration camps. With the S.S. Verfügungstruppen they formed the nucleus of the Waffen S.S.

Colonel-General von Brauchitsch has promised me to bring the war against Poland to a close within a few weeks. Had he reported to me that he needs two years or even only one year, I should not have given the command to march and should have allied myself temporarily with England instead of Russia for we cannot conduct a long war. To be sure a new situation has arisen. I experienced those poor worms Daladier and Chamberlain in Munich. They will be too cowardly to attack. They won't go beyond a blockade. Against that we have our autarchy and the Russian raw materials.

Poland will be depopulated and settled with Germans. My pact with the Poles was merely conceived of as a gaining of time. As for the rest, gentlemen, the fate of Russia will be exactly the same as I am now going through with in the case of Poland. After Stalin's death—he is a very sick man—we will break the Soviet Union. Then there will begin the dawn of the German rule of the earth. . . .

The opportunity is as favourable as never before. I have but one worry, namely that Chamberlain or some other such pig of a fellow ('Saukerl') will come at the last moment with proposals or with ratting ('Umfall'). He will fly down the stairs, even if I shall personally have to trample on his belly in the eyes of the photographers.

No, it is too late for this. The attack upon and the destruction of Poland begins Saturday[2] early. I shall let a few companies in Polish uniform attack in Upper Silesia or in the Protectorate. Whether the world believes it is quite

indifferent ('Scheissegal'). The world believes only in success.

For you, gentlemen, fame and honour are beginning as they have not since centuries. Be hard, be without mercy, act more quickly and brutally than the others. The citizens of Western Europe must tremble with horror. That is the most human way of conducting a war. For it scares the others off.

The new method of conducting war corresponds to the new drawing of the frontiers. A war extending from Reval, Lublin, Kaschau to the mouth of the Danube. The rest will be given to the Russians. Ribbentrop has orders to make every offer and to accept every demand. In the West I reserve to myself the right to determine the strategically best line. Here one will be able to work with Protectorate regions, such as Holland, Belgium and French Lorraine.

And now, on to the enemy, in Warsaw we will celebrate our reunion.

The speech was received with enthusiasm. Göring jumped on a table, thanked bloodthirstily and made bloodthirsty promises. He danced like a wild man. The few that had misgivings remained quiet. (Here a line of the memorandum is missing in order no doubt to protect the source of information.)[3]

During the meal which followed Hitler said he must act this year as he was not likely to live very long. His successor however would no longer be able to carry this out. Besides, the situation would be a hopeless one in two years at the most.

---

[2]August 26.

[3]This sentence in parentheses forms part of the original typescript.

---

5 The Fall of France

On May 10, 1940, Hitler launched his offensive in the west with an invasion of neutral Belgium, Holland, and Luxembourg. French troops rushed to Belgium to prevent a breakthrough, but the greater menace lay to the south, on the French frontier. Meeting almost no resistance, German panzer divisions had

moved through the narrow mountain passes of Luxembourg and the dense Forest of the Ardennes in southern Belgium. On May 12, German units were on
French soil near Sedan. Thinking that the Forest of the Ardennes could not be
penetrated by a major German force, the French had only lightly fortified the
western extension of the Maginot Line, the immense fortifications designed to
hold back a German invasion.

The battle for France turned into a rout. Whole French divisions were cut off
or in retreat. On June 10, Mussolini also declared war on France. With authority breaking down and resistance dying, the French cabinet appealed for an
armistice, which was signed on June 22 in the same railway car in which Germany had agreed to the armistice ending World War I.

Several reasons explain the collapse of France. It is likely that the Germans
and the French (including the British planes based in France) had some three
thousand planes each. But many French planes—in what still remains a mystery—stayed on the airfields. The planes were available, but the high command
either did not use them or did not deploy them properly. Unlike the Germans,
the French did not comprehend or appreciate the use of aviation in modern
warfare. As for tanks, the French had as many as the Germans, and some were
superior. Nor was German manpower overwhelming. France met disaster
largely because its military leaders, unlike the Germans, had not mastered the
psychology and technology of motorized warfare. "The French commanders,
trained in the slow-motion methods of 1918, were mentally unfitted to cope
with Panzer pace, and it produced a spreading paralysis among them," says
British military expert Sir Basil Liddell Hart. One also senses a loss of will
among the French people: a consequence of internal political disputes dividing
the nation, poor leadership, the years of appeasement and lost opportunities,
and German propaganda, which depicted Nazism as irresistible and the Führer
as a man of destiny. It was France's darkest hour.

Heinz Guderian
"FRENCH LEADERSHIP . . . COULD NOT GRASP THE SIGNIFICANCE OF THE TANK IN MOBILE WARFARE"

After the war, General Heinz Guderian (1888–1954), whose panzer divisions
formed the vanguard of the attack through the Ardennes into France, analyzed
the reasons for France's collapse.

The First World War on the Western Front, after being for a short time a war of movement,
soon settled down to positional warfare. No
massing of war material, on no matter how vast
a scale, had succeeded in getting the armies
moving again until, in November 1916, the enemy's tanks appeared on the battlefield. With
their armour plating, their tracks, their guns
and their machine-guns, they succeeded in carrying their crews, alive and capable of fighting,
through artillery barrages and wire entanglements, over trench systems and shell craters,

into the centre of the German lines. The power of the offensive had come back into its own.

The true importance of tanks was proved by the fact that the Versailles Treaty forbade Germany the possession or construction of armoured vehicles, tanks or any similar equipment which might be employed in war, under pain of punishment.

So our enemies regarded the tank as a decisive weapon which we must not be allowed to have. I therefore decided carefully to study the history of this decisive weapon and to follow its future development. For someone observing tank theory from afar, unburdened by tradition, there were lessons to be learned in the employment, organisation and construction of armour and of armoured units that went beyond the doctrines then accepted abroad. After years of hard struggle, I had succeeded in putting my theories into practice before the other armies had arrived at the same conclusions. The advance we had made in the organisation and employment of tanks was the primary factor on which my belief in our forthcoming success was based. Even in 1940 this belief was shared by scarcely anybody in the German Army.

A profound study of the First World War had given me considerable insight into the psychology of the combatants. I already, from personal experience, knew a considerable amount about our own army. I had also formed certain opinions about our Western adversaries which the events of 1940 were to prove correct. Despite the tank weapons to which our enemies owed in large measure their 1918 victory, they were preoccupied with the concepts of positional warfare.

France possessed the strongest land army in Western Europe. France possessed the numerically strongest tank force in Western Europe. The combined Anglo-French forces in the West in May 1940 consisted of some 4,000 armoured vehicles: the German Army at that time had 2,800, including armoured reconnaissance cars, and when the attack was launched only 2,200 of these were available for the operation. We thus faced superiority in

numbers, to which was added the fact that the French tanks were superior to the German ones both in armour and in gun-calibre, though admittedly inferior in control facilities and in speed. Despite possessing the strongest forces for mobile warfare the French had also built the strongest line of fortifications in the world, the Maginot Line. Why was the money spent on the construction of those fortifications not used for the modernisation and strengthening of France's mobile forces?

The proposals of de Gaulle, Daladier and others along these lines had been ignored. From this it must be concluded that the highest French leadership either would not or could not grasp the significance of the tank in mobile warfare. In any case all the manœuvres and large-scale exercises of which I had heard led to the conclusion that the French command wanted its troops to be trained in such a way that careful movement and planned measures for attack or for defence could be based on definite, pre-arranged circumstances. They wanted a complete picture of the enemy's order of battle and intentions before deciding on any undertaking. Once the decision was taken it would be carried out according to plan, one might almost say methodically, not only during the approach march and the deployment of troops, but also during the artillery preparation and the launching of the attack or the construction of the defence as the case might be. This mania for planned control, in which nothing should be left to chance, led to the organisation of the armoured forces within the army in a form that would destroy the general scheme, that is to say their assignment in detail to the infantry divisions. Only a fraction of the French armour was organised for operational employment.

So far as the French were concerned the German leadership could safely rely on the defence of France being systematically based on fortifications and carried out according to a rigid doctrine: this doctrine was the result of the lessons that the French had learned from the First World War, their experience of positional warfare, of the high value they attached to fire power, and of their underestimation of movement.

These French strategic and tactical principles, well known to us in 1940 and the exact contrary of my own theories of warfare, were the second factor on which my belief in victory was founded.

By the spring of 1940 we Germans had gained a clear picture of the enemy's dispositions, and of his fortifications. We knew that somewhere between Montmédy and Sedan the Maginot Line changed from being very strong indeed to being rather weaker. We called the fortifications from Sedan to the Channel 'the prolonged Maginot Line.' We knew about the locations and, usually, about the strength of the Belgian and Dutch fortifications. They all faced only towards Germany.

While the Maginot Line was thinly held, the mass of the French army together with the British Expeditionary Force was assembled in Flanders, between the Meuse and the English Channel, facing northeast; the Belgian and Dutch troops, on the other hand, were deployed to defend their frontiers against an attack from the east.

From their order of battle it was plain that the enemy expected the Germans to attempt the Schlieffen Plan once again, and that they intended to bring the bulk of the allied armies against this anticipated outflanking movement through Holland and Belgium. A sufficient safeguard of the hinge of their proposed advance into Belgium by reserve units—in the area, say, of Charleville and Verdun—was not apparent. It seemed that the French High Command did not regard any alternative to the old Schlieffen Plan as even conceivable.

Our knowledge of the enemy's order of battle and of his predictable reactions at the beginning of the German advance was the third factor that contributed to my belief in victory.

In addition there were a number of other aspects in our general evaluation of the enemy which, though of less reliability, were still worth taking into consideration.

We knew and respected the French soldier from the First World War as a brave and tough fighter who had defended his country with stubborn energy. We did not doubt that he would show the same spirit this time. But so far as the French leaders were concerned, we were amazed that they had not taken advantage of their favourable situation during the autumn of 1939 to attack, while the bulk of the German forces, including the entire armoured force, was engaged in Poland. Their reasons for such restraint were at the time hard to see. We could only guess. Be that as it may, the caution shown by the French leaders led us to believe that our adversaries hoped somehow to avoid a serious clash of arms. The rather inactive behavior of the French during the winter of 1939–40 seemed to indicate a limited enthusiasm for the war on their part.

From all this I concluded that a determined and forcibly led attack by strong armoured forces through Sedan and Amiens, with the Atlantic coast as its objective, would hit the enemy deep in the flank of his forces advancing into Belgium; I did not think that he disposed of sufficient reserves to parry this thrust; and I therefore believed it had a great chance of succeeding and, if the initial success were fully exploited, might lead to the cutting off of all the main enemy forces moving up into Belgium.

REVIEW QUESTIONS

1. According to Heinz Guderian, why was it an error for French military strategy to rely so heavily on the Maginot Line?
2. How did World War I demonstrate the importance of tanks in modern warfare?
3. What mistaken lessons did the French draw from their experience in World War I?

6 The Battle of Britain

Hitler expected that after his stunning victories in the West, Britain would make peace. The British, however, continued to reject Hitler's overtures, for they envisioned a bleak future if Nazi Germany dominated the Continent. With Britain unwilling to come to terms, Hitler proceeded in earnest with invasion plans. A successful crossing of the English Channel and the establishment of beachheads on the English coast depended on control of the skies. In early August 1940, the Luftwaffe began massive attacks on British air and naval installations. Virtually every day during the Battle of Britain, hundreds of planes fought in the sky above Britain as British pilots rose to the challenge. On September 15, the Royal Air Force (RAF) shot down sixty aircraft; two days later Hitler postponed the invasion of Britain "until further notice." The development of radar by British scientists, the skill and courage of British fighter pilots, and the inability of Germany to make up its losses in planes saved Britain in its struggle for survival. With the invasion of Britain called off, the Luftwaffe concentrated on bombing English cities, industrial centers, and ports. Almost every night for months, the inhabitants of London sought shelter in subways and cellars to escape German bombs, while British planes rose time after time to make the Luftwaffe pay the price. British morale never broke during the "Blitz."

Winston Churchill
"BLOOD, TOIL, TEARS, AND SWEAT"

Churchill, at the age of sixty-six, proved to be an undaunted leader, sharing the perils faced by all and able by example and by speeches to rally British morale. When he first addressed Parliament as prime minister on May 13, 1940, he left no doubt about the grim realities that lay ahead. Excerpts from his speeches in 1940 follow.

May 13, 1940

I would say to the House, as I said to those who have joined this Government: "I have nothing to offer but blood, toil, tears, and sweat." We have before us an ordeal of the most grievous kind. We have before us many, many long months of struggle and suffering. You ask: "What is our policy?" I will say: "It is to wage war by sea, land, and air with all our might, and with all the strength that God can give us; to wage war against a monstrous tyranny, never surpassed in the dark lamentable catalogue of human crime." That is our policy.

You ask: "What is our aim?" I can answer in one word: "Victory!" Victory at all costs, victory in spite of all terror, victory however long and hard the road may be; for without victory there is no survival.

When Churchill spoke next, on May 19, the Dutch had surrendered to the Germans, and the French and British armies were in retreat. Still, Churchill promised that "conquer we shall."

May 19, 1940

This is one of the most awe-striking periods in the long history of France and Britain. It is also beyond doubt the most sublime. Side by side, unaided except by their kith and kin in the great Dominions and by the wide Empires which rest beneath their shield—side by side, the British and French peoples have advanced to rescue not only Europe but mankind from the foulest and most soul-destroying tyranny which has ever darkened and stained the pages of history. Behind them—behind us—behind the armies and fleets of Britain and France—gather a group of shattered states and bludgeoned races: the Czechs, the Poles, the Norwegians, the Danes, the Dutch, the Belgians—upon all of whom the long night of barbarism will descend unbroken even by a star of hope, unless we conquer, as conquer we must; as conquer we shall.

By early June the Belgians had surrendered to the Germans, and the last units of the British Expeditionary Force in France had been evacuated from Dunkirk; the French armies were in full flight. Again Churchill spoke out in defiance of events across the Channel.

June 4, 1940

We shall not flag or fail. We shall go on to the end. We shall fight in France, we shall fight on the seas and oceans, we shall fight with growing confidence and growing strength in the air. We shall defend our island, whatever the cost may be. We shall fight on the beaches, we shall fight on the landing-grounds, we shall fight in the fields and in the streets, we shall fight in the hills. We shall never surrender; and even if, which I do not for a moment believe, this island or a large part of it were subjugated and starving, then our Empire beyond the seas, armed and guarded by the British Fleet, would carry on the struggle, until, in God's good time, the New World, with all its power and might, steps forth to the rescue and liberation of the Old.

By June 18 the battle of France was lost; on June 22 France surrendered. Now Britain itself was under siege. Churchill again found the right words to sustain his people:

June 18, 1940

What General [Maxime] Weygand [commander of the French army] called the Battle of France is over. . . . The Battle of Britain is about to begin. Upon this battle depends the survival of Christian civilization. Upon it depends our own British life and the long continuity of our institutions and our Empire. The whole fury and might of the enemy must very soon be turned upon us. Hitler knows that he will have to break us in this island or lose the war.

If we can stand up to him, all Europe may be free and the life of the world may move forward into broad sunlit uplands. But if we fail, then the whole world, including the United States, including all that we have known and cared for, will sink into the abyss of a new Dark Age made more sinister and perhaps more prolonged by the lights of a perverted science.

Let us therefore brace ourselves to our duty and so bear ourselves that if the British Empire and Commonwealth last for a thousand years, men will still say, "This was their finest hour."

With Britain unwilling to come to terms, Hitler proceeded in earnest with invasion plans. Crossing the English Channel and establishing beachheads on the English coast depended on control of the skies. Starting in early August 1940, the Luftwaffe began massive attacks on British air and naval installations. Heavy losses in aircraft forced Hitler on September 17 to call off the invasion. While the Battle of Britain raged, Churchill lauded the courage of British airmen who rose to the challenge.

August 20, 1940

The gratitude of every home in our island, in our Empire, and indeed throughout the world, except in the abodes of the guilty, goes out to the British airmen who, undaunted by odds, unwearied in their constant challenge and mor-

tal danger, are turning the tide of world war by their prowess and by their devotion. Never in the field of human conflict was so much owed by so many to so few. All hearts go out to the fighter pilots whose brilliant actions we see with our own eyes day after day.

REVIEW QUESTIONS

1. According to Winston Churchill, what would a Nazi victory mean for Europe?
2. On whose help did Churchill ultimately count for the liberation of Europe?
3. Both Hitler and Churchill were gifted orators. Compare their styles.

---

7 Nazi Propaganda: for Volk, Führer, and Fatherland

After World War II, Germans maintained that the Wehrmacht (the German army) was an apolitical professional fighting force that remained free of Nazi ideology and was uninvolved in criminal acts perpetrated by Heinrich Himmler's SS, the elite units responsible for the extermination of Jews. It is now known that units of the German army assisted the SS in the rounding up of Jews and at times participated in mass murder. Recently historians have also argued that the regular army, far from being apolitical, was imbued with Nazi ideology, and that many German officers and soldiers, succumbing to Nazi indoctrination, viewed the war, particularly on the eastern front, as a titanic struggle against evil and subhuman Jewish-led Bolsheviks who threatened the very existence of the German Volk.

THE INDOCTRINATION OF THE GERMAN SOLDIER

The following excerpts from German army propaganda and letters written by soldiers show how Nazi ideology influenced ordinary German troops. The first is a news-sheet published by the High Command of the Armed Forces in the spring of 1940, and distributed to all army units, which expressed quasi-religious fervor for the Führer.

THE FÜHRER AS SAVIOR

Behind the battle of annihilation of May 1940 stands in lone greatness the name of the Führer.

All that has been accomplished since he has taken the fate of our people into his strong hands!

. . . He gave the people back its unity, smashed the parties and destroyed the hydra of the organizations . . . he decontaminated the body of our people from the Jewish subversion, created a stock-proud, race-conscious *Volk,* which had overcome the racial death of diminishing births and was granted renewed [abundance of childbirths] as a carrier of the great future of the Fatherland. He subdued the terrible plight of unemployment and granted to millions of people who had already despaired of the *Volk* a new belief in the *Volksgemeinschaft* [community of the people] and happiness in a new Fatherland. . . .

His genius, in which the whole strength of Germandom is embodied with ancient powers, has animated the souls of 80,000,000 Germans, has filled them with strength and will, with the storm and stress *(Sturm und Drang)* of a renewed young people; and, himself the first soldier of Germany, he has entered the name of the German soldier into the book of immortality.

All this we were allowed to experience. Our great duty in this year of decision is that we do not accept it as observers, but that we, enchanted, and with all the passion of which we are capable, sacrifice ourselves to this Führer and strive to be worthy of the historical epoch molded by a heaven-storming will.

This same religious devotion to Hitler and Nazi ideology was expressed in literature given to company commanders to assist them in indoctrinating their troops.

Only the Führer could carry out what had not been achieved for a thousand years. . . . [He has] brought together all the German stock . . . for the struggle for freedom and living space . . . [and] directed all his thoughts and efforts toward the National Socialist education of the *Volk,* the inner cohesion of the state, the armament and offensive capability of the Wehrmacht. . . . When the German Eastern Armies fought an unparalleled battle during the winter of 1941–42 in the snow and ice of the Russian winter, he said: "Any weakling can put up with victories. Only the strong can stand firm in battles of destiny. But heaven gives the ultimate and

highest prize only to those who are capable of withstanding battles of destiny." In the difficult winter of 1942–43 the strength of the Führer was demonstrated once more, when . . . he called upon the German *Volk* at the front and in the homeland to stand firm and make the supreme effort. The Führer . . . clearly sees the goal ahead: a strong German Reich as the power of order in Europe and a firm root of the German *Lebensraum.* This goal will be achieved if the whole *Volk* remains loyal to him even in difficult times and as long as we soldiers do our duty.

Such words were not without their impact on German soldiers. In November 1940, one soldier expressed his feelings about Hitler in a letter home.

The last words of the Führer's radio address are over and a new strength streams through our veins. It is as if he spoke to each individual, to everyone of us, as if he wanted to give everyone new strength. With loyalty and a sense of duty, we must fight for our principles and endure to the end. Our Führer represents our united German Fatherland. . . . What we do for him, we do for all of you; what we sacrifice in foreign lands, we sacrifice for our loved ones. When the Führer speaks on these festive occasions, I feel deep in my soul that you at home also feel that we must be ready to make all sacrifices. . . . German victory is as certain as our love for each other. Just as we believe in our love, so we believe in our final victory and in the future of our people and our Fatherland.

Similar sentiments were voiced by a private in a letter to his brother.

The Führer has grown into the greatest figure of the century, in his hand lies the destiny of the world and of culturally-perceptive humanity. May his pure sword strike down the Satanic monster. Yes, the blows are still hard, but the horror will be forced into the shadows through the inexorable Need, through the command which derives from our National Socialist idea. This [battle] is for a new ideology, a new belief, a new life! I am glad that I can participate, even if as a tiny cog, in this war of light against darkness.

BOLSHEVIKS AND JEWS AS DEVILS

German propaganda described Jews and Russian communists in racial and religious terms, calling them a morally depraved form of humanity in the service of Satan. A tract from SS headquarters illustrates the mythical quality of Nazism.

Just as night rises up against the day, just as light and darkness are eternal enemies, so the greatest enemy of world-dominating man is man himself. The sub-man—that creature which looks as though biologically it were of absolutely the same kind, endowed by Nature with hands, feet and a sort of brain, with eyes and mouth—is nevertheless a totally different, a fearful creature, is only an attempt at a human being, with a quasi-human face, yet in mind and spirit lower than any animal. Inside this being a cruel chaos of wild, unchecked passions: a nameless will to destruction, the most primitive lusts, the most undisguised vileness. A sub-man—nothing else! . . . Never has the sub-man granted peace, never has he permitted rest. . . . To preserve himself he needed mud, he needed hell, but not the sun. And this underworld of sub-men found its leader: the eternal Jew!

The news-sheet distributed to regular army units used similar language.

Anyone who has ever looked at the face of a red commissar knows what the Bolsheviks are like. Here there is no need for theoretical expressions. We would insult the animals if we described these mostly Jewish men as beasts. They are the embodiment of the Satanic and insane hatred against the whole of noble humanity. The shape of these commissars reveals to us the rebellion of the *Untermenschen* [sub-men] against noble blood. The masses, whom they have sent to their deaths [in this war against Germany] by making use of all means at their disposal such as ice-cold terror and insane incitement, would have brought an end to all meaningful life, had this eruption not been dammed at the last moment.

In October 1941, Walter von Reichenau, commander of the sixth army, appealed to his men in the language of Nazi racial ideology.

The essential goal of the campaign against the Jewish-Bolshevik system is the complete destruction of its power instruments and the eradication of the Asiatic influence on the European cultural sphere. . . . Therefore the soldier must have *complete* understanding for the necessity of the harsh, but just atonement of Jewish subhumanity.

In November 1941, General von Manstein, commander of the eleventh army, used much the same language.

Since 22 June the German *Volk* is in the midst of a battle for life and death against the Bolshevik system. This battle is conducted against the Soviet army not only in a conventional manner according to the rules of European warfare. . . .

Judaism constitutes the mediator between the enemy in the rear and the still fighting remnants of the Red Army and the Red leadership. It has a stronger hold than in Europe on all key positions of the political leadership and administration, it occupies commerce and trade and further forms cells for all the disturbances and possible rebellions.

The Jewish-Bolshevik system must be eradicated once and for all. Never again may it interfere in our European living space.

The German soldier is therefore not only charged with the task of destroying the power instrument of this system. He marches forth also as a carrier of a racial conception and as an avenger of all the atrocities which have been committed against him and the German people.

The soldier must show understanding for the harsh atonement of Judaism, the spiritual carrier of the Bolshevik terror.

And in that same month, Colonel-General Hoth also interpreted the war as a struggle between racial superiors and inferiors.

It has become increasingly clear to us this summer, that here in the East spiritually unbridgeable conceptions are fighting each other: German sense of honor and race, and a soldierly tradition of many centuries, against an Asiatic mode of thinking and primitive instincts, whipped up by a small number of mostly Jewish intellectuals: fear of the knout [whip used for flogging], disregard of moral values, levelling down, throwing away of one's worthless life.

More than ever we are filled with the thought of a new era, in which the strength of the German people's racial superiority and achievements entrust it with the leadership of Europe. We clearly recognize our mission to save European culture from the advancing Asiatic barbarism. We now know that we have to fight against an incensed and tough opponent. This battle can only end with the destruction of one or the other; a compromise is out of the question.

The frontline soldier was affected by ideological propaganda.

I have received the "Stürmer" [a notoriously anti-Semitic newspaper] now for the third time. It makes me happy with all my heart. . . . You could not have made me happier. . . . I recognized the Jewish poison in our people long ago; how far it might have gone with us, this we see only now in this campaign. What the Jewish-regime has done in Russia, we see every day, and even the last doubters are cured here in view of the facts. We must and we will liberate the world from this plague, this is why the German soldier protects the Eastern Front, and we shall not return before we have uprooted all evil and destroyed the center of the Jewish-Bolshevik "world-do-gooders."

REVIEW QUESTIONS

1. How did Nazi propaganda depict Hitler? Germans? Jews? Russians?
2. Why was such propaganda effective?

---

8 Stalingrad: A Turning Point

In July 1942, the Germans resumed their advance into the U.S.S.R. begun the previous summer, seeking to conquer Stalingrad, a vital transportation center located on the Volga River. Germans and Russians battled with dogged ferocity over every part of the city; 99 percent of Stalingrad was reduced to rubble. A Russian counteroffensive in November trapped the German Sixth Army. Realizing that the Sixth Army, exhausted and short of weapons, ammunition, food, and medical supplies, faced annihilation, German generals pleaded in vain with Hitler to permit withdrawal before the Russians closed the ring. On February 2, 1943, the remnants of the Sixth Army surrendered. More than a million people—Russian civilians and soldiers, Germans and their Italian, Hungarian, and Romanian allies—perished in the epic struggle for Stalingrad. The Russian victory was a major turning point in the war.

William Hoffman
DIARY OF A GERMAN SOLDIER

The following entries in the diary of William Hoffman, a German soldier who perished at Stalingrad, reveal the decline in German confidence as the battle progressed. While the German army was penetrating deeply into Russia, he believed that victory was not far away and dreamed of returning home with medals. Then the terrible struggles in Stalingrad made him curse the war.

Today, after we'd had a bath, the company commander told us that if our future operations are as successful, we'll soon reach the Volga, take Stalingrad and then the war will inevitably soon be over. Perhaps we'll be home by Christmas.

July 29 1942. . . . The company commander says the Russian troops are completely broken, and cannot hold out any longer. To reach the Volga and take Stalingrad is not so difficult for us. The Führer knows where the Russians' weak point is. Victory is not far away. . . .

August 2. . . . What great spaces the Soviets occupy, what rich fields there are to be had here after the war's over! Only let's get it over with quickly. I believe that the Führer will carry the thing through to a successful end.

August 10. . . . The Führer's orders were read out to us. He expects victory of us. We are all convinced that they can't stop us.

August 12. We are advancing towards Stalingrad along the railway line. Yesterday Russian "katyushi" [small rocket launchers] and then

tanks halted our regiment. "The Russians are throwing in their last forces," Captain Werner explained to me. Large-scale help is coming up for us, and the Russians will be beaten.

This morning outstanding soldiers were presented with decorations. . . . Will I really go back to Elsa without a decoration? I believe that for Stalingrad the Führer will decorate even me. . . .

August 23. Splendid news—north of Stalingrad our troops have reached the Volga and captured part of the city. The Russians have two alternatives, either to flee across the Volga or give themselves up. Our company's interpreter has interrogated a captured Russian officer. He was wounded, but asserted that the Russians would fight for Stalingrad to the last round. Something incomprehensible is, in fact, going on. In the north our troops capture a part of Stalingrad and reach the Volga, but in the south the doomed divisions are continuing to resist bitterly. Fanaticism. . . .

August 27. A continuous cannonade on all sides. We are slowly advancing. Less than twenty miles to go to Stalingrad. In the daytime we can see the smoke of fires, at night-time the bright glow. They say that the city is on fire; on the Führer's orders our Luftwaffe [air force] has sent it up in flames. That's what the Russians need, to stop them from resisting . . .

September 4. We are being sent northward along the front towards Stalingrad. We marched all night and by dawn had reached Voroponovo Station. We can already see the smoking town. It's a happy thought that the end of the war is getting nearer. That's what everyone is saying. If only the days and nights would pass more quickly . . .

September 5. Our regiment has been ordered to attack Sadovaya station—that's nearly in Stalingrad. Are the Russians really thinking of holding out in the city itself? We had no peace all night from the Russian artillery and aeroplanes. Lots of wounded are being brought by. God protect me . . .

September 8. Two days of non-stop fighting. The Russians are defending themselves with insane stubbornness. Our regiment has lost many men from the "katyushi," which belch out terrible fire. I have been sent to work at battalion H.Q. It must be mother's prayers that have taken me away from the company's trenches . . .

September 11. Our battalion is fighting in the suburbs of Stalingrad. We can already see the Volga; firing is going on all the time. Wherever you look is fire and flames. . . . Russian cannon and machine-guns are firing out of the burning city. Fanatics . . .

September 13. An unlucky number. This morning "katyushi" attacks caused the company heavy losses: twenty-seven dead and fifty wounded. The Russians are fighting desperately like wild beasts, don't give themselves up, but come up close and then throw grenades. Lieutenant Kraus was killed yesterday, and there is no company commander.

September 16. Our battalion, plus tanks, is attacking the [grain storage] elevator, from which smoke is pouring—the grain in it is burning, the Russians seem to have set light to it themselves. Barbarism. The battalion is suffering heavy losses. There are not more than sixty men left in each company. The elevator is occupied not by men but by devils that no flames or bullets can destroy.

September 18. Fighting is going on inside the elevator. The Russians inside are condemned men; the battalion commander says: "The commissars have ordered those men to die in the elevator."

If all the buildings of Stalingrad are defended like this then none of our soldiers will get back to Germany. I had a letter from Elsa today. She's expecting me home when victory's won.

September 20. The battle for the elevator is still going on. The Russians are firing on all sides. We stay in our cellar; you can't go out into the street. Sergeant-Major Nuschke was killed today running across a street. Poor fellow, he's got three children.

September 22. Russian resistance in the elevator has been broken. Our troops are advancing towards the Volga. . . .

. . . Our old soldiers have never experienced such bitter fighting before.

September 26. Our regiment is involved in constant heavy fighting. After the elevator was taken the Russians continued to defend themselves just as stubbornly. You don't see them at all, they have established themselves in houses and cellars and are firing on all sides, including from our rear—barbarians, they use gangster methods.

In the blocks captured two days ago Russian soldiers appeared from somewhere or other and fighting has flared up with fresh vigour. Our men are being killed not only in the firing line, but in the rear, in buildings we have already occupied.

The Russians have stopped surrendering at all. If we take any prisoners it's because they are hopelessly wounded, and can't move by themselves. Stalingrad is hell. Those who are merely wounded are lucky; they will doubtless be at home and celebrate victory with their families. . . .

September 28. Our regiment, and the whole division, are today celebrating victory. Together with our tank crews we have taken the southern part of the city and reached the Volga. We paid dearly for our victory. In three weeks we have occupied about five and a half square miles. The commander has congratulated us on our victory. . . .

October 3. After marching through the night we have established ourselves in a shrub-covered gully. We are apparently going to attack the factories, the chimneys of which we can see clearly. Behind them is the Volga. We have entered a new area. It was night but we saw many crosses with our helmets on top. Have we really lost so many men? Damn this Stalingrad!

October 4. Our regiment is attacking the Barrikady settlement. A lot of Russian tommy-gunners have appeared. Where are they bringing them from?

October 5. Our battalion has gone into the attack four times, and got stopped each time. Russian snipers hit anyone who shows himself carelessly from behind shelter.

October 10. The Russians are so close to us that our planes cannot bomb them. We are preparing for a decisive attack. The Führer has ordered the whole of Stalingrad to be taken as rapidly as possible.

October 14. It has been fantastic since morning: our aeroplanes and artillery have been hammering the Russian positions for hours on end; everything in sight is being blotted from the face of the earth. . . .

October 22. Our regiment has failed to break into the factory. We have lost many men; every time you move you have to jump over bodies. You can scarcely breathe in the daytime: there is nowhere and no one to remove the bodies, so they are left there to rot. Who would have thought three months ago that instead of the joy of victory we would have to endure such sacrifice and torture, the end of which is nowhere in sight? . . .

The soldiers are calling Stalingrad the mass grave of the Wehrmacht [German army]. There are very few men left in the companies. We have been told we are soon going to be withdrawn to be brought back up to strength.

October 27. Our troops have captured the whole of the Barrikady factory, but we cannot break through to the Volga. The Russians are not men, but some kind of cast-iron creatures; they never get tired and are not afraid of fire. We are absolutely exhausted; our regiment now has barely the strength of a company. The Russian artillery at the other side of the Volga won't let you lift your head. . . .

October 28. Every soldier sees himself as a condemned man. The only hope is to be wounded and taken back to the rear. . . .

November 3. In the last few days our battalion has several times tried to attack the Russian positions, . . . to no avail. On this sector also the Russians won't let you lift your head. There have been a number of cases of self-inflicted wounds and malingering among the men. Every day I write two or three reports about them.

November 10. A letter from Elsa today. Everyone expects us home for Christmas. In Germany everyone believes we already hold Stalingrad. How wrong they are. If they could only see what Stalingrad has done to our army.

November 18. Our attack with tanks yesterday had no success. After our attack the field was littered with dead.

November 21. The Russians have gone over to the offensive along the whole front. Fierce fighting is going on. So, there it is—the Volga, victory and soon home to our families! We shall obviously be seeing them next in the other world.

November 29. We are encircled. It was announced this morning that the Führer has said: "The army can trust me to do everything necessary to ensure supplies and rapidly break the encirclement."

December 3. We are on hunger rations and waiting for the rescue that the Führer promised.

I send letters home, but there is no reply.

December 7. Rations have been cut to such an extent that the soldiers are suffering terribly from hunger; they are issuing one loaf of stale bread for five men.

December 11. Three questions are obsessing every soldier and officer: When will the Russians stop firing and let us sleep in peace, if only for one night? How and with what are we going to fill our empty stomachs, which, apart from 3½-7 ozs of bread, receive virtually nothing at all? And when will Hitler take any decisive steps to free our armies from encirclement?

December 14. Everybody is racked with hunger. Frozen potatoes are the best meal, but to get them out of the ice-covered ground under fire from Russian bullets is not so easy.

December 18. The officers today told the soldiers to be prepared for action. General Manstein is approaching Stalingrad from the south with strong forces. This news brought hope to the soldiers' hearts. God, let it be!

December 21. We are waiting for the order, but for some reason or other it has been a long time coming. Can it be that it is not true about Manstein? This is worse than any torture.

December 23. Still no orders. It was all a bluff with Manstein. Or has he been defeated at the approaches to Stalingrad?

December 25. The Russian radio has announced the defeat of Manstein. Ahead of us is either death or captivity.

December 26. The horses have already been eaten. I would eat a cat; they say its meat is also tasty. The soldiers look like corpses or lunatics, looking for something to put in their mouths. They no longer take cover from Russian shells; they haven't the strength to walk, run away and hide. A curse on this war! . . .

Anton Kuzmich Dragan
A SOVIET VETERAN RECALLS

Anton Kuzmich Dragan, a Russian soldier, describes the vicious street fighting in Stalingrad during late September 1942.

'The Germans had cut us off from our neighbours. The supply of ammunition had been cut off; every bullet was worth its weight in gold. I gave the order to economize on ammunition, to collect the cartridge-pouches of the dead and all captured weapons. In the evening the enemy again tried to break our resistance, coming up close to our positions. As our numbers grew smaller, we shortened our line of defence. We began to move back slowly towards the Volga, drawing the enemy after us, and the ground we occupied was invariably too small for the Germans to be able easily to use artillery and aircraft.

'We moved back, occupying one building after another, turning them into strongholds. A soldier would crawl out of an occupied position only when the ground was on fire under him and his clothes were smouldering. During the day the Germans managed to occupy only two blocks.

'At the crossroads of Krasnopiterskaya and Komsomolskaya Streets we occupied a three-storey building on the corner. This was a good position from which to fire on all comers and it became our last defence. I ordered all entrances to be barricaded, and windows and embrasures to be adapted so that we could fire through them with all our remaining weapons.

'At a narrow window of the semi-basement we placed the heavy machine-gun with our emergency supply of ammunition—the last belt of cartridges. I had decided to use it at the most critical moment.

'Two groups, six in each, went up to the third floor and the garret. Their job was to break down walls, and prepare lumps of stone and beams to throw at the Germans when they came up close. A place for the seriously wounded was set aside in the basement. Our garrison consisted of forty men. Difficult days began. Attack after attack broke unendingly like waves against us. After each attack was beaten off we felt it was impossible to hold off the onslaught any longer, but when the Germans launched a fresh attack, we managed to find means and strength. This lasted five days and nights.

'The basement was full of wounded; only twelve men were still able to fight. There was no water. All we had left in the way of food was a few pounds of scorched grain; the Germans decided to beat us with starvation. Their attacks stopped, but they kept up the fire from their heavy-calibre machine-guns all the time.

'We did not think about escape, but only about how to sell our lives most dearly—we had no other way out. . . .

'The Germans attacked again. I ran upstairs with my men and could see their thin, blackened and strained faces, the bandages on their wounds, dirty and clotted with blood, their guns held firmly in their hands. There was no fear in their eyes. Lyuba Nesterenko, a nurse, was dying, with blood flowing from a wound in her chest. She had a bandage in her hand. Before she died she wanted to help to bind someone's wound, but she failed . . .

'The German attack was beaten off. In the silence that gathered around us we could hear the bitter fighting going on for Mameyev Kurgan and in the factory area of the city.

'How could we help the men defending the city? How could we divert from over there even a part of the enemy forces, which had stopped attacking our building?

'We decided to raise a red flag over the building, so that the Nazis would not think we had given up. But we had no red material. Understanding what we wanted to do, one of the men who was severely wounded took off his bloody vest and, after wiping the blood off his wound with it, handed it over to me.

'The Germans shouted through a megaphone: "Russians! Surrender! You'll die just the same!"

'At that moment a red flag rose over our building.'

'"Bark, you dogs! We've still got a long time to live!" shouted my orderly, Kozhushko.

'We beat off the next attack with stones, firing occasionally and throwing our last grenades. Suddenly from behind a blank wall, from the rear, came the grind of a tank's caterpillar tracks. We had no anti-tank grenades. All we had left was one anti-tank rifle with three rounds. I handed this rifle to an anti-tank man, Berdyshev, and sent him out through the back to fire at the tank point-blank. But before he could get into position he was captured by German tommy-gunners. What Berdyshev told the Germans I don't know, but I can guess that he led them up the garden path, because an hour later they started to attack at precisely that point where I had put my machine-gun with its emergency belt of cartridges.

'This time, reckoning that we had run out of ammunition, they came impudently out of their shelter, standing up and shouting. They came down the street in a column.

'I put the last belt in the heavy machine-gun at the semi-basement window and sent the whole of the 250 bullets into the yelling, dirty-grey Nazi mob. I was wounded in the hand but did not leave go of the machine-gun. Heaps of bodies littered the ground. The Germans still alive ran for cover in panic. An hour later they led our anti-tank rifleman on to a heap of ruins and shot him in front of our eyes, for having shown them the way to my machine-gun.

'There were no more attacks. An avalanche of shells fell on the building. The Germans stormed at us with every possible kind of weapon. We couldn't raise our heads.

'Again we heard the ominous sound of tanks. From behind a neighbouring block stocky German tanks began to crawl out. This, clearly, was the end. The guardsmen said good-bye to one another. With a dagger my orderly scratched on a brick wall: "Rodimtsev's guardsmen fought and died for their country here." The battalion's documents and a map case containing the Party and Komsomol cards of the defenders of the building had been put in a hole in a corner of the basement. The first salvo shattered the silence. There were a series of blows, and the building rocked and collapsed. How much later it was when I opened my eyes, I don't know. It was dark. The air was full of acrid brickdust. I could hear muffled groans around me. Kozhushko, the orderly, was pulling at me:

'"You're alive . . ."

'On the floor of the basement lay a number of other stunned and injured soldiers. We had been buried alive under the ruins of the three-storey building. We could scarcely breathe. We had no thought for food or water—it was air that had become most important for survival. I spoke to the soldiers:

'"Men! We did not flinch in battle, we fought even when resistance seemed impossible, and we have to get out of this tomb so that we can live and avenge the death of our comrades!"

'Even in pitch darkness you can see somebody else's face, feel other people close to you.

'With great difficulty we began to pick our way out of the tomb. We worked in silence, our bodies covered with cold, clammy sweat, our badly-bound wounds ached, our teeth were covered with brickdust, it became more and more difficult to breathe, but there were no groans or complaints.

'A few hours later, through the hole we had made, we could see the stars and breathe the fresh September air.

'Utterly exhausted, the men crowded round the hole, greedily gulping in the autumn air. Soon the opening was wide enough for a man to crawl through. Kozhushko, being only relatively slightly injured, went off to reconnoitre. An hour later he came back and reported:

'"Comrade Lieutenant, there are Germans all round us; along the Volga they are mining the bank; there are German patrols nearby . . ."

'We took the decision to fight our way through to our own lines.'

Joachim Wieder
MEMORIES AND REASSESSMENTS

In 1962, Joachim Wieder, a German officer who had survived Stalingrad and Russian captivity, wrote *Stalingrad: Memories and Reassessments,* in which he described his feelings as the Russians closed the ring on the trapped Sixth

Army. Wieder recalled his outrage at Hitler's refusal to allow the Sixth Army to break out when it still had a chance. As the German army faced decimation, he reflected on the misery and death the invading German forces had inflicted on other people and the terrible retribution Germany would suffer.

A foreboding I had long held grew into a terrible certainty. What was happening here in Stalingrad was a tragic, senseless self-sacrifice, a scarcely credible betrayal of the final commitment and devotion of brave soldiers. Our innocent trust had been misused in the most despicable manner by those responsible for the catastrophe. We had been betrayed, led astray and condemned. The men of Stalingrad were dying in betrayed belief and in betrayed trust. In my heart the bitter feeling of '. . . and all for nothing' became ever more torturing.

In my soul arose again the whole abysmal disaster of the war itself. More clearly than ever before I appreciated the full measure of misery and wretchedness of the other countries in Europe to which German soldiers and German arms had brought boundless misfortune. Had not we, so far the victors, been all too prone to close our eyes and our hearts and to forget that always and everywhere, the issues were living human beings, their possessions and their happiness?

Probably only a few among us had entertained the thought that the suffering and dying being caused by our sorry profession of war would one day be inflicted upon us. We had carried our total war into one region of Europe after another and thereby destructively interfered in the destinies of foreign nations. Far too little had we asked the reason why, the necessities and the justifications for what was happening or reflected on the immeasurability of our political responsibility that these entailed. Misery and death had been initiated by us and now they were inexorably coming home to roost. The steppe on the Don and the Volga had drunk streams of precious human blood. Here in their hundreds of thousands had Germans, Roumanians, Italians, Russians and members of other Soviet peoples found their common grave.

The Russians were certainly also making cruelly high blood sacrifices in the murderous battle of Stalingrad. But they, who were defending their country against a foreign aggressor, knew better than we why they were risking their lives.

Several thousand Red Army prisoners suffering hunger and misery behind barbed wire at Voroponovo and doomed to share our downfall were particularly to be pitied. In my broodings which constantly haunted and tortured me, I began to realise just how much our feelings had atrophied towards the continual boundless disregard and violation of human dignity and human life. At the same time my horror and revulsion of the Moloch[1] of war, to whom ethical-religious conscience had stood in irreconcilable opposition from the very beginning, grew.

And so as the last days of our army were drawing to a close, a deep moral misery gnawed at the hearts of the men helplessly doomed to destruction. Added to their indescribable external suffering were the violent internal conflicts caused by the voice of conscience, and not only with regard to the question of the unconditional duty to obey. Wherever I went and observed I saw the same picture. And what I learned about the matter later on only confirmed the impressions I had gained. Whoever was still unclear about the contexts and reasons for the catastrophe sensed them in dark despair.

Many officers and commanders now began to oppose the insane orders emanating from Führer Headquarters and being passed on by Army Command. By this they began to reject the long eroded military concepts of honour and discipline to which the Army leadership had

---

[1]In the Old Testament Moloch was the god of the Ammonites and the Phoenicians to whom children were sacrificed.

clung until the end. In the unconditional obe-dience, such as was fatally being upheld here at Stalingrad, they no longer saw a soldierly stance but rather a lack of responsibility. . . .

How shocked had we been then at the very outset of the eastern campaign, about two in-humane orders of the day that had been in open breach of international law and of true, decent German soldiery itself! These were the uneth-ical 'commissar order' that required the phys-ical extermination of the regulators of the Bolshevik ideology in the Red Army, and the 'Barbarossa order' dealing with military tri-bunals, that abolished mandatory prosecution of crimes by German soldiers against civilians in the eastern theatre. Even if these orders had only been acknowledged by our staffs on the front and evaded as far as possible, was it not guilt enough to have accepted and tolerated them in silence like so much else?

And what had gone on in the rear of the fighting troops? Many an ugly rumour had come to one's ears, many an ugly picture had come before one's eyes. I had heard of brutal acts of retribution which had struck the in-nocent with the guilty. On a drive through the occupied area I had on one occasion seen in Minsk, with its dozens of public gallows, scenes of shameful inhumanity. Were all these excesses and evils not bound to rebound on us sooner or later? . . .

Now, faced with the imminently impend-ing final catastrophe, the question about the sense of what was happening that had plagued me so often during the war seized me again with cruel force. Hundreds of thousands of flowering human lives were suddenly being senselessly snuffed out here in Stalingrad. What an immeasurable wealth of human hap-piness, human plans, hopes, talents, fertile possibilities for the future were thereby being destroyed for ever! The criminal insanity of an irresponsible war management with its super-stitious belief in technology and its utter lack of feeling for the life, value and dignity of man, had here prepared a hell on earth for us. Of what importance was the individual in his uniqueness and distinctiveness? He felt him-self as if extinguished and used up as raw ma-terial in a demonic machine of destruction. Here war showed itself in its unmasked brutal-ity. Stalingrad appeared to me as an unsur-passed violation and degeneration of the human essence. I felt myself to be locked into a gigantic, inhuman mechanism that was run-ning on with deadly precision to its own disso-lution and destruction. . . .

In the sad events on the Volga I saw not only the military turning-point of the war. In the experiences behind me I felt and apprehended something else as well; the anticipation of the final catastrophe towards which the whole na-tion was reeling. In my mind's eye I suddenly saw a second Stalingrad, a repetition of the tragedy just lived through, but of much greater, more terrible proportions. It was a vast pocket battle on German soil with the whole German nation fighting for life or death inside. And were the issues not the same as those of the final months of our Sixth Army? In the sacrifice thus already ordained, would insight, the power of decision and the strength either to break out or to surrender be able to mature?

In our helpless abandonment, to feel our own fate and destruction breaking in on our country, was a crushing mental burden that was to become virtually unbearable in the times ahead.

REVIEW QUESTIONS

1. What were the expectations of William Hoffman as he marched with the German army in July and August? How did he view Hitler and the war?
2. How did the hard fighting at Stalingrad alter Hoffman's conception of the war and his attitude toward the Russians?
3. What does Anton Kuzmich Dragan's account reveal about the resolve of the Russian soldiers at Stalingrad?

4. What kinds of doubts attacked Joachim Wieder when the Sixth Army was trapped at Stalingrad?

9 The Holocaust

Over conquered Europe the Nazis imposed a "New Order" marked by exploitation, torture, and mass murder. The Germans took some 5.5 million Russian prisoners of war, of whom more than 3.5 million perished; many of these prisoners were deliberately starved to death. The Germans imprisoned and executed many Polish intellectuals and priests and slaughtered vast numbers of Gypsies. Using the modern state's organizational capacities and the instruments of modern technology, the Nazis murdered six million Jews, including one and a half million children—two-thirds of the Jewish population of Europe. Gripped by the mythical, perverted world-view of Nazism, the SS, Hitler's elite guard, carried out these murders with dedication and idealism; they believed that they were exterminating subhumans who threatened the German nation.

Hermann Graebe
SLAUGHTER OF JEWS IN THE UKRAINE

While the regular German army penetrated deeply into Russia, special SS units, the *Einsatzgruppen,* rounded up Jews for mass executions. Aided by Ukranian, Lithuanian, and Latvian auxiliaries, and contingents from the Romanian army, the Einsatzgruppen massacred 1 to 1.4 million Jews. Hermann Graebe, a German construction engineer, saw such a mass slaughter in Dubno in the Ukraine. He gave a sworn affidavit before the Nuremberg tribunal, a court at which the Allies tried Nazi war criminals after the end of World War II.

Graebe had joined the Nazi party in 1931 but later renounced his membership, and during the war he rescued Jews from the SS. Graebe was the only German citizen to volunteer to testify at the Nuremberg trials, an act that earned him the enmity of his compatriots. Socially ostracized, Graebe emigrated to the United States, where he died in 1986 at the age of eighty-five.

On October 5, 1942, when I visited the building office at Dubno, my foreman told me that in the vicinity of the site, Jews from Dubno had been shot in three large pits, each about 30 metres long and 3 metres deep. About 1,500 persons had been killed daily. All the 5,000 Jews who had still been living in Dubno before the pogrom were to be liquidated. As the shooting had taken place in his presence, he was still much upset.

Thereupon, I drove to the site accompanied by my foreman and saw near it great mounds of earth, about 30 metres long and 2 metres high. Several trucks stood in front of the mounds. Armed Ukrainian militia drove the people off the trucks under the supervision of an S.S.

man. The militiamen acted as guards on the trucks and drove them to and from the pit. All these people had the regulation yellow patches on the front and back of their clothes, and thus could be recognized as Jews.

My foreman and I went directly to the pits. Nobody bothered us. Now I heard rifle shots in quick succession from behind one of the earth mounds. The people who had got off the trucks—men, women and children of all ages—had to undress upon the orders of an S.S. man, who carried a riding or dog whip. They had to put down their clothes in fixed places, sorted according to shoes, top clothing and underclothing. I saw a heap of shoes of about 800 to 1,000 pairs, great piles of underlinen and clothing.

Without screaming or weeping, these people undressed, stood around in family groups, kissed each other, said farewells, and waited for a sign from another S.S. man, who stood near the pit, also with a whip in his hand. During the fifteen minutes that I stood near I heard no complaint or plea for mercy. I watched a family of about eight persons, a man and a woman both about fifty with their children of about one, eight and ten, and two grown-up daughters of about twenty to twenty-nine. An old woman with snow-white hair was holding the one-year-old child in her arms and singing to it and tickling it. The child was cooing with delight. The couple were looking on with tears in their eyes. The father was holding the hand of a boy about ten years old and speaking to him softly; the boy was fighting his tears. The father pointed to the sky, stroked his head, and seemed to explain something to him.

At that moment the S.S. man at the pit shouted something to his comrade. The latter counted off about twenty persons and instructed them to go behind the earth mound. Among them was the family which I have mentioned. I well remember a girl, slim and with black hair, who, as she passed close to me, pointed to herself and said "23." I walked around the mound and found myself confronted by a tremendous grave. People were closely wedged together and lying on top of each other so that only their heads were visible. Nearly all had blood running over their shoulders from their heads. Some of the people shot were still moving. Some were lifting their arms and turning their heads to show that they were still alive. The pit was already two-thirds full. I estimated that it already contained about 1,000 people.

I looked for the man who did the shooting. He was an S.S. man, who sat at the edge of the narrow end of the pit, his feet dangling into the pit. He had a tommy-gun on his knees and was smoking a cigarette. The people, completely naked, went down some steps which were cut in the clay wall of the pit and clambered over the heads of the people lying there, to the place to which the S.S. man directed them. They lay down in front of the dead or injured people; some caressed those who were still alive and spoke to them in a low voice.

Then I heard a series of shots. I looked into the pit and saw that the bodies were twitching or the heads lying motionless on top of the bodies which lay before them. Blood was running from their necks. I was surprised that I was not ordered away, but I saw that there were two or three postmen in uniform nearby. The next batch was approaching already. They went down into the pit, lined themselves up against the previous victims and were shot.

When I walked back round the mound, I noticed another truckload of people which had just arrived. This time it included sick and infirm persons. An old, very thin woman with terribly thin legs was undressed by others who were already naked, while two people held her up. The woman appeared to be paralyzed. The naked people carried the woman around the mound. I left with my foreman and drove in my car back to Dubno.

On the morning of the next day, when I again visited the site, I saw about thirty naked people lying near the pit—about 30 to 50 metres away from it. Some of them were still alive; they looked straight in front of them with a fixed stare and seemed to notice neither the chilliness of the morning nor the workers of my firm who stood around. A girl of about twenty spoke to me and asked me to give her clothes and help her escape. At that moment we heard a fast car approach and I noticed that it was an S.S. detail. I moved away to my site. Ten minutes later we heard shots from the vicinity of the pit. The Jews alive had been ordered to throw the corpses into the pit, then they had themselves to lie down in it to be shot in the neck.

Rudolf Hoess
COMMANDANT OF AUSCHWITZ

To speed up the "final solution of the Jewish problem," the SS established death camps in Poland. Jews from all over Europe were crammed into cattle cars and shipped to these camps to be gassed or worked to death. At Auschwitz, the most notorious of the concentration camps, the SS used five gas chambers to kill 9,000 or more people a day. Special squads of prisoners, called *Sonderkommandos,* were forced to pick over the corpses for gold teeth, jewelry, and anything else of value for the German war effort. Some 1.3 million Jews perished at Auschwitz. In the following passage from *Commandant of Auschwitz,* Rudolf Hoess (1900–1947), who commanded the camp and was executed by Poland after the war, recalled the murder process when he was in a Polish prison.

In the spring of 1942 the first transports of Jews, all earmarked for extermination, arrived from Upper Silesia.

They were taken from the detraining platform to the "cottage"—to bunker I—across the meadows where later building site II was located. The transport was conducted by Aumeier and Palitzsch and some of the block leaders. They talked with the Jews about general topics, inquiring concerning their qualifications and trades, with a view to misleading them. On arrival at the "cottage," they were told to undress. At first they went calmly into the rooms where they were supposed to be disinfected. But some of them showed signs of alarm, and spoke of death by suffocation and of annihilation. A sort of panic set in at once. Immediately all the Jews still outside were pushed into the chambers, and the doors were screwed shut. With subsequent transports the difficult individuals were picked out early and most carefully supervised. At the first signs of

unrest, those responsible were unobtrusively led behind the building and killed with a small-caliber gun, that was inaudible to the others. The presence and calm behavior of the Special Detachment [of *Sonderkommandos*] served to reassure those who were worried or who suspected what was about to happen. A further calming effect was obtained by members of the Special Detachment accompanying them into the rooms and remaining with them until the last moment, while an SS man also stood in the doorway until the end.

It was most important that the whole business of arriving and undressing should take place in an atmosphere of the greatest possible calm. People reluctant to take off their clothes had to be helped by those of their companions who had already undressed, or by men of the Special Detachment.

The refractory ones were calmed down and encouraged to undress. The prisoners of the Special Detachment also saw to it that the process of undressing was carried out quickly, so that the victims would have little time to wonder what was happening. . . .

Many of the women hid their babies among the piles of clothing. The men of the Special Detachment were particularly on the lookout for this, and would speak words of encouragement to the woman until they had persuaded her to take the child with her. The women believed that the disinfectant might be bad for their smaller children, hence their efforts to conceal them.

The smaller children usually cried because of the strangeness of being undressed in this fashion, but when their mothers or members of the Special Detachment comforted them, they became calm and entered the gas chambers, playing or joking with one another and carrying their toys.

I noticed that women who either guessed or knew what awaited them nevertheless found the courage to joke with the children to encourage them, despite the mortal terror visible in their own eyes.

One woman approached me as she walked past and, pointing to her four children who were manfully helping the smallest ones over the rough ground, whispered:

"How can you bring yourself to kill such beautiful, darling children? Have you no heart at all?"

One old man, as he passed by me, hissed:

"Germany will pay a heavy penance for this mass murder of the Jews."

His eyes glowed with hatred as he said this. Nevertheless he walked calmly into the gas chamber, without worrying about the others.

One young woman caught my attention particularly as she ran busily hither and thither, helping the smallest children and the old women to undress. During the selection she had had two small children with her, and her agitated behavior and appearance had brought her to my notice at once. She did not look in the least like a Jewess. Now her children were no longer with her. She waited until the end, helping the women who were not undressed and who had several children with them, encouraging them and calming the children. She went with the very last ones into the gas chamber. Standing in the doorway, she said:

"I knew all the time that we were being brought to Auschwitz to be gassed. When the selection took place I avoided being put with the able-bodied ones, as I wished to look after the children. I wanted to go through it all, fully conscious of what was happening. I hope that it will be quick. Goodbye!"

From time to time women would suddenly give the most terrible shrieks while undressing, or tear their hair, or scream like maniacs. These were immediately led away behind the building and shot in the back of the neck with a small-caliber weapon.

It sometimes happened that, as the men of the Special Detachment left the gas chamber, the women would suddenly realize what was happening, and would call down every imaginable curse upon our heads.

I remember, too, a woman who tried to throw her children out of the gas chamber, just as the door was closing. Weeping, she called out:

"At least let my precious children live."

There were many such shattering scenes, which affected all who witnessed them.

During the spring of 1942 hundreds of vigorous men and women walked all unsuspecting to their death in the gas chambers, under the blossom-laden fruit trees of the "cottage" orchard. This picture of death in the midst of life remains with me to this day.

The process of selection, which took place on the unloading platforms, was in itself rich in incident.

The breaking up of families, and the separation of the men from the women and children, caused much agitation and spread anxiety throughout the whole transport. This was increased by the further separation from the others of those capable of work. Families wished at all costs to remain together. Those who had been selected ran back to rejoin their relations. Mothers with children tried to join their husbands, or old people attempted to find those of their children who had been selected for work, and who had been led away.

Often the confusion was so great that the selections had to be begun all over again. The limited area of standing room did not permit better sorting arrangements. All attempts to pacify these agitated mobs were useless. It was often necessary to use force to restore order.

As I have already frequently said, the Jews have strongly developed family feelings. They stick together like limpets. . . .

Then the bodies had to be taken from the gas chambers, and after the gold teeth had been extracted, and the hair cut off, they had to be dragged to the pits or to the crematoria.

Then the fires in the pits had to be stoked, the surplus fat drained off, and the mountain of burning corpses constantly turned over so that the draught might fan the flames. . . .

It happened repeatedly that Jews of the Special Detachment would come upon the bodies of close relatives among the corpses, and even among the living as they entered the gas chambers. They were obviously affected by this, but it never led to any incident.[1]

---

[1]On October 7, 1944, the *Sonderkommandos* attacked the SS. Some SS guards were killed, and one crematorium was burned. Most of the prisoners who escaped were caught and killed.

Y. Pfeffer
CONCENTRATION CAMP LIFE AND DEATH

Jews not immediately selected for extermination faced a living death in the concentration camp, which also included non-Jewish inmates, many of them opponents of the Nazi regime. The SS, who ran the camps, took sadistic pleasure in humiliating and brutalizing their helpless Jewish victims. In 1946, Y. Pfeffer, a Jewish survivor of Majdanek concentration camp in Poland, described the world created by the SS and Nazi ideology.

You get up at 3 A.M. You have to dress quickly, and make the "bed" so that it looks like a matchbox. For the slightest irregularity in bed-making the punishment was 25 lashes, after which it was impossible to lie or sit for a whole month.

Everyone had to leave the barracks immediately. Outside it is still dark—or else the moon is shining. People are trembling because of lack of sleep and the cold. In order to warm up a bit, groups of ten to twenty people stand together, back to back so as to rub against each other.

There was what was called a wash-room, where everyone in the camp was supposed to wash—there were only a few faucets—and we were 4,500 people in that section (no. 3). Of course there was neither soap nor towel or even a handkerchief, so that washing was theoretical rather than practical. . . . In one day, a person there [be]came a lowly person indeed.

At 5 A.M. we used to get half a litre of black, bitter coffee. That was all we got for what was called "breakfast." At 6 A.M.—a headcount (*Appell* in German). We all had to stand at attention, in fives, according to the barracks, of which there were 22 in each section. We stood there until the SS men had satisfied their game-playing instincts by "humorous" orders to take off and put on caps. Then they received their report, and counted us. After the headcount—work.

We went in groups—some to build railway tracks or a road, some to the quarries to carry stones or coal, some to take out manure, or for potato-digging, latrine-cleaning, barracks—or sewer—repairs. All this took place inside the camp enclosure. During work the SS men beat up the prisoners mercilessly, inhumanly and for no reason.

They were like wild beasts and, having found their victim, ordered him to present his backside, and beat him with a stick or a whip, usually until the stick broke.

The victim screamed only after the first blows, afterwards he fell unconscious and the SS man then kicked at the ribs, the face, at the most sensitive parts of a man's body, and then, finally convinced that the victim was at the end of his strength, he ordered another Jew to pour one pail of water after the other over the beaten person until he woke and got up.

A favorite sport of the SS men was to make a "boxing sack" out of a Jew. This was done in the following way: Two Jews were stood up, one being forced to hold the other by the collar, and an SS man trained giving him a knockout. Of course, after the first blow, the poor victim was likely to fall, and this was prevented by the other Jew holding him up. After the fat, Hitlerite murderer had "trained" in this way for 15 minutes, and only after the poor victim was completely shattered, covered in blood, his teeth knocked out, his nose broken, his eyes hit, they released him and ordered a doctor to treat his wounds. That was their way of taking care and being generous.

Another customary SS habit was to kick a Jew with a heavy boot. The Jew was forced to stand to attention, and all the while the SS man kicked him until he broke some bones. People who stood near enough to such a victim, often heard the breaking of the bones. The pain was so terrible that people, having undergone that treatment, died in agony.

Apart from the SS men there were other expert hangmen. These were the so-called Capos. The name was an abbreviation for "barracks police." The Capos were German criminals who were also camp inmates. However, although they belonged to "us," they were privileged. They had

a special, better barracks of their own, they had better food, better, almost normal clothes, they wore special red or green riding pants, high leather boots, and fulfilled the functions of camp guards. They were worse even than the SS men. One of them, older than the others and the worst murderer of them all, when he descended on a victim, would not revive him later with water but would choke him to death. Once, this murderer caught a boy of 13 (in the presence of his father) and hit his head so that the poor child died instantly. This "camp elder" later boasted in front of his peers, with a smile on his beast's face and with pride, that he managed to kill a Jew with one blow.

In each section stood a gallows. For being late for the headcount, or similar crimes, the "camp elder" hanged the offenders.

Work was actually unproductive, and its purpose was exhaustion and torture.

At 12 noon there was a break for a meal. Standing in line, we received half a litre of soup each. Usually it was cabbage soup, or some other watery liquid, without fats, tasteless. That was lunch. It was eaten—in all weather—under the open sky, never in the barracks. No spoons were allowed, though wooden spoons lay on each bunk—probably for show, for Red Cross committees. One had to drink the soup out of the bowl and lick it like a dog.

From 1 P.M. till 6 P.M. there was work again. I must emphasize that if we were lucky we got a 12 o'clock meal. There were "days of punishment"—when lunch was given together with the evening meal, and it was cold and sour, so that our stomach was empty for a whole day.

Afternoon work was the same: blows, and blows again. Until 6 P.M.

At 6 there was the evening headcount. Again we were forced to stand at attention. Counting, receiving the report. Usually we were left standing at attention for an hour or two, while some prisoners were called up for "punishment parade"—they were those who in the Germans' eyes had transgressed in some way during the day, or had not been punctilious in their performance. They were stripped naked publicly, laid out on specially constructed benches, and whipped with 25 or 50 lashes.

The brutal beating and the heart-rending cries—all this the prisoners had to watch and hear.

Richard von Weizsäcker
"WE SEEK RECONCILIATION"

In a speech during a commemorative ceremony on May 8, 1985, Richard von Weizsäcker (b. 1920), president of the Federal Republic of Germany, reflected on the Holocaust and the need for remembrance.

May 8th is a day of remembrance. Remembering means recalling an occurrence honestly and undistortedly so that it becomes a part of our very beings. This places high demands on our truthfulness.

Today we mourn all the dead of the war and tyranny. In particular we commemorate the six million Jews who were murdered in German concentration camps. . . .

At the root of the tyranny was Hitler's immeasurable hatred of our Jewish compatriots. Hitler had never concealed this hatred from the public, and made the entire nation a tool of it. Only a day before his death, on April 30, 1945, he concluded his so-called "will" with the words: "Above all, I call upon the leaders of the nation and their followers to observe painstakingly the race laws and to oppose ruthlessly the poisoners of all nations: international Jewry." Hardly any country has in its history always remained free from blame for war or violence. The genocide of the Jews is, however, unparalleled in history.

The perpetration of this crime was in the hands of a few people. It was concealed from the eyes of the public, but every German was able to experience what his Jewish compatriots had to suffer, ranging from plain apathy and hidden intolerance to outright hatred. Who could remain unsuspecting after the burning of the synagogues, the plundering, the stigmatization with the Star of David, the deprivation of rights, the ceaseless violation of human dig-

nity? Whoever opened his eyes and ears and sought information could not fail to notice that Jews were being deported. The nature and scope of the destruction may have exceeded human imagination, but in reality there was, apart from the crime itself, the attempt by too many people, including those of my generation, who were young and were not involved in planning the events and carrying them out, not to take note of what was happening. There were many ways of not burdening one's conscience, of shunning responsibility, looking away, keeping mum. When the unspeakable truth of the Holocaust then became known at the end of the war, all too many of us claimed that they had not known anything about it or even suspected anything.

There is no such thing as the guilt or innocence of an entire nation. Guilt is, like innocence, not collective, but personal. There is discovered or concealed individual guilt. There is guilt which people acknowledge or deny. Everyone who directly experienced that era should today quietly ask himself about his involvement then.

The vast majority of today's population were either children then or had not been born. They cannot profess a guilt of their own for crimes that they did not commit. No discerning person can expect them to wear a penitential robe simply because they are Germans. But their forefathers have left them a grave legacy.

All of us, whether guilty or not, whether old or young, must accept the past. We are all affected by its consequences and liable for it. The young and old generations must and can help each other to understand why it is vital to keep alive the memories. It is not a case of coming to terms with the past. That is not possible. It cannot be subsequently modified or made undone. However, anyone who closes his eyes to the past is blind to the present. Whoever refuses to remember the inhumanity is prone to new risks of infection.

The Jewish nation remembers and will always remember. We seek reconciliation. Precisely for this reason we must understand that there can be no reconciliation without remembrance. The experience of millionfold death is part of the very being of every Jew in the world, not only because people cannot forget such atrocities, but also because remembrance is part of the Jewish faith.

"Seeking to forget makes exile all the longer; the secret of redemption lies in remembrance." This oft quoted Jewish adage surely expresses the idea that faith in God is faith in the work of God in history. Remembrance is experience of the work of God in history. It is the source of faith in redemption. This experience creates hope, creates faith in redemption, in reunification of the divided, in reconciliation. Whoever forgets this experience loses his faith.

If we for our part sought to forget what has occurred, instead of remembering it, this would not only be inhuman. We would also impinge upon the faith of the Jews who survived and destroy the basis of reconciliation. We must erect a memorial to thoughts and feelings in our own hearts.

Elie Wiesel
REFLECTIONS OF A SURVIVOR

Elie Wiesel (b. 1928), survivor of Auschwitz, author of numerous books and articles on the Holocaust and Jewish culture, human rights activist, and the 1986 Nobel Peace laureate, has also stressed the need for remembrance. In November 1987, Wiesel spoke at a conference center built inside the shell of the destroyed Reichstag, the German parliament during the Nazi era. The following is a journalistic report of his speech.

GHOSTS IN THE PARLIAMENT OF DEATH

. . . Elie Wiesel . . . delivered this speech from the rostrum of the Reichstag building in West Berlin. . . . The occasion was a planning conference for a museum to be built at Wannsee, the Berlin suburb where the formal decision to murder European Jewry was taken 45 years ago.

Elie Wiesel began his address in Yiddish. A literal translation follows:

"Hush, hush, let us be silent; tombs are growing here. Planted by the foe, they are green and turning to blue. . . . Hush, my child, don't cry, crying won't do us any good; the foe will never understand our plight. . . ."

This lullaby was written in the ghetto by Shmelke Katchegirsky. Grieving Jewish mothers would chant it, trying to put to sleep their hungry, weakened and agonizing children.

Tombs? These children—these innocent little children, perhaps the best our people ever had—were deprived of everything; their lives and even a burial place.

And so, hush, little children, one million of you, hush, come: we invite you. We invite you into our memory.

(The rest of Wiesel's speech was in English.)

Yiddish in the Reichstag? There is symbolism in using this warm, melancholy and compassionate language in a place where Jewish suffering and Jewish agony—some 50 years ago—aroused neither mercy nor compassion.

Yiddish was the tongue of many if not most of the Jewish victims who perished during the dark period when the Angel of Death seemed to have replaced God in too many hearts in this country.

There is symbolism, too—as there is irony and justice—in my speaking to you this afternoon from this very rostrum where my own death, and the death of my family, and the death of my friends, and the death of my teachers and the death of my entire people, was decreed and predicted by the legally elected leader of Germany.

I would betray the dead were I not to remind you that his poisonous words did *not* make him unpopular with his people. Most applauded with fervor; some, very few, remained silent. Fewer still objected.

How many Jews found shelter in how many German homes during the Kristallnacht? How many Germans tried to help extinguish the synagogues in flames? How many tried to save holy scrolls?

In those days and nights, humanity was distorted and twisted in this city, the capital of a nation proud of its distant history, but struggling with its recent memories.

Everything human and divine was perverted then. The law itself became immoral. Here, in this city, on this rostrum, it was made legal and commendable to humiliate Jews simply for being Jews—to hunt down children simply because they were Jewish children.

It became legal and praiseworthy to imprison, shame and oppress and, ultimately, to destroy human beings—sons and daughters of an ancient people—whose very existence was considered a crime.

The officials who participated in the Wannsee conference knew they acted on behalf of their government and in the name of the German people.

The atrocities committed under the law of the Third Reich *must* not and *will* not be forgotten; nor will they be forgiven.

I have no right to forgive the killers for having exterminated six million of my kinsmen. Only the dead can forgive, and no one has the right to speak on their behalf.

Still, not all Germans alive then were guilty. As a Jew, I have never believed in collective guilt. Only the guilty were guilty.

Children of killers are not killers but children. I have neither the desire nor the authority to judge today's generation for the unspeakable crimes committed by the generation of Hitler.

But we may—and we must—hold it responsible, not for the past, but for the way it remembers the past. And for what it does with the memory of the past.

Memory is the keyword. To remember is to forge links between past and present, between past and future.

It is in the name of memory that I address myself to Germany's youth. "Remember" is the commandment that dominates the lives of young Jews today; let it dominate your lives as well. Challenged by memory, we can move forward together. Opposed to memory, you will remain eternally opposed to us and to all we stand for.

I understand: of course, I understand: it is not easy to remember. It may be even more difficult for you than it is for us Jews. We try to remember the dead, you must remember those who killed them. Yes—there is pain involved in both our efforts. Not the same pain. Open yourselves to yours, as we have opened ourselves to ours.

You find it hard to believe that your elders did these deeds? So do I. Think of the tormentors as I think of their victims. I remember every minute of their agony. I see them constantly. I am afraid: if I stop seeing them, they will die. I keep on seeing them, and they died nevertheless.

I remember: 1942, in my childhood town, somewhere in the Carpathian Mountains. Jewish children were playing in the snow, others studied hard at school. They were already decreed dead here in Berlin, and they did not know it.

There is something in all this I do not understand—I never will. Why such obstinacy on the part of the killer to kill so many of my people? Why the old men and women? Why the children?

You, young men and women in Germany, must ask yourselves the same questions.

A people that has produced Goethe and Schiller, Bach and Beethoven, chose suddenly to put its national genius at the service of evil—to erect a monument to its dark power called Auschwitz.

A community that contributed to culture and education, as few nations have, called all of culture and education into question. After all: many of the killers had college degrees. And were products of the best universities in Germany. Many came from distinguished families.

Although I often wonder about the theological implications of Auschwitz, I must recognize that Auschwitz was not sent down from heaven. Auschwitz was conceived and built by human beings.

After Auschwitz, hope itself is filled with anguish.

But after Auschwitz, hope is necessary. Where can it be found? In remembrance alone.

How was remembrance handled after the war? Admit it, it took many Germans far too long to begin to confront their past.

Teachers did not teach, and pupils did not learn, the most tragic and important chapter in German and world history. Too painful, came the explanation.

It took the Eichmann trial in Jerusalem for German courts to indict 88 murderers who, after the war, had quietly returned to their homes and resumed their trades—as if nothing had happened.

True, the situation in East Germany is worse. Unlike the Federal Republic, which did make a serious effort, under Konrad Adenauer, to compensate the survivors and to help Israel, East Germany is hostile to Israel and refused to pay reparations. East Germany, like Austria, shows not the slightest trace of remorse.

The Federal Republic has chosen a more honest and enlightened course. In just a few decades, you have traveled from brutal totalitarianism to true democracy.

The freedom of the individual is respected here. Your commitment to the Western alliance is firm.

Among you are individuals and groups to whom we feel especially close. They have been seeking atonement, in word and in deed; some have gone to work in Israel; others are involved in religious dialogues.

Writers, artists, poets, novelists, statesmen: there are among them men and women who refuse to forget—and, make no mistake, the best books by German authors deal with the trauma of the past.

Now the museum. . . . What will it be?

Show pictures of Jews before they died.

Show the cold brutality of those who killed them.

Show the passivity, the cowardly indifference of the bystanders.

Remember the Jewishness of the Jewish victims, remember the uniqueness of their tragedy. True, not all victims were Jews, but all Jews were victims.

Be the conscience of your nation. And remember, a conscience that does not speak up when injustices are being committed is betraying itself. A mute conscience is a false conscience.

In remembering, you will help your own people vanquish the ghosts that hover over its history. Remember: a community that does not come to terms with the dead will continue to traumatize the living.

We remember Auschwitz and all that it symbolizes because we believe that, in spite of the past and its horrors, the world is worthy of salvation; and salvation, like redemption, can be found only in memory.

REVIEW QUESTIONS

1. What do the accounts of Hermann Graebe, Rudolf Hoess, and Y. Pfeffer reveal about the capacity of people to inflict oppression? How did the SS view their victims?
2. What do these accounts reveal about the ways in which people respond to overwhelmingly hopeless oppression?
3. Compare the views of the Holocaust of the German Richard von Weizsäcker and the Jew Elie Wiesel. What do they have to say about collective guilt, about the implications of forgetfulness and remembrance, and about the possibility of redemption, reconciliation, and salvation?
4. In your opinion what is the meaning of the Holocaust for Western civilization? For Jews? For Christians? For Germans?

---

10 D-Day, June 6, 1944

On June 6, 1944, the Allied forces launched their invasion of Nazi-occupied France. The invasion, called Operation Overlord, had been planned with meticulous care. Under the supreme command of General Dwight D. Eisenhower (1890–1969), the Allies organized the biggest amphibious operation of the war. It involved 5,000 ships of all kinds, 11,000 aircraft, and 2 million soldiers, 1.5 million of them Americans, all equipped with the latest military gear. Two artificial harbors and several oil pipelines stood ready to supply the troops once the invasion was under way.

Historical Division, War Department
OMAHA BEACHHEAD

Allied control of the air was an important factor in the success of D-Day. A second factor was the fact that the Germans were caught by surprise. Although expecting an invasion, they did not believe that it would take place in the Normandy area of France, and they dismissed June 6 as a possible date because weather conditions were unfavorable.

Ultimately the invasion's success depended on what happened during the first few hours. If the Allies had failed to secure beachheads, the operation would have ended in disaster. As the following reading illustrates, some of the hardest fighting took place on Omaha Beach, which was attacked by the Americans. The extract, published in 1945, comes from a study prepared in the field by the 2nd Information and Historical Service attached to the First Army, and by the Historical Section, European Theater of Operations.

As expected, few of the LCVP's and LCA's [amphibious landing craft] carrying assault infantry were able to make dry landings. Most of them grounded on sandbars 50 to 100 yards out, and in some cases the water was neck deep. Under fire as they came within a quarter-mile of the shore, the infantry met their worst experiences of the day and suffered their heaviest casualties just after touchdown. Small-arms fire, mortars, and artillery concentrated on the landing area, but the worst hazard was produced by converging fires from automatic weapons. Survivors from some craft report hearing the fire beat on the ramps before they were lowered, and then seeing the hail of bullets whip the surf just in front of the lowered ramps. Some men dove under water or went over the side to escape the beaten zone of the machine guns. Stiff, weakened from seasickness, and often heavily loaded, the debarking troops had little chance of moving fast in water that was knee deep or higher, and their progress was made more difficult by uneven footing in the runnels crossing the tidal flat. Many men were exhausted before they reached shore, where they faced 200 yards or more of open sand to cross before reaching cover at the sea wall or shingle bank. Most men who reached that cover made it by walking, and under increasing enemy fire. Troops who stopped to organize, rest, or take shelter behind obstacles or tanks merely prolonged their difficulties and suffered heavier losses. . . .

Perhaps the worst area on the beach was Dog Green, directly in front of strongpoints guarding the Vierville draw [gully] and under heavy flanking fire from emplacements to the west, near Pointe de la Percée. Company A of the 116th was due to land on this sector with Company C of the 2d Rangers on its right flank, and both units came in on their targets. One of the six LCA's carrying Company A foundered about a thousand yards off shore, and passing Rangers saw men jumping overboard and being dragged down by their loads. At H+6[1] minutes the remaining craft grounded in water 4 to 6 feet deep, about 30 yards short of the outward band of obstacles. Starting off the craft in three files, center file first and the flank files peeling right and left,

the men were enveloped in accurate and intense fire from automatic weapons. Order was quickly lost as the troops attempted to dive under water or dropped over the sides into surf over their heads. Mortar fire scored four direct hits on one LCA, which "disintegrated." Casualties were suffered all the way to the sand, but when the survivors got there, some found they could not hold and came back into the water for cover, while others took refuge behind the nearest obstacles. Remnants of one boat team on the right flank organized a small firing line on the first yards of sand, in full exposure to the enemy. In short order every officer of the company, including Capt. Taylor N. Fellers, was a casualty, and most of the sergeants were killed or wounded. The leaderless men gave up any attempt to move forward and confined their efforts to saving the wounded, many of whom drowned in the rising tide. Some troops were later able to make the sea wall by staying in the edge of the water and going up the beach with the tide. Fifteen minutes after landing, Company A was out of action for the day. Estimates of its casualties range as high as two-thirds. . . .

As headquarters groups arrived from 0730 on, they found much the same picture at whatever sector they landed. Along 6,000 yards of beach, behind sea wall or shingle embankment, elements of the assault force were immobilized in what might well appear to be hopeless confusion. As a result of mislandings, many companies were so scattered that they could not be organized as tactical units. At some places, notably in front of the German strongpoints guarding draws, losses in officers and noncommissioned officers were so high that remnants of units were practically leaderless. . . .

There was, definitely, a problem of morale. The survivors of the beach crossing, many of whom were experiencing their first enemy fire, had seen heavy losses among their comrades or in neighboring units. No action could be fought in circumstances more calculated to heighten the moral effects of such losses. Be-

---

[1]H indicates the start of an operation.

hind them, the tide was drowning wounded men who had been cut down on the sands and was carrying bodies ashore just below the shingle. Disasters to the later landing waves were still occurring, to remind of the potency of enemy fire. . . .

At 0800, German observers on the bluff sizing up the grim picture below them might well have felt that the invasion was stopped at the edge of the water. Actually, at three or four places on the four-mile beachfront, U.S. troops were already breaking through the shallow crust of enemy defenses.

The outstanding fact about these first two hours of action is that despite heavy casualties, loss of equipment, disorganization, and all the other discouraging features of the landings, the assault troops did not stay pinned down behind the sea wall and embankment. At half-a-dozen or more points on the long stretch, they found the necessary drive to leave their cover and move out over the open beach flat toward the bluffs. Prevented by circumstance of mislandings from using carefully rehearsed tactics, they improvised assault methods to deal with what defenses they found before them. In nearly every case where advance was attempted, it carried through the enemy beach defenses. . . .

Various factors, some of them difficult to evaluate, played a part in the success of these advances. . . . But the decisive factor was leadership. Wherever an advance was made, it depended on the presence of some few individuals, officers and noncommissioned officers, who inspired, encouraged, or bullied their men forward, often by making the first forward moves. On Easy Red a lieutenant and a wounded sergeant of divisional engineers stood up under fire and walked over to inspect the wire obstacles just beyond the embankment. The lieutenant came back and, hands on hips, looked down disgustedly at the men lying behind the shingle bank. "Are you going to lay there and get killed, or get up and do something about it?" Nobody stirred, so the sergeant and the officer got the materials and blew the wire. On the same sector, where a group advancing across the flat was held up by a marshy area suspected of being mined, it was a lieutenant of engineers who crawled ahead through the mud on his belly, probing for mines with a hunting knife in the absence of other equipment. When remnants of an isolated boat section of Company B, 116th Infantry, were stopped by fire from a well-concealed emplacement, the lieutenant in charge went after it single-handed. In trying to grenade the rifle pit he was hit by three rifle bullets and eight grenade fragments, including some from his own grenade. He turned his map and compass over to a sergeant and ordered his group to press on inland. . . .

. . . Col. George A. Taylor arrived in the second section at 0815 and found plenty to do on the beach. Men were still hugging the embankment, disorganized, and suffering casualties from mortar and artillery fire. Colonel Taylor summed up the situation in terse phrase: "Two kinds of people are staying on this beach, the dead and those who are going to die—now let's get the hell out of here." Small groups of men were collected without regard to units, put under charge of the nearest noncommissioned officer, and sent on through the wire and across the flat, while engineers worked hard to widen gaps in the wire and to mark lanes through the minefields.

REVIEW QUESTIONS

1. What disadvantages did Allied troops face while attempting the amphibious landing at Omaha Beach? Why were casualties so heavy?
2. According to the Historical Division study, many of the Allied soldiers at Omaha Beach were experiencing their first enemy fire. How did the officers who survived manage to rally these shaken and demoralized soldiers?

11 The End of the Third Reich

In January 1945, the Russians launched a major offensive, which ultimately brought them into Berlin. In February, American and British forces were battling the Germans in the Rhineland, and in March they crossed the Rhine into the interior of Germany. In April, the Russians encircled Berlin. After heavy artillery and rocket-launchers inflicted severe damage on the besieged city, Russian infantry attacked and engaged in vicious street fighting. The siege took the lives of some 125,000 Berliners, many of them suicides. Russian dead, wounded, and missing totaled about 305,000. From his underground bunker near the chancellery in Berlin, a physically exhausted and emotionally unhinged Hitler engaged in wild fantasies about new German victories.

The last weeks of the war were chaotic and murderous. Many German soldiers fought desperately against the invaders of the Fatherland, particularly the Russians, who had been depicted by Nazi propaganda as Asiatic barbarians. SS officers, still loyal to Hitler and National Socialism, hunted down and executed reluctant fighters as a warning to others. The misery of the Jews never abated. As the Russians neared the concentration camps, the SS marched the inmates into the German interior. It was a death march, for many of them, already human skeletons, could not endure the long trek, the weather, and the brutality of guards who shot stragglers.

Nerin E. Gun
THE LIBERATION OF DACHAU

In the closing weeks of the war, the Allies liberated German concentration camps, revealing the full horror of Nazi atrocities to a shocked world. On April 29, 1945, American soldiers entered Dachau. One of the liberated prisoners was Nerin E. Gun, a Turkish Catholic journalist, who had been imprisoned by the Nazis during the war for his reports about the Warsaw ghetto and his prediction that the German armies would meet defeat in Russia. Gun described the liberation of Dachau in *The Day of the Americans* (1966), from which the following selection is taken.

The first wave of Americans had been followed by a second, which must have broken into the camp either through the crematorium or through the marshaling-yard, where the boxcars loaded with thousands of corpses had been parked. For, as soon as they saw the SS men standing there with their hands on their heads, these Americans, without any other semblance of trial, without even saying a warning word, turned their fire on them. Most of the inmates applauded this summary justice, and those who had been able to get over the ditch rushed out to strip the corpses of the Germans. Some even hacked their feet off, the more quickly to be able to get their boots. . . .

The detachment under the command of the American major had not come directly to the Jourhaus. It had made a detour by way of the marshaling yard, where the convoys of deportees normally arrived and departed. There they found some fifty-odd cattle cars parked on the tracks. The cars were not empty.

"At first sight," said [Lieutenant Colonel Will] Cowling, "they seemed to be filled with rags, discarded clothing. Then we caught sight of hands, stiff fingers, faces. . . ."

The train was full of corpses, piled one on the other, 2,310 of them, to be exact. The train had come from Birkenau, and the dead were Hungarian and Polish Jews, children among them. Their journey had lasted perhaps thirty or forty days. They had died of hunger, of thirst, of suffocation, of being crushed, or of being beaten by the guards. There were even evidences of cannibalism. They were all practically dead when they arrived at Dachau Station. The SS men did not take the trouble to unload them. They simple decided to stand guard and shoot down any with enough strength left to emerge from the cattle cars. The corpses were strewn everywhere—on the rails, the steps, the platforms.

The men of the 45th Division had just made contact with the 42nd, here in the station. They too found themselves unable to breathe at what they saw. One soldier yelled: "Look, Bud, it's moving!" He pointed to something in motion among the cadavers. A louse-infested prisoner was crawling like a worm, trying to attract attention. He was the only survivor.

"I never saw anything like it in my life," said Lieutenant Harold Mayer. "Every one of my men became raving mad. We turned off toward the east, going around the compound, without even taking the trouble to reconnoiter first. We were out to avenge them." . . .

The ire of the men of the First Battalion, 157th Regiment, was to mount even higher as they got closer to the Lager of the deportees. The dead were everywhere—in the ditches, along the side streets, in the garden before a small building with chimneys—and there was a huge mountain of corpses inside the yard of this building, which they now understood to be the crematorium. And finally there was the ultimate horror—the infernal sight of those thousands and thousands of living skeletons, screaming like banshees, on the other side of the placid poplars.

When some of the SS men on the watchtowers started to shoot into the mobs of prisoners, the Americans threw all caution to the winds. They opened fire on the towers with healthy salvos. The SS men promptly came down the ladders, their hands reaching high. But now the American GI saw red. He shot the Germans down with a telling blast, and to make doubly sure sent a final shot into their fallen bodies. Then the hunt started for any other Germans in SS uniforms. Within a quarter of an hour there was not a single one of the Hitler henchmen alive within the camp.

In the SS refectory, one soldier had been killed while eating a plate of beans. He still held a spoonful in his hand. At the signal center, the SS man in charge of the switchboard was slumped over his panel, blood running down to the receiver, the busy signal from Munich still ringing in his unheeding ear. At the power plant, the SS foreman had been beaten to death with shovels by a Polish prisoner and his Czech assistant. After that, they had been able to cut the high-voltage current from the barbed-wire fences around the camp.

Joseph Goebbels
"THE MORALE OF THE GERMAN PEOPLE, BOTH AT HOME AND AT THE FRONT, IS SINKING EVER LOWER"

In his diary, Joseph Goebbels (1897–1945), the cynical and sinister head of the propaganda ministry, recorded his impressions of Germany in the last weeks of the war. The following selections from his diary show Goebbels' concern with German morale, particularly as affected by devastating air raids.

March 8 {1945}

During the last 24 hours the air war has again raged over Reich territory with devastating effect. It was the turn of Magdeburg and even more of Dessau. The greater part of Dessau is a sheet of flame and totally destroyed; yet another German city which has been largely flattened. In addition reports coming in from towns recently attacked, Chemnitz in particular, make one's hair grow grey. Yet once more it is frightful that we have no defence worth mentioning with which to oppose the enemy air war.

The Party Chancellery is now planning a special operation to raise the troops' morale. . . . Evidence of demoralization is now to be seen. . . . Desertions have reached a considerable level. . . . Again and again one hears that the enemy air bombardment is at the bottom of it all. It is understandable that a people which has been subjected for years to the fire-effect of a weapon against which it has no defence, should gradually lose its courage.

March 12

The morale of the German people, both at home and at the front, is sinking ever lower. The Reich propaganda agencies are complaining very noticeably about this. The people thinks that it is facing a perfectly hopeless situation in this war. Criticism of our war strategy does not now stop short even of the Führer himself. . . . It must always be pointed out,

however, that the present level of morale must not be confused with definite defeatism. The people will continue to do their duty and the front-line soldier will defend himself as far as he has a possibility of doing so. These possibilities are becoming increasingly limited, however, primarily owing to the enemy's air superiority. The air terror which rages uninterruptedly over German home territory makes people thoroughly despondent. One feels so impotent against it that no one can now see a way out of the dilemma. The total paralysis of transport in West Germany also contributes to the mood of increasing pessimism among the German people.

March 13

. . . [P]eople in Eisenhower's headquarters are clear that they still face a titanic struggle in the West. They declare that on both sides war is being waged without mercy and that there is no question whatsoever of the German Wehrmacht yielding. Above all people in Eisenhower's headquarters are deeply impressed by the fact that all German prisoners of war still have faith in victory and—as they explicitly state—believe in Hitler with well-nigh mystical fanaticism. . . .

The Jews are re-emerging. Their spokesman is the well-known notorious Leopold Schwarzschild [former newspaper editor, who had emigrated to America]; he is now arguing in the American press that under no circumstances should Germany be given lenient treatment. Anyone in a position to do so should kill these Jews off like rats. In Germany, thank God, we have already done a fairly complete job. I trust that the world will take its cue from this.

March 16

Mail received testifies to a deep-seated lethargy throughout the German people degenerating almost into hopelessness. There is very sharp criticism of the Luftwaffe but also of the entire national leadership. The latter is accused of being over-ambitious in its policy and strategy, of having been negligent in its conduct of the war, particularly in the air, and this is given as the main reason for our misfortunes.

March 21

The number killed in air raids up to December inclusive is reported as 353,000—a horrifying figure which becomes even more terrible when one adds the 457,000 wounded. This is a war within a war, sometimes more frightful than the war at the front. The homeless are simply innumerable. The air war has turned the Reich into one great heap of ruins. In the last 24 hours a further crazy series of air raids has been reported, particularly on the west of the Reich.

March 23

The letters I receive envince profound apathy and resignation. All refer quite openly to the leadership crisis. All the letter-writers show marked aversion to Göring, Ley and Ribbentrop.[1] Unfortunately even the Führer is now more frequently referred to in critical terms. I get off somewhat more lightly in the letters I receive but that must not be over-estimated. Everything must be looked at relatively. I think that my work too is no longer being totally effective today. A fateful development

seems to me to be that now neither the Führer in person nor the National-Socialist concept nor the National-Socialist movement are immune from criticism. Many Party members, moreover, are now beginning to waver. All our set-backs are unanimously ascribed to Anglo-American air superiority.

March 26

As we know, the Americans succeeded in taking our Saar front in rear. The Army fighting on the Siegfried Line was withdrawn too late and largely fell into enemy hands. The troops' morale was correspondingly low. That of the civil population was even worse; in many places people opposed the troops and placed obstacles in the way of the defence. To a great extent the tank barriers constructed in the hinterland were captured by the enemy without a fight. I [blame] Slesina [head of the propaganda office in Westmark] with the fact that not a single symbol of resistance has emerged in the West, like Breslau or Königsberg, for instance, in the East. His explanation is that people in the West have been so worn down by the months and years of enemy air raids that they prefer an end to this horror rather than an endless horror.

March 29

The military situation in the West is characterised mainly by sinking morale both among the civil population and among the troops. This loss of morale implies great danger for us since a people and an army no longer prepared to fight cannot be saved, however great the reinforcements in men and weapons. In Siegburg, for instance, a women's demonstration took place outside the Town Hall demanding the laying down of arms and capitulation.

March 30

As far as morale is concerned, I am firmly convinced that, now that the Führer has removed from me the impediment of the Reich Press Officer, I can get going again. I shall very quickly purge the Press Section of refractory and defeatist elements and can now carry on

---

[1] Reichsmarschall Hermann Goring headed the German airforce. Robert Ley headed the Nazi German Labor Front. Joachim von Ribbentrop was the Nazi foreign minister from 1938 to 1945.

propaganda against the West which will be in no way inferior to that against the East. Anti-Anglo-American propaganda is now the order of the day. Only if we can demonstrate to our people that Anglo-American intentions towards them are no different from those of the Bolshevists will they adopt a different attitude to the enemy in the West. If we succeeded in stiffening the German people against the bolshevists and instilling hatred into them, why should we not succeed in doing so against the Anglo-Americans!

Marie Neumann
"WE'RE IN THE HANDS OF A MOB, NOT SOLDIERS, AND THEY'RE ALL DRUNK OUT OF THEIR MINDS"

As Russian troops advanced into Germany, many terrified German civilians fled westward, and not without reason. The invading Russians, seeking vengeance for the misery and ruin the Nazis had inflicted on their homeland and kinfolk, committed numerous atrocities against the conquered enemy. It quickly became official Soviet policy to prevent the perpetration of such personal acts of revenge and mayhem.

Marie Neumann of Baerwalde in Pomerania was one of the victims of this "terrible revenge." She put her nightmare in writing in 1948. Thirty years later, after reading *Nemesis at Potsdam* by Alfred-Maurice de Zayas, she sent the author her story. Following an exchange of letters and two personal visits, de Zayas was convinced she was telling the truth and later incorporated her testimony into a book about the postwar fate of Germans in Eastern Europe. Frau Neumann eventually left the Soviet zone of occupation and began a new life in West Germany. Unlike many others, she survived the acts of cruelty carried out against her and her family, described in the following passages from her 1948 account.

. . . My sister was on one side of the house with her seven-year-old daughter, and I was on the other side with her two other children and my husband. Someone had pressed a burning candle into his hand. My sister and I were raped again and again. The beasts lined up for us. During this time one of the military policemen held the door shut. I saw this because I was finally left alone before my sister was. Once she and her daughter both screamed in a most unnatural way, so that I thought they were being killed; and I wanted to go over to them when the policeman standing guard burst into our room and knocked my husband to the ground with his rifle. My niece Ilschen was crying and threw herself on my husband while the boy and I held the policeman's arm crying loudly, otherwise he would probably have killed my husband.

When we were finally granted a little peace and my husband had regained his senses, my sister came over to us and begged my husband to help her, asking, "Karl, what's going to happen to us?" My husband said, "I can't help any of you; we're in the hands of a mob, not soldiers, and they're all drunk out of their minds." I said, "Karl has to hide himself or they'll beat him to death; they've already beaten him half to death." My husband agreed with me and wanted to hide, but Grete held him back and begged him to think of her poor children. My husband then answered: "Grete, I just can't help anybody, but I'll stay with you; all we can do is hide, all of us, out in the hayloft." No sooner said than done. But just as we were climbing up into the loft, three men appeared; since there was snow outside, they had seen our tracks. We had to climb down; the two little girls were kissed and their mother raped again. She and her children cried so that it broke my heart. She cried out desperately: "O God, O God, why is this happening?" The men left, and my husband said: "They're going to kill me, they're going to kill all of you, and what they'll do to the children you can well imagine." My husband said that hiding now made no sense, we don't have any time to do it. I said: "Everybody get up there. I'll lock all the doors and they'll have to break them down first," hoping that it would give us the time to hide ourselves. But I had forgotten in the excitement that the yard gates had been broken down already because we had been closing them whenever we could. We had just gotten into the loft when there came a howling and yelling of rabble in our yard, shooting like crazy into the ground, and then they came after us. It had gotten dark in the meantime and they had flashlights. They were civilians and some military wearing cornered hats with pompoms. What happened next I can barely write down, the pen sticks in my hand. They hanged us all in that hayloft, from the rafters, except for the children. The mob strangled them by hand with a rope.

Later I was told by the people who had taken shelter in the Hackbarth family's cellar on Polziner Street that they had heard our unnatural screams, even down in the cellar; but no one had the courage to come for us, they were all fighting for their own lives at the time. I came to on the floor, lying next to my loved ones. I didn't know yet what had happened to them, although I had a good idea, it was the details I lacked. Because I was first thrown to the floor when the mob caught us, hit on the head and raped, after which I was hanged. I had lost conciousness immediately. Later I heard voices. I was lying on the floor, four men kneeling around me. They said, "Frau komm," and when I tried to stand, I fell down at once. Later I found myself in the yard being held up by two men. They took me inside and laid me on a bed. One of the four men, a civilian, a Pole, stayed by me and asked: "Frau, who did?" I said: "The Russians." Then he hit me and said: "Russians, good soldiers. German SS, pigs, hang women and children." I fell into a fit of crying; it was impossible to stop. Then the other three came back in, but when they saw me, they left my apartment. Shortly thereafter a Russian came in carrying a whip, constantly yelling at me. Apparently he wanted me to be still, but I just couldn't. So he hit me once with the whip, then kept hitting the side of the bed. When that didn't work, he gave up and left my house. Then I heard voices in front of the house and got more scared than I was ever before or since. Seized by a cold panic I ran out to the little creek next to our garden, where the geese used to swim. I wanted to drown myself and tried for a long time until I was faint. But even that didn't bring my life to an end.

How I got through all this I don't know to this day. In any case someone had hauled me out of the creek. When I regained my senses I made my way to Fraulein Bauch's room on the ground floor of Schmechel's, the shopkeeper. Dear God how I was freezing because there were no windows or doors left in the place, and my clothes were wet; it was the night of March 4th to 5th and there was still snow and ice about. After a while I saw there was a bed in the room, so I laid down thinking I was alone in the place. But I quickly saw that someone had been sitting at the table and was now standing up, coming over to my bed, and, oh no, it was a Russian. Suddenly my whole miserable plight came before my eyes. I cried again and begged him if he wouldn't please shoot me. He shined a flashlight into my face, took off his coat and showed me his medals, saying that he was a first lieutenant and that I need not be afraid. He took a hand towel down from the wall and began to rub me dry. When he saw my throat, he asked: "Who did?" I said, "the Russians." "Yes, yes," he said, "Was the Bolsheviks, but now not Bolsheviks, now White Russians; White Russians good." He then took his bayonet and cut off my panties, whereupon I again was ready to die, for I didn't know what to expect anymore. He rubbed my legs dry; but I was still freezing and didn't know what I should do if I had frostbite. But then he took off my wedding ring and put it in his pocket. He asked me where my husband was, and then raped me in spite of my miserable condition. Afterwards he promised to send me to a German doctor. I was happy about that, but then I remembered there were no more German doctors in our area.

Shortly after he left four 18- to 20-year-old Russians appeared. Totally drunk, they pulled me out of bed and raped me in an unnatural way. In my condition I wasn't able to do more and fell beside the bed, so they kicked me with their boots, getting me just in the worst spot. I fainted again. When I came to, I crawled back into the bed. Then two more such bums showed up, but they left me alone as I was more dead than alive. I learned back then how much a human being can endure; I couldn't talk, couldn't cry, couldn't even utter a sound. They hit me a bit, which didn't matter to me since I couldn't feel anything, and then left me alone. I fell asleep out of sheer exhaustion.

When I awoke very early next morning, I realized again where I was. I quickly noticed an open wardrobe door, and inside was a dress. There was also a shirt and some underwear. So even though the things were much too small, I put them on; what was left of my clothes was still wet. I had to put the dress on leaving the back unfastened, to make it fit. There were no stockings to be found; mine had been wound up so tight they were like bones. Then I was visited by the Russians again. First one who apparently thought the room was empty, because when he saw me in bed, he left the room immediately. He came back with three more

men; that first one wanted to hit me, but the officer wouldn't let him. So the first man pointed to the Hitler portrait on the wall which was full of bullet holes, and he said I was a Hitler fascist. I said, "No! This isn't my house." He said, "Come! Go your house!" I had to walk ahead of them to my house and must have been a pretty sight. When I got there I saw a truck parked in front, and Russian soldiers were loading my slaughtered livestock into a car. The soldiers almost laughed themselves to death when they saw me. They indicated to their officer, their fingers tapping their heads, that I was probably crazy, and when four female soldiers appeared, they wanted to shoot me. But the officer didn't permit it. He asked about my neck, and I said, "Russian soldiers; my husband, sister, children, too." When he heard the word children, he was shocked. I asked him to come to the barn with me but he didn't want to, and I wasn't allowed to go back either. So I asked to go to the commandant. He agreed at once with that and sent a soldier with me. But when we got to the corner by Kollatz, he indicated to me that I should continue along Neustettiner Street by myself. There were several men already in the marketplace, clearing things away. When I got to the butcher, Albert Nass's place, a Russian soldier told me to go in: Commander's Headquarters.

Inside the courtyard. . . .

[A] Russian soldier said, "German woman! Stairs there, go up." I was immediately made a prisoner for my effort, locked into a room with others.

When evening arrived, it was hell itself. One woman after another in our group was hauled out. The shoemaker's wife, Frau Graf, who was in her last month of pregnancy, was taken, also a woman from Wusterhausen, and the Peters' daughter Frau Schmidt. They were driven away by some soldier. The women screamed as they were being forced into the car, and the prisoners' room was full of screaming. Our nerves were raw. Then we heard the motor revving up, the Russians shone searchlights into the room through the window, so bright that several women screamed out that they were using flame throwers against us. The children cried miserably; it was horrible. Toward morning the women came back. Two came into the room and collapsed; the other woman was raped once more by the door before they let her in. They came to get me once during the night. I was taken into the slaughterhouse and assaulted on a feather bed right on the soil. When I came to, my neighbor Herr Held was crying over me. My neck had swollen so much over the past hours that I had trouble moving my mouth, and I was spitting blood.

Adolf Hitler
POLITICAL TESTAMENT

On April 30, 1945, with the Russians only blocks away, Hitler took his own life. In his political testament, which is printed below, he again resorted to the vile lie.

More than thirty years have now passed since I in 1914 made my modest contribution as a volunteer in the first world-war that was forced upon the Reich.

In these three decades I have been actuated solely by love and loyalty to my people in all my thoughts, acts, and life. They gave me the strength to make the most difficult decisions which have ever confronted to mortal man. I have spent my time, my working strength, and my health in these three decades.

It is untrue that I or anyone else in Germany wanted the war in 1939. It was desired and instigated exclusively by those international statesmen who were either of Jewish descent or worked for Jewish interests. I have made too many offers for the control and limitation of armaments, which posterity will not for all time be able to disregard for the responsibility for the outbreak of this war to be laid on me. I have further never wished that after the first fatal world war a second against England, or even against America, should break out. Centuries will pass away, but out of the ruins of our towns and monuments the hatred against those finally responsible whom we have to thank for everything, International Jewry and its helpers, will grow.

Three days before the outbreak of the German-Polish war I again proposed to the British ambassador in Berlin a solution to the German-Polish problem—similar to that in the case of the Saar district, under international control. This offer also cannot be denied. It was only rejected because the leading circles in English politics wanted the war, partly on account of the business hoped for and partly under influence of propaganda organized by international Jewry.

I also made it quite plain that, if the nations of Europe are again to be regarded as mere shares to be bought and sold by these international conspirators in money and finance, then that race, Jewry, which is the real criminal of this murderous struggle, will be saddled with the responsibility. I further left no one in doubt that this time not only would millions of children of Europe's Aryan peoples die of hunger, not only would millions of grown men suffer death, and not only hundreds of thousands of women and children be burnt and bombed to death in the towns, without the real criminal having to atone for this guilt, even if by more humane means.

After six years of war, which in spite of all set-backs, will go down one day in history as the most glorious and valiant demonstration of a nation's life purpose, I cannot forsake the city which is the capital of this Reich. As the forces are too small to make any further stand against the enemy attack at this place and our resistance is gradually being weakened by men who are as deluded as they are lacking in initiative, I should like, by remaining in this town, to share my fate with those, the millions of others, who have also taken upon themselves to do so. Moreover I do not wish to fall into the hands of an enemy who requires a new spectacle organized by the Jews for the amusement of their hysterical masses.

I have decided therefore to remain in Berlin and there of my own free will to choose death at the moment when I believe the position of the Fuehrer and Chancellor itself can no longer be held.

I die with a happy heart, aware of the immeasurable deeds and achievements of our soldiers at the front, our women at home, the achievements of our farmers and workers and the work, unique in history, of our youth who bear my name.

That from the bottom of my heart I express my thanks to you all, is just as self-evident as my wish that you should, because of that, on no account give up the struggle, but rather continue it against the enemies of the Fatherland, no matter where, true to the creed of the great Clausewitz.[1] From the sacrifice of our soldiers and from my own unity with them unto death, will in any case spring up in the history of Germany, the seed of a radiant renaissance of the National-Socialist movement and thus of the realization of a true community of nations.

Many of the most courageous men and women have decided to unite their lives with mine until the very last. I have begged and finally ordered them not to do this, but to take part in the further battle of the Nation. I beg

the heads of the Armies, the Navy and the Air Force to strengthen by all possible means the spirit of resistance of our soldiers in the National-Socialist sense, with special reference to the fact that also I myself, as founder and creator of this movement, have preferred death to cowardly abdication or even capitulation.

May it, at some future time, become part of the code of honour of the German officer—as is already the case in our Navy—that the surrender of a district or of a town is impossible, and that above all the leaders here must march ahead as shining examples, faithfully fulfilling their duty unto death.

Before my death I expel the former Reichsmarschall Hermann Goering from the party and deprive him of all rights which he may enjoy by virtue of the decree of June 29th, 1941, and also by virtue of my statement in the Reichstag on September 1st, 1939, I appoint in his place Grossadmiral Doenitz, President of the Reich and Supreme Commander of the Armed Forces.

Before my death I expel the former Reichsfuehrer-SS and Minister of the Interior, Heinrich Himmler, from the party and from all offices of State. In his stead I appoint Gauleiter Karl Hanke as Reichsfuehrer-SS and Chief of the German Police, and Gauleiter Paul Giesler as Reich Minister of the Interior.

Goering and Himmler, quite apart from their disloyalty to my person, have done immeasurable harm to the country and the whole nation by secret negotiations with the enemy, which they conducted without my knowledge and against my wishes, and by illegally attempting to seize power in the State for themselves.

In order to give the German people a government composed of honourable men,—a government which will fulfill its pledge to continue the war by every means—I appoint the following members of the new Cabinet as leaders of the nation:

President of the Reich: Doenitz.

Chancellor of the Reich: Dr. Goebbels.

Party Minister: Bormann. . . .

---

[1]Karl von Clausewitz (1780–1831), a Prussian general whose classic treatise *On War* greatly influenced military strategy and tactics in the nineteenth and twentieth centuries.

Several other appointees are listed; then the text resumes.

Although a number of these men, such as Martin Bormann, Dr. Goebbels, etc., together with their wives, have joined me of their own free will and did not wish to leave the capital of the Reich under any circumstances, but were willing to perish with me here, I must nevertheless ask them to obey my request, and in this case set the interests of the nation above their own feelings. By their work and loyalty as comrades they will be just as close to me after death, as I hope that my spirit will linger among them and always go with them. Let them be hard, but never unjust, above all let them never allow fear to influence their actions, and set the honour of the nation above everything in the world. Finally, let them be conscious of the fact that our task, that of continuing the building of a National Socialist State, represents the work of the coming centuries, which places every single person under an obligation always to serve the common interest and to subordinate his own advantage to this end. I demand of all Germans, all National Socialists, men, women and all the men of the Armed Forces, that they be faithful and obedient unto death to the new government and its President.

Above all I charge the leaders of the nation and those under them to scrupulous observance of the laws of race and to merciless opposition to the universal poisoner of all peoples, international Jewry.

Given in Berlin, this 29th day of April 1945. 4:00 A.M.

Adolf Hitler.

Witnessed by
Dr. Josef Fuhr.   Wilhelm Buergdorf.
Martin Bormann.   Hans Krebs.

REVIEW QUESTIONS

1. According to Nerin E. Gun, how did the American soldiers react when they discovered conditions at Dachau?
2. What signs did Goebbels remark on as evidence of sinking German morale? What did he consider the primary reason for this failure of nerve?
3. What do atrocities such as those described by Marie Neumann reveal about the nature of warfare? Do you think it is possible to wage war without awakening barbaric instincts in soldiers? Explain why or why not.
4. Compare Hitler's final testament with his speech to his generals in 1939 (see page 374). How had his views and expectations changed by the end of the war?

CHAPTER 14

Western Europe:
The Dawn of a New Era

WHEN THE WAR IN EUROPE ENDED in May 1945, many areas lay devastated, none more so than the once-picturesque German city of Dresden, in which at least 50,000 people had perished in a terror bombing by Allied planes in February 1945. Europe was faced with the awesome task of reconstructing a continent in ruins. *(Sovfoto/Eastfoto)*

At the end of World War II, Winston Churchill lamented: "What is Europe now? A rubble heap, a charnel house, a breeding ground for pestilence and hate." Everywhere the survivors counted their dead. War casualties were relatively light in Western Europe. Britain and the Commonwealth suffered 460,000 casualties; France, 570,000; and Italy, 450,000. War casualties were heavier in the east: 5 million people in Germany, 6 million in Poland (including 3 million Jews), 1 million in Yugoslavia, and more than 25 million in the Soviet Union. The material destruction had been unprecedentedly heavy in the battle zones of northwestern Europe, northern Italy, and Germany, growing worse farther east, where Hitler's and Stalin's armies had fought without mercy to people, animals, or the environment. Industry, transportation, and communication had come to a virtual standstill. Now members of families searched for each other; prisoners of war made their way home; Jews from extermination camps or from hiding places returned to open life; and displaced persons by the millions sought refuge. Yet Europe did recover from this blight, and with astonishing speed.

The war produced a shift in power arrangements. The United States and the Soviet Union emerged as the two most powerful states in the world. The traditional Great Powers—Britain, France, and Germany—were now dwarfed by these superpowers. The United States had the atomic bomb and immense industrial might; the Soviet Union had the largest army in the world and was extending its dominion over eastern Europe. With Germany defeated, the principal incentive for Soviet-American cooperation had evaporated.

After World War I, nationalist passions intensified. After World War II, Western Europeans progressed toward unity. The Hitler years convinced many Europeans of the dangers inherent in extreme nationalism, and fear of the Soviet Union prodded them toward greater cooperation.

Some intellectuals, shocked by the irrationality and horrors of the Hitler era, drifted into despair. To these thinkers, life was absurd, without meaning; human beings could neither comprehend nor control it. In 1945, only the naive could have faith in continuous progress or believe in the essential goodness of the individual. The future envisioned by the philosophes seemed more distant than ever. Nevertheless, this profound disillusionment was tempered by hope. Democracy had, in fact, prevailed over Nazi totalitarianism and terror. Moreover, fewer intellectuals were now attracted to antidemocratic thought. The Nazi dictatorship convinced many of them, even some who had wavered in previous decades, that freedom and human dignity were precious ideals and that liberal constitutional government, despite its imperfections, was the best means of preserving these ideals. Perhaps, then, democratic institutions and values would spread throughout the globe, and the newly established United Nations would promote world peace.

1   The Aftermath: Devastation and Demoralization

In 1945 European cities everywhere were in rubble; bridges, railway systems, waterways, and harbors destroyed; farmlands laid waste; livestock killed; coal mines wrecked. Homeless and hungry people wandered the streets and roads. Europe faced the gigantic task of rebuilding.

Stephen Spender
EUROPEAN WITNESS

The English poet and critic Stephen Spender (1909–1995) traveled through Germany (with a side-trip to France) in the summer and fall of 1945. His mission was to assess German intellectual life and to inquire into the conditions in German libraries. His book, based on a journal he kept during his travels, was published in 1946. It offers an eyewitness account of the ruined country and its demoralized people under Allied occupation.

In the selection below, Spender describes the devastation of the heavily bombed city of Cologne.

My first impression on passing through [Cologne] was of there being not a single house left. There are plenty of walls but these walls are a thin mask in front of the damp, hollow, stinking emptiness of gutted interiors. Whole streets with nothing but the walls left standing are worse than streets flattened. They are more sinister and oppressive.

Actually, there are a few habitable buildings left in Cologne; three hundred in all, I am told. One passes through street after street of houses whose windows look hollow and blackened— like the open mouth of a charred corpse; behind these windows there is nothing except floors, furniture, bits of rag, books, all dropped to the bottom of the building to form there a sodden mass.

Through the streets of Cologne thousands of people trudge all day long. These are crowds who a few years ago were shop-gazing in their city, or waiting to go to the cinema or to the opera, or stopping taxis. They are the same people who once were the ordinary inhabitants of a great city when by what now seems an un-believable magical feat of reconstruction in time, this putrescent corpse-city was the hub of the Rhineland, with a great shopping centre, acres of plate-glass, restaurants, a massive business street containing the head offices of many banks and firms, an excellent opera, theatres, cinemas, lights in the streets at night.

Now it requires a real effort of the imagination to think back to that Cologne which I knew well ten years ago. Everything has gone. In this the destruction of Germany is quite different from even the worst that has happened in England (though not different from Poland and from parts of Russia). In England there are holes, gaps and wounds, but the surrounding life of the people themselves has filled them up, creating a scar which will heal. In towns such as Cologne and those of the Ruhr, something quite different has happened. The external destruction is so great that it cannot be healed and the surrounding life of the rest of the country cannot flow into and resuscitate the city which is not only battered but also dismembered and cut off from the rest of Germany and from Europe. The ruin of the city is reflected in the internal ruin of its inhabitants who, instead of being lives that can form a scar over the city's wounds, are parasites sucking at a dead [carcass], digging among the ruins for hidden food, doing business at their black market near the cathedral—the commerce of destruction instead of production.

The people who live there seem quite dissociated from Cologne. They resemble rather a tribe of wanderers who have discovered a ruined city in a desert and who are camping there, living in the cellars and hunting amongst the ruins for the booty, relics of a dead civilization.

The great city looks like a corpse and stinks like one also, with all the garbage which has not been cleared way, all the bodies still buried under heaps of stones and iron. Although the streets have been partly cleared, they still have many holes in them and some of the side streets are impassable. The general impression is that very little has been cleared away. There are landscapes of untouched ruin still left.

. . . But it is the comparatively undamaged cathedral which gives Cologne what it still retains of character. One sees that this is and was a great city, it is uplifted by the spire of the cathedral from being a mere heap of rubble and a collection of walls, like the towns of the Ruhr. Large buildings round the cathedral have been scratched and torn, and, forming a kind of cliff beneath the spires, they have a certain dignity like the cliffs and rocks under a church close to the sea.

. . . In the destroyed German towns one often feels haunted by the ghost of a tremendous noise. It is impossible not to imagine the rocking explosions, the hammering of the sky upon the earth, which must have caused all this.

The effect of these corpse-towns is a grave discouragement which influences everyone living and working in Germany, the Occupying Forces as much as the German. The destruction is *serious* in more senses than one. It is a climax of deliberate effort, an achievement of our civilization, the most striking result of co-operation between nations in the twentieth century. It is the shape created by our century as the Gothic cathedral is the shape created by the Middle Ages. Everything has stopped here, that fusion of the past within the present, integrated into architecture, which forms the organic life of a city, a life quite distinct from that of the inhabitants who are, after all, only using a city as a waiting-room on their journey through time: that long, gigantic life of a city has been killed. The city is dead and the inhabitants only haunt the cellars and basements. Without their city they are rats in the cellars, or bats wheeling around the towers of the cathedral. The citizens go on existing with a base mechanical kind of life like that of insects in the crannies of walls who are too creepy and ignoble to be destroyed when the wall is torn down. The destruction of the city itself, with all its past as well as its present, is like a reproach to the people who go on living there. The sermons in the stones of Germany preach nihilism.

Bruno Foa
EUROPE IN RUINS

Shortly after the end of World War II, international economic experts in Europe and the United States began to evaluate the difficulties posed by social and economic dislocation and material destruction. The following report, authored by Bruno Foa, a specialist in Inter-American Affairs and member of the Board of Governors of the Federal Reserve System, isolated the central challenges to

European recovery. His conclusions proved prescient; the European Recovery Program announced by Secretary of State Marshall only two years later was formulated to address the problems that Foa pointed out so clearly.

The present situation of the liberated countries of Europe is governed, to an overwhelming extent, by facts and realities from which there is no escape. These facts are hunger, unemployment, economic dislocation of unprecedented scope, and destruction and damage on an appalling scale. . . .

. . . [I]t is already clear that the economic and social disturbances which followed the last war were child's play in comparison with the crisis Europe is now facing. . . . [T]he experiences of this war, and of the new dark age which began on January 30, 1933, have destroyed old frames of references and created conditions favorable to nihilism and despair.

The lights which Sir Edward Grey saw dimming all over Europe in the fateful August of 1914, and which went out once more twenty-five years later, are being rekindled over a desolate landscape of death and ruins. The living skeletons who are emerging from German concentration camps, and the millions of "displaced persons" to whom liberation means rescue from certain death but holds no promise of real life and happiness, symbolize the depths to which Europe has fallen. . . .

ECONOMIC CONSEQUENCES OF WAR

It is unnecessary to dwell on the dreary catalogue of the economic consequences of war for the liberated countries of Europe. There have been the effects of actual war damage and destruction. There have been the effects of the ruthless economy of spoliation and slavery enforced by the Germans. . . .

War Damage and Destruction

The physical destruction wrought by this war is beyond description. It is reported that in France over a million buildings have been de-

stroyed or badly damaged, a number considerably in excess of the damage produced in World War I. In France thousands of bridges have also been demolished. Railroad equipment, both fixed installations and rolling stock, has suffered great destruction and depletion. Practically all major French ports have been either destroyed or badly damaged. Italy has suffered perhaps even more—countless cities, towns and villages from Salerno to Bologna are heaps of ruins; extensive damage has been wreaked on such great cities as Milan, Genoa, Naples and Turin. Bridges and railroad lines were sabotaged by the Germans in the course of their slow retreat across the Italian peninsula. First reports from liberated Holland, although less catastrophic than expected, are grim. As to eastern Europe and the Balkans, the tale of destruction due to actual fighting, guerrilla warfare and enemy ruthlessness is now generally familiar. . . .

It can be confidently predicted that, in some areas at least, reconstruction will be carried on with vigor and speed. This was the case after World War I, although it must be noted that the damage caused by World War II is far in excess of anything previously experienced. Among other things destruction of railroad lines and equipment has been incomparably heavier, and their rebuilding will require massive imports of expensive and specialized equipment and materials. Reconstruction of permanent port installations in places like Antwerp, Rotterdam, Bordeaux, Marseilles, Genoa and Naples will entail enormous cost and effort. . . .

Impact on Human Potential

The war and German occupation have had an incalculable impact on the human potential of the subjugated lands of Europe. German policies have followed a single criminal pattern—a slave Europe ruled by the *Herrenvolk.* These policies have been implemented in varying ways and degrees in the different countries. Extermination was applied against the Jews of all occupied territories, and millions of Poles, Russians and other peoples of eastern Europe were murdered. By holding in bondage over two and a half million young Frenchmen for five years, the Germans struck a heavy blow at France's birth rate. Outright starvation killed hundreds of thousands, and indeed millions, in Greece, Poland and the Balkans. In most occupied countries malnutrition, tuberculosis and a high rate of infant mortality have sapped the human potential. All this is bound to have lasting effects not only on population statistics but also on the vitality, the physical and mental balance, and the productivity of at least two generations.

German Depredation

German depredation varied in degree and methods in different countries, but was uniformly far-reaching. In Poland and Russia it took the form of outright robbery, confiscation, and the dismantlement and removal to Germany of industrial and productive assets. In Czechoslovakia the ownership of most basic industries was transferred to German hands, and Germans penetrated into practically the entire economic life of the country. In Italy depredation and destruction of foodstuffs, cattle, etc., were extensive. In western and northern Europe spoliation was thinly clothed under financial and other manipulations, which deceived no one. . . .

Heavy occupation costs and other equivalent contributions were levied on France, Belgium, Holland, Czechoslovakia, Norway and Poland. The most significant case in point was that of France, which paid to Germany for occupation costs . . . the enormous sum of 860 billion francs—the equivalent of more than $17 billion. The amounts levied by Germany on other countries, although lower, were proportionately even heavier. . . . [T]he damaging effects

of these tributes, in terms of inflation and public finance, are irreparable. . . .

Hunger: Legacy of War

With few exceptions, liberated Europe is starving or semi-starving. The situation is worse in Greece, Yugoslavia and Poland, but also disastrous in Italy, France—with the exception of a few well-stocked rural districts such as Normandy—Belgium and Holland. The average caloric intake of people in Greece, France and Italy is far below the minimum subsistence level. Death rates have risen to exceptionally high levels, in particular infant mortality, which in France and Italy is said to exceed 50 per cent. Even those who escape outright starvation are suffering from the effects of an unbalanced diet and deficiencies in fats, iron, calcium and vitamins. . . .

Coal and Transportation

Everywhere in liberated western Europe coal and transportation are pressing problems of the day, on which almost everything else depends. . . .

Prices, Wages, and Black Markets

Europe [is], from one end to the other, a single, giant black market. . . .

[T]here is no incentive at present for a worker to stick to his job or look for a new one. For, wages being what they are, the worker is better off . . . supplementing his income by engaging in black-market or other illegal activity which lends itself to exploitation of the consumer. In general, and this applies both to entrepreneurs and to laborers, there is hardly a legitimate activity that pays. While some of these illegal activities—such as outright racketeering, dealings in Allied stolen properties, etc.—are still considered criminal by a majority of the people, the line of demarcation between what is legal and what is illegal has become increasingly blurred. To survive, one has literally to push around, cheat or exploit the other fellow. It is the law of the jungle. The white collar, professional and lower middle classes are the hardest hit; and the proletarianization of large strata of the population, which played havoc with central Europe in the early twenties and contributed powerfully to the rise of Hitler, is spreading throughout the continent.

REVIEW QUESTIONS

1. How did the destruction that Stephen Spender witnessed in Cologne differ from what he had seen in England?
2. According to Bruno Foa's report, how were the problems of farm production and transportation crucial to recovery and reconstruction in Europe after World War II?
3. Why do black markets flourish in wartime and in ruined postwar economies?

---

2 Germany Confronts Its Past

Until the 1960s, German secondary school history courses generally ended with the beginning of the twentieth century. Few teachers discussed the Nazi regime, and appropriate books about Nazism and the Holocaust were lacking. Moreover, many teachers found the subject uncomfortable, for only a few years earlier they had faithfully served the Third Reich and embraced its ideology. Distressed by a sudden outburst of anti-Semitic incidents that afflicted Germany in 1959, notably desecrated cemeteries and swastikas smeared on the walls of synagogues, German educational authorities made a concerted effort to teach young people about the Nazi past.

Hannah Vogt
THE BURDEN OF GUILT

These same anti-Semitic outrages moved Hannah Vogt, a civil servant concerned principally with education, to write a book for students about the Nazi past. Published in 1961, *The Burden of Guilt,* became a widely used text in secondary schools. In the Preface, Vogt stated the book's purpose:

> [S]elf-examination and a repudiation of false political principles are the only means we have of winning new trust among those peoples who were forced to suffer fearful things under Hitler's brutal policy of force. . . . Only if we draw the right conclusions from the mistakes of the past and apply them to our thought and action can we win new trust. . . . Anyone who makes an effort to understand recent political history will learn that in politics not every means is just [and] that law and the dignity of man are not empty phrases.

The book's conclusion, excerpted below, showed a sincere effort of German schools to come to grips with the darkest period in German history.

A nation is made up of individuals whose ideas—right or wrong—determine their actions, their decisions, and their common life, and for this reason a nation, too, can look back at its history and learn from it. As Germans, we should not find it too difficult to understand the meaning of the fourteen years of the Weimar Republic and the twelve years of the Hitler regime.

The ancient Greeks already knew and taught that no state can remain free without free citizens. If the citizens of a commonwealth are not prepared to make sacrifices for their liberty, to take matters into their own hands and participate in public affairs, they deliver themselves into the hands of a tyrant. They do not deserve anything but tyrannical rule: "A class which fails to make sacrifices for political affairs may not make demands on political life. It renounces its will to rule, and must therefore be ruled." These words of a German liberal about the educated class are valid for people everywhere.

The Greeks called a man who abstained from politics "idiotēs." The Oxford English Dictionary translates this as "private person," "ignorant," "layman," or "not professionally learned." And what are we to call those who have learned nothing from our recent history but the foolish slogan "without me" *(Ohne mich)*? Are they not like fish who expect to improve their condition by jumping from the frying pan into the fire?

We have paid dearly once before for the folly of believing that democracy, being an ideal political arrangement, must function automatically while the citizens sit in their parlors berating it, or worrying about their money. Everybody must share in the responsibility and must be prepared to make sacrifices. He must also respect the opinions of others and must curb his hates, which are too blinding to be good guides for action. In addition, we need to be patient, we must have confidence in small advances and abandon the belief in political miracles and panaceas.

Only if the citizens are thoroughly imbued with democratic attitudes can we put into practice those principles of political life which were achieved through centuries of experience, and which we disregarded to our great sorrow. The first such principle is the need for a continuous and vigilant control of power. For this, we need not only a free and courageous press but also some mechanism for shaping a vital political opinion in associations, parties, and other organizations. Equally necessary are clearly drawn lines of political responsibility, and a strong and respected political opposition. Interest groups must not be diffused too widely but must aim at maximum cohesiveness. Present developments appear to indicate that we are deeply aware of at least this necessity.

More than anything else we must base our concept of law on the idea of justice. We have had the sad experience that the principle "the law is the law" does not suffice, if the laws are being abused to cover up for crimes and to wrap injustices in a tissue of legality. Our actions must once again be guided by that idea which is the basis of just life: no man must be used as a means to an end.

This principle must also be applied to our relationships with other nations. Although, on the international scene, there is as yet no all-inclusive legal body that would have enough power to solve all conflicts peacefully, still there are legal norms in international affairs which are not at all the "sound and smoke" (Faust) Hitler had presumed them to be. In no other matter was he as divorced from reality as in his belief that it was shrewd to conclude treaties today and "to break them in cold blood tomorrow," and that he could undo 2000 years of legal evolution without having such action recoil upon him. He considered force the one and only means of politics, while, in reality, it had always been the worst. Hitler's so-called *Realpolitik* was terrifyingly unreal, and brought about a catastrophe which has undone the gains Bismarck had made through moderation.

Bismarck gave Germany its unity. Hitler, goaded by his limitless drive for world power, divided Germany and destroyed the work of generations.

Thus we are now faced with the difficult task of regaining, by peaceful means, the German unity that Hitler has gambled away. We must strive for it tirelessly, even though it may take decades. At the same time, we must establish a new relationship, based on trust, with the peoples of Europe and the nations of the world. Our word must again be believed, our commitment to freedom and humanity again be trusted. Our name has been used too much for lies and treachery. We cannot simply stretch out our hands and hope that all will be forgotten.

These are the questions which should touch the younger generation most deeply: What position could and should we have among the nations? Can we restore honor to the German name? Can we shape a new and better future? Or shall we be burdened with the crimes of the Hitler regime for generations to come?

However contradictory the problem may look at first sight, there can be no shilly-shallying, but only a clear Yes to these questions. The past cannot be erased, but the future is free. It is not predetermined. We have the power to re-examine our decisions and mend our wrong ways; we can renounce force and place our trust in peaceful and gradual progress; we can reject racial pride. Instead of impressing the world with war and aggression, we can strive for world prestige through the peaceful solution of conflicts, as the Swiss and the Scandinavians have done for centuries to their national glory. For us, the choice is open to condemn Hitler's deluded destructiveness and to embrace Albert Schweitzer's message—respect for life.

If we are really serious about this new respect for life, it must also extend to the victims of the unspeakable policy of extermination. Ever since human beings have existed, respect for life has included respect for the dead. Everywhere it is the duty of the living to preserve the memory of the dead. Should we listen to insinuations that the time has come to forget crimes and victims because nobody must incriminate himself? Is it not, rather, cowardly, mean, and miserable to deny even now the dead the honor they deserve, and to forget them as quickly as possible?

We owe it to ourselves to examine our consciences sincerely and to face the naked truth, instead of minimizing it or glossing over it. This is also the only way we can regain respect in the world. Covering up or minimizing crimes will suggest that we secretly approve of them. Who will believe that we want to respect all that is human if we treat the death of nearly six million Jews as a "small error" to be forgotten after a few years?

The test of our change of heart should be not only the dead but the living. There are 30,000 Jewish fellow-citizens living among us. Many of them have returned only recently from emigration, overwhelmed with a desire for their old homeland. It is up to all of us to make sure that they live among us in peace and without being abused, that their new trust in us, won after much effort, is not destroyed by desecrated cemeteries, gutter slogans, or hate songs. Those who will never learn must not be allowed to take refuge in the freedom of opinion. A higher value is at stake here, the honor of the dead, and respect for the living. But it is not up to the public prosecutor to imbue our lives with new and more humane principles. This is everybody's business. It concerns us all! It will determine our future.

REVIEW QUESTIONS

1. According to Hannah Vogt, what lessons should Germans learn from the Nazi era?
2. How did she suggest that Germans now confront the Holocaust?

3 The Cold War

After World War II the first Western statesman to express his alarm over Soviet expansionism was Winston Churchill, the doughty and articulate wartime leader of Great Britain. While noting, on a visit to America, that the United States stood "at the pinnacle of world power," he warned of the Soviet challenge. It threatened the liberties that were a traditional part of Western democracy. Prompted by the failure of the attempt to appease Hitler and by the war experience, he urged military strength and political cooperation between Western Europe and the United States in order to stem the communist advance.

In the United States, George Kennan, a foreign service officer with extensive experience in Eastern Europe and Moscow, soon followed Churchill's lead, advocating the thwarting of Soviet ambitions by a policy of containment. Churchill and Kennan formulated the Western outlook in what came to be called "the Cold War." At his first major Party Congress, Nikita Khrushchev, Stalin's successor in the Soviet Union, set forth the Soviet position, foreseeing the victory of communism by peaceful means. By 1956 the ideological positions of the chief antagonists in the Cold War had been fixed.

Winston Churchill
THE "IRON CURTAIN"

In a famous speech at Fulton, Missouri, in early March 1946, when he was no longer in office, Churchill (1874–1965) articulated his views on the duty of Western democracies in the face of Soviet expansion. Significant passages from that speech, in which the term *iron curtain* was first used, follow.

A shadow has fallen upon the scenes so lately lighted by the Allied victory. Nobody knows what Soviet Russia and its Communist international organization intends to do in the immediate future, or what are the limits, if any, to their expansive and proselytizing tendencies. I have a strong admiration and regard for the valiant Russian people and for my wartime comrade, Marshal Stalin. There is sympathy and good will in Britain—and I doubt not here also—toward the peoples of all the Russias and a resolve to persevere through many differences and rebuffs in establishing lasting friendships. We understand the Russian need to be secure on her western frontiers from all

renewal of German aggression. We welcome her to her rightful place among the leading nations of the world. Above all we welcome constant, frequent and growing contacts between the Russian people and our own people on both sides of the Atlantic. It is my duty, however, to place before you certain facts about the present position in Europe—I am sure I do not wish to, but it is my duty, I feel, to present them to you.

From Stettin in the Baltic to Triest in the Adriatic, an iron curtain has descended across the Continent. Behind that line lie all the capitals of the ancient states of central and eastern Europe. Warsaw, Berlin, Prague, Vienna,

454   *Part Three Western Civilization in Crisis*

Budapest, Belgrade, Bucharest and Sofia, all these famous cities and the populations around them lie in the Soviet sphere and all are subject in one form or another, not only to Soviet influence but to a very high and increasing measure of control from Moscow. . . . The Communist parties, which were very small in all these eastern states of Europe, have been raised to preeminence and power far beyond their numbers and are seeking everywhere to obtain totalitarian control. Police governments are prevailing in nearly every case. . . . Turkey and Persia are both profoundly alarmed and disturbed at the claims which are made upon them and at the pressure being exerted by the Moscow government. An attempt is being made by the Russians in Berlin to build up a quasi-Communist party in their zone of occupied Germany. . . . Whatever conclusions may be drawn from these facts—and facts they are—this is certainly not the liberated Europe we fought to build up. Nor is it one which contains the essentials of permanent peace. . . . What we have to consider here today while time remains, is the permanent prevention of war and the establishment of conditions of freedom and democracy as rapidly as possible in all countries. Our difficulties and dangers will not be removed by closing our eyes to them. They will not be removed by mere waiting to see what happens; nor will they be relieved by a policy of appeasement. What is needed is a settlement and the longer this is delayed the more difficult it will be and the greater our dangers will become. From what I have seen of our Russian friends and allies during the war, I am convinced that there is nothing they admire so much as strength, and there is nothing for which they have less respect than for military weakness. . . . If the western democracies stand together in strict adherence to the principles of the United Nations Charter, their influence for furthering these principles will be immense and no one is likely to molest them. If, however, they become divided or falter in their duty, and if these all-important years are allowed to slip away, then indeed catastrophe may overwhelm us all.

Nikita S. Khrushchev
REPORT TO THE TWENTIETH PARTY CONGRESS

After World War II, the Korean War, and the escalation of the nuclear arms race into the deployment of hydrogen bombs, the Soviets perceived themselves to be in a worldwide struggle with the Western capitalists. In the Soviet view, the socialist system was advancing, whereas the capitalist system was in decline; the Cold War represented a desperate effort to preserve capitalism. Communists especially attacked the American desire to deal with the socialist countries from a position of superior strength.

Soviet international policy gave special attention to the aspirations of "the people of the East," the Asians and Africans emerging from colonial rule. Soviets described American aid to developing countries as a new form of imperialism, whereas Soviet aid was pictured as humanitarian assistance in the struggle against colonialism.

Nikita Khrushchev (1894–1971) summed up the Soviet perspective on world affairs for the benefit of a new generation of Soviet citizens. As first secretary of the Communist party, he delivered a report to the Twentieth Party Congress in February 1956, on the eve of his famous denunciation of the crimes of the Stalin era (see page 322). He sounded an optimistic but militant note. Alarmed by the progress of the arms race, Khrushchev gave vigorous support to an old Soviet plea for the peaceful coexistence of the two competing sociopolitical systems— a coexistence in which victory would inevitably go to communism.

Soon after the Second World War ended, the influence of reactionary and militarist groups began to be increasingly evident in the policy of the United States of America, Britain and France. Their desire to enforce their will on other countries by economic and political pressure, threats and military provocation prevailed. This became known as the "positions of strength" policy. It reflects the aspiration of the most aggressive sections of present-day imperialism to win world supremacy, to suppress the working class and the democratic and national-liberation movements; it reflects their plans for military adventures against the socialist camp.

The international atmosphere was poisoned by war hysteria. The arms race began to assume more and more monstrous dimensions. Many big U.S. military bases designed for use against the U.S.S.R. and the People's Democracies [East European countries under Soviet control] were built in countries thousands of miles from the borders of the United States. "Cold war" was begun against the socialist camp. International distrust was artificially kindled, and nations set against one another. A bloody war was launched in Korea; the war in Indo-China dragged on for years.

The inspirers of the "cold war" began to establish military blocs, and many countries found themselves, against the will of their peoples, involved in restricted aggressive alignments—the North Atlantic bloc, Western European Union, SEATO (military bloc for South-East Asia) and the Baghdad pact.

The organizers of military blocs allege that they have united for defence, for protection against the "communist threat." But that is sheer hypocrisy. We know from history that when planning a redivision of the world, the imperialist powers have always lined up military blocs. Today the "anti-communism" slogan is again being used as a smokescreen to cover

up the claims of one power for world domination. The new thing here is that the United States wants, by means of all kinds of blocs and pacts, to secure a dominant position in the capitalist world for itself, and to reduce all its partners in the blocs to the status of obedient executors of its will. . . .

The winning of political freedom by the peoples of the former colonies and semi-colonies is the first and most important prerequisite of their full independence, that is, of the achievement of economic independence. The liberated Asian countries are pursuing a policy of building up their own industry, training their own technicians, raising the living standards of the people, and regenerating and developing their age-old national culture. History-making prospects for a better future are opening up before the countries which have embarked upon the path of independent development. . . .

[T]he colonial powers . . . have recourse to new forms of colonial enslavement under the guise of so-called "aid" to underdeveloped countries, which brings colossal profits to the colonialists. Let us take the United States as an example. The United States renders such "aid" above all in the form of deliveries of American weapons to the underdeveloped countries. This enables the American monopolies to load up their industry with arms orders. . . . States receiving such "aid" in the form of weapons, inevitably fall into dependence. . . .

Naturally, "aid" to underdeveloped countries is granted on definite political terms, terms providing for their integration into aggressive military blocs, the conclusion of joint military pacts, and support for American foreign policy aimed at world domination, or "world leadership," as the American imperialists themselves call it. . . .

[In contrast,] the exceptionally warm and friendly welcome accorded the representatives of the great Soviet people has strikingly demonstrated the deep-rooted confidence and love the broad masses in the Eastern countries have for the Soviet Union. Analyzing the sources of this confidence, the Egyptian *Al Akhbar* justly wrote: "Russia does not try to buy the conscience of the peoples, their rights and liberty. Russia has extended a hand to the peoples and said that they themselves should decide their destiny, that she recognizes their rights and aspirations and does not demand their adherence to military pacts or blocs." Millions of men and women ardently acclaim our country for its uncompromising struggle against colonialism, for its policy of equality and friendship among all nations and for its consistent peaceful foreign policy. *(Stormy, prolonged applause.)*

. . . The Leninist principle of peaceful coexistence of states with different social systems has always been and remains the general line of our country's foreign policy. . . . To this day the enemies of peace allege that the Soviet Union is out to overthrow capitalism in other countries by "exporting" revolution. It goes without saying that among us Communists there are no supporters of capitalism. But this does not mean that we have interfered or plan to interfere in the internal affairs of countries where capitalism still exists. . . . It is ridiculous to think that revolutions are made to order. We often hear representatives of bourgeois countries reasoning thus: "The Soviet leaders claim that they are for peaceful co-existence between the two systems. At the same time they declare that they are fighting for communism, and say that communism is bound to win in all countries. Now if the Soviet Union is fighting for communism, how can there be any peaceful co-existence with it?". . .

When we say that the socialist system will win in the competition between the two systems—the capitalist and the socialist—this by no means signifies that its victory will be achieved through armed interference by the socialist countries in the internal affairs of the capitalist countries. Our certainty of the victory of communism is based on the fact that the socialist mode of production possesses decisive advantages over the capitalist mode of production. Precisely because of this, the ideas of Marxism-Leninism are more and more capturing the minds of the broad masses of the working people in the capitalist countries, just as they have captured the minds of millions of men and women in our country and the People's Democracies. *(Prolonged applause)*. We believe that all working men in the world, once they have become convinced of the advantages communism brings, will sooner or later take the road of struggle for the construction of socialist society.

REVIEW QUESTIONS

1. Where did Winston Churchill observe evidence of Soviet expansionism? Find on a map of Europe and Asia the areas he mentioned.
2. What were Churchill's recommendations for countering Soviet expansionism?
3. What, according to Nikita Khrushchev, were the "imperialist powers" (the United States, England, and France) trying to accomplish in their pursuit of a "position of strength"?
4. How did Khrushchev describe the aims of American policy in regard to the Soviet Union?
5. What were Khrushchev's hopes for the future? What were his reasons for viewing socialism as superior to capitalism?

4 Communist Repression

When at the end of World War II the Soviet armies pursued the retreating Germans deep into central Europe, they subjected all of Eastern Europe to Soviet domination. By 1948 all countries except Yugoslavia had fallen under Stalin's iron grip. Soviet domination was buttressed by the Warsaw Pact, the military alliance of all countries within the Soviet bloc formed in 1955 to counter the North Atlantic Treaty Organization (NATO). It was further strengthened by the Council for Mutual Economic Assistance (COMECON), created in 1958 in response to the emerging European Economic Community; it tried to weld the disparate economies of Eastern Europe into a viable unit for the benefit of the Soviet boss.

Yet Soviet rule did not take firm root. The peoples under Soviet domination traditionally had looked westward, benefiting from economic, religious, and cultural ties with Western Europe. They also carried over from their past a strong nationalist ambition for independence. As Western Europe recovered from World War II, the discrepancy between the poverty of the Soviet bloc and the prosperity of its Western neighbors, especially the Federal Republic of Germany, added a further source of anti-Soviet agitation.

Inevitably the craving for independence and freedom caused mounting tensions in Soviet-controlled Eastern Europe. Within each country Soviet lackeys struggled against the reformers who were asserting, however cautiously, the yearnings of their peoples. Tensions occasionally erupted in dramatic protests, as evidenced in Hungary in 1956.

Milovan Djilas
THE NEW CLASS

Milovan Djilas's book *The New Class: An Analysis of the Communist System* (1957), from which the following excerpts are taken, provides helpful insights into the explosion of discontent in Hungary, Czechoslovakia, and Poland under Soviet control. Djilas (1911–1995), a Yugoslav author and political commentator, became a communist after finishing his studies in 1933. Although he began as a close friend of Marshal Tito, the all-powerful leader of Yugoslavia, in 1953 he turned critic, not only of his friend, but also of communist practice and ideology. Jailed for his heresies in 1956, he wrote his assessment of the communist system, showing its connection to the unprecedented new class of political bureaucrats dominating state and society. Under communism the state did not wither away, as early theorists had expected. On the contrary, it grew more powerful, thanks to that highly privileged "exploiting and governing class." Aware of the dynamics of nationalism at work underneath each communist regime, Djilas pointed to the weaknesses of communist rule and the growing desire for national self-assertion among the peoples of the Soviet satellite states.

Earlier revolutions, particularly the so-called bourgeois ones, attached considerable significance to the establishment of individual freedoms immediately following cessation of the revolutionary terror. Even the revolutionaries considered it important to assure the legal status of the citizenry. Independent administration of justice was an inevitable final result of all these revolutions. The Communist regime in the U.S.S.R. is still remote from independent administration of justice after forty years of tenure. The final results of earlier revolutions were often greater legal security and greater civil rights. This cannot be said of the Communist revolution. . . .

In contrast to earlier revolutions, the Communist revolution, conducted in the name of doing away with classes, has resulted in the most complete authority of any single new class. Everything else is sham and an illusion. . . .

This new class, the bureaucracy, or more accurately the political bureaucracy, has all the characteristics of earlier ones as well as some new characteristics of its own. Its origin had its special characteristics also, even though in essence it was similar to the beginnings of other classes. . . . The new class may be said to be made up of those who have special privileges and economic preference because of the administrative monopoly they hold. . . .

The mechanism of Communist power is perhaps the simplest which can be conceived, although it leads to the most refined tyranny and the most brutal exploitation. The simplicity of this mechanism originates from the fact that one party alone, the Communist Party, is the backbone of the entire political, economic, and ideological activity. The entire public life is at a standstill or moves ahead, falls behind or turns around according to what happens in the party forums. . . .

. . . Communist control of the social machine . . . restricts certain government posts to party members. These jobs, which are essential in any government but especially in a Communist one, include assignments with police, especially the secret police; and the diplomatic and officers corps, especially positions in the information and political services. In the judiciary only top positions have until now been in the hands of Communists. . . .

Only in a Communist state are a number of both specified and unspecified positions reserved for members of the party. The Communist government, although a class structure, is a party government; the Communist army is a party army; and the state is a party state. More precisely, Communists tend to treat the army and the state as their exclusive weapons.

The exclusive, if unwritten, law that only party members can become policemen, officers, diplomats, and hold similar positions, or that only they can exercise actual authority, creates a special privileged group of bureaucrats. . . .

The entire governmental structure is organized in this manner. Political positions are reserved exclusively for party members. Even in non-political governmental bodies Communists hold the strategic positions or oversee administration. Calling a meeting at the party center or publishing an article is sufficient to cause the entire state and social mechanism to begin functioning. If difficulties occur anywhere, the party and the police very quickly correct the "error." . . .

The classes and masses do not exercise authority, but the party does so in their name. In every party, including the most democratic, leaders play an important role to the extent that the party's authority becomes the authority of the leaders. The so-called "dictatorship of the proletariat," which is the beginning of and under the best circumstances becomes the authority of the party, inevitably evolves into the dictatorship of the leaders. In a totalitarian government of this type, the dictatorship of the proletariat is a theoretical justification, or ideological mask at best, for the authority of some oligarchs. . . .

Freedoms are formally recognized in Communist regimes, but one decisive condition is a prerequisite for exercising them: freedoms must be utilized only in the interest of the system of "socialism," which the Communist leaders represent, or to buttress their rule. This practice, contrary as it is to legal regulations, inevitably had to result in the use of exceptionally severe and unscrupulous methods by police and party bodies. . . .

. . . It has been impossible in practice to separate police authority from judicial authority. Those who arrest also judge and enforce punishments. The circle is closed: the executive, the legislative, the investigating, the court, and the punishing bodies are one and the same. . . .

Communist parliaments are not in a position to make decisions on anything important. Selected in advance as they are, flattered that they have been thus selected, representatives do not have the power or the courage to debate even if they wanted to do so. Besides, since their mandate does not depend on the voters, representatives do not feel that they are answerable to them. Communist parliaments are justifiably called "mausoleums" for the representatives who compose them. Their right and role consist of unanimously approving from time to time that which has already been decided for them from the wings. . . .

Though history has no record of any other system so successful in *checking* its opposition as the Communist dictatorship, none ever has *provoked* such profound and far-reaching discontent. It seems that the more the conscience is crushed and the less the opportunities for establishing an organization exist, the greater the discontent. . . .

In addition to being motivated by the historical need for rapid industrialization, the Communist bureaucracy has been compelled to establish a type of economic system designed to insure the perpetuation of its own power. Allegedly for the sake of a classless society and for the abolition of exploitation, it has created a closed economic system, with forms of property which facilitate the party's domination and its monopoly. At first, the Communists had to turn to this "collectivistic" form for objective reasons. Now they continue to strengthen this form—without considering whether or not it is in the interest of the national economy and of further industrialization—for their own sake, for an exclusive Communist class aim. They first administered and controlled the entire economy for so-called ideal goals; later they did it for the purpose of maintaining their absolute control and domination. That is the real reason for such far-reaching and inflexible political measures in the Communist economy. . . .

A citizen in the Communist system lives oppressed by the constant pangs of his conscience, and the fear that he has transgressed. He is always fearful that he will have to demonstrate that he is not an enemy of socialism, just as in the Middle Ages a man constantly had to show his devotion to the Church. . . .

. . . Tyranny over the mind is the most complete and most brutal type of tyranny; every other tyranny begins and ends with it. . . .

History will pardon Communists for much, establishing that they were forced into many brutal acts because of circumstances and the need to defend their existence. But the stifling of every divergent thought, the exclusive monopoly over thinking for the purpose of defending their personal interests, will nail the Communists to a cross of shame in history. . . .

In essence, Communism is only one thing, but it is realized in different degrees and manners in every country. Therefore it is possible to speak of various Communist systems, i.e., of various forms of the same manifestation.

The differences which exist between Communist states—differences that Stalin attempted futilely to remove by force—are the result, above all, of diverse historical backgrounds. . . . When ascending to power, the Communists face in the various countries different cultural and technical levels and varying social relationships, and are faced with different national intellectual characters. . . . Of the former international proletariat, only words and empty dogmas remained. Behind them stood the naked national and international interests, aspirations, and plans of the various Communist oligarchies, comfortably entrenched. . . .

. . . The Communist East European countries did not become satellites of the U.S.S.R. because they benefited from it, but because they were too weak to prevent it. As soon as they become stronger, or as soon as favorable conditions are created, a yearning for independence and for protection of "their own people" from Soviet hegemony will rise among them.

The subordinate Communist governments in East Europe can, in fact must, declare their independence from the Soviet government. No one can say how far this aspiration for independence will go and what disagreements will result. The result depends on numerous unforeseen internal and external circumstances. However, there is no doubt that a national Communist bureaucracy aspires to more complete authority for itself. This is demonstrated . . . by the current unconcealed emphasis on "one's own path to socialism," which has recently come to light sharply in Poland and Hungary. The central Soviet government has found itself in difficulty because of the nationalism existing even in those governments which it installed in the Soviet republics (Ukraine, Caucasia), and still more so with regard to those governments installed in the East European countries. Playing an important role in all of this is the fact that the Soviet Union was unable, and will not be able in the future, to assimilate the economies of the East European countries.

The aspirations toward national independence must of course have greater impetus. These aspirations can be retarded and even made dormant by external pressure or by fear on the part of the Communists of "imperialism" and the "bourgeoisie," but they cannot be removed. On the contrary, their strength will grow.

Andor Heller
THE HUNGARIAN REVOLUTION, 1956

After Stalin's death in 1953, the rigid political controls in Hungary were relaxed, leading to an unstable balance between Soviet-oriented hard-liners and patriotic reformers willing to grant greater freedom to the spirit of nationalism and individual enterprise stirring among the people. In 1956, the year of Khrushchev's attack on Stalin, the Hungarian yearning for escape from Soviet domination exploded. On October 23 a student demonstration in Budapest, the capital, provided the spark. Throughout the country, communist officials were ousted and the Soviet troops forced to withdraw. A coalition government under Imre Nagy was formed to restore Hungary's independence; it even appeared that the country would withdraw from the newly formed Warsaw Pact controlled by Moscow. In Budapest especially, the popular excitement over the country's liberation from the Soviet yoke knew no bounds, as described in the following eyewitness account.

Deep dejection followed the anger caused by the Soviet counterattack that killed thousands of people and drove 200,000 into exile. A new "peasant-worker government" under János Kádár boasted of having saved the country from "fascist counter-revolution." Subsequently, however, Kádár transformed his country's economy. Dubbed "goulash communism" for its mixture of state and private enterprise, it became the freest in the Soviet bloc and a model for Gorbachev's *perestroika*.

I saw freedom rise from the ashes of Communism in Hungary: a freedom that flickered and then blazed before it was beaten down—but not extinguished—by masses of Russian tanks and troops.

I saw young students, who had known nothing but a life under Communist and Russian control, die for a freedom about which they had only heard from others or from their own hearts.

I saw workers, who had been pushed to the limit of endurance by their hopeless existence under Communism, lay down their tools and take up arms in a desperate bid to win back freedom for our country.

I saw a girl of fourteen blow up a Russian tank, and grandmothers walk up to Russian cannons.

I watched a whole nation—old and young, men and women, artists and engineers and doctors, clerks and peasants and factory workers—become heroes overnight as they rose up in history's first successful revolt against Communism.

Tuesday, October 23, 1956

No Hungarian will forget this day. . . .

. . . In spite of the cold and fog, students are on the streets early in the morning, marching and singing. No one shows up for classes at the universities. After a decade of Communist control over our country, we are going to show our feelings spontaneously, in our own way—something never allowed under Communist rules.

The students carry signs with slogans that until now we have never dared express except to members of our own family—and not in every family. The slogans read:

RUSSIANS GO HOME!

LET HUNGARY BE INDEPENDENT!

BRING RAKOSI TO JUSTICE!

WE WANT A NEW LEADERSHIP!

SOLIDARITY WITH THE POLISH PEOPLE!

WE TRUST IMRE NAGY—BRING IMRE
     NAGY INTO THE GOVERNMENT!

The walls of Budapest are plastered with leaflets put up by the students during the night. They list the fourteen demands adopted at the stormy meetings held at the universities:

1. Withdrawal of all Soviet troops from Hungary.
2. Complete economic and political equality with the Soviet Union, with no interference in Hungary's internal affairs.
3. Publication of Hungary's trade agreements, and a public report on Hungary's reparations payments to the U.S.S.R.
4. Information on Hungary's uranium resources, their exploitation, and the concessions given to the U.S.S.R.
5. The calling of a Hungarian Communist Party congress to elect a new leadership.
6. Reorganization of the government, with Imre Nagy as Premier.
7. A public trial of Mihaly Farkas and Matyas Rakosi [notorious Stalinists].
8. A secret general multi-party election.
9. The reorganization of Hungary's economy on the basis of her actual resources.
10. Revision of the workers' output quotas, and recognition of the right to strike.
11. Revision of the system of compulsory agricultural quotas.
12. Equal rights for individual farmers and cooperative members.
13. Restoration of Hungary's traditional national emblem and the traditional Hungarian army uniforms.
14. Destruction of the giant statue of Stalin.

During the morning a radio announcement from the Ministry of Interior bans all public meetings and demonstrations "until further notice," and word is sent to the universities that the student demonstrations cannot be held. At that moment the students decide that the will to freedom is greater than the fear of the A.V.H.—the Russian-controlled Hungarian secret police. The meeting will be held! . . .

At 3 P.M. there are 25,000 of us at the Petofi Monument. We weep as Imre Sinkovits, a young actor, declaims the *Nemzeti Dal* ("National Song"), Sandor Petofi's [a great Hungarian poet and revolutionary hero in the anti-Austrian rebellion of 1848–1849] ode to Hungary and our 1848 "freedom revolution." With tears in our eyes, we repeat the refrain with Sinkovits: . . .

"We swear, we swear, we will no longer remain slaves."

The student voices are tense with feeling. No policeman or Communist official is in sight. The young people are keeping order on their own.

. . . [W]e have swelled to some 60,000. Someone grabs a Hungarian flag and cuts out the hated hammer and sickle that the Communists had placed at its center.

One after another of the purified Hungarian flags appear. Suddenly someone remembers to put the old Kossuth [Lajos Kossuth was the leader of the Hungarian uprising of 1848–1849] coat-of-arms on the flag, in place of the Communist emblem.

We have created a new flag of freedom!

Meantime we all sing the . . . *Appeal to the Nation,* and the *Hungarian National Hymn* that begins "God Bless the Magyar"—both of which had been banned under the Communist rule.

We cannot get enough. The actor Ferenc Bessenyei recites the *National Song* again, and follows once more with *Appeal to the Nation.* Peter Veres, the head of the Hungarian Writers' Federation, leaps to the top of a car equipped with a loudspeaker. He reads the Hungarian writers' demands for more freedom—many of them the same as those in the fourteen points of the students.

The day is ending. We begin to march toward the Parliament Building. The crowds are peaceful, marching in orderly lines. We carry the new Hungarian flag.

As we march we are joined by workers leaving their jobs. By the time we arrive in Kossuth Lajos Square there are at least 150,000 of us, in front of the Parliament Building. On the square, the traffic stops. . . .

Suddenly everyone makes torches of newspapers, and lights them. It is a marvelous spectacle—ten thousand torches burning in the Square before the Parliament Building. . . .

But finally, Imre Nagy appears on the balcony. "Comrades!" he begins, but the crowd interrupts him with a roar: "There are no more comrades! We are all Hungarians!" . . .

The crowd grows still bigger, and we head for the Stalin statue. Now the demonstration has spread so large that it is going on simultaneously in three places: at the Parliament Building: in Stalin Square, where the crowd is trying to pull down the huge Stalin statue with tractors and ropes; and at the building of Radio Budapest, where part of the crowd has gone to demand the right of patriots to be heard over the air. . . .

I go with the group that heads for Stalin Square. Some of the workers have got hold of acetylene torches. They and the students are trying to cut down the dictator's twenty-five-foot metal figure. At the edge of the crowd the first Russian tanks appear, but at the moment they are only onlookers. The crowd pulls hard at the cables that have been attached to the Stalin statue. It leans forward, but is still held by its boots—a symbol, we feel. The cables are now being pulled by tractors, and the men with the torches work feverishly. The statue, though still in one piece, begins to bend at the knees. The crowds burst into cheers. . . .

. . . [W]e watch the Stalin statue, cut off at the knees, fall to the ground with a thunderous crash. . . .

Suddenly shooting breaks out from all sides. The security police—the A.V.H.—are firing into the crowds. In minutes the streets are strewn with the dying and wounded. News of the A.V.H. attack spreads. All over Budapest the workers and students are battling the hated A.V.H.

The peaceful demonstrations of the youth and the workers have been turned by Communist guns into a revolution for national freedom.

For four days—from October 31 to November 3, 1956—Hungary was free. Although the Russian forces were still in our country, they had withdrawn from the cities and the fighting had stopped. The whole nation recognized the

Imre Nagy government, which, knowing it had no other alternative, was ready to carry out the will of the people. . . .

On November 3, Radio Free Kossuth summed up: "The over-whelming weight of Hungarian public opinion sees the result of the revolution as the establishment of a neutral, independent and democratic country, and just as it was ready to sweep out Stalinist tyranny, so it will protect with the same determination and firmness its regained democratic achievement.". . .

In those four days of freedom, political liberty came quickly to life. . . .

Before October 23 there had been only five newspapers in Budapest, all under complete Communist control. On November 4 there were twenty-five. Neither news nor opinions could be suppressed any longer.

Plans for a free general election were speeded.

Religious freedom, like political freedom, came back to strong life in those four days. . . .

In the countryside, the peasants and their spokesmen were mapping the changes of the farm laws and regulations. All were agreed on the goal of a free farm economy based on the individual working farmers and peasants. Peasants would be free to join or leave the farm collectives. If the collectives were dissolved, the land, tools and stock were to be distributed to the individual peasants. Compulsory deliveries at government fixed prices were abolished.

The factory committees and workers' groups were putting forward the needs and demands of the workers, not the government. The right to strike—a criminal act under the Communists—was upheld. Wages, prices, pension rights, working conditions were eagerly discussed and debated.

The economy was slowly getting on its feet. Everyone wanted to be on the streets together. . . .

Return of the Russians

At dawn on November 4, 1956, Soviet Russia attacked Hungary with 6,000 tanks, thousands of guns and armored cars, squadrons of light bombers, 200,000 soldiers—and a tidal wave of lies.

REVIEW QUESTIONS

1. How did Milovan Djilas characterize the "new class"? What were its qualities? How did it wield its power?
2. Why, according to Djilas, would the communist governments in Eastern Europe sooner or later declare their independence from the Soviet government?
3. What would you say was the climax of the Budapest demonstration on October 23?
4. What was at stake for the workers and farmers of Hungary in the anti-Soviet uprising?
5. How did the Hungarians in those crucial October days assert their freedom? What evidence of nationalism did you observe in the anti-Soviet demonstrations?

5 The Twilight of Imperialism

World War II accelerated the disintegration of Europe's overseas empires. The European states could hardly justify ruling over Africans and Asians after they had fought to liberate European lands from German imperialism. Nor could they ask their people, exhausted by the Hitler years and concentrating all their energies on reconstruction, to fight new wars against Africans and Asians pressing for independence. In the years just after the war, Great Britain surrendered India, France lost Lebanon and Syria, and the Dutch departed from Indonesia. In the 1950s and 1960s, virtually every colonial territory gained independence. In those instances where the colonial power resisted independence for the colony, the price was bloodshed.

Frantz Fanon
THE EVILS OF COLONIALISM

One of the keenest modern critics of colonialism was Frantz Fanon (1925–1961). A black from the French West Indies, Fanon was familiar with racial discrimination, and he was influenced by Marxism. He was trained in France as a psychiatrist and decorated for valor in World War II. In the 1950s he sided with the Algerian rebels in their fight for independence from France and became an embattled advocate of African decolonization. In his book *The Wretched of the Earth,* published in 1961 when colonial rule in Africa, although on the wane, still persisted, he examined the relations between the colonial masters and their subject peoples with the keen eye of a psychoanalyst. Reflecting the tensions built up under colonialism and the fury of the Algerian war, Fanon focused on the oppressive and dehumanizing aspects of imperialism. He did not even spare the Christian churches from criticism, although they had often trained those who eventually led the anticolonial struggles.

Fanon also anticipated the ambitions of the emerging African leaders. As he observed, "The colonised man is an envious man," who wanted what the masters possessed—wealth and power in an independent state. Rejection of colonial domination did not rule out imitation of the colonial masters' way of life—an attitude that sometimes brought a new dependence, branded as neo-colonialism. Yet the memory of colonial exploitation that Fanon so vividly described persists, kept alive by the poverty and powerlessness of the new African states. In the following passage from *The Wretched of the Earth,* Fanon starkly compares the two realms of the colonial world: ruler and ruled.

The colonial world is a world cut in two. The dividing line, the frontiers are shown by barracks and police stations. In the colonies it is the policeman and the soldier who are the official, instituted go-betweens, and spokesmen of the settler and his rule of oppression. In capitalist societies the educational system, whether lay or clerical, the structure of moral reflexes handed down from father to son, the exemplary honesty of workers who are given a medal after fifty years of good and loyal service, and the affection which springs from harmonious relations and good behaviour—all these esthetic expressions of respect for the established order serve to create around the exploited person an atmosphere of submission and of inhibition which lightens the task of policing considerably. . . . In the colonial countries . . . the policeman and the soldier, by their immediate presence and their frequent and direct action, maintain contact with the native and advise him by means of rifle-butts and napalm not to budge. It is obvious here that the agents of government speak the language of pure force. . . .

The zone where the natives live is not complementary to the zone inhabited by the settlers. The two zones are opposed, but not in the service of a higher unity. . . .

. . . No conciliation is possible, for of the two terms, one is superfluous. The settlers' town is a strongly-built town, all made of stone and steel. It is a brightly-lit town; the streets are covered with asphalt, and the garbage-cans swallow all the leavings, unseen, unknown and hardly thought about. . . . The settler's town is a well-fed town, an easy-going town; its belly is always full of good things. The settler's town is a town of white people, of foreigners.

The town belonging to the colonised people, or at least the native town, the negro village, the medina,[1] the reservation, is a place of ill fame, peopled by men of evil repute. They are born there, it matters little where or how; they die there, it matters not where, nor how. It is a world without spaciousness; men live there on top of each other, and their huts are built one on top of the other. The native town is a hungry town, starved of bread, of meat, of shoes, of coal, of light. The native town is a crouching village, a town on its knees, a town wallowing in the mire. It is a town of niggers and dirty arabs. . . . The look that the native turns on the settler's town is a look of lust, a look of envy; it expresses his dreams of possession—all manner of possession: to sit at the settler's table, to sleep in the settler's bed, with his wife if possible. The colonised man is an envious man. And

this the settler knows very well; when their glances meet he ascertains bitterly, always on the defensive "They want to take our place." It is true, for there is no native who does not dream at least once a day of setting himself up in the settler's place.

This world divided into compartments, this world cut in two is inhabited by two different species. . . . When you examine at close quarters the colonial context, it is evident that what parcels out the world is to begin with the fact of belonging to or not belonging to a given race, a given species. In the colonies. . . . you are rich because you are white, you are white because you are rich. . . .

. . . As if to show the totalitarian character of colonial exploitation the settler paints the native as a sort of quintessence of evil. . . . Native society is not simply described as a society lacking in values. It is not enough for the colonist to affirm that those values have disappeared from, or still better never existed in, the colonial world. The native is declared insensible to ethics; he represents not only the absence of values, but also the negation of values. He is, let us dare to admit, the enemy of values, and in this sense he is the absolute evil. . . .

. . . I speak of the Christian religion, and no one need be astonished. The Church in the colonies is the white people's Church, the foreigner's Church. She does not call the native to God's ways but to the ways of the white man, of the master, of the oppressor. . . .

. . . [Colonialism] dehumanises the native, or to speak plainly it turns him into an animal. In fact, the terms the settler uses when he mentions the native are zoological terms. He speaks of the yellow man's reptilian motions, of the stink of the native quarter, of breeding swarms, of foulness, of spawn, of gesticulations. When the settler seeks to describe the native fully in exact terms he constantly refers to the bestiary. The . . . native, who knows what is in the mind of the settler, guesses at once what he is thinking of.

---

[1]The term *medina* here connotes a quarter of a North African city inhabited by indigenous people; the Saudi Arabian city of Medina is the sacred center of the Islamic faith.

Jawaharlal Nehru
INDIA'S RESENTMENT OF THE BRITISH

Born into a wealthy Indian family, Jawaharlal Nehru (1889–1964) received a privileged education and legal training in England, practicing law on his return to India in 1912. In 1919, after the Amritsar massacre (see page 241), he joined Gandhi in organizing resistance to British rule. Nehru was frequently arrested and jailed, and during his longest prison term (August 1942–March 1945) he wrote *The Discovery of India,* from which the following passages are selected. His book shows admiration for Western culture combined with recognition of India's backwardness. But he also blamed British arrogance and economic exploitation for his county's continued poverty; the British, he said, had failed to advance their Indian subjects. Nehru's book contributed the patriotic thrust that led to Indian independence in 1947 under his leadership.

Independence disproved Nehru's (and Gandhi's) charge that British rule was responsible for India's poverty. Standards of living in the Indian subcontinent are still among the lowest in the world.

The impact of Western culture on India was the impact of a dynamic society, of a "modern" consciousness, on a static society wedded to medieval habits of thought, which, however sophisticated and advanced in its own way, could not progress because of its inherent limitations. And yet, curiously enough, the agents of this historic process were not only wholly unconscious of their mission in India but, as a class, actually represented no such process. In England their class fought this historic process, but the forces opposed to them were too strong for them and could not be held back. In India they had a free field and were successful in applying the brakes to that very change and progress which, in the larger context, they represented. They encouraged and consolidated the position of the socially reactionary groups in India, and opposed all those who worked for political and social change. If change came, it was in spite of them or as an incidental and unexpected consequence of their other activities. The introduction of the steam engine and the railway was a big step toward a change of the medieval structure, but it was intended to consolidate their rule and facilitate the exploitation, for their own benefit, of the interior of the country. This contradiction between the deliberate policy of the British authorities in India and some of its unintended consequences produces a certain confusion and masks that policy itself. Change came to India because of this impact of the West, but it came almost in spite of the British in India. They succeeded in slowing down the pace of that change to such an extent that even today the transition is very far from complete.

The feudal landlords and their kind who came from England to rule over India had the landlord's view of the world. To them India was a vast estate belonging to the East India Company, and the landlord was the best and the natural representative of his estate and his tenants. That view continued even after the East India Company handed over its estate of India to the British crown, being paid very handsome compensation at India's cost. . . . The millions of people who lived and functioned in India were just some kind of landlord's tenants who had to pay their rents and cesses [local taxes] and to keep their place in the natural feudal order. For them a challenge to that order was an offense against the very moral basis of the universe and a denial of a divine dispensation. . . .

This sense of identifying India with their own interests was strongest in the higher administrative services, which were entirely British. In later years these developed in that close and well-knit corporation called the Indian Civil Service, "the world's most tenacious trade union," as it has been called by an English writer. They ran India, they were India, and anything that was harmful to their interests must of necessity be injurious to India. From the Indian Civil Service and the kind of history and record of current events that was placed before them, this conception spread in varying degrees to the different strata of the British people. The ruling class naturally shared it in full measure, but even the worker and the farmer were influenced by it to some slight extent and felt, in spite of their own subordinate position in their own country, the pride of possession and empire. That same worker or farmer if he came to India inevitably belonged to the ruling class here. He was totally ignorant of India's history and culture and he accepted the prevailing ideology of the British in India for he had no other standards to judge by or apply. At the most a vague benevolence filled him, but that was strictly conditioned within that framework. For a hundred years this ideology permeated all sections of the British people and became, as it were, a national heritage, a fixed and almost unalterable notion which governed their outlook on India and imperceptibly affected even their domestic outlook. . . .

I remember that when I was a boy the British-owned newspapers in India were full of official news and utterances; of service news, transfers, and promotions; of the doings of English society, of polo, races, dances, and amateur theatricals. There was hardly a word about the people of India, about their political, cultural, social, or economic life. Reading them, one would hardly suspect that they existed. . . .

English clubs in India usually have territorial names—the Bengal Club, the Allahabad Club, etc. They are confined to Britishers, or rather to Europeans. There need be no objection to territorial designation or even to a group of persons having a club for themselves and not approving of outsiders joining it. But this designation is derived from the old British habit of considering that they are the real India that counts, the real Bengal, the real Allahabad. Others are just excrescences, useful in their own way, if they know their place, but otherwise a nuisance. The exclusion of non-Europeans is far more a racial affair than a thoroughly justifiable way for people having cultural affinities meeting together in their leisure moments for play and social intercourse, and disliking the intrusion of other elements. For my part I have no objection to exclusive English or European clubs, and very few Indians would care to join them. But when this social exclusiveness is clearly based on racialism and on a ruling class always exhibiting its superiority and unapproachability, it bears another aspect. In Bombay there is a well-known club which did not allow, and so far as I know, does not allow, an Indian (except as a servant) even in its visitors' room, even though he might be a ruling prince or a captain of industry.

Racialism in India is not so much English versus Indian. It is European as opposed to Asiatic. In India every European, be he German or Pole or Rumanian, is automatically a member of the ruling race. Railway carriages, station retiring rooms, benches in parks, are marked "For Europeans Only." This is bad enough in South Africa or elsewhere, but to have to put up with it in one's own country is a humiliating and exasperating reminder of our enslaved condition. . . .

The English are a sensitive people, and yet when they go to foreign countries, there is a strange lack of awareness about them. In India, where the relation of ruler and ruled makes mutual understanding difficult, this lack of awareness is peculiarly evident. Almost, one would think, it is deliberate, so that they may see only what they want to see and be blind to all else. But facts do not vanish because they are ignored, and when they compel attention, there is a feeling of displeasure and resentment at the unexpected happening, as of some trick having been played.

In this land of caste the British, and more especially the Indian Civil Service, have built up a caste which is rigid and exclusive. Even the Indian members of the service do not really belong to that caste, though they wear its insignia and conform to its rules. That caste has developed something in the nature of a religious faith in its own paramount importance, and round that faith has grown an appropriate mythology which helps to maintain it. A combination of faith and vested interests is a powerful one, and any challenge to it arouses the deepest passions and fierce indignation. . . .

The chief business of the East India Company in its early period, the very object for which it was started, was to carry Indian manufactured goods—textiles, etc., as well as spices and the like—from the East to Europe, where there was a great demand for these articles. With the developments in industrial techniques in England a new class of industrial capitalists rose there demanding a change in this policy. The British market was to be closed to Indian products and the Indian market opened to British manufactures. The British parliament, influenced by this new class, began to take a greater interest in India and the working of the East India Company. To begin with, Indian goods were excluded from Britain by legislation, and as the company held a monopoly in the Indian export business, this exclusion influenced other foreign markets also. This was followed by vigorous attempts to restrict and crush Indian manufactures by various measures and internal duties which prevented the flow of Indian goods within the country itself. British goods meanwhile had free entry. The Indian textile industry collapsed, affecting vast numbers of weavers and artisans. The process was rapid in Bengal and Bihar; elsewhere it spread gradually with the expansion of British rule and the building of railways. It continued throughout the nine-teenth century, breaking up other old industries also, shipbuilding, metalwork, glass, paper, and many crafts.

To some extent this was inevitable as the older manufacturing came into conflict with the new industrial technique. But it was hastened by political and economic pressure, and no attempt was made to apply the new techniques to India. Indeed every attempt was made to prevent this happening, and thus the economic development of India was arrested and the growth of the new industry prevented. Machinery could not be imported into India. A vacuum was created in India which could only be filled by British goods, and which also led to rapidly increasing unemployment and poverty. The classic type of modern colonial economy was built up, India becoming an agricultural colony of industrial England, supplying raw materials and providing markets for England's industrial goods.

The liquidation of the artisan class led to unemployment on a prodigious scale. What were all these scores of millions, who had so far been engaged in industry and manufacture, to do now? Where were they to go? Their old profession was no longer open to them; the way to a new one was barred. They could die of course; that way of escape from an intolerable situation is always open. They did die in tens of millions. The English governor-general of India, Lord Bentinck, reported in 1834 that "the misery hardly finds a parallel in the history of commerce. The bones of the cotton-weavers are bleaching the plains of India." . . .

This, then, is the real, the fundamental cause of the appalling poverty of the Indian people, and it is of comparatively recent origin. Other causes that contribute to it are themselves the result of this poverty and chronic starvation and undernourishment—like diseases and illiteracy. . . .

Long subjection of a people and the denial of freedom bring many evils, and perhaps the greatest of these lies in the spiritual sphere—demoralization and sapping of the spirit of the people. It is hard to measure this, though it may be obvious. It is easier to trace and measure the economic decay of a nation, and as we look back on British economic policy in India, it seems that the present poverty of the Indian people is the ineluctable consequence of it. There is no mystery about this poverty; we can see the causes and follow the processes which have led to this present condition. . . .

Nearly all our major problems today have grown up during British rule and as a direct result of British policy: the princes; the minority problem; various vested interests, foreign and Indian; the lack of industry and the neglect of agriculture; the extreme backwardness in the social services; and, above all, the tragic poverty of the people. The attitude to education has been significant. In Kaye's *Life of Metcalfe* it is stated that "this dread of the free diffusion of knowledge became a chronic disease . . . continually afflicting the members of Government with all sorts of hypochondriacal day-dreams and nightmares, in which visions

of the Printing Press and the Bible were making their flesh creep, and their hair to stand erect with horror. It was our policy in those days to keep the natives of India in the profoundest state of barbarism and darkness, and every attempt to diffuse the light of knowledge among the people, either of our own or of the independent states, was vehemently opposed and resented."

Imperialism must function in this way or else it ceases to be imperialism. The modern type of finance imperialism added new kinds of economic exploitation which were unknown in earlier ages. The record of British rule in India during the nineteenth century must necessarily depress and anger an Indian, and yet it illustrates the superiority of the British in many fields, not least in their capacity to profit by our disunity and weaknesses. A people who are weak and who are left behind in the march of time invite trouble and ultimately have only themselves to blame.

Ndabaningi Sithole
IMPERIALISM'S BENEFITS
BY AN ANTI-IMPERIALIST AFRICAN

Born in the British colony of Rhodesia, the Rev. Ndabaningi Sithole (1920–2000) was one of the prominent westernized Africans who led the transition from European rule to independence. He was educated at a missionary school and worked as a teacher before entering the Andover Newton Theological Seminary near Boston, Massachusetts, where he studied for the ministry from 1955 to 1958. Those years in America, he wrote, were "among the happiest in my life," because, in contrast to his inferiority under British rule, he was accepted "as a human being." On his return he published in 1959 his book *African Nationalism,* from which the passages printed below are taken. As a congregational minister and school principal, he then joined the campaign for African independence. After years of struggle and detention by British jailers he helped guide the transition from Rhodesia to independent Zimbabwe in the late 1970s. Bitterly opposed to "the white man's keep-down-the-nigger policy" of shamelessly exploiting African resources, he yet remained grateful to the missionaries who had educated him. An optimist about Africa's future when he wrote this book, he was able to see the constructive side of imperialism. His subsequent career in Zimbabwean politics was troubled by exile in the United States. Following his return he won a seat in Parliament in 1995, but in 1997 he was convicted of conspiring to assassinate Prime Minister Mugabe, and sentenced to two years in jail. Sithole was released pending his appeal, and he died in the United States where he had gone to seek medical treatment.

One of the blessings of the advent of European powers in Africa was the suppression of slavery and the slave-trade.[1] The gigantic wave of humanitarianism that was sweeping across the whole continent of Europe coincided with European expansion to Africa. The abolition of slavery in Africa was one of the practical expressions of this European humanitarianism. . . .

With the passing away of slavery, slaves were accorded new human status. Let it be noted in passing that the general outlook of a slave on life is different from that of a free man. His potential capacities are crippled, stunted, and pushed into the background. The emancipation of slaves therefore opened a new world to thousands upon thousands of African slaves; hence, it can rightly be said that European colonial powers, by dealing slavery a deathblow, set the whole continent of Africa on a new venture of freedom and human dignity. . . .

The advent of European powers in Africa not only saw slavery coming to an end, but also the terrible tribal wars. What are now the Republic of South Africa, Rhodesia, Nigeria, Ghana, Portuguese, and French-speaking Africa were torn with countless tribal wars so that the chief occupation of most able-bodied African men was that of raiding other tribes. Europe itself was of course a war-torn, war-cursed country. But the European powers, whose weapons were superior to those of the Africans, were able to impose peace on the African people, and this was to the general good of the peoples of Africa. Something more creative took the place of destructive tribal wars. It is obvious, however, that with the European dictator of peace at the top, the African soon gained peace and good order but lost the control of his country. The European powers, although they had failed to keep peace in Europe, were soon regarded by most native tribes as 'peace-makers', bearers of 'deeds of humanity', and 'bringers of enlightenment'. Indeed, it has been rightly asserted by both Africans and Europeans that the European occupation of Africa, although it deprived people of their independence, helped to direct the minds and activities of the native peoples away from destructive to constructive programmes of action.

. . . The reader should note these four things, among others, that the coming of the European power, brought to Africa: the coming together of different tribes; better communications; a new economic system; and the creation of new classes among the African people. . . .

With the coming of mines, towns, and cities the different tribes of Africa found themselves thrown together. Tribesmen who had never had anything to do with one another, found themselves living together in one area, working side by side with one another, and the need to get along with one another became imperative. For instance, in the Johannesburg goldmines members of tribes from the whole of South and Central Africa, and even East Africa, are to be found in large numbers. . . . Eventually the African regarded himself not so much as a tribesman; but as a worker. A common language, a kind of *lingua franca,* soon developed, and thus communication was facilitated among members of different tribes. Down in the mine, in the factories, in the police force,

---

[1]Despite the efforts of the imperialist powers to suppress slavery, Africans continued into the early twentieth century to enslave other Africans for local use and for export to Arab lands.

in domestic service, on the farm, in the store, hospital, clinic, and a host of other European-introduced institutions and occupations, no tribal barriers existed or were encouraged. People just mixed freely. Tribalism among urbanized Africans was on its way out. . . .

With the construction of good roads, bridges, and railroads, and with the introduction of motor-cars, lorries, buses, trains, and aeroplanes, the African people have become highly mobile. Mobility of the population has greatly accelerated the exchange of ideas. The dissemination of all kinds of information has been unprecedented in African history. Even illiterate people are now better educated and better trained than ever before. Radio and, more recently, television have revolutionized African outlooks. Different parts of Africa and, indeed, the world, have now been brought to the very doors of the radio-owning African. With the rise of literacy African populations have become a vital reading public and the press has appeared. Africans read not only their own thoughts but those of others separated by vast stretches of water. What happens in Europe, Asia, America, and Australasia has become of real interest to the African people.

It is seen, then, that colonialism has created a radio-audience and a television-audience. It has created a reading public. It has created a press-writing and reading public. It has created a travelling-public by land, sea, and air. All these four kinds of African public are still growing every year. The tendency has been the creation of a comparatively well-informed and enlightened African public, and a focussing of the world's problems on the public consciousness of the African people. The African public that existed before the introduction of the radio, the press, the train, and the motor-car was highly localized. Particularism is now in many places giving way to universalism. Colonialism gave birth to a new brand of African, a non-tribal African: in short, a national African. . . .

The last of the four points raised is the new social and economic stratification of the African peoples. New armies of African bakers, butchers, cobblers, tailors, storekeepers, clerks, mechanics, builders, carpenters, and a chain of others have made their appearance on the scene, and they are changing the whole African social pattern. In relation to industry and commerce, the African acquired class consciousness as a worker. He wanted his voice to be heard in industry and commerce. The birth of African trade unions was really that of the new African who believed in economic justice and who was prepared to fight lawfully to achieve this end. European trade unionism has been transferred to the African scene. . . .

It has been seen that colonialism gave to Africa a new vigorous industrial pattern, a new social and industrial consciousness, a new way of organizing and doing things, new skills, new insights, new dreams and visions. It created a new climate, a new environment. It annihilated many tribal, linguistic, ethnic barriers and divisions. It was largely responsible for the unification of African tribes, where previously tribal divisions had made for weakness rather than for strength. It brought Africa into international light, and this was very helpful if Africa was to keep pace with the rest of the world. Since colonialism fertilized, stimulated, invigorated, and shaped African nationalism, it is understandable when African observers say, 'The twentieth-century African nationalism is indeed the child of European colonialism be it within or outside wedlock.' . . .

White supremacy produced two groups of people in Africa—the dominator and the dominated. It divided Africa into two hostile camps. . . . The white people were conscious that they ruled as a white group, and the African people also became conscious that they were ruled as an African group. They suffered as a racial group. . . .

The overall European policy in Africa may be summed up in these two words—white supremacy, and this is what the African means when he says, 'White people, from Cape to Cairo, are the same.' That is, they have a mania to rule Africa. This European policy was a great challenge to Africa, and since it is the nature of human existence to respond to challenge, the African peoples, despite their great geographical, linguistic, and ethnic differences, were united by this challenge. So long as the challenge remained, the African continued to respond positively and persistently by every conceivable means to overthrow white domination.

An examination of the ingredients that make up African nationalism may be enumerated as the African's desire to participate fully in the central government of the country; his desire for economic justice that recognizes fully the principle of 'equal pay for equal work' regardless of the skin colour; his desire to have full political rights in his own country; his dislike of being treated as a stranger in the land of his birth; his dislike of being treated as a means for the white man's end; and his dislike of the laws of the country that prescribed for him a permanent position of inferiority as a human being. It was this exclusive policy of white supremacy that brought to the fore the African's 'consciousness of kind'.

REVIEW QUESTIONS

1. Why did Frantz Fanon think that no conciliation is possible between the colonial masters and their subjects?
2. How did Fanon define the "totalitarian character" of colonial exploitation?
3. In saying that colonized people are envious, does Fanon reject what colonial exploitation stands for?
4. What, according to Nehru, were the features of British racialism in India?
5. What did Nehru believe to be the causes of India's poverty and backwardness? Did he give a clear assessment of the causes?
6. How did Sithole balance the benefits and drawbacks of white rule in Africa?

CHAPTER 15

The West in an Age of Globalism

WORLD TRADE CENTER TOWERS burn after terrorist attack on September 11, 2001. *(©Corbis/Sygma)*

The most important developments in recent European history were the collapse of communism and the end of the Cold War. With the decline of Soviet power and the discrediting of Marxism, the countries of Eastern Europe, and Russia itself, struggled to adapt to Western democratic forms and the free market. The transition to laissez-faire capitalism proved particularly difficult in Russia, which remains plagued with corruption, organized crime, and a declining standard of living.

In the closing decade of the twentieth century, ethnic conflicts grew more acute. In France, Britain, Germany, Austria, and other lands, right-wing parties protested against immigration, particularly from African, Middle Eastern, and Asian lands, complaining that the essential character of their nation was being destroyed. At times, right-wing extremists, often neo-Nazis, employed violence against immigrants. Yugoslavia was torn apart by the worst ethnic violence since World War II.

In the twenty-first century, globalization continues relentlessly; the world is being knit ever closer together by the spread of Western ideals, popular culture (particularly American), free market capitalism, and technology. Government officials and business and professional people all over the world dress in Western clothes. Women follow Western fashions in dress and makeup. People line up to eat at McDonalds, see a Hollywood movie, or attend a rock concert. Everywhere people are eager to adopt the latest technology that originated in the West but is now also manufactured in other, particularly Asian, lands.

Advanced technology intensifies the means of communication, not only through television and radio, but also with faxes, e-mail, cellular phones, or the Internet—all means of instantaneous individual communication that have become commonplace in the past decade.

These developments promote shared interests among individuals and businesses, some of them multinational corporations, throughout the globe, reducing the importance of national frontiers. All these factors combined are reshaping non-Western societies in a relentless adjustment that causes both deep hardships and possibilities for a better life.

The ideals of freedom and democracy, historical accomplishments of Western civilization, exert a powerful influence worldwide; they are also part of the process of westernization. Unlike technology, they cannot be easily put into practice outside the countries of their origin. However, they inspire human ambitions everywhere. They have even become part of the rhetoric of dictatorships.

At the same time, strong cultural traditions still divide the world. The hatred of radical Muslims for the West, which they see as a threat to traditional Islam, is a striking example of the clash of cultures. These Muslim militants, organized in an international network, Al Qaeda, with well-financed cells in dozens of countries, including the United States, were behind the bombing of the World Trade Center and the Pentagon, the worst terrorist attacks in history. Their ultimate aims are the destruction of Western civilization, which they see as immoral and an affront to God, the restoration of the Islamic empire that existed in the Middle Ages, and the imposition of strict Islamic law in all Islamic lands. Often fortified by a fundamentalist theology, these militants represent a radical attack on freedom and secularism, two hallmarks of modernity.

1 The Collapse of Communism

Throughout the 1970s and early 1980s the discrepancy between Soviet ambition and deteriorating economic conditions became apparent in the Soviet Union and satellite countries of Eastern Europe. Economic productivity declined just when increasing contact with democratic and prosperous Western countries raised consumer expectations. In addition, loyalty toward the Soviet Union in the satellite countries had been steadily eroded by nationalist resentment against communist repression.

The reforms instituted by Mikhail Gorbachev in 1986 led to a groundswell of support for liberation in Eastern Europe. Agitation for self-determination, democracy, and the end of communist rule spread and was not suppressed as it had been in the past. During 1989, Soviet power crumbled as, one by one, the Eastern European countries declared their sovereignty and ousted their communist governments. By the end of the year, all communist regimes there, except in Albania, had been overthrown. (Communist rule in Albania ended in 1991.) In the Soviet Union itself the communist empire collapsed at the end of 1991. Within three years, the once-mighty superpower had disintegrated unexpectedly and in a remarkably peaceful manner. The Cold War was over.

Vaclav Havel
THE FAILURE OF COMMUNISM

Established as a sovereign state at the end of World War I, Czechoslovakia enjoyed two decades of independence until it fell under Hitler's rule in 1938–1939; in World War II it was brutally occupied by the German army. After Czechoslovakia's liberation by Soviet soldiers, Stalin ruthlessly turned it into a communist state in 1948.

In 1968, enlightened party members, with the support of the Czech people, sought to loosen the oppressive restraints of the communist order and reestablish ties with Western Europe. Under the leadership of Alexander Dubček the country was intoxicated with the air of freedom. Seeking a humane version of Marxism, the reformers rehabilitated the victims of the Stalinist past and stopped censorship.

Suddenly, on August 21, 1968, Soviet troops invaded the country. Although they avoided the bloodshed that had accompanied their suppression of the Hungarian uprising in 1956, the Soviet leaders stopped Dubček's reforms; liberalization in Czechoslovakia endangered their own political system. "Socialism with a human face," as Dubček's program was called, came to an end.

Yet twenty years later, in December 1989, the communist regime dissolved in the "Velvet Revolution." Vaclav Havel, a frequently imprisoned dissident playwright and a lively intellectual, was elected president. In his 1990 New Year's Day address, excerpted below, Havel told the Czech people how the communist regime had abused its power.

THE TRUTH, UNVARNISHED

For 40 years you have heard on this day from the mouths of my predecessors, in a number of variations, the same thing: how our country is flourishing, how many more millions of tons of steel we have produced, how we are all happy, how we believe in our Government and what beautiful prospects are opening ahead of us. I assume you have not named me to this office so that I, too, should lie to you.

Our country is not flourishing. The great creative and spiritual potential of our nation is not being applied meaningfully. Entire branches of industry are producing things for which there is no demand while we are short of things we need.

The state, which calls itself a state of workers, is humiliating and exploiting them instead. Our outmoded economy wastes energy, which we have in short supply. The country, which could once be proud of the education of its people, is spending so little on education that today, in that respect, we rank 72d in the world. We have spoiled our land, rivers and forests, inherited from our ancestors, and we have, today, the worst environment in the whole of Europe. Adults die here earlier than in the majority of European countries. . . .

LEARNING TO BELIEVE AGAIN

The worst of it is that we live in a spoiled moral environment. We have become morally ill because we are used to saying one thing and thinking another. We have learned not to believe in anything, not to care about each other, to worry only about ourselves. The concepts of love, friendship, mercy, humility or forgiveness have lost their depths and dimension, and for many of us they represent only some sort of psychological curiosity or they appear as long-lost wanderers from faraway times, somewhat ludicrous in the era of computers and space ships. . . .

COGS NO LONGER

The previous regime, armed with a proud and intolerant ideology, reduced people into the means of production, and nature into its tools. So it attacked their very essence, and their mutual relations. . . . Out of talented and responsible people, ingeniously husbanding their land, it made cogs of some sort of great, monstrous, thudding, smelly machine, with an unclear purpose. All it can do is slowly but irresistibly, wear itself out, with all its cogs.

If I speak about a spoiled moral atmosphere I don't refer only to our masters. . . . I'm speaking about all of us. For all of us have grown used to the totalitarian system and accepted it as an immutable fact, and thereby actually helped keep it going. None of us are only its victims; we are all also responsible for it.

It would be very unwise to think of the sad heritage of the last 40 years only as something foreign; something inherited from a distant relative. On the contrary, we must accept this heritage as something we have inflicted on ourselves. If we accept it in such a way, we shall come to understand it is up to all of us to do something about it.

Let us make no mistake: even the best Government, the best Parliament and the best President cannot do much by themselves. Freedom and democracy, after all, mean joint participation and shared responsibility. If we realize this, then all the horrors that the new Czechoslovak democracy inherited cease to be so horrific. If we realize this, then hope will return to our hearts.

Everywhere in the world, people were surprised how these malleable, humiliated, cynical citizens of Czechoslovakia, who seemingly believed in nothing, found the tremendous strength within a few weeks to cast off the totalitarian system, in an entirely peaceful and dignified manner. We ourselves are surprised at it.

And we ask: Where did young people who had never known another system get their longing for truth, their love of freedom, their political imagination, their civic courage and civic responsibility? How did their parents, precisely the generation thought to have been lost, join them? How is it possible that so many people immediately understood what to do and that none of them needed any advice or instructions? . . .

RECALLING RUINED LIVES

Naturally we too had to pay for our present-day freedom. Many of our citizens died in prison in the 1950's. Many were executed. Thousands of human lives were destroyed. Hundreds of thousands of talented people were driven abroad. . . . Those who fought against totalitarianism during the war were also persecuted. . . . Nobody who paid in one way or another for our freedom could be forgotten.

Independent courts should justly evaluate the possible guilt of those responsible, so that the full truth about our recent past should be exposed.

But we should also not forget that other nations paid an even harsher price for their present freedom, and paid indirectly for ours as well. All human suffering concerns each human being. . . . Without changes in the Soviet Union, Poland, Hungary, and the German Democratic Republic, what happened here could hardly have taken place, and certainly not in such a calm and peaceful way.

Now it depends only on us whether this hope will be fulfilled, whether our civic, national and political self-respect will be revived. Only a man or nation with self-respect, in the best sense of the word, is capable of listening to the voices of others, while accepting them as equals, of forgiving enemies and of expiating sins. . . .

A HUMANE REPUBLIC

Perhaps you are asking what kind of republic I am dreaming about. I will answer you: a republic that is independent, free, democratic, a republic with economic prosperity and also social justice, a humane republic that serves man and that for that reason also has the hope that man will serve it. . . .

THE PEOPLE HOLD SWAY

My most important predecessor started his first speech by quoting from Comenius.[1] Permit me to end my own first speech by my own paraphrase. Your Government, my people, has returned to you.

---

[1]Comenius was a Czech theologian and educator of the seventeenth century. The quotation was used by Tomáš Masaryk (1850–1937), the first President of Czechoslovakia which was created after World War I. "I, too, believe before God that, when the storms of wrath have passed, to thee shall return the rule over thine own things, O Czech people."

REVIEW QUESTION

1. What did Vaclav Havel mean when he said the Czechs had lived in a "spoiled moral environment" for the past forty years?

---

2 The New Russia: The Trauma of Transition from Communism

The collapse of communist power led to attempts at constructing not only Western-style democracy but also free markets. Socialist regimes throughout the Eastern Bloc had earlier experimented with limited private enterprise, achieving notable success in some cases, e.g., Hungary and East Germany. Now, however, post-communist governments undertook "shock therapy," the wholesale marketization and privatization of their economic infrastructures, often at the urging of Western academics and consultants. The results, at best, were mixed. In general, the countries of Eastern Europe negotiated the transition more smoothly than post-Soviet Russia, where a Stalinist command economy had been firmly entrenched for well over half a century. In particular, the return of state property to private ownership in Russia turned out to be disappointingly counterproductive; the chief beneficiaries of the changeover were the same elites that had controlled the economy during the Soviet era. In addition, the introduction of a market economy sometimes seemed only to replace socialism's benefits with capitalism's ills. Fixed prices and guaranteed welfare gave way to ruinous inflation and hand-to-mouth subsistence. A new middle class was in the making, but many of its members had amassed their wealth by questionable means, sometimes by criminal methods. In sum, the achievement of economic security, no less than the attainment of participatory democracy, was likely to be a long and painful process.

Georgi Arbatov
THE NEGATIVE CONSEQUENCES OF "SHOCK THERAPY" CAPITALISM

In the following selection, Russian economist Georgi Arbatov discusses the negative consequences of the "shock therapy program" launched in 1992 "to inject laissez-faire capitalism immediately into the Russian economy."

The economic system created by the Soviet Union, and inherited by Russia, was inefficient and wasteful. It was unable to provide proper economic development of the country and a decent standard of living for its citizens. By the time Boris Yeltsin took charge, the problems with the "administrative-command" system were quite obvious and the main subject of political debate.

Different groups of economists prepared possible programs that were openly debated. But the country was taken by surprise by the "Chicago School" program prepared by Yegor Gaidar, and approved in haste by President Yeltsin. On January 2, 1992, Gaidar launched the shock therapy program to inject laissez-faire capitalism immediately into the Russian economy. The West cheered, perhaps for ideological reasons. Influential Western experts . . . all gave their blessings. . . .

The poorly conceived transition program resulted in an unprecedented decline of the national economy. By 1998 Russian GDP was only about one-half its 1990 level, with the crisis spread to virtually all areas of production. Russian industry found itself unable to compete even in its own domestic markets. All of this was accompanied by a sharp reduction in investment and a disintegration of scientific and technological potential. We are now witnessing processes of pauperization and de-intellectualization, accompanied by criminalization, as Russia increasingly takes on the appearance of a Third World republic.

The standard of living of most Russians has decreased dramatically. Rampant inflation has eliminated the savings of much of the population, while the increase of salaries and pensions has lagged far behind the price rises. The mortality rate has grown, and the birthrate has plummeted. As a result, Russia has been losing more than one-half million in population each year.

The sharp decline in the standard of living of the overwhelming majority is not only expressed in the obvious fact that diet, health, and elementary conditions of life have become worse for millions of people, but also in the loss of social benefits. The customary summer camp for all children has now become an unusual lux-

ury. Few can still afford to vacation at a resort, be it a most modest one. Such previously expected amenities have become unaffordable because of large increases in railway and airplane ticket prices, making it hardly feasible to visit relatives. People who settled in the Far North or Far East have become "hostages" of these distant places. Because of high tariffs on long-distance telephone calls, for many the usual means of communication with relatives and friends has become a rare luxury.

Life has become especially hard for the millions of people who are dependent on pensions, many of whom now live in impoverished conditions. Their savings were practically eliminated by inflation, and the level of pensions is below the minimum necessary, even by the official calculations, for bare survival. Their situation is aggravated by the tremendous increase in the prices of medicines and the lower quality and reduced availability of subsidized health care. In addition, there is a traditionally Russian concern: when you die who will bury you and with what money?

Though the sheer fact of being young makes life look not so hopeless, the situation of Russian youth is also very difficult. Education has deteriorated drastically. Higher education is not free anymore and is unaffordable for many. Even more serious are the problems of unemployment and the financial difficulty that a young family has in getting a house and raising children.

Russians now have less access to culture—books and magazines, museums, libraries, arts, theaters, and music. During the past five years, the overall number of published books fell by 65 percent, circulation of newspapers by 80 percent, and the number of copies of published magazines by over 90 percent. Theater tickets, music concerts, CDs, and traditional records have also become unavailable for the majority. The futures of many theaters, music schools, and the large national libraries are in question.

Faced with overwhelming difficulties and misfortunes, ordinary people have become helpless. Government agencies, which in the past cared about them, at least to a minimal degree, disappeared or continued in name only with the decline of the state and its power. The old pseudo trade unions, which represented the state, also disappeared. New ones have just started to be organized. As a result, only spontaneous protests are possible against extreme circumstances such as long overdue payment of salaries.

The way of life for ordinary Russians has deteriorated remarkably. The majority are fully immersed in the day-to-day fight for survival. This is now the major subject that people think and talk about. Friends and colleagues meet each other less frequently and rarely travel. Staying at home is also encouraged by the unprecedented rise in crime, which has made big cities and many of the smaller towns dangerous places. . . . Today most people have little hope for improvement. . . .

In a time span of five years, especially during a period of sharp economic decline, it is difficult for a person to prosper in an honest way. There is a practically unanimous belief, to a large degree correct, that the country is being robbed of its wealth. The increasingly obvious growth of crime and corruption have been practically accepted as an inevitable fact of life by the government, which appears to do little to fight back.

Svetlana P. Glinkina, Andre Grigoriev, and Vakhtang Yakobidze
CRIME AND CORRUPTION

The liberalization of the Soviet economy and the breakup of the Soviet Union provided opportunities for government officials and top managers to enrich themselves through illegal activities. Several oligarchs acquired former state-owned enterprises, from which they now reap huge profits, and gained control of banks "that operate in a pathological fashion." Furthermore, as law enforcement deteriorated, organized crime became a major force in Russian life. In the selection below, three Russian economists describe the impact of corruption and criminalization on Russian life.

The Russian economy has been transformed into a highly corrupt and criminalized economic system. Rampant crime and corruption have degraded everyday life, obstructed legitimate business activity, and impaired the functioning of government. The most valuable of state assets have been transferred to a small number of "oligarchs," who compose a politically connected business elite largely oriented toward plunder. Though the proclivity for corruption and illegality predates the economic transition, primary blame resides with the reform strategy. . . .

ORGANIZED CRIME

Taking advantage of weak law enforcement, mafia influences have become prominent in all facets of Russian life. An estimated 200,000 active criminal groups existed in Russia by the mid-1990s, including 5,500 large organizations. In addition to extortion, their activities included burglary, embezzlement, and criminal misappropriation of both public and business funds.

Retail markets in every Russian city are controlled by gangsters who collect a share of the revenues of each vendor. This system is so well established that payments are calculated on the basis of records that the vendor is required to maintain. Gangsters may even agree to defer payments in light of special circumstances, creating, through force of habit, the impression that they are reasonable partners performing a needed security function.

Cities are divided into spheres of influence. For example, rival mafia groups divided the northern city of Arkhangelsk into two parts. It was not possible to start a business in that city without permission from the criminal group in control of the particular locale.

Organized crime has also been active in theft and exportation of fuels and metals. It is estimated that from 1992 to 1994, over 20 percent of the petroleum output and one-third of metals production were smuggled out of the country. So much of this contraband passed through Estonia that this resource-scarce country became a major exporter of natural resources. At one point, 70 percent of the raw materials shipped from Russia by rail through Lithuania never reached their legal destination, the Russian city of Kaliningrad. Disappearance of trainloads of oil was a daily occurrence. Railway personnel and customs officials conspired in these operations.

Apart from corruption in the primary export industries, nearly every small business or street kiosk had felt the mafia presence by the first year of the transition period. Nevertheless, opportunity for embezzlement from these small businesses could in no way compare with the wealth that could be taken from the state budget. The vast sums of money appropriated by opportunistic Soviet officials attracted the attention of these gangsters, who quickly ter-

rorized them and took over their enterprises. Government information indicates that roughly 70 to 80 percent of banks, as well as state and private companies, make payments to racketeers and corrupt officials. Other data show three-quarters of businessmen routinely make payoffs, and ordinary citizens are also frequently forced to give bribes.

The gangsters did end their terror campaigns against those businessmen who were the most well connected in government. Criminals depended on businessmen to invest their wealth. Businessmen, in turn, made use of gangsters in forcing clientele to honor their obligations. All the while, corrupt officials approved their projects in return for hefty bribes.

Their alliance, of course, soon grew to envelop more than debt collection services. The potential to eliminate unwanted competitors and coerce business partners to soften their terms was a fact that was not lost on the gangsters. Indeed, the large number of murders of businessmen and bankers reflects a general moral breakdown. Due to the availability of former KGB operatives and the fact that law enforcement is lax, the cost of a professional murder in Russia is low.

PRIVATIZATION

The privatization process was key to the transfer of the nation's wealth to a tainted minority. Most enterprises were privatized by the mid-1990s, with employees and managers holding more than 50 percent of all shares of privatized firms. However, employee shares were mostly locked in trusts controlled by management, effectively giving ownership to managers.

The first phase of "official" privatization entitled individual Russians to vouchers that were redeemable for cash or a share of industry. Conversion of vouchers into shares was of little consequence, since dividends were rarely paid and investors had little say in the decision-making process. For those who were able to obtain a large quantity, however, the vouchers were extremely useful. Quick to see the rewards of such a program, criminal and commercial elements soon began to collect vouchers from transients, alcoholics, and gullible citizens who were promised high dividends in television advertisements. With the vast amounts they collected, these groups bought up the most desirable enterprises at giveaway prices. Often the enterprises were quickly shut down as the new owners made gains by simply selling off real estate. . . .

Corrupt privatization aggravated Russia's financial woes, as the state disposed of valuable assets at extremely low prices. Uralmash, the giant machine-building plant in Sverdlovsk, and the Cheliabinsk Metallurgical Combine went for around $4 million each. The Kovrovsky Mechanical Factory, which supplied the Russian military with firearms, sold for under $3 million. Telephone companies were sold for $100 per line compared to about $650 in North America. The power company United Energy Systems was sold for $200 million, whereas a company with similar kilowatt production would be worth $50 billion in the United States. . . .

THE OLIGARCHS

A young, unscrupulous economic elite known as the "oligarchs" now controls much of the Russian economy, including the nation's natural wealth. They also control banks that operate in a pathological fashion, industries that owe billions in unpaid taxes, and media empires. Through their use of money and media to sway elections, as well as by provision of bribes and sinecures, they have influenced all branches and levels of government. While they certainly have influence on government rules, their primary mode of operation is to circumvent them. Overseeing the tainted transfer of government assets and the corrupt allocation

of government funds, the oligarchs have been integral to the creation of Russian-style kleptocracy. . . .

From the outset, the oligarchs have been reluctant to invest to modernize production. Little has been accomplished in the way of upgrading the plants, oil companies, banks, and steamship lines that they acquired so cheaply. . . .

In addition to bribery, the oligarchs have employed blackmail in order to influence government appointments. . . .

The oligarchs not only used state funds for their own ends by utilizing and often embezzling money through their own banks, but, as it became clear after the crisis of August 1998, these leaders of Russian business also cheated a great number of their compatriots who entrusted their savings to the banks. . . .

The oligarchs hardly qualify as the Russian version of the "robber barons" who helped to industrialize the United States. Instead of creating and building new industries, they have shunted the wealth of Russia abroad. Rather than transform their profits into domestic investment, they have expatriated them. Illegal capital flight has also helped them shield their gains from taxation, undermining the capacity of government to finance itself adequately.

CONCLUSION

Corruption and criminalization in Russia have created a corrosive economic environment. Productive economic activity is inhibited while the siphoning off of the nation's resources continues. Potential investors are fearful that criminals and corrupt officials will impose unforeseen costs and even expropriate their investments. Forced or enticed to join forces with criminal structures, managers are not inclined toward company strategies that are optimal for the long run. A plundering oligarchic elite, with strong influence over the media and politicians, has had a noxious influence on government. . . .

Russian reality—not only the lack of rule of law but also weak economic policy—may well continue to provide opportunities for the parasitic existence of criminal structures. In the final analysis, the future of any country is jeopardized by swindling of the state and criminal interference with market competition. So long as such activity is not only possible, but acceptable, Russia's prospects will be dim.

REVIEW QUESTIONS

1. According to Arbatov, how did the advent of capitalism in Russia lead to a decline in the quality of life for most Russians?
2. How did the transition to a market economy offer the opportunity for "a politically connected business elite" to take over Russian business and industry? Why have industries under the control of the oligarchs failed to flourish?
3. How is the weakness of the Russian legal system and the rule of law linked to Russia's economic woes?

---

3 Ethnic Minorities

Beginning at least as early as the French Revolution, the gradual movement in Europe toward the creation of nation-states established specific criteria for citizenship ranging from language, to ethnicity, to residency. Yet virtually no European state community has been able to make a serious claim to homogeneity. Moreover, by the 1960s Western European states had become new homes for an increasing number of people from outside of the Continent. In the case of West Germany, most came as guest workers, largely from Turkey; in France and Great Britain, these new residents came from former colonial possessions in North and sub-Saharan Africa, and from South Asia and the Caribbean, respectively; in these and other states, people came as asylum-seekers from regimes that had violated their human rights. Members of these new ethnic minorities brought with them very different cultural influences and often new languages, providing a truly cosmopolitan influence on host country residents, who reacted with a range of sentiment, from openness, to reluctant acceptance, to xenophobia. As long as the economies were healthy, Europeans generally expressed rather few xenophobic concerns. However, when competition for scarce jobs, competing claims on health and welfare services, and criminality increased during periods of recession, these foreigners often found themselves the objects of criticism, even physical attacks. The creation of the European Union has been successful thus far in promoting greater understanding and a sense of commonality among its member communities, but the place of ethnic minorities in these states is far from uniformly secure.

Enoch Powell
BRINGING THE IMMIGRATION ISSUE
TO THE CENTER OF POLITICS

Fear of being overwhelmed by immigrants from former British colonies in the West Indies, Africa, and South Asia became a serious political issue in Great Britain during the later 1960s, and the chief spokesman of those in favor of suspending immigration and assisting in re-immigration was the Conservative politician Enoch Powell. Powell was anything but a fire-breathing xenophobe along the lines of Jean-Marie Le Pen or Jörg Haider. Nonetheless, he was a darling of staunch British Tories, both because of his oratorical skill and his willingness to challenge the Labour government's progressive Race Relations Bill (1968) through a clear association of ethnic homogeneity with a stable Britain.

Powell delivered the following speech in Birmingham on April 20, 1968, against the impending vote on the Race Relations Bill. It set off an uproar in Britain and overseas, and he was bitterly attacked. Yet at the same time it touched a nerve among British people uncomfortable about sharing their small country with peoples of different colors, religions, and languages. Powell conjured up the image of a United Kingdom overrun by people of color and warned that his country might come to suffer the same ethnic problems as the United States if measures were not taken to prevent an influx of foreigners.

A week or two ago I fell into conversation with a constituent, a middle-aged, quite ordinary working man employed in one of our nationalised industries. After a sentence or two about the weather, he suddenly said: 'If I had the money to go, I wouldn't stay in this country.' I made some deprecatory reply, to the effect that even this government wouldn't last for ever; but he took no notice, and continued: 'I have three children, all of them been through grammar school and two of them married now, with family. I shan't be satisfied till I have seen them all settled overseas. In this country in fifteen or twenty years time the black man will have the whip hand over the white man.'

I can already hear the chorus of execration. How dare I say such a horrible thing? How dare I stir up trouble and inflame feelings by repeating such a conversation? The answer is that I do not have the right not to do so. Here is a decent, ordinary fellow Englishman, who in broad daylight in my own town says to me,

his Member of Parliament, that this country will not be worth living in for his children. I simply do not have the right to shrug my shoulders and think about something else. What he is saying, thousands and hundreds of thousands are saying and thinking—not throughout Great Britain, perhaps, but in the areas that are already undergoing the total transformation to which there is no parallel in a thousand years of English history.

In fifteen or twenty years, on present trends, there will be in this country 3½ million Commonwealth immigrants and their descendants. That is not my figure. That is the official figure given to Parliament by the spokesman of the Registrar General's office. There is no comparable official figure for the year 2000; but it must be in the region of 5–7 million, approximately one-tenth of the whole population, and approaching that of Greater London. . . . Whole areas, towns and parts of towns across England will be occupied by different sections of the immigrant and immigrant-descended population.

As time goes on, the proportion of this total who are immigrant descendants, those born in England, who arrived here by exactly the same route as the rest of us, will rapidly increase. . . .

The natural and rational first question with a nation confronted by such a prospect is to ask: 'how can its dimensions be reduced?' . . . The answers to the simple and rational question are equally simple and rational: by stopping, or virtually stopping, further inflow, and by promoting the maximum outflow. Both answers are part of the official policy of the Conservative Party.

It almost passes belief that at this moment twenty or thirty additional immigrant children are arriving from overseas in Wolverhampton alone every week—and that means fifteen or twenty additional families of a decade or two hence. Those whom the gods wish to destroy, they first make mad. We must be mad, literally mad, as a nation to be permitting the annual inflow of some 50,000 dependents, who are for the most part the material of the future growth of the immigrant-descended population. It is like watching a nation busily engaged in heaping up its own funeral pyre. So insane are we that we actually permit unmarried persons to immigrate for the purpose of founding a family with spouses and fiancés whom they have never seen. Let no one suppose that the flow of dependents will automatically tail off. On the contrary, even at the present admission rate of only 5000 a year by voucher, there is sufficient for a further 25,000 dependents per annum *ad infinitum,* without taking into account the huge reservoir of existing relations in this country—and I am making no allowance at all for fraudulent entry. In these circumstances nothing will suffice but that the total inflow for settlement should be reduced at once to negligible proportions, and that the necessary legislative and administrative measures be taken without delay. I stress the words 'for settlement'. This has nothing to do with the entry of Commonwealth citizens, any more than of aliens, into this country for the purposes of study or of improving their qualifications, like (for instance) the Commonwealth doctors who, to the advantage of their own countries, have enabled our hospital service to be expanded faster than would otherwise have been possible. These are not, and never have been, immigrants.

I turn to re-emigration. If all immigration ended tomorrow, the rate of growth of the immigrant and immigrant-descended population would be substantially reduced, but the prospective size of this element in the population would still leave the basic character of the national danger unaffected. This can only be tackled while a considerable proportion of the total still comprises persons who entered this country during the last ten years or so. Hence the urgency of implementing now the second element of the Conservative Party's policy: the encouragement of re-emigration. Nobody can make an estimate of the numbers which, with generous grants and assistance, would choose either to return to their countries of origin or to go to other countries anxious to receive the manpower and the skills they represent. Nobody knows, because no such policy has yet been attempted. I can only say that, even at present, immigrants in my own constituency from time to time come to me, asking if I can find them assistance to return home. If such a policy were adopted and pursued with the determination which the gravity of the alternative justifies, the resultant outflow could appreciably alter the prospects for the future.

It can be no part of any policy that existing families should be kept divided; but there are two directions in which families can be reunited, and if our former and present immigration laws have brought about the division of families, albeit voluntary or semi-voluntary, we ought to be prepared to arrange for them to be reunited in their countries of origin. In short, suspension of immigration and encouragement of re-emigration hang together, logically and humanly, as two aspects of the same approach.

The third element of the Conservative Party's policy is that all who are in this country as citizens should be equal before the law and that there shall be no discrimination or difference made between them by public authority. As Mr. Heath[1] has put it, we will have no 'first-class citizens' and 'second-class citizens'. This does not mean that the immigrant and his descendants should be elevated into a privileged or special class or that the citizen should be denied his right to discriminate in the management of his own affairs between one fellow-citizen and another or that he should be subjected to inquisition as to his reasons and motives for behaving in one lawful manner rather than another. . . .

The other dangerous delusion from which those who are willfully or otherwise blind to realities suffer, is summed up in the word 'integration'. To be integrated into a population means to become for all practical purposes indistinguishable from its other members. Now, at all times, where there are marked physical differences, especially of colour, integration is difficult though, over a period, not impossible. There are among the Commonwealth immigrants who have come to live here in the last fifteen years or so, many thousands whose wish and purpose is to be integrated and whose every thought and endeavour is bent in that direction. But to imagine that such a thing enters the heads of a great and growing majority of immigrants and their descendants is a ludicrous misconception, and a dangerous one to boot. . . .

Now we are seeing the growth of positive forces acting against integration, of vested interests in the preservation and sharpening of racial and religious differences, with a view to the exercise of actual domination, first over fellow-immigrants and then over the rest of the population. The cloud no bigger than a man's hand, that can so rapidly overcast the sky, has been visible recently in Wolverhampton and has shown signs of spreading quickly. The words I am about to use, verbatim as they appeared in the local press on 17 February, are not mine, but those of a Labour Member of Parliament who is a Minister in the present Government. 'The Sikh community's campaign to maintain customs inappropriate in Britain is much to be regretted. Working in Britain, particularly in the public services, they should be prepared to accept the terms and conditions of their employment. To claim special communal rights (or should one say rites?) leads to a dangerous fragmentation within society. This communalism is a canker; whether practised by one colour or another it is to be strongly condemned.' All credit to John Stonehouse for having had the insight to perceive that, and the courage to say it.

For these dangerous and divisive elements the legislation proposed in the Race Relations Bill is the very pabulum they need to flourish. Here is the means of showing that the immigrant communities can organise to consolidate their members, to agitate and campaign against their fellow citizens, and to overawe and dominate the rest with the legal weapons which the ignorant and the ill-informed have provided. As I look ahead, I am filled with foreboding. Like the Roman, I seem to see 'the River Tiber foaming with much blood'. That tragic and intractable phenomenon which we watch with horror on the other side of the Atlantic but which there is interwoven with the history and existence of the States itself, is coming upon us here by our own volition and our own neglect. Indeed, it has all but come. In numerical terms, it will be of American proportions long before the end of the century. Only resolute and urgent action will avert it even now. Whether there will be the public will to demand and obtain that action, I do not know. All I know is that to see, and not to speak, would be the great betrayal.

---

[1]Edward Heath—Conservative politician and prime minister from 1970 to 1974.

Joachim Krautz
VIOLENCE AND XENOPHOBIA IN GERMANY

During the early 1960s, the economy of the Federal Republic of Germany experienced enormous growth—the era of the so-called economic miracle. There was more work than could be done by Germans alone, prompting the West German government to enter into labor recruitment agreements with Spain, Italy, Greece, Yugoslavia, and Turkey. Up until the recession of 1973 and the onset of widespread unemployment, there was ample work for these "guest workers"; it was also expected that at some point they would return home. Turkish guest workers proved the most reluctant to leave Germany and the most willing to bring their families with them to their new residences.

In 1961, the non-German population comprised 1.2 percent of the FRG's entire population, with the Turkish minority representing only 1 percent of that foreign total; by 1970 this number had increased to a non-German population of 4.3 percent, of which the Turkish minority constituted 16.5 percent. By 1992, the numbers had increased to 8 percent and more than 28.5 percent, respectively. When recruitment of foreign labor ended in 1973, this Turkish-dominated body of guest workers became a resident minority overnight. Today, approximately 10 percent of all residents of Germany are considered foreigners, and the overwhelming majority of them are of Turkish origin.

While Germany is not the only country to experience racist violence against foreigners in recent years, the specter of neo-Nazism has led the international media to focus much of their attention upon xenophobia and crimes against foreigners by ultra-rightists in the Federal Republic. Since reunification in 1990, some 49 foreigners—almost all of them Turks, Africans, or Asians—have been killed by neo-Nazis in firebombings of guest-worker or refugee dwellings, or as a result of beatings and stabbings. In the following selection, published in October 1993, the journalist Joachim Krautz seeks the causes of violence and xenophobia in the post-reunification malaise of unemployment, inflation, and economic dislocation, particularly in Eastern Germany.

The arsonists came at night. Fully aware of the likelihood that people might be in their bedrooms they set fire to the apartment house, in which—according to the nameplates near the doorbells—a couple of Turkish families lived. The fact that Turks were the sole inhabitants of that house had been the precise reason for the murderers' choice of their target. In the night from Saturday to Whitsunday five people—all of them women and girls—became the victims of this treacherous crime which took place in

Solingen, a small, until then very ordinary town in the west of Germany. It was the climax of a whole series of violent attacks against foreigners since the reunification of Germany. A deadly series which claimed 49 lives so far. All these assaults had in common that the perpetrators were led by racist or right-extremist motives. Pictures went around the world showing young men with tattooed arms and closely shorn haircuts, instigated by beer and rock music with explicitly fascist texts, hurling petrol bombs at houses while honest citizens stood by and watched. And the politicians, apparently, are not able or—as terrified foreigners in Germany claim—not willing to halt this development. Chancellor Helmut Kohl did not even think it appropriate to be present at the memorial ceremonies. What is happening in Germany at the moment? Has Nazism risen from its grave? Or will Germany turn once more into the scourge of Europe?

The current events make up a very complex issue. Over the past few years facts and statistics with regard to foreigners, aggressors and right-extremism in Germany have been perpetually blurred and distorted—both at home and abroad—to serve various interest groups. Right-extremism, nationalism and the ugly face of racism are by no means confined to Germany. But because of her historical peculiarity these phenomena have always been ascribed a specific significance in the country which made Auschwitz happen. . . .

For the majority of the young Germans who grew up in the sixties, seventies, and early eighties nationalism was out. And so were all its symbols like the national flag or the national anthem. It would have been unthinkable to sing the latter in school or to play it in cinemas after the performance as it is the custom in some other countries. Intoxicated fans bawled the national anthem and waved the country's flag in the football stadiums. But young (West) Germans who wanted to be politically fashionable defined their politics by the absence of patriotism and their national pride consisted of criticism of their country—if they were proud of it at all.

The situation in the other German state was different from the start. There the Communist government by definition had seen themselves as not having any links with the brown-shirted [Nazi] past. As a result there had never been any attempt at dealing with the past as there had been in the West.

Consequently, the notion of the nation had retained its positive connotation for the people in the former German Democratic Republic. National pride for socialist achievements was not only condoned but even encouraged by the government. After all, one lived in the better part of the two Germanies. The general public, however, saw it differently. After having been fed—or rather brainwashed—with West German advertisements and TV commercials for decades they, indeed, imagined paradise, the land of milk and honey, as the epitomy of German ingeniousness—but on the other side of the Wall. Whether identifying themselves with or rebelling against the system and embracing the world view of the class enemy— none of the generations in East Germany ever felt obliged to suppress the sentiment of patriotism. . . .

No wonder the enticers of West German right-extremist groups met with such a fertile ground for their propaganda when the Wall fell in November 1989. While the legal right-wing parties NPD and the Republikaner (Republicans—REP) have tried to attract conservative petitbourgeois citizens the group which openly profess their loyalty to National Socialism have recruited their followers among East German skinheads and hooligans (a social phenomenon, by the way, which had been anything but unknown in the former German Democratic Republic). . . .

In spite of the fact that there were hardly any foreigners living in East Germany the various right-wing fringe groups and splinter parties were highly successful in spreading their message of the threat of 'foreignization'. In 1989 less than 200,000 foreign workers and students lived in the East—representing a mere 1.2 per cent of the entire population— compared to 5.2 million foreigners in the West—i.e. 8.2 per cent of the population there. And yet the first violent assaults against Vietnamese workers and Polish tourists in the East were reported as early as December 1989. Shocking pictures of attacks against hostels for asylum seekers in Hoyerswerda (in September 1991) and in Rostock (in August 1992) seemed only to confirm the worst prejudices

West Germans hold against their brethren in the East: their society had been inferior, they are not used to hard work in a capitalist world, and now they even turn out to be prone to long-buried ideologies of hatred and violence.

However, the spectacular events of Mölln, a West German town where neo-Nazis murdered three Turks by setting their house alight in November last year, or of Solingen now, showed that all is not well in the old Republic either. But the good citizens in the West are only too willing to lay the blame on the sudden popularity of nationalist and neo-Nazi ideas in the East, to call West German evildoers 'imitators', and to lament a spread of xenophobia coming from the former internationalist workers' paradise. On the one hand the East: a hotbed for terror and violence because of all its deficiencies? On the other hand the West: a natural realm of tolerance and understanding because of the long-standing dialogue and exchange of views in its society? Does this picture hold good?

A recent poll among A-level candidates in the West German city of Minich showed that the majority of them believed the actual rate of asylum seekers among the population amounted to a menacing 30 per cent or more, whereas in fact it is less than 1 per cent. Those interviewed were neither neo-Nazis nor skinheads but they belonged to the intellectual elite of the young generation. Such grossly wrong estimates about figures concerning asylum seekers, refugees, and foreigners in general are 'common knowledge' nowadays. This cannot be the work of a few splinter parties alone. . . .

Until May this year Germany had the world's most liberal legislation granting every political refugee an individual right to political asylum. The experience of the Nazi-dictatorship encouraged the Founding Fathers of the Federal Republic of Germany to write down this right into the German constitution. As a result of the political changes and upheavals in Eastern Europe and of the growing misery in the Third World but also because

of improved international transportation the numbers of asylum seekers from all over the world have been increasing over the past few years.

Soon the right-extremist parties focused their attention on this alleged threat to society. At first, coming up with completely arbitrary figures, a differentiation was made between 'genuine' political refugees and 'economic migrants'. Using very emotional language the latter were denigrated as 'scroungers' or even as 'parasites'. Then, right-wing propaganda tried to create an atmosphere of fear using the absolute numbers of asylum seekers arriving in Germany every year. A horror scenario was conjured up claiming that within a few years foreigners would outnumber the native population. According to these figures from 1989 to 1991 alone about 650,000 refugees applied for political asylum.

But these statistics are faulty. . . . But above all these figures grossly misrepresent the increase of the number of foreigners living in Germany because they do not take into account that in the same period of time almost 1.5 million foreigners left Germany for good. With other groups of migrants coming to the country—relatives of foreign workers, members of EC countries, etc., and because children born of foreign parents in Germany are nevertheless foreigners due to an atavistic law concerning nationality, the overall 'foreign' population is, however, still slightly on the rise.

Right-wing groups have constantly dwelt upon these statistics using terrifying images of 'floods of asylum parasites', etc. Germany has been compared to a 'boat [which] is full'. Appealing to basic instincts like fear and distrust, providing easy answers to complex problems, offering a clear profile of the enemy to project one's hate and frustration on—all this won them wide sympathies at a time when cries abound. . . .

Of all the immigrant nationalities the Turks have a culture the most foreign to German sensibilities. And yet it is not only their Muslim religion and their extremely patriarchal family structure but their sheer number—with 1.8 million the Turks represent the largest minority in Germany—which has kindled a subliminal anxiety within many Germans. The foreign loses its exotic fascination if it become common and usual. It needs malicious incitement, however, to turn this anxiety into fear and hatred: fear of losing one's own cultural identity and hatred of those who appear to threaten this culture. . . .

The subconscious fear of an uncertain national identity has resulted in a concept of citizenship based upon descent ('ius sanguinis') or upon the profession of German culture reflecting the definition given by the Nazi-German's Home Secretary, Wilhelm Frick, in 1939. This can lead to the absurd situation that a Latvian SS-man's grandson who does not speak a single word of German but whose grandfather had proclaimed his loyalty to German culture by joining the SS can be entitled to German nationality. On the other hand a young Turk, who has been born in Germany and who speaks German better than Turkish, still has no right to it. This law governing nationality ensures a steady increase in 'homemade' foreigners. . . .

The damage right-extremist violence has done to Germany's image abroad is tremendous. Big business has long since realized that the current development runs against their interest. The tourist trade fears losses, export figures plummeted already, and Japanese investments fell off to a record low in 1992. And they reacted swiftly: companies started to fire employees who molested foreign workmates in word or in deed (measures which the women's rights movement has been fighting for for years). It was mainly their initiative which brought about the large turnout of concerned citizens protesting against xenophobia at the nationwide candlelight vigils last December. All this reminded one of the 'public breast-beating contests', as Max Horkheimer used to call the mass abjurations after World War II. And while honest middle-class citizens—in accordance with the government—call the perpetrators 'a few demented criminals', the

Left—in accordance with the press abroad—is busy in conjecturing the scare of reviving Nazism. Who is right?

It is a fact that since the reunification right-extremist terror and aggression have claimed at least 49 lives. The victims were not only foreigners; 15 homeless and disabled were among them. Pretending to feel a call to 'cleanse' Germany from its 'impurities' the young perpetrators insist that they only perform the will of the majority. And in a horrifying way they are right. Xenophobic, racist, and eugenic ideas and prejudices are widespread even if they mostly remain tacit. Although there have always been violent crimes committed by youths the nature of the tidal wave of aggression currently sweeping over Germany is altogether different. Above all, it is the brutality of the assaults which is shocking. The youths—two out of three are younger than 21—aim at maiming and killing their victims. Where does their readiness to commit acts of violence stem from? . . .

Frustration and disappointment prevail with unemployment soaring in a country whose citizens had not known anything but full employment for 40 years and whose self-respect had always been based upon work. Only anti-social elements, who refused to work, used to be without a job. Furthermore, despite the snooper activities of the 'Stasi' (the former East German Secret Service) there has been a sense of solidarity among the citizens against the bigwigs and party bosses of the ruling SED. Now with jobs scarce and uncertainty everywhere mistrust and envy govern people's minds. Young people are deprived of any perspective for the future. Besides, now that the euphoria about the reunification has long since abated and its true costs are presented by an only too evasive government, East Germans feel more and more excluded as second-class citizens by West Germans. They in their turn exclude those whom they deem even further down on the social scale. And so they fall back on the only identity which they think they can be sure of, i.e., their national identity: Germany for the Germans! . . .

What would be the cure of this crisis? First, it would be necessary to focus the attention of the masses on Germany's real problems: the decline of ethical standards, the devastation of the environment, the decrease of work, and the reunification which has virtually failed. Equally important would be to restrain the media from offering a forum for the perpetrators. The former were often rightly accused of depicting the crimes as if there were no victims or rather of portraying the aggressors, the 'misled youths', as the actual victims. Assaulting people is a safe bet to make it into the headlines of nationwide newspapers—but only if the motives are right-extremist. Some TV teams have been rumoured of having even paid Nazi hooligans to hurl stones or raise their arms with the illegal Hitler salute.

Jörg Haider
MULTICULTURALISM AND LOVE OF ONE'S COUNTRY

Jörg Haider (b. 1952) is currently the most successful right-wing political leader in Western Europe. Raised by parents who embraced National Socialism in the 1930s and 1940s, Haider emerged as leader of the far-right Austrian Freedom Party in the mid-1980s. On the strength of his personality—a blend of crowd-pleasing demagogue, rugged outdoorsman, and slippery, glib political talk-show guest—the Freedom Party's popularity increased. Yet Haider's xenophobic rhetoric and his praise of the employment policies of the Nazi regime (for which he subsequently apologized) aroused criticism. In 1993 he called for a tightening of restrictions on immigrants, but his "Austria first" initiative, described in the selection below, was met with candlelight vigils in favor of tolerance in major Austrian cities and towns.

Despite setbacks, the Freedom Party received the second-largest share of votes in the Austrian general election of 1999, the strongest showing by a far-right party in Western Europe since World War II. Its success was due not only to the telegenic Haider, but also to a general feeling that the entrenched coalition of Social Democratic and People's Parties was unresponsive to the concerns of ordinary Austrians.

Dismay in Europe increased when the Freedom Party formed a coalition government with the People's Party and ousted the Social Democrats. Alarmed, the European Union imposed sanctions on Austria for one year. Haider stepped down as party leader in order to improve the Freedom Party's international reputation. Although the party's share of the vote has diminished, Haider remains an influential figure in Austrian politics and currently holds the post of Governor of the province of Carinthia.

The concept of a "multi-cultural society" has become an ideology. After the pitiful Socialist utopia of a classless society proved itself to be a flop, a new dogma pops up to force us to be "happy." Since the Left failed to convert people to Marxist Socialism it has been in search of a new ideology, and new enemies. They found their new ideology in the idea of a multi-cultural society which to some has the same appeal as a classless society. But the experiment of a multi-cultural society has never worked anywhere in practice. Wherever and whenever it was tried, immense social problems, ghettos, slums, crime and social unrest ensued. The USA is the best example of this. In the American "melting pot" neither a social nor a cultural balance has been successful. The disturbances in Los Angeles are just an example of many. Every immigration wave creates an "elbow society"—discrimination and social injustice are never far behind.

Order in a state requires a minimal consensus on basic values. This is endangered when incompatible norms meet each other in an enclosed area. This is the crux of the problem of a multi-cultural society. This is most plain the more diverse the cultures and values are. In many European cities this is best illustrated by immigrants of Islamic faith. In France there are over three million Moslems, in Britain about a million, in Germany roughly 1.7 million. The social order of Islam is diametrically opposed to Western values. Our concept of human rights and democracy are about as compatible with the Moslem teachings as equal rights for women. The individual and freedom, as perceived by us, count for nothing, the fight for the faith, the Jihad, is everything. No religion on earth is spreading so fast at the moment as Islam. The German *Süddeutsche Zeitung* only recently asked whether "700 years after the crusades, Arabic Muslims would stage a counter-attack and storm the citadels of affluence, freedom and democracy."

However one assesses the danger of Islamic fundamentalism, the problems posed by the encounter of two very different cultural spheres remain. This is not easy to overcome as we could see from the dispute in France over whether Islamic schoolgirls should wear headscarves. In Austria there was an outcry when Islamic parents demanded that the crucifix be removed from schoolrooms because it offended the religious feelings of their children!

This is the kernel of the problem of a would-be multi-cultural society. It is not the immigrants who integrate into the society and culture they find themselves in; instead they expect from the natives that they should accept their customs. Peaceful integration on these terms is not likely.

A society which does not rest on a shared value system leads inexorably into chaos and the breakup of law and order. This may be alright for the fans of leftist teaching with its anarchist tendencies. For citizens who want to live in peace in their country, such "utopian" dreams quickly turn into a nightmare. The arguments of the advocates of a multi-cultural society are not only naive and divorced from the real world but for the most part are plain cynical. This is especially true for the argument that we need large immigration to offset the decline in the birth rate. The same people who are for abortion on demand and constantly devalue the family justify unrestricted immigration to compensate for the results.

The mismanaged family policy of recent decades has meant that decisions to have children or not are taken largely for financial reasons. For the poor it is a question of survival, while for the affluent it means a decline in their standard of living and less leisure time. We need action which will make it attractive to say "yes" to children and "yes" to the family.

Both the extreme Left and Right have debauched the question of immigration and abuse it for their own dogma. The extreme Left hope for a new class struggle and the extreme Right for a new race warfare. These apologists for civil war have to be resolutely opposed. Whoever thinks the immigration problem can be solved with violence is either politically or emotionally unstable. The state must counter them with all the means at its disposal in no uncertain terms.

Every democratic, responsible politician is confronted with the question: How many foreigners can we take in without endangering social peace and security? Who gives us the right to make people strangers in their own country? When we mounted our popular initiative "Austria first" the argument was made that immigration was not an issue you should put to a vote. It was not "suitable".

Those who opposed the idea of an initiative on immigration thus implied that Austrians were either not competent enough to judge or hostile to foreigners. The historic facts prove the contrary. Austrians took in refugees fleeing from Hungary during the revolution in 1956 as they did for Czechs in 1968 when the Prague Spring was crushed. The same generosity was shown after the military putsch in Poland. No other country has taken in so many refugees from former Yugoslavia as Austria. Humanitarian aid for Slovenia, Croatia, and above all for Bosnia, has served as a model for all Europe.

In the discussion on immigration and multiculturalism two factors stand out—the refugee problem on the one hand and the question of economic immigrants on the other. Austria was, and is, an exemplary country when it comes to providing asylum for those being persecuted. Austria, however, is not and cannot be a land of immigration. We are simply not in the position to let everyone who is in search of social and economic benefits settle here. We are, as the Austrian president Thomas Klestil put it, "a country of hospitality but no beaten track for unnecessary transit traffic and no dropping off point for all those without hope on our continent. . . . It would be a false understanding of humanity to keep the borders open for so long that social stability will be endangered".

We can only accept immigrants to the degree that we can offer jobs, apartments, and schools for their children. The German sociologist Horst Afheldt believes that Europe should only take in as many people as it can integrate in its social structures. That way it has a better chance of achieving harmony than a basically open society with ongoing immigration evoking fear amongst ethnic groups of being overwhelmed by others. "This can only lead to aggression", he said.

The question is, who should decide which path to take? In my opinion: the people. Whoever doubts the role of the people as the highest sovereign questions the very essence of democracy. People have the right not just to go to the polls every four years but are entitled to have a say in questions which are decisive for the future of their country. For this reason I and my party introduced at the beginning of 1993 the popular initiative "Austria first", which included the following 12 points:

1. *A constitutional provision: "Austria is no country of immigration".* . . .
2. *An end to immigration until a satisfactory solution to the problem of illegal foreigners has been found, until the accommodation shortage has been resolved and until unemployment goes down to 5%.*

In Vienna about 100,000 foreigners live illegally. This puts extra pressure on the labor market and accommodation. Only through an end to immigration can further social conflicts between the indigenous population and foreigners be prevented.

3. *An ID requirement for foreign employees at the work place which should be presented for the work permit and for registration for health insurance.*

Only controls can put a stop to the illegal hiring of foreigners, which has meant not only tax evasion and the bypassing of compulsory social insurance contributions, but has also led to a decline in wage levels. The need for an appropriate regulation was acknowledged by the government in the 1990 program but it now rejects its implementation.

4. *An expansion of the police-force (aliens and criminal branches) as well as better pay and resources to trace illegal foreigners and to effectively combat crime, especially organized crime.* . . .

5. *Immediate creation of permanent border controls (customs-police) in place of the army. . . .*

6. *A reduction of tension in schools by limiting the percentage of pupils with a foreign mother tongue in elementary and vocational schools to a maximum of 30%; in case of more than 30% of foreign speaking children, special classes for foreigners should be set up.*

The preservation of our cultural identity, the achievement of educational goals and the need for integration all make a limitation on the percentage of foreign-speaking children in classes indispensable.

7. *Reduction of tension in schools through participation in regular education only by those with adequate knowledge of German.*

In preparatory classes children of school age with a foreign mother tongue should be taught German in order to enable them to take part in education in the regular school classes.

8. *No right to vote for foreigners in general elections.*

The opposite demand of the government coalition and the Greens is primarily aimed at new votes, gaining to compensate for recent losses.

9. *No premature granting of Austrian citizenship.*

We demand that the 10 year period laid down in the law should be kept and exceptions should be kept to a minimum.

10. *Rigorous measures against illegal business activities of foreigners and the abuse of social benefits.*

Many associations of foreigners run restaurants and clubs which do not meet commercial, health or legal requirements. Some serve as centres for the black market.

11. *Immediate deportation and residence ban for foreign offenders of the law.*

The crime rate among foreigners, especially in Vienna, has soared, making it necessary to provide extra detention cells. In practice deportees cannot be detained because of the acute lack of cells.

12. *The establishment of an Eastern Europe Foundation to prevent migration.*

The lasting improvement of conditions of life in Eastern European countries should be provided by specially targeted economic help to prevent emigration for economic reasons.

Commission for the Abolishment of Sexual Mutilations
AFRICAN IMMIGRANTS IN FRANCE: THE CONTROVERSY OVER FEMALE CIRCUMCISION

Language barriers, skin color, religion, diet, and practices such as the wearing of head scarves are among the most prominent of the cultural differences marking immigrants to Western Europe from Africa, the Middle East, South Asia, or the Caribbean. In recent years, the practice of female circumcision—also referred to as female genital mutilation (or FGM) by critics—has met with careful scrutiny. Supporters of the procedure claim that it prevents adultery, offers health benefits, and is an initiation rite, but many human rights organizations have denounced the practice because it can cause severe pain and health risks, sometimes leading to death, in women. Since inflicting mutilation on a person was made a crime in the 1980s, some twenty FGM cases have been heard by French criminal courts. The following report, prepared by the Commission for the Abolishment of Sexual Mutilations, demonstrates the lack of understanding between French society and a number of African immigrants when it comes to this contentious cultural practice.

France is the only country to date to engage in legal proceedings when a child has been excised, providing that the case is reported to the police or to a Judge. It has now been over fifteen years that the French authorities have been compelled to deal with FGM.

It all began with three-month-old Bobo Traore's death in July 1982 who died of severe hemorrhage as a result of excision performed in a Parisian suburb, at her parents' request. The infant had bled for two days. The parents said that they did not seek medical care for their child, being aware that the practice was forbidden in France. This tragedy caused public outcry. . . . Doctors and social workers in contact with the African population started asking for guidelines from the authorities. Statistics showed a great number of African little girls had been mutilated and brought to hospitals.

The French Penal Code punishes violence all the harder when the victim is a child under the age of fifteen. When the violences cause permanent infirmity or a mutilation, it is a major criminal offense. The penalty incurred goes up to ten years of imprisonment, and is increased when the persons responsible for the harm done to the child are its own parents.

Linda Weil-Curiel, a lawyer, established that the mutilation of an African infant is a major criminal offense falling within the jurisdiction of the Criminal Court and convinced the Court to rule that excision should be punished no matter the motives invoked. The first penalties consisted in suspended prison sentences for the parents (three to five years) but they are harsher now and in 1991 an excisor was condemned to serve five years. One objective was to give visibility to that issue by numerous press reports of the trials.

The parents pleaded that they only had done what was expected of good parents among their kinfolks pleading the cultural gap. The fact is that this is not legally valid; all families in France including African families are required to visit childcare centers with their babies/children where they receive information from the doctors that it is unlawful to excise children in France.

At the trials in France many testimonies have been heard of how the young African girls react when they learn that they have been submitted to the practice by their parents. They feel humiliated to have been mutilated without their consent, and they are full of anger as they understand that they will never regain what has been taken from them.

The next excision trial scheduled will take place this autumn because a young girl has complained to a Judge about her mutilation and that of her sisters and gave the name of her excisor, who is now in prison. She will ask for damages in court. She feels she has been abused and betrayed by those who should have protected and taken the best care of her, that is to say her own parents.

The younger generation is now in favor of prosecution in excision cases. They want examples to be set and harsh punishment for those who won't respect their integrity and their right to live. . . . Since 1984, when an excisor was put in jail and African families acknowledged that prison might really lie ahead, the number of excisions has decreased in France: prosecution equals protection in the excision cases. A woman from Mali living in France when a journalist after a trial asked her: 'Is it acceptable to bring all these parents to trial?' answered: 'What is not acceptable is to allow children to be tortured.'

REVIEW QUESTIONS

1. Why did Enoch Powell see immigrants as a drain on the resources of Britain? Is there a contradiction in his proposal that they should re-emigrate to countries "anxious to receive the manpower and the skills they represent"?
2. According to Joachim Krautz, how did reunification lead to a resurgence of nationalism in Germany? How did it contribute to the growth of right-wing extremism?
3. In Jörg Haider's view, why does multiculturalism represent a threat to the continued existence of Austrian culture and the Austrian national identity? How does the American model of multiculturalism differ?
4. Consider the debate over female circumcision. Should the principle of respect for cultural differences sometimes give way to the effort to protect universal human rights? How are these rights determined?

---

4   Ethnic Cleansing: Slaughter in Yugoslavia

One of the most tragic conflicts of the final decade of the twentieth century occurred in the former Yugoslavia. Successfully administered as a one-party state by Marshal Tito until his death in 1980, Yugoslavia thereafter began to unravel along its major ethnic and religious fault lines. The Eastern Orthodox Serbs were at odds with the Roman Catholic Croats, and both groups hated the Muslims, who were Slavs like both the Serbs and the Croats, but had converted to Islam during the Ottoman conquest of the late Middle Ages. In 1992, conflict flared up in Bosnia, a multi-ethnic microcosm of Yugoslavia divided between Serbs, Croats, and Muslims.

Serbia sought to realize its long-standing territorial ambitions by making common cause with Bosnian Serbs. They seized large areas of Bosnia and subjected the Bosnian capital, Sarajevo, to a cruel siege. They also engaged in ethnic cleansing, expelling the Muslim population from conquered territory. Meanwhile, the Croation government began to evict Serbs from its territory and seize parts of Bosnia inhabited by a majority of Croats. At the same time, the Muslim government of Bosnia created its own army and fought to preserve its territory from the incursions of both Serbs and Croats. This ruthless civil war claimed 100,000 lives by 1994 and turned millions of others into refugees. Only in 1995 did the international community, through NATO, utilize military force to halt Serb aggression. The treaty signed in 1996 reunited Bosnia, if only on paper, and restored peace.

At the end of the war, Radovan Karadzic, the Bosnian Serb leader, and his military commander, General Ratko Mladic, were indicted on charges of genocide and crimes against humanity by the United Nations International Criminal

Tribunal for the Former Yugoslavia in The Hague, Netherlands. Warrants for their arrest were issued in 1995, but both men are still at large, as are several dozen other war criminals in Yugoslavia.

Yugoslav President Slobodan Milosevic remained in office and once again resorted to ethnic cleansing in the Yugoslav province of Kosovo in 1999, driving 1.5 million ethnic Albanians out of the country. After a protracted NATO bombing campaign had inflicted widespread damage upon his country, he capitulated and accepted a peace accord. At the same time the U.N. Tribunal indicted him for crimes against humanity committed in Kosovo.

A fraudulent reelection campaign in September 2000 sparked widespread protests and forced Milosevic from office. He was arrested in June 2001 and transferred to the custody of the U.N. Tribunal to face the above charges, as well as charges of genocide and other crimes committed in the Bosnian war. Despite his contempt for the legality of the Tribunal, his trial began in 2002.

David Rieff
"THE ENEMY IS NOT HUMAN"

The following selection is drawn from the book Slaughterhouse—Bosnia and the Failure of the West (1995), by David Rieff. While Rieff concedes that all sides in the war committed atrocities, he comes down particularly hard on Serb leaders and on Western nations for failing to curb their aggression.

The slaughter of Bosnia is the story of a defeat. I say slaughter because to refer to what has happened there as a war is to distort and, more gravely, to dignify the real nature of what has occurred. War, for all its bestiality, has its dignity and its laws, and soldiers, at least when they are faithful to their codes, rightly claim theirs to be an honorable as well as a terrible calling. To think otherwise is to imagine that nothing is worth dying for, and if Bosnia proves anything it is that such a statement is a shameful lie.

But about what the Serbs have done in Bosnia no such claims can or should be made. This is what happened. Two hundred thousand Bosnian Muslims died, in full view of the world's television cameras, and more than 2 million other people were forcibly displaced. A state formally recognized by the European Community, by the United States, and by the United Nations was allowed to be destroyed.

This slaughter was led by a group of extreme Bosnian Serb nationalists, well supplied by their allies and mentors in Serbia proper. They succeeded through a combination of skillful propaganda and terror in rallying the majority of Bosnian Serbs to the cause of Greater Serbia.

Ethnic cleansing in Bosnia has been as much about methodically humiliating a people and destroying their culture as it has been about killing them. The Serb assault on the Ottoman and Islamic architectural legacy throughout the country was not a by-product of the fighting—collateral damage, as soldiers say—but an important war aim. For the Bosnian Serb leadership, the Serbianization of areas of Bosnia that had been ethnically mixed before the fighting started could not be accomplished simply by driving out many of the non-Serbs who lived in villages. The massacres at the beginning of the fighting in the spring of 1992 had only been the start. The process and program that was ethnic cleansing of necessity involved the rewriting of the Bosnian past as well.

A crucial factor in the success of ethnic cleansing was the prevailing belief among Serbs that they were the injured parties, engaged in a defensive war. In interview after interview, Radovan Karadzic, the leader of the Bosnian Serbs, would make this point with varying degrees of eloquence and hyperbole. "We Serbs are only defending ourselves against Muslim attacks," was one of his catchphrases. A fallback was to use the horrors of the war— "It is civil war," he once said, "what do you expect?"—to prove that Serbs and Muslims could not live together in Bosnia, and that, in fact, what the Serbs were trying to accomplish was in the interests of the Muslims as well, whether they realized it or not.

In Karadzic's formulation, Serbian-ness, Croatian-ness, and Muslim-ness were essences— unchanging and immutable. . . . The savagery of the war he had unleashed made what otherwise might have appeared to be his mad ideas convincing to people; and more than that, made them appear to have been confirmed by their experience. The fact that they had had these experiences because of plans conceived by Karadzic, Serbian president Slobodan Milosevic, and their colleagues did not alter the fact that people were now likely to feel in their guts that the ideas had been true all along. As Zdravko Grebo, a Sarajevo law professor and longtime political opponent of Karadzic, quipped, "Radovan Karadzic is the greatest genius Bosnia has ever produced. He says something that at the time is a complete lie. And two years later it becomes the truth."

Whatever Karadzic might claim, Serbs had not always believed that they could not get on with Muslims and Croats. They had been neighbors for generations. They had gone to school with one another, worked together, and, to a surprising extent, had intermarried—particularly in the urban areas of Bosnia-Herzegovina. It took a lot of propaganda to make them first begin to fear one another—the war

started in fear and only ended in genocide— and then slaughter one another. And yet once the killing had begun, the violence was taken by many to confirm the justice of Karadzic's original diagnosis. This was often as true for many of the Bosnian Serb leader's bitterest adversaries as it was for those Serbs who had reluctantly begun to follow him.

Trying to make sense of what was going on in Bosnia by talking to Karadzic was, as the successive waves of United Nations officials both civilian and military who were sent to deal with him all learned eventually, a hopeless exercise. . . . There appeared to be no limits to how far he was willing to go, whether it was claiming, before the imposition of NATO's so-called "no fly" zone over Bosnia-Herzegovina, that no Bosnian Serb Army aircraft were conducting bombing raids or transporting troops; or denying that the Serb shells raining down on Sarajevo were coming from his positions ("It is the Muslims," he said over and over again, "who shell themselves. They hope to gain the sympathy of the world"); or even claiming that there was no such thing as ethnic cleansing, a term Karadzic himself had resuscitated. And why not? What Karadzic and the other Serb leaders learned over the course of the two years in which they conquered Bosnia was that whatever they did, the United Nations and the great powers were not going to lift a finger to stop them. And if their deeds brought no retaliation down on their heads, why should their words have any consequences?

With the world community supine, the Serb leaders knew that the only propaganda war they had to win was among their own people. In this, they were astonishingly successful.

Traveling through Bosnian Serb–controlled territory, it was common enough to meet Serbs who were sick of the war and horrified by the way in which Bosnia had been shattered. But it was all but impossible to find anyone who believed the Serb side had started the conflict, or that the Serbs were anything but misunderstood victims. Ordinary Serbs spoke with genuine bewilderment about the attitude of the Western powers. "I used to love America," a high school teacher told me in the Sarajevo suburb of Ilidza during the summer of 1993, the tears welling up in her eyes. "For a while, I told myself that you American people had been duped, but now I realized that you are all our enemies, and that I must learn to think of you that way—even though I don't want to. I see what you write about us, the lies, and I just don't understand."

I asked her why, if the Serbs were the true victims of the war, they continued to shell Sarajevo pitilessly, and why Sarajevan children had to die at the hands of Serb snipers. She just sighed and shook her head. "It is not true," she said, softly reproving. "If we shell the city, it is only because the Muslims shoot at us first. Don't we have the right to defend ourselves? Don't you think that every human being has that right, even we evil, evil Serbs? I am sure that if they would stop firing, we would stop too, right away. Nobody wants war."

"And the sniper fire?" I asked, the memories of the maimed children of the Kosevo pediatrics ward coming, terrible and unbidden, to mind.

She looked at me coldly. "I think you are mistaken," she said. "Sniping is a coward's weapon. Serbs are incapable of behaving in this dishonorable way. I come from Sarajevo. I was thrown out of my home by Muslims. Our soldiers, many of them, come from the city also. They would not kill children. If kids are being killed, it must be the Muslims who are doing this to blame the Serbian people."

Anyone who had spent time in the bowl of Sarajevo, where the snipers can see and pick out their victims, and where, throughout the siege, even to stand at your window was to risk your life, might have been tempted to question her sanity. But her sincerity was beyond question. Perhaps it should not have been surprising. The only information about the fighting this woman had received in more than a year, except through chance encounters with foreign journalists and aid workers whom she already

had written off as being pro-Muslim, was what was dished out each night on Bosnian Serb television and radio. Her only source was what the fighters returning from the front chose to tell her.

And the fighters themselves were capable of similar leaps of faith and fancy. In a sand-bagged revetment on a hill above Sarajevo, not too far from the no-man's-land of the city's Jewish cemetery, a bearded Serb fighter said to me, "Before this summer ends we will have driven the Turkish army out of the city, just as they drove us from the field of Kossovo in 1389. That was the beginning of Turkish domination of our lands. This will be the end of it, after all these cruel centuries."

Like the woman I had met in Ilidza, he too had been a high school teacher in a Sarajevo suburb, and later that evening he would ask me what I thought of the novels of John Updike. But when this man looked down at the city of Sarajevo, into which he had been shooting his 50-caliber machine gun for the better part of a year, he did not see what had once been a rich city by world standards, the Balkan capital of rock'n roll, but rather the campsite of the Turkish army that had conquered the Balkans in the 14th and 15th centuries. Somewhere he must have known that the people he was shooting at were civilians—already, after a year of the siege, thirty-five hundred of the dead were children—but imaginatively he could not see anyone in that urban bowl below except armed invaders. His job was not to murder them. One cannot murder invaders; one defends oneself against them, repels them. "We Serbs are saving Europe," he boasted, "even if Europe does not appreciate our efforts, even if it condemns them." . . .

Getting individuals to kill is not that difficult. There is savagery in every civil war, and rarely any moral bottom. (Paradoxical though it may appear, the Bosnian conflict has been *both* a civil war and a war of aggression; it has been as ruthless as the former and as one-sided as the latter.) Once the blood has flowed, the individual fighter thirsts as much for revenge as for victory. And since in the former Yugoslavia atrocities have been committed by all sides, the desire for vengeance has taken the form of further atrocities. But, from the beginning, such excesses were also a Serb war aim. The more terrified the Muslims could be made to feel, the more likely they were not simply to flee but to resist ever returning to lands the Serbs had taken.

On reflection, atrocities were one logical consequence of ethnic cleansing. If you keep repeating on television and radio and in every address to your troops, as the Serbs have done, that the enemy is not human; that you may have grown up with the man, and you may think you know him, but in reality you don't; in short, that you are confronting a devil, then the results are all but foreordained. It is no longer a question of whether there will be killing, only of how long the bloodletting will go on.

Thus not only propagandists insisted that the Muslims were less than human. Those who carried out the ethnic cleansing almost invariably behaved as if the atrocities they perpetrated were somehow justified. The aggrieved innocence so commonly and unaffectedly displayed by individual fighters made it clear that they felt themselves and not those they were killing or displacing to be the real victims of the war. And like victims everywhere, they thirsted for what they usually called justice but were sometimes willing to categorize as revenge. When Serb forces took possession of conquered lands, houses, and farm animals, they were likely to burn the houses and slaughter the livestock, even though they obviously realized that their actions made it impossible for their fellow Serbs to start farming them themselves. But they thought the price worth paying, so deep-seated was the Serb feeling of being the injured party.

In the villages, radical military operations were often accompanied by equally radical cognitive ones. "We've liberated Radovac," a Serb fighter in Banja Luka told me one afternoon. . . .

"We've liberated Radovac," he repeated, practically bellowing at me, apparently believing that I hadn't heard him the first time. He then flashed a thumbs-up. I nodded. "It was a hard fight," he shouted, "but we got it back." Only later would I learn that Radovac had always been an entirely Muslim village. For the Serb, though, such considerations were secondary. For him, the Muslims of Radovac were not and could not be the village's real inhabitants. However long their tenancy, it could never be long enough, in the Bosnian Serb version of history, to justify their presence.

It was a variant of the same story each time the Serbs attacked somewhere. If the area in question was not full of Serbs being oppressed or killed by Muslims, the Serbs were only trying to protect Serb parts of the area. This was how Karadzic justified the shelling of Sarajevo throughout the war, when, with a straight face, he insisted that there was no siege, only Serb forces trying to protect Serbs who just happened to live in all the neighborhoods that ringed the city. Karadzic said more or less the same thing when the city of Gorazde in eastern Bosnia became a major target in April 1994. And when neither of these claims would do, the Serbs would fall back on history, and insist that the area in question had once been Serb, until some Muslim or Croat massacre had upset its proper demographic future.

The Bosnian Serb forces tailored their tactics to the kind of area in which they were operating. It was one thing to lay siege to Sarajevo, but in the ethnically mixed villages of Bosnia, the fighters could not pursue ethnic cleansing successfully on their own. They had to transform those local Serbs who were either still undecided about joining the fight or frankly opposed to it into their accomplices. The natural impulse for self-preservation was the fighters' greatest ally, providing they could summon the necessary ruthlessness.

One common method was for a group of Serb fighters to enter a village, go to a Serb house, and order the man living there to come with them to the house of his Muslim neighbor. As the other villagers watched, he was marched over and the Muslim brought out. Then the Serb would be handed a Kalashnikov assault rifle or a knife—knives were better—and ordered to kill the Muslim. If he did so, he had taken that step across the line the Chetniks (Serb soldiers) had been aiming for. But if he refused, as many did, the solution was simple. You shot him on the spot. Then you repeated the process with the next Serb householder. If he refused, you shot him. The Chetniks rarely had to kill a third Serb. But in most places, this kind of raw terror was not enough. More than killing or making people accomplices to murder, it was engendering a deep fear that was required. From the start, fear had lain at the heart of the Bosnian catastrophe. The fear of the future that the collapse of the Yugoslav economy in the late '80s began to produce in ordinary people had made them lose faith in each other. Only the old atavistic notions of identity seemed to offer any sanctuary from this fear. It was not that people had only felt themselves to be Serbs, or Croats, or Muslims before—or that Tito's slogan, "Brotherhood and Unity," had been only an imposed sham—but rather that the failure of cosmopolitanism, of Yugoslavism, or, more properly, its murder at the hands of political leaders like Slobodan Milosevic, had breathed such new energy into the old national feelings and national grievances. Ethnic nationalism was no more inevitable in Germany in the 1930s. It was one possibility—inevitable only in the sense that everything that happens is inevitable in hindsight.

In reality, the victory of the ethnic nationalists was not inevitable. They won in Serbia because of what they did, and because of what others did not do—particularly in the West—not because history was on their side. They won because Slobodan Milosevic was far and away the ablest politician in the former Yugoslavia, because the idea of Greater Serbia was coherent in a way that the idea of the Bosnian state never succeeded in becoming, and because the Serb fighters in Bosnia had a hundred heavy guns for every one the Bosnian side had. They won because they knew how to take old fears and old complaints, repackage them, and cause otherwise decent Serbs, people from a national community with no more of an innate predilection for murder than any other national community, to commit genocide.

Once that genocide began, however, the fear had to be fed. Had the Bosnian Serb leadership not put a particular effort into propaganda, it is at least possible that ordinary Serbs, having defeated the Bosnian government forces and seized most of the territory they had been taught to covet in the first half year of the fighting, might have been less eager subsequently to go along with the seemingly endless further rounds of killings and displacements. But if every living Muslim remained a threat, then the ethnic cleansing had to go on. What began as a tactic of pure massacre and terror in villages had evolved within six months into a sophisticated system for the destruction of a people, by Serb fighters who believed themselves to be retaliating for Muslim atrocities. If you are told over and over again that your comrades are being castrated, roasted alive on spits, and drowned in their own blood, and you have no sources of information from which you might learn a different story, it is a foregone conclusion that before too long you will, as you imagine it anyway, reply in kind.

REVIEW QUESTIONS

1. What part did government propaganda play in the war in Bosnia? What historical events and cultural mythology informed the actions of the Bosnian Serbs?

2. Why do the perpetrators of ethnic cleansing often deny the humanity of the targeted group? According to Rieff, why were atrocities a calculated part of the war aims of the Serbs?

---

5 Genocide in Rwanda: Western Inaction

After World War II and the revelation of the extermination of European Jewry, the West pledged that never again would it permit such inhumanity. In December 1948, the General Assembly of the United Nations adopted the Genocide Convention, which obliged its signatories "to prevent and to punish . . . acts committed with intent to destroy, in whole or in part, a national, ethnical, racial or religious group." In 1994, genocide took place in Rwanda, and Western nations (and the rest of the world) did nothing to stop the slaughter.

The central African country of Rwanda became a Belgian colony after World War I. Although Hutus from the south and Tutsis from the north had lived together and intermarried, the Belgian rulers enforced a separation. They found the physical appearance of the taller Tutsis more congenial than that of the stocky, Bantu Hutus, and despite the Tutsis' minority status, gave them preference in education as well as in administrative, military, and political jobs. In 1962 Rwanda became independent, and thereafter clashes erupted between the two groups every few years.

In 1993 President Habyarimana, a Hutu, signed a peace accord with the Tutsi army, the Rwandan Patriotic Front. To ensure that the provisions of the accord were observed in Rwanda, the United Nations sent a peacekeeping force, UNAMIR (United Nations Assistance Mission in Rwanda). Early in 1994 Major General Dellaire, the commander of UNAMIR, informed the UN Headquarters in New York that a group called Hutu Power was planning a massacre of Tutsis. The UN played down Dellaire's message as no more alarming than reports from other peacekeeping missions around the world.

On April 6, 1994, an airplane carrying President Habyarimana was shot down. One hour later Hutu Power began its planned massacre of the Tutsi population throughout Rwanda; 800,000 Tutsis were killed by machete-wielding Hutus in the following hundred days.

Mahmood Mamdani
PRIESTS, DOCTORS, AND TEACHERS TURN GENOCIDAL

Mahmood Mamdani, a prominent African intellectual, observes that local officials in Rwanda recruited ordinary people to kill their neighbors by convincing them that they were engaged in clearing the land of aliens, a necessary community project. To further this end, the perpetrators employed "the language of 'customary' obligation. . . . Right from the first massacre, . . . local officials were instructed to kill Tutsi as part of their communal work obligation. . . . Killings came to be referred to as umuganda (communal work), chopping up men as 'bush clearing,' and slaughtering women and children as 'pulling out the roots of bad weeds.'"

A particularly distressing feature of the massacres was the willing, if not eager, participation of priests, physicians, nurses, teachers, and human rights officials, people associated with professions that value and nurture life. Sometimes they hacked to death innocents, including children; other times they turned their charges over to others who did the bloody work. Mamdani discusses this troubling phenomenon.

. . . [E]ven if we can never know the numbers of those who killed, there is no escaping the disturbing fact that many did enthusiastically join in the killing. The genocide was not simply a state project. Had the killing been the work of state functionaries and those bribed by them, it would have translated into no more than a string of massacres perpetrated by death squads. Without massacres by machete-wielding civilian mobs, in the hundreds and thousands, there would have been no genocide. We now turn to the social underbelly of the genocide: the participation of those who killed with a purpose, for whom the violence of the genocide and its target held meaning. . . .

KILLINGS SANCTIFIED

Just as the killing in Rwanda was not done by shadowy death squads but by mobs of ordinary people guided by armed militia and trained infantrymen, the killing also did not happen in secluded but in public places. Most often, the killings happened in places of worship. Contrary to Gérard Prunier's contention that "the bystanders were mostly the churches," the church was a direct participant in the genocide. Rather than a passive mirror reflecting tensions, the Church was more of an epicenter radiating tensions.

Like the middle class of which they were a prominent part, priests were also divided between those who were targeted in the killings and those who led or facilitated the killings.

Here, too, there was hardly any middle ground. A Lutheran minister recalled what the gangs told him: "You can have religion afterwards." Explaining why he walked around with a club, the minister told a reporter: "Everyone had to participate. To prove that you weren't RPF [Rwandan Patriotic Front, the Tutsi army], you had to walk around with a club. Being a pastor was not an excuse." Priests who had condemned the government's use of ethnic quotas in education and the civil service were among the first victims of the massacres. In all, 105 priests and 120 nuns, "at least a quarter of the clergy," are believed to have been killed. But priests were not only among those killed, they were also among the killers. Investigators with the UN Center for Human Rights claimed "strong evidence" that "about a dozen priests actually killed." Others were accused of "supervising gangs of young killers. . . ."

How low the moral terpitude of the clergy had sunk is illustrated by a story Jean Carbonnarre, honorary president of the Paris-based NGO Survie, narrated to correspondents of the Inter-Press Service: "André Karamaga, president of the Anglican Church in Rwanda, told me that he went to the Taba commune near Kigali to settle a dispute between two priests quarreling over who should run the parish. The first priest told Karamaga that he was more deserving because the second priest had killed 15 people. When Karamaga challenged the second priest, he admitted the killings, but still maintained that he deserved to run the parish as, he said, the other priest had killed even more." Father Wenceslas Munyashyaka, the curate of Sainte-Famille church, sheltered eight thousand refugees but provided the militia members with lists of those he alleged had expressed sympathy for the RPF and agreed to let them come and pick off those they wanted. . . .

How could it be that most major massacres of the genocide took place in churches? How could all those institutions that we associate with nurturing life—not only churches, but schools and even hospitals—be turned into places where life was taken with impunity and facility? Médecins sans Frontières, a medical charity, pulled out of the University Hospital in Kigali after its patients kept disappearing. *The British Medical Journal* quoted the testimony of Dr. Claude-Emile Rwagasonza: "The extremist doctors were also asking patients for their identity cards before treating them. They refused to treat sick Tutsis. Also, many people were coming to the hospital to hide. The extremist doctors prevented many of these people from hiding in the hospital." A medical doctor, a member of the hospital staff, directed the militia into the hospital in Kibeho and shut off the power supply so that the massacre may proceed in darkness. Some of "the most horrific massacres occurred in maternity clinics, where people gathered in the belief that no one would kill mothers and new-born babies." "The percentage of doctors who became 'killers par excellence' was very high," concluded African Rights on the basis of extensive investigations. They included persons as highly qualified as Dr. Sosthène Munyemana, a gynecologist at the University Hospital of Butare, Rwanda's principal teaching hospital. "A huge number of the most qualified and experienced doctors in the country, men as well as women—including surgeons, physicians, paediatricians, gynaecologists, anaesthetists, public health specialists and hospital administrators—participated in the murder of their own Tutsi colleagues, patients, the wounded and terrified refugees who had sought shelter in their hospitals, as well as their neighbours and strangers." In a sector as small as Tumba, three doctors played a central part. Of these, one was a doctor at Groupe Scolaire Hospital, and the other, her husband, was the health director for Butare. "Two of the most active assassins in Tumba" were a medical assistant and his wife, a nurse.

Close on the heels of priests and doctors as prime enthusiasts of the genocide were teachers, and even some human rights activists. When I visited the National University at Butare in 1995, I was told of Hutu staff and students who betrayed their Tutsi colleagues and joined in their physical elimination. Teachers commonly denounced students to the militia or killed students themselves. A Hutu teacher told a French journalist without any seeming compunction: "A lot of people got killed here. I myself killed some of the children. . . . We had eighty kids in the first year. There are twenty-five left. All the others, we killed them or they have run away." African Rights compiled a fifty-nine-page dossier charging Innocent Mazimpaka, who was in April 1994 the chairman of the League for the Promotion and Defence of Human Rights in Rwanda (LIPRODHOR) and simultaneously an employee of a Dutch aid organization, SNV, with responsibility for the genocide. Along with his younger brother, the *burgomaster* of Gatare commune, he was charged with the slaughter of all but twenty-one of Gatare's Tutsi population of 12,263. Rakiya Omaar pointed out that "several members of human rights groups are now known to have participated" in the killings, refuting "the notion that an independent civil society—of which the educated and the political opposition were the backbone—resisted the project of genocide."

That victims looking for a sanctuary should seek out churches, schools and hospitals as places for shelter is totally understandable. But that they should be killed without any let or hindrance—even lured to these places for that purpose—is not at all understandable. As places of shelter turned into slaughterhouses, those pledged to heal or nurture life set about extinguishing it methodically and deliberately.

That the professions most closely associated with valuing life—doctors and nurses, priests and teachers, human rights activists—got embroiled in taking it is probably the most troubling question of the Rwandan genocide.

REVIEW QUESTIONS

1. In your opinion, what led people associated with professions that value and nurture life to engage in mass murder?
2. Compare the genocide in Rwanda with the slaughter of six million European Jews during the Holocaust (see page 393). What similarities and differences do you find?

---

6 The Lingering Appeal of Fascism

Although fascism was widely discredited in the wake of World War II and the crimes against humanity perpetrated by the National Socialist regime and its minions, a small core of obdurate extremists continued to harbor xenophobic and racist views well after 1945. Once the dynamic economic growth associated with reconstruction was tempered by serious recession in the early 1970s, radical right-wing rumblings were discernible in much of Western Europe. Targets of rightist anger included a wide range of "outsiders": foreign-born laborers (the so-called guest workers), immigrants from former colonial possessions, Jews, and the domestic Left. Additionally, an increasingly dangerous phenomenon into the 1980s and 1990s was the emergence of extremism among the younger generation. Usually unemployed or under-employed youth who resented the welfare state's inability to provide the level of comfort and security they demanded, these young people began to flock to established far-right political organizations. They also organized their own new parties, formed new Neo-Nazi groups, or expressed themselves through outbursts of skinhead violence against "outsiders," whom they regarded as parasites draining away scarce resources and diluting the "national character" of their respective host countries. As unrepentant members of the wartime generation felt comfortable reasserting their fascist convictions and younger, postwar rightists joined in the chorus of hate-mongering, Western European societies were forced to come to terms with the most sinister threat to both domestic stability and human rights since the 1930s and 1940s.

Ingo Hasselbach
INSIDE THE NEO-NAZI SCENE

The son of members of the Communist elite in East Germany, Ingo Hasselbach spent much of his adolescence in jail for petty crimes. After sharing a cell with the former Dresden Gestapo chief and hearing the old man blame Germany's division and weakness on the stale, but still emotionally appealing, myth of a global Jewish conspiracy, Hasselbach formed East Germany's first neo-Nazi party upon his release in 1988. Over the next five years, first in the East and then in the newly unified Germany, he led a violent, extremist group that engaged in street violence and organized and indoctrinated a small, but tightly organized cadre. The neo-Nazi movement's activities increased dramatically after unification, as splinter groups in the East and the West knitted together and began to plan terrorist attacks against foreigners and leftist opponents.

After confronting the human cost of the movement's activities—i.e., the fire-bombing of foreign refugee hostels in Solingen and Mölln—Hasselbach underwent a change of heart. He renounced neo-Nazi activities in 1993 and dedicated himself to working with German youths to steer them away from hatred and violence. The following selection details the depth of organization of the movement, sheds light on its support network within Germany and Austria, and describes the violent groundwork deemed necessary for the creation of a "Fourth Reich."

I happened to arrive in the United States from Germany for the first time two days before the bombing in Oklahoma City in April 1995. I was sitting in a hotel room in the middle of Manhattan finishing work on the pages that follow. It was one of the first times I'd had a chance to rest and pause in the two years since I'd left the neo-Nazi movement. America represented everything I'd come to love since quitting—a society of all nationalities, a strong democracy, a land of liberty—everything I'd worked to destroy when I was in the Movement.

The news in the weeks that followed linked the bombing with the existence of a far-right subversive movement, fueled by paranoid conspiracy theories and hatred of the federal government. That there was such a movement didn't come as news to me. As the founder of the former East Germany's first neo-Nazi political party, I'd been the main contact for several American far-right organizations in Europe and one of the main distributors of their propaganda. Before I got out of the Movement in 1993, I organized teach-ins, ran paramilitary camps, and indoctrinated young people at marches and meetings.

I began developing right-wing extremist ideas in 1987, when I was nineteen years old

and sitting in an East German prison for shouting "the Wall must fall!" in a public place. When I got out, I began working secretly with a small militant group opposed to the Communist government.

After the government fell, I didn't simply quit being a troublemaker and rejoice in my newfound freedom. Prison, youthful rebellion, and the intense study of the most evil ideology known to mankind had already begun to change me. The peaceful revolution going on in the streets of Berlin in November 1989 had nothing to do with the violent revolution going on in my head. I didn't want a part of this capitalist West Germany where I could buy a Walkman or a bunch of bananas. I wanted the German empire a former Gestapo officer had told me about in prison, the one whose medals and slogans and insignia were the ultimate taboos in both East and West Germany—and whose embrace confirmed my opposition to both those systems. . . .

. . . Those looking for a new Führer saw me as a pure "blond beast" risen from the ashes of the Iron Curtain, and, along with the drug of never-ending rebellion, I began to crave the fix of power I got from handing out hate literature, planning attacks, and standing at the head of hundreds of other equally angry young people, egging them on, pushing them further over the edges of decency.

I made contact with a flourishing international network of neo-Nazis and racist movements and began building up caches of weapons and starting paramilitary camps. Like the extremists in America, the common attitude we shared was a hatred for the government (especially federal government agents), a belief that our freedoms and traditions as white men (or, as we said, Aryans) were being infringed on by a multicultural society, and a general anti-Semitism that held that the Jews ran a conspiracy that emanated from New York and Washington.

While most of these ideas could have come from European anti-Semitic tracts from before World War II, they didn't. Virtually all of our propaganda and training manuals came from right-wing extremist groups in Nebraska and California. Such materials are legal to print in the United States under the First Amendment. In Germany they are not, under the Constitution passed after the defeat of the Third Reich.

We also received illegal materials from our friends in Nebraska—the world headquarters of the NSDAP/AO, the successor to the original National Socialist German Workers' Party, or Nazi Party—like a U.S. Army training manual entitled *Explosives and Demolitions,* which has since been copied and circulated (still with the TOP SECRET stamp across the title page) to thousands of right-wing extremists all over Europe. A computer program we received from the NSDAP/AO, entitled "A Movement in Arms," described how to build bombs and wage a war of right-wing terrorism against a democratic government. Before I quit, I'd become the leader of an NSDAP/AO terrorist cell, taking my orders directly from Lincoln, Nebraska.

I'd had plenty of contact with America. But it was an America populated by men who hated their country and found the swastika a more appealing symbol than the Statue of Liberty, who saw great affinities between their Founding Fathers and Adolf Hitler. It was an America oddly obsessed with Germany and the Third Reich. . . .

I don't know if whoever blew up the Alfred P. Murrah Federal Building in Oklahoma read the army manual we worked from. If they didn't, I'm sure we had some other reading material in common. The right-wing extremist movement is a loose network of people with a great deal of hatred and potential for violence, and all over the world they are constantly exchanging information. Of course, lots of people in the Movement may have been horrified by the sight of burned children in the Oklahoma bombing, but my experience as a neo-Nazi taught me that enough militant ideology and conspiracy thinking can destroy even the most basic human sympathy.

I began the slow and difficult process of getting out of the Movement after the fatal fire-bombing in 1992 of a Turkish family in the city of Mölln in northern Germany by two young men in the middle of the night. It had killed two young girls and the grandmother of one of the girls. My group had had nothing to do with the attack, but for the first time the deadly potential of our rhetoric was driven home to me. The police investigation showed that the perpetrators had connections with and had received propaganda from a group like mine in Hamburg, as well as from an American neo-Nazi group. Yet in prosecuting the case the authorities viewed these connections as secondary and treated the bombing as a case of isolated, if deadly, juvenile delinquency.

I never personally built a bomb or set fire to anyone's house. I justified my role in the Movement much as the leaders of the American militias or any of the other militant groups do. I was trying to "defend" my society against rampant crime, too much immigration, racial and cultural "alienation," and control by a world conspiracy. I organized paramilitary camps and taught guerrilla warfare only to prepare Germans to defend themselves and the cultural traditions of northern Europeans. I knew the arguments well, and I taught them to many others.

I know now that during all that time I was deceiving myself. Morally, I was just as responsible as anyone who planted a fuse or drove a truck with explosives in it—because my messages of hatred against the larger society influenced who knows how many potentially violent young men. The first step for me in rejoining the civilized world was realizing that. . . .

Hasselbach describes the movement's contact with old Nazis still loyal to Hitler and Nazi Party principles.

While the backbone of our organization was young men in their teens and twenties, we also got many visits from older people (our oldest member was seventy, an old Nazi, now, of course, retired). They often provided us with propaganda from the Third Reich that they'd carefully saved at home. These old Nazis— some from the SS, others from the Wehrmacht—would speak about the principles of national socialism in a way that made the concepts seem real and immediate. They could convey an enthusiasm for the SS, Hitler, and the Cause that simply could not be duplicated by someone who had not lived through the time.

These were not "important" Nazis, by and large, but that didn't matter. They were the living embodiment of not only Nazi glory but *German* glory. I came to realize then how fully Hitler had succeeded in merging the concepts of nationalism and Nazism in Germany and what a benefit that was to us. . . .

One man who came to us had belonged to the SS Leibstandarte, the elite SS bodyguards who were always around Adolf Hitler. This man educated us about race, about the system of national socialism and its entire program, about everything. He was still completely fixated on Hitler.

. . . He came to our organization through the West Berlin neo-Nazis, and he was probably about eighty years old.

[The old SS man] began our race education by making us aware of the racial characteristics of others. We started to pay attention to the size of everyone's head, the shades of color in their eyes, the shape of their hands. We learned to recognize the typical features of a Jew. For example, [he] taught us that a short back of the hand is typical for Jews and that a Jew will never have a straight body. Such things.

For the neo-Nazis, the Jew was still the main enemy. There was more violence against foreigners simply because Jews were harder to find. You would not see any recognizable Jews nowadays in the street. I thought I'd met a few people who were Jews—I wondered about it and tried to check the signs—but I couldn't be sure. There were hardly any Jews left in Germany, so we got little chance to practice our knowledge. But our Movement was always about the past and the future more than the present. It was important to learn about the racial characteristics of Jews in order to be able to understand the original Nazism, the history of our Movement, and it was also important for the future, when we might need to spot and segregate Jews again. The present was merely a stepping-stone between the Third and Fourth Reichs. . . .

If we really needed money badly, a telephone call to a well-to-do "friend" was all it took. One time there was a transport problem: one call, and the next day I had 5,000 marks in hand to buy a car.

This money was the gift of an elderly woman whose husband had been very influential in the National Socialists but had died during the war. These Nazi widows were usually well off because they got pensions from the State; in the case of the more fervent ones, their husbands had usually been rather high-ranking Nazis, and, as pensions were based on rank, this made them very rich indeed. It is an irony of the West German system that the widows of resistance fighters often didn't get any pension at all, while the widows of SS generals lived in luxury.

These old ladies all treated Michael Kühnen with great respect. He'd stop by their meetings, which would take place in individual homes or rented rooms, where they'd always serve coffee and lots of sweet cakes; the atmosphere was dainty compared to the meetings of the establishment professionals in the German Cultural Community.

Kühnen would stop by to shake the old ladies' hands and to gossip with them about their health and the Jews. And they would gawk like a movie star was in their presence, for they knew Kühnen was the Führer of the Movement, even if he wasn't their Führer, because that title would forever remain in the hands of their girlhood passion—Adolf Hitler, the *Führer!* In return, Kühnen had a deep respect for these militant Nazi widows. Partly because of this, he founded an organization called the HNG—the Help Organization for National Prisoners—to give old Nazi widows something useful to do: take care of young neo-Nazis sitting in prison.

The HNG WAS explicitly devoted to the rights and comforts of imprisoned neo-Nazis. . . .

These Nazi widows send prisoners food and cigarettes and keep them supplied with propaganda material. In dark moments, they encourage them to hang on so they can fight the Jew another day. The HNG also publishes a monthly newsletter, the *HNG News,* which is distributed to all "political prisoners"—only neo-Nazis, not Communists, of course—to keep them abreast of all the goings-on in the scene. . . .

[T]hese old ladies were actually ideologically harder and more ruthless than most neo-Nazis of my generation.

In their youth, they had been hard-core Nazis, and they held stubbornly to this ideology. Bitterness and old age had only further hardened their love of the Führer and hatred of the Jews. A meeting with them was no ordinary coffee klatch. When these women began

to gossip, they would talk about Auschwitz— or rather, the "Auschwitz lie"—and about the Jews and foreign pigs and Communists who should all be kicked out of Germany.

But first and always, they talked about Jews. Hatred of Jews was their deepest conviction, and Jews were their favorite topic of conversation. I don't think I ever talked about Jews as much as with these venomous little old ladies.

But they didn't just talk. They distributed propaganda and Holocaust denial literature— and they had a distinct advantage in that they were inconspicuous. They also worked as secret agents and spies for the Movement. They did come under surveillance, and about once a year some action was taken against the HNG. But usually the authorities would simply take the propaganda material away from an HNG member and tell her to stop passing it out in the future. It was a tough call for the cops because one couldn't very well put old ladies behind bars, though many of them really belonged there.

For one thing, they also held big meetings in which they would give speeches not *directly* calling for arson. But they might say, "It's about time something is done against foreigners, something our cowardly, corrupt democratic government in Bonn has neither the will nor the morality to do. . . ." Officially they would oppose the bombings and fires, while praising the young men who set foreigners' shelters on fire as being brave and patriotic in a land of cowardly democrats and multicultural mongrels.

And eventually they would express regret that they had to fight foreigners instead of the Jews. They'd say, "Nowadays there are only the foreigners, it is important to fight them . . . but we should not forget the Jews! We should not forget the Jews," they would always add, hopefully. . . .

Somehow, it seemed more natural for young people to have these beliefs. I know that sounds crazy. But it is a uniquely sinister sensation to be sitting next to an eighty-year-old woman who is eating a piece of cake and dribbling coffee onto her blouse, and saying, "We absolutely should desecrate more Jewish cemeteries this month." And somehow I hated them for trying to incite a young person like me to do such things. . . .

Military training and ideological indoctrination were cardinal concerns of the movement.

By far the most serious war games I observed were in Austria. They were organized by . . . trainers from the Austrian Federal Army, the Bundesheer. I went as an observer for the north German neo-Nazis. We took video cameras so we could film their camp for our own training exercises. What I saw in Austria made me realize that our exercises had all been childish games.

The exercises were held in Langleuten, a town where the far-right Austrian Freedom Party was very strong. The Austrian trainees arrived on Friday evening and practiced until Sunday afternoon—without sleep. It was total round-the-clock paramilitary training. During the day they practiced target shooting, grenade attacks, and laying explosives.

At night more specialized training took place. Night marches were accompanied by hand-to-hand combat in the dark and training in the art of silent killing. . . .

. . . What was unusual were the straw dummies used for the killing exercises. These were all dressed as concentration camp inmates, with striped uniforms and yellow Jewish stars on their breasts.

The Austrians would line up a row of these macabre scarecrows, and by the end of the practice there'd be little left of them. They practiced shooting them, stabbing them, and then, when they were mostly destroyed, putting them into a pile and blowing them up with grenades or timed charges.

The sadistic nostalgia for concentration camp tortures could hardly have been lost on anyone, but everyone participated cheerfully, taking the costumes as an amusing joke.

"Jews die!" a row of troops would scream as they led a bayonet charge against the scarecrows or shot them. Before blowing them up, there was simply mechanical efficiency, because it was a purely "technical" operation and they were clocking one another. They seemed to have an infinite supply of these striped concentration camp uniforms. I have no idea where they got them. . . .

The basic requirement for indoctrination was youth. We accepted older members, of course, but far fewer and treated them differently. It was assumed that if you joined an organization like ours when you were over, say, twenty-two, you were aware of what the Movement's history and implications were. You had at the very least the foundation of hatred and loyalty, a basic understanding of who the enemy was and why you wanted to fight him. This is not to say that older members weren't indoctrinated—in the Movement it was a permanent, ongoing process; you were never too old to indoctrinate or to be indoctrinated—but we focused on indoctrinating teenagers. . . .

. . . We taught them about Germany in their grandparents' era, Germany the last time it had been a great power in the world—and we gave them a map of Europe at the time.

Together we'd look at the map showing Germany in 1937 and Germany today, and I'd say, "Look at the Poles, they took this from us . . . the Czechs took this . . . and Austria too belonged to the German Reich. All this is gone. It was stolen, taken unlawfully from us Germans." You inflamed the recruit's feeling of injustice. And you began to draw all the strings connecting everything to the Jews. The land was gone because the Jews had stabbed Germany in the back in the First World War and then created the lie of the Holocaust in the Second. We'd begin to spend a lot of time on the *results* of the Holocaust lie, even before proving it was a lie. That way you first established Jewish guilt and made the idea suspect without having to confront the evidence. The Holocaust myth was simply a way to weaken Germans, as well as how the

Jews had swindled Germany into financing the State of Israel.

And you could watch a fourteen-year-old quickly develop a total feeling of injustice. This could have been someone who'd never thought about the Jews before, and in a way that was even better, because he'd had no time to develop perspective or counterarguments.

What you wanted was a fresh tablet upon which to write. With the exception of someone whose grandparents had been concentration camp guards and who had been a ruthless Jew-hating Nazi from the cradle on, anyone who had thought much about the Holocaust before you got to him was basically disqualified from indoctrination. We didn't want to waste our time on him because he'd have too many questions in his head, too many doubts. But if you took a real blank slate and you worked on him, the result would often be someone who was soon filled with hate and prepared to either commit violent acts or at least express his anger in some other way.

REVIEW QUESTIONS

1. In Ingo Hasselbach's account, how was the neo-Nazi movement in Germany influenced by elderly Nazis who had supported or participated in the Third Reich?
2. Why did neo-Nazis seek teenagers who could serve as a "blank slate" for their teachings?

---

7 Globalization: Patterns and Problems

The interaction between the West and the non-Western world initiated during the Age of Exploration in the fifteenth and sixteenth centuries accelerated with the emergence of European imperialism in the late nineteenth century. Today the world is being knit ever closer together by the spread of Western ideals, free-market capitalism, and technology. But globalization has also created a backlash among people who regard westernization as a threat to revered traditions. The most dramatic and dangerous reaction against Western values has occurred in Muslim lands, which have witnessed a surge of religious fundamentalism designed to counter Western influence. In their struggle against modernization and westernization, Islamic fundamentalists have resorted to terrorism, culminating in the attack on the World Trade Center and the Pentagon on September 11, 2001.

Thomas L. Friedman
GLOBALIZATION AS AN INTERNATIONAL SYSTEM

In his bestselling *The Lexus and the Olive Tree*, Thomas L. Friedman, foreign affairs columnist for *The New York Times*, maintains that globalization is "an international system . . . that has now replaced the old Cold War system, and, like that Cold War system, globalization has its own rules and logic that today directly or indirectly influence the politics, environment, geopolitics and economics of virtually every country in the world." In the following excerpt from this work, Friedman elaborates on this view.

While there are a lot of similarities in kind between the previous era of globalization and the one we are now in, what is new today is the degree and intensity with which the world is being tied together into a single globalized marketplace and village. What is also new is the sheer number of people and countries able to partake of today's globalized economy and information networks, and to be affected by them. The pre-1914 era of globalization may have been intense, but many developing countries in that era were left out of it. The pre-1914 era may have been large in scale relative to its time, but it was minuscule in absolute terms compared to today. Daily foreign exchange trading in 1900 was measured in the millions of dollars. In 1992, it was $820 billion a day, according to the New York Federal Reserve, and by April 1998 it was up to $1.5 trillion a day, and still rising. Around 1900, private capital flows from developed countries to developing ones could be measured in the hundreds of millions of dollars and relatively few countries were involved. By 2000, it was being measured in the hundreds of billions of dollars, with dozens of countries involved. This new era of globalization, compared to the one before World War I, is turbocharged.

But today's era of globalization is not only different in degree; in some very important ways it is also different in kind—both technologically and politically. Technologically speaking, it is different in that the previous era of globalization was built around falling transportation costs. Thanks to the invention of the railroad, the steamship and the automobile, people could get to a lot more places faster and cheaper and they could trade with a lot more places faster and cheaper. But as *The Economist* has noted, today's era of globalization is built around falling telecommunications costs—thanks to microchips, satellites, fiber optics and the Internet. These new information technologies are able to weave the world together even tighter. These technologies mean that developing countries don't just have to trade their raw materials to the West and get finished products in return; they mean that developing countries can become big-time producers as well. These technologies also allow companies to locate different parts of their production, research and marketing in different countries, but still tie them together through computers and teleconferencing as though they were in one place. Also, thanks to the combination of computers and cheap telecommunications, people can now offer and trade services globally—from medical advice to software writing to data processing—services that could never really be traded before. And why not? A three-minute call (in 1996 dollars) between New York and London cost $300 in 1930. Today it is almost free through the Internet.

These technologies are making it possible not only for traditional nation-states and corporations to reach farther, faster, cheaper and deeper around the world than ever before, but also for individuals to do so. I was reminded of this point close to home, when in the summer of 1998 my then seventy-nine-year-old mother, Margaret Friedman, who lives in Minneapolis, called me sounding very upset. "What's wrong, Mom?" I asked. "Well," she said, "I've been playing bridge on the Internet with three Frenchmen and they keep speaking French to each other and I can't understand them." When I chuckled at the thought of my card-shark mom playing bridge with three Frenchmen on the Net, she took a little umbrage. "Don't laugh," she said, "I was playing bridge with someone in Siberia the other day."

Friedman describes globalization "as an international system—the dominant international system that replaced the Cold War system after the fall of the Berlin Wall."

When I say that globalization has replaced the Cold War as the defining international system, what exactly do I mean?

I mean that, as an international system, the Cold War had its own structure of power: the balance between the United States and the U.S.S.R. The Cold War had its own rules: in foreign affairs, neither superpower would encroach on the other's sphere of influence; in economics, less developed countries would focus on nurturing their own national industries, developing countries on export-led growth, communist countries on autarky and Western economies on regulated trade. The Cold War had its own dominant ideas: the clash between communism and capitalism, as well as detente, nonalignment and perestroika. The Cold War had its own demographic trends: the movement of people from east to west was largely frozen by the Iron Curtain, but the movement from south to north was a more steady flow. The Cold War had its own perspective on the globe: the world was a space divided into the communist camp, the Western camp, and the neutral camp, and everyone's country was in one of them. The Cold War had its own defining technologies: nuclear weapons and the second Industrial Revolution were dominant, but for many people in developing countries the hammer and sickle were still relevant tools. The Cold War had its own defining measurement: the throw weight of nuclear missles. And lastly, the Cold War had its own defining anxiety: nuclear annihilation. When taken all together the elements of this Cold War system influenced the domestic politics, commerce and foreign relations of virtually every country in the world.

Today's era of globalization is a similar international system, with its own unique attributes, which contrast sharply with those of the Cold

War. To begin with the Cold War system was characterized by one overarching feature—division. The world was a divided-up, chopped-up place and both your threats and opportunities in the Cold War system tended to grow out of who you were divided from. Appropriately, this Cold War system was symbolized by a single word: the *wall*—the Berlin Wall. One of my favorite descriptions of that world was provided by Jack Nicholson in the movie *A Few Good Men.* Nicholson plays a Marine colonel who is the commander of the U.S. base in Cuba, at Guantánamo Bay. In the climactic scene of the movie, Nicholson is pressed by Tom Cruise to explain how a certain weak soldier under Nicholson's command, Santiago, was beaten to death by his own fellow Marines: "You want answers?" shouts Nicholson. "You want answers?" I want the truth, retorts Cruise. "You can't handle the truth," says Nicholson. "Son, we live in a world that has walls and those walls have to be guarded by men with guns. Who's gonna do it? You? You, Lieutenant Weinberg? I have a greater responsibility than you can possibly fathom. You weep for Santiago and you curse the Marines. You have that luxury. You have the luxury of not knowing what I know—that Santiago's death, while tragic, probably saved lives. And my existence, while grotesque and incomprehensible to you, saves lives. You don't want the truth because deep down in places you don't talk about at parties, you want me on that wall. you need me on that wall."

The globalization system is a bit different. It also has one overarching feature—integration. The world has become an increasingly interwoven place, and today, whether you are a company or a country, your threats and opportunities increasingly derive from who you are connected to. This globalization system is also characterized by a single word: the *Web.* So in the broadest sense we have gone from a system built around division and walls to a system increasingly built around integration and webs. In the Cold War we reached for the "hotline," which was a symbol that we were all divided but at least two people were in charge—

the United States and the Soviet Union—and in the globalization system we reach for the Internet, which is a symbol that we are all increasingly connected and nobody is quite in charge.

This leads to many other differences between the globalization system and the Cold War system. The globalization system, unlike the Cold War system, is not frozen, but a dynamic ongoing process. That's why I define globalization this way: it is the inexorable integration of markets, nation-states and technologies to a degree never witnessed before—in a way that is enabling individuals, corporations and nation-states to reach around the world farther, faster, deeper and cheaper than ever before, and in a way that is enabling the world to reach into individuals, corporations and nation-states farther, faster, deeper, cheaper than ever before. This process of globalization is also producing a powerful backlash from those brutalized or left behind by this new system.

The driving idea behind globalization is free-market capitalism—the more you let market forces rule and the more you open your economy to free trade and competition, the more efficient and flourishing your economy will be. Globalization means the spread of free-market capitalism to virtually every country in the world. Therefore, globalization also has its own set of economic rules—rules that revolve around opening, deregulating and privatizing your economy, in order to make it more competitive and attractive to foreign investment. In 1975, at the height of the Cold War, only 8 percent of countries worldwide had liberal, free-market capital regimes, and foreign direct investment at the time totaled only $23 billion, according to the World Bank. By 1997, the number of countries with liberal economic regimes constituted 28 percent, and foreign investment totaled $644 billion.

Unlike the Cold War system, globalization has its own dominant culture, which is why it tends to be homogenizing to a certain degree. In previous eras this sort of cultural homogenization happened on a regional scale—the Romanization of Western Europe and the Mediterranean world, the Islamification of Central Asia, North Africa, Europe and the Middle East by the Arabs and later the Ottomans, or the Russification of Eastern and Central Europe and parts of Eurasia under the Soviets. Culturally speaking, globalization has tended to involve the spread (for better and for worse) of Americanization—from Big Macs to iMacs to Mickey Mouse.

Globalization has its own defining technologies: computerization, miniaturization, digitization, satellite communications, fiber optics and the Internet, which reinforce its defining perspective of integration. Once a country makes the leap into the system of globalization, its elites begin to internalize this perspective of integration, and always try to locate themselves in a global context.

The nation states, says Friedman, particularly the Soviet Union and the United States, were the focal point of the Cold War. The new globalization system deviates from this pattern.

Last, and most important, globalization has its own defining structure of power, which is much more complex than the Cold War structure. The Cold War system was built exclusively around nation-states. You acted on the world in that system through your state. The Cold War was primarily a drama of states confronting states, balancing states and aligning with states. And, at a system, the Cold War was balanced at the center by two superstates: the United States and the Soviet Union.

The globalization system, by contrast, is built around three balances, which overlap and affect one another. The first is the traditional balance between nation-states. In the globalization system, the United States is now the sole and dominant superpower and all other nations are subordinate to it to one degree or another. The balance of power between the United States and the other states, though, still matters for the stability of this system. And it can still explain a lot of the news you read on the front page of the papers, whether it is the containment of Iraq in the Middle East or the expansion of NATO against Russia in Central Europe.

The second balance in the globalization system is between nation-states and global markets. These global markets are made up of millions of investors moving money around the world with the click of a mouse. I call them "the Electronic Herd," and this herd gathers in key global financial centers, such as Wall Street, Hong Kong, London and Frankfurt, which I call "the Supermarkets." The attitudes and actions of the Electronic Herd and the Supermarkets can have a huge impact on nation-states today, even to the point of triggering the downfall of governments. Who ousted Suharto in Indonesia in 1998? It wasn't another state, it was the Supermarkets, by withdrawing their support for, and confidence in, the Indonesian economy. You will not understand the front page of newspapers today unless you bring the Supermarkets into your analysis. Because the United States can destroy you by dropping bombs and the Supermarkets can destroy you by downgrading your bonds. In other words, the United States is the dominant player in maintaining the globalization gameboard, but it is not alone in influencing the moves on that gameboard. This globalization gameboard today is a lot like a Ouija board—sometimes pieces are moved around by the obvious hand of the superpower, and sometimes they are moved around by hidden hands of the Supermarkets.

The third balance that you have to pay attention to in the globalization system—the one that is really the newest of all—is the balance between individuals and nation-states. Because globalization has brought down many of the walls that limited the movement and reach of people, and because it has simultaneously wired the world into networks, it gives more power to individuals to influence both markets and na-

tion-states than at any time in history. Individuals can increasingly act on the world stage directly—unmediated by a state. So you have today not only a superpower, not only Supermarkets, but, as will be demonstrated later in the book, you now have Super-empowered individuals. Some of these Super-empowered individuals are quite angry, some of them quite wonderful—but all of them are now able to act directly on the world stage.

Without the knowledge of the U.S. government, Long-Term Capital Management—a few guys with a hedge fund in Greenwich, Connecticut—amassed more financial bets around the world than all the foreign reserves of China. Osama bin Laden, a Saudi millionaire with his own global network, declared war on the United States in the late 1990s, and the U.S. Air Force retaliated with a cruise missile attack on him (where he resided in Afghanistan) as though he were another nation-state. Think about that. The United States fired 75 cruise missiles, at $1 million apiece, at a person! That was a superpower against a Super-empowered angry man. Jody Williams won the Nobel Peace Prize in 1997 for her contribution to the international ban on landmines. She achieved that ban not only without much government help, but in the face of opposition from all the major powers. And what did she say was her secret weapon for organizing 1,000 different human rights and arms control groups on six continents? "E-mail."

Nation-states, and the American superpower in particular, are still hugely important today, but so too now are Supermarkets and Super-empowered individuals. You will never understand the globalization system, or the front page of the morning paper, unless you see it as a complex interaction between all three of these actors: states bumping up against states, states bumping up against Supermarkets, and Supermarkets and states bumping up against Super-empowered individuals.

Abbas Amanat
ISLAMIC TERRORISM

On September 11, 2001, nineteen Muslim Arabs, fifteen of them from Saudi Arabia, hijacked four planes; two of them they crashed into the World Trade Center in New York, bringing down both towers; a third plane rammed into the Pentagon in Washington, D.C., causing severe damage; the fourth plane apparently was headed for the White House, but when passengers attacked the hijackers, it crashed in a field in Pennsylvania. In all, more than 3,000 people perished in the September 11 attacks. The meticulously planned operation was the work of Al Qaeda, an international terrorist network of militant Muslims.

The leader of Al Qaeda, Osama bin Laden, scion of an immensely wealthy Saudi Arabian family, operated from Afghanistan with the protection and support of the radical fundamentalist Taliban who ruled the country. When Taliban leaders refused to turn bin Laden over to the United States, President George W. Bush, supported by a coalition of many states, launched a military campaign whose ultimate goal was the destruction of international terrorism. Local Afghan forces opposed to the Taliban, assisted by American air power, which proved decisive, defeated the Taliban in a few weeks.

The new leaders of Afghanistan would no longer permit their country to serve as a haven and training center for radical Islamic terrorists. But with Al Qaeda cells located in scores of countries—and bin Laden still unaccounted for—the war against international terrorism was not over. On numerous occasions, President Bush and his chief advisors declared that the attack on Afghanistan was directed against "evildoers" and not against Muslims in general and the Islamic faith. However, bin Laden and his followers viewed their struggle against the United States as a holy war against the infidel. In 1998, bin Laden told his followers that the stationing of American troops in Saudi Arabia, "the land of the two holy Mosques," demonstrated that America "had spearheaded the crusade against the Islamic nation." To be sure, the actions of bin Laden and his followers violated core Islamic teachings. At the same time, however, terrorists found religious justification for their actions in Islamic tradition. The early followers of Muhammad, says the Middle Eastern Scholar Bernard Lewis, divided the world

> into two houses: the House of Islam, in which a Muslim government ruled and Muslim law prevailed, and the House of War, the rest of the world . . . ruled by infidels. Between the two, there was to be a perpetual state of war until the entire world either embraced Islam or submitted to the rule of the Muslim state. . . . For Osama bin Laden, 2001 marks the resumption of the war for the religious dominance of the world that began in the seventh century. For him and his followers, this is a moment of opportunity. Today, America exemplifies the civilization and embodies the leadership of the House of War, and it . . . has become degenerate and demoralized, ready to be overthrown.

Bin Laden is a religious fanatic, an absolutist who cannot tolerate pluralism, and a theocrat who hoped to use the state's power to impose a narrow, intolerant version of Islam on others. He and his followers were true believers convinced that they were doing God's will, for which they would be richly rewarded in Paradise. This helps to explain why Al Qaeda had little difficulty recruiting people willing, if not eager, to engage in suicidal attacks against the enemies of God and their centers of evil.

In the following selection, Abbas Amanat analyzes the roots of Islamic radicalism, focusing on the resentment many Muslims have against the West.

To this author, a historian of the Middle East who grew up in that part of the world, bin Laden's message of violence comes as a sobering reminder of what has become of the Middle East. This is not only because an outrage of unprecedented magnitude has been committed by some Middle Easterners against the U.S., which is both demonized in that region and seductive to many who live there. Nor is it because such an act confirmed the worst stereotypes of violence and fanaticism long associated with Islam and the Middle East. It was also because the outrage revealed much about the undeniable and alarming growth of religious extremism in the Muslim world, a trend that has been deeply intertwined with the tortured historical experience of becoming modern. . . .

1.

The emergence of the construct we call Islamic extremism, with its penchant for defiance, resentment, and violence, has its roots in the history of the Muslim sense of decline and its unhappy encounter with the dominant West. It is sobering to remind ourselves how frequently the Middle East, as one part of the Muslim world, has been visited by waves of violence in its recent history. Since the end of the Second World War, the area extending from Egypt and Turkey in the west to Afghanistan in the northwest and Yemen in the south has suffered at least ten major wars—and that's not counting the U.S. engagement in Afghanistan after September 11. Casualties have run into millions. Populations have been uprooted, societies torn up by their roots, political structures demolished—all on a massive scale.

Three of the region's wars were fought with Western powers (Britain's and France's attacks on Egypt during the Suez crisis in 1956; the Soviet Union's long, losing effort to subjugate Afghanistan in the 1980s; the American-led campaign to liberate Kuwait from Iraq in 1990–91); Israel and its Arab neighbors waged five wars (1948, 1956, 1967, 1973 and 1982); Yemen and Lebanon have suffered prolonged civil wars; and Iraq and Iran fought for eight years. The transforming effects of these crises haunted the last several generations in the Middle East. Throughout the region people have become ever more disillusioned with the deeply-entrenched dictatorships in their own countries, with the collapse of democratic institutions, hollow nationalistic rhetoric, and with their failing economies.

In the minds of many, Western powers shared the blame, both directly and indirectly. Whether based on historical reality or faulty perception, holding the Western powers responsible made special sense against the backdrop of a powerful West and a powerless Middle East. From the days of the European colonial powers in the 19th century to the more recent interventions of the superpowers, there has been a pattern of diplomatic, military and economic presence tying the fate of the Middle East and its resources to the West. Whether motivated by oil, grand strategy or support for Israel, the Western powers were either involved in, or perceived to be behind, most of the region's political crises.

As a result, for new generations of Middle Easterners perceptions of the West, and particularly of the U.S., dramatically changed for the worse. Long gone were the images of well-wishing Yankees who established schools, universities and hospitals, distributed food, and supported nationalist endeavors. Instead, fascination with a luster of American popular culture was only heightened thanks to Hollywood and American high tech—computers, video games, and satellite dishes. Yet in a paradoxical turn, as the lines of visa-seekers in front of U.S. consulates grew longer, a cloud of mistrust and resentment against the U.S. also settled over the region. The people in the Middle East began to view American society through the lenses of sitcoms and softwares. To many unaccustomed eyes, the U.S. seemed like the center of a greedy, materialistic and uncaring world obsessed with violence and promiscuity. The U.S.'s unreserved support for Israel, its backing of unpopular regimes, and its fighter jets over Middle Eastern skies only added to anti-American feelings.

2.

Mistrust toward the West deepened as a result of the problematic way the Middle East improvised its own version of modernity. Since the beginning of the 20th century, Westernization has transformed lifestyles and expectations. Yet, despite an undeniable measure of growth and material improvement, today's Middle East by most economic indicators is still one of the least developed regions in the world. It is grappling endlessly with failed centralized planning, high birthrates, lopsided distribution of wealth, high unemployment, widespread corruption, inefficient bureaucracies, and environmental and health problems. The frustration endemic among the young urban classes—often the children of rural migrants who came to the cities in search of a better life and a higher income—is a response to these conundrums.

For the population of the Middle East, progressively younger because of high birthrates, uprooted from their traditional setting, and deprived of illusive privileges that they can see around them and on television screens but cannot have, the familiar and comforting space of Islam offers a welcoming alternative. Daily

prayers, Friday sermons, Koranic study groups, Islamic charities—these are all part of that space. But so are the street demonstrations and the clandestine pamphlets, with their fiery anti-establishment, anti-secular, and anti-Zionist message.

In dealing with these restive multitudes, the governments of the Middle East and their associated ruling elites have little to offer. They are themselves part of the problem as they contribute to the public perception of powerlessness. In the period right after World War II, nationalist ideologies were highly effective in mobilizing the public against the European colonial presence. But over time they often hindered the growth of democratic institutions and the emergence of an enduring civil society. The army officers who came to power in Egypt, Syria, Iraq, and elsewhere through military coups, and prolonged their leadership through repressive means, invested heavily in anti-Western rhetoric. Yet facing the erosion of their own legitimacy, they learned to pay a lip service to the rising Islamic sentiments in their societies, exploiting them as a cushion between the elite and the masses and to suppress individual freedoms.

The predictable victims of this appeasement were the modernizing urban middle classes of the Middle East. Though small and vulnerable, these middle classes were crucial conduits for modernizing even as they preserved a sense of national culture. Egypt, Iraq, Syria, Turkey, and Iran, in their rush for an illusive economic growth, and greater equity, purposely undermined the economic bases of their middle classes. They did so through heavy-handed state planning and the mindless nationalization programs. The middle classes in the Middle East today, besieged and intimidated, are no longer willing or able to take up the cause of democratic reforms. They have instead given rise to a spoiled crust of the politically silenced and submissive class whose voice of protest is heard, increasingly, through extremist causes.

Out of this milieu came Mohamed Atta [who crashed the hijacked plane into the

World Trade Center], a failed son of an affluent Egyptian lawyer. Another example is bin Laden's chief lieutenant, Ayman al-Zawahiri, a physician from a celebrated Egyptian family.

This staggering reorientation toward radical Islam needs to be understood in light of a deeper crisis of identity in the Arab world. In the post-colonial period, most nation-states in that region had to improvise their own ideologies of territorial nationalism in order to hold together what were often disjointed local and ethnic identities. At the same time they had to remain loyal to the ideology of pan-Arabism—the notion, or dream, that all Arab peoples make up one supernation—a project that was destined to fail dismally. Egypt came out of the colonial experience with what might have been the basis for its own Egyptian nationalism, but under Gamal Abdel Nasser, it traded that away for leadership of the pan-Arab cause. Yet the experiences of secular pan-Arabism, whether that of the Nasser era in the 1950s and 60s or the Ba'thist regimes of Iraq and Syria in the 1960s and 1970s, proved illusory to the intellectuals who championed it. It was even more unrewarding to the Arab masses who for decades were exposed to the state-run propaganda machines and to the often demagogic street politics. The harsh realities of the military and paramilitary regimes of the Arab world sobered even the most ardent supporters of Arab nationalism.

It was in this environment of despair that the disempowered Arab masses came to share the common cause of confronting Zionism. Resistance to the establishment of the Jewish homeland since the end of World War I and to the creation of the state of Israel in 1947 offered the Arab world a rallying point of great symbolic power. The subsequent experiences of multiple defeats in wars against Israel revived in the Arab psyche memories of prolonged colonial domination. From the Arab nationalist perspective, Zionism was not merely another form of imagined nationalism rooted in the 19th century, but a project designed by the West to perpetuate its imperial presence and protect its vested interests in the region—the latest manifestation of centuries of enmity against the Muslim peoples. For many in the Arab world it was comforting to believe that the reason why hundreds of millions of Arabs could not defeat Israel was because Western powers were protecting it. And more often than not there was ample evidence to convince them of the validity of their claim.

3.

Not surprisingly, the sense of despair toward repressive regimes at home and helplessness against the consolidation of the neighboring Zionist state engendered a new spirit of Islamic solidarity. It was radical in its politics, monolithic in its approach, and defiant toward the West.

The decisive shift came not inside the Arab world but with the 1979 revolution in Iran. The establishment of an Islamic republic under the leadership of the uncompromising Ayatollah Khomeini evoked throughout the Muslim world the long-cherished desire for creating a genuine Islamic regime. Even though it was preached by a radical Shi'a clergy who committed enormous atrocities against his own people, the Iranian model of revolutionary Islam was viewed as pointing the way to an "authentic" and universalist Islam. Through cassette tapes and demonstrations, Iranian revolutionaries managed to topple the Shah and the mighty Pahlavi regime despite its vast military arsenal, secularizing program, and Western backing. Even more empowering was the revolution's anti-imperialist rhetoric.

After his followers besieged the American embassy and held its staff hostage in 1980–81, Khomeini labeled the U.S. as the Great Satan for backing the "Pharaonic" powers—a label for the shah and conservative rulers elsewhere in the region—and for repressing the "disinherited" of the earth.

The Iraq-Iran War of 1980–88 further established the appeal of the paradigm of martyrdom that had long been deeply rooted in Shi'a Islam. That conflict was portrayed as an apocalyptic jihad between the forces of truth and falsehood. In addition to defending their own nation, the Iranians believed they were exporting their revolution. As the slogan on the banners declared and as the battle cries of many teenage volunteers confirmed, the path of Islamic liberation stretched across the battlefields to the Shi'a holy cities of Karbala' and Najaf in Iraq all the way to Jerusalem.

Even if the Iranian revolution failed to take root elsewhere, the celebration of martyrdom found resonance far and wide. The revolutionary Shiites of Lebanon's Hezbollah, and later the young Palestinians who eagerly volunteered for suicide bombings on behalf of the Hamas and Islamic Jihad, saw martyrdom as a way of empowerment. It is not difficult to see the same traits among the hijackers of September 11.

The accelerated pace of Islamic radicalism in the early 1980s, whether inspired by the Iranian revolution or reacting to it, helped shape the outlook of a generation from which came the extremism of Osama bin Laden himself. In his twenties, he was a pious, though uninspiring, student in Jidda University in Saudi Arabia. He came from a superrich family with close connections to the Saudi royalty. In November 1979, he must have witnessed the siege of the Grand Mosque of Mecca and the revolt under the leadership of a messianic figure who claimed to have received direct authority from the Prophet to render justice. The quick suppression of this revolt by the Saudi authorities came only a month after the signing of the Camp David peace agreement between Israel and Egypt. The treaty was received by the Islamic activists throughout the Arab world as a betrayal to the Arab and Islamic causes. Only a year later, in October 1980, the Egyptian president, Anwar al-Sadat, was assassinated by a splinter group of the Muslim Brothers with Ayman al-Zawahiri, bin Laden's future lieutenant, was associated.

The Mecca uprising and Sadat's assassination were both inspired by a tradition of religious radicalism going back to the Society of the Muslim Brothers in the 1920s and 30s and be-

fore that to the Wahhabi movement that began in the late 18th century. The central doctrine of Wahhabism was a return to the way of "virtuous ancestors," a highly regressive, monolithic interpretation of Islam known as Salafiyya, a doctrinal propensity that for centuries encouraged strict adherence to puritanical principles.

In the early 20th century, the Salafiyya played a central part in the shaping of Saudi Arabia as an Islamic state. It also served as the guiding doctrine for the Muslim Brother's goal of moral and political reconstruction. Inspired by the ideas of Sayyid Qutb, a leader of the Muslim Brothers—who was executed in 1966 by the Nasser regime—this ideology received a new lease on life. A true believer was required to "renounce" the dark sacrilege of his secular surroundings. The primary targets were the regimes of the Arab world, whose secularism was labeled a return to the "paganism" of pre-Islamic times. . .

The doctrine of Salafiyya and its articulation by Sayyid Qutb gained an overwhelming currency among Islamic radicals in the early 1980s. But the wilderness that might serve as a refuge for them could not be recreated in the oil-rich Saudi Arabia of bin Laden or in the tourist-infested Egypt of al-Zawahiri. Instead, Afghanistan beckoned. The burgeoning resistance movement against the occupying Soviet forces there was highly appealing to radical and moderate sentiments alike. It could unite activists of all Islamic persuasions for a common cause of fighting the spread of the godless communism.

Amanat then discusses how Osama bin Laden and other Arabs from Morocco to Yemen devoted to militant Wahhabism fought in Afghanistan where they came to be known as Arab Afghans. In Afghanistan, bin Laden and his cohorts drew up plans for the creation of a world Islamic state governed by Islamic law, a revival of the medieval Caliphate. After the defeat of the Soviets, bin Laden returned to Saudi Arabia and then went to Sudan, now ruled by a militant Islamic regime. The Gulf War fueled his anti-Americanism, for he regarded as an affront to Wahhabi Islam the stationing of infidel American troops in Saudi Arabia, the home of Islam's holiest shrines.

4.

. . . Bin Laden's personal odyssey further affirmed his anti-American resolve. In 1994, under American pressure, the Saudi authorities revoked his passport and froze his assets. Two years later Washington succeeded in pressuring Sudan to deny him the safe haven he had enjoyed there. As a last resort he sought refuge with the Taliban, who had taken control of Kabul in 1996, in exchange for his financial and logistic support.

The Taliban was the other side of the al Qaeda coin. The Wahhabi propaganda campaign, which went on under Saudi auspices for at least two decades, was the chief factor behind the emergence of this militant student movement that eventually took over Afghanistan. In the 1980s and 90s through patronage and missionary work, financing the construction of new communal mosques from Indonesia and the Philippines to sub-Saharan Africa and Central Asia, training young students of many nationalities in pro-Wahhabi subsidized seminaries, making available to the public the Wahhabi literature, establishing interest-free charity and scholarships for the poor, facilitating the transfer of the Hajj pilgrims, and backing conservative clerical elements with Wahhabi proclivities, the Saudi establishment built a strong and growing network that is now changing the face of Islam throughout the towns and villages of the Muslim world. Inadvertently, this network proved to be a fertile ground for garnering support for bin Laden from Pakistan and southern Afghanistan to Central Asia, Africa and Southeast Asia.

The Taliban movement took root among the dislocated and deprived children of the Afghan refugees trained in the religious schools of Pakistan financed by private Saudi funding. Armed with Wahhabi fervor for jihad and lit-tle else, under the auspices of the Pakistani army intelligence these seminarians were organized into a fighting force. The political lacuna that came about as a result of the devastating Afghan civil war opened the way for the Taliban's gradual advance and eventual takeover. The regime they established embodied all the neo-Wahhabi zeal that was preached in the Peshawar schools. It revived and imposed a strict patriarchal order deeply hostile to women and their education and public presence. It allowed battering, even killing, of women by their male relatives, enforced facial veiling, and closed most girls schools. It displayed extraordinary intolerance toward Shiites and other minorities, obliterated even the most primitive symbols of a modern culture, and undermined all human and individual rights. In the name of purging Afghanistan of factionalism and ending the civil war, the Taliban turned it into a miserable fortress whose people suffered from starvation and isolation.

In the year that bin Laden arrived in Afghanistan, he issued a fatwa, or religious ruling, that called upon all Muslims to kill Americans as a religious duty. The 1998 bombing of the American embassies in Nairobi and Dar es Salaam was, as far as we know, his first attempt to put his own ruling into practice. This came at the time when al Qaeda's merger with Egyptian Islamic Jihad—led by Ayman al-Zawahiri, who had recently masterminded the killing of fifty-eight tourists in Luxor, Egypt—and other terrorist organizations drastically increased bin Laden's capacity to wreak havoc. The U.S. tried to punish him for the embassy bombings by firing missiles into his camps. His emerging unscathed gave him greater confidence and enhanced his reputation for invincibility in the eyes of his followers.

For bin Laden and his al Qaeda associates, the terrorist war against the U.S. was a struggle rooted in Islam's noble past and ensured of victory by God. In this context, the attack on giant structures representing American economic and military might was a largely symbolic act that would, they hoped, miraculously subdue their enemies, just as the infidels of early Islam eventually succumbed to the Prophet's attacks on their caravans. This theory of terror, violent and indiscriminate, though utterly against the mainstream interpretation of Islam, attracted a small but committed group of devotees who also saw self-sacrifice as a permissible avenue toward symbolic achievement of their goals.

In several respects, however, bin Laden's apocalyptic vision was grounded in reality and geared to the possible. He and his associates were men of worldly capabilities who could employ business administration models to generate revenue, invest capital in the market, create a disciplined leadership, recruit volunteers, incorporate other extremist groups, organize and maintain new cells, issue orders and communicate through a franchised network of semi-autonomous units on a global scale. This mix of the messianic and the pragmatic allowed al Qaeda to tailor its rhetoric to the grievances of its growing audience and to carry out recruitment and indoctrination on a wider scale.

The vast majority of Muslims do not approve of bin Laden's terrorism, nor do they share his ambition to build a monolithic community based on a pan-Islamic order. Yet there is an undeniable sympathy for the way he has manipulated grievances and symbols. The contrasting images of the "pagan" America and the "authentic" Islam find currency in wide and diverse quarters. One example is the young boys among Afghan and Pakistani refugees who were brainwashed in the Saudi-funded Wahhabi seminaries of Peshawar—and from whose ranks rose the Taliban (the word itself means "students"). Another is the new generation of Western-educated Arab middle classes who were recruited to the al Qaeda's suicide cells in Europe.

We can read in the testament of Mohamed Atta, the Egyptian ringleader of the September 11 attacks, the typical obsessive enthusiasm of a born-again Muslim. As a reward for his resort to massive terror and destruction, which he carried out with resolve and precision, Atta

seeks the Koranic promise of heavenly recompense especially reserved for martyrs. His literal reading of the sacred text is imbued with sexual references. "Know," he promises his accomplices, "that the gardens of paradise are waiting for you in all their beauty. And the women of paradise are waiting, calling out, 'Come hither, friends of God.' They are dressed in their most beautiful clothing." This is all the more glaring, and perversely pathetic, when contrasted with Atta's final encounters in a Florida strip club. One can only imagine that he was gazing at the barely-clad strippers of this world in anticipation of the houris—beautiful maidens awaiting the brave and virtuous—in paradise. This was the reward he expected for his martyrdom in the "battle for the sake of God," which he was waging, as he himself reminded us, in the "way of the pious forefathers." This surreal mix of the pious and the profane, backed by a litany of Koranic verses, reveals a discomfiting pseudomodern crust over the hard core of extremism.

As for bin Laden himself, he came into the spotlight after September 11 having shrouded himself and his cause in an apocalyptic aura. His October 7 statement broadcast on television, both in tone and content, alluded to a seminal narrative of Islam. Above all, he said, he placed his total trust in God as he waged the struggle of true believers against infidels, confident of the ultimate reward of martyrdom. His references to the impending fall of the "hypocrites"—those Muslim individuals and governments who were not supportive of his cause—and to the sure victory of the righteous on horseback and armed with swords— presumably in contrast to the sophisticated weaponry of his enemies—all have resonance in the encoded story of early Islam. In a statement at the same time, bin Laden's chief lieutenant, al-Zawahiri, referred to the catastrophic loss of Muslim Spain at the end of the 15th century. This, too, was meant to remind Muslims of the greater days of Islam before its defeat by Christianity, hence complementing bin Laden's vision of the glorious past.

5.

That al-Qaeda effectively communicates to a wide audience far beyond its own extremist circle there can be no doubt. In doing so, it has found abundant opportunities, thanks to the global media, and thanks to complacency and ignorance of Western intelligence services and law enforcement agencies. The dilemmas and inconsistencies of U.S. foreign policy in the region also provided al Qaeda with its weapons of choice to appeal to the frustration and anger of the mainstream Muslims worldwide.

At the core of the resentment so widespread in the Arab and Islamic world is Israel and its treatment of the Palestinians in the occupied territories. Hundreds of millions of Arabs, and increasingly other Muslims as well, are now more then ever informed through media about the Palestinians' unending confrontations with the Israeli security forces. . . .

Broadcast through the Arab networks, and more recently on the global al-Jazeerah television network based in Qatar—the outlet of choice for bin Laden himself—these tragic depictions are increasingly intermingled with symbols of Islamic defiance: the suicidal missions of Hamas and Islamic Jihad against Israeli targets, the fiery anti-American and anti-Israeli slogans and sermons in Friday congregations. Added to this is the enormous level of Islamic radical pamphleteering with anti-American and anti-Zionist content, not infrequently laced in the Arabic textbooks with flagrant anti-Jewish racial references.

The politically repressive regimes of most Arab countries permit anti-Zionist (and even anti-Jewish) expressions as a safety valve. This further adds to the symbolic value of the Palestinian cause as a powerful expression of Arab unity with growing Islamic coloring. Since the Intifada of 1986 and the 1993 Oslo Peace Accord, the thrust of Arab public opinion has been directed toward the fate of the Palestinians in the occupied territories rather than against the very existence of Israel. Yet the oppressive Arab regimes still use the hypocritical rhetoric of national security as an impediment to the growth of democracy in their own countries. In such a repressive environment the mosque often functions as a political forum. There the differentiation between Israeli conduct and American foreign policy fades. Arab public opinion widely believes that the Jewish lobby in the U.S. is the sole determinant of American policy in the region and therefore makes little distinction between U.S. foreign policy and Israeli abuse of the Palestinians.

Proponents of Muslim piety also hold American "corrupting influences" responsible for the erosion of the assumed "authentic" mores of Islamic austerity and devotion. These influences are widely associated with the worst clichés of American popular culture and lifestyle. In this world of misperceptions, the globally permeating images of promiscuity, ostentatious wealth, organized crime, random violence, drug use, gluttony and wastefulness contrast sharply with the idealized Islamic virtues of moral outrage, self-sacrifice, otherworldliness, brotherhood, and piety. The extremists eagerly and skillfully sell these contrasts to the ill-informed Muslim masses, who more than ever now rely on visual images thanks to the power of the electronic media.

To Muslim viewers around the world these exaggerated contrasts offer an elusive comfort, since they seem to explain the root cause of the perceived malfunction of their own government and societies. They are all the more suggestive because they are shrewdly tied up with the story of sufferings of the Palestinian people at the hands of the Israelis and those of the Iraqi people under U.S.-upheld sanctions. On top of that, they are constantly reminded of the "defiling" of the Islamic holy lands by the presence of American troops in Saudi Arabia.

Bin Laden is a master at exploiting these symbolic references. The U.S. and its Western allies have tried to convince the world, and especially the Muslim world, that the campaign against bin Laden and al Qaeda is not directed at Islam but at terrorism. However, that differentiation won't carry much weight in the minds of many Muslims so long as bin Laden, "dead or alive," has at his disposal such potent propaganda weapons. The issue is not only the danger that he or people like him will turn their extremist dream into a religious war between Islam and the West. Equally important is that they will provoke an escalating conflict between militant neo-Wahhabi Islam and the retreating forces and quavering voices of moderation and tolerance in the Muslim world. Bin Laden presents to much of his audience the image of a messianic prophet. Even if he is killed for his cause, he will, in their eyes, have died a martyr's death.

Jacques Ellul
THE BETRAYAL OF THE WEST

Jacques Ellul (1912–1994), a French sociologist with a pronounced moralist bent, is known for his study of the impact of technology and bureaucracy on the modern world. In the following passages from *The Betrayal of the West* (1978), he assessed the historical uniqueness and greatness of Western civilization; twenty-five years later his insights still apply.

. . . I am not criticizing or rejecting other civilizations and societies; I have deep admiration for the institutions of the Bantu and other peoples (the Chinese among them) and for the inventions and poetry and architecture of the Arabs. I do not claim at all that the West is superior. In fact, I think it absurd to lay claim to superiority of any kind in these matters. What criterion would you apply? What scale of values would you use? I would add that the greatest fault of the West since the seventeenth century has been precisely its belief in its own unqualified superiority in all areas.

The thing, then, that I am protesting against is the silly attitude of western intellectuals in hating their own world and then illogically exalting all other civilizations. Ask yourself this question: If the Chinese have done away with binding the feet of women, and if the Moroccans, Turks, and Algerians have begun to liberate their women, whence did the impulse to these moves come from? From the West, and nowhere else! Who invented the "rights of man"? The same holds for the elimination of exploitation. Where did the move to socialism originate? In Europe, and in Europe alone. The Chinese, like the Algerians, are inspired by western thinking as they move toward socialism. Marx was not Chinese, nor was Robespierre an Arab. How easily the intellectuals forget this! The whole of the modern world, for better or for worse, is following a western model; no one imposed it on others, they have adopted it themselves, and enthusiastically.

I shall not wax lyrical about the greatness and benefactions of the West. Above all, I shall not offer a defense of the material goods Europe brought to the colonies. We've heard that kind of defense too often: "We built roads, hospitals, schools, and dams; we dug the oil wells. . . ." And the reason I shall say nothing of this invasion by the technological society is that I think it to be the West's greatest crime, as I have said at length elsewhere. The worst thing of all is that we exported our rationalist approach to things, our "science," our conception of the state, our bureaucracy, our nationalist ideology. It is this, far more surely than anything else, that has destroyed the other cultures of the world and shunted the history of the entire world onto a single track.

But is that all we can say of the West? No, the essential, central, undeniable fact is that the West was the first civilization in history to focus attention on the individual and on freedom. Nothing can rob us of the praise due us for that. We have been guilty of denials and betrayals (of these we shall be saying something more), we have committed crimes, but we have also caused the whole of mankind to take a gigantic step forward and to leave its childhood behind.

This is a point we must be quite clear on. If the world is everywhere rising up and accusing the West, if movements of liberation are everywhere under way, what accounts for this? Its sole source is the proclamation of freedom that the West has broadcast to the world. The West, and the West alone, is responsible for the movement that has led to the desire for freedom and to the accusations now turned back upon the West.

Today men point the finger of outrage at slavery and torture. Where did that kind of indignation originate? What civilization or culture cried out that slavery was unacceptable and torture scandalous? Not Islam, or Buddhism, or Confucius, or Zen, or the religions and moral codes of Africa and India! The West alone has defended the inalienable rights of the human person, the dignity of the individual, the man who is alone with everyone against him. But the West did not practice what it preached? The extent of the West's fidelity is indeed debatable: the whole European world has certainly not lived up to its own ideal all the time, but to say that it has never lived up to it would be completely false.

In any case, that is not the point. The point is that the West originated values and goals that spread throughout the world (partly through conquest) and inspired man to demand his freedom, to take his stand in the face of society and affirm his value as an individual. I shall not be presumptuous enough to try to "define" the freedom of the individual. . . .

. . . The West gave expression to what man—every man—was seeking. The West turned the whole human project into a conscious, deliberate business. It set the goal and called it freedom, or, at a later date, individual freedom. It gave direction to all the forces that were working in obscure ways, and brought to light the

value that gave history its meaning. Thereby, man became man.

The West attempted to apply in a conscious, methodical way the implications of freedom. The Jews were the first to make freedom the key to history and to the whole created order. From the very beginning their God was the God who liberates; his great deeds flowed from a will to give freedom to his people and thereby to all mankind. This God himself, moreover, was understood to be sovereignly free (freedom here was often confused with arbitrariness or with omnipotence). This was something radically new, a discovery with explosive possibilities. The God who was utterly free had nothing in common with the gods of eastern and western religions; he was different precisely because of his autonomy.

The next step in the same movement saw the Greeks affirming both intellectual and political liberty. They consciously formulated the rules for a genuinely free kind of thinking, the conditions for human freedom, and the forms a free society could take. Other peoples were already living in cities, but none of them had fought so zealously for the freedom of the city in relation to other cities, and for the freedom of the citizen within the city.

The Romans took the third step by inventing civil and institutional liberty and making political freedom the key to their entire politics. Even the conquests of the Romans were truly an unhypocritical expression of their intention of freeing peoples who were subject to dictatorships and tyrannies the Romans judged degrading. It is in the light of that basic thrust that we must continue to read Roman history. Economic motives undoubtedly also played a role, but a secondary one; to make economic causes the sole norm for interpreting history is in the proper sense superficial and inadequate. You cannot write history on the basis of your suspicions! If you do, you only project your own fantasies.

I am well aware, of course, that in each concrete case there was darkness as well as light, that liberty led to wars and conquests, that it rested on a base of slavery. I am not concerned here, however, with the excellence or defects of the concrete forms freedom took; I am simply trying to say (as others have before me) that at the beginning of western history we find the awareness, the explanation, the proclamation of freedom as the meaning and goal of history.

No one has ever set his sights as intensely on freedom as did the Jews and Greeks and Romans, the peoples who represented the entire West and furthered its progress. In so doing, they gave expression to what the whole of mankind was confusedly seeking. In the process we can see a progressive approach to the ever more concrete: from the Jews to the Greeks, and from the Greeks to the Romans there is no growth in consciousness, but there is the ongoing search for more concrete answers to the question of how freedom can be brought from the realm of ideas and incarnated in institutions, behavior, thinking, and so on.

Today the whole world has become the heir of the West, and we Westerners now have a twofold heritage: we are heirs to the evil the West has done to the rest of the world, but at the same time we are heirs to our forefathers' consciousness of freedom and to the goals of freedom they set for themselves. Other peoples, too, are heirs to the evil that has been inflicted on them, but now they have also inherited the consciousness of and desire for freedom. Everything they do today and everything they seek is an expression of what the western world has taught them. . . .

. . . Everything used to be so organized that wealth and poverty were stable states, determined (for example) by the traditional, accepted hierarchy, and that this arrangement was regarded as due to destiny or an unchangeable divine will. The West did two things: it destroyed the hierarchic structures and it did away with the idea of destiny. It thus showed the poor that their state was not something inevitable. This is something Marx is often credited with having done, but only because people are ignorant [of history]. It was Christianity that did away with the idea of destiny and fate. . . .

Once Christianity had destroyed the idea of destiny or fate, the poor realized that they were poor, and they realized that their condition was not inevitable. Then the social organisms that had made it possible to gloss over this fact were challenged and undermined from within.

Against all this background we can see why the whole idea of revolution is a western idea. Before the development of western thought, and apart from it, no revolution ever took place. Without the individual and freedom and the contradictory extremes to which freedom leads, a society cannot engender a revolution. Nowhere in the world—and I speak as one with a knowledge of history—has there ever been a revolution, not even in China, until the western message penetrated that part of the world. Present-day revolutions, whether in China or among the American Indians, are the direct, immediate, unmistakable fruit of the western genius. The entire world has been pupil to the West that it now rejects. . . .

. . . I wish only to remind the reader that the West has given the world a certain number of values, movements, and orientations that no one else has provided. No one else has done quite what the West has done. I wish also to remind the reader that the whole world is living, and living almost exclusively, by these values, ideas, and stimuli. There is nothing original about the "new" thing that is coming into existence in China or Latin America or Africa: it is all the fruit and direct consequence of what the West has given the world.

In the fifties it was fashionable to say that "the third world is now entering upon the stage of history." The point was not, of course, to deny that Africa or Japan had a history. What the cliché was saying, and rightly saying, was that these peoples were now participating in the creative freedom of history and the dialectic of the historical process. Another way of putting it is that the West had now set the whole world in motion. It had released a tidal wave that would perhaps eventually drown it. There had been great changes in the past and vast migrations of peoples; there had been planless quests for power and the building of gigantic empires that collapsed overnight. The West represented something entirely new because it set the world in movement in every area and at every level; it represented, that is, a coherent approach to reality. Everything—ideas, armies, the state, philosophy, rational methods, and social organization—conspired in the global change the West had initiated.

It is not for me to judge whether all this was a good thing or bad. I simply observe that the entire initiative came from the West, that everything began there. I simply observe that the peoples of the world had abided in relative ignorance and [religious] repose until the encounter with the West set them on their journey.

Please, then, don't deafen us with talk about the greatness of Chinese or Japanese civilization. These civilizations existed indeed, but in a larval or embryonic state; they were approximations, essays. They always related to only one sector of the human or social totality and tended to be static and immobile. Because the West was motivated by the ideal of freedom and had discovered the individual, it alone launched society in its entirety on its present course.

Again, don't misunderstand me. I am not saying that European science was superior to Chinese science, nor European armies to Japanese armies; I am not saying that the Christian religion was superior to Buddhism or Confucianism; I am not saying that the French or English political system was superior to that of the Han dynasty. I am saying only that the West discovered what no one else had discovered; freedom and the individual, and that this discovery later set everything else in motion. Even the most solidly established religions could not help changing under the influence. . . .

It was not economic power or sudden technological advances that made the West what it is. These played a role, no doubt, but a negligible one in comparison with the great change— the discovery of freedom and the individual— that represents the goal and desire implicit in the history of all civilizations. That is why, in speaking of the West, I unhesitatingly single out freedom from the whole range of values. After all, we find justice, equality, and peace everywhere. Every civilization that has attained a certain level has claimed to be a civilization of justice or peace. But which of them has ever spoken of the individual? Which of them has been reflectively conscious of freedom as a value?

The decisive role of the West's discovery of freedom and the individual is beyond question, but the discovery has brought with it . . . tragic consequences. First, the very works of the West now pass judgment on it. For, having proclaimed freedom and the individual, the West played false in dealing with other peoples. It subjected, conquered, and exploited them, even while it went on talking about freedom. It made the other peoples conscious of their enslavement by intensifying that enslavement and calling it freedom. It destroyed the social structures of tribes and clans, turned men into isolated atoms, and shaped them into a worldwide proletariat, and all the time kept on talking of the great dignity of the individual: his autonomy, his power to decide for himself, his capacity for choice, his complex and many-sided reality. . . .

. . . Reason makes it possible for the individual to master impulse, to choose the ways in which he will exercise his freedom, to calculate the chances for success and the manner in which a particular action will impinge upon the group, to understand human relations, and to communicate. Communication is the highest expression of freedom, but it has little meaning unless there is a content which, in the last analysis, is supplied by reason. . . . Here precisely we have the magnificent discovery made by the West: that the individual's whole life can be, and even is, the subtle, infinitely delicate interplay of reason and freedom.

This interplay achieved its highest form in both the Renaissance and classical literature since the Enlightenment. No other culture made this discovery. We of the West have the most rounded and self-conscious type of man.

For, the development of reason necessarily implied reason's critique of its own being and action as well as a critique of both liberty and reason, through a return of reason upon itself and a continuous reflection which gave rise to new possibilities for the use of freedom as controlled by new developments of reason. . . .

Let me return to my main argument. It was the West that established the splendid interplay of freedom, reason, self-control, and coherent behavior. It thus produced a type of human being that is unique in history: true western man. (I repeat: the type belongs neither to nature nor to the animal world; it is a deliberate construct achieved through effort.) I am bound to say that I regard this type as superior to anything I have seen or known elsewhere. A value judgment, a personal and subjective preference? Of course. But I am not ready on that account to turn my back on the construction and on the victory and affirmation it represents. Why? Because the issue is freedom itself, and because I see no other satisfactory model that can replace what the West has produced.

REVIEW QUESTIONS

1. According to Friedman, how did globalization shift from reliance on falling transportation costs to reliance on falling telecommunications costs?
2. How are globalization and free-market capitalism linked? How do global investors wield power over nation-states?
3. Acording to Abbas Amanat, what grievances do Muslims have against the West in general and the United States in particular?
4. If you were having a discussion with an Arab who shared these grievances, how would you respond?
5. What contribution, according to Jacques Ellul, did the West make to human life everywhere?
6. According to Ellul, what was the West's "greatest crime"?
7. Ellul asserts on one hand that he does "not claim at all that the West is superior," and on the other he characterizes Chinese or Japanese civilization as existing only "in a larval or embryonic state." Compare these statements in the context of the entire passage. Are they contradictory?

Credits continued from page iv.

Chapter 1 continued

Section 3 P. 12: From *The Prince* by Niccolò Machiavelli, translated by Luigi Ricci, revised by E.R.P. Vincent (1935), pp. 92–93, 97–99, 101–103, by permission of Oxford University Press. *Section 4* P. 17: Reprinted from *Luther's Works,* Volume 44, edited by James Atkinson, copyright © 1966 Fortress Press and Volume 31, edited by Harold Grimm, copyright © 1957 Muhlenberg Press. Used by permission of Augsburg Fortress. P. 19: "The Interpretation of the Bible" from Luther, *What Luther Says: An Anthology,* edited by Ewald Plass. Copyright © 1959 by Concordia Publishing House. Used with permission. *Section 5* P. 20: From *Select Statutes and Other Constitutional Documents Illustrative of the Reigns of Elizabeth and James I,* 3rd ed., ed. G.W. Prothero (Oxford: Clarendon Press, 1906), pp. 400–401, 293–294. *Section 6* P. 22: From *The English Works of Thomas Hobbes of Malmesbury: Leviathan, or the Matter Form and Power of a Commonwealth Ecclesiastical and Civil,* collected and ed. Sir William Molesworth (London: John Bohn, 1839), III, 110–113, 116, 117, 154, 157–158, 160–161. *Section 7* P. 26: From *Select Documents of English Constitutional History,* ed. George Burton Adams and M. Morse Stephens (New York: Macmillan Company, 1902), pp. 464–465.

Chapter 2

Section 1 P. 32: From Nicolaus Copernicus, *On the Revolutions,* translated by Edward Rosen, edited by Jerry Dbrzycki, pp. 3–5. Reprinted with permission of Macmillan Ltd. Copyright by Macmillan Ltd. All rights reserved. P. 35: Maurice A. Finocchiaro, ed. *Galileo Affair: A Documentary History,* pp. 67–68. Copyright © 1989 by The Regents of the University of California. Reprinted by permission of the University of California Press. *Section 2* P. 36: From *Discoveries and Opinions of Galileo Galilei* by Galileo Galilei. Copyright © 1957 by Stillman Drake. Used by permission of Doubleday, a division of Bantam Doubleday Dell Publishing Group, Inc. *Section 3* P. 39: Galileo Galilei, *Dialogue Concerning the Two Chief World Systems: The Ptolemaic and Copernican, 2nd revised edition,* translated and edited by Stillman Drake. Copyright © 1962 by the Regents of the University of California. Reprinted by permission of the Regents of the University of California and the University of California Press. *Section 4* P. 43: From *The Philosophy of Francis Bacon,* ed. and trans. Benjamin Farrington (Liverpool University Press, 1970), pp. 114–115. P. 43: From *The Works of Francis Bacon,* ed. Spedding, Ellis, and Heath (Boston: Taggard and Thompson, 1863), VIII, 67–69, 71–72, 74, 76–79, 142. *Section 5* P. 45: From *Discourse on Method* by René Descartes, translated by Laurence J. Lafleur, pp. 3–7, 9–12, 20–21. Copyright © 1960. Reprinted by permission of Macmillan Ltd. *Section 6* P. 49: From Sir Issac Newton, *The Mathematical Principles of Natural Philosophy, Book III,* trans. Andrew Motte (London: H.D. Symonds, 1803), II, 160–162, 310–314.

Chapter 3

Section 1 P. 54: From *The Philosophy of Kant,* by Immanuel Kant, trans. by Carl J. Friedrich. Copyright © 1949 by Random House, Inc. *Section 2* P. 56: From John Locke, *Two Treatises on Civil Government* (London: 1688, 7th reprinting by J. Whiston et al., 1772), pp. 292, 315–316, 354–355, 358–359, 361–362. P. 58: First printing of the Declaration of Independence, July 4, 1776, Papers of the Continental Congress No. 1, Rough Journal of Congress, III. *Section 3* P. 60: From *Candide and Other Writings* by Voltaire, edited by Haskell M. Block, copyright © 1956 and renewed 1984 by Random House, Inc. Used by permission of Random House, Inc. *Section 4* P. 64: From Thomas Paine, *Age of Reason being an Investigation of True and Fabulous Theology* (New York: Peter Eckler, 1892), pp. 5–11. P. 65: From Paul Heinrich Dietrich Baron d'Holbach, *Good Sense or Natural Ideas opposed to Ideas that are Supernatural* (New York: G. Vale, 1856), pp. vii–xi. *Section 5* P. 67–71: © Oxford University Press 1989. Reprinted from John Locke: *Some Thoughts Concerning Education* edited with an introduction, notes, and critical apparatus by John W. and Jean S. Yalton (The Clarendon Edition of the Works of John Locke, 1989) by permission of Oxford University Press. P. 71: Helvétius, *Essays on the Mind and Its Several Faculties,* trans. from the French (London: J.M. Richardson, 1809), pp. 391–363. P. 73: From Jean Jacques Rousseau, *Émile,* trans. Barbara Foxley, pp. 80–84, Everyman's Library Series, reprinted by permission of J.M. Dent and Everyman's Library as publishers. *Section 6* P. 75: From Denis Diderot, *The Encyclopedia Selections,* ed. and trans. Stephen J. Gendzier, pp. 92–93, 104, 124–125, 134, 136, 153, 183–187, 199, 229–230. Reprinted by permission of Stephen J. Gendzier. *Section 7* P. 78: From Jean Jacques Rousseau, *The Social Contract* in *The Social Contract and Discourses,* trans. G.D.H. Cole, pp. 8–9, 13–15, 18–19, 23 and 26–28. Reprinted by permission of J.M. Dent & Sons and Everyman's Library. *Section 8* P. 81: *On Crimes and Punishments* by Beccaria, translated by H. Paolucci, © 1963. Reprinted by permission of Prentice-Hall, Inc., Upper Saddle River, NJ. P. 83: John Howard, *The State of Prisons in England and Wales with Preliminary Observations, and an Account of Some Foreign Prisons.* (London: Warrington, 1777). *Section 9* P. 85: From Denis Diderot, *The Encyclopedia Selections,* ed. and trans. Stephen J. Gendzier, pp. 92–93, 104, 124–125, 134, 136, 153, 183–187, 199, 229–230. Reprinted by permission of Stephen J. Gendzier. *Section 10* P. 88: From Denis Diderot, *The Encyclopedia Selections,* ed. and trans. Stephen J. Gendzier, pp. 92–93, 104, 124–125, 134, 136, 153, 183–187, 199, 229–230. Reprinted by permission of Stephen J. Gendzier. P. 89: Copyright © 1996 by St. Martin's Press, Inc. From *The French Revolution and Human Rights: A Brief Documentary History* by Lynn Hunt, ed. Reprinted with permission of St. Martin's Press, Inc. P. 90: John Wesley, *Thoughts upon Slavery* (London: R. Hawes, 1774), pp. 29–30, 34–35, 38–44, 47–49, 52–53. *Section 11* P. 93: From Marie Jean Antoine de Condorcet, *Sketch for a Historical Picture of the Progress of the Human Mind,* translated by June Barraclough, pp. 4–5, 9–10, 128, 136, 140–142, 173–175, 179. Reprinted by permission of the publisher, Weidenfeld & Nicolson.

Chapter 4

Section 1 P. 100: From Arthur Young, *Travels During the Years 1787, 1788, and 1789* (London: Printed for W. Richardson, 1792), pp. 533–540. P. 102: *What is the Third Estate?*, Emmanuel Sieyès, trans. by M. Blondel. Copyright © 1964 by Frederick A. Praeger, Inc., Publishers. All rights reserved. © Pall Mall Press, Ltd. 1963. Reproduced with permission of Greenwood Publishing Group, Inc. Westport, CT. **Section 2** P. 106: From Thomas Paine, *Rights of Man* (New York: Peter Eckler, 1892), pp. 94–96. **Section 3** P. 108: From Mary Wollstonecraft, *Vindication of the Rights of Woman*. P. 111: Copyright © 1996 by St. Martin's Press, Inc. From *The French Revolution and Human Rights* by Lynn Hunt, ed. Reprinted with permission of St. Martin's Press, Inc. **Section 4** P. 115: Reprinted with the permission of Macmillan College Publishing Company from *A Documentary Survey of the French Revolution* by John Hall Stewart. Copyright © 1951 by Macmillan College Publishing Company, renewed 1979 by John Hall Stewart. P. 116: "Republic of Virtue" by Maximilien Robespierre from *The French Revolution*, edited by Paul H. Beik. Copyright © 1971 by Paul H. Beik. Reprinted by permission of HarperCollins Publishers, Inc. P. 118: E.L. Higgins, ed., *The French Revolution as Told by Contemporaries* (Boston: Houghton Mifflin, 1938), p. 301. **Section 5** P. 119: Gracchus Babeuf, *The Defense of Gracchus Babeuf before the High Court of Vendome*, ed. and trans. by John Anthony Scott, pp. 44–47, 51–52, 54–58. Copyright © 1972. Reprinted by permission of John A. Scott. **Section 6** P. 122–126: Diary passages from *The Corsican: A Diary of Napoleon's Life in His Own Words*, ed. R.M. Johnston (Boston & New York: Houghton Mifflin, The Riverside Press, Cambridge, 1910), pp. 140, 143–145, 166, 189, 322. P. 123: Stewart, John Hall, *A Documentary Survey of the French Revolution,* © 1979, pp. 672–673. Reprinted by permission of Prentice-Hall, Upper Saddle River, New Jersey. P. 125: Lesson VII from *The Constitutions and other Select Documents Illustrative of the History of France, 1789–1907*, ed. Frank Malloy Anderson (Minneapolis: H.W. Wilson, 1908), pp. 312–313. P. 125: Letter to Fouché from *Napoleon: Was He the Heir of the Revolution?* ed. David L. Dowd (New York: Holt, Rinehart and Winston, 1966), p. 41. P. 126: From *Letters of Napoleon,* trans. and ed. J.M. Thompson, pp. 207–208. Reprinted by permission of Basil Blackwell.

Chapter 5

Section 1 P. 129: From Edward Baines, *The History of the Cotton Manufacture in Great Britain* (London: Fisher, Fisher and Jackson, 1835), pp. 84–89. P. 132: From J.R. McCulloch (London: Ward Lock, n.d.), pp. 19, 20, 22. **Section 2** P. 133: From Samuel Smiles, *Self-Help; with Illustrations*

of Conduct and Perseverance (London: John Murray, 1897), pp. 1–3. P. 134: From Samuel Smiles, *Thrift* (New York: A.L. Burt n.d.), pp. 6, 14, 18–21. **Section 3** P. 136: From A. Schroter and Walter Becker, *Die deutsche Maschinenbau industrie in der industriellen Revolution* in S. Pollard and C. Holmes, *Documents of European Economic History,* pp. 534–536. Reprinted by permission of S. Pollard and Colin Holmes. **Section 4** P. 138: From Report from the Committee on the Bill to Regulate the Labour of Children in the Mills and Factories of the United Kingdom, *British Sessional Papers, 1831–1832,* House of Commons, XV, 5–6, 95–96, 99–100. **Section 5** P. 141: From Adam Smith, *An Inquiry into the Nature and Causes of the Wealth of Nations;* reprint of the edition of 1813, ed. J. R. McCulloch (London: Ward Lock, n.d.), pp. 352, 354, 544–545. P. 143: From Thomas Robert Malthus, *First Essay on Population, 1798,* reprinted for the Royal Economic Society (London: Macmillan & Co. Ltd., 1926), pp. 7, 11–14, 16–17.

Chapter 6

Section 1 P. 148: William Wordsworth, "Tables Turned," *The Poetical Works of William Wordsworth* (London: Edward Moxon, Son and Co., 1869), p. 361. P. 149: From William Blake, *Milton: A Poem in Two Books* (London: Printed by William Blake, 1804), pp. 42–44. **Section 2** P. 151: From Edmund Burke, *Reflections on the Revolution in France* (London: Printed for J. Dodsley, 1791), pp. 51–55, 90–91, 116–117, 127–129. P. 152: From The Odious Ideas of the Philosophes. P. 153: From Joseph de Maistre, *On God and Society: Essay on the Generative Principle of Political Constitutions,* ed. Elisha Greifer and trans. with the assistance of Laurence M. Porter, pp. 3, 12–14, 29–30, 33, 40, 45, 51, 54, 86. Reprinted by permission of Regnery-Gateway. **Section 3** P. 155: From John Stuart Mill, *On Liberty* (Boston: Ticknor and Fields, 1863), pp. 22–23, 27–29, 35–36. **Section 4** P. 157: From Ernst Moritz Arndt, *The War of Liberation,* © 1913. P. 159: From *Metternich's Europe,* ed. Mack Walker, pp. 45–47. Copyright © 1968. P. 159: From Great Britain, *Annual Register,* 1819, pp. 159–160. **Section 5** P. 161: From Anatole G. Mazour, *The First Russian Revolution, 1825.* Copyright © 1937 by The Regents of the University of California. Reprinted by permission of the University of California Press. **Section 6** P. 163: From *Joseph Mazzini: His Life, Writings, and Political Principles* (New York: Hurd and Houghton, 1872), pp. 62, 69, 71–74. **Section 7** P. 165: From *The Recollections of Alexis de Tocqueville,* trans. A.T. De Mattos (New York: Macmillan, 1896), pp. 14, 187–189, 197–200. P. 167: From *The Reminiscences of Carl Schurz* (New York: The McClure Co., 1907), I, 112–117.

Chapter 7

Section 1 P. 172: George J. Becker, ed.; *Documents of Modern Literary Realism.* Copyright © 1963 by Princeton University Press. Reprinted by permission of Princeton University Press. P. 172: From Emile Zola, *The Experimental Novel and Other Essays,* trans. Belle M. Sherman (New York: The Lassell Publishing Co., 1893), pp. 20–21, 23,

25. P. 174: Charles Dickens, *Hard Times,* pp. 22, 63, 265. Copyright © 1854. *Section 2* P. 176: From Charles Darwin, *His Life Told in an Autobiographical Chapter and in a Selected Series of his Published Letters,* edited by his son Francis Darwin (New York: D. Appleton, 1893), pp. 41–43, 45, 49. P. 177: From Charles Darwin, *The Origin of the Species* (New York: D. Appleton, 1872), I, 77, 79, 98, 133–134. P. 179: From Charles Darwin, *The Descent of Man* (New York: D. Appleton, 1876), pp. 606–607, 619. *Section 3* P. 180: From Andrew D. White, *A History of the Warfare of Science with Theology in Christendom* (New York: Appleton, 1896), Vol. 1, pp. 70–74, 78–81, 86. *Section 4* P. 183: From *Manifesto of the Communist Party,* Authorized English Translation, ed. and annotated by Frederick Engels, pp. 8–11, 16–20, 21–25, 28–29, 31–34, 48. Reprinted by permission of the Charles B. Kerr Company. *Section 5* P. 190: L.T. Hobhouse, *Liberalism* (Westport, Connecticut: Greenwood Press, 1980), pp. 83–84. P. 191: From Herbert Spencer, *The Man versus the State* (London: William & Norgate, 1884), pp. 28, 33, 34, 38, 39, 41, 107.

Chapter 8
Section 1 P. 197: G.J. Shaw Lefevre, Peel and O'Connell: A Review of the Irish Policy of Parliament from the Act of Union to the Death of Sir Robert Peel (London: Kegan Paul, 1887), pp. 288–289. P. 198: "The Famine in Skibereen" by Nicholas Cummins from *The Great Hunger* by Cecil Woodham-Smith. Copyright © 1962 by Cecil Woodham-Smith. Reprinted by permission of Harper-Collins Publishers, Inc. *Section 2* P. 200: From Mark Traugott (ed.), *The French Worker: Autobiographies from the Early Industrial Era,* pp. 345–349, 353–354, 369. Copyright © 1993 by The Regents of the University of California. Reprinted by permission of The Regents of the University of California and the University of California Press, and Mark Traugott. P. 202: From Alfred Kelly, *German Worker: Working-Class Autobiographies from the Age of Industrialization,* pp. 164–65, 168, 172, 175. Copyright © 1987 by the Regents of the University of California. Reprinted by The Regents of the University of California and the University of California Press. P. 205: From William Booth, *In Darkest England* and *The Way Out* (London: International Headquarters of the Salvation Army, 1890), pp. 9, 11–16, 18–20. P. 208: M.I. Pokzovskaya, *Jus Suffragii,* 6, February 1, 1914, translated by Sonia Lethes. Used with permission. *Section 4* P. 219: From John Stuart Mills, *The Subjection of Women,* 1929, pp. 3–6. 10–12, 15, 60–61, 64, 73, 82, 161–164, 214–215. P. 221: From Emmeline Pankhurst, October 21, 1913, *Speech, Suffrage and the Pankhursts,* ed. Jane Marcus, pp. 153–157, 159–161. Reprinted by permission of Routledge & Kegan Paul Ltd. P. 224: From *Pages from the Goncourt Journal,* edited and translated by Robert Baldick, pp. 18, 27. Copyright © 1984. Reprinted by permission of Oxford University Press, England. P. 225: Almroth E. Wright, The Unexpurgated Case Against Woman Suffrage. (London: Constable, 1913). *Section 5* P. 229: Excerpt from *Rehearsal for Destruction: A Study of Political*

Anti-Semitism in Imperial Germany by Paul W. Massing. Copyright 1949 by The American Jewish Committee. Reprinted by permission of HarperCollins Publishers, Inc. P. 232: From Edouard Drumont, *La France Juive. Essai d'Histoire Contemporaine,* Vol. 1, 50th ed., orig. pub. in 1886, trans. Theodore H. Von Laue (Paris: C. Marpon & E. Flammarion, n.d.), from the Intro. & Ch. 1. P. 233: Die zur Erforschung der Pogrom Eingesetzten Kommission, Die Judenpogrome in Russland: Herausgegeben im Auftrage des Zionistischen Hilfsfonds in London, Vol. 2, Einzeldarstellungen, trans. Theodore H. Von Laue (Köln: Judischer Verlag GmbH, 1910), pp. 11–24. P. 236: From Theodor Herzl, *The Jewish State: An Attempt at a Modern Solution of the Jewish Question* (New York: American Zionist Emergency Council, 1946), pp. 76–77, 85–86, 91–93, 96. Reprinted by permission of the American Zionist Federation.

Chapter 9
Section 1 P. 242: From *Cecil Rhodes* by John E. Flint. Copyright © 1974 by John Flint. By permission of Little, Brown and Company. (Inc.) P. 244: From Joseph Chamberlain, *Foreign and Colonial Speeches* (London: G. Routledge and Sons, 1897), pp. 102, 131–133, 202, 244–246. P. 246: From Karl Pearson, *National Life from the Standpoint of Science* (London: Adam and Charles Black, 1905), pp. 21, 23–27, 36–37, 44, 46–47, 60–61, 64. P. 248: From J. A. Hobson, *Imperialism* (London: James Nisbet & Co., Ltd., 1902), pp. 132–134, 139, 234–235, 295–297. *Section 2* P. 251: Friedrich Fabri, *Bedarf Deutschland der Kolonien? Eine Politischökonomische Betrachtung* (Gotha, Germany: Perthes, 1879). Translated by T.H. Von Laue. P. 253: Paul Leroy-Beaulieu, *De la colonisation chez les peuples modernes,* 5th edition (Paris, Guillaumin, 1902). The text is from the Preface, which appeared originally in the 2nd edition, 1885. Translation by T. H. Von Laue. *Section 3* P. 256: From *Cecil Rhodes* by John E. Flint. Copyright © 1974 by John E. Flint. By permission of Little, Brown and Company. (Inc.) P. 258: Quoted from E.D. Morel, *The Black Man's Burden* (London: National Labour Press, 1920), pp. 34–35. P. 260: From Colonel R. Meinertzhagen, *Kenya Diary, 1902–1906.* Copyright © 1957. Reprinted by permission of the Estate of Colonel R. Meinertzhagen. P. 264: From: *Out of My Life and Thought: An Autobiography,* © 1933, 1949 by Henry Holt & Company, Inc. © 1990 by Rhena Scweitzer Miller, Translation © 1990 by Antje Bultmann Lemke. Reprinted by permission of Henry Holt and Company, LLC. *Section 4* P. 268: Excerpted in Betty Balfour, ed., *The History of Lord Lytton's Indian Administration, 1876–1880, compiled from letters and official papers* (London: Longmans, Green Co., 1899), pp. 510–513. P. 269: From *Hind Swaraj, or Indian Home Rule* by Mohandas K. Gandhi. Copyright © 1939. Reprinted by permission of Navajivan Trust.

Chapter 10
Section 1 P. 273: From *The Will to Power* by Friedrich Nietzsche, translated by Walter Kaufmann & R.J. Holling-

dale. Copyright © 1967 by Walter Kaufmann. Reprinted by permission of Random House, Inc. P. 276: From *Twilight of the Idols/The Anti-Christ* by Friedrich Nietzsche, translated by R.J. Hollingdale, pp. 115–118, 125, 128, 131, 156–157. Copyright © 1968. Reprinted by permission of Penguin Books Ltd., UK. **Section 2** P. 278: From *The Collected Papers,* Volume 4, by Sigmund Freud. Authorized translation under the supervision of Joan Riviere. Published by Basic Books, Inc. by arrangement with The Hogarth Press, Ltd. and The Institute of Psycho-Analysis, London. Reprinted by permission of Basic Books, a member of Perseus Books, L.L.C. P. 279: From *Five Lectures on Psycho-Analysis* by Sigmund Freud, translated by James Strachey. Translation copyright © 1961 by James Strachey. Reprinted by permission of W.W. Norton & Company, Inc., and by arrangement with Mark Patterson & Associates. P. 281: From *Civilization and its Discontents* by Sigmund Freud, translated by James Strachey. Translation copyright © 1961 by James Strachey, renewed 1989 by Alix Strachey. Reprinted by permission of W.W. Norton & Company, Inc. **Section 3** P. 283: Reprinted with the permission of The Free Press, a Division of Simon & Schuster, Inc., from *Reflections on Violence,* by Georges Sorel, translated by T.E. Holme and J. Roth. Copyright © 1950, copyright renewed 1978 by The Free Press. P. 286: Gustave Le Bon, *The Crowd: A Study of the Popular Mind* (New York: Macmillan Co., 1896), pp. 3, 6–13, 22–24, 49, 55–57, 59, 63–65, 112–113, 118–119, 126–128.

Chapter 11

Section 3 P. 301: Roland Doregelès, "After Fifty Years," in George A. Panichas, ed., *Promise of Greatness* (New York: John Day, 1968), pp. 13–15. P. 302: From Stefan Zweig, *The World of Yesterday,* pp. 222–224, 226–227. English translation copyright © 1943, renewed © 1970 by The Viking Press, Inc. Reprinted by permission of William Verlag AG. P. 304: From *The Making of New Germany: The Memoirs of Philipp Scheidemann,* translated by James Edward Michell, vol. II. pp. 310–312, 316–317, 319. Copyright © 1929. Reproduced by permission of Hodder and Stoughton Limited. P. 305: From Bertrand Russell, *The Autobiography of Bertrand Russell, 1914–1944, Vol. 2,* 1956. pp. 3–7, 41. Copyright © 1956. Reprinted by permission of Unwin Hyman. **Section 4** P. 307: *All Quiet on the Western Front* by Erich Maria Remarque. *Im Westen Nichts Neues,* copyright © 1928 by Ullstein A.G.; copyright renewed 1956 by Erich Maria Remarque. *All Quiet on the Western Front* copyright © 1929, 1930 by Little, Brown and Company; copyright renewed © 1957, 1958 by Erich Maria Remarque. All Rights Reserved. P. 309: "Base Details," from *Collected Poems of Siegfried Sassoon* by Siegfried Sassoon. Copyright 1918, 1920 by E.P. Dutton. Copyright 1936, 1946, 1947, 1948 by Siegfried Sasson. Used by permission of Viking Penguin, a division of Penguin Putnam Inc. P. 310: From *Poems* by Wilfred Owen, 1920, 1963, p. 32. **Section 5** P. 313: Magda Trott, "Opposition to Female Employment," from Marilyn Shervin-Coetzee, eds., *World War I and European Society—*

A Sourcebook. Copyright © 1995 by Houghton Mifflin Company. Used by permission. **Section 6** P. 315: From *The Public Papers of Woodrow Wilson: War and Peace,* Part III (New York: Harper, 1927), I, pp. 50–51, 159–161, 182–183, 199, 326, 363–364, 398–399. P. 317: From Georges Clemenceau, *The Grandeur and Misery of Victory,* pp. 105, 107–108, 115–117, 271–281. Reprinted by permission of Georges P. Clemenceau. P. 319: From *A History of the Peace Conference of Paris,* ed. H.W.V. Temperley, Vol. II (London: Oxford University Press, 1920), pp. 256–259, 266–268. **Section 7** P. 324: From *The Russian Revolution, 1917,* by N.N. Sukhanov, edited and translated by Joel Carmichael, pp. 584–585. Copyright © 1955. Reprinted by permission of Oxford University Press. P. 326: From *Collected Works of V.I. Lenin,* Vol. 26, pp. 234–235. Copyright © 1964. **Section 8** P. 327: Excerpts from *Variety* by Paul Valéry, translated by Malcolm Cowley, copyright 1927 by Harcourt, Inc. and renewed 1954 by Malcolm Cowely, reprinted by permission of the publisher. Copyright © 1927 by Harcourt Brace & Company and renewed 1954 by Malcolm Cowley, reprinted by permission of Harcourt Brace & Company. P. 328: *All Quiet on the Western Front* by Erich Maria Remarque. *Im Westen Nichts Neues,* copyright © 1928 by Ullstein A.G.; copyright renewed 1956 by Erich Maria Remarque. *All Quiet on the Western Front* copyright © 1929, 1930 by Little, Brown and Company; copyright renewed © 1957, 1958 by Erich Maria Remarque. All Rights Reserved. P. 329: From by Theodore H. Von Laue, trans., *Die Geachteten,* (Berlin: Ernst Rowohlt Verlag, 1931), pp. 28–30, 34–35. Reprinted by permission of Sanford J. Greenburger Associates, Inc. P. 330: From *The Collected Papers, Volume 4 by Sigmund Freud.* Authorized translation under the supervision of Joan Riviere. Published by Basic Books, Inc. by arrangement with The Hogarth Press, Ltd. and The Institute of Psycho-Analysis, London. Reprinted by permission of Basic Books, a member of Perseus Books, L.L.C.

Chapter 12

Section 1 P. 337: From Joseph Stalin, *Leninism: Selected Writings,* pp. 199–200. Reprinted by permission of International Publishers. **Section 2** P. 338: From Joseph Stalin, *Leninism: Selected Writings,* pp. 160–163. Reprinted by permission of International Publishers. P. 339: Pages 226, 234–235, 248–251 from *The Education of a True Believer* by Lev Kopelev and translated by Gary Kern. English translation copyright © 1980 by Harper & Row, Publishers, Inc. Reprinted by permission of HarperCollins Publishers, Inc. **Section 3** P. 343: From *Execution by Hunger: The Hidden Holocaust* by Miron Dolot. Copyright © 1985 by Miron Dolot. Used by permission of W.W. Norton & Company, Inc. **Section 4** P. 347: Reprinted with the permission of Simon & Schuster, Inc., from *Stalin: Great Lives Observed* by T.H. Rigby. Copyright © 1966 by Prentice-Hall, Inc.; copyright renewed © 1994 by T.H. Rigby. P. 348: From *A Precocious Autobiography* by Yevgeny Yevtushenko, translated by Andrew R. MacAndrew, copyright © 1963 by Yevgeny Yevtushenko, renewed 1991 by Yevgeny Yevtushenko. Translation copyright © 1963 by E.P. Dutton, renewed 1991 by Penguin USA. Used by permission of Dutton, a division of Penguin Putnam, Inc. **Section 5** P. 350: From *The Anti-Stalin Campaign and International Communism,* 1956, ed. Columbia University, Russian Institute, pp. 10, 12–13, 17–18, 22, 31–34. Copyright © 1956 Columbia University Press. Reprinted by permission of the publisher. P. 352: From Lev Razgon, *True Stories,* translated by John Crowfoot, pp. 25–27, 29–30, 170–172, 191–193. Copyright © 1997. Reprinted by permission of Ardis. **Section 6** P. 358: From Benito Mussolini, *The Political and Social Doctrine of Fascism,* No. 305, pp. 7–10, 12–13, 15–17. Reprinted by permission of the Carnegie Endowment for International Conciliation. **Section 7** P. 360: Excerpts from *Mein Kampf* by Adolf Hitler, translated by T. Von Laue. Central Publishers of the NSDAP, Franz Eher Nachf., Munich. All rights reserved. Copyright Vol. I 1925, Vol. II 1927 by Franz Eher Nachf. Verlag Gmblt, Munich. P. 364: From Kurt G.W. Ludecke, *I Knew Hitler—The Story of a Nazi who Escaped the Blood Purge,* 1937. P. 365: From *Order of the Day* by Thomas Mann, trans. by H.T. Lowe-Porter. Copyright © 1942 and renewed 1970 by Alfred A. Knopf, Inc. Reprinted by permission of the publisher. **Section 8** P. 368: Ernst Huber, *Ver fassungsrecht des grossdeutschen Reiches,* 1939. **Section 9** P. 369: Dr. Alice Hamilton, "The Youth Who Are Hitler's Strength," *The New York Times Magazine,* October 8, 1933. Copyright © 1933 by The New York Times Co. Reprinted by permission. P. 372: From *Nazi Culture,* ed. by George L. Mosse, pp. 206–207. Copyright © 1966 by the Estate of George L. Mosse. Reprinted by permission of the Estate of George L. Mosse. P. 373: From *Nazi Culture,* ed. by George L. Mosse, pp. 206–207. Copyright © 1966 by the Estate of George L. Mosse. Reprinted by permission of the Estate of George L. Mosse. P. 374: From *The Goebbels Diaries: 1942–1943* by Goebbels, copyright 1948 by The Fireside Press, Inc. Used by permission of Doubleday, a division of Random House, Inc. **Section 10** P. 376: Das Tagebuch der Hertha Nathorff-Berlin—New York. Herfreichmungen 1933 lis 1945 © 1987 by R. Oldenbourg Verlag GmbH, Munich. P. 378: Marta Appel, "Memoirs of a Jewish German Woman" from undated manuscript, excerpted in Monkia Richarz, ed., *Jewish Life in Germany—Memoirs from Three Centuries,* pp. 351–356. Copyright © 1991. Reprinted by permission of the publisher, Indiana University Press. **Section 11** P. 381: From *The Revolt of the Masses* by Jose Ortega y Gasset. Copyright 1932 by W. W. Norton & Company, Inc., renewed © 1960 by Teresa Carey. Used by permission of W. W. Norton & Company, Inc. P. 383: "I Was Ripe to be Converted" by Arthur Koestler from *The God that Failed,* edited by Richard H.S. Crossman. Copyright 1949 by Richard Crossman, renewed © 1977 by Anne Crossman. Reprinted by permission of HarperCollins Publishers Inc. P. 385: From Nicolas Berdyaev, *The Fate of Man in the Modern World.* Copyright © 1961. Reprinted by permission of the publisher, The University of Michigan Press.

Chapter 13

Section 1 P. 390: Horace Rumbold, *Documents in British Foreign Policy 1919–1939, 2nd Series, Vol. V* (1933), ed. by E.L. Woodward and Rohan Butler, 1956, pp. 47–51, 53–55. **Section 2** P. 395: From Stefan Zweig, *The World of Yesterday,* pp. 222–224, 226–227. English translation copyright © 1943, renewed © 1970 by The Viking Press, Inc. Reprinted by permission of William Verlag AG. **Section 3** P. 397: From *In Search of Peace* by Neville Chamberlain. Copyright © 1939. P. 399: Winston Churchill, *Parliamentary Debates, House of Commons v339, 12th vol. of session 1837–1938,* 1938, pp. 361–369, 373. **Section 4** P. 402: Adolf Hitler, *Documents on British Foreign Policy, 1919–1939, 2nd Series, Vol. VII,* 1939, pp. 258–260. **Section 5** P. 404: From *Panzer Leader* by Guderian, translated by Constantine Fitzgibbon, copyright 1952 by Heinz Guderian. Used by permission of Dutton, a division of Penguin Putnam Inc. **Section 6** P. 407: Reproduced with permission of the Curtis Brown Ltd., London on behalf of the Estate of Sir Winston S. Churchill. Copyright Winston S. Churchill. **Section 7** P. 409: From *Hitler's Army: Soldiers, Nazis, and War in the Third Reich* by Omer Bartov, copyright © 1992 by Oxford University Press, Inc. Used by permission of Oxford University Press, Inc. Copyright © Alfred-Maurice de Zayas From: *A Terrible Revenge: The Ethnic Cleansing of the East European Germans* by: Alfred-Maurice de Zayas. Reprinted with permission of Palgrave. **Section 8** P. 413, 416: From Vasili Chuikov, *The Battle for Stalingrad,* pp. 248–254. Reprinted by permission of Grafton Books, a Division of HarperCollins Publishers Ltd. P. 418: From Joachim Wieder and Heinrich Graf von Einsiedel, *Stalingrad: Memories and Reassessments,* translated by Helmut Bugler, 1993, pp. 112–113, 117–118, 120, 131. Copyright © 1993. Reprinted by permission of Cassell PLC. **Section 9** P. 423: From *Commandant of Auschwitz* by Rudolph Hoess, pp. 164–168. Reprinted by permission of Weidenfeld & Nicholson, publisher. P. 425: From Yehuda Bauer, *History of the Holocaust,* 1982, pp. 211–213. Copyright © 1982. Reprinted by permission of Franklin Watts, Inc. Reprinted by permission of Grolier Publishing Company. P. 428: From *The Kingdom of Memory,* by Elie Wiesel. Copyright © 1990 by Elirion Associates, Inc. Reprinted by permission of Georges Borchardt, Inc. on behalf of the author. **Section 11** P. 434: From *The Day of the Americans* by Nerin E. Gun, 1966. P. 436: *From Final Entries 1945: The Diaries of Joseph Goebbels* by Joseph Goebbels, edited by Hugh Trevor-Roper, translated by Richard Barry, copyright © 1978 by Martin Secker & Warberg Ltd and G.P. Putnam's Sons. Original German copyright © 1977 by Hoffman und Campe Verlag. Used by permission of G.P. Putnam's Sons, a division of Penguin Putnam, Inc.

Chapter 14

Section 1 P. 446: "European Witness" by Stephen Spender. Reprinted by permission of Ed Victor Limited. P. 447: Bruno Foa, *Foreign Policy Reports,* vol. XXI, no. 7,

Principles of Macroeconomics

W·W·NORTON & COMPANY·INC· NEW YORK

Principles of Macroeconomics

EDWIN MANSFIELD

WHARTON SCHOOL / UNIVERSITY OF PENNSYLVANIA

Copyright © 1974 by W. W. Norton & Company, Inc.

First Edition

Library of Congress Cataloging in Publication Data

Mansfield, Edwin.
    Principles of macroeconomics. ③ New York, W. W. Norton ⌐C1974⌐ ⌐xvi, 476 p. ⓔ
illus. ② 24 cm.
1. Macroeconomics. I. Title. II. t; macroeconomics, Principles of.
HB171.5.M2715 1974b   339   74–1224
ISBN 0–393–09275–5

Permission from the following sources to reprint photographs is hereby
gratefully acknowledged:
Mansell Collection (pp. 17, 332); Time-LIFE Picture Agency (p. 25, photo-
graph by Stephen Northrup; p. 363, photograph by Walter Sanders; p. 553,
photograph by Hank Walker); The Department of the Treasury (p. 106);
United Press International (p. 195); Board of Governors of the Federal
Reserve System (p. 287); Ford Archives (p. 412); German Information
Center (pp. 632, 699); Swiss Bank Corporation (p. 655).

To Walena,
who prefers people to rats,
and Dick,
who cools the tepid air.

CONTENTS

6 • **Government Expenditures, Taxation, and the Public Debt**　　　　**92**

7 • **The Business Firm: Organization, Motivation, and Technology**

PART THREE

NATIONAL OUTPUT, INCOME, AND EMPLOYMENT

8 • **Unemployment, Inflation, and National Output**　　　　**133**

9 • The Determination of National Output 158

10 • Fiscal Policy and National Output 185

11 • Business Fluctuations and Economic Forecasting 208

PART FOUR

MONEY, BANKING, AND STABILIZATION POLICY

PREFACE

As economists extend the reach of their discipline into more and more areas of practical concern, opportunities multiply to shape economics courses along new lines. And yet, many introductory texts continue to protect much of economics from contamination by actual events. I think that this is a mistake. Economics has its share of elegant theories; but their elegance is enhanced, not diminished, by application to real problems of the economy.

Although drawn from my text, *Economics: Principles, Problems, Decisions,* this is a self-contained introduction to macroeconomics. It can be used in conjunction with its companion volume, *Principles of Microeconomics,* for a full-year principles course, or it may be used separately. I have taken pains in this volume, as in my intermediate text (*Microeconomics: Theory and Applications*) to blend theory with case studies and relevant empirical matter. In teaching the principles course over the past decade, I have found student interest

invariably heightened when time is taken to demonstrate how the principles of economics can be, and have been, used by decision makers, both in the public and private sectors.

In keeping with this emphasis on the real world, primary attention in this book is focused on social issues. The problems of unemployment, inflation, poverty, economic growth, environmental pollution, the less developed countries, and international trade and finance are what make economics so fascinating. While most discussions are well within the mainstream of economic thought, consideration is also given to present-day Marxist, radical, and conservative thought—not because anyone wants to indoctrinate the student one way or another, but because a subject retains its vitality by allowing and responding to criticism, dissent, and change.

In most elementary texts the decisions of firms and consumers seem to be regarded as problems almost too trivial for analysis. In contrast, I try to

XV

inject at numerous points some idea of how economics can improve private decision making, for what may appear to be low-level problems actually are of great importance to society.

Similarly, more attention is devoted here to modern tools of economic analysis, such as econometric forecasting models. To ignore these techniques or to confine them to cryptic appendices is to give the student an incomplete and somewhat distorted idea of current economic practice. Unusually complete descriptions of these techniques are provided, but at a level that requires no mathematics beyond high-school algebra. Indeed, the very few sections requiring any high-school mathematics at all are written so that they can be skipped; these are identified by footnotes.

There are other departures. Unusually complete treatments are given to the nature of the decision-making process in government and business and the role and importance of incomes policy in the modern economy. Further, the energy crisis, so much in the news, figures in several chapters. And an entire chapter is devoted to the economics of environmental pollution. These topics ordinarily are slighted or omitted in elementary texts. In view of their importance, I believe that they deserve a better fate.

As supplements to this text, I have prepared both a book of readings and a workbook containing problems and exercises. *Principles of Macroeconomics: Readings, Issues, and Cases* is designed to acquaint the student with a wide range of economic analysis, spanning the spectrum from the classics to the present-day radicals. The emphasis, as in the text, is on integrating theory, measurement, and applications. *Economic Problems* contains problems, concepts, cases, and tests, as well as brief answers to practically all of them. This volume should be helpful to the student as a device for self-evaluation and practice. It also provides the instructor with material for quizzes and for other uses.

Finally, it is a pleasure to acknowledge the debts that I owe to the many teachers at various colleges and universities who have commented in detail on various parts of the manuscript. Without question, this book has benefited greatly from the advice I received from the following distinguished economists, none of whom is responsible, of course, for the outcome: Bela Balassa, Johns Hopkins; Robert Baldwin, University of Wisconsin (Madison); William Branson, Princeton; Martin Bronfenbrenner, Duke; Richard Cooper, Yale; Robert Dorfman, Harvard; James Duesenberry, Harvard; David Fand, Wayne State; Robert Gordon, Northwestern; Herschel Grossman, Brown; Albert Hirschman, Harvard; Ronald Jones, Rochester; John Kareken, Minnesota; Ann Krueger, Minnesota; Simon Kuznets, Harvard; Raymond Lubitz, Columbia and the Federal Reserve; Sherman Maisel, University of California (Berkeley); Thomas Mayer, University of California (Davis); Arthur Okun, Brookings Institution; and David Schulze, Florida.

I would like to thank Elisabeth Allison of Harvard University for contributing the inserts that appear (over her initials) in various chapters, and Donald S. Lamm of W. W. Norton for his efficient handling of the editorial and publishing end of the work. Above all, my wife, Lucile, has contributed an enormous amount to the completion of this book. She encouraged and helped and even read the book—which, for a clinical psychologist, means paying the ultimate price.
Philadelphia, 1974

E. M.

PART ONE

Introduction to Economics

CHAPTER 1

Economic Problems, Policies, and Decisions

John Ruskin, the famous nineteenth-century English author and critic, had a point when he said, "Life being short, and the quiet hours of it few, we ought to waste none of them in reading valueless books." You have a right to expect some convincing evidence that economics is important enough to warrant your spending the time to master the material in this book. This is doubly true when you recognize that economics is a fairly technical subject and that, although it hurts to say so, no introductory economics text, including this one, can hold a candle to a Hemingway or Dostoevski novel as sheer entertainment.

Introductory texts often begin by defining economics, and one standard definition is this one: *economics is concerned with the way resources are allocated among alternative uses to satisfy human wants.* Such definitions may help get you oriented, but being chock-full of vague words like "resources" and "human wants," they communicate little of the power and usefulness of economics. Really,

1

the only way you can get an idea of what economics is all about is by looking at some of the problems it can help you solve. This introductory chapter will describe seven fairly typical problems economics can help with. Although this is only a small sample of the problems where economics is useful, it gives you a reasonable first impression of the nature of economics and its relevance to the real world. After considering this sample, you will be better able to judge for yourself whether this is one of those "valueless books" Ruskin warned against.

Unemployment and Inflation

The history of the American economy is for the most part a story of growth. Our output—the amount of goods and services we produce annually—has grown rapidly over the years, giving us a standard of living that could not have been imagined a century ago. For example, output per person in the United States was about $6,000 in 1973; in 1909 it was about $1,840. Nonetheless, the growth of output has not been steady or uninterrupted; instead, our output has tended to fluctuate—and so has unemployment. In periods when output has fallen, thousands, even millions, of people have been thrown out of work. In the Great Depression of the 1930s, for example, over 20 percent of the labor force was unemployed (see Figure 1.1). Unemployment on this scale results in enormous economic waste and social misery.

The first of our sample of economic problems is: *what determines the extent of unemployment in the American economy, and what can be done to reduce it?* This problem is complicated by a related phenomenon: the level of prices tends to rise when we reduce the level of unemployment. In other words, inflation occurs. Thus, the problem is not only to curb unemployment, but to do this without producing an inflation so ruinous to the nation's economic health that the cure proves more dangerous than the ailment. As Figure 1.2 shows, we have experienced considerable inflation between 1929 and 1972. The dollar has lost about ⅔ of its purchasing power during this period.

Figure 1.1
Unemployment Rates, United States, 1929–72

The unemployment rate has varied substantially from year to year. In the Great Depression, it reached a high of about 25 percent.

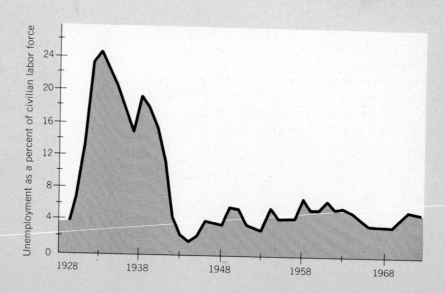

Figure 1.2
Changes in Price Level, United States, 1929–72

The price level has increased steadily since the 1930s, and is now over 3 times as high as it was in 1935.

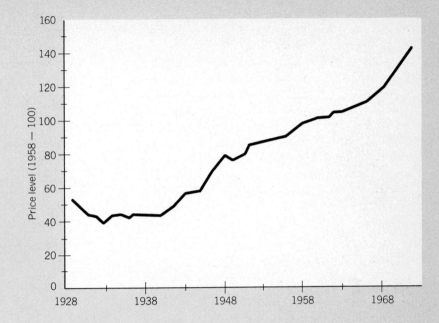

During the past 50 years, economists have learned a great deal about the factors that determine the extent of unemployment. Since, contrary to earlier opinion, our economy has no automatic regulator that keeps it moving quickly and dependably toward minimal unemployment with stable prices, the American people, as well as people in other lands, have given their government the responsibility of promoting full employment[1] without serious inflation. Economists have developed useful techniques to help the government do this job. In particular, they have shown how government can use its control over the money supply and interest rates, as well as its power to spend and tax, to promote full employment with reasonably stable prices. As a responsible citizen, you must be interested in this matter. To judge how well Congress and the president are doing their jobs, and to determine how you should vote, you must know what the government can do to reduce unemployment and how much it is doing.

In recent years, the United States has experienced very substantial inflation. In 1971 and again in 1973, President Nixon imposed price controls in an attempt to stem the rapid rate of inflation. The federal government has established one anti-inflation program after another, the newest program in 1973 being designated Phase IV. Yet the price level has continued to rise. For example, food prices jumped by about 25 percent during a single year, 1973. To understand the reasons for this inflation, and the ways that the government can reduce the rate of inflation, you must understand some economics.

Government Regulation of Business

The 100 largest manufacturing firms control about

[1] By full employment, we mean a minimal level of unemployment, recognizing that there will always be some frictional and structural unemployment of the sort described in Chapter 8.

½ of all manufacturing assets in the United States (and their share of total assets seems to have increased since World War II). In certain industries, like automobiles and aluminum, the four largest firms account for over 90 percent of the market (see Table 1.1). Nonetheless, although the large corporations obviously wield considerable power in their markets, the American economic system is built on the idea that firms should compete with one another. In particular, the producers of steel, automobiles, oil, toothpicks, and other goods are expected to set their prices independently and not to collude. Certain acts of Congress, often referred to as the antitrust laws, make it illegal for firms to get together and set the price of a product.

Table 1.1

Market Share of 4 Largest Firms, Selected Manufacturing Product Markets, United States

Industry	Market share of 4 largest firms (percent)
Automobiles	99
Aluminum	96
Cigarettes	80
Soap	72
Tires	70
Aircraft	59
Blast furnaces and steel plants	50

Source: *Concentration Ratios in Manufacturing Industry*, Senate Judiciary Committee, 1967.

Our second example of an economic problem is: *why is competition of this sort socially desirable?* More specifically, why should we be in favor of the antitrust laws? What reasons are there to believe that such laws will result in a more efficient economic system? (And what do we mean by "efficient"?) To a business executive, lawyer, government official, or judge, these questions are very important, since it is likely that at one time or another these people will be concerned with an antitrust case. But these issues matter to every citizen, because they deal with the basic rules of the game for firms in our economy. Of course, one reason why Americans have traditionally favored competition over collusion, and relatively small firms over giant ones, is that they have mistrusted the concentration of economic power, and obviously, this mistrust was based on both political and economic considerations. But beyond this, you should know how the price system works, and why economists generally favor competitive markets.

One way that society has attempted to control the economic power of corporations that dominate an entire industry is through public regulation. Take the case of radio and TV. The Federal Communications Commission, a government agency, monitors the activities of broadcasting stations and networks to prevent misuse of the airwaves. Other regulatory commissions supervise the activities of the power companies, the airlines, the railroads, and other industries where it is felt that competition cannot be relied on to produce socially desirable results.

The regulatory commissions and the principles they use are currently a subject of tremendous controversy: Many observers feel that they tend to be lax, or, worse still, to be captured by the industries they are supposed to regulate. Since these regulated industries produce about 8 percent of national income, we all have a big stake in understanding how they operate and whether they are being regulated properly. This is another aspect of the same general problem of how industries should be organized.

The Elimination of Poverty

As pointed out by Philip Wicksteed, a prominent twentieth-century British economist, "A man can be neither a saint, nor a lover, nor a poet, unless he has comparatively recently had something to eat." Although relatively few people in the United States lack food desperately, over 24 million American people, about 12 percent of the population of the United States, live in what is officially designated as poverty. These people have frequently been called invisible in a nation where the average yearly income per person is about $6,000; but the poor are invisible only to those who shut their eyes, since they exist in ghettos in the wealthiest American cities, like New York, Chicago, and Los Angeles, as well as near Main Street in thousands of small towns. They can also be found in areas where industry has come and gone, as in the former coal-mining towns of Pennsylvania and West Virginia, and in areas where decades of farming have depleted the soil.

Table 1.2 shows the distribution of income in the United States in 1972. Clearly, there are very substantial differences among families in income level. Indeed, the cats and dogs of the very rich eat better than some human beings. You as a citizen and a human being need to understand the social mechanisms underlying the distribution of income,

Table 1.2

Percentage Distribution of Families, by Income, United States, 1972

Money income	Percent of all families
Under $2,000	4
2,000– 3,999	8
4,000– 5,999	10
6,000– 7,999	11
8,000– 9,999	11
10,000–14,999	26
15,000–24,999	23
25,000 and over	7
Total	100

Source: Department of Commerce.

both in the United States and in other countries, and how reasonable and just they are. Our third economic problem is: *why does poverty exist in the world today, and what can be done to abolish it?* To help the poor effectively, we must understand the causes of poverty. Does it make sense, for example, to pour billions of dollars into programs often denounced by politicians and even the recipients themselves as a "welfare mess"?

Since poverty is intimately bound up with our racial problems and the decay of our cities, the success or failure of measures designed to eradicate poverty may also help us determine whether we can achieve a society where equality of opportunity is more than a slogan and where people do not have to escape to the suburbs to enjoy green space and fresh air. Nor does the economist's concern with poverty stop at our shoreline. One of the biggest problems of the world today is the plight of the poor countries of Asia, Africa and Latin America—the so-called "less developed countries." The industrialized countries of the world, like the United States, Western Europe, Japan, and the Soviet Union, are really just rich little islands surrounded by seas of poverty. Over 2 billion people live in countries where income per person is less than $500 per year. These countries lack equipment, technology, and education; sometimes (but by no means always) they also suffer from overpopulation. Economists have devoted considerable attention to the problems of the less developed countries, and to developing techniques to assist them.

Environmental Pollution

The poor seem always to be with us; and in our industrialized world, so too is pollution. For many years, people in the United States paid relatively little attention to the environment and what they were doing to it, but this attitude has changed markedly in the past decade. Now the public is really concerned about environmental pollution.

Table 1.3

Water Pollution for Major Drainage Areas, United States, 1970 and 1971

Major watershed	Stream miles	Polluted miles 1970	Polluted miles 1971	Change
Ohio	28,992	9,869	24,031	+ 14,162
Southeast	11,726	3,109	4,490	+ 1,381
Great Lakes	21,374	6,580	8,771	+ 2,191
Northeast	32,431	11,895	5,823	− 6,072
Middle Atlantic	31,914	4,620	5,627	+ 1,007
California	28,277	5,359	8,429	+ 3,070
Gulf	64,719	16,605	11,604	− 5,001
Missouri	10,448	4,259	1,839	− 2,420
Columbia	30,443	7,443	5,685	− 1,758
United States	260,324	69,739	76,299	+ 6,560

Source: Council on Environmental Quality, *Third Annual Report,* August 1972.

You may have seen the considerable air pollution in Los Angeles, New York, or many other cities. Chances are that a river near you is no longer fit for swimming or an abundant fish life, even if it is not as badly polluted as Cleveland's Cuyahoga, which was so full of wastes that it literally caught fire in 1969. You can get an idea of the scope of the water pollution problem from Table 1.3. In response to the pollution problem, the government and interested groups of private citizens are trying to control pollution, whether from auto exhausts, combustion of fossil fuels, solid waste disposal, or the noise of sirens and jackhammers. But this is a difficult task, not unlike the job performed by Hercules in the Augean stables.

Our fourth example of an economic problem is: *what causes environmental pollution, and how can we reduce it to the proper levels?* Consider as an example, Richmond, a village south of Albany, New York, on the Hudson River.[2] It is situated at a place where the river is polluted very badly: the water is brown with the human and industrial

[2] The names Richmond and Smith are fictitious; otherwise, this is a factual account.

wastes of Albany, Troy, and other cities upstream, as well as with the wastes dumped into the river locally. In the area immediately around Richmond, two of the principal polluters are the village of Richmond itself and the Smith Paper Company. The village's sewer mains dump their contents into the river, and the Smith Paper Company discharges its untreated wastes into a creek that flows into the river. The people of Richmond have dragged their heels about building a sewage treatment system, feeling that unless the towns upstream took action their own efforts would be fruitless. The Smith Paper Company, for other reasons, has also been slow to do anything about water pollution.

In a situation of this sort, what should be done? For example, should the village of Richmond and the Smith Paper Company be required by the federal government to treat their wastes in certain ways? If so, how pure should the water be, and who should pay for the treatment costs—the village and the Smith Paper Company, or the general public? Or, instead of imposing such standards, should the government charge a fee for pollution, and if so, how high should it be? Economists have devoted substantial attention to questions like this in recent years. To a considerable extent, the problem of environmental pollution is an economic problem—and economics must play an important role in any attempted solution.

The Planned Economies

Roughly ⅓ of the world's people live and work under a set of economic rules quite different from ours. The object of the game—achieving material prosperity and living the good life—may be broadly similar, but differences in how it is played account for a distinct cleavage between Communist and capitalist countries. Some of these differences can be spotted at once. For example, the steel mills of the Soviet Union are owned and operated by the government, whereas the steel mills of Gary, Indiana, or Pittsburgh belong to private corporations that compete against each other for sales, striving to make the profits that will fuel their further growth and insure a favorable return to their owners—the hundreds of thousands of people who have invested in their stocks. The Communist nations believe that factories, mines, and other such productive units should be owned by the state; most Americans believe that they should be owned by individuals.

Under the Communist system, the productive activities of a country are planned by a small group of bureaucrats in government ministries. In the capitalist world, industrial decision making is dispersed among many firms, each sizing up the demand for its products and choosing its own methods of production. Much is made of these contrasts in the economic life of the Communist and the capitalist nations, and rightly so. But it is important to recognize that neither the Communist nor the capitalist system is quite as pristine pure as its more zealous admirers would have us believe. For example, when the American government provides huge loans to a giant defense contractor faced with bankruptcy, this can hardly be regarded as a triumph of pure capitalism. And when the Soviet planners adopt various capitalist techniques, some people do not regard it as a triumph of pure communism.

Our fifth example of an economic problem is: *what are the various ways in which our mixed capitalist system differs from a planned economy like the Soviet Union, and does our kind of economic system seem to be out-performing theirs?* Economics helps you understand the differences between communism and capitalism. Of course there are political, social, and cultural differences as well, but a major part of the differences is economic—and economists, here and in the Communist countries, have devoted considerable time and effort to studying each other's economic systems, in the process laying to rest many pernicious myths. This is all to the good, because sensible dealings with other nations must rest on fact, not myth. It will be a long time before the tensions between the Communist and capitalist blocs are eliminated, but a realistic understanding of the Communist systems is bound to promote the chances of harmonious international relations.

Rational Decision Making

The problems discussed in previous sections are problems that concern our entire society. Obviously, they merit study by economists. But much of economics deals with narrower problems, such as the operations of the business firm. Consider for example, the cost calculations that must be made by the management of Continental Air Lines, to determine how many flights to run between Houston and Los Angeles. Or take the case of the International Business Machines Corporation (IBM), which must decide how to make, market, and price its next generation of electronic computers. These firms face very difficult problems, often involving millions of dollars. It is important, both to the firms themselves and to society at large, that they make the best decisions possible.

This is our sixth example of an economic problem: *how should a firm decide what to produce, how much to produce, and how to produce it?* Suppose that a metalworking firm has signed a contract to remove impurities from 100 square feet of sheet metal per week, at a price of $10 per square foot. There are three processes the firm can use. Process A requires 2 manhours of labor and 1 hour of machine time to remove the defects from 1 square foot of sheet metal, Process B requires 1.5 manhours of labor and 1.5 hours of machine time for the same job, and Process C can do it with 1.1 manhours of labor and 2.2 hours of machine time. The same kind of machine is used for each process. The firm must pay $3 per manhour for labor and $2 for an hour of machine time.

Given these circumstances, what process should the firm use to satisfy its contract? Should it use one process for all 100 square feet of sheet metal per week? Or should it use Process A to remove the defects from 50 square feet and Process B for the other 50 square feet? Or some other combination of processes? Which of the myriad possibilities will yield the firm the highest profits? You may not care much about sheet metal, but if you are interested in managing or working for a business firm, you should want to know how to solve this type of problem, for of course the same principles apply to many other fields. (Answer: Process B used for all 100 square feet will return the highest profits.)

Economics is divided into two parts: macroeconomics and microeconomics. **Macroeconomics** deals with the behavior of economic aggregates like national output, the price level, and the level of unemployment, while **microeconomics** deals with the economic behavior of individual units like consumers, firms, and resource owners. This volume is concerned primarily with macroeconomics, but since one must know some microeconomics to understand macroeconomics, we include some microeconomics as well. However, the economic problem cited in this section is too purely microeconomic in nature to be taken up in detail here. For a more intensive discussion of this sort of problem, see the companion volume to this one, *Principles of Microeconomics.*

The Energy Crisis

Since World War II, Americans have had relatively little experience with shortages—situations where, at the going price, the quantity demanded of particular commodities exceeds the quantity supplied. In 1973, our affluent society was jolted by shortages in a number of areas, particularly in the production and distribution of fossil fuels like oil. The "energy crisis" hit the headlines, and stayed there for some time. Responding to apparently serious fuel shortages, the United States set out to expand domestic supplies of energy.

Our seventh example of an economic problem is: *what factors are responsible for our energy problems, and how can these problems be solved?* In later chapters, we shall examine how shortages of this sort can occur, and discuss a variety of issues pertaining to our energy problems. Among other things, we shall look at the behavior of our oil imports, the economics of coal research and development, and the nature of some rationing schemes considered in 1973. To comprehend our energy problems, one must understand these matters.

Economic Problems:
Some Common Threads

Even this brief sample of economic problems shows certain important characteristics they tend to have in common. First, economic problems generally involve *choice*. There are often a number of alternative ways to handle a problem, and the question is which is best. What is the best way to reduce unemployment without causing inflation? Or the best way to deal with poverty in the United States? To throw light on such questions, one must examine the costs and benefits associated with each alternative feasible solution, and choose the solution whose benefits are greatest relative to its costs. This is often a complicated and subtle business, since neither the costs nor the benefits may be easy to conceptualize and measure. Economists have spent a great deal of time and energy developing sophisticated ways to help solve such problems of choice.

To illustrate problems of choice, let's return to our earlier example of the metalworking firm that has to decide which process to use to remove impurities from a certain quantity of sheet metal per week. To solve this problem, the firm must consider the costs and benefits of each alternative process. This sounds easy, but there are many pitfalls, since costs and benefits often are overlooked, misinterpreted, or miscalculated. Any economist worth his salt can entertain you with horror stories of major corporations that have gone astray in estimating the costs of alternative manufacturing processes. This is quite understandable, because unlike the simple problem confronting the metalworking firm, many of the problems faced by these corporations are very complicated indeed. Nonetheless, the basic principles of economics can be surprisingly effective in guiding you to a solution.

A second characteristic of many economic problems is that, to choose among a number of feasible solutions, one must *forecast what will occur* if each solution is adopted. This emphasis on the future necessarily entails some uncertainty. For example, in a period of substantial unemployment, the government can reduce the extent of unemployment in a variety of ways: it can reduce taxes, increase its expenditures, or increase the amount of money in circulation, among other methods. Which measure is best depends on the magnitude and nature of the effects of each one, which must be forecasted. Unfortunately, economic forecasting is by no means an exact science, but there is no way to avoid making such forecasts. One way or another, a choice will be made, and any choice involves a forecast, explicit or implicit. Each year, thousands of studies are carried out by economists in an effort to improve their ability to forecast various phenomena.

Judging by the available evidence, these efforts have been paying off, and economic forecasting has become increasingly reliable.

A third characteristic of many economic problems is that they involve choices concerning *the role of government* in economic affairs. Consider the problem of stemming inflation. Should the government impose wage and price controls, or should the government leave prices and wages to private bargaining and markets? Or how much government intervention to reduce pollution should be accepted? Should the Environmental Protection Agency be given the power to impose regulations of various kinds on the extent to which any firm or individual can pollute the environment, or should we allow firms and individuals to make these decisions themselves?

Turn to a different area: the antitrust laws, which are designed to stimulate and preserve competition and to discourage monopoly. In the Von's Grocery case of 1965, the Supreme Court disallowed a merger between two supermarkets that together had less than 8 percent of the Los Angeles market. Is this carrying government intervention too far? Or consider the regulation of natural gas prices by the Federal Power Commission. When it instructed the Commission to regulate these prices, the Supreme Court said that the producers of natural gas had appreciable power over the market; but there are thousands of natural gas producers, and many observers believe that the industry is highly competitive. Is governmental regulation of this sort justified?

A fourth noteworthy characteristic of many economic problems is their *interdependence*. Often they cannot be considered in isolation, because attempts to solve one problem may worsen another problem. For example, measures designed to reduce the rate of inflation may increase unemployment, unless the government is very careful. Similarly, stepping up the rate of increase of national output may also increase environmental pollution, and attempts to reduce pollution may worsen the poverty problem, because the antipollution programs may hurt the poor more than the rich.

Needless to say, an attempt to solve a particular problem does not always aggravate another problem. However, since it *may* make another problem worse, we must determine its side effects before we act.

The Role of Economics in Public Policy

The problems we have touched on are only a sample of the ways economics affects your life as a citizen, administrator, worker, investor, or consumer. But even this small sample makes it clear that some economic problems are problems facing our entire society. For example, avoiding excessive unemployment is not a task that can be assigned to a particular individual, family, or firm. It requires the concerted effort of our entire society. In other words, it is a problem of public policy—a problem that is considered and debated in the political arena. As citizens, we are all entitled to take part in making public policy—and we are all affected by the policies adopted.

Economics, and economists, play an extremely important role in the formulation of public policy. Skim through the articles in a daily newspaper. Chances are that you will find a report of an economist testifying before Congress, perhaps on the costs and benefits of a program to reduce unemployment among black teenagers in the Bedford-Stuyvesant area of New York City, or on the steps that can be taken to make American goods more competitive with those produced by Japan or West Germany. In the financial pages, you may read about an economist who has explained to a group of bankers why higher interest rates may be necessary to curb inflation. Still another economist may crop up on the sports page, arguing that professional athletes should be allowed to sell their talents to any team, not merely the team that has acquired the right to negotiate with them through a players' draft.

Economics and economists play a key role at the highest levels of our government. Consider the package of proposals concerning trade agreements with foreign countries that President Nixon submitted to Congress in April 1973. This package was devised in large part by economists, inside and outside the government, and the work was coordinated by George P. Shultz, Secretary of the Treasury and chairman of the President's Council on Economic Policy, a distinguished economist who was formerly professor of economics at M.I.T. and the University of Chicago. Some idea of the range of issues economists deal with is suggested by the fact that, in early April, Shultz "negotiated with European finance ministers, with Soviet leaders, with key Republican and Democratic lawmakers, and with AFL-CIO President George Meany on such diverse subjects as [the preceding] February's dollar devaluation; the Soviet exit fees on Jewish emigrants, the legislation to extend Nixon's authority [to impose wage and price controls], and, of course, the trade package." [3]

In addition, economics plays a very important role in the decisions made by individual government agencies. For example, in April 1973 the Environmental Protection Agency decided to allow automobile manufacturers a one-year extension in meeting the 1975 emission standards for pollutants, but to establish relatively stringent interim standards for 1975. This decision required the auto makers, like General Motors, Ford, and Chrysler, to use catalyst systems, mufflerlike devices in the exhaust system that convert polluting gases into less harmful vapors. The car makers argued that such major changes in engine design would be very costly and risky, and have tried to show that less stringent standards should be imposed. Both the Environmental Protection Agency and the auto companies relied on economic evidence and opinion in arguing their sides of this important question.

In the Congress, too, economics plays a major role. Economists are frequent witnesses before congressional committees, staff members for the committees, and advisers to individual congressmen and senators. Many congressional committees focus

[3] *Business Week,* April 14, 1973, p. 26.

largely on economic matters. For example, some, including the powerful Ways and Means Committee of the House of Representatives, deal with taxes. In recent years, tax reform has been a hot subject, as the public has clamored for the reduction of various loopholes in the tax laws, such as the oil depletion allowance, a boon to the petroleum industry. These loopholes frequently favor the rich at the expense of the poor. The Congress also decides how much the government will spend each year on various programs. There is frequently considerable politicking over the size and distribution of government expenditures. For example, in 1973 many congressmen fought hard against President Nixon's attempt to keep a tight lid on government spending, and there was considerable debate over the adequacy of the amounts allotted for antipoverty, health, and educational programs.

Finally, perhaps the most dramatic evidence of the importance of economics in the formulation of public policy is provided during presidential elections, when each candidate—with his or her own cadre of economic advisers supplying ideas and reports—stakes out a position on the major economic issues of the day. This position can be of crucial importance in determining victory or defeat, and you, the citizen, must know some economics to understand whether a candidate is talking sense or nonsense (or merely evading an issue). For example, if a candidate promises to increase government expenditures, lower taxes, and reduce the federal deficit, you can be pretty certain that he is talking through his hat. This may not be obvious now, but it should be later on.

The Role of Economics in Private Decision Making

Not all economic problems affect all, or a major part, of our society: some affect a particular individual, household, or firm, and are largely a matter of private decision making. Because these problems tend to be narrow and localized, they are some-times viewed as less important or interesting than those involving public policy. But this is not the case. If individuals, households, and firms do a reasonably good job of solving their own problems, many social problems are solved automatically. Moreover, most of us spend most of our lives wrestling with these narrower questions. Thus, we all have an interest in learning how to cope better with them.

Economics and economists play an extremely important role in private decision making. Their role in the decision-making process in business firms is particularly great, since many of the nation's business executives have studied economics in college or in postgraduate programs, and many of the nation's larger corporations hire professional economists to forecast their sales, reduce their costs, increase their efficiency, negotiate with labor and government, and carry out a host of other tasks. Judging from the fancy salaries business economists are paid, the firms seem to think they can deliver the goods; and in fact the available evidence seems to indicate that they do provide important guidance to firms in many areas of their operations.

As an illustration, consider the Magnavox Company, a major manufacturer of television sets. In 1971, Magnavox's president, Robert Platt, decided to move slowly in converting Magnavox's TV sets from electron tubes to all solid-state sets, because he did not believe that the solid-state sets would catch on quickly with the public, and because he wanted to wait until an improved picture tube was available in 1973 before making the transition. This was a mistake. Consumers rushed to buy the solid-state sets, and Magnavox's sales fell to $226 million in 1972, down 36 percent from their peak in 1968. Economics is concerned with decisions of this sort, and although it cannot insure success or prevent mistakes, it can shed important light on the way such decisions should be made.

In addition, economics is essential to firms in their dealings with the government. For example, IBM, the huge producer of electronic computers and other business machines, has been charged with violation of the antitrust laws. In 1972 the

Justice Department accused IBM of monopolizing the market for general-purpose electronic computers and employing its "market power" to maintain its dominance. The outcome of the case will determine the shape of the computer industry for years to come, as well as the health and vitality of IBM. IBM's economists have been trying to punch holes in the government's case, just as the government's economists have been trying to strengthen it. To understand what this and similar cases are all about, and to argue the pros and cons, economics is essential.

Finally, economics and economists influence the decision making of households as well as firms. Few households—other, perhaps, than the Rockefellers and the Gettys—can afford to hire their own professional economist, but this does not mean that many households do not receive and use a considerable amount of economic advice. On the contrary, most households take magazines and newspapers that contain a great deal of economic information. *The Wall Street Journal* is packed with it; so are the financial pages of the *New York Times* and other leading newspapers. Even a general news magazine like *Time* now has a board of economic advisers—and puts an economist on its cover from time to time. Based on information provided in such publications, households can make more informed decisions on their investments and expenditures. Through this channel, among others, economics can play a major role in their decision making.

Economics: A Social Science

In previous sections, we have tried to indicate the practical importance of economics. But economics is much more than a bag of techniques for solving practical problems. *Like any other natural or social science, it is concerned with explaining and predicting observed phenomena, whether or not these explanations and predictions have any immediate practical application.* One need only look at some of the books economists write for each other—books bristling with complicated mathematical formulas and highly theoretical arguments—to realize that not all economics is a search for immediate answers to the world's ailments. Instead, many fields of economics pursue abstract truth, immediately useful or not.

Thus much economic research is directed at questions like these: what determines the level of national output? (Why did the total amount of goods and services produced in the United States plummet by about 30 percent between 1929 and 1933?) What determines the price of various commodities? (Why are lamb chops more expensive than hot dogs?) What determines the overall price level? (Why is the average level of prices so much higher now than it was 40 years ago?) What determines how much a worker makes? (Why are brain surgeons paid more than pipefitters?) What determines the rate of increase of per capita output? (Why has Japan's per capita output increased so much more rapidly than other industrialized countries' in recent years?) What determines how a consumer allocates his or her income among various commodities? (How will an increase in the price of honeydew melons influence the quantity you buy?) What determines the goods a country exports and those it imports? (Why do we export electronic computers and import transistor radios?) What determines the value of foreign money? (Why was a British pound worth about $2.50 in 1973?)

As these questions and their parenthetical accompaniments stand, they are not in the form of practical problems. Yet a knowledge of the answers to these questions is obviously of interest and of value. In this respect, many branches of economics recall mathematics. Pure mathematics is not concerned with day-to-day affairs, but various branches of mathematics are very valuable in solving practical problems, and some knowledge of mathematics is indispensable for understanding the world around us and for professional and technical training. Or think of physics. Although many of its branches are rather far removed from practical application, a general knowledge of physics has proved necessary to solve many types of practical problems; and certain branches, like solid-state physics, have had enormous practical impact on technology and industry.

The crucial consideration is that *economics is a science*. Like other sciences, it formulates and tests basic propositions that can be used to predict and explain the phenomena we observe in the world around us. This does not mean it cannot be useful; but because it is a science—a social science—economics goes beyond problem-solving *to deal with the basic principles and mechanisms that make economic systems work as they do.*

Finally, it is important to recognize that economics, although probably the most highly developed of the social sciences, is still far from being able to solve many of the pressing social issues we face. Nor will a knowledge of economics insure that your bank balance will soar. Economics can help solve important social problems, and it can help you come to better decisions, but it is no panacea. As you will see in subsequent chapters, there are many economic questions that are unsettled and debated by the experts. Consequently, one should not expect too much. But even Ruskin would probably admit that, to be valuable, a book need not provide reliable answers to all interesting questions.

Summary

Economics helps you to understand the nature and organization of our society (and other societies), the arguments underlying many of the great public issues of the day, and the operation and behavior of business firms and other economic decision-making units. It is no exaggeration to say that everyone must know something about economics to function responsibly and effectively as a citizen, administrator, worker, or consumer. According to one standard definition, economics is concerned with the way resources are allocated among alternative uses to satisfy human wants. Perhaps the best way to become acquainted with what economics is all about is to look at some of the problems it can help solve. Some of these are matters of public policy, whereas others concern private decisions.

Seven representative problems that economics deals with are: (1) What determines the extent of unemployment, and what can be done to reduce it? (2) Why should we expect competition among firms to produce socially desirable effects? (3) Why does poverty exist, and what can be done to abolish it? (4) What causes environmental pollution, and how can we reduce it to the proper levels? (5) How do the economic systems of the Communist nations work, and how does their economic performance stack up against ours? (6) How should a firm decide what to produce, how much to produce, and how to produce it? (7) What factors are responsible for our energy problems, and how can these problems be solved? This is only a sample—and a very small sample at that—of the questions to which economics relates. Many more will be discussed in subsequent chapters.

Although economics plays an important role in helping to solve basic social and private problems, you should not jump to the conclusion that economics is wholly a bag of techniques designed to solve practical problems; this is far from the case. Economics—like any natural or social science—is concerned with explaining and predicting observed phenomena, whether or not these explanations or predictions have any immediate application to practical problems. Also, it is important to recognize that, although economics can help solve social and private problems, it is no panacea. Nor is economics able to answer every important question about the workings of the economic system. As we shall see, our understanding of some questions is far from adequate. Nonetheless, a knowledge of economics is very useful and important in understanding the world around us.

CONCEPTS FOR REVIEW

Economics
Unemployment
Inflation
Forecasting

Choice
Government regulation
Poverty
Pollution

Planned economy
Interdependence

QUESTIONS FOR DISCUSSION AND REVIEW

1. According to Charles Schultze, "Modern economics can and has successfully prescribed the means of preventing large-scale unemployment without bringing on major inflation." What does this statement mean? Is it a matter worth worrying about?

2. According to Robert Heilbroner, "Relevance is a word that makes professors of economics wince these days." Is economics relevant to the major social issues and private problems of the day? Why or why not?

3. In Communist nations, about all of the factories, mines, and equipment are publicly owned. True or False?

4. At present, yearly income per capita in the United States is about:
   a. $2,000. b. $4,000. c. $6,000. d. $10,000.

CHAPTER 2

Economic Analysis: Models and Measurement

As a formal field of study, economics is a Johnny-come-lately. Copernicus paved the way for modern astronomy 400 years ago, and Newton started his revolution in physics in the seventeenth century. By contrast, modern economics is generally said to have begun in 1776, the same year as the American Revolution, with the publication of Adam Smith's *The Wealth of Nations,* and to have developed into a science only a century or so ago. But despite its relative youth, economics has influenced generations of statesmen, philosophers, and ordinary citizens, and played a significant role in shaping our society today. To understand the great ideas that underlie important parts of our civilization and to appreciate great segments of our intellectual heritage, you must understand some economics.

Apart from its value as an intellectual discipline, economics provides keys that help to interpret the broad sweep of the world's history. Economic forces have strongly influenced the course of human events. It would be a gross oversimplification to

15

argue that taxes levied by the British on the American colonies were the sole cause of the American Revolution; yet the movement for independence cannot be understood without some knowledge of the economic ties of the colonies to the mother country. Few historians would call the triumph of Nazism in the 1930s solely a consequence of raging inflation; yet Hitler used the economic plight of Germany as a lever in his rise to power.

In 1960, John F. Kennedy's pledge "to get the economy moving ahead" scored effectively at the political box office. In 1972, Richard Nixon's campaign appealed to the majority of voters who, rightly or wrongly, seemed to mistrust the economic proposals of his opponent, Senator George McGovern. It is safe to say that many elections have turned on economic issues, that many wars have resulted from economic causes, and that many revolutions have occurred because of economic discontent. Of course, economics is only one key to history; political, social, religious, and cultural factors are extremely important too. But to understand much about history—either the history of ideas or the history of events—you need to know something about economics.

Since economic factors are closely intertwined with social, psychological, and political factors, it is worth pointing out that there is no well-defined border between economics and the other social sciences—sociology, anthropology, psychology, and political science. To understand many problems in society, one must consider the sociological and political, as well as economic angles. For example, noneconomic factors are important in explaining why some countries are richer than others. Even in solving narrower problems, such as why consumers buy a particular product, psychological as well as economic factors must be considered. Thus, the economist must continually keep abreast of the advances made in other fields, since they can help him solve his own problems. Conversely, political scientists, psychologists, and other social scientists can often use economic techniques in their work. Just as such cross-fertilization of disciplines is mutually helpful to professionals, so you too should relate what you learn in economics to your knowledge of these other fields.

Adam Smith, Father of Modern Economics

As pointed out in the previous section, Adam Smith (1723–90) is often called the father of modern economics. Smith, who was one of the first scholars to understand many of the central mechanisms of a free, or unplanned, economy, lived in Great Britain at the time when our forefathers were fighting for their independence. They were tough days, in Great Britain and elsewhere. Of course, a small segment of society led rich lives in city drawing rooms or on country estates, but the great bulk of the population lived in abject poverty. To take one small example, in some coal mines, both men and women worked, often half-naked, for long hours; children worked in the mines too—and some seldom saw daylight for months. In the factory towns, as in the mines, the hours were long, and children often spent their early years at work. Shifts of 10 to 12 hours a day were not uncommon, and wages were very low.

Smith spent much of his life as professor of moral philosophy at the University of Glasgow in Scotland. He was a popular lecturer and a very distinguished author—as well as one of the most absent-minded men of his (or any other) day. In 1759, he published *The Theory of Moral Sentiments,* which established him as one of Britain's foremost philosophers, but this was not the book for which he is famous today. His masterpiece, published in 1776 (while the American colonists were brewing rebellion), was *The Wealth of Nations,*[1] a long, encyclopedic book 12 years in the writing. It was not an instant success, but the laurels it eventually won undoubtedly compensated for its early neglect. It is unquestionably one of the most influential books ever written.

[1] Adam Smith, *The Wealth of Nations,* New York: Modern Library, 1937.

Adam Smith
on the "Invisible Hand" and Specialization

It is only for the sake of profit that any man employs [his] capital in the support of industry, and he will always, therefore, endeavor to employ it in the support of that industry of which the produce is likely to be of the greatest value, or to exchange for the greatest quantity either of money or of other goods. But the annual revenue of every society is always precisely equal to the exchangeable value of the whole annual produce of its industry, or rather is precisely the same thing with that exchangeable value. As every individual, therefore, endeavors as much as he can both to employ his capital in the support of domestic industry, and so to direct that industry that its produce may be of the greatest value, every individual necessarily labors to render the annual revenue of the society as great as he can: He generally, indeed, neither intends to promote the public interest, nor knows how much he is promoting it....He intends only his own security; and by directing that industry in such a manner as its produce may be of the greatest value, he intends only his own gain, and *he is in this, as in many other cases, led by an invisible hand to promote an end which was no part of his intention.* Nor is it always the worse for the society that it was no part of it. *By pursuing his own interest he frequently promotes that of the society more effectually than when he really intends to promote it.* I have never known much good done by those who affected to trade for the public good. It is an affectation, indeed, not very common among merchants, and very few words need be employed in dissuading them from it...

It is the maxim of every prudent master of a family, never to attempt to make at home what it will cost him more to make than to buy. The tailor does not attempt to make his own shoes, but buys them of the shoemaker. The shoemaker does not attempt to make his own clothes, but employs a tailor. The farmer attempts to make neither the one nor the other, but employs those different artificers. All of them find it for their interest to employ their whole industry in a way in which they have some advantage over their neighbors, and to purchase with a part of its produce, or with the price of a part of it, whatever else they have occasion for.

Adam Smith, *The Wealth of Nations,* London: George Routledge, 1900, p. 345. Originally published in 1776. (Italics added.)

Much of *The Wealth of Nations* seems trite today, because it has been absorbed so thoroughly into modern thought, but it was not trite when it was written. On the contrary, Smith's ideas were revolutionary. *He was among the first to describe how a free, competitive economy can function— without central planning or government interference—to allocate resources efficiently. He recognized the virtues of the "invisible hand" that leads the private interests of firms and individuals toward socially desirable ends, and he was properly suspicious of firms that are sheltered from competition, since he recognized the potentially undesirable effects on resource allocation.*

In addition, Smith—with the dire poverty of his times staring him in the face—was interested in the forces that determined the evolution of the economy—that is, the forces determining the rate of growth of average income per person. Although Smith did not approve of avarice, he felt that saving was good because it enabled society to invest in machinery and other forms of capital. Accumulating more and more capital would, according to Smith, allow output to grow. In addition, he emphasized the importance of increased specialization and division of labor in bringing about economic progress. Moreover, he recognized that the rate of population increase was an important determinant of a country's economic development.

All in all, Smith's views were relatively optimistic, in keeping with the intellectual climate of his time—the era of Voltaire, Diderot, Franklin, and Jefferson, the age of the Enlightenment, when men believed in rationality. Leave markets alone, said Smith, and beware of firms with too much economic power and government meddling. If this is done, there is no reason why considerable economic progress cannot be achieved.

How Successful Are Economics and Economists?

Economics has come a long way since Adam Smith. Due to the efforts of such great figures as David Ricardo, Thomas Malthus, John Stuart Mill, Alfred Marshall, and John Maynard Keynes, as well as the work of countless other talented people, our understanding of the workings of the economic system has improved continually and significantly. But you may still have some doubts about how much of a science economics is, and whether it will give you valid, useful answers, or just ivory-tower concoctions with little or no applicability to the real world. These questions deserve an answer, although finding a concise one is not easy. One reason for the difficulty is that some aspects of economics are not as well understood as others, in part because less research has been done on them. Any discipline—physics, chemistry, or biology, for example—has such areas. Another reason is that all scientific predictions contain some error. Thus, the real question isn't whether economic predictions and propositions are accurate, but how accurate they are.

Even in this more meaningful form, the question is not easy to answer, however, since, as noted above, some economic predictions and propositions are much more accurate than others. For example, advances in economics and related disciplines in the postwar period have allowed economists to figure out more efficient ways for firms to run many aspects of their operations. Linear programming and related economic techniques have been applied to petroleum refineries, for example, to determine the minimum-cost blend of gasoline stocks and the most profitable outputs of regular and premium gasoline, enabling firms to increase their profits substantially. Short-range forecasting of changes in business conditions is another area where economics has proved very useful. Such forecasts are used by the government, as well as a host of business firms, to guide major decisions involving billions of dollars.

On the other hand, economic knowledge in other areas is very limited. For example, economists are still uncertain about many effects of the government's monetary and fiscal policies. Most economists believe that both *monetary policy* (the government's policy concerning the money supply and interest rates) and *fiscal policy* (the government's policy concerning spending and taxes) play an important role in determining the size of national output, the extent of unemployment, and the rate of inflation. But an influential minority of the economics profession believes monetary policy to be far more important than fiscal policy, and the available evidence is too weak to show conclusively whether they are right or wrong. Our knowledge of the modern process of inflation is also limited. This the Nixon administration found out in the late 1960s when it tried to control the inflation occurring then. The standard remedies it applied did not work as many distinguished economists predicted they would.

However, even though economic knowledge in some areas is much more limited than we would like, you should recognize this important fact: *judging from all available evidence, a knowledge of economics will enable you to solve economic problems better than you would without it. Even though economic predictions and propositions are not always very precise, they tend to work better than predictions and propositions not based on economics.* And this is really the crucial consideration.

One important signal that economics has become a full-fledged science is the establishment in 1969 of a Nobel Prize in economics. The beginning of these awards was an indication that economics was the first of the social sciences to "arrive." The first Nobel Prizes went to Professors Ragnar Frisch of Norway and Jan Tinbergen of Holland. Paul Samuelson, Simon Kuznets, Kenneth Arrow, and Wassily Leontief of the United States, as well as England's Sir John Hicks, received subsequent prizes. All these scholars have contributed greatly to economics, but each in a quite different way: Samuelson, Arrow, and Hicks have been responsible primarily for theoretical advances, while Kuznets has done basic empirical work, and Frisch, Tinbergen, and Leontief have pioneered in the blending of theoretical and statistical techniques. Like any science, economics requires advances of many types —theoretical, empirical, statistical—to develop and flourish.

Another clear signal that economics has become a useful science is the very high salaries economists pull down in industry and government. Years ago, the taunt may have been: "If you're so smart, why aren't you rich?" Today the reply could be: "Those economists who are interested in making money seem to be doing very well indeed!" For example, Pierre Rinfret, an economic consultant and adviser to President Nixon, has an income in excess of $150,000 per year; and Arthur Okun, chairman of President Johnson's Council of Economic Advisers, reportedly said that it would not be difficult for him to make twice as much. Of course, this does not mean that most economists in universities are making loads of money. Like other academic scientists, they are willing to earn less than they could in industry or government in order to enjoy the freedom to do research and teach. But if an economist wants to make lots of money, he certainly has the opportunity.

Model Building and the Methodology of Economics

By now, you may think it worthwhile to devote a little time to economics, but you still don't know anything about how economists approach their subject or the methods they use. To complete this chapter, we will provide a general description of the methodology of economics. Like other types of scientific analysis, economics is based on the formulation of **models.** *A model is a theory. It is composed of a number of assumptions from which conclusions—or predictions—are deduced.* If an astronomer wants to formulate a model of the solar system, he might represent each planet by a point in space and assume that each would change position in accord with certain mathematical equations. Based on this model, he might predict when an eclipse would occur, or estimate the probability of a planetary collision. The economist proceeds along similar lines when he sets forth a model of economic behavior.

There are several important aspects of models. First, *to be useful, a model must in general simplify and abstract from the real situation.* The assumptions made by a model need not be exact replicas of reality. If they were, the model would be too complicated to use. The basic reason for using a model is that the real world is so complex that masses of detail often obscure underlying patterns. The economist faces the familiar problem of seeing the forest, as distinct from just the trees. Other scientists must do the same; physicists work with simplified models of atoms, just as economists work with simplified models of markets. However, this does not mean that *all* models are good or useful. A model may be so oversimplified and distorted that it is utterly useless. The trick is to construct a model so that irrelevant and unimportant considerations and variables are neglected, but the major factors —those that seriously affect the phenomena the model is designed to predict—are included.

Second, the purpose of a model is to make predictions about the real world, and in many respects the most important test of a model is how well it predicts. In this sense, a model that predicts the price of copper within plus or minus $.01 a pound is better than a model that predicts it within plus or minus $.02 a pound. Of course, this does not mean that a model is useless if it cannot predict very accurately. We do not always need a very accurate prediction. For example, a road map is a model that can be used to make predictions about the route a driver should take to get to a particular destination. Sometimes, a very crude map is good enough to get you where you want to go, but such a map would not, for instance, serve the hiker who needs to know the characteristics of the terrain through which he plans to walk. How detailed a map you need depends on where you are going and how you want to get there.

Third, if one wants to predict the outcome of a particular event, he will be forced to use the model that predicts best, even if this model does not predict very well. The choice is not between a model and no model; it is between one model and another. After all, if one must make a forecast, he will use the most accurate device available—and any such device is a model of some sort. Consequently, when economists make simplifying assumptions and de-

rive conclusions that are only approximately true, it is somewhat beside the point to complain that the assumptions are simpler than reality or that the predictions are not always accurate. This may be true, but if the predictions based on the economists' model are better than those obtained on the basis of other models, their model must, and will, be used until something better comes along. Thus, if a model can predict the price of copper to within plus or minus $.01 per pound, and no other model can do better, this model will be used even if those interested in the predictions bewail the model's limitations and wish it could be improved.

Economic Measurement

To utilize and test economic models, economists need facts of many kinds. As Lord William Beveridge said almost 40 years ago, "There can be no science of society until the facts about society are available . . . It matters little how wrong we are with our existing theories, if we are honest and careful with our observations." As economics has become more of a science, more and more economists have spent more and more time digging out the facts and seeing what their implications are. Each economic model yields predictions, and to determine whether these predictions are accurate enough to be worth anything, economists must continually collect data to see how accurate the predictions are. For example, if a model predicts that the price of copper should be $.03 a pound higher in 1974 than in 1973, it is important to determine what price change really occurred, and how close the model's predictions were to reality.

At the outset, note that, to a very large extent, economics is not an experimental, or laboratory, science. In other words, economists, unlike physicists, chemists, or biologists, cannot generally carry out experiments under carefully controlled conditions. Consequently, they usually cannot study the effects of varying one factor, while holding constant other factors that may influence the outcome. Such controlled experiments are common in the natural sciences and in technology. For example, a controlled experiment might be performed in agriculture to learn the effect of various amounts of fertilizer on the amount of wheat produced on an acre of land. A sample of plots of ground might be planted with wheat, the amount of fertilizer varying from plot to plot. Then the yield obtained from each plot might be related to the amount of fertilizer used on that plot.

Since controlled experimentation of this sort is often, but not always, impossible in economics, economists must rely on data generated by the economic system. To test a certain model of consumer behavior, an economist may set out to estimate the effect of a household's income on the amount of money it spends per year on clothing. To make such an estimate, the economist cannot perform an experiment in which he varies the in-

come of a household and sees the effect on its clothing expenditures. Instead, he must gather data concerning the incomes and clothing expenditures of a large number of households, and study the relationship between them. The relationship he finds may, for example, resemble that shown in Figure 2.1: The line AA' represents an average relationship between household income and household clothing expenditure. Each family is represented by a dot. Clearly, the relationship, AA' does not fit all families exactly, since all the points do not fall on the line. AA' does, however, give the average clothing expenditure for each level of income: it is an average relationship. Most economic relationships are like AA' in the sense that they are relationships that hold on the average, but that do not fit every case exactly.

Based on the study of relationships of this sort, economists determine how well various models fit

Figure 2.1
Relationship between Annual Clothing Expenditures and Annual Household Income

The line *AA'* represents an average relationship. Each family is a dot. Clearly, *AA'* does not fit all families exactly, since all the points do not fall on the line. *AA'* does give average clothing expenditure for each income level.

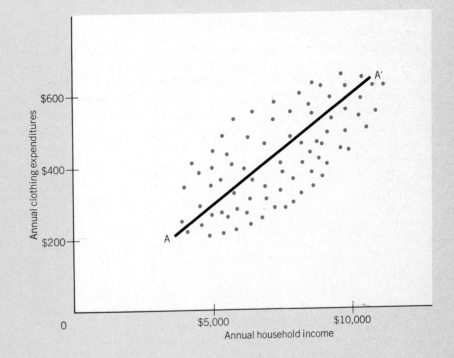

reality. In other words, they perform statistical tests to see whether a particular model is satisfactory. Two types of error can be made: they can reject a satisfactory model, or they can accept an unsatisfactory one. Which of these errors is more important will depend, of course, on the costs involved. For example, if the cost of accepting an unsatisfactory model is low, while the cost of rejecting a satisfactory model is high, then one should worry more about the latter type of error than the former. Using standard statistical methods, economists formulate their tests so that the probability that they will commit each type of error is roughly commensurate with the costs. Generally, it is impossible to eliminate completely the probability of error; the costs of doing so would be prohibitive.

Measurements like those in Figure 2.1 enable economists to *quantify* their models: in other words, they enable them to construct models that predict *how much* effect one variable has on another. For example, economists could be content with a model that predicts that higher household income results in higher household clothing expenditures; but this model would not be interesting or useful, since you don't need an economist to tell you that. A more valuable model is one that is quantitative, that predicts *how much* clothing expenditure will increase if household income increases by a certain amount. A model of this sort might predict that clothing expenditures tend to increase by $60 when income increases by $1,000. Judging by Figure 2.1, such a model would be reasonably accurate, at least for households with incomes between $5,000 and $10,000 per year. Such quantitative models, tested against data like those in Figure 2.1, can be extremely valuable to firms that sell clothing and related products, to government agencies concerned with consumer expenditures, and to economists and other social scientists interested in consumer behavior.[2]

[2] It is worth noting that, although it is useful to see how well a model would have fit the historical facts, this is no substitute for seeing how well it will predict the future. As a distinguished mentor of mine once observed, "It's a darned poor person who can't predict the past."

Simple Economic Models: A Case Study

To illustrate the nature and practical importance of economic models, consider the situation faced by the Boston and Maine Railroad in the early 1960s. The Boston and Maine wanted to discontinue its unprofitable railroad passenger commuter service into Boston. According to the railroad, the revenues it obtained from its commuter operations did not and could not meet the costs of providing the service. However, the Mass Transportation Commission of Massachusetts was not at all sure that such service had to be unprofitable for the Boston and Maine. The commission thought that lowering the price of commuter tickets might increase the service's profitability. This issue was of considerable importance both to the railroad and to Boston commuters.

To understand the Commission's view, we need the concept of a demand curve. Assuming that the incomes and tastes of the Boston commuting public, as well as the cost of commuting by alternative means of transportation, remain constant, it is extremely likely that the number of commuter tickets sold by the Boston and Maine will be inversely related to the price it charges for a ticket. In other words, holding constant these other factors, the lower the price, the greater the quantity of tickets sold. *This relationship between price and quantity of tickets sold can be represented graphically by a demand curve, which shows the number of tickets that will be sold at each price.*

The Commission suspected that the demand curve might be shaped like BB' in Figure 2.2, in which case the quantity of tickets sold would increase very substantially in response to a price cut. If BB' is the demand curve, and if the price of a ticket is reduced from $1 to $.75, the quantity of tickets sold per day increases from 1 million to 2 million, with the result that the railroad's total revenue from suburban passenger service increases from $1 million per day (if the ticket price is $1)

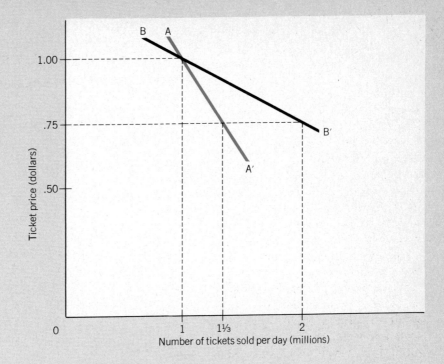

Figure 2.2
Demand Curve for Commuter Tickets, the Commission's View and the Skeptics' View

The commission suspected the demand curve might be *BB'*; the skeptics thought it might be *AA'*.

to $1.5 million per day (if the ticket price is $.75).[3] Since the extra $500,000 per day in revenue is greater than the extra cost of carrying the extra million passengers per day, such a price reduction would increase the railroad's profits. Indeed, according to the Commission, it might increase the Boston and Maine's profits enough to push its suburban passenger service into the black.

On the other hand, skeptics had a different model of the situation. According to their model, the demand curve was shaped like *AA'* in Figure 2.2, in which case the quantity of tickets sold does not increase very much in response to price cuts. For example, if the price of a ticket is reduced from $1 to $.75, the quantity of tickets sold per day increases only from 1 million to 1⅓ million, with

[3] The total revenue equals 1 million tickets times $1 when the price is $1, and 2 million tickets times 75 cents when the price is 75 cents. Thus, it is $1 million in the former case and $1.5 million in the latter. Of course, the demand curves in Figure 2.2 (and the other numbers in this example) are hypothetical, but they illustrate the essential point.

the result that the total revenues of the railroad remain constant at $1 million per day. Since it will cost the railroad more to transport 1⅓ million people than 1 million people per day, it follows that the railroad will make less money by reducing the price of a ticket. Thus, according to the skeptics, a price cut of this sort would not make the Boston and Maine's suburban passenger service profitable. On the contrary, it would make it more unprofitable.

Which model was correct, the Commission's or the skeptics'? As in any science, a question of this sort must be answered by an appeal to facts. Measurements must be made, and data gathered to shed light on the shape of this demand curve. Once such data are in hand, statistical tests can be carried out to see which model is closer to reality. The Commission asked the Boston and Maine to experiment with a reduction in ticket prices to see its effect on the quantity of tickets sold. This experiment, made in 1963, indicated that the skeptics' model was more nearly correct than the Commission's, and the railroad continued with its petition to terminate commuter passenger service when the experiment ended. However, public subsidies eventually were instituted to keep the service from terminating.

The models used in the Boston and Maine case were very simple, relative to most others employed by economists. All economic models are not this straightforward. Moreover, in this brief sketch we cannot do justice to all the subtleties and nuances involved in interpreting and testing these models: there are lots of problems and pitfalls. Yet, even so, this case study is a useful introduction to the construction and use of economic models.

The Use of Economic Models: Another Case Study

Turning to more complicated economic models, let's look at how such models were used by the Kennedy administration in the early 1960s to reduce unemployment and stimulate economic growth. When the Kennedy administration took office in 1961, it was confronted with a relatively high unemployment rate (about 7 percent of the labor force was unemployed in mid-1961), and a widespread feeling that the United States was not increasing its average income per person as fast as it should. These two problems—unemployment and inadequate economic growth—were regarded as among the most important ones facing the new administration.

Decades of research by many economists all over the world had produced models that indicated the factors influencing the unemployment rate, as well as the factors influencing the rate of growth of average income per person. Thus, when the Kennedy administration took office, it could draw on some reasonably well-formulated economic models to help in the framing of its policies. The economists advising the president and the Congress did not have to make up entirely new models to describe the phenomena they were interested in. Models already existed. These models indicated a number of ways in which the government could reduce the unemployment rate and increase the rate of growth of per capita income. One such way was to reduce taxes. Having made its own evaluation of the advantages and disadvantages of each approach, the Kennedy administration decided to press for the tax cut. It also proposed a variety of policies to increase the nation's investment in research and development, education, and plant and equipment, policies which, according to these models, would increase the rate of growth of per capita income.

Led by economists like Walter W. Heller, Chairman of President Kennedy's Council of Economic Advisers, the administration argued strongly for the adoption of the tax cut and other policies; and in 1964, the tax cut was passed by Congress. Without question, modern economics—and the reasonably sophisticated models at hand—played an important role in the formulation and passage of these measures. And most important of all, the measures seemed to work. As the models predicted, unemployment fell and the rate of growth of per capita income increased. Of course, the models used by Heller and his colleagues may have been wrong; perhaps unemployment fell and the growth rate increased for reasons other than the measures adopted by the government. One cannot rule out this possibility, but it seems unlikely.[4]

Values and Decisions

Economists make an important distinction between positive economics and normative economics. *Positive economics contains descriptive statements, propositions, and predictions about the world.* For

[4] However, it should be noted that some prominent economists—the monetarists—feel that the models used by Heller and his colleagues were wrong, at least in part. To understand this issue, you need to know more about fiscal and monetary policy, discussed in Chapters 10 and 14.

Arthur Okun and George Shultz

As any baseball player who ever took a third strike knows, many distinctions are clearer in theory than they appear in practice. The distinction between positive and normative economics is no exception.

The first Nixon victory in 1968 formally ended the reign of the liberal economists in Washington. Arthur Okun, chairman of the Council of Economic Advisers and a former Yale professor, prepared a final Economic Report for Lyndon Johnson and packed his bags. His final year had been brightened by passage of a tax surcharge, a measure designed to give the economy a strong dose of anti-inflationary medicine; yet the inflationary fever persisted.

Among the economists who came to Washington with the Nixon administration was George Shultz, former dean of the Business School of the University of Chicago and the new Secretary of Labor. A staunch advocate of government restraint in economic policy making, Shultz ultimately was to become Secretary of the Treasury and head of the Office of Management and the Budget. From the start, he was a chief administration spokesman on economic affairs.

Within a year, Okun and Shultz locked verbal horns over the proper course of national economic policy: Okun became an avid advocate of wage and price policies for curbing the post-Vietnam inflation; Shultz the public defender of the original administration policy of keeping the government's hands off prices and wages. Why this disagreement between two distinguished economists? In part, the disagreement was one over values. Okun, one of the most steadfastly liberal Keynesians, regarded unemployment of 6 percent falling upon the minorities and the young as a very heavy burden. He had no reservations about a massive government presence in the economy. Indeed, he worried that "the most serious consequence of the 1968–69 disappointment is that it [may] make economists lose their nerve." Shultz was more inclined to count the costs of inflation. He had declared himself skeptical of the federal government's ability to manage affairs better than private citizens and private business.

ARTHUR OKUN **GEORGE SHULTZ**

But it is worth noting that this disagreement on values was in part predicated on a disagreement as to facts. The two economists disagreed as to the nature of the markets to be controlled. Shultz looked at the American economy and tended to see thousands of competitive markets. Okun looked at the same economy and saw it in the grip of big business, like General Motors, on one side of the bargaining table, and big labor, like the Auto Workers and the Electrical Workers, on the other. Although there is considerable agreement among economists about most aspects of positive economics, there is by no means complete agreement. In part, the differences between these two distinguished economists stemmed from their different views of the way the economy works, interacting with their values, to produce different policy conclusions.   E.A.

instance, an economic model may predict that the price of copper will increase by a penny a pound if income per person in the United States rises by 10 percent; this is positive economics. Positive economics tells us only what will happen under certain circumstances. It says nothing about whether the results are good or bad—or about what we should do. **Normative economics,** *on the other hand, makes statements about what ought to be, or about what a person, organization, or nation ought to do.* For instance, a model might say that Chile should nationalize its copper industry and use the profits to reduce poverty; this is normative economics.

Clearly positive economics and normative economics must be treated differently. Positive economics is science in the ordinary sense of the word. Propositions in positive economics can be tested by an appeal to the facts. Needless to say, in a non-experimental science like economics, it is sometimes difficult to get the facts you need to test particular propositions. For example, if income per person in the United States does not rise by 10 percent, it may be difficult to tell what the effect of such an increase would be on the price of copper. Moreover, even if per capita income does increase by this amount, it may be difficult to separate the effect of the increase in income per person on the price of copper from the effect of other factors. But nonetheless, we can, in principle, test propositions in positive economics by an appeal to the facts.

In normative economics, however, this is not the case. *In normative economics, the results you get depend on your values or preferences.* For example, if you believe that reducing unemployment is more important than maintaining the purchasing power of the dollar, you will get one answer to certain questions; whereas if you believe that maintaining the purchasing power of the dollar is more important than reducing unemployment, you are likely to get a different answer to the same questions. This is not at all strange. After all, if people desire different things (which is another way of saying that they have different values), they may

well make different decisions and advocate different policies. It would be strange if they did not.

People sometimes make fun of economists because they disagree, and their differences are sometimes held up as evidence that economics is really not a science at all. In truth, of course, they prove nothing of the kind. *Because economists—like physicists, mathematicians, lawyers, and plumbers —differ in their preferences and values, they come to different conclusions when they enter the realm of normative economics.* Thus, liberal economists often differ from conservative economists in their conclusions on public policy, and the disagreements can be over means as well as ends. *However, there is very substantial agreement on most of the propositions of positive economics.* Of course, this does not mean that everything is settled, but the areas of disagreement are generally relatively narrow. And this, it should be noted, is the important thing, since the pure science of economics is positive economics.

This book will spend a lot of time on the principles of positive economics—the principles and propositions concerning the workings of the economic system about which practically all economists tend to agree. Also, normative economics will be treated as well, since we must discuss questions of policy—and all policy discussions involve individual preferences, not solely hard facts. In these discussions, we shall try to indicate how the conclusions depend on one's values. Then you can let your own values be your guide. The purpose of this book is not to convert you to a particular set of values. It is to teach you how to obtain better solutions to economic problems, whatever set of values you may have.

Methodological Hazards in Economics

There are lots of impediments to straight thinking in economics that are not present in other disciplines like chemistry or biology. To begin with, people have preconceptions about economic matters that they don't have about chemical or biological matters. Few people have a long-standing bias against two hydrogen atoms combining with an oxygen atom to form water, but some people grow up with the idea that profits are a bad thing or that unions are a social evil. These biases get in the way of objective analysis, because people tend to believe what they want to believe. If you want to learn any economics, you must respect facts, unpleasant though they may be at times.

Another hazard in economics is the use of loaded, emotional words. Unless you school yourself to look carefully at what words mean—and don't mean—you can be gulled by misleading terminology. For example, Marxists often refer to the exploitation of labor by capitalists, which sounds bad, since no one can be in favor of exploitation. But you must remember that labels can be misleading. What the Marxists call exploitation, most Western economists do not regard as exploitation at all.

Social scientists are often and justly accused of using unfamiliar words, or jargon, to describe common phenomena. Economists do not escape this charge. You would probably not refer to your checking account in a bank as a demand deposit: economists do. What is more, economists define some terms in a different way from the man on the street. You will find out that rent to the economist is not an amount paid each month for an apartment, but a payment for a resource that is fixed in supply. Of course, economists have a right to define terms as they please, but you can be confused if you assume that seemingly familiar terms mean what you think they mean.

Still another pitfall is to assume that, because one event follows another, the former event is caused by the latter. The Romans had a phrase for this kind of reasoning: *post hoc ergo propter hoc* (after this, therefore because of this). This fallacy occurs all the time. Consider the people who attributed a spell of bad weather that occurred after the first moon landing to the astronauts' trip to the moon. The bad weather followed the lunar trip—therefore it must have been caused by it. Needless to say, this sort of reasoning is treacherous indeed, since many events occur on the heels of other events without being caused by them. To jump to the conclusion that an event following another event is caused by the earlier event is clearly to court disaster.

Still another common pitfall to sound economic reasoning is the fallacy of composition. Some people assume that what is true of part of a system must be true for the whole system. This can be quite wrong. For example, it may be true that a farmer will gain from producing a larger crop. But it may not be true that farmers as a whole will gain if all produce a larger crop. Or consider another case: a business firm will go bankrupt by continuing to spend more than it takes in, but it does not follow that an entire nation will go bankrupt if its government spends more than it takes in. The fallacy of composition—that what is true of the part must be true of the whole—lies in wait for the unwary student of economics, and for the experienced economist too. Grievous errors can be avoided by keeping clear of this fallacy's clutches.

Summary

Economics—and economists—have played a significant role in shaping the present nature of society. A knowledge of economics is necessary to understand the history of human events, and the masterpieces of economics produced in the past are important segments of our intellectual heritage. The methodology used by economists is much the same as that used in any other kind of scientific analysis. The basic procedure is the formulation and testing of models. A model must in general simplify and abstract from the real world. Its purpose is to make predictions concerning phenomena in the real world, and in many respects the most important test of a model is how well it predicts these phenomena. One illustration of the construction and use of an economic model was the discussion concerning the Boston and Maine's decision to discontinue suburban passenger service. Another example of the use of economic models was the decision made by the Kennedy administration to press for a tax cut to reduce unemployment.

To test and quantify their models, economists gather data and utilize various statistical techniques. Economists often distinguish between positive economics and normative economics. Positive economics contains descriptive statements, propositions, and predictions about the world, whereas normative economics contains statements about what ought to be, or about what a person, organization, or nation ought to do. In normative economics, the results you get depend on your basic values and preferences; in positive economics, the results are testable, at least in principle, by an appeal to the facts.

CONCEPTS FOR REVIEW

Model	Demand curve	Normative economics
Measurement	Positive economics	Fallacy of composition

QUESTIONS FOR DISCUSSION AND REVIEW

1. Suppose that you wanted to construct a model to explain and predict the breakfast cereal that your father will choose tomorrow. What factors would you include? How well do you think you could predict?

2. Suppose that you were given the job of estimating the demand curve for commuter tickets in metropolitan Boston. How would you proceed? What sorts of difficulties would you anticipate?

3. There is almost complete agreement with regard to most of the propositions of normative economics. True or False?

4. To be useful a model must
   a. have assumptions that are close to exact replicas of reality.
   b. predict better than any other that is available.
   c. predict very accurately or it is useless.
   d. have few assumptions and be as simple as possible.

PART TWO

The Private Sector and
the Public Sector:
An Overview

CHAPTER 3

The American Economy: Our Mixed Capitalist System

The economy of the United States is the richest in the world. The typical American family has plenty of food, clothing, housing, appliances, and luxuries of many kinds, and the typical American worker is well-educated and well-trained. American agriculture is enormously efficient and productive, American industry is known the world over for its productivity, and American engineers and scientists are in the forefront of science and technology. Yet, despite these successes, the American economy faces serious problems. A substantial minority of our citizens live in what most Americans would regard as poverty. There are obvious and far-reaching problems of discrimination and urban decay. Industrial pollution literally brings tears to the eyes of some city dwellers, and a weekend exodus to the country may involve battling traffic bottlenecks only to reach lakes and ocean beaches contaminated by agricultural and industrial wastes. In the early 1970s, a rash of shortages broke out in several industries, including oil, paper, and lumber.

31

And in world markets, American firms were facing stiff competition from foreign producers.

As a first step toward understanding why we are so well off in some respects and so lacking in others, we need to understand how our economy works. Of course, this is a big task. Indeed, you could say that this whole book is devoted to discussing this subject. So we will not try to present a detailed picture of the operation of the American economy at this point. All we shall do now is give a preliminary sketch, a basic blueprint of some of the highlights. The details will be provided later, as they are needed.

The American Economy:
Some Salient Facts

A good way to begin studying practically any subject is to get a few facts about it. The difference between wise men and fools is that the former respect and heed the facts whereas the latter reject or ignore them. Here are some salient facts about the American economy. First, it is huge. The United States contains over 200 million people, about 90

Table 3.1

Population, 1970, Selected Countries

Country	Population (millions of people)
United States	205
Soviet Union	243
Japan	103
France	51
United Kingdom	56
Italy	54
Sweden	8

Source: United Nations.

million of whom are in the labor force. Table 3.1 shows how large our population is, relative to other major industrialized nations. In addition, the American economy contains over 10 million business firms, and thousands of local and state governments, as well as the enormous federal government with its many departments and agencies. By practically any standard, ours is the biggest economic show on earth.

Second, the American economy is very rich and productive. In 1973, our income per capita was about $6,000 per year. In other words, if you take the total amount of income that Americans made that year and divide by the number of Americans in existence (including all ages), the result equals about $6,000. As shown in Table 3.2, this figure is higher than for any other country. Moreover, the United States produces an enormous amount of such basic products as steel, petroleum, chemicals, electric power, automobiles, electronic computers, and a myriad of other goods. For example, Tables 3.3–3.5 show that we lead the world in steel production, electric energy production, and computer production, three basic indices of industrial might.

Third, the American economy is based on freedom of choice. Consumers can buy what they like, and reject what they do not like; workers can take jobs when and where they please, and quit if they please; firms can produce whatever products they want to produce, and use whatever techniques they want to use. Of course, this freedom is not unlimited. For example, there are laws to prevent people and firms from engaging in antisocial dealings. Moreover, this freedom is not all it might be. For example, it is sometimes difficult for a firm to enter a market, or for a person to get a particular type of job. Yet relative to other countries, our economy is very free.

Fourth, the American economy is organized for the basic purpose of satisfying human wants. Human wants are the goods, services, and circumstances people desire. Wants vary greatly among individuals, and, for a given individual, they vary greatly over time. Some people like to ride horseback, others like to read. Some want to carouse

Table 3.2

Income Per Capita, 1973, Selected Countries

Country	Income per capita (dollars)
United States	6,000
Canada	4,900
Sweden	4,900
Germany	3,800
France	3,700
United Kingdom	2,700
Japan	2,600
Italy	2,100
Soviet Union	1,800
Brazil	500
India	100
China	100

These estimates are rough, because of problems in converting other currencies into dollars, and for other reasons. Nonetheless, they should provide reasonable indications of relative orders of magnitude.

Table 3.3

Steel Production, Selected Countries, 1970

Country	Steel production (million short tons)
United States	131
Belgium	14
Canada	12
China	19
France	26
Germany	50
Italy	19
Japan	103
Soviet Union	128
United Kingdom	31

Source: Statistical Abstract of the United States.

Table 3.4

Electric Energy Production, Selected Countries, 1969

Country	Electric energy production (millions of kilowatt hours)
United States	1,553
Soviet Union	659
United Kingdom	222
Japan	306
Germany	211
Canada	190
France	132
Italy	106
China	50
India	55

Source: World Almanac.

Table 3.5

Production of Electronic Computers, Selected Countries, 1965

Country	Production of computers ($ millions)
United States	3,200
France	240
Germany	200
United Kingdom	190
Italy	135
Sweden	8
Denmark	5

Source: Organization for Economic Cooperation and Development, 1969.

until 3 A.M., others follow Ben Franklin's maxim of early to bed, early to rise. An individual's desire for a particular good during a particular period of time is not infinite, but in the aggregate human wants seem to be insatiable. Besides the basic desires for food, shelter, and clothing, which must be fulfilled to some extent if the human organism is to maintain its existence, wants arise from cultural factors. To some extent, wants are encouraged and manufactured by advertising, social pressures, education, and emulation of other people.

Fifth, the American economy is rich in resources. Resources are the materials and services used to produce goods that can be used to satisfy wants. **Economic resources** are scarce, while **free resources,** such as air, are so abundant that they can be obtained without charge. The test of whether a resource is an economic resource or a free resource is price: economic resources command a nonzero price but free resources do not. Economists often classify economic resources into three categories: land, labor and capital. **Land** is a shorthand expression for natural resources. **Labor** is human effort, both physical and mental. **Capital** includes equipment, buildings, inventories, raw materials, and other nonhuman producible resources that contribute to the production, marketing, and distribution of goods and services. Relative to other countries, the United States is rich in all three of these types of resources.

Finally, the American economy is noted for its sophisticated and advanced technology. **Technology** is society's pool of knowledge concerning the industrial arts. It includes knowledge, needed in industry, of the principles of social and physical phenomena (such as the laws of motion and the properties of fluids); knowledge regarding the application of these principles to production (such as applying various aspects of genetic theory to the breeding of new plants); and knowledge regarding the day-to-day operation of productive processes (such as the rules of thumb of the skilled craftsman). Note that technology is different from the techniques in use, since not all that is known is likely to be in use. Also, technology is different

from pure science, although the distinction is not very precise. Pure science is directed toward understanding, whereas technology is directed toward use. Table 3.6 shows that, according to data collected by the Organization for Economic Cooperation and Development, the United States has been responsible for a very large share of the major new processes and products introduced since World War II.

The Tasks of an Economic System

The statistics concerning the American economy make an impressive score card, but we cannot evaluate how well an economic system (or any system) is working unless we know what it is meant to do. Basically, there are four things that any economic system—*ours or any other*—must do. *First, it must determine the level and composition of society's output*. It must answer questions such as these: To what extent should society's resources be used to produce new destroyers and missiles? To what extent should they be used to produce sewage plants to reduce water pollution? To what extent should they be used to produce swimming pools for the rich? To what extent should they be used to produce low-cost housing for the poor? Pause for a moment to think about how important—and how vast—this function is. Most people simply take for granted that somehow it is decided what we as a society are going to produce, and far too few people really think about the social mechanisms that determine the answers to such questions.

Second, *an economic system must determine how each good and service is to be produced*. Given existing technology, a society's resources can be used in various ways. Should the skilled labor in Birmingham, Alabama be used to produce cotton or steel? Should a particular machine tool be used to produce aircraft or automobiles? The way questions of this sort are answered will determine the way each good and service is produced. In other words, it will determine which resources are used to produce which goods and services. If this func-

Table 3.6

Location of First Commercial Exploitation of 110 Significant Technological Innovations (New Products and Processes) Occurring since 1945

Country	Plastics	Metal working	Non-ferrous metals	Electric power	Computers	Instruments	Semiconductors	Electronic consumer goods	Other	Total
United States	15	4	5	2	10	10	16	—	11	74
Belgium	—	1	—	—	—	—	—	—	—	1
France	—	1	—	—	1	—	—	—	—	2
Germany	3	3	1	—	1	3	—	—	3	14
Italy	2	—	1	—	—	—	—	—	—	3
Netherlands	—	—	—	—	—	—	—	—	—	—
Sweden	—	1	—	2	—	—	—	—	1	4
Switzerland	1	1	—	2	—	—	—	—	—	4
United Kingdom	1	4	2	1	2	2	1	—	5	18
Japan	—	—	—	—	—	1	—	2	1	4
Austria	—	1	—	—	—	—	—	—	—	1
Total[a]	17	12	9	7	14	16	17	2	16	

Source: Organization for Economic Cooperation and Development, 1970.
[a] The sum of the figures for individual countries does not necessarily equal the total number of innovations, since innovations sometimes originate in two or more countries at the same time.

tion is performed badly, society's resources are put to the wrong uses, resulting in less output than if this function is performed well.

Third, *an economic system must determine how the goods and services that are produced are to be distributed among the members of society.* In other words, how much of each type of good and service should each person receive? Should there be a considerable amount of income inequality, the rich receiving much more than the poor? Or should incomes be relatively equal? Take your own case: somehow or other, the economic system determines how much income you will receive. In our economic system, your income depends on your skills, the property you own, how hard you work, and prevailing prices, as we shall see in succeeding chapters. But in other economic systems, your income might depend on quite different factors. This function of the economic system has generated, and will continue to generate, heated controversy. Some people favor a relatively egalitarian society where the amount received by one family varies little from that received by another family of the same size. Other people favor a less egalitarian society where the amount a family or person receives varies a great deal. Few people favor a thoroughly egalitarian society, if for no other reason than that some differences in income are required to stimulate workers to do certain types of work.

Fourth, an economic system must maintain and provide for an adequate rate of growth of per capita income. The goal of economic growth is a relatively new one, there having been less emphasis on growth many years ago. Regardless of its newness, however, it has come to be regarded as an extremely important function, particularly in the less developed countries of Africa, Asia, and Latin America. There is very strong pressure in these countries for changes in technology, the adoption of superior techniques, increases in the stock of capital resources, and better and more extensive education and training of the labor force. These are viewed as some of the major ways to promote the growth of per capita income. In the industrialized nations, the goal of economic growth has become somewhat more controversial. Some observers claim that we have become rich enough, while others point out that since so many of the world's people, here and abroad, are poor, it seems hard to believe that extra output would not be useful.

The Product Transformation Curve and the Determination of What Is Produced

In the previous chapter, we said that economists use models to throw light on economic problems. At this point, let's try our hand at constructing a simple model to illuminate the basic functions any economic system, ours included, must perform. You will recall that these functions are: (1) It must determine the level and composition of society's output. (2) It must determine how each good and service is to be produced. (3) It must determine how the goods and services that are produced are to be distributed among the members of society. (4) It must maintain and provide for an adequate rate of growth of per capita income.

To keep things simple, suppose that society produces only two goods, food and tractors. This, of course, is unrealistic, but, as we stressed in the previous chapter, a model does not have to be realistic to be useful. Here, by assuming that there are only two goods, we eliminate a lot of unnec-

essary complexity and lay bare the essentials. In addition, we suppose that society has at its disposal a certain amount of resources, and that this amount is fixed for the duration of the period in question. This assumption is quite realistic. So long as the period is relatively short, the amount of a society's resources is relatively fixed (except, of course, under unusual circumstances, such as if a country annexes additional land). Finally, we suppose as well that society's technology is fixed. So long as the period is relatively short, this assumption too is realistic.

Under these circumstances, it is possible to figure out the various amounts of food and tractors that society can produce. Let's begin with how many tractors society can produce if all resources are devoted to tractor production: According to Table 3.7, the answer is 15 million tractors. Next, let's consider the opposite extreme, where society devotes all its resources to food production: According to Table 3.7, it can produce 12 million tons of food in this case. Next, let's consider cases where both products are being produced: Such cases are represented by possibilities B to F in the table. Clearly the more of one good that is produced, the less of the other good can be produced. This is reasonable enough: to produce more of one good, resources must be taken away from the production of the other good,

Table 3.7
Alternative Combinations of Outputs of Food and Tractors That Can Be Produced

Possibility	Food (millions of tons)	Tractors (millions)
A	0	15
B	2	14
C	4	12
D	6	10
E	8	7
F	10	4
G	12	0

lessening the amount of the other good produced.

Figure 3.1 shows the various production possibilities society can attain. It is merely a different way of presenting the data in Table 3.7; the output of food is plotted on the horizontal axis and the output of tractors on the vertical axis. The curve in Figure 3.1, which shows the various combinations of output of food and tractors that society can produce, is called a **product transformation curve.** Economists are fond of inelegant labels of this sort: like Eliza Doolittle, heroine of *My Fair Lady* (and *Pygmalion,* in her earlier incarnation), economics is sometimes guilty of "cold-blooded murder of the English tongue." But so are other sciences. You just have to roll with the punches—and learn what these strange-sounding terms mean.

The product transformation curve is a useful indicator of the economic tasks facing any society. It shows the various production possibilities open to society. For example, in Figure 3.1, society can choose to produce 4 million tons of food and 12 million tractors (point *C*), or 6 million tons of food and 10 million tractors (point *D*), but it cannot choose to produce 6 million tons of food and 12 million tractors (point *H*). Point *H* is inaccessible with this society's resources and technology: Perhaps it will become accessible if the society's resources increase or if its technology improves, but for the present, point *H* is out of reach.

Since society must wind up somewhere on the product transformation curve, it is clear that *the first function of any economic system—to determine the level and composition of society's output—is really a problem of determining at what point along the product transformation curve society should be.* Should society choose point *A, B, C, D, E, F,* or *G*? In making this choice, one thing is obvious from the product transformation curve: *you cannot get more of one good without giving up some of the other good.* In other words, you cannot escape the problem of choice. So long as

Figure 3.1
Product Transformation Curve

This curve shows the various combinations of outputs that can be produced efficiently with given resources and technology. Point *H* is unattainable; point *K* is inefficient.

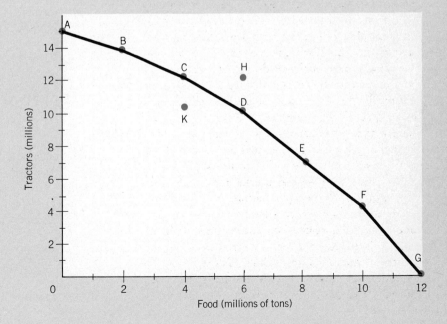

resources are limited and technology is less than magic, you must reckon with the fact that more of one thing means less of another. Once you see this, it is clear that more of anything always entails a cost—the cost being the reduction in something else. The old saw that you don't "get something for nothing" is hackneyed, but true, so long as resources are fully and efficiently utilized.

The Product Transformation Curve and the Determination of How Goods Are Produced

Let's turn now to the second basic function of any economic system: to determine how each good and service should be produced. In Table 3.7, we assumed implicitly that society's resources would be fully utilized and that the available technology would be applied in a way that would get the most out of the available resources. In other words, we assumed that the firms making food and tractors were as efficient as possible and that there was no unemployment of resources. But if there is widespread unemployment of people and machines, will society still be able to choose a point on the product transformation curve? Clearly, the answer is no. Since society is not using all of its resources, it will not be able to produce as much as if it used them all. Thus, *if there is less than full employment of resources, society will have to settle for points inside the product transformation curve.* For example, the best society may be able to do under these circumstances is to attain point K in Figure 3.1. Clearly, K is a less desirable point than C or D—but that is the price of unemployment.

Suppose, on the other hand, that there is full employment of resources but that firms are inefficient. Perhaps they promote relatives of the boss, regardless of their ability; perhaps the managers are lazy or not much interested in efficiency; or perhaps the workers like to take long coffee breaks

and are unwilling to work hard. Whatever the reason, will society still be able to choose a point on the product transformation curve? Again, the answer is no. Since society is not getting as much as it could out of its resources, it will not be able to produce as much as it would if its resources were used efficiently. Thus, *if resources are used inefficiently, society will have to settle for points inside the product transformation curve.* Perhaps in these circumstances, too, the best society can do may be point K in Figure 3.1. This less desirable position is the price of inefficiency.

At this point, it should be obvious that our model at least partially answers the question of how each good and service should be produced. The answer is to *produce each good and service in such a way that you wind up on the product transformation curve, not on a point inside it.* Of course, this is easier said than done, but at least our model indicates a couple of villains to watch out for: unemployment of resources and inefficiency. When these villains are present, we can be sure that society is not on the product transformation curve. Also, the old saw is wrong and it is possible to "get something for nothing" when society is inside the product transformation curve. That is, society can increase the output of one good without reducing the output of another good in such a situation. Society need not give up anything—in the way of production of other goods—to increase the production of this good under these circumstances.

This simple model helps illuminate the sequence of events in various countries at the beginning of World War II. In certain countries, like the Soviet Union, the war effort meant a substantial decrease in the standard of living on the home front. Resources had to be diverted from the production of civilian goods to the production of military goods, and the war struck a severe blow at the living standards of the civilian population. In other countries, like the United States, it was possible to increase the production of military goods without making such a dent in the living standards of the civilian population. This happened because the United States at the beginning of World War II

Figure 3.2
Effect of Increased Production of War Goods at the Beginning of World War II

Because the United States was at a point inside its product transformation curve, we could increase our production of war goods without reducing production of civilian goods. Because the Russians were on their product transformation curve, they could increase their output of war goods only by reducing ouput of civilian goods.

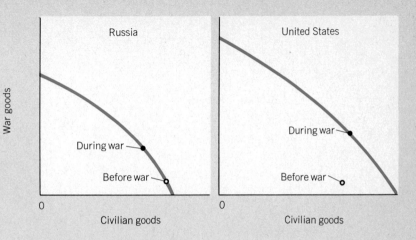

was still struggling to emerge from the Great Depression, and several million people were still unemployed. The same was not true in the Soviet Union. Thus, we could increase the production of both guns and butter, whereas they could not.

Suppose that we divide all goods into two classes: war goods and civilian goods. Then, as shown in Figure 3.2, *we were inside our product transformation curve at the beginning of the war, while the Russians were not.* Consequently, for the reasons discussed above, we could increase our production of war goods without reducing our production of civilian goods, while the Russians could not. (Note that in Figure 3.2, the two goods are war goods and civilian goods, not food and tractors.)

The Product Transformation Curve, Income Distribution, and Growth

Let's return now to the case where our economy produces food and tractors. The third basic function of any economic system is to distribute the goods and services that are produced among the members of society. Each point on the product transformation curve in Figure 3.1 represents so-

ciety's total pie, but to deal with the third function, we must know how the pie is divided up among society's members. Since the product transformation curve does not tell us this, it cannot shed light on this third function.

Fortunately, the product transformation curve is of more use in analyzing the fourth basic function of any economic system: to maintain and provide for an adequate rate of growth of per capita income. Suppose that this society invests a considerable amount of its resources in developing improved processes and products. For example, it might establish agricultural experiment stations to improve farming techniques and industrial research laboratories to improve tractor designs. As shown in Figure 3.3, the product transformation curve will be pushed outward. This will be the result of improved technology, enabling more food and/or more tractors to be produced from the same amount of resources. Thus, one way for an economy to increase its output—and its per capita income—is to invest in research and development.

Another way is by devoting more of its resources to the production of capital goods rather than consumers' goods. *Capital goods* consist of plant and equipment that are used to make other goods; *consumers' goods* are items that consumers purchase

Figure 3.3
Effect of Improvement in Technology on Product Transformation Curve

An improvement in technology results in an outward shift of the product transformation curve.

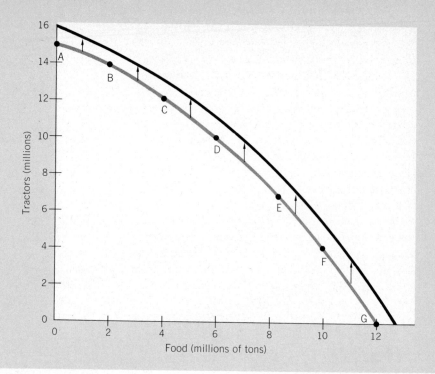

like clothing, food, and drink. Since capital goods are themselves resources, a society that chooses to produce lots of capital goods and few consumers' goods will push out its product transformation curve much farther than a society that chooses to produce lots of consumers' goods and few capital goods.

To illustrate this point, consider our simple society that produces food and tractors. The more tractors (and the less food) this society produces, the more tractors it will have in the next period; and the more tractors it has in the next period, the more of both goods—food and tractors—it will be able to produce then. Thus, the more tractors (and the less food) this society produces, the further out it will push its product transformation curve—and the greater the increase in output (and per capita income) that it will achieve in the next period. For example, if this society chooses point F in Figure 3.1, the effect will be entirely different than if it chooses point C. If it chooses point F, it produces 4 million tractors, which we assume

to be the number of tractors worn out each year. Thus, if it chooses point F, it adds nothing to its stock of tractors: it merely replaces those that wear out. Since it has no more tractors in the next period than in the current period, the product transformation curve does not shift out at all if point F is chosen. On the other hand, if point C is chosen, the society produces 12 million tractors, which means that it has 8 million additional tractors at the beginning of the next period. Thus, as shown in Figure 3.4, the product transformation curve is pushed outward. By producing more capital goods (and less consumers' goods) our society has increased its production possibilities and its per capita income.

What Is Capitalism?

The particular kind of economic system the United States has adopted to carry out these four basic economic functions is **capitalism.** Capitalism is one of those terms that is frequently used but seldom defined, and even less frequently understood. Exactly what does it mean? Let us begin with one of its important characteristics: *private ownership of capital.* In other words, you or I can buy the tools of production. We can own factories, equipment, inventories, and other forms of capital. In a capitalistic system, somebody owns each piece of capital—and receives the income from it. Each piece of equipment has some sort of legal instrument indicating to whom it belongs. If it belongs to a corporation, its owners basically are the stockholders who own the corporation. Moreover, each piece of capital has a money market value. This system is in marked contrast to a Communist or socialist state where the government owns the capital. In these states, the government decides how much and what kinds of capital goods will be produced; it owns the capital goods; and it re-

ceives and distributes the income they produce. In the Soviet Union or China, no one can buy or put up a new steel plant: it simply isn't allowed.

The United States is basically a capitalistic system, but there are certain areas where the government, not individuals, owns capital, and where individual property rights are limited in various ways by the government. The government owns much of the tooling used in the defense industries; it owns dams and the Tennessee Valley Authority; and it owns research laboratories in such diverse fields as atomic energy, space exploration, and health. Further, the government determines how much of a man's assets can go to his heirs when he dies. (The rest goes to the government in the form of estate and inheritance taxes.) Also, the government can make a person sell his property to allow a road or other public project to be built. There are many such limitations on property

**Figure 3.4
Effect of Increase in Capital Goods on Product Transformation Curve**

An increase in the amount of capital goods results in an outward shift of the product transformation curve. The choice of point *C* means the production of more capital goods than the choice of point *F*.

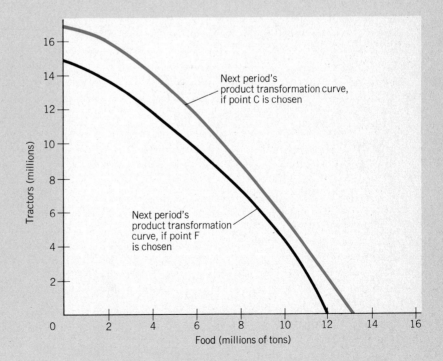

rights. Ours is basically a capitalistic system, but it must be recognized that the government's role is important. More will be said on this score in subsequent sections.

Private ownership of capital is but one of the important characteristics of capitalism. Another is freedom of choice and freedom of enterprise. **Freedom of choice** means that consumers are free to buy what they please and reject what they please; that laborers are free to work where, when, and if they please; and that investors are free to invest in whatever property they please. By **freedom of enterprise,** we mean that firms are free to enter whatever markets they please, obtain resources in whatever ways they can, and organize their affairs as best they can. Needless to say, this does not mean that firms can run roughshod over consumers and workers. Even the strongest champions of capitalism are quick to admit that the government must set "rules of the game" to prevent firms from engaging in sharp or unfair practices. But granting such limitations, the name of the game under capitalism is economic freedom.

Freedom to do what? Under capitalism, individuals and firms are free to pursue their own self-interest. Put in today's idiom, each individual or firm can do his, her, or its own thing. However, it is important to note that this freedom is circumscribed by one's financial resources. Consumers in a capitalistic system can buy practically anything they like—if they have the money to pay for it. Similarly, workers can work wherever or whenever they please—if they don't mind the wages. And a firm can run its business as it likes—if it remains solvent. Thus, an important regulator of economic activity under capitalism is the pattern of income and prices that emerges in the marketplace.

Still another important characteristic of capitalism is **competition.** Firms compete with one another for sales. Under perfect competition, there are a large number of firms producing each product; indeed, there are so many that no firm controls the product's price. Because of this competition, firms are forced to jump to the tune of the consumer. If a firm doesn't produce what consumers

want—at a price at least as low as other firms are charging—it will lose sales to other firms. Eventually, unless it mends its ways, such a firm will go out of business. Of course, in real-life American markets, the number of producers is not always so large that no firm has any control over price. (Much more will be said on this score below.) But in the purest form of capitalism, such imperfections do not exist. Also, lest you think that competition under capitalism is confined to producers, it must be remembered that owners of resources also compete. They are expected to offer their resources—including labor—to the buyer who gives them the best deal, and buyers of resources and products are supposed to compete openly and freely.

Finally, *still another very important characteristic of capitalism is its reliance upon markets. Under pure capitalism, the market—the free market—plays a central role. Firms and individuals buy and sell products and resources in competitive markets. Some firms and individuals make money and prosper; others lose money and fail. Each of these economic actors is allowed freedom to pursue his interests in the market place, while the government guards against shady and dishonest dealings. Such is the nature of the economic system under pure capitalism.*

Some of the major countries of the world operate with an economic system that is completely different from capitalism. In particular, the economic system in the Communist countries, such as the Soviet Union and China, is vastly different from the capitalist system. In these economies, capital is owned by the state, not by individuals or private firms. To determine what is produced, the Russian and Chinese governments formulate plans indicating what they want the people to produce. There is much less freedom for the consumer, the producer, or the resource owner (including laborers) in the Communist economies than under capitalism.

When we compare institutional characteristics and basic suppositions there is obviously a considerable gap between the Communist economies and a purely capitalistic economy. Most of the non-Communist nations of the world are somewhere between these two extremes. Even the United States, which is basically capitalistic, has adopted a mixed form of capitalism that combines the basic elements of capitalism with considerable government intervention. As will become evident, if it is not evident already, the American economy is by no means a purely capitalistic one, but it is closer to pure capitalism than many of the non-Communist nations of the world. In many of the other non-Communist nations, the economic system can be described as democratic, or liberal socialism. In such nations, there is much more government intervention than under pure capitalism, but much less than under communism; and there is much more economic freedom (and reliance on free markets) than under communism, but much less than under pure capitalism.

How Does Capitalism Perform the Four Basic Economic Tasks?

The *price system* lies at the heart of any capitalist economy. In a purely capitalist economy, it is used to carry out the four basic economic functions discussed above. The price system is a way to organize an economy. Under such a system, every commodity and every service, including labor, has a price. Everyone receives money for what he sells, including labor, and uses this money to buy the goods and services he wants. If more is wanted of a certain good, the price of this good tends to rise; if less is wanted, the price of the good tends to fall. Producers base their production decisions on the prices of commodities and inputs. Thus, increases in a commodity's price generally tend to increase the amount of it produced, and decreases generally tend to decrease the amount produced. In this way, firms' output decisions are brought into balance with consumers' desires.

The very important question of how the price system performs the basic economic functions we discussed above will be answered in some detail in the next chapter. All we can do here is provide a preliminary sketch of the way the price system carries out each of these four tasks. First, consider the determination of what the society will produce. In a substantially capitalistic economy, such as ours, consumers choose the amount of each good that they want, and producers act in accord with these decisions. The importance consumers attach to a good is indicated by the price they are willing to pay for it. Of course, the principle of *consumer sovereignty*—producers dancing to the tune of consumers' tastes—should not be viewed as always and completely true, since producers do attempt to manipulate the tastes of consumers through advertising and other devices, but it is certainly a reasonable first approximation.

In its second fundamental task, the price system helps determine how each good and service will be produced by indicating the desires of workers and the relative value of various types of materials and equipment as well as the desires of consumers. For example, if plumbers are scarce relative to the demand for them, their price in the labor market —their wage—will be bid up, and they will tend to be used only in the places where they are productive enough so that their employers can afford to pay them the higher wages. The forces that push firms toward actually carrying out the proper decisions are profits and losses. Profits are the carrot and losses are the stick used to eliminate the less efficient and alert firms and to increase the more efficient and the more alert.

How does the price system accomplish its third task, of determining how much in the way of goods and services each member of the society is to receive? In general, an individual's income depends largely on the quantities of resources of various kinds that he owns and the prices he gets for them. For example, if a man both works and rents out farm land he owns, his income is the number of hours he works per year times his hourly wage rate plus the number of acres of land he owns times the annual rental per acre. Thus, the distribution of income depends on the way resource ownership—including talent, intelligence, training, work habits, and, yes, even character—is distributed among the population. Also, to be candid, it depends on just plain luck.

Finally, how does the price system provide for an adequate rate of growth of per capita income? A nation's rate of growth of per capita income depends on the rate of growth of its resources and the rate of increase of the efficiency with which they are used. In our economy, the rate at which labor and capital resources are increased is motivated, at least in part, through the price system. Higher wages for more skilled work are an incentive for an individual to undergo further education and training. Capital accumulation occurs in response to the expectation of profit. Increases in efficiency, due in considerable measure to the advance of technology, are also stimulated by the price system.

Our Mixed Capitalist System and the Role of Government

Since the days of Adam Smith, economists have been fascinated by the features of a purely capitalistic economic system—an economy that relies entirely on the price system. Smith, and many generations of economists since, have gone to great pains to explain that in such an economic system, *the price system, although it is not controlled by any person or small group, results in economic order, not chaos.* The basic economic tasks any economy must perform can, as we have said, be carried out in such an economic system by the price system. It is an effective means of coordinating economic activity through decentralized decision making based on information disseminated through prices and related data.

But does this mean that the American economy is purely capitalistic? As we have stressed repeatedly in previous sections, the answer is no. A purely capitalistic system is a useful model of reality, not a description of our economy as it exists now or in the past. It is useful because a purely capitalistic economy is, for some purposes, a reasonably close fit to our own. However, this does not mean that such a model is useful for all purposes. Many American markets are not entirely competitive and never will be; they are dominated by a few producers or buyers who can influence price and thus distort the workings of the price system. Moreover, *the American economy is a mixed capitalistic economy, an economy where both government and private decisions are important.* The role of the government in American economic activity is very large indeed. Although it is essential to understand the workings of a purely capitalistic system, any model that omits the government entirely cannot purport to be adequate for the analysis of many major present-day economic issues.

To create a more balanced picture of the workings of the American economy, we must recognize that, although the price system plays an extremely important role, it is not permitted to solve all of the basic economic problems of our society. Consumer sovereignty does not extend—and cannot realistically be extended—to all areas of society. For example, certain public services cannot be left to private enterprise. The provision of fire protection, the operation of schools, and the development of weapons systems are examples of areas where we rely on political decision making, not the price system alone. Moreover, with regard to the consumption of commodities like drugs, society imposes limits on the decisions of individuals.

In addition, certain consequences of the price system are, by general agreement, unacceptable. Reliance on the price system alone does not assure a just or equitable or optimal distribution of income. It is possible, for example, that one person will literally have money to burn while another person will live in degrading poverty. Consequently, the government modifies the distribution of income by imposing taxes that take more from the rich than the poor, and by "welfare" programs that try to keep the poor from reaching the point where they lack decent food, adequate clothing, or shelter. Besides providing public services and maintaining certain minimum income standards, the government also carries out a variety of regulatory functions. Industries do not police the actions of their constituent firms, so it falls to the government to establish laws that impose limits on the economic behavior of firms. For example, these laws say that firms must not misrepresent their products, that child labor must not be employed, and that firms must not collude and form monopolies to interfere with the proper functioning of the price system. In this way, the government tries, with varying effectiveness, to establish the "rules of the game"— the limits within which the economic behavior of firms (and consumers) should lie.

Capital, Specialization, and Money: Other Characteristics of the American Economy

Finally, we must point out three additional characteristics of the American economy: the use of a great deal of capital per worker, specialization, and the use of money. These characteristics are common to all modern, industrialized nations, not just the United States, and they are so obvious that you may take them for granted. But they are too important to be ignored.

First, consider the enormous amount of capital American labor has to work with. Think of the oil refineries in New Jersey and Philadelphia, the blast furnaces and open hearths in Pittsburgh and Cleveland, the railroad yards in Chicago and Wichita, the aircraft plants in California and Georgia, the skyscrapers in New York, and the host of additional types of capital that we have and use in this country. To understand this idea fully, stop and think about what we mean by capital. As noted earlier in this chapter, to the economist capital is not the same as money. A man with a hot-dog stand who has $100 in his pocket may say that he has $100 in capital. But his definition is different from that of the economist, who

would also include in the man's capital the value of his stand, the value of his equipment, the value of his inventories of hot dogs, buns, and mustard, and the value of other nonlabor resources (other than land) that he uses.

Defining capital as economists do, it is evident that American workers have an enormous amount of capital to work with. And it is evident as well that this enormous amount of capital, together with an advanced technology and a well-trained labor force, is responsible for the tremendous amount of goods and services the American economy produces. All this capital contributes to increased production because it is often more efficient to adopt **roundabout methods of production.** For example, it is often more efficient to build a blast furnace and open hearth to produce steel rather than to try to produce steel directly. On the other hand, harking back to our discussion of Figure 3.4, it is also true that the production of capital goods means that less consumers' goods can be produced. In other words, although a greater amount of capital means greater production, consumers must be willing— or forced—to forgo current consumption of goods and services to produce this capital.

Next, consider the tremendous amount of specialization in the American economy. You may decide to specialize in tax law (and a particular branch of tax law at that), a classmate may specialize in brain surgery, another may specialize in repairing hi-fi sets, and another in monitoring certain types of equipment in an oil refinery. In contrast to more primitive economies, where people specialize much less, the American economy is characterized by an intricate web of specialization. What does it accomplish? As stressed by Adam Smith over two centuries ago, it results in much greater output than if people attempted to be jacks-of-all-trades. Because of this specialization, people can concentrate on the tasks they do best. For example, Bobby Fischer, the world champion chess player, can concentrate on chess and leave the hi-fi repairs to people who understand more about woofers and tweeters. However, it should be recognized that this specialization also results in great interdependence. Because each of us performs such specialized tasks, each of us depends on others for most of the things he needs. For example, unless you are much better at farming than I am, you would lose a lot of weight—and not because you wanted to—if farmers decided that they no longer wanted to provide us city folks with the fruits (and vegetables) of their labor.

Finally, the use of money is another important characteristic of all modern economies, including the American economy. Unquestionably you take the use of money as much for granted as you do the fact that the moon revolves about the earth. But money is a social invention. There is no evidence that Adam and Eve were created with the idea of money. They, or their descendants, had to think it up themselves, and this took time, as evidenced by the fact that extremely primitive cultures resorted to barter, which meant that to get a particular commodity, you had to swap a commodity that you owned for it. Since the exchange of commodities and services by barter was very difficult, the use of money has made trade and exchange much, much easier and facilitated the specialization of labor.

Summary

The American economy is the richest in the world. Based on freedom of enterprise, the American economy is rich in resources—land, labor, and capital —and American technology is among the most advanced in the world. The American economy, like any economic system, must perform four basic tasks: (1) It must determine the level and composition of society's output. (2) It must determine how each good and service is to be produced. (3) It must determine how the goods and services that are produced are to be distributed among the members of society. (4) It must maintain and provide for an adequate rate of growth of per capita income.

The product transformation curve, which shows the various production possibilities a society can attain, is useful in indicating the nature of the economic tasks any society faces. The task of determining the level and composition of society's output is really a problem of determining at what point along the product transformation curve society should be. Society, in performing this task, has to recognize that it cannot get more of one good without giving up some of another good, if resources are fully and efficiently used. However, if they are not fully and efficiently used, society will have to settle for points inside the product transformation curve—and it will be possible to obtain more of one good without giving up some of another good. Clearly, the task of determining how each good and service should be produced is, to a considerable extent, a problem of keeping society on its product transformation curve, rather than at points inside the curve. The product transformation curve does not tell us anything about the distribution of income, but it does indicate various ways that a society can promote growth in per capita income. By doing lots of research and development, or by producing lots of capital goods (rather than consumers' goods), society can push its product transformation curve outward, thus increasing per capita income.

Ours is a capitalistic economy, an economic system in which there is private ownership of capital, freedom of choice, freedom of enterprise, competition, and reliance upon markets. Many countries do not have a capitalistic economy, and even ours is not a purely capitalistic system. Under pure capitalism, the price system is used to perform the four basic economic tasks. Although it is not controlled by any person or small group, the price system results in order, not chaos. A purely capitalistic system is a useful model of reality, not a description of our economy as it exists now or in the past. The American economy is a mixed capitalistic economy, in which both government and private decisions are important. For example, certain public services, like fire protection and schools, cannot be left to private enterprise. In addition, society has said that certain consequences of the price system—like the existence of abject poverty —are unacceptable. Moreover, the government carries out a bewildering array of additional functions, many of which are described in Chapter 5.

CONCEPTS FOR REVIEW

Economic resources	Product transformation	Capitalism
Free resources	curve	Capital
Technology	Capital goods	Consumer sovereignty
	Consumers' goods	Money

QUESTIONS FOR DISCUSSION AND REVIEW

1. Suppose that you were appointed to the position of philosopher-king in a small country. In what way would you dictate that each of the four tasks of the economic system be carried out? Would you rely on the price system? Why or why not? Would you permit private ownership of capital? Why or why not?

2. As philosopher-king, would you find the concept of the product transformation curve useful? If not, why not; and if so, how?

3. Suppose that a society's product transformation curve is as follows:

Output (per year)

Possibility	Food (millions of tons)	Tractors (millions)
A	0	30
B	4	28
C	8	24
D	12	20
E	16	14
F	20	8
G	24	0

a. Is it possible for the society to produce 30 million tons of food per year?
b. Can it produce 30 million tractors per year?
c. Suppose this society produces 20 million tons of food and 6 million tractors per year. Is it operating on the product transformation curve? If not, what factors might account for this?

4. Which of the following is *not* a characteristic of capitalism?
   a. Competition
   b. General denial of self-interest for the public good
   c. Private ownership of capital
   d. Freedom of enterprise

CHAPTER 4

The Price System: Consumers, Firms, and Markets

Capitalist economies use the price system to perform the four basic tasks any economic system must carry out. Of course, as we pointed out in the previous chapter, the American economy is a mixed capitalist system, not a pure one. But this does not mean that the price system is unimportant. On the contrary, the price system plays a vital role in the American economy, and to obtain even a minimal grasp of the workings of our economic system, one must understand how the price system operates. This chapter takes up the nature and functions of the price system, as well as some applications of our theoretical results to real-life problems. For example we show how the price system determines the quantity produced of a commodity like wheat, and how the pricing policies of the Broadway theater hurt show business in a variety of ways. These applications should help illustrate the basic theory and indicate its usefulness.

Consumers

We begin by describing and discussing consumers and firms, the basic building blocks that make up the private, or nongovernmental, sector of the economy. What is a consumer? Sometimes—for example, when a man buys himself a beer on a warm day—the consumer is an individual. In other cases —for example, when a family buys a new car—the consumer may be an entire household. Consumers purchase the goods and services that are the ultimate end-products of the economic system. When a man buys tickets to a ball game, he is a consumer; when he buys himself a Coke at the game, he is a consumer; and when he buys his wife a book on baseball for their twentieth wedding anniversary, he is also a consumer.

Consumers—whether individuals or households —are an extremely varied lot. To get some idea of the variation, let's look at two families, the Onassises and the Ríoses. First, consider Aristotle Onassis, the Greek shipping and industrial magnate, and his wife, the former Mrs. John F. Kennedy. According to one reporter, Mr. and Mrs. Onassis were spending money during the first year of their marriage at the rate of $20 million per year. Mr. Onassis maintains fully staffed homes in Monte Carlo, Paris, Montevideo, Athens, New York, and the island of Skorpios, as well as hotel suites and a yacht. He has over 200 servants. Certainly Mr. Onassis is an extraordinary consumer, a man who consumes on a mammoth scale. Given his rate of expenditure, one might expect him to wind up in the poorhouse. But since he is estimated to be worth between $500 million and $1 billion, even if he put his money in a savings bank at 5 percent interest, he would have more than $20 million per year coming in. Clearly, Mr. Onassis has kept the wolf at a remarkable distance from the door!

In contrast, let's look at the Ríoses, a Puerto Rican family living in La Esmeralda, a slum section of San Juan. There are three branches of the Ríos family. One is headed by a man who works as a messenger and makes about $1,700 a year,

another by a woman who works as a barmaid and makes about $1,500 a year, and another by a woman who makes about $500 a year. The Ríoses consume relatively little. They live in crowded quarters with inadequate sanitary facilities, none of them has a refrigerator, and the average number of years spent in school by the members of the family is about 4 years. Excluding clothing, the total value of the possessions of these households is $436, $149, and $120; and the total value of each household's clothing is $496, $70, and $53.[1] Clearly, the Ríos family, which is quite typical of the families in La Esmeralda, is an example of abject poverty. To compare the level of consumption of the Onassises with that of the Ríoses is to compare an ocean liner with a frail canoe: yet both are consumers.

Firms

There are over 10 million firms in the United States. About $9/10$ of the goods and services produced in this country are produced by firms. (The rest are provided by government and not-for-profit institutions like universities and hospitals.) A firm is an organization that produces a good or service for sale. In contrast to not-for-profit organizations, firms attempt to make a profit. It doesn't take great analytical power to see that an economy like ours is centered around the activities of firms.

Like consumers, firms are extremely varied in size, age, power, and purpose. Consider two examples, Peter Amacher's drugstore on Chicago's South Side and the General Motors Corporation. The Amacher drugstore, started in 1922 by Mr. Amacher's father-in-law, is known in the retail drug trade as an independent, because it has no affiliation with a chain-store organization. Mr. Amacher and two other pharmacists keep the store open for business 13 hours a day, except on Sundays. The store sells about $150,000 worth

[1] Oscar Lewis, *La Vida*, New York: Random House, 1966.

of merchandise per year. Prescriptions account for about 25 percent of total sales, and cosmetics and greeting cards are the other principal sales items. Amacher's drugstore is an example of the small-business segment of the American business community.

In contrast, General Motors is one of the giants of American industry. It is the largest manufacturer of automobiles in the United States, its sales in 1971 being over $28 billion. Besides cars, it makes trucks, locomotives, aircraft engines, household appliances, and other products. Its total assets amounted to over $18 billion in 1971; and its total employment was over 700,000. General Motors, which was formed by merger, was set up as a holding company in 1908 by William C. Durant, owner of the Buick Motor Car Company. Durant acquired about 50 auto companies and parts manufacturers and put them all together as General Motors. Its present share of the market is greater than it was in 1908, when it produced about 25 percent of all cars in this country. In 1971, for example, it produced about 55 percent of all domestically produced cars.[2]

Markets

Consumers and firms come together in a market. The concept of a market is not quite as straightforward as it may seem, since most markets are not well defined geographically or physically. For example, the New York Stock Exchange is an atypical market because it is located principally in a particular building. For present purposes, *a market can be defined as a group of firms and individuals that are in touch with each other in order to buy or sell some good.* Of course, not every person in a market has to be in contact with every other person in the market. A person or firm is part of a market even if it is in contact with only a subset of the other persons or firms in the market.

[2] L. Weiss, *Economics and American Industry,* New York: Wiley, 1961, p. 329; and *Moody's Industrials,* annual.

Markets vary enormously in their size and procedures. For some toothpastes, most people who have their own teeth (and are interested in keeping them) are members of the same market; while for other goods like Picasso paintings, only a few dealers, collectors, and museums in certain parts of the world may be members of the market. And for still other goods, like lemonade sold by neighborhood children for a nickel a glass at a sidewalk stand, only people who walk by the stand—and are brave enough to drink the stuff—are members of the market. Basically, however, all markets consist primarily of buyers and sellers, although third parties like brokers and agents may be present as well.

Markets also vary in the extent to which they are dominated by a few large buyers or sellers. For example, in the United States, there was for many years only one producer of aluminum. Clearly this firm, the Aluminum Corporation of America, had great power in the market for aluminum. In contrast, the number of buyers and sellers in some other markets is so large that no single buyer or seller has any power over the price of the product. This is true in various agricultural markets, for example. When a market for a product contains so many buyers and sellers that none of them can influence the price, economists call the market *perfectly competitive.* In these introductory chapters, we make the simplifying assumption that markets are perfectly competitive. We will relax that assumption later.

The Demand Side of a Market

There are two sides of every market, just as there are of every argument. A market has a demand side and a supply side. *The **demand** side can be represented by a market demand curve, which shows the amount of the commodity buyers demand at various prices.* Consider Figure 4.1, which shows the demand curve for wheat in the American market during the early 1960s, as estimated by Iowa

**Figure 4.1
Market Demand Curve for
Wheat, Early 1960s**

The curve shows the amount of
wheat buyers would demand at
various prices.

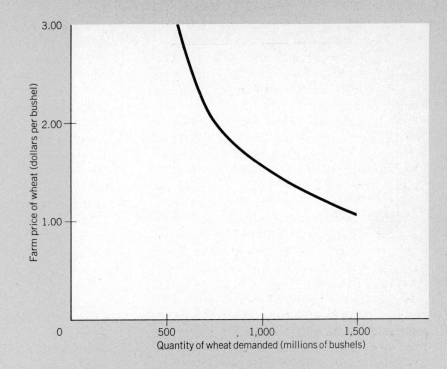

State's Karl Fox.[3] The figure shows that about 550 million bushels of wheat will be demanded annually if the farm price is $3 per bushel, about 700 million bushels will be demanded annually if the farm price is $2 per bushel, and about 1,500 million bushels will be demanded annually if the farm price is $1 per bushel. The total demand for wheat is of several types: to produce bread and other food products for domestic use, as well as for feed use, for export purposes, and for industrial uses. The demand curve in Figure 4.1 shows the total demand—including all these components— at each price. Any demand curve pertains to a particular period of time, and its shape and position depend on the length of this period.

[3] Karl Fox, "Commercial Agriculture: Perspectives and Prospects" in K. Fox, V. Ruttan, and L. Witt, *Farming, Farmers, and Markets for Farm Goods,* Committee for Economic Development, 1962. Of course, these estimates are only rough approximations, but they are good enough for present purposes.

Take a good look at the demand curve for wheat in Figure 4.1. This simple, innocent-looking curve influences a great many people's lives. After all, wheat is the principal grain used for direct human consumption in the United States. To states like Kansas, North Dakota, Oklahoma, Montana, Washington, Nebraska, Texas, Illinois, Indiana, and Ohio, wheat is a mighty important cash crop. Note that the demand curve for wheat slopes downward to the right. In other words, the quantity of wheat demanded increases as the price falls. This is true of the demand curve for most commodities: they almost always slope downward to the right. This makes sense: only the most obtuse of our citizenry would expect increases in a good's price to result in a greater quantity demanded.

What determines the position of the demand curve for a commodity? Why isn't the demand curve for wheat higher or lower, and what factors will cause it to shift? Although the position of the demand curve for a commodity depends on a host of factors, several are generally of primary importance. First, there are the tastes of consumers. If consumers show an increasing preference for a product, the demand curve will shift to the right; that is, at each price, consumers will desire to buy more than previously. On the other hand, if consumers show a decreasing preference for a product, the demand curve will shift to the left, since, at each price, consumers will desire to buy less than previously. Take wheat. If consumers become convinced that foods containing wheat prolong life and promote happiness, the demand curve may shift, as shown in Figure 4.2; and the greater the shift in preferences, the larger the shift in the demand curve.

Second, the demand curve for a commodity is affected by the income level of consumers. For some types of products, the demand curve shifts to the right if per capita income increases; whereas for other types of commodities, the demand curve shifts to the left if per capita income rises. Economists can explain why some goods fall into one category and other goods fall into the other, but, at present, this need not concern us. All that is important here is that changes in per capita income affect the demand curve, the size and direction of this effect varying from product to product. For example, in the case of wheat, a 10 percent increase in per capita income would probably have a relatively small effect on the demand curve, as shown in Figure 4.3.

Third, the demand curve for a commodity is affected by the number of consumers in the market. Compare Austria's demand for wheat with America's. Austria is a small country with a population of about 7 million; the United States is a huge country with a population of over 200 million. Clearly, at a given price of wheat, the quantity demanded by American consumers will greatly exceed the quantity demanded by Austrian consumers, as shown in Figure 4.4. Even if consumer tastes, income, and other factors were held constant, this would still be true simply because the United States has so many more consumers in the relevant market.[4]

Fourth, the demand curve for a commodity is affected by the level of other prices. For example, since wheat can be substituted to some extent for corn as livestock feed, the quantity of wheat demanded depends on the price of corn as well as on the price of wheat. If the price of corn is high, more wheat will be demanded since it will be profitable to substitute wheat for corn. If the price of corn is low, less wheat will be demanded since it will be profitable to substitute corn for wheat. Thus, as shown in Figure 4.5, increases in the price of corn will shift the demand curve for wheat to the right, and decreases in the price of corn will shift it to the left.

The Supply Side of a Market

So much for our first look at demand. What about the other side of the market: supply? *The supply side of a market can be represented by a market supply curve that shows the amount of the commodity sellers will supply at various prices.* Let's continue with the case of wheat. Figure 4.6 shows the supply curve for wheat in the United States in the early 1960s, based on estimates made informally by government experts.[5] According to the figure, about 1,750 million bushels of wheat would be supplied if the farm price were $3 per bushel, about 1,400 million bushels if the farm price were $2 per bushel, and about 750 million bushels if the farm price were $1 per bushel.

Look carefully at the supply curve shown in Figure 4.6. Although it looks innocuous enough, it summarizes the potential behavior of thousands of American wheat farmers—and their behavior plays an important role in determining the pros-

[4] Note that no figures are given along the horizontal axis in Figure 4.4. This is because we do not have reasonably precise estimates of the demand curve in Austria. Nonetheless, the hypothetical demand curves in Figure 4.4 are close enough to the mark for present purposes.

[5] I am very much indebted to officials of the U.S. Department of Agriculture for providing me with these estimates. Of course, they are only rough approximations, but they are good enough for present purposes.

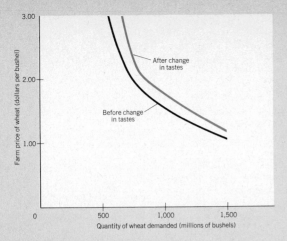

Figure 4.2
Effect of Increased Preference for Wheat on Market Demand Curve

An increased preference would shift the demand curve to the right.

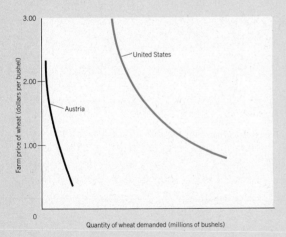

Figure 4.4
Market Demand Curves for Wheat, Austria and United States

Since the United States has far more consumers than Austria, the demand curve in the United States is far to the right of Austria's.

Figure 4.3
Effect of Increase in Income on Market Demand Curve for Wheat

An increase in income would shift the demand curve for wheat to the right, but only slightly.

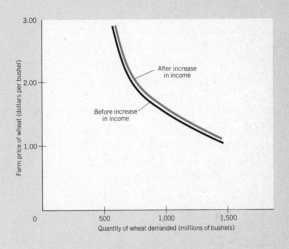

Figure 4.5
Effect of Price of Corn on Market Demand Curve for Wheat

Price increases for corn will shift the demand curve to the right.

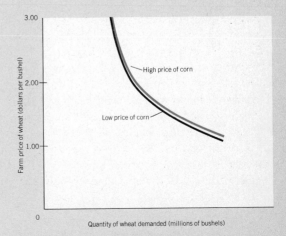

54

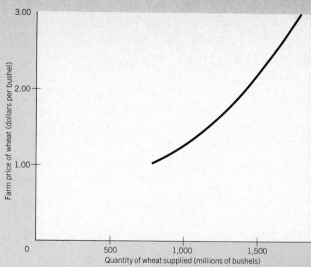

Figure 4.6
Market Supply Curve for Wheat, Early 1960s

The curve shows the amount of wheat sellers would
supply at various prices.

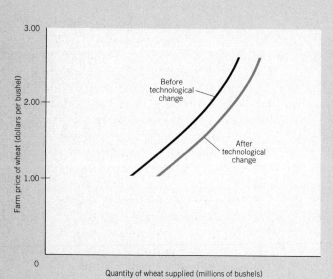

Figure 4.7
Effect of Technological Change on Market Supply
Curve for Wheat

Improvements in technology often shift the supply
curve to the right.

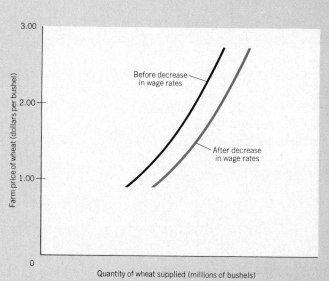

Figure 4.8
Effect of Decrease in Farm Wage Rates on Market
Supply Curve for Wheat

A reduction in the wage rate might shift the supply
curve to the right.

perity of many states and communities. Note that the supply curve for wheat slopes upward to the right. In other words, the quantity of wheat supplied increases as the price increases. This seems plausible, since increases in price give a greater incentive for farms to produce wheat and offer it for sale. Empirical studies indicate that the supply curves for a great many commodities share this characteristic of sloping upward to the right.

What determines the position of the supply curve for a commodity? As you might expect, it depends on a host of factors. But several stand out. First, there is the state of technology, defined in the previous chapter as society's pool of knowledge concerning the industrial arts. As technology progresses, it becomes possible to produce commodities more cheaply, so that firms often are willing to supply a given amount at a lower price than formerly. Thus, technological change often causes the supply curve to shift to the right. For example, this certainly has occurred in the case of wheat, as shown in Figure 4.7. There have been many important technological changes in wheat production, ranging from advances in tractors to the development of improved varieties like semidwarf wheats.

Second, the supply curve for a commodity is affected by the prices of the resources (labor, capital, and land) used to produce it. Decreases in the price of these inputs make it possible to produce commodities more cheaply, so that firms may be willing to supply a given amount at a lower price than they formerly would. Thus, decreases in the price of inputs may cause the supply curve to shift to the right. On the other hand, increases in the price of inputs may cause it to shift to the left. For example, if the wage rates of farm labor decrease, the supply curve for wheat may shift to the right, as shown in Figure 4.8.

The Equilibrium Price

The two sides of a market, demand and supply, interact to determine the price of a commodity.

Recall from the previous chapter that prices in a capitalistic system play a central role in determining what is produced and how, who receives it, and how rapidly per capita income grows. It behooves us, therefore, to look carefully at how prices themselves are determined in a capitalist system. As a first step toward describing this process, we must define the equilibrium price of a product. At various points in this book, you will encounter the concept of an equilibrium, which is very important in economics, as in many other scientific fields.

Put briefly, an *equilibrium is a situation where there is no tendency for change:* in other words, it is a situation that can persist. Thus, *an equilibrium price is a price that can be maintained.* Any price that is not an equilibrium price cannot be maintained for long, since there are basic forces at work to stimulate a change in price. The best way to understand what we mean by an equilibrium price is to take a particular case, such as the wheat market. Let's put both the demand curve for wheat (in Figure 4.1) and the supply curve for wheat (in Figure 4.6) together in the same diagram. The result, shown in Figure 4.9, will help us determine the equilibrium price of wheat.

We begin by seeing what would happen if various prices were established in the market. For example, if the price were $3 per bushel, the demand curve indicates that 550 million bushels of wheat would be demanded, while the supply curve indicates that 1,750 million bushels would be supplied. Thus, if the price were $3 a bushel, there would be a mismatch between the quantity supplied and the quantity demanded per year, since the rate at which wheat is supplied would be greater than the rate at which it is demanded. Specifically, as shown in Figure 4.9, there would be an *excess supply* of 1,200 million bushels. Under these circumstances, some of the wheat supplied by farmers could not be sold, and as inventories of wheat built up, suppliers would tend to cut their prices in order to get rid of unwanted inventories. Thus, a price of $3 per bushel would not be maintained for long—and for this reason, $3 per bushel is not an equilibrium price.

56

Figure 4.9
Determination of the
Equilibrium Price of Wheat
in a Free Market, Early 1960s

The equilibrium price is $1.40
per bushel, and the equilibrium
quantity is 1,100 million bushels.
At a price of $3.00 per bushel,
there would be an excess supply
of 1,200 million bushels. At a
price of $1.00 per bushel, there
would be an excess demand of
750 million bushels.

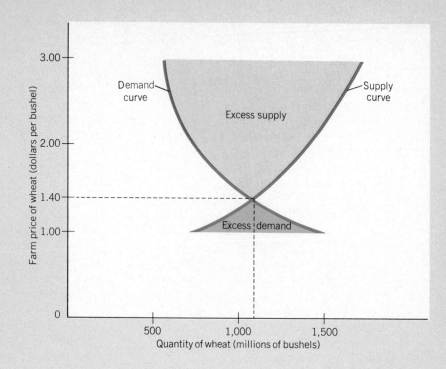

If the price were $1 per bushel, on the other hand, the demand curve indicates that 1,500 million bushels would be demanded, while the supply curve indicates that 750 million bushels would be supplied. Again we find a mismatch between the quantity supplied and the quantity demanded per year, since the rate at which wheat is supplied would be less than the rate at which it is demanded. Specifically, as shown in Figure 4.9, there would be an *excess demand* of 750 million bushels. Under these circumstances, some of the consumers who want wheat at this price would have to be turned away empty-handed. There would be a shortage. And given this shortage, suppliers would find it profitable to increase the price, and competition among buyers would bid the price up. Thus, a price of $1 per bushel could not be maintained for long—so $1 per bushel is not an equilibrium price.

Under these circumstances, the equilibrium price must be the price where the quantity demanded equals the quantity supplied. Obviously, this is the only price at which there is no mismatch between the quantity demanded and the quantity supplied; and consequently the only price that can be maintained for long. In Figure 4.9, the price at which the quantity supplied equals the quantity demanded is $1.40 per bushel, the price where the demand curve intersects the supply curve. Thus, $1.40 per bushel is the equilibrium price of wheat under the circumstances visualized in Figure 4.9, and 1,100 million bushels is the equilibrium quantity.

Actual Price versus Equilibrium Price

The price that counts in the real world, however, is the actual price, not the equilibrium price, and it is the actual price that we set out to explain. In general, economists simply assume that the actual price will approximate the equilibrium price, which seems reasonable enough, since the basic forces at work tend to push the actual price toward the equilibrium price. Thus, if conditions remain fairly stable for a time, the actual price should move toward the equilibrium price.

To see that this is the case, consider the market for wheat, as described by Figure 4.9. What if the price somehow is set at $3 per bushel? As we saw in the previous section, there is downward pressure on the price of wheat under these conditions. Suppose the price, responding to this pressure, falls to $2.50. Comparing the quantity demanded with the quantity supplied at $2.50, we find that there is still downward pressure on price, since the quantity supplied exceeds the quantity demanded at $2.50. The price, responding to this pressure, may fall to $2.00, but comparing the quantity demanded with the quantity supplied at this price, we find that there is still a downward pressure on price, since the quantity supplied exceeds the quantity demanded at $2.00.

So long as the actual price exceeds the equilibrium price, there will be downward pressure on price. Similarly, so long as the actual price is less than the equilibrium price, there will be an upward pressure on price. Thus there is always a tendency for the actual price to move toward the equilibrium price. But it should not be assumed that this movement is always rapid. Sometimes it takes a long time for the actual price to get close to the equilibrium price. Sometimes the actual price never gets to the equilibrium price because by the time it gets close, the equilibrium price changes. All that safely can be said is that the actual price will move toward the equilibrium price. But of course this information is of great value, both theoretically and practically. For many purposes, all that is needed is a correct prediction of the direction in which the price will move.

Changes in the Demand and Supply Curves

Heraclitus, the ancient Greek philosopher, said you cannot step in the same stream twice: everything changes, sooner or later. One need not be a disciple of Heraclitus to recognize that demand curves and supply curves shift. Indeed, we have already seen that demand curves shift in response to changes in tastes, income, population, and prices of other products, and that supply curves shift in response to changes in technology and input prices. Any supply-and-demand diagram like Figure 4.9 is essentially a snapshot of the situation during a particular period of time. The results in Figure 4.9 are limited to a particular period because the demand and supply curves in the figure, like any demand and supply curves, pertain only to a certain period.

What happens to the equilibrium price of a product when its demand or supply curve changes? This is an important question because it sheds a good deal of light on how the price system works. Suppose that consumer tastes shift in favor of foods containing wheat, causing the demand curve for wheat to shift to the right. This state of affairs is shown in Figure 4.10, where the demand curve shifts from DD' to D_1D_1'. It is not hard to see the effect on the equilibrium price of wheat. When DD' is the demand curve, the equilibrium price is OP. But when the demand curve shifts to D_1D_1', a shortage of (OQ_2-OQ) develops at this price: that is, the quantity demanded exceeds the quantity supplied at this price by (OQ_2-OQ). Consequently, suppliers raise their prices. After some testing of market reactions and trial-and-error adjustments, the price will tend to settle at OP_1, the new equilibrium price, and quantity will tend to settle at OQ_1. On the other hand, suppose that consumer demand for wheat products falls off, perhaps because of a great drop in the price of corn products. The demand for wheat now shifts to the left. Specifically, as shown in Figure 4.11, it shifts from DD' to D_2D_2'. What will be the effect on the equilibrium price of wheat? Clearly, the new equilibrium price will be OP_2, where the new demand curve intersects the supply curve.

In general, a shift to the right in the demand curve results in an increase in the equilibrium price, and a shift to the left in the demand curve results in a decrease in the equilibrium price. This

Figure 4.10
Effect on the Equilibrium Price of a Shift to the Right of the Market Demand Curve

A shift to the right from *DD'* to *D₁D₁'* results in an increase in the equilibrium price from *OP* to *OP₁* and an increase in the equilibrium quantity from *OQ* to *OQ₁*.

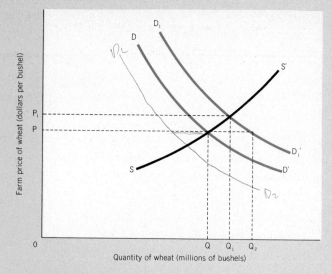

Figure 4.11
Effect on the Equilibrium Price of a Shift to the Left of the Market Demand Curve

A shift to the left from *DD'* to *D₂D₂'* results in a decrease in the equilibrium price from *OP* to *OP₂* and a decrease in the equilibrium quantity.

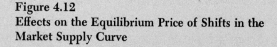

Figure 4.12
Effects on the Equilibrium Price of Shifts in the Market Supply Curve

A shift to the right from *SS'* to *S₁S₁'* results in a decrease in the equilibrium price from *OP* to *OP₃*. A shift to the left from *SS'* to *S₂S₂'* increases the equilibrium price from *OP* to *OP₄*.

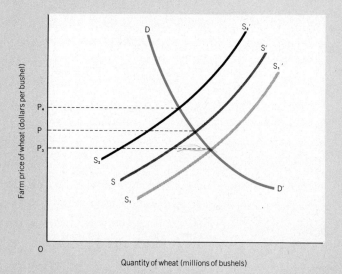

is the lesson of Figures 4.10 and 4.11. Of course, this conclusion depends on the assumption that the supply curve slopes upward to the right, but, as we noted in a previous section, this assumption is generally true.

At this point, since all of this is theory, you may be wondering how well this theory works in practice. In 1972 and 1973, there was a vivid demonstration of the accuracy of this model in various agricultural markets, including wheat. Because of poor harvests abroad and greatly increased foreign demand for American wheat, the demand curve for wheat shifted markedly to the right. What happened to the price of wheat? In accord with our model, the price increased spectacularly, from about $1.35 a bushel in the early summer of 1972 to over $4 a year later. Anyone who witnessed this phenomenon could not help but be impressed by the usefulness of this model.

Let's turn now to changes in the supply curve. Suppose that, because of technological advances in wheat production, wheat farmers are willing and able to supply more wheat at a given price than they used to. Specifically, suppose that the supply curve shifts from SS' to S_1S_1' in Figure 4.12. What will be the effect on the equilibrium price? Clearly, it will fall from OP (where the SS' supply curve intersects the demand curve) to OP_3 (where the S_1S_1' supply curve intersects the demand curve). On the other hand, suppose that the weather is poor, with the result that the supply curve shifts to the left. Specifically, suppose that the supply curve shifts from SS' to S_2S_2' in Figure 4.12. Clearly, the equilibrium price will increase from OP (where the SS' supply curve intersects the demand curve) to OP_4 (where the S_2S_2' supply curve intersects the demand curve).

In general, a shift to the right in the supply curve results in a decrease in the equilibrium price, and a shift to the left in the supply curve results in an increase in the equilibrium price. Of course, this conclusion depends on the assumption that the demand curve slopes downward to the right, but, as we noted in a previous section, this assumption is generally true.

The Price System and the Determination of What Is Produced

Having described how prices are determined in free markets, we can now describe more adequately how the price system goes about performing the four basic tasks that face any economic system. (In the previous chapter, we sketched out the functions of the price system, but in a very cursory manner.) Let's begin by considering the determination of what society will produce: how does the price system carry out this task? As pointed out in the previous chapter, consumers indicate what goods and services they want in the marketplace, and producers try to meet these wants. More specifically, the demand curve for a product shows how much of that product consumers want at various prices. If consumers don't want much of it at a certain price, its demand curve will indicate that fact by being positioned close to the vertical axis at that price. In other words, the demand curve will show that, at this price for the product, the amount consumers will buy is small. On the other hand, if consumers want lots of the product at this price, its demand curve will be far from the vertical axis.

A product's demand curve is an important determinant of how much firms will produce of the product, since it indicates the amount of the product that will be demanded at each price. From the point of view of the producers, the demand curve indicates the amount they can sell at each price. In a capitalist economy, firms are in business to make money. Thus, the manufacturers of any product will turn it out only if the amount of money they receive from consumers exceeds the cost of putting the product on the market. Acting in accord with the profit motive, firms are led to produce what the consumers desire. For example, we saw in the previous section that if consumers' tastes shift in favor of foods containing wheat, the demand curve for wheat will shift to the right, which will result in an increase in the price of wheat. This increase will stimulate farmers to produce more wheat. For example, when the demand curve shifts from DD' to D_1D_1' in Figure 4.10, the equilibrium quantity produced increases from OQ to OQ_1. Given the shift in the demand curve, it is profitable for firms to step up their production. Acting in their own self-interest, they are led to make production decisions geared to the wants of the consumers.

Thus, the price system uses the self-interest of the producers to get them to produce what consumers want. Consumers register what they want in the marketplace by their purchasing decisions— i.e., their demand curves. Producers can make more money by responding to consumer wants than by ignoring them. Consequently, they are led to produce what consumers want—and are willing to pay enough for to cover the producers' costs. Note that costs as well as demand determine what will be produced, and that producers are not forced by anyone to do anything. They can produce air conditioners for Eskimos if they like—and if they are prepared to absorb the losses. The price system uses prices to communicate the relevant signals to producers, and metes out the penalties and rewards in the form of losses or profits.

The Price System and the Determination of How Goods Are Produced

Next, consider how society determines how each good and service is produced. How does the price system carry out this task? As pointed out in the previous chapter, the price of each resource gives producers an indication of how scarce this resource is, and how valuable in other uses. Clearly, firms should produce goods and services at minimum cost. Suppose that there are two ways of producing tables: Technique A and Technique B. Technique A requires 4 manhours of labor and $10 worth of

wood per table, whereas Technique B requires 5 manhours of labor and $8 worth of wood. If the price of a manhour of labor is $4, Technique A should be used since a table costs $26 with this technique, as opposed to $28 with technique B.[6] In other words, Technique A uses fewer resources per table.

The price system nudges producers to opt for Technique A rather than Technique B through profits and losses. If each table commands a price of $35, then by using Technique A, producers make a profit of $35 − $26 = $9 per table. If they use Technique B, they make a profit of $35 − $28 = $7 per table. Thus producers, if they maximize profit, will be led to adopt Technique A. Their desire for profit leads them to adopt the techniques that will enable society to get the most out of its resources. No one commands firms to use particular techniques. Washington officials do not order steel plants to substitute the basic oxygen process for open hearths, or petroleum refineries to substitute catalytic cracking for thermal cracking. It is all done through the impersonal marketplace.

You should not, however, get the idea that the price system operates with kid gloves. Suppose all firms producing tables used Technique B until this past year, when Technique A was developed: in other words, Technique A is based on a new technology. Given this technological change, the supply curve for tables will shift to the right, as we saw in a previous section, and the price of a table will fall. Suppose it drops to $27. If some firm insists on sticking with Technique B, it will lose money at the rate of $1 a table; and as these losses mount, the firm's owners will become increasingly uncomfortable. The firm will either switch to Technique A or go bankrupt. The price system leans awfully hard on producers that try to ignore its signals.

---

[6] To obtain these figures, note that the cost with Technique A is 4 manhours times $4 plus $10, or $26, while the cost with Technique B is 5 manhours times $4 plus $8, or $28.

The Price System and the Determination of Who Gets What

Let's turn now to how society's output will be distributed among the people: how does the price system carry out this task? How much a person receives in goods and services depends on his money income, which in turn is determined under the price system by the amount of various resources that he owns and by the price of each resource. Thus, under the price system, each person's income is determined in the marketplace: he comes to the marketplace with certain resources to sell, and his income depends on how much he can get for them.

The question of who gets what is solved at two levels by the price system. Consider an individual product—for example, the tables discussed in the previous section. For the individual product, the question of who gets what is solved by the equality of quantity demanded and quantity supplied. If the price of these tables is at its equilibrium level, the quantity demanded will equal the quantity supplied. Consumers who are willing and able to pay the equilibrium price (or more) get the tables, while those who are unwilling or unable to pay it do not get them. It is just as simple—and as impersonal—as that. It doesn't matter whether you are a nice guy or a scoundrel, or whether you are a connoisseur of tables or someone who doesn't know good workmanship from poor: all that matters is whether you are able and willing to pay the equilibrium price.

Next, consider the question of who gets what at a somewhat more fundamental level. After all, whether a consumer is able and willing to pay the equilibrium price for a good depends on his money income. Thus, Aristotle Onassis can pay the equilibrium price for an astonishing variety of things, whereas the Ríos family can scrape up the equilibrium price for very little. As we have already seen, a consumer's money income depends on the amount of resources of various kinds that he owns and the price that he can get for them. Some

people have lots of resources: they are endowed with skill and intelligence and industry, or they have lots of capital or land. Other people have little in the way of resources. Moreover, some people have resources that command a high price, while others have resources that are of little monetary value. The result is that, under the price system, some consumers, like Aristotle Onassis, get a lot more of society's output than other consumers, like the Ríos family.

The Price System and Economic Growth

Let's turn now to the task of providing for an adequate rate of growth of per capita income. How does the price system do this? As pointed out in the previous chapter, a nation's rate of increase of per capita income depends on the rate of growth of its resources and the rate of increase of the efficiency with which they are used. First, consider the rate of growth of society's resources. The price system controls the amount of new capital goods produced much as it controls the amount of consumer goods produced. Similarly, the price system influences the amount society invests in educating, training, and upgrading its labor resources. To a considerable extent, the amount invested in such resource-augmenting activities is determined by the profitability of such investments, which is determined in turn by the pattern of prices.

Next, consider the rate of increase of the efficiency with which a society's resources are used. Clearly, this factor depends heavily on the rate of technological change. If technology is advancing at a rapid rate, it should be possible to get more and more out of a society's resources. But if technology is advancing rather slowly, it is likely to be difficult to get much more out of them. The price system affects the rate of technological change in a variety of ways: it influences the profitability of investing in research and development, the profitability of introducing new processes and products into commercial practice, and the profitability of accepting technological change—as well as the losses involved in spurning it.

The price system establishes strong incentives for firms to introduce new technology. Any firm that can find a cheaper way to produce an existing product, or a way to produce a better product, will have a profitable jump on its competitors. Until its competitors can do the same thing, this firm can reap higher profits than it otherwise could. Of course, these higher profits will eventually be competed away, as other firms begin to imitate this firm's innovation. But lots of money can be made in the period during which this firm has a lead over its competitors. These profits are an important incentive for the introduction of new technology.

The Price System in Action behind Enemy Lines

Just as general discussions of tennis will take a neophyte only so far, after which he or she must watch and participate in a few matches, so a general discussion of the price system will take a student only so far. Then he should look at real-life examples of the price system at work. Our first illustration of the price system in operation is a prisoner-of-war camp in World War II. This case is not chosen because of its inherent importance, but because of its simplicity. Just as certain elementary forms of life illustrate important biological principles in a simple way, so the economic organization of a prisoner-of-war camp is an elementary form of economic system that illustrates certain important economic principles simply and well.

The prisoner-of-war camp was so elementary because no goods were produced there. All commodities were provided by the country running the camp, by the Red Cross, and by other outside donors. Each prisoner received an equal amount of food and supplies—canned milk, jam, butter, cookies, cigarettes, etc. In addition, private parcels of clothing, cigarettes, and other supplies were re-

ceived, with different prisoners, of course, receiving different quantities. Because no goods were produced in the prisoner-of-war camp, the first two tasks of an economic system (What will be produced? How will it be produced?) were not relevant; neither was the fourth task (What provision is to be made for growth?).

All that did matter in this elementary economic system was the third task: to determine who would consume the various available goods. At first blush, the answer may seem obvious: each prisoner would consume the goods he received from the detaining country, the Red Cross, and private packages. But this assumes that prisoners would not trade goods back and forth ("I'll swap you a cigarette for some milk"), which is clearly unrealistic. After all, some prisoners smoked cigarettes, others did not; some liked jam and didn't like canned beef, others liked canned beef and didn't like jam. Thus, there was bound to be exchange of this sort, and the real question is in what way and on what terms such exchange took place.

How did the prisoners go about exchanging goods? According to one observer, the process developed as follows:

> Starting with simple direct barter, such as a non-smoker giving a smoker friend his cigarette issue in exchange for a chocolate ration, more complex exchanges soon became an accepted custom . . . Within a week or two, as the volume of trade grew, rough scales of exchange values came into existence. [Some prisoners], who had at first exchanged tinned beef for practically any other foodstuff, began to insist on jam and margarine. It was realized that a tin of jam was worth one half lb. of margarine plus something else, that a cigarette issue was worth several chocolate issues, and a tin of diced carrots was worth practically nothing . . . By the end of the month, there was a lively trade in all commodities and their relative values were well known, and expressed not in terms of one another—one didn't quote [jam] in terms of sugar—but in terms of cigarettes. The cigarette became the standard of value.[7]

[7] R. A. Radford, "The Economic Organization of a Prisoner of War Camp," reprinted in E. Mansfield, *Economics: Readings, Issues, and Cases*, New York: Norton, 1974.

Thus, the prisoners used the price system to solve the problem of allocating the available supply of goods among consumers. A market developed for each good. This market had, of course, both a demand and a supply side. Each good had its price—but this price was quoted in cigarettes, not dollars and cents. These markets were not started in a self-conscious, deliberate way. No one said, "Let's adopt the price system to allocate available supplies," or "Let's vote on whether or not to adopt the price system." Instead, the system just evolved. . . and it worked.

To see how the supply of a particular good—jam, say—was allocated, look at Figure 4.13, which shows the market supply curve for jam, SS'. In the short run, this supply was fixed, so SS' is a vertical line. Figure 4.13 also provides the market demand curve for jam, DD', which shows the amount of jam the prisoners wanted to consume at various prices of jam—expressed in terms of cigarettes. For example, DD' shows that the prisoners wanted OQ_1 tins of jam when a tin of jam cost OP_1 cigarettes, and OQ_2 tins of jam when a tin of jam cost OP_2 cigarettes. For the quantity demanded to equal the available supply, the price of a tin of jam had to be OP cigarettes: one tin of jam had to exchange for OP cigarettes. At this price, the available supply of jam was rationed, without resort to fights among prisoners or intervention by the prison authorities. Those prisoners who could and would pay the price had the jam—and there were just enough such consumers to exhaust the available supply. Moreover, this held true for each of the other goods (including cigarettes) as well.

Figure 4.13
Determinants of Equilibrium Price of a Tin of Jam (in Terms of Cigarettes) in a Prisoner-of-War Camp

The market supply for jam is fixed at *OS* tins. The market demand curve is *DD'*. Thus the equilibrium price of a tin of jam is *OP* cigarettes. If the price were *OP₁*, *OQ₁* tins would be demanded; if the price were *OP₂*, *OQ₂* tins would be demanded.

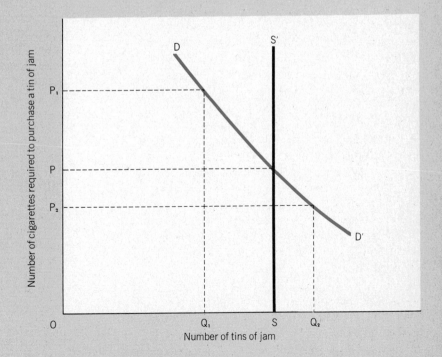

The Price System in Action on the Great White Way

It is a long way from a prisoner-of-war camp to the Broadway theater, but economics, like any good tool of analysis, applies to a very wide variety of problems. In this section, we discuss the theater's pricing problems—and the role of the price system in helping to solve these problems. Prices for tickets to Broadway shows are established at levels that are much the same whether the show is a success or a flop. For example, an orchestra ticket to *Kelly* (which managed to hold out for one performance before closing) cost about as much as an orchestra ticket to such hits as *Hair* or *A Little Night Music*. And once a play opens, the price of a ticket remains much the same whether the play is greeted with universal praise or with discontented critics and customers.

Because of these pricing methods, the Broadway theater has been beset for many years by serious problems. Here they are described by two veteran observers of the Broadway stage:

> For centuries the sale of theater tickets has brought on corruption and confusion. When there are more buyers than sellers, a black market results. The so-called "retail" price, the price printed on the ticket, becomes meaningless. Speculation doubles, triples, or quadruples the "real" as opposed to the "legal" asking price. A smash hit on Broadway means "ice" —the difference between the real and legal prices— a well-hidden but substantial cash flow that is divided among shadowy middlemen. Ticket scandals break out in New York as regularly as the flu. The scenario is familiar. A play opens and becomes a superhit. Tickets become difficult, then impossible, to obtain. There are letters to the newspapers . . . Shocking corruption is discovered. Someone . . . is convicted of overcharging and accepting illegal gratuities. Someone may even go to jail. The black market, valiantly scotched, *never stops for a single moment.*[8]

[8] S. Little and A. Cantor, *The Playmakers*, New York: Norton, 1970, p. 220.

Besides enriching crooked box-office men and managers, as well as other shadowy elements of society, the black market for theater tickets has the additional undesirable effect of excluding the authors, composers, directors, and stars of the play from participation in the premium revenue. Almost all of these people receive a percentage of the play's revenues; and if the revenues at the box office are less than the customers pay for their seats (because of "ice"), these people receive less than they would if no black market existed. The amount of "ice" can be substantial. For example, Rodgers and Hammerstein estimated that, at one performance of their play, *South Pacific*, the public probably paid about $25,000 for tickets with a face value of $7,000, the amount turned in at the box office.

To focus on the problem here, let's look at the market for tickets to a particular performance of *My Fair Lady* (one of Broadway's all-time big hits) when it was at the height of its popularity. Since the supply of tickets to a given performance is fixed, the market supply curve, SS' in Figure 4.14, is a vertical line at the quantity of tickets corresponding to the capacity of the theatre. The price set officially on the price of a ticket was $8. But because the show was enormously popular, the market demand curve was DD' in Figure 4.14, and the equilibrium price for a ticket was $50.[9]

Figure 4.14 makes the nature of the problem apparent: at the official price of $8, the quantity of tickets demanded is much greater than the quantity supplied. Supply and demand don't match. Obviously, there is an incentive for people to buy the tickets from the box office at $8 and sell them at the higher prices customers are willing to pay. There is also an incentive for box-office men to sell them surreptitiously at higher prices and turn in only $8. The price system cannot play the role it did in the prisoner-of-war camp for jam and other goods. It cannot act as an effective rationing device because, to do so, the price of tickets would have to increase to its equilibrium level, $50.

[9] This figure is an estimate based on an article in *Variety*.

Figure 4.14
Equilibrium Price for Tickets to
My Fair Lady

The market supply for tickets is fixed at *OS* per performance. If the demand curve is *DD'*, the equilibrium price of a ticket is $50. (If the demand curve is *D₁D₁'*, the equilibrium price is $7.) If the demand curve is *DD'* and the price of a ticket is $8, the quantity of tickets demanded will far exceed the quantity supplied.

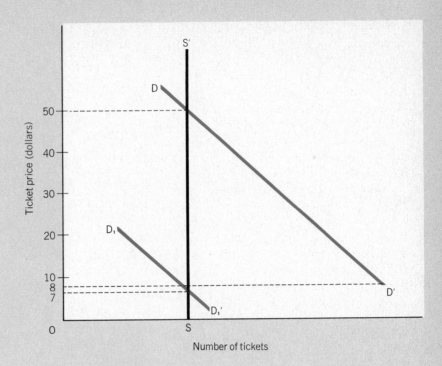

Many theater experts believe that the solution to Broadway's pricing problems lies in allowing the price system to work more effectively by permitting ticket prices to vary depending on a show's popularity. For example, the official ticket price would be allowed to rise to $50 for *My Fair Lady*. On the other hand, if *My Fair Lady* had been much less popular and its market demand curve had been *D₁D₁'* in Figure 4.14, its official ticket price would have been allowed to fall to $7. In this way, the black market for tickets would be eliminated, since the equilibrium price—which equates supply and demand—would be the official price. "Ice" would also be eliminated, since there would be no difference between the official and the actual price paid, and the people responsible for the show would receive its full receipts, not share them with crooked box-office men and illegal operators.

Rationing, Coupons, and All That

During national emergencies, the government sometimes puts a lid on prices, not allowing them to reach their equilibrium levels. For example, during World War II, the government did not allow the prices of various foodstuffs to rise to their equilibrium levels, because it felt that this would have been inequitable (and highly unpopular). Under such circumstances, the quantity demanded of a product exceeds the quantity supplied. In other words, the situation is like that in Figure 4.14, where the quantity demanded of tickets for *My Fair Lady* exceeds the quantity supplied. There is a shortage.

Since the price system is not allowed to perform its rationing function, some formal system of rationing or allocating the available supply of the product may be required. Thus, in World War II,

66

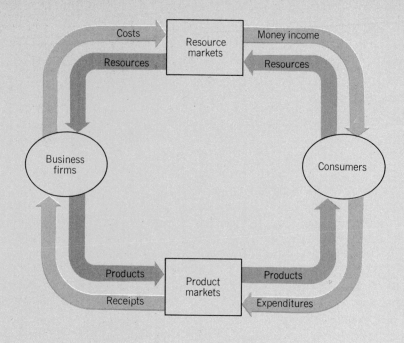

**Figure 4.15
The Circular Flows of Money
and Products**

In product markets, consumers exchange money for products and firms exchange products for money. In resource markets, consumers exchange resources for money and firms exchange money for resources.

families were issued ration coupons which determined how much they could buy of various commodities. And in late 1973, when supplies of gasoline seemed to be cut by the curtailment of Arab exports of oil to the United States, there was serious talk that gasoline and oil might be rationed in a similar way. Such rationing schemes may be justified in emergencies (of reasonably short duration), but they can result eventually in serious distortions, since prices are not allowed to do the job normally expected of them. More will be said on this score in Chapter 15.

The Circular Flows of Money and Products

So far we have been concerned largely with the workings of a single market—the market for wheat or tables or jam or tickets to *My Fair Lady*. But how do all of the various markets fit together? This is a very important question. Perhaps the

best way to begin answering it is to distinguish between product markets and resource markets. As their names indicate, *product markets are markets where products are bought and sold; and resource markets are markets where resources are bought and sold.* Let's first consider product markets. As shown in Figure 4.15, firms provide products to consumers in product markets, and receive money in return. The money the firms receive is their receipts; to consumers, on the other hand, it represents their expenditures.

Next, let's consider resource markets. Figure 4.15 shows that consumers provide resources—including labor—to firms in resource markets, and receive money in return. The money the consumers receive is their income; to firms, on the other hand, it represents their costs. Note that the flow of resources and products in Figure 4.15 is counterclockwise: that is, *consumers provide resources to firms which in turn provide goods and services to consumers.* On the other hand, the flow of money in Figure 4.15 is clockwise: that is, *firms pay money for resources to consumers who in turn use the money to buy goods and services from the firms.* Both flows—that of resources and products, and that of money—go on simultaneously and repeatedly.

So long as consumers spend all their income, the flow of money income from firms to consumers is exactly equal to the flow of expenditure from consumers to firms. Thus, these circular flows, like Ole Man River, just keep rolling along. As a first approximation, this is a perfectly good model. But as we pointed out in Chapter 1, capitalist economies have experienced periods of widespread unemployment and severe inflation that this model cannot explain. Also, note that our simple economy in Figure 4.15 has no government sector. In the following chapter, we shall bring the government into the picture. Under pure capitalism, the government would play a limited role in the economic system, but in the mixed capitalistic system we have in the United States, the government plays an important role indeed.

Summary

Consumers and firms are the basic units comprising the private sector of the economy. Consumers, whether individuals or households, purchase the goods and services that are the ultimate end-products of the economic system. Consumers are obviously an extremely varied lot, as a brief comparison of Aristotle Onassis and the Ríos family indicates. A firm is a unit that produces a good or service for sale. About 9/10 of the goods and services produced in the United States are produced by firms, which number in the millions. Like consumers, they are extremely varied in size, age, power, and purpose, as illustrated by a comparison of Amacher's drugstore and General Motors. A market is a group of firms and individuals that are in touch with each other in order to buy or sell some commodity or service. When a market for a homogeneous product contains so many buyers and sellers that none of them can influence the price, economists call it a perfectly competitive market.

There are two sides of every market: the demand side and the supply side. The demand side can be represented by the market demand curve, which almost always slopes downward to the right and whose location depends on consumer tastes, the number and income of consumers, and the prices of other commodities. The supply side of the market can be represented by the market supply curve, which generally slopes upward to the right and whose location depends on technology and resource prices. The equilibrium price and equilibrium quantity of the commodity are given by the intersection of the market demand and supply curves. If conditions remain reasonably stable for a time, the actual price and quantity should move close to the equilibrium price and quantity. Changes in the position and shape of the demand curve—in response to changes in consumer tastes, income, population, and prices of other commodities—result in changes in the equilibrium price and equilibrium output of a product. Similarly, changes in the position and shape of the supply curve—in response to changes in technology and resource prices, among other things—also result in changes in the equilibrium price and equilibrium output of a product.

To determine what goods and services society will produce, the price system sets up incentives for firms to produce what consumers want. To the extent that they produce what consumers want and are willing to pay for, firms reap profits; to the extent that they don't, they experience losses. Similarly, the price system sets up strong incentives for firms to produce these goods at minimum cost. These incentives take the form of profits for firms that minimize costs and losses for firms that operate with relatively high costs. To determine who gets what, the price system results in each person's receiving an income that depends on the quantity of resources he owns and the prices that they command. The price system also establishes incentives for activities that result in increases in a society's per capita income. The very simple case of a prisoner-of-war camp and the more complicated case of the Broadway theater provide real illustrations of the price system in action.

There are circular flows of money and products in a capitalist economy. In product markets, firms provide products to consumers and receive money in return. In resource markets, consumers provide resources to firms, and receive money in return.

The flow of resources and products is as follows: consumers provide resources to firms which in turn provide goods and services to consumers. The flow of money is as follows: firms pay money for resources to consumers who in turn use the money to buy goods and services from firms. Both flows go on simultaneously and repeatedly.

CONCEPTS FOR REVIEW

Consumer	Supply	Equilibrium price
Firm	Perfect competition	Product market
Market	Market demand curve	Resource market
Demand	Market supply curve	Actual price

QUESTIONS FOR DISCUSSION AND REVIEW

1. According to W. Allen Wallis, "Not only do prices convey information on how an individual should act, but they provide at the same time a powerful inducement for him to do so." Do you agree? If you do, explain why it is true. If you don't, explain where it is wrong.

2. Suppose that you were appointed head of a blue-ribbon commission to recommend changes in pricing practice for the entertainment industry. Would you recommend a free market for tickets for Broadway shows? For tickets to the San Francisco Opera? For the Dallas Cowboys games? In each case, why or why not?

3. If consumers show a decreasing preference for a product, this will cause the demand curve to shift to the right. True or False?

4. The demand curve for a commodity is *not* likely to be affected by
   a. number of consumers.
   b. changes in per capita income.
   c. prices of the resources used to produce the product.
   d. prices of other commodities.

CHAPTER 5

The Economic Role of the Government

To state that the United States is a mixed capitalist system, in which both government decisions and the price system play important roles, is hardly to provoke a controversy. But going a step beyond, as we shall in this chapter, takes us into areas where viewpoints often diverge. The proper functions of government and the desirable size and nature of government expenditures and taxes are not matters on which all agree. Indeed, the question of how big government should be, and what its proper functions are, is hotly debated by conservatives and liberals throughout the land. Of course, this is only a preliminary airing of many of these issues. As the base of economic analysis is broadened in subsequent chapters, much more will be said on these matters, and you will be in a far better position to judge them for yourself.

In the latter part of this chapter, we describe the nature and causes of our farm problem, and indicate the extent to which government programs seem to have solved this problem. This is an interesting application of the supply and demand theory presented in the previous chapter, as well as an example of the economic role of the government. Whether you are from the city or the country, you should be interested in the nature and success of our farm programs—if for no other reason than that you and your tax-paying and food-consuming friends and relatives pay for them.

Limitations of the Price System

Despite its many advantages, the price system suffers from serious limitations. Critics of capitalism never tire of citing them, and of arguing that the price system should be replaced by some other mechanism for solving our society's basic economic problems. But the important limitations of the price system do not mean that it should be scrapped—and in fact we have not scrapped it. Instead, we have charged the government with the responsibility for correcting many of its shortcomings. Thus, to a considerable extent, the government's role in the economy has developed in response to the limitations of the price system.

What are these limitations? First, *there is no reason to believe that the distribution of income generated by the price system is fair or, in some sense, best.* Aristotle Onassis obviously receives much more income in a day than the Ríos family does in a year. Most people feel that the distribution of income generated by the price system should be altered to suit humanitarian needs; in particular, that help should be given to the poor. Both liberals and conservatives tend to agree on this score, although there are arguments over the extent to which the poor should be helped and the conditions under which they should be eligible for help. But the general principle that the government should step in to redistribute income in favor of the poor is generally accepted in the United States today.[1]

Second, *some goods and services cannot be provided through the price system because there is no way to exclude a citizen from consuming the good whether he pays for it or not.* For example, there is no way to prevent a citizen from benefiting from national expenditures on defense, whether he pays money toward defense or not. Consequently, the price system cannot be used to provide such goods; no one will pay for them since they will receive them whether they pay or not. Such goods are called **public goods.** It is generally agreed that the government must provide public goods. Such goods are consumed collectively or jointly, and are indivisible in the sense that their benefits cannot be priced in a market.

Third, *in cases where the production or consumption of a good by one firm or consumer has adverse or beneficial uncompensated effects on other firms or consumers, the price system will not operate effectively.* An **external economy** is said to occur when consumption or production by one person or firm results in uncompensated benefits to another person or firm. A good example of an external economy exists where fundamental research carried out by one firm is used by another firm. (To cite one such case, there were external economies from the Bell Telephone Laboratories' invention of the transistor.) Where external economies exist, it is generally agreed that the price system will produce too little of the good in question and that the government should supplement the amount produced by private enterprise. This is the basic rationale for much of the government's huge investment in basic science. An **external diseconomy** is said to occur when consumption or production by one person or firm results in uncompensated costs to another person or firm. A good example of an external diseconomy occurs when a firm dumps pollutants into a stream and makes the water unfit for use by firms and people

---

[1] Also, because the wealthy have more "dollar votes" than the poor, the sorts of goods and services that society produces will reflect this fact. Thus, luxuries for the rich may be produced in larger amounts and necessities for the poor may be produced in smaller amounts than some critics regard as sensible and equitable. This is another frequently encountered criticism of the price system.

downstream. Where activities result in external diseconomies, it is generally agreed that the price system will tolerate too much of the activity and that the government should curb it. For example, as we shall see in Chapter 18, the government, in keeping with this doctrine, is involving itself increasingly in environmental protection and the reduction of air and water pollution.[2]

What Functions Should the Government Perform?

There are wide differences of opinion on the proper role of government in economic affairs. Although it is generally agreed that the government should redistribute income in favor of the poor, provide public goods, and offset the effects of external economies and diseconomies, there is considerable disagreement over how far the government should go in these areas, and what additional areas the government should be responsible for. Some people feel that "Big Government" is already a problem; that government is doing too much. Others believe that the public sector of the economy is being undernourished and that government should be allowed to do more. This is a fundamental question, and one that involves a great deal more than economics.

On the one hand, conservatives, such as the University of Chicago's distinguished economist, Milton Friedman, believe that the government's role should be limited severely. They feel that economic and political freedom is likely to be undermined by excessive reliance on the state. Moreover, they tend to be skeptical about the government's ability to solve the social and economic problems at hand. They feel that the prevailing faith in the government's power to make a substantial dent in these

problems is unreasonable, and they call for more and better information concerning the sorts of tasks government can reasonably be expected to do—and do well. They point to the slowness of the government bureaucracy, the difficulty in controlling huge government organizations, the inefficiencies political considerations can breed, and the difficulties in telling whether government programs are successful or not. On the basis of these considerations, they argue that the government's role should be carefully circumscribed.

The flavor of the conservative position on this question, as well as a generous helping of sarcasm and wit, is evident in the remarks of George Stigler, another distinguished economist at the University of Chicago:

> I consider myself courageous, or at least obtuse, in arguing for a reduction in governmental controls over economic life. You are surely desirous of improving this world, and it assuredly needs an immense amount of improvement. No method of displaying one's public-spiritedness is more popular than to notice a problem and pass a law. It combines ease, the warmth of benevolence, and a suitable disrespect for a less enlightened era. What I propose is, for most people, much less attractive: close study of the comparative performance of public and private economy, and the dispassionate appraisal of special remedies that is involved in compassion for the community at large.[3]

To such remarks, liberals respond with very telling salvos of their own. Just as conservatives tend to be skeptical of the government's ability to solve important social and economic problems, so liberals tend to be skeptical about the price system's ability to solve these problems. They point to the important limitations of the price system, discussed above, and they assert that the government can accomplish a great deal that will benefit the nation and the world.

[2] The effects of external economies and diseconomies can also be taken care of by legal arrangements that assign liabilities for damages and compensate for benefits. However, such arrangements often are impractical or too costly to be used.

[3] G. Stigler, "The Government of the Economy," *A Dialogue on the Proper Economic Role of the State,* University of Chicago, Graduate School of Business, Selected Paper no. 7, reprinted in E. Mansfield, *Economics: Readings, Issues, and Cases,* New York: Norton, 1974. Also, see M. Friedman, *Capitalism and Freedom,* Chicago: University of Chicago Press, 1962.

According to some distinguished liberals, like Harvard's John Kenneth Galbraith, the public sector of the economy is being starved of needed resources, while the private sector is catering to relatively unimportant wants. In his best-selling book, *The Affluent Society,* Galbraith argues that consumers are led by advertising and other promotional efforts to purchase more and more goods of marginal significance to them. On the other hand, in his opinion, the nation is suffering because too little is spent on government services like education, transportation, and urban renewal.[4] In the next chapter, we shall discuss this proposition in more detail.

Liberals tend to be less concerned than conservatives about the effects of greater governmental intervention in the economy on personal freedom. They point out that the price system also involves coercion, since the fact that the price system awards the available goods and services to those who can pay their equilibrium price can be viewed as a form of coercion. Moreover, some people are awarded only a pittance by the price system: in a real sense, they are coerced into discomfort and malnutrition.[5] The relationship between government intervention and personal freedom is a tricky and controversial one that involves a great deal more than economics. Your own feelings on this score are likely to depend on your political and ethical philosophy.

A Legal, Social, and Competitive Framework

Although there is considerable disagreement over the proper role of the government, both conservatives and liberals agree that it must do certain things. The first of these is to establish the "rules of

[4] J. K. Galbraith, *The Affluent Society,* Boston: Houghton Mifflin, 1958.
[5] See P. Samuelson, "The Economic Role of Private Activity," *A Dialogue on the Proper Economic Role of the State,* University of Chicago, Graduate School of Business, Selected Paper no. 7, reprinted in E. Mansfield, *Economics: Readings, Issues, and Cases.*

the game"—that is, a legal, social, and competitive framework enabling the price system to function as it should. Specifically, the government must see to it that contracts are enforced, that private ownership is protected, and that fraud is prevented. Clearly, these matters must be tended to if the price system is to work properly. Also, the government must maintain order (through the establishment of police and other forces), establish a monetary system (so that money can be used to facilitate trade and exchange), and provide standards for the weight and quality of products.

As an example of this sort of government intervention, consider the Pure Food and Drug Act. This act, originally passed in 1906 and subsequently amended in various ways, protects the consumer against improper and fraudulent activities on the part of producers of foods and drugs. It prohibits the merchandising of impure or falsely labeled food or drugs, and it forces producers to specify the quantity and quality of the contents on labels. These requirements strengthen the price system. Without them, the typical consumer would be unable to tell whether food or drugs are pure or properly labeled. Unless the consumer can be sure that he is getting what he is paying for, the basic logic underlying the price system breaks down. Similar regulation and legislation have been instituted in fields other than food and drugs—and for similar reasons.

Besides establishing a legal and social framework that will enable the price system to do its job, the government must also see to it that markets remain reasonably competitive. Only if they are will prices reflect consumer desires properly. If, on the other hand, markets are dominated by a few sellers (or a few buyers), prices will be "rigged" by these sellers (or buyers) to promote their own interests. For example, if a single firm is the sole producer of aluminum, it is a safe bet that this firm will establish a higher price than if there were many aluminum producers competing among themselves. The unfortunate thing about prices determined in noncompetitive markets—rigged prices, if you will —is that they give incorrect signals concerning what consumers want and how scarce resources and commodities are. Producers, responding to these incorrect signals, do not produce the right things in the right quantities. Consumers respond to these incorrect signals by not supplying the right resources in the right amounts, and by not consuming the proper amounts of the goods that are produced. Thus the price system is not permitted to solve the four basic economic problems properly in the absence of reasonable competition.

To try to encourage and preserve competition, the Congress has enacted a series of antitrust laws, such as the Sherman Antitrust Act and the Clayton Act, and has established the Federal Trade Commission. The antitrust laws make it illegal for firms to collude or to attempt to monopolize the sale of a product. Both conservative and liberal economists, with some notable exceptions, tend to favor the intent and operation of the antitrust laws. In addition, the government tries to control the activities of firms in markets where competition cannot be expected to prevail (as in the telephone industry, where efficient operations would be destroyed if more than a very few firms got in the act). In industries of this sort, the government often establishes commissions to regulate prices and standards of services. Such regulatory commissions are common in the communications, transportation, electric, and gas industries.

Redistribution of Income

We have already noted at several points the general agreement that the government should redistribute income in favor of the poor. In other words, it is usually felt that help should be given to people who are ill, handicapped, old and infirm, disabled, and unable for other reasons to provide for themselves. To some extent, the nation has decided that income—or at least a certain minimum income—should be divorced from productive services. Of course, this doesn't mean that people who are too lazy to work should be given a handout. It does

mean that people who cannot provide for themselves should be helped. To implement this principle, various payments are made by the government to needy people—including the aged, the handicapped, the unemployed, pensioners, and veterans.

These welfare payments are to some extent a "depression baby," for they grew substantially during the Great Depression of the 1930s, when relief payments became a necessity. But they also represent a feeling shared by a large segment of the population that human beings should be assured that, however the Wheel of Fortune spins and whatever number comes up, they will not starve and their children will not be deprived of a healthy environment and basic schooling. Of course, someone has to pay for this. Welfare payments allow the poor to take more from the nation's output than they produce. In general, the more affluent members of society contribute some of their claims on output to pay for these programs, their contributions being in the form of taxes. By using its expenditures to help certain groups and by taxing other groups to pay for these programs, the government accomplishes each year, without revolt and without bayonets, a substantial redistribution of income. This is a crucial aspect of the government's role in our economy.

It should not be assumed, however, that all government programs transfer income from the rich to the poor. On the contrary, some programs, intentionally or unintentionally, soak the poor to give to the rich. Some government programs fatten the purses of rich farmers, some tax loopholes allow the affluent to dodge taxes through the creation of trusts and other legal devices, and some important taxes—such as sales taxes—hit the poor harder than the rich. Nonetheless, the best available evidence indicates that, when all its activities are taken into account, the government does take from the rich to give to the poor. In other words, taking account of both its expenditures and the taxes it levies, the government redistributes income in favor of the poor. Whether it goes as far as it should in this direction is a more nettlesome question, the answer to which will depend on your own ethical values.

Economic Stabilization

It is also generally agreed that the government should see to it that the economy maintains reasonably full employment with reasonably stable prices. Capitalist economies have tended to alternate between booms and depressions in the past. The Great Depression of the 1930s hit the American economy—and the world economy—a particularly devastating blow, putting millions of people out of work and in desperate shape. When World War II ended, the American people vowed that they would not let a depression of this sort occur again. The Congress passed the Employment Act of 1946, which stated that it was the responsibility of the federal government to maintain full employment in the United States. In particular, the federal government was not supposed to tolerate unemployment of the sort that materialized during severe depressions in the past.

Of course, it is one thing to charge the federal government with the responsibility for maintaining full employment and quite another thing to tell the federal government how to achieve this goal. Without a good deal of economic knowledge, this law would have been as empty as Atlantic City in December. After all, it is useless to tell the federal government to do something no one knows how to do. Fortunately, however, advances in economic knowledge during the 1930s made it much more likely that the federal government could carry out the responsibility of maintaining full employment. The man who contributed much of this new economic knowledge was John Maynard Keynes, one of the great figures of modern economics, whom we will continue to encounter in subsequent chapters.

Besides maintaining full employment, the government must also maintain a reasonably stable price level. No economy can function well if prices are gyrating wildly. Through its control of the money supply and its decisions regarding expenditures and taxation, the government has considerable impact on the price level, as well as on the level of employment.

Public Goods and Externalities

As we have indicated, most people agree that the government must provide public goods. Let's consider the nature of public goods in more detail. They often are relatively indivisible: they come in such big units that there is no way to break them into pieces that can be bought or sold in ordinary markets. Also, they are consumed by society as a whole. Once such goods are produced, there is no way to bar certain citizens from consuming them. Whether or not a citizen contributes toward their cost, he benefits from them. As pointed out in a previous section, this means that the price system cannot be used to handle the production and distribution of such goods.

An obvious example of a public good is a lighthouse. There might be general agreement that the cost of building a particular lighthouse would be more than justified by the benefits (saving of lives, fewer shipwrecks, cheaper transportation). Nonetheless, no firm or person would build and operate such a lighthouse because they could not find any way to charge the ships using the lighthouse for the service. Nor would any single user gain enough from the lighthouse to warrant constructing and operating it. Moreover, voluntary contributions are very unlikely to support such a lighthouse because each user is likely to feel that his contribution will not affect the outcome and that he will be able to use the lighthouse whether or not he contributes. Consequently, the lighthouse will be established and operated only if the government intervenes.

National defense is another example. The benefits of expenditure on national defense extend to the entire nation. There is no way of preventing a citizen from benefiting from them, whether he contributes to their cost or not. Thus, there is no way to use the price system to provide for national defense. Since it is a public good, national defense must be provided by the government. Similarly with flood control, roads, police and fire protection, public parks, and a host of other such services. In each case, although the people who benefit may not contribute to the costs of these services voluntarily, they may feel better off when the government taxes them to make such services possible.

Other services, such as education and health, can be provided by private enterprise on a fee basis, but much of the population feels that the government should intervene to see to it that everyone, regardless of income level, receives a certain minimum amount of education and health care. Free public education has, of course, been an important and conspicuous part of American society, and in recent years the government has begun to play a more significant role in the health field. Both in health and education, an important argument for government intervention has been that the social benefits of these services exceed the private benefits. However, opponents of such intervention assert that it is paternalistic and that it results in less efficiency in education and health. This is an area of controversy.

Essentially, deciding how much to produce of a public good is a political decision. The citizens of the United States elect senators and congressmen who decide how much should be spent on national defense or education, and how it should be spent. However, it is important to recognize that there are many special-interest groups that lobby hard for the production of certain public goods. For example, an alliance of military and industrial groups presses for increased defense expenditures, and other interested groups promote expenditures on highways, health, education, and other functions.

The tax system is used to pay for the production of public goods. In effect, the government says to each citizen: "Fork over a certain amount of money to pay for the expenses incurred by the government." The amount a particular citizen is assessed may depend on his income (as in the income tax), the value of all or specific types of his property (as in the property tax), the amount he spends on certain types of goods and services (as in the sales tax), or on still other criteria.

Finally, it is generally agreed that the government should encourage the production of goods and services that entail external economies and discourage the production of those that entail external diseconomies. Take the pollution of air and water. When a firm or individual dumps wastes into the water or air, other firms or individuals often must pay all or part of the cost of putting the water or air back into a usable condition. Thus the disposal of these wastes entails external diseconomies. Unless the government prohibits certain kinds of pollution, or enforces air and water quality standards, or charges polluters in accord with the amount of waste they dump into the environment, there will be socially undesirable levels of pollution. In recent years, the government has begun to do more to protect the environment in these ways.

Government Production and "Creeping Socialism"

As we pointed out in the previous section, it is generally accepted that, in the case of public goods and in situations where there are important externalities, the government should intervene to influence their production. But this does not mean that the government must actually produce the good in question. On the contrary, *the government does not produce most of the goods and services it provides.* For example, the federal government supports over ½ of the research and development carried out in the United States, but only about 20 percent of federally supported research and development is carried out in government laboratories. The rest is carried out by firms and universities working under government contracts.[6]

Some of the areas in which our government actually becomes involved in the production of goods and services are familiar. In the United States the post office, the airports, and many water, gas, and electric companies are publicly owned and operated. In these cases it would be inefficient to have many producers, and since competition is not feasible, the courts have held that such industries must be publicly owned or regulated. But there is

[6] Edwin Mansfield, *The Economics of Technological Change,* New York: Norton, 1968, Chapter 6.

no very clear line between them and other industries that have not been publicly owned. For example, many other countries have publicly owned telephone, telegraph, railroad, airline, and broadcasting industries. The reasons why these industries are not under public ownership in the United States are partly historical and cultural. Also, many people feel that public ownership tends to result in too much bureaucracy and inefficiency, and this country has been suspicious of anything smacking of "creeping socialism."

As we explained in Chapter 3, socialism means government ownership and operation of plants, farms, and mines. Clearly, *there has been little movement toward public ownership in the United States,* despite occasional cries to the contrary on the hustings and in the press. Perhaps the most important and controversial area where government ownership has been extended appreciably in the last 40 years has been in electric power. During the administration of Franklin D. Roosevelt, the Tennessee Valley Authority, Bonneville Dam, and Hoover Dam, among others, were established. But this was hardly a widespread thrust toward public ownership—and it took place several decades ago.

However, although there has been little movement toward government ownership and operation, *there has been a tendency in certain fields for the boundaries between the private sector and the public sector to become extremely blurred.* Particularly in the field of defense, it is difficult to know how to categorize some organizations. To what extent is a firm like Lockheed Aircraft Corporation really part of the private sector? Although it is privately owned, most of its output (92 percent in 1971) goes to a single customer—the government. Much of its supply of tools is provided by the government, and government officials play an important role in influencing its decisions, auditing its books, regulating its profits, and so forth. The same tendency toward blurred boundaries between the private and public sectors has occurred in atomic energy, space exploration, and other areas. To a certain extent, it appears that—in the words of Don Price, dean of Harvard's school of public administration—the

government "has learned to socialize without assuming ownership."[7] This blurring of the boundaries between the private and public sectors is an important recent development, with repercussions on many aspects of our daily life.

How Big Is the Government?

Up to this point, we have been concerned primarily with the reasons why the government must intervene in our economy—and the types of role it should play—but we have made little or no attempt to describe its role in quantitative terms. It is time now to turn to some of the relevant facts. One useful measure of the extent of the government's role in the American economy is the size of government expenditures, both in absolute terms and as a percent of our nation's total output. This measure makes it clear that the government's role is large.

The sum total of government expenditures—federal, state, and local—was about $400 billion in 1973. Since our nation's total output was about $1.2 trillion, this means that government expenditures are about one-third of our total output. The ratio of government expenditures to total output in the United States has not always been this large, as Figure 5.1 shows. In 1929, the ratio was about 10 percent, as contrasted with about 30 percent in 1973. (Of course, the ratio of government spending to total output is smaller now than during World War II, but in a wartime economy, one would expect this ratio to be abnormally high.)

There are many reasons why government expenditures have grown so much faster than total output. Three of these are particularly important. First, the United States did not maintain anything like the kind of military force in pre-World War II days that it does now. In earlier days, when weapons were relatively simple and cheap, and when we viewed our military and political responsibilities much more narrowly than we do now, our

[7] Don Price, *The Scientific Estate,* Cambridge, Mass.: Belknap Press, 1965, p. 43.

**Figure 5.1
Government Spending as a
Percent of Total Output,
United States.**

Government expenditures—
federal, state, and local—totaled
about $400 billion in 1973. These
expenditures, which include
transfer payments, have grown
more rapidly than total output in
this period.

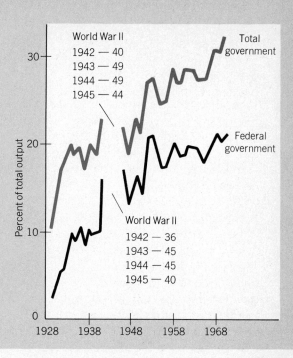

military budget was relatively small. The cost of being a superpower in the days of nuclear weaponry is high by any standards. Second, there has been a long-term increase in the demand for the services provided by government, like more and better schooling, more extensive highways, more complete police and fire protection, and so forth. As incomes rise, people want more of these services. Third, *government transfer payments*— payments in return for no products or services— have grown substantially. For example, various types of welfare payments have increased markedly. Since transfer payments do not entail any reallocation of resources from private to public goods, but a transfer of income from one private citizen or group to another, Figure 5.1 is, in some respects, an overstatement of the role of the public sector.

When in Table 5.1 we compare the size of government spending in the United States (relative to total output) with that in other countries, we learn that the governments of Sweden, France, West Germany, and the United Kingdom spend more—as a percent of total output—than we do.

In part, of course, this is because of the extensive welfare programs in Sweden and the United Kingdom. It is interesting, however, that, despite our huge military programs, we do not spend more

Table 5.1

Taxes as Percentages of Total Output, 1970

Country	Percentage
Sweden	41
France	39
West Germany	35
United Kingdom	33
Canada	29
United States	29
Japan	21
India	13
Spain	12
Mexico	10
Nigeria	9

(relative to total output) than these countries. It is also noteworthy that poor countries like Nigeria —ones with little industry and at a relatively early stage of economic development—spend the least on government services. This is understandable, since such countries must devote more of their output to the basic necessities of life. In many cases, as we saw in Chapter 1, they have a rough time merely feeding their populations.

What the Federal, State, and Local Governments Spend Money On

There are three levels of government in the United States—federal, state, and local. The state governments spend the least, while the federal government spends the most. This was not always the case. Before World War I, the local governments spent more than the federal government. In those days, the federal government did not maintain the large military establishment it does now, nor did it engage in the many programs in health, education, welfare, and other areas that it currently does. Figure 5.1 shows that federal spending is now a much larger percentage of the total than it was 40 years ago. Table 5.2 shows how the federal government spends its money. *About ⅓ of the federal expenditures goes for defense and other items connected with international relations and national security. About ⅓ goes for health, labor, and welfare. The rest goes to support farm, transportation, housing, and other such programs, as well as to run Congress, the courts, and the executive branch of the federal government.*

What about the local and state governments? On what do they spend their money? Table 5.3 shows that *the biggest expenditure of the local governments is on schools*. After the end of World War

---

Table 5.2

Federal Expenditures, United States, Fiscal 1973

Purpose	Amount (billions of dollars)	Percent of total
National defense	78	32
International affairs and finance	4	2
Veterans' benefits	12	5
Space research and technology	3	1
Agriculture and agricultural resources	7	3
Education	11	4
Health, labor, and welfare	88	36
Natural resources	2	1
Commerce and transportation	12	5
Housing and community development	5	2
Interest	21	9
General government and other	3	1
Total*	246	100

* Because of rounding errors, the figures may not sum to the totals.
Source: U.S. Bureau of the Budget, *The Budget in Brief.*

Table 5.3

Expenditures of State and Local Governments, United States, 1970

Type of Expenditure	State Amount (billions of dollars)	State Percent of total	Local Amount (billions of dollars)	Local Percent of total
Education	30.9	40	39.0	47
Highways	13.5	17	5.4	7
Natural resources	2.2	3	0.6	1
Health and hospitals	5.4	7	5.0	6
Public welfare	13.2	17	6.7	8
Housing and urban renewal	0.1	b	2.1	2
Interest on debt	1.5	2	2.9	3
Other	10.9	14	21.5	25
Total[a]	77.6	100	83.2	100

[a] Because of rounding errors, the figures may not sum to the totals.
[b] Less than 1 percent.
Source: *Statistical Abstract of the United States.*

II, these expenditures increased greatly because of the "baby boom"—the increase in the number of school-age children. Traditionally, schools in the United States have been a responsibility of local governments—cities and towns. *State governments spend most of their money on highways, welfare, old age, and unemployment benefits, and providing help to localities to cover the cost of education, as well as supporting education directly.* In addition, the local and state governments support hospitals, redevelopment programs, recreation and natural resource programs, and courts, police, and fire departments.

Changes in Views of Government Responsibilities

We have already seen that government expenditures in the United States have grown considerably,

both in absolute amount and as a percentage of our total output. It must be recognized that this growth in government expenditure has been part of a general trend in the United States toward a different view of the government's role. Two hundred years ago, it was not uncommon for people to believe in the slogan: "That government governs best which governs least." There was considerable suspicion of government interference and meddling, freedom was the watchword, and governments were viewed as potential tyrants. In the nineteenth century, the United States prospered mightily under this laissez-faire system, but gradually—and not without considerable protest—the nation began to interpret the role of the government more broadly.

Responding to the dangers of noncompetitive markets, states were given the power to regulate public utilities and railroads. The Interstate Commerce Commission was established in 1887 to regulate railroads operating across state lines; and the Sherman Antitrust Act was passed in 1890 to curb monopoly and promote competition. To help control recurring business fluctuations and financial panics, banking and finance were regulated. In 1913, the Federal Reserve System was established as a central bank controlling the member commercial banks. In 1933, the Federal Deposit Insurance Corporation was established to insure bank deposits. And in 1934, the Securities and Exchange Commission was established to watch over the financial markets. Responding to the "buyer-beware" attitudes of unscrupulous and careless sellers, the Pure Food and Drug Act was passed by Congress in 1906 to insure proper quality for drugs and food.

In addition, the government's role in the fields of labor and welfare expanded considerably. For example, in the 1930s, minimum wage laws were enacted, old-age pensions and unemployment insurance were established, and the government became an important force in collective bargaining and labor relations. Furthermore, the power of government has been used increasingly to insure that citizens will not fall below a certain economic level. Food-stamp programs and programs that provide aid to dependent children have been established. *In general, the broad trend in the United States in the past century has been for the government to be used to a greater and greater extent to achieve social objectives.*

Recall from your study of American history the programs of Theodore Roosevelt, Franklin D. Roosevelt, John F. Kennedy, and Lyndon B. Johnson. Although they were quite different sorts of presidents faced with quite different sorts of situations, they all had one thing in common: they promoted a broader view of government responsibilities. Theodore Roosevelt's "Square Deal," Franklin D. Roosevelt's "New Deal," John F. Kennedy's "New Frontier," and Lyndon B. Johnson's "Great Society" all extended government responsibilities. Some of these extensions were highly controversial at the time. For example, the ill-feeling generated by FDR's "wild-eyed schemes" is legendary. Yet when the Republicans took office subsequently, these schemes were not repudiated. This has been the typical pattern. Although the rate at which government involvement has grown has depended heavily on who was in power, neither political party has reversed the direction of change. As you would expect, conservatives view this trend with suspicion and alarm, while liberals view it with favor and satisfaction. Your own view will depend inevitably on your own political beliefs and preferences.

What the Federal, State, and Local Governments Receive in Taxes

To get the money to cover most of the expenditures discussed in previous sections, governments collect taxes from individuals and firms. As Table 5.4 shows, at the federal level the personal income tax is the biggest single money raiser. It brings in almost ½ of the tax revenue collected by the federal government. The next most important taxes at the federal level are the social security, payroll, and employment taxes, and the corporation income tax. Other important taxes are excise taxes—levied on the sale of tobacco, liquor, imports, and certain

Table 5.4

Federal Tax Receipts, by Tax, Fiscal 1973

Type of tax	Amount (billions of dollars	Percent of total
Personal income tax	99	44
Corporation income tax	34	15
Employment taxes	65	29
Excise taxes	16	7
Estate and gift taxes	5	2
Other revenues	7	3
Total[a]	225	100

[a] Because of rounding errors, the figures may not sum to the totals.
Source: *Economic Report of the President*, 1973.

Table 5.5

State and Local Tax Revenues, by Source, 1970

Source	State Revenues (billions of dollars)	Percent of total	Local Revenues (billions of dollars)	Percent of total
General sales tax	14	29	2	5
Property tax	1	2	33	85
Selective excise taxes	13	27	1	3
Personal income tax	9	19	2	5
Corporate income tax	4	8	—	
Motor vehicle licenses	3	6	—	
Estate and gift taxes	1	2	—	
Other taxes	4	8	1	3
Total[a]	48	100	39	100

[a] Because of rounding errors, the figures may not sum to the totals.
Source: Statistical Abstract of the United States.

other items—and death and gift taxes. (Even when the Grim Reaper shows up, the Tax Man is not far behind.)

At the local level, on the other hand, the most important form of taxation and source of revenue is the property tax. (See Table 5.5.) This is a tax levied primarily on real estate. Other important local taxes—although dwarfed in importance by the property tax—are local sales taxes and local income taxes. Many cities—for example, New York City—levy a sales tax, equal to a certain percent— 3 percent in New York City—of the value of each retail sale. The tax is simply added on to the amount charged the customer. Also, many cities— for example, Philadelphia and Pittsburgh—levy an income (or wage) tax on their residents and even on people who work in the city but live outside it. At the state level, sales (and excise) taxes are the biggest money raisers, followed by income taxes and highway user taxes. Highway user taxes include taxes on gasoline and license fees for vehicles and

drivers. Often they exceed the amount spent on roads, and the balance is used for a variety of non-highway uses.

The Role of Government in American Agriculture: A Case Study

Thus far, we have been discussing the government's role in the American economy in rather general terms. Now we need to consider in some detail a particular example of the economic programs carried out by our government. The government's farm programs are a logical choice, because they illustrate the usefulness of the supply-and-demand analysis presented in the previous chapter. It is important to recognize at the outset that these farm programs are not being held up as a representative sample of what the government does. There are a host of other government economic programs—poverty programs, urban programs, defense programs, research programs, education programs, transportation programs, fiscal programs, monetary programs, and many more. Most of these programs will be discussed at some point in this book.

Agriculture is an enormously important sector of the American economy. Even though its size is decreasing steadily—and this contraction has been going on for many decades—agriculture still employs about 4 million Americans. Its importance, moreover, cannot be measured entirely by its size. You need only think about how difficult it would be to get along without food to see the strategic role agriculture plays in our economic life. Also, when it comes to technological change, agriculture is one of the most progressive parts of the American economy. Output per manhour has grown more rapidly there than in any other major sector of the American economy, in considerable part because of government-financed agricultural research programs. The efficiency of American agriculture is admired throughout the world.

Nonetheless, it is widely acknowledged that American agriculture has had serious problems. Perhaps the clearest indication of these problems is shown by a comparison of per capita income of American farmers with per capita income among the rest of the population. It is clear that farm incomes have tended to be much lower than nonfarm incomes. For example, in 1970, per capita income on the farms was about 20 percent below that for the nonfarm population. Moreover, a large proportion of the rural population is poor. Thus, the National Advisory Commission on Rural Poverty found that "rural poverty is so widespread, and so acute, as to be a national disgrace."[8] Of course, this does not mean that all farmers are poor: on the contrary, many do very well indeed. But a large percentage of the nation's farmers are poor by any standard.

[8] National Advisory Committee on Rural Poverty, *The People Left Behind*, Washington, 1967, part of which is reprinted in E. Mansfield, *Economics: Readings, Issues, and Cases,* New York: Norton, 1974.

This farm problem is nothing new. During the first two decades of the twentieth century, farmers enjoyed relatively high prices and relatively high incomes. But in 1920, the country experienced a sharp depression that jolted agriculture as well as the rest of the economy. Whereas the Roaring Twenties saw a recovery and boom in the nonfarm sector of the economy, agriculture did not recover as completely, and the 1930s were dreadful years; the Great Depression resulted in a sickening decline in farm prices and farm incomes. World War II brought prosperity to agriculture, but in the postwar period, farm incomes continually have been well below nonfarm incomes. Thus, all in all, agriculture has been experiencing difficulties for several decades. In 1973, as we shall see, prosperity began to return to the farms. How long-lived it will be is anyone's guess.

Causes of the Farm Problem

In Chapter 1, we claimed that relatively simple economic models are of considerable use in understanding important public and private problems. To back up this claim, we will apply the simple models of market behavior presented in the previous chapter—the models involving market demand curves and market supply curves—to explain the basic causes of the problems that, until 1973, besieged agriculture. Let's start with the market demand curve for farm products. If you think about it for a moment, you will agree that this market demand curve must have two important characteristics. First, its shape must reflect the fact that food is a necessity and that the quantity demanded will not vary much with the price of food. Second, the market demand curve for food is unlikely to shift to the right very much as per capita income rises, because consumption of food per capita faces natural biological and other limitations.

Next, consider the market supply curve for farm products. Again, you should be aware of two important characteristics of this market supply curve. First, the quantity of farm products supplied tends to be relatively insensitive to price, because the farmers have only limited control over their output. (Weather, floods, insects, and other such factors are very important.) Second, because of the rapid technological change emphasized in the previous section, the market supply curve has been shifting markedly and rapidly to the right.

If you understand these simple characteristics of the market demand curve and market supply curve for farm products, it is no trick at all to understand why we had the sort of farm problem just described. Figure 5.2 shows the market demand and market supply curves for farm products at various points in time. As you would expect, the market demand curve for farm products shifts rather slowly to the right as incomes (and population) grow over time. Specifically, the market de-

mand curve shifted from DD' in the first period to D_1D_1' in the second period to D_2D_2' in the third period. On the other hand, the market supply curve for farm products shifted rapidly to the right as technology improved over time. Specifically, it shifted from SS' in the first period to S_1S_1' in the second period to S_2S_2' in the third period.

What was the consequence of these shifts in the market demand and supply curves for food products? Clearly, *the equilibrium price of food products fell (relative to other products)*. Specifically, the equilibrium price fell from OP to OP_1 to OP_2 in Figure 5.2. This price decrease was, of course, a large part of the farm problem. If we correct for changes in the general level of prices (which have tended to rise over time), there was, until 1973, a declining trend in farm prices. That is, agricultural prices generally fell, relative to other prices, in the last 60 years. Moreover, *given this fall in*

**Figure 5.2
Shifts over Time in Market
Demand and Supply Curves
for Farm Products**

The market demand curve has shifted rather slowly to the right (from DD' to D_1D_1' to D_2D_2'), whereas the market supply curve has shifted rapidly to the right (from SS' to S_1S_1' to S_2S_2'), with the result that the equilibrium price has declined (from OP to OP_1 to OP_2).

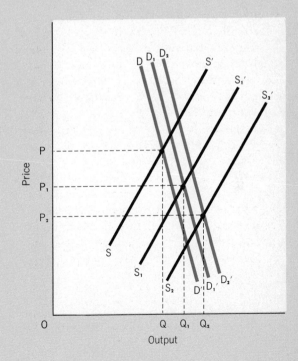

farm prices, farm incomes tended to fall, because, although lower prices were associated with greater amounts sold, the reduction in price was much greater than the increase in quantity sold, as shown in Figure 5.2.[9]

Thus the simple model of market behavior described in the previous chapter makes it possible to explain the fact that, until recently, farm prices and farm incomes have tended to fall in the United States. Certainly there is nothing mysterious about these trends. Given the nature and characteristics of the market demand curve and market supply curve for farm products, our simple model shows that these trends are as much to be expected as parades on the Fourth of July. However, one additional fact must be noted to understand the farm problem: *people and nonhuman resources have been relatively slow to move out of agriculture in response to these trends.* Recall from the previous chapter that the price system uses such trends —lower prices and lower incomes—to signal producers that they should use their resources elsewhere. Unfortunately, farmers have been loath to move out of agriculture, even though they often could make more money elsewhere. This has been a crucial cause of the farm problem. If more people and resources had left farming, agricultural prices and incomes would have risen, and ultimately farm incomes would have come closer to nonfarm incomes. Poor education and color have, of course, been significant barriers to migration.

Nonetheless, even though farmers have been slow to move out of agriculture, they have left the farm in the long run. For example, in 1930 the farm population was about 30 million, or 25 percent of the total population; in 1950, it was about 23 million, or 15 percent of the total population; and in 1970, it was about 10 million, or 5 percent of the total population. Thus, the price system has

[9] The amount farmers receive is the amount they sell times the price. Thus, in Figure 5.2, the amount farmers receive in income is $OP \times OQ$ in the first period, $OP_1 \times OQ_1$ in the second period, and $OP_2 \times OQ_2$ in the third period. Clearly, since the price is decreasing much more rapidly than the quantity is increasing, farm incomes are falling.

had its way. Resources have been moving out of agriculture in response to the signals and pressures of the price system. This movement of people and nonhuman resources unquestionably has contributed to greater efficiency and production for the nation as a whole. But during most of the past 40 years, we have continued to have a "surplus" of farmers—and this has been the root of the farm problem.

Government Aid to Agriculture

Traditionally, farmers have had a disproportionately large influence in Congress; and faced with declining economic fortunes, they have appealed to the government for help. They have extolled the virtues of rural life, emphasized that agriculture is a competitive industry, and claimed that it was unfair for their prices to fall relative to the prices they have had to pay. In addition, they have pointed out that the movement of resources out of agriculture has entailed large human costs, since this movement, although beneficial to the nation as a whole, has been traumatic for the farm population. For reasons of this sort, they have argued that the government should help farmers; and in particular, that the government should act to bolster farm prices and farm incomes.

Their voices have been heard. In the Agricultural Adjustment Act of 1933, the Congress announced the concept of parity as the major objective of American farm policy. This concept has acquired great importance—and must be clearly understood. Put in its simplest terms, the concept of *parity* says that a farmer should be able to exchange a given quantity of his output for as much in the way of nonfarm goods and services as he could at some time in the past. For example, if a farmer could take a bushel of wheat to market in 1912 and get enough money to buy a pair of gloves, today he should be able to get enough money for a bushel of wheat to buy a pair of gloves.

To see what the concept of parity implies for

farm prices, suppose that the price of gloves triples. Obviously, if parity is to be maintained, the price of wheat must triple too. Thus, the concept of parity implies that farm prices must increase at the same rate as the prices of the goods and services farmers buy. Of course, farmers buy lots of things besides gloves, so in actual practice the parity price of wheat or other farm products is determined by the changes over time in the average price of all the goods and services farmers buy.

Several things should be noted about parity. First, to use this concept, one must agree on some base period, such as 1912 in the example above, during which the relationship of farm to nonfarm prices is regarded as equitable. Obviously, the higher farm prices were relative to nonfarm prices in the base period, the higher farm prices will be in subsequent periods if parity is maintained. It is interesting to note that 1910–14 is used as the base period (with some recent modifications). Since this was a period of relatively high farm prices and of agricultural prosperity, the farm bloc must have wielded considerable political clout on this issue. Second, note that the concept of parity is an ethical, not a scientific proposition. It states what the relative economic position of a bushel of wheat ought to be—or more precisely, it states one particular view of what the relative economic position of a bushel of wheat should be. It must also be noted that price parity is not the same thing as income parity. If price parity is maintained while productivity is increasing considerably, farm incomes will rise more rapidly than income parity would call for.

Price Supports and Surplus Controls

During the past 40 years, the concept of parity has been the cornerstone of a system of government price supports. In many cases, the government has not supported farm prices at the full 100 percent of parity. For example, Congress may have enacted a bill saying that the Secretary of Agriculture can establish a price of wheat, corn, cotton, or some other product that is between 65 and 90 percent of parity. But whatever the exact level of the price supports, the idea behind them is perfectly simple: it is to maintain farm prices above the level that would result in a free market.

Using the simple supply-and-demand model developed in the previous chapter, we can see more clearly the effects of these price supports. The situation is shown in Figure 5.3. A support price, OP', was set by the government. Since this support price was above the equilibrium price, OP, the public bought *less* of farm products (OQ_2 rather than OQ) and paid a *higher* price for them. Farmers gained from the price supports, since the amount they received for their crop under the price support was equal to $OP' \times OQ_1$, a greater amount than what they would have received in a free market, which was $OP \times OQ$.

Note, however, that since the support price exceeded the equilibrium price, the quantity supplied of the farm product, OQ_1, exceeded the quantity demanded, OQ_2. That is, *there was a surplus of the farm product in question,* which the government had to purchase, since no one else would. These surpluses were an embarrassment, both economically and politically. They showed that society's scarce resources were being utilized to produce products consumers simply did not want at existing prices. Moreover the cost of storing these surpluses was very large indeed: in some years, these storage costs alone hit the $1 billion mark.

To help reduce these surpluses, the government followed two basic strategies. First, it tried to restrict output of farm products. In particular, the government established an acreage allotment program, which said that farmers had to limit the number of acres they planted in order to get price supports on their crops. The Department of Agriculture estimated how much of each product would be demanded by buyers (other than the government) at the support price, and tried to cut back the total acreage planted with this crop to the point where the quantity supplied equaled the quantity de-

Figure 5.3
Effects of Farm Price Support Program

The support price, *OP′*, is above the equilibrium price, *OP*, so the public buys *OQ₂*, farmers supply *OQ₁* units of output, and the government buys the difference ($OQ_1 - OQ_2$).

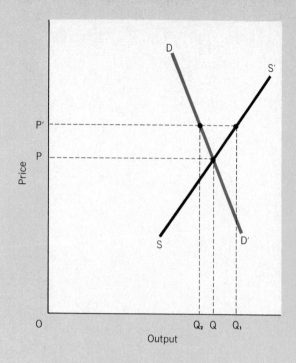

manded. These output restrictions did not eliminate the surpluses, because farmers managed to increase the yields from acreage they were allowed to plant, but undoubtedly they reduced the surpluses. With these restrictions, the situation was as shown in Figure 5.4, where OQ_3 was the total output that could be grown on the acreage that could be planted with the crop. Because of the imposition of this output control, the surplus—which the government had to purchase—was reduced from $OQ_1 - OQ_2$ to $OQ_3 - OQ_2$. Farmers continued to benefit from price supports because the amount they received for their crop—$OP' \times OQ_3$—was still greater than they would have received in a free market, because the amount demanded of farm products was not very sensitive to their price.

Second, the government tried to shift the demand curve for farm products to the right. An effort was made to find new uses for various farm products.

Also, various antipoverty programs, such as the food-stamp program, used our farm surpluses to help the poor. In addition, the government tried to expand the export markets for American farm products. Western Europe and Japan have been increasing their demand for food, and the Communist countries have been purchasing our farm products to offset their own agricultural deficiencies. Moreover, the less developed countries were permitted by Public Law 480 to buy our farm products with their own currencies, rather than dollars. The result was a reduction in farm surpluses, as shown in Figure 5.5. Since the market demand curve for farm products shifted from DD' to D_1D_1', the surplus was reduced from $OQ_3 - OQ_2$ to $OQ_3 - OQ_4$. Because of these demand-augmenting and output-restricting measures, surpluses during the late 1960s and early 1970s were considerably smaller than they were during the late 1950s and early 1960s.

The 1973 Changes in the Farm Program

In 1973, farm prices increased markedly, due partly to very great increases in foreign demand for American agricultural products. This increase in foreign demand was due partly to poor harvests in the Soviet Union, Australia, Argentina, and elsewhere, as well as to devaluations of the dollar. As a result, farm incomes reached very high levels, farm surpluses disappeared, and for the first time in 30 years the government was trying to stimulate farm production rather than restrict it.

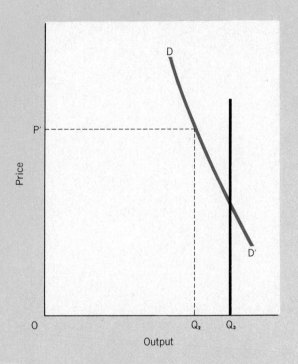

Figure 5.4
Effects of Price Supports and Output Restrictions

The government restricts output to OQ_3, with the result that it buys $(OQ_3 - OQ_2)$ units of output.

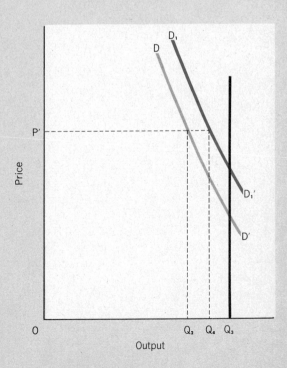

Figure 5.5
Effects of Price Supports, Output Restrictions, and a Shift to the Right in the Demand Curve for Farm Products

By shifting the demand curve from DD' to D_1D_1', the government reduces the surplus from $(OQ_3 - OQ_2)$ to $(OQ_3 - OQ_4)$ units of output.

Taking advantage of this new climate, Congress passed a new farm bill which ended price supports. Instead, agricultural prices will be allowed to fluctuate freely in accord with supply and demand. However, the government will make cash payments to farmers if prices fall below certain "target" levels established by the law. These target levels are above the prices that generally prevailed in the past, but they are far below the record prices prevailing in 1973.

A program of this kind was originally proposed in 1949 by Charles F. Brannan, who was Secretary of Agriculture under President Truman. Farm organizations and their supporters in Congress succeeded in killing the proposal. One important reason why it was passed in 1973 was that farm prices were so high. This meant that a program of this sort would cost little or nothing, so long as prices remained above the "target" levels.

The Wheat Program: A Case Study

To get a better idea of how price supports and output restrictions have worked in agriculture, we will narrow our focus to the case of wheat. In the previous chapter, we described how the price of wheat would be determined in a free market. But the market for wheat has been influenced by government programs for many decades. Let's begin our brief account of the wheat program with the situation after World War II. During the war, a rural political coalition succeeded in getting guarantees of 100 percent of parity price. After the war, there was some movement away from rigid price supports by important government officials, including President Eisenhower's Secretary of Agriculture, Ezra Taft Benson, who wanted the government to reduce its involvement in the farm economy, both because he felt that the government's programs were not succeeding and because he wanted to see a reversal of "the trend toward government invasion of farm freedoms."[10]

During Secretary Benson's eight years in office (1952–60), there was a chronic mismatch between the quantity supplied and quantity demanded of wheat. Because of rapid advances in agricultural technology, wheat farmers were able to maintain production in the face of serious droughts, production controls, and moderate reductions in wheat prices. The government was forced to buy up enormous surpluses of wheat. A big issue in the 1950s was whether price supports should remain at the high levels established during World War II. Rural interests, which included commercial wheat farmers, wanted price supports to stay high: specifically, they wanted them to be at least 90 percent of parity. Secretary Benson, on the other hand, wanted to institute flexible support levels so that they could be used to help reduce overproduction. He succeeded in reducing price support levels—as well as in alienating farmers, farm leaders, and many political liberals.

In 1960, with the election of John F. Kennedy as president, Orville Freeman became Secretary of Agriculture. In contrast to Benson, Secretary Freeman felt that the government should play a major role in American agriculture. Faced with the prospect of continuing large surpluses of wheat, he pushed for great reductions in acreage, which was held at little more than half its postwar high. Also, he urged the export of wheat to the less developed countries, both to help promote their economic growth and to stave off famine. Rather than attempt to maintain 90 percent of parity, Freeman adopted the more modest goal of maintaining 100 percent of parity prices *on the production used for domestic food* (less than half the total crop yield in the 1960s).

The Cotton-Wheat Act of 1964 established a voluntary wheat-marketing certificate program for 1964 and 1965, later extended with only limited changes to 1969. Under this program, farmers who complied with acreage allotments and agreed to participate in a land-diversion program received price supports, marketing certificates, and payments

[10] D. Hadwiger, *Federal Wheat Commodity Programs*, Ames: Iowa State University Press, 1970, Chapter 8.

for land diversion, but farmers who did not comply did not receive benefits. During 1964 to 1969, the price of wheat ranged from about $1.15 to $1.74 per bushel. However, the total price to farmers was more than this, because participants in the wheat program also got direct marketing certificate payments amounting to 65 cents per bushel in 1969. During the early 1970s, the wheat program remained conceptually the same, although some modifications were made.[11]

In August 1973, the wheat program, like other agricultural programs, changed drastically. Price supports were ended, and, as we know from the previous section, the government pledged to make cash payments to farmers if prices fall below certain "target" levels. (However, there is a maximum amount of $20,000 that a farmer can receive per year.) The price of wheat exceeded $4 per bushel in 1973, and was well above the "target" level. In contrast to previous years, the Secretary of Agriculture imposed no restrictions on the acreage that wheat farmers could plant in 1974. Given the enormous increase in the demand for American wheat, the emphasis was on expanding, not curtailing, production.

Evaluation of Government Farm Programs

It is obviously hard to evaluate the success of the government's farm programs. Farmers will certainly take a different view of price supports and other measures than their city cousins. Nonetheless, from the point of view of the nation as a whole, these farm programs have received considerable criticism. To understand these criticisms, we must hark back to our discussion earlier in this chapter of the proper functions of government, and ask what justification there is for the government's

[11] See G. Shepherd and G. Futrell, *Marketing Farm Products,* Ames: Iowa State University Press, 1969, p. 417; and W. Rasmussen and G. Baker, "Programs for Agriculture, 1933–1965," *Agricultural Economics Research,* July, 1966.

intervening in this way in agriculture. Perhaps the most convincing justification is that the government ought to help the rural poor. As we saw in previous sections, most people agree that the government should redistribute income in this way.

Unfortunately, however, *our farm programs have done little for the farmers most in need of help,* because the amount of money a farmer has gotten from price supports has depended on how much he produced. Thus, the big farmer has gotten the lion's share of the subsidies—and he, of course, needed help least. On the other hand, the small farmer, the farmer who is mired most deeply in poverty, has received little from these programs. Recognizing this fact, many observers have pointed out that, if these programs are really aimed at helping the rural poor, it would be more sensible to channel the money to them through direct subsidies, than to finance programs where much of the benefits go to prosperous commercial farmers.

It must also be recognized that *our farm programs have not dealt with the basic causes of the farm problem.* In the past at least, we have had too many people and resources in agriculture. This, as we stressed in previous sections, is why farmers' incomes have tended to be low. Yet the government's farm programs have been directed more toward supporting farm prices and incomes (and stabilizing a sector of the economy that historically has been unstable), rather than toward promoting the needed movement of people and resources out of agriculture. Indeed, some people would say that the government's farm programs have made it more difficult for the necessary adjustments to take place.

Given these defects, many proposals have been made to alter our farm programs. In the view of many observers, agriculture should return to something more closely approximating free markets: the price system should be allowed to work more freely. The changes that occurred in 1973 are in that direction, but it is important to note that the government is still intervening heavily in agriculture. (Moreover, if farm prices recede from their record 1973 levels, the taxpayers may have to pay very heavy subsidies to farmers, according to the new law.) Although further movements toward a free market in agriculture may not be popular among many farm groups, there are signs that such changes may occur in the years ahead.

Finally, before closing this chapter, we must point out a fundamental moral of our farm programs: *the government, like the price system, can bungle the job of organizing a nation's economic activities.* We began this chapter by stressing the fact that the price system breaks down under some circumstances, and that the government must intervene. It is also worth stressing that the government sometimes intervenes when it shouldn't—and that even when it should intervene, it sometimes does so in a way that wastes resources. This, of course, doesn't mean that the government should play no part in the American economy. On the contrary, the government must—and does—play an enormously important role. What it does mean is that, just as the price system is no all-purpose cure-all, neither is the government.

Summary

The price system, despite its many virtues, suffers from serious limitations. There is no reason to believe that the distribution of income generated by the price system is equitable or optimal. Also, there is no way for the price system to handle public goods, and because of external economies or diseconomies, the price system may result in too little or too much of certain goods being produced. To a considerable extent, the government's role in the economy has developed in response to these limitations of the price system. There is considerable agreement that government should redistribute income in favor of the poor, provide public goods, and offset the effects of external economies and diseconomies. Also, it is generally felt that the government should establish a proper legal, social, and competitive framework for the price system, and that it should see to it that the economy maintains relatively full employment with reasonably stable prices. Beyond this, however, there are wide dif-

ferences of opinion on the proper role of government in economic affairs. Conservatives tend to be suspicious of "big government" while liberals are inclined to believe that the government should do more.

In the past 50 years, government spending has increased considerably, both in absolute terms and as a percent of total output. (It is now about one-third of our total output.) To a large extent, this increase has been due to our greater military responsibilities, as well as to the fact that, as their incomes have risen, our citizens have demanded more schools, highways, and other goods and services provided by government. The growth in government expenditures has also been part of a general trend in the United States whereby, more and more, the power of the government has been used to achieve social objectives. To get the money to cover most of these expenditures, governments collect taxes from individuals and firms. At the federal level, the most important is the personal income tax.

One example of the role of government in the American economy is the farm program. American agriculture has been plagued by relatively low incomes. Until 1973, the demand for farm products grew slowly, while rapid technological change meant that the people and resources currently in agriculture could supply more and more farm products. Because people and resources did not move out of agriculture as rapidly as the price system dictated, farm incomes tended to be relatively low. In response to political pressures from the farm blocs, the government set in motion a series of programs to aid farmers. A cornerstone of these programs was the concept of parity, which said that the prices farmers receive should increase at the same rate as the prices of the goods and services farmers buy. The government instituted price supports to keep farm prices above their equilibrium level. But since the support prices exceeded the equilibrium prices, there was a surplus of the commodities that the government had to purchase and store. To help reduce these surpluses, the government tried to restrict the output of farm products and expand the demand for them.

These farm programs received considerable criticism. From the point of view of income redistribution, they suffered from the fact that they did little for the farmers most in need of help. As tools of resource allocation, they suffered because they dealt more with the symptoms of the farm problem than with its basic causes. In 1973, price supports were ended, but the government pledged to make cash payments to farmers if farm prices fall below certain "target" levels. The government's farm programs illustrate the fact that government intervention, like the price system, has plenty of limitations. Neither the price system nor government intervention is an all-purpose cure-all.

CONCEPTS FOR REVIEW

Public goods	Welfare payments	Public sector
External economy	Price supports	Income tax
External diseconomy	Parity	Sales tax
Transfer payments	Depression	Property tax
Antitrust laws	Private sector	

QUESTIONS FOR DISCUSSION AND REVIEW

1. According to George Stigler, "The state never knows when to quit." What does he mean? Do you agree or disagree?

2. According to Paul Samuelson, "Libertarians fail to realize that the price system is, and ought to be, a method of coercion." What does he mean? Do you agree or disagree?

3. The distribution of income generated by the price system is not necessarily equitable or optimal. True or False?

4. Consumption or production by one firm or person resulting in uncompensated costs to another is called
   a. external economy. b. external diseconomy. c. public good. d. economic stabilization.

CHAPTER 6

Government Expenditures, Taxation, and the Public Debt

The government plays an extremely important role in the American economy. It is obvious that it influences our economic lives and fortunes in countless ways. At this point, we must look in detail at how decisions are made concerning the level and distribution of government expenditures. Also, we must discuss the principles of taxation. These topics are of central importance in understanding the public sector of our economy.

In addition, we must discuss some of the salient issues concerning the public sector, including the so-called military-industrial complex, tax reform, and revenue sharing. Further, we must describe in some detail the nature, size, and burden of the public debt, a subject that has been surrounded by as many myths as any in economics.

The Federal Budgetary Process

Determining how much the federal government should spend is a mammoth undertaking, involving literally thousands of people and hundreds of thousands of manhours. Decisions on expenditures are part of the budgetary process. The *budget* is a statement of the government's anticipated expenditures and revenues. The federal budget is for a fiscal year, from July 1 to June 30. Let's consider the budget for the fiscal year beginning July 1, 1973. In the summer of 1972, the various agencies of the federal government began to prepare their program proposals. By the fall they had made detailed budget requests which the president, with his Office of Management and Budget, went over from October to December 1972. Since the agencies generally wanted more than the president wanted to spend, he usually cut down their requests.

In January 1973, the president submitted his budget to Congress. Often the proposals for expenditures are first examined by the committee responsible for overseeing the particular program —for example, the Military Affairs Committee— and then by the entire Congress. The oversight committee must recommend new legislation if it is needed; it must vote authorizations for programs. Then the Appropriations Committees and the House of Representatives and Senate must vote the appropriations of money. The appropriations may be less than the authorizations, since the Appropriations Committees tend to be less generous than the oversight committees. The Congress voted these appropriations—reducing some of the president's requests, increasing others—in the spring and summer of 1973. The appropriations allowed the president to spend the allotted amounts of money, which he usually, but not always, does.

Three things should be noted about the budgetary process. First, it is a long procedure. Second, although it appears rigid, it is more flexible than it looks. If conditions change, the president usually can go to Congress for supplementary appropriations, or he can refuse to spend money already appropriated. Third, the decision-making process in Congress is fragmented. Separate committees and subcommittees of the Appropriations Committees consider various parts of the president's recommended budget, making it hard to establish any overall policy for total government expenditure. Of course, evaluation of the entire budget must be broken down into parts, since it is too big a job for any single committee, but it is also important that the total be more than the sum of largely uncoordinated parts.

Benefit-Cost Analysis and Program Budgeting

How much should the government spend on various activities and services? Basically, the answer must be provided by the nation's political processes. For example, with regard to the provision of public goods

> Voting by ballot must be resorted to in place of dollar voting . . . [D]ecision making by voting becomes a substitute for preference revelation through the market. The results will not please everybody, but they will approximate—more or less perfectly, depending on the efficiency of the voting process and the homogeneity of preferences—the community's preferences in the matter.[1]

Under certain circumstances, particular types of economic analysis can prove helpful in determining how much the government should spend on various programs. Let's begin by supposing that we can measure the benefits and costs of each such program. What is the optimal amount to spend on each one? The answer, clearly enough, is that *spending on the program should be pushed to the point where the extra benefit from an extra dollar spent is at least equal to the dollar of cost.* This would insure that the amount spent on each government program yields a benefit at least as great as the value of output forgone in the private

[1] Richard and Peggy Musgrave, *Public Finance in Theory and Practice,* New York: McGraw Hill, 1973, p. 8.

sector. This would also make sure that one government program is not being expanded at the expense of other programs that would yield greater benefits if they were expanded instead.

The principle that extra benefit should be compared with extra cost is valuable—and, as we shall see in the next section, widely applicable—but it can solve only a small part of the problem of allocating resources in the public sector. Why? Because it is impossible to measure the benefits from defense or police protection or the courts in dollars and cents. Only in certain cases can benefits be quantified at all precisely. And it is not only a question of the amount of the benefits and costs; it is also a question of who benefits and who pays. Nonetheless, it is difficult to see how rational choices can be made without paying attention to costs and benefits—even if they are measured imprecisely, and are by no means the whole story.

In recent years, there has been a noteworthy attempt to increase the use of economic analysis to help promote better decision making regarding government spending. In 1965, President Johnson established a Planning-Programming-Budgeting System throughout the federal government. This system, similar to one already established in the Department of Defense, had several objectives. It encouraged more precise identification of the goals of various programs and promoted the search for alternative means of reaching these goals, thus making it more likely that they would be fulfilled economically. It also required officials to try to obtain better measures of the true cost and output of various programs. But the PPB System encountered a number of obstacles, including the failure of agency heads to use it, lack of interest in Congress, and opposition by some private interest groups. Critics of the system have pointed to a number of failures. Its advocates, while they do not deny the problems, claim that the system has improved the decision-making process.

The PPB system has also been adopted by various state governments; the first to do so was Wisconsin in 1964. In Wisconsin, needs or goals are classified within broad functional areas, like educa-

tion, commerce, environmental resources, human relations and resources, and general operations. For example, within the human relations and resources category, a specific goal may be to provide education and related training to crippled children. Then the alternative means of accomplishing this goal, such as financial aid to individuals, aid to orthopedic schools, orthopedic hospitals, or transportation aids, are considered. After their costs and effectiveness are examined, proposals are made for the techniques to use to achieve this goal. Some local governments, like New York City, have also adopted the PPB system. However, PPB is still not used in any comprehensive way by most state and local governments.[2]

Benefit-Cost Analysis: A Case Study[3]

Despite the difficulties involved, in recent years more and more benefit-cost analyses have been carried out to help guide public policy. For example, consider the following study, by the University of Wisconsin's Burton Weisbrod, of a program to reduce the dropout rate in a high school in St. Louis. In this program, potential dropouts were given counseling and help in getting part-time jobs. It cost over $500 per student. The question, of course, was whether the program did enough good to be worth the cost. To help answer this question, the experience of the students in the program was compared with the experience of a control group of comparable students who were not included in

[2] For an excellent discussion of the PPB system, see Charles Schultze, *The Politics and Economics of Public Spending*, Washington: Brookings Institution, 1968. Also, see Bernard Herber, *Modern Public Finance*, Homewood, Ill.: Irwin, 1971, pp. 389–91.

[3] This section is based on Burton Weisbrod, "Preventing High School Dropouts," in Robert Dorfman (editor), *Measuring Benefits of Government Investments*, Washington: Brookings Institution, 1965. A brief discussion of this study is also provided in Otto Eckstein, *Public Finance*, Englewood Cliffs, N.J.: Prentice-Hall, 1967.

the program. It turned out that, despite the help they received, 44 percent of the students in the program dropped out of school before graduation, while 52 percent of the students in the control group dropped out before graduation. Thus the program seemed to reduce the dropout rate by 8 percentage points.

How much was this benefit worth? Weisbrod pointed out that one principal gain was the increased income earned by students who complete high school. A high school graduate earns about $2,750 more than a dropout over a lifetime. Let us use this figure—$2,750—as a measure of the benefit of preventing a student from dropping out. Was the program worthwhile? Since the program reduced the probability of dropping out by 8 percentage points, the average benefit per student was .08 times $2,750, or $220. Since this was less than the cost per student, the program did not seem worthwhile. Of course, one can object that the measure of the benefit from preventing a student from dropping out is incomplete. It does not include the psychic and social benefits from putting people in a position to earn their own keep rather than to be prime candidates for public assistance, and even perhaps jail. Nonetheless, this study raised important questions and had significant effects.

Benefit-cost analyses have proved useful in many areas of government. In particular, they have been used for many years in the Department of Defense. Decisions to develop one weapons system rather than another, or to procure a certain amount of a given weapon, have been based in part on such studies. Other areas where benefit-cost analyses have been used extensively are water projects (irrigation, flood control, hydroelectric and other projects), transportation projects, and urban renewal, recreation, and health projects. For example, in water projects, benefit-cost analysis has frequently been used by the Corps of Engineers and others to determine whether it is worthwhile to spend additional money on flood control, and if so, how much extra expenditure is justified.

A highly simplified example of a benefit-cost

Table 6.1

Benefit-Cost Analysis for Constructing a Dam

Alternative policies	Annual cost	Annual benefit
Build a low dam	$100,000	$150,000
Build a high dam	$250,000	$350,000

analysis of the construction of a dam is shown in Table 6.1. The alternative policies are to build a low dam or a high dam. Table 6.1 shows the annual costs and benefits associated with each of these policies. Clearly, the high dam should be built because the extra cost involved ($150,000 more than for the low dam) is more than outweighed by the extra benefits received ($200,000 more than for the low dam). Note, however, that this is a very simple case. In general, data on costs and benefits are not laid out so straightforwardly. Instead, there are very wide bands of uncertainty about the relevant benefits and costs.

Government Expenditures and the Problem of Social Balance

It is not easy to decide how large government expenditures should be. As we saw in Chapter 5, opinions differ widely on the proper role of government in economic affairs, and it is often impossible to measure the costs and benefits of government programs with dependable accuracy. Nonetheless, some economists—led by Harvard's John Kenneth Galbraith—believe that the public sector of the economy is being starved of needed resources, whereas the private sector is catering to relatively unimportant wants. For example, in *The Affluent Society*, Galbraith argues that consumers are led by advertising and other promotional efforts to purchase more and more goods of marginal significance to them. On the other hand, in his opinion, the nation is suffering from too little spending on government services. Thus he writes:

> In the years following World War II, the papers of any major city . . . told daily of the shortages and shortcomings in the elementary municipal and metropolitan services. The schools were old and overcrowded. The police force was understrength and underpaid. The parks and playgrounds were insufficient. Streets and empty lots were filthy, and the sanitation staff was underequipped and in need of men. Access to the city by those who work there was uncertain and painful and becoming more so. Internal transportation was overcrowded, unhealthy, and dirty. So was the air. Parking on the streets had to be prohibited, and there was no space elsewhere. These deficiencies were not in new and novel services, but in old established ones.[4]

Many economists agree with Galbraith. Particularly among liberals, there is a widespread feeling that resources are being mal-allocated, too much going for deodorants, comic books, and mouth wash, and too little going for schools and public services. But this feeling is not shared by all economists. Galbraith's critics point out that expenditures often benefit particular interest groups, which lobby hard for them in federal and state legislatures. The result is that spending programs may be carried beyond the optimal point. Further, they point out that Galbraith's assertion that private wants are becoming more and more trivial and synthetic is not scientifically verifiable and that, in any case, it ignores the large number of people living in very modest circumstances, indeed even in dire poverty.

Economic theory alone cannot settle this basic question. It is obviously a matter of politics as well as economics. However, in trying to reach an opinion, bear in mind that both sides may be partly correct. For certain types of government services, you may agree with Galbraith and his

followers that too little is being spent, but for other types of government services you may agree with his critics that too much is being spent. For example, you may feel that too little is being spent on pollution control and urban problems, but that too much is being spent on agricultural subsidies (many of which go to wealthy farmers) and subsidies to the merchant marine (which are meant to keep the American shipping industry competitive with other nations).

Finally, it is important to distinguish between decisions concerning the *scope* of government activities and decisions concerning the *efficiency* of government. Thus far in this section we have been discussing the proper scope of government. Assume that we can divide all goods into public goods and private goods, and that Figure 6.1 shows the society's product transformation curve. In other words, as you recall from Chapter 3, Figure 6.1 shows the maximum amount of public goods that can be produced, given each quantity produced of private goods. Then the question that we have been discussing is: At what point along the product transformation curve should society be? For example, should society choose point A (where more public goods and less private goods are produced) or point B (where less public goods and more private goods are produced)?

But there is another important question: How can we attain a point *on* the product transformation curve, rather than one (like point C) that is *inside* it? As we know from Chapter 3, inefficiency will result in society's being on a point inside the product transformation curve. Thus, to attain a point on the product transformation curve, government officials (and others) must do their best to eliminate inefficiency. By doing so, society can get more from the available resources. For example, it can attain points A or B rather than point C. Whether society wants to use its added efficiency to attain point A or point B is then a political question. However, regardless of how this question is decided, society is better off to eliminate inefficiency.

[4] John Kenneth Galbraith, *The Affluent Society,* Boston: Houghton Mifflin, 1958, p. 252. Incidentally, Galbraith opposed the tax cut of 1964 because he felt that government spending should be increased instead.

Figure 6.1
Product Transformation Curve,
Public versus Private Goods

At Point B, society produces less public goods and more private goods than at Point A. Thus, a movement from Point A to Point B reduces government expenditures by reducing the *scope* of government services. At Point C, society is producing inefficiently, and a movement from Point C to Point B or Point A can be attained by increasing the *efficiency* of government (and/or private) operations

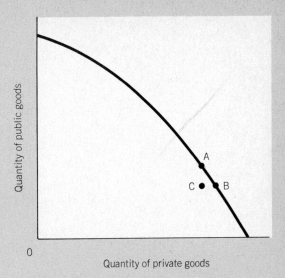

Military Spending and the Military-Industrial Complex

At this point, it is worthwhile to look briefly at two federal agencies, the Department of Defense and the Office of Coal Research. Although these two agencies cannot be held up as typical, they do represent interesting case studies. On the one hand, the Department of Defense has repeatedly been charged with overspending. But since it is hard to tell what level of defense capability is optimal, it is equally difficult to tell whether defense spending is too much or too little. However, there can be no doubt about the enormous size of our defense expenditures. In 1970, American military expenditures were more than $80 billion, which means that they constituted over 40 percent of the total federal budget and about 10 percent of national output. Moreover, this underestimates the costs of our military establishment, because it does not include defense-related expenditures by the Atomic Energy Commission and National Aeronautics and Space Administration. Some people claim that this exaggerates the cost of defense, because if defense expenditures were cut appreciably, our national out-

put would fall. But this assumes that other forms of government spending would not be substituted for defense, or that fiscal and monetary policies could not keep the economy at a high employment level without defense spending—both very unrealistic assumptions.

However, some forms of defense and space spending, particularly on research and development, do provide important benefits to the civilian economy. The electronic computer, numerical control, integrated circuits, atomic energy, synthetic rubber, and many other significant inventions stemmed at least partly from military R and D. Moreover, there is undoubtedly considerable opportunity for such spillover from current military and space R and D. Nonetheless, there seems to be a widespread feeling that the spillover per dollar of military-space R and D is unlikely to be as great as in the past, because the capabilities that are being developed and the environment that is being probed are less intimately connected with civilian activities than formerly. For example, the devices needed to send a man to the moon may have relatively little applicability in the civilian economy because they "oversatisfy" civilian requirements and few people or firms are willing to pay for them.

There is considerable evidence that the weapons acquisition process has not been as efficient as it might have been. There have been spectacular overruns in development and production costs. For example, the cost of the Lockheed C5A transport plane increased from the $3.4 billion estimated in 1965 to $5.3 billion in 1968. To some extent, such cost increases reflect the fact that new weapons systems tend to push the state of the art, so that unexpected problems must be expected. But in addition, the firms that develop and produce these weapons systems often submit unrealistically low bids to get a contract, knowing that they are likely to get approval for cost increases later on. According to some observers, like Merton J. Peck of Yale University and F. M. Scherer of the International Institute of Management, these cost overruns have also been due to "inadequate attention to the efficient utilization of technical, production, and administrative manpower—areas in which major cost reductions are possible."[5]

In addition, some observers believe that the major defense contractors, in conjunction with the military services, apply undue political pressure in support of high defense budgets. For example, President Dwight D. Eisenhower, himself a distinguished military commander, warned of the dangers involved in this "military-industrial complex." In his last speech to the nation as president, he said, "In the councils of government, we must guard against the acquisition of unwarranted influence, whether sought or unsought, by the military-industrial complex. The potential for the disastrous rise of misplaced power exists and will persist." It seems unlikely that there is any real conspiracy, but military contractors, with their political allies, are undoubtedly a powerful lobby for defense spending.

[5] M. J. Peck and F. M. Scherer, *The Weapons Acquisition Process*, Cambridge: Harvard University Press, 1962 p. 594.

The Office of Coal Research: Another Case Study

Just as it is sometimes charged that certain agencies, like the Department of Defense, may have been spending too much, so it is sometimes charged that other agencies, like the Office of Coal Research, may have been spending too little. In recent years, there has been considerable discussion and alarm over the so-called "energy crisis," a situation where a marked shortage seems to have arisen in clean domestic fuels. One way to avoid such a crisis is to develop new technologies to convert our relatively plentiful coal supplies into a clean gas or other forms of fuel that would be less polluting than coal. The Office of Coal Research is responsible for financing research of this kind, and in accord with President Nixon's energy message of June 4, 1971, it is charged with accelerating the coal gasification program to develop a process or processes to produce clean, high-quality gas from coal on a commercial scale by 1980.

The expenditures of the Office of Coal Research (OCR) have increased very substantially in recent years. Its budget was about $52 million in 1974, about $30 million in 1972, and about $15 million in 1970. Much of this money is spent for coal gasification work; about $30 million was spent in 1973 on this program, 2/3 to be funded by OCR and about 1/3 by industry. The Office of Coal Research has helped to finance several approaches to coal gasification, including the Institute of Gas Technology's HYGAS pilot plant, the Consolidation Coal Company's CO_2 Acceptor pilot plant, FMC Corporation's COED pilot plant, and others. Each of these pilot plants costs millions of dollars. Because it is felt that the social returns from the information gained from them will exceed the private returns to the companies operating them, the government subsidizes this research and development.

Despite the increase in OCR's expenditures, many knowledgeable people feel that such work should be expanded more rapidly. For example, in 1973 Senator Henry Jackson of Washington called for a 10-year R and D program on coal gasification costing $660 million (60 percent to be paid for by government, 40 percent by industry), and a 12-year R and D program on coal liquefaction costing $750 million (75 percent to be paid for by government). Also, the Office of Science and Technology's Energy Advisory Panel called in 1972 for an expanded R and D program for coal liquefaction, as well as continued emphasis on coal gasification. In June 1973, President Nixon asked for an increase in the amount of resources devoted to such programs. It seems likely that more will be spent for these purposes.

The Federal Tax Legislative Process

It is one thing for the federal government to decide how much to spend and on what; it is another to raise the money to underwrite these programs. This section describes how the federal government decides how much to tax. Of course, this problem is not solved from scratch every year. Instead, the government takes the existing tax structure as given and changes it from time to time as seems desirable. Often the initiative leading to a change in the tax laws comes from the president, who sometimes requests tax changes in his State of the Union message, his budget message, or a special tax message. Much of the spadework underlying his proposals will have been carried out by the Treasury Department, particularly the Treasury's Office of Tax Analysis, Office of the Tax Legislative Counsel, and Internal Revenue Service.

The proposal of a major tax change generally brings about considerable public debate. Representatives of labor, industry, agriculture, and other economic and social groups present their opinions. Newspaper articles, radio shows, and television commentators analyze the issues. By the time the Congress begins to look seriously at the proposal, the battle lines between those who favor the change and those who oppose it are generally pretty clearly drawn. The tax bill incorporating the change is first considered by the Ways and Means Committee of the House of Representatives, a very powerful committee composed of 25 members drawn from both political parties. After public hearings, the committee goes into executive session and reviews each proposed change with its staff and with the Treasury staff. After careful study, the committee arrives at a bill it recommends—though this bill may or may not conform to what the president asked for. Then the bill is referred to the entire House of Representatives for approval. Only rarely is a major tax bill recommended by the committee turned down by the House.

Next, the bill is sent to the Senate. There it is referred to the Finance Committee, which is organized like the House Ways and Means Committee. The Finance Committee also holds hearings, discusses the bill at length, makes changes in it, and sends its version of the bill to the entire Senate, where there frequently is considerable debate. Ultimately, it is brought to a vote. If it does not pass, that ends the process. If it does pass (and if it differs from the House version of the bill, which is generally the case), then a conference committee must be formed to iron out the differences between the House and Senate versions. Finally, when this compromise is worked out, the result must be passed by both houses and sent to the president. The president rarely vetoes a tax bill, although it has occasionally been done.[6]

[6] For an excellent discussion of the federal tax legislative process, see J. Pechman, *Federal Tax Policy*, revised edition, New York: Norton, 1971, part of which is reprinted in E. Mansfield, *Economics: Readings, Issues, and Cases*, New York: Norton, 1974.

Principles of Taxation

According to the English political philosopher, Edmund Burke, "To tax and to please, no more than to love and to be wise, is not given to men." What constitutes a rational tax system? Are there any generally accepted principles to guide the nation in determining who should pay how much? The answer is that there are some principles most people accept, but they are so broad and general that they leave plenty of room for argument and compromise. Specifically, two general principles of taxation command widespread agreement. First, *there is the principle that people who receive more in benefits from a certain government service should pay more in taxes to support it.* Certainly few people would argue with this idea. Second, *there is the principle that people should be taxed so as to result in a socially desirable redistribution of income.* In practice, this has ordinarily meant that the wealthy have been asked to pay more than the poor. This idea, too, has generally commanded widespread assent—although this, of course, has not prevented the wealthy from trying to avoid its application to them.

It follows from these principles that if two people are in essentially the same circumstances (their income, purchases, utilization of public services are the same), then they should pay the same taxes. This is an important rule, innocuous though it may seem. It says that equals should be treated equally—*whether one is a Republican and the other is a Democrat, or whether one is a friend of the president and the other is his enemy, or whether one has purely salary income and the other has property income, they should be treated equally.* Certainly, this is a basic characteristic of an equitable tax system.

It is easy to relate most of the taxes in our tax structure to these principles. For example, the first principle—the benefit principle—is the basic rationale behind taxes on gasoline and license fees for vehicles and drivers. Those who use the roads are asked to pay for their construction and upkeep. Also, the property tax, levied primarily on real estate, is often supported on these grounds. It is argued that property owners receive important benefits—fire and police protection, for example—and that the extent of the benefits is related to the extent of their property.

The personal income tax is based squarely on the second principle—ability to pay. A person with a large income pays a higher proportion of income in personal income taxes than does a person with a smaller income. For example, in 1973, if a couple's income (after deductions but before exemptions) were $5,000, their federal income tax would be $535, whereas if their income were $20,000, their federal income tax would be $3,960. (However, the wealthy can avoid taxes in various perfectly legal ways, as we shall see in a later section.) Also, estate and inheritance taxes hit the rich much harder than the poor; but again, it is possible to take some of the sting out of them if you have a good lawyer.

The principles cited above are useful and important, but they do not take us very far toward establishing a rational tax structure. They are too vague and leave too many questions unanswered. For example, if I use about the same amount of public services as you do, but my income is twice yours, how much more should I pay in taxes? Twice as much? Three times as much? Fifty percent more? These principles throw no real light on many of the detailed questions that must be answered by a real-life tax code.

The Personal and Corporate Income Taxes

The federal personal income tax brings in almost $100 billion a year. Yet a great many people are perhaps unaware of just how much they are contributing because it is deducted from their wages each month or each week, so that they owe little extra when April 15 rolls around. (Indeed, they may even be due a refund.) This pay-as-you-go scheme reduces the pain, but, of course, it does

Table 6.2

Federal Personal Income Tax, Couple without Children, 1973

Income (after deductions but before exemptions)	Personal income tax	Average tax rate (percent)	Marginal tax rate (percent)
Below $1500	$ 0	0	0
$3000	215	7.2	15
5000	535	10.7	17
10,000	1,490	14.9	22
20,000	3,960	19.8	28
50,000	16,310	32.6	50
100,000	44,280	44.3	60
1,000,000	669,930	67.0	70

not eliminate it: taxes are never painless.

Obviously, how much a family has to pay in personal income taxes depends on the family's income. The tax schedule as of 1973, is as shown in Table 6.2. The second column shows how much a couple would have to pay if their income was the amount shown in the first column. For example, at an income of $5,000, their income tax would be $535; at an income of $20,000, their income tax would be $3,960. Clearly, the percentage of income owed in income tax increases as income increases, but this percentage does not increase indefinitely. As shown in the third column of Table 6.2, the percentage of income going for personal income taxes never exceeds 70 percent, no matter how much money the couple makes. (And on income from wages and personal effort, it never exceeds 50 percent.)

It is instructive to look further at how the "tax bite" increases with income. In particular, let's ask ourselves what proportion of an *extra* dollar of income the couple will have to pay in personal income taxes. In other words, what is the **marginal tax rate**—the tax on an extra dollar of income? The fourth column of Table 6.2 shows that the marginal tax rate is 17 percent if the couple's income is $5,000, 28 percent if the couple's income is $20,000, 50 percent if the couple's income is $50,000, and 70 percent if the couple's income is $1 million. Thus, the greater the couple's income, the greater the proportion of an extra dollar that goes for personal income taxes.

Clearly, the personal income tax tends to reduce the inequality of after-tax income, since the rich are taxed more heavily than the poor. However, the personal income tax does not bear down as heavily on the rich as one might surmise from Table 6.2. This is because, as we shall see in a subsequent section, there are a variety of perfectly legal ways for people to avoid paying taxes on their incomes. In addition, of course, there is some illegal tax evasion, such as underreporting of income, fake expenses, and imaginary dependents. But evasion is much less important than legal tax avoidance, despite Will Rogers's quip that the income tax has made more liars among the American public than golf.

The federal government imposes a tax on the incomes of corporations as well as of people. Corporations must pay 22 percent of their first $25,000 of annual net earnings and 48 percent of the rest as corporate income tax. For example, a corporation with annual profit of $125,000 would pay $53,500 in corporate income tax—$5,500 (22 percent of the first $25,000) plus $48,000 (48 percent of the remaining $100,000). The corporate income tax involves "double taxation." The federal government taxes a corporation's earnings both through the corporate income tax (when the corporation earns the profits) and through the personal income tax (when the corporation's earnings are distributed to the stockholders as dividends).

It is generally agreed that the personal income tax is paid by the person whose income is taxed: he or she cannot shift this tax to someone else. But the incidence of the corporate income tax is not so clear. To some extent, corporations may pass along some of their income tax bill to customers in the form of higher prices or to workers in the form of lower wages. Some economists feel that a corporation shifts much of the tax burden in this way; others disagree. This is a controversial issue that has proved very difficult to resolve.

The Property Tax and the Sales Tax

The *property tax* is the fiscal bulwark of our local governments. The way it works is simple enough. Most towns and cities estimate the amount they will spend in the next year or two, and then determine a property tax based on the assessed property values in the town or city. For example, if there is $500 million in assessed property values in the town and the town needs to raise $5 million, the tax rate will be 1 percent of assessed property value. In other words, each property owner will have to pay 1 percent of the assessed value of his property. There are well-known problems in the administration of the property tax. First, assessed values of property often depart significantly from actual market values; the former are typically much lower than the latter. And the ratio of assessed to actual value is often lower among higher-priced pieces of property; thus wealthier people tend to

Table 6.3

State Retail Sales Tax Rates, 1970

State	Percentage	State	Percentage	State	Percentage
Alabama	4	Louisiana	2	Oklahoma	2
Arizona	3	Maine	5	Pennsylvania	6
Arkansas	3	Maryland	4	Rhode Island	5
California	4	Massachusetts	3	South Carolina	4
Colorado	3	Michigan	4	South Dakota	4
Connecticut	5	Minnesota	3	Tennessee	3
District of Columbia	4	Mississippi	5	Texas	3¼
Florida	4	Missouri	3	Utah	4
Georgia	3	Nebraska	2½	Vermont	3
Hawaii	4	Nevada	2	Virginia	3
Idaho	3	New Jersey	3	Washington	4½
Illinois	4	New Mexico	4	West Virginia	3
Indiana	2	New York	3	Wisconsin	4
Iowa	3	North Carolina	3	Wyoming	3
Kansas	3	North Dakota	4		
Kentucky	5	Ohio	4		

Source: Advisory Commission on Intergovernmental Relations.

get off easier. Second, there is widespread evasion of taxes on *personal property*—securities, bank accounts, and so on. Many people simply do not pay up. Third, the property tax is not very flexible: assessments and rates tend to change rather slowly.

The *sales tax,* of course, is a bulwark of state taxation. It provides a high yield with relatively low collection costs. As Table 6.3 indicates, most of the states have some form of general sales tax, the rate being usually between 3 and 5 percent. Retailers add to the price of goods sold to consumers an amount equal to 3 to 5 percent of the consumer's bill. This extra amount is submitted to the state as the general sales tax. Some states exempt food purchases from this tax, and a few exempt medical supplies. Where they exist, these exemptions help reduce the impact of the sales tax on the poor; but in general the sales tax imposes a greater burden relative to income on the poor than on the rich, for the simple reason that the rich save a larger percentage of their income. Practically all of a poor family's income may be subject to sales taxes; a great deal of a rich family's income may not be, because it is not spent on consumer goods, but saved.

Who really pays the property tax or the sales tax? To what extent can these taxes be shifted to other people? The answer is not as straightforward as one might expect. For the property tax, the owner of unrented residential property swallows the tax, since there is no one else to shift it to. But the owner of rented property may attempt to pass along some of the tax to the tenant. In the case of the sales tax, the extent to which it can be shifted to the consumer depends on the demand and supply curves for the taxed commodity. For example, if the demand curve were a vertical line, the whole tax would be passed along to the consumer, whereas if the supply curve were a vertical line, the tax would be absorbed entirely by the producer or seller.

Tax Reform

Because the tax structure of the United States con-

tains so many exemptions and loopholes, there is continual pressure for tax reform. Senator George McGovern, in his bid for the presidency in 1972, stressed the importance of tax reform, stating: "The tax code fills hundreds of pages. It is riddled with loopholes, special exemptions, and shelters, available to those with access to wealth and legal talent. Income which is earned on an assembly line or in an office should no longer be more heavily taxed than profits from oil or securities." In particular, there are questions about the equity of the relatively low tax rates on capital gains, the tax-free status of interest on state and local bonds, the depletion allowances, and other aspects of the tax code.

Because there are so many exemptions, exclusions, and deductions, a surprisingly small percentage of all income is subject to the federal personal income tax. In 1960, only about $3/7$ of personal income in the United States was subject to the income tax. This erosion of the tax base, lamented frequently by experts on public finance, means that tax rates must be higher than they would be if the tax base were broader. In other words, if a larger proportion of all income were subject to the personal income tax, a smaller tax could be imposed on each dollar of income subject to tax. Many tax experts feel strongly that the erosion of the tax base should be stopped, and that the tax base should be broadened appreciably. But it is difficult to take away the various exemptions and deductions that have been granted in the past.

Current tax laws are favorable to homeowners, who can deduct the payment of local real estate taxes and the interest on their mortgage from their income to get the adjusted level of income on which they pay income taxes. Also, money a person makes on the stock market or from some other situation where his assets go up in value, known as a *capital gain,* is subject to lower personal income tax rates than other income. Interest paid by state and local governments on their bonds are not taxable at all by the federal government. Moreover, certain industries, particularly the oil industry, receive preferential tax treatment. In 1913, the

Congress, believing that the sale of minerals involves the sale of a firm's assets, allowed industries selling natural resources to deduct a small proportion of their revenues from their taxable income. This deduction is called a *depletion allowance.* Over the years, this proportion has been increased, until now this preferential treatment results in a tax saving of well over a billion dollars to these industries.

When the time seems ripe for a change in tax rates to stabilize the economy, there is often a tendency to try to accomplish tax reform as well. For example, if a tax cut seems advisable to reduce excessive unemployment, there may be an attempt to combine tax reform with tax reduction. Although the attempt to kill two birds—economic stabilization and tax reform—with one stone seems laudable in theory, in practice it can spell trouble. For example, here is how Thomas Dernburg of Oberlin College and Duncan McDougall of the University of Kansas describe the attempts in the early 1960s to mix tax reduction and tax reform:

> During the debate of the early 1960's, the Treasury proposed that the tax bill contain a comprehensive package of reform. Aware that congressmen cannot be interested in reforms that penalize wealthy constituents and potential campaign contributors, the Treasury attempted to tack the reform package onto the tax reduction proposed by the President. The hope was that the tasty carrot of a tax reduction might be strong enough to drag along the refractory donkey of reform. Tax reform got nowhere in Congress. Realizing that the entire bill was in jeopardy, the Administration eventually gave up on reform, and the final bill represented rate reduction and not much else. Undoubtedly, the attempt to gain reform was one factor making for delay in obtaining passage of the tax bill.[7]

State and Local Finance and Revenue Sharing

It is important to recognize that there are several levels of government in the United States—federal, state, and local—and that each level of government spends and taxes. Thus, all levels of government, not just the federal government, play a role in our economic affairs. Unfortunately, however, there has been limited coordination between the spending and tax decisions of the federal government and those of the state and local governments. From the point of view of promoting full employment without inflation, it would be desirable for the federal, state, and local governments to work in unison, or at least in the same direction, to fight excessive unemployment or inflation. But in fact they often have worked at cross purposes.

In this country the state and local governments are traditionally entrusted with the responsibility for some of the services that have had to be expanded most rapidly—education, highways, municipal facilities, and so forth. Yet the kinds of taxes the state and local governments rely on—notably sales and property taxes—do not provide a yield that increases very rapidly with increases in income. Thus a basic question arises: how can the state and local governments get the money they need to expand their services at the desired rate? Presently, the state and local governments are caught in a fiscal bind. Their expenditures are being pushed up more rapidly than their revenues. On the other hand, because the personal income tax generates a great deal of additional money as income increases, the federal government is in the fortunate position of having its revenues increase at a relatively rapid rate.

Recognizing that it has access to greater sources of revenue, the federal government has been making more and more grants to states and—on a smaller scale—to local governments. These grants have been earmarked primarily for highways, welfare, and education, the major expenditure areas for state and local governments. One effect of these grants is to offset the considerable regional differences in income. Since some states—particularly those in the South—are poor, less tax revenue is

[7] Thomas Dernburg and Duncan McDougall, *Macroeconomics,* New York: McGraw-Hill, 1972, p. 414.

generated there than in richer states even if tax rates are the same. Thus, to equalize the extent and quality of public services, the federal government in effect takes from the richer states—like New York and California—and gives to the poorer states —like Mississippi and Alabama.

In recent years, a great deal of attention has been given to *revenue sharing*—large and unconditional grants by the federal government to the state and local governments. Initially suggested by Walter W. Heller of the University of Minnesota and Joseph Pechman of the Brookings Institution, this idea was accepted by the Nixon administration, and eventually by Congress. At first it was opposed on the grounds that those who spend money should have the responsibility of raising it, since the divorce of expenditure from financing responsibilities might lead to wasteful expenditures. Initially, other objections were raised

as well. But the fiscal plight of the state and local governments is serious and undesirable: there is a mismatch between their responsibilities and their resources. Recognizing that some device must be adopted to help the local and state governments, Congress passed the first revenue sharing bill in 1972.

The National Debt: Size and Growth

No subject in economics has more confused the public than the national debt. When the federal government spends more than it receives in taxes, it borrows money to cover the difference. The national debt—composed of bonds, notes, and other government IOUs of various kinds—is the result of such borrowing. These IOUs are held by in-

Figure 6.2
Size of the National Debt, United States, 1929–72

The national debt, currently about $450 billion, is due largely to World War II.

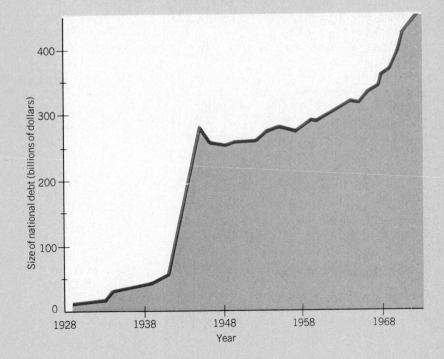

The Department of the Treasury and the National Debt

The average U.S. citizen has very little direct contact with the Department of the Treasury. If he works for the federal government, he receives a bimonthly check; if he is so fortunate as to have overpaid his income tax, he may receive a lovely green refund check. In fact, the processing of checks is (at least, to the nonrecipient economist) much less important than many other functions of the Treasury. Should Congress or the president wish technical advice on the effect of a new tax measure, the Treasury Department will supply the analysis. In addition, it represents American interests in negotiations over international monetary arrangements with other countries; and, through the Internal Revenue Service and the Customs Service, it collects most federal taxes.*

But from an economist's point of view, one of the most interesting tasks the Treasury performs may be the management of the national debt. Imagine yourself with a debt of over $325 billion (held by the public), with a few billion coming due each week. Obviously, much of the Treasury's time must be spent scratching for new Peters in order to pay old Pauls. This may not sound like an easy task; and, in fact, it isn't. Over the years the Treasury has developed a bewildering array of devices—refinancing Series E bonds, U.S. savings bonds, short-term bills, long-term bonds—for coaxing new lenders to release their cash, or persuading old lenders to defer collection.

The most important of these instruments is U.S. Treasury bills, which in 1973 amounted to almost $103 billion. (Should you ever have a spare $10,000, the smallest denomination in which Treasury bills are sold, their current prices can be found in the financial pages of any major newspaper.)

Almost every month the Undersecretary of the Treasury for Monetary Affairs must decide in what form the portion of the debt coming due should be refinanced. Are interest rates going up? If so, he might refinance by selling long-term bonds, locking up money at the present low rate. Will interest rates fall? If so, he might prefer the 90-day bill. Before an issue is floated, he gets a reading of market conditions from committees of the American Bankers Association and the Investment Bankers Association. But cost is not his only problem. He must also worry about the effect of Treasury operations on financial markets and must have developed future refunding policies. In any case, an elaborate financial network of banks, big insurance companies, pension funds, and investment houses is always waiting to respond to the Treasury's next offering.

E.A.

*Moreover, faithful television fans may realize that, through its Bureau of Customs, the Treasury is responsible for controlling the importation of narcotics.

Figure 6.3
National Debt as a Percent of
National Output, United
States, 1929–72

As a percent of national output,
the national debt has declined
steadily since World War II.

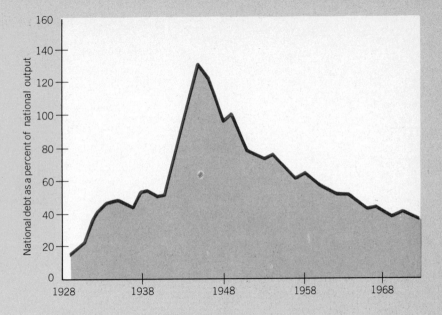

dividuals, firms, banks, and public agencies. There is a large and very important market for government securities, which are relatively riskless and highly liquid. If you look at the *New York Times* or *Wall Street Journal*, for example, you can find each day the prices at which each of a large number of issues of these bonds, notes, and bills are quoted.

How large is the national debt? In 1972, as shown in Figure 6.2, it was almost $450 billion. This certainly seems to be a large amount, but it is important to relate the size of the national debt to the size of our national output. After all, a $450 billion debt means one thing if our annual output is $1 trillion, and another thing if our annual output is $100 billion. As a percent of output, the national debt is smaller now than in 1939, and no larger now than shortly after the Civil War. In 1972, the debt was about 40 percent of output; in 1939, it was about 50 percent of output; and in 1868, it was about 40 percent of output. The debt —expressed as a percentage of output—is shown in

Figure 6.3. Surely the figures do not seem to provide any cause for alarm. The popular misconception that the national debt is growing at a dangerous rate seems hard to square with the facts.

It is obvious from Figure 6.2 that the size of our national debt is due largely to one thing: World War II. In 1939, the national debt was less than $50 billion; by 1945, it was close to $300 billion. This huge increase occurred to finance the war. Since 1945, the national debt has not grown fast. Indeed, as a percent of national output, it has decreased substantially since 1945. Consequently, as Richard and Peggy Musgrave point out, "The specter of an ever-rising debt to [output] ratio, which so agitated the public only a few decades ago, has become of more or less anthropological interest, a striking example of the demise of a once burning issue."[8]

[8] Richard and Peggy Musgrave, *op. cit.*, p. 587. Note too that much of the public debt is in the hands of government agencies, not held by the public. For example, in 1971 only about $325 billion was held by the public.

Burdens and Advantages of the National Debt

When I was a boy and the national debt was increasing to the "incredible" level of about $47 billion, my grandfather used to warn me repeatedly that the debt was a burden his generation was thrusting on my generation. I believed it then, but I don't believe it now. Without trying to show where my grandfather may have been led astray —after all, who needs a smart-aleck grandson!— it is worth pointing out that a public debt is not like your debt or mine, which must be paid off at a certain time in the future. In practice, new government debt is floated to pay off maturing public debt. There never comes a time when we must collectively reach into our pockets to pay off the debt. And even if we did pay it off, the same generation would collect as the one that paid.

Of course, this does not mean that the debt is of no economic consequence. On the contrary, to the extent that the debt is held by foreigners, we must send goods and services overseas to pay the interest on it. This means that less goods and services are available for our citizens. Even if the debt is internally held, there are additional effects as well. Taxes must be collected from the public at large to pay interest to the holders of government bonds, notes, and other obligations. To the extent that the bondholders receiving the interest are wealthier than the public as a whole, there is thus some redistribution of income from the poor to the rich. To the extent that the taxes needed to obtain the money to pay interest on the debt reduce incentives, the result may be a smaller national output.

Beyond this, the existence of all those government bonds, notes, and so forth in the portfolios of people and firms may make them feel richer, and this may make them spend more. Whether this is good or bad depends upon whether we are at less than full employment. If so, it is a good thing; if not, it is bad. In addition, the existence of a large, broadly marketed national debt enables the Federal Reserve System to buy and sell government securities to help stabilize the economy, as we shall see in Chapter 14. (However, problems can arise if the government forces the Federal Reserve System to keep down the interest costs on the debt—this may result in some destabilization of the economy, as in 1946–51.)

If the government's revenues fall short of its expenditures, the difference is called a **deficit.** Borrowing is not the only method the government can use to finance a deficit. It can also create new money to cover the difference between expenditures and revenues. In other words, rather than selling bonds and other types of IOUs to the public to obtain the amount needed to cover the deficit, the government can print new currency, or create additional money in other ways. According to many economists, a deficit will have a less expansionary effect on output and employment if it is financed by borrowing from the public than if it is financed by creating new money. Much more will be said in Chapter 12 about the effects on output and employment of changes in the quantity of money.

A final word should be added about the idea that the national debt imposes a burden on future generations. *The principal way in which one generation can impose such a burden on another is by using up some of the country's productive capacity or by failing to add a normal increment to this capacity.* This, of course, is quite different from incurring debt. For example, World War II would have imposed a burden on subsequent generations whether or not the national debt was increased. However it was financed, the war would have meant that our resources had to be used for tanks and warplanes rather than for keeping up and expanding our productive capacity during 1941–45. And this imposed a burden, a real burden, on Americans living after 1945—as well, of course, as on those living during the war!

Summary

The spending decisions of the federal government take place in the context of the budgetary process.

The president submits his budget, which is a statement of anticipated expenditures and revenues, to Congress, which votes appropriations. Basically, the amount that the government spends on various activities and services must be decided through the nation's political processes. Voting by ballots must be substituted for dollar voting. In making such decisions, it is important to distinguish between changes in government expenditure that alter the scope of government and changes in government expenditures due to changes in efficiency.

Benefit-cost analysis and program budgeting have proved useful in decision making on government expenditures. Spending on each government program should be pushed to the point where the extra benefit from an extra dollar spent is at least equal to the dollar of cost. The PPB system has encouraged more precise identification of the goals of various programs and promoted the search for alternative means of fulfilling these goals. In some areas, benefit-cost analyses have proved useful in determining which of a variety of projects can accomplish a particular goal most economically, and whether any of them is worth carrying out. However, accurate measurement of the relevant benefits and costs is frequently difficult.

The Ways and Means Committee of the House of Representatives and the Senate Finance Committee play important roles in the federal tax legislative process. It is generally agreed that people who receive more in benefits from a certain government service should pay more in taxes to support it. It is also generally agreed that people should be taxed so as to result in a socially desirable redistribution of income, and that equals should be treated equally. But these general principles, although useful, cannot throw light on many of the detailed questions a real-life tax code must answer. The personal and corporate income taxes are very important sources of federal revenue, the sales tax is an important source of state revenues, and the property tax is an important source of local revenues. In recent years, there has been continual pressure for tax reform, since the tax structure of the United States contains many exemptions and loopholes. Also, recognizing the mismatch between the responsibilities and resources of the state and local governments, the federal government has begun a program of revenue sharing.

When the government spends more than it receives in revenues, the difference is called a deficit. The national debt is the result of previous deficits, since the government borrows money to cover a deficit. It could simply print money for this purpose, but it has chosen to borrow a considerable proportion of what was needed. Despite much public worry about the size of the national debt, as a percentage of national output it has been declining over the past 25 years. There are important differences between government debt and private debt. Although the size of the debt is certainly of consequence, it is not true that it somehow transmits a serious burden to future generations or that it may lead to bankruptcy.

CONCEPTS FOR REVIEW

Planning-Programming-Budgeting system	Tax reform	Capital gains
Benefit-cost analysis	Benefit principle	Depletion allowance
Revenue sharing	Personal income tax	Public debt
Military-industrial complex	Sales tax	Tax evasion
	Ability to pay	Tax avoidance
	Marginal tax rate	

QUESTIONS FOR DISCUSSION AND REVIEW

1. Is it possible to test Galbraith's proposition that too little is being spent on government services? What sorts of tests would you propose? In 1973, President Nixon proposed a greatly expanded program of energy research and development. What sorts of information would you look at in order to decide whether the president's proposal should be accepted or rejected?

2. Make a detailed set of recommendations concerning changes that should be made in the American tax system. With regard to every change that you propose, state your reasons for advocating the change.

3. In 1960, less than half of personal income in the United States was subject to the income tax. True or False?

4. The national debt
   a. transmits a burden to future generations.
   b. is the result of previous deficits.
   c. as a percentage of GNP, has remained relatively constant over the past 25 years.
   d. if not decreased, may lead to bankruptcy.

CHAPTER 7

The Business Firm: Organization, Motivation, and Technology

It is hard to overstate the importance of business firms in the American economy. They produce the bulk of our goods and services, hire most of the nation's workers, and issue stocks and bonds that represent a large percentage of the nation's wealth. Judged by any yardstick—even less complimentary ones like the responsibility for environmental pollution—business firms are an extremely important part of the American economy. In this chapter, we discuss the various types of business firms, such as proprietorships and corporations. Then we describe the various types of securities—common stock, bonds, and so forth—issued by firms, and discuss the workings of the stock market. Next, we take up the motivation and structure of firms, as well as their technology. Finally, we provide some essential elements of accounting. This material is a necessary introduction to the workings of the business enterprise, absolutely essential to anyone who works for, manages, or invests in a firm.

111

General Motors: A Case Study

In Chapter 4, when we first discussed the role of the business firm in the American economy, we cited two examples of American business firms: Peter Amacher's drugstore and the General Motors Corporation. Now that we are considering the operations of the business firm in more detail, let's look more closely at the General Motors Corporation. A description of its formation and vicissitudes should give you a better feel for what firms do and the sorts of problems they face.

General Motors was formed in 1908 by Wil-

liam C. Durant, an energetic and imaginative businessman who made over a million dollars in the carriage business before he was 40. Having taken over the bankrupt Buick Motor Company in 1904, Durant built it into a very successful operation. Then, in 1908, he gained control of a number of small automobile companies (including Cadillac and Olds), several truck firms, and 10 parts and accessory firms. The resulting amalgamation was General Motors.

In 1910, General Motors' sales fell below scheduled production, and Durant lacked the funds to pay his work force and suppliers. To get the

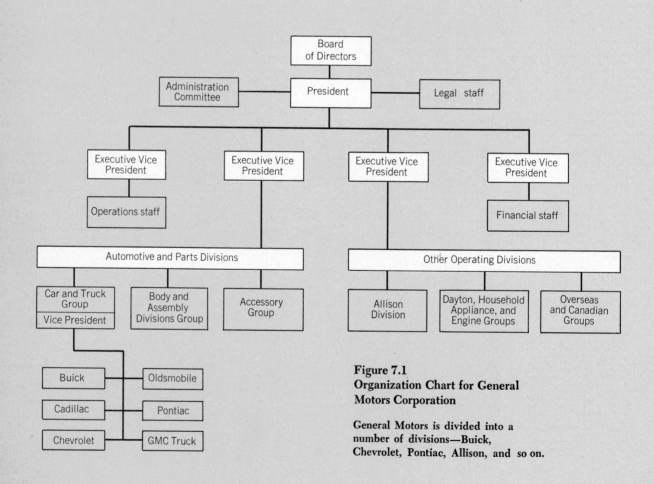

Figure 7.1
Organization Chart for General Motors Corporation

General Motors is divided into a number of divisions—Buick, Chevrolet, Pontiac, Allison, and so on.

money he needed, he went to a banking syndicate, which lent him $15 million—but required him to turn over the management of the company to them. By 1915, Durant had acquired another auto producer, Chevrolet, and had picked up formidable financial allies in the Du Ponts, the owners of the famous chemical firm. Using both these levers, Durant regained full control of General Motors in 1916; and between 1916 and 1920, he concentrated on expanding the productive capacity of the General Motors Corporation. A man of extraordinary vision, he recognized, as did few of his contemporaries, a great potential demand for moderately priced cars, and devoted his energy to putting General Motors in a position to satisfy this demand.

Although Durant was a man of great vision, he was not the sort of administrator who created a tidy organizational structure. The General Motors Corporation under Durant was a very large agglomeration of companies in a variety of product lines, with somewhat tangled lines of communication and diffuse control. When automobile sales did not come up to expectations in 1920, the firm suffered a reduction in profits. The ensuing crisis resulted in Durant's retirement as president of General Motors, and the adoption by the firm of a new organizational plan created by Alfred Sloan, a young M.I.T.-trained engineer, who soon became president. This plan divided General Motors into a number of divisions: the Buick division, the Chevrolet division, the accessory division, and so forth. Each division was given considerable freedom, but more attention was devoted to central control and coordination than under Durant's more anarchical organization. Sloan's organizational plan, an important innovation in its day, has remained in effect with little change from 1920 to the present: Figure 7.1 shows the organization of General Motors today.

During the 1920s General Motors prospered: its sales rose from $600 million in 1920 to $1,500 million in 1929, and its profits rose from about $38 million in 1920 to about $248 million in 1929. The next decade was different: the 1930s were the years of the Great Depression, when sales and profits of most firms, including General Motors, were hard hit. But during the 1940s General Motors entered another period of prosperity and growth. Its sales rose from about $1.8 billion in 1940 to about $5.7 billion in 1949, and its profits rose from about $196 million in 1940 to about $656 million in 1949. The 1950s and 1960s saw the prosperity of General Motors continue. Of course there were short intervals when sales and profits fell, but the trend was upward—in part because of population growth and because higher incomes have meant bigger sales of automobiles. The firm has experienced no prolonged period of low profits or considerable excess capacity, as was the case in the 1930s. By 1971, General Motors had sales of over $28 billion. The somewhat jumbled organization William Durant assembled in 1908 had become the biggest industrial company in the United States, a symbol of industrial might around the world.

Characteristics of American Firms: Some Salient Facts

General Motors is an economic colossus—America's biggest industrial firm. Of course it is not typical of American business firms. If we broaden our focus to take in the entire population of business firms in the United States, the first thing we note is their tremendous number; according to government statistics, there are over 10 million. The vast majority of these firms, as one would expect, are very small. There are lots of grocery stores, gas stations, auto dealers, drugstores (like Mr. Amacher's), clothing shops, restaurants, and so on. You see hundreds of them as you walk along practically any downtown city street. But these small firms, although numerous, do not control the bulk of the nation's productive capacity. The several hundred largest firms have great economic power, measured by their sales, assets, employment, or other such indexes. The small firms tend to be weak and short-lived. On the average, they tend to go out of busi-

Table 7.1

Number and Receipts of Business Firms, by Industry, United States

Industry	Number of firms (millions)	Receipts of firms (millions of dollars)
Agriculture, forestry and fisheries	3.4	52
Mining	.1	16
Construction	.8	98
Manufacturing	.4	645
Transportation, communication[a]	.4	117
Wholesale trade	.5	235
Retail trade	2.1	344
Financial	1.0	164
Services	2.8	102
Total	11.5	1,773

Source: *Statistical Abstract of the United States.*
[a] Includes electric and gas.

ness before they have been in existence 7 years.

The next thing to note is that most of the nation's business firms are engaged in agriculture, services, and retail trade. Table 7.1 shows that almost ¾ of the firms in the United States are in these industries, an understandable figure since these industries tend to have lots and lots of small businesses. Although manufacturing firms constitute only about 4 percent of all American firms, they account for more than ⅓ of all business receipts. On the other hand, agriculture (including forestry and fisheries) includes about 30 percent of the nation's business firms, but accounts for only 3 percent of the total receipts. Clearly, this is because manufacturing firms tend to be much bigger, in terms of receipts, employment, and assets, than agricultural firms. Think, for example, of the steel plants in Pittsburgh or Cleveland, or of the aircraft plants in California or Georgia. They dwarf the typical farm—and they are only parts of a manufacturing firm.

Finally, note that most of the nation's business firms are proprietorships: indeed, almost ⅘ fall into this category, while about 13 percent are corporations, and about 8 percent are partnerships. You often hear the terms "proprietorship," "partnership," "corporation." What do these terms mean?

Proprietorships

A proprietorship is a legal form of business organization—the most common form, as we saw in the previous section, and also the simplest. Specifically, a *proprietorship* is a firm owned by a single individual. A great many of the nation's small businesses are proprietorships. For example, the corner drugstore may well be one. If so, it has a single owner. He hires the people he needs to wait on customers, deliver orders, do the bookkeeping, and so forth. He borrows, if he can, whatever money he feels he needs. He reaps the profits, or incurs the losses. All his personal assets—his house, his furniture, his car—can be taken by creditors to meet the drugstore's bills: that is, he has unlimited liability for the debts of the business.

What Lincoln said about the common man applies as well to proprietorships: God must love them, or He wouldn't have created so many of them. If proprietorships didn't have advantages over other legal forms of business organization under many sorts of circumstances, there wouldn't be so many of them. What are these advantages? First, the owner of a proprietorship has complete control over the business. He doesn't have to negotiate with partners or other co-owners. He is the boss—and the only boss. Anyone who has been in a position of complete authority knows the joy it can bring: many proprietors treasure this feeling of independence. Second, a proprietorship is easy and inexpensive to establish: all you have to do is hang out your shingle and announce you are in business. This too is a great advantage.

But proprietorships have important disadvantages as well—and for this reason, they are seldom found in many important industries. One disadvantage is that it is difficult for a proprietor to put together enough financial resources to enter industries like automobiles or steel. No one in the world has enough money to establish, by himself, a firm of General Motors' present size. Another disadvantage is that the proprietor is liable for all of the debts of the firm. If his business fails, his personal assets can be taken by his creditors, and he can be completely wiped out.

Partnerships

A *partnership* is somewhat more complicated than a proprietorship. As its name implies, it is a form of business organization where two or more people agree to own and conduct a business. Each partner agrees to contribute some proportion of the capital and labor used by the business, and to receive some proportion of the profits or losses. There are a variety of types of partnerships. In some cases, one or more of the partners may be "silent partners," who

put up some of the money, but have little or nothing to do with the operations of the firm. The partnership is a common form of business organization in some industries and professions, like the law. But as we saw in a previous section, partnerships are found less frequently than proprietorships or corporations in the United States.

A partnership has certain advantages. Like a proprietorship, it can be established without great expense or legal red tape. (However, if you ever go into partnership with someone, you would be well advised to have a good lawyer draw up a written agreement establishing such things as the salaries of each partner and how profits are to be shared.) In addition, a partnership can avoid some of the problems involved in a proprietorship. It can usually put together more financial resources and specialized know-how than a proprietorship— and this can be an important advantage.

But the partnership also has certain drawbacks. First, each partner is liable without limit for the bills of the firm. For example, even if one partner of a law firm has only a 30 percent share of the firm, he may be called upon to pay all the firm's debts if the other partners cannot do so. Second, there is some red tape in keeping a partnership in existence. Whenever a partner dies or withdraws, or whenever a new partner is admitted, a new partnership must be established. Third, like the proprietorship, the partnership is not a very effective way to obtain the large amounts of capital required for some modern industries. A modern automobile plant may cost $500 million, and not many partnerships could assemble that much capital. For these reasons, as well as others discussed in the next section, the corporation has become the dominant form of business organization.

Corporations

A far more complicated form of business organization than either the proprietorship or partnership, the *corporation* is a fictitious legal person, separate and distinct from its owners. A businessman forms a corporation by having his lawyer draw up the necessary papers stating (in general terms) what sorts of activities he and the other owners of the corporation intend to engage in. The owners of the corporation are the stockholders. **Stock,** pieces of paper signifying ownership of the corporation, is issued to the owners, generally in exchange for their cash. Ordinarily, each **share** of stock gives its owner one vote. The corporation's **board of directors,** which is responsible for setting overall policy for the firm, is elected by the stockholders. Any of the firm's owners can, if he is dissatisfied with the company's policies or thinks he has better opportunities elsewhere, sell his stock to someone else, assuming, of course, that he can find a buyer.

The corporation has many advantages over the partnership or proprietorship. In particular, each of the corporation's owners has limited, not unlimited, liability. If I decide to become one of the owners of General Motors and if a share of General Motors common stock sells for $65 a share, I can buy 10 shares of General Motors stock for $650. And I can be sure that, if General Motors falls on hard times, I cannot lose more than the $650 I paid for the stock. There is no way that I can be assessed beyond this. Moreover, the corporation, unlike the partnership or proprietorship, has unlimited life. If several stockholders want to withdraw from the firm, they simply sell their stock. The corporation goes on, although the identity of the owners changes. For these reasons, the corporation is clearly a better device for raising large sums of money than the partnership or proprietorship. This is a very important advantage of the corporation, particularly in industries like automobiles and steel, which could not otherwise finance their operations.

Without question, the corporation is a very important social invention. It permits people to assemble the large quantities of capital required for efficient production in many industries. Without limited liability and the other advantages of the corporation, it is doubtful that the opportunities and benefits of large-scale production could have been reaped. However, this does not mean that the corporate form will work for all firms. In many cases, a firm requires only a modest amount of capital, and there is no reason to go to the extra trouble and expense of establishing a corporation. Moreover, one disadvantage of the corporation is **double taxation of income,** since, as you will recall from Chapter 6, corporations pay income taxes —and the tax rate is often about ½ of every extra dollar earned. Thus, every dollar earned by a corporation and distributed to stockholders is taxed twice by the federal government—once when it is counted as income by the corporation, and once when the remainder is counted as income by the stockholders. This disadvantage of the corporation must be balanced against the advantage that the top tax rates for corporations are less than those that may apply to unincorporated businesses.

Corporate Securities

The corporation raises money by issuing various kinds of securities; of these, three kinds—common stock, preferred stock, and bonds—are particularly significant. Each of these types of securities is important to the workings of the corporation and to people's investment decisions. As you know from the previous section, **common stock** is the ordinary certificate of ownership of the corporation. A holder of common stock is an owner of the firm. He shares in the firm's profits—and in its losses as well. At frequent intervals, the board of directors of the firm may declare a dividend of so much per share for the common stockholders. For example, the common stockholders of General Motors received dividends of $3.40 per share in 1970. **Dividends** are thus the income the owners of common stock receive. (In addition, of course, common stockholders can make money by selling their stock for more than they paid for it; such income is called **capital gains.**) Common stock is generally regarded as more risky than preferred stock or bonds, for reasons that will be explained.

Preferred stock is a special kind of certificate of ownership that pays at most a stated dividend. For example, owners of one type of General Motors preferred stock receive $5 a share per year, as long as the firm makes enough to pay this dividend. To protect the owners of preferred stock, it is stipulated that no dividends can be paid on the common stock unless the dividends on the preferred stock are paid in full. Since the common stockholders cannot receive their dividends unless the preferred stock's dividends have been paid, common stock is obviously more risky than preferred stock. But by the same token, the amount preferred stockholders have to gain if the company prospers is less than the amount common stockholders have to gain, since however high its profits may be, the firm will pay only the stated dividend—for example, $5 per share per year in the case of General Motors—to the owners of preferred stock.

Bonds are quite different from both common and preferred stocks. **Bonds** are debts of the firm; in other words, they are IOUs issued by the firm. In contrast to stockholders, the bondholders are not owners of a firm: they are its creditors, and receive interest, not dividends. Specifically, a bond is a certificate bearing the firm's promise to pay the interest every 6 months until the bond matures, at which time the firm also promises to pay the bondholder the principal (the amount he lent the firm) as well. Often, bonds are sold in $1,000 denominations. For example, one type of bond issued by General Motors is a 3¼ percent bond, due in 1979. The owner of each such bond receives $32.50 per year in interest, and General Motors promises to pay him the principal of $1,000 when the bond falls due in 1979. A firm must pay the interest on the bonds and the principal when it is due, or it can be declared bankrupt. In other words, the bondholders are legally entitled to receive what is due them before the stockholders can get anything.

Thus, from the point of view of the investor, bonds are generally considered less risky than preferred stock, and preferred stocks are considered less risky than common stock. But we have ig-

nored another fact: inflation. The tendency for the price level in the United States to increase over time has meant that owners of common stocks have reaped substantial capital gains, while bondholders have been paid off with dollars that were worth less than those they lent. For this reason and others, many investors in recent years have tended to favor common stocks. During the 1960s and early 1970s, a "cult of equities" developed; it became fashionable to buy common stock. To understand why, it is necessary to look briefly at the workings of the stock market.

The Stock Market

In general, large corporations do not sell stock directly to the investor. Instead, the investor buys stock on the stock market. Two major stock exchanges in the United States are the New York Stock Exchange and the American Stock Exchange, both in New York City. On these and similar exchanges in other cities, the common stocks of thousands of corporations are bought and sold. The price of each common stock fluctuates from day to day, indeed from minute to minute. Basically, the factors responsible for these price fluctuations are the shifts in the demand curve and supply curve for each kind of common stock. For example, if a strike breaks out at a General Motors plant, this may cause the demand curve for General Motors stock to shift downward to the left, since the strike is liable to mean lower profits for General Motors. Because of this downward, or leftward, shift in the demand curve, the price of General Motors common stock will tend to fall.

Occasionally, the stock market gets a case of jitters over economic conditions, stock prices tumble, and old investors think back to the Great Crash of 1929. The 1920s witnessed a feverish interest in investing in the stock market. Along with raccoon coats, Stutz Bearcats, and the Charleston, common stocks were the rage. Both the professionals on Wall Street and the neophytes on Main Street bought common stocks and more common stocks. Naturally, as the demand curves for common stocks shifted upward to the right, their prices rose, thus whetting the appetites of investors for still more common stocks. This upward spiral continued until 1929, when the bubble burst. Suddenly the prices of common stocks fell precipitously —and continued to drop during the early 1930s. The most famous average of industrial stock prices, the Dow-Jones average, fell from 381 in 1929 to 41 in 1933. Many investors, large and small, were wiped out.

The Great Crash made investors wary of common stocks for many years. But by the 1960s confidence in them was fully restored, and there certainly was no tendency for investors to shy away from them. Judging from historical experience, the public's taste for common stocks seems to be justified. Studies show that, during the course of a lifetime, the typical investor would have done better to invest in common stocks than in the best-quality bonds, because stock prices have tended to rise. This tended to apply in a great many cases, even for investors who lived through the Great Crash. And it has certainly been borne out during the past 40 years. Thus, although common stocks are riskier in some respects than bonds or preferred stocks, they seem to have performed better, on the average, at least in recent times.

During periods when the average of stock prices is going up, such as the 1920s and much of the 1950s and 1960s, it is relatively easy to be a financial wizard, whether by luck or calculation. A much more exacting test of your financial acumen is how well you can pick which stocks will outperform the averages. If you can predict that increases will occur in a certain firm's profits, and if other people don't predict the same thing, you may be able to pass this test. However, the sobering truth is that "playing the stock market" is much more an art than a science. The stock market is affected by psychological as well as economic considerations. Moreover, when you try to spot stocks that will increase in price, you are pitting your knowledge and experience against those of skilled professionals with big research staffs and with friends and acquaintances working for the companies in question. And even these professionals can do surprisingly poorly at times.

Do economists have a nose for good investments? John Maynard Keynes was an extremely successful speculator who made millions of dollars. Other economists have been far less successful. Certainly, a knowledge of basic economics is not sufficient to enable you to make money on the stock market, but insofar as the market reflects economic realities, a knowledge of basic economics should be helpful.

The Giant Corporation

Much of the trading on the stock market centers around the relatively small number of giant corporations that control a very substantial percentage of the total assets and employment in the American economy. And well it might, for the largest 100 manufacturing corporations control about ½ of this country's manufacturing assets. These firms have tremendous economic and political power. They include the giant automobile manufacturers (General Motors, Ford, and Chrysler), the big oil firms (Exxon, Gulf, Standard Oil of Indiana, Mobil, Standard Oil of California, Texaco, Atlantic-Richfield), the big steel firms (U. S. Steel, Bethlehem, Jones and Laughlin, Armco), the big computer and office machinery producers (IBM and Xerox), the leading tobacco firms (American Brands, R. J. Reynolds, Philip Morris), and many others.

An interesting and important feature of the large corporation is the fact that it is owned by many, many people, practically all of whom have little or no detailed information about the firm's operations. For example, the owners of the American Telephone and Telegraph Company, the giant public utility, number several million but most of them know relatively little about what is going on in the firm. Moreover, because of the wide diffusion of ownership, working control of a large corporation can often be maintained by a group with only ⅓ or less of all the voting stock. The result is a *separation of ownership from control.* In other words, the owners control the firm in only a limited and somewhat sporadic sense.

So long as a firm's management is not obviously incompetent or corrupt, it is difficult for insurgent stockholders to remove the management from office. Most stockholders do not go to the annual meetings to vote for members of the firm's board of directors. Instead, they receive *proxies,* which, if returned, permit the management to exercise their votes. Usually enough shareholders mail in their proxies to give management the votes it needs to elect a friendly board of directors. In recent years, the Securities and Exchange Commission, which oversees and regulates the financial markets, has attempted to make the giant corporations more democratic by enabling insurgent groups to gain access to mailing lists of stockholders and so forth. But there is still a noteworthy and widespread separation of ownership from control.

The large corporation is generally organized into various operating divisions. We saw in Figure 7.1 how General Motors is divided along various product lines. An automotive division like Buick is part of the Car and Truck Group, the head of which reports to an executive vice president, who reports in turn to the president of General Motors. Usually, the president is the chief operations officer in the firm, although sometimes the chairman of the board of directors fills this role. As for the board of directors, some members are chosen for their reputations and contacts, while others are chosen for their knowledge of the firm, the industry, or some profession or specialty. Usually, the board contains at least one representative of the financial community, and a university president or former government official is often included. Members of GM's board include James Killian, Chairman of M.I.T.; John Connor, a former Secretary of Commerce; and Leon Sullivan, pastor of Zion Baptist Church of Philadelphia. The board of directors is concerned with overall policy. Since it meets only a few times a year, it seldom becomes involved in day-to-day decisions; and it usually goes along with management's policies, so long as management retains the board's confidence.

The New Industrial State

The large corporation is a subject of considerable debate among economists. Many feel that bigness can be a detriment to society, whereas others are more impressed by its virtues. One view of the large corporation that has received considerable attention in recent years can be found in John Kenneth Galbraith's *The New Industrial State.*[1] Galbraith is less concerned than most economists with the disadvantages of the large corporation; indeed, he feels that large corporations are required for much of society's business. According to Galbraith, the large corporation is free of most of the restraints imposed by the marketplace. It can, by a judicious mixture of advertising and other devices, influence the demand for its own products. Indeed, according to Galbraith, it can control its demand curve to a very considerable extent. In addition, the management of the large corporation is, in Galbraith's view, largely emancipated from the control of the stockholders, since there is a considerable separation of ownership from control. Moreover, the large corporation is free from the obligation to borrow in the capital markets, since it can reinvest its own earnings.

Under these circumstances, who runs the large corporation, and for what purpose? Galbraith's answer is that the large corporation is run by the *"technostructure"*—the professional managers, engineers, and technicians that are the corporate bureaucracy—and the large corporation's overriding goal is its own survival and autonomy. Consequently, the large corporation tries to avoid risk, and emphasizes planning and stability. It is interested in corporate growth, even if this means some sacrifice of profits. Moreover, it is often interested

[1] John Kenneth Galbraith, *The New Industrial State,* Boston: Houghton Mifflin, 1967.

in technological leadership. Galbraith does not view this situation as bad. Instead, he regards it as inevitable since, in his view, modern technology requires that huge amounts of money and huge organizations dominate the modern economy. Whether you like it or not, he says, this is the way it must be.

Although Galbraith's book has generated much useful and interesting discussion, it has not escaped criticism by the economics profession. For one thing, as Robert Solow of M.I.T. has pointed out, the large corporation does not dominate many parts of the American economy. Nor is it at all clear that modern technology requires very large firms in many industries. Nor is Galbraith's assumption that firms attempt to maximize their rate of growth of sales necessarily better than the more conventional assumption that firms maximize their profits. As we shall see, most economists seem to regard profit maximization as the more fruitful assumption.

Profit Maximization

What determines the behavior of the business firm? As a first approximation, *economists generally assume that firms attempt to maximize* **profits,** *which are defined as the difference between the firm's revenue and its costs.* In other words, economists generally assume, contrary to Galbraith, that firms try to make as much money as possible. This assumption certainly does not seem unreasonable: most businessmen appear to be interested in making money. Nonetheless, the assumption of profit maximization oversimplifies the situation. Although businessmen certainly want profits, they are interested in other things as well. For example, some firms claim that they want to promote better cultural activities or better racial relations in their community. At a less lofty level, other firms say that their aim is to increase their share of the market. Whether or not one takes these self-proclaimed goals very seriously, it is clear that firms are not

interested *only* in making money—often for the same reason that Dr. Johnson gave for not becoming a philosopher: "because cheerfulness keeps breaking in."[2]

In a large corporation, there are some fairly obvious reasons why firms may not maximize profits. Various groups within such firms develop their own party lines, and intrafirm politics is an important part of the process determining firm behavior. Whereas in a small firm it may be fairly accurate to regard the goals of the firm as being the goals of the proprietor, in the large corporation the decision on the goals of the firm is a matter of politics, with various groups within the organization struggling for power. In addition, because of the separation of ownership from control, top management usually has a great deal of freedom as long as it seems to be performing reasonably well. Under these circumstances, the behavior of the firm may be dictated in part by the interests of the management group, resulting in higher salaries, more perquisites, and a bigger staff for their own benefit than would otherwise be the case.

Also, in a world of risk and uncertainty, it is difficult to know exactly what profit maximization means, since the firm cannot be sure that a certain level of profit will result from a certain action. Instead, the best the firm can do is to estimate that a certain probability distribution of profit levels will result from a certain action. Under these circumstances, the firm may choose less risky actions, even though they have a lower expectation of profit than other actions. In a world where ruin is ruinous, this may be perfectly rational policy.

Nonetheless, profit maximization remains the standard assumption in economics—in large part because it is a close enough approximation to reality for many of the economist's most important purposes. As we agreed in our discussion of model building in Chapter 2, to be useful models need

[2] This quote is taken from R. Solow, "The New Industrial State or Son of Affluence," *The Public Interest,* Fall 1967. Since footnotes are so often used to cite dreary material, it seems worthwhile to use them occasionally to cite humor as well.

not be exact replicas of reality. Economic models based on profit maximization are clearly not exact replicas of reality, but they have been very useful indeed. For one thing, they help to show how the price system functions. For another, in the real world, they suggest how a firm should operate if it wants to make as much money as possible. Even if a firm does not want to maximize profit, these theories can be utilized. For example, they can show how much the firm is losing by taking certain courses of action. In recent years, the theory of the profit-maximizing firm has been studied more and more for the sake of determining profit-maximizing rules of business behavior.

Technology and Inputs

The decisions a firm should make in order to maximize its profits are determined by the current state of technology. Technology, it will be recalled from Chapter 3, is the sum total of society's knowledge concerning the industrial arts. Just as the consumer is limited by his income, the firm is limited by the current state of technology. If the current state of technology is such that we do not know how to produce more than 40 bushels of corn per year from an acre of land and 2 manyears of labor, then this is as much as the firm can produce from this combination of land and labor. In making its decisions, the firm must take this into account.

In constructing his model of the profit-maximizing firm, the economist must somehow represent the state of technology and include it in his model. As a first step toward this end, we must define an **input.** Perhaps the simplest definition of an input is that it is anything the firm uses in its production process. For example, some of the inputs of a farm producing corn might be seed, land, labor, water, fertilizer, various types of machinery, as well as the time of the people managing the farm. In analyzing production processes, we suppose that all inputs can be classified into two categories: fixed and variable inputs.

A *fixed input* is one whose quantity cannot change during the period of time under consideration. This period will vary: it may be 6 months for one problem, 6 years for another. Among the most important inputs often included as "fixed" are the firm's plant and equipment—that is, its factory and office buildings, its machinery, its tooling, and its transportation facilities. A *variable input* is one whose quantity can be changed during the relevant period. For example, it is generally possible to increase or decrease the number of workers engaged in a particular activity (although this is not always the case, since they may have long-term contracts). Similarly, it frequently is possible to alter the amount of raw material that is used.

The Short Run and the Long Run

Whether an input is considered variable or fixed depends on the length of the period under consideration. The longer the period, the more inputs are variable, not fixed. Although the length of the period varies from problem to problem, economists have found it useful to focus special attention on two time periods: the short run and the long run. The *short run* is defined as the period of time in which some of the firm's inputs are fixed. More specifically, since the firm's plant and equipment are among the most difficult inputs to change quickly, *the short run is generally understood to mean the length of time during which the firm's plant and equipment are fixed. On the other hand, the long run is that period of time in which all inputs are variable.* In the long run, the firm can make a complete adjustment to any change in its environment.

To illustrate the distinction between the short run and the long run, let's return to the General Motors Corporation. Any period of time during which GM's plant and equipment cannot be altered freely is the short run. For example, a period of one year is certainly a case of the short run, because in a year GM could not vary the quantity of its plant and equipment. It takes longer than a year to construct an automotive plant, or to alter an existing plant to produce a new kind of automobile. For example, the tooling phase of the model changeover cycle currently takes about 2 years. On the other hand, any period of time during which GM can vary the quantity of all inputs is the long run: for example, a period of 50 years is certainly a case of the long run. Whether a shorter period of time—10 years, say—is a long-run situation depends on the problem at hand. If all the relevant inputs can be varied, it is a long-run situation; if not, it is a short-run situation.

The Production Function

Having defined an input and distinguished between the short and long runs, we can now describe how economists represent the state of technology. The basic concept economists use for this purpose is the production function. For any commodity, *the production function is the relationship between the quantities of various inputs used per period of time and the maximum quantity of the commodity that can be produced per period of time.* More specifically, the production function is a table, a graph, or an equation showing the maximum output rate that can be achieved from any specified set of usage rates of inputs. The production function summarizes the characteristics of existing technology at a given point in time. It shows the technological constraints the firm must reckon with.

To see more clearly what we mean by a production function, consider the Milwaukee Machine Company, a hypothetical machine shop that produces a simple metal part. Suppose that we are dealing with the short run. The firm's basic plant and equipment are fixed, and the only variable input is the amount of labor used by the machine shop. Suppose that the firm collects data showing the relationship between the quantity of its output and the quantity of labor it uses. This relationship, shown in Table 7.2, is the firm's production function. It shows that, when one worker is employed, 100 parts are produced per month; when 2 workers are employed, 210 parts are produced per month; and so on.

To illustrate what a production function looks like in a real case, let's consider a crude oil pipeline that transports petroleum from oilfields and storage areas over hundreds of miles to major urban and industrial centers. We begin by noting that the output of such a pipeline is the amount of oil carried per day, and that the two principal inputs are the diameter of the pipeline and the horsepower applied to the oil carried. These inputs are important. Clearly, the bigger the diameter of the pipe, the more oil the pipeline can carry, holding constant the horsepower applied. And the greater the horsepower applied, the more oil the pipeline can carry, holding constant the diameter of the pipeline.

The production function shows the maximum output rate that can be derived from each com-

---

Table 7.2

Production Function, Milwaukee Machine Company

Quantity of labor used per month (number of men employed)	Output per month (number of parts)
0	0
1	100
2	210
3	315
4	415
5	500

Table 7.3

Production Function, Crude Oil Pipeline[a]

Line diameter (inches)	Horsepower (thousands)				
	20	30	40	50	60
	Output rate (thousands of barrels per day)				
14	70	90	95	100	104
18	115	140	155	165	170
22	160	190	215	235	250
26	220	255	290	320	340

Source: Leslie Cookenboo, *Crude Oil Pipe Lines and Competition in the Oil Industry,* Cambridge: Harvard University Press, 1955.

[a] The output rates given in this table are only approximate, since they were read from Cookenboo's graph on p. 16.

bination of input rates. Thus, in this case, the production function shows the maximum amount of oil carried per day as a function of the pipeline's diameter and the amount of horsepower applied. On the basis of engineering estimates, one can derive the production function for crude oil pipelines. For example, Leslie Cookenboo of Standard Oil of New Jersey derived such a production function, assuming that the pipeline carries Mid-Continent crude, has ¼-inch pipe throughout the lines, has lines 1,000 miles in length with a 5 percent terrain variation, and no net gravity flow in the line.[3] Some of his results are shown in Table 7.3. For example, the production function shows that if the diameter of the pipeline is 22 inches and the horsepower is 40,000, the pipeline can carry 215,000 barrels per day. Certainly, any firm operating a pipeline or considering the construction of one is vitally interested in such information. The production function plays a strategic role in the decision making of any firm.

[3] L. Cookenboo, *Crude Oil Pipe Lines and Competition in the Oil Industry,* Cambridge: Harvard University Press, 1955.

Elements of Accounting: The Firm's Balance Sheet

In a previous section, we stated that economists generally assume that firms attempt to maximize profits. Viewed as a first approximation, this assumption does not seem too hard to swallow, but exactly what do we mean by profit? This is an important question, of interest to businessmen and investors as well as to economists. The accounting profession provides the basic figures that are reported in the newspapers and in a firm's annual reports to its stockholders. If General Motors reports that it made $1.5 billion last year, this figure is provided by GM's accountants. How do the accountants obtain this figure? What are its limitations?

Basically, accounting concepts are built around two very important statements: the balance sheet and the profit and loss statement. *A firm's* **balance sheet** *shows the nature of its assets, tangible and intangible, at a certain point in time.* For example, let us return to the Milwaukee Machine Company. Its balance sheet might be as shown in Table 7.4.

Table 7.4

Balance Sheet, Milwaukee Machine Company, as of December 31, 1974

Assets		Liabilities and net worth	
Current assets:		Current liabilities:	
Cash	$ 10,000	Accounts payable	$ 10,000
Inventory	60,000	Notes payable	20,000
Fixed assets:		Long-term liabilities:	
Equipment	80,000	Bonds	80,000
Buildings	90,000		
		Net worth:	
		Preferred stock	50,000
		Common stock	50,000
		Surplus	30,000
Total	$240,000	Total	$240,000

The left-hand side of the balance sheet shows the assets of the firm as of December 31, 1974. **Current assets** are assets that will be converted into cash relatively quickly (generally within a year), whereas **fixed assets** generally will not be liquidated quickly. The firm has $10,000 in cash, $60,000 in inventory, $80,000 in equipment, and $90,000 in buildings. At first glance, these figures may seem more accurate than they are likely to be. It is very difficult to know how to value various assets. For example, should they be valued at what the firm paid for them, or at what it would cost to replace them? More will be said about these problems in the next section.

The right-hand side of the firm's balance sheet shows the claims by creditors on the firm's assets and the value of the firm's ownership. For example, in Table 7.4, the Milwaukee Machine Company has total liabilities—or debts—of $110,000. There is $30,000 in **current liabilities,** which come due in less than a year; and $80,000 in **long-term liabilities,** which come due in a year or more. Specifically, there is $10,000 in **accounts payable,** which are bills owed for goods and services that

the firm bought; $20,000 in **notes payable,** short-term notes owed to banks or finance companies; and $80,000 in **bonds payable,** or bonds outstanding.

The difference between the value of a firm's assets and the value of its liabilities is its **net worth,** which is the value of the firm's owners' claims against the firm's assets. In other words, the value of the firm to its owners is the total value of its assets less the value of the debts owed by the firm. Since

total value of assets − total liabilities = net worth,

it follows that

total value of assets = total liabilities + net worth.

That is, the sum of the items on the left-hand side of the balance sheet must equal the sum of the items on the right-hand side. This, of course, must be true because of the way we define net worth. In the case of the Milwaukee Machine Company, the firm's net worth—the difference between its assets and its liabilities—is $130,000. Specifically, there is $50,000 worth of preferred stock and $50,000 worth of common stock; there is also $30,000 in surplus, which we shall explain below.

The Firm's Profit and Loss Statement

A firm's **profit and loss statement** *shows its sales during a particular period, its costs incurred in connection with these sales, and its profits during this period.* Table 7.5 shows the Milwaukee Machine Company's profit and loss statement during the period January 1, 1975 to December 31, 1975. Sales during this period were $120,000. The cost of manufacturing the items made during this period was $55,000—$15,000 for materials, $20,000

for labor, $17,000 for depreciation (discussed below), and $3,000 for miscellaneous operating expenses. However, because the firm has reduced its inventories from $60,000 to $55,000 during the period, the cost of manufacturing the items *made* during the period does not equal the cost of manufacturing the items *sold* during the period. To find the *cost of goods sold*—which is the amount that logically should be deducted from sales to get the profits made from the sale of these goods—we must add the decrease in the value of inventories to the total manufacturing cost. Or, putting it another way, we must add the beginning inventory and subtract the closing inventory, as shown in Table 7.5. The resulting figure for cost of goods sold is $60,000.

But manufacturing costs are not the only costs the firm incurs. To estimate the firm's profits, we must also deduct from sales its selling and adminis-

Table 7.5

Profit and Loss Statement, Milwaukee Machine Company, January 1, 1975 to December 31, 1975

Net sales		$120,000
Manufacturing cost of goods sold		60,000
Materials	$15,000	
Labor	20,000	
Depreciation	17,000	
Miscellaneous operating cost	3,000	
Total	$55,000	
Plus beginning inventory	60,000	
Less closing inventory	− 55,000	
Adjusted total	60,000	
Selling and administrative costs		10,000
Fixed interest charges and state and local taxes		5,000
Net earnings before income taxes		$ 45,000
Corporation income taxes		20,000
Net earnings after taxes		$ 25,000
Dividends on preferred stock		2,000
Net profits of common stockholders		$ 23,000
Dividends paid on common stock		10,000
Addition to surplus		$ 13,000

trative expenses, its interest charges and state and local taxes, as well as its federal income taxes. Table 7.5 shows that the Milwaukee Machine Company's aftertax earnings during 1975 were $25,000. This is the amount left for the owners of the business. The profit and loss statement also shows what the owners do with what is left. For example, Table 7.5 shows that the Milwaukee Machine Company used $2,000 to pay dividends to holders of preferred stock. When this was done, the holders of common stock were free to distribute some of the profits to themselves. According to Table 7.5, they distributed $10,000 to themselves in dividends on the common stock, and plowed the rest—$13,000—back into the business.

Before leaving the profit and loss statement, we should explain one element of manufacturing cost —*depreciation.* While the other elements of manufacturing cost are self-explanatory, this one is not. The idea behind depreciation is that the buildings and equipment will not last forever; eventually will have to be replaced. Clearly, it would be foolish to charge the entire cost of replacing them to the year when they are replaced. Instead, a

better picture of the firm's true profitability will be drawn if the cost of replacing them is spread gradually over the life of buildings and equipment, thus recognizing that each year's output has a hand in wearing them out. One frequently used technique is so-called *straight-line depreciation,* which spreads the cost of buildings and equipment (less their scrap value) evenly over their life. Thus, if the Milwaukee Machine Company buys a piece of equipment for $10,000 and if it is expected to last 10 years (its scrap value being zero), it would charge depreciation of $1,000 per year for this machine for 10 years after its purchase. The $17,000 charge for depreciation in Table 7.5 is the sum of such charges. Clearly, this is only a rough way to estimate the true depreciation charges, but it is good enough for many purposes.

Relationship between Balance Sheet and Profit and Loss Statement

The balance sheet and profit and loss statement are closely related. To see the relationship, let's com-

Table 7.6

Balance Sheet, Milwaukee Machine Company, as of December 31, 1975

Assets		Liabilities and net worth	
Currents assets:		Current liabilities:	
Cash	$ 18,000	Accounts payable	$ 5,000
Inventory	55,000	Notes payable	20,000
Fixed assets		Long-term liabilities	
Equipment	85,000	Bonds	80,000
Buildings	90,000		
		Net worth:	
		Preferred stock	50,000
		Common stock	50,000
		Surplus	43,000
Total	$248,000	Total	$248,000

pare the Milwaukee Machine Company's balance sheet at the end of the period covered by the profit and loss statement in Table 7.5 with the balance sheet at the beginning of this period. The balance sheet at the beginning of the period was shown in Table 7.4. The balance sheet at the end of the period is now given in Table 7.6. At first glance, it may not be obvious how the two balance sheets and the profit and loss statement are related; but after a little reflection, it should be clear that the firm's net worth as shown by the end-of-period balance sheet must equal the firm's net worth as shown by the beginning-of-period balance sheet plus the addition to surplus shown in the profit and loss statement.

The reason for this lies in the definition of ***addition to surplus.*** This is the amount the common stockholders plow back into the firm; in other words, the amount they add to the net worth of the firm. Since this is so, the increase (or decrease, if addition to surplus is negative) in the net worth of the firm must equal the addition to surplus (assuming, of course, that the net worth of the firm is not changed by altering the amount of stock outstanding).[4] Thus, for example, in the case of the Milwaukee Machine Company, the firm's net worth had to increase by $13,000 during 1974; and since it was $130,000 at the beginning of 1974, it must have been $143,000 at the end of 1974. Where on the balance sheet does this $13,000 show up? What part of net worth increased by $13,000? The answer is that ***surplus,*** which shows the total amount that the stockholders have plowed back into the firm in the past, went up by $13,000.

Economic versus Accounting Profits

The previous sections described the nature of profit, as defined by accountants. This is the concept on

which practically all published figures in business reports are based. But economists define profits somewhat differently. In particular, the economist does not assume that the firm attempts to maximize the current, short-run profits measured by the accountant. Instead he assumes that the firm will attempt to maximize the sum of profits over a long period of time.[5] Also, when the economist speaks of profits, he means profit after taking account of the capital and labor provided by the owners. Thus, suppose that the owners of the Milwaukee Machine Company, who receive profits but no salary or wages, put in long hours for which they could receive $15,000 in 1974 if they worked for someone else. Also suppose that if they invested their capital somewhere other than in this firm, they could obtain a return of $11,000 on it in 1974. Under these circumstances, economists would say that the firm's aftertax profits in 1974 were $25,000 − $15,000 − $11,000, or − $1,000, rather than the $25,000 shown in Table 7.5. In other words, the economist's concept of profit includes only what the owners make above and beyond what their labor and capital employed in the business could have earned elsewhere. In this case, that amount is negative.

To a considerable extent, the differences between the concepts used by the accountant and the economist reflect the difference in their functions. The accountant is concerned with controlling the firm's day-to-day operations, detecting fraud or embezzlement, satisfying tax and other laws, and producing records for various interested groups. On the other hand, the economist is concerned primarily with decision making and rational choice among prospective alternatives. Although the figures published on profits almost always conform to the accountant's, not the economist's, concept, the economist's concept is the more relevant one for many kinds of decisions. (And this, of course, is recognized by sophisticated accountants.) For example, suppose the owners of the Milwaukee Machine Company are trying to decide whether they should continue

---

[4] This statement also makes some other assumptions—e.g., that all changes in surplus occur through changes in earned surplus. For more complete treatments, see any college accounting textbook.

[5] The profits earned at various points in time should be *discounted* before being added together, but, for simplicity's sake, we neglect this point here.

in business. If they are interested in making as much money as possible, the answer depends on the firm's profits as measured by the economist, not the accountant. If the firm's economic profits are greater than zero, the firm should continue in existence; otherwise, it should not. Thus, the Milwaukee Machine Company should not stay in existence if 1974 is a good indicator of its future profitability.

The Financial Statements of General Motors: A Case Study

To conclude this chapter, let's return once again to General Motors, and examine its financial statements—its balance sheet and profit and loss state-

ment. These are a bit more detailed than the hypothetical statements of the Milwaukee Machine Company, but they are constructed on the same principles. Each year, General Motors issues an annual report to its stockholders, which includes these financial statements. Table 7.7 reproduces GM's balance sheet as of December 31, 1970; and Table 7.8 reproduces GM's profit and loss statement for 1970. Take a close look at these tables, and see if you understand what each item means. For example, Table 7.7 says that GM had $1,726 million in accounts receivable at the end of 1970. What are accounts receivable? (Bills its customers owe General Motors.) It also says that GM had $184 million in preferred stock at the end of 1970. What is preferred stock? (If you don't recall, turn back to the section on "Corporate Securities.") Turning to Table 7.8, GM incurred depreciation

Table 7.7

Balance Sheet, General Motors Corporation, as of December 31, 1970

Assets ($ million)		Liabilities and net worth ($ million)	
Current assets:		Current liabilities:	
Cash	323	Accounts payable	1,660
Government securities	71	Taxes owed	1,561
Accounts receivable	1,726	Other	3
Inventories	4,115		
		Long-term liabilities	
Fixed Assets:		Bonds	281
		Other[b]	815
Investments[a]	1,202		
Real estate, plant, and equipment	6,396	Net worth:	
Other	341	Preferred stock	284
		Common stock	479
		Surplus	9,091
Total	14,174	Total	14,174

[a] This is included neither as a current nor as a fixed asset, but as a separate classification in General Motors' annual report.
[b] Includes reserves.

THE BUSINESS FIRM: ORGANIZATION, MOTIVATION, AND TECHNOLOGY

Table 7.8

Profit and Loss Statement, General Motors Corporation, January 1, 1970 to December 31, 1970

Net sales (and other income)		18,879
Manufacturing cost of goods sold		17,094
Materials, labor, and miscellaneous operating costs	15,949	
Depreciation	1,499	
Total	17,448	
Plus beginning inventory	3,761	
Less closing inventory	−4,115	
Adjusted total	17,094	
Selling and administrative costs (and interest charges)		1,007
Net earnings before U.S. and foreign taxes		778
U.S. and foreign taxes		169
Net earnings after taxes		609
Dividends on preferred stock		13
Net profits of common stockholders		596
Dividends paid on common stock		971
Addition to surplus		−375

costs of $1,499 million in 1970. What is depreciation? (Turn back to "The Firm's Profit and Loss Statement" if you need to.) Also, GM's addition to surplus was negative in 1970. What does this mean? (See the section on "Relationship Between Balance Sheet and Profit and Loss Statement.")

Financial analysts spend an enormous amount of time poring over the financial statements of various companies to estimate whether their stock is a good or bad investment. Banks look at a firm's financial statements when they decide whether or not to grant the firm a loan. The financial pages of the major newspapers, as well as magazines specializing in financial and business news, are sprinkled liberally with summaries of these financial statements. You would do well to make sure you understand the basic definitions and principles of accounting presented in previous sections. In dealing with practical problems, this information will serve you well.

Summary

There are three principal types of business firms: proprietorships, partnerships, and corporations. The corporation has many advantages over the other two—limited liability, unlimited life, and greater ability to raise large sums of money. The corporation raises money by issuing various kinds of securities, of which three kinds—common stock, preferred stock, and bonds—are particularly important. A relatively small number of giant corporations control a very substantial proportion of the total assets and employment in the American economy. In the large corporation, ownership and control tend to be separated. So long as a firm's management is not obviously incompetent or corrupt, it is difficult for insurgent stockholders to remove the management from office.

As a first approximation, economists generally assume that firms attempt to maximize profits. In large part, this is because it is a close enough approximation to reality for many of the most important purposes of economics. Also, economists are interested in the theory of the profit-maximizing firm because it provides rules of behavior for firms that do want to maximize profits. In constructing his model of the profit-maximizing firm, the economist must somehow represent the state of technology and include it in his model. He classifies inputs used by the firm into two categories: fixed and variable. He also differentiates between the short run and the long run. Then, to summarize the characteristics of existing technology at a given point in time, he uses the concept of the production function, which shows the maximum output rate of a given commodity that can be achieved from any specified set of usage rates of inputs.

Accounting concepts are built around two very important statements: the balance sheet and the profit and loss statement. The balance sheet shows the nature of the firm's assets and liabilities at a given point in time. The difference between its assets and its liabilities is its net worth, which is the value of the firm's owners' claims against its assets. A firm's profit and loss statement shows its sales during a particular period, its costs incurred in connection with these sales, and its profits during the period. The balance sheet and the profit and loss statement are closely related. Economists define profits somewhat differently than accountants do. In particular, the economist excludes from profit the value of the capital and labor provided by the owners, and he is interested in longer periods than those to which accounting statements apply. Although the profit figures that are published almost always conform to the accountant's concept, the economist's concept is the more relevant one for many kinds of decisions.

CONCEPTS FOR REVIEW

Proprietorship	Common stock	Fixed input	Fixed assets
Partnership	Preferred stock	Variable input	Profit and loss
Corporation	Bond	Production function	statement
Liability	Profit	Balance sheet	Depreciation
Board of directors	Input	Current assets	

QUESTIONS FOR DISCUSSION AND REVIEW

1. Do you think that General Motors maximizes profits? What do you think that William C. Durant would have replied if you had asked him this question? For economic models to be useful, must firms maximize profits?

2. Suppose that a friend offered to sell you some stock in a small company. How would the firm's balance sheet and profit and loss statement be useful in evaluating how much the stock is worth?

3. In a partnership, though one partner has only a 25 percent share of the firm, he may be liable for all the firm's debts if the other partners cannot pay them. True or False?

4. A firm's assets which can be converted into cash fairly quickly are called _____ assets.   a. tangible b. intangible c. current d. fixed

PART THREE

National Output, Income, and Employment

CHAPTER 8

Unemployment, Inflation, and National Output

Three of the most important indicators of the health of any nation's economy are its unemployment rate, its rate of inflation, and the size of its national output. Every government, including our own, watches these indicators with great interest. Moreover, most societies today are committed to policies designed to influence each of them, in particular to keeping unemployment and inflation to a reasonable minimum, and to promoting the growth of national output. These social goals certainly seem sensible, since high rates of unemployment can cause enormous social waste and private hardship. Also, most societies seem to believe that the benefits of greater national output outweigh the costs, and that serious inflation should not be tolerated.

In this chapter, we begin to study unemployment, inflation, and national output. Our first objective is to describe the nature of unemployment and inflation, and how the rate of inflation is related to the rate of unemployment. Then we turn to a detailed examination of how national output is measured, our purpose being to describe such concepts as gross national product and its components: consumption, investment, government spending, and net exports. Finally, we discuss how the gap between actual and potential output is related to the level of unemployment.

Unemployment

Almost a century ago, Pope Leo XIII said: "Among the purposes of a society should be to arrange for a continuous supply of work at all times and seasons."[1] The word "unemployment" is one of the most frightening in the English language—and for good reason. Unemployed people (defined by the U.S. Government as all those 16 years old or more who do not have a job and are looking for one) become demoralized, suffer loss of prestige and status, and their families tend to break apart. Sometimes they are pushed toward crime and drugs; often they feel terrible despair. Their children are innocent victims too. Indeed, perhaps the most devastating effects of unemployment are on children, whose education, health, and security may be ruined. After a few minutes' thought, most people would agree that in this or any other country every citizen who is able and willing to work should be able to get a job.

Of course we are not saying that all unemployment, whatever its cause or nature, should be eliminated. Some unemployment is *frictional,* which means that it is related to the entrance of new workers into the labor market and the movement of workers from one position to another. For example, Tom Smith may quit his job after the boss calls him a fathead. It may take him a month to find another job, perhaps because he is unaware of job opportunities or perhaps because the boss was right. During this month, he is numbered among the unemployed. It would not make much

[1] Pope Leo XIII, *Encyclical Letter on the Conditions of Labor,* May 15, 1891.

sense to try to eliminate all such temporary unemployment. On the contrary, a free labor market could not function without a certain amount of frictional unemployment.

Another type of unemployment, called *structural unemployment,* exists when jobs are available for qualified workers, but the unemployed do not have the necessary qualifications. This sort of unemployment results from a mismatch between job requirements and the skills of the unemployed, as in the case of a 58-year-old cotton picker thrown out of work by the introduction of mechanical cotton pickers and lacking the skills needed to get a job in another field. To some extent, structural unemployment can be reduced by monetary and fiscal policies of the sort described in the following chapters. But in many cases, the principal way to attack it is by retraining workers whose skills are no longer in demand for jobs in other occupations, industries, or areas.

Still another type is *cyclical unemployment,* which is associated with business fluctuations, or the so-called business cycle. Industrialized capitalistic economies have been subject to fluctuations, with booms often succeeding busts and vice versa. Before World War II the American economy periodically went through serious depressions, during which unemployment was very high. The Great Depression of the 1930s was particularly long and severe, and when World War II ended, the American people resolved that the gigantic social costs of the enormous unemployment of the 1930s must not be repeated in the postwar period. To avoid this, Congress passed the Employment Act of 1946, which says:

> It is the continuing policy and responsibility of the Federal Government to use all practicable means . . . [to create and maintain] conditions under which there will be afforded useful employment opportunities, including self-employment, for those able, willing, and seeking to work and to promote maximum employment, production, and purchasing power.

The Employment Act of 1946 was an extremely important piece of legislation, for it committed the

Figure 8.1
Unemployment Rates, United States, 1929–72

The unemployment rate has varied substantially. Fortunately, since World War II it has not approached the very high levels of the Great Depression of the 1930s.

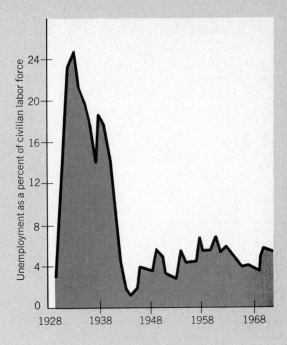

How Much Unemployment
Is There?

federal government to combat cyclical unemployment.

How Much Unemployment Is There?

To get some idea of the extent of unemployment, we can consult Figure 8.1, which shows the percent of the labor force unemployed during each year from 1929 to 1972. Note the wide fluctuations in the unemployment rate, and the very high unemployment rates during the 1930s. Fortunately, unemployment since World War II has never approached the tragically high levels of the Great Depression of the 1930s. In 1949 and 1950, and again in 1954, the unemployment rate pushed up toward 6 percent, but in general it remained at about 4 percent or less until 1958, when it increased to almost 7 percent. Between 1958 and 1964, it

averaged about 6 percent, and then declined steadily until it fell below 4 percent in 1966–69. In 1970–72, it bounced back up to 5 or 6 percent. Although these variations in the unemployment rate may seem small, they are by no means unimportant. Any administration, Democratic or Republican, watches these figures closely, and tries to avoid significant increases in unemployment.

The importance of unemployment statistics makes it worthwhile to see how they are collected. The federal government periodically conducts a scientific survey of the American people, asking a carefully selected sample of the population whether they have a job, and, if not, whether they are looking for one. According to most expert opinion, the resulting figures are quite reliable within certain limits. One of these is that they do not indicate the extent to which people are **underemployed.** Some people work only part-time, or at jobs well below their level of education or skill, but the government figures count them as fully employed. Also, some people have given up look-ing for a job and are no longer listed among the unemployed, even though they would be glad to get work if any was offered. To count as unem-ployed in the government figures, one must be actively seeking employment.

In addition, aggregate figures on unemployment cover up very substantial differences among groups within a society. Unemployment rates among blacks and other minorities are much higher than among whites. Also, unemployment rates among teenagers and women tend to be very high. For example, in 1972, although the unemployment rate for all workers was 5.6 percent, it was 16.2 percent among people 16 to 19 years of age and 10.0 percent among nonwhites. Consequently, since unemploy-ment tends to be concentrated in particular seg-ments of the population, overall unemployment rates can be somewhat misleading.

Unemployment: A Case Study

Since general descriptions of the plight of the un-employed often have relatively little impact, a real-life case study may give you a better feel for what unemployment is like. Consider Joseph Torrio, a New Haven factory worker who was laid off after 18 years on the job. He describes in his own words how he spent several mornings:

> Up at seven, cup of coffee, and off to Sargent's. Like to be there when the gang comes to work, the lucky devils. Employment manager not in. Waited in his outer office. . . . Three others waiting, two reporting for compensation. Other one laid off two weeks ago and said he called at office every day. He inquired what I was doing and when I said "looking for work" he laughed. "You never work here? No? What chance you think you got when 400 like me who belong here out?" Employment manager showed up at 9:30. I had waited two hours. My time has no value. A pleasant fellow; told me in a kind but snappy way business was very bad. What about the future, would he take my name? Said he referred only to the present. Nothing

more for me to say, so left. Two more had drifted into office. Suppose they got the same story. Must be a lot of men in New Haven that have heard it by now.

> [On May 21], interview with sales manager of the Real Silk Hosiery Mills. Had seen their ads for salesmen in the paper. Sales manager ap-proached me with his hand sticking out, the first one who had offered to shake hands with me. I told him my name and inquired about the position. He took me into his private office, well furnished, and asked me if I had had any selling experience. I told him that I hadn't any but I thought I could do the work. . . . Asked me to report at 9 A.M. the next morning for further instructions. . . . [On May 22], I kept my appointment with the sales manager. Spent the morning learning about different kinds of stockings. Made another appoint-ment for the afternoon which I did not keep because he wanted me to bring along $6 as security on a bag and some stock. I did not have the $6.[2]

No single case study can give you an adequate picture of the impact on people of being without a job. There are a wide variety of responses to unemployment. Some people weather it pretty well, others sink into despair; some people have sub-stantial savings they can draw on, others are hard pressed; some people manage to shield their fami-lies from the blow, others allow their misfortunes to spread to the rest of the family. But despite these variations, being without work deals a heavy blow to a person's feeling of worth. It hits hard at a person's self-image, indicating that he or she is not needed, cannot support a family, is not really a full and valuable member of society. It can strike a cruel blow at men and women alike, since many women are vitally interested in achievement out-side the home, sometimes because they are the family breadwinner. The impact of widespread and persistent unemployment is most clearly visible at present among the blacks and other racial minori-ties, where unemployment rates are much higher than among the white population. Unquestion-ably, the prevalence of unemployment among

[2] E. W. Bakke, *The Unemployed Worker*, Hamden, Conn.: Archon, 1969, pp. 168, 169, 174, and 175.

blacks greatly influences how the blacks view themselves, as well as the way they interact with the rest of the community.

Inflation

Almost everyone has heard the term "inflation," since it appears regularly in the press and on television. *Inflation is a general upward movement of the prices of both products and inputs.* In other words, inflation means that goods and services that currently cost $1 are marked up to $1.20 or $1.50, and wages and other input prices increase as well. It is essential to distinguish between the movements of individual prices and the movement of the entire price level. As we saw in Chapter 4, the price of an individual commodity can move up or down with shifts in the commodity's demand or supply curve. If the price of a particular good—corn, say —goes up, this need not be inflation, since the prices of other goods may be going down at the same time, so that the overall price level—the general average level of prices—remains much the same. Inflation occurs only if most prices for goods and services in the society move upward—that is, if the average level of prices increases.

Inflation may seem no more than a petty annoyance: after all, most people care about relative, not absolute, prices. For example, if wages (the price of labor) increase at the same rate as prices, a family may be no better or worse off under inflation than under a constant price level. But this view ignores the people—civil service employees, teachers, people living on pensions, and many others—who cannot increase their wages to compensate for price increases because they work under long-term contracts, among other reasons. These people take a considerable beating from inflation.

Also, inflation hurts lenders and benefits borrowers, since it results in the depreciation of money. A dollar is worth what it will buy, and what it will buy is determined by the price level. If the price

level increases, a dollar is worth less than it was before. Consequently, if you lend Bill Jones $100 in 1972 and he pays you $100 in 1980—when a dollar will buy much less than in 1972—you are losing on the deal. In terms of what the money will buy, he is paying you less than what he borrowed. Of course, if you expect this amount of inflation, you may be able to recoup by charging him a high enough interest rate to offset the depreciation of the dollar, but it is not so easy to forecast the rate of inflation and protect yourself.

Unlike unemployment, inflation (at least in small doses) does not seem to reduce national output: in the short run, output may increase. The principal effect of inflation is on the distribution of income and wealth. Many inflations are not anticipated; and even if they are, we have just noted that many people are not knowledgeable enough to protect themselves.[3] The poor worker who has put aside some money for his old age, only to find that it will buy a fraction of what he hoped, has been victimized by inflation. Why should he bear this loss? As Arthur Okun, former chairman of President Johnson's Council of Economic Advisers, has put it, " 'sharpies' . . . make sophisticated choices and often reap gains on inflation which do not seem to reflect any real contribution to economic growth. On the other hand, the unsophisticated saver who is merely preparing for the proverbial rainy day becomes a sucker."[4]

Citizens and policy makers generally agree that inflation, like unemployment, should be minimized. However, this feeling has not prevented the United States from suffering from considerable inflation. As shown in Figure 8.2, the price level has tended to increase considerably in the United States during the past 40 years. Substantial inflation followed World War II; the price level increased by about

---

[3] Economists often distinguish between anticipated and unanticipated inflation because if inflation is anticipated, people may be able to compensate for it by charging higher interest rates and by similar devices.

[4] Arthur Okun, "The Costs of Inflation" in his *The Battle Against Unemployment* (revised edition), New York: Norton, 1972.

Figure 8.2
The Price Level, United States,
1929–72

The price level has increased
considerably in the United States
during the past 40 years. In recent
years, inflation has been a
stubborn problem.

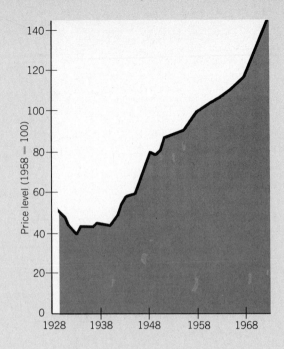

33 percent between 1945 and 1948. Bursts of inflation recurred during the Korean war and then during the Vietnam war. And in the 1960s and early 1970s, despite the government's efforts, inflation has continued. Our government's policy is to avoid both excessive unemployment and excessive inflation, but this goal, like many desirable social objectives, is by no means easy to achieve. Indeed, under certain circumstances, it may be impossible to have both stable prices and high employment, as we shall see in the next section.

The Relationship between Inflation and Unemployment

There seems to be a reasonable amount of evidence that in the short run the unemployment rate is inversely related to the rate of inflation: that is, the lower the unemployment rate, the higher the rate of inflation. This relationship is by no means fixed

and immutable, and the factors underlying its shape and position are still matters of debate. But, as a first approximation, we assume that this relationship is like that shown in Figure 8.3. In Chapter 15, we shall discuss in detail why this relationship seems to exist. At this point, it is sufficient to point out that, as the unemployment rate decreases, it is easier for unions and unorganized labor to get higher wages, and for firms to pass along these wage increases to consumers in the form of price increases. As the unemployment rate decreases, demand tends to press against capacity, prompting firms and resource owners to raise prices.

Figure 8.4, which shows the aggregate supply curve for an economy, provides further insight into this relationship. Note that, up to a point (Q_1), total output increases, dollar for dollar, with total spending. But beyond that point total output does not increase by the same amount as total spending. Indeed, when output reaches Q_2, increases in total spending can tease no more production out of the

Figure 8.3
Relationship between
Unemployment Rate and
Rate of Inflation

There seems to be an inverse short-run relationship between the unemployment rate and the rate of inflation. If the relationship is as shown here, a 4 percent unemployment rate means a 3 percent rate of inflation, a 5 percent unemployment rate means a 1.5 percent rate of inflation, and a 6 percent unemployment rate means a 0.5 percent rate of inflation.

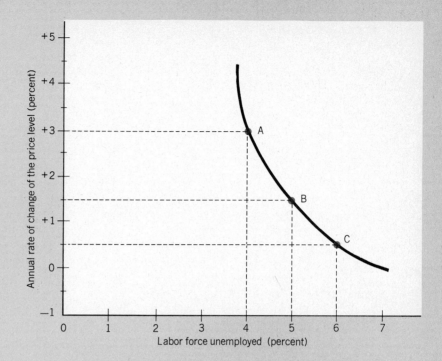

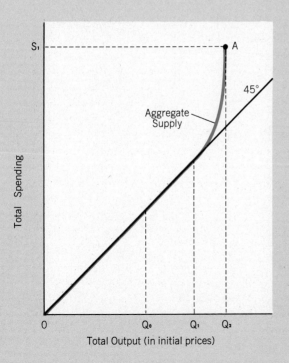

Figure 8.4
Aggregate Supply Curve

Total output increases, dollar for dollar, with total spending until it reaches Q_1, after which increases in spending do not result in equal increases in output. (The 45-degree line shows the locus of points where spending and output are equal.) If output equals Q_0, there will be considerable unemployment. As output increases, there will be less unemployment, but when output exceeds Q_1, there will be more and more inflation.

economy. This is quite reasonable, since, as you will recall from our discussion of the product transformation curve in Chapter 3, any economy can only produce so much, given its resources and the existing technology. In Figure 8.4 the maximum output level, if all the economy's resources are fully and efficiently employed, is Q_2.

On the basis of Figure 8.4, one can see why there is likely to be an inverse relationship between the unemployment rate and the rate of inflation. If actual output is much less than Q_2, say Q_0, there will be considerable unemployment, since output is much less than required to employ fully the available work force. As spending and output increase, the unemployment rate falls. Eventually, as spending and output increase further, inflation begins to occur. If output is between Q_1 and Q_2, total spending exceeds the total value of output at initial prices. In other words, as the economy approaches its maximum output, the price level begins to rise. Consumers, firms, and the government bid up the prices of goods and services. There are "too many dollars chasing too few goods." Also, as the economy approaches full employment, bottlenecks occur in some parts of the economy, and labor pushes harder for wage increases and firms are more likely to jack up prices. The result is the inverse relationship between the unemployment rate and the inflation rate shown in Figure 8.3.

The Menu of Policy Choices

The curve in Figure 8.3 is a fascinating tool. For example, suppose that you want to stabilize the price level. What level of unemployment would be required to prevent prices from rising? According to Figure 8.3, if unemployment is about 7 percent, prices will not increase. Thus 7 percent seems to be the answer. On the other hand, if you are interested in reducing unemployment to about 4 percent, what will be the effect on the rate of inflation? According to Figure 8.3, a 4 percent unemploy-

ment rate means that the price level will rise by about 3 percent per year. Of course, the curve in Figure 8.3 is an oversimplification, and it would be a mistake to assume that the relationship between unemployment and inflation is this cut and dried. But for present purposes, it is a reasonable first approximation, at least in the short run.

Suppose that the economy is faced by the kind of alternatives described by the curve in Figure 8.3: what sorts of choices are available to the government's policy makers? Obviously, the government can choose where along the curve in Figure 8.3 it wants to be. For example, it may choose point C, with an unemployment level of 6 percent and a rate of price increase of ½ percent. Or it may choose an unemployment level of 4 percent and a rate of price increase of 3 percent—in other words, point A.

Needless to say, government policy makers do not sit down and specify a point on a graph like Figure 8.3. The policy making process is neither so simple nor so neat nor so self-conscious. But policy makers do make choices—explicit or implicit —about where on such a curve they want to operate. Some administrations are more inclined than others to tolerate more unemployment in order to stem inflation. Some are more willing than others to tolerate inflation in order to reduce unemployment. Of course, in their public statements, politicians often refuse to acknowledge that any choice of this sort is required. They often claim that they will reduce *both* unemployment *and* inflation. But this can't be done, unless they shift the curve in Figure 8.3.

In fact, it is possible for the government to shift this curve, through programs to train manpower, increase labor mobility, reduce discrimination, and change people's expectations. With such programs, as well as various kinds of incomes policies, the government can push the curve downward and to the left, as shown in Figure 8.5. In this way, the government can reduce both unemployment and inflation. The curve can also shift for reasons other than government action. For expository purposes, however, it is convenient to assume temporarily that

**Figure 8.5
Shift in Relationship between
Unemployment Rate and Rate
of Inflation**

The relationship between the
unemployment rate and the
inflation rate shifts in response to
a variety of factors, including
people's expectations. The
government would like to push it
downward and to the left, as
shown here.

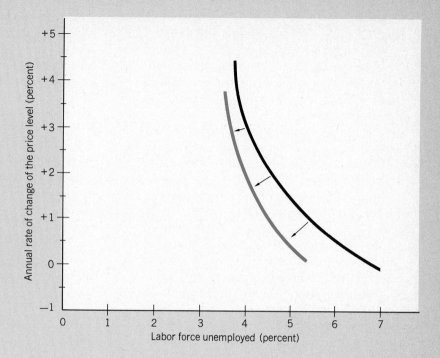

the curve in Figure 8.3 is fixed. In Chapter 15, when we discuss incomes policies and related matters, this assumption will be relaxed.

Given this assumption, society is faced in the short run with the menu of policy choices in Figure 8.3. Your political preferences and values determine where along the curve in Figure 8.3 you feel society should be. A commonly accepted target is point A, with 4 percent unemployment, but in the 1970s the Nixon administration has shown some tendency to accept point B, where unemployment is 5 percent, as a goal. The target one chooses depends, of course, on his evaluation of the relative social costs associated with unemployment and inflation. The more importance you give to the costs of unemployment, and the less importance to the costs of inflation, the farther up the curve you will want to be. The more importance you attach to the costs of inflation, and the less to the costs of unemployment, the farther down on the curve you will want to be.

Estimates of Gross National Product: Uses and History

Having discussed unemployment and inflation, we must turn next to national output, which is most commonly measured by the concept of gross national product. Almost everyone talks about the gross national product, and for good reason. This statistical measure tells us a great deal about how well our economy is performing, and has become a major indicator of the nation's economic condition. Put in the simplest terms, *the gross national product*—or *GNP, as it is often called—is a measure of the total amount of goods and services produced by our economy during a particular period of time.*

Both the government and the business community watch the GNP figures like hawks. Government officials, from the president down, are interested because these figures indicate how prosperous we are, and because they are useful in forecasting the future health of the economy. Politicians are well aware that the political party in power generally gets clobbered when GNP falls substantially. Business executives are also extremely interested in the GNP figures because the sales of their firms are related to the level of GNP, and so the figures are useful in forecasting the future health of their businesses. All in all, it is no exaggeration to say that the gross national product is one of the most closely watched numbers in existence.

In view of their importance, it is noteworthy that estimates of the gross national product are of comparatively recent vintage. The Department of Commerce first made such estimates in 1932, after experiments at various universities and at the National Bureau of Economic Research. A leading pioneer in this field was Nobel Laureate Simon Kuznets, then at the University of Pennsylvania. The concepts that Kuznets and others developed are often called the **national income accounts,** and the National Income Division of the U.S. Department of Commerce compiles these figures on a continuing basis. Just as the accounts of a firm are used to describe and analyze its financial health, so the national income accounts are used to describe and analyze the economic health of the nation as a whole.

Measuring Gross National Product

The American economy produces millions of types of goods and services. How can we add together everything from lemon meringue pie to helicopters, from books to houses? The only feasible answer is to use money as a common denominator and to make the price of a good or service—the amount the buyer is willing to pay—the measure of value. In other words, we add up the value in money terms of the total output of goods and services in the economy during a certain period, normally a year, and the result is the gross national product during that period.

At the outset, we must note several important points about the gross national product. First, it does not include the value of *all* goods and services produced: it includes only the value of *final* goods and services produced. **Final goods and services** are goods and services to be used by the ultimate user. For example, bread purchased by a housewife is a final good, but flour to be used in manufacturing bread is an **intermediate good,** not a final good. Clearly, we would be double counting if we counted both the bread and the flour used to make the bread as output. Flour bought by housewives for use in domestic cooking is, on the other hand, a final good. To avoid double counting, we include only the value of final goods and services in gross national product.

Second, some final goods and services that must be included in gross national product are not bought and sold in the marketplace, so they are valued at what they cost. For example, consider the services performed by government—police protection, fire protection, the use of the courts, defense, and so forth. Such services are not bought and sold in any market (despite the old saw about the New Jersey judge who was "the best that money could buy"). Yet they are an important part of our economy's final output. Economists and statisticians have decided to value them at what they cost the taxpayers. This is by no means ideal, but it is the best practical solution advanced to date.

Third, it is necessary for practical reasons to omit certain types of final output from gross national product. In particular, some nonmarketed goods and services, such as the services performed by housewives, are excluded from the gross national product. This is not because economists fail to appreciate these services, but because it would be extremely difficult to get reasonably reliable estimates of the money value of a housewife's services. At first glance, this may seem to be a very important weakness in our measure of total output, but so long as the value of these services does not change much (in relation to total output), the variation in gross national product will provide a reasonably accurate picture of the variation in total output—and, for many purposes, this is all that is required.

Fourth, purely financial transactions are excluded from the gross national product. Such financial transactions include government transfer payments, private transfer payments, and the sale and purchase of securities. **Government transfer payments** are payments made by the government to individuals who do not contribute to production in exchange for them. Payments to welfare recipients are a good example of government transfer payments. Since these payments are not for production, it would be incorrect to include them in GNP. **Private transfer payments** are gifts or other transfers of wealth from one person or private organization to another. Again these are not payments for production, so there is no reason to include them in GNP. The sale and purchase of securities are not payments for production, as you will recall from our discussion in Chapter 7, so they too are excluded from GNP.

Finally, the sale of secondhand goods is also excluded from the gross national product. The reason for this is clear. When a good is produced, its value is included in GNP. If its value is also included when it is sold on the secondhand market, it will be counted twice, thus leading to an overstatement of the true GNP. For example, suppose that you buy a new bicycle and resell it a year later. The value of the new bicycle is included in GNP when the bicycle is produced. But the resale value of the bicycle is not included in GNP; to do so would be double counting.

Gross National Product: Adjusting for Price Changes

In discussing inflation, we stressed that the general price level has changed over time. Since gross national product values all goods and services at their current prices, it is bound to be affected by changes in the price level as well as by changes in total output. If all prices doubled tomorrow, this would produce a doubling of gross national product. Clearly, if gross national product is to be a reliable measure of changes in total output, we must correct it somehow to eliminate the effects of changes in the price level.

Fortunately, economists have devised ways to do this—at least approximately. They choose some **base year** and express the value of all goods and services in terms of their prices during the base year. For example, if 1960 is taken as the base year and if the price of beef was $1 per pound in 1960, beef is valued at $1 per pound in all other years. Thus, if 200 million pounds of beef were produced in 1965, this total output is valued at $200 million even though the price of beef in 1965 was actually higher than $1 per pound. In this way, distortions caused by changes in the price level are eliminated.

It is customary to express gross national product either in current dollars or in constant dollars. Figures expressed in **current dollars** are actual dollar amounts, whereas those expressed in **constant dollars** are corrected in this way for changes in the price level. Expressed in current dollars, gross national product is affected by changes in the price level. Expressed in constant dollars, gross national product is not affected by the price level because the prices of all goods are maintained at their base-year level. In recent years, inflation has caused gross national product expressed in current dollars to increase more rapidly than gross national product in constant dollars, as shown in Figure 8.6.

It is often useful to have some measure of how much prices have changed over a certain period of time. One way to obtain such a measure is to divide the value of a set of goods and services expressed in current dollars by the value of the same set of goods and services expressed in constant (or base-year) dollars. For example, suppose that a set of goods and services costs $100 when valued at 1972 prices, but $70 when valued at 1960 prices. Apparently, prices have risen an average of 43 percent for this set of goods between 1960 and 1972. How do we get 43 percent? The ratio of the cost in 1972 prices to the cost in 1960 prices is 100 ÷

Figure 8.6
Gross National Product,
Expressed in Current Prices
and in 1958 Prices, United
States, 1929–72

Because of inflation, GNP
expressed in current dollars has
increased more rapidly in recent
years than GNP in constant (1958)
dollars.

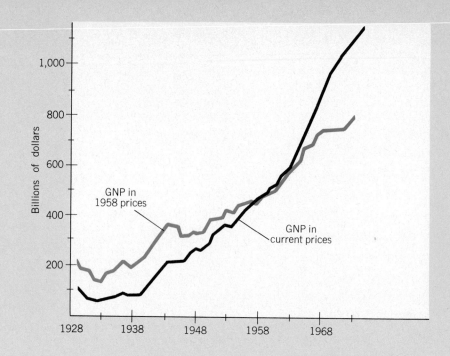

70 = 1.43; thus, prices must have risen on the average by 43 percent for this set of goods.

The ratio of the value of a set of goods and services in current dollars to the value of the same set of goods and services in constant (base-year) dollars is a *price index.* Thus, 1.43 is a price index in the example above. An important function of a price index is to convert values expressed in current dollars into values expressed in constant dollars. This conversion, known as *deflating,* can be achieved simply by dividing values expressed in current dollars by the price index. For example, in the illustration above, values expressed in 1972 dollars can be converted into constant (i.e., 1960) dollars by dividing by 1.43. This procedure is an important one, with applications in many fields other than the measurement of gross national product. For example, firms use it to compare their output in various years. To correct for price changes, they deflate their sales by a price index for their products.

To illustrate how a price index can be used to solve problems of this sort, suppose that we want to determine the extent to which the output of bread has increased in real terms between 1970 and 1974. We know that the value of output of bread in current dollars during each year was as shown in the first column of Table 8.1, and that the price of bread during each year was as shown in the second column. To determine the value of output of bread in 1970 dollars, we form a price index with 1970 as base year, as shown in the third column. Then dividing the figures in the first column by this price index, we get the value of output of bread during each year in 1970 dollars, shown in the fourth column. Thus, the fourth column shows how much the output of bread has grown in real terms. For example, the real output of bread has increased by 19 percent—(1,900 − 1,600) ÷ 1,600—between 1970 and 1974.

Table 8.1

Use of Price Index to Convert from Current to Constant Dollars

Year	(1) Output of bread in current prices	(2) Price of bread	(3) Price index (price ÷ 1970 price)	(4) Output of bread in 1970 dollars[1]
1970	$1,600 million	$0.50	1.00	$1,600 million
1971	1,768 million	$0.52	1.04	1,700 million
1972	1,980 million	$0.55	1.10	1,800 million
1973	2,090 million	$0.55	1.10	1,900 million
1974	2,204 million	$0.58	1.16	1,900 million

[1] This column was derived by dividing column 1 by column 3.

Intermediate Goods, Value-Added, and Net National Product

We have pointed out that gross national product includes the value of only the final goods and services produced. Obviously, however, the output of final goods and services is not due to the efforts of only the producers of the final goods and services. The total value of an automobile when it leaves the plant, for example, represents the work of many industries besides the automobile manufacturers. The steel, tires, glass, and many other components of the automobile were not produced by the automobile manufacturers. In reality, the automobile manufacturers only added a certain amount of value to the value of the intermediate goods—steel, tires, glass, etc.—they purchased. This point is basic to an understanding of how the gross national product is calculated.

To measure the contribution of a firm or industry to the final output, we use the concept of value-added. **Value-added** means just what it says: the amount of value added by a firm or industry to the total worth of the product. It is a measure in money terms of the extent of production taking place in a particular firm or industry. Suppose that $160 million of bread was produced in the United States in 1974. To produce it, farmers harvested $50 million of wheat, which was used as an intermediate product by flour mills, which turned out $80 million of flour. This flour was used as an intermediate product by the bakers who produced the $160 million of bread. What is the value-added at each stage of the process? For simplicity, assume that the farmers did not have to purchase any materials from other firms in order to produce the wheat. Then the value-added by the wheat farmers is $50 million, the value-added by the flour mills is $30 million ($80 million − $50 million); and the value-added by the bakers is $80 million ($160 million − $80 million). Of course, the total of the value-added at all stages of the process ($50 million + $30 million + $80 million) must equal the value of the output of final product ($160 million).

Table 8.2 shows the value-added by various industrial groups in the United States in 1972. Since the total of the value-added by all industries must equal the value of all final goods and sources, which, of course, is gross national product, it follows that $1,155 billion—the total of the figures in Table 8.2—must have been equal to gross national product in 1972. It is interesting to note that most of the value-added in the American economy in 1972 was not contributed by manufacturing, mining, construction, transportation, communication, or electricity or gas. Instead, most of it came from

Table 8.2

Value-added by Various Industries, United States, 1972

Industry	Value-added (billions of dollars)
Agriculture, forestry, and fisheries	37
Mining	18
Construction	56
Manufacturing	291
Transportation	46
Communication	28
Electricity, gas, and sanitation	28
Wholesale and retail trade	194
Finance, insurance, and real estate	164
Other services	133
Government[1]	153
Rest of the world	7
Gross national product	1,155

[1] Equals wages and salaries of government workers.
Source: Survey of Current Business, July 1973.

services—wholesale and retail trade, finance, insurance, real estate, government services, and other services. This is a sign of a basic change taking place in the American economy, which is turning more and more toward producing services, rather than goods.

Gross national product has one drawback as a measure that must now be faced: it does not take into account the fact that plant and equipment wear out with use. Economists have therefore developed another measure, net national product (or NNP), that allows for the fact that some of the nation's plant and equipment and structures are used up during the period. In other words, net national product recognizes what every accountant knows—the relevance of depreciation. (Recall the discussion in Chapter 7.) Specifically, *net national product* equals gross national product minus depreciation. To obtain net national product, government statisticians estimate the amount of depreciation—the amount of the nation's plant, equipment, and structures that are worn out during the period—and deduct it from gross national product. Net national product is a more accurate measure of the economy's output than gross national product because it takes depreciation into account, but estimates of net national product contain whatever errors are made in estimating depreciation (which is not easy to measure). As we shall see in succeeding chapters, data on gross national product are more often used, even if net national product may be a somewhat better measure. Actually, since GNP and NNP move together quite closely, which one you use doesn't matter much for most practical purposes.

The Limitations of Gross National Product and Net National Product

It is essential that the limitations of both gross national product and net national product be understood. Although they are very useful, they are by no means ideal measures of economic well-being. At least five limitations of these measures must always be borne in mind. First, GNP and NNP are not very meaningful unless one knows the size of the population of the country in question. For example, the fact that a particular nation's GNP equals $50 billion means one thing if the nation has 10 million inhabitants, and quite another thing if it has 500 million inhabitants. To correct for the size of the population, GNP per capita—GNP divided by the population—is often used as a rough measure of output per person in a particular country.

Second, GNP and NNP do not take account of one of man's most prized activities, leisure. During the past century, the average workweek in the United States has decreased substantially. It has gone from almost 70 hours in 1850 to about 40 hours today. As people have become more affluent, they have chosen to substitute leisure for increased production. Yet this increase in leisure time, which surely contributes to our well-being, does not show up in GNP or NNP. Neither does the personal satisfaction (or displeasure and alienation) people get from their jobs.

Third, GNP and NNP do not take adequate account of changes in the quality of goods. An improvement in a product is not reflected accurately in GNP and NNP unless its price reflects the improvement. For example, if a new type of drug is put on the market at the same price as an old drug, and if the output and cost of the new drug are the same as the old drug, GNP will not increase, even though the new drug is twice as effective as the old one. Because GNP and NNP do not reflect such increases in product quality, it is sometimes argued that the commonly used price indexes overestimate the amount of inflation, since, although prices may have gone up, quality may have gone up too.

Fourth, GNP and NNP say nothing about the social desirability of the composition and distribution of the nation's output. Each good and service produced is valued at its price. If the price of a

Bible is $5 and the price of a pornographic novel is $5, both are valued at $5, whatever you or I may think about their respective worth. Moreover, GNP and NNP measure only the total quantity of goods and services produced. They tell us nothing about how this output is distributed among the people. If a nation's GNP is $500 billion, this is its GNP whether 90 percent of the output is consumed by a relatively few rich families or whether the output is distributed relatively equally among the citizens.

Finally, GNP and NNP do not reflect some of the social costs arising from the production of goods and services. In particular, they do not reflect the environmental damage resulting from the operation of our nation's factories, offices, and farms. It is common knowledge that the atmosphere and water supplies are being polluted in various ways by firms, consumers, and governments. Yet these costs are not deducted from GNP or NNP, even though the failure to do so results in an overestimate of our true economic welfare.

Economists are beginning to correct the GNP figures to eliminate some of these problems. For example, William Nordhaus and James Tobin at Yale University have tried to correct the GNP figures to take proper account of the value of leisure, the value of housewife's services, and the environmental costs of production, among other things.[5] They have found that, when these corrections were made, the increase in economic welfare since World War II has been much less than is indicated by the growth of uncorrected GNP per capita. Unquestionably, more work along this line is needed, and will be done. However, it is also worth noting that many of these adjustments and corrections are necessarily quite rough, since there is no accurate way to measure the relevant values and costs.

---

[5] W. Nordhaus and J. Tobin, "Is Growth Obsolete?", *Fiftieth Anniversary Colloquium,* National Bureau of Economic Research, 1972.

Gross National Income

We have been dealing with the measurement of national product, or output. We must also recognize *the identity between gross national product and gross national income*. **Gross national income** is the total annual flow of income paid out (or owed) as wages, rent, interest, and profits, plus two other items: indirect business taxes and depreciation. **Indirect business taxes** are sales taxes, excise taxes, and other such taxes that firms view as part of their costs. Thus, gross national income exactly equals the total claims on output—the sum total of the wages of the workers who participated in the productive efforts, the interest paid to the investors who lent money to the firms who produced the output, the profits of the owners of the firms who produced the output, and the rents paid the owners of land used to produce the output, as well as indirect business taxes and depreciation. If you think back to the circular flows of money and products described in Chapter 4, you can see why gross national income must equal gross national product.

Table 8.3

Sales, Costs, and Profit, General Electric Company, 1970

Sales ($ million)		Costs and profit ($ million)	
Sales:	$8,834	Employee compensation	$3,776
		Interest	101
		Depreciation	335
		Indirect business taxes	89
		Intermediate products bought from other firms	3,978
		Total costs	8,279
		Profits	555
Total	8,834	Total	8,834

Source: General Electric Company, 1970 Annual Report.

Table 8.4

Value-added and Claims Against Output, General Electric Company, 1970

Value-added ($ million)			Claims against output	
	Sales:	$8,834	Employee compensation	$3,776
			Interest	101
Subtract:	Intermediate products bought from other firms:	3,978	Profits	555
			Depreciation	335
	Value-added	4,856	Indirect business taxes	89
			Total	4,856

Source: General Electric Company, 1970 Annual Report.

To make sure that you understand this, let's start with a single firm, the General Electric Corporation, a huge producer of electrical equipment, appliances, and other products. By the simple rules of accounting discussed in Chapter 7,

$$\text{profit} = \text{sales} - \text{costs.} \qquad (8.1)$$

Thus it follows that

$$\text{sales} = \text{costs} + \text{profit.} \qquad (8.2)$$

Suppose we put the value of General Electric's output (i.e., its sales) on the left-hand side of Table 8.3 and its costs and profits on the right-hand side. Clearly, by Equation (8.2), the total of the right-hand side must equal the total of the left-hand side.

Now suppose that we deduct one element of costs, "Intermediate products bought from other firms," from both sides of Table 8.3, and present the results in Table 8.4. Since the left-hand total equals the right-hand total in Table 8.3, the same must hold in Table 8.4. The total of the left-hand side of Table 8.4 equals value-added, since General Electric's value-added equals its sales minus its expenditures on intermediate goods bought from other firms. The total of the right-hand side of Table 8.4 equals the total claims against General Electric's output, which is the total of income paid out (or owed) by the firm—wages, interest, rent, profits—plus indirect business taxes and depreciation. And, as pointed out above, the total of the left-hand side must equal the total of the right-hand side of Table 8.4.

Next, imagine constructing a table like Table 8.4 for each employer in the economy, putting sales less intermediate products bought from other firms on the left and costs plus profits less intermediate products bought from other firms on the right. For every employer, the total of the left side must equal the total of the right side. Thus, if we add up the total of the left-hand sides for all employers in the economy, the result must equal the total of the right-hand sides for all the employers in the

economy. But what is the total of the left-h. sides for all employers in the economy? It is t. sum of value-added for all employers, which, a. we saw in a previous section, equals gross national product. And the total of the right-hand sides for all employers in the economy is the total of all income paid out (or owed) in the economy—wages, interest, rent, profits—plus indirect business taxes and depreciation. Consequently, gross national product must equal the total of all income paid out (or owed) in the economy plus indirect business taxes and depreciation.

Table 8.5 shows the total amounts of various types of income paid out (or owed) in the American economy during 1972. It also shows depreciation and indirect business taxes. You can see for yourself that the total of these items equals gross national product. Besides helping to prove the point stated at the beginning of this section, this table is an interesting description of the relative importance of various types of income. For example, it shows the great importance of wages and salaries in the total income stream in the United States. About

Table 8.5

Gross National Income, United States, 1972

Type of claim on output	Amount of claim (billions of dollars)
Employee compensation	707
Rental income	24
Net interest	45
Income of proprietors and professionals	74
Corporate profits	91
Indirect business taxes	109
Depreciation	102
Statistical discrepancy	3
Gross national income	1,155

Source: Survey of Current Business, July 1973.

ational income is paid out in
d this percentage has re-
ng the past 30 years.

Income, Personal Income,
Disposable Income

There is more to gross national income than the total amount of income paid out (or owed) by employers (including government). As noted in the previous section, it also includes indirect business taxes and depreciation. We are sometimes interested only in the total amount of income paid out (or owed) by employers, an amount called *national income.* Clearly, it is easy to derive national income if you know gross national income. All you have to do is subtract indirect business taxes and depreciation from gross national income. Or putting it another way, all you have to do is subtract indirect business taxes from net national product, since gross national income minus depreciation equals net national product.[6] Table 8.6 shows the result for 1972.

For some purposes, we also need to know how much the people of a nation receive in income. This is *personal income,* and it differs from national income in two ways. First, some people who have a claim on income do not actually receive it. For example, although all a firm's profits belong to the owners, not all of its profits are paid out to them. As we saw in Chapter 7, part of the profits are plowed back into the business, and part go to the government for corporate income taxes. Also, wage earners do not actually receive the amounts they and their employers pay currently for Social

[6] Two other small items must also be taken into account. As shown in Table 8.6, we must subtract *business transfer payments*—pensions and other payments made by firms that are transfer payments—and add *subsidies less surpluses of government enterprises,* which corrects for the fact that some government agencies pay out more to income recipients than they produce in value-added. In addition, of course, there is a statistical discrepancy that must be recognized. It is purely a statistical matter.

Security. Second, some people receive income that is not obtained in exchange for services rendered. You will recall from an earlier section that government transfer payments are made to welfare recipients, people receiving unemployment compensation or Social Security, and so forth. Also, there are business transfer payments—pensions and other payments made by firms that are not in exchange for current productive services.

Table 8.6

Gross National Product, Net National Product, National Income, Personal Income, and Disposable Income, United States, 1972

Measure	Amount (billions of dollars)
Gross national product	1,155
Subtract: Depreciation	102
Net national product	1,053
Subtract: Indirect business taxes	109
Business transfers	5
Statistical discrepancy	−1
Add: Subsidies less surpluses of government enterprises	2
National income	942
Subtract: Corporate profits	91
Contributions for social insurance	74
Add: Government transfers to persons	98
Dividends	26
Interest paid by government	33
Business transfers	5
Personal income	939
Subtract: Personal taxes	142
Disposable personal income	797

Source: Survey of Current Business, July 1973.

If you know national income, it is easy to derive personal income. You begin by subtracting profits from national income and adding dividends to the result. This will correct for the fact that profits not distributed as dividends do not actually enter people's hands. Then you must deduct contributions for social insurance, and add government and business transfer payments. (Note that interest paid by governments on their debt is regarded as a transfer payment, on the grounds that it is not a payment for current goods and services.) These calculations are shown in detail in Table 8.6.

Finally, it is also useful for many purposes to know how much the people of a nation receive in income and get to keep after personal income taxes. This is *disposable income.* If you know what personal income is, you can easily obtain disposable income by deducting personal income taxes from personal income, as shown in Table 8.6. Disposable income plays a very important role in subsequent chapters because it has a major influence on how much consumers spend. According to Table 8.6, disposable income equaled about 69 percent of gross national product (gross national income) in 1972.

Consumption, Investment, and Government Expenditure

Up to this point, we have been concerned with national output and national income, Now we take up *national expenditure.* At the outset, note that, if we include business spending for increased inventories as a form of expenditure, *the total amount spent on final goods and services must equal the total value of final goods and services produced.* In other words, *gross national expenditure must equal gross national product,* because all goods produced must either be bought by someone or added to the producer's inventories. In either case, the value of the goods is included in gross national expenditure.

The total amount spent on final goods and serv-ices is generally broken down into four parts. First, there is *consumption,* the amount spent by households on durable goods, nondurable goods, and services. For example, consumption includes your expenditures on meals and clothing, and your parents' expenditures on the family car or on an electric washer and dryer. Table 8.7 shows that in 1972 consumption accounted for about 63 percent of the total amount spent on final goods and services in the United States. Expenditure on consumer durable goods is clearly much less than on consumer nondurable goods or services.

Second, there is *investment,* the amount spent by firms for new plant and equipment, new housing, and increases in inventories, as well as the

Table 8.7

Expenditure on Final Goods and Services, United States, 1972

Type of Expenditure		Amount (billions of dollars)
Personal consumption		727
Durable goods	118	
Nondurable goods	300	
Services	309	
Gross private domestic investment		178
Expenditures on plant and equipment	118	
Residential structures	54	
Increase in inventories	6	
Net exports		−5
Exports	73	
Imports	78	
Government expenditures		255
Federal	104	
State and local	151	
Gross national product		1,155

Source: Survey of Current Business, July 1973.

amount spent by households for new housing. (Owner-occupied houses are treated as investment goods because they can be rented out.) Table 8.7 shows that in 1972 investment accounted for about 15 percent of the total amount spent on final goods and services in the United States. This is *gross investment,* the gross amount of money spent on new plant, equipment, buildings, and extra inventory, not the net amount. Why? Because during the period in question, some plant, equipment, and so forth wore out: there was depreciation. Thus, to determine net investment we must deduct depreciation from gross investment. Net investment is a good measure of how fast the nation's capital goods are increasing. If net investment is positive, the nation's productive capacity, as gauged by its capital stock, is growing. If net investment is negative, the nation's productive capacity, as gauged by its capital stock, is declining.

Third, there are *government purchases of goods and services.* They include the expenditures of the federal, state, and local governments for the multitude of functions they perform: defense, education, police protection, and so forth. They do not include transfer payments, since they are not payments for current production. Table 8.7 shows that government spending in 1972 accounted for about 22 percent of the total amount spent on final goods and services in the United States. State and local expenditures are bigger than federal expenditures. As you recall from Chapter 5, much of the expenditures of the federal government are connected with national defense, while at the state and local levels the biggest expenditure is for education.

Finally, there are *net exports of goods and services,* which equal the amount spent by foreigners on our goods and services less the amount we spent on other nations' goods and services. Obviously, this factor must be included since some of our national output is destined for foreign markets, and since we import some of the goods and services we consume. There is no reason why this component of spending cannot be negative, since imports can exceed exports. The quantity of net exports tends to be quite small. Table 8.6 shows that net exports in 1972 were negative, and equal to about $\frac{4}{10}$ of 1 percent of the total amount spent on final goods and services in the United States. Because net exports are so small, we shall generally ignore them until Chapters 19 and 20, when we shall focus attention exclusively on international trade and finance.

Three Basic Facts

The measures of national output, national income, and national expenditure discussed above are some of the basic figures economists look at when trying to analyze the state of the economy. Using these measures, it is easy to demonstrate the following three facts, each of which will be needed in succeeding chapters. First, disposable income, although it goes up and down with gross national product, does not fluctuate as much as gross national product. This is shown in Figure 8.7. As we shall soon see, disposable income has a smoother path because our tax system and our social insurance programs, as well as other mechanisms, tend to dampen the effect of changes in gross national product on disposable income. When total output declines, the amount of aftertax income people receive does not go down so much; and when total output increases, the amount of aftertax income they receive does not go up so much. This, of course, cushions the effect of changes in gross national product.

Second, consumption expenditure seems to depend closely on—and vary directly with—disposable income. This observation, shown in Figure 8.8, is neither strange nor surprising. On the contrary, it would be odd if the amount households spend on goods and services were *not* closely related to their aftertax income, for consumers can do only two things with their aftertax income: spend it or save it.

Third, investment varies much more than the other components of total spending. Figure 8.9 shows that investment goes up and down, while

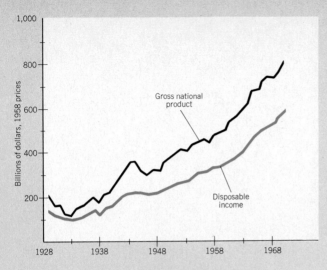

Figure 8.7
Relationship between Disposable Income and Gross National Product, United States, 1929–72

Disposable income, although it goes up and down with gross national product, does not fluctuate as much as GNP.

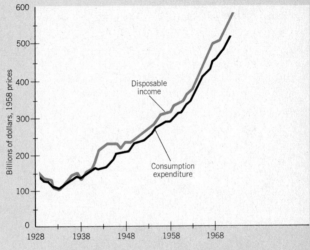

Figure 8.8
Relationship between Consumption and Disposable Income, United States, 1929–72

Consumption expenditure seems to depend closely on, and vary directly with, disposable income.

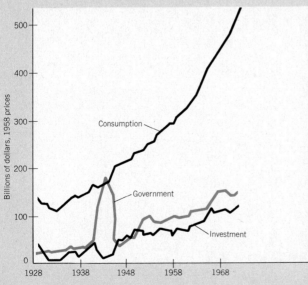

Figure 8.9
Consumption Expenditure, Gross Private Domestic Investment, and Government Expenditures, United States, 1929–72

Investment varies more than the other components of total spending. Also, because of wars, government spending moves up and down rather erratically.

consumption moves along with only slight bumps and dips, and government expenditures do not move up and down very much except when war breaks out.[7] (Note the bulges in government spending during World War II, the Korean war, and the Vietnamese war.) The volatility of investment is an important factor in explaining the changes in national output over time. Also, the wartime bulges in government spending have been major causes of changes in national output. We shall have considerably more to say on this score in the next few chapters.

The Gap between Actual and Potential Output

Gross national product is a measure of the value of final goods and services produced in a given period: in other words, GNP measures actual output. Besides being concerned about actual output, economists are also interested in potential output. Specifically, they are interested in estimating how high the gross national product could have been *if the unemployment rate had been quite low, say 4 percent* (which is a common definition of full employment)? An economy's potential output is determined by the size of its labor force, the average number of hours a worker is on the job per year, and the average amount of goods and services a worker can produce per hour. The average amount of goods and services a worker can produce per hour depends in turn on the extent and quality of the capital he has to work with, the level of technology, and his skill and schooling.

More specifically, the *potential GNP* is estimated by multiplying 96 percent of the labor force times the normal hours of work per year times the average output per manhour at the relevant time. In the past few years, there has been some criticism of this definition of potential GNP on the grounds that an unemployment rate of 4.5 or 5 percent is a more realistic measure of full employment than 4

percent because there now are more young people, women, and minority workers in the labor force. All of these groups find it relatively difficult to find jobs. Since this debate is unresolved, we shall stick with the conventional definition, but the apparent difficulties in this measure should be noted.

If potential GNP is defined in this way, the gap between actual and potential GNP depends on the difference between the actual unemployment rate and 4 percent. Specifically, the gap will grow larger and larger as the unemployment rate exceeds 4 percent by greater and greater amounts. According to Arthur Okun, who served as chairman of the Council of Economic Advisers under President Johnson, the relationship is as follows:

$$\text{potential GNP} - \text{actual GNP} =$$
$$3 \times (\text{unemployment rate} - .04) \times \text{actual GNP}.$$

In this equation, the number 3 in the formula is derived by fitting the equation to historical data.[8]

Needless to say, it is not easy to measure potential GNP. Consequently, as Okun is the first to emphasize, one should view this equation as only a rough predictor. But rough predictors are better than none, and this equation is a handy device to estimate the gap between actual and potential output at various levels of unemployment. For example, if the unemployment rate were 7 percent, the gap between actual and potential output would be 3 times .03 (the difference between .07 and .04) times the actual gross national product. In other words, the gap would equal 9 percent of actual gross national product. Figure 8.10 shows the estimated size of the gap between actual and potential GNP from 1955 to 1972. Note that both actual and potential GNP are expressed in 1958 prices.

The gap between actual and potential output is an extremely important measure of what it costs society to tolerate an unemployment rate above 4 percent. Besides the psychic costs of unemployment described in a previous section, society produces less than it could, so that human wants

---

[7] Net exports are excluded from Figure 8.9. They were almost always under $10 billion during this period.

[8] Arthur Okun, *The Political Economy of Prosperity*, New York: Norton, 1970.

Figure 8.10
Actual and Potential Output,
United States, 1955–72

The gap measures what it costs society each year, in output forgone, to tolerate an unemployment rate above 4 percent.

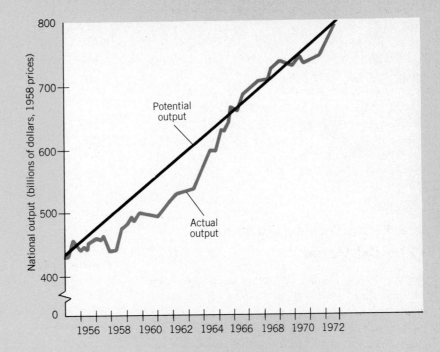

are less effectively fulfilled than they could be. For example, consider the period from 1958 to 1963. During this period, unemployment tended to be relatively high, and actual GNP was considerably less than potential GNP. Using Okun's equation, it is possible to estimate the gap between actual and potential GNP in each of these years. All one needs to do is insert the actual unemployment rates and actual figures for GNP in the equation. Based on such calculations, Okun has concluded that

> The United States could have produced a total of nearly $200 billion more output [if there had been a] 4% unemployment rate. This is two-thirds of the amount spent for national defense in the period and far more than the expenditure for public education. It is fair to conclude that tolerance of idle resources has been America's outstanding extravagance and waste [during this period.][9]

[9] Arthur Okun, *The Battle Against Unemployment,* New York: Norton, 1965, p. 22.

Clearly we must learn to curb the forces responsible for such waste. The following chapters will discuss some of the basic factors that cause excessive unemployment and excessive inflation, as well as various measures that can be taken to combat them.

Summary

Unemployment inflicts enormous social costs. Recognizing this fact, the Congress passed the Employment Act of 1946, which commits the federal government to combat excessive unemployment. Inflation is a general upward movement of prices. Since inflation results in an arbitrary and often inequitable redistribution of income, government policymakers attempt to curb inflation. Unfortunately, there appears to be an inverse relationship between the unemployment rate and the rate of inflation, because it is easier for unions and unorganized labor to increase wages and for firms to increase prices when there is little unemployment. Thus government policymakers, if they reduce unemployment, often create inflationary pressures, whereas if they attack inflation, they often increase unemployment. What you regard as the optimal combination of unemployment and inflation depends on your political preferences and values. The relationship between unemployment and inflation is by no means fixed, and one way out of this difficulty is for the government to try to shift this relationship downward and to the left.

Besides unemployment and inflation, another very important indicator of the health of any economy is its gross national product, which measures the total value of the final goods and services it produces in a particular period. Since gross national product is affected by the price level, it must be deflated by a price index to correct for price level changes. Gross national product is the sum of value-added by all industries. Net national product is gross national product minus depreciation. It indicates the value of net output when account is taken of capital used up.

Gross national product equals gross national income. Gross national income equals the sum of the total claims against output, including indirect business taxes and depreciation. National income is the total amount of income paid out (or owed) by employers; personal income is the total amount

people actually receive in income; and disposable income is the total amount they get to keep after taxes.

Gross national product also equals gross national expenditure. Gross national expenditure equals the total amount spent on final goods and services, including business spending for increased inventories. The total amount spent on final goods and services is generally broken down into four parts: consumption, investment, government purchases, and net exports.

Based on the official data, investment appears to vary much more over time than other types of expenditure. As we shall see, this volatility is an important clue to the causes of change in national output. Also, there have been large variations in government expenditures associated with wars; these too have caused major changes in national output.

Estimates have been made of how the gap between actual and potential output is related to the unemployment rate. For example, if Okun's results are accepted, output could be expanded about 9 percent if the unemployment rate is reduced from 7 to 4 percent. Clearly, one of the major social costs of unemployment is the fact that less goods and services are produced than could be produced with full employment. According to Okun, this cost totaled nearly $200 billion over the 5-year period 1958–63 alone.

CONCEPTS FOR REVIEW

Frictional unemployment
Structural unemployment
Cyclical unemployment
Gross national product
Intermediate good

Current dollars
Constant dollars
Price index
Value added
Net national product
Gross national income
Personal income

Transfer payments
Disposable income
Inflation
National income
Consumption
Investment
Net exports

QUESTIONS FOR DISCUSSION AND REVIEW

1. According to the September 1932, issue of *Fortune* magazine, "About 1,000,000 out of [New York City's] 3,200,000 working population are unemployed." What effect did this have on the city's population? During the past 30 years, has this experience been repeated? About how many New Yorkers are presently unemployed?

2. Suppose that you were given the job of estimating the gross national product of Monaco. How would you proceed?

3. Inflation occurs whenever the price of an individual commodity moves up significantly. True or False?

4. The type of unemployment where jobs are available for qualified workers, but the unemployed do not have the necessary qualifications is called
   a. frictional. b. cyclical. c. structural.

CHAPTER 9

The Determination of National Output

In early 1973, the American economy was in the midst of a boom. Gross national product was moving ahead rapidly, the unemployment rate was receding, and inflationary pressures were evident practically everywhere. In 1970, on the other hand, GNP was declining, the unemployment rate was increasing, and there was less upward pressure on the price level. Why the pronounced difference between these two periods? To answer this question, as well as to understand the causes of severe unemployment and inflation, and what can be done to avoid these problems, we must understand how the level of a nation's output is determined.

In this chapter, we show how national output is determined in a purely market economy without government spending or taxation. The resulting model is interesting in its own right, as well as a useful step toward the more complete analysis provided in Chapter 10. In this chapter, national output is defined as net national product, since it is the best measure of how much the economy is producing when depreciation is taken into account. But since net national product and gross national product differ by relatively little, and since they move up and down together, this theory is also useful in explaining movements in gross national product. Indeed, as we shall see, it has been used to help forecast GNP.

The Classical View of Unemployment

Until the 1930s, most economists were convinced that the price system, left to its own devices, would hold unemployment to a reasonable minimum. Thus, most of the great names of economics in the nineteenth and early twentieth centuries—including John Stuart Mill, Alfred Marshall, and A. C. Pigou[1]—felt that there was no need for government intervention to promote a high level of employment. To be sure, they recognized that unemployment was sometimes large, but they regarded these lapses from high employment as temporary aberrations that the price system would cure automatically. Although economists today look at this matter differently, we must understand why the classical economists felt that this was the case.

Basically, their view was founded on the assertion that total spending was unlikely to be too small to purchase the high-employment level of output, because of the operation of a law propounded by the nineteenth-century French economist, J. B. Say. According to **Say's Law**, the production of a certain amount of goods and services

results in the generation of an amount of income precisely sufficient to buy that output. In other words, supply creates its own demand, since the total amount paid out by the producers of the goods and services to resource owners must equal the value of the goods and services. (Recall the circular flow discussed in Chapter 4.) However, as the classical economists recognized, there could be a fly in the ointment. If some of the owners of resources did not spend their income, but saved some of it instead, how would the necessary spending arise to take all the output off the market?

The answer the classical economists offered is that each dollar saved will be invested. Therefore, investment (made largely by business firms) will restore to the spending stream what resource owners take out through the saving process. Recall that the economist's definition of investment is different from the one often used in common parlance. To the economist, investment means expenditure on plant, equipment, and other productive assets. The classical economists believed that the amount invested would automatically equal the amount saved because the interest rate—the price paid for the use of money—would fluctuate in such a way as to maintain equality between them. In other words, there is a market for loanable funds, and the interest rate will vary so that the quantity of funds supplied equals the quantity demanded. Thus, since funds are demanded to be used—that is, invested—the amount saved will be invested.

Further, the classical economists said that the amount of goods and services businessmen can sell depends upon the prices businessmen charge, as well as on total spending. For example, $1 million in spending will take 400 cars off the market if the price is $2,500 per car, and 500 cars off the market if the price is $2,000 per car. Recognizing this, the classical economists argued that firms would cut prices to sell their output. Competition among firms would prod them to reduce their prices in this way, with the result that the high-employment level of output would be taken off the market.

Looking at this process more closely, it is obvious that the prices of resources must also be reduced under such circumstances. Otherwise firms would they would be getting less for ... paying no less for resources. The ... ts believed that it was realistic ... es of resources to decline in such ... eed they were quite willing to as- ... wage rate—the price of labor— ... ble in this way. They expected this flexibl... ause of competition among laborers. Through the processes of competition, they felt that wage rates would be bid down to the level where everyone who really wanted to work could get a job.

The Views of Karl Marx

Quite a different view of unemployment was held by Karl Marx (1818–83), the intellectual father of communism. A man of unquestioned genius, he became an object of quasi-religious devotion to a large part of the world and a hated (and sometimes feared) revolutionary figure to another large part of the world. Because Marx the revolutionary has had such an enormous effect on modern history, it is difficult to discuss Marx the economist. But he was a very profound and influential economist. A meticulous German scholar who spent much of his life in poverty-ridden circumstances in Britain, he wrote a huge, four-volume work on economics, *Das Kapital*.[2] Eighteen years in the making, it is one of the most influential books ever written.

To understand Marx, we need to know something about the times in which he lived. The period was characterized by revolutionary pressures against the ruling classes. In most of the countries of Europe, there was little democracy, as we know it. The masses participated little, if at all, in the world of political affairs, and very fully in the world of drudgery. For example, at one factory in Manchester, England, in 1862, people worked an average of about 80 hours per week. For these incredibly long hours of toil, the workers generally received small wages. They often could do little

[2] Karl Marx, *Das Kapital*, New York: Modern Library, 1906.

more than feed and clothe themselves. Given the circumstances of the times, it is little wonder that revolutionary pressures were manifest.

Marx, viewing the economic system of his day, believed that capitalism was doomed to collapse. He believed that the workers were exploited by the capitalists—the owners of factories, mines, and other types of capital. And he believed that the capitalists, by introducing new labor-saving technology, would throw more and more workers into unemployment. This army of unemployed workers, by competing for jobs, would keep wages at a subsistence level. As machinery was substituted for labor, Marx felt that profits would fall. Unemployment would become more severe. Big firms would absorb small ones. Eventually the capitalistic system was bound to collapse.

To get the flavor of his reasoning and emotions, consider the following passage from *Das Kapital*, a famous passage describing his vision of the death knell of the capitalist system:

> Along with the constantly diminishing number of the magnates of capital, who usurp and monopolize all advantages of this process of transformation, grows the mass of misery, oppression, slavery, degradation, exploitation; but with this too grows the revolt of the working-class, a class always increasing in numbers, and disciplined, united, organized by the very mechanism of the process of capitalist production itself . . . Centralization of the means of production and socialization of labor at last reach a point where they become incompatible with their capitalist integument. This integument bursts asunder. The knell of capitalist private property sounds. The expropriators are expropriated.[3]

According to Marx, the inevitable successor to capitalism would be socialism, an economic system with no private property. Instead, property would be owned by society as a whole. Socialism, constituting a "dictatorship of the proletariat," would be only a transitional step to the promised land of communism. Marx did not spell out the characteristics of communism in detail. He was sure that it

[3] Karl Marx, *Das Kapital*, *op. cit.*, pp. 836–7, reprinted in E. Mansfield, *Economics: Readings, Issues, and Cases*, New York: Norton, 1974.

would be a classless society where everyone worked and no one owned capital, and he was sure that the state would "wither away," but he did not attempt to go much beyond this in his blueprint for communism. While this is not the place to examine Marx's doctrines (and their limitations) in detail, it should be clear that the classical view did not go unchallenged, even in the nineteenth century.

John Maynard Keynes and the Great Depression

The man who was responsible for much of the modern theory of the determination of national product was John Maynard Keynes (1883–1946). Son of a British economist who was justly famous in his own right, Keynes was enormously successful in a variety of fields. He published a brilliant book on the theory of probability while still a relatively young man. Working for a half-hour in bed each morning, he made millions of dollars as a stock market speculator. He was a distinguished patron of the arts and a member of the Bloomsbury set, a group of London intellectuals who were the intellectual pace-setters for British society. He was a faculty member at Cambridge University, and a key figure at the British Treasury. In short, he was an extraordinarily gifted and accomplished man.

Keynes lived and worked almost a century after Marx. His world was quite different from Marx's world; and Keynes himself—polished, successful, a member of the elite—was quite different from the poverty-stricken, revolutionary Marx. But the two great economists were linked in at least one important respect: both were preoccupied with unemployment and the future of the capitalistic system. As we saw in the previous section, Marx predicted that unemployment would get worse and worse, until at last the capitalist system would collapse. In the 1930s, when Keynes was in his heyday, the Great Depression seemed to many people to be proving Marx right.

In 1936, while the world was still in the throes of this economic disaster, Keynes published his masterpiece, *The General Theory of Employment, Interest, and Money*.[4] His purpose in this book was to explain how the capitalist economic system could get stalled in the sort of depressed state of equilibrium that existed in the 1930s. He also tried to indicate how governments might help to solve the problem. Contrary to the classical economists, Keynes concluded that no automatic mechanism in a capitalistic society would generate a high level of employment—or, at least, would generate it quickly enough to be relied on in practice. Instead, the equilibrium level of national output might for a long time be below the level required to achieve high employment. His reasons for believing that this could be the case are discussed in detail in this and subsequent chapters.

To push the economy toward a higher level of employment, Keynes advocated the conscious, forceful use of the government's power to spend and tax. As we shall see in Chapter 10, many years passed before these powers became accepted tools of national economic policy, but it was Keynes who provided much of the intellectual stimulus. And in so doing, he helped falsify the predictions of Marx. Keynes and his many followers showed how severe unemployment could be tamed, and how a capitalistic economy could be managed to avoid the sorts of debacles Marx predicted. It is no exaggeration to say that Keynes made a major contribution to saving the capitalist system.

Flaws in the Classical View

There were at least two basic flaws in the classical model, as Keynes and his followers pointed out. First, *the people and firms who save are often not the same as the people and firms who invest, and they often have quite different motivations.* In particular, a considerable amount of saving is done by families who want to put something aside for a

[4] John Maynard Keynes, *The General Theory of Employment, Interest, and Money*, New York: Harcourt, Brace, 1936.

Figure 9.1
Relation between Family
Expenditures on Consumption
and Family Disposable Income,
United States, 1960

Families with higher incomes
spend more on consumption than
families with lower incomes.

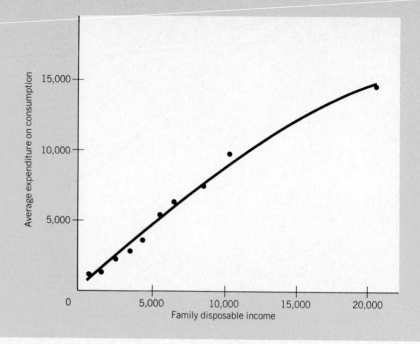

rainy day or for a car or appliance. On the other hand, a considerable amount of investment is done by firms that are interested in increasing their profits by expanding their plants or by installing new equipment. There is no assurance that desired saving will equal desired investment at a level insuring high employment. For one thing, saving may be used to increase money balances, not to support investment. Thus a purely capitalist economic system, in the absence of appropriate government policies, has no dependable rudder to keep it clear of the shoals of serious unemployment or of serious inflation.

Second, *Keynes and his followers pointed out the unreality of the classical economists' assumption that prices and wages are flexible.* Contrary to the classical economists' argument, the modern economy contains many departures from perfect competition that are barriers to downward flexibility of prices and wages. In particular, many important industries are dominated by a few producers who try hard to avoid cutting price. Even in the face of a considerable drop in demand, such industries have sometimes maintained extraordi-

narily stable prices. Moreover, the labor unions fight tooth and nail to avoid wage cuts. In view of these facts of life, the classical assumption of wage and price flexibility seems unrealistic indeed. And it seems unlikely that price and wage reductions can be depended on to maintain full employment.

The Great Depression of the 1930s struck a severe blow against the classical view. When it continued for years, and millions and millions of people continued to be unemployed, it became increasingly difficult to accept the idea that unemployment was only a temporary aberration that the market economy would cure automatically in a reasonable length of time. Nonetheless, the classical economists did not change their tune. They claimed that the economy would get back to high employment if the labor unions would allow more wage flexibility, if the big corporations would allow more price flexibility, and if President Franklin D. Roosevelt and his New Dealers would quit interfering with free markets.

Finally, when Keynes's *General Theory* appeared in 1936, it seemed to offer a more satisfactory model, even though, at first, only a minority of the econom-

**Figure 9.2
Relationship between
Consumption Expenditure and
Disposable Income, United
States, 1929–72**

There is a very close relationship
between consumption expenditure
and disposable income in the
United States.

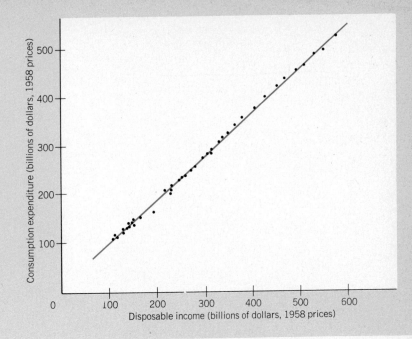

ics profession was converted to the Keynesian view. Within 10 or 15 years of its publication, most economists were convinced that Keynes's theory was essentially sound; and his ideas now are generally accepted, although they have been refined and extended by his followers. Whether Republican or Democrat, any modern economist relies heavily on Keynesian ideas and concepts. But, of course, not all economists share Keynes's views on proper public policy. Moreover, as we shall see in subsequent chapters, under certain circumstances, more complicated models are likely to outperform the simple Keynesian model presented in this and the following chapters.

The Modern Theory: The Consumption Function

Keynes's *General Theory of Employment, Interest, and Money* is impenetrable for the general reader. Even among professional economists, it is not noted for its lucidity or liveliness. But the basic ideas

that Keynes presented—and that subsequent economists have refined, extended, and reworked—are really quite simple. In the remainder of this chapter, we shall describe and discuss the determinants of national output, according to the modern view. The first thing to note is that *consumption expenditures—whether those of a single household or the total consumption expenditures in the entire economy—are influenced heavily by income.* For individual households, Figure 9.1 shows that families with higher incomes spend more on consumption than families with lower incomes. Of course, individual families vary a good deal in their behavior; some spend more than others even if their incomes are the same. But, on the average, a family's consumption expenditure is tied very closely to its income.

What is true for individual families also holds for the entire economy: total consumption expenditures are closely related to disposable income. This fact, noted in the previous chapter, is shown in detail in Figure 9.2, a "scatter diagram" that plots total consumption expenditure in each year (from 1929 to 1972) against disposable income in the

164

Figure 9.3
**Figure 9.3
Shift in the Consumption
Function**

The consumption function
describes the total amount of
consumption expenditure at each
level of disposable income. The
consumption function may shift
upward (from *A* to *B*) if changes
occur in the public's assets, its expectations, or in other variables.

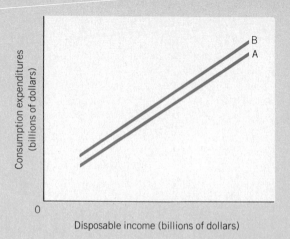

same year (from 1929 to 1972). The points fall
very near the straight line drawn in Figure 9.2,
but not right on it. For most practical purposes,
however, we can regard the line drawn in Figure
9.2 as representing the relationship between total
consumption expenditures and disposable income.

*This relationship between consumption spending
and disposable income is the* **consumption function.**
The consumption function, the importance of
which was stressed by John Maynard Keynes, is at
the heart of the modern theory of the determination of national output. It is a working tool that is
used widely and often by economists to analyze
and forecast the behavior of the economy. There
have been many statistical studies of the consumption function. Some of these studies have been
based on cross-section data—comparisons of the
amount spent on consumption by families at various income levels. (Figure 9.1 is based on cross-
section data.) Others have been based on time-series
data—comparisons of the total amount spent on
consumption in the economy with total income over
various periods of time. (Figure 9.2 is based on
time-series data.)

Like most things in the world, the consumption
function does not remain fixed, but changes from

time to time, because variables other than disposable income affect consumption expenditures.
Some of the most important of these variables are
changes in income distribution, changes in population, changes in the amount of assets in the hands
of the public, changes in the ease and cheap-
ness with which consumers can borrow money, and
changes in their price expectations. For example,
consumption expenditure is likely to be higher—
holding disposable income constant—if income is
more equally distributed, if the population is
greater, if people are holding large amounts of
government bonds and other liquid assets, or if
consumers can borrow money easily and cheaply.
Under any of these conditions, the consumption
function is likely to shift upward, as indicated by
the movement from position *A* to position *B* in
Figure 9.3.

The Marginal Propensity to Consume

Suppose that we know what the consumption function for a given society looks like at a particular
point in time. For example, suppose that it is given

by the figures for disposable income and consumption expenditure in the first two columns of Table 9.1. Based on our knowledge of the consumption function, we can determine the *extra* amount families will spend on consumption if they receive an *extra* dollar of disposable income. *This amount— the fraction of an extra dollar of income that is spent on consumption—is called the* **marginal propensity to consume.** For reasons discussed in subsequent sections of this chapter, the marginal propensity to consume, shown in column 4 of Table 9.1, plays a major role in the modern theory of national output determination.

To make sure that you understand exactly what the marginal propensity to consume is, consult Table 9.1. What is the marginal propensity to consume when disposable income is between $1,000 billion and $1,050 billion? The second column

shows that, when income rises from $1,000 billion to $1,050 billion, consumption rises from $950 billion to $980 billion. Consequently, the fraction of the extra income—$50 billion—that is consumed is $30 billion ÷ $50 billion, or 0.60. Thus, the marginal propensity to consume is 0.60.[5] Based on similar calculations, the marginal propensity to consume when disposable income is between $1,050 billion and $1,100 billion is 0.60; the marginal propensity to consume when disposable income is between $1,100 billion and $1,150 billion is 0.60; and so forth.

[5] Students with some knowledge of mathematics will recognize that this is an approximation since $50 billion is a substantial change in income, whereas the marginal propensity to consume pertains to a small change in income. But this is an innocuous simplification. Similar simplifications are made below.

Table 9.1

The Consumption Function

Disposable income (billions of dollars)	Consumption expenditure	Average propensity to consume	Marginal propensity to consume	Saving (billions of dollars)	Marginal propensity to save
1,000	950	.95		50	
			$\frac{30}{50} = .60$		$\frac{20}{50} = .40$
1,050	980	.93		70	
			$\frac{30}{50} = .60$		$\frac{20}{50} = .40$
1,100	1,010	.92		90	
			$\frac{30}{50} = .60$		$\frac{20}{50} = .40$
1,150	1,040	.90		110	
			$\frac{30}{50} = .60$		$\frac{20}{50} = .40$
1,200	1,070	.89		130	
			$\frac{30}{50} = .60$		$\frac{20}{50} = .40$
1,250	1,100	.88		150	
			$\frac{30}{50} = .60$		$\frac{20}{50} = .40$
1,300	1,130	.87		170	

There are several things to note about the marginal propensity to consume. First, it can differ, depending on the level of disposable income. Only if the consumption function is a straight line, as in Figure 9.2 and Table 9.1, will the marginal propensity to consume be the same at all levels of income. Second, the marginal propensity to consume will not in general equal the *average propensity to consume,* which is the proportion of disposable income that is consumed. For example, in Table 9.1, the average propensity to consume when disposable income is $1,100 billion is 0.92; but the marginal propensity to consume when disposable income is between $1,050 billion and $1,100 billion is 0.60. The point is that the marginal propensity to consume is the proportion of *extra* income consumed, and this proportion generally is quite different from the proportion of *total* income consumed. Third, the marginal propensity to consume can be interpreted geometrically as the slope of the consumption function. The slope of any line is, of course, the ratio of the vertical change to the horizontal change when a small movement occurs along the line. Thus, the steeper the consumption function, the higher the marginal propensity to consume.

The Saving Function and the Marginal Propensity to Save

If people don't devote their disposable income to consumption expenditure, what else can they do with it? Of course, they can save it. When families refrain from spending their income on consumption goods and services—that is, when they forgo present consumption to provide for larger consumption in the future—they save. Thus we can derive from the consumption function the total amount people will save at each level of disposable income. All we have to do is subtract the total consumption expenditure at each level of disposable income from disposable income. This will give us the total amount of saving at each level of disposable income, as shown in Table 9.1. Then we can plot the total amount of saving against disposable income, as shown in Figure 9.4. The resulting relationship between total saving and disposable income is called the *saving function.* Like the consumption function, it plays a major role in the modern theory of national output determination.

If we know the saving function, we can calculate the marginal propensity to save at any level of disposable income. The *marginal propensity to save is the proportion of an extra dollar of disposable income that is saved.* To see how to calculate it, consult Table 9.1 again. The fifth column shows that, when income rises from $1,000 billion to $1,050 billion, saving rises from $50 billion to $70 billion. Consequently, the fraction of the extra income—$50 billion—that is saved is $20 billion ÷ $50 billion, or 0.40. Thus, the marginal propensity to save is 0.40. Similar calculations show that the marginal propensity to save when disposable income is between $1,050 billion and $1,100 billion is 0.40; the marginal propensity to save when disposable income is between $1,100 billion and $1,150 billion is 0.40; and so forth.

Note that, at any particular level of disposable income, the marginal propensity to save plus the marginal propensity to consume must equal one. By definition, the marginal propensity to save equals the proportion of an extra dollar of disposable income that is saved, and the marginal propensity to consume equals the proportion of an extra dollar of income that is consumed. The sum of these two proportions must equal one, for, as stated above, the only things that people can do with an extra dollar of disposable income are consume it or save it. Table 9.1 shows this fact quite clearly. At every level of disposable income, the marginal propensity to consume plus the marginal propensity to save equals one. Finally, it is worth noting that the marginal propensity to save equals the slope of the saving function—just as the marginal propensity to consume is the slope of the consumption function. As pointed out above, the slope of a line equals the vertical distance between

**Figure 9.4
The Saving Function**

The saving function describes the total amount of saving at each level of disposable income.

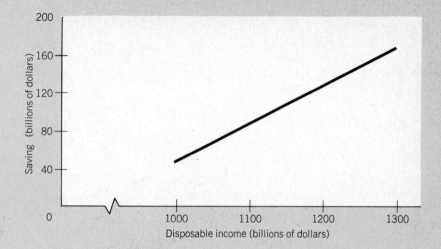

Determinants of Investment

Next, consider the factors determining the level of net investment. As you recall from the previous chapter, investment consists largely of the amount firms spend on new buildings and factories, new equipment, and increases in inventories. Net investment equals gross investment less depreciation. A host of factors influence the level of net investment. First, there is the *rate of technological change.* When new products are developed, firms often must invest in new plant and equipment in order to produce them. For example, Du Pont, after successfully developing nylon in 1938, had to invest millions of dollars in new plant and equipment to produce it. Moreover, the invention of new processes, as well as products, makes it profitable for firms to invest in new plant and equipment. For example, after the invention of the continuous wide strip mill by Armco in the 1920s,

American steel producers invested huge sums in new rolling mills to replace the old hand mills.

Second, the level of investment is influenced by *the level of sales and the stock of capital goods needed to produce the output to be sold.* As a firm's sales go up, its need for plant, equipment, and inventories clearly goes up as well. Beyond some point, increases in sales result in pressure on the capacity of existing plant and equipment, so that the firm finds it profitable to invest in additional plant and equipment. Clearly, the crucial relationship is between a firm's sales and its stock of capital goods—that is, its stock of plant, equipment, and inventories. If its sales are well below the amount it can produce with its stock of capital goods, there is little pressure on the firm to invest in additional capital goods. But if its sales are at the upper limit of what can be produced with its capital goods, the firm is likely to view the purchase of additional capital goods as profitable.

Third, the level of investment is influenced heavily by the *expectations of businessmen.* If businessmen believe that their sales are about to drop, they will be unlikely to invest much in additional capital goods. On the other hand, if they believe that their sales are about to increase greatly, they may be led to invest heavily in capital goods. Firms must make investment decisions on the basis of forecasts. There is no way any firm can tell exactly what the future will bring, and the investment decisions it makes will be influenced by how optimistic or pessimistic its forecasts are. This in turn will depend on existing business conditions, as well as on many other factors. Sometimes government actions and political developments have an important impact on business expectations. Sometimes unexpected changes in the fortune of one industry have a major effect on expectations in other industries.

Fourth, the level of investment is affected by the **rate of interest,** the price an investor must pay for the use of money. Since the cost of an investment is bound to increase with increases in the rate of interest, a given investment will be less profitable when the interest rate is high than when it is low. For example, a firm may find it profitable to invest in a new machine if it can borrow the money needed to purchase the machine at 8 percent interest per year, but it may not find it profitable if the interest rate is 15 percent.

In most of the rest of this chapter, we shall assume that the total amount of desired investment is independent of the level of net national product. This, of course, is only a rough simplification, since, as we noted above, the amount firms invest will be affected by the level of output in the economy. But this simplification is very convenient and not too unrealistic. Moreover, as we shall show at the end of this chapter, it is relatively easy to extend the model to eliminate this assumption.

The Determination of the Equilibrium Level of National Output

We are now ready to show how net national product is determined. At the outset, however, we must make several assumptions. First, we assume that there are no government expenditures and that the economy is closed (no exports or imports). Thus *total spending on final output—that is, net national product—in this simple case equals consumption expenditure plus net investment.* Needless to say, in subsequent chapters we shall relax the assumptions that there are no government expenditures and that the economy is closed. Second, we assume that there are no taxes and no government transfer payments (and no undistributed corporate profits). Thus, *net national product equals disposable income in this simple case.* In subsequent chapters, we shall also relax this assumption.

Under these assumptions, suppose that firms decide that they want to invest $90 billion (net of depreciation) next year regardless of the level of net national product. Suppose too that the consumption function is as shown in Table 9.1. What will be the equilibrium level of net national product—the level of net national product that eventually will be attained, allowing some time for the basic forces to work themselves out? To answer this question, let's construct a table showing the amount consumers and firms desire to spend at various levels of NNP. Since NNP equals disposable income in this simple case, the consumption function in Table 9.1 shows the level of desired consumption expenditure at each level of NNP. These data are shown in columns 1 and 2 of Table 9.2. The level of desired saving at each level of NNP, which can be derived by subtracting desired consumption expenditures from NNP in this simple case, is shown in column 3. Desired investment expenditure is shown in column 4, while total desired spending, which equals desired consumption expenditure plus desired investment, is shown in column 5.

The equilibrium level of net national product will be at the point where desired spending on NNP equals NNP: no other level of NNP can be maintained for any considerable period of time. Let's see why this very important statement is true.

The easiest way to show this is to show that, if desired spending on NNP is *not* equal to NNP,

Table 9.2

Determination of Equilibrium Level of Net National Product

(1) Net national product (= dis- posable income)	(2) Desired consumption expenditure	(3) Desired saving	(4) Desired investment	(5) Total desired spending (2) + (4)	(6) Tendency of national output
1,000	950	50	90	1,040	Upward
1,050	980	70	90	1,070	Upward
1,100	1,010	90	90	1,100	No change
1,150	1,040	110	90	1,130	Downward
1,200	1,070	130	90	1,160	Downward
1,250	1,100	150	90	1,190	Downward

NNP is *not* at its equilibrium level. If desired spending on NNP is greater than NNP, what will happen? Since the total amount that will be spent on final goods and services exceeds the total amount of final goods and services produced (the latter being, by definition, NNP), firms' inventories will be reduced. Consequently, firms will increase their output rate to restore their inventories to their normal level and to bring their output into balance with the rate of aggregate demand. Since an increase in the output rate means an increase in NNP, it follows that NNP will tend to increase if desired spending on NNP is greater than NNP—reflecting the fact that NNP is not at its equilibrium level.

On the other hand, what will happen if desired spending on NNP is less than NNP? Since the total amount that will be spent on final goods and services falls short of the total amount of final goods and services produced (the latter being, by definition, NNP), firms' inventories will increase. As inventories pile up unexpectedly, firms will cut back their output to bring it into better balance with aggregate demand. Since a reduction in output means a reduction in NNP, it follows that NNP will tend to fall if desired spending on NNP is less than NNP—reflecting the fact that NNP is not at its equilibrium level.

Thus, if NNP tends to increase when desired spending on NNP is greater than NNP, and if NNP tends to decrease when desired spending on NNP is less than NNP, clearly NNP will be at its equilibrium level only if desired spending on NNP is equal to NNP.

The Process Leading Toward Equilibrium: A Tabular Analysis

In the previous section, we described the general nature of the process leading toward equilibrium. But this process is much clearer if we consider a specific numerical example, such as that contained in Table 9.2. To get a better idea of why NNP tends to the level where desired spending on NNP equals NNP, consider three possible values of NNP—$1,050 billion, $1,100 billion, and $1,150 billion—and see what would happen in our simple economy if these values of NNP prevailed. First, let's consider an NNP of $1,050 billion. What would happen if firms were to produce $1,050 billion of final goods and services? Given our assumptions, disposable income would also equal $1,050 billion (since disposable income equals NNP), so that consumers would spend $980 billion on consumption goods and services. (This follows from the nature of the consumption function: see column 2 of Table 9.2). Since firms want to invest $90 billion, total desired spending would be $1,070 billion ($980 billion + $90 billion, as shown in column 5). But the total amount spent on final goods and services under these circumstances would exceed the total value of final goods and services produced by $20 billion ($1,070 billion − $1,050 billion), so that firms' inventories would be drawn down by $20 billion. Clearly, this situation could not persist very long. As firms become aware that their inventories are becoming depleted, they would step up their production rates, so that the value of output of final goods and services—NNP —would increase.

Second, what would happen if $1,150 billion were the value of NNP—if firms were to produce $1,150 billion of final goods and services? Given our assumptions, disposable income would also equal $1,150 billion (since disposable income equals NNP), with the result that consumers would spend $1,040 billion on consumption goods and services. (This follows from the consumption function: see column 2 of Table 9.2.) Since firms want to invest $90 billion, total spending would be $1,130 billion ($1,040 billion + $90 billion, as shown in column 5). But the total amount spent on final goods and services under these circumstances would fall short of the total value of final goods and services produced by $20 billion ($1,150 billion − $1,130 billion), so that firms' inventories would increase by $20 billion. Clearly, this situation, like the previous one, could not continue very long. When firms see that their inventories are increasing, they reduce their production rates, causing the value of output of final goods and services— NNP—to decrease.

Finally, consider what would happen if NNP were $1,100 billion—if firms were to produce $1,100 billion of final goods and services? Disposable income would also equal $1,100 billion (since disposable income equals NNP), so that consumers would spend $1,010 billion on consumption goods and services. (This follows from the consumption function: see column 2 of Table 9.2.) Since firms want to invest $90 billion, total spend-

ing would be $1,100 billion ($1,010 billion + $90 billion, as shown in column 5). Thus, the total amount spent on final goods and services under these circumstances would exactly equal the total value of final goods and services produced. Consequently, there would be no reason for firms to alter their production rates. Thus, this would be an equilibrium situation—a set of circumstances where there is no tendency for NNP to change—and the equilibrium level of NNP in this situation would be $1,100 billion.

These three cases illustrate the process that pushes NNP toward its equilibrium value. So long as NNP is below its equilibrium value, the situation is like that described in our first case. So long as NNP is above its equilibrium value, the situation is like that described in our second case. Whether NNP is below or above its equilibrium value, there is a tendency for production rates to be altered so that NNP moves toward its equilibrium value. Eventually, NNP will reach its equilibrium value, and the situation will be like that described in our third case. The important aspect of the third case—the equilibrium situation —is that, for it to occur, desired spending on NNP must equal NNP. (Of course, the equilibrium value of NNP will change if the consumption function or the level of desired investment changes.)

A Graphical Analysis

Some people see things more clearly when they are presented in graphs rather than tables. Let's show again that the equilibrium level of NNP is at the point where desired spending on NNP equals NNP, but now using a graph. Since disposable income equals net national product in this simple case, we can plot consumption expenditure (on the vertical axis) versus net national product (on the horizontal axis), as shown in Figure 9.5. This is the consumption function. Also, we can plot the sum of consumption expenditures and investment expenditures against NNP, as shown in Figure

Figure 9.5
Determination of Equilibrium Value of Net National Product

The consumption function is **C**, and the sum of consumption and investment expenditure is **C + I**. The equilibrium value of NNP is at the point where the **C + I** line intersects the 45-degree line, here $1,100 billion. The **C + I** line shows aggregate demand and the 45-degree line shows aggregate supply.

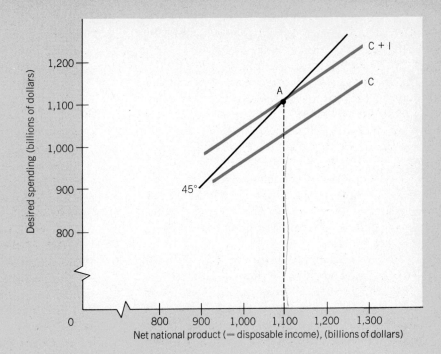

9.5. This relationship, shown by the *C + I* line, indicates the level of total desired spending on net national product for various amounts of NNP. Finally, we can plot a 45-degree line, as shown in Figure 9.5. This line contains all points where total desired spending on net national product equals net national product.

The equilibrium level of net national product will be at the point where total desired spending on NNP equals NNP. Consequently, the *equilibrium level of NNP will be at the point on the horizontal axis where the C + I line intersects the 45-degree line—$1,100 billion in Figure 9.5.* Under the conditions assumed here, no other level of NNP can be maintained for any considerable period of time. Let's begin by proving that the point where the *C + I* line intersects the 45-degree line is indeed the point where desired spending on NNP equals NNP. This is easy, since a 45-degree line is, by construction, a line that includes all points where the amount on the horizontal axis equals the

amount on the vertical axis. In this case, desired spending on NNP is on the vertical axis and NNP is on the horizontal axis. Thus, at point A, the point where the *C + I* line intersects the 45-degree line, desired spending on NNP must equal NNP, because such a point is on the 45-degree line.

Next, let's see why the equilibrium level of NNP must be at $1,100 billion, the point on the horizontal axis where the *C + I* line intersects the 45-degree line. If NNP exceeds $1,100 billion, the *C + I* line lies below the 45-degree line. Since the *C + I* line shows how much people desire to spend with a particular level of disposable income, this shows that total desired spending on NNP is less than NNP. Consequently, some production will not be sold, inventories will build up, production will be cut back, and NNP will decrease. If NNP is less than $1,100 billion, the *C + I* line lies above the 45-degree line, which shows that total desired spending on NNP is greater than NNP. Consequently, inventories will decrease, production will be stepped up, and NNP will increase. Thus, since NNP tends to fall when it exceeds $1,100 billion, and to rise when it falls short of $1,100 billion, its equilibrium value must be $1,100 billion.

Saving and Investment: Desired and Actual

Another way to describe the conditions under which NNP is at its equilibrium level is to say that *desired saving must equal desired investment.* This is just another way to say that desired spending on NNP must equal NNP. To see this, note that desired spending on NNP equals desired consumption plus desired investment. This is obvious from Figure 9.5, since the desired spending line $(C + I)$ equals the desired consumption line (C) + the desired investment line (I). Thus, if we subtract desired consumption from desired spending on NNP, we get desired investment. Next, note that NNP equals desired consumption plus desired saving. This is obvious from the fact, noted in a previous section, that people must save whatever

amounts of their income they do not consume. Thus, if we subtract desired consumption from NNP, we get desired saving. Consequently, if desired spending on NNP equals NNP, it follows that desired spending on NNP minus desired consumption must equal NNP minus desired consumption—which means that desired investment must equal desired saving.

From this proposition, it follows that we can find the equilibrium value of NNP by plotting the saving function and finding the value of NNP where desired saving equals desired investment. For example, based on the situation described in Table 9.2, the savings function (SS') is as shown in Figure 9.6. The value of desired investment is $90 billion, which is represented by the horizontal line II'. Clearly, desired saving is equal to desired investment at point B, where NNP is equal to $1,100 billion. Of course, whether we use the sort of analysis shown in Figure 9.5 (based on the equilibrium condition that desired spending on NNP must equal NNP) or the sort shown in Figure 9.6 (based on the equilibrium condition that desired investment must equal desired saving), the answer —the equilibrium level of NNP—must be the

Figure 9.6
Determination of Equilibrium Value of Net National Product

The saving function is *SS'* and the investment function is *II'*. The equilibrium value of NNP is at the point where *SS'* interects *II'*, which here is $1,100 billion.

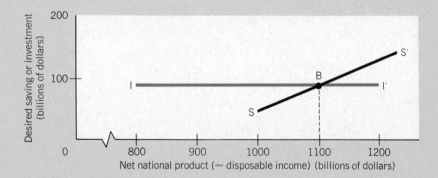

same (in this case, $1,100 billion).[6]

Why bother to look at the determination of NNP in terms of desired saving and desired investment? After all, as we just stated, we can get the same answer by comparing desired spending on NNP with actual NNP. One important reason for looking at the determination of NNP in terms of desired saving and desired investment is that it helps to lay bare the reasons why equilibrium NNP may be different from the level of NNP that would result in reasonably full employment at reasonably stable prices. As we pointed out in our discussion of the flaws in the classical view of unemployment, these reasons revolve about the fact that desired saving and desired investment are carried out by different parts of society and for different reasons. Households do much of the saving. They abstain from consuming now in order to provide for retirement, college educations for their children, emergencies, and other ways of consuming later. Firms, on the other hand, do most of the investing. They build plants and equipment and expand their inventories in response to profit opportunities. Because of this cleavage between the savers and the investors, there is no assurance that desired saving will equal desired investment at a level of NNP that results in reasonably full employment at reasonably stable prices.

Finally, it must be recognized that, whether or not desired saving equals desired investment, *actual saving must always equal actual investment*. In other words, although the amount people *set out to save* during a particular year may not equal the amount firms *set out to invest*, the *actual amount saved* will always equal the *actual amount invested*.

This must be true because, as pointed out in the previous chapter, NNP has to equal consumption plus net investment;[7] and it also has to equal consumption plus saving. Subtracting consumption from each of these expressions for NNP, saving must equal investment. To see why, consider the case where NNP is $1,050 billion. In this case, desired saving is $70 billion but desired investment is $90 billion. How does it turn out that actual saving equals actual investment? As pointed out in the previous section, there is an unintended **disinvestment** (i.e., negative investment) of − $20 billion in inventories if NNP is $1,050 billion. (Recall from Chapter 8 that a buildup of inventories is a form of investment, so a $1 billion increase in inventories equals $1 billion of investment.) Thus, the actual investment is $90 billion (in intended investment) minus $20 billion (in unintended disinvestment), or $70 billion. Actual saving equals desired saving, or $70 billion. Thus, actual saving equals actual investment.

To check your understanding, see if you can describe the process whereby actual investment is brought into equality with actual saving in the case where NNP is $1,150 billion. The answer is given below (footnote 8).[8] If you arrived at the right solution, you worked out for yourself one of the important conclusions of national income theory: actual saving must equal actual investment even though desired saving does not equal desired investment.

[6] To prove to yourself that this must be the case, note three things. (1) The saving function in Figure 9.6 plots the vertical distance between the 45-degree line and the consumption function in Figure 9.5, since saving here equals NNP less consumption. (2) The investment function in Figure 9.6 plots the vertical distance between the $C + I$ line and the consumption function in Figure 9.5, since $C + I$ less C obviously is I. (3) In Figure 9.5, the equilibrium value of NNP is at the point where these two vertical distances are equal, which means it must be at the point where the saving and investment functions intersect.

[7] Recall from Chapter 8 that net national product equals consumption plus government expenditures plus net exports plus net investment. Since government expenditures and net exports are assumed to be zero, it follows that net national product equals consumption plus net investment.

[8] In the case where NNP equals $1,150 billion, desired saving is $110 billion. This is shown in Table 9.2. Desired investment is $90 billion, but there is an unintended increase in inventories of $20 billion. Thus, actual investment turns out to equal $110 billion, which equals actual saving.

Note that we assume here that actual saving will equal desired saving and that unintended changes in inventories will make actual investment conform to actual and desired saving. There are other ways for adjustments to take place. The important thing is that, one way or another, actual saving will equal actual investment.

The Multiplier: A Geometric Formulation

In Chapter 8, we pointed out that investment is a particularly volatile form of expenditure. It is subject to large variations from year to year. For example, in 1955, net private investment was close to $80 billion, and in 1958, it fell to about $60 billion. Looking at the highly simplified model we have constructed, what is the effect of a change in the amount of desired investment? Specifically, if firms increase their desired investment by $1 billion, what effect will this increase have on the equilibrium value of net national product?

Let's begin by noting once again that, if NNP is at its equilibrium level, desired saving must equal desired investment. Then let's apply the sort of graphical analysis that we used in the previous section to determine equilibrium NNP. If the saving function in our simplified economy is SS' in Figure 9.7 and desired investment is shown by the horizontal line II', what will be the effect of a $1 billion increase in desired investment on equilibrium NNP? Before the increase in desired investment,

equilibrium NNP was equal to Y_0. The increase of $1 billion in desired investment will shift the II' line up by $1 billion, to the new position shown in Figure 9.7. This shift in the II' line will increase the equilibrium level of NNP, but by how much?

The resulting increase in equilibrium NNP, ΔY, can be derived by the following geometrical reasoning. First, the slope of SS' times the change in equilibrium NNP must equal the increase in desired investment, $1 billion. This follows from the definition of the slope of a line: The slope of SS' equals the vertical distance between any two points on SS' divided by the horizontal difference between them. The vertical distance between points A and B in Figure 9.7 is the increase in desired investment (ΔI), and the horizontal distance between points A and B is the change in equilibrium NNP (ΔY). Consequently, the change in equilibrium NNP must equal the increase in desired investment divided by the slope of SS'. Since the slope of SS' is the marginal propensity to save—as pointed out in a previous section—it follows that *the change in equilibrium NNP equals the increase in desired investment divided by the marginal propensity to save*. Thus, a $1 billion increase in desired invest-

**Figure 9.7
The Multiplier**

If investment increases by ΔI, the equilibrium value of NNP increases by ΔY. Clearly $\dfrac{\Delta I}{\Delta Y}$ equals the slope of the saving function between A and B. Since this slope equals the marginal propensity to save (MPS), $\dfrac{\Delta I}{\Delta Y} = MPS$. Thus, $\Delta Y = \dfrac{\Delta I}{MPS}$ and if $\Delta I = 1$, $\Delta Y = \dfrac{1}{MPS}$.

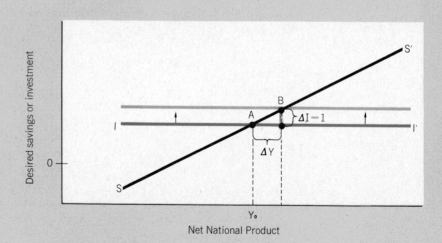

ment will result in an increase in equilibrium NNP of $\left(\frac{1}{MPS}\right)$ billions of dollars, where MPS is the marginal propensity to save.

This is a very important conclusion. To understand more clearly what it means, let's consider a couple of numerical examples. For example, if the marginal propensity to save is ⅓, a $1 billion increase in desired investment will increase equilibrium NNP by 1 ÷ ⅓ billion dollars; that is, by $3 billion. Or take a somewhat more complicated case. If the consumption function is as shown in Table 9.1, what is the effect of an increase in desired investment from $90 billion to $91 billion? The first step in answering this question is to determine the marginal propensity to consume —which is 0.60 in Table 9.1. Then it is a simple matter to determine the marginal propensity to save—which must be 1 − 0.60 or 0.40. Finally, since the marginal propensity to save is 0.40, it follows from the previous paragraph that a $1 billion increase in desired investment must result in an increase in equilibrium NNP of $\frac{1}{0.40}$ billion dollars. That is, equilibrium NNP will increase by $2½ billion.

Since a dollar of extra desired investment results in $\left(\frac{1}{MPS}\right)$ dollars of extra NNP, $\left(\frac{1}{MPS}\right)$ is called the **multiplier.** If you want to estimate the effect of a given increase in desired investment on NNP, all you have to do is multiply the increase in desired investment by $\left(\frac{1}{MPS}\right)$: the result will be the resulting increase in NNP. Moreover, it is easy to show that the same multiplier holds for decreases in desired investment as well as for increases. That is, a dollar less of desired investment results in $\left(\frac{1}{MPS}\right)$ dollars less of NNP. Consequently, if you want to estimate the effect of a given change in desired investment (positive or negative) on NNP, all you have to do is multiply the change in desired investment by $\left(\frac{1}{MPS}\right)$.

It is important to note that, since MPS is less than one, the *multiplier must be greater than one.* In other words, an increase in desired investment of $1 will result in an increase in NNP of more than $1. This means, of course, that NNP is relatively sensitive to changes in desired investment. Moreover, since the multiplier is the reciprocal of the marginal propensity to save, the smaller the marginal propensity to save, the higher the multiplier—and the more sensitive is NNP to changes in desired investment. As we shall see, this result has important implications for public policy. For example, because our system of taxes and transfer payments tends to increase the marginal propensity to save out of NNP, the destabilizing effect of a sharp change in investment expenditures is reduced.

The Multiplier: An Algebraic Interpretation[9]

Equations speak more clearly to some than words, and so for those with a taste for (elementary) algebra, we will show how the results of the previous section can be derived algebraically. If you have trouble with equations, or if you feel that you already understand the material, go on to the next section. We begin by recalling that the equilibrium value of NNP is attained at the point where NNP equals desired spending on NNP. This condition can be expressed in the following equation:

$$NNP = C + I, \tag{9.1}$$

which says that NNP must equal desired expenditure on consumption goods (C) plus desired investment (I). Since desired consumption expenditures plus desired investment equals desired spending on NNP, it follows that this equation states that NNP must equal desired spending on NNP.

Next, let's introduce a friend from a few pages back, the consumption function. The consumption function in Table 9.1 can be represented by the

[9] This section is optional and can be omitted without loss of continuity.

Figure 9.8
Consumption Function

The consumption function is
derived from the data in Table
9.1. The marginal propensity to
consume is 0.6, so the slope is 0.6.

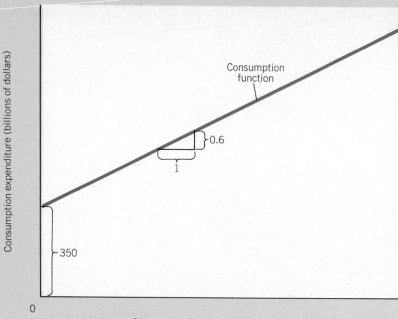

following equation:

$$C = 350 + 0.6D \tag{9.2}$$

which says that desired consumption equals $350
billion plus 0.6 times disposable income (D). Figure 9.8 shows the consumption function. As you
can see, $350 billion is the intercept on the vertical
axis, while 0.6 is the slope of the consumption
function. Since—as we noted in a previous section
—the slope of the consumption function equals
the marginal propensity to consume, 0.6 equals the
marginal propensity to consume.

The next step is to substitute the right-hand side
of equation (9.2)—350 + .6D—for C in Equation
(9.1). The result is:

$$NNP = 350 + 0.6D + I. \tag{9.3}$$

But recall that disposable income is equal to NNP
in our simplified economy. Consequently, we can
substitute NNP for D in this equation, to get

$$NNP = 350 + 0.6NNP + I. \tag{9.4}$$

And going a step further, we can subtract 0.6
times NNP from both sides of Equation (9.4),
which gives

$$NNP - 0.6NNP = 350 + I, \tag{9.5}$$

or, collecting terms,

$$0.4NNP = 350 + I. \tag{9.6}$$

Finally, dividing both sides by 0.4, we have

$$NNP = \frac{350}{0.4} + \frac{I}{0.4}. \tag{9.7}$$

Now we can see what happens to NNP if there
is a $1 billion increase in I. In other words, suppose that I is increased from some amount, X bil-

lion, to $(X + 1)$ billion. How much will this increase NNP? From Equation (9.7), it is clear that NNP will equal

$$\frac{350}{0.4} + \frac{X}{0.4}$$

if desired investment equals $X billion. It is also clear from Equation (9.7) that NNP will equal

$$\frac{350}{0.4} + \frac{(X + 1)}{0.4}$$

if desired investment is equal to $(X + 1)$ billion. Consequently the increase in NNP due to the $1 billion increase in desired investment is equal to

$$\left[\frac{350}{0.4} + \frac{(X + 1)}{0.4}\right] - \left[\frac{350}{0.4} + \frac{X}{0.4}\right]$$
$$= \frac{X + 1}{0.4} - \frac{X}{0.4} = \frac{X}{0.4} + \frac{1}{0.4} - \frac{X}{0.4} = \frac{1}{0.4}$$

That is, a $1 billion increase in desired investment will result in an increase of $\frac{1}{0.4}$ billion dollars in NNP. Recalling that 0.6 is the marginal propensity to consume—and that the sum of the marginal propensity to consume and the marginal propensity to save equals one—it follows that *a $1 billion increase in desired investment will result in an increase of* $\left(\frac{1}{MPS}\right)$ *billions of dollars in NNP, where MPS is the marginal propensity to save—0.4 in this case.*

This is precisely the same conclusion we arrived at in the previous section. Thus, we have derived the value of the multiplier by an algebraic route rather than the geometric route used before.

The Multiplier and the Spending Process

Having shown in two ways that the multiplier equals $\frac{1}{MPS}$, we are in danger of beating a dead horse to death if we show it in still a third way. However, we don't yet have much feel for the process that results in the multiplier's being what it is. In other words, leaving the realm of graphs and equations, what process in the real world insures that a $1 billion change in desired investment results in a change of $\left(\frac{1}{MPS}\right)$ billions of dollars in equilibrium NNP? It is worthwhile spelling this out in some detail.

If there is a $1 billion increase in desired investment, the effects can be divided into a number of stages. In the first stage, firms spend an additional $1 billion on plant and equipment. This extra $1 billion is received by workers and suppliers as extra income, which results in a second stage of extra spending on final goods and services. How much of their extra $1 billion in income will the workers and suppliers spend? If the marginal propensity to consume is 0.6, they will spend 0.6 times $1 billion, or $.6 billion. This extra expenditure of $.6 billion is received by firms and disbursed to workers, suppliers, and owners as extra income, bringing about a third stage of extra spending on final goods and services. How much of this extra income of $.6 billion will be spent? Since the marginal propensity to consume is 0.6, they will spend 60 percent of this $.6 billion, or $.36 billion. This extra expenditure of $.36 billion is received by firms and disbursed to workers, suppliers, and owners as extra income, which results in a fourth stage of spending, then a fifth stage, a sixth stage, and so on.

Table 9.3 shows the total increase in expenditure on final goods and services arising from the original $1 billion increase in desired investment. The total increase in expenditures is the increase in the first stage, plus the increase in the second stage, plus the increase in the third stage, etc. Since there is an endless chain of stages, we cannot list all the increases. But because the successive increases in spending get smaller and smaller, we can determine their sum, which in this case is $2.5 billion. Thus, the $1 billion increase in desired investment results—after all stages of the spending

Table 9.3

The Multiplier Process

Stage	Amount of extra spending
1	$1.00 billion
2	.60 billion
3	.36 billion
4	.22 billion
5	.13 billion
6	.08 billion
7	.05 billion
8	.03 billion
9 and beyond	.03 billion
Total	$2.50 billion

and re-spending process have worked themselves out—in a $2.5 billion increase in total expenditures on final goods and services. In other words, it results in a $2.5 billion increase in NNP.

It is important to note that this spending and re-spending process results in the same multiplier as indicated in previous sections. This happens because, if 0.6 is the marginal propensity to consume, a $1 billion increase in desired investment will result in increased total spending of $(1 + .6 + .6^2 + .6^3 + \ldots)$ billions of dollars. This is evident from Table 9.3, which shows that the increased spending in the first stage is $1 billion, the increased spending in the second stage is $.6 billion, the increased spending in the third stage is $.6^2$ billion, and so on. But it can be shown that $(1 + .6 + .6^2 + .6^3 + \ldots) = \frac{1}{1 - .6}$.[10] Consequently, since $(1 - .6)$ is equal to the marginal propensity to save, a $1 billion increase in desired investment results in an increase of $\left(\frac{1}{MPS}\right)$ billions of dollars in NNP. Thus, however we look at it, the answer remains the same: the multiplier equals $\left(\frac{1}{MPS}\right)$.

Application of the Multiplier: A Case Study [11]

Having discussed the modern theory of the determination of NNP in the abstract, it is time to look at a specific application of this theory. Consider a famous incident that occurred at the end of World War II. Economists, using the best models then available, had been able to forecast the pace of the economy reasonably well during the war. When the war was coming to an end, they were charged with forecasting the level of national product in 1946, the year immediately after the war. This was an important task, since the government was worried that the economy might suffer severe postwar unemployment. The Great Depression of the 1930s was a recent—and still bitter—memory.

A group of economists in Washington was given the responsibility for this forecast. They made it in terms of gross national product, not net national product, but they used essentially the same theory as that discussed in previous sections. To forecast

[11] This account is based on Michael Sapir, "Review of Economic Forecasts for the Transition Period," *Conference on Research in Income and Wealth,* Volume XI, National Bureau of Economic Research, 1949; and Lawrence Klein, "A Post-Mortem on Transition Predictions of National Product," *Journal of Political Economy,* August 1946.

[10] To see this, let's divide 1 by $(1 - m)$, where m is less than 1. Using the time-honored rules of long division, we find that

$$1 - m \overline{\smash{\big)}\ 1} \quad \begin{array}{l} 1 + m + m^2 + m^3 + \cdots \\ \hline \end{array}$$

$$\begin{array}{r} 1 - m \\ \hline m \\ m - m^2 \\ \hline m^2 \\ m^2 - m^3 \\ \hline m^3 \\ m^3 - m^4 \\ \hline m^4 \\ \vdots \end{array}$$

Thus, letting $m = 0.6$, it follows that 1 divided by $(1 - .6)$ equals $1 + .6 + .6^2 + .6^3 + \ldots$

gross national product in 1946, these Washington economists began by using prewar data to estimate the consumption function. Then they estimated the amount of investment that would take place in 1946. Finally, to forecast gross national product in 1946, they performed the sort of calculations shown in Equation (9.7). In other words, they computed the multiplier $\left(\dfrac{1}{MPS}\right)$ and multiplied it by their estimate of investment for 1946. Then they added an amount analogous to the first term on the right-hand side of Equation (9.7); and since their model—unlike ours—included government spending and taxes, other calculations, which will be discussed in Chapter 10, had to be made as well. The result was a forecast of a gross national product in 1946 of about $170 billion. This forecast received considerable attention and publicity inside and outside the government.

Before discussing the accuracy of this forecast, an important empirical question must be considered: in real-world studies like this, what is the estimated value of the multiplier? Judging from our findings in the previous sections, we would guess a figure of at least 2½, since the marginal propensity to consume should be at least 0.6. But these results are based on the assumption of no taxation. For reasons discussed in Chapter 10, the multiplier will be lower if there is taxation. Including the effects of taxation, most estimates of the multiplier seem to center around a value of 2. But these estimates can vary considerably, depending, of course, on the shape of the consumption function and other factors.

Multiplier Effects of Shifts in the Consumption Function

Before discussing the accuracy of this forecast, we must also look at the effects of shifts in the consumption function. So far, we have been concerned only with the effects of changes in desired investment on NNP. We have shown—repeatedly and

in various ways—that changes in desired investment have an amplified effect on NNP, the extent of the amplification being measured by the multiplier. But it is important to note at this point that a shift in the consumption function will also have such an amplified effect on NNP. For example, in Figure 9.9, if the consumption function shifts from CC' to $\phi\phi'$, this means that, at each level of disposable income, consumers desire to spend $1 billion more on consumption goods and services than they did before. It is easy to show that *this $1 billion upward shift in the consumption function will have precisely the same effect on equilibrium NNP as a $1 billion increase in desired investment.*

For those of more mathematical bent, it may be worthwhile to prove that this is the case. Others can skip this paragraph without loss of continuity. Let's recall that in Equation (9.7), we showed that the equilibrium value of NNP equals

$$\frac{350}{0.4} + \frac{I}{0.4},$$

where 350 is the intercept on the vertical axis of the consumption function, 0.4 is the marginal propensity to save, and I is desired investment. A $1 billion shift upward in the consumption function causes the intercept to increase from its former amount, $350 billion, to $351 billion. What is the effect of this increase in the intercept on the equilibrium value of NNP? If the intercept is $350 billion, the equilibrium value of NNP will equal

$$\frac{350}{0.4} + \frac{I}{0.4}.$$

If the intercept is $351 billion, the equilibrium value of NNP will equal

$$\frac{351}{0.4} + \frac{I}{0.4}.$$

Consequently, the increase in NNP from the $1 billion upward shift in the consumption function is

180

Figure 9.9
Shift in the Consumption Function

If the consumption function shifts from *CC′* to *øø′* this means that, at each level of disposable income, consumers desire to spend $1 billion more on consumption goods and services. Such a *shift* is quite different from a *movement along* a given consumption function, such as from *A* to *B*.

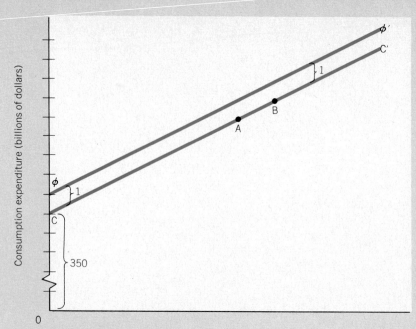

$$\left[\frac{351}{0.4} + \frac{I}{0.4}\right] - \left[\frac{350}{0.4} + \frac{I}{0.4}\right] = \frac{351}{0.4} - \frac{350}{0.4} = \frac{1}{0.4}.$$

That is, a $1 billion upward shift in the consumption function results in an increase of $\frac{1}{0.4}$ billions of dollars in NNP. Recalling that $0.4 = MPS$, it follows that *a $1 billion upward shift in the consumption function will result in an increase of* $\left(\frac{1}{MPS}\right)$ *billions of dollars in NNP.*

Since a $1 billion increase in desired investment also results in an increase of $\left(\frac{1}{MPS}\right)$ billions of dollars in NNP, the effect of a $1 billion change in desired investment is the same as a $1 billion shift in the consumption function. Both have the same multiplier effects. Thus, shifts in the consumption function—from changes in tastes, assets, prices, population, etc.—will have a magnified effect on NNP. In other words, NNP is sensitive

to shifts in the consumption function in the same way that it is sensitive to changes in desired investment. This is an important point. Finally, to prevent misunderstanding, it must be clear that a *shift* in the consumption function is quite different from a *movement along* a given consumption function. (An example of the latter would be the movement from point *A* to point *B* in Figure 9.9.) We are concerned here with shifts in the consumption function, not movements along a given consumption function.

The Accuracy of the Postwar Forecasts

We can now pick up the account of the GNP forecasts in 1946 where we left off several paragraphs back. The government forecasters' estimate of a GNP of about $170 billion caused a severe chill in many parts of the government, as well as among businessmen and consumers. A GNP of only about $170 billion would have meant a great deal of unemployment in 1946. Indeed, according to some predictions, about 8 million people would have been unemployed in the first quarter of 1946.

Unfortunately for the forecasters—but fortunately for the nation—the GNP in 1946 turned out to be not $170 billion, but about $190 billion. And unemployment was only about ⅓ of the forecasted amount. These are very large errors in practically anyone's book—so big that they continue to embarrass the economics profession 30 years later. Of course, our knowledge of the economy has expanded considerably over the past 30 years, and an error of this magnitude is much less likely now. Moreover, even at the end of World War II, some economists forecasted GNP in 1946 pretty well. Not everyone, by any means, agreed with the forecast of $170 billion. But it is worth bearing this notable mistake in mind when considering economic forecasts of this sort. Economics is not as exact a science as physics or chemistry—and mischief can result if one assumes otherwise.

What went wrong in the Washington economists' forecasts? To a considerable extent, the answer lies in the topic of the previous section: a shift in the consumption function. When World War II ended, households had a great deal of liquid assets on hand. They had saved money during the war. There had been rationing of many kinds of goods, and other goods—like automobiles or refrigerators—could not be obtained at all. When the war ended and these goods flowed back on the market, consumers spent more of their income on consumption goods than in the previous years. In other words, there was a pronounced upward shift of the consumption function.

To see why this shift in the consumption function caused the forecasters to underestimate GNP in 1946, recall from the previous section that an upward shift of $1 billion in the consumption function will result in an increase of $\left(\dfrac{1}{MPS}\right)$ billions of dollars in national product. Bearing this in mind,

suppose the forecasters assumed that the consumption function remained fixed, when in fact there was a $8 billion shift upward. Then if the multiplier—$\dfrac{1}{MPS}$—were 2½, national product would turn out to be $20 billion higher than the forecasters would expect. (Since $\dfrac{1}{MPS}$ is assumed to be 2½, national product will increase $2.5 billion for every $1 billion shift in the consumption function, so an $8 billion shift in the consumption function will result in a $20 billion increase in national product.) Of course, these figures—a multiplier of 2½ and an $8 billion shift in the consumption function—are only illustrative, not precise estimates of the actual situation. For one thing, as noted above, the multiplier is wrong because it assumes no taxation. But they indicate the sort of thing that occurred, and they show dramatically the effects of a shift in the consumption function.

Induced Investment

Before concluding this chapter, one final point is worth noting. In previous sections, we have assumed that desired net investment is a certain amount, regardless of the level of NNP. This assumption has been reflected in the fact that the investment function—for example, in Figures 9.6 and 9.7—is horizontal. Although this assumption may be a useful first approximation, it neglects the fact that firms are much more likely to invest in plant and equipment when NNP is high than when it is low. After all, NNP measures output; and the greater the output of the economy, the greater the pressure on the capacity of existing plant and equipment—and the greater the pressure to expand this capacity by investing in additional plant and equipment.

It is relatively simple to extend the theory to take account of the fact that, to some extent, increases in NNP may increase desired investment. Rather than portraying the investment function

182

**Figure 9.10
Determination of Equilibrium
Value of Net National Product,
with Induced Investment**

If the level of investment depends
on NNP, the investment function,
II', is positively sloped, and the
equilibrium level of NNP is at the
point where *II'* intersects *SS'*,
the saving function.

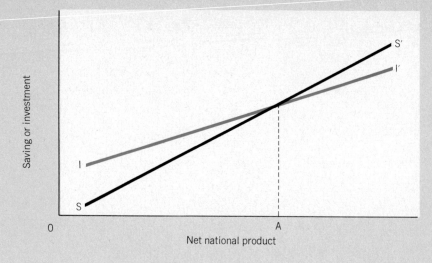

as a horizontal line, we need only assume that it
is positively sloped, as in Figure 9.10. Then, as
before, the equilibrium level of NNP is at the
point where the saving function intersects the investment function—that is, at point A, the point
where desired saving equals desired investment.
Much more will be said about *induced investment*
—investment stimulated by increases in NNP—
in Chapter 11.

Summary

Until the 1930s, most economists were convinced
that the price system, left to its own devices, would
insure the maintenance of full employment. They
thought it unlikely that total spending would be
too small to purchase the full-employment level of
output, and argued that prices would be cut if any
problem of this sort developed. A notable exception
was Karl Marx, who felt that the capitalistic system would suffer from worse and worse unemployment, leading to its eventual collapse. John
Maynard Keynes, in the 1930s, developed a theory
to explain how the capitalist economic system remained mired in the Great Depression, with its

tragically high levels of unemployment. Contrary
to the classical economists, Keynes concluded that
there was no automatic mechanism in a capitalistic
system to generate and maintain full employment—
or, at least, to generate it quickly enough to be
relied on in practice. Keynes's ideas form the core
of the modern theory of output and employment.

The consumption function—the relation between
consumption expenditures and disposable income—
is at the heart of this theory. There have been
many studies of the consumption function, some
based on cross-section data, some based on time-
series data. From the consumption function, one
can determine the marginal propensity to consume, which is the proportion of an extra dollar
of income that is spent on consumption, as well as
the saving function (the relationship between
total saving and disposable income) and the marginal propensity to save (the proportion of an
extra dollar of income that is saved).

The equilibrium level of net national product
will be at the point where desired spending on
NNP equals NNP. If desired spending on NNP
exceeds NNP, NNP will tend to increase. If
desired spending on NNP falls short of NNP,
NNP will tend to fall. Another way to describe
this equilibrium condition is to say that NNP is
at its equilibrium level if desired saving equals

desired investment. Because of the cleavage between savers and investors, there is no assurance that desired saving will equal desired investment at a level of NNP that results in reasonably full employment at stable prices. But actual saving and actual investment always must turn out to be equal.

A $1 billion change in desired investment will result in a change in equilibrium NNP of $\left(\frac{1}{MPS}\right)$ billions of dollars, where MPS is the marginal propensity to save. In other words, the multiplier is $\frac{1}{MPS}$. The multiplier can be interpreted in terms of—and derived from—the successive stages of the spending process. An example of the use of the multiplier was the formulation at the end of World War II of GNP forecasts for 1946. A shift in the consumption function will also have an amplified effect on NNP, a $1 billion shift in the consumption function resulting in a change of $\left(\frac{1}{MPS}\right)$ billions of dollars in NNP. To a considerable extent, the large error in government forecasts of GNP in 1946 was due to an unanticipated shift in the consumption function. Responding to large accumulated wartime savings and pent-up wartime demands, consumers spent more of their income on consumption goods than in previous years.

CONCEPTS FOR REVIEW

Consumption function
Marginal propensity to consume
Average propensity to consume

Saving function
Marginal propensity to save
Multiplier
Induced investment

Shifts in the consumption function
Investment function
45-degree line

QUESTIONS FOR DISCUSSION AND REVIEW

1. Describe in detail the mechanisms that push NNP toward its equilibrium value. Must the equilibrium value be such that full employment results? Why or why not?

2. What assumptions are made in this chapter concerning the economy's position on the aggregate supply curve? Explain the significance of these assumptions.

3. Assume that the consumption function is as follows:

Disposable Income (billions of dollars)	Consumption Expenditure (billions of dollars)
900	750
1,000	800
1,100	850
1,200	900
1,300	950
1,400	1,000

a. How much will be saved if disposable income is $1,000 billion?
b. What is the average propensity to consume if disposable income is $1,000 billion?
c. What is the marginal propensity to consume if disposable income is between $1,000 billion and $1,100 billion?
d. What is the marginal propensity to save if disposable income is between $1,000 billion and $1,100 billion?

4. Including the effects of taxation, most estimates of the multiplier are around 5. True or False?

CHAPTER 10

Fiscal Policy and National Output

During the past 40 years, the idea that the government's power to spend and tax should be used to stabilize the economy—that is, to reduce unemployment and fight inflation—has gained acceptance throughout the world. In many countries, including the United States, this acceptance was delayed by a fear of government deficits and of increases in the public debt, but with the passage of time these fears have receded or been put in proper perspective. However, time has also revealed that fiscal policy is no panacea. Witness the severe inflationary pressures that have plagued the American economy in recent years. Both the power and the limitations of fiscal policy must be recognized.

This chapter presents a first look at fiscal policy, in the context of the simplest Keynesian model. In effect, we assume here that the money supply is fixed, and that the interest rate is not affected by changes in total desired spending (or that, if it is affected, it has little effect on total desired spending). In Chapter 15, a more sophisticated analysis of fiscal policy is presented, money and financial assets being included in the model.

Government Expenditures and Net National Product

In the previous chapter, we showed how the equilibrium level of net national product was determined in a simplified economy without government spending or taxation. We must now extend this theory to include government spending and taxation, an important extension in view of the large amounts of government spending and taxes in the modern economy. As we shall see, the results form the basis for much of our nation's past and present economic policy. In this section, we incorporate government spending into the theory of the determination of net national product. In so doing, we assume that government spending will not affect the consumption function or the level of desired investment. In other words, we assume that government spending does not reduce or increase private desires to spend out of each level of income. (Government includes here federal, state, and local.)

Suppose that the government purchases $50 billion worth of goods and services and that it will purchase this amount whatever the level of NNP. (Note that only government purchases, not transfer payments, are included here.) Clearly, adding this public expenditure to the private expenditures on consumption and investment results in a higher total level of desired spending. In an economy with government spending (but no net exports), total desired spending on NNP equals desired consumption expenditure plus desired in-

Figure 10.1 Determination of Net National Product, Including Government Expenditure

The consumption function is *C*, the sum of consumption and investment expenditures is *C + I*, and the sum of consumption, investment, and government expenditures is *C + I + G*. The equilibrium value of NNP is at the point where the *C + I + G* line intersects the 45-degree line, which here is $1,225 billion. The *C + I + G* line shows aggregate demand, and the 45-degree line shows aggregate supply.

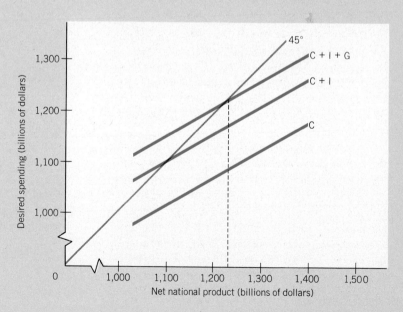

Figure 10.2
Effects on Equilibrium Net National Product of $5 Billion Increase and Decrease in Government Expenditure

A $5 billion increase raises the equilibrium value of NNP from $1,225 billion to $1,237.5 billion. A $5 billion decrease reduces the equilibrium value of NNP from $1,225 billion to $1,212.5 billion.

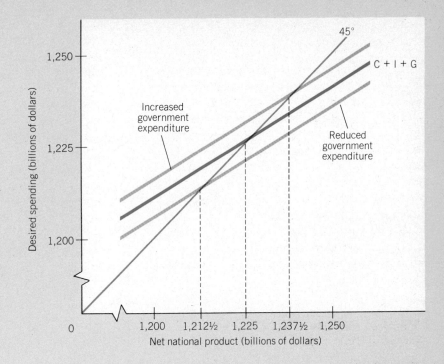

vestment expenditure plus desired government expenditure. Thus, since an increase in government expenditure (like increases in consumption or investment expenditure) results in an increase in desired spending on NNP, and since the equilibrium value of net national product is at the point where desired spending on NNP equals NNP, it follows that an increase in government expenditure, as well as the induced increase in private spending, brings about an increase in the equilibrium value of NNP.

To see the effects of government expenditure on the equilibrium value of NNP, we can use a simple graph similar to those introduced in the previous chapter. We begin by plotting the consumption function, which shows desired consumption expenditure at each level of NNP (since NNP equals disposable income under our assumptions): the result is line C in Figure 10.1. Then, as in Figure 9.5, we can plot the sum of desired consumption expenditure and investment expenditure

at each level of NNP: the result is line $C + I$. Next, we plot the sum of desired consumption expenditure, investment expenditure, and government expenditure at each level of NNP, to get line $C + I + G$. Since the $C + I + G$ line shows total desired spending on NNP, and since, as we stressed in the previous chapter, the equilibrium value of NNP is at the point where desired spending on NNP equals NNP, it follows that the equilibrium value of NNP is $1,225 billion, since this is the point at which the $C + I + G$ line intersects the 45-degree line.

What happens to the equilibrium level of NNP if government expenditure increases? Figure 10.2 shows the results of a $5 billion increase in government spending. Obviously, the increased government expenditure will raise the $C + I + G$ line by $5 billion, as the figure shows. Since the $C + I + G$ line must intersect the 45-degree line at a higher level of NNP, increases in government expenditure result in increases in the equilibrium level of NNP. In Figure 10.2, the $5 billion increase in government expenditure raises the equilibrium value of NNP from $1,225 billion to $1,237.5 billion. Figure 10.2 also shows what happens when government spending goes down by $5 billion. Obviously, the $C + I + G$ line must be lowered by $5 billion. Since the $C + I + G$ line must intersect the 45-degree line at a lower level of NNP, decreases in government expenditure result in decreases in the equilibrium level of NNP. In Figure 10.2, the $5 billion decrease in government expenditure reduces the equilibrium value of NNP from $1,225 billion to $1,212.5 billion.

It is essential to learn how sensitive the equilibrium level of NNP is to changes in government spending. In the previous chapter, we found that a $1 billion change in desired investment—or a $1 billion shift in the consumption function—results in a change in equilibrium NNP of $\left(\frac{1}{MPS}\right)$ billions of dollars, where MPS is the marginal propensity to save. The effect of a $1 billion change in government expenditure is exactly the same. In other words, *it will result in a change in equilibrium NNP of* $\left(\frac{1}{MPS}\right)$ *billion dollars. Thus, a change in government expenditure has the same multiplier effect on NNP as a change in investment or a shift in the consumption function.* For example, if the marginal propensity to consume is 0.6, an extra $1 billion in government expenditure will increase equilibrium NNP by $2.5 billion.

The mathematically inclined reader may be interested in proving that a $1 billion change in government expenditure will result in a change in equilibrium NNP of $\left(\frac{1}{MPS}\right)$ billions of dollars: Others can skip to the next section without loss of continuity. To prove this proposition, recall that the equilibrium value of NNP is at the point where desired spending—$C + I + G$—equals NNP. Thus,

$$NNP = C + I + G. \tag{10.1}$$

Assuming that the consumption function is as given in Table 9.1, it follows that

$$C = 350 + 0.6 \; NNP \tag{10.2}$$

where 0.6 is the marginal propensity to consume.[1] Substituting the right-hand side of Equation (10.2) for C in Equation (10.1), we have

$$NNP = 350 + 0.6 \; NNP + I + G \tag{10.3}$$

Thus,

$$(1 - 0.6) \; NNP = 350 + I + G$$
$$NNP = \frac{350}{0.4} + \frac{I}{0.4} + \frac{G}{0.4}. \tag{10.4}$$

What happens to NNP when G increases from $X billion to $(X + 1)$ billion? How much will this increase the equilibrium value of NNP? From Equation (10.4), it is clear that equilibrium NNP will be

$$\frac{350}{0.4} + \frac{I}{0.4} + \frac{X}{0.4}$$

if government expenditure equals $X billion. And it is equally clear from Equation (10.4) that NNP will equal

$$\frac{350}{0.4} + \frac{I}{0.4} + \frac{(X + 1)}{0.4}$$

if government expenditure is $(X + 1)$ billion. Consequently the increase in NNP due to the $1 billion increase in government spending is

$$\left[\frac{350}{0.4} + \frac{I}{0.4} + \frac{(X + 1)}{0.4}\right] - \left[\frac{350}{0.4} + \frac{I}{0.4} + \frac{X}{0.4}\right],$$

which equals

$$\frac{X + 1}{0.4} - \frac{X}{0.4} = \frac{1}{0.4}.$$

That is, a $1 billion increase in government expenditure will result in an increase of $\frac{1}{0.4}$ billion dollars of NNP—which is equal to $\left(\frac{1}{MPS}\right)$ billions

[1] Note that NNP equals disposable income. This is because there are no taxes, no transfer payments, and no undistributed corporate profits. Taxes are brought into the picture in the next section.

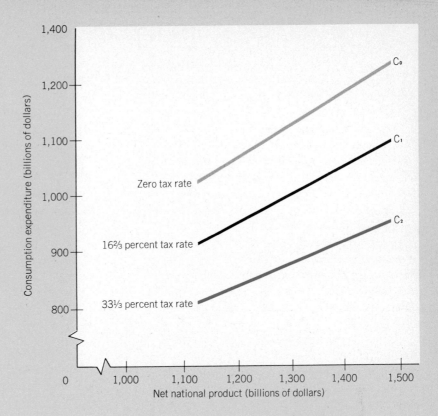

Figure 10.3
Relationship between Consumption Expenditure and Net National Product, Given Three Tax Rates

If taxes are zero, C_0 is the relationship betwen consumption expenditure and NNP. If consumers pay $16\frac{2}{3}$ percent of their income in taxes, C_1 is the relationship; and if consumers pay $33\frac{1}{3}$ percent of their income in taxes, C_2 is the relationship. Clearly, the higher the tax rate, the less consumers spend on consumption from a given NNP.

of dollars of NNP, since $0.4 = MPS$. This is what we set out to prove.

Taxation and Net National Product

The previous section added government expenditures to our theory, but it did not include taxes. Here we assume taxes to be net of transfer payments. For simplicity, it is assumed that all tax revenues stem from personal taxes. How do tax collections influence the equilibrium value of net national product? For example, if consumers pay $16\frac{2}{3}$ percent of their income to the government in taxes, what effect does this have on NNP? Clearly, the imposition of this tax means that, for each level of NNP, people have less disposable income

than they would with no taxes. In particular, disposable income now equals $83\frac{1}{3}$ percent of NNP, whereas without taxes it equaled NNP. Thus, the relationship between consumption expenditure and NNP is altered by the imposition of the tax. Before the tax was levied, the relationship was given by line C_0 in Figure 10.3; after the imposition of the tax, it is given by line C_1.

The relationship between consumption expenditure and NNP changes in this way because consumption expenditure is determined by the level of disposable income. For instance, in the case in Figure 10.3, consumption expenditure equals $350 billion plus 60 percent of disposable income. Thus, since the tax reduces the amount of disposable income at each level of NNP, it also reduces the amount of consumption expenditure at each level of NNP. In other words, since people have less aftertax income to spend at each level of NNP, they spend less on consumption goods and services at each level of NNP. This seems eminently reasonable. It is illustrated in Figure 10.3, where, at each level of NNP, consumption expenditure after the tax (given by line C_1) is less than before the tax (given by line C_0).

Because the imposition of the tax influences the relationship between consumption expenditure and NNP, it also influences the equilibrium value of NNP. As we have stressed repeatedly, the equilibrium value of NNP is at the point where desired spending on NNP equals NNP. Lines C_0 and C_1 in Figure 10.3 show desired consumption expenditure at each level of NNP, before and after the tax. Adding desired investment and government

expenditure to each of these lines, we get the total desired spending on NNP before and after the tax. The results are shown in Figure 10.4, under the assumption that the sum of desired investment and government spending equals $140 billion. The $C_0 + I + G$ line shows desired spending on NNP before the tax, while the $C_1 + I + G$ line shows desired spending on NNP after the tax.

Note that the equilibrium level of NNP is lower after the imposition of the tax than before. Specifically, as shown in Figure 10.4, it is $980 billion after the imposition of the tax and $1,225 billion before. The tax reduced the equilibrium level of NNP because it lowered the $C + I + G$ line from $C_0 + I + G$ to $C_1 + I + G$. It did this because, as pointed out above, it reduced the amount people

Figure 10.4
Determination of Equilibrium Value of Net National Product, with Zero and 16⅔ Percent Tax Rates

The tax rate influences the relationship between consumption expenditure and NNP. (C_0 is this relationship with a zero tax rate, while C_1 is the relationship with a 16⅔ percent tax rate. See Figure 10.3.) The $C_0 + I + G$ line shows total desired spending at each level of NNP if the tax rate is zero, and the $C_1 + I + G$ line shows total desired spending at each level of NNP if the tax rate is 16⅔ percent. Consequently, the equilibrium value of NNP is $1,225 billion if the tax rate is zero, and $980 billion if it is 16⅔ percent.

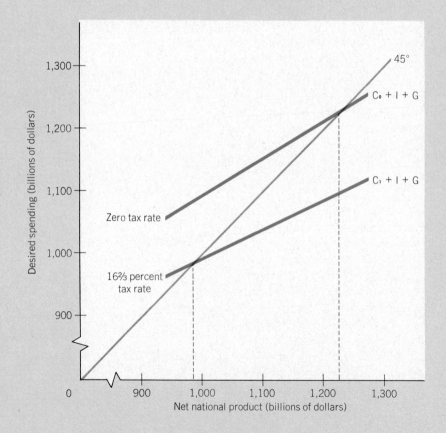

**Figure 10.5
Determination of Equilibrium
Value of Net National Product,
with 16⅔ Percent and 33⅓
Percent Tax Rates**

The $C_1 + I + G$ line shows total
desired spending at each level of
NNP if the tax rate is 16⅔
percent, and the $C_2 + I + G$ line
shows total desired spending at
each level of NNP if the tax rate
is 33⅓ percent. Consequently,
the equilibrium value of NNP is
$980 billion if the tax rate is
16⅔ percent and $816⅔ billion
if it is 33⅓ percent.

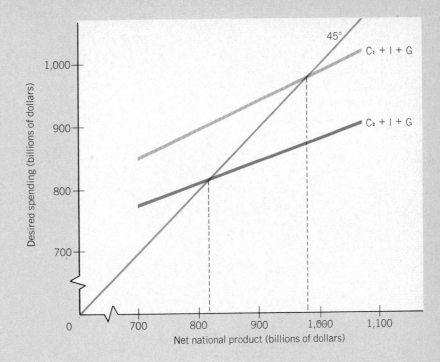

wanted to spend on consumption goods at each
level of NNP. People still wanted to spend the
same amount *from each (after-tax) income level,*
but because of the tax their spending decisions had
to be based on a *reduced (after-tax) income,* so
that they spent less on consumption goods and
services at each level of NNP.

Going a step further, *the higher the tax rate, the
lower the equilibrium value of NNP; and the
lower the tax rate, the higher the equilibrium
value of NNP.* This is a very important proposition, as we shall see in subsequent sections. To
demonstrate it, let's see what will happen to the
equilibrium value of NNP when the tax rate is
increased from 16⅔ percent of NNP to 33⅓ percent of NNP. If the tax rate is 33⅓ percent, the
desired spending on NNP at each level of NNP
will be given by line $C_2 + I + G$ in Figure 10.5.
Since the equilibrium value of NNP will be at
the point where the $C_2 + I + G$ line intersects the
45-degree line, the equilibrium value of NNP will

be $816⅔ billion, rather than $980 billion (which
was the equilibrium value when the tax rate was
16⅔ percent). Thus, the increase in the tax rate
will reduce the equilibrium value of NNP. By reducing the amount people want to spend on consumption at each level of NNP, it will lower the
$C + I + G$ line from $C_1 + I + G$ to $C_2 + I + G$.

On the other hand, suppose that the tax rate is
lowered from 16⅔ percent of NNP to a lesser
amount. What will happen to the equilibrium
value of NNP? If the tax rate is less than 16⅔
percent, the desired spending on NNP at each
level of NNP will be given by a $C + I + G$ line
that lies between $C_0 + I + G$ and $C_1 + I + G$ in
Figure 10.4. Since the equilibrium value of NNP
will be at the point where this line intersects the
45-degree line, the equilibrium value of NNP will
be greater than $980 billion. Thus, the decrease
in the tax rate will increase the equilibrium value
of NNP. By increasing the amount people want
to spend on consumption at each level of NNP, it

will raise the $C + I + G$ line from $C_1 + I + G$ to a higher level.[2]

The Nature and Objectives of Fiscal Policy

Our discussions in previous sections make it easy to understand the basic ideas underlying modern fiscal policy. For example, suppose that the economy is suffering from an undesirably high unemployment rate. What should the government do? Since actual NNP is too low to result in full employment, the economy needs increased spending. In other words, as shown in Figure 10.6, the economy needs an upward shift of the $C + I + G$ line, which by increasing NNP will increase employment as well. There are three ways that the government can try to bring this about. First, it can reduce taxes, which, as shown in a previous section, will shift the relation between consumption expenditure and NNP —and consequently the $C + I + G$ line—upward. Second, it can increase government expenditures, which will also shift the $C + I + G$ line upward. Third, the government can encourage firms to invest more, perhaps by enacting tax credits to make investment more profitable for them; an increase in desired investment will shift the $C + I + G$ line upward too.

On the other hand, perhaps we are suffering from an undesirably high rate of inflation. What should the government do? Since total spending

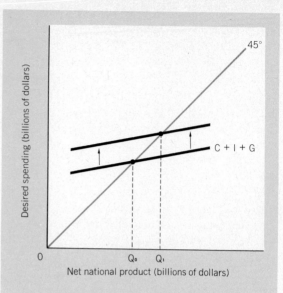

Figure 10.6
Expansionary Fiscal Policy

At Q_0, NNP is too low to result in high employment. By pushing the $C + I + G$ line upward, the government can increase NNP to Q_1, thus increasing real output and reducing unemployment.

[2] Note that the slope of the relationship between consumption and NNP increases as the tax rate decreases. This means that the "marginal propensity to consume out of NNP" increases as the tax rate decreases. Consequently, the multiplier—the amount by which NNP changes if desired investment changes (or the consumption function shifts, or government expenditures change) —increases as the tax rate goes down, and conversely decreases as the tax rate goes up. In other words, as the tax rate increases, NNP becomes less sensitive to changes in investment, government spending, and the consumption function.

To see this, the mathematically inclined reader is encouraged to work through the following proof. Suppose that the consumption function is a straight line:
$$C = \alpha + \beta(1 - T)Y,$$
were $Y = $ NNP and T equals the tax rate, i.e., the proportion of NNP consumers pay in taxes. Also, by definition,
$$Y = C + I + G.$$
Thus, substituting for C,
$$Y = \alpha + \beta(1 - T)Y + I + G,$$
which means that
$$[1 - \beta(1 - T)]Y = \alpha + I + G,$$
or
$$Y = \frac{\alpha}{1 - \beta(1 - T)} + \frac{I}{1 - \beta(1 - T)} + \frac{G}{1 - \beta(1 - T)};$$
Thus, a \$1 billion increase in α, I, or G results in an increase of $\left[\dfrac{1}{1 - \beta(1 - T)}\right]$ billions of dollars in NNP. In other words, the multiplier is $\left[\dfrac{1}{1 - \beta(1 - T)}\right]$. But $\left[\dfrac{1}{1 - \beta(1 - T)}\right]$ gets bigger as T gets smaller; and conversely, $\left[\dfrac{1}{1 - \beta(1 - T)}\right]$ gets smaller as T gets bigger. This completes the proof.

exceeds the value at initial prices of maximum output, the economy needs reduced spending. In other words, what is required is a downward shift of the $C + I + G$ line, as shown in Figure 10.7. The government has three ways to try to bring this about. First, it can increase taxes; this, as shown in a previous section, will shift the relation between consumption expenditure and NNP—and consequently the $C + I + G$ line—downward. Second, it can cut government expenditures, which will also shift the $C + I + G$ curve downward. Third, it can change the tax laws and do other things to discourage firms from investing in plant and equipment or inventories; a decrease in desired investment will shift the $C + I + G$ line downward too.

Certainly, these ideas do not seem very hard to understand. Put bluntly, all we are saying is that, *if there is too much unemployment, the government should promote, directly or indirectly, additional public and/or private spending, which will* result *in additional output and jobs.* On the other hand, *if there is too much inflation, the government should reduce, directly or indirectly, spending (public and/or private); this will curb the inflationary pressure on prices.* Surely these propositions seem reasonable enough. And they are useful —although by themselves they cannot deal as effectively as one would like with times like the early 1970s, when excessive unemployment and inflation have occurred together. We shall discuss such situations in detail in Chapter 15.

Perhaps the most surprising thing about these ideas is that they have been understood and accepted only very recently. Until the appearance of John Maynard Keynes's work in the 1930s, the economics profession really did not understand the effects of fiscal policy at all well. And once Keynes showed his fellow economists the way, it took over 20 years to convince congressmen, presidents, and other officials that these ideas were valid. Moreover, the educational process is still going on. Per-

Figure 10.7
Contractionary Fiscal Policy

For simplicity, assume that Q_2 is the *maximum* value of *real* NNP (*in initial prices*) that can be achieved; thus, any increase of *money* NNP above Q_2 is due entirely to inflation. The existing $C + I + G$ line is too high, resulting in a money NNP of Q_3, which means considerable inflation. (A money NNP of Q_3 can be achieved only by an increase in prices since at initial prices Q_2 is the maximum value of money NNP.) By pushing the $C + I + G$ line downward, the government can ease the upward pressure on prices.

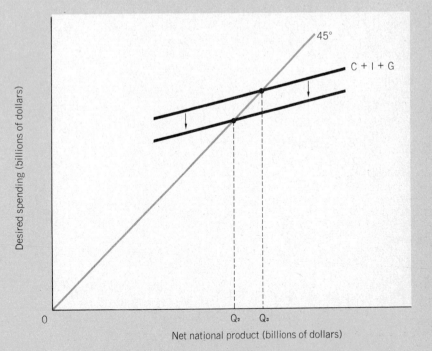

haps the most important reason why it has been so difficult to get across such simple ideas is that, until recently, the conventional wisdom passed down from father to son was that the government should balance its budget. In other words, it should spend no more than what it collects in taxes. This proposition is at odds with the ideas presented above. If those ideas are accepted, it may be necessary for the government to run a deficit or a surplus, depending on the economic situation. A *deficit* occurs when the government spends more than it collects in taxes; a *surplus* occurs when it spends less. It has taken a long time to convince people that full employment and stable prices—not a balanced budget—should be our goals. Some people still believe that the road to economic destruction is lined with unbalanced budgets.

Makers of Fiscal Policy

When you go to a ball game, you generally get a program telling you who on each team is playing each position. To understand the formulation and implementation of fiscal policy in the United States we need the same kind of information. Who are the people who establish our fiscal policy? Who decides that, in view of the current and prospective economic situation, tax rates or government expenditures should be changed? This is not a simple question because lots of individuals and groups play an important role. In the Congress, the House and Senate appropriations committees—as well as their numerous subcommittees—have enormous power over the size and direction of federal expenditure. The House Ways and Means Committee and the Senate Finance Committee have the same sort of power over federal tax matters. In addition, another congressional committee is of great importance—the Joint Economic Committee of Congress. Established by the Employment Act of 1946, this committee goes over the annual Economic Report of the President on the state of the economy, and, through its hearings, provides an important forum for review of economic issues.

In the executive branch of government, the most important person in the establishment of fiscal policy is, of course, the president. Although he must operate in the context of the tax and expenditure laws passed by Congress, he and his advisers are the country's principal analysts of the need for fiscal expansion or restraint and its leading spokesmen for legislative changes to meet these needs. Needless to say, he doesn't pore over the latest economic data and make the decisions all by himself. The Office of Management and Budget, which is part of the Executive Office of the President, is a very powerful adviser to the president on expenditure policy, as is the Treasury Department on tax policy. In addition, there is the **Council of Economic Advisers,** which is part of the Executive Office of the President. Established by the Employment Act of 1946, its job is to help the president carry out the objectives of that act.

During the past 20 years, the Council of Economic Advisers, headed by a series of very distinguished economists who left academic and other posts to contribute to public policy, has become a very important economic adviser to the president. Its position has been well described by Stanford's G. L. Bach:

> Fundamentally, it is responsible for overseeing the state of the economy, for continually checking on the appropriateness of government policies for stable economic growth, and for working intimately with the President and other parts of the executive branch in developing overall legislative policy in the economic field. Some Council chairmen have worked closely with Congressional committees; others have remained more in the background as Presidential advisers. But for macroeconomic policy, the Council is now perhaps the President's most important single advisory group. It is *his* council and more specifically *his* part of the government than are the regular executive branch departments.[3]

[3] G. L. Bach, *Making Monetary and Fiscal Policy,* Washington, D.C.: Brookings Institution, 1971, pp. 30–31. The Chairmen of the Council of Economic Advisers have been Herbert Stein, Paul McCracken, Arthur Okun, Gardner Ackley, Walter Heller, Raymond Saulnier, Arthur Burns, Leon Keyserling, and Edwin Nourse.

The Council of Economic Advisers

Before World War II, there was relatively little place in the government for economists. The Treasury had a small number, the antitrust division of the Justice Department a handful, but there was no place for economists who aspired to give advice on broad policy matters. The Employment Act of 1946 changed that situation by creating a council to "gather timely and authoritative information . . . to develop and recommend to the President national economic policies . . . and to make and furnish studies . . . as the President may request."

But, as demonstrated by the first chairman, Edwin Nourse, the Act was really a hunting license for a chairman to peddle his good counsel. Nourse, who believed that the Council's role was to "interpret literal facts . . . without becoming involved in any way in the advocacy of particular measures," found that such services were rarely required by the president. It is hard to find any trace of the Nourse era on the economic policies of the late forties.

Nourse's successor, Leon Keyserling, hunted so avidly that Congress almost suspended his license. Keyserling was temperamentally and politically inclined to activism. His advocacy of expansionist policies to a conservative Congress and a president concerned primarily with containing the Korean war inflation led to a bill reducing the CEA's budget by 25 percent. The Council was saved by the persuasiveness of a new chairman, Arthur F. Burns, and the support of a few senators. But the limits of independent advocacy had been established.

The Eisenhower years were quiet years for the Council. Even the election of John F. Kennedy, who was eager to increase the U.S. rate of economic growth, did not insure the Council's future. Kennedy, a C-student in economics at Harvard, was inclined to fiscal conservatism and less interested in domestic than in foreign affairs. It was Walter Heller, the new chairman under Kennedy, who made the CEA an integral part of the New Frontier. The tax cut of 1964, which Heller sold to a president committed to balanced budgets, is a tribute to his success in making a body without formal powers or legislative prerogatives an integral part of the policy-making process. The new-found status of the Council was acknowledged in Washington by the establishment of a Quadriad, made up of representatives of the Council, the Bureau of the Budget, the Treasury, and the Federal Reserve, which met periodically to discuss economic affairs.

THE FIRST COUNCIL OF ECONOMIC ADVISERS. EDWIN NOURSE, CHAIRMAN, AT LEFT.

The Council's influence has risen and ebbed in recent years with both the state of the economy and with other pressures on the president. In 1966, as Vietnam heated up, the Council urged a tax increase; Lyndon Johnson, more attuned to the political realities, did not take action on the proposal until 1967. The Council's position in the Nixon administration further exemplified this process. Led by Paul McCracken and Herbert Stein, the Council successfully championed restraint in fiscal and monetary policies early in Nixon's first term, and let the Kennedy-Johnson price-wage guideposts lapse. But faced with mounting inflationary pressures, the Council members reluctantly joined other administration economists in setting up wage and price controls. As one economic game plan after another was tried and modified, economists who had favored relaxing government reins on the economy found themselves tugging hard to keep inflation in check.

E.A.

Automatic Stabilizers

Now that we have met some of the major players, we must point out that they get help from some *automatic stabilizers*—some structural features of our economy that tend to stabilize NNP. Although these automatic stabilizers cannot do all that is required to keep the economy on an even keel, they help a lot. As soon as the economy turns down and unemployment mounts, they give the economy a helpful shot in the arm. As soon as the economy gets overheated and inflation crops up, they tend to restrain it.

There are several automatic stabilizers. First, there are automatic changes in tax revenues. One of the major points emphasized in Chapter 5 was that our federal tax system relies heavily on the income tax. The amount of income tax collected by the federal government goes up with increases in NNP and goes down with decreases in NNP. Moreover, because the income tax is progressive, the average tax rate goes up with increases in NNP, and goes down with decreases in NNP. This, of course, is just what we want to occur! When NNP falls off and unemployment mounts, tax collections fall off too, so disposable income falls less than NNP. This means less of a fall in consumption, which tends to brake the fall in NNP. When NNP rises too fast and the economy begins to suffer from serious inflation, tax collections rise too—which tends to brake the increase in NNP. Of course, corporation income taxes, as well as personal income taxes, play a significant role here.

Second, there are unemployment compensation and welfare payments. Unemployment compensation is paid to workers who are laid off, according to a system that has evolved over the past 40 years. When an unemployed worker goes back to work, he stops receiving unemployment compensation. Thus, when NNP falls off and unemployment mounts, the tax collections to finance unemployment compensation go down (because of lower employment), while the amount paid out to un-employed workers goes up. On the other hand, when NNP rises too fast and the economy begins to suffer from serious inflation, the tax collections to finance unemployment compensation go up, while the amount paid out goes down because there is much less unemployment. Again, this is just what we want to see happen! Spending is bolstered when unemployment is high and curbed when there are serious inflationary pressures. Various welfare programs have the same kind of stabilizing effect on the economy.

Third, there are corporate dividends and family saving. Since corporations tend to maintain their dividends when their sales fall off, and moderate the increase in their dividends when their sales soar, their dividend policy tends to stabilize the economy. This is very important. Also, to the extent that consumers tend to be slow to raise or lower their spending in response to increases or decreases in their income, this too tends to stabilize the economy. Finally, there are the agricultural support programs, described in Chapter 5. The government has buttressed farm prices and incomes when business was bad and unemployment was high. When output was high and inflation occurred, the government distributed the commodities in its warehouses and received dollars. In both cases, these programs acted as stabilizers.

Having painted such a glowing picture of the economy's automatic stabilizers, we are in danger of suggesting that they can stabilize the economy all by themselves. It would be nice if this were true, but it isn't! All the automatic stabilizers do is *cut down* on variations in unemployment and inflation, not *eliminate* them. Discretionary programs are needed to supplement the effects of these automatic stabilizers. Some economists wish strongly that it were possible to set well-defined rules for government action, rather than leave things to the discretion of policy makers. Indeed, Milton Friedman, among others, forcefully argues for greater reliance on such rules, but most economists feel that it is impossible to formulate a set of rules flexible and comprehensive enough to let us do away with the discretionary powers of policy makers.

The Tools of Discretionary Fiscal Policy

Having discussed the automatic stabilizers, let's get back to the players—the people responsible for the formulation and implementation of discretionary fiscal policy—and the tools they have to work with. For example, suppose that the Council of Economic Advisers, on the basis of information concerning recent economic developments, believes that NNP may decline soon and that serious unemployment is likely to develop. Suppose that other agencies, like the Treasury and the Federal Reserve System (discussed in Chapter 14), agree. What specific measures can they recommend that the government take under such circumstances?

First, the government can vary its expenditure for public works and other programs. If increased unemployment seems to be in the wind, it can step up expenditures on roads, urban reconstruction, and other public programs. Of course, these programs must be well thought out and socially productive. There is no sense in pushing through wasteful and foolish public works programs merely to make jobs. Or if, as in 1969, the economy is plagued by inflation, it can (as President Nixon ordered) stop new federal construction programs temporarily.

Second, the government can vary welfare payments and other types of transfer payments. For example, a hike in Social Security benefits may provide a very healthy shot in the arm for an economy with too much unemployment. An increase in veterans' benefits or in aid to dependent children may do the same thing. The federal government has sometimes helped the states to extend the length of time that the unemployed can receive unemployment compensation; this too will have the desired effect. On the other hand, if there is full employment and inflation is a dangerous problem, it may be worthwhile to cut back on certain kinds of transfer payments. For example, if it is agreed that certain kinds of veterans' benefits should be reduced, this reduction might be timed to occur during a period when inflationary pressures are evident.

Third, the government can vary tax rates. For example, if there is considerable unemployment, the government may cut tax rates, as it did in 1964. Or if inflation is the problem, the government may increase taxes, as it did in 1968 when, after considerable political maneuvering and buckpassing, the Congress was finally persuaded to put through the 10 percent tax surcharge to try to moderate the inflation caused by the Vietnam war. We shall show in the next sections the processes leading up to the 1964 tax cut and the 1968 tax increase.

Of course there are advantages and disadvantages in each of these tools of fiscal policy. One of the big disadvantages of public works and similar spending programs is that they take so long to get started. Plans must be made, land must be acquired, and preliminary construction studies must be carried out. By the time the expenditures are finally made and have the desired effect, the dangers of excessive unemployment may have given way to dangers of inflation, so that the spending, coming too late, does more harm than good. To some extent, this problem may be ameliorated by having a backlog of productive projects ready to go at all times. In this way, at least a portion of the lag can be eliminated. But it is necessary to recognize that the supply of public services should be determined by public demand, and that considerations of stabilization policy are only one of many factors to be considered.

In recent years, there has been a widespread feeling that government expenditures should be set on the basis of their long-run desirability and productivity and not on the basis of short-term stabilization considerations. The optimal level of government expenditure is at the point where the value of the extra benefits to be derived from an extra dollar of government expenditure is at least equal to the dollar of cost. This optimal level is unlikely to change much in the short run, and it would be wasteful to spend more—or less—than this amount for stabilization purposes when tax changes could be used instead. Thus, many economists believe that tax cuts or tax increases should be the primary fiscal weapons to fight unemployment or inflation.

However, one of the big problems with tax changes is that it is difficult to get Congress to take speedy action. There is often considerable debate over a tax bill, and sometimes it becomes a political football. Another difficulty with tax changes is that it generally is much easier to reduce taxes than it is to get them back up again. To politicians, lower taxes are attractive because they are popular, and higher taxes are dangerous because they may hurt a politician's chances of reelection. In discussing fiscal policy (or most other aspects of government operations, for that matter), to ignore politics is to risk losing touch with reality.

The Tax Cut of 1964:
An Application of Modern
Economic Analysis

Knowing something about the players and the plays they can call, we can look now at two examples of fiscal policy in action. When the Kennedy administration took office in 1961, it was confronted with a relatively high unemployment rate—about 7 percent in mid-1961. By 1962, although unemployment was somewhat lower (about 6 percent), the president's advisers, led by Walter W. Heller, Chairman of the Council of Economic Advisers, pushed for a tax cut to reduce unemployment further. The president, after considerable discussion of the effects of such a tax cut, announced in June 1962 that he would propose such a measure to the Congress; and in January 1963, the bill was finally sent to Congress.

The proposed tax bill was a victory for modern ideas on fiscal policy. Even though it would mean a deliberately large deficit, the president had been convinced to cut taxes to push the economy closer to full employment. But the Congress was not so easily convinced. Many congressmen labeled the proposal irresponsible and reckless. Others wanted to couple tax reform with tax reduction. It was not until 1964, after President Kennedy's death, that the tax bill was enacted. It took a year from the time the bill was sent to Congress for it to be passed, and during this interval, there was a continuous debate in the executive branch and the Congress. The Secretary of the Treasury, Douglas Dillon, the Chairman of the Federal Reserve Board, William M. Martin, and numerous congressmen—all powerful and all initially cool to the proposal—were eventually won over. The result was a tax reduction of about $10 billion per year.

The effects of the tax cut are by no means easy to measure, but in line with the theory presented in earlier sections, consumption expenditure did increase sharply during 1964. Moreover, the additional consumption undoubtedly induced additional investment. According to estimates provided by Arthur Okun, Chairman of the Council of Economic Advisers under President Johnson, the tax cut resulted in an increase in GNP of about $24 billion in 1965 and more in subsequent years.[4] The unemployment rate, which had been about 5½ to 6 percent during 1962 and 1963, fell to 5 percent during 1964 and to 4.7 percent in the spring of 1965. It is fair to say that most economists were extremely pleased with themselves in 1965. Fiscal policy based on their theories seemed to work very well indeed! Unfortunately, however, this pleasure did not last very long, there being another, and sadder, tale to tell.

The Impact of Vietnam:
Another Case Study

In late July 1965, President Johnson announced that the United States would send 50,000 more men to Vietnam. From fiscal 1965 to fiscal 1966, defense expenditures rose from $50 billion to $62

[4] Arthur Okun, "Measuring the Impact of the 1964 Tax Reduction," in Walter W. Heller, *Perspectives on Economic Growth,* New York: Random House, 1968, p. 33.

billion—a large increase in government expenditure, and one that took place at a time of relatively full employment. Clearly, on the basis of the theory presented earlier in this chapter, such an increase in government expenditure would be expected to cause inflationary pressures. Equally clearly, one way to eliminate undesirable pressures of this sort was to raise taxes (and, where possible, cut other kinds of government expenditure). The president was told by his economic advisers in late 1965 that an increase in income taxes was desirable to cut down on inflationary pressures, but he would not ask for such an increase at that time.

In fiscal 1967, the situation got no better. Because of the large military buildup in that year, military expenditure was $10 billion higher than estimated in the January 1966 budget. This was a large increase in government spending at a time when inflationary pressures were strong. The effects of these pressures were becoming clearer and clearer. During 1965, the general price level—as measured by the GNP deflator—had gone up by about 3 percent; during 1966, it had gone up by about 4 percent; and during 1967, it rose again by about 4 percent. The inflation was bubbling along merrily . . . and unfortunately, little was being done by fiscal policy makers to stop it.

Even in 1967, the Congress was unwilling to raise taxes. The case for fiscal restraint was, it felt, not clear enough. Moreover, the pressure from the general public was certainly not for an increase in the amount they would have to pay Uncle Sam. As for the president, he recognized that the Vietnam war was not popular. Consequently, as he himself put it, "It is not a popular thing for a President to do . . . to ask for a penny out of a dollar to pay for a war that is not popular either."[5] Finally, in mid-1968, when prices were rising by well over 4 percent per year, a 10 percent surcharge on income taxes, together with some restraint on government spending, was enacted. This was almost a year after the surtax had been requested.

[5] Arthur Okun, *The Political Economy of Prosperity,* New York: Norton, 1970, p. 88.

This increase in taxes was obviously the right medicine, but it was at least two years too late, and its effects were delayed. Certainly, the record of 1965–68 was disappointing. Government spending was highly destabilizing, and tax changes were painfully slow to come. One moral of this episode is that, although we know a great deal more than we used to about how fiscal policy should be used to avoid inflation or considerable unemployment, there is no guarantee that it will be used in this way. In the early 1960s, policy makers seemed to make the right choices; in the later 1960s, they did not.

Deficit and Surplus Financing

Now that you have studied the basic elements of fiscal policy, let's see how well you would fare with some of the problems that confront our nation's top policy makers. Suppose that, through some inexplicable malfunctioning of the democratic process, you are elected President of the United States. Your Council of Economic Advisers reports to you that, on the basis of various forecasts (based on models like those discussed in Chapter 11), NNP is likely to drop next year, and unemployment is likely to be much higher. Naturally, you are concerned; and having absorbed the ideas presented in this chapter, you ask your advisers—the Council of Economic Advisers, the Treasury, and the Office of Management and Budget—what sort of fiscal policy should be adopted to head off this undesirable turn of events. On the basis of their advice, you suggest to Congress that taxes should be cut and government expenditures should be increased.

When they receive your message, a number of key congressmen point out that if the government cuts taxes and raises expenditures it will operate in the red. In other words, government revenue will fall short of government spending—there will be a deficit. They warn that such fiscal behavior is irresponsible, since it violates the fundamental tenet of public finance that the budget should be balanced: income should cover outgo. For further clarification on this point, you call in your advisers, who deny that the budget should be balanced each year. They point out that if a deficit is run in a particular year, the government can borrow the difference; and they claim that the national debt is in no sense dangerously large in the United States at present. Whose advice would you follow —that of your economic advisers or that of the congressmen?

Or suppose your advisers tell you that inflation is a growing problem and that you should cut back government spending and raise taxes. Since this advice seems eminently sensible, based on the principles set forth in this chapter, you propose this course of action to Congress. Some prominent newspapers point out that by raising taxes and cutting expenditures, the government will take in more than it spends. In other words, there will be a surplus. They say that there is no reason for the government to take more money from the people than it needs to pay for the services it performs, and argue that taxes should not be increased because the government can cover its expenditures without such an increase. Whose advice would you follow—that of your economic advisers or that of the newspapers?

You would be wise to go along with your economic advisers in both cases. Why? Because there is nothing particularly desirable about a balanced budget. Although it may well be prudent for individuals and families not to spend more than they earn, this does not carry over to the federal government. When we need to stimulate the economy and raise NNP, it is perfectly legitimate and desirable for the federal government to run a deficit, provided it gets its full money's worth for what is spent. All that happens is that the government borrows the difference, and—as we pointed out in Chapter 6—there is no indication that the national debt is dangerously large. Thus, in the first case, you should not have been worried by the fact that a deficit would result. And in the second case, while it is true that the government could support its expenditures with lower taxes,

this would defeat your purpose. What you want to do is to cut total spending, public and private, and raising taxes will cut private spending.

Deficit Spending in the 1930s: A Case Study

Some people—fewer than there used to be, but still some—are dead set against deficit spending by the government. Many, when pressed to explain their opposition, retort that it was tried by Franklin D. Roosevelt during the Great Depression of the 1930s and that it failed to eliminate the high levels of unemployment that prevailed then. This is both bad history and bad economics. The federal government did spend more than it took in during the Roosevelt administration, but the deficit was far too small to have much effect. GNP fell from about $100 billion in 1929 to less than $60 billion in 1933. Federal deficits in the 1930s were only a few billion dollars per year at most, and in many years these deficits were offset by surpluses run by the state and local governments. The situation somewhat resembled that described by the columnist Heywood Broun, when he wrote: "I have known people to stop and buy an apple on the corner and then walk away as if they had solved the whole unemployment problem."[6]

In a careful study of the effects of fiscal policy in the 1930s, Professor E. Cary Brown of M.I.T. concluded that fiscal policy "seems to have been an unsuccessful recovery device in the thirties—not because it did not work, but because it was not tried."[7] For those who know something of the political history of the period, this is not surprising.

[6] Heywood Broun, It Seems to Me, 1933. Of course, I am not implying that the Roosevelt administration did not attempt to reduce unemployment. What I am saying is that the history of the period is not a very good test of the effectiveness of deficit spending.

[7] E. Cary Brown, "Fiscal Policy in the Thirties: A Reappraisal," American Economic Review, December 1956, pp. 865–66.

Few government officials of that day understood the power and effects of fiscal policy. The federal government did run a deficit, but largely in spite of itself. In that era, the golden rule of fiscal responsibility was a balanced budget, and deficits were regarded as unfortunate aberrations. If you contrast this attitude with the attitude of the federal government toward the tax cut of 1964, you will see how far the nation has come in its understanding of fiscal policy.

Alternative Budget Policies

At least three policies concerning the government budget are worthy of detailed examination. The first policy says that the government's budget should be balanced each and every year. This is the philosophy that generally prevailed, here and abroad, until the advent of Keynesian economics in the 1930s. Superficially, it seems eminently reasonable. After all, won't a family or firm go bankrupt if it continues to spend more than it takes in? Why should the government be any different? However, the truth is that the government has economic capabilities, powers, and responsibilities that are entirely different from those of any family or firm, and it is misleading—sometimes even pernicious—to assume that what is sensible for a family or firm is also sensible for the government.

If this policy of balancing the budget is accepted, the government cannot use fiscal policy as a tool to stabilize the economy. Indeed, if the government attempts to balance its budget each year, it is likely to make unemployment or inflation worse rather than better. For example, suppose that severe unemployment occurs because of a drop in NNP. Since incomes drop, tax receipts drop as well. Thus if the government attempts to balance its budget, it must cut its spending and/or increase tax rates, both of which will tend to lower, not raise, NNP. On the other hand, suppose that inflation occurs because spending increases too rapidly. Since incomes increase, tax receipts increase too. Thus, for the government to balance its budget, it must in-

crease its spending and/or decrease tax rates, both of which will tend to raise, not lower, spending.[8]

A second budgetary philosophy says that the government's budget should be balanced over the course of each "business cycle." As we shall see in Chapter 11, the rate of growth of NNP tends to behave cyclically. As shown in Figure 8.6, it tends to increase for a while, then drop, increase, then drop. Unemployment also tends to ebb and flow in a similar cyclical fashion. This is the so-called business cycle. According to this second budgetary policy, the government is not expected to balance its budget each year, but is expected to run a big enough surplus during periods of high employment to offset the deficit it runs during the ensuing period of excessive unemployment. This policy seems to give the government enough flexibility to run the deficits or surpluses needed to stabilize the economy, while at the same time allaying any public fear of a chronically unbalanced budget. It certainly seems to be a neat way to reconcile the government's use of fiscal policy to promote noninflationary full employment with the public's uneasiness over chronically unbalanced budgets.

Unfortunately, however, it does contain one fundamental flaw: there is no reason to believe that the size of the deficits required to eliminate excessive unemployment will equal the size of the surpluses required to moderate the subsequent inflation. For example, suppose that NNP falls

[8] In sophisticated circles, there is some support for this philosophy of a balanced budget, based on the idea that it makes it much easier for the Office of Management and Budget to keep expenditures within reasonable limits. Once this philosophy is abandoned completely, it is feared that the individual departments and agencies of the government can challenge OMB's estimate of how big a surplus or deficit is appropriate, and argue that more spending on their part would be a good thing. In other words, it makes it easier to control spending.

Another point that is frequently made is that the government, through inappropriate fiscal or monetary policies, is often responsible for problems of unemployment and inflation. To many economists, the practical problem seems to be how to prevent the government from creating disturbances, rather than how to use the government budget (and monetary policy) to offset disturbances arising from the private sector. Unfortunately, as we noted in connection with the inflation arising from the Vietnam war, there is sometimes a good deal of truth to this.

sharply, causing severe and prolonged unemployment; then regains its full-employment level only briefly; then falls again. In such a case, the deficits incurred to get the economy back to full employment are likely to exceed by far the surpluses run during the brief period of full employment. Thus there would be no way to stabilize the economy without running an unbalanced budget over the course of this business cycle. If this policy were adopted, and if the government attempted to balance the budget over the course of each business cycle, this would interfere with an effective fiscal policy designed to promote full employment with stable prices.

Finally, a third budgetary policy says that the government's budget should be set so as to promote whatever attainable combination of unemployment and inflation seems socially optimal, even if this means that the budget is unbalanced over considerable periods of time. This policy is sometimes called *functional finance.*[9] Proponents of functional finance point out that, although this policy may mean a continual growth in the public debt, the problems caused by a moderate growth in the public debt are small when compared with the social costs of unemployment and inflation.

Certainly, the history of the past 40 years has been characterized by enormous changes in the nation's attitude toward the government budget. Forty years ago, the prevailing attitude was that the government's budget should be balanced. The emergence of the modern theory of the determination of national output and employment shook this attitude, at least to the point where it became respectable to advocate a balanced budget over the business cycle, rather than in each year. Then, as modern ideas regarding fiscal policy have become accepted by more and more people, the idea that the budget should be balanced over the business cycle has been largely abandoned, and the government budget is now viewed as a means to reduce undesirable unemployment and inflation.

[9] See Abba Lerner, *Economics of Control,* New York: Macmillan, 1944.

The Full-Employment Budget

Some of the misconceptions about budget deficits and surpluses can be avoided by the use of the *full-employment budget,* which shows the difference between tax revenues and government expenditures that would result if we had full employment, which is generally defined as 4 percent unemployed. For example, in 1958, the Eisenhower administration ran a deficit of over $10 billion—a reasonably large deficit by historical standards. Basically, the reason for this deficit was that, with the unemployment rate at about 7 percent, there was a substantial gap between actual and potential output. Net national product fell from 1957 to 1958, and, as a result, incomes and federal tax collections fell, and the government ran a deficit. But this $10 billion deficit was entirely due to the high level of unemployment the country was experiencing.

Had we been at full employment, there would have been a surplus of about $5 billion in 1958. NNP, incomes, and federal tax receipts would all have been higher. Government spending and the tax rates in 1958 were not such as to produce a deficit if full employment had been attained. On the contrary, the full-employment budget shows that, if full employment had prevailed, tax receipts would have increased so that federal revenues would have exceeded expenditure by about $5 billion. It is important to distinguish between the full-employment budget and the actual budget. When, as in 1958, the actual budget shows a deficit but the full-employment budget does not, most economists feel that fiscal policy is not too expansionary, since at full employment the federal government would be running a surplus.

Recognizing these considerations, President Nixon officially adopted the full-employment budget as his measure of the stabilization impact of the budget. As you can see in Figure 10.8, he ran a full-employment surplus during his first term in office to combat inflation. During the late 1950s and early 1960s there was also a substantial full-employment surplus because, with continued

Figure 10.8
Full-Employment and Actual Budget Deficits and Surpluses, 1956–72

The full-employment budget shows the difference between tax revenues and government expenditures that would result if there was full employment, which is generally defined as 4 percent unemployed. The Nixon administration has officially adopted the full-employment budget as a measure of the stabilization impact of the budget.

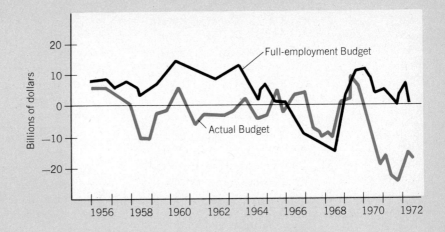

growth in NNP, federal tax receipts grew each year—and this growth in tax receipts was considerable! Unless taxes are reduced or government expenditures increase, a full-employment surplus will develop and grow, with deflationary results. This automatic growth in tax receipts in a growing economy with progressive taxes is called *fiscal drag.* This drag is beneficial if there are inflationary pressures (as in the late 1960s and early 1970s), but under healthy full-employment conditions, it tends to push the economy toward less than full employment. One way to look at the 1964 tax cut is as a device to eliminate the effects of fiscal drag. (As you can see in Figure 10.8, the full-employment surplus was largely eliminated by the tax cut.) Unfortunately, the Vietnam war resulted in a large—and inflationary—full-employment deficit in 1966–68.

Recent American Experience with Fiscal Policy

It should be evident by now that much more is known today about the impact of fiscal policy than at the time when the economy was staggered by the Great Depression. During the 1930s, the ideas presented here were relatively new and by and large not accepted. In fact, the federal government did run a deficit, but—as we saw in a previous section—it was far too small to make a significant dent in the high unemployment levels of the Great Depression. During the 1940s, the ideas presented here began to gain wider acceptance. World War II showed beyond any reasonable doubt the power of government spending to increase output and generate full employment. Unfortunately, it also showed that an expansionary fiscal policy can produce inflation.

During the 1950s, modern ideas on fiscal policy had become strongly entrenched in the intellectual community, but were less accepted in the business community and some parts of the government. However, the makers of fiscal policy took these ideas into account in responding to the increases in unemployment during 1953–54 and 1957–58. During the 1960s, modern views on fiscal policy came to be widely accepted by practically all parts of the community. The tax cut of 1964 was a major victory for modern economics, but as we have observed, the later 1960s were marred by the destabilizing effects of greatly increased military spending on Vietnam, and the inflationary consequences remained with us afterward.

The hard choices faced by economists in the top councils of government can be demonstrated by a close inspection of the recent efforts to keep the economy on an even keel. When the Nixon administration took office, it inherited an economy suffering from considerable inflation, in part because of the fiscal policies pursued in the mid-1960s. In response to this inflation, the administration pursued a restrictive fiscal policy designed to keep a tight rein on spending. During 1969 and 1970, the administration restricted government expenditures and tried to run a surplus. For example, in his Economic Report in 1970, President Nixon said: "Our purpose has been to slow down the rapid expansion of demand firmly and persistently, but not to choke off demand so abruptly as to injure the economy. . . . The growth of total spending, public and private, which was the driving force of the inflation, slowed markedly, from 9.4 percent during 1968 to 6.8 percent during 1969."[10]

As the administration's restrictive fiscal policies took hold, the nation's level of real output began to rise more slowly; and in 1970, gross national product in constant dollars fell below its 1969 level. Unemployment, which had been only 3.5 percent of the civilian labor force in 1969, rose to 4.9 percent in 1970 and to 5.9 percent in 1971. During 1970 and 1971, many liberal economists criticized the administration's fiscal policies on the grounds that they were too restrictive. They accused the administration of being so absorbed with reducing inflation that it was creating serious unemployment. Yet despite the administration's efforts, the rate of inflation was not decreasing as fast as desired. Between 1969 and 1970, the index of consumer prices rose by about 6 percent. During the first half of 1971, it rose at an annual rate of about 4½ percent. Although there was improvement, the inflationary process was proving difficult to quell.

In August 1971, the Nixon administration, reversing its previous attitudes, established controls on prices, wages, and rents. At the same time, the administration switched to a more expansionary

fiscal policy in order to reduce the relatively high level of unemployment. Specifically, the president called for a tax reduction of about $7 or $8 billion. Included in his tax package was an investment tax credit, which encouraged investment by business firms, as well as a reduction in personal income taxes. Commenting on his fiscal policy decisions, the president said in 1972:

> 6 percent unemployment is too much, and I am determined to reduce that number significantly in 1972. To that end I proposed the tax reduction package of 1971. Federal expenditures will rise by $25.2 billion between last fiscal year and fiscal 1972. Together these tax reductions and expenditure increases will leave a budget deficit of $38.8 billion this year. If we were at full employment in the present fiscal year, expenditures would exceed receipts by $8.1 billion. This is strong medicine, and I do not propose to continue its use, but we have taken it in order to give a powerful stimulus to employment.[11]

Of course, this New Economic Policy also was the subject of criticism, both from the left and the right. Some economists welcomed the shift to a more expansionary policy as long overdue; others viewed it as a mistake. Also, both the tax reduction and the controls were criticized on the grounds that they benefited business more than labor. Fortunately, both the rate of inflation and the unemployment rate fell during 1972. This was good news. But both remained undesirably high: the unemployment rate was about 5½ percent in late 1972 and the rate of inflation was about 3 percent during the year.

After his reelection in November 1972, President Nixon indicated that he wanted to keep a tight lid on government spending, both to reduce inflation and to trim some programs that he regarded as secondary or of dubious value. In particular, he stressed the desirability of a $250 billion ceiling on federal spending. Critics of the president's economic policies claimed that his emphasis on restricting public expenditures was a mistake. In

---

[10] Economic Report of the President, 1970, Washington, D.C.: Government Printing Office, p. 6.

[11] Economic Report of the President, 1972, op cit., p. 5.

early 1973, the president phased out the wage and price controls he had imposed in 1971. Inflation, which never had been quelled, increased after the phaseout of the controls, and during early 1973 the economy was in the midst of a boom. In June 1973, the president imposed another price freeze, this time for 60 days. Then he instituted the so-called "Phase IV" program which attempted to limit price increases to an amount equal to cost increases.

Clearly, judging from our recent history, fiscal policy is no panacea. Policy makers are continually confronted with difficult choices, and the tools of fiscal policy, at least as they are currently understood and used, are not sufficient to solve or dispel many of the problems at hand. However, it is important to recognize that fiscal policy is not the only available means by which policy makers attempt to stabilize the economy. There is also monetary policy, which we shall discuss in detail in Chapter 14. Really, a sensible fiscal policy can be formulated only in conjunction with monetary policy, and although it is convenient to discuss them separately, in real life they must be coordinated. Also, lest you become overly pessimistic, you should note that, despite the problems that remain unsolved, our improved understanding of fiscal and monetary policy has enabled us to steer a better and more stable course than in the days before World War II. So far at least, we have managed to avoid either disastrous unemployment or disastrous inflation.

Improving the Workings of Fiscal Policy[12]

What measures might be adopted to improve the workings of fiscal policy? Several have been widely discussed. First, tax rates might vary automatically in response to changes in economic conditions. For example, tax rates might fall by a specified amount

[12] Much of this section is based on Dernburg and McDougall, *op. cit.*, pp. 420–23.

if unemployment exceeded a certain percentage of the labor force, or if industrial production fell from one quarter to the next. Similarly, tax rates might increase by a specified amount if the index of consumer prices rose by more than a certain amount during a year. The advantage of such an automatic change in tax rates would be in eliminating the long lag that often occurs while a change in fiscal policy is being pushed through.

Despite the apparent attractiveness of such an approach, critics have pointed out that it suffers from a number of problems. For one, it is difficult to develop rules that can be counted on to be sensible. For another, in some situations these rules could indicate contradictory signals. For example, if we applied such rules to the early 1970s, unemployment might be high enough to trigger a tax cut, while inflation might be high enough to trigger a simultaneous tax increase. For still another thing, there is no indication that Congress would be willing to give up some of its power over taxation. After all, such automatic changes in tax rates would have to be approved by Congress, which thereafter would have less discretionary power over taxes.

Second, Congress might give the president some discretionary power over taxes. For example, the president might be empowered to reduce or stop tax collections for a specified period of time, or to establish increases in tax rates of up to a certain percentage. This too might eliminate the long lag that often occurs while a change in fiscal policy is being pushed through. But it runs into the same difficulty as the previous suggestion: there is no indication that the Congress will give up any substantial portion of its power over the purse. On the contrary, the Congress seems very intent on keeping its existing power in this area.

Third, Congress might revise the way it makes fiscal decisions. Some people argue that the Congress should play a more active role in fiscal policy, rather than merely react to initiatives from the executive branch. Others point to the fragmented nature of the decision-making process in Congress. As we saw in a previous chapter, decisions on government expenditures are made by a number of separate appropriations subcommittees that set the level of spending for individual government agencies. The decisions made by these subcommittees are largely uncoordinated, and the total level of expenditure may not correspond with what is appropriate from the point of view of rational fiscal policy.

According to some conservative economists, this fragmentation of congressional decision making results in excessive government spending. For example, Herbert Stein, chairman of President Nixon's Council of Economic Advisers, believes that "our biggest difficulties in achieving a stabilizing budget policy lie in Congress. Every candid Congressman will agree with that. The whole Congressional procedure is so fragmented that Congress is permitted and encouraged to escape any discipline on total spending. . . . The great need is for improved procedure within the Congress that will force more disciplined action." Needless to say, liberal economists do not agree that there is any tendency toward excessive government spending: witness the views of John Kenneth Galbraith. But conservatives and liberals alike seem to see a need for congressional reform in this area.

Summary

The equilibrium level of net national product is the level where desired consumption plus desired investment plus desired government spending equals net national product. A $1 billion change in government expenditure will result in a change in equilibrium NNP of the same amount as a $1 billion change in desired investment or a $1 billion shift in the relation between consumption expenditures and NNP. In any of these cases, there is a multiplier effect. An increase in the tax rate shifts the relationship between consumption expenditure and NNP downward, thus reducing the equilibrium value of NNP. A decrease in the tax rate shifts the relationship upward, thus increasing the equilibrium value of NNP.

Policy makers receive a lot of help in stabilizing the economy from our automatic stabilizers—automatic changes in tax revenues, unemployment compensation and welfare payments, corporate dividends, family saving, and farm aid. However, the automatic stabilizers can only cut down on variations in unemployment and inflation, not eliminate them. Discretionary programs are needed to supplement the effects of these automatic stabilizers. Such discretionary actions include changing government expenditure on public works and other programs, changing welfare payments and other such transfers, and changing tax rates. An important problem with some of these tools of fiscal policy is the lag in time before they can be brought into play.

At least three policies concerning the government budget have received considerable attention. First, the budget can be balanced each and every year. Second, the budget can be balanced over the course of the business cycle. Third, the budget can be set in a way that will promote full employment with stable prices whether or not this means that the budget is unbalanced over considerable periods of time. The history of the past 40 years has seen enormous changes in the public's attitude toward the government budget. Forty years ago, the prevailing doctrine was that the budget should be balanced each year; now the attitude seems to be that the budget should be used as a tool to reduce unemployment and inflation. Some of the popular misconceptions concerning budget deficits and budget surpluses can be avoided by the use of the full-employment budget, which shows the difference between tax revenue and government expenditure that would result if we had full employment.

CONCEPTS FOR REVIEW

$C + I + G$ line
Deficit
Surplus
Automatic stabilizers

Full-employment
  budget
Fiscal drag
Functional finance

Discretionary fiscal
  policy
Balanced budget

QUESTIONS FOR DISCUSSION AND REVIEW

1. According to Joseph Pechman, "Among taxes, the federal individual income tax is the leading [automatic] stabilizer." Explain why, and discuss the significance of this fact. He also says that "on the expenditure side, the major built-in stabilizer is unemployment compensation." Again, explain why, and discuss the significance of this fact.

2. According to Maurice Stans, "The federal government should have a balanced budget; its expenditures, especially in times like these, should not exceed its income." Do you agree?

3. A $1 billion change in government expenditures will result in a change in equilibrium NNP of $\dfrac{1}{MPS}$ billions of dollars. True or False?

4. Most economists would feel that fiscal policy is not too expansionary when
a. the actual budget shows a deficit, but the full-employment budget shows no deficit.
b. both the actual and full-employment budgets show huge deficits.
c. the price level is increasing at 10 percent per year.
d. the actual and full-employment budgets both show deficits of $20 billion.

CHAPTER 11

Business Fluctuations and Economic Forecasting

The American economy has not grown at a constant rate: instead, output has grown rapidly in some periods, and little, if at all, in others. Our history indicates that national output, employment, and the price level tend to fluctuate. These fluctuations, often mild, sometimes violent, are frequently called business cycles. The average citizen, as well as the government official or the business executive, needs to know why these fluctuations occur and whether they can be avoided. This chapter summarizes some of the leading theories advanced to answer these questions.

We also take up a related question of great practical importance: can business fluctuations be forecasted? More and more, economic models are being used by government and industry to forecast changes in GNP and other economic variables. Economic forecasting has become a very important part of the economist's job. Although no reputable economist would claim that economic forecasting is very precise or reliable, some of the more sophisti-

**Figure 11.1
Gross National Product (in
1958 Dollars), United States,
1918–72, Excluding World
War II**

Real GNP has not grown steadily.
Instead, it has tended to approach
its full-employment level, then to
falter and fall below this level,
then to rise once more, and so on.
This movement of national output
is sometimes called the business
cycle.

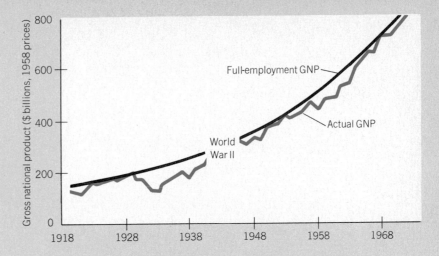

cated models have forecasted quite well in recent years. In the latter part of this chapter, we describe some of the more widely used forecasting techniques, and see how accurate they have proved in the past.

Business Fluctuations

To illustrate what we mean by "business fluctuations"—or the "business cycle"—let's look at how national output has grown in the United States since World War I. Figure 11.1 shows the behavior of real GNP (in constant dollars) in the United States since 1919. It is clear that output has grown considerably during this period; indeed, GNP is more than 5 times what it was 50 years ago. It is also clear that this growth has not been steady. On the contrary, although the long-term trend has been upward, there have been periods— like 1919–21, 1929–33, 1937–38, 1944–46, 1948– 49, 1953–54, 1957–58, and 1969–70—when national output has declined.

Let's define the full employment-level of GNP as the total amount of goods and services that could have been produced if there had been full em-

ployment. Figure 11.1 shows that national output tends to rise and approach its full-employment level for a while, then falter and fall below this level, then rise to approach it once more, then fall below it again, and so on. For example, output remained close to the full-employment level in the prosperous mid-1920s, fell far below this level in the depressed 1930s, and rose again to this level once we entered World War II. This movement of national output is sometimes called the *business cycle*, but it must be recognized that these cycles are far from regular or consistent. On the contrary, they are very irregular.

Each cycle can be divided by definition into four phases, as shown in Figure 11.2. The *trough* is the point where national output is lowest relative to its full-employment level. *Expansion* is the subsequent phase during which national output rises. The *peak* occurs when national output is highest relative to its full-employment level. Finally, *recession* is the subsequent phase during which national output falls.[1] Besides these four phases, two other

[1] More precisely, the peak and trough are generally defined in terms of deviations from the long-term trend of NNP, rather than in terms of deviations from the full-employment level of NNP. But the latter definition tends to be easier for beginners to grasp.

Figure 11.2
Four Phases of Business Fluctuation

Each cycle can be divided into four phases: trough, expansion, peak, and recession.

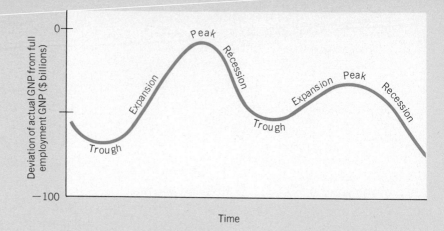

terms are frequently used to describe stages of the business cycle. A *depression* is a period when national output is well below its full-employment level; it is a severe recession. Depressions are, of course, periods of excessive unemployment. *Prosperity* is a period when national output is close to its full-employment level. Prosperity, if total spending is too high relative to potential output, can be a time of inflation. Of course, in some business cycles, the peak may not be a period of prosperity because output may be below its full-employment level, or the trough may not be a period of depression because output may not be far below its full-employment level.

Since World War II, peaks have occurred in 1948, 1953, 1957, 1960, and 1969, while troughs have occurred in 1949, 1954, 1958, 1961, and 1970. None of these recessions has been very long or very deep. We have done better since the war at avoiding and cushioning recessions, partly because of improvements in economic knowledge of the causes and cures of business cycles. Note that, although these cycles have certain things in common, they are highly individualistic. For certain classes of phenomena, it may be true that "if you've seen one, you've seen them all," but not for business cycles; they vary too much in length and nature.

Moreover, the basic set of factors responsible for the recession and the expansion differs from cycle to cycle.[2] This means that any theory designed to explain them must be broad enough to accommodate their idiosyncracies.

It is also worth stressing that investment seems to be the component of total spending that varies most over the course of a business cycle. Investment goes down markedly during recessions and increases markedly during expansions; on the other hand, consumption generally moves along with only slight bumps and dips.[3] The volatility of investment, together with the reasons for this volatility, are important clues to the cause of many business cycles. We shall see that this variation in

[2] For example, there is some evidence that every so often, a business boom, or peak, takes place at about the same time as a boom in building construction; thus such a peak is buoyed further by this favorable conjuncture—and every so often, a trough is lowered by it. These long swings in building (and other phenomena), lasting 15 to 25 years, are called Kuznets cycles after Harvard's Nobel Laureate, Simon Kuznets, who has devoted considerable study to them. See Alvin Hansen, *Business Cycles and National Income,* New York: Norton, 1962.

[3] However, expenditure on consumer durables is more volatile than other consumption expenditure. Moreover, the consumption function can shift, as it did after World War II. (Recall the discussion of this shift in Chapter 9.)

investment plus our old friend (of Chapter 9), the multiplier, can produce the sorts of business fluctuations that have occurred in the United States.

Government Spending and Expectations

Government expenditures too can sometimes cause business fluctuations. When we discussed fiscal policy, we described how government spending might be used to stabilize the economy. The unfortunate fact is that in the past the government's spending—particularly during and after wars—has sometimes been a major destabilizing force, resulting in business fluctuations. Recall from Chapter 8 the great bulge in government spending during World War II and the lesser bulges during the Korean and Vietnamese wars. These increases in spending produced strong inflationary pressures. The price level rose over 50 percent during 1940–46 (World War II), and major inflationary spurts also occurred during the wars in Korea and Vietnam. In Chapter 10, we discussed in some detail the destabilizing effects of the Vietnamese military buildup.

Government spending has been a destabilizing force after, as well as during, wars. The recession in 1953–54 was caused primarily by the reduction in government expenditures when the Korean war came to a close. When hostilities terminated, government expenditures were reduced by more than $10 billion. Government spending sometimes has also had the same destabilizing effect in other than wartime or postwar situations. The recession in 1957–58 was aggravated by a drop in defense expenditures in late 1957. Faced with this drop, the defense contractors cut their inventories and expenditures for plant and equipment.

Another factor is the nature and behavior of expectations. For example, in the recession of 1957, businessmen's expectations became decidedly more pessimistic. Capital spending was cut by over $7 billion and inventory investment by over $8 bil-

lion. (Fortunately, the recession was short, and the economy began to move upward in late 1958.) Such expectations play a significant role in business fluctuations. Decisions made at any point in time depend on expectations concerning the future. For example, when a firm builds a new warehouse, it has certain expectations concerning the extent of its sales in the future, the price it will have to pay for labor and transportation, and so on. In forming their expectations, businessmen often tend to follow the leader. As more and more businessmen and analysts predict a rosy future, others tend to jump on the bandwagon. This means that, as the economy advances from a trough, optimistic expectations concerning sales and profits tend to spread, slowly at first, then more and more rapidly. These expectations generate investment, which in turn increases NNP. Thus, the rosy expectations are self-fulfilling, at least up to a point. (In this area, even if "wishing won't make it so," expecting may turn the trick!) The result is that the expansion is fueled by self-fulfilling and self-augmenting expectations.

Eventually, however, these expectations are not fulfilled, perhaps because full-employment ceilings cause NNP to grow at a slower rate, perhaps because the government cuts back its spending (as in 1953–54), perhaps for some other reason. Now the process goes into reverse. Pessimistic expectations appear; and as NNP begins to decline, these expectations spread more and more rapidly. These expectations also tend to be self-fulfilling. Businessmen, feeling that the outlook for sales and profits is unfavorable, cut back on their investing, which in turn reduces NNP. Thus, the recession is made more serious by the epidemic of gloom. In any theory of business fluctuations, it is necessary to recognize the importance of expectations.

The Acceleration Principle

Investment in plant and equipment, as we know, varies considerably over the course of the business cycle. One of the most important reasons for this variation is illustrated by the following example. Suppose that the Johnson Shoe Corporation, a maker of women's shoes, requires 1 machine to make 50 pairs of shoes per year. Since each machine (and related plant and facilities) costs $1,000 and each pair of shoes costs $10, it takes $2 worth of plant and equipment to produce $1 worth of output per year. In 1965, we suppose that the quantity of the firm's plant and equipment was exactly in balance with its output. In other words, the firm had no excess capacity; sales were $10,000 and the actual stock of capital was $20,000. The firm's sales in subsequent years are shown in Table 11.1. For example, in 1966 its sales increased to $12,000; in 1967 they increased to $14,000; and so forth.

Table 11.1 also shows the amount the firm will have to invest each year in order to produce the amount it sells. Let's begin with 1966. To produce $12,000 worth of product, the firm must have $24,000 worth of capital. This means that it must increase its stock of capital from $20,000—the

amount it has in 1965—to $24,000.[4] In other words, it must increase its stock of capital by $4,000, which means that its net investment in plant and equipment must equal $4,000. But this is not the same as its gross investment—the amount of plant and equipment the firm must buy—because the firm must also replace some plant and equipment that wears out. Suppose that $1,000 of plant and equipment wear out each year: then gross investment in 1966 must equal net investment ($4,000) plus $1,000, or $5,000.

Next, let's look at 1967. The firm's sales in that year are $14,000. To produce this much output, the firm must have $28,000 of capital, which means that it must increase its stock of capital by $4,000 —from $24,000 to $28,000. In addition, there is $1,000 of replacement investment to replace plant and equipment that wear out in 1967. In all, the firm's gross investment must be $5,000. In 1968, the firm's sales are $15,000. To produce this output,

[4] Note that the firm's stock of capital is an entirely different concept than its common stock or preferred stock. See Chapter 7.

Table 11.1

Relationship between Sales and Investment, Johnson Shoe Corporation

Year	Sales (thousands of dollars)	Needed stock of capital (thousands of dollars)	Actual stock of capital (thousands of dollars)	Replacement investment (thousands of dollars)	Net investment (thousands of dollars)	Gross investment (thousands of dollars)
1965	10	20	20	1	0	1
1966	12	24	24	1	4	5
1967	14	28	28	1	4	5
1968	15	30	30	1	2	3
1969	16	32	32	1	2	3
1970	16	32	32	1	0	1
1971	15	30	31	0	0	0
1972	15	30	30	0	0	0
1973	15	30	30	1	0	1
1974	17	34	34	1	4	5

the firm must have $30,000 of capital, which means that it must increase its stock of capital by $2,000—from $28,000 to $30,000. In addition, there is $1,000 of replacement investment. In all, the firm's gross investment must be $3,000. Table 11.1 shows the results for subsequent years.

What conclusions can be drawn from Table 11.1? First, *changes in sales can result in magnified percentage changes in investment.* For example, between 1965 and 1966 sales went up by 20 percent, whereas gross investment went up by 400 percent. Between 1973 and 1974, sales went up by about 13 percent, whereas gross investment went up by 400 percent. The effect of a decrease in sales is even more spectacular because it tends to drive net investment to zero. Indeed, even gross investment may be driven to zero, as in 1971, if the firm wants to reduce the value of its plant and equipment. To accomplish this, the firm simply does not replace the plant and equipment that wear out.

Second, *the amount of gross investment depends on the rate of increase of sales.* In particular, for gross investment to remain constant year after year, the rate of increase of sales must also remain constant. You can see this in 1966 and 1967. In each of these years, since sales increased from the previous year by the same amount ($2,000), gross investment remained constant at $5,000 per year. It is very important to note that *gross investment will fall when sales begin to increase at a decreasing rate.* The fact that sales are increasing does not insure that gross investment will increase; on the contrary, if sales are increasing at a decreasing rate, gross investment will fall. This is a very important point.

This effect of changes in sales on gross investment is often called the **acceleration principle,** since changes in sales result in accelerated, or magnified, changes in investment, and since an increase in investment results from an increase in the growth rate (an **acceleration**) of sales. The acceleration principle applies to kinds of investment other than plant and equipment. For example, it is easy to show that it applies to inventories and

housing as well. Thus, firms often try to maintain a certain amount of inventory for each dollar of sales —just as they often maintain a certain amount of plant and equipment for each dollar of sales.

The Interaction between the Acceleration Principle and the Multiplier

Economists—led by Nobel Laureates Paul Samuelson and Sir John Hicks[5]—have shown that the acceleration principle combined with the multiplier may produce business cycles like those experienced in the real world. The basic idea is easy. Suppose that the economy is moving up toward full employment, NNP is increasing, and sales are increasing at an increasing rate. Because of the acceleration principle, the increases in sales result in a high level of investment. And via the multiplier, the high level of investment promotes further increases in NNP. Thus, the accelerator and multiplier tend to reinforce one another, resulting in a strong upward movement of NNP. The economy is in an expansion. It is a good time to be president of the United States, president of a major corporation, or an average citizen.

Eventually, however, the economy nears full employment; and since we have only a certain amount of land, labor, and capital, it simply is impossible to increase NNP at the rate experienced during the recovery. Consequently, sales cannot increase forever at the same rate; instead, they begin to increase more slowly. But as we saw in the previous section, the reduction in the rate of increase of sales is the kiss of death for investment. Even though sales continue to increase, the drop in the rate of increase means decreasing investment. And this reduction in investment sounds the death

[5] Paul A. Samuelson, "The Interaction between the Multiplier Analysis and the Acceleration Principle," *Review of Economics and Statistics,* 1939; and John Hicks, *A Contribution to the Theory of the Trade Cycle,* Oxford, 1950. Also, see R. F. Harrod, *The Trade Cycle,* Oxford, 1936.

knell for the boom, since it reduces NNP directly and via the multiplier. The reduction in NNP means a reduction in sales, and the reduction in sales means a drastic reduction in investment, through the acceleration principle. The drastic reduction in investment means a further reduction in NNP. The economy is in a recession. Everything is moving downward, with the notable exception of unemployment. People are getting increasingly nervous—including the president of the United States, the presidents of major corporations, and many average citizens.

Eventually, however, firms reduce their stock of capital to the point where it is in balance with their reduced sales. In other words, they go through the sort of process shown in Table 11.1 during 1971–72, when the Johnson Shoe Corporation reduced its stock of capital by refusing to replace worn-out plant and equipment. At the end of this process, the stock of capital is in balance with sales. To keep this balance, firms must now replace worn-out equipment, which means an increase in gross investment. Via the multiplier, this increase in investment results in an increase in national product, which means an increase in sales. Via the acceleration principle, this increase in sales results in an increase in investment, which in turn increases national product. The economy is once again in the midst of a recovery. It is again a good time to be president of the United States, president of a major corporation, or an average citizen. As moviegoers put it, this is where we came in.

This theory, although highly simplified, provides a great many insights into the nature of business fluctuations. One aspect of the theory in particular should be noted: business cycles are self-starting and self-terminating. Recession, trough, recovery, peak—each phase of the business cycle leads into the next. This theory shows that one need not look outside the economic system for causes of the upper and lower turning points—that is, the points where the economy begins to turn down after a recovery or begins to turn up after a recession. These turning points can occur for the reasons we have just indicated.

Inventory Cycles

Inventories also play an important role in business fluctuations. Indeed, the "minor" or "short" business cycle, lasting about 2 to 4 years, is sometimes called an *inventory cycle* because it is often due largely to variations in inventories. This cycle proceeds as follows. Businessmen, having let their inventories decline during a business slowdown, find that they are short of inventories. They increase their inventories, which means that they produce more than they sell. This investment in inventories has a stimulating effect on NNP. So long as the rate of increase of their sales holds up, firms continue to increase their inventories at this rate.[6] Thus, inventory investment continues to stimulate the economy. But when their sales begin to increase more slowly, firms begin to cut back on their inventory investment. This reduction in inventory investment has a depressing effect on NNP. As their sales decrease, firms cut back further on their inventory investment, further damping NNP. Then when inventories are cut to the bone, the process starts all over again.

As an illustration, consider the recession of 1948–49, which was primarily the result of reduction of inventory investment. After World War II, there was a period of stockpiling. Inventories were built up very substantially during 1948: indeed, they increased by $5 billion during that year. In 1949, on the other hand, inventories were cut by about the same amount. Thus, there was a $10 billion decrease in inventory investment between 1947 and 1948. This meant a considerable cutback in production. Not only did firms stop producing more—$5 billion more—than they sold, they started producing less—$5 billion less—than they sold, and they cut wages and income. This was a major cause of the recession of 1948–49.

---

[6] As noted above, the acceleration effect discussed in previous sections applies to inventories as well as plant and equipment, since firms often try to maintain inventories equal to a certain percentage of sales. Thus, the *rate of increase* of sales will affect the rate of investment in inventories as well as plant and equipment.

Innovations and Random External Events

Let's turn now to a different sort of explanation of business fluctuations. Clearly, the acceleration principle is only one factor influencing gross investment. Since a firm will invest in any project where the returns exceed the costs involved, many investment projects are not triggered by changes in sales. For example, a new product may be invented, and large investments may be required to produce, distribute, and market it. Consider the automobile industry, currently one of America's largest industries. It took big investments by the pioneers in the auto business to get the automobile to the point where it was an important item in the average consumer's budget. Or consider nylon, which Du Pont spent several million dollars to develop. It took large investments before nylon was on its way.

Major innovations do not occur every day; neither do they occur at a constant rate. There are more in some years than in others, and sheer chance influences the number of innovations in a given year. Similarly, chance greatly influences the timing of many other types of events that bear on the level of output and investment. These include crop failures, hurricanes, and other such natural disasters, as well as man-made events, like strikes in major industries and financial panics, which also affect output and investment.

Let's suppose that these events—innovations and other occurrences that have a major effect on investment—occur more or less at random. Because so many factors influence the timing of each such event, we cannot predict how many will occur in a particular year. Instead, the number is subject to chance variation, like the number thrown in a dice game or the number of spades in a poker hand. In particular, suppose that the chance that one of these events occurs in one year is about the same as in another year.

If this is the case, economists—led by Norway's Nobel Laureate, Ragnar Frisch[7]—have shown that business cycles are likely to result. The basic idea is simple enough. The economy, because of its internal structure, is like a pendulum or rocking chair. If it is subjected to random shocks—like pushing a rocking chair every now and then—it will move up and down. These random shocks are the bursts of investment that arise as a consequence of a great new invention or of the development of a new territory, or for some other such reason. These bursts play the role of the forces hitting the pendulum or the rocking chair. To a considerable extent, they may be due to noneconomic events or forces, but whatever their cause, they bang into the economy and shove it in one direction or another.

Of course, the occurrence of these shocks is not the whole story. Business fluctuations in this model do not occur only because of the random events that affect investment. In addition, the economy must respond to—and amplify—the effects of these stimuli. The economy must be like a rocking chair, not a sofa. (If you whack a sofa every now and then, you are likely to hurt your hand, but not to move the sofa much.) Frisch showed that the economy is likely to respond to, and amplify, these shocks. This model explains the fact, stressed in a previous section, that although cycles bear some family resemblance, no two are really alike. Thus the model has the advantage of not explaining more than it should. It does not imply that business fluctuations are more uniform and predictable than they are.

This theory provides valuable insight into the nature of business fluctuations. Like the theory of the interaction of the acceleration principle and the multiplier, it contains important elements of truth, although it obviously is highly simplified. Each of these theories focuses on factors that may be partly responsible for business fluctuations. They complement one another, in the sense that both processes—the interaction of the multiplier and the acceleration principle, and the random external stimuli to investment—may be at work. There is

[7] Ragnar Frisch, "Propagation Problems and Impulse Problems in Dynamic Economics," *Economic Essays in Honor of Gustav Cassel,* London: George Allen and Unwin, 1933.

no need to choose between these theories: both help to explain business fluctuations, and both are far from the whole truth.

Monetary Factors

Finally, we must stress that *monetary factors are of great importance in causing business fluctuations.* For example, monetary factors were of the utmost importance in slowing down the boom of the late 1960s, as we shall see in Chapter 14. The fact that we have not yet taken up these factors is no indication that they are unimportant. On the contrary, they are so important that we shall devote the next several chapters entirely to them. For pedagogical reasons, it seems advisable to discuss them after the topics taken up in Chapters 9–11. You should constantly bear in mind that monetary policy can be of enormous importance in moderating business fluctuations and in promoting reasonably full employment with reasonably stable prices. In economics as in other aspects of life, money counts.

Can Business Fluctuations Be Avoided?

Having looked at some theories designed to explain business fluctuations, we are led to ask whether they (the fluctuations, not the theories) can be avoided in the future. To some extent, a discussion of this question is premature, since we have not yet taken up monetary policy. But there is no reason to postpone answering it in general terms, waiting for subsequent chapters to provide more detailed discussions of various aspects of the answer.

On the basis of our increased knowledge of the reasons for business fluctuations and the growing acceptance of modern monetary and fiscal policy, some people seem to think the business cycle has been licked. That is, they feel that we can now use monetary and fiscal policy to head off a recession

or a boom, and in this way offset the processes and events that destabilize the economy. This is a rather optimistic view, although the evidence does indicate that we have been able to reduce the severity and frequency of major recessions in recent years. Our record in this regard has been distinctly better than in pre-World War II days.

In particular, the fact that we managed to maintain uninterrupted economic expansion for most of the 1960s was an unparalleled achievement—although, as pointed out in previous chapters, our record on inflation during the later 1960s was not so awe-inspiring. This improvement in performance must be attributed partly to better economic knowledge and partly to the fact that the nation, recognizing that depressions are not inevitable, expects the government to take the actions required to prevent them.

Unfortunately, this does not mean that a major depression—like that experienced in the 1930s—is impossible, although the chance of its occurrence must be regarded as very small. Even though we now know how to prevent a depression, one could still occur through stupidity or some weird sequence of events. But the probability of such a depression is very, very small, given our automatic stabilizers and the fact that policy makers—and the electorate —know now that fiscal policy (Chapter 10) and monetary policy (Chapter 14) can be used to push the economy toward full employment.

It seems unlikely, however, that the small recessions—the "dips" and "pauses"—are a thing of the past. There will be ups and downs in spending on plant and equipment, there will be fluctuations in inventories, there will be military buildups and cutbacks, and changes in government spending and in tax rates. All these things can be destabilizing, and existing economic knowledge is not sufficiently precise to allow policy makers to iron out the resulting small deviations of NNP from its long-term upward trend. Although there has been a certain amount of optimistic talk about "fine-tuning" of the economy, the truth is that we lack the knowledge or the means to do it.

Finally, the prospect for inflation is not so bright. The recent record of the United States has not been particularly encouraging. We have just about learned that a balanced budget is not the touchstone of fiscal policy, but we have not yet learned how to maintain reasonably full employment with reasonably stable prices. This is a very difficult problem, and an important one, which we shall discuss in much greater detail in Chapters 12, 14, and 15.

Can Business Fluctuations Be Forecasted?

Having studied important aspects of the modern theory of the determination of national product, as well as various reasons for business fluctuations, you may well ask how useful these theories are in forecasting NNP. This is a perfectly reasonable question. After all, when you study physics or chemistry, you want to come away with certain theories or principles that will enable you to predict physical or chemical phenomena. To the extent that economics is a science, you have a right to expect the same thing, since an acid test of any science is how well it predicts.

This question is also of great practical importance. Government officials are enormously interested in what NNP is likely to be in the next year or so, since they must try to anticipate whether excessive unemployment or serious inflationary pressures are developing. Business executives are equally interested, since their firms' sales, profits, and needs for equipment depend on NNP. For these reasons, forecasting is one of the principal jobs of economists in government and industry.

The first thing that must be said is that, in forecasting as in most other areas, economics is not an exact science. If an economist tells you he can predict exactly what NNP will be next year, you can be pretty sure that he is talking through his hat. Of course, by luck, he may be able to predict correctly, but lucky guesses do not a science make. However, although economic forecasting is not perfectly accurate, economic forecasts are still useful. Since governments, firms, and private individuals must continually make decisions that hinge on what they expect will happen, there is no way that they can avoid making forecasts, explicit or implicit. Really the only question is how best to make them.

There is considerable evidence that, even though forecasts based on economic models are sometimes not very good, they are better—on the average—than those made by noneconomists. There is no substitute for economic analysis in accurate forecasting over the long haul. Of course, this really isn't very surprising. It would be strange if economists, whose profession it is to study and predict economic phenomena, were to do worse than those without this training—even if the others are tycoons or politicians. Further, it would be strange if government and industry were to hire platoons of economists at fancy prices—which they do—if they couldn't predict any better than anyone else.

In the realm of economic forecasting, what is a good batting average? According to M.I.T.'s Paul Samuelson,

> In economic forecasting of the direction of change, we ought to be able to do at least .500 just by tossing a coin. And taking advantage of the undoubted upward trend in all modern economies, we can bat .750 or better just by parrot-like repeating, "Up, Up." The difference between the men and the boys, then, comes between an .850 performance and an .800 performance. Put in other terms, the good forecaster, who must in November make a point-estimate of GNP for the calendar year ahead, will over a decade, have an average error of perhaps one percent, being in a range of $12 billion with reality being $6 billion on either side of the estimate. And a rather poor forecaster may, over the same period, average an error of 1½ percent. When we average the yearly results for a decade, it may be found that in the worst year the error was over 2 percent, compensated by rather small errors in many of the years not expected to represent turning points.[8]

[8] Paul A. Samuelson, "Economic Forecasting and Science," in his *Readings in Economics*, New York: McGraw-Hill, 1970, pp. 112–113, and reprinted in E. Mansfield, *Economics: Readings, Issues, and Cases*, New York: Norton, 1974.

Economists have no single method for forecasting NNP or GNP. They vary in their approach just as physicians, for example, differ in theirs. But reputable economists tend to use one of a small number of forecasting techniques, each of which is described in a subsequent section. Of course, many economists do not restrict themselves to one technique, but rely on a combination of several, using one to check on another.

Leading Indicators

Perhaps the simplest way to forecast business fluctuations is to use *leading indicators,* which are certain economic series that typically go down or up before NNP does. The National Bureau of Economic Research, founded by Wesley C. Mitchell (1874–1948), has carried out detailed and painstaking research to examine the behavior of various economic variables over a long period of time, in some cases as long as 100 years. The Bureau has attempted to find out whether each variable goes down before, at, or after the peak of the business cycle, and whether it turns up before, at, or after the trough. Variables that go down before the peak and up before the trough are called *leading series.* Variables that go down at the peak and up at the trough are called *coincident series.* And those that go down after the peak and up after the trough are called *lagging series.*

It is worthwhile examining the kinds of variables that fall into each of these three categories, since they give us important facts concerning the anatomy of the cycle. According to the Bureau, some important leading series are business failures, new orders for durable goods, average work week, building contracts, stock prices, certain wholesale prices, and new incorporations. These are the variables that tend to turn down before the peak and turn up before the trough.[9] Coincident series include employment, industrial production, corporate prof-

[9] Of course, business failures turn *up* before the peak and *down* before the trough.

its, and gross national product, among many others. Some typical lagging series are retail sales, manufacturers' inventories, and personal income.

Economists sometimes use leading series as forecasting devices. There are good economic reasons why these series turn down before a peak or up before a trough. In some cases, they indicate changes in spending in strategic areas of the economy, while in others they indicate changes in businessmen's and investors' expectations. Both to guide the government in determining its economic policies and to guide firms in their planning, it is important to try to spot turning points—peaks and troughs—in advance. This, of course, is the toughest part of economic forecasting. Economists sometimes use these leading indicators as evidence that a turning point is about to occur. If a large number of leading indicators turn down, this is viewed as a sign of a coming peak. If a large number turn up, this is thought to signal an impending trough.

Unfortunately, the leading indicators are not very reliable. It is true that the economy has never turned down in recent years without a warning from these indicators. This is fine. But unfortunately these indicators have turned down on several occasions—1952 and 1962, for example—when the economy did not turn down subsequently. Thus, they sometimes provide false signals. Also, in periods of expansion, they sometimes turn down too long before the real peak. And in periods of recession, they sometimes turn up only a very short while before the trough, so that we've turned the corner before anything can be done. Nonetheless, these indicators are not worthless. They are watched closely and used to supplement other, more sophisticated forecasting techniques.

Simple Keynesian Models

Leading indicators are used primarily to spot turning points—peaks and troughs. They are of little or no use in predicting GNP (or NNP). To forecast GNP, we need a more sophisticated approach, one more firmly rooted in economic theory. (Leading indicators are largely the product of strictly empirical analysis.) To forecast GNP, it is worthwhile bringing into play the theory we described in Chapters 9 and 10. After all, if the theory is any good, it should help us to forecast GNP. This theory can be used in a variety of ways to help prepare such forecasts, and a first course in economics can provide no more than the most basic introduction to these methods.

One simple way of trying to forecast GNP is to treat certain components of total spending as given and to use these components to forecast the total. This method is sometimes used by the Council of Economic Advisers, among others. For example, suppose that we decide to forecast private investment and government expenditures as a first step, after which we will use these forecasts to predict GNP.[10] Private investment is made up of three parts: expenditures on plant and equipment, residential construction, and changes in inventories. The most important of these parts is expenditure on plant and equipment. To forecast it, the results of surveys of firms' expenditure plans for the next year are helpful. The Department of Commerce and the Securities and Exchange Commission send out questionnaires at the beginning of each year to a large number of firms, asking them how much they plan to spend on plant and equipment during the year. The results, which appear in March in the *Survey of Current Business,* are pretty accurate. For example, the average error in 1951–63 was only about 3 percent.

This survey can help us forecast business expenditures on plant and equipment, but what about the other parts of private investment—residential construction and changes in inventories? Lots of techniques are used to forecast them. Some people use construction contracts and similar indicators as the basis for forecasts of residential construction. For inventory changes, some people watch the surveys carried out by *Fortune* magazine and the Com-

merce Department, which ask companies about their inventory plans.

Next, we need a forecast of government expenditures. At the federal level, it is possible to forecast government expenditures on the basis of the president's proposed budget or Congress's appropriations (although, as indicated by our discussion of the Vietnam buildup in Chapter 10, these forecasts can sometimes be quite wrong). At the state and local level, it is often possible to extrapolate spending levels reasonably well.

Suppose that, having studied as many relevant factors as we can, we finally conclude that in our best estimate private investment plus government expenditure will equal $400 billion next year. How do we go from this estimate to an estimate of GNP? Suppose that consumers in the past have devoted about 90 percent of their disposable income to consumption expenditure, and that disposable income has been about 70 percent of GNP. Assuming that this will also be true again next year, it follows that consumption expenditure will equal 63 percent (90 percent times 70 percent) of GNP. In other words,

$$C = .63Y, \tag{11.1}$$

where C is consumption expenditure and Y is GNP. Also, by definition,

$$Y = C + I + G,$$

where I is gross private investment and G is government expenditure. Since $I + G = 400$, it follows that

$$Y = C + 400. \tag{11.2}$$

Substituting the right-hand side of Equation (11.1) for C,

$$Y = .63Y + 400,$$

---

[10] We continue to ignore net exports in this part of the book because they are quite small. Chapters 19–20 will study them in some detail.

or

$$Y - .63Y = 400$$
$$.37Y = 400$$
$$Y = \frac{400}{.37}$$
$$= 1081.$$

Thus, our forecast for GNP next year is $1,081 billion.

At this point, our job may seem to be over. But it really isn't; we must check this forecast in various ways. For example, it implies that consumption expenditures next year will be $681 billion. (Since $C = .63Y$, according to Equation (11.1), and Y equals 1081, C must equal 681.) Does this seem reasonable? For example, how does it compare with the latest results of the survey of consumer buying plans carried out at the Survey Research Center at the University of Michigan? Also, the forecasted level of GNP must be compared with the physical capacity of the economy. Do we have the physical capacity to produce this much at stable prices? To what extent will the general price level be pushed upward? Moreover, our assumptions concerning I and G must be reexamined in the light of our forecast of GNP. If GNP is $1,081 billion, is it reasonable to assume that I will be the amount we initially forecasted? Or do we want to revise our forecast of I? A great many steps must be carried out before we finally put forth a GNP forecast, if we are conscientious and professional in our approach. Moreover, even after the forecast is made, it is often updated as new information becomes available, so the process goes on more or less continuously.

Econometric Models

In recent years, more and more emphasis has been placed on econometric models. Twenty years ago, econometric models were in their infancy, but now the Council of Economic Advisers, the Treasury, the Federal Reserve Board, and other parts of the federal government pay attention to the forecasts made by econometric models—and sometimes construct their own econometric models. Business firms too hire economists to construct econometric models for them, to forecast both GNP and their own sales. *Econometric models* are systems of equations estimated from past data that are used to forecast economic variables. There are many kinds of econometric models. For example, some are designed to forecast wage rates; others are designed to forecast the sales of a new product; and still others are designed to forecast a particular company's share of the market. We are concerned here only with econometric models designed to forecast GNP.

The essence of any econometric model is that it blends theory and measurement. It is not merely a general, nonquantitative theory. Useful as such a theory may be, it does not in general permit quantitative or numerical forecasts. Nor is an econometric model a purely empirical result based on little or no theoretical underpinning. Useful as such results may be, they generally are untrustworthy once the basic structure of the economic situation changes. Most econometric models designed to forecast GNP are built, at least in part, on the theoretical foundations described in previous chapters. In other words, they contain a number of equations, one of which is designed to explain consumption expenditures, one to explain investment expenditures, and so forth.

To see what is involved in the construction of an econometric model, let's consider just one of the equations, the consumption equation. The first step in formulating this equation is to ask ourselves what variables influence consumption expenditure. We know from Chapter 9 that one important determinant of consumption expenditure is disposable income. Thus, if the ratio of disposable income to GNP remains constant, consumption expenditure should be closely related to GNP. To keep things simple, let's suppose that this is the only factor determining consumption expenditure. Needless to say, this is not the case, but it makes it easier to see what is involved in constructing an

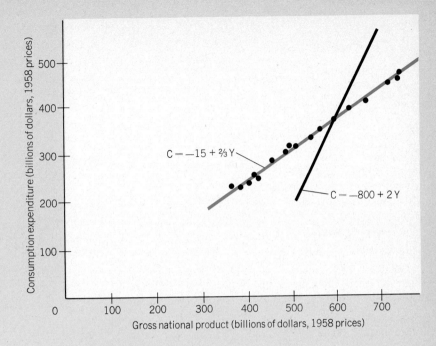

Figure 11.3
Relationship between Consumption Expenditure and Gross National Product, 1950–70

The line $C = -15 + \frac{2}{3}Y$ fits the data (indicated by the dots) far better than the line $C = -800 + 2Y$. (C is consumption expenditure and Y is GNP.) No one needs a Ph.D. in mathematical statistics to see this.

econometric model.

Economic theory—and hunch and intuition based on experience and insight—suggest the explanatory variables to be used in an equation, but they alone cannot supply the numbers to be used. For example, if the relationship between consumption expenditure and GNP is linear, it follows that

$$C = a + bY, \qquad (11.3)$$

where C is consumption expenditure and Y is gross national product. But what are the numerical values of a and b? At this point, statistical techniques of various sorts come into play. In the simple case considered here, we can plot consumption expenditure (C) against gross national product (Y) in various years in the past, as shown in Figure 11.3. Then we can pick the values of a and b that fit the data best. For example, as shown in Figure 11.3, an equation based on $a = -800$ and $b = 2$ does not fit the data at all well, while an

equation based on $a = -15$ and $b = \frac{2}{3}$ does much better. There are standard statistical methods, known as regression techniques, that can be used to determine which values of a and b fit the data best. These values, once determined, can be inserted into Equation (11.3).

A Small Econometric Model[11]

Econometric models, like many of the good things in life, come in various sizes. Some are composed of lots of equations; some contain only a few. Bigger models are not necessarily to be preferred to smaller ones, or vice versa. The sort of model that is best for a particular purpose depends on which one predicts best and how costly it is to operate. The best way to get a feel for the nature of an

[11] This section, and the following one, are optional and can be omitted without loss of continuity.

econometric model is to examine one. Let's take a look at a small one designed by Wharton's Irwin Friend and Paul Taubman.[12] Because it contains only 5 equations, it is an easy one for a student to begin on. More complicated models are discussed in the next section.

Although the discussion in this section and the next one is at an elementary level, the nature of the analysis requires familiarity with the idea of, and notation for, a set of equations. Readers who do not have this familiarity can skip these two sections without losing the thread of the argument.

One of the hardest things to keep track of in econometric models is what each symbol stands for. Let's begin by spelling this out for the Friend-Taubman model. There are 9 variables used in the model, and the symbol for each is as follows:

Y = gross national product
C = consumption expenditure
E = plant and equipment expenditures
E^e = expected plant and equipment expenditures, according to surveys
H = residential construction expenditure
L = housing starts (lagged a quarter)
I = inventory investment
S^e = expected business sales, according to surveys
G = government expenditure plus net exports.

$Y, C, E, E^e, H, I, G,$ and S^e are measured in billions of 1954 dollars. L is measured in hundreds of thousands of units. Another symbol that must be explained is Δ, which means the change in a particular variable. For example, ΔY means "the change in Y," or since Y is GNP, it means "the change in GNP." Still another symbol is the subscript $_{-1}$. Any variable with a subscript $_{-1}$ means the value of the variable in the preceding period. Thus, a change with a subscript $_{-1}$ means a change occurring between the previous two periods. For example, ΔC_{-1} means the change in consumption expenditure between the last period

[12] Irwin Friend and Paul Taubman, "A Short-Term Forecasting Model," *Review of Economics and Statistics,* August 1964. This model has been revised since publication, and is presented for illustrative purposes only.

and the period before. In this model, each period is 6 months.

Having disposed of the preliminaries, let's look at the model. The first equation explains ΔC, the change in consumption expenditure between this period and last period. According to this equation,

$$\Delta C = 2.18 + .37\Delta Y + .10\Delta C_{-1}. \quad (11.4)$$

In other words, the change in consumption expenditures equals 2.18 billion (1954) dollars plus .37 times the change in GNP between this period and last period plus .10 times the change in consumption expenditures between last period and the period before. Certainly it is reasonable to expect that the change in consumption will be directly related to the change in GNP. This follows from our discussion of the consumption function in Chapter 9. It is also reasonable to expect that the change in consumption between this period and the last will depend on the change in consumption between the last period and the one before. Basically the reason for this is that there is likely to be a lag in adjustment. The numbers in Equation (11.4), like those in all the equations in the model, were estimated from past data.

The second equation explains ΔE, the change in expenditures on plant and equipment between this period and the last period. According to this equation,

$$\Delta E = -.82 + .63(E^e - E_{-1}) + .08(\Delta Y + \Delta Y_{-1}). \quad (11.5)$$

In other words, the change in expenditure on plant and equipment equals $-.82$ billion (1954) dollars plus .63 times the difference between expected expenditure on plant and equipment (based on surveys) and actual expenditure on plant and equipment in the previous period, plus .08 times the sum of the change in GNP between this period and the last period and the change in GNP between the last period and the previous period. One would suppose, of course, that the change in actual expenditure on plant and equipment would be directly related to the change indicated by businessmen's expectations concerning their expenditures on plant and equipment. Also, based on the acceleration principle, one would suppose that the amount spent on plant and equipment would be directly related to the rate of change of GNP. Both suppositions are included in Equation (11.5) because neither theory by itself does as well historically as a mixture of both.

The third equation explains ΔH, the change in residential construction between this period and last period. According to this equation,

$$\Delta H = .35 + .58\Delta L + .06(\Delta Y - \Delta Y_{-1}) \\ - .16(E^e - E_{-1}). \quad (11.6)$$

In other words, the change in expenditure on residential construction equals .35 billion (1954) dollars plus .58 times the change in housing starts (lagged a quarter) plus .06 times the change in the rate of change of GNP minus .16 times the expected change in expenditure on plant and equipment (based on surveys). One would suppose, of course, that the change in expenditure on construction would be directly related to the change in housing starts (lagged a quarter). Also, from the acceleration principle, one would suppose that the amount spent on residential construction would be directly related to the rate of change of GNP. Thus, the change in the amount spent on residential construction would be assumed to vary directly with the change in the rate of change of GNP, which of course equals $\Delta Y - \Delta Y_{-1}$. Finally, the change in residential construction is likely to be inversely related to the change in expected expenditures on plant and equipment because if there is a great increase (decrease) in the latter, this will mean higher (lower) interest rates and greater (less) competition for resources which may discourage (encourage) residential construction.

The fourth equation explains ΔI, the change in inventory investment between this period and the last period. According to this equation,

$$\Delta I = 1.51 + .025\Delta S^e + 1.70(E^e - E_{-1}) \\ - 1.15I_{-1}. \quad (11.7)$$

In other words, the change in inventory investment equals 1.51 billion (1954) dollars plus .25 times the change in total sales expected by businessmen (as given by surveys) plus 1.70 times the difference between expected expenditure on plant and equipment (as given by surveys) and actual expenditure on plant and equipment in the previous period minus 1.15 times the inventory investment in the previous period. The authors of the model argue that the change in inventory investment will be directly related to the change in expected sales, since firms generally want to keep their inventories more or less proportional to their sales. Also, they believe that the change in inventory investment will be directly related to the expected change in expenditure on plant and equipment, since the latter is a good indicator of the general economic outlook. In addition, they state that the change in inventory investment will be inversely related to the level of inventory investment in the previous period. According to their model, if inventory investment was high (low) in the previous period, there will be a smaller (bigger) change in inventory investment than if it was low (high) in the previous period.

Finally, the fifth equation merely states the obvious fact that the change in GNP must equal the change in consumption expenditures plus the change in each of the parts of gross private investment (expenditures on plant and equipment, residential construction, and inventories) plus the change in government expenditures (plus net exports). In other words,

$$\Delta Y = \Delta C + \Delta E + \Delta H + \Delta I + \Delta G. \quad (11.8)$$

This must be true because $Y =$ consumption + gross private investment + government expenditures (plus net exports). Since gross private investment equals $E + H + I$, it follows that $Y = C + E + H + I + G$. Thus, the change in Y must equal the sum of the changes in C, E, H, I, and G.

Econometric models—even small ones like this —are fairly complicated. It is easy to get so engrossed in the details of each equation that we lose sight of the basic purpose of the model—to forecast GNP, in this case. How can we use this model to forecast GNP? As a first step, let's substitute the right-hand side of Equation (11.4) for ΔC in Equation (11.8). Also, let's substitute the right-hand side of Equation (11.5) for ΔE in Equation (11.8). Let's substitute the right-hand side of Equation (11.6) for ΔH in Equation (11.8), and the right-hand side of Equation (11.7) for ΔI in Equation (11.8). All of these substitutions give us an expression for ΔY. In particular,

$$\Delta Y = 3.22 + 2.00\Delta G + 4.34(E^e - E_{-1}) \\ - 2.30 I_{-1} + .05\Delta S^e + 1.15\Delta L + .037\,\Delta Y_{-1} \\ + .19\Delta C_{-1}. \quad (11.9)$$

This equation can be used to forecast ΔY—the change in gross national product between the *next* period and the *present* period. To do so, one must insert the appropriate values of ΔC_{-1}, ΔY_{-1}, $(E^e - E_{-1})$, ΔL, ΔS^e, I_{-1}, and ΔG into Equation (11.9). For example, if the change in consumption between this period and the last period was $1 billion, we would substitute 1 for ΔC_{-1} in Equation (11.9). And if the change in gross national product between this period and the last period was $2 billion, we would substitute 2 for ΔY_{-1}, and so on for the other variables on the right-hand side of Equation (11.9). When the value of each of the variables has been inserted into Equation (11.9), we are the proud possessor of a forecast of ΔY—the change in gross national product between the next period and the present period.

Econometric Models, Big and Bigger

The econometric model just presented is a small one designed to forecast changes in GNP over the next 6 months. The economists who constructed it did not intend it to be used to estimate the effects of government policy—for example, changes in tax rates or government expenditures—or to forecast prices, income distribution, unemployment, capital utilization, and so forth. In recent years, there has been a remarkable amount of activity in the economics profession here and abroad, aimed at the construction of larger econometric models, which may be able to represent the behavior of the economy in richer and more complete detail. The leading figure in the development of such models has been Lawrence Klein of the University of Pennsylvania. Two of the models that he has constructed—or helped to construct—are known as the Wharton model and the Brookings model.

The Wharton model, published in 1967, contained about 50 equations: 3 equations that explain various components of consumer spending (consumer nondurable goods, automobiles, and other consumer durable goods), 6 equations to explain various components of private investment (expenditure on plant and equipment, residential housing, and inventory changes), 4 explaining depreciation, 4 explaining tax receipts and transfer payments, 5 explaining the level of output in various sectors of the economy, 7 explaining price level changes in various sectors of the economy, and other equations explaining hours worked, wage rates, unemployment, interest rates, profits, and other variables. This model was used to make quarterly forecasts of GNP, unemployment, changes in the price level, and other variables a year or more ahead. It was also used to forecast the effects on the economy of alternate government policies—for example, to estimate the effects of changes in tax rates on GNP and unemployment. Its forecasts were watched closely and publicized widely in the business community and in government.[13] In recent years, the Wharton model has been extended and refined in numerous ways.

The Brookings model—more formally, the Brookings Quarterly Econometric Model of the United States—was the "big daddy" of the econometric models. Composed of well over 200 equa-

[13] Michael Evans and Lawrence Klein, *The Wharton Econometric Forecasting Model*, Philadelphia: University of Pennsylvania, 1967.

Table 11.2

Predictive Record of Some Leading Economic Forecasting Techniques

Year	Actual GNP	Error (in billions of dollars)				
		Average general forecast (Federal Reserve Bank of Philadelphia)	Council of Economic Advisers	Michigan model	Friend-Taubman model	Wharton model
1959	484	−13	—	−19	—	
1960	504	4	—	−10	—	
1961	520	− 7	—	2	—	
1962	560	4	14	4	—	
1963	591	−11	− 6	− 6	4	1
1964	632	− 7	− 4	− 4	5	1
1965	685	−10	− 6	−14	−3	−4
1966	748	− 7	−10	− 7	—	−4
1967	790	4	6	13	—	3
Average error (1963–67)		7.8	6.4	8.8	4.0	2.8

Source: Michael Evans, *Macroeconomic Activity*, New York: Harper & Row, 1969, p. 516.

tions, it was the product of a team of over 20 well-known economists, headed by Klein and Harvard's James Duesenberry. Work on this model went on for over 10 years, and although it was designed largely for experimental purposes, it provided economists with many useful results.[14] Another very large model was the Federal Reserve Board–Massachusetts Institute of Technology–Pennsylvania model, which contained over 125 equations. It too was largely experimental in nature, although it has been used to generate some forecasts of the effects of alternate government policies.[15]

[14] J. Duesenberry, G. Fromm, L. Klein, and E. Kuh, *The Brookings Quarterly Econometric Model of the United States,* Chicago: Rand McNally, 1965.
[15] Some econometric models, such as those developed at the Federal Reserve Bank of St. Louis, have been built largely on monetary factors. In the following three chapters, we shall discuss the effects of monetary factors on national output, employment, and the price level.

Econometric Forecasts: The Track Record

How well can econometric models forecast? Table 11.2 compares the success of the Wharton model, the Friend-Taubman model, and a model constructed at the University of Michigan's Research Seminar in Quantitative Economics in predicting GNP during 1959–67 with the forecasts of the Council of Economic Advisers and a composite forecast of GNP from about 50 economists which is tabulated each year by the Federal Reserve Bank of Philadelphia. With the exception of the Friend-Taubman model, these forecasts were made at the end of the previous year. The Friend-Taubman forecasts were made in mid-March.

In this period, the econometric models seemed to do better than the average forecast of general economists. While the general economists were off, on the average, by about $8 billion during the period, the econometric models were off by an average of about $5 billion. The performance of the Wharton model in this period was particularly impressive. Its average error was only about $3 billion—or less than ½ of 1 percent. In this ball game, that is a very fancy batting average: recall Samuelson's remarks quoted earlier.

However, before you jump to the conclusion that the problem of economic forecasting is now solved, note several things. First, it is much easier to forecast GNP during a period of sustained prosperity like 1963–67—or a sustained downswing—than at a turning point of the business cycle. Unfortunately, the turning points are most significant to policy makers. Second, for some purposes, the components of GNP—like inventory changes or expenditures on consumer durables—are more important than GNP. Unfortunately, it is easier to forecast GNP than to forecast components of GNP. Third, the assumption underlying any econometric model is that the basic structure of the economy— the numbers in the equations of the model—will not change. If this assumption does not hold, the model is in trouble. After all, any econometric model is powered by past data, not magic.

The Economic Forecasts for 1972: A Case Study

To illustrate the nature, accuracy, and impact of economic forecasts, consider the situation at the end of 1971. The federal government was faced with both excessive unemployment and excessive inflation. With an election approaching in November 1972, the administration was clearly concerned about the economic picture in 1972. Would GNP grow rapidly enough to reduce the unemployment rate? Would it grow too rapidly, and provoke further inflationary pressures? The best answers available were the forecasts made by leading economists, inside and outside the government. As you can see in Table 11.3, these forecasts tended to agree

with one another: the outlook was for a 1972 GNP in current dollars of about $1,150 billion, which would mean an unemployment rate of about 5½ percent.

Businessmen, as well as government officials, were vitally interested in what GNP would be. From past experience, firms have a pretty good idea of the relationship between GNP and their own sales and profits. Thus, if they know what GNP is likely to be, they can make better estimates of what their sales and profits will be. As an indication of the importance of such forecasts to business executives, leading business magazines and newspapers are continually keeping the business community informed of the latest forecasts. For example, *Business Week* published the forecasts in Table 11.3 in its December 25, 1971 issue, together with a long article on what they added up to.

As it turned out, GNP in 1972 was about $1,155 billion, unemployment was about 5.6 percent, and the price level increased by about 3.4 percent, which meant that these forecasts were darned good. Further, most private economists predicted GNP in the previous year, 1971, quite accurately, even though the official government forecast was far too optimistic. At the end of 1970, practically all economists, conservative or liberal, predicted that GNP in 1971 would be about $1,050 billion, although the administration insisted that it would be $1,065 billion. In part, the administration's forecast may have been wishful thinking because it wanted a more vigorous expansion to reduce unemployment. In any event, the economists' forecasts were very close to the mark. In contrast to the administration's expectations, GNP in 1971 was $1,047 billion.

Economic forecasts play an important role in the decision-making process, both in government and industry. For example, in the recession of 1953–54, President Eisenhower asked Arthur Burns, Chairman of the Council of Economic Advisers, to appear at every meeting of the Cabinet until further notice, and summarize developments and prospects. During the 1960s and 1970s, Presidents Kennedy, Johnson, and Nixon also paid close at-

Table 11.3

Forecasts of Gross National Product in 1972, as well as Price Increase and Unemployment

	1972 GNP (billions of current dollars)	1972 price increase	1972 average unemployment
Economists:			
Robert Johnson—Paine, Webber, Jackson & Curtis	$1,159	4.0%	5.4%
James O'Leary—U.S. Trust	1,157	4.0	5.3
A. Gary Shilling—Estabrook	1,156	2.7	5.0
Eleanor Daniel—Mutual of New York	1,154	3.8	5.4
Donald R. Conlan—Dean Witter	1,150	3.5	5.4
William Freund—New York Stock Exchange	1,150	3.5	5.5
Tilford C. Gaines—Manufacturers Hanover	1,150	3.2	5.6
Walter W. Heller—University of Minnesota	1,150	3.3	5.6
Raymond Jallow—United California Bank	1,150	2.9	5.4
Roy L. Reierson—Bankers Trust	1,150	4.0	5.6
Daniel Suits—University of California (Santa Cruz)	1,150	3.8	5.0
Robert Ortner—Bank of New York	1,149	3.5	5.6
Robert Parks—Eastman Dillon, Union Securities	1,148	3.0	5.5
Albert T. Sommers—The Conference Board	1,148	3.4	5.4
Guy E. Noyes—Morgan Guaranty	1,147	3.0	5.3
Bohdan Kekish—Moody's	1,146	3.2	5.5
Morris Cohen—Schroder, Naess & Thomas	1,145	3.0	5.5
Martin Gainsbrugh—The Conference Board	1,145	3.3	5.4
Saul Klaman—National Association of Mutual Savings Banks	1,145	3.5	5.1
Francis Schott—Equitable Life	1,145	3.5	5.4
Beryl Sprinkel—Harris Trust & Savings	1,145	3.1	5.4
Kenneth Wright—Life Insurance Association of America	1,145	3.2	5.6
Raymond J. Saulnier—Barnard College	1,140	3.0	5.5
George W. McKinney, Jr.—Irving Trust	1,139	3.9	5.4
Sally Ronk—Drexel Firestone	1,139	3.3	6.0
Leonard Santow—Aubrey G. Lanston	1,137	3.3	5.5
Econometric models:			
General Electric, MAPCAST	1,151	3.3	5.6
Wharton, EFA	1,150	3.6	5.4
University of California (Los Angeles)	1,148	3.7	5.5
Data Resources	1,147	3.2	5.7
Townsend-Greenspan	1,147	3.1	5.5
Chase Econometrics	1,152	3.1	5.4
University of Michigan, RSQE	1,144	2.9	5.3

Source: Business Week, December 25, 1971.

tention to economic forecasts. So do most corporation presidents. This isn't because these forecasts are always very good. It's because they are the best available. As Thomas Huxley put it, "If a little knowledge is dangerous, who is the man who has so much as to be out of danger?"

Summary

Changes in sales can result in magnified or accelerated changes in investment, the amount of gross investment depending on the rate of increase of sales. The fact that sales are increasing does not insure that gross investment will increase. On the contrary, if sales are increasing at a decreasing rate, gross investment is likely to fall. This effect of sales on investment is called the acceleration principle. The interaction of the acceleration principle with the multiplier can cause business cycles. Thus, turning points can be generated within the economic system. Investment is also determined by many events that occur more or less at random, like innovations, wars, and so on. The effects of these random shocks can also cause business fluctuations. The short cycles are generally inventory cycles. The acceleration principle also applies to inventories.

Although we are not in a position to erase the small dips and pauses in economic activity, it seems extremely unlikely that we will have another depression of the severity of the 1930s. The reason is that policy makers—and the electorate—know that monetary and fiscal policy can be used to push the economy back toward full employment. However, the prospect for price stability is not so bright.

Although economics is by no means an exact science, economic forecasts are useful for many purposes. This does not mean that these forecasts are always very accurate. It means only that they are better than noneconomists' forecasts.

Economists have a number of techniques for forecasting. One makes use of leading indicators—variables that historically have turned up or down before GNP. Although of some use, these leading indicators are not very reliable. Another technique is based on the use of simple Keynesian models plus surveys and other data. For example, investment and government expenditures (and net exports) are sometimes estimated as a first step. Then, using the historical relationship between consumption and GNP, it is possible to forecast GNP. A third technique is based on econometric models, which are systems of equations estimated from past data. Econometric models blend theory and measurement.

Econometric models may be big or small. An example of a small model is the Friend-Taubman model; an example of a fairly large model is the Wharton model; and an example of a very large model is the Brookings model. During the period for which comparisons have been made, econometric models seemed to do somewhat better than the average forecasts of general economists. Some did very well indeed. However, it is important to recognize that econometric models—like any forecasting device in the social sciences—are quite fallible. We should also note that economic forecasts receive considerable attention from heads of state and heads of firms. This isn't because these forecasts are always very good: it's because they are the best available.

CONCEPTS FOR REVIEW

Business cycle	Prosperity	Coincident series
Trough	Inventory cycle	Lagging series
Expansion	Net investment	Econometric models
Peak	Gross investment	Expectations
Recession	Acceleration principle	
Depression	Leading indicators	

QUESTIONS FOR DISCUSSION AND REVIEW

1. Suppose that the president gave you the job of forecasting GNP for the next year. What techniques would you use? What range of probable error would you expect? Use these techniques as best you can to produce an actual numerical forecast.

2. According to Paul Samuelson, "A good scientist should be good at *some* kind of prediction. But it need not be flat prediction about future events." Do you agree? Why or why not?

3. It is much easier to forecast GNP during a turning point of the business cycle than during periods of sustained prosperity or sustained downswing. True or False?

4. Important factors in business fluctuations are:
a. inventories
b. expectations
c. innovations
d. changes in money supply and interest rates
e. all of the above

PART FOUR

Money, Banking, and Stabilization Policy

CHAPTER 12

The Role and Importance of Money

According to the maxim of an ancient Roman, "Money alone sets all the world in motion." Although a statement that leaves so little room for the laws of physics or astronomy may be a mite extravagant, no one would deny the importance of money in economic affairs. The quantity of money is a very significant factor in determining the health and prosperity of any economic system. Inadequate increases in the quantity of money may bring about excessive unemployment, while excessive increases in the quantity of money may result in serious inflation. To some economists, a discussion of business fluctuations and economic stabilization that ignores the money supply is like a performance of *Hamlet* that omits the prince. Most economists would not go quite that far, but almost all would agree that the money supply is very important.

In this chapter, we are concerned with the nature and value of money, as well as with the relationship between a nation's money supply and the extent of unemployment and inflation. In particular, we consider questions like: What is money? What determines its value? What factors influence the demand for money, and what factors influence its quantity? What is the relationship between the quantity of money and the price level? What is the relationship between the quantity of money and the level of net national product? To understand the workings of our economy and the nature of our government's economic policies, you must be able to answer these questions.

What Is Money?

We must begin by defining money. At first blush, it may seem natural to define it by its physical characteristics. You may be inclined to say that money consists of bills of a certain size and color with certain words and symbols printed on them, as well as coins of a certain type. But this definition would be too restrictive, since money in other societies has consisted of whale teeth, wampum, and a variety of other things. Thus it seems better to define money by its functions than by its physical characteristics. Like beauty, money is as money does.

Money's first function is to act as a *medium of exchange.* People exchange their goods and services for something called money, and then use this money to buy the goods and services they want. To see how important money is as a medium of exchange, let's suppose that it did not exist. To exchange the goods and services they produce for the goods and services they want to consume, people would resort to *barter,* or direct exchange. If you were a wheat farmer, you would have to go to the people who produce the meat, clothes, and other goods and services you want, and swap some of your wheat for each of these goods and services. Of course this would be a very cumbersome procedure, since it would take lots of time and effort to locate and make individual bargains with each

of these people. To get some idea of the extent to which money greases the process of exchange in any highly developed economy, consider all the purchases your family made last year—cheese from Wisconsin and France, automobiles from Detroit, oil from Texas and the Middle East, books from New York, and thousands of other items from all over the world. Imagine how few of these exchanges would have been feasible without money.

Second, money acts as a *standard of value.* It is the unit in which the prices of goods and services are measured. How do we express the price of coffee or tea or shirts or suits? In dollars and cents, of course. Thus money prices tell us the rates at which goods and services can be exchanged. For example, if the money price of a shirt is $5 and the money price of a tie is $1, a shirt will exchange for 5 ties. Put differently, a shirt will be "worth" 5 times as much as a tie.

Money also acts as a *store of value.* A person can hold on to money and use it to buy things later. You often hear stories about people who hoard a lot of money under their mattresses or bury it in their back yards. These people have an overdeveloped appreciation of the role of money as a store of value. But even those of us who are less miserly often use this function of money by carrying some money with us, and keeping some in the bank to make future purchases.

Finally, it should be recognized that money is a social invention. It is easy to assume that money has always existed, but this is not the case. Someone had to get the idea, and people had to come to accept it. Nor has money always had the characteristics it has today. In ancient Greece and Rome, money consisted of gold and silver coins. By the end of the seventeenth century, paper money was established in England; but this paper currency, unlike today's currency, could be exchanged for gold. Only recently has the transition been made to money that is not convertible into gold or silver. But regardless of its form or characteristics, anything that is a medium of exchange, a standard of value, and a store of value is money.

Three Kinds of Money

Like Caesar's Gaul, all money in modern economies is divided into three parts—coins, currency, and demand deposits. *Coins* are not really a very large proportion of the total quantity of money in the United States. In all, they amount to only about $6 billion, or about 2 percent of the total money supply. This is mainly because coins come in such small denominations. It takes a small mountain of pennies, nickels, dimes, quarters, and half-dollars to make even a billion dollars. Of course, the metal in each of these coins is worth less than the face value of the coin; otherwise people would melt them down and make money by selling the metal. In the 1960s, when silver prices rose, the government stopped using silver in dimes and quarters to prevent coins from meeting this fate.

Currency—paper money like the $5 and $10 bills everyone likes to have on hand—constitutes a far larger share of the total money supply than coins. Together, currency and coins outstanding totaled about $50 billion in 1972, as shown in Table 12.1. The Federal Reserve System, described in a later section, issues practically all of our currency in the form of Federal Reserve Notes. Before 1933, it was possible to exchange currency for gold, but this is no longer the case. All American currency (and coin) is presently "fiat" money. It is money because the government says so and because the people accept it. There is no real metallic backing of the currency anymore. But this does not mean that we should be suspicious of the soundness of our currency, since gold backing is not what gives money its value. (In fact, to some extent, cause and effect work the other way: the use of gold to back currencies has in the past increased the value of gold.) Basically, the value of currency depends on its acceptability by people and on its scarcity.

Third, bank deposits subject to payment on demand—so-called *demand deposits*—are quantitatively by far the biggest part of our money supply, as shown in Table 12.1. At first you may question whether these demand deposits—or checking accounts, as you probably call them—are money at all. In everyday speech, they often are not considered money. But economists include demand deposits as part of the money supply, and for good reason. After all, you can pay for goods and services just as easily by check as with cash. Indeed, the public pays for more things by check than with cash. This means that checking accounts are just as much a medium of exchange—and just as much a standard of value and a store of value— as cash. Thus, since they perform all of the functions of money, they should be included as money.

Figure 12.1 shows how the money supply—the sum total of coins, paper currency, and demand deposits—has behaved since World War II. You can see that the quantity of money has generally increased from one year to the next, and that the increase has been at an average rate of about 3 percent per year. However, the rate of increase of the quantity of money has by no means been constant. In some years, like 1968, the quantity of money increased by about 8 percent; in others, like 1960, it decreased slightly. A great deal will be said later about the importance and determinants of changes in the quantity of money.

Table 12.1

Money Supply, December 31, 1972, Seasonally Adjusted

	Amount (billions of dollars)
Demand deposits	$190.0
Currency and coins	56.9
Total	$246.9

Source: Economic Report of the President, 1973.

**Figure 12.1
Behavior of Money Supply,
United States, 1947–72**

The money supply, about $250
billion in 1972, has generally
increased from year to year, but
the rate of increase has by no
means been constant.

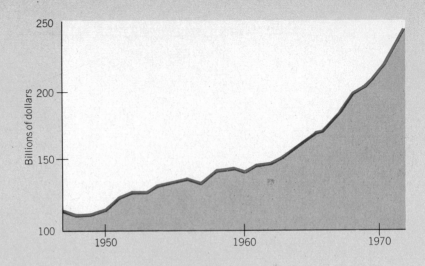

Near-Monies

We have just stated that all money is of three kinds—coins, currency, and demand deposits. This is the money supply, narrowly defined. It is not the only definition. There is also the money supply, broadly defined, which includes time or savings deposits as well as coins, currency, and demand deposits. The money supply, narrowly defined, is often called M_1, while the money supply, broadly defined, is often called M_2. Although economists usually use the narrow definition—and when we refer to the money supply in this book, we shall mean this definition—it is sometimes useful to work with the broad definition as well.

Time or savings deposits are excluded from the narrow definition of money because you cannot pay directly for anything with them. For example, suppose that you have a savings account at a commercial bank. You cannot draw a check against it, as you can with a demand deposit. To withdraw your money from the account, you may have to give the bank a certain amount of notice (although in practice this right may be waived and the bank will ordinarily let you withdraw your money when you want).

On the other hand, economists who use the broad definition feel that time or savings deposits

should be included in the money supply because time or savings deposits can so readily be transformed into cash. You may intend to buy a house sometime in the next year and you may want to keep $5,000 on hand to use as a down payment. You could leave this $5,000 in your checking account, or you could put it in a savings account, where it would earn some interest. Because ordinarily you can withdraw the money from a savings account on short notice, you may decide on this alternative. Since this savings account can so readily be transformed into cash, it is almost like a checking account. Not quite, but almost. Although time deposits or savings deposits cannot be used as a medium of exchange, they can be transformed into cash quite readily.

Many other assets can also be transformed into cash without much difficulty—though not quite as easily as savings deposits. For example, it is not difficult to convert government bonds into cash. There is no simple way to draw a hard-and-fast dividing line between money and nonmoney, since many assets have some of the characteristics of money. Consequently, there are still other definitions of the money supply that are more inclusive than M_2. But most economists feel that, although assets like government bonds have some of the properties of money, it would be stretching things too far to include them in the money supply. (For one thing, their price varies as interest rates change.)

Economists call such assets **near-money**, and recognize that the amount of near-money in the economy has an important effect on spending habits. There is some disagreement among economists as to exactly what is and what isn't near-money, but this needn't concern us here. The major point we want to make is that any dividing line between money and nonmoney must be arbitrary.

The Value of Money

Let's go back to one very important point that was mentioned briefly in a previous section: there is no gold backing for our money. In other words, there is no way that you can exchange a $10 bill for $10 worth of gold. If you look at a $10 bill, you will see that it says that the United States will pay the bearer on demand ten dollars. But all this means is that the government will give you another $10 bill in exchange for this one. Currency and demand deposits are really just debts, or IOUs. Currency is the debt of the government, while demand deposits are the debts of the commercial banks. Intrinsically, neither currency nor demand deposits have any real value. A $10 bill is merely a small piece of paper, and a demand deposit is merely an entry in a bank's accounts. And, as we have seen, even coins are worth far less as metal than their monetary value.

All this may make you feel a bit uncomfortable. After all, if our coins, currency, and demand deposits have little or no intrinsic value, doesn't this mean that they can easily become worthless? To answer this question, we must realize that basically, *money has value because people will accept it in payment for goods and services*. If your university will accept your check in payment for your tuition, and your grocer will accept a $20 bill in payment for your groceries, your demand deposit and your currency have value. You can exchange them for goods and services you want. And your university

or your grocer accepts this money only because they have confidence that they can spend it for goods and services they want.

Thus, money is valuable because it will buy things. But how valuable is it? For example, how valuable is $1? Clearly, *the value of a dollar is equivalent to what a dollar will buy. And what a dollar will buy depends on the price level.* If all prices doubled, the value of a dollar would be cut in half, because a dollar would be able to buy only half as many goods and services as it formerly could. On the other hand, if all prices were reduced by 50 percent, the value of a dollar would double, because a dollar would be able to buy twice as many goods and services as it formerly could. You often hear people say that today's dollar is worth only $.50. What they mean is that it will buy only half what a dollar could buy at some specified date in the past.

It is interesting and important to see how the value of the dollar, as measured by its purchasing power, has varied over time. Figure 12.2 shows how an index of the price level in the United States has changed since 1779. Over time, prices have fluctuated sharply, and the greatest fluctuations have resulted from wars. For example, the price level fell sharply after the Revolutionary War, and our next war—the War of 1812—sent prices skyrocketing, after which there was another postwar drop in prices. The period from about 1820 to about 1860 was marked by relative price stability, but the Civil War resulted in an upward burst followed by a postwar drop in prices. After a period of relative price stability from 1875 to 1915, there was a doubling of prices during World War I and the usual postwar drop. World War II also caused an approximate doubling, but there was no postwar drop in prices.

Clearly, the value of money is inversely related to the price level. The value of money decreases when the price level increases, and increases when the price level decreases. Thus, the wartime periods when the price level rose greatly were periods when the value of the dollar decreased greatly. The doubling of prices during World War II meant

238

Figure 12.2
Index of Wholesale Prices,
United States, 1779–1970
(1910–14 = 100)

The price level has fluctuated
considerably, sharp increases
generally occurring during wars.
Since World War II, the price
level has tended to go only one
way—up.

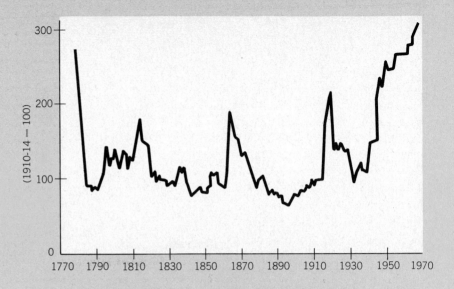

that the value of the dollar was chopped in half.
Similarly, the postwar periods when the price
level fell greatly were periods when the value of
the dollar increased. The 50 percent decline in
prices after the Civil War meant a doubling in
the value of the dollar. Given the extent of the
variation of the price level shown in Figure 12.2,
it is clear that the value of the dollar has varied
enormously during our history.

Runaway Inflation and the
Value of Money

In periods of inflation, the value of money is
reduced. Since inflation means an increase in the
price level, and since an increase in the price level
means a reduction in the value of money, this
proposition seems clear enough. But remember
that inflations vary in severity: *runaway inflations*
wipe out the value of money quickly and thoroughly, while *creeping inflations* erode its value
gradually and slowly. There is a lot of difference

between a runaway inflation and a creeping inflation.

The case of Germany after World War I is a
good example of runaway inflation. Germany was
required to pay large reparations to the victorious
Allies after the war. Rather than attempting to
tax its people to pay these amounts, the German
government merely printed additional quantities of
paper money. This new money increased total
spending in Germany, and the increased spending
resulted in higher prices because the war-devastated
economy could not increase output substantially.
As more and more money was printed, prices rose
higher and higher, reaching utterly fantastic levels.
By 1923, it took a *trillion* marks (the unit of German currency) to buy what one mark would buy
before the war. The effect of this runaway inflation
was to disrupt the economy. Prices had to be adjusted from day to day. People rushed to the
stores to spend the money they received as soon as
possible, since very soon it would buy much less.
Speculation was rampant. This inflation was a
terrible blow to Germany. The middle class was
wiped out; its savings became completely worthless.

It is no wonder that Germany has in recent years been more sensitive than many other countries to the evils of inflation.

Needless to say, this is not the only case in history of runaway inflation. Our own country suffered from runaway inflations during the Revolutionary War and the Civil War. You may have heard the expression that something is "not worth a continental." It comes from the fact that the inflated dollars in use during the Revolutionary War were called "continentals." There have also been runaway inflations in China and Eastern Europe and other parts of the world. Generally, such inflations have occurred because the government increased the money supply at an enormously rapid rate. It is not hard to see why a tremendous increase in the quantity of money will result in a runaway inflation. Other things held constant, increases in the quantity of money will result in increases in total desired spending, and once full employment is achieved, such increases in desired spending will bring about more and more inflation. Eventually, when the inflation is severe enough, households and businesses may refuse to accept money for goods and services because they fear that it will depreciate significantly before they have a chance to spend it. Instead, they may insist on being paid in merchandise or services. Thus, the economy will turn to barter, with the accompanying inconveniences and inefficiency.

To prevent such an economic catastrophe, the government must manage the money supply responsibly. As we have stressed in previous sections, the value of money depends basically on the public's willingness to accept it, and the public's willingness to accept it depends on money's being reasonably stable in value. If the government increases the quantity of money at a rapid rate, thus causing a severe inflation and an accompanying precipitous fall in the value of money, public confidence in money will be shaken, and the value of money will be destroyed. The moral is clear: *The government must restrict the quantity of money, and conduct its economic policies so as to maintain a reasonably stable value of money.*

Creeping Inflation and the Value of Money

For the past 40 years, the price level in the United States has tended to go one way only—up. Year after year, prices have risen. Since 1950, there hasn't been a single year when the price level has fallen, and in the 1940s it fell only in 1949. Certainly, this has not been a runaway inflation, but it has resulted in a very substantial erosion in the value of the dollar. Like a beach slowly worn away by the ocean, the dollar has slowly lost a considerable portion of its value. Specifically, prices now tend to be over 3 times what they were about 40 years ago. Thus, the dollar now is worth less than $\frac{1}{3}$ of what it was worth then. Although a creeping inflation of this sort is much less harmful than a runaway inflation, it has a number of unfortunate social consequences.

For one thing, people with fixed incomes are hit hard by inflation. Although a creeping inflation does not hurt them as much as a runaway inflation, its cumulative effect over a period of years can be substantial. Old people often suffer, since they tend to have fixed incomes derived from Social Security, private pensions, and interest on their savings. In addition, as we pointed out in Chapter 8, inflation hurts lenders and savers. The results can be both devastating and inequitable. The family that works hard and saves for retirement (and a rainy day) finds that its savings are worth far less, when it finally spends them, than the amount it saved. For example, consider the well-meaning souls who invested $1,000 of their savings in United States savings bonds in 1939. By 1949, these bonds were worth only about 800 1939 dollars, including the interest received in the 10-year period. Thus, these people had $200 taken away from them, in just as real a sense as if someone picked their pockets.

Although a mild upward creep of prices at the rate of 1 or 2 percent per year is not likely to result in very disastrous social consequences, any major inflation is a real social problem. In recent years, because it has proved difficult to bring inflation under control, some people have argued that inflation is not as bad as it looks. This, of course, seems quite sensible to those who have gained from inflation. But it does not do justice to the many people, including a disproportionate number of the elderly, who have been "suckered" by inflation. Why should these people have been subjected to such an arbitrary and inequitable tax on their savings and incomes? Moreover, this is not the only consideration. According to some respected economists, inflation tends to feed on itself. That is, a 2 percent rate of inflation tends to grow to a 3 percent rate of inflation, which tends to grow to a 4 percent rate of inflation, and so on. Although the available evidence is too weak to demonstrate this proposition, the possibility should nonetheless be borne in mind.

Inflation has a bad name, both among economists and with the general public. The novelist Ernest Hemingway, overstating his case more than a bit, wrote: "The first panacea for a mismanaged nation is inflation of currency: the second is war. . . . Both are the refuge of political and economic opportunists."[1] Yet we must recognize that, under some conditions, full employment can be achieved only if a moderate amount of inflation is tolerated. For example, as we shall see, this seems to have been the case in the early 1970s. Under such circumstances, the nation is faced with a painful decision: should it allow a moderate amount of inflation in order to promote full employment? The importance of maintaining full employment was described in detail in Chapter 8. The answer you give to this question will depend on your own ethical values and political preferences.

Unemployment and the Quantity of Money

In the last two sections, we have been concerned primarily with what happens when the quantity of money grows too rapidly. As we have seen, the result is inflation. But this is only part of the story. The quantity of money can grow too slowly as well as too rapidly; and when this happens the result is increased unemployment. If the money supply grows very slowly, or decreases, there will be a tendency for total desired spending to grow very slowly or decrease. This in turn will cause NNP to grow very slowly or decrease, thus causing unemployment to increase. The result will, of course, be the social waste and human misery associated with excessive unemployment.

Looking back over past business fluctuations, many economists believe that an inadequate rate of increase in the quantity of money was responsible, at least in part, for many recessions. For example, according to Harvard's James Duesenberry: "Every major depression has been accompanied by a substantial decline in the money supply, and often by a complete collapse of the banking system. Among the many causes responsible for our major depressions, money and banking difficulties have always been prominent."[2] Recall that in our discussion of business fluctuations in the previous chapter, we stressed the importance of monetary factors. In this chapter, as well as Chapters 13–15, we will study these factors in detail.

Determinants of the Quantity of Money

Judging from our discussion thus far, it is clear that to avoid excessive unemployment or excessive inflation, the quantity of money must not grow too slowly or too fast. But what determines the quantity of money? We have already seen that money is of three types: coins, paper currency, and demand deposits. Let's begin by considering the quantity of coins and paper currency in circulation. They make up about ⅓ of the total, a pro-

[1] Ernest Hemingway, "Notes on the Next War," *Esquire*, September 1935.

[2] J. S. Duesenberry, *Money and Credit: Impact and Control*, Englewood Cliffs, N.J.: Prentice-Hall, 1972, p. 3.

THE ROLE AND IMPORTANCE OF MONEY □ 241

portion that has remained fairly stable over time. Practically all the currency is Federal Reserve Notes, issued by the Federal Reserve Banks. When the United States was on the gold standard, the amount of money in circulation was determined by the amount of monetary gold in the country. When gold flowed into the country, the money supply increased; when it flowed out, the money supply decreased. This is no longer the case, since we are no longer on the gold standard—and neither is any other major nation.

If gold doesn't determine the amount of coins and currency in circulation, what does? The answer is that this amount responds to the needs of firms and individuals for cash to use or hoard. When people want more coins and currency, they go to their banks and exchange their demand deposits for coins and currency: in other words, they convert part of their checking accounts into cash. When they want less coins and currency, they take their cash to the banks and exchange it for demand deposits, thus converting some of their cash into checking accounts. The government allows the share of money in coin and currency to be determined by the public's wishes.

Next, consider the quantity of demand deposits, which is of obvious importance, since the bulk of our money supply is composed of demand deposits, not coin and paper currency. Demand deposits are created by commercial banks.[3] The question of how much money banks can create is both fundamental and complicated, and most of the next chapter will be required to present an adequate answer. For the moment, it is sufficient to say that the Federal Reserve System and other government agencies limit the amount of demand deposits the banks can create.

[3] Of course, banks do not create money all by themselves. The public's preferences and actions, as well as bank behavior, influence the amount of demand deposits. Also, commercial banks may not be as unique in this respect as it appears at first sight. See James Tobin, "Commercial Banks as Creators of Money" in D. Carson (ed.), *Banking and Monetary Studies,* Homewood, Ill. Richard D. Irwin, 1963.

The Federal Reserve System

The Federal Reserve System—or "Fed," as it is called by the cognoscenti—plays a central role in the American banking system and in the economy as a whole. After a severe financial panic in 1907, when a great many banks failed, there was strong public pressure to do something to strengthen our banking system. At the same time, there was great fear of centralized domination of the nation's banks. The result—after 6 years of negotiation and discussion—was the establishment by Congress of the *Federal Reserve System* in 1913. As shown in Figure 12.3, the organization of this system can be viewed as a triangle. At the base are the commercial banks that belong to the system—the *member banks.* All *national banks* (so called because they receive their charter from the federal government) have to be members, and many of the larger *state banks* (chartered by the states) are members too. Member banks, which number about 6,000 out of the nation's 14,000 commercial banks, hold about 85 percent of the nation's demand deposits.

In the middle of the triangle in Figure 12.3 are the 12 Federal Reserve Banks, each located in a Federal Reserve district. The entire nation is divided into 12 Federal Reserve districts, with Federal Reserve Banks in New York, Chicago, Philadelphia, San Francisco, Boston, Cleveland, St. Louis, Kansas City, Atlanta, Richmond, Minneapolis, and Dallas. Each of these banks is a corporation owned by the member banks, but, despite this fact, the member banks do not in any sense act as "owners" of the Federal Reserve Bank in their district. Instead, each Federal Reserve Bank is a public agency. These Federal Reserve Banks act as "bankers' banks," performing much the same sorts of functions for commercial banks that commercial banks perform for the public. That is, they hold the deposits of member banks and make loans to them. In addition, as noted in previous sections, the Federal Reserve Banks perform a function no commercial bank can perform: they issue Federal

Figure 12.3
Organization of Federal Reserve System

The Federal Reserve System contains over 6,000 commercial banks, the 12 regional Federal Reserve Banks, and the Board of Governors, as well as the Federal Open Market Committee and various advisory councils and committees.

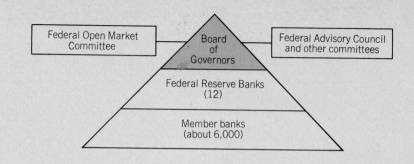

Reserve Notes, which are the nation's currency.

At the top of the triangle in Figure 12.3 is the Board of Governors of the Federal Reserve System. Located in Washington, this board—generally called the Federal Reserve Board—has 7 members appointed by the president for 14 year terms. The board, which coordinates the activities of the Federal Reserve System, is supposed to be independent of partisan politics and to act to promote the nation's general economic welfare. It is responsible for supervising the operation of the money and banking system of the United States. The board is assisted in important ways by the Federal Open Market Committee, which establishes policy concerning the purchase and sale of government securities. The Federal Open Market Committee is composed of the board plus 5 presidents of Federal Reserve Banks. The Board is also assisted by the Federal Advisory Council, a group of 12 commercial bankers that advises the board on banking policy.

The Federal Reserve Board, with the 12 Federal Reserve Banks, constitute the "central bank" of the United States. Every major country has a central bank: for example, England has the Bank of England, and France has the Bank of France. **Central banks** are very important organizations, whose most important function is to help control the quantity of money. One interesting feature of our central

bank is that its principal allegiance is to Congress, not to the executive branch of the federal government. This came about because Congress wanted to protect the Fed from pressure by the president and the Treasury Department. Thus, the Fed was supposed to be independent of the executive branch. In fact, although the Fed has sometimes locked horns with the president, it has generally cooperated with him and his administration, as we shall see in Chapter 14.

To repeat, any central bank's most important function is to control the money supply. But this is not its only function: a central bank also handles the government's own financial transactions, and coordinates and controls the country's commercial banks. Specifically, the Federal Reserve System is charged with these responsibilities: First, the Federal Reserve Banks hold deposits, or reserves, of the member banks. As we shall see in the following chapters, these reserves play an important role in the process whereby the Fed controls the quantity of money. Second, the Federal Reserve System provides facilities for check collection. In other words, it enables a bank to collect funds for checks drawn on other banks. Third, the Federal Reserve Banks supply the public with currency. As we have already pointed out, they issue Federal Reserve Notes. Fourth, the Federal Reserve Banks act as fiscal agents for the federal government—

they hold some of the checking accounts of the U.S. Treasury, and aid in the purchase and sale of government securities. Finally, the Federal Reserve Banks supervise the operation of the member commercial banks. More will be said about the nature of bank supervision and regulation in the next chapter.

Commercial Banks in the United States

In 1970, there were over 13,000 commercial banks in the United States. This testifies to the fact that, in contrast to countries like England, where a few banks with many branches dominate the banking scene, the United States has promoted the growth of a great many local banks. In part, this has stemmed from a traditional suspicion in this country of "big bankers." ("Eastern bankers" are a particularly suspect breed in some parts of the country.) Most of our banks are state, not national, banks: there are about 9,000 state banks, but only about 4,600 national banks.

Commercial banks have two primary functions. First, *banks hold demand deposits and permit checks to be drawn on these deposits.* This function is familiar to practically everyone. Most people have a checking account in some commercial bank, and draw checks on this account. Second, *banks lend money to industrialists, merchants, homeowners, and other individuals and firms.* At one time or another, you will probably apply for a loan to finance some project for your business or home. Indeed, it is quite possible that some of the costs of your college education are being covered by a loan to you or your parents from a commercial bank.

In addition, commercial banks perform a number of other functions. Often they hold time or savings accounts. You will recall that these accounts bear interest and, although technically one must give a certain amount of notice before withdrawal, in practice they can usually be withdrawn whenever

their owner likes. Commercial banks also sell money orders and traveler's checks, and handle estates and trusts. Because of their work with trusts, some banks—for example, the First Pennsylvania Bank and Trust Company, a large Philadelphia bank—include the word "trust" in their title. In addition, commercial banks rent safe-deposit boxes and provide a variety of services for customers.

Despite the number of these subsidiary activities, the principal functions of a commercial bank are to accept deposits and to make loans and investments. It is essential that these loans and investments be safe and reasonably easily turned into cash, because the bank must be able to meet its depositors' demands for cash. Otherwise it will be insolvent and fail. Until about 40 years ago, banks used to fail in large numbers during recessions, causing depositors to lose their money. Even during the prosperous 1920s, over 500 banks failed per year. It is no wonder that the public viewed the banks with less than complete confidence. Since the mid-1930s, bank failures have been rare, in part because of tighter standards of regulation by federal and state authorities. For example, bank examiners audit the books and practices of the banks. In addition, confidence in the banks was strengthened by the creation in 1934 of the Federal Deposit Insurance Corporation, which insures over 99 percent of all commercial bank deposits. At present, each deposit is insured up to $20,000.

Needless to say, commercial banks are not the only kind of financial institution. Mutual savings banks and savings and loan associations hold savings and time deposits; "consumer finance" companies lend money to individuals; insurance companies lend money to firms and governments; "factors" provide firms with working capital; and investment bankers help firms sell their securities to the public. All these types of financial institutions play an important role in the American economy. In general, they all act as intermediaries between savers and investors; that is, they all turn over to investors moneys that they received from savers. As we saw in Chapter 9, this process of converting savings into investment is very important in determining net national product.[4]

The Demand for Money

Turning now to the demand for money, let us recall money's various functions: it is a medium of exchange, a standard of value, and a store of value. Consider money from the point of view of the individual family or firm. Why does a family or firm want to hold money? Clearly, a family can be wealthy without holding much money. We all know stories about very rich men who have very little money, since virtually all of their wealth is tied up in factories, farms, and other nonmonetary assets. So why do people and firms want to hold money, rather than these other kinds of assets?

First, there is the *transactions demand* for money. People and firms like to keep some money on their person and in their checking accounts to buy things. (It is extremely inconvenient to want to buy something and not to have any money—even if you are rich.) Of course, the higher a person's annual income—in dollar, not real terms—the more money he will want to hold for transaction purposes. For example, in 1973, when a doctor makes about $50,000 a year, the average physician will want to keep more money on hand for transaction purposes than in the days—many, many years ago—when a doctor made perhaps $10,000 a year.

Second, there is a *precautionary demand* for money. Unpredictable events require money: for example, people get sick, and houses need repairs. To meet such contingencies, people and firms like to put a certain amount of their wealth into money

and near-money. Also, there is a *speculative demand* for money. People and firms like to keep a certain amount of their wealth in a form in which they can be sure of its monetary value and can take advantage of future price reductions. The amount of money individuals or firms keep on hand for precautionary or speculative purposes will vary with the extent to which they feel that prices and interest rates will go up or down in the future, the degree to which they are uncertain about future income or expenses, and their aversion to or preference for risk.

Up to this point, we have discussed why individuals and firms want to hold money. But we must recognize that there are disadvantages, as well as advantages, in holding money. One is that the real value of money will fall if inflation occurs. Another is that an important cost of holding money is the interest or profit one loses, since instead of holding the money, one might have invested it in assets that would have yielded interest or profit. For example, the cost of holding $5,000 in money for one year, if one can obtain 6 percent on existing investments, is $300, the amount of interest or profit forgone.

Figure 12.4 shows the demand curve for money, with the interest rate as the "price" of holding money. Like other demand curves, this one slopes downward to the right, because the cost of holding money increases as the interest rate or yield on existing investments increases. For example, if the interest rate were 7 percent rather than 6 percent, the cost of holding $5,000 in money for one year would be $350 rather than $300. Thus, as the interest rate or profit rate increases, people try harder to minimize the amount of money they hold. So do firms: big corporations like General Motors or U. S. Steel are very conscious of the cost of holding cash balances. Consequently, with NNP constant, *the amount of money held by individuals and firms is inversely related to the interest rate: the higher the interest rate, the smaller the amount of money demanded.* The demand curve for money, shown in Figure 12.4, is often called the *liquidity preference function.*

---

[4] If President Nixon's recommendations (of August 1973) are accepted, some of the differences between commercial banks and other financial institutions will narrow. According to his recommendations (based on the report of the so-called Hunt Commision), federally chartered thrift institutions could offer checking accounts. Also, the interest ceilings on time and savings deposits would be removed (over a 5½ year period).

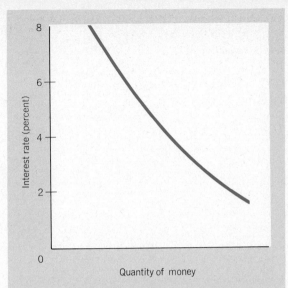

8

6

4

2

0

Interest rate (percent)

Quantity of money

Figure 12.4 The Demand Curve for Money, or Liquidity Preference Function

Holding NNP constant, the amount of money demanded by individuals and firms is inversely related to the interest rate, since the cost of holding money is the interest or profit forgone.

The Role of Money in the Keynesian Model

We began this chapter by saying that the quantity of money has an important effect on the health and prosperity of the economy. Now we can show how changes in the quantity of money affect net national product. Recall our conclusion that the amount of money people want to hold is inversely related to the interest rate. Thus, if the money supply increases, the interest rate will tend to fall, in order to induce people to hold the extra money, since at the existing interest rate they would not have been willing to hold more money. (They would have spent it instead.) Similarly, if the

money supply decreases, interest rates will tend to rise. The relationship between the interest rate and the quantity of money is shown in the liquidity preference function in Figure 12.4.[5]

Given the liquidity preference function, it is a simple matter to show how the money supply can be inserted into the Keynesian models in Chapters 9 and 10. For example, let's trace the effects of an increase in the money supply from $200 billion to $250 billion. The first effect is to decrease the interest rate from d percent to c percent, as shown by the liquidity preference function in panel A of Figure 12.5. This decrease in the interest rate in turn affects the investment function. Because it is less costly to invest—and because credit is more available[6]—the investment function will shift upward, as shown in panel B of Figure 12.5. This occurs because at each level of net national product, firms will want to invest more, since investment is more profitable (because of the cut in the interest rate) and funds are more readily available. This shift in the investment function then affects the equilibrium level of net national product. As shown in panel C of Figure 12.5, the equilibrium level of net national product will increase from D to E, in accord with the principles discussed in Chapter 9. (Recall that the equilibrium value of NNP is at the point where the $C + I + G$ line intersects the 45° line.) Thus, *the effect of the increase in the money supply is to increase net national product.*

Next, let's trace the effects of a decrease in

[5] However, this relationship between the quantity of money and the interest rate is only short-run. In the long run, increases in the money supply, if they result in increased inflation, may *raise* interest rates, because lenders will require a greater return to offset the greater rate of depreciation of the real value of the dollar. Still, however, the *real* rate of interest—the rate of interest adjusted for inflation—may decline.

[6] Note that it is not just a matter of interest rates: Availability of credit is also important. In times when money is tight, some potential borrowers may find that they cannot get a loan, regardless of what interest rate they are prepared to pay. In times when money is easy, people who otherwise might find it difficult to get a loan may be granted one by the banks. To repeat, both availability and interest rates are important.

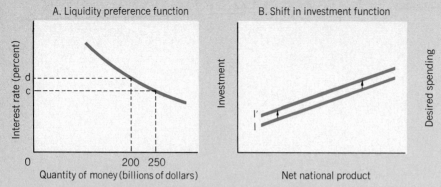

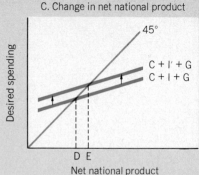

A. Liquidity preference function

Interest rate (percent)

0   200   250

Quantity of money (billions of dollars)

B. Shift in investment function

Investment

Net national product

C. Change in net national product

Desired spending

45°

$C + I' + G$

$C + I + G$

D   E

Net national product

Figure 12.5   **Effect of an Increase in the Money Supply.**

If the money supply increases from $200 billion to $250 billion, the interest rate drops from *d* percent to *c* percent (panel A). Because of the decrease in the interest rate, the investment function shifts upward (panel B), and the equilibrium level of NNP increases from *D* to *E* (panel C).

the money supply from $200 billion to $160 billion. The first effect is to increase the interest rate from *d* percent to *e* percent, as shown by the liquidity preference function in panel A of Figure 12.6. This increase in the interest rate affects the investment function. Because it is more costly to invest—and more difficult to obtain credit—the investment function will shift downward, as shown in panel B of Figure 12.6. This shift occurs because, at every level of net national product, firms want to invest less. This shift in the investment function has an effect in turn on the equilibrium level of net national product. As shown in panel C of Figure 12.6, the equilibrium level of net national product will decrease from D to F. Thus, *the effect of the decrease in the money supply is to decrease net national product.*[7]

This, in simplified fashion, is how changes in

the money supply affect NNP, according to the Keynesian model.[8] To summarize, increases in the money supply tend to increase NNP, and decreases in the money supply tend to reduce NNP. Obviously, these results are of great importance in understanding why our economy behaves the way it does. For example, we can now understand more completely why vast increases in the quantity of money will result in runaway inflation. Total spending will be pushed upward at a very rapid rate, driving the price level out of sight. Similarly, we can now see that an inadequate rate of growth of the money supply can lead to excessive unemployment, for an insufficient growth of the money supply prevents NNP from reaching its full employment level.

[7] Many firms depend to a considerable extent on retained earnings to finance their investment projects. Thus, since they do not borrow externally, the effect on their investment plans of changes in interest rates and credit availability is slight. This factor may reduce the effects of changes in the money supply.

[8] Changes in the money supply, interest rates, and credit availability affect the consumption function and government spending, as well as the investment function. For example, *increases (decreases) in interest rates shift the consumption function and the level of government spending downward (upward).* These factors augment the effect of monetary policy described in the text. We focus attention on the investment function in Figures 12.5 and 12.6 merely because this simplifies the exposition.

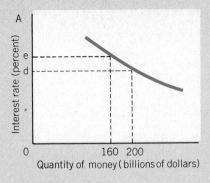
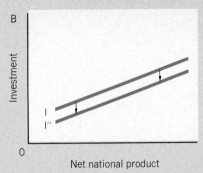
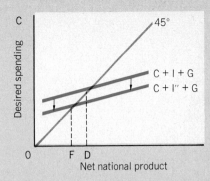

Figure 12.6 Effect of a Decrease in the Money Supply

If the money supply decreases from $200 billion to $160 billion, the interest rate increases from *d* percent to *e* percent (panel A). Because of the increase in the interest rate, the investment function shifts downward (panel B) and the equilibrium level of NNP decreases from *D* to *F* (panel C).

Money Makes a Comeback

Economists in the late 1930s, 1940s, and 1950s tended to play down the importance of the money supply as a determinant of net national product and to rely exclusively on the Keynesian model, in which the quantity of money plays a part, but the starring roles go to investment, government spending, and the multiplier. The quantity of money, which before the Keynesian revolution had occupied the center of the stage in economic models of this sort, was largely pushed to the wings. In recent years, however, there has been a great revival of interest in it. Some prominent economists, led by Milton Friedman of the University of Chicago, have emphasized the importance of the relationship between the quantity of money and nominal, or money, NNP. Undoubtedly this has been a healthy development; the significance of money was underestimated 20 or 30 years ago.

However, the monetarists—the name commonly given to Professor Friedman and his followers—go beyond saying that money matters. In their view, the quantity of money is a much more effective tool

for forecasting or controlling nominal NNP than the Keynesian model described in Chapters 9 and 10. They view the rate of growth of the money supply as the principal determinant of nominal, or money, net national product. Indeed, they go so far as to say that fiscal policy, although it will alter the composition of net national product, will have no permanent effect on the size of nominal NNP unless it influences the money supply. This latter view, explained in more detail in Chapter 15, is not now accepted by most economists.

The monetarists have had a great impact on economic thought in the postwar period, even though theirs remains a minority view. Professor Friedman's most severe critics admit that his research in this area has been path-breaking and extremely important. According to his findings,

the rate of change of the money supply shows well-marked cycles that match closely those in economic activity in general and precede the latter by a long interval. On the average, the rate of change of the money supply has reached its peak nearly 16 months before the peak in general business and

248

Figure 12.7
Relationship between Money Supply and National Product, United States, 1929–70

There is a reasonably close relationship between the money supply and the money value of national product. As one goes up, the other tends to go up too.

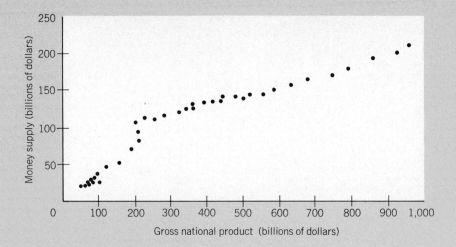

has reached its trough over 12 months before the trough in general business.[9]

Clearly, findings of this sort must be taken seriously. Moreover, research carried out at the Federal Reserve Bank of St. Louis has shown a close relationship between short-run changes in the quantity of money and short-run changes in NNP. Based on this relationship, the St. Louis Bank has constructed some simple econometric models that have had some success in forecasting NNP. These results have also strengthened the hand of the monetarists.

The Velocity of Money and the Equation of Exchange

The monetarists have revived interest in the so-called quantity theory of money. In previous sections, we defined the money supply; and in Figure 12.1, we saw how the money supply has varied over time. Now let's look at the money supply and nominal, or money, national product to determine what, if any, is the relationship between these two variables. Figure 12.7 shows that *there is a definite*

relationship between the money supply in the United States and our nominal national product.[10] *In general, as the money supply has increased, national product has increased as well.* Indeed, the rate of increase of national product during 1929–70 was about the same as the rate of increase of the money supply: both increased by about 700 or 800 percent.

To see why this relationship exists, it is useful to begin by defining a new term: the velocity of circulation of money. The **velocity of circulation of money** is the rate at which the money supply is used to make transactions for final goods and services. That is, it equals the average number of times per year that a dollar was used to buy the final goods and services produced by the economy. In other words,

$$V = \frac{NNP}{M}, \qquad (12.1)$$

where V is velocity, NNP is the nominal net national product, and M is the money supply. For example, if our nominal net national product is

[9] Milton Friedman, testimony before the Joint Economic Committee, The Relationship of Prices to Economic Stability and Growth, 85th Congress, 2nd Session, 1958.

[10] In Figure 12.7, the data refer to gross national product, not net national product. But, as noted in previous chapters, there is little difference between them and they are highly correlated.

$1 trillion and our money supply is $200 billion, the velocity of circulation of money is 5, which means that, on the average, each dollar of our money consummates $5 worth of purchases of net national product.[11]

Nominal net national product can be expressed as the product of real net national product and the price level: In other words,

$$NNP = P \times Q, \qquad (12.2)$$

where P is the price level—the average price at which final goods and services are sold—and Q is net national product in real terms. Substituting this expression for NNP in Equation (12.1), we have

$$V = \frac{P \times Q}{M}. \qquad (12.3)$$

That is, velocity equals the price level (P) times real NNP (Q) divided by the money supply (M). This is another way to define the velocity of circulation of money—a way that will prove very useful.

At the beginning of this section, we set out to explain why nominal national product is related to the money supply. Having defined the velocity of circulation of money, our next step is to present the so-called equation of exchange. The **equation of exchange** is really nothing more than a restatement, in somewhat different form, of our definition of the velocity of circulation of money. To obtain the equation of exchange, all we have to do is multiply both sides of Equation (12.3) by M. The result, of course, is

$$MV = PQ. \qquad (12.4)$$

To understand exactly what this equation means, let's look more closely at each side. Clearly, the

right-hand side equals the amount received for final goods and services during the period, because Q is the output of final goods and services during the period and P is their average price. Thus, the product of P and Q must equal the total amount received for final goods and services during the period—or nominal NNP.

Whereas the right-hand side of Equation (12.4) equals the *amount received for* final goods and services during the period, the left-hand side equals the *amount spent on* final goods and services during the period, since the left-hand side equals the money supply—M—times the average number of times during the period that a dollar was spent on final goods and services—V. Obviously, the result—$M \times V$—must equal the amount spent on final goods and services during the period. Thus, since the *amount received* for final goods and services during the period must equal *the amount spent* on final goods and services during the period, the left-hand side must equal the right-hand side.

The equation of exchange—Equation (12.4)—is what logicians call a tautology: it holds by definition. As pointed out above, it is nothing more than a restatement of the definition of the velocity of circulation of money. Yet it is not useless. On the contrary, economists regard the equation of exchange as very valuable, because it sets forth some of the fundamental factors that influence net national product and the price level.

The Crude Quantity Theory of Money and Prices

The classical economists discussed in Chapter 9 assumed that both V and Q were constant. They believed that V was constant because it was determined by the population's stable habits of holding money, and they believed that Q would remain constant at its full employment value. On the basis of these assumptions, they propounded

[11] This concept of velocity is often called the *income velocity of money*. Another velocity concept is the *transactions velocity of money*, defined as the ratio of the total volume of transactions per year to the quantity of money.

the *crude quantity theory* of money and prices, a theory that received a great deal of attention and exerted considerable influence in its day. If these assumptions hold, it follows from the equation of exchange—Equation (12.4)—that the price level (P) must be proportional to the money supply (M), because V and Q have been assumed to be constant. (In the short run, the full employment level of real net national product will not change much.) Thus, we can rewrite Equation (12.4) as

$$P = \left(\frac{V}{Q}\right) M, \qquad (12.5)$$

where (V/Q) is a constant. So P must be proportional to M if these assumptions hold.

The crude quantity theory is true to its name: it is only a crude approximation to reality. One important weakness is its assumption that velocity is constant. Another is its assumption that the economy is always at full employment, which we know from previous chapters to be far from true. But despite its limitations, the crude quantity theory points to a very important truth: if the government finances its expenditures by a drastic increase in the money supply, the result will be drastic inflation. For example, if the money supply is increased tenfold, there will be a marked increase in the price level. If we take the crude quantity theory at face value, we would expect a tenfold increase in the price level; but that is a case of spurious accuracy. Perhaps the price level will go up only eightfold. Perhaps it will go up twelvefold. The important thing is that it will go up a lot!

There is a great deal of evidence to show that the crude quantity theory is a useful predictor during periods of runaway inflation, such as in Germany after World War I. The German inflation occurred because the German government printed and spent large bundles of additional money. You often hear people warn of the dangers in this country of the government's "resorting to the printing presses" and flooding the country with a vast increase in the money supply. It is a danger in any country. And one great value of the crude

quantity theory is that it predicts correctly what will occur as a consequence: rapid inflation.

There is also considerable evidence that the crude quantity theory works reasonably well in predicting long-term trends in the price level. For example, during the sixteenth and seventeenth centuries, gold and silver were imported by the Spanish from the New World, resulting in a great increase in the money supply. The crude quantity theory would predict a great increase in the price level, and this is what occurred. Or consider the late nineteenth century, when the discovery of gold in the United States, South Africa, and Canada brought about a considerable increase in the money supply. As the crude quantity theory would lead us to expect, the price level rose considerably as a consequence.

A More Sophisticated Version of the Quantity Theory

The crude quantity theory was based on two simplifying assumptions, both of which are questionable. One assumption was that real net national product (Q) remains fixed at its full employment level; the other was that the velocity of circulation of money (V) remains constant. A more sophisticated version of the quantity theory can be derived by relaxing the first assumption. This version of the quantity theory recognizes that the economy is often at less than full employment and consequently that real net national product (Q) may vary a good deal for this reason.

So long as velocity remains constant, the equation of exchange—Equation (12.4)—can be used to determine the relationship between net national product in current dollars and M, even if Q is allowed to vary. On the basis of the equation of exchange, it is obvious that $P \times Q$ should be proportional to M, if the velocity of circulation of money (V) remains constant. Since $P \times Q$ is the net national product *in current dollars,* it follows that, if this assumption holds, *the nominal net national product should be proportional to the money supply.* In other words,

$$NNP = aM, \qquad (12.6)$$

where NNP is the nominal net national product and V is assumed to equal a constant—a.

If velocity is constant, this version of the quantity theory should enable us to predict nominal net national product if we know the money supply. Also, if velocity is constant, this version of the quantity theory should enable us to control nominal net national product by controlling the money supply. Clearly, if velocity is constant, Equation (12.6) is an extremely important economic relationship—one that will go a long way toward accomplishing the goals of Chapters 9, 10, and 11, which were to show how net national product could be forecasted and controlled. But is velocity constant? Since Equation (12.6) is based on this assumption, we must find out.

Figure 12.8[12] shows how the velocity of circulation of money has behaved since 1920. Obviously velocity has not been constant. But on the other hand, it has not varied enormously. Excluding the war years, it has generally been between 2.5 and 4.5 in the United States. Over the long run, it has been reasonably stable, but it has varied a good deal over the business cycle. As shown in Figure 12.8, velocity tends to decrease during depressions and increase during booms. *All in all, one must certainly conclude that, although velocity is fairly stable over the long run, it is not so stable that Equation (12.6) alone can be used in any precise way to forecast or control net national product.*

However, this does not mean that Equation

[12] The velocity figures in Figure 12.8 are based on gross national product, not net national product. But for the reasons given in note 10, this makes little real difference.

Figure 12.8
Velocity of Circulation of Money, United States, 1920–70

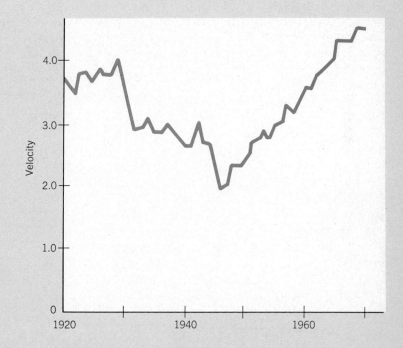

The velocity of circulation of money has generally been between 2.5 and 4.5, except during World War II.

(12.6) is useless, or that the more sophisticated quantity theory is without value. On the contrary, this version of the quantity theory points out a very important truth, which is that *the money supply has an important effect on net national product (in money terms): increases in the quantity of money are likely to increase net national product, while decreases in the quantity of money are likely to decrease net national product.* Because velocity is not constant, the relationship between the money supply and net national product is not as neat and simple as that predicted by Equation (12.6), but there is a relationship. And it may be possible to predict V as a function of other variables, like the frequency with which people are paid and the level of business confidence. Time will tell how far this tack may take us. (At present, most economists feel that changes in V reflect, rather than cause, changes in NNP.)

Now let's return to our original question: why is there a relationship (in Figure 12.7) between the money supply and national product (in money terms)? Given the discussion in the last few sections, the answer is obvious: the velocity of circulation of money has remained relatively stable over the long run—not so stable that the money supply and national product moved in locked steps, but stable enough so that there is a reasonably close relationship.

Two Alternative Models

At this point, you may have the uneasy feeling that two theories have been dished up to explain the same thing. If so, you are right. Earlier in this chapter when we discussed Figures 12.5 and 12.6, as well as in Chapters 9–11, we presented the Keynesian model, which uses changes in income and expenditure to explain changes in NNP. In the last few sections, we have presented the quantity theory, which uses changes in the money supply to explain changes in NNP. You have a

perfect right to ask which model is better. At present, there is a controversy over this question. The monetarists believe that the latter theory is better, while the Keynesians argue for the former theory. This is one of the most important debates in economics at present.

While recognizing the existence and importance of this debate, we must underscore one major point on which these two alternative models agree: *the effect of the money supply on net national product is qualitatively the same in both the Keynesian and monetarist models.* More specifically, whatever theory you look at, you get the same result: increases in the money supply would be expected to increase nominal net national product, and decreases in the money supply would be expected to decrease nominal net national product. Thus, whether the Keynesian (majority) view of the world or the monetarist (minority) view of the world is correct, it is important that you understand the topics taken up in the next two chapters—the banking system, the factors determining the money supply, and the ways the government tries to alter the money supply in order to promote full employment with stable prices.

Also, no matter which view is accepted, if the economy is at considerably less than full employment, increases in the money supply would be expected to increase real national product, while decreases in the money supply would be expected to reduce real national product. However, once full employment is approached, increases in the money supply result more and more in increases in the price level, as distinct from increases in real output. These expectations are shared both by the monetarists and the Keynesians, which is fortunate since they underlie a great deal of monetary theory.

In Chapter 15 we shall discuss the theoretical and policy differences between the monetarists and the Keynesians in considerable detail. Before we do, we must describe how banks create money and how the Federal Reserve controls the money supply. These are the principal topics of the next two chapters.

Summary

Money performs several basic functions. It serves as a medium of exchange, a standard of value, and a store of value. There are three kinds of money —coins, currency, and demand deposits. Economists include demand deposits as part of the money supply because you can pay for goods and services about as easily by check as with cash. Besides this narrow definition of money, a broader definition includes saving and time deposits. Of course, there are lots of other assets—for example, government bonds—that can be transformed without much difficulty into cash. It is not easy to draw a line between money and nonmoney, since many assets have some of the characteristics of money.

America's history has seen many sharp fluctuations in the price level. Wars have generally been periods of substantial inflation, and prices have dropped in the postwar periods. Since World War II, prices have tended to go one way only—up. Although a mild upward creep of prices at the rate of 1 or 2 percent per year is not likely to result in very disastrous social consequences, runaway inflation is a real social evil that disrupts the economy very seriously. Generally, such inflations have occurred because the government expanded the money supply far too rapidly. However, too small a rate of growth of the money supply can also be a mistake, resulting in excessive unemployment.

The Federal Reserve System is responsible for regulating and controlling the money supply. Established in 1913, the Fed is composed of the member banks, twelve regional Federal Reserve Banks, and the Federal Reserve Board, which coordinates the activities of the system. The Federal Reserve System is the central bank of the United States. Commercial banks have two primary functions. First, they hold demand deposits and permit checks to be drawn on them. Second, they lend money to firms and individuals. In the course of carrying out these activities, banks create and destroy money.

Most economists believe that the lower the interest rate, the greater the amount of money demanded. Thus, increases in the quantity of money result in lower interest rates, which result in increased investment (and other types of spending), which results in a higher NNP. Conversely, decreases in the quantity of money result in higher interest rates, which result in decreased investment (and other types of spending), which results in a lower NNP. This is the Keynesian approach. Another, contrasting approach is based on the equation of exchange. The equation of exchange is $MV = PQ$, where M is the money supply, V is velocity, P is the price level, and Q is net national product in real terms. The velocity of circulation of money is the rate at which the money supply is used to make transactions for final goods and services. Specifically, it equals NNP in money terms divided by the money supply.

If the velocity of circulation of money remains constant and if real net national product is fixed at its full employment level, it follows from the equation of exchange that the price level will be proportional to the money supply. This is the crude quantity theory, which is a reasonably good approximation during periods of runaway inflation, and works reasonably well in predicting long-term trends in the price level. A more sophisticated version of the quantity theory recognizes that real net national product is often at less than full employment, with the result that Q is not fixed. Thus, if velocity remains constant, net national product in money terms should be proportional to the money supply. In fact, nominal net national product has been fairly closely related to the money supply. However, velocity has by no means remained stable over time. The monetarists, led by Milton Friedman, adopt the more sophisticated version of the quantity theory. There are many important disagreements between the monetarists and the Keynesians, but both approaches agree that increases in the money supply will increase NNP (in money terms) while decreases in the money supply will decrease NNP (in money terms).

CONCEPTS FOR REVIEW

Demand deposits

Currency

Time deposits

Near-money

Runaway inflation

Transactions demand

Precautionary demand

Speculative demand

Velocity of circulation

Equation of exchange

Crude quantity theory

Liquidity preference
  function

Federal Reserve Notes

Federal Reserve System

Federal Reserve Board

Federal Deposit Insurance Corporation

QUESTIONS FOR DISCUSSION AND REVIEW

1. According to Milton Friedman, the monetarists "have always stressed that money matters a great deal for the development of nominal [i.e., money] magnitudes, but not over the long run for real magnitudes." What does he mean? Do you agree or disagree?

2. Describe how the quantity of money influences nominal and real NNP according to (a) the Keynesion model, (b) the crude quantity theory, and (c) the more sophisticated quantity theory. What sorts of tests might be performed to determine which of these models works best?

3. Once full employment is reached, increases in the money supply result primarily in increases in the price level. True or False?

4. $MV = PQ$ is called

a. the equation of exchange.

b. a tautology.

c. a restatement of the velocity of circulation.

d. all of the above.

e. none of the above.

CHAPTER 13

The Banking System and the Quantity of Money

Banking is often viewed as a colorless, dull profession whose practitioners are knee-deep in deposit slips and canceled checks. Also, when the time comes to reject a loan application, the banker is often viewed as a heartless skinflint—even if he advertises that "you have a friend at Chase Manhattan." Yet despite these notions, most people recognize the importance of the banks in our economy, perhaps because the banks deal in such an important and fascinating commodity—money.

In this chapter, we look in detail at how commercial banks operate. We begin by discussing the nature of their loans and investments, as well as the important concept of reserves. Then, after looking into legal reserve requirements, we describe how commercial banks create money—a very important and commonly misunderstood process. Finally, we take up the effects of currency withdrawals and excess reserves on our results. The purpose of this chapter is to introduce you to the operations of the banking system, which is neither as colorless nor as mysterious as is sometimes assumed.

The Bank of America: A Case Study

We can learn something about banking in the United States from the history of a particular bank —the Bank of America, the nation's largest commercial bank. In 1904, Amadeo Peter Giannini, a 34-year-old son of an Italian immigrant, founded the Bank of Italy in the Italian district of San Francisco. Giannini was a man of enormous energy and drive. At the age of 12, he had gone to school by day, while working in his stepfather's produce firm for much of each night. At 19, he was a full-fledged member of the produce firm, and at 31 had become rich enough to retire from the produce business—and eventually to turn to banking.

Giannini showed the sort of entrepreneurial zeal in banking that would be expected from his previous track record. As an illustration, consider the following episode:

> In 1906, the city of San Francisco was rocked by earthquake and swept by fire. As the flames approached the little Bank of Italy, the young banker piled his cash and securities into a horse-drawn wagon and with a guard of two soldiers took them to his home at San Mateo, twenty miles from San Francisco, where he buried them in the garden; and then while the ruins of the city were still smoking he set up a desk in the open air down by the waterfront, put up a sign over the desk which read BANK OF ITALY, and began doing business again—the first San Francisco bank to resume.[1]

Clearly, Giannini was a banker who did not observe banker's hours.

Giannini's bank prospered and grew. By the time he was 50, it had over 25 branches. During

[1] Frederick Lewis Allen, *The Lords of Creation,* New York: Harper and Bros., 1935, p. 320. Much of this section is based on Allen's account.

the 1920s, he acquired more and more branches, until old-line California bankers began to realize that the Bank of Italy had become a factor to be reckoned with. They did their best to prevent its further expansion, but to no avail. A man who can turn an earthquake to his advantage is unlikely, after all, to submit to such pressures. Indeed, by 1929, Giannini had 453 banking offices in California alone, as well as a considerable number elsewhere. His was the fourth largest commercial bank in the country.

In 1930, Giannini's bank was renamed the Bank of America. The 1930s were not particularly kind to it, any more than they were to the rest of the economy. But in the past 35 years, the Bank of

Table 13.1

The Ten Largest Commercial Banks in the United States in Terms of Deposits, December 31, 1971

Bank and location	Deposits (billions of dollars)
Bank of America, San Francisco	29.0
First National City Bank, New York	24.4
Chase Manhattan Bank, New York	20.4
Manufacturers Hanover Trust Company, New York	12.2
Morgan Guaranty Trust Company, New York	10.7
Chemical Bank, New York	10.5
Bankers Trust Company, New York	8.9
Security Pacific National Bank, Los Angeles	8.5
Continental Illinois National Bank and Trust Company, Chicago	8.5
First National Bank, Chicago	7.2

Source: Moody's, 1972.

America has grown and grown. In 1940, its loans (and discounts) totaled $778 million; in 1950, $3,257 million; in 1960, $6,699 million; and in 1970, $15,951 million. Clearly, the Bank of America was on the move. By the end of 1971, it had deposits of almost $30 billion, and was the largest commercial bank in the United States. (The 10 largest banks in the United States, in terms of deposits, are listed in Table 13.1.) Certainly it had come a long way since the days of the open-air desk on the waterfront.

How Banks Operate

The Bank of America, the biggest in the country, is hardly a typical commercial bank. It has had a remarkable history and a gifted founder. Many commercial banks are very small, as you would guess from the fact that there are over 13,000 of them in the United States. But regardless of their size, what do banks do? Their function and activities vary considerably. Some are principally for firms; they do little business with individuals. Others are heavily engaged in lending to consumers. Nonetheless, although it is difficult to generalize about the operations of commercial banks because they vary so much, certain principles and propositions generally hold.

First, *banks generally make loans to both firms and individuals, and invest in securities, particularly the bonds of state and local governments, as well as federal government bonds.* The relationship between a business firm and its bank is often a close and continuing one. The firm keeps a reasonably large deposit with the bank for long periods of time, while the bank provides the firm with needed and prudent loans. The relationship between an individual and his or her bank is much more casual, but banks like consumer loans because they tend to be relatively profitable. In addition, besides lending to firms and individuals, banks buy large quantities of government bonds. For example, in the early 1970s, commercial banks held

about $60 billion of state and local government bonds.

Second, *banks, like other firms, are operated to make a profit.* They don't do it by producing and selling a good, like automobiles or steel. Instead, they perform various services, including lending money, making investments, clearing checks, keeping records, and so on. They manage to make a profit from these activities by lending money and making investments that yield a higher rate of interest than they must pay their depositors. For example, the Bank of America may be able to get 9 percent interest on the loans it makes, while it must pay only 5 percent interest to its depositors. (Commercial banks do not pay interest on demand deposits, but they do pay interest on time deposits. Also, they provide services at less than cost to holders of demand deposits.) If so, it receives the difference of 4 percent, which goes to meet its expenses—and to provide it with some profits.

Third, *banks must constantly balance their desire for high returns from their loans and investments against the requirement that these loans and investments be safe and easily turned into cash.* Since a bank's profits increase if it makes loans or investments that yield a high interest rate, it is clear why a bank favors high returns from its loans and investments. But those that yield a high interest rate often are relatively risky, which means that they may not be repaid in full. Because a bank lends out its depositors' money, it must be careful to limit the riskiness of the loans and investments it makes. Otherwise it may fail.

The Balance Sheet of an Individual Bank

A good way to understand how a bank operates is to look at its balance sheet. Figure 13.1 shows the Bank of America's balance sheet as of the beginning of 1970. The left-hand side shows that the total assets of the Bank of America were $25.6 billion, and that these assets were made up as fol-

Figure 13.1 Balance Sheet, Bank of America, January 1, 1970

Assets ($ billions)		Liabilities and net worth ($ billions)	
Cash	4.8	Demand deposits	9.1
Securities	4.2	Savings and time deposits	13.1
Loans	14.6	Other liabilities	2.0
Other assets	2.0	Net worth	1.4
Total	25.6	Total	25.6

Source: Bank of America.

lows: $4.8 billion in cash, $4.2 billion in bonds and other securities, $14.6 billion in loans, and $2.0 billion in other assets. In particular, note that the loans included among the assets of the Bank of America are the loans it made to firms and individuals. As we just said, lending money is one of the major functions of a commercial bank.

The right-hand side of the balance sheet says that the total liabilities—or debts—of the Bank of America were $24.2 billion, and that these liabilities were made up of $22.2 billion in deposits (both demand and time), and $2.0 billion in other liabilities. Note that the deposits at the Bank of America are included among its liabilities, since the Bank of America owes the depositors the amount of money in their deposits. It will be recalled from the previous chapter that maintaining these deposits is one of the major functions of a commercial bank. Returning to the balance sheet of the Bank of America, the difference between its total assets and its total liabilities—$1.4 billion —is, of course, its net worth.

One noteworthy characteristic of any bank's balance sheet is the fact that *a very large percentage of its liabilities must be paid on demand.* For example, if all the depositors of the Bank of America withdrew their demand deposits, over ⅓ of its liabilities would be due on demand. Of course, the chance of everyone wanting to draw out his or her money at once is infinitesimally small. Instead, on a given day some depositors withdraw some money, while others make deposits, and most neither withdraw nor deposit money. Consequently, any bank can get along with an amount of cash to cover withdrawals that is much smaller than the total amount of its demand deposits. For example, the Bank of America's cash equaled about ½ of its total demand deposits. Note that "cash" here includes the bank's deposit with the Federal Reserve System and its deposits with other banks, as well as cash in its vault.

The Bank of America's practice of holding an amount of cash—including its deposits with the Federal Reserve and with other banks—much less than the amount it owes its depositors may strike you as dangerous. Indeed, if you have a deposit at the Bank of America, you may be tempted to go over and withdraw the money in your account and deposit it in some bank that does have cash equal to the amount it owes its depositors. But you won't be able to do this because *all banks hold much less cash than the amount they owe their depositors.* Moreover, this is a perfectly sound banking practice, as we shall see.

Fractional-Reserve Banking

To understand the crucial significance of *fractional-reserve banking,* as this practice is called,

THE BANKING SYSTEM AND THE QUANTITY OF MONEY   ☐   259

Figure 13.2   Bank Balance Sheet: Case where Reserves Equal Demand Deposits

Assets		Liabilities and net worth	
Reserves	$2,000,000	Demand deposits	$2,000,000
Loans and investments	500,000	Net worth	500,000
Total	$2,500,000	Total	$2,500,000

let's compare two situations—one where a bank must hold as reserves an amount equal to the amount it owes its depositors, another where its reserves do not have to match the amount it owes its depositors. In the first case, the bank's balance sheet might be as shown in Figure 13.2, if demand deposits equal $2 million. The bank's loans and investments in this case are made entirely with funds put up by the owners of the bank. To see this, note that loans and investments equal $500,000, and that the bank's net worth also equals $500,000. Thus, if some of these loans are not repaid or if some of these investments lose money, the losses are borne entirely by the bank's stockholders. The depositors are protected completely because every cent of their deposits is covered by the bank's reserves.

Now let's turn to the case of fractional-reserve banking. In this case, the bank's balance sheet might be as shown in Figure 13.3, if deposits equal $2 million. Some of the loans and investments made by the bank are not made with funds put up by the owners of the bank, but with funds deposited in the bank by depositors. Thus, though depositors deposited $2 million in the bank, the reserves are only $400,000. What happened to the remaining $1.6 million? Since the bank (in this simple case) only has two kinds of assets, loans (and investments) and reserves, the bank must have lent out (or invested) the remaining $1.6 million.

The early history of banking is the story of an evolution from the first to the second situation. The earliest banks held reserves equal to the amounts they owed depositors, and were simply places where people stored their gold. But as time went on, banks began to practice fractional-reserve banking. It is easy to see how this evolution could take place. Suppose that you owned a bank of the first type. You would almost certainly be struck by the fact that most of the gold entrusted to you was not demanded on any given day. Sooner or later, you might be tempted to lend out some of the gold and obtain some interest. Eventually, as

Figure 13.3   Bank Balance Sheet: Fractional Reserves

Assets		Liabilities and net worth	
Reserves	$400,000	Demand deposits	$2,000,000
Loans and investments	2,100,000	Net worth	500,000
Total	$2,500,000	Total	$2,500,000

experience indicated that this procedure did not inconvenience the depositors, you and other bankers might make this practice common knowledge.

You might use several arguments to defend this practice. First, you would probably point out that none of the depositors had lost any money. (To the depositors, this would be a rather important argument!) Second, you could show that the interest you earned on the loans made it possible for you to charge depositors less for storing their gold. Consequently, you would argue that it was to the depositors' advantage (because of the savings that accrued to them) for you to lend out some of the gold. Third, you would probably argue that putting the money to work benefited the community and the economy. After all, in many cases, firms can make highly productive investments only if they can borrow the money, and by lending out your depositors' gold, you would enable such investments to be made.

Legal Reserve Requirements

Arguments of this sort have led society to permit fractional-reserve banking. In other words, a bank is allowed to hold less in reserves than the amount it owes its depositors. But what determines the amount of reserves banks hold? For example, the Bank of America, according to Figure 13.1, held cash equal to about 20 percent of its total deposits. Probably it could get away with holding much less in reserves, so long as there is no panic among depositors and it makes sound loans and investments. One reason why the Bank of America held this much cash is very simple: *the Federal Reserve System requires every commercial bank that is a member of the system to hold a certain percentage of its deposits as reserves.* This percentage varies with the size of the bank. As of late 1973, each member bank had to hold as reserves 8 percent of its first $2 million of demand deposits, 10½ percent of its next $8 million, 12½ percent of its next $90 million, 13½ percent of its next $300 million,

and 18 percent of its demand deposits in excess of $400 million. These are *legal reserve requirements;* they exist for time deposits too, but are lower than for demand deposits.

The Federal Reserve System in recent years has dictated that the average bank should hold about $1 dollar in reserves for every $6 of demand deposits. Most of these reserves are held in the form of deposits by banks at their regional Federal Reserve Bank. Thus, for example, a great deal of the Bank of America's reserves are held in its deposit with the Federal Reserve Bank of San Francisco. In addition, some of any bank's reserves are held in cash on the bank's premises. However, its legal reserves are less than the "cash" entry on its balance sheet since its deposits with other banks do not count as legal reserves. Of course, these legal reserve requirements are binding only on members of the Federal Reserve System, and, as we noted in the previous chapter, although all national banks are members, not all state banks are. But the banks outside the Federal Reserve System hold only a small percentage of the nation's deposits, and the Fed seems to believe that it includes a large enough proportion of the banks to accomplish its goals.

The most obvious reason why the Fed imposes these legal reserve requirements would seem to be to keep the banks safe, but in this case the obvious answer isn't the right one. Instead, *the most important reason for legal reserve requirements is to control the money supply.* It will take some more discussion before this becomes clear.

To close with a historical sidelight, until 1972 legal reserve requirements were higher for big-city banks than for small-town banks. Back when the Federal Reserve System was formed, big-city banks often held the reserves of the small-town banks, and thus it seemed reasonable to enforce higher reserve requirements for the big-city banks. But nowadays reserves of all member banks—in big cities or in small towns—are held by the Federal Reserve Banks. Consequently, this difference in legal reserve requirements was like the human appendix and wisdom teeth: a somewhat illogical and useless inheritance from the past. Finally, in 1972, it was jettisoned.

The Safety of the Banks

We have just argued that the reserve requirements imposed by the Federal Reserve System exceed what would be required under normal circumstances to insure the safety of the banks. To support our argument, we might cite some authorities who claim that a bank would be quite safe if it only had reserves equal to about 2 percent of its deposits. Under these circumstances it would be able to meet its depositors' everyday demands for cash. Obviously this level of reserves is much lower than the legally required level. We must, however, recognize that the safety of a bank depends on many factors besides the level of its reserves. In particular, a bank must make prudent investments.

For example, suppose that a bank lends money to every budding inventor with a scheme for producing perpetual-motion machines—and that it grants particularly large loans to those who propose to market these machines in the suburbs of Missoula, Montana. This bank is going to fail eventually, even if it holds reserves equal to 20 percent—or 50 percent for that matter—of its demand deposits. It will fail simply because the loans it makes will not be repaid, and eventually these losses will accumulate to more than the bank's net worth. In other words, if the bank is sufficiently inept in making loans and investments it will lose all the owners' money and some of the depositors' money besides.

In addition, even if the bank makes sensible loans and investments, it must protect itself against short-term withdrawals of large amounts of money. Although larger-than-usual withdrawals are not very likely to occur, the bank must be prepared to meet a temporary upswing in withdrawals. One way is to invest in securities that can readily be turned into cash. Such securities are near-money, in the jargon of the previous chapter. For example, the bank may invest in short-term government securities that can readily be sold at a price that varies only moderately from day to day.

There can be no doubt that banks are much safer today than they were 50 or 100 years ago. The reason is that the government has put its power squarely behind the banking system. It used to be that "runs" occurred on the banks. Every now and then, depositors, frightened that their banks would fail and that they would lose some of their money, would line up at the tellers' windows and withdraw as much money as they could. Faced with runs of this sort, banks were sometimes forced to close because they could not satisfy all demands for withdrawals. Needless to say, no fractional-reserve banking system can satisfy demands for total withdrawal of funds.

Runs on banks are a thing of the past, for several reasons. One is that the government—including the Federal Deposit Insurance Corporation (FDIC), the Fed, and other public agencies—has made it clear that it will not stand by and tolerate the sorts of panics that used to occur periodically in this country. The FDIC insures the accounts of depositors in practically all banks so that, even if a bank fails, the depositor will get his money back—up to $20,000. Another reason is that the banks themselves are better managed and regulated. For example, bank examiners are sent out to look over the bankers' shoulders and see whether they are solvent. It is a far cry from the situation sixty-odd years ago that led to the creation of the Federal Reserve System.

The Lending Decision: A Case Study

To get a better feel for the workings of a bank, let's look at an actual decision faced by Robert Swift, the assistant vice president of the Lone Star National Bank of Houston, Texas. Mr. Swift received a call from Ralph Desmond, president of the Desmond Engineering Corporation. Mr. Desmond wanted to change his bank; he was dissatisfied with the amount he could borrow from his present bank. He wanted to borrow $30,000 from the Lone Star to pay what he owed to his present bank, pay some bills coming up, and buy some material needed to fulfill a contract. Mr. Swift asked Mr. Desmond to come to his office with various financial statements regarding the Desmond Engineering Corporation and its prospects. These included recent profit and loss statements and balance sheets, as well as a variety of other data, including information indicating how rapidly the firm collected its bills and the quality of the debts owed the firm.

Mr. Swift forwarded Mr. Desmond's loan application to the credit department of the bank for further analyses. The credit department added comments on the Desmond Engineering Corporation's solvency and prospects. Besides being secured by a mortgage on some equipment owned by the Desmond Engineering Corporation, this loan was to be personally endorsed by Mr. Desmond and another principal stockholder in the firm. Consequently, Mr. Swift obtained information on the extent and nature of the personal assets of Mr. Desmond and the other stockholder. This information was used, together with all the other data on the firm, to determine whether the bank would make the loan. After a reasonable amount of time, Mr. Swift recommended the acceptance of Mr. Desmond's loan application. In his view, Mr. Desmond had a very good chance of repaying the loan.[2]

Note two things about this decision. First, if the bank grants Mr. Desmond the loan, it will create a demand deposit for him. In other words, it will create some money. Second, the bank can do this only if it has reserves exceeding the legal reserve requirements. Both of these points are important enough to dwell on for a while.

[2] This case comes from Leonard Marks and Alan Coleman, *Cases in Commercial Bank Management*, New York: McGraw-Hill, 1962, pp. 168–76. However, the outcome is purely conjectural.

Two Ways Banks Cannot Create Money

Genesis tells us that God created heaven and earth. Economists tell us that banks create money. To many people, the latter process is at least as mysterious as the former. Even bankers themselves have been known to fall into serious error by claiming that they do not create money. Yet the way banks create money is a relatively simple process, which the next few sections will describe in detail. Suppose that someone receives $10,000 in newly printed currency and deposits it in his local bank. Before we see how the bank can create more than $10,000 from this deposit, we will describe two ways in which banks *cannot* create new money. Since people often jump to the conclusion that one or the other of these two processes is the correct one, it is a good idea to kill off these heresies at the outset.

First, suppose that ours is not a fractional-reserve banking system. In other words, assume that every bank has to maintain reserves equal to its deposits. In this case, the bank receiving the $10,000 deposit cannot create any new money. You may be inclined to think that it can be done, but it can't. To see why not, consider the changes in the bank's balance sheet, shown in Figure 13.4. When the $10,000 is deposited in the bank, the bank's deposits go up by $10,000. Since the bank must hold $10,000 in reserves to back up the new 10,000 deposit, it must put the $10,000 it receives from the depositor into its reserves. Thus, the bank's demand deposits go up by $10,000, and its reserves go up by $10,000. Since demand deposits are on the right-hand side of the balance sheet and reserves are on the left-hand side, the balance sheet continues to balance. *No new money is created. All that happens is that the depositor gives up $10,000 in one form of money—currency—and receives $10,000 in another form of money—a demand deposit.*

Next, let's turn to a second way banks cannot create money. Suppose that we have a fractional-reserve banking system and that the legal reserve requirement is 16⅔ percent. In other words, the bank must hold $1 in reserves for every $6 of demand deposits. Suppose that the bank decides to take the crisp, new $10,000 in currency that is deposited and add it to its reserves, thus increasing its reserves by $10,000. Then suppose it reasons (incorrectly) that it can increase its deposits by $50,000, since it has $10,000 in additional reserves. Why $50,000? Because the $10,000 in additional reserves will support $60,000 in demand deposits; and since the person who deposited the $10,000 has a demand deposit of $10,000, this means that it can create additional demand deposits of $60,000 minus $10,000, or $50,000.

The bank will create these additional demand deposits simply by making loans or investments. Thus, when a person comes in to the bank for a loan, all the banker has to do is give him a demand deposit—a checking account—that didn't exist before. In other words, the banker can say to his staff: "Establish a checking account of $50,000 for Mr. Smith. We have just lent him this amount to buy a new piece of equipment to be used in his business." At first, this whole process looks a bit like black magic, perhaps even larceny. After all, how can checking accounts be established out of thin air? But they can, and are. In essence, this is how banks create money.

But we prefaced this example by saying that it contains an error: the error is the supposition that the bank can create an additional $50,000 of demand deposits on the basis of the $10,000 deposit.

To see why this won't work, consider the changes in the bank's balance sheet, shown in Figure 13.5. After the bank received the $10,000 deposit, its demand deposits and its reserves both increased by $10,000, as shown in the first panel of Figure 13.5. Then, as we noted above, the bank made a $50,000 loan and (in the process of making the loan) created $50,000 in new deposits, as shown in the second panel. So far, so good. The bank's balance sheet continues to balance—in accord with common sense and accounting (in that order). The bank's reserves are ⅙ of its demand deposits; they satisfy the legal reserve requirements established by the Fed.

So what is the problem? None, unless the money lent by the bank is spent. If the man who received the loan—Mr. Smith—never used the money he borrowed, the bank could act this way and get away with it. But people who borrow money are in the habit of spending it; why pay interest on money one doesn't use? Even if Mr. Smith, the recipient of this loan, spent the money, the bank could act in accord with this example and get away with it if the people who received the money from Mr. Smith deposited it in this same bank. But the chances of this occurring are very small. The equipment Mr. Smith plans to buy is likely to be produced by a firm in some other city; and even if it is located in the same city, the firm may well have an account at another bank.

To see the problem that results when the loan

Figure 13.4   Changes in Bank Balance Sheet, where Reserves Equal Demand Deposits

Assets		Liabilities and net worth	
Reserves	+$10,000	Demand deposits	+$10,000
Loans and investments	No change	Net worth	No change
Total	+$10,000	Total	+$10,000

Figure 13.5   Changes in Bank Balance Sheet: Fractional Reserves

	Assets		Liabilities and Net Worth	
Bank receives deposit	Reserves	+$10,000	Demand deposits	+$10,000
	Loans and investments	No change	Net worth	No change
	Total	+$10,000	Total	+$10,000
Bank makes loan	Reserves	No change	Demand deposits	+$50,000
	Loans and investments	+$50,000	Net worth	No change
	Total	+$50,000	Total	+$50,000
Mr. Smith spends $50,000	Reserves	−$50,000	Demand deposits	−$50,000
	Loans and investments	No change	Net worth	No change
	Total	−$50,000	Total	−$50,000
Total effect	Reserves	−$40,000	Demand deposits	+$10,000
	Loans and investments	+ 50,000	Net worth	No change
	Total	+$10,000	Total	+$10,000

is spent in this way, suppose that Mr. Smith spends the $50,000 on a machine produced by the Acme Corporation, which has an account at the First National Bank of Boston. He sends the Acme Corporation a check for $50,000 drawn on our bank. When the Acme Corporation receives Mr. Smith's check, it deposits this check to its account at the First National Bank of Boston, which, using the facilities of the Federal Reserve System, presents the check to our bank for payment. Our bank must then fork over $50,000 of its cash—its reserves—to the First National Bank of Boston. Consequently, once the $50,000 check is paid, the effect on our bank's balance sheet is as shown in the third panel of Figure 13.5. Taken as a whole, the bank's demand deposits have increased by $10,000, and its reserves have decreased by $40,000, as shown in the bottom panel of Figure 13.5.

At this point, the error in this example is becoming clear. *If the bank was holding $1 in reserves for every $6 in demand deposits before the $10,000 deposit was made, these transactions must cause the bank to violate the legal reserve requirements.* This is simple to prove. Suppose that, before the $10,000 deposit, our bank had $X in demand deposits and $\$\frac{X}{6}$ in reserves. Then, after the transactions described above, it must have ($X + $10,000) in demand deposits and $\left(\$\frac{X}{6} - \$40,000\right)$ in reserves. Certainly, the reserves—$\$\frac{X}{6} - \$40,000$ —are now less than ⅙ of the demand deposits— $X + $10,000. This must be true whatever value X has. (Try it and see.) Thus, no bank can create money in this way because, if it did, it would violate the legal reserve requirements after the newly created demand deposits were used. However, as we shall see later, a monopoly bank— that is, the only bank in the country—could create money like this. But monopoly banks do not exist in the United States.

How Banks Can Create Money

Now that you have learned two ways that banks *cannot* create money, let's describe how they *can* create money. Imagine the following scenario. First, suppose once again that someone deposits $10,000 of newly printed money in our bank, which we'll call Bank A. Second, suppose that Bank A lends Mr. Smith $8,333, and that Mr. Smith uses this money to purchase some equip-

ment from Mr. Jones, who deposits Mr. Smith's check in his account at Bank B. Third, Bank B buys a bond for $6,941 from Mr. Stone, who deposits the check from Bank B to his account at Bank C. Fourth, Bank C lends $5,784 to Mr. White, who uses the money to buy a truck from the local General Motors dealer, Mr. Black, who deposits Mr. White's check for $5,784 to his account at Bank D. Fifth, Bank D lends Mr. Cohen $4,820 which Mr. Cohen uses to buy some lumber from Mr. Palucci, who deposits Mr. Cohen's check to his account at Bank E. Admittedly, this is a somewhat complicated plot with a substantial cast of characters, but life is like that.

The first step in our drama occurs when someone deposits $10,000 in newly printed money in Bank A. The effect of this deposit is shown in the first panel of Figure 13.6: Bank A's demand deposits

Figure 13.6 Changes in Bank A's Balance Sheet

	Assets		Liabilities and net worth	
Bank receives deposit	Reserves	+$10,000	Demand deposits	+$10,000
	Loans and investments	No change	Net worth	No change
	Total	+$10,000	Total	+$10,000
Bank makes loan	Reserves	No change	Demand deposits	+$ 8,333
	Loans and investments	+$ 8,333	Net worth	No change
	Total	+$ 8,333	Total	+$ 8,333
Mr Smith spends $8,333	Reserves	−$ 8,333	Demand deposits	−$ 8,333
	Loans and investments	No change	Net worth	No change
	Total	−$ 8,333	Total	−$ 8,333
Total effect	Reserves	+$ 1,667	Demand deposits	+$10,000
	Loans and investments	+$ 8,333	Net worth	No change
	Total	+$10,000	Total	+$10,000

and its reserves both go up by $10,000. Now Bank A is far too smart to pull the sort of trick described in the last section. It does not try to make a $50,000 loan, lest it wind up with less reserves than dictated by the legal reserve requirements. When Mr. Smith asks one of the loan officers of the bank for a loan to purchase equipment, the loan officer approves a loan of $8,333, not $50,000. Mr. Smith is given a checking account of $8,333 at Bank A.

How can Bank A get away with this loan of $8,333 without winding up with less than the legally required reserves? The answer to this question lies in the second panel of Figure 13.6, which shows what happens to Bank A's balance sheet when Bank A makes the $8,333 loan and creates a new demand deposit of $8,333. Obviously, both demand deposits and loans go up by $8,333. Next, look at the third panel of Figure 13.6, which shows what happens when Mr. Smith spends the $8,333 on equipment. As pointed out above, he purchases this equipment from Mr. Jones. Mr. Jones deposits Mr. Smith's check to his account in Bank B which presents the check to Bank A for payment. After Bank A pays Bank B (through the Federal Reserve System), the result—as shown in the third panel—is that Bank A's deposits go down by $8,333 since Mr. Smith no longer has the deposit. Bank A's reserves also go down by $8,333 since Bank A has to transfer these reserves to Bank B to pay the amount of the check.

As shown in the bottom panel of Figure 13.6, the total effect on Bank A is to increase its deposits by the $10,000 that was deposited originally and to increase its reserves by $10,000 minus $8,333, or $1,667. In other words, reserves have increased by ⅙ as much as demand deposits. This means that Bank A will meet its legal reserve requirements. To see this, suppose that before the deposit of $10,000, Bank A had demand deposits of $X and

reserves of $ $\frac{X}{6}$. Then after the full effect of the transaction occurs on Bank A's balance sheet, Bank A's demand deposits will equal ($X + $10,000)

and its reserves will equal $\left(\$\frac{X}{6} + \$\frac{10,000}{6} \right)$, since $1,667 = $\frac{\$10,000}{6}$. Thus Bank A continues to hold $1 in reserves for every $6 in demand deposits, as required by the Fed.

Impact on Other Banks

It is important to recognize that *Bank A has now created $8,333 in new money*. To see this, note that Mr. Jones winds up with a demand deposit of this amount that he didn't have before; and this is a net addition to the money supply, since the person who originally deposited the $10,000 in currency still has his $10,000, although it is in the form of a demand deposit rather than currency. But this is not the end of the story. The effects of the $10,000 deposit at Bank A are not limited to Bank A. Instead, as we shall see, other banks can also create new money as a consequence of the original $10,000 deposit at Bank A.

Let's begin with Bank B. Recall from the previous section that the $8,333 check made out by Mr. Smith to Mr. Jones is deposited by the latter in his account at Bank B. This is a new deposit of funds at Bank B. As pointed out in the previous section, Bank B gets $8,333 in reserves from Bank A when Bank A pays Bank B to get back the check. Thus the effect on Bank B's balance sheet, as shown in the first panel of Figure 13.7, is to increase both demand deposits and reserves by $8,333. Bank B is in much the same position as was Bank A when the latter received the original deposit of $10,000. Bank B can make loans or investments of $6,941. (The way we derive $6,941 is explained in the next paragraph.) Specifically, it decides to buy a bond for $6,941 from Mr. Stone, who deposits the check from Bank B to his account in Bank C. Thus, as shown in the second panel of Figure 13.7, the effect of this transaction is to increase Bank B's investments by $6,941 and to increase its demand deposits by $6,941 when

Figure 13.7 Changes in Bank B's Balance Sheet

	Assets		Liabilities and net worth	
Bank receives deposit	Reserves	+$8,333	Demand deposits	+$8,333
	Loans and investments	No change	Net worth	No change
	Total	+$8,333	Total	+$8,333
Bank buys bond	Reserves	No change	Demand deposits	+$6,941
	Loans and investments	+$6,941	Net worth	No change
	Total	+$6,941	Total	+$6,941
Mr. Stone deposits money in Bank C	Reserves	−$6,941	Demand deposits	−$6,941
	Loans and investments	No change	Net worth	No change
	Total	−$6,941	Total	−$6,941
Total effect	Reserves	+$1,392	Demand deposits	+$8,333
	Loans and investments	+$6,941	Net worth	No change
	Total	+$8,333	Total	+$8,333

Bank B bought the bond. This transaction increases Bank B's demand deposits by $6,941 because the bank creates a demand deposit of $6,941 to pay for the bond. In other words, the bank in effect creates a deposit for itself and uses it to pay Mr. Stone for the bond. Then Bank B's demand deposits and its reserves are decreased by $6,941 when it transfers this amount of reserves to Bank C to pay for the check. When the total effects of the transaction are summed up, Bank B—like Bank A—continues to meet its legal reserve requirements, as shown in the bottom panel of Figure 13.7.

Bank B has also created some money—$6,941 to be exact. Mr. Stone has $6,941 in demand deposits that he didn't have before; and this is a net addition to the money supply since the person who originally deposited the currency in Bank A still has his $10,000, and Mr. Jones still has the $8,333 he deposited in Bank B. And this is still not the end of the story. Bank C has experienced an increase of $6,941 in its demand deposits and in its reserves. Thus it—like Banks A and B before it—can increase its loans and investments. By how much? At this point, the pattern is becoming clear: *it can lend the amount by which its reserves exceed the legally required reserves.* In other words, since Bank C must hold $\frac{6,941}{6}$, or $1,157, in legally required reserves against the new deposit of $6,941, it can lend $6,941 minus $1,157, or $5,784.

According to our plot, Bank C lends $5,784 to Mr. White, who buys a truck from the local General Motors dealer, Mr. Black. Mr. Black deposits Mr. White's check for $5,784 to his account at

Figure 13.8   Changes in Bank C's Balance Sheet

	Assets		Liabilities and net worth	
Bank receives deposit	Reserves	+$6,941	Demand deposits	+$6,941
	Loans and investments	No change	Net worth	No change
	Total	+$6,941	Total	+$6,941
Bank makes loan	Reserves	No change	Demand deposits	+$5,784
	Loans and investments	+$5,784	Net worth	No change
	Total	+$5,784	Total	+$5,784
Mr. White spends $5,784	Reserves	−$5,784	Demand deposits	−$5,784
	Loans and investments	No change	Net worth	No change
	Total	−$5,784	Total	−$5,784
Total effect	Reserves	+$1,157	Demand deposits	+$6,941
	Loans and investments	+ 5,784	Net worth	No change
	Total	+$6,941	Total	+$6,941

Bank D. Figure 13.8 traces out the effects on Bank C's balance sheet. The top panel shows the original increase in its demand deposits and in its reserves of $6,941. The second panel shows the increase of $5,784 in its loans stemming from its loan to Mr. White, as well as the accompanying increase in its demand deposits of $5,784 representing the demand deposit it gave to Mr. White. The third panel shows the $5,784 decrease in demand deposits when Mr. White checked out the whole of his account, and the $5,784 decrease in reserves when Bank C transferred this amount of reserves to Bank D to pay for the check. The bottom panel shows the total effect. As in the case of Banks A and B, Bank C continues to meet the legal reserve requirements when the full effects of the transaction have made themselves felt.

Bank C also has created some money—$5,784, to

be exact. To see why, note that Mr. Black has $5,784 in demand deposits that he didn't have before; and this is a net addition to the money supply since the original depositor in Bank A still has his $10,000, Mr. Jones still has the $8,333 in Bank B, and Mr. Stone still has the $6,941 in Bank C. But this is still not the end of the story. Bank D has experienced an increase of $5,784 in its demand deposits and its reserves. Thus, it—like Banks A, B, and C before it—can increase its loans and investments by the amount of its **excess reserves** (those in excess of legal requirements). Since it must hold $\frac{\$5,784}{6} = \$964$ as legal reserves against its increase in deposits of $5,784, its excess reserves are $5,784 minus $964, or $4,820. Thus Bank D can increase its loans and investments by $4,820. As we saw at the beginning of this saga, it decides

Figure 13.9   Changes in Bank D's Balance Sheet

	Assets		Liabilities and net worth	
Bank receives deposit	Reserves Loans and investments Total	_____	Demand deposits Net worth Total	_____
Bank makes loan	Reserves Loans and investments Total	_____	Demand deposits Net worth Total	_____
Mr. Cohen spends $4,820	Reserves Loans and investments Total	_____	Demand deposits Net worth Total	_____
Total effect	Reserves Loans and investments Total	+$ 964 + 4820 +$5784	Demand deposits Net worth Total	+$5784 No change +$5784

to lend Mr. Cohen $4,820 to buy some lumber from Mr. Palucci. Mr. Cohen pays Mr. Palucci with a check for $4,820 drawn on Bank D and Mr. Palucci deposits the check to his account at Bank E. As shown in Figure 13.9, Bank D winds up with no excess reserves after it transfers reserves to Bank E to pay for the check. (To check your grasp of the material in this section, see if you can fill in the numbers in the top three panels of Figure 13.9.)[3] But Mr. Palucci winds up with a demand deposit of $4,820 that he didn't have before. Thus *Bank D also creates some money—$4,820, to be exact.*

---

[3] The answer is:

	Assets		Liabilities and net worth	
Bank receives deposit	Reserves Loans and investments Total	+$5,784 No change +$5,784	Demand deposits Net worth Total	+$5,784 No change +$5,784
Bank makes loan	Reserves Loans and investments Total	No change +$4,820 +$4,820	Demand deposits Net worth Total	+$4,820 No change +$4,820
Mr. Cohen spends $4,820	Reserves Loans and investments Total	−$4,820 No change −$4,820	Demand deposits Net worth Total	−$4,820 No change −$4,820

The Total Effect of the Original $10,000 Deposit

How big an increase in the money supply can the entire banking system support as a consequence of the original $10,000 deposit in Bank A? Clearly, the effects of the original deposit spread from one bank to another, since each bank hands new reserves (and deposits) to another bank, which in turn hands them to another bank. For example, Bank E now has $4,820 more in deposits and reserves and so can create $4,017 [4] in new money by making a loan or investment of this amount. This process goes on indefinitely, and it would be impossible to describe each of the multitude of steps involved. Fortunately, it isn't necessary to do so. We can figure out the total amount of new money the entire banking system can support as a consequence of the original $10,000 deposit in Bank A without going through all these steps.

We do this by computing how much new money each bank creates. Besides the original $10,000, Bank A creates $8,333—which is $5/6$ of $10,000. Then Bank B creates an additional $6,941—$(5/6)^2$ of $10,000. Then Bank C creates an additional $5,784—$(5/6)^3$ of $10,000. Then Bank D creates an additional $4,820—$(5/6)^4$ of $10,000. Then Bank E creates an additional $4,017—$(5/6)^5$ of $10,000. The amount of money created by each bank is less than that created by the previous bank, so that the total amount of new money created by the original $10,000 deposit—$10,000 + $8,333 + $6,941 + $5,784 + $4,820 + $4,017 + · · · —tends to a finite limit as the process goes on and on. Elementary algebra tells us what this sum of terms will be. *When the process works itself out, the entire banking system can support $60,000 in money as a consequence of the original $10,000 deposit of new funds.*[5] For demonstrations of this fact, see Table 13.2 and Figure 13.10. Table 13.2 shows the amount of new demand deposits created at each

Table 13.2

Increase in Money Supply Resulting from $10,000 Increase in Reserves

Source	Amount
Original deposit	$10,000
Created by Bank A	8,333
Created by Bank B	6,941
Created by Bank C	5,784
Created by Bank D	4,820
Created by Bank E	4,017
Created by Bank F	3,347
Created by Bank G	2,789
Created by Bank H	2,324
Created by Bank I	1,937
Created by Bank J	1,614
Created by other banks	8,094
Total	60,000

stage of this process, while Figure 13.10 plots the cumulative expansion in demand deposits.

We must note that the banking system as a whole has accomplished what we said in a previous section than an individual bank—Bank A—could not do. It has created an additional $50,000 of demand deposits on the basis of the original $10,000 deposit. In other words, given the additional $10,000 in reserves, the banking system can create $60,000 in money. Certainly this seems sensible, since each $1 of reserves can back up $6 in demand deposits. But for the reasons discussed in a previous section, an individual bank cannot do this, unless, of course, it is a monopoly bank. If it is, it need have no fear of losing reserves to other banks, because there are no other banks; so it can behave this way.

---

[4] Why $4,017? Because it must hold $\frac{\$4,820}{6} = \$803$ as reserves to support the new demand deposit of $4,820. Thus, it has excess reserves of $4,017, and it can create another new demand deposit of this amount.

[5] The proof of this is as follows: the total amount of money supported by the $10,000 in reserves is $10,000 + $8,333 + $6,941 + $5,784 + · · · , which equals $10,000 + 5/6 × $10,000 + $(5/6)^2$ × $10,000 + $(5/6)^3$ × $10,000 + . . . , which equals $10,000 × $(1 + 5/6 + (5/6)^2 + (5/6)^3 + . . .) = \$10{,}000 \times \frac{1}{1-(5/6)} = \$60{,}000$, since $1 + 5/6 + (5/6)^2 + (5/6)^3 + . . . = \frac{1}{1-(5/6)}$.

However, banking in the United States is not monopolized.

In general, *if a certain amount of additional reserves is made available to the banking system, the banking system as a whole can increase the money supply by an amount equal to the amount of additional reserves multiplied by the reciprocal of the required ratio of reserves to deposits.* In other words, to obtain the total increase in the money supply that can be achieved from a certain amount of additional reserves, multiply the amount of additional reserves by the reciprocal of the required ratio of reserves to deposits—or, what amounts to the same thing, *divide the amount of additional reserves by the legally required ratio of reserves to deposits.* Putting it in still another way, the banking system as a whole can increase the money supply by $(1/r)$ dollars—where r is the required ratio of reserves to deposits—for every \$1 increase in reserves.[6]

[6] The total amount of money supported by \$1 of additional reserves is

$$1 + (1 - r) + (1 - r)^2 + (1 - r)^3 + \cdots = \frac{1}{1 - (1 - r)} = \frac{1}{r}$$

We reach this conclusion by the same method we used in note 5.

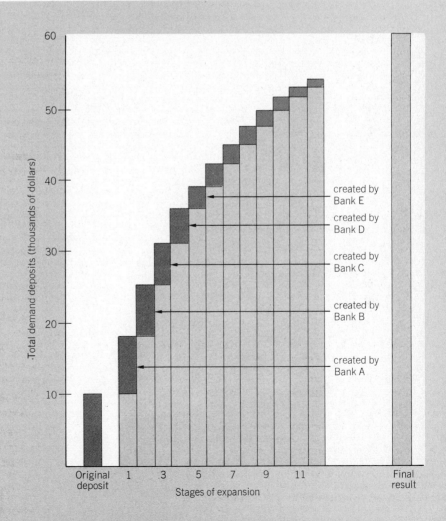

Figure 13.10
Cumulative Expansion in Demand Deposits on Basis of \$10,000 of New Reserves and Legal Reserve Requirement of 16⅔ Percent

The original deposit was \$10,000. In the first stage of the expansion process, Bank A created an additional \$8,333. In the second stage, Bank B created an additional \$6,941. In the third stage, Bank C created an additional \$5,784. This process goes on until the final result is \$60,000 of demand deposits.

Let's apply this proposition to a couple of specific cases. Suppose that the banking system's reserves increase by $10,000 and that the required ratio of reserves to deposits is ⅙. To determine how much the banking system can increase the money supply, we must divide the amount of the additional reserves—$10,000—by the required ratio of reserves to deposits—⅙—to get the answer, $60,000. Note, with proper satisfaction, that this answer checks with our earlier results. Now suppose that the required ratio of reserves to deposits is ⅕. By how much can the banking system increase the money supply? Dividing $10,000 by ⅕, we get the answer: $50,000. Note that the higher the required ratio of reserves to deposits, the smaller the amount by which the banking system can increase the money supply on the basis of a given increase in reserves. More will be said about this in the next chapter.

Finally, an increase in reserves generally affects a great many banks at about the same time. For expository purposes, it is useful to trace through the effect of an increase in the reserves of a single bank—Bank A in our case. But usually this is not what happens. Instead, lots of banks experience an increase in reserves at about the same time. Thus, they all have excess reserves at about the same time, and they all make loans or investments at about the same time. The result is that, when the people who borrow money spend it, each bank tends both to gain and lose reserves. Thus, on balance, each bank need not lose reserves. In real life the amount of bank money often expands simultaneously.

The Effect of a Decrease in Reserves

Up to this point, we have been talking only about the effect of an increase in reserves. What happens to the quantity of money if reserves decrease? For example, suppose that you draw $10,000 out of your bank and hold it in the form of currency, perhaps by sewing it in your mattress. You thus reduce the total reserves of the banking system by $10,000. Let us begin with the effect on your bank. Clearly, it will experience a $10,000 decrease in deposits (because of your withdrawal) and, at the same time, a $10,000 decrease in reserves. Thus, if it was holding $1 in reserves for every $6 in deposits before you withdrew the money, it now holds less than the legally required reserves. If its deposits go down by $10,000, its reserves must go down by $1,667, not $10,000, if the 6:1 ratio between deposits and reserves is to be maintained. To observe the legal reserve requirements, your bank must increase its reserves by $10,000 minus $1,667, or $8,333. It has several ways to get this money, one being to sell securities. It may sell a municipal bond to Mrs. Cherrytree for $8,333. To pay for the bond, she writes a check on her bank, Bank Q, for the $8,333. Thus, as shown in Figure 13.11, your bank's investments decrease by $8,333, and its reserves increase by $8,333 when Bank Q transfers this amount to your bank to pay for the check.

But this is not the end of the story. Because Bank Q has lost $8,333 in deposits and $8,333 in reserves, its reserves are now less than the legal minimum. Since its deposits have gone down $8,333, its reserves should have gone down $\frac{\$8,333}{6}$, or $1,392. Thus, Bank Q must increase its reserves by $8,333 minus $1,392, or $6,941. To do so, it might sell a bond it holds for $6,941. But when the person who buys the bond gives Bank Q his check for $6,941 drawn on Bank R, Bank R loses $6,941 in deposits and $6,941 in reserves. Thus, Bank R's reserves are now below the legal requirement. Since its deposits have gone down $6,941, its reserves should have gone down $\frac{\$6,941}{6}$, or $1,157. So Bank R must increase its reserves by $6,941 minus $1,157, or $5,784. And on and on the process goes.

Let us consider the overall effect on the money supply of the $10,000 decrease in reserves. Your bank's demand deposits decreased by $10,000, Bank Q's demand deposits decreased by $8,333 (⅚ of $10,000), Bank R's demand deposits decreased by $6,941 ((⅚)² of $10,000), and so on. The total de-

Figure 13.11   Change in Your Bank's Balance Sheet

	Assets		Liabilities and net worth	
You withdraw deposit	Reserves	−$10,000	Demand deposits	−$10,000
	Loans and investments	No change	Net worth	No change
	Total	−$10,000	Total	−$10,000
Bank sells bond and gets funds from Bank Q	Reserves	+$ 8,333	Demand deposits	No change
	Loans and investments	−$ 8,333	Net worth	No change
	Total	No change	Total	No change
Total effect	Reserves	−$ 1,667	Demand deposits	−$10,000
	Loans and investments	−$ 8,333	Net worth	No change
	Total	−$10,000	Total	−$10,000

crease in the money supply—$10,000 + $8,333 + $6,941 + · · ·—tends to a finite limit as the process goes on and on. This limit is $60,000. Thus, *when the process works itself out, the entire banking system will reduce the money supply by $60,000 as a consequence of a $10,000 decrease in reserves.* More generally, *if the banking system's reserves decrease by a certain amount, the banking system as a whole will reduce demand deposits by an amount equal to the reduction in reserves multiplied by the reciprocal of the required ratio of reserves to deposits.*

In other words, to obtain the total decrease in demand deposits resulting from a reduction in reserves, *divide the reduction in reserves by the legally required ratio of reserves to deposits.* Putting it another way, the banking system as a whole will reduce demand deposits by (1/r) dollars—where r is the required ratio of reserves to deposits—for every $1 decrease in reserves. Of course, there is

often a simultaneous contraction of money on the part of many banks, just as there is often a simultaneous expansion. But this doesn't affect the result.

Let's apply this proposition to a particular case. Suppose that the banking system experiences a decrease in reserves of $10,000 and that the required ratio of reserves to deposits is ⅙. Applying this rule, we must divide the reduction in reserves—$10,000 —by the required ratio of reserves to deposits—⅙— to get the answer, which is a $60,000 reduction in demand deposits. This answer checks with the result in the previous paragraph. The effect of a $1 decrease in reserves is equal in absolute terms to the effect of a $1 increase in reserves. Whether the change is an increase or a decrease, a $1 change in reserves leads to a $(1/r) change in demand deposits. Or, more precisely, this is the case if certain assumptions, discussed in the next section, are true. To complete our discussion of how banks create money, we turn now to these assumptions.

Currency Withdrawals and Excess Reserves

In discussing the amount of additional demand deposits that can be created by the banking system as a result of injecting $10,000 of new reserves, we made the important assumption that everyone who received the new demand deposits—from Mr. Palucci back to the person who originally deposited his money in Bank A—wants to keep this money in the form of demand deposits rather than currency. However, this clearly may not be the case. Some people who receive new demand deposits may choose to withdraw some part of this money as currency. For example, Mr. Palucci may decide to withdraw $1,000 of his new demand deposit in cash.

It is fairly obvious what effect this withdrawal of currency will have on the amount of demand deposits the banking system can create. This withdrawal of currency from the entire banking system reduces the reserves of the banking system by $1,000. Applying the results of the previous section, this means that the banking system can create $6,000 less in demand deposits ($1,000 divided by ⅙) than it could if the currency had not been withdrawn. Consequently, the banking system can create $60,000 minus $6,000, or $54,000, from the combination of the original $10,000 injection of reserves and the $1,000 withdrawal of currency. In other words, the banking system can create an amount of demand deposits equal to the amount of additional reserves *left permanently with the banking system* ($10,000 minus $1,000, or $9,000 in this case) divided by the required ratio of reserves to demand deposits.

Similarly, in discussing how much demand deposits will be reduced as a consequence of a $10,000 reduction in reserves, we made the important assumption that everyone who buys a security from a bank pays the bank by check. But some people may pay partly or in full with currency, and this will affect how much the amount of demand deposits must be reduced by the banking system. If somebody pays $1,000 in currency to one of the banks,

this restores $1,000 of the $10,000 in reserves that the banking system lost. Thus, the banking system really loses $9,000, not $10,000. Then, applying the rule set forth in the previous section, the banking system must reduce its demand deposits by $54,000 ($9,000 divided by ⅙), not $60,000 ($10,000 divided by ⅙). In general, whether the change in reserves is an increase or a decrease, the change in demand deposits equals the change in reserves *left permanently with the banking system* ($9,000 in these cases) divided by the required ration of reserves to demand deposits. Thus, *whether or not a change in reserves has the maximum effect on demand deposits depends on how much of these reserves the public leaves in the banking system.*[7]

Another important assumption lies behind our discussion of the effects of $10,000 of additional reserves—or a $10,000 reduction in reserves—on the amount of demand deposits: *we have assumed that no bank holds excess reserves.* In other words, we have assumed that, whenever a bank has enough reserves to make a loan or investment, it will do so. Recall Bank A, which received a new deposit of $10,000. The new deposit enabled Bank A to increase its loans and investments by $8,333 without winding up with less than the legally required reserves. Thus, we assumed that it would go ahead and make this much in additional loans and investments. In general, this seems to be a reasonable assumption, for the simple reason that loans and investments bring profits (in interest) into the bank while excess reserves bring none. But the matter is not as simple as all that. If a bank cannot find loans and investments it regards as attractive, it

---

[7] Note too that people can convert demand deposits into time deposits, and vice versa. There are legal reserve requirements against time deposits, but they are lower than those against demand deposits. The conversion of demand deposits into time deposits will influence how much money can be supported by a certain amount of reserves. Thus, the banking system can support an amount of demand deposits equal to the amount of additional reserves divided by the legally required ratio of reserves to demand deposits (no more, no less) only if there is no conversion of demand deposits into time deposits. In other words, we assume that all the demand deposits created by the banking system are converted into neither cash nor time deposits.

may decide to make no such loans. After all, there isn't much profit to be made on a loan that is not repaid. Also, if interest rates are very low, the bank may feel that it isn't losing much by not lending money. During the Great Depression of the 1930s, for example, banks held large excess reserves for this reason. In addition, banks can benefit by maintaining excess reserves, since they constitute insurance against deposit losses.

What difference does it make whether banks hold excess reserves? If, for example, Bank A decides to lend less than the full $8,333, this will mean that an increase in reserves will have a smaller effect on the amount of demand deposits than we indicated previously. Similarly, if banks hold excess reserves, a decrease in reserves is likely to have a smaller effect on the amount of demand deposits than we indicated above. Thus, *whether or not a change in reserves has the maximum effect on demand deposits depends on the lending policies of the bankers. If they do not lend out as much as they can, the effect on demand deposits will be diminished accordingly.*

Summary

Most of our money supply is not coin and paper currency, but bank money—demand deposits. This money is created by banks. Whereas the earliest banks held reserves equal to demand deposits, modern banks practice fractional-reserve banking: that is, their reserves equal only a fraction of their demand deposits. The Federal Reserve System requires every commercial bank that is a member of the system to hold a certain percentage of its demand deposits as reserves; the percentage varies with the size of the bank. Although they increase the safety of the banks, the major purpose of these legal reserve requirements is to control the money supply. Banks have become much safer in recent years, due in part to better management and regulation, as well as to the government's stated willingness to insure and stand behind their deposits.

A bank creates money by lending or investing its excess reserves. If banks had to keep reserves equal to their deposits, they could not create money. A bank cannot lend or invest more than its excess reserves, unless it is a monopoly bank, because it will wind up with less than the legally required reserves. However, the banking system as a whole can support demand deposits equal to its total reserves divided by the legally required ratio of reserves to deposits. Thus, if reserves somewhere in the banking system increase by a certain amount, the banking system as a whole can increase demand deposits by the amount of the increase in reserves divided by the legally required ratio of reserves to deposits.

Similarly, if there is a decrease in reserves somewhere in the banking system, the system as a whole must decrease demand deposits by the amount of the decrease in reserves divided by the legally required ratio of reserves to deposits. Demand deposits are decreased by banks' selling securities or refusing to renew loans, just as demand deposits are increased by banks' making loans and investments.

Our argument so far has assumed that when additional reserves were made available to the banking system, there was no withdrawal of part of them in the form of currency, and that when reserves are decreased, no currency is deposited in banks. If such changes in the amount of currency take place, the change in demand deposits will equal the change in reserves left permanently with the banking system divided by the legally required ratio of reserves to deposits. We have also assumed that the banks hold no excess reserves. Since banks make profits by lending money and making investments, this assumption is generally sensible. But when loans are risky and interest rates are low— for example, in the Great Depression of the 1930s —banks have been known to hold large excess reserves. Clearly, changes in reserves will not have their full, or maximum, effect on demand deposits if the banks do not lend and invest as much as possible.

CONCEPTS FOR REVIEW

Fractional-reserve banking
Legal reserve requirements

Excess reserves
Simultaneous expansion

QUESTIONS FOR DISCUSSION AND REVIEW

1. Describe the way in which the banking system can create money if there is a single monopoly bank in the nation.

2. Suppose that you were the president of the Bank of America. What rules would you ask your executives to follow in making loans? In other words, what information should they look at, and how should they use this information, to decide whether or not to grant a particular loan?

3. Demand deposits are increased by banks by their calling in loans and selling investments. True or False?

4. On the basis of additional reserves of $5,000, the banking system as a whole can support how much in demand deposits, if the legal reserve requirement is 20 percent of deposits?
a. $5,000 b. $10,000 c. $25,000 d. $50,000

Monetary Policy

During the middle and late 1960s, strong inflationary pressures were generated by the increase in government expenditures associated with the Vietnam war and by the government's failure to increase taxes until 1968. Clearly, fiscal policy was a destabilizing rather than a stabilizing force in the economy. Under these circumstances, it was fortunate that government policy makers had other means to hold down the increasing price level and to stabilize the economy. As we shall see, monetary policy was ultimately called on to restrain an economy that seemed to be getting out of hand. Like fiscal policy, monetary policy is no panacea, but it is a very important tool for stabilization of the economy.

In this chapter, we are concerned with a variety of basic questions about monetary policy: Who makes monetary policy? What sorts of tools can be employed by monetary policy makers? How does monetary policy affect our national output and the price level? What are some of the problems involved in formulating effective monetary policy? What has been the nature of monetary policy in

277

the United States in recent decades? These questions are very important, since the economic health of any nation depends on its monetary policies.

The Aims and Role of Monetary Policy

Monetary policy is concerned with the money supply and interest rates. We described in Chapter 12 how the money supply influences net national product and the price level. If the economy is at considerably less than full employment, increases in the money supply tend to increase real national product, and decreases in the money supply tend to decrease real national product, with little or no effect on the price level. As full employment is approached, increases in the money supply tend to affect the price level, as well as real output. Finally, once full employment is reached, increases in the money supply result primarily in increases in the price level, since real output cannot increase appreciably.

In formulating monetary policy, the government's objectives are to attain and maintain reasonably full employment without excessive inflation. In other words, when a recession seems imminent and business is soft, the monetary authorities are likely to increase the money supply and push down interest rates. That is, they will "ease credit" or "ease money," as the newspapers put it. This tends to increase net national product. On the other hand, when the economy is in danger of overheating and serious inflation threatens, the monetary authorities will probably rein in the money supply and push up interest rates—in newspaper terms, they will "tighten credit" or "tighten money." This tends to reduce spending, and thus curb the upward pressure on the price level.

At this point, you may be muttering to yourself: "But the aims of monetary policy are essentially the same as those of fiscal policy!" And, of course you are right. Monetary policy and fiscal policy are both aimed at promoting full employment without inflation. But they use different methods to attain this goal. Fiscal policy uses the spending and taxing powers of the government, whereas monetary policy uses the government's power over the money supply.

Before we go on, let us review the processes by which changes in the money supply affect national product and the price level. You will recall from Chapter 12 that there is a difference of view about these processes. On the one hand, monetarists use the quantity theory of money to link changes in the money supply directly with changes in nominal net national product. Although the velocity of circulation of money is by no means constant, nominal NNP does seem to have been fairly closely related to the money supply. Keynesians explain this relationship in different terms. They believe that an increase (decrease) in the money supply decreases (increases) the interest rate, which in turn shifts the investment function upward (downward). This shift in the investment function tends to increase (decrease) national product. They also recognize that spending by consumers and governments, as well as investment, is likely to be affected by changes in the quantity of money.

Let's be a little more specific about how the monetary authorities can promote their aims. In particular, how can they influence the money supply? The answer is: *by managing the reserves of the banking system.* For example, perhaps the monetary authorities think a recession is about to develop. To head it off, they want to increase the money supply more rapidly than they would otherwise. To realize this objective, they can increase the reserves of the banks. As we saw in the previous chapter, an increase in bank reserves enables the banks to increase the money supply. Indeed, we learned that if there were no excess reserves and no currency withdrawals, the banks could increase the money supply by $6 for every $1 of additional reserves.[1] The ways in which the monetary authori-

[1] Of course, this assumes that the legal reserve requirement is 16⅔ percent. If the legal reserve requirement were 20 percent, a $5 increase in the money supply could be supported by $1 of additional reserves. Also, this assumes that banks hold no excess reserves and that no currency is withdrawn. As pointed out in the previous chapter, a much smaller increase in the money supply may result from an extra dollar of reserves if banks hold excess reserves and if currency is withdrawn.

ties can increase the reserves of the banking system are discussed at length in subsequent sections.

On the other hand, suppose that the monetary authorities smell a strong whiff of unacceptable inflation in the economic wind, and so decide to cut back on the rate of increase of the money supply. To do so, they can slow down the rate of increase of bank reserves. As we saw in the previous chapter, this will force the banks to cut back on the rate of increase of the money supply. Indeed, if the monetary authorities go so far as to reduce the reserves of the banking system, this will tend to reduce the money supply. Under the assumptions made in the previous chapter, the banks must cut back the money supply by $6 for every $1 reduction in reserves.

Makers of Monetary Policy

Who establishes our monetary policy? Who decides that, in view of the current and prospective economic situation, the money supply should be increased (or decreased) at a certain rate? As in the case of fiscal policy, this is not a simple question to answer; many individuals and groups play an important role. Certainly, however, *the leading role is played by the Federal Reserve System—in particular, by the members of the Federal Reserve Board and the Federal Open Market Committee.* The Chairman of the Federal Reserve Board is often the chief spokesman for the Federal Reserve System. The recent chairmen—Arthur F. Burns and William McChesney Martin—undoubtedly have had considerable influence over monetary policy.

Although the Federal Reserve is responsible to Congress, Congress has established no clear guidelines for its behavior. Thus, the Federal Reserve has had wide discretionary powers over monetary policy. But the Federal Reserve System is a huge organization, and it is not easy to figure out exactly who influences whom and who decides what. Formal actions can be taken by a majority of the board and of the Federal Open Market Committee (which is composed of the 7 members of the board plus 5 of the presidents of the 12 regional banks). However, this obviously tells only part of the story.

To get a more complete picture, it is essential to recognize that many agencies and groups other than the Fed have an effect on monetary policy, although it is difficult to measure their respective influences. The Treasury frequently has an important voice in the formulation of monetary policy. Indeed, as we shall see, the Federal Reserve was largely subservient to the Treasury during the 1940s. Also, Congressional committees hold hearings and issue reports on monetary policy and the operations of the Federal Reserve. These hearings and reports cannot fail to have some effect on Fed policy. In addition, it is sometimes argued that the policies of the Fed are influenced by the commercial banks. In this connection, it is interesting to note that, of the 9 directors of each regional Bank, 3 may be bankers, 3 must represent industry and agriculture in the region, and 3 are appointed by the Federal Reserve Board to represent the general public. Finally, the President may attempt to influence the Federal Reserve Board. To keep the board as free as possible from political pressure, members are appointed for long terms—14 years—and a term expires every 2 years.

Tools of Monetary Policy: Open Market Operations

We know from a previous section that the Federal Reserve controls the money supply largely by controlling the quantity of member banks' reserves. The most important means the Federal Reserve has to exercise this control are **open market operations,** the purchase and sale by the Fed of U.S. government securities in the open market. As we saw in Chapter 6, the market for government securities is huge and well developed. The Federal Reserve is part of this market. Sometimes it buys government securities; sometimes it sells them. Whether it is buying or selling—and how much —can have a heavy impact on the quantity of bank reserves.

Figure 14.1   Effect of Fed's Purchasing $1 Million of Government Securities

A. Effect on Fed's balance sheet:

Assets		Liabilities and net worth	
Government securities	+$1 million	Member bank reserves	+$1 million

B. Effect on balance sheet of the Chase Manhattan Bank:

Assets		Liabilities and net worth	
Reserves	+$1 million	Demand deposits	+$1 million

Suppose that the Federal Reserve *buys* $1 million worth of government securities in the open market, and that the seller of these securities is General Motors.[2] To determine the effect of this transaction on the quantity of bank reserves, let's look at the effect on the balance sheet of the Fed and on the balance sheet of the Chase Manhattan Bank, General Motors' bank.[3] In this transaction, the Fed receives $1 million in government securities and gives General Motors a check for $1 million. When General Motors deposits this check to its account at the Chase Manhattan Bank, the bank's demand deposits and reserves increase by $1 million. Thus, as shown in Figure 14.1, the left-hand side of the Fed's balance sheet shows a $1 million increase in government securities, and the right-hand side shows a $1 million increase in bank reserves. The left-hand side of the Chase Manhattan Bank's balance sheet shows a $1 million increase in reserves, and the right-hand side shows a $1 million increase in demand deposits. Clearly, *the Fed has added $1 million to the banks' reserves*. The situation is entirely analogous to the $10,000 deposit at Bank *A* in the previous chapter.

Now consider the opposite situation, where the Federal Reserve *sells* $1 million worth of government securities in the open market. They are bought by Merrill Lynch, Pierce, Fenner, and Smith, a huge brokerage firm. What effect does this transaction have on the quantity of bank reserves? To find out, let's look at the balance sheet of the Fed and the balance sheet of Merrill Lynch's bank, which we again assume to be the Chase Manhattan. When Merrill Lynch buys the government securities from the Fed, the Fed gives Merrill Lynch the securities in exchange for Merrill Lynch's check for $1 million. When the Fed presents this check to the Chase Manhattan Bank for payment, Chase Manhattan's demand deposits and reserves decrease by $1 million. Thus, as shown in Figure 14.2, the left-hand side of the Fed's balance sheet shows a $1 million decrease in government securities, and the right-hand side shows a $1 million decrease in reserves. The left-hand side of the Chase Manhattan Bank's balance sheet shows a $1 million decrease in reserves, and the right-hand side shows a $1 million decrease in demand deposits. Clearly, *the Fed has reduced the reserves of*

[2] Large corporations often hold quantities of government securities.

[3] For simplicity, we assume that General Motors has only one bank, the Chase Manhattan Bank. Needless to say, this may not be the case, but it makes no difference to the point we are making here. We make a similar assumption regarding the investment firm of Merrill Lynch in the next paragraph.

Figure 14.2   Effect of Fed's Selling $1 Million of Government Securities

A. Effect on Fed's balance sheet:

Assets		Liabilities and net worth	
Government securities	−$1 million	Member bank reserves	−$1 million

B. Effect on balance sheet of the Chase Manhattan Bank:

Assets		Liabilities and net worth	
Reserves	−$1 million	Demand deposits	−$1 million

the banks by $1 million.

Thus, the Federal Reserve adds to bank reserves when it buys government securities and reduces bank reserves when it sells them. Obviously, the extent to which the Federal Reserve increases or reduces bank reserves depends on the amount of government securities purchased or sold. The greater the amount, the greater the increase or decrease in bank reserves. As noted above, open market operations are the Fed's most important technique for controlling the money supply. The power to decide on the amount of government securities the Fed should buy or sell at any given moment rests with the *Federal Open Market Committee.* This group wields an extremely powerful influence over bank reserves and the nation's money supply. Every few weeks, the Federal Open Market Committee meets to discuss the current situation and trends, and gives instructions to the Manager of the Open Market Account at the Federal Reserve Bank of New York, who actually buys and sells the government securities.

To get some insight into the nature of these discussions, consider the meeting of the Federal Open Market Committee (FOMC) that was held on May 26, 1970. According to Sherman Maisel, a former member of the Federal Reserve Board and one of the participants, much of the meeting was devoted to a discussion of whether the money supply was increasing too rapidly.

> The money supply and bank credit had grown far faster than appeared consistent with the 4 percent growth rate set as policy by prior votes [of the Committee]. The FOMC would now have to make a choice. . . . If the money supply were held to a 4 percent growth rate, interest rates would continue to rise and perhaps at an accelerating rate. . . . Was this what the Committee wanted, or would it prefer to allow reserves and money to grow more rapidly in order to avoid the unsettling effect of a still more rapid run-up in interest rates? . . . As in many similar situations, the Committee was sharply divided in its views. . . . The FOMC finally agreed that it would not change its basic policy stance. Monetary growth above 4 percent was not desirable.[4]

Although no single meeting can be regarded as typical, this brief description gives you some idea of the sort of discussion that takes place every few weeks in the meetings of the Federal Open Market Committee.

[4] Sherman Maisel, *Managing the Dollar,* New York: Norton, 1973. A section of this book dealing with Federal Reserve decision making is reprinted in E. Mansfield, *Economics: Readings, Issues, and Cases,* New York: Norton, 1974.

Changes in Legal Reserve Requirements

Open market operations are not the only means the Federal Reserve has to influence the money supply. Another way is *to change the legal reserve requirements.* In other words, *the Federal Reserve Board can change the amount of reserves banks must hold for every dollar of demand deposits.* In 1934, Congress gave the Federal Reserve Board the power to set—within certain broad limits—the legally required ratio of reserves to deposits for both demand and time deposits. From time to time, the Fed uses this power to change legal reserve requirements. For example, in 1960 it cut the legally required ratio of reserves to deposits in big-city banks from 17½ percent to 16½ percent, and the ratio remained there until 1968, when it was raised to 17 percent.

The obvious effect of an increase in the legally required ratio of reserves to deposits is that banks must hold larger reserves to support the existing amount of demand deposits. This in turn means that banks with little or no excess reserves will have to sell securities, refuse to renew loans, and reduce their demand deposits to meet the new reserve requirements. For example, suppose that a member bank has $1 million in reserves and $6 million in demand deposits. If the legal reserve requirement is 16 percent, it has excess reserves of $1 million minus $960,000 (.16 × $6 million), or $40,000. It is in good shape. If the legal reserve requirement is increased to 20 percent, this bank now needs $1,200,000 (.20 × $6 million) in reserves. Since it only has $1,000,000 in reserves, it must sell securities or refuse to renew loans.

Consider now what happens to the banking system as a whole. Clearly, an increase in the legally required ratio of reserves to deposits means that, with a given amount of reserves, the banking system can maintain less demand deposits than before. For example, if the banking system has $1 billion in total reserves, it can support $\frac{\$1 \text{ billion}}{.16}$, or $6.25 billion in demand deposits when the legal reserve requirement is 16 percent. But it can support only $\frac{\$1 \text{ billion}}{.20}$, or $5 billion in demand deposits when the legal reserve requirement is 20 percent. Thus, *increases in the legal reserve requirement tend to reduce the amount of demand deposits—bank money—the banking system can support.*

What is the effect of a decrease in the legally required ratio of reserves to deposits? Obviously, it means that banks must hold less reserves to support the existing amount of demand deposits, which in turn means that banks will suddenly find themselves with excess reserves. For example, if the banking system has $1 billion in reserves and $5 billion in demand deposits, there are no excess reserves when the legal reserve requirement is 20 percent. But suppose the Federal Reserve lowers the legal reserve requirement to 16 percent. Now the amount of legally required reserves is $800 million ($5 billion × .16), so that the banks have $200 million in excess reserves—which means that they can increase the amount of their demand deposits. Thus, *decreases in the legal reserve requirements tend to increase the amount of demand deposits—bank money—the banking system can support.*

Changes in legal reserve requirements are a rather drastic way to influence the money supply —they are to open market operations as a cleaver is to a scalpel, and so are made infrequently. For example, for over 7 years—from December 1960 to January 1968—no change at all was made in legal reserve requirements for demand deposits. Nonetheless, the Fed can change legal reserve requirements if it wants to. And there can be no doubt about the potential impact of such changes. Large changes in reserve requirements can rapidly alter bank reserves and the money supply.

Changes in the Discount Rate

Still another way that the Federal Reserve can influence the money supply is through changes in the discount rate. To understand this method, one needs to know that the commercial banks that are members of the Federal Reserve System can borrow from the Federal Reserve when their reserves are low (if the Fed is willing). This is one of the functions of the Federal Reserve. The interest rate the Fed charges the banks for loans is called the *discount rate,* and the Fed can increase or decrease the discount rate whenever it chooses. Increases in the discount rate discourage borrowing from the Fed, while decreases in the discount rate encourage it.

The discount rate can change substantially and fairly often. For example, take 1968: the discount rate was changed from 4½ to 5 percent in March, from 5 to 5½ percent in April, and from 5½ to 5¼ percent in August. When the Fed increases the discount rate, it obviously makes it more expensive for banks to augment their reserves in this way; hence it tightens up a bit on the money supply. On the other hand, when the Fed decreases the discount rate, it is cheaper for banks to augment their reserves in this way, and hence the money supply eases up a bit. However, note that the Fed is largely passive in these relations with the banks. It cannot make the banks borrow. It can only set the discount rate and see how many banks show up at the "discount window" to borrow. Also, it must be recognized that the Fed will not allow banks to borrow on a permanent or long-term basis. They are expected to use this privilege only to tide themselves over for short periods.

Most economists agree that changes in the discount rate have relatively little direct impact, and that the Fed's open market operations can and do offset easily the amount the banks borrow. Certainly changes in the discount rate cannot have anything like the direct effect on bank reserves of open market operations or changes in legal reserve requirements. *The principal importance of changes in the discount rate lies in their effects on people's expectations.* When the Fed increases the discount rate, this is generally interpreted as a sign that the Fed will tighten credit and the money supply. A cut in the discount rate is generally interpreted as

a sign of easier money and lower interest rates. For example, when in 1969 the Federal Reserve announced an increase in the discount rate, the effect was a sharp drop in the prices of stocks and bonds. People interpreted this increase in the discount rate as a sure sign that the Fed was going to keep the money supply under tight reins to fight inflation.

Other Tools of Monetary Policy

In addition, the Federal Reserve has several other tools it can use. The first is *moral suasion,* a fancy term to describe various expressions of pleasure or displeasure by the Fed. In other words, the Fed tells the banks what it would like them to do or not do, and exhorts them to go along with its wishes. It may appeal to the patriotism of the bankers, or it may make some statements that could be regarded as threats. Of course, the Fed does not have the power to force banks to comply with its wishes, but the banks don't want to get into difficulties with the Fed. Consequently, moral suasion can have a definite impact, particularly for short periods. But banks are profit-oriented enterprises, and when the Fed's wishes conflict strongly with the profit motive, moral suasion may not work very well.

Second, the Fed can vary the maximum interest rates commercial banks can pay on time deposits. No commercial banks are permitted to pay interest on demand deposits, according to a law Congress passed during the depression of the 1930s.[5] For time or savings deposits, the Fed has the power, under *Regulation Q,* to establish a ceiling on the interest rates commercial banks can pay. And the level at which this ceiling is set can influence the flow of funds into time deposits, savings and loan associations, and other financial institutions. (For example, when savings and loan associations began

[5] Some people felt that many of the banks' problems in the 1920s and 1930s were due to too much competition: hence this law. It is easy to see why bankers felt that their earnings would be improved if none of them were allowed to compete for deposits by paying interest, but this is hardly consistent with a competitive philosophy.

to pay higher interest rates than commercial banks could pay on time deposits, people began to take their money out of time deposits and put it into savings and loan associations.) In recent years, the Fed, using Regulation Q, has increased the ceiling on interest rates on time deposits. In 1966 and 1970 this regulation had an important effect on interest rates and credit. Many economists would like to see such ceilings abolished because they interfere with the functioning of free markets for funds.

Another of the Fed's tools is to vary the margin requirements for the purchase of stocks. **Margin requirements** set the maximum percentage of the price of stocks that a person can borrow. For example, in the early 1960s, you could borrow 50 percent of the cost of such securities from your broker, but in late 1972, you could borrow only 35 percent from your broker. This is an example of a **selective credit control**—a control aimed at the use of credit for specific purposes. It may seem odd that margin requirements for the purchase of stocks were singled out for special treatment, but the severity of the stock market crash in 1929 was attributed partly to the fact that people in those days could borrow a large percentage—sometimes even 90 percent—of the value of the stock they purchased. (When stock prices slid, their small equity vanished quickly, and they had to sell out.) Consequently, after the crash, margin requirements were imposed.

Finally, during and immediately after World War II, the Fed also had two other powers—regulation of mortgage terms and of installment contracts. Until 1953, the Fed could vary the size of down payments for houses and the number of years mortgages could run. This was an effective tool to influence the pace of residential construction. Increases in the size of down payments and decreases in the length of mortgages tended to discourage construction, while decreases in the size of down payments and increases in the length of mortgages tended to encourage construction. Until 1952, the Fed, under "Regulation W," could also establish minimum amounts a person had to put up when he bought appliances, automobiles, and other items; and it could impose other restrictions on installment buying. After the Korean war, these restrictions became unpopular, and this power of the Fed was not continued.

When Is Monetary Policy Tight or Easy?

Everyone daydreams about being powerful and important. It is a safe bet, however, that few people under the age of 21 daydream about being members of the Federal Reserve Board or the Federal Open Market Committee. Yet the truth is that the members of the board and the committee are among the most powerful people in the nation. Suppose you were appointed to the Federal Reserve Board. As a member, you would have to decide—month by month, year by year—exactly how much government securities the Fed should buy or sell, as well as whether and when changes should be made in the discount rate, legal reserve requirements, and the other instruments of Federal Reserve policy. How would you go about making your choices?

Obviously you would need lots of data. Fortunately, the Fed has a very large and able research staff to provide you with plenty of the latest information about what is going on in the economy. But what sorts of data should you look at? Clearly, one thing you would want is some information on the extent to which monetary policy is inflationary or deflationary—that is, the extent to which it is "tight" or "easy." This is not simple to measure, but there is general agreement that the members of the Federal Reserve Board—and other members of the financial and academic communities—have often used the following four variables as measures.

First, the Federal Reserve Board has looked at the level of short-term interest rates. High interest rates are interpreted as meaning that monetary policy is tight; low interest rates are usually thought to mean that monetary policy is easy. The Fed can influence the level of interest rates through its open market operations and other policies. The level of interest rates has been used by the Fed and by the financial and academic communities as a major indicator of the effect of monetary policy on the economy, and the Fed has set as a target increases, decreases, or stability in interest rates. However, to know what the proper interest rate is, you need a forecast of the strength or weakness of investment demand, and an estimate of the extent to which a high interest rate is required to offset inflation. Thus, the level of interest rates may be an ambiguous indicator.

Second, the Federal Reserve Board has looked at the rate of increase of the money supply. When the money supply is growing at a relatively slow rate (much less than 4 percent per year), this is often interpreted as meaning that monetary policy is tight. A relatively rapid rate of growth in the money supply (much more than 4 percent per year) is often taken to mean that monetary policy is easy. During the 1960s and 1970s, this has become an increasingly important indicator of the effects of monetary policy on the economy. Its popularity is due to the influence of the monetarists. This indicator has the disadvantage of being influenced by the decisions of the banks and the public about how they want to hold their assets.

Third, the Federal Reserve Board can also examine the rate of increase of the **monetary base,** which by definition equals bank reserves plus currency outstanding. The monetary base is important because the total money supply is dependent upon —and made from—it. Moreover, as an indicator of the effects of monetary policy, the monetary base has the advantage of being almost completely under the control of the Federal Reserve. A relatively slow growth rate in the monetary base (much less than 4 percent per year) is often interpreted as a sign of tight monetary policy. A relatively rapid rate of growth (much more than 4 percent per year) is often taken to mean that monetary policy is easy. This indicator is currently influential, particularly among the monetarists. Before 1960, it was seldom emphasized.

Fourth, the Federal Reserve Board has looked at *free reserves,* the excess reserves of the banks minus the amounts borrowed by the banks from the Federal Reserve.[6] When free reserves are negative, and the banks owe more to the Fed than they have in excess reserves, this has been used as an indicator that monetary policy is tight. Large and positive free reserves have been used as an indicator that monetary policy is easy. During the 1950s, the Fed used the amount of free reserves as its principal indicator of the effect of monetary policy on the economy, but this method is much less important today. Its shortcomings have been pointed out by many observers. In particular, the banks can influence the amount of free reserves by their lending and borrowing policies.

Decision Making at the Fed: A Case Study

Let's continue to assume that you have been appointed to the Federal Reserve Board, and that the economy suddenly is confronted with what seems to be a dangerously inflationary situation. What sort of action would you recommend? One appropriate action would be to sell a considerable amount of government securities, which would reduce bank reserves. You might also recommend an increase in the discount rate or even an increase in legal reserve requirements. To see how well you were doing, you would watch the variables discussed in the previous section. Specifically, you would look at the rate of increase of the money supply, as well as the rate of increase of the monetary base, and try to reduce both. At the same time you would try to increase interest rates.

Let's compare your recommendations with what the Fed really did in a similar situation. You will recall that the large military buildup associated

[6] Another measure of "money market conditions" is the interest rate on Federal funds, the interest rate banks receive when they make an overnight loan of reserves to another bank.

with the Vietnam war created strong inflationary pressures during the middle and late 1960s. Fiscal policy was not used to curb this inflation, since government spending was highly destabilizing and tax changes were painfully slow in coming. Consequently, much of the responsibility for fighting inflation fell to the Federal Reserve. What actions did it take?

In July 1965, when President Johnson announced that 50,000 more men would be sent to Vietnam, it was evident that inflationary pressures would mount unless appropriate fiscal or monetary policies were adopted. William M. Martin, chairman of the Federal Reserve Board, discussed these dangers with administration policy makers during the summer and fall of 1965, and argued publicly for a tax increase. But no such tax increase was in the cards. On December 4, 1965, the Fed decided to fire a highly visible volley against inflation. *The Federal Reserve Board voted to increase the discount rate from 4 to 4½ percent.* President Johnson and many Democrats in Congress were openly critical of this action, but many businessmen and economists agreed with the board's decision to act against inflation.

During 1965, the price level rose by 3 percent. During 1966, inflationary pressures continued unabated, and the government's large expenditures on Vietnam and domestic programs led to a huge budget deficit. As the hopes for a tax increase became dimmer, the Federal Reserve began to resort to sterner and more powerful measures to stem the inflationary tide. During early 1966, the Fed tried to tighten money, but there was a controversy within the Board over the proper indicator. Using interest rates as an indicator, money was tight; but the money supply seemed to indicate that money was easy.[7] By the summer of 1966, *the Fed allowed no increase in the monetary base, and the rate of increase in the money supply was cut to zero.* In other words, the Fed did not permit the money supply to increase at all. *Interest rates*

[7] For an interesting account of the controversy within the Fed by one of the members of the Federal Reserve Board at that time, see S. Maisel, *Managing the Dollar, op. cit.*

climbed to very high levels, in part because of an increase in the demand for credit as people and firms began to fear that soon they would be unable to get credit. Money became extremely tight.

The effects on the financial and housing markets were devastating. Money for mortgages was extremely scarce, and for a time virtually no buyers could be found for municipal bonds. Knowledgeable people began to talk about an impending financial panic. By September 1966, when a crisis seemed imminent, the Fed assured all banks that it would lend them reserves so long as they made only legitimate and socially desirable loans. In addition, the Fed used its open market operations to increase bank reserves, and thus allow some increase in the money supply. By late September, the financial markets were operating reasonably well again.

Clearly, the Fed did pretty much what you would have recommended, and its policies had the intended effect. Indeed, this episode—the so-called "credit crunch of 1966"—indicates dramatically the potency of monetary policy. For that matter, according to some economists, the Fed may have gone too far. The job of the Fed is often described as "leaning against the wind," and in this case it leaned so heavily that it may almost have caused a panic. However, in its defense it must be pointed out that the Fed was faced with the problem of undoing the mischief caused by inadequate fiscal policies. It was dealt a very bad hand by the fiscal policy makers.

Monetary Policy in the 1950s and 1960s

For a more complete—and more balanced—picture of monetary policy in the United States, let's look briefly at the formulation of monetary policy in the past two decades. When the Eisenhower administration took office in 1952, the economy was prosperous, but the Korean war was ending and

William McChesney Martin and Arthur F. Burns

According to an old saying, "where you stand depends on where you sit." This is no less true at 20th and Constitution, the location of the Federal Reserve Board, than elsewhere in Washington. But while internal and external constraints determine the broad outlines of monetary policy, whatever baggage the chairman brings to the job weighs also in setting the Fed's stance vis-à-vis the rest of the government and its stand on specific issues. Consider, for example, former Chairman William McChesney Martin and present Chairman Arthur F. Burns.

WILLIAM MCCHESNEY MARTIN ARTHUR F. BURNS

Martin associated himself with the New York financial community. Indeed he had served as president of the New York Stock Exchange during the thirties. He believed that good monetary policy required a "feel" for credit markets, an instinct presumably inbred and possibly cultivated, but certainly not acquired by examining thousands of statistics on M_1 and M_2.

More importantly, Martin held that the primary responsibility of the Fed was to preserve a sound currency: to stand firm while others were pandering to popular sentiment and calling for cheap money. While elected officials played to the crowd with promises of more employment, the Fed would fight the good fight—the fight against inflation. In order to assure the independence necessary to pursue such a course, Martin virtually removed the Fed from all but the most formal and infrequent contact with the Treasury, the CEA, and Budget Bureau during the Eisenhower administration.

Burns brought a different set of baggage to his new job. Having spent much of his professional life as an economist at Columbia University and with the National Bureau of Economic Research, he was at home, not in a Wall Street club, but with a page of statistics. Thus, his chairmanship has meant much more systematic collection and analysis of data on money markets and interest rate movements. (One veteran banker commented, "They may not be making better policy now, but they can certainly tell you better why they're making it.") More significantly, under Burns the Fed became a more active member of the Quadriad and he himself has given informal economic counsel to President Nixon. In contrast to Martin, Burns has tried to maintain a more stable growth in money hoping that this would increase stability in GNP more than would large contracyclical swings in interest rates.

The Fed under Burns has taken the position that its proper role does not call for it to veto the official stance of the government. On several notable occasions, the Fed under Martin followed the opposite policy. For example, in June 1965 Martin spoke at Columbia University, drawing parallels between the 1965 economy and the pre-Depression economy, noting that "some experts seem resolved to ignore the lessons of the past!" (The Dow-Jones industrial stock average dropped 9 points after his speech.) In December, after his warnings had been ignored by the Johnson administration, the Federal Reserve took matters into its own hands, and against the wishes of the administration, raised the discount rate.

E.A.

the economy would soon have to adapt to peace-time conditions. At first, the Federal Reserve viewed inflation as the big danger, and in January 1953 it raised the discount rate and used open market operations to cut bank reserves. But by the middle of 1953, the Fed changed its course and increased bank reserves by its open market operations and by reducing the legal reserve requirements. This was fortunate because the reduction in government expenditures on the war helped to push the economy into a recession in mid-1953. During this recession, the Fed maintained a stimulative monetary policy.

The economy came out of the recession in 1954. By late 1954 and 1955, inflation began to reappear, and in late 1955 the Fed moved toward credit restraint. In the middle of 1957, the economy turned down again, partly because of a drop in investment and defense expenditures. Once this became evident, the Fed quickly eased credit. The money supply was permitted to increase more rapidly, and interest rates fell. The recession was short-lived, and by late 1958 the economy was rising once more. But almost as soon as the recovery was under way, both the monetary and fiscal authorities began to put on the brakes. Interest rates rose substantially during much of 1958 and all of 1959. As a consequence of these monetary (and fiscal) policies, the economy began to turn soft once more, and in 1960 another recession began. In early 1960, the Federal Reserve began to ease credit somewhat.

When the Kennedy administration took office in 1961, it inherited a soft economy. To stimulate it, the Federal Reserve added to bank reserves, thus permitting rapid growth in the money supply. However, monetary policy did not play a leading role in economic policy in the Kennedy years. Instead, as described in Chapter 10, the Kennedy administration pushed hard for the tax cut, which was the cornerstone of its economic policy. Monetary policy played a supporting role. Leading administration economists felt that the money supply should grow in such a way as to accommodate the desired growth in national product, but that the growth in national product was to be brought about

largely by the tax cut.[8] In fact, the Federal Reserve expanded the money supply during the early 1960s at a substantially higher average annual rate than during the late 1950s. In later years, some monetarists—like Milton Friedman—were to argue that this increase in the money supply, and not the tax cut, was responsible for the growth of national product in the mid-1960s.

When government spending in Vietnam began to skyrocket in 1965, monetary policy began to push itself to the fore. As described in the previous section, the Federal Reserve Board, faced with strong inflationary pressures stemming from a highly destabilizing fiscal policy, committed itself to a strong deflationary stance. The result, as we have seen, was the "credit crunch of 1966," after which the Fed eased credit considerably. Indeed, in a rapid about-face, the Fed began to expand credit very rapidly in 1967 and 1968. In the latter part of 1967, the money supply was increasing at 10 percent per year. The tax surcharge was expected (incorrectly) to reduce spending so much that the Fed was encouraged to increase the money supply to offset it partially. Alarmed by this apparent shift to an inflationary posture, critics in Congress and elsewhere belabored the Fed for its "stop-go" policies.

Monetary Policy under the Nixon Administration

When the Nixon administration came into office in 1968, inflation was unquestionably the nation's principal economic problem. Moreover, it was generally agreed that the rapid increase in the

[8] During much of the 1960s, monetary policy was formulated with one eye on the balance of payments, discussed in Chapter 20. If the Fed had attempted to stimulate the economy, interest rates would have fallen, and capital would have gone abroad in response to higher yields there. The result would have been a worsening of our balance of payments problems. In Chapter 20, we discuss the effect of our balance of payments problems on our domestic economic policy.

money supply in 1968 had been a mistake. Thus, practically everyone, both Republicans and Democrats, agreed that monetary policy should be tight during 1969. In accord with this view, the Federal Reserve kept a close rein on the money supply during 1969. In the latter part of 1969, the quantity of money grew at an annual rate of only about 2 percent. Clearly, the nation's money managers were out to curb inflation. The result, however, was to slow the growth of national output and to increase unemployment (as would be expected from Figure 8.3).

Early in 1970, the Federal Reserve stated that it would adhere to a policy of maintaining steady growth in the money supply. Apparently the target was a 4 percent annual increase in the quantity of money. This decision was in part a reaction to the many criticisms of the Fed's previous "stop-go" policies. During most of 1970, the Fed succeeded in expanding the money supply at this relatively constant rate, but this meant that interest rates did not go down much. In the latter part of 1970, bank reserves increased considerably and interest rates fell sharply, but the money supply increased more slowly. Apparently, the Fed felt that money was sufficiently easy. During the first half of 1971, the money supply was allowed to expand rapidly: from January to June 1971, the quantity of money increased at a rate of 12 percent. But the second half of 1971 saw little growth in the money supply.

In August 1971, President Nixon announced his New Economic Policy, which, as you will recall from Chapter 10, entailed direct controls of prices, wages, and rents, as well as an expansionary fiscal policy. In line with the more expansionary tone of his economic policies, the president announced in early 1972, that "The Federal Reserve has taken steps to create the monetary conditions necessary for rapid economic expansion." Also, the Council of Economic Advisers stated in early 1972 that

> the steady, strong expansion we seek and expect will require support from monetary policy. An abundant supply of money and other liquid assets, and favorable conditions in money markets, should

encourage an expansion of outlays by consumers, businesses, and State and local governments. This process would involve a more rapid rise of currency and demand deposits than occurred in the second half of 1971. Steps have been taken by the Federal Reserve System to start this acceleration.[9]

In fact, the money supply grew by about 8 percent in 1972.

After price and wage controls were largely removed in 1973, open inflation occurred with a vengeance. In the *single month* of June 1973, wholesale prices increased by 2.4 percent. President Nixon responded by slapping a 60-day freeze on most prices (but not wages) beginning in mid-June of 1973. And the Federal Reserve tightened money considerably. For example, on June 8, 1973, the Fed raised the discount rate to 6½ percent, its highest level since 1921. When it did this, the Fed announced that "the action was taken in recognition of increases that have already occurred in other short-term interest rates, the recent growth in money and bank credit, and the continuing rise in the general price level."

Problems in Formulating Monetary Policy

Before attempting to evaluate the Fed's record, we must recognize the three major problems it must confront. First, the Fed must continually try to figure out whether the economy is sliding into a recession, being propelled into an inflationary boom, or growing satisfactorily. As we saw in Chapter 11, there is no foolproof way to forecast the economy's short-term movements. Recognizing the fallibility of existing forecasting techniques all too well, the Fed must nonetheless use these techniques as best it can to guide its actions.

Second, having come to some tentative conclusion about the direction in which the economy is heading, the Fed must decide to what extent it

[9] *Economic Report of the President,* 1972, pp. 5 and 106.

should tighten or ease money. The answer depends on the Fed's estimates of when monetary changes will take effect and the magnitude of their impact, as well as on its forecasts of the economy's future direction. Also, the answer depends on the Fed's evaluation of the relative importance of full employment and price stability as national goals. If it regards full employment as much more important than price stability, it will probably want to err in the direction of easy money. On the other hand, if it thinks price stability is at least as important as full employment, it may want to err in the direction of tight money.

Finally, once the Fed has decided what it wants to do, it must figure out how to do it. Should open market operations do the whole job? If so, how big must be the purchase or sale of government securities? Should a change be made in the discount rate, or in legal reserve requirements? How big a change? Should moral suasion be resorted to? These are the operational questions the Fed continually must answer.

In answering these questions, the Fed must reckon with two very inconvenient facts, both of which make life difficult. First, *there is often a long lag between an action by the Fed and its effect on the economy.* Although the available evidence indicates that monetary policy affects some types of expenditures more rapidly than others, it is not uncommon for the bulk of the total effects to occur a year or more after the change in monetary policy.[10] Thus the Fed may act to head off an imminent recession, but find that some of the consequences of its action are not felt until later, when inflation—not recession—is the problem. Conversely, the Fed may act to curb an imminent inflation, but find that the consequences of its action are not felt until some time later, when recession, not inflation, has become the problem. In either case, the Fed can wind up doing more harm than good.

[10] For example, see Frank de Leeuw and Edward Gramlich, "The Channels of Monetary Policy: A Further Report on the Federal Reserve—MIT Econometric Model," *Federal Reserve Bulletin,* June 1969.

Second, *experts disagree about which of the available measures—such as interest rates, the rate of increase of the money supply, or the rate of increase of the monetary base—is the best measure of how tight or easy monetary policy is.* Fortunately, these measures often point in the same direction; but when they point in different directions, the Fed can be misled. For example, during 1967–68, the Fed wanted to tighten money somewhat. Using free reserves and interest rates as the primary measures of the tightness of monetary policy, it reduced free reserves and increased interest rates. However, at the same time, it permitted a substantial rate of increase in the money supply and the monetary base. By doing so, the Fed—in the eyes of many experts—really eased, not tightened, money.

The Fed's Relations with the Treasury

In making its decisions, the Federal Reserve must also take into account the problems of the Treasury, which is faced with the task of selling huge amounts of government securities each year. As you know from Chapter 6, the United States has a national debt of about $450 billion, and each year a part of this debt must be paid off. To pay off the bonds and notes that come due, as well as to borrow new amounts, the Treasury floats new securities on the market. Like any borrower, the Treasury has generally liked to reduce its interest costs; and in view of its responsibilities, it has had a major interest in finding a market for this vast amount of government securities. As a public body, the Federal Reserve System has worked closely with the Treasury, and the Treasury's interest in financing the public debt has sometimes had an important effect on Federal Reserve policy making.

During World War II, the government financed only about ⅓ of the cost of the war through taxes. The rest was financed by borrowing, much of it from the banks. The Federal Reserve used open market operations—that is, it bought government securities in the open market—to provide the banks with added reserves. Then the banks could increase their demand deposits by a multiple of the added reserves (such being the nature of a fractional-reserve banking system), and use the new demand deposits to pay for government securities. This, of course, was inflationary: the Fed was creating new money—new bank money—to be used by the Treasury. This creation of new money was just as real as if the Fed had printed up lots of new currency, but policy makers felt that wartime pressures justified this procedure.

After the war, the Fed was faced with an enormous headache. Inflationary forces were strong, and it would have liked to cut bank reserves and increase interest rates. But this would have caused the price of government securities to drop; and both the Treasury and President Truman, recalling that the drop in government bond prices after World War I had caused a considerable public outcry, were dead set against such a development. However, if the Fed maintained the price of government securities (by buying them whenever their price fell), banks could readily turn their vast holdings of government securities into reserves. Thus, so long as it maintained the price of government securities, the Fed really could not fight inflation.

Until 1951, the Fed supported the price of government securities, but by 1951 the Fed and the Treasury were in open conflict. On January 21, 1951, President Truman asked the Federal Open Market Committee to come to the White House to discuss the situation. This meeting created further conflict. On March 4, 1951, a so-called "accord" was worked out, stating that the Fed would no longer support the price of government securities. Thus the Fed was much freer to use monetary policy to tighten money and credit, and as we have seen in previous sections, it has used this power repeatedly in the 20 years since then. But this does not mean that the Fed turns its back on the Treasury's financing problems. On the contrary, in formulating monetary policy, the Fed must continually take account of the Treasury's problems. But the days are long gone when the Fed's policies are dictated by the Treasury's financing needs. Witness, for example, the "credit crunch of 1966!"

How Well Has the Fed Performed?

Given the difficult problems the Federal Reserve faces and the fact that its performance cannot be measured by any simple standard, it would be naive to expect that its achievement could be graded like an arithmetic quiz. Nonetheless, just as war is too important to be left to the generals, so monetary policy is too important to be left unscrutinized to the monetary authorities. According to recent studies of Federal Reserve policy making, what have been the strengths and weaknesses of the Fed's decisions?

First, if one takes into account the limitations in existing forecasting techniques, the Fed seems to have done a reasonably good job in recent years of recognizing changes in economic conditions. As noted in previous sections, it sometimes was a bit slow to see that the economy was sinking into a recession, or that inflationary pressures were dominant. But hindsight is always much clearer than foresight, which is why Monday morning quarterbacks make so few mistakes—and get paid so little. The lag between changes in economic conditions and changes in policy was consequently rather short, particularly when compared with the lag for fiscal policy.

Second, the Fed does not seem to have taken much account of the long—and seemingly quite variable—lags between changes in monetary policy and their effects on the economy. Instead, it simply reacted quickly to changes in business conditions. As pointed out in a previous section, such a policy can in reality be quite destabilizing. For example, the Fed may act to suppress inflationary pressures, but find that the consequences of its action are not felt until some time later when recession—not

Is There an Independent Federal Reserve? Should There Be?

A MEETING OF THE FEDERAL OPEN MARKET COMMITTEE.

Some say the Fed is responsible to Congress. Its enabling legislation was passed by Congress in 1913, and it could presumably be reorganized should it sufficiently rouse Congress's wrath. But Congress moves with nothing if not deliberate speed, and not since 1935 has it sought to influence the Federal Reserve through new legislation. The president fills vacancies on the Board of Governors, but since terms on the Board run for 14 years, presidents have had to wait until their second terms to appoint a majority of the Board.

In fact, as knowledgeable observers often agree, there are two groups that, without appearing prominently on the organization chart, exercise considerable influence over the policies of the Fed. One is the business community—a group with a definite interest in preserving the value of a dollar. The second is the Board's professional staff of senior economists. Administrations come and go, but the staff economist remains, and his uniquely detailed knowledge of the workings of the Fed assures him a hearing at 20th and Constitution.

Does it matter that the Fed is a focal point for the forces in the economy who fear inflation and are willing to accept somewhat higher unemployment in the hopes prices will not rise as rapidly? It may matter less than the formal structure suggests. Virtually since its inception, the Federal Reserve has had a crop of antagonistic observers in Congress. Former Secretary of the Treasury John Connally compared one of the Fed's perennial congressional foes to a cross-eyed discus thrower: "He'll never set any records for distance but he certainly keeps the crowd on its toes."

Both William McChesney Martin and the present chairman, Arthur Burns, have been sensitive to the ultimate vulnerability of the Fed's independence, and so have been reluctant to buck administration policy too dramatically. The slow increase in interest rates in the 1973 inflation was a compromise between the banker's feeling for sound money and a politician's unwillingness to be the "fall guy" in the fight against inflation. Whether the Federal Reserve's current procedures can survive the general call for more accountability is an open question.   E.A.

inflation—is the problem. Unfortunately, the truth is that, despite advances in knowledge in the past decade, economists do not have a firm understanding of these lags. Thus, the Fed is only partly to blame.

Third, with a few notable exceptions, there generally seems to have been reasonably good coordination between the Federal Reserve and the executive branch (the Treasury and the Council of Economic Advisers, in particular). This is important because monetary policy and fiscal policy should work together, not march off in separate directions. Of course, the fact that the Fed and the executive branch have generally been aware of one another's views and probable actions does not mean that there has always been agreement between them. Nor does it mean that, even when they agreed, they could always point monetary and fiscal policy in the same direction. But at least the left hand had a pretty good idea of what the right hand was doing.

Fourth, the Fed has been criticized for paying too much attention during the 1950s to free reserves and interest rates as measures of the tightness or looseness of monetary policy, and giving too little attention to the rate of growth of the money supply and the monetary base. During the 1960s and 1970s, however, the Fed has paid much more attention to the rate of growth of the money supply and the monetary base. Again, the fault is only partly the Fed's, since the experts cannot agree on the relative importance that should be attached to each measure. But wherever the fault, if any, may lie, the Fed's performance is bound to suffer if it acts on the basis of unreliable measures.

Fifth, the Fed is often criticized for putting too much emphasis on preventing inflation and too little on preventing unemployment. According to various studies, it probably is true that the Fed has been more sensitive to the dangers of inflation than has the Congress or the administration. Liberals, emphasizing the great social costs of excessive unemployment, tend to denounce the Fed for such behavior. Without question, the costs of unemployment are high, as stressed in Chapter 8.

Conservatives, on the other hand, often claim that governments are tempted to resort to inflation in order to produce short-term prosperity. In the short run (which is when the next election is decided), unemployment is much more likely than inflation to result in defeat at the polls. Whether you think that the Fed has put too much emphasis on restraining inflation will depend on the relative importance that you attach to reducing unemployment, on the one hand, and reducing inflation, on the other.[11]

Should the Fed Be Governed by a Rule?

As we have just seen, important criticisms can be made of Federal Reserve policy making. The monetarists, led by Milton Friedman, go so far as to say that the Fed's attempts to "lean against the wind"—by easing money when the economy begins to dip and tightening money when the economy begins to get overheated—really do more harm than good. In their view, the Fed actually intensifies business fluctuations by changing the rate of growth of the money supply. Why? Partly because the Fed sometimes pays too much attention to interest rates (and free reserves) rather than to the money supply or the monetary base. But more fundamentally, because the Fed tends to overract to ephemeral changes, and because the effects of changes in the money supply on the economy occur with a long and highly variable lag. In their view, this lag is so unpredictable that the Fed—no matter how laudatory its intent—tends to intensify business fluctuations.

Instead, Professor Friedman and his followers want the Fed to abandon its attempts to "lean

[11] For a good discussion of recent monetary and fiscal policy, see G. L. Bach, *Making Monetary and Fiscal Policy*, Washington: Brookings Institution, 1971. Also, see the papers by Milton Friedman and Walter W. Heller in E. Mansfield, *Economics: Readings, Issues and Cases*, New York: Norton, 1974.

against the wind." *They propose that the Fed conform to a rule that the money supply should increase at some fixed, agreed-upon rate, such as 4½ percent per year. The Fed's job would be simply to see that the money supply grows at approximately this rate.* The monetarists do not claim that a rule of this sort would prevent all business fluctuations, but they do claim that it would work better than the existing system. In particular, they feel that it would prevent the sorts of major depressions and inflations we have experienced in the past. Without major decreases in the money supply (such as occurred during the crash of 1929–33), major depressions could not occur. Without major increases in the money supply (such as occurred during World War II), major inflations could not occur. Of course, it would be nice if monetary policy could iron out minor business fluctuations as well, but in their view this simply cannot be done at present.

This proposal has received considerable attention from both economists and politicians. A number of studies have been carried out to try to estimate what would have happened if Friedman's rule had been used in the past. The results, although by no means free of criticism, seem to indicate that such a rule might have done better than discretionary action did in preventing the Great Depression of the 1930s and the inflation during World War II. But in the period since World War II, the evidence in favor of such a rule is less persuasive. Most economists seem to believe that it would be a mistake to handcuff the Fed to a simple rule of this sort. They think that a discretionary monetary policy can outperform Friedman's rule.

Nonetheless, the debate over rules versus discretionary action goes on, and the issues are still very much alive. Professor Friedman has been able to gain important converts, including the Federal Reserve Bank of St. Louis and members of the Joint Economic Committee of Congress. Indeed, after the Fed's "stop-go" policies of 1966–68 (when the Fed tightened money sharply in 1966 and loosened it rapidly in 1967–8), the Joint Economic Committee urged the Fed to adopt a rule of the sort advocated by Friedman. In 1968, the committee complained that its advice was not being followed, and special hearings were held. The Council of Economic Advisers and the Secretary of the Treasury sided with the Fed against adopting such a rule. Some academic economists favor such a rule, others oppose it, and considerable economic research is being carried out to try to clarify and resolve the questions involved.

Monetary Policy: Advantages and Disadvantages

Just as sensible wine drinkers value both Bordeaux and Burgundy (and both France and California), so most economists believe that both monetary and fiscal policy can and should play an important role in our nation's economic stabilization policies. However, this does not mean, of course, that monetary policy does not have certain advantages over fiscal policy, and vice versa. One disadvantage of monetary policy, according to many economists, is that it may be less dependable than fiscal policy when the government wants to stimulate the economy. All that monetary policy can do is to increase bank reserves. The monetary authorities cannot make the banks lend out the excess reserves—as illustrated by the situation during the 1930s when banks held huge excess reserves. And if the banks don't lend them out or invest them, there is little or no stimulation to the economy. Thus, monetary policy may be less effective as a stimulant than as a rein on the economy. However, under current circumstances (not the 1930s), this assymetry may be less pronounced than has sometimes been assumed.

On the other hand, one of the most important advantages of monetary policy is that the monetary authorities can react much more quickly to changed economic conditions than can the fiscal authorities. Changes in monetary policy can be put into effect relatively quickly if the Fed wants to do so, but no matter what the Treasury, the Council of Economic Advisers, and other administration officials want to do, changes in tax and expenditure policy must be approved by the Congress. Proposed fiscal policies can be delayed and even made into a political football, as happened to the tax surcharge of 1968, which had been kicked around for a couple of years before it finally was enacted.

According to some observers, another advantage of monetary policy is that it is nondiscriminatory. In other words, the Fed does not favor particular classes of borrowers or activities; it just tightens or eases money and credit, and lets the market determine which people and industries will be benefited or hurt. But other observers retort that monetary policy is highly discriminatory, since it can hit a particular group or industry or type of borrower harder than anyone would intend. For example, the home construction industry has sometimes been clobbered by tight monetary policy. Because of the importance of mortgage funds to the construction industry, tight money can really have a big impact on its output and profits.

Monetary Policy and Private Decision Making

Up to this point, we have discussed monetary policy strictly from the point of view of society as a whole. It is important to look at things from this vantage point, but it must also be recognized that an understanding of monetary policy is a great help, and sometimes absolutely essential, in making decisions about your personal finances and your firm's problems. For example, suppose that you have $10,-000 in cash and are thinking about investing it in bonds, which currently yield a return of 7 percent per year. Should you invest it now, or wait? The answer depends on whether you think interest rates will rise. If so, you may be better off to hold the $10,000 in cash, and invest it in bonds later, when you can get a higher return.

But whether or not interest rates will rise depends upon the sort of monetary policy pursued by the Fed. Thus, to make an informed judgment about whether you should invest now or wait, you have to have some understanding of what the Fed is likely to do. Will it tighten money, and push interest rates up? Or will it ease money, and push interest rates down? Based on your appraisal of the current economic climate, as well as the published opinions of experts, you should be able to come to a reasoned conclusion on this score.

Or take another example. Suppose you own a small business, and will soon need to borrow some money to buy some new equipment. Is this a good time to apply for a bank loan? The answer depends in part on how tight money is now, and on how tight it is likely to be in the future. But to understand the current monetary situation, and the likely changes in the near future, you must understand what monetary policy is all about. You must be able to understand what the Federal Reserve has been doing in the recent past, and what it is likely to do in the future.

Or suppose that you are thinking of buying a house. The rate of interest you pay on the mortgage has a big effect on the total cost of the house. For example, the payments on a $40,000 mortgage are almost $4,000 higher over the 25-year life of the mortgage if the interest is 7½ percent than if it is 7 percent. Thus, since interest rates are influenced by monetary policy, an understanding of monetary policy is useful in figuring out whether and when it is a good time to buy.

Summary

Monetary policy is concerned with the money supply and interest rates. Its purpose is to attain and maintain full employment without inflation. When a recession seems imminent and business is soft, the monetary authorities are likely to increase the money supply and reduce interest rates. On the other hand, when the economy is in danger of "overheating" and inflation threatens, the monetary authorities are likely to rein in the money supply and push up interest rates. Monetary policy and fiscal policy are aimed at much the same goals, but they use different methods to promote them. One advantage of monetary policy is that the lag between decision and action is relatively short. In view of the time involved in getting tax (and spending) changes enacted, this is an important point.

Although monetary policy is influenced by Congress, the Treasury, and other parts of the government and the public at large, the chief responsibility for the formulation of monetary policy lies with the Federal Reserve Board and the Federal Open Market Committee. To a considerable extent, monetary policy operates by changing the quantity of bank reserves. The most important tool of monetary policy is open market operations, which involve the buying and selling of government securities in the open market by the Federal Reserve. When the Fed buys government securities, this increases bank reserves. When the Fed sells government securities, this reduces bank reserves. The Fed can also tighten or ease money by increasing or decreasing the discount rate or by increasing or decreasing legal reserve requirements. In addition, the Fed can use moral suasion, and it has power over maximum interest rates on time deposits and margin requirements for the purchase of stock.

As indicators of how tight or easy monetary policy is, the Fed has looked at the level of short-term interest rates, the quantity of free reserves, the rate of growth of the money supply, and the rate of growth of the monetary base. During the 1950s, the Fed paid most attention to the first two indicators; in the 1960s and 1970s, the Fed increased the amount of attention paid to the last two. To provide some idea of how monetary policy has been used, we presented a brief description of the nature and course of monetary policy during the past two decades. Also, to provide a richer picture of the use of monetary policy to stem inflation, we described in some detail the "credit crunch of 1966." This episode is a dramatic example of the potency of monetary policy.

The Federal Reserve is faced with many difficult problems in formulating and carrying out monetary policy. It must try to see where the economy is heading, and whether—and to what extent—it should tighten or ease money to stabilize the economy. This task is made very difficult by the fact that there is often a long—and highly variable—lag between an action by the Fed and its effect on the economy. There is also considerable disagreement over the best way to measure how tight or easy monetary policy is. In addition, the Fed's job is complicated by the fact that, although it is independent of the executive branch, it must take account of the Treasury's problems in financing the public debt. During the 1940s and early 1950s, the Fed's policies were dictated largely by such financing matters.

There has been criticism of various kinds regarding the performance of the Federal Reserve. Often, the Fed is criticized for paying too little attention to the long lags between its actions and their effects on the economy. Also, some critics claim that the Fed puts too much emphasis on fighting inflation and too little on preventing unemployment. Some monetarists, led by Milton Friedman, believe that monetary policy would be improved if discretionary policy were replaced by a rule that the Fed should increase the money supply at some fixed, agreed-on rate, such as 4½ percent per year. The Fed, the Council of Economic Advisers, the Treasury, and many academic economists have argued against the adoption of such a rule, but Friedman's proposal has won some support in the Joint Economic Committee and elsewhere. The debate over rules versus discretionary policy goes on, and is one of the liveliest in present-day economics.

CONCEPTS FOR REVIEW

Monetary policy	Changes in legal reserve requirements	Free reserves
Federal Reserve Board		Monetary base
Federal Open Market Committee	Easing money	Margin requirements
	Moral suasion	Credit crunch
Open market operations	Selective credit control	Tightening money
Discount rate		

QUESTIONS FOR DISCUSSION AND REVIEW

1. According to Henry Wallich, although "monetary policy has so often been wrong that it [may seem] preferable to deprive it of discretion and subject it to a fixed rule, . . . this reasoning is fallacious." Do you agree? Why or why not? How would you go about testing this proposition?

2. According to Sherman Maisel, William McChesney Martin, former Chairman of the Federal Reserve Board, felt "that the primary function of the Federal Reserve Board was to determine what was necessary to maintain a sound currency . . . [To Martin] it is as immoral for a country today to allow the value of its currency to fall as it was for kings of old to clip coinage." Do you agree with Martin's views? Why or why not?

3. The Fed's task is made more difficult by the fact that there is often a long lag between an action by the Fed and its effect on the economy. True or False?

4. In order to decide whether monetary policy is inflationary or deflationary and what should be done in this regard, the Federal Reserve Board would probably *not* consider
a. short-term interest rates.
b. the size of the national debt.
c. the rate of increase of the money supply.
d. the rate of increase of the monetary base.

CHAPTER 15

Problems of Economic Stabilization Policy

Despite the advances in economic knowledge during the past 40 years, we, like other countries, find it very difficult to achieve full employment with stable prices. Monetary policy is an important means toward that end. And in the eyes of most economists, so is fiscal policy. Yet, despite the power of monetary and fiscal policies, we are still a long way from the desired degree of economic stability. Judging from the experience of the past 40 years, we have learned how to avoid very serious depressions, but we have not yet learned how to attain full employment with stable prices. Excessive unemployment and excessive inflation persist.

Two important reasons why our performance has been less than satisfactory are evident. First, economists are still uncertain about many effects of monetary and fiscal policies. For one thing, as pointed out in previous chapters, the views of the monetarists differ from those of the Keynesians. Second, if some of the inflationary pressures in our society stem from an upward push of costs (or profits), some form of incomes policy may be needed to quell undesirable inflation. In this chapter, we discuss both of these problems at length.

The General Problem of Achieving Economic Stability

As a first step, let's review how fiscal and monetary policies can be used to promote full employment without inflation. We begin with fiscal policy. With a given level of potential output or capacity, actual net national product is determined by desired spending. Fiscal policy uses the government's expenditures and taxes to influence desired spending. Specifically, when NNP is at less than its full-employment level, increases in government expenditures or reductions in taxes can be used to push it up to this level, and thus reduce excessive unemployment. Or when there is excessive inflation, decreases in government expenditures or increases in taxes can reduce total spending, and thus curb inflation.

Monetary policy uses the government's power over the quantity of money to influence NNP. Increases in the money supply tend to increase the money value of NNP, whereas reductions in the money supply tend to reduce the money value of NNP. The route by which the quantity of money has this effect on NNP is a subject of controversy. The majority, or Keynesian, view is that increases in the money supply reduce interest rates, which stimulates investment, which increases NNP. Conversely, decreases in the money supply increase interest rates, which cuts investment, which reduces NNP. Many Keynesians, at least in more recent years, also recognize that changes in the money supply influence the net worth of consumers, and thus have an impact on consumption expenditures. Monetarists, relying heavily on the quantity theory of money, relate changes in the money supply more directly to changes in nominal, or money, NNP.

The controversy between the monetarists and the

Keynesians has received so much attention in recent years that one might think that, if it were resolved, the problem of formulating monetary and fiscal policies to achieve full employment with stable prices would be licked. This is by no means true. However the controversy is resolved, no existing economic model can give policy makers reliable quantitative estimates of how much the money supply should be altered, or government expenditures should be changed, or tax rates should be modified, to achieve full employment with stable prices. To a considerable extent, the knowledge we have is qualitative, not quantitative. Until we can better estimate the quantitative effects of policy changes of various magnitudes, it will be unreasonable to expect that monetary and fiscal policies can be used with precision to achieve our national goals.

In addition, it must be emphasized that both the Keynesian and the monetarist models are just that—models. In other words, they are convenient and useful simplifications; and, as such, they abstract from many important aspects of reality. In particular, they take little or no notice of the possibility that inflation may arise because of an upward push of costs, and they tell us very little about what to do when there is both excessive unemployment and excessive inflation. Nor do they say much about the extent of the lags between the time when policy makers want to act and the time when such action is approved and taken, or the lags between the time when action is taken and the time when its economic effects are felt.

Further, it must be recognized that government decisions are not dictated by considerations of economic stabilization alone. Thus, even if economic models were completely accurate and the government knew how to achieve full employment at stable prices, it would not always choose to do so. For example, the political party in power may be committed to a particular policy designed to alleviate a certain social ill, like poverty or discrimination. To carry out this objective, it may increase government expenditures at a time when, from the point of view of economic stabilization, it would be better to reduce them. Or in wartime, modern military needs require enormous outlays, but the political party in power may not be willing to take the unpopular step of raising taxes, even though this would be desirable for economic stabilization. Or consider an upcoming presidential election. The incumbent president may initiate or expand programs to make people feel prosperous in the short run, even though this may be destabilizing in the longer run. After all, the important thing is to win the election and prevent that other fellow, whoever he may be, from ruining the country!

Monetarists versus Keynesians

The debate between the monetarists and the Keynesians has not been limited to the classroom and scholarly gatherings. It has spilled over onto the pages of the daily newspapers and aroused considerable interest in Congress and other parts of the government. At heart, the argument is over what determines the level of output, employment, and prices. The Keynesians put more emphasis on the federal budget than do the monetarists, who put more emphasis on the money supply than do the Keynesians. To understand this debate fully, we need to know something about the recent development of economic thought. Up until the Great Depression of the 1930s, the prevailing theory was that NNP, expressed in real terms, would tend automatically to its full-employment value. (Recall from Chapter 9 the classical economists' reasons for clinging to this belief.) Moreover, the prevailing theory was that the price level could be explained by the crude quantity theory of money. In other words, the price level, P, was assumed to be proportional to the quantity of money, M, because $MV = PQ$, and real NNP, Q, and the velocity of money, V, were thought to be essentially constant.

During the Great Depression of the 1930s, this body of theory was largely discredited and abandoned. Clearly, NNP was not tending automatically toward its full-employment level. And the crude quantity theory seemed to have little value. In contrast, Keynes's ideas, which stressed the importance of fiscal policy, seemed to offer the sort of theoretical guidance and policy prescriptions that were needed. Keynesians did not neglect the use of monetary policy entirely, but they felt that it played a subsidiary role. Particularly in depressions, monetary policy seemed to be of relatively little value, since "you can't push on a string." In other words, monetary policy can make money available, but it cannot insure that it will be spent.

During the 1940s, 1950s, and early 1960s, the Keynesian view was definitely predominant, here and abroad. But by the mid-1960s, it was being challenged seriously by the monetarists, led by Professor Milton Friedman and his supporters. The monetarist view harked back to the pre-Keynesian doctrine in many respects. In particular, it emphasized the importance of the equation of exchange as an analytical device and the importance of the quantity of money as a tool of economic policy. The monetarist view gained adherents in the late 1960s. Partly responsible was the long delay in passing the surtax of 1968, for the reluctance of the administration to propose and of Congress to enact the new levy vividly illustrated some of the difficulties in using fiscal policy for stabilization. In contrast, monetary policy seemed to assure only a short lag between policy decisions and their implementation. Another factor favoring the monetarists was that the economy was plagued by inflation, not unemployment. Monetary policy, by controlling the quantity of money, can quite effectively restrain inflation, even if, under certain circumstances, it may not be so effective in reducing unemployment. "You may be able to pull on a string," even if "you can't push on a string."

The Monetarist View of the Role of Money

Given its recent prominence, the monetarist view deserves a closer look. The monetarists believe that the velocity of money, V, is relatively stable or so predictable that changes in M will have a predictable effect on PQ. Suppose that people and firms want to hold a quantity of money equal to 20 percent of nominal, or money, NNP. Then if NNP is $1,000 billion, they will want to hold $200 billion of money; if NNP is $1,200 billion, they will want to hold $240 billion of money; and if NNP is $1,400 billion, they will want to hold $280 billion of money. According to the monetarists, there is a stable and predictable relationship of this sort between NNP and the quantity of money people and firms want to hold.

To the monetarists, this relationship determines the equilibrium level of NNP. Continuing our example (where firms and people want to hold 20 percent of NNP in the form of money), suppose that NNP is $1,000 billion (which means that the public wants to hold $200 billion in money), but that the Federal Reserve makes $240 billion in money available. What will happen? Since the public has more money on hand than it wants, it will spend away its unwanted excess cash. Firms will invest in plant, equipment, inventories, or other items. Individuals too, having more cash on hand than they want, will step up their spending. The result, of course, will be an increase in NNP, since the increased spending will boost NNP.

By how much will NNP increase? So long as NNP is less than $1,200 billion, the public will have more money than it wants to hold. Its $240 billion of money is more than the 20 percent of NNP it wants to hold in money. Consequently, for the amount of money to be the amount people want to hold, NNP must be five times the quantity of money, or $5 \times \$240$ billion in this case. Thus, NNP must rise to $1,200 billion. So long as NNP is less than $1,200 billion, there is a disequilibrium, since people have more money than they want to hold. The result will be that they spend the excess cash and increase NNP. Only when NNP rises to $1,200 billion will an equilibrium be achieved.

Similarly, suppose that NNP is $1,000 billion, but that the Federal Reserve makes only $160

billion of money available. Since NNP is $1,000 billion, the public would like to hold $200 billion (20 percent of NNP) in money. The public holds less money than it wants to; and in order to return to its desired relationship between NNP and the quantity of money furnished by the Fed, the public cuts down its spending. In other words, firms reduce their expenditures on plant, equipment, and other items in an attempt to build up their money balances. Similarly, individuals reduce their spending to try to build up their money balances. The result, of course, is a decline in NNP, since the reduced spending will reduce NNP.

By how much will NNP fall? For the amount of money to be the amount people want to hold, NNP must be five times the quantity of money, or $5 \times \$160$ billion in this case. Thus, NNP must fall to 800 billion. So long as NNP is above $800 billion, there is a disequilibrium, since people have less money than they want to hold. Consequently, they will cut back on their spending in an effort to build up their money balances, and NNP is reduced. Only when NNP falls to $800 billion will an equilibrium be achieved.

Following this line of reasoning, the monetarists conclude that increases in the quantity of money will increase NNP. If the economy is not at full employment, much of this increase in NNP will represent an increase in real output; but if full employment exists, it will represent an increase in the price level. Similarly, the monetarists conclude that decreases in the quantity of money will decrease NNP. Unless such a decrease in NNP offsets existing inflationary pressures, it will, of course, represent a decrease in real output. The monetarists provide considerable statistical evidence that, in their eyes at least, backs up these conclusions. For example, they point out that the money supply seemed to fall just before various depressions of the past. And they explain why the increase in taxes in 1968 had less than the expected contractionary effect on NNP by citing the fact that the money supply continued to increase at a relatively rapid rate.

The Debate over Stabilization Policy

From these theoretical and empirical foundations, the monetarists and the Keynesians reach quite different conclusions about how economic stabilization policies should be carried out. For one thing, the monetarists attack the Keynesian view that fiscal policy works in the way we described in Chapter 10. According to the monetarists, whether the government runs a surplus or a deficit has no permanent effect on NNP, except insofar as the government finances the surplus or deficit in a way that affects the stock of money.

For example, if the government runs a deficit and finances it by borrowing from the public, the money supply will be unchanged. Thus the monetarists would argue that such a deficit has no expansionary effect on NNP. On the other hand, if the government finances its deficit by increasing the money supply, the monetarists would expect NNP to increase, but as a result of the expansion of the money supply, not of the deficit. Thus, the monetarists claim that the expansion of NNP after the tax cut of 1964 was due to considerable increases in the money supply, not to the tax cut.

Another important difference between the monetarists and the Keynesians is that many, but not all, leading monetarists advocate the establishment of a rule to govern monetary policy. In the previous chapter, we discussed the arguments of Friedman and his supporters for such a rule. You will recall their charge that the Federal Reserve's monetary policies have often caused economic instability. Because of the difficulties in forecasting the future state of the economy and the fairly long and variable time lag in the effect of changes in the money supply, the Fed, in the eyes of many leading monetarists, has caused excessive inflation or unemployment by its discretionary policies. According to the monetarists, we would be better off with a rule stipulating that the money supply should grow steadily at a rate fixed somewhere between 4 and 5 percent per year.

Needless to say, the Keynesians—or the New Economists, as they have sometimes been called—have plenty of counterarguments against the monetarists. They believe that the monetarists take too simple and highly aggregated a view of the economy. The Keynesians point out that many factors impinge significantly on the economy and that, in their view, it is overly simplistic to concentrate so single-mindedly on one variable, the quantity of money. For example, desired spending may be influenced heavily by people's expectations, which may be unrelated to the quantity of money. The Keynesians also believe that the monetarists sometimes tend to mix up cause and effect. Changes in desired spending may bring about a greater demand for money, which in turn causes the money supply to increase. Under these circumstances, the line of causation may be the opposite of that posited by the monetarists.

In addition, the Keynesians tend to feel that the interest rate is far more important than the monetarists realize. According to the Keynesians, the money supply has an important influence on NNP, but its influence is felt largely through its impact on the interest rate, which in turn affects spending. Thus the Keynesians are more inclined than the monetarists to use the level of interest rates to measure whether money is tight or easy. To the monetarists, the change in the quantity of money, not the level of interest rates, is important. The Keynesians have presented evidence of various kinds to demonstrate, at least to their own satisfaction, that their view is the correct one.[1]

The Keynesians have also attacked the monetarists' contention that the velocity of money is relatively stable. Data we have seen (recall Figure 12.8) confirm that velocity is far from constant. For one thing, it varies with interest rates and with people's expectations. However, sophisticated monetarists would say that the velocity function—a functional relationship derived from the demand for money—is stable. This is different from saying that velocity as a calculated number is stable.

[1] For some of the arguments on both sides, see the papers by Walter W. Heller, Milton Friedman, and Arthur Okun in E. Mansfield, *Economics: Readings, Issues, and Cases*, New York: Norton, 1974.

Milton Friedman versus Walter W. Heller

Seldom do the *New York Times,* the *Wall Street Journal,* and *Vogue* cover a debate between two economists. That they covered the seventh annual Arthur K. Salomon Lecture at New York University in November 1968 is a tribute to the impact each of the protagonists—Milton Friedman and Walter W. Heller—has had on presidents, potential presidents, and public opinion in the monetary versus fiscal debate.

Friedman, a professor at the University of Chicago, has written on as wide a range of subjects as any living economist. A staunch conservative, he neverthe-less originated such "liberal" proposals as the educational voucher (now being used experimentally in Vermont and North Dakota districts) and the negative income tax. In keeping with his conservative philosophy, he has attacked the evils of Social Security and the minimum wage, praised the virtues of abolishing li-

FRIEDMAN—HELLER DEBATE, NOVEMBER 1968.

censing of professions, and argued the intimate connection between capitalism and freedom. Although never a full-time government employee since his World War II stint with the Treasury Department, he has served in his spare time as economics adviser to presidential candidate Barry Goldwater and to President Nixon (before Nixon left the faith and imposed price and wage controls).

But Friedman is most prominently identified, at least within the economics profession, as the defender (and in large part the creator) of monetarism. While Keynesianism triumphant swept the economics profession in the postwar years, Friedman and a few University of Chicago colleagues were investigating the historical connection be-

tween money and U.S. economic history, eventually persuading the Federal Reserve Bank of St. Louis to gather and publish statistics using their concepts and fortifying the monetarist arguments until the inflation of the late sixties made monetarism fashionable again.

By contrast, Walter W. Heller, a professor at the University of Minnesota, has been a liberal and a political activist (at least by economists' standards). As chairman of the Council of Economic Advisers under both Presidents Kennedy and Johnson, he was a principal architect of the 1962 investment tax credit and the 1964 tax cut. He enjoyed a close and sympathetic relationship with the New Frontiersmen, and as a consequence, the Council assumed a broader, more activist role than it has enjoyed before or since. He was a leading spokesman for the use of fiscal and monetary policies, not merely to avoid major depressions and inflations, but to smooth out the smaller fluctuations in the economy.

In their debate, Heller posed many basic questions concerning monetarism: "Which money-supply indicator do you believe? Can one read enough from money supply without weighing also shifts in demand and interest rates? Don't observed variations in monetary time lags and velocity cast serious doubt on any simple relation between money supply and GNP? Can a rigid monetary rule find happiness in a world beset with rigidities and rather limited adjustment capabilities? That is, is the rigid Friedman rule perhaps a formula made in heaven, that will work only in heaven?" These questions are of great importance, and they continue to be debated, here and abroad.

E.A.

As for the monetarists' contention that monetary policy should be governed by a rule, the Keynesians retort that such a rule would handcuff the monetary authorities and contribute to economic instability, since discretionary monetary policies are required to keep the economy on a reasonably even keel. The Keynesians grant that the Fed sometimes makes mistakes, but they assert that things would be worse if the Fed could not pursue the policies that a given set of circumstances seems to call for.

The debate between the monetarists and the Keynesians is important and illuminating. It has forced the entire economics profession to review its thinking about the effects of monetary and fiscal policies. This is the sort of ferment that keeps a discipline healthy and vital. Chances are that it will be many years before the issues are completely resolved, but in the past decade, considerable strides have been taken toward achieving a synthesis of these two views. Having focused attention on the differences between them, let's look now at this new synthesis.

Elements of a New Synthesis

The Keynesian theory says that the economy will be in equilibrium only when consumers are spending at the rate they desire, given their income, and when firms are investing at the rate they desire. The monetarist theory says that the economy will be in equilibrium only when consumers and firms are willing to hold the existing quantity of money, given their income and the quantity of other assets that they hold. In truth, of course, both these conditions for equilibrium must be fulfilled: neither alone is sufficient to guarantee equilibrium. This fact suggests that a more complete model than either the Keynesian or the monetarist model may be needed to analyze many problems effectively.

For example, what happens when the government increases the quantity of money by handing out some newly printed money to the public? Let's begin with the public's asset holdings. Since the public has more money than before, it will rearrange its portfolio of assets, assuming that it had the portfolio it desired prior to the increase in the money supply. Consumers and firms, finding themselves with more money than they want to hold, will exchange money for other types of assets. In other words, they will spend some of their money holdings—and will continue to spend money until, once again, their portfolio of assets is balanced so as to maximize their satisfaction.

Second, consider how the increase in the public's income due to the increase in the money supply will affect spending. The people who receive the newly printed money, finding that their disposable incomes have risen, want to spend more on consumption goods. Firms that receive the new money are also likely to want to increase their investment expenditures. Both consumers and firms will continue to spend more until, once again, their expenditures are in the desired relationship to their incomes. Note that this adjustment process, stressed by Keynesian theory, goes on simultaneously with the adjustment process described in the previous paragraph, which is related to the monetarist theory.

Once one recognizes that both processes go on simultaneously, it is easy to see that much of the debate between the Keynesians and monetarists is really over which of two simplifications is more fruitful—or does less violence to reality. According to the Keynesians, the multiplier is more stable than the velocity of money, so that changes in taxes or government spending have a more predictable effect on total spending than changes in the quantity of money. According to the monetarists, the velocity of money is more predictable than the multiplier, which means that the effects of changes in the quantity of money on total spending are more predictable than changes in taxes or government spending. Much econometric work is being done at present to try to resolve this issue. Although the evidence as yet is inconclusive, it is reasonable to expect that in the foreseeable future we will be much better able to answer this question.

Figure 15.1
The *IS* Curve

The *IS* curve shows, for each level of the interest rate, the level of NNP that will satisfy the equilibrium condition that desired saving must equal desired investment.

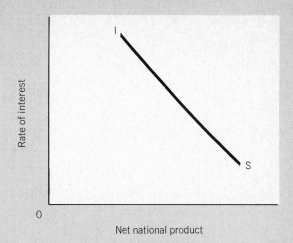

Figure 15.2
The *LM* Curve

The *LM* curve shows, for each level of the interest rate, the level of NNP that will satisfy the equilibrium condition that the public be satisfied to hold the existing quantity of money.

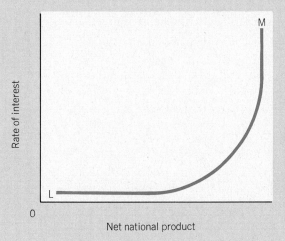

The IS and LM Curves[2]

Now that we recognize that equilibrium requires both that households and firms be spending the desired amount relative to their incomes and that they be satisfied to hold the existing quantity of money, it is worthwhile to show, in somewhat more detail, how net national product is determined. To do this, we draw two curves, *IS* and *LM,* both of which are constructed on the assumption that the money supply and the price level are fixed and that the public has a fixed demand curve for real money balances, a fixed consumption function, and a fixed investment function.

[2] This section, which is somewhat more advanced than the rest of this chapter, can be omitted without losing the thread of the argument.

The *IS* curve in Figure 15.1 shows, for each possible level of the interest rate, the level of NNP that will satisfy the equilibrium condition that desired saving equal desired investment (see Chapter 9). This equilibrium condition is equivalent to saying that the public must be spending the desired amount relative to its income. The *IS* curve slopes downward to the right because the higher the interest rate, the lower the amount of investment (as we know from Chapter 9); and the lower the amount of investment, the lower the equilibrium level of NNP (as we also know from Chapter 9). If the level of NNP is to satisfy the equilibrium condition that desired saving must equal desired investment, it must fall on the *IS* curve in Figure 15.1.

The *LM* curve, provided in Figure 15.2, shows,

for each possible level of the interest rate, the level of NNP that will satisfy the equilibrium condition that the public be satisfied to hold the existing quantity of money. The *LM* curve slopes upward to the right because the higher the interest rate, the less money the public will want to hold (as we know from Chapter 12). So the level of NNP will have to rise to offset this effect (since increases in NNP raise the amount of money the public wants to hold). If the level of NNP is to satisfy the equilibrium condition that the public be satisfied to hold the existing quantity of money, it must fall on the *LM* curve in Figure 15.2.

Since the equilibrium level of NNP must fall on both the *IS* and *LM* curves, *the equilibrium level of NNP must be at the intersection of the IS and LM curves,* as shown in Figure 15.3. That is, the equilibrium level of NNP must be X, and the equilibrium level of the interest rate must be i. This is the only combination of NNP and interest rate that will satisfy both equilibrium conditions, given that the money supply, the public's demand curve for money, its consumption function, and its investment function remain fixed.

Suppose, however, that all these conditions do not remain fixed. In particular, assume that fiscal policy is expansionary, thus stimulating spending by the public. This will shift the *IS* curve to the right, because spending at each level of the interest rate will be greater than before. As Figure 15.4 indicates, the result will be a higher equilibrium level of NNP and a higher rate of interest, so long as NNP is between X_0 and X_2. (Specifically, the equilibrium point shifts from A to B.) If NNP is at X_2, a shift of the *IS* curve to the right only increases the interest rate; it does not affect NNP. (The equilibrium point shifts from C to D.) This is the so-called **classical range,** where fiscal policy cannot increase NNP because the velocity of money is constant at its upper limit. Most economists do not consider such a situation very likely. If NNP is below X_0, a rightward shift of the *IS*

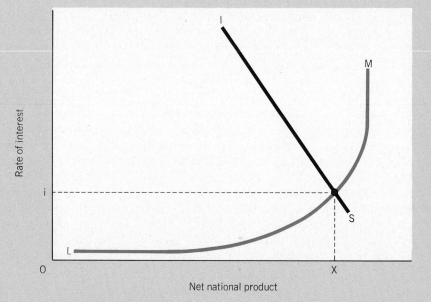

**Figure 15.3
Determination of Equilibrium
NNP and Interest Rate**

The equilibrium level of NNP (and of the interest rate) must be at the intersection of the *IS* and *LM* curves. The equilibrium NNP equals X, and the equilibrium interest rate equals i.

Figure 15.4
Effects of an Expansionary
Fiscal Policy

An expansionary fiscal policy shifts the *IS* curve to the right, resulting in a higher equilibrium level of NNP and of the interest rate, so long as NNP is between X_0 and X_2. For example, if I_1S_1 is the existing curve, which shifts to the right, the equilibrium shifts from A to B. On the other hand, if I_2S_2 is the existing curve, which shifts to the right, the equilibrium shifts from C to D. This is the *classical range*. Or if I_0S_0 is the existing curve, which shifts to the right, the equilibrium shifts from E to F. This is the *liquidity-trap range*.

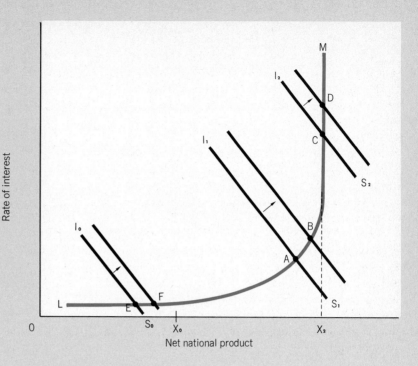

curve will not affect the interest rate, although it will increase NNP. (The equilibrium point shifts from E to F.) This is the so-called **liquidity-trap range**, which is also unlikely to occur, except in severe depressions.

Assume next that the monetary authorities increase the money supply. Since the interest rate that equates the demand and supply of money (at any given level of NNP) must be lower if the quantity of money increases, this expansionary monetary policy results in a shift of the *LM* curve downward and to the right. As shown in Figure 15.5, the result will be a higher equilibrium level of NNP and a lower rate of interest, as long as the economy is not in the range of the liquidity trap. (Specifically, the equilibrium point shifts from G to H.) If we are in the liquidity trap, although the *LM* curve shifts, the portion of the curve below X_0 remains fixed, with the result that the equilibrium level of NNP and the interest rate are unchanged (at point K). A liquidity trap occurs

when the interest rate is so low that people expect it to rise, and they are willing to hold more cash at existing interest rates. Such a situation is very unlikely to occur, except perhaps in very deep depressions. But if it does occur, monetary policy is unable to influence NNP.

Figures 15.4 and 15.5 show that the effects of monetary or fiscal policy on NNP depend on the shape of the *IS* and *LM* curves. For example, the closer the *LM* curve is to being vertical in the relevant range, the less impact fiscal policy will have, and the closer the economy is to the liquidity trap, the less effect monetary policy will have. These diagrams, originated by Oxford's Nobel Laureate, Sir John Hicks, are extremely useful in putting the debate between the monetarists and the Keynesians into proper perspective. To a considerable extent, this debate, when stripped of its semantic and rhetorical aspects, is over the shape of the *IS* and *LM* curves. This, of course, is an empirical question that requires careful statistical and

Figure 15.5
Effects of an Expansionary
Monetary Policy

An expansionary monetary policy
shifts the *LM* curve downward
and to the right, the result being
a higher equilibrium level of NNP
and a lower rate of interest, so
long as the economy is not in the
liquidity trap. Specifically, the
equilibrium shifts from *G* to *H*.
If we are in the liquidity trap,
the equilibrium remains at *K*.

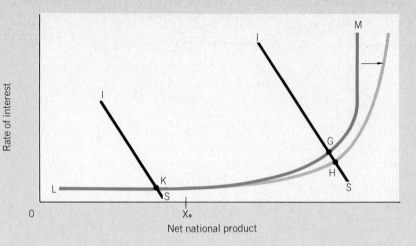

Demand-Pull and
Cost-Push Inflation

Whether they lean toward the monetarist or the
Keynesian route to economic stability, policy makers
have found inflation to be a stubborn foe. In previous chapters, we described *demand-pull inflation,*
a situation in which there is too much aggregate
spending. The $C + I + G$ line is too high, resulting in inflationary pressure. Or, put in terms of the
equation of exchange, $M \times V$ is too high, so that
P is pushed up: too much money is chasing too
few goods. This kind of inflation stems from the
demand or spending behavior of the nation's consumers, firms, and government. We have had many
inflations of this kind. The major inflations during
the Revolutionary and Civil wars were basically
caused by demand-pull factors; and so, much more
recently, was the inflation arising from the Vietnam
war.

econometric work to resolve. As we noted, considerable work of this sort is currently in progress. Regardless of how this work turns out, an understanding of the *IS* and *LM* curves provides us with much
additional insight into the real differences and
similarities between the monetarists and Keynesians.

However, in the view of many economists, demand-pull inflation is not the only kind of inflation. There is also a different kind—*cost-push inflation.* The process underlying cost-push inflation
is not as well understood as it should be, but, according to many economists, it works something
like this: costs are increased, perhaps because
unions push up wages, and in an attempt to protect their profit margins, firms push up prices.
These price increases affect the costs of other
firms and the consumer's cost of living. As the cost
of living goes up, labor feels entitled to, and obtains, higher wages to offset the higher living costs.
Firms again pass on the cost increase to the consumer in the form of a price increase. This so-called
wage-price spiral is at the heart of cost-push inflation.

Basically, in cost-push inflation, *the culprits are
unions and firms with considerable market power.*
In a world of perfect competition, both in product
and input markets, cost-push inflation could not
occur. In such a world, labor could not increase
wages in the face of appreciable unemployment.
If it tried, competition would bring wages back
down. Nor could firms increase prices to protect
their profits. Competition would put a tight ceiling
on their pricing policy. Under perfect competition,
inflation could occur (make no mistake about that),

but it would have to be of the demand-pull type. Whether big labor or big business initiates the wage-price spiral is very difficult to determine in practice, and may well vary from case to case. But whoever makes the first move, the result is inflation.

Generally it is difficult, if not impossible, to sort out cost-push inflation from demand-pull inflation. However, one case of fairly pure cost-push inflation occurred in the late 1950s. This was a period of considerable slack in the economy. You will recall from Chapter 11 that a recession occurred in 1957–58. By 1958 6.8 percent of the labor force was unemployed. Nonetheless, wage increases took place during the late 1950s—and at a rate in excess of the rate of increase of labor productivity (output per manhour).[3] For example, average earnings (outside agriculture) went up by 4 percent between 1957 and 1961, while labor productivity went up by 2½ percent. Moreover, prices increased each year—by 3 percent from 1956 to 1957, and by 2 percent from 1957 to 1958.

Certainly this seemed to be a different phenomenon than the demand-pull inflation described in previous chapters. There was no evidence that too much money was chasing too few goods. Instead, this was apparently a case of cost-push inflation. Commenting on the situation in the middle and late 1950s, the Council of Economic Advisers concluded: "The movement of wages during this period reflected in part the power exercised in labor markets by strong unions and the power possessed by large companies to pass on higher wage costs in higher prices."[4]

The Phillips Curve

What determines the rate at which labor can push up wages? If you think about it for a while, you

will probably agree that *labor's ability to increase wages depends on the level of unemployment. The more unemployment, the more difficult it is for labor to increase wages.* Although perfect competition by no means prevails in the labor market, there is enough competition so that the presence of a pool of unemployed workers puts some damper on wage increases. In nonunion industries and occupations, workers are much less inclined to push for wage increases—and employers are much less inclined to accept them—when lots of people are looking for work. In unionized industries and occupations, unions are less likely to put their members through the hardship of a strike—and firms have less to lose from a strike—when business is bad and unemployment is high.

Because wages tend to be increased at a greater rate when unemployment is low, one would expect the rate of increase of wages in any year to be inversely related to the level of unemployment. This expectation is borne out by the available evidence. Figure 15.6 shows how the rate of increase in wages in a particular period tends to be related to the level of unemployment. According to this figure, which is based on hypothetical, but reasonable, numbers, wages tend to rise by about 3 percent per year when 7 percent of the labor force is unemployed, by about 4½ percent per year when 5 percent of the labor force is unemployed, and by about 6 percent per year when 4 percent of the labor force is unemployed. *The relationship between the rate of increase of wages and the level of unemployment is the Phillips curve.* It was named after A. W. Phillips, the British economist who first called attention to it.

Given the Phillips curve in Figure 15.6 it is a simple matter to determine the relationship between the rate of inflation and the level of unemployment. It can easily be shown that the rate of increase of prices equals the rate of increase of total cost per manhour minus the rate of increase of labor productivity. If C is the total cost—wage and nonwage—per manhour, the total cost per unit of output equals $C \times M \div O$, where M is the total number of manhours worked and O is total output.

[3] In the next section, we shall discuss the importance of the rate of increase of output per manhour. For present purposes, it is sufficient to note that the greater the rate of increase of output per manhour, the larger the rate of increase of cost per manhour that can be absorbed without an increase in unit cost.

[4] 1962 *Annual Report of the Council of Economic Advisers*, Washington, D.C.: Government Printing Office, p. 175.

**Figure 15.6
The Phillips Curve**

The Phillips curve shows the
relationship between the rate of
increase of wages and the level
of unemployment.

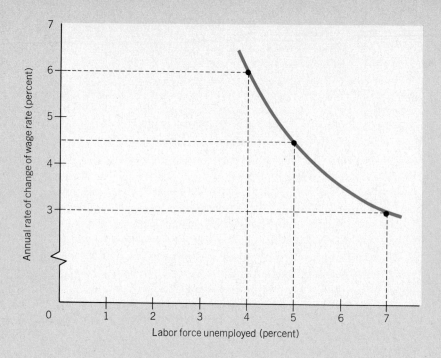

**Figure 15.7
Relationship between Unem-
ployment Rate and Rate of
Inflation**

This relationship can, under the
conditions specified in the text,
be deduced from the Phillips
curve.

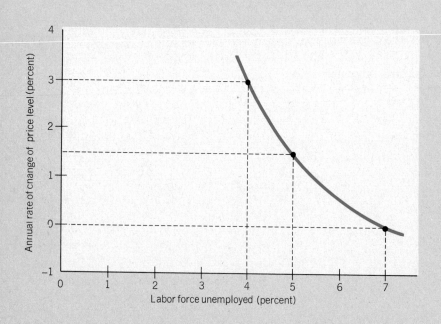

This says no more than that total cost per unit of output equals total cost per manhour times the number of manhours divided by the number of units of output. But $C \times M \div O$ equals $C \div (O/M)$. Thus, total cost per unit of output equals total cost per manhour divided by output per manhour.

Since the rate of increase of a ratio is the rate of increase of the numerator minus the rate of increase of the denominator, it follows that the rate of increase of total cost per unit of output equals the rate of increase of total cost per manhour minus the rate of increase of output per manhour. To see the implications of this result suppose that the rate of increase of total cost per manhour equals the rate of increase of wages, and that the rate of increase of labor productivity is 3 percent per year. Then the rate of increase of prices equals the rate of increase of wages minus 3 percent. Consequently, the relationship between the rate of increase in prices and the level of unemployment is as shown in Figure 15.7.

There is, of course, a simple relationship between the curve in Figure 15.6 and the curve in Figure 15.7. The curve in Figure 15.7 (which shows the relationship between *price* increases and unemployment) is always 3 percentage points below the curve in Figure 15.6 (which shows the relationship between *wage* increases and unemployment). Why? Because the rate of increase of prices—under the assumptions set forth above—always equals the rate of increase of wages minus 3 percent.

At this point it should be clear that the curve in Figure 15.7 is none other than the curve encountered before, in Figure 8.3. Our present discussion has added an account of how this relationship is related to, and based on, the Phillips curve.

Shifts in the Phillips Curve

Before we get too impressed by the apparent accuracy of the Phillips curve, we must remind ourselves that the world is more complicated than Figure 15.7 indicates. In fact, predictions based on this curve may be quite wrong. Why? Because the Phillips curve can shift over time. For example, it may shift from position 1 to position 2 in Figure 15.8, (on the next page) thus causing the relationship between the rate of price increase and unemployment to shift from position 1 to position 2 in Figure 15.9. If you make a prediction based on the curve's being in position 1 in Figure 15.9, when in fact it is in position 2, you can make a substantial mistake. For example, suppose that you want to predict the rate of price increase if unemployment is 5 percent. Assuming that the curve is in position 1, you will predict a 1 percent increase in prices, but in fact there will be a 3 percent increase. The moral is clear enough: we need to look at the factors that can cause the Phillips curve to move.

One of the most important factors that can shift the Phillips curve is education or training. As more and more of the labor force is trained and equipped with relevant and basic skills, there is less upward pressure on wages at any level of unemployment. An important reason why wages are pushed upward as unemployment falls is that the economy tends to run out of skilled workers, so that poorly educated and untrained workers constitute a large percentage of the unemployed. When aggregate demand gets strong enough to absorb these workers, other workers experience so strong a demand that their wages are pushed up. Thus it follows that programs to train the labor force, particularly the unemployed, will shift the Phillips curve downward. That is, the rate of increase of wages associated with a given level of unemployment will fall.

Increased mobility of workers will also shift the Phillips curve. As the labor force becomes able and willing to move from place to place, there is less pressure on wages at any level of unemployment. Thus it follows that measures designed to increase the mobility of workers—such as employment services and preferential tax treatment of moving expenses—tend to shift the Phillips curve downward. Still another factor that will shift the Phillips curve is reduced discrimination against blacks, women, and others who historically have fared poorly in the labor force. With intense discrimina-

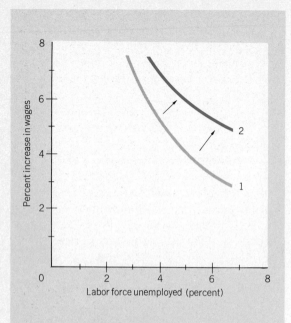

Figure 15.8
Shift in Phillips Curve

The Phillips curve can shift over time, as from position 1 to position 2.

mands of labor (and the pricing policies of management). Thus, wages will rise more rapidly at a given unemployment level than if people expect less inflation. In other words, the more inflation people expect, the further upward and out from the origin the Phillips curve is likely to be. And the less inflation people expect, the further downward and close to the origin the Phillips curve will be. If we experience a great deal of inflation—as we did in the late 1960s—the Phillips curve is likely to be pushed upward because it is likely that people will come to expect inflation to continue. This phenomenon undoubtedly was important in explaining our experience with high unemployment and high rates of inflation in the early 1970s.

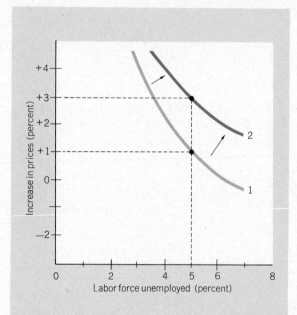

Figure 15.9
Shift in Relationship between Price Increase and Unemployment Rate.

If the Phillips curve shifts, as in Figure 15.8, the relationship between the unemployment rate and the rate of inflation will shift from position 1 to position 2.

tion, labor markets must be very tight (and wages must be under considerable upward pressure) to make employers willing to hire women, blacks, and other minorities. With less discrimination, there is less upward pressure on wages at any level of unemployment, because the minorities are now in a position to compete on a more equal basis with other workers. Thus, reductions in discrimination tend to shift the Phillips curve downward. The Phillips curve can also be shifted by changes over time in the demographic composition of the labor force (such as the proportion of women, teenagers, or blacks), as well as by changes in the bargaining power of unions.

Last but by no means least, another important factor in shifting the Phillips curve is the nature of people's expectations. If people expect a great deal of inflation, this will be reflected in the wage de-

Given these and other factors, the Phillips curve in one economy is likely to differ from that in another economy. It is interesting that, during the early 1960s, the annual rate of increase of prices was about 5 percent in Italy, about 3½ percent in Austria, and about 2 percent in Belgium. Yet all three countries had about 3 or 4 percent of the labor force unemployed. Apparently, the Phillips curve was higher in Italy than in Austria, and higher in Austria than in Belgium, in part because of the effects of the factors discussed in this section.

The Phillips Curve: Short versus Long Run

According to some economists, among them Milton Friedman of the University of Chicago and Edmund Phelps of Columbia, the Phillips curve in Figure 15.6 is only a short-run relationship. In the long run, the Phillips curve is vertical, as shown in panel A of Figure 15.10. Thus, expansionary monetary and fiscal policies that result in inflation will only reduce unemployment temporarily. The only

permanent way to reduce it is through manpower and training policies that will make the unemployed better suited to the available jobs. This is because labor comes to recognize that its wage gains are being eroded by inflation, so that it builds its expectations of inflation into its wage demands, thus pushing the Phillips curve upward and outward from the origin. Eventually, labor bargains with reference to the real, not the money wage.

This challenge to the conventional Phillips curve has itself been challenged by many economists. (This entire area is one of continuing controversy.) As indicated by panel B of Figure 15.10, there may be a range of unemployment, perhaps above 5 percent, where an inverse relationship exists in the long run betweeen unemployment and inflation; but below this range, the Phillips curve may be essentially vertical. This view has been put forth by Yale's James Tobin and Northwestern University's Robert Gordon, among others. According to Gordon, "There is a danger zone, perhaps between 4 and 5 percent unemployed. In that zone, monetary and fiscal policies are no longer the right tools to reduce unemployment." Manpower and retraining programs should be used instead.

Figure 15.10
The Phillips Curve, Short and Long Run

Some economists argue that the long-run Phillips curve is vertical, as in panel A; others argue that it is shaped like that in panel B.

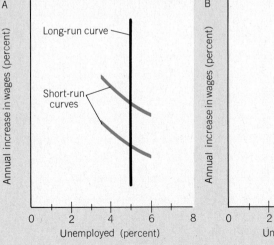
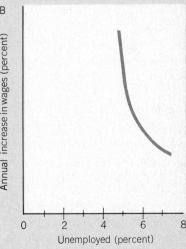

Price Controls and the Reduction of Market Power: Two Suggested Remedies

The government would, of course, like to shift the Phillips curve downward, for example from position C to position D in Figure 15.11. Programs to train manpower, increase labor mobility, reduce discrimination, and change expectations can have this effect. Unfortunately, however, programs of this sort take a considerable amount of time to make an impact, and the evidence of recent years seems to indicate that because young people and women make up a larger share of the labor force, the Phillips curve may have shifted upward, not downward. Consequently, the government has been forced to take more direct action in an attempt to shift the Phillips curve.

During World War II—and other wartime emergencies—the government has imposed controls on wages and prices. In other words, the government intervened directly in the market place to see that wages and prices did not increase by more than a certain amount. Some distinguished economists argue that price and wage controls should also be used to control cost-push inflation in peacetime. According to a former president of the American Economic Association:

A complete attack on inflation requires that both causes of inflation—both the excess of demand or spending, and the wage-price spiral—be brought under control. . . . The defense against the wage-price spiral (i.e., cost-push inflation) . . . is the direct control over prices and wages. These direct controls are not a substitute for a strong fiscal policy; they perform a different task. . . . To tie down the wage-price spiral, with reasonable justice and equity, we need to do three things. They are (1) Effectively stabilize basic living costs. This is necessary if wages are to be stabilized. (2) Maintain a general ceiling on wages and prices in that part of the economy where wages are determined by collective-bargaining contracts and where prices normally move in response to wage movements. I have reference here to what may properly

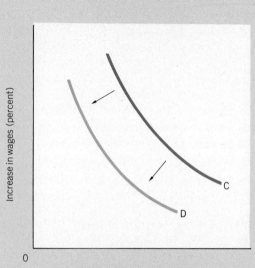

Figure 15.11
Shift in Phillips Curve

The government would like to shift the Phillips curve downward, as from position C to position D.

be called the great industrial core of the American economy—the steel, automobile, electrical goods, construction, transport, and like industries. (3) As a contribution to over-all stability, place firm ceiling prices on basic raw materials.[5]

But most economists do not share this view. The economics profession has little enthusiasm for direct controls of wages and prices, for several reasons. First, such controls are likely to result in a distortion of the allocation of resources. Recall from Chapter 3 our discussion of the functions of the price system in allocating resources. Price and wage controls do not permit prices to perform these functions, and the result is inefficiency and waste.

[5] J. Kenneth Galbraith, Testimony before the Joint Committee on the Economic Report, 82nd Congress, 1st Session.

Second, such controls are likely to be expensive to administer. For example, during the Korean war, the Economic Stabilization Agency had 16,000 employees; and even so, it was difficult to prevent violation or evasion of the controls. Third, there is widespread opposition to detailed government regulation and control of this sort, on the grounds that it impairs our economic freedom. The Council of Economic Advisers undoubtedly spoke for most of the economics profession when it said in 1968:

> The most obvious—and least desirable—way of attempting to stabilize prices is to impose mandatory controls on prices and wages. While such controls may be necessary under conditions of an all-out war, it would be folly to consider them as a solution to the inflationary pressures that accompany high employment under any other circumstance. . . . Although such controls may be unfortunately popular when they are not in effect, the appeal quickly disappears once people live under them.[6]

Another approach to the problem of cost-push inflation is to reduce the market power of unions and firms. Since this market power is the basic cause of cost-push inflation, it would seem logical to attack cost-push inflation in this way. To some extent, the government is, of course, committed to a policy of this sort. Antitrust policy is a basic part of our nation's economic policy.

Antitrust policy, however, is not designed to root out market power in all forms and degrees. This would be foolish in any case, because economies of scale and other considerations require that firms in many industries—to be efficient and innovative—must have a certain amount of market power. Moreover, even when the existing size of firms or concentration of industries cannot be defended on these grounds, the government is not seriously attempting to break up existing firms. Some economists would favor such a policy, both to quell cost-push inflation and to obtain the other advantages (such as greater efficiency in resource use) of a competitive economy. But it does not

[6] 1968 *Annual Report* of the Council of Economic Advisers, Washington, D.C.: Government Printing Office, p. 119.

seem at all likely that such a radical—and politically difficult—policy will be adopted.

Peacetime Wage and Price Controls under the Nixon Administration

Despite the disadvantages of price controls, the United States was forced to adopt them in the summer of 1971 to stem an inflationary surge that threatened to get out of hand. Though the Nixon administration had been trying to use monetary and fiscal policies to halt inflation, wholesale prices were rising at about 5 percent per year. The wage-price spiral was very much in evidence. Collective bargaining agreements were reached calling for wage increases far in excess of productivity increases, and there was no question but that firms would boost prices in an attempt to cover the resulting increase in costs. Since it took office in 1969, the Nixon administration had been opposed to wage and price guidelines, or wage and price controls, although a number of congressmen and others had suggested the adoption of controls or some form of incomes policy.

However, in August 1971, President Nixon reversed his previous stand. He froze wages and prices for a 3-month period. Then he appointed a 15-member Pay Board and a 7-member Price Commission, both of which were supervised by the government's Cost of Living Council. The Pay Board was given the responsibility of administering wage controls, and the Price Commission was to administer price controls. In November 1971, these two bodies announced their initial policies. The Pay Board stated that pay increases had to be kept under 5.5 percent per year. A company could increase some employees' pay by more than this amount, but other employees would have to get less since total increases could not exceed this figure. The Price Commission ruled that price increases had to be kept under 2.5 percent. Both for prices and wages, exceptions could be made in some areas. Large firms were required to notify the Pay Board and Price Commission of intended wage or price increases. The government tried to avoid constructing a large bureaucracy to enforce the controls by giving the task of enforcing them to the Internal Revenue Service.

During the wage and price freeze in the latter part of 1971, both wages and prices continued to rise, but much more slowly than during early 1971. After the freeze ended, and the system of wage and price controls began to function, inflation seemed to go on at a lower rate than before the freeze. It was by no means stopped (the consumer price index rose by about 3 percent during 1972); but it was less severe than during 1970 or the early part of 1971.[7] In January 1973, the Pay Board and the Price Commission became part of the Cost of Living Council, headed by Harvard's labor economist, John Dunlop. And controls were eliminated or relaxed for most prices and wages, with the major exceptions of health, food, and construction industries. To a considerable extent, the Nixon administration phased out the first peacetime wage and price controls in our history.

Unfortunately, inflation occurred subsequently at a bewildering pace. During the first half of 1973, wholesale prices of farm products and processed foods and feeds rose at the unbelievable rate of 48 percent per year. At the same time, the prices of lumber, fuel, and other industrial goods rose at alarming rates. President Nixon responded by imposing a 60-day freeze on prices (but not wages), beginning in mid-June of 1973. This was only a breather, an interim measure designed to give the administration some time to deal with the serious inflationary pressures that were evident throughout the economy. In August 1973, the administration unveiled its so-called Phase IV program which said that price increases could not exceed cost increases. And in September 1973, steel and auto executives, among others, appeared before the Cost of Living Council to try to justify price increases. How much effect the Phase IV program will have on inflation is difficult at present to say.

Incomes Policies

Most economists regard neither direct controls nor the reduction of market power as effective, practical devices to fight cost-push inflation. Faced with this fact, there has been considerable interest, both here and abroad, in using incomes policies to stem cost-push inflation. According to one common definition, an *incomes policy* contains three elements. *First, it has some targets for wages (and other forms of income) and prices for the economy as a whole.* For example, the target may be to stabilize the price level, or to permit the consumer price index to increase by less than 2 percent per year, or to allow wage increases not exceeding a certain percentage.

Second, an incomes policy gives particular firms and industries some more detailed guides for decision making on wages (and other forms of income) and prices. These guides are set in such a way that the overall targets for the entire economy will be fulfilled. For example, if the aim is price stability, these guides tell firms and unions what kinds of decisions are compatible with this target. To be useful, the guides must be specific and understandable enough to be applied in particular cases. There obviously is little point in telling firms and unions to avoid "inflationary" wage and price decisions if they don't know whether a particular decision is "inflationary" or not.

Third, an incomes policy contains some mechanisms to get firms and unions to follow the guides. An incomes policy differs from price and wage controls in that it seeks to induce firms and unions to follow these guides voluntarily. But if it is to have any effect, clearly the government must be prepared to use certain forms of "persuasion" beyond moral suasion. In fact, governments sometimes have publicly condemned decisions by firms

[7] In particular, see B. Bosworth, "Phase II: The U.S. Experiment with an Incomes Policy" and R. Gordon, "Wage-Price Controls and the Shifting Phillips Curve" in *Brookings Papers on Economic Activity,* 1972, No. 2.

and unions that were regarded as violating the guides. Government stockpiles of materials and government purchasing policies have also been used to penalize or reward particular firms and industries. Other pressures too have been brought to bear in an attempt to induce firms to follow the established guides.

An example of an incomes policy in the United States was the so-called Kennedy-Johnson guidelines. Although earlier administrations (for example, the Eisenhower and Truman administrations) had often appealed to business and labor to limit wage and price increases, the first systematic attempt at a fairly specific incomes policy in the United States occurred during the Kennedy administration. In 1961, President Kennedy's Council of Economic Advisers issued the following wage-price guidelines:

> The general guide for noninflationary wage behavior is that the rate of increase in wage rates (including fringe benefits) in each industry be equal to the trend rate of *over-all productivity advance*. General acceptance of this guide would maintain stability of labor cost per unit of output for the economy as a whole—though not of course for individual industries. The general guide for noninflationary price behavior calls for price reduction if the industry's rate of productivity increase exceeds the overall rate—for this would mean declining unit labor costs; it calls for an appropriate increase in price if the opposite relationship prevails; and it calls for stable prices if the two rates of productivity increase are equal.[8]

To see just what this meant, let's consider prices and wages in the auto industry. Suppose that labor productivity in the economy as a whole was increasing at 3.2 percent per year. Then according to the guidelines, *wages in the automobile industry should increase by 3.2 percent per year*. If labor productivity in the auto industry increased by 4.2 percent per year, then, applying the results of a previous section, the labor cost of producing a unit

of output would decrease by 1 percent per year in the auto industry (since the 3.2 percent rate of increase of wages minus the 4.2 percent rate of increase of labor productivity equals −1 percent). Thus, the guidelines specified that *prices in the auto industry should decrease*, perhaps by about 1 percent per year.

The Council of Economic Advisers specified several situations where these general guidelines would have to be modified. In particular, if there was a shortage of labor in a particular industry or if an industry's wages were lower than those earned elsewhere by similar labor, higher wage increases (than specified in general) would be warranted. Or if an industry's profits were insufficient to attract needed infusions of capital, or if an industry's nonwage costs rose greatly, higher price increases than specified in general would be justified. However, the Council did not attempt to set forth detailed, quantitative provisions about the extent to which higher wages or prices would be warranted under these circumstances.

The Steel Price Increase of 1962: A Case Study

To conform to our definition of an incomes policy, the Kennedy-Johnson wage-price policy had to have an overall target, more detailed guides for wage and price decisions, and a mechanism to get firms and unions to observe these guides. The overall target was the stabilization of prices, and the more detailed guides for price and wage decisions were described in the previous section. But what about the mechanisms to induce acceptance of these guides? How did the government get industry and labor to go along?

The famous confrontation in 1962 between President Kennedy and the steel industry is an interesting case study of how pressure was brought to bear. Before the wage-price guidelines were issued, President Kennedy asked the major steel companies to avoid raising prices, and no price increases occurred. Then after the issuance of the

[8] 1962 *Annual Report of the Council of Economic Advisers*, Washington, D.C.: Government Printing Office, p. 189.

guidelines, he asked the steel union for restraint in the wage negotiations coming up in March 1962. Arthur Goldberg, Kennedy's Secretary of Labor, played an important role in persuading the union to accept a 2.5 percent increase in compensation, which was clearly noninflationary. At this point, government and the press felt quite optimistic about the apparent success of the President's program.

In the week following the wage agreement, however, the United States Steel Corporation increased all its prices by 3½ percent, and most of the major steel companies followed suit. The price increase was clearly a violation of the president's guidelines. It almost seemed as if the steel companies were trying to demonstrate once and for all that pricing was up to them, and them alone. Their action elicited a wrathful speech by the president publicly denouncing them. Roger M. Blough, chairman of the United States Steel Corporation, tried to rebut the president's arguments by claiming that U. S. Steel's profits were too low to attract new capital.

Three of the major steel producers—Armco, Inland, and Kaiser—did not follow U. S. Steel's lead in the day or so after its price increase. Government officials, noting this fact as well as prior public arguments against price increases by Inland officials, quickly began to apply pressure on these three producers to hold their prices constant. Government officials who knew executives of these firms called them and tried to persuade them to do so. The firms were also informed that government contracts would be directed to firms that held their prices constant. Apparently, the government's campaign succeeded. Inland and Kaiser made public statements that they would not raise prices. Faced with this fact, the other steel companies had no choice but to rescind the price increase.

This is an example of how presidential pressure can induce firms to go along with the guidelines. Often the Council of Economic Advisers tried to head off price increases before they were announced. In one way or another, sometimes from the companies themselves, the Council often learned of an impending price increase. The Council then asked the firms to meet to discuss the situation. In these meetings, the Council explained the importance of price stability and both parties discussed the proposed increase. It is difficult, of course, to measure the impact of such discussions, but, according to the Council, they sometimes resulted in the postponement or reduction of the planned price increases.

The Kennedy-Johnson Guidelines: Criticism and Experience

Soon after the announcement of the guidelines, critics began to point out problems in them. The criticism was of several types. First, some observers feared that the guidelines would result in inefficiency and waste. In a free-enterprise economy, we rely on price changes to direct resources into the most productive uses and to signal shortages or surpluses in various markets. If the guidelines were accepted by industry and labor, prices would not be free to perform this function. Of course, the guidelines specified that modifications of the general rules could be made in case of shortages, but critics of the guidelines felt that this escape hatch was too vague to be very useful.

Second, many observers were concerned about the reduction in economic freedom. Of course, the guidelines were presented in the hope that they would be observed voluntarily. But a time was sure to come when they would be in serious contradiction with the interests of firms and unions. In such a situation, what would happen if the firms or unions decided not to follow them? To the extent that the government applied pressure on the firms or unions, there would certainly be a reduction in economic freedom; and to some observers, it seemed likely that the next step might well be direct government controls. Moreover, the non-legislated character of the guidelines and the arbitrary choice of whom to pursue by the government raised important questions of a political nature.

Third, many people felt that the guidelines really

were not workable. In other words, even if the public would go along with them, in many cases they would be impossible to use, because accurate and relevant data on changes in labor productivity in particular industries were often unobtainable, and the situations where exceptions were allowed were so vaguely specified.

Fourth, some economists felt that reliance on the guidelines was dangerous because it focused attention on symptoms rather than causes, of inflation. In their view, inflation was largely the result of improper monetary and fiscal policies. In other words, the basic causes had to be laid at the government's own door. But by setting up guidelines, the government seemed to be saying that the fault lay with industry and labor. Thus, some critics felt that the guidelines tended to cloud the real issues and to let the government escape responsibility for its actions.

After the government's bout with the steel industry in 1962, there was no major public fight over wages and prices for a couple of years; and the government claimed that the guideposts were working well. To a considerable extent, this may have been because the economy still had considerable slack, as well as because of the noninflationary expectations of firms and individuals engendered by several years of relative price stability. By 1965, as labor markets tightened and prices rose in response to the Vietnam buildup (see Chapter 10), it became much more difficult to use the guidelines. Union leaders fought the guidelines tooth and nail, mainly because consumer prices were rising. In various important labor negotiations, unions demanded and got higher wage increases than the guidelines called for. For example, the airline machinists got a 4.9 percent increase in 1966. By 1968, the guidelines were dead: no one was paying any attention to them.

What effect did the guidelines have? Some people claim that they had no real effect at all, while others claim that they reduced cost-push inflation in the early 1960s by a considerable amount. Since it is difficult to separate the effects of the guidelines from the effects of other factors, there is considerable dispute over the question. Considering the level of unemployment in the early 1960s, wages increased less rapidly then than in earlier or later periods. Prices too increased less rapidly during that period—holding unemployment constant—than earlier or later. But whether these developments were due to the guidelines, or to noninflationary expectations or some other factor, is very hard to say.

Perhaps the most important reason why the guidelines broke down was that they could not deal with the strong demand-pull inflation of the late 1960s. Even the strongest defenders of the guidelines are quick to point out that they were no substitute for proper monetary and fiscal policy. *If fiscal or monetary policy is generating strong inflationary pressures, such as existed in the late 1960s, it is foolish to think that guidelines can save the situation.* Perhaps they can cut down on the rate of inflation for a while; but in the long run, the dike is sure to burst. If the guidelines are voluntary, as in this case, firms and unions will ignore them, and the government will find it difficult, if not impossible, to do anything about it. *Even price and wage controls are no adequate antidote to strong inflationary pressures generated by an overly expansive fiscal or monetary policy. Such controls may deal temporarily with the symptoms of inflation, but over the long haul these inflationary pressures will have an effect.*

Economic Stabilization: Where We Stand

Where do we stand in the struggle to achieve full employment without inflation? Clearly, we know much more than we did 40 years ago about how to use monetary and fiscal policies to attain this objective. Given the more advanced state of economics, it is very, very unlikely that a catastrophe like the Great Depression of the 1930s will occur again. But on the other hand, economists were overly optimistic in the mid-1960s when they talked about "fine-tuning" the economy. Our experience since then makes it clear that we have a long way to go before we understand the workings of the economy well enough to achieve continuous full employment without inflation. Equally important, we have seen that, even if the advice of its economists were always correct, the government might still pursue destabilizing policies, as it did in the late 1960s.

Pressed by events, government policy makers have turned to some form of incomes policy to supplement monetary and fiscal policy. Very little is known about the effects of various kinds of incomes policies, and what little we know is not very encouraging. As M.I.T.'s Robert Solow puts it, they "are not the sort of policy you would invent if you were inventing policies from scratch. They are the type of policy you back into as you search for ways to protect an imperfect economy from the worst consequences of its imperfect behavior."[9] Much more research is needed to illuminate the effects of various kinds of incomes policies, as well as the nature of cost-push inflation. In addition, we need more research to clarify the debate between the monetarists and the Keynesians on the effects of monetary and fiscal policy.

Finally, it must be reiterated that the game is well worth the candle. In recent years, it has become fashionable to say that our society's most pressing economic problems are not the attainment of full employment without inflation, but our urban problems, our pollution problems, our racial problems, and our poverty problems. Clearly, these are more visible, but it is hard to see how we can go about solving them with more than patchwork measures if we cannot achieve reasonably full employment with reasonably stable prices. In other words, economic stabilization, although it will not solve all our economic and social problems, is a necessary condition for solving many of them.

[9] R. Solow, "The Case Against the Case Against the Guideposts," reprinted in E. Mansfield, *Economics: Readings, Issues, and Cases,* New York: Norton, 1974. Also, see the papers by Friedman and Burns in the same volume.

Summary

There are many important differences between the policy recommendations of the monetarists and the Keynesians. The monetarists attack the Keynesian view that fiscal policy works as described in Chapter 10. According to the monetarists, whether the government runs a surplus or a deficit does not affect NNP, except insofar as the government finances the deficit or surplus in a way that alters the quantity of money. Also, many leading monetarists favor the establishment of a rule to govern monetary policy, an idea most Keynesians oppose. The Keynesians, on the other hand, attack the monetarist contention that the velocity of money is relatively stable, and argue that the interest rate is more important than the monetarists realize. In general, the Keynesians believe that the monetarists take too simple a view of the economy and that they tend to mix up cause and effect.

An important barrier to achieving economic stability through monetary and fiscal policy is cost-push inflation. The Phillips curve shows the relationship between the rate of increase of wages and the level of unemployment. As might be expected, the rate of increase of wages in any year seems to be inversely related to the level of unemployment. Given the Phillips curve, it is a simple matter to determine the relationship between the rate of inflation and the level of unemployment. If the Phillips curve remains fixed, it poses an awkward dilemma for policy makers. To the extent that they use fiscal and monetary policy to fight unemployment, they fuel the fires of inflation; to the extent that they use monetary and fiscal policy to fight inflation, they contribute to greater unemployment.

The only escape from this dilemma is, of course, to shift the Phillips curve, which is easier said than done. The Phillips curve shifts in response to increased education or training of the work force, increased mobility of workers, reduced discrimination, demographic changes, changes in union bargaining power, and changes in people's expectations. Also, it can shift, at least temporarily, in response to various government policies, such as wartime controls on wages and prices. Although a few economists favor such controls during peacetime, most do not agree. Such controls are likely to distort the allocation of resources, to be difficult and expensive to administer, and to run counter to our desire for economic freedom.

Another way to shift the Phillips curve is to attack market power, but although many economists favor some such action, it does not seem practically or politically feasible. In addition, many countries have experimented with various kinds of incomes policies. An incomes policy contains targets for wages and prices for the economy as a whole, more detailed guides for wage and price decisions in particular industries, and some mechanisms to get firms and unions to follow these guides. The Kennedy-Johnson guidelines were one form of incomes policy.

In the summer of 1971, President Nixon imposed a 3-month freeze on wages and prices. This was the first time the United States had resorted to direct wage and price controls in peacetime. After the freeze, he appointed a Pay Board to administer wage increases and a Price Commission to administer price increases. In the period after the freeze, inflation continued, but at a more modest rate than in previous years. This experiment with price and wage controls was an attempt to shift the Phillips curve. In January 1973, the Nixon administration dismantled most of this system of direct controls over prices and wages. But inflation accelerated at a rapid rate in the first half of 1973, causing the administration to impose another price freeze in June 1973. In August 1973, the administration began its so-called Phase IV program which said that price increases are not supposed to exceed cost increases.

CONCEPTS FOR REVIEW

Monetarists	Classical range	Wage-price spiral	Pay Board
Keynesians	Liquidity trap	Phillips curve	Cost of Living
IS curve	Demand-pull inflation	Incomes policy	Council
LM curve	Cost-push inflation	Price Commission	Price freeze

QUESTIONS FOR DISCUSSION AND REVIEW

1. According to Juanita Kreps, "It is the function of manpower programs to improve the terms of the tradeoff—that is, to shift the Phillips curve to the left." Suggest as many kinds of manpower programs as you can that might help in this regard. What sorts of manpower programs have been launched in this country?

2. According to Milton Friedman, "It is far better that inflation be open than that it be suppressed [by price guidelines]." Do you agree? Why or why not?

3. The Kennedy-Johnson guidelines for noninflationary price behavior called for price reduction if the industry's rate of productivity increase exceeded the overall rate. True or False?

4. The inflations arising from the Revolutionary, Civil, and Vietnam wars were largely   a. cost-push. b. demand-pull. c. liquidity-trap.

5. According to *Business Week*, monetarists believe "that the economy itself is inherently stable, that as long as interest rates are kept relatively stable the demand for money will remain stable. . . ." Do you agree? Suggest ways to test this proposition.

PART FIVE

Economic Growth and the Environment

CHAPTER 16

Economic Growth

Until fairly recently in human history, poverty was the rule, not the exception. As Sir Kenneth Clark puts it in his famous lectures on *Civilization*:

> Poverty, hunger, plagues, disease: they were the background of history right up to the end of the nineteenth century, and most people regarded them as inevitable—like bad weather. Nobody thought they could be cured: St. Francis wanted to sanctify poverty, not abolish it. The old Poor Laws were not designed to abolish poverty but to prevent the poor from becoming a nuisance. All that was required was an occasional act of charity.[1]

Clearly, the human condition has changed considerably during the past century, at least in the industrialized nations of the world. Rising living standards have brought a decline in poverty, though by no means its disappearance. How has this increase in per capita output been achieved?

[1] K. Clark, *Civilization*, New York: Harper & Row, 1970.

325

This question has fascinated economists for a long time. Although we still are far from completely understanding the process of economic growth, our knowledge has increased considerably through the efforts of economic researchers, here and abroad. In this chapter, we discuss the process of economic growth in industrialized countries. A discussion of economic growth in less developed countries will be presented in Chapter 21.

What Is Economic Growth?

There are two common measures of the rate of economic growth. The first is the rate of growth of a nation's real gross national product (or net national product),[2] which tells us how rapidly the economy's total real output of goods and services is increasing. The second is the rate of growth of *per capita* real gross national product (or net national product), which is a better measure of the rate of increase of a nation's standard of living. We shall use the second measure unless we state otherwise.

Two aspects of the rate of growth of per capita real gross national product should be noted from the start. First, *this measure is only a very crude approximation to the rate of increase of economic welfare*. For one thing, gross national product does not include one good that people prize most highly —leisure. For another, gross national product does not value at all accurately new products and improvements in the quality of goods and services, and does not allow properly either for noneconomic changes in the quality of life, nor for the costs of environmental pollution. Nor does gross national product take account of how the available output is distributed. Clearly, it makes a difference whether the bulk of the population gets a reasonable share of the output, or whether it goes largely to a favored few.

[2] Either net national product or gross national product will do. As pointed out in Chapter 8, NNP has certain conceptual advantages, but GNP is more frequently used. It makes little difference since they do not differ by much. We use gross national product in this chapter, because data on GNP are more easily available.

favored few.

Second, *small differences in the annual rate of economic growth can make very substantial differences in living standards a few decades hence.* For example, per capita GNP in the United States was about $4,800 in 1970. If it grows at 2 percent per year, it will be about $8,700 (1970 dollars) in the year 2000, whereas if it grows at 3 percent per year, it will be about $11,600 (1970 dollars) in the year 2000. Thus an increase of 1 percentage point in the growth rate means a $2,900—or 30 percent—increase in per capita GNP in the year 2000. Even an increase of ¼ of 1 percentage point can make a considerable difference. If the growth rate increases from 1¾ percent to 2 percent per year, per capita GNP in the year 2000 will increase from $8,100 to $8,700. Of course, this is no more than simple arithmetic, but that doesn't make it any less important.

Economic Growth as a Policy Objective

Following World War II, governments throughout the world became much more involved in trying to stimulate economic growth. In the United States, the government was not much inclined to influence the growth rate before the war. Of course, the government did many things that had some effect on the rate of economic growth, and in a general sort of way was interested in promoting economic growth. But it was normally taken for granted that, left to its own devices, our economy would manage to grow at more or less the proper rate. In the late 1950s and early 1960s, the climate of opinion began to change. To a considerable extent, this was because the U.S. rate of economic growth during the 1950s was rather low compared to that of other industrialized nations. From 1950 to 1959, per capita GNP grew by about 2 percent per year in the United States, whereas it grew by about 6 percent in Japan, 5 percent in Italy and Germany, 4 percent in France, and 3 percent in the

Netherlands, Norway, and Sweden. Moreover, our growth rate seemed to be less than that of the Soviet Union, the leading economic power in the Communist world.

During the late 1950s and early 1960s, many American economists and politicians drew attention to these facts, and called for an explicit public policy designed to increase our growth rate. In response, President Kennedy set as a target the attainment of a 4½ percent annual increase in total output during the 1960s. Three principal arguments were given at that time for government stimulation of the rate of economic growth. First, it was argued that we had to increase our rate of economic growth to stay ahead of the Communist countries, the Soviet Union in particular. Economic growth was regarded as important for national defense and national prestige. In 1958, a report by the Rockefeller Brothers Fund concluded that growth was the most feasible way to provide for the defense outlays it envisioned as necessary in the future.

Second, it was argued that we should increase our rate of economic growth in order to increase public expenditures for schools, urban renewal, transportation, hospitals, and other such services. As we saw in Chapter 6, some observers, led by John Kenneth Galbraith, believe that there is serious underinvestment in the public sector. Since it is very difficult politically to increase the percentage of GNP devoted to such services, it was felt that the only realistic way to remedy the situation was to increase the GNP. Then the absolute amount spent on the public sector could increase even if its percentage of GNP remained much the same.

Third, it was argued that we should increase our rate of economic growth in order to impress the neutral nations, many of which are relatively poor, with the benefits of our type of society. The emphasis here, as in the first argument, was on economic competition with the Communist world. According to many observers, the neutral countries were watching the growth rates of the Communist and capitalist countries, and the results

would help decide which way these countries jumped. As the Council of Economic Advisers put it in 1962, "The less developed nations . . . need a further demonstration of the ability of a free economy to grow."[3]

Not all economists and policy makers agree that the government should alter the growth rate. Particularly in the past few years, there has been a growing feeling among economists (as well as the public at large) that economic growth should not be force-fed. Those who feel this way fall into two broad groups. One school of economists—including people like the University of Rochester's W. Allen Wallis, a prominent adviser to Presidents Nixon and Eisenhower—believes that the proper rate of economic growth is that which would emerge from private decisions. In their view, there is no reason to "force" growth on the economy, since there is no real possibility that the USSR will catch up with us soon, and the "unmet social needs" argument is little more than a slogan.

Another group of economists—led by E. J. Mishan of the London School of Economics—feels that economic growth, as usually measured, is a mirage. In their view, it has resulted in the degradation of the environment, the congestion and noise of our cities, the ugliness of some of the countryside, and the dullness of much of our work. They argue that the added production is not really of much value to society, and that people must be convinced by producers (through advertising and other sales techniques) that they want it. This viewpoint has appealed to many young people in recent years. However, it should be noted that if we are to reduce poverty, clean up the environment, and improve the quality of life, we shall need productive capacity, and economic growth is an important way to get it.

Whether or not the government should increase the rate of economic growth is, of course, a political decision; and your opinion of such a government policy will depend on many things, including

[3] 1962 *Annual Report of the Council of Economic Advisers*, Washington, D.C.: Government Printing Office, p. 110.

your attitude toward present sacrifice for future material gain. As we shall see in subsequent sections, *a more rapid rate of growth can often be achieved only if consumers are willing to give up some consumption now so that they and their children can have more goods and services in the future.* To the extent that you believe that private decisions place too little weight on the future and too much weight on the present, you may be inclined to support a government policy designed to increase the growth rate. Otherwise you may not favor such a policy. In the next chapter, we shall discuss the pros and cons of economic growth in much more detail. Here we are concerned with its determinants.

Economic Growth, the Product Transformation Curve, and the Aggregate Production Function

To represent the process of economic growth, it is convenient to use the product transformation curve which, as you will recall from Chapter 3, shows all efficient combinations of output an economy can produce. For example, suppose that a society produces only two goods, food and tractors. Then if this society has at its disposal a fixed amount of resources and if technology is fixed, the product transformation curve (like the one in Figure 16.1) shows the maximum quantity of food that can be

Figure 16.1
Product Transformation Curve

The product transformation curve shows all efficient combinations of output an economy can produce.

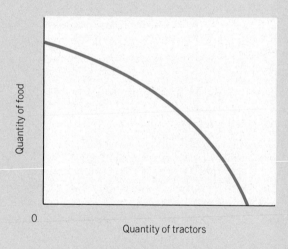

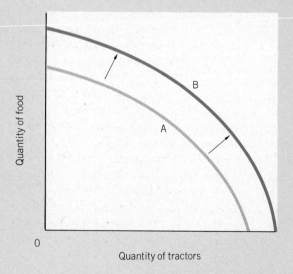

Figure 16.2 Outward Shift of Product Transformation Curve

A nation's potential output increases when its product transformation curve shifts outward, for example, from position *A* to position *B*.

produced, given each amount of tractors produced.

Clearly, *a nation's potential output increases when its product transformation curve shifts outward,* for example, from position *A* to position *B* in Figure 16.2. This happens because the society can produce (and consume) more of one good without having to produce (and consume) less of the other good. Thus, its productive capacity must be greater. If the product transformation curve shifts outward, if the economy is efficient, and if population remains constant, per capita GNP increases and economic growth occurs. Moreover, the faster the product transformation curve shifts outward, the greater the rate of economic growth.

In addition, economic growth can occur if unemployment or inefficiency is reduced. If a nation allows some of its resources to be unemployed or under-utilized because of an insufficiency of desired spending, this will cause the economy to operate at a point *inside* the product transformation curve rather than *on* the curve. The same thing will happen if a nation allocates its resources inefficiently. Clearly, a nation can achieve some economic growth by getting closer to the product transformation curve through a reduction in unemployment or inefficiency.

A nation's potential output is directly related to the amount of resources it possesses and the extent to which they are used. These resources, or inputs, are of various kinds, including labor, capital, and land. The relationship between the amount used of each of these inputs and the resulting amount of potential output is often called the **aggregate production function.** It is analogous to the production function discussed in Chapter 7, which is the relationship between a firm's inputs and its output. However, the aggregate production function pertains to the entire economy, not a single firm.

Given that a nation's potential output depends on the amount of labor, capital, and land it uses, then the rate of growth of a nation's potential output must depend, in part at least, on the changes that occur in the amount of each of these inputs that is used. For example, if a nation invests heavily in additional capital, we would expect this to result in a substantial increase in potential output. Thus, *a nation's rate of economic growth depends on the extent of the changes in the amounts of the various inputs used.* In addition, *a nation's rate of economic growth depends on the rate of technological change.* The aggregate production function is constructed on the assumption that technology is fixed. Changes in technology result in shifts in the production function, since more output is obtained from a given amount of resources.

The Law of Diminishing Marginal Returns

If a nation's land, labor, and capital increase, one would certainly expect its output to increase as well. But suppose the nation cannot increase the amount used of all of its resources at the same rate. Instead, suppose it can increase the quantity of one resource, say labor, while the amount of other resources, like land, is held constant. In this situation, what will be the effect on output of more and more increases in the amount of the resource that can be augmented? This is an important question, which occurs both in the present context and in the study of the production processes of the business firm.

To help answer it, economists have formulated the famous law of *diminishing marginal returns,* which states that, *if more and more of a resource is used, the quantities of other resources being held constant, the resulting increments of output will decrease after some point has been reached.* Note several important things about this law. First, at least one resource must be fixed in quantity. The law of diminishing marginal returns does not apply to cases where there is a proportional increase in all resources. Second, technology is assumed to be fixed. Third, the law of diminishing marginal returns is an empirical generalization that seems to hold in the real world, not a deduction from physical or biological laws.

Table 16.1

The Law of Diminishing Marginal Returns

(1) Manhours of labor (millions)	(2) Bushels of corn (millions)	(3) Marginal product of labor (bushels per manhour)	(4) Average product of labor (bushels per manhour)
1	1.5		1.50
		2.0	
2	3.5		1.75
		2.5	
3	6.0		2.00
		3.0	
4	9.0		2.25
		2.0	
5	11.0		2.20
		2.0	
6	13.0		2.17
		1.0	
7	14.0		2.00
		0.0	
8	14.0		1.75
9	13.0		

To illustrate the workings of this law, consider Table 16.1, which shows the total output—or GNP —of a simple agricultural society under a set of alternative assumptions concerning the number of manhours of labor used. For simplicity, we assume that this society produces only one product, corn, so that total output can be measured in bushels of corn. Also, we assume that the amount of land and capital that can be used is fixed in quantity. Column 1 in the table shows various alternative numbers of manhours of labor that can be used with this fixed amount of land and capital. Column 2 shows the total output in each case.

Column 3 shows the additional output resulting from the addition of an extra manhour of labor; this is called the **marginal product of labor.** For example, if the quantity of labor is between 2 million manhours and 3 million manhours, the marginal product of labor is 2.5 bushels per manhour of labor, because each extra manhour of labor results in an extra 2.5 bushels of output.

In Table 16.1, the marginal product of labor increases as more and more labor is used, but only up to a point: beyond 4 million manhours of labor, the marginal product of labor goes down as more and more labor is used. Specifically, the marginal product of labor reaches a maximum of 3.0 bushels per manhour when between 3 and 4 million manhours of labor are used. Then it falls to 2.0 bushels per manhour when between 4 and 5 million manhours of labor are used, remains at 2.0 bushels per manhour when between 5 and 6 million manhours of labor are used, and falls once again to 1.0 bushel per manhour when between 6 and 7 million manhours of labor are used.

Thus, as predicted by the law of diminishing marginal returns, the marginal product of labor eventually declines. Moreover, as shown in Column 4 of Table 16.1, the **average product** of labor, which is defined as total output per manhour, also falls beyond some point as more and more labor is used with a fixed amount of other resources. This too stems from the law of diminishing marginal returns.

It is easy to see why the law of diminishing marginal returns must be true. For example, imagine what would happen in the simple economy of Table 16.1 if more and more labor were applied to a fixed amount of land. Beyond a point, as more and more labor is used, the extra labor has to be devoted to less and less important tasks, and it is increasingly difficult to prevent the workers from getting in one another's way. For such reasons, one certainly would expect that, beyond some point, extra amounts of labor would result in smaller and smaller increments of output. This is true as well as sensible: there is a lot of evidence for the validity of the law of diminishing marginal returns.

Thomas Malthus and Population Growth

A nation's rate of economic growth depends on, among other things, how much the quantities of inputs of various kinds increases. To illuminate the nature of the growth process, we discuss the effect on the rate of economic growth of increasing each kind of input, holding the others constant. We begin by looking at the effects of changes in the quantity of labor. Economists have devoted a great deal of attention to the effects of population growth on the rate of economic growth. The classic work was done by Thomas Malthus (1776–1834), a British parson who devoted his life to academic research. The first professional economist, he taught at a college established by the East India Company to train its administrators—and was called "Pop" by his students behind his back. Whether "Pop" stood for population or not, Malthus's fame is based on his theories of population growth.

Malthus believed that the population tends to grow at a geometric rate. In his *Essay on Population,* published in 1798, he pointed out the implications of such a constant rate of growth:

If any person will take the trouble to make the calculation, he will see that if the necessities of life could be obtained without limit, and the number of people could be doubled every twenty-five years, the population which might have been produced from a single pair since the Christian era, would have been sufficient, not only to fill the earth quite full of people, so that four should stand in every

square yard, but to fill all the planets of our solar system in the same way, and not only them but all the planets revolving around the stars which are visible to the naked eye, supposing each of them . . . to have as many planets belong to it as our sun has.[4]

In contrast to the human population, which tends to increase at a geometric rate,[5] the supply of land can increase slowly if at all. And land, particularly in Malthus's time, was the source of food. Consequently, it seemed to Malthus that the human population was in danger of outrunning its food supply: "Taking the whole earth," he wrote, ". . . and supposing the present population to be equal to a thousand millions, the human species would increase as the numbers 1, 2, 4, 8, 16, 32, 64, 128, 256, and subsistence as 1, 2, 3, 4, 5, 6, 7, 8, 9. In two centuries, the population would be to the means of subsistence as 256 to 9; in three centuries as 4096 to 13, and in two thousand years the difference would be incalculable."[6]

Certainly, Malthus's view of humanity's prospects was bleak, as he himself acknowledged (in a masterpiece of British understatement) when he wrote that "the view has a melancholy hue." Gone is the optimism of Adam Smith: according to Malthus, the prospects for economic progress are very limited. Given the inexorable increase in human numbers, the standard of living will be kept at the minimum level required to keep body and soul together. If it exceeds this level, the population will increase, driving the standard of living back down. On the other hand, if the standard of living is less than this level, the population

---

[4] T. Malthus, *Essay on Population,* as quoted by R. Heilbroner, *The Worldly Philosophers,* New York: Simon and Schuster, 1961, p. 71. For those who would like to read more concerning the history of economic thought, Heilbroner's book is highly recommended.

[5] Of course, it does not matter to Malthus's argument whether the population doubles every 25 years or every 40 years: the important thing is that it increases at a geometric rate.

[6] T. Malthus, "The Principle of Population Growth," as reprinted in E. Mansfield, *Economics: Readings, Issues, and Cases,* New York: Norton, 1974.

Thomas Malthus
on Population

Throughout the animal and vegetable kingdoms Nature has scattered the seeds of life abroad with the most profuse and liberal hand; but has been comparatively sparing in the room and the nourishment necessary to rear them.... Necessity, that imperious, all-pervading law of nature, restrains them within the prescribed bounds. The race of plants and the race of animals shrink under this great restrictive law; and man cannot by any efforts of reason escape from it.

In plants and irrational animals, the view of the subject is simple.... The effects of this check on man are more complicated.

It may safely be pronounced that population, when unchecked, goes on doubling itself every twenty-five years, or increases in a geometrical ratio. The rate according to which the productions of the earth may be supposed to increase, will not be so easy to determine. Of this, however, we may be perfectly certain, that the ratio of their increase in a limited territory must be of a totally different nature from the ratio of the increase of population. A thousand millions are just as easily doubled every twenty-five years by the power of population as a thousand. But the food to support the increase from the greater number will by no means be obtained with the same facility. Man is necessarily confined in room. When acre has been added to acre til all the fertile land is occupied, the yearly increase of food must depend upon the melioration of the land already in possession. This is a fund, which, from the nature of all soils, instead of increasing, must be gradually diminishing. But population, could it be supplied with food, would go on with unexhausted vigor; and the increase of one period would furnish the power of a greater increase the next, and this without any limit....

It may be fairly pronounced, therefore, that considering the present average state of the earth, the means of subsistence, under circumstances the most favorable to human industry, could not possibly be made to increase faster than in an arithmetical ratio.... The ultimate check to population appears then to be a want of food, arising necessarily from the different ratios according to which population and food increase.

Thomas Malthus, *An Essay on the Principle of Population,* London: Reeves and Turner, 1888, pp. 4–6. Originally published in 1798.

**Figure 16.3
Diminishing Marginal Returns
and the Effect of Population
Growth**

According to Malthus, the labor
force will tend to *OP* because, if
output per worker exceeds *OA*,
population will increase, and if
output per worker is less than
OA, starvation will reduce the
population.

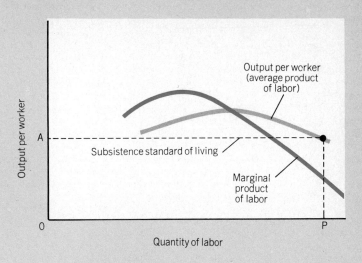

will decline because of starvation. Certainly, the long-term prospects were anything but bright. Thomas Carlyle, the famous historian and essayist, called economics "the dismal science." To a considerable extent, economics acquired this bad name through the efforts of Parson Malthus.

Malthus's theory can be interpreted in terms of the law of diminishing marginal returns. Living in what was still largely an agricultural society, he emphasized the role of land and labor as resources, and assumed a relatively fixed level of technology. Since land is fixed, increases in labor—due to population growth—will eventually cause the marginal product of labor to get smaller and smaller because of the law of diminishing marginal returns. In other words, because of this law, the marginal product of labor will behave as shown in Figure 16.3, with the result that continued growth of the labor force will ultimately bring economic decline —that is, a reduction in output per worker. This happens because as the marginal product of labor falls with increases in the labor force, the average product of labor will eventually fall as well—and the average product of labor is another name for output per worker.

Of course, Malthus recognized that various devices could keep the population down—war, fam-

ine, birth control measures, among others. In fact, he tried to describe and evaluate the importance of various checks on population growth. For example, suppose that population tends to grow to the point where output per worker is at a subsistence level—just sufficient to keep body and soul together. If this is the case, and if the subsistence level of output per worker is *OA*, then the labor force will tend to equal *OP* in Figure 16.3. Why? Because, as noted above, Malthus believed that if the standard of living rises appreciably above *OA*, population will increase, thus forcing it back toward *OA*. On the other hand, if the standard of living falls below *OA*, some of the population will starve, thus pushing it back toward *OA*.

Effects of Population Growth

Was Malthus right? Among the less developed nations of the world, his analysis seems very relevant today. During the past 30 years, the population of the less developed nations has grown very rapidly, in part because of the decrease in death rates attributable to the transfer of medical advances from the industrialized countries to the less developed coun-

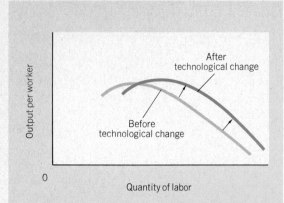

Figure 16.4
Shift over Time in the Marginal Product of Labor

Technological change has shifted the marginal-product-of-labor curve to the right.

tries. Between 1940 and 1970, the total population of Asia, Africa, and Oceania almost doubled. There has been a tendency for growing populations to push hard against food supplies in some of the countries of Africa, Latin America, and Asia; and the Malthusian model can explain important elements of the situation.

However Malthus's theory seems far less relevant or correct for the industrialized countries. In contrast to his model, population has not increased to the point where the standard of living has been pushed down to the subsistence level. On the contrary, the standard of living has increased dramatically in all of the industrialized nations. The most important mistake Malthus made was to underestimate the extent and importance of technological change. Instead of remaining fixed, the marginal-product-of-labor curve in Figure 16.3 moved gradually to the right, as new methods and new products increased the efficiency of agriculture. In other words, the situation was as shown in Figure 16.4. Thus, as population increased, the marginal product of labor did not go down. Instead, technological

change prevented the productivity of extra agricultural workers from falling.

Among the industralized nations, have countries with relatively high rates of growth of population had relatively low—or relatively high—rates of economic growth? In general, there seems to be little or no relationship between a nation's rate of population increase and its rate of economic growth. For example, Figure 16.5 plots the rate of population increase against the rate of growth of output per manyear in 11 industrialized nations between 1913 and 1959. The results suggest that there is little or no relation between them; and the relationship that exists appears to be direct rather than inverse.

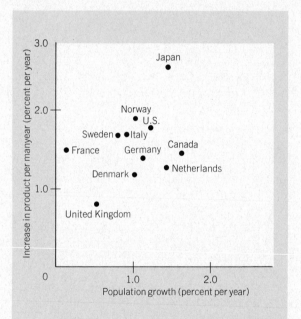

Figure 16.5
Relationship between Population Growth and Increases in National Product per Manyear, 11 Industrialized Nations, 1913–59

In industrialized nations, there is little or no relationship between a nation's rate of population growth and its rate of economic growth.

David Ricardo: Trade and Economic Growth

A contemporary and good friend of Malthus who also contributed to the theory of economic growth was David Ricardo (1772–1823). Of all the titans of economics, he is probably least known to the general public. Smith, Malthus, Marx, and Keynes are frequently encountered names. Ricardo is not, although he made many brilliant contributions to economic thought. An extremely successful stockbroker who retired at the age of 42 with a very large fortune, he devoted much of his time to highly theoretical analyses of the economic system and its workings. In contrast to Malthus, who was reviled for his pessimistic doctrines, Ricardo and his writings were widely admired in his own time. He was elected to the House of Commons and was highly respected there.

Ricardo was concerned in much of his work with the distribution of income. Unlike Adam Smith, who paid much less attention to the conflict among classes, Ricardo emphasized the struggle between the industrialists—a relatively new and rising class in his time—and the landowners —the old aristocracy that resisted the rise of the industrial class. This clash was reflected in the struggle in Britain around 1800 over the so-called Corn Laws ("corn" being a general term covering all types of grain). Because of the increase in population, the demand for grain increased in Britain, causing the price of grain to rise greatly. This meant higher profits for the landowners. But the industrialists complained bitterly about the increase in the price of food, because higher food prices meant that they had to pay higher wages. As the price of grain increased, merchants began to import cheap grain from abroad. But the landowners, who dominated Parliament, passed legislation—the Corn Laws—to keep cheap grain out of Britain. In effect, the Corn Laws imposed a high tariff or duty on grain.

According to Ricardo's analysis, the landlords were bound to capture most of the benefits of economic progress, unless their control of the price of grain could be weakened. As national output increased and population expanded, poorer and poorer land had to be brought under cultivation to produce the extra food. As the cost of producing grain increased, its price would increase too—and so would the rents of the landlords. The workers and the industrialists, on the other hand, would benefit little, if at all. As the price of grain increased, the workers would have to get higher wages—but only high enough to keep them at a subsistence level (since Ricardo agreed entirely with his friend Malthus on the population issue). Thus, the workers would be no better off; and neither would the industrialists, who would wind up with lower profits because of the increase in wage rates.

Ricardo felt that the Corn Laws should be repealed and that free trade in grain should be permitted. In a beautiful piece of theoretical analysis that is still reasonably fresh and convincing 150 years after its publication, he laid out the basic principles of international trade and pointed out the benefits to all countries that can be derived by specialization and free trade. For example, suppose that England is relatively more efficient at producing textiles, and France is relatively more efficient at producing wine. Then, on the basis of Ricardo's analysis, it can be shown that each country is likely to be better off by specializing in the product it is more efficient at producing—textiles in England, wine in France—and trading this product for the one the other country specializes in producing. In Chapter 19, we shall discuss this argument in considerable detail; it is a very important part of economics.

Ricardo's View of Capital Formation

Let's turn now to the effect on economic growth of increases in physical capital, holding other inputs and technology fixed. Ricardo constructed some interesting theories concerning the effects of capi-

Figure 16.6
Marginal Product of Capital

This curve shows the marginal product of capital, under various assumptions concerning the total amount of capital. For example, if there is $100 billion of capital, the marginal product of capital is $A, whereas if there is $150 billion of capital, the marginal product of capital is $B.

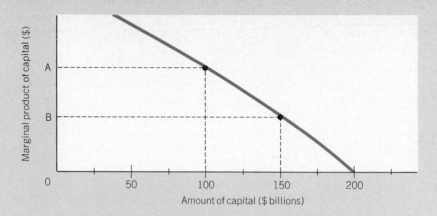

tal formation—i.e., investment in plant and equipment—on economic growth. Other things held constant, a nation's output depends on the amount of plant and equipment that it has and operates. Moreover, one can draw a curve showing the marginal product of capital—the extra output that would result from an extra dollar's worth of capital—under various assumptions about the total amount of capital in existence. This curve will slope downward to the right, as shown in Figure 16.6, because of the law of diminishing marginal returns. As more and more capital is accumulated, its marginal product eventually must decrease. For example, if $100 billion is the total investment in plant and equipment (or total capital), the extra output to be derived from an extra dollar of investment is worth $A; whereas if the total investment is increased to $150 billion, the economy must resort to less productive investments, and the extra output to be derived from an extra dollar of investment is only worth $B.

The curve in Figure 16.6 leads to the conclusion that investment in plant and equipment, although it will increase the growth rate up to some point, will eventually be unable to increase it further. As more and more is invested in new plant and equipment, less and less productive projects must be undertaken. Moreover, when all the productive projects have been carried out, further investment in plant and equipment will be useless. At this

point—$200 billion of total capital in Figure 16.6 —further investment in plant and equipment will not increase output at all.

This kind of analysis led Ricardo to the pessimistic conclusion that the economy would experience decreases in the profitability of investment in plant and equipment, and eventual termination of economic growth. Also, he expected increases in the ratio of capital to output, because he expected increases in the total amount of capital to be accompanied by decreases in the marginal product of capital. To illustrate this, suppose that an economy's output equals $1 trillion and its total capital is $3 trillion. Suppose too that $100 billion of extra capital will result in $30 billion in extra output, another $100 billion of extra capital will result in $20 billion in extra output, and still another $100 billion in extra capital will result in $10 billion in extra output. Then the capital-output ratio will be $(3,000 + 100)/(1,000 + 30)$ if $100 billion is invested, $(3,000 + 200)/(1,000 + 50)$ if $200 billion is invested, and $(3,000 + 300)/(1,000 + 60)$ if $300 billion is invested. Since the marginal product of capital is decreasing, the capital-output ratio is increasing—from 3 to 3.01 to 3.05 to 3.11.

Was Ricardo right? Have we experienced increases in the capital-output ratio, decreases in the profitability of investment in plant and equipment, and eventual termination of economic growth? Clearly, no. Ricardo, like Malthus, was led astray by underestimating the extent and impact of future changes in technology. Suppose that, because of the development of major new products and processes, lots of new opportunities for profitable investment arise. Obviously, the effect on the curve in Figure 16.6 is to shift it to the right, because there are more investment opportunities than before above a certain level of productivity. But if this curve shifts to the right, as shown in Figure 16.7, we may be able to avoid Ricardo's pessimistic conclusions.

To see how this can occur, note that, if XX' in Figure 16.7 is the relevant curve in a particular year and if $100 billion is the total amount of capital, an extra dollar of investment in plant and equipment would have a marginal product of $C. A decade later, if YY' is the relevant curve and if the total amount of capital has grown to $150 billion, the marginal product of an extra dollar of investment in plant and equipment is still $C. Thus, there is no reduction in the productivity of investment opportunities despite the 50 percent increase in the total amount of capital. Because of technological change and other factors, productive

and profitable new investment opportunities are opened up as fast as old ones are invested in.

The history of the United States is quite consistent with this sort of shift in investment opportunities over time. Even though we have poured an enormous amount of money into new plant and equipment, we have not exhausted or reduced the productivity or profitability of investment opportunities. The rate of return on investment in new plant and equipment has not fallen. Instead, it has fluctuated around a fairly constant level during the past 70 years. Moreover, the capital-output ratio has remained surprisingly constant. It has not increased.

Effects of Capital Formation

To see more clearly the role of investment in the process of economic growth, let's extend the Keynesian model we discussed in Chapter 9. Suppose we ignore the government and consider only the private sector of the economy. Suppose that the full-employment, noninflationary NNP this year

**Figure 16.7
Effects of Technological
Change on the Marginal
Product of Capital**

Technological change has shifted
the marginal-product-of-capital
curve to the right.

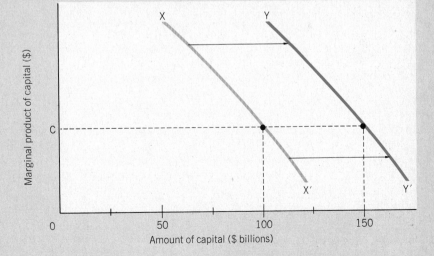

is $1,000 billion, and that the consumption function is such that consumption expenditure is $900 billion if NNP is $1,000 billion. If desired investment this year is $100 billion, with the result that NNP is in fact $1,000 billion, *next year's full-employment NNP will increase because this year's investment will increase the nation's productive capacity.* In other words, this year's investment increases next year's full-employment NNP. The amount of the increase in full-employment NNP depends on the **capital-output ratio,** which is the number of dollars of extra investment required to produce an extra dollar of output. For example, if the capital-output ratio is 2, $2 of investment is required to increase full-employment NNP by $1.

Let's look more closely at the effect of investment on full-employment NNP. If the capital-output ratio is 2, full-employment NNP will increase by $50 billion as a consequence of the $100 billion of investment: thus, full-employment NNP next year is $1,050 billion. On the other hand, suppose that this year's investment is $200 billion rather than $100 billion, and that the consumption function is such that consumption expenditure is $800 billion rather than $900 billion if NNP is $1,000 billion. What will full-employment NNP be next year? If the capital-output ratio is 2, it will be $1,100 billion. Thus, the full-employment NNP will be larger if investment is $200 billion than if it is $100 billion.

In general, the greater the percent of NNP that the society devotes to investment this year, the greater will be the increase in its full-employment NNP. Thus, *so long as the economy sustains noninflationary full employment and the capital-output ratio remains constant, the rate of growth of national output will be directly related to the percent of NNP devoted to investment.*[7]

[7] It can be shown that the rate of growth of NNP equals s/b, where s is the proportion of NNP that is saved (and invested), and b is the capital-output ratio, assuming that both s and b are constant and that full employment is maintained. For example, if b is 2 and $s = .10$, NNP will grow at 5 percent per year, since $.10/2 = .05$. This result is part of the so-called Harrod-Domar growth model developed by Sir Roy Harrod of Oxford and Evsey Domar of M.I.T. Although useful, this result must be used with caution since it is based on highly simplified assumptions.

Table 16.2

Rate of Growth of Output per Man and Percent of GNP Invested in Physical Capital, 1955–64

Nation	Rate of growth of output per man	Percent of GNP invested
Annual Average		
France	4.7%	15.7%
Germany	4.4	20.1
Italy	5.7	16.9
Japan	8.8	30.2
United Kingdom	2.6	13.7
United States	1.9	13.9

Source: Angus Maddison, *Lloyds Bank Review,* January 1966 and E. Phelps, *The Goal of Economic Growth,* revised edition, Norton, 1969.

Certainly, this result seems sensible enough. If a country wants to increase its growth rate, it should produce more blast furnaces, machine tools, and plows, and less cosmetics, household furniture, and sports cars. But all this is theory. What do the facts suggest? Table 16.2 shows the rate of investment and the growth rate in the six major industrialized nations of the non-Communist world in 1955–64. The growth rate was highest in Japan, so was the investment rate. The growth rates were lowest in the United States and the United Kingdom, and so were the investment rates. Of course, this does not prove that there is any simple cause-and-effect relationship between the investment rate and the growth rate, but it certainly is compatible with the view that investment influences growth.

Turning to the historical record of the United States, between 1929 and 1947 the amount of U.S. plant and equipment increased at about the same rate as the labor force. On the other hand, between 1947 and 1965, the amount of U.S. plant and equipment increased much more rapidly than the labor force. These facts would lead one to expect that the rate of economic growth would be more rapid in the latter period; and, in keeping with the theory, this turns out to be true. Again, one must be cautious about interpreting such comparisons. Lots of other things besides the investment rate were different in 1947–65 than in 1929–47, and these other things, not the investment rate, may have been responsible for the difference in growth rates. However, it seems likely that the difference in investment rates was at least partially responsible.

The Role of Human Capital

A nation's rate of economic growth is influenced by the rate at which it invests in human capital as well as physical capital. It may seem odd to speak of *human* capital, but every society builds up a certain amount of human capital through investments in formal education, on-the-job training, and health programs. You often hear people talk about investing in their children's future by putting them through college. For the economy as a whole, the expenditure on education and public health can also be viewed—at least partly—as an investment, because consumption is sacrificed in the present in order to make possible a higher level of per capita output in the future.

The United States invests in human capital on a massive scale. For example, in 1960 expenditures for schools at all levels of education were about $25 billion, or about 5 percent of our gross national product. Moreover, our total investment in the education of the population—the "stock" of educational capital—has grown much more rapidly than has the stock of plant and equipment. For example, whereas the stock of physical capital was about 4 times as big in 1956 as in 1900, the stock of educational capital was about 8 times as big. These enormous and rapidly growing investments in human capital have unquestionably increased the productivity, versatility, and adaptability of our labor force. They have certainly made a

major contribution to economic growth.

Income tends to rise with a person's education. Using this relationship to measure the influence of education on a person's productivity, some economists, notably the University of Chicago's Theodore Schultz and Gary Becker, have tried to estimate the profitability, both to society and to the person, of an investment in various levels of education. For example, Becker has tried to estimate the rate of return from a person's investment in a college education. According to his estimates, the typical urban white male in 1950 received about a 10 percent return (after taxes) on his investment in tuition, room, books, and other college expenses (including the earnings he gave up by being in college rather than at work). This was a relatively high return—much higher, for example, than if the student (or his family) simply put the equivalent amount of money in a savings bank or in government bonds.

The Role of Technological Change

A nation's rate of economic growth depends on the rate of technological change, as well as on the extent to which quantities of inputs of various kinds increase. Indeed, the rate of technological change is perhaps the most important single determinant of a nation's rate of economic growth. Recall from Chapter 3 that technology is knowledge concerning the industrial and agricultural arts. Thus, technological change often takes the form of new methods of producing existing products, new designs that make it possible to produce goods with important new characteristics, and new techniques of organization, marketing, and management. Two examples of technological change are new ways of producing power (for example, atomic energy) and new fibers (for example, nylon or dacron).

We have already seen that technological change can shift the curves in both Figure 16.4 and 16.7, thus warding off the law of diminishing marginal returns. But note that new knowledge by itself has little impact. *Unless knowledge is applied, it has little effect on the rate of economic growth.* A change in technology, when applied for the first time, is called an **innovation,** and the firm that first applies it is called an **innovator.** Innovation is a key stage in the process leading to the full evaluation and utilization of a new process or product. The innovator must be willing to take the risks involved in introducing a new and untried process, good, or service; and in many cases, these risks are high. Once a change in technology has been applied for the first time, the **diffusion process**—the process by which the use of the innovation spreads from firm to firm and from use to use—begins. How rapidly an innovation spreads depends heavily on its economic advantages over older methods or products. The more profitable the use of the innovation is, the more rapidly it will spread.

Joseph Schumpeter, Harvard's distinguished economist and social theorist, stressed the important role played by the innovator in the process of economic growth. In Schumpeter's view, the innovator is the mainspring of economic progress, the man with the foresight to see how new things can be brought into being and the courage and resourcefulness to surmount the obstacles to change. For his trouble, the innovator receives profit; but this profit eventually is whittled down by competitors who imitate the innovator. The innovator pushes the curves in Figure 16.4 and 16.7 to the right, and once his innovation is assimilated by the economy, another innovator may shove these curves somewhat further to the right. For example, one innovator introduces vacuum tubes, a later innovator introduces semiconductors, one innovator introduces the steam locomotive, a later innovator introduces the diesel locomotive. This process goes on and on—and is a main source of economic growth.

The Electronic Computer: A Case Study[8]

To get a better feel for the nature of technological change and the process of innovation, let's consider one of the most important technological advances of the twentieth century—the electronic computer. Many of the basic ideas underlying the computer go back to Charles Babbage, a brilliant nineteenth-century British inventor; but not until 1946 was the first electronic computer, the ENIAC, designed and constructed. John Mauchly and J. Presper Eckert, both professors at the Moore School of Electrical Engineering at the University of Pennsylvania, were responsible for the ENIAC's design and construction. The work was supported by the U.S. Army. John von Neumann, a famous mathematician at the Institute for Advanced Study at Princeton, added the important concepts of stored programming and conditional transfer.

After the war, Mauchly and Eckert established a small firm to produce electronic computers. Their firm was acquired by Remington Rand, which in 1951 marketed the Univac I, a machine used by the Census Bureau. The International Business Machines Corporation (IBM), the leading company in office machinery and data processing, which before this had been cautious about the potential market for computers, was spurred into action by Remington Rand's success. Once it entered the field, IBM's financial resources, strong marketing organization, and engineering strength enabled it to capture a very large share of the computer market, here and abroad. In the United States, IBM's share of the market grew to about 90 percent during the 1960s.

The electronic computer has been an extremely important stimulus to economic growth. By 1966, the total number of computers installed in the Western world exceeded 50,000 at a total value of about $20 billion. These computers have had important effects on production techniques in many industries. For example, in the chemical, petroleum, and steel industries, digital computers are the latest step in the evolution of control techniques. Com-

[8] This and the following section are based to a considerable extent on E. Mansfield, *The Economics of Technological Change,* New York: Norton, 1968; and my paper in the International Economic Association's *Science and Technology in Economic Growth,* London: Macmillan, 1973.

puters help to determine and enforce the best conditions for process operation, as well as act as data loggers. They can also be programmed to help carry out the complex sequence of operations required to start up or shut down a plant. They have increased production, decreased waste, improved quality control, and reduced the chance of damage to equipment. In another quite different industry, banking, computers have had an important effect too. They have made it possible to eliminate conventional machines and processes for sorting checks, balancing accounts, and computing service charges. With high-speed sorters, it is possible now to process more than 1,500 checks per minute.

Obviously, the electronic computer has enabled us to produce more output from a given amount of resources. In other words, it has enabled us to push the product transformation curve outward, thus increasing our rate of economic growth. But it must be recognized that the process by which the computer has had this effect has by no means been simple or straightforward. Many people in many countries were involved in the development of the basic ideas. Many organizations, public and private, funded the experimental work. Firms of various types were the innovators with respect to particular aspects of the modern computer. And countless individuals and organizations had to be willing to accept, work with, and invest in computers.

Technological Change: Determinants and Measurement

What determines the rate of technological change and the rate at which changes in technology are applied and spread? Clearly, the nature and extent of a nation's scientific capability, and the size and quality of its educational system are of fundamental importance. The first thing that must be said about the influence of a nation's scientific capability on its rate of technological change is that science and technology are two quite different things that have drawn together only recently. Until the twentieth

century, it simply was not true that technology was built on science. Even today, many technological advances rely on little in the way of science. However, in more and more areas of the economy (such as aircraft, electronics, and chemicals), the rapid application of new technology has come to depend on a strong scientific base. Merely to imitate or adapt what others have developed, a firm in these areas needs access to high-caliber scientists.

A nation's educational system also has a fundamental influence on the rate of technological change. First, and perhaps most obviously, it determines how many scientists and engineers are graduated, and how competent they are. Clearly, the rate of technological change depends on the quantity and quality of scientific and engineering talent available in the society. Second, the educational system influences the inventiveness and adaptability of the nation's work force. The effective use of modern technology depends on the skills and educational level of the work force; so does the extent to which inventions and improvements are forthcoming from the labor force. The closer links between technology and science should not lead one to believe that workers and independent inventors are no longer important sources of invention. On the contrary, they remain very important in many areas. The educational system also influences the rate of technological change and innovation via the training of managers.

Industrial managers are a key agent in the innovative process. We must emphasize that the proper management of innovation is much more than establishing and maintaining a research and development laboratory that produces a great deal of good technical output. In many industries, most important innovations are not based in any significant degree on the firms' research and development. And even when the basic idea does come from a firm's own R and D, the coupling of R and D with marketing and production is crucial. Many good ideas are not applied properly because the potential users do not really understand them, and many R and D projects are technically successful but commercially irrelevant because they were not designed with sufficient comprehension of market realities. Typically, successful technological innovations seem to be stimulated by perceived production and marketing needs, not by technological opportunities. In other words, most of the time it takes a market-related impetus to prompt work on a successful innovation.

In addition, the rate of technological change depends on the organization of industry and the nature of markets. Although a certain amount of industrial concentration may promote more rapid technological change, increases in concentration beyond a moderate level probably reduce rather than increase the rate of technological change. The rate of technological change also depends on the scale and sophistication of available markets. The scale of the market influences the extent to which a firm can spread the fixed costs of developing and introducing an innovation. This factor has often been cited as a reason for America's technological lead over many other countries. Finally, it is extremely important to note that a country that is not a technological leader can still achieve considerable technological change by borrowing and transferring technology from the leaders.

It is difficult to measure the rate of technological change. Perhaps the most frequently used measure is the rate of growth of labor productivity—that is, the rate of growth of output per manhour. Unfortunately, this measure is influenced by lots of other factors besides the rate of technological change. Nonetheless, despite its inadequacies, it is worthwhile to look briefly at how rapidly productivity has increased in the United States over the long run. Since about 1890, the nation's real output per manhour increased by about 2 percent per year—and these productivity gains were widely diffused, real hourly earnings growing about as rapidly, on the average, as output per manhour.

In part because of differing rates of technological change, there have been considerable differences among industries in the rate of growth of output per manhour. As shown in Table 16.3, labor productivity increased in some industries—like rubber—by more than 4 percent per year,

Table 16.3

Average Annual Rates of Increase of Labor Productivity, Manufacturing Industries, 1899–1953

Industry	Productivity increase (percent per year)
Foods	1.8
Beverages	1.6
Tobacco	5.1
Textiles	2.5
Apparel	1.9
Lumber	1.2
Furniture	1.3
Paper	2.6
Printing	2.7
Chemicals	3.5
Petroleum	3.8
Rubber	4.3
Leather	1.3
Glass	2.7
Primary metals	2.3
Fabricated metals	2.7
Machinery, nonelectric	1.8
Machinery, electric	2.4
Transportation equipment	3.7

Source: John Kendrick, *Productivity Trends in the United States,* Princeton University Press, 1961.

and in other industries—like lumber products—by only about 1 percent per year. To some extent, these differences can be explained by interindustry differences in the amount spent on *research and development.* In addition, a number of other factors—like the amount spent by *other industries* to improve the capital goods and other inputs the industry uses, the extent of *competition* in the industry, the attitudes of *unions* toward change, and the quality of *management*—undoubtedly played an important role too in explaining these interindustry differences in productivity increase.

Entrepreneurship and the Social Environment

Still another set of basic factors influencing a nation's level of potential output and its rate of economic growth is the economic, social, political, and religious climate of the nation. It is difficult, if not impossible, to measure the effect of these factors, but there can be no doubt of their importance. Some societies despise material welfare and emphasize the glories of the next world. Some societies are subject to such violent political upheavals that it is risky, if not foolish, to invest in the future. Some societies are governed so corruptly that economic growth is frustrated. And some societies look down on people engaged in industry, trade, or commerce. Obviously, such societies are less likely to experience rapid economic growth than others with a more favorable climate and conditions.

The relatively rapid economic growth of the United States was undoubtedly stimulated in part by the attitude of its people toward material gain. It is commonplace to note that the United States is a materialistic society, a society that esteems business success, that bestows prestige on the rich, that accepts the Protestant ethic (which, crudely stated, is that work is good), and that encourages individual initiative. The United States has been criticized over and over again for some of these traits—often by nations frantically trying to imitate its economic success. Somewhat less obvious is the fact that, because the United States is a young country whose people came from a variety of origins, it did not inherit many feudal components in the structure of society. This too was important.

The United States has also been characterized by great economic and political freedom, by institutions that have been flexible enough to adjust to change, and by a government that has encouraged competition in the marketplace. This has meant fewer barriers to new ideas. Also, the United States has for a long time enjoyed internal peace, order, and general respect for property rights. There have been no violent revolutions since the Civil War, and for many years we were protected from strife in other lands by two oceans—which then seemed much broader than they do now. All these factors undoubtedly contributed to rapid economic growth.

The American economy also seems to have been able to nurture a great many entrepreneurs and a vast horde of competent businessmen. During the nineteenth century, American entrepreneurs were responsible for such basic innovations as the system of interchangeable parts, pioneered by Eli Whitney and others. In many areas, the United States gained a technological lead over other nations, and the available evidence seems to indicate that, to a significant extent, this lead has been maintained. It must be recognized that much of this lead has come from superior management as well as superior technological resources. For example, the Organization for Economic Cooperation and Development recently concluded: "In the techniques of *management,* including the management of research, and of combined technological and market forecasting, the United States appears to have a significant lead."[9]

The Gap between Actual and Potential Output

Up to this point, our discussion of economic growth has centered on the factors that determine how rapidly a nation's potential output grows—factors like technological change, increased education, investment in plant and equipment, and increases in the labor force. Now we must examine the factors that determine how close a nation's actual output comes to its potential output. As we already know, a nation's potential output is its output under full employment. Thus, as we also know, whether or not the economy operates close to full employment is determined by the level of $C + I + G$. If the $C + I + G$ line is too low, the economy will operate with considerable unemploy-

[9] Organization for Economic Cooperation and Development, *Technology Gap: General Report,* Paris, 1968, p. 25.

ment, and actual output will be substantially below potential output. Or, in terms of the equation of exchange, if $M \times V$ is too small, the economy will operate with considerable unemployment, and actual output will be substantially below potential output.

From previous chapters, we also know how the government can use fiscal and monetary policies to push actual output close to potential output. Cuts in tax rates, increases in government spending, incentives for private investment in plant and equipment, increases in the money supply, reductions in interest rates; all these devices can be used to push actual output closer to potential output. Such devices promote economic growth, in the sense that actual per capita output is increased. However, only so much growth can be achieved by squeezing the slack out of the economy. For example, if there is a 7 percent unemployment rate, output per capita can be increased by perhaps 9 percent simply by reducing the unemployment rate to 4 percent, as we saw in Chapter 8. *But this is a one-shot improvement.* To get any further growth, the nation must increase its potential output.

Of course this doesn't mean that it isn't important to maintain the economy at close to full employment. On the contrary, as we stressed in Chapter 8, one of the major objectives of public policy must be full employment, and a reduction of unemployment will have a significant effect on the rate of economic growth in the short run. (Much of the economic growth in the United States in the early 1960s was caused by the transition to full employment.) But the point we are making is that, once the economy gets to full employment, no further growth can occur by this route. If a nation wants further growth, it must influence the factors responsible for the rate of growth of potential output.

Japan: A Case Study of Rapid Economic Growth

Japan has experienced a very high rate of economic growth for a long time. Especially after World War II, the Japanese economy increased per capita GNP very rapidly. For example, between 1955 and 1964 gross national product per man increased at an average rate of 8.8 percent per year. Some of the most important reasons for this rapid growth are as follows:[10]

First, after World War II, the rate of investment in plant and equipment was extremely high. For example, in 1954 the Japanese devoted over 20 percent of their GNP to the formation of physical capital; and in 1961 and 1964, they devoted 35 and 33 percent, respectively. While this high rate of capital formation was due, particularly in the early postwar years, to the dislocations caused by the war, this was not the only reason. To a considerable extent, the rate was high because Japan was catching up with technological developments elsewhere in the world. Japan invested heavily in newer industries based on innovations in other countries—television, electronic devices, synthetics, and others—as well as in older industries like steel, machinery, and chemicals.

A second very important contributor to Japan's economic growth was the borrowing and application of technology developed in other countries. The Japanese were skilled borrowers of Western technology. Their success illustrates a very important point often overlooked by nations interested in increasing their growth rates. To benefit from technology, a nation does not have to develop or invent it. Conversely, because a country develops or invents a new product or process, it does not follow that the product or process will do much for its rate of economic growth. If another country is quicker to apply and exploit the innovation, it may get more of the economic benefits. The Japanese concentrated their energies and resources on transferring Western technology rather than developing or inventing their own. This strategy paid off well.

Japan has also had an abundant supply of edu-

[10] For further discussion, see K. Ohkawa and H. Rosovsky, "Recent Japanese Growth in Historical Perspective," *American Economic Review,* May 1963, pp. 578–88.

cated labor, which has made it much easier to assimilate new technology. The importance of such an investment in human capital has been emphasized in previous sections. And Japan undoubtedly benefited from the fact that its burden of national defense was largely assumed by the United States, so that Japanese resources could be devoted to economic development rather than to defense. Last, Japan's level of per capita GNP was lower than that of most of the nations with which it is generally compared. It is often argued that countries at a relatively low level of economic development find it easier to achieve a high growth rate than do more affluent societies. In other words, a high rate of growth may be easier to achieve from a low economic base.

Summary

Economic growth is measured by the increase of per capita real gross national product, an index that does not measure accurately the growth of economic welfare, but is often used as a first approximation. In recent years, many economists and politicians have called for an explicit public policy designed to increase our growth rate. A nation's rate of economic growth depends on the increase in the quantity and quality of its resources (including physical and human capital) and the rate of technological change. In addition, the rate of economic growth depends on the extent to which a society maintains full employment and on the efficiency with which its resources are allocated and managed.

One factor that may influence a nation's rate of economic growth is the rate at which its population grows. In Malthus's view, population growth, unless checked in some way, ultimately meant economic decline, since output could not grow in proportion to the growth in population. The law of diminishing marginal returns insured that beyond some point, increases in labor, holding the quantity of land constant, would result in smaller and smaller increments of output. However, Malthus underestimated the extent and importance of technological change, which offset the law of diminishing marginal returns.

Another factor that determines whether per capita output grows rapidly or slowly is the rate of expenditure on new plant and equipment. Without technological change, more and more of this sort of investment would result in increases in the capital-output ratio and decreases in the profitability of investment in plant and equipment, as Ricardo pointed out. But because of technological change, none of these things has occurred. According to the available evidence, a nation's rate of economic growth seems directly related to its rate of investment in plant and equipment.

To a considerable extent, economic growth here and abroad has resulted from technological change. A change in technology, when applied for the first time, is called an innovation, and the firm that first applies it is called an innovator. Innovation is a key stage in the process leading to the full evaluation and utilization of a new process or product. Unless knowledge is used, it has little effect on the rate of economic growth. The rate of technological change and the rate at which new technology is applied depend on a number of factors, including the nature and extent of a nation's scientific capability, the size and quality of its educational system, the quality of its managers, the attitude and structure of its firms, the organization of its industries, and the nature of its markets.

Another factor with an important effect on a nation's rate of economic growth is the rate at which it invests in human capital. The United States invests in human capital on a massive scale, and these enormous and rapidly growing investments have unquestionably increased the productivity, versatility, and adaptability of our labor force. Still another set of basic factors influencing the rate of economic growth is the economic, social, and political climate of the nation. Some societies despise material welfare, are subject to violent political upheavals, and are governed by corrupt groups. Such societies are unlikely to have a high rate of economic growth. Finally, the rate of economic growth is also affected by the extent and behavior of the gap between actual and potential GNP. However, once a nation gets to full employment, it cannot grow further by reducing this gap.

CONCEPTS FOR REVIEW

Economic growth	Average product of	Innovation
Capital formation	labor	Innovator
Population increase	Law of diminishing	Diffusion process
Marginal product of	marginal returns	Aggregate production
labor	Technological change	function

QUESTIONS FOR DISCUSSION AND REVIEW

1. In 1971, Herbert Stein wrote, "During the past 4 years the rates of growth in productivity . . . slowed down." What are some possible reasons why this occurred? What is the significance of this slowdown?

2. Describe in as much detail as you can the ways in which capital formation, population growth, technological change, and education are interrelated. Show how these interrelationships make it difficult to sort out the effect of each of these factors on the rate of economic growth.

3. Malthus thought that output would increase only in proportion to the growth in population. True or False?

4. In the United States during the twentieth century the capital-output ratio has a. increased steadily. b. remained fairly constant. c. decreased steadily. d. fluctuated markedly up and down.

CHAPTER 17

American Economic Growth: History, Policies, Problems, and Prospects

About a century ago, Benjamin Disraeli, the famous British prime minister, said that "increased means and increased leisure are the two civilizers of man." Although one might add to Disraeli's list of "civilizers," there can be little doubt that economic growth has helped to improve man's lot. Since World War II, the rate of economic growth has become a major index, both here and abroad, of how well an economy is performing; and many governments have tried to increase their rate of economic growth. In 1960 John F. Kennedy ran for president on a platform emphasizing the need for faster economic growth in the United States; and in subsequent elections—here and abroad— economic growth frequently has been a campaign issue.

However, bigger may not always be better. More and more often, observers in recent years have stressed that economic growth may not be an unalloyed blessing. It too has its costs. Indeed, the pros and cons of more rapid economic growth have been the subject of much debate. In this chapter, we are concerned with four basic questions about economic growth in the United States. What has been our rate of economic growth in the past? What are the advantages and disadvantages of a faster rate of economic growth? If faster growth is desired, what measures can the government take to promote it? And, assuming that present trends continue, what rate of economic growth can we expect in the future?

Economic Growth in the United States

Let's begin by looking at the salient facts about the rate at which the American economy has grown in the past. Soon after its emergence as an independent nation, the United States reached a relatively high level of economic development. By 1840, it ranked fourth in per capita income, behind England, France, and Germany. During the next 30 years, the United States experienced relatively rapid economic growth. By 1870, it ranked second only to England in per capita income. In the next 40 years, the American economy continued to grow

rapidly. National product per person employed grew by about 2.2 percent per year between 1871 and 1913. This growth rate was higher than for practically any other major industrialized nation; and well before the turn of the century, income per capita was greater in the United States than in any other nation in the world.

Between 1913 and 1959, the American growth rate was somewhat lower than in previous years. National product per person employed grew by about 1.8 percent per year. Nonetheless, although we grew less rapidly than in earlier years, we pulled further ahead of most other industrialized countries, because we continued to grow faster than they did. Of course, our rate of economic growth varied from decade to decade: economic growth does not proceed at a steady rate. In some decades (like the 1920s), our economy grew rapidly, while in others (like the 1930s), it grew little, if at all. During periods of recovery and prosperity, the growth rate was high; during depressions, it was low. In the 1950s, the growth rate in the United States was lower than in many other countries. As pointed out in the previous chapter, this caused considerable controversy and some alarm.

During the 1960s, our growth rate increased perceptibly. But our present growth rate is by no

---

Table 17.1

Average Annual Growth Rates of Per Capita Real GNP, Selected Industrialized Countries

Country	1870–1964	1929–1964	1950–1964
United States	1.9%	1.7%	1.8%
Canada	1.7	1.8	1.8
France	1.5	1.4	3.8
Germany	1.7	2.8	5.9
Italy	1.4	2.2	5.2
Japan	—	—	8.7
United Kingdom	1.3	1.7	2.4

Source: U.S. Department of Commerce, *Long-Term Economic Growth,* 1966.

means the highest among the major industrialized nations. That honor belongs to Japan, which, as we saw in the previous chapter, has long experienced rapid economic growth. Table 17.1 shows the annual rates of growth of per capita real GNP in the United States and other major industrialized countries during various periods in the last century. You can see that, for the period as a whole, per capita real GNP in the United States grew at an average rate of about 2 percent per year. Compared with Germany, France, Italy, Canada, and the United Kingdom, our growth rate was quite impressive. In recent years, however, many industrialized countries have shown growth rates larger than or equal to ours.

Population and Human Resources

As we have seen, a nation's rate of economic growth is influenced, among other things, by its rate of population growth and the extent of its investment in human capital. As shown in Figure 17.1, the population of the United States has grown substantially during our history, because of a fairly high birth rate as well as considerable immigration from other parts of the world.[1] Indeed, our population in 1970 was about double what it was in 1920, and almost triple what it was in 1900.

In the past 15 or 20 years, the birth rate has fallen considerably, due partly to changes in attitudes toward women's role in society. However, according to official forecasts, the American population will continue to grow for at least the next 10 or 20 years, and perhaps for much longer. Of course, increases in population do not necessarily bring about economic growth. As we saw in the

[1] As shown in Figure 17.1, the percent of the population in the labor force does not remain constant over time, and changes in this percentage can, of course, influence a country's rate of economic growth. Increases in the number of years of schooling and more liberal attitudes toward working wives, as well as changes in the age distribution of the population and in income levels, will influence this percentage.

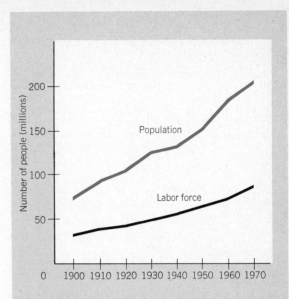

Figure 17.1
Population and Labor Force, United States, 1900–70.

The American population in 1970 was about double what it was in 1920, and almost triple what it was in 1900.

previous chapter, population increases, carried beyond a certain point, can lower per capita GNP, unless they are offset by other factors, such as advances in technology.

Equally important, it is not sheer numbers alone that count. The quality as well as the quantity of the population determines how much is produced. Measured by its education and skill, the quality of the American population is among the highest in the world. Moreover, as indicated by Table 17.2, the educational level of the population has increased dramatically during the past 70 years. To a considerable extent, our economic growth seems to have been due to this large investment in human capital.

Is it possible to make any quantitative estimate of the contribution of increased education to eco-

Table 17.2

Percent of 17-Year-Olds that Graduated from High School, United States, 1900–1980

Year	Percent graduated from high school
1900	6.4
1920	16.8
1940	50.8
1950	59.0
1960	65.1
1970	78.0
1980 (projected)	82.5

Source: Statistical Abstract of the United States, 1972.

Table 17.3

Estimated Sources of Growth in Real National Income in the United States, 1909–57

Source	Period 1909–29	1929–57
	[Percent of total growth]	
Increase in quantity of labor	39	27
Increase in quantity of capital	26	15
Improved education and training	13	27
Technological change	12	20
Other factors	10	11
Total	100	100

Source: E. Denison, The Sources of Economic Growth in the United States, Committee for Economic Development, 1962.

nomic growth in the United States? Because the effects of education, technological change, and investment in plant and equipment intertwine in various ways, it is very difficult to sort out any one of them. Yet it is worthwhile to give the best estimates currently available. According to Edward Denison of the Brookings Institution, increased education seemed to account for about ⅛ of the growth in real output in the United States during 1909–29, and for about ¼ of this growth during 1929–57. Thus, if these estimates, shown in Table 17.3, can be trusted, increased education has been a major contributor to economic growth in the United States.

Technological Change

America's economic growth has also been due in very considerable part to technological change. For example, as shown in Table 17.3, Denison concludes that the "advance of knowledge" contributed about ⅛ of the growth in real output during 1909–29, and about ⅓ of this growth during 1929–57. Such estimates are rough, but useful. It is very difficult to separate the effects on economic growth of technological change from those of investment in physical capital, since to a considerable extent new technology must be embodied in physical capital—new machines and equipment—to be used. For example, a nuclear power plant must obviously be built to take advantage of nuclear power plant technology. Nor can the effects of technological change easily be separated from those of education. After all, the returns from increased education are enhanced by technological change, and, as we saw in the previous chapter, the rate of technological change is influenced by the extent and nature of a society's investment in education.

In interpreting America's economic growth, we must recognize that the United States has long been a technological leader. Even before 1850, scattered evidence gives the impression that the United States was ahead of other countries in many technological areas. And after 1850, the available evidence indicates that productivity was higher in the United States than in Europe, that the United States had a strong export position in technically progressive industries, and that Europeans tended to imitate American techniques. Needless to say, the United States did not lead in all fields, but it appears to have held a technological lead in many important aspects of manufacturing. This was in contrast to pure science where, until World War II, the United States was not a leader.

Toward the end of the nineteenth century, as the connection between science and technology gradually became closer, commercial research laboratories began to appear. The first organized research laboratory in the United States was established by Thomas Edison in 1876. Eastman Kodak (1893), B. F. Goodrich (1895), General Electric (1900), DuPont (1902), and the Bell Telephone System (1907) were some of the earliest firms to establish laboratories. The industrial R and D laboratory constituted a significant departure from the past, when invention was mainly the work of independent inventors like Eli Whitney (inter-changeable parts and cotton gin), Robert Fulton (steamboat), Samuel Morse (telegraph), Charles Goodyear (vulcanization of rubber), and Cyrus McCormick (reaper). These men were responsible for a very rich crop of inventions, some of which established whole new industries. Since the advent of the industrial laboratory, the relative importance of independent inventors seems to have declined, but they continue to produce a significant share of the important inventions in many areas. For example, xerography was invented by an independent inventor, Chester Carlson.

Recent decades have witnessed a tremendous growth in the amount spent on research and development. Table 17.4 shows that R and D expenditures in the United States in 1972 were about 19 times what they were in 1945. Although the bulk of these expenditures go for rather minor improvements rather than major advances, this vast increase in research and development has generated much economic growth. But, as the table shows, the federal government is the source of most R and D funds, which are heavily concentrated on defense and space technology. In the eyes of many economists, this vast investment in R and D would

Table 17.4

Expenditures on Research and Development, United States, 1945–70

| Year | Total R and D expenditure | Sources of funds | | |
		Government	Industry	Universities and nonprofit institutions
		(millions)		
1945	$ 1,520	$ 1,070	$ 430	$ 20
1950	2,870	1,610	1,180	80
1955	6,270	3,490	2,510	270
1960	13,710	8,720	4,510	480
1965	20,439	13,033	6,539	867
1972°	28,000	15,210	11,320	1,470

Source: *Statistical Abstract of the United States,* 1970, and National Science Foundation, *National Patterns of R and D Resources,* 1972.
° Estimated by National Science Foundation.

probably have had a bigger impact on the rate of economic growth if more of it had been directed at civilian rather than military and political objectives.

Capital Formation and Natural Resources

As pointed out in the previous chapter, a nation's rate of economic growth depends partially on how much of its GNP is invested in new plant and equipment. In recent years, we have devoted over 10 percent of our GNP to this purpose. In the United States, the average worker has more equipment to work with than his counterpart in any other country of the world. In manufacturing, for example, the average American worker has at his disposal about $30,000 worth of plant and equipment. Moreover, the government has invested huge amounts in highways, harbors, dams, and other forms of social capital; and the public has invested heavily in residential construction.

America's great natural resources have also been an important factor underlying our economic growth. We have an abundance of fertile soil and of various kinds of ores and minerals, a reasonably good climate, and coal, oil, and other sources of power. Few nations have as plentiful a supply of natural resources, and obviously they have been a great boon to our economic development. Although countries with limited natural resources can offset this limitation by importing raw materials, by irrigation and drainage projects, and by the use of modern technology, a good supply of natural resources is a valuable asset in achieving rapid economic growth.

In recent years, some fear has been expressed that, if the world economy continues to grow at current rates, we shall begin to run out of basic raw materials. For example, in 1972 Jay Forrester and his colleagues at M.I.T. conducted a study sponsored by the Club of Rome on *The Limits of Growth,*[2] in which they concluded that unless we curb our growth rate the world will run out of raw materials in the foreseeable future. However, this ignores the fact that the price system encourages producers to conserve raw materials as they become increasingly scarce, and that it provides a strong incentive for producers to invent and adopt new techniques that use less of these resources. The price system accomplishes these things simply by seeing to it that the price of a raw material increases as it becomes scarcer.

The history of technology seems to indicate that Forrester's view is oversimplified and overly pessimistic. As Peter Passell and Leonard Ross of Columbia University point out

> Before we run out of Arabian oil, we will begin extracting petroleum from the vast reserves of oil-shale rocks and tar sands. And long before we run out of those reserves, cars will be powered with other sources of energy. Appeals to faith in technical change are more than a cheap debating trick to counter the Forrester school. The technology of substituting plentiful materials for scarce ones grows every day. Silicates made from sand replace copper and silver radio circuitry; European cattle feeds are enriched with nutrients made of natural gas converted by bacteria; mattresses are filled with polyurethane which never was closer to a Liberian rubber tree than Bayonne, N.J.[3]

The Social and Entrepreneurial Environment, the GNP Gap, and Allocative Efficiency

As we stressed in the previous chapter, America's relatively rapid long-term economic growth has also been a result of its social and entrepreneurial environment. In general, American society places con-

[2] For example, see Donella Meadows, Dennis Meadows, J. Randers, and William Behrens, "The Limits to Growth," reprinted in E. Mansfield, *Economics: Readings, Issues, and Cases,* New York: Norton, 1974.
[3] P. Passell and L. Ross, "Don't Knock the $2-Trillion Economy," *New York Times,* March 5, 1972.

siderable emphasis on materialistic considerations, values hard work, allows a great deal of economic and political freedom, and is flexible enough to adjust to change. Also, the United States has not been wracked (in the past century) by internal armed conflict or widespread confiscation of private property. These factors have been important in promoting economic growth. In addition, the price system, which has been relied on to channel resources into the proper uses, seems to have worked quite well. It has provided the incentives required to get labor, land, and capital to move from less productive to more productive uses.

However, not all aspects of the American economy have been conducive to rapid economic growth. For one thing, as we saw in Chapter 8, in many periods actual GNP fell short of potential GNP because desired spending was too low. For example, in the Great Depression of the 1930s, actual GNP was far below our potential GNP. When a large gap develops between actual and potential GNP, this reduces the growth rate, as we saw in the previous chapter. Moreover, it has indirect as well as direct effects. As this gap grows, and there is substantial unemployment, firms are discouraged from investing in new technology or capital formation, and unions are more inclined to resist adopting new techniques that might replace men with machines, so that the growth rate in subsequent years may be reduced as well.

Another factor that can reduce our economic growth rate is the growth of monopolistic elements that prevent resources from being allocated efficiently. For example, some labor unions resist the adoption of new techniques that would increase productivity and growth. Thus, the compositors' union has restricted the use of the teletypesetter by requiring that the machine be operated by a journeyman printer or apprentice. Also, groups that are adversely affected by changes that would promote economic growth often try to convince the government to stop or offset them. For example, the farm programs discussed in Chapter 5 impeded past economic growth by making it more difficult to transfer resources out of agriculture and

into more productive uses. Also, many industries that cannot compete with foreign producers lobby for and obtain tariffs, with the result that resources are misallocated.

Finally, if resources tend to be more immobile, this too will hamper economic growth. As tastes, technology, and population change, resources often should move from one use or location to another, if society's output is to be maximized. But there are many barriers to the mobility of resources. In the case of labor, people often are reluctant to pick up stakes, sever their ties to friends, family, and neighbors, and move to another location. Similarly, they often are unwilling or unable to learn a new occupation or trade, even though it might increase their income. The immobility of capital is even more obvious. A particular piece of capital is built for specific purposes—for example, to cut metal or to refine oil—and cannot be used for other purposes. However, when this piece of capital wears out, it can be replaced with capital of another type.

Past and Present Views of Economic Growth

Despite an imperfect record, the American economy has strongly adhered to a pattern of growth. Should we try to increase our rate of economic growth? Some economists answer yes, some answer no. Before presenting the issues, several points should be noted about the attitudes of economists, past and present, toward economic growth. First, the great economists of the past were deeply concerned with the poverty and economic misery of their times; and they tried in various ways to help set humanity on a course whereby output per capita might rise. Smith, Malthus, and Ricardo all wanted to ameliorate the meager lot of the average Englishman of their day; Marx was distressed and angered by the misery of the working classes; and Keynes spent much of his time and energy trying to find a way out of the poverty and misery arising from the Great Depression.

Second, except for Smith and Keynes, these great economists of the past were not very optimistic about how much output per capita could be increased. Malthus and Ricardo were about as pessimistic as one reasonably could get. In their view, population would expand whenever the standard of living poked its head above the subsistence level, with the result that more and more people would be working a relatively fixed amount of land. Given the law of diminishing marginal returns, it appeared certain to them that output per capita would eventually fall. As for Marx, we have seen that he believed the capitalistic system was headed for collapse, and that the bulk of the population was doomed to increased misery so long as capitalism survived.

With all the advantages of hindsight, it is relatively easy to see where the pessimists went wrong, at least for the industrialized nations. As pointed out in the previous chapter, Malthus and Ricardo vastly underestimated the power of technological change. They could not visualize the sorts of innovations that were to occur. New techniques and new products were destined to offset the dreaded law of diminishing marginal returns and to allow food supplies to more than keep pace with increases in population. Moreover, because of innovations in birth control and changes in attitudes, population has not grown as rapidly as many people forecasted. Marx could not visualize the sorts of changes that were to occur in capitalism. Nor could he avoid the consequences of certain basic flaws in his economic analysis that have led to many modifications of Marxian theory as applied by Communist countries.

It is important to recognize that, for a variety of reasons, the attitude of most economists today is quite different from the attitudes of their great predecessors. Of course, the difference does not lie in a lack of concern for the underprivileged. Most economists today are just as interested in eradicating poverty as were Smith or Marx. *The big difference is that today's economists are reasonably confident that we can increase output per capita. Indeed, they expect, almost as a matter of course,* *that output per capita will increase in the industrialized nations of the world.* Of course, some wish that it could be made to increase a little faster (and some would like to slow it down) but, in general, the present view is decidedly optimistic.

The Case for Economic Growth

Having reached a level of affluence that would have astonished Smith, Ricardo, Malthus, or Marx (but not Keynes), the industrialized nations are now at a point where some observers question the wisdom of further economic growth. For example, in the United States, the attitude toward economic growth has changed perceptibly in the decade or so since President Kennedy made it a target of public policy. More emphasis is placed today on the "costs" of economic growth. There are more statements to the effect that we really are rich enough, and more questions about the desirability of technological change, which is one of the principal mainsprings of economic growth.

In making the case for rapid economic growth, three basic arguments are employed. First, it is argued that economic growth means a higher standard of living, which is important in and of itself. But before accepting this uncritically, one should stress the limitations of the customary growth measures. A decade or so ago, people tended uncritically to accept increases in per capita GNP as a measure of increases in economic welfare, despite the many warnings of economists. People now are more conscious of the frailties of the GNP—the fact that it does not count as "product" many benefits that are provided as part of the productive process (such as increased leisure) and that it does not count as "costs" many problems (such as the human and environmental costs) that arise as a consequence of the productive process. Some economists are currently trying to improve the statistics to take better account of some of these factors, such as environmental pollution (see Chapter 8). But since it is unlikely that we will ever have very precise measures of economic welfare, the available figures need to be treated with caution.

Second, it is argued that economic growth provides the means to reduce poverty and attain other national objectives. In the words of Peter Passell and Leonard Ross, "Growth is the only way that America will ever reduce poverty. . . . While the relative share of income that poor people get seems to be frozen, their incomes do keep pace with the economy. . . . Even allowing for inflation, the average income of the bottom 10th of the population has increased about 55 percent since 1950. Twenty more years of growth could do for the poor what the Congress won't do."[4] Also, it is argued that economic growth makes it easier to achieve other national goals, because they can be achieved without reducing the production and consumption of other goods and services.

Third, many maintain that economic growth contributes to national prestige and national defense. As pointed out in the previous chapter, this was one of the most important reasons for the emphasis on economic growth in the early 1960s. People were worried that we were losing the "growth race" to the Soviet Union, and that Premier Khrushchev's claim that the Russians would "bury" us economically might be more than an idle boast. In recent years, as our relations with the Communist countries have improved, these reasons for economic growth have been given less importance, but they still are cited by some proponents of economic growth.

The Case against Economic Growth

Basically, there are four arguments made by those who question the wisdom of further economic growth in our society. First, it is argued that increases in per capita GNP really will not make us any happier: on the contrary, they will only be achieved by reducing the quality of our lives. For

example, according to E. J. Mishan of the London School of Economics, economic growth results in "the appalling traffic congestion in our towns, cities, and suburbs, . . . the erosion of the countryside, the 'uglification' of coastal towns, . . . and a wide heritage of natural beauty being wantonly destroyed."[5] In his view, to strain for further economic growth is simply to put ourselves on a meaningless treadmill, since it prevents us from enjoying what we have. Relatively few economists share this rather extreme view.

Second, it is argued that economic growth is likely to result in additional environmental pollution. Of course, increases in per capita GNP do not necessarily have to entail increases in pollution. On the contrary, as we shall see in the next chapter, it is possible to increase output without increasing pollution. Nonetheless, the fact seems to be that economic growth in the past has been associated with increases in pollution, and some observers feel that this association is likely to persist in the future. Thus they regard increases in environmental pollution as a likely "cost" of economic growth. Among those who argue against further economic growth on environmental grounds is biologist Barry Commoner of Washington University, who concludes that:

> In most of the technological displacements which have accompanied the growth of the economy since 1946, the new technology has an appreciably greater environmental impact than the technology which it has displaced, and the postwar technological transformation of productive activities is the chief reason for the present environmental crisis. . . . If we are to survive economically as well as biologically, much of the technological transformation of the United States economy since 1946 will need to be, so to speak, redone in order to bring the nation's productive technology much more closely into harmony with the inescapable demands of the ecosystem.[6]

[4] Passell and Ross, *op. cit.*

[5] E. Mishan, *Technology and Growth*, New York: Praeger, 1969.
[6] B. Commoner, "The Environmental Costs of Economic Growth," in R. and N. Dorfman, *Economics of the Environment*, New York: Norton, 1972.

Third, it is argued that economic growth is not the solver of social problems that its proponents claim. For example, critics point out that we are rich enough now to solve the problem of poverty in the United States. In their view, what we need is the will and courage to eliminate poverty, not extra output. In reply to the argument that economic growth is needed for reasons of national prestige and defense, the critics retort that it is not the size of a country's GNP, but its composition, that counts in determining military strength. For example, the Soviet Union's military strength is roughly equal to ours, although its GNP is about 50 percent smaller. Moreover, the critics question whether the less developed countries are much impressed by a simple comparison of our growth rate with that of the Soviet Union.

Fourth, it is pointed out that, to increase our growth rate, it may be necessary for us to make sacrifices now. For example, we may have to sacrifice leisure or postpone the consumption of goods and services in order to invest in capital goods. Many economists have stressed that one cannot make the naive assumption that more growth is costless, or that it will always be worth the sacrifices involved. According to some economists, there is no reason to "force" growth on the economy. To them, the proper rate of economic growth is that which would emerge from private decisions. Whether the increase in the growth rate is worth the sacrifices depends upon the tastes and preferences of the people: it is a political issue.

Public Policies to Stimulate Economic Growth

Although the critics of growth have made some headway, there has been no renunciation of economic growth as a goal of public policy. On the contrary, most government officials, in the United States and elsewhere, continue to press for further economic growth. All nations have important social objectives that seem more likely to be attained if they can increase per capita output. Thus, most would like to effect such an increase, notwithstanding Mishan's views concerning the hollowness of it all. But the more sophisticated question of how far the government should go in promoting or forcing growth is not easy to answer. And as you would expect, there are very substantial differences of opinion on this score among politicians in this country (and other countries as well).

Whether or not we should stimulate growth is essentially a political question, and your own view will depend on your political preference. As Robert Solow puts it, "The pro-growth-man is someone who is prepared to sacrifice something useful and desirable right now so that people should be better off in the future; the anti-growth-man is someone who thinks that is unnecessary or undesirable."

But whether you are for or against the stimulation of growth, you should know how the government's policies can influence the growth rate. Suppose that the American people, registering their opinions through the proper democratic process, indicate that they want to increase the nation's rate of economic growth. Suppose that you are a United States Senator and that you feel that, regardless of your own preferences, you should advocate programs to further the people's objectives—in this case, to increase the nation's rate of economic growth. What sorts of programs would you support?

First, you would probably want to *increase expenditures on research and development* (R and D), since increases in such expenditures are likely to increase the rate of technological change, which in turn will increase the growth rate.[7] The government can either increase R and D expenditures by directly financing more R and D, or it can provide tax credits or other inducements to get private firms to increase their R and D expenditures. It is important to recognize, however, that the added R and D must be carried out in areas

[7] It is interesting to contrast this attitude toward R and D with the view of the French revolutionaries, who said, as they led the famous scientist, Lavoisier, to the guillotine: "The Republic has no need of scientists." Clearly, scientists are viewed differently—and treated more gently—today.

where the social payoffs are high: otherwise there will be little impact on the growth rate. Moreover, we must also note that the government can stimulate the growth rate by encouraging the application and diffusion of existing technology, as well as by encouraging the development of new technology.

Second, you would probably want to *increase investment in education and training.* We saw in the previous chapter that, according to various experts, there may be a high rate of return from such an investment. Increased education and training may increase the nation's potential output considerably. To foster such increases, the federal government could spend larger amounts on scholarships and provide loans for potential students. Many people argue that loans should be made available to students who plan to enter highly paid occupations, since the student could pay back the loan from his extra earnings. Also, the government could provide more financial support to the nation's colleges and universities.

Third, you would probably want to *increase aggregate investment in plant and equipment.* Increases in such investment will increase the growth rate, assuming, of course, that the extra investment is in areas of high productivity. Again, we must recognize that this policy, like the others described above, imposes costs. Increases in investment can occur—under full employment—only at the expense of current consumption. Assuming that the people understand these costs and are willing to pay them, the government can increase investment in plant and equipment by keeping interest rates low (to encourage investment) and personal tax rates high (to choke off consumption). Also, the government can give tax credits for investment in plant and equipment and allow firms to depreciate their plant and equipment more rapidly.[8]

[8] A tax credit is a device whereby a firm's income tax liability is smaller if it invests a great deal in plant and equipment than if it invests little. Obviously, such a tax credit increases the profitability of investing in plant and equipment. More rapid depreciation of plant and equipment also encourages investment because, if a firm can write off a new piece of equipment more rapidly for tax purposes, the new piece of equipment is more profitable to the firm than it otherwise would be.

Fourth, if the economy is operating at considerably less than full employment, you would probably want *to narrow the gap between actual and potential output.* As we saw in the previous chapter, this can be a very effective way to grow, at least in the short run. To do it, the government must use its fiscal and monetary policies to reduce unemployment. The goal of full employment is widely accepted—more widely, for that matter, than the goal of increasing the rate of economic growth. Unfortunately, however, when the economy approaches full employment, there is a tendency for the goal of full employment to conflict with the goal of price stability, as we saw in Chapter 8. Thus, an attempt to close completely the gap between actual and potential output may lead to undesirable inflationary pressures.

Policies for Economic Growth in the Early 1960s: A Case Study

As we have noted, in the early 1960s, the Kennedy administration set out to spur the rate of economic growth in the United States. We now can take a closer look at the set of economic policies designed to accomplish this goal. These policies were formulated by members of the Council of Economic Advisers, and others, inside and outside the government. To be put into effect, some of these policies and programs had to be approved by the Congress.

For research and development, the Kennedy administration proposed a Civilian Industrial Technology program to encourage and support additional R and D in industries that it regarded as lagging technologically. It also proposed an industrial extension service—analogous to the agricultural extension service that distributes technological information and advice—to increase the rate of diffusion of innovations. Congress eventually approved the industrial extension service,[9] but not the Civilian

[9] The industrial extension service, embodied in the State Technical Services Act, was passed in 1965, but was later killed.

Industrial Technology program. An important reason for its defeat was that some industrial groups feared that government sponsorship of industrial R and D could upset existing competitive relationships.

In the field of education too, the administration proposed new measures. For example, in his 1962 Economic Report, President Kennedy stated:

> Public education has been the great bulwark of equality of opportunity in our democracy for more than a century. . . . There can be no better investment in equity and democracy—and no better instrument for economic growth. For this reason, I urge action by the Congress to provide Federal aid for more adequate public school facilities, higher teachers' salaries, and better quality in education. I urge early completion of congressional action on the bill to authorize loans for construction of college academic facilities and to provide scholarships for able students who need help. The talent of our youth is a resource which must not be wasted.[10]

To encourage investment in plant and equipment, the administration pushed through an "investment tax credit" that permitted firms to deduct from their income tax statements 7 percent of the amount they invested in new plant and equipment. Obviously, this made such investment more profitable. Also, the administration revised the depreciation schedules so that firms could write off such investments more quickly for tax purposes, thus increasing their profitability still more. But it did not lower interest rates or increase taxes to choke off consumption. In its 1962 Annual Report, the Council of Economic Advisers recognized that such actions might promote growth, but felt that other considerations, such as our balance of payments (discussed in Chapter 20), ruled them out.

Finally, turning to the reduction of the gap between actual and potential output, the administration used fiscal and monetary policies to push the economy toward full employment. An important part of this policy in the eyes of most economists was the tax cut of 1964, described in Chap-

[10] *Economic Report of the President*, 1962, Washington, D.C.: Government Printing Office, p. 10.

ter 10. Between 1962 and 1966, the United States achieved a high rate of growth, in considerable part because of the reduction of the gap between actual and potential output.

Thus, taken as a whole, the Kennedy administration's policies to stimulate economic growth conformed to the elementary principles discussed in this and the previous chapter. In the area of growth policy—just as in fiscal, monetary, and incomes policy—the basic principles of economics take you a long way toward understanding the policies of government, whether Democratic or Republican.

Technological Unemployment

Up to now, we have stressed that rapid technological change is an important stimulus to economic growth. But this stimulus to growth can be offset, at least partially, if rapid technological change results in technological unemployment. Economists have long recognized that new technology can throw people out of work. Karl Marx, in particular, gave technological change—and technological unemployment—a significant role in his theoretical system. (As we saw in Chapter 9, he believed that capitalists would adopt new technologies that would result in more and more technological unemployment.) Workers too have long recognized and feared technological unemployment. As long ago as the mid-1700s, a mob of worried English spinners entered James Hargreaves's mill and smashed the first workable multispindle frames.

Although the dread of technology-induced mass unemployment is not new, it was revived with great effect in the late 1950s and early 1960s. The new scare word was "automation." For example, Professor Crossman of Oxford University, addressing an international conference in 1964, said that "unemployment due to automation will grow steadily over the next four decades, perhaps centuries, and in the end it is likely to reach a very high figure, say 90 percent of the labor force, unless radical changes are made in the present pattern of working."[11] Although *automation* means different things to different people, it generally refers to processes designed to mechanize the human cognitive, conceptual, and informational processes.

Do increases in the rate of technological change necessarily result in increases in aggregate unemployment? To make a long story short, the answer is *no*. Rapid technological change need not have this effect if the government increases total spending at the proper rate. When total spending rises too slowly, increased aggregate unemployment takes place. If it rises too rapidly and resources are already fully employed, inflation will result. As we know, the job of choosing and carrying out appropriate fiscal and monetary policies is not easy; but used with reasonable finesse, such policies should prevent any large increase in aggregate unemployment from technological change.

To see how large-scale technological unemployment can occur—and how it can be avoided—consider Figure 17.2, which shows the $C + I + G$ line at a particular point in time. (If you are a bit hazy about the meaning and significance of this line, review Chapter 10.) Since this line intersects the 45-degree line at point A, the equilibrium level of net national product is $400 billion. If the high-employment level of net national product is also $400 billion, the economy enjoys a high level of employment. Now suppose that there is a significant amount of technological change. What will be the result? To begin with, the advance in technology will almost certainly result in an increase in productivity. In other words, it will enable the labor force to produce more than it formerly could. Thus, the high-employment level of net national product will increase—say to $450 billion. Given this increase, it is obvious that there will be substantial unemployment if the $C + I + G$ line stays put. This is obvious enough. After all, if output remains the same and output per manhour increases, fewer workers will be needed and there

[11] Organization for Economic Cooperation and Development, *The Requirements of Automated Jobs*, Paris, 1965, p. 21.

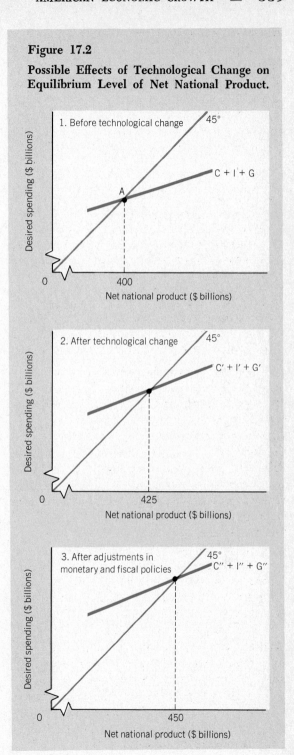

Figure 17.2

Possible Effects of Technological Change on Equilibrium Level of Net National Product.

will be unemployment.

But there is no reason why the C + I + G line should remain constant. The advance in technology itself may increase the profitability of investment, thus raising *I*. Moreover, the advance in technology may result in new consumer products, which prompt consumers to spend more of a given level of income, thus raising *C*. Suppose that, by virtue of these changes in *C* and *I*, the *C + I + G* line shifts to *C′ + I′ + G′* (shown in panel 2 of Figure 17.2). The new equilibrium level of net national product is $425 billion, as shown in panel 2. Unfortunately, in this particular case (but not necessarily in other cases), the new equilibrium level of NNP is less than the new high-employment level of NNP. Thus, without some change in public policy, there would be some technological unemployment. But as we know, the Federal Reserve can increase *I* by increasing the money supply and reducing interest rates, and the government can push *C* upward by reducing tax rates and increase *G* by increasing its own expenditures. Thus, there is no reason why the government cannot raise the *C + I + G* line to the point where it intersects the 45-degree line at $450 billion. For example, the government might nudge the *C + I + G* line up to *C″ + I″ + G″* in panel 3 of Figure 17.2. And if it does this, the equilibrium level of net national product equals the high-employment level of net national product. Thus it should be possible to avoid large amounts of technological unemployment, although transitional problems, discussed in a subsequent section, will remain.

Structural Unemployment

The considerable concern during the 1950s and early 1960s that technological change would result in massive technological unemployment was heightened by fears that workers and jobs were becoming more and more mismatched. According to one group of economists, technological change and other factors were increasing the skill and educational requirements of available jobs, and making it more likely that shortages of highly educated workers would coexist with unemployed pools of unskilled workers. Unemployment of this sort—unemployment that occurs because the workers available for employment do not possess the qualities that employers require—is called **structural unemployment.** The economists who asserted that structural unemployment was growing in the late 1950s and early 1960s were often called the structuralists.

In opposition to the structuralists, another large group of economists denied that structural unemployment was increasing. An important and lively debate took place, both inside and outside the government, over the important question of how unemployment would respond to an increase in total spending. If an increase in total spending would reduce unemployment, then evidently at least that much unemployment was not structural. If it would fail to reduce unemployment, then the unemployment that remained could be called structural. To put the issue to a test, attempts were made to compare various periods when the general pressure of total spending was about the same, to see whether the level of unemployment was higher or more strongly concentrated in certain skill categories, industries, or regions in more recent periods than in the past.

Although neither side had a monopoly on the truth, the results of these tests, as well as the course of events since the 1964 tax cut, provided little support for the structuralist view. There was no evidence that unemployment was becoming more concentrated in particular geographic regions. Moreover, after adjusting for the effect of the overall unemployment rate on the unemployment rate in particular occupations and industries, very few occupations or industries showed an unambiguous tendency for unemployment to increase with time. Also, after adjusting for the effects of the overall unemployment rate, there was no significant tendency for unemployment rates among blacks to rise during the late 1950s and early 1960s. Thus, although a substantial portion of all unemployment may have been structural, there was no evidence that unemployment of this type increased greatly during that period.

Labor Displacement

Economic growth often occurs as a consequence of innovation and the redeployment of resources, which in turn means that *people*—workers, managers, owners of capital—*must adapt to these innovations and redeployments of resources.* Some people lose their jobs, some must move to other places, and some must enter new occupations. For example, consider the movement of people from agricultural to urban areas in the United States—a movement that has been part of the process of economic growth. During the postwar period, the number of farm owners and farm workers declined by over 40 percent. Innovations in agriculture—ranging from chemical fertilizers and insecticides to the mechanical cotton picker and huge harvesting combines—have contributed to this exodus, although they are by no means the only reason. Of those who left agriculture, many wound up in urban ghettos, many lacked the skills and education needed to fill urban jobs, and many who adapted to their new surroundings did so at considerable cost in psychological and emotional terms. Such human costs do not show up in the gross national product. Yet they are important costs, or disadvantages, of economic growth.

Although an adequate level of total spending can go a long way toward assuring that aggregate unemployment will not exceed a socially acceptable minimum, it cannot prevent labor from being displaced from particular occupations, industries, and regions, and being drawn to others. Nor would we want to eliminate all such movements of labor, without which it would be impossible to adjust to changes in technology, population, and consumer tastes. However, regardless of the long-run benefits of this adjustment process, important problems may arise in the short run, and great distress may be imposed on the workers who are displaced. These movements of labor must be carried out as efficiently and painlessly as possible.

The most serious adjustment problems have occurred when massive displacement has occurred in isolated areas among workers with specialized skills and without alternative sources of employment. Coal miners are a good example. About ⅔ of the nation's bituminous coal miners in 1960 were located in West Virginia, Pennsylvania, and Kentucky, and most of the coal mining was concentrated in isolated towns. Employment in bituminous coal started to decline after World War II, partly because of shifting demand and the adoption of new techniques. Between 1947 and 1959, total employment in the industry declined by more than 60 percent, leading to an unemployment rate of roughly 10 percent of the labor force in 5 major bituminous coal areas during most of the 1950s. In 25 smaller areas where there were few job opportunities outside coal mining, the unemployment rate was even higher.

Displaced older workers have encountered particularly serious problems. Seniority rights have helped hold down the displacement of older workers; but once unemployed, they are less likely than younger workers to be reemployed. For example, one year after the shutdown of the Packard automobile plant in Detroit, 77 percent of the workers under 45 were working at another job, whereas the percentages were 67 for the 45-to-54 age group and 62 for the 55-to-64 age group. Even if skill is held constant, the older workers had more serious unemployment problems than the younger workers, at least as measured by length of unemployment. Another study obtained similar results for a period when the general level of employment was higher than in the Packard case. It is easy to understand why older workers have more trouble finding another job. Many of their skills are specific to a particular job, and much of their income and status may be due to seniority, so that they cannot command as high a wage on the open market as they previously earned. Moreover, employers naturally are reluctant to invest in hiring and training a worker who will only be available for a relatively few years and who often has relatively limited education. Finally, because of their roots in the community, older workers are less likely to move to other areas where jobs are more plentiful.

Displaced black workers seem to find it even more difficult than older workers to obtain suitable reemployment at their previous status and earnings. For example, among workers who had been earning the same wage at Packard, blacks experienced a higher average length of unemployment than whites. Moreover, the prestige and economic level of the new job were more likely to be lower for blacks than whites. Needless to say, prejudice often plays an important role in preventing displaced blacks from obtaining new jobs.

Manpower and Training Policies

Beyond insuring an adequate level of total spending, perhaps the most important way that the government can facilitate adjustment to the adoption of new techniques is by promoting the necessary adaptability of the labor force through education and training. Education can increase the versatility and flexibility of the work force and increase its ability to adjust to change. It can open up greater opportunities and improve the productivity of workers at any level of skill or ability. The available evidence indicates the importance of a broad-based, secondary education rather than a narrow vocational education. The training for many—perhaps most—specific jobs can and should be done on the job.

Turning from the education of tomorrow's work force to the retraining of today's, it is generally agreed that the government should help workers who are casualties of technological (and other) change to obtain the skills required to return to productive employment. A coordinated, integrated system of adult retraining, which takes proper account of nationwide needs and supplies and reaches the underprivileged and hard-core unemployed, is useful and important. However, it should be recog-

nized that industry quite properly plays the predominant role in the vocational training and retraining of the work force, and that the government plays only a residual role. The difficulties faced by government-sponsored training programs are considerable, given the limitations of capacity of the vocational education system and the lack of basic education among the trainees.

The government can also promote greater efficiency of labor markets and better adjustment to change by providing better labor market information and by experimenting, in its role as employer, with new adjustment techniques. Job seekers typically have relatively little information about alternative job openings. The federal government should do what it can to expand the amount and quality of available information—keeping in mind that the costs incurred must bear a reasonable relationship to the benefits attained. As well as exploring new ways of disseminating information to those who need and want work, the government might also investigate new education technologies to recognize individual potential and to promote faster and better learning.

Visions of the Economic Future

Finally, let's turn to the rate of economic growth in the future. What sort of economic growth rate is the United States likely to experience between now and the year 2000? Long-range economic forecasting is a hazardous business—unless, of course, the forecaster is so old and the forecast so far in the future that he can be sure of being dead before anyone can tell whether the forecast was right or wrong. As we saw in Chapter 11, it is difficult enough to forecast what will happen next year, let alone 25 years from now. Nonetheless, for some purposes, long-range economic forecasts are useful and need to be made. What do they indicate about the future rate of economic growth in the United States?

In 1967, Herman Kahn, the well-known physicist and strategic theorist, collaborated with sociolo-

John Maynard Keynes
on "Economic Possibilities for Our Grandchildren"

Let us, for the sake of argument, suppose that a hundred years hence we are all of us, on the average, eight times better off in the economic sense than we are today. Assuredly there need be nothing here to surprise us.

Now it is true that the needs of human beings may seem to be insatiable. But they fall into two classes—those needs which are absolute in the sense that we feel them whatever the situation of our fellow human beings may be, and those which are relative in the sense that we feel them only if their satisfaction lifts us above, makes us feel superior to, our fellows. Needs of the second class, those which satisfy the desire for superiority, may indeed be insatiable; for the higher the general level, the higher still are they. But this is not so true of the absolute needs—a point may soon be reached, much sooner perhaps than we are all of us aware of, when these needs are satisfied in the sense that we prefer to devote our further energies to non-economic purposes.

Now, for my conclusion, which you will find, I think, to become more and more startling to the imagination the longer you think about it.

I draw the conclusion that, assuming no important wars and no important increase in population, the *economic problem* may be solved, or be at least within sight of solution, within a hundred years. This means that the economic problem is not—if we look into the future—*the permanent problem of the human race.*

Why, you may ask, is this so startling? It is startling because—if, instead of looking into the future we look into the past—we find that the economic problem, the struggle for subsistence, always has been hitherto the primary, most pressing problem of the human race—not only of the human race, but of the whole of the biological kingdom from the beginnings of life in its most primitive forms.

Thus we have been expressly evolved by nature —with all our impulses and deepest instincts— for the purpose of solving the economic problem. If the economic problem is solved, mankind will be deprived of its traditional purpose.

Will this be a benefit? If one believes at all in the real values of life, the prospect at least opens up the possibility of benefit. Yet I think with dread of the readjustment of the habits and instincts of the ordinary man, bred into him for countless generations, which he may be asked to discard within a few decades.

John Maynard Keynes, *Essays in Persuasion,* London: Macmillan, 1933. Originally published in 1930.

gist Anthony Wiener to produce some forecasts of what the world will be like by the year 2000. In their view, economic growth will probably have resulted in a per capita gross national product of at least $10,000 (in terms of 1965 prices) in the United States. This is a very, very high standard of living. For comparison, recall that per capita GNP in 1970 was about $4,800. Thus, Kahn and Weiner believe that per capita GNP will be more than twice as high in 2000 as in 1970. In their view the United States will have become a "post-industrial society". There will be a reduction in society's emphasis on efficiency and production, less attention paid to traditional work-oriented values, much more leisure, and a much looser relationship between work and income.[12]

Certainly, if these are truly the characteristics of the future, it is not at all what was anticipated by many of the great economists of the past. Malthus and Ricardo never dreamed of such affluence, and Marx never dreamed it could happen under capitalism. Only Keynes, who lived much later than the others, could see the handwriting on the wall. In a famous article written in 1930, he concluded that, "assuming no important wars and no important increase in population, the *economic problem* may be solved, or be at least within sight of solution, within a hundred years."[13] Specifically, he hazarded the guess that we might then be 8 times better off economically than at the time he was writing.

At first glance, it may seem that if Keynes and Kahn and Wiener are right, we are on the threshold of solving practically all our problems. But upon closer examination, one cannot escape the feeling that there are likely to be important problems in adjusting to such a level of affluence. As Keynes put it so well:

> I think with dread of the readjustment of the habits and instincts of the ordinary man, bred into him for countless generations, which he may be asked

to discard within a few decades. . . . (For) the first time since his creation man will be faced with his real, his permanent problem—how to use his freedom from pressing economic cares, how to occupy his leisure, which science and compound interest will have won for him, to live wisely and agreeably and well.

Nonetheless, one must be very pessimistic about the intelligence and imagination of our people if he regards such problems as outweighing the benefits of this economic freedom. Admittedly, the rich have their problems, but there are few poor people who wouldn't trade places with them. In time, is it too much to expect that we will learn how to use these riches to build a better life than we, or others, have known before? I think not. In time, is it too much to expect that we will become more willing and able to share these riches with the poorer nations of the world? I hope not. On this latter point, it is important to understand that the forecasts of milk and honey by the year 2000 are for the industrialized countries, not the less developed countries. The prospects for the latter are less cheerful, as we shall see in Chapter 21.

Summary

Compared with that of other major industrial countries, America's rate of economic growth has been quite impressive over the past century, although in recent years many industrialized countries have experienced higher growth rates than we have. Our relatively rapid economic growth has been due to a variety of important factors, such as rapid technological change, increases in education and training, investment in plant and equipment, plentiful natural resources, and our social and entrepreneurial climate. However, not all aspects of the American economy have been conducive to rapid economic growth. Actual GNP has fallen short of potential GNP, and monopolies and immobilities have prevented efficient resource allocation.

Having reached a level of affluence that would have astonished Smith, Ricardo, Malthus, or Marx (but not Keynes), the industrialized nations are

[12] Herman Kahn and Anthony J. Weiner, *The Year 2000,* New York: Macmillan, 1967.
[13] John Maynard Keynes, "Economic Possibilities for our Grandchildren," reprinted in *Essays in Persuasion,* London: Macmillan, 1933.

now at a point where some observers question the wisdom of further economic growth. The critics of growth assert that more output does not bring more happiness, that economic growth is likely to result in additional environmental pollution, that we are rich enough now to solve our major social problems, and that extra growth is not worth the sacrifices it requires. On the other hand, the proponents of growth argue that it will bring higher living standards, that it will enable us to solve such national problems as poverty, and that it is important for reasons of national defense and national prestige. Although the critics of growth have made some headway, there has been no renunciation of economic growth as a goal of public policy. To stimulate the rate of economic growth, governments can encourage investment in technology, education, and plant and equipment, as well as reduce the gap between actual and potential GNP.

Although rapid technological change is an important stimulus to economic growth, it can also result in technological unemployment. If the government increases total spending at the proper rate, there is no reason why technological unemployment should be large. But an adequate level of total spending cannot prevent labor from being displaced from particular occupations, industries, and regions, and being drawn to others. This adjustment process, which results in long-run benefits, may impose great distress on the workers who are involved. It is important than these movements of labor be carried out as efficiently and painlessly as possible. Through its manpower and training policies, the government can help to distribute the "costs of change" more equitably. According to various long-term forecasts, per capita real GNP in the United States is likely to be more than twice as high in 2000 as in 1970. If this turns out to be true, many economic problems will be solved, but many will still remain.

CONCEPTS FOR REVIEW

Benefits from economic growth   Automation   Investment tax
Costs of economic growth   Structural unemployment   credit
Limits to economic growth   Technological unemployment

QUESTIONS FOR DISCUSSION AND REVIEW

1. According to E. J. Mishan, "If the moving spirit behind economic growth were to speak, its motto would be 'Enough does not suffice.'" Do you agree?

2. According to Robert Solow, "The Doomsday Models [by Forrester et al., say that continued economic growth is, possible . . . because (a) the earth's natural resources will soon be used up; (b) increased industrial production will soon strangle us in pollution; and (c) increased population will eventually outrun the world's capacity to grow food." Do you agree with these models?

3. Increases in the rate of technological change necessarily result in increases in aggregate unemployment. True or False?

4. In order to stimulate economic growth the government probably would *not*
a. increase expenditures on research and development.
b. increase investment in education and training.
c. decrease aggregate investment in plant and equipment.
d. decrease the gap between actual and potential output.

CHAPTER 18

Environmental Pollution

According to many scientists and social observers, one of the costs of economic growth is environmental pollution. For many years, people in the United States paid relatively little attention to the environment and what they were doing to it, but this attitude has changed markedly in the last decade. Now the public seems genuinely concerned about environmental pollution. Even television stars ask that we be kind to the environment. However, in the effort to clean up the environment, choices are not always clear, nor solutions easy. For example, the "energy crisis" that surfaced in the fall of 1973 has brought home the fact that a cleaner environment is not costless. There are major tasks here for the economist, since most environmental issues ultimately come down to questions of economics.

In this chapter, we discuss the nature and causes of environmental pollution, as well as its relationship to the rate of economic growth. After describing the extent of the various kinds of pollution today, we show that excessive pollution results from certain defects in the economic system. Basically, as we shall see, it occurs because of external diseconomies in waste disposal. We also discuss various ways in which public policy might help to solve the problem, with particular attention to direct regulation, effluent fees, and tax credits. Finally, we describe the nature and extent of existing pollution control programs in the United States.

The Nature and Extent
of Environmental Pollution

To see what we mean by environmental pollution, let's begin with one of the most important parts of man's environment, our water supplies. As a result of human activities, large amounts of pollutants are discharged into streams, lakes, and the sea. Chemical wastes are released by industrial plants and mines, as well as by farms and homes when fertilizers, pesticides, and detergents run off into waterways. Oil is discharged into the waters by tankers, sewage systems, oil wells, and other sources. (A spectacular example occurred in California in 1969, when an offshore oil well blew out in the Santa Barbara channel, fouling beaches and killing fish and birds for miles around.) Organic compounds enter waterways from industrial plants and farms, as well as from municipal sewage plants; and animal wastes, as well as human wastes, contribute substantially to pollution.

To reduce the ill effects of water pollution, waste water is sometimes subjected to a treatment process, in which the water is separated from the solid waste, and both are treated so as to protect public health and in-stream life. Generally, the treatment occurs in one or two phases. Primary treatment takes large particles out of the water and lets some of the smaller particles settle out as sludge before releasing the water to a nearby stream or river. Secondary treatment employs a controlled sequence of aeration and settling processes. According to a 1962 survey, 20 percent of the waste water in communities with sewage sys-

tems was untreated, and 28 percent received only primary treatment.

Obviously, we cannot continue to increase the rate at which we dump wastes into our streams, rivers, and oceans. A river, like everything else, can bear only so much. The people of Cleveland know this well: in 1969, the Cuyahoga River, which flows through Cleveland, literally caught fire, so great was its concentration of industrial and other wastes. Of course, the Cuyahoga is an extreme case, but many of our rivers, including the Hudson and the Ohio, are badly polluted, as Table 18.1 shows. Water pollution is a nuisance and perhaps a threat: for example, according to the Public Health Service, we may be approaching a crisis with respect to drinking water.[1]

If clean water is vital to man's survival, so too is clean air. Yet the battle being waged against air pollution in most of our major cities has not been won. Particles of various kinds are spewed into the air by factories that utilize combustion processes, grind materials, or produce dust. Motor vehicles release lead compounds from gasoline and rubber particles worn from tires, helping to create that unheavenly condition known as smog. Citizens of Los Angeles are particularly familiar with smog, but few major cities have escaped at least periodic air pollution. No precise measures have been developed to gauge the effects of air pollution on public health and enjoyment, but some rough estimates suggest that perhaps 25 percent of all deaths from respiratory disease could be avoided by a 50 percent reduction in air pollution.

One of the most important contributors to air pollution is the combustion of fossil fuels, particularly coal and oil products: by-products of combustion comprise about 85 percent of the total amount of air pollutants in the United States. Most of these pollutants result from impure fuels or inefficient burning. Among the more serious pollutants are sulfur dioxide, carbon monoxide, and various

[1] See *Fortune,* February 1970, and D. Rohrer, D. Montgomery, M. Montgomery, D. Eaton, and M. Arnold, *The Environment Crisis,* Skokie, Ill.: National Textbook Company, 1970.

Table 18.1

Water Pollution for Major Drainage Areas, United States, 1970 and 1971

Major watershed	Stream miles	Polluted miles 1970	1971	Change
Ohio	28,992	9,869	24,031	+14,162
Southeast	11,726	3,109	4,490	+ 1,381
Great Lakes	21,374	6,580	8,771	+ 2,191
Northeast	32,431	11,895	5,823	− 6,072
Middle Atlantic	31,914	4,620	5,627	+ 1,007
California	28,277	5,359	8,429	+ 3,070
Gulf	64,719	16,605	11,604	− 5,001
Missouri	10,448	4,259	1,839	− 2,420
Columbia	30,443	7,443	5,685	− 1,758
United States	260,324	69,739	76,299	+ 6,560

Source: Council on Environmental Quality, *Third Annual Report,* August 1972.

oxides of nitrogen. Table 18.2 shows the total amount of major air pollutants emitted by various sources, and Figure 18.1 shows the upward trend in the amount of these emissions. According to some observers, the worst air pollution threat for the future lies in the tremendous growth of the electric power industry. Some technologists hope that nuclear energy, which does not pollute the air, will provide the power the American economy needs. However, it will be a long time before nuclear energy is likely to supply most of the nation's energy, and even then, the environment may be subjected to hazards. Nuclear reactors can cause thermal pollution of rivers and streams, and radiation may be a threat despite various preventive measures.

At present, the automobile is the principal source of air pollution in the United States. According to some estimates, human activities pump into the air over 200 million tons of waste each year, and automobiles can be credited with the dubious honor of contributing about 40 percent of this figure. Spurred on by the public interest in pollution control, some technologists have been hard at work on substitutes for the internal combustion engine.

Attempts have been—and are being—made to devise economical and convenient electric and steam-driven automobiles. To date, however, these efforts have not succeeded. Thus it seems likely that, in the near future at least, we shall have to rely heavily on modifications of the internal combustion engine and its fuel to reduce air pollution.[2] (More use of nonpolluting transport like bicycles and feet would help too.)

Unfortunately, the air and water are not the only parts of man's environment that are being polluted. Each year, we produce an enormous amount of solid waste. Junk heaps testify to the quantity of superannuated cars left, like mechanical corpses, to mar the scenery. Each year industry produces literally mountains of waste and refuse. And picnic lovers and beer drinkers the world over are engaged in what sometimes seems a conspiracy to distribute cans, bottles, and other trash in every conceivable quarter. (Indeed, they sometimes even deposit some in a trash basket!) And it must be noted that the problem is not merely an aesthetic one. Our nation's cities are buckling under the

[2] Ibid. Also, see L. Lave and E. Seskin, "Air Pollution and Human Health," *Science,* August 21, 1970.

Table 18.2

Estimated Emissions of Air Pollutants by Weight, Nationwide, 1970

Source	Carbon monoxide	Particulates	Sulfur oxides	Hydrocarbons	Nitrogen oxides
		(millions of tons per year)			
Transportation	110.0	0.7	1.0	19.5	11.7
Fuel combustion in stationary sources	0.8	6.8	26.5	0.6	10.0
Industrial processes	11.4	13.1	6.0	5.5	0.2
Solid waste disposal	7.2	1.4	0.1	2.0	0.4
Miscellaneous	16.8	3.4	0.3	7.1	0.4
Total	147.2	25.4	33.9	34.7	22.7

Source: Council on Environmental Quality, *Third Annual Report,* August 1972.

Figure 18.1
Weight of Emission of Air Pollutants, United States, 1940–70

Among the most serious air pollutants are carbon monoxide, sulfur oxides, nitrogen oxides, particulates, and hydrocarbons. In the past 30 years, the amount of these pollutants emitted in the United States has increased.

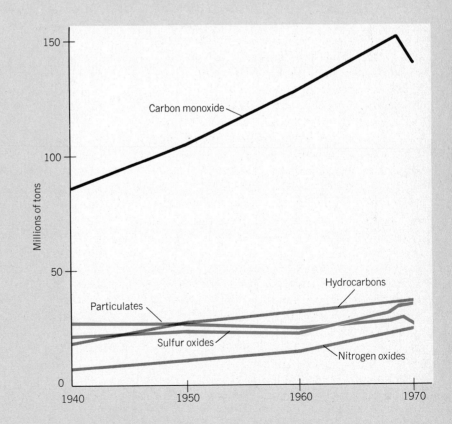

strain of disposing of all the solid waste generated by the affluent society.

There are other problems too. In many of our cities, the noise level is annoying and perhaps dangerous. Then there is thermal pollution. Water is used to cool machinery, particularly in electric power plants; in the process, the water is heated and when discharged, raises the water temperature in the stream or lake into which it flows. Thus, the solubility of certain substances may rise, the water may become more toxic and unable to hold as much oxygen, and the behavior patterns and reproductive capacities of fish may be altered. As for fish, so perhaps for man. There are questions about the extent to which man's production and disposal of wastes may render the earth uninhabitable for various kinds of life. To be sure, many of the most pessimistic and shocking predictions are probably little more than science fiction, but the questions are too important to be dismissed without careful consideration.

The Important Role of External Diseconomies

The reason why our economic system has tolerated pollution of the environment lies largely in the concept of external diseconomies, which we mentioned in Chapter 5. An *external diseconomy* occurs when one person's (or firm's) use of a resource damages other people who cannot obtain proper compensation. When this occurs, a market economy is unlikely to function properly. The price system is based on the supposition that the full cost of using each resource is borne by the person or firm that uses it. If this is not the case and if the user bears only part of the full costs, then the resource is not likely to be directed by the price system into the socially optimal use.

To understand why, we might begin by reviewing briefly how resources are allocated in a market economy. As we saw in Chapter 4, resources are used in their socially most valuable way because

they are allocated to the people and firms who find it worthwhile to bid most for them, assuming that prices reflect true social costs. For example, under these circumstances, a paper mill that maximizes its profits will produce the socially desirable output of paper and use the socially desirable amounts of timber, labor, capital, and other resources.

Suppose, however, that because of the presence of external diseconomies people and firms do not pay the true social costs for resources. For example, suppose that some firms or people can use water and air for nothing, but that other firms or people incur costs as a consequence of this prior use. In this case, the *private costs* of using air and water differ from the *social costs: the price paid by the user of water and air is less than the true cost to society.* In a case like this, users of water and air are guided in their decisions by the private cost of water and air—by the prices they pay. Since they pay less than the true social costs, water and air are artificially cheap to them, so that they will use too much of these resources, from society's point of view.

Note that the divergence between private and social cost occurs if and only if the use of water or air by one firm or person imposes costs on other firms or persons. Thus, if a paper mill uses water and then treats it to restore its quality, there is no divergence between private and social cost. But when the same mill dumps wastes into streams and rivers (the cheap way to get rid of its by-products), the towns downstream that use the water must incur costs to restore its quality. The same is true of air pollution. An electric power plant uses the atmosphere as a cheap and convenient place to dispose of wastes, but people living and working nearby may incur costs as a result, since the incidence of respiratory and other diseases may increase.

We said above that pollution-causing activities that result in external diseconomies represent a malfunctioning of the market system. Let's examine this statement at greater length. *Firms and people dump too much waste material into the water and the atmosphere. The price system does not provide the proper signals because the polluters are induced to use our streams and atmosphere in this socially undesirable way by the artificially low price of disposing of wastes in this manner. Moreover, because the polluters do not pay the true cost of waste disposal, their products are artificially cheap, so that too much is produced of them.*

Consider two examples. Electric power companies do not pay the full cost of disposing of wastes in the atmosphere. They charge an artificially low price, and the public is induced to use more electric power than is socially desirable. Similarly, since the owners of automobiles do not pay the full cost of disposing of exhaust and other wastes in the atmosphere, they pay an artificially low price for operating an automobile, and the public is induced to own and use more automobiles than is socially desirable.[3]

The Polluted Hudson and the Tin Can: Two Case Studies[4]

Richmond is a village of about 2,000 people about 10 miles south of Albany. It is situated at a very badly polluted place on the Hudson River. The water is brown with the human and industrial wastes of Albany, Troy, and other cities upstream, as well as with the wastes dumped into the river locally. In the area immediately around Richmond, two of the principal polluters are the village of Richmond itself and the Smith Paper Company. The village's sewer mains dump their contents into the river, and the Smith Paper Company discharges its untreated wastes into a creek that flows into the river.

[3] L. Ruff, "The Economic Common Sense of Pollution," *The Public Interest,* Spring 1970; R. Solow, "The Economist's Approach to Pollution and Its Control," *Science,* August 6, 1971; and M. Goldman, *Controlling Pollution,* Englewood Cliffs, N.J.: Prentice-Hall, 1967.
[4] The names Richmond and Smith are fictitious, but otherwise the case study given in the first part of this section, taken from an article in the *New York Times,* May 4, 1970, is factual.

The people of Richmond have dragged their heels about building a sewage treatment system because they have felt that unless towns upstream took action, their own efforts would be fruitless. After some prodding by New York State, a referendum was held in 1968 to vote on a sewer district, but it was turned down by the voters. Needless to say, part of the reason was that the people of the village would have to pay about $85 per family per year for the water treatment system. Despite the state's nudging, the officials of Richmond admit that it will be a long time before the problem is taken care of.

The Smith Paper Company has also been slow to do anything about water pollution. State health officials ordered it to clean up its effluent by July 1970, but the Company did not formulate a preliminary plan for a treatment system until April 1970. According to many reports, the Company was not in healthy financial condition, and Smith's treatment costs, according to some of its engineers, could run as high as $300,000—or about 10 percent of the value of its plant. Obviously, one reason why this plant remains in business is that it does not pay the full social costs of waste disposal. Obviously, too, the price of its paper is artificially low for this reason. This is no criticism of the Company. In a free enterprise economy, firms are expected to be motivated by profit. The problem is that, because of external diseconomies, the market system does not insure that the private costs of waste disposal equal the social costs. The result is a polluted river.

Richmond is an example of one type of pollution. To understand how external diseconomies can result in another type of pollution, consider the cans and bottles that are so conspicuous a part of our nation's litter problem. Years ago, beer, soft drinks, and other such liquids came in relatively expensive bottles on which there was a deposit. Typically, when you purchased a bottle of beverage, you had to deposit $.05 for the bottle. If you didn't bring back the bottle, you didn't get the $.05 back. If someone else found—or stole—your bottle, he could take it back and get the

Figure 18.2
Beer Containers by Type,
United States, 1957–76

In recent years, metal cans and nonreturnable bottles have captured a much larger share of the market, while returnable bottles, which result in less trash and litter, have become far scarcer.

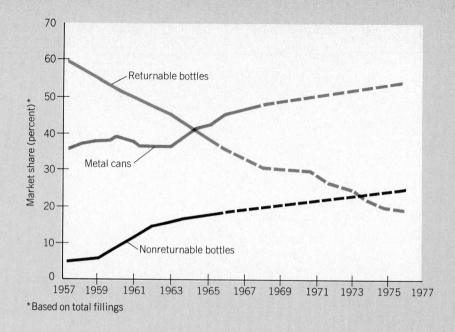

money. Since $.05 was a significant amount in those days, there were few bottles lying around as unsightly litter. Kids—and more than a few adults—were only too glad to pick them up and take them back to the store to get the deposit. Thus, in those days, the system worked in such a way that the purchaser of the beverage paid for the cost of bringing the bottle back to the store. Either he took it back himself (and got his deposit back), or in effect he paid someone else $.05 to do it for him.

But this situation changed abruptly about 40 years ago, when producers of beer and soft drinks introduced a packaging innovation: the can. Unlike the old-fashioned bottle, there was no deposit on the can. Indeed, one of the advantages to consumers was that they didn't have to bother to take the cans back; they could simply throw them away. Consumers preferred the can for its convenience, and bottle manufacturers were forced to develop a cheaper no-deposit bottle to compete with cans. (Figure 18.2 shows the increase in recent years in the percentage of beer containers

that are metal cans or nonreturnable bottles.) The result has been trash and litter, because there is no longer the same incentive to pick up cans and bottles or to return them to stores or manufacturers. Moreover, since bottles are no longer used over and over, there are more bottles and cans to dispose of.

It is important to note that, once the cans and no-deposit bottles were introduced, the consumer of beverages no longer had to pay for the cost of disposing of the cans or bottles. Basically, this was the reason for the litter problem. In other words, there was now an external diseconomy, since purchasers and consumers of beverages imposed costs on other people, who had to bear the expense of disposing of the litter. Of course, this was not always the case, since many people were public-spirited enough to dispose of their own cans and bottles, even without financial incentive. But our highways and parks testify to the fact that many people are not so public-spirited; as a result, certain states and localities have recently passed laws requiring the sale of deposit bottles.

Economic Growth and Environmental Pollution

According to many authorities, economic growth—defined as increases in total economic output per capita—has been associated with increases in the level of environmental pollution. This is not very surprising, since practically all the things that are produced must eventually be thrown away in one form or another. Thus, as output per capita goes up, the level of pollution is likely to go up as well. For example, as we grow more affluent and increase the number of automobiles per capita, we also increase the amount of such air pollutants as nitrogen oxide and tetraethyl lead, both of which are emitted by automobiles. We also increase the number of automobiles that eventually must be scrapped.

But it is important to recognize that pollution is not tied inextricably to national output. Although increases in national output in the past have been associated with increases in pollution, there is no reason why this correlation must continue unchanged in the future. Clearly, we can produce things that are heavy polluters of the environment —like electric power and automobiles—or we can produce things that do not pollute the environment nearly so much—like pianos and bicycles.

In recent years, some people have suggested that we curtail our economic growth in order to reduce pollution: **Zero Economic Growth** is their goal. Very few economists seem to favor such a policy. Opponents of Zero Economic Growth point out that more productive capacity would help produce the equipment required to reduce pollution. As we shall see, this equipment will not be cheap. Moreover, with proper public policies, we should be able to increase output without increasing pollution, if this is what our people want. In addition, as pointed out by Walter Heller of the University of Minnesota:

> Short of a believable threat of extinction, it is hard to believe that the public would accept the tight controls, lowered material living standards, and large income transfers required to create and man-age a [no-growth] state. Whether the necessary shifts could be accomplished without vast unemployment and economic dislocation is another question. It may be that the shift to a no-growth state would throw the fragile ecology of our economic system so out of kilter as to threaten its breakdown. Like it or not, economic growth seems destined to continue.[5]

Some people have also argued that technological change is the real villain responsible for pollution, and that the rate of technological change should be slowed. Certainly, technological change has made people more interdependent, and brought about more and stronger external diseconomies. Technological change also results in ecological changes, some of which are harmful. For example, detergents contain phosphate, which induces water pollution by causing heavy overgrowths of algae.

But technological change is also a potential hero in the fight against pollution, because the creation of new technology is an important way to reduce the harmful side effects of existing techniques—assuming, of course, that we decide to use our scientists and engineers to this end. Contrary to some people's views, pollution is not the product of some mindless march of technology, but of human action and inaction. There is no sense in blaming technology, when pollution is due basically to economic, social, and political choices and institutions.

Finally, it is frequently suggested that, as our population increases, we must expect more pollution. Many who advocate a policy of **Zero Population Growth** advance the argument that it would help reduce the level of pollution. The available evidence indicates some relationship between a nation's population and its pollution levels. But there are important differences in the amount of pollution generated by people in various countries. The average American is responsible for much more pollution than the average citizen of most other countries, because the average American is a much bigger user of electric power, detergents, pesticides,

[5] W. Heller, "Economic Growth and Ecology—An Economist's View," *Monthly Labor Review*, November 1971.

and other such products. It has been estimated that the United States, with less than $\frac{1}{10}$ of the world's population, produces about $\frac{1}{3}$ of the wastes discharged into the air and water. Clearly, much more than economics is involved in the discussion of the optimal level of population. Although it is only one of a number of important factors, a nation's population does affect the level of pollution; but as we shall see in subsequent sections, pollution can be reduced considerably even if our population continues to grow.[6]

Public Policy toward Pollution

Pollution is caused by defects in our institutions, not by malicious intent, greed, or corruption. In cases where waste disposal causes significant external diseconomies, economists generally agree that government intervention may be justifiable. But how can the government intervene? Perhaps the simplest way is to issue certain regulations for waste disposal. For example, the government can prohibit the burning of trash in furnaces or incinerators, or the dumping of certain materials in the ocean; and make any person or firm that violates these restrictions subject to a fine, or perhaps even imprisonment. Also, the government can ban the use of chemicals like DDT, or require that all automobiles meet certain regulations for the emission of air pollutants. Further, the government can establish quality standards for air and water.

The government can also intervene by establishing effluent fees. An *effluent fee* is a fee a polluter must pay to the government for discharging waste. In other words, a price is imposed on the disposal of wastes into the environment; and the more a firm or individual pollutes, the more he must pay. The idea behind the imposition of effluent fees is

that they can bring the private cost of waste disposal closer to the true social costs. Faced with a closer approximation to the true social costs of his activities, the polluter will reduce the extent to which he pollutes the environment. Needless to say, many practical difficulties are involved in carrying out this seemingly simple scheme, but many economists believe that this is the best way to deal with the pollution problem.[7]

Still another way for the government to intervene is to establish tax credits for firms that introduce pollution-control equipment. There are, of course, many types of equipment that a plant can introduce to cut down on pollution—for example, "scrubbers" for catching poisonous gases, and electrostatic precipitators for decreasing dust and smoke. But such pollution-control equipment costs money, and firms are naturally reluctant to spend money on purposes where the private rate of return is so low. To reduce the burden, the government can allow firms to reduce their tax bill by a certain percentage of the amount they spend on pollution-control equipment. Tax incentives of this sort have been discussed widely in recent years, and some have been adopted.

Direct Regulation

Let's look more closely at the advantages and disadvantages of each of these major means by which the government can intervene to remedy the nation's pollution problems. At present we rely mostly on direct regulation of waste disposal (and the quality of the environment); and despite the many problems involved, it has undoubtedly done much good. As Allen Kneese, one of the country's top experts in this area, says about water pollution,

---

[6] It must also be noted that pollution is not confined to capitalist countries; the Soviet Union and other Communist countries are afflicted by serious pollution problems. Nor is pollution anything new: for example, the ancient Romans complained of water pollution.

[7] Another possibility is for the government to issue a certificate or license to pollute. The government might issue a limited number of certificates, to be auctioned off to the highest bidders. Although it has theoretical possibilities, this technique is not being used to any appreciable extent at present.

"The control of water discharges through administrative orders regulating individual waste disposers has been a useful device and cannot be abandoned until we have a better substitute."[8]

However, economists agree that direct regulation suffers from some serious disadvantages. First, such regulations have generally taken the form of general, across-the-board rules. For example, if two factories located on the same river dump the same amount of waste material into the river, such regulations would probably call for each factory to reduce its waste disposal by the same amount. Unfortunately, although this may appear quite sensible, it may in fact be very inefficient. Suppose, for example, that it is much less costly for one factory to reduce its waste disposal than for the other. Clearly, in such a case, it would be more efficient to ask the factory that could reduce its wastes more cheaply to cut down more on its waste disposal than the other factory. For reasons of this sort, reductions in pollution are likely to be accomplished at more than minimum cost, if they are accomplished by direct regulation.

Second, to formulate such regulations in a reasonably sensible way, the responsible government agencies must have access to much more information than they are likely to obtain or assimilate. Unless the government agencies have a detailed and up-to-date familiarity with the technology of hundreds of industries, they are unlikely to make sound rules. Moreover, unless the regulatory agencies have a very wide jurisdiction, their regulations will be evaded by the movement of plants and individuals from localities where regulations are stiff to localities where they are loose. In addition, the regulatory agencies must view the pollution problem as a whole, since piecemeal regulation may simply lead polluters to substitute one form of pollution for another. For example, New York and Philadelphia have attempted to reduce water pollution by more intensive sewage treatment. However, one result has been the production of a lot of

[8] A. Kneese, "Public Policy Toward Water Pollution," in E. Mansfield, *Microeconomics: Selected Readings,* New York: Norton, 1971, p. 467.

biologically active sludge that is being dumped into the ocean—and perhaps causing problems there.[9]

Effluent Fees

The use of effluent fees is the approach most economists seem to prefer, for the following reasons. First, it obviously is socially desirable to use the cheapest way to achieve any given reduction in pollution. A system of effluent fees is more likely to accomplish this objective than direct regulation, because the regulatory agency cannot have all the relevant information (as we noted above), whereas polluters, reacting in their own interest to effluent fees, will tend to use the cheapest means to achieve a given reduction in pollution.

To see why this is the case, consider a particular polluter. Faced with an effluent fee—that is, a price it must pay for each unit of waste it discharges—the polluter will find it profitable to reduce its discharge of waste to the point where the cost of reducing waste discharges by one unit equals the effluent fee. Why? Because, if the cost of reducing its waste disposal (i.e., its pollution) by an additional unit is less than the effluent fee, the firm can increase its profits by discharging less waste. On the other hand, if the cost of reducing its waste disposal (i.e., its pollution) by an additional unit is greater than the effluent fee, the firm can increase its profits by discharging more waste. Thus, if the firm is maximizing profit, the cost of reducing its waste disposal by an additional unit must equal the effluent fee.

It follows that, since the effluent fee is the same for all polluters, the cost of reducing waste discharges by one extra unit must be the same for all polluters. But if this is so, the total cost of achieving the resulting decrease in pollution must be a minimum. Why? Because the total cost of achieving a certain decrease in pollution is a mini-

[9] Solow, *op. cit.*

mum if the decrease is carried out so that the cost of reducing waste discharges by one extra unit is the same for all polluters. To see this, suppose that the cost of reducing waste discharges by an additional unit is *not* the same for all polluters. Then there is a cheaper way to reduce pollution to its existing level—by getting polluters whose cost of reducing waste discharges by an additional unit is low to reduce their waste disposal by an additional unit, and by allowing polluters whose cost of reducing waste discharges by an additional unit is high to increase their pollution commensurately.

Economists also favor effluent fees because this approach requires far less information in the hands of the relevant government agencies than does direct regulation. After all, when effluent fees are used, all the government has to do is meter the amount of pollution a firm or household produces (which admittedly is sometimes not easy) and charge accordingly. It is left to the firms and households to figure out the most ingenious and effective ways to cut down on their pollution and save on effluent fees. This is also a spur to inventive activities aimed at developing more effective ways to reduce pollution. Also, economists favor the use of effluent fees because financial incentives are likely to be easier to administer than direct regulation. Witness the case of Richmond, which illustrates the gap between regulation and enforceable performance.

To illustrate how effluent fees can produce more efficient ways to reduce pollution, consider a recent proposal by the state of Washington for reducing emission of sulfur oxides. The proposed regulation would oblige copper smelters to control 90 percent of the sulfur content of ore entering smelters. There is considerable disagreement over the cost of the regulation. The state says it would cost the smelters about $.02 per pound of copper to comply, whereas the smelters say it is technologically impossible to comply. Some people have suggested that one way to resolve this controversy might be to impose a fee equivalent to $.03 per pound of copper if the emission of sulfur oxide were not controlled. Then if the smelters could achieve 90

percent control for $.02 per pound, they would have every incentive to do so, thus increasing their profits. If they could not reach the goal, they would have an incentive to adopt other control measures or to develop new and less costly control devices.

While economists tend to favor the use of effluent fees, they are not always against direct regulation. Some ways of disposing of certain types of waste are so dangerous that the only sensible thing to do is to ban them. For example, a ban on the disposal of mercury or arsenic in places where human beings are likely to consume them—and die—seems reasonable enough. In effect, the social cost of such pollution is so high that a very high penalty—imprisonment—is put on it. In addition, of course, economists favor direct regulation when it simply is not feasible to impose effluent fees—for example, in cases where it would be prohibitively expensive to meter the amount of pollutants emitted by various firms or households.

The Ruhr: A Case Study[10]

Let's consider a well-known case of effluent fees in use—the Ruhr valley in West Germany. The Ruhr is one of the world's most industrialized areas. It includes about ⅓ of West Germany's industrialized capacity, and about 70 to 90 percent of West Germany's coal, coke, and iron and steel outputs. It contains about 10 million people and about 4,300 square miles. Water supplies in the Ruhr are quite limited: five small rivers supply the area. The amazing amount of waste materials these rivers carry is indicated by the fact that the average annual natural low flow is less than the volume of effluent discharged into the rivers. Yet the local water authorities have succeeded in making this small amount of water serve the needs of the firms and households of this tremendous industrial area, and at the same time the streams

[10] This section is based on A. Kneese and B. Bower, *Managing Water Quality: Economics, Technology, Institutions* (Resources for the Future, 1968), Chapter 12.

have been used for recreation. Moreover, all this has been achieved at a remarkably low cost. The success of water management in the Ruhr seems to be due in considerable part to institutional arrangements that allowed the German water managers to plan and operate a relatively efficient regional system. Collective water quality improvement measures are used. Water quality is controlled by waste treatment in over 100 plants, regulation of river flow by reservoir, and a number of oxidation lakes in the Ruhr itself.

Effluent fees are an integral part of the institutional arrangements governing water quality. The amount a firm has to pay depends upon how much waste—and what kind—it pumps into the rivers. A formula has been devised to indicate how much a polluter must pay to dispose of a particular type of waste. In simple terms, the formula bases the charge on the amount of clean water needed to dilute the effluent in order to avoid harm to fish. Using this formula, the local authorities can determine, after testing the effluent of any firm, the amount the firm should pay. Specifically, the amount depends on the amount of suspended materials that will settle out of the effluent, the amount of oxygen consumed by bacteria in a sample of effluent, the results of a potassium permanganate test, and the results of a fish toxicity test. You need not understand the nature or specific purposes of these measurements and tests. The important thing is that you understand their general aim—which is to measure roughly the amount of pollution caused by various kinds of wastes. Having made these measurements and tests, the local authorities use their formula to determine how much a firm must pay in effluent fees.

Tax Credits for Pollution-Control Equipment

Many tax inducements to encourage firms and individuals to install pollution-control equipment have been proposed. A typical suggestion is that the government offer a tax credit equal to 20 percent of the cost of pollution-control equipment, and allow a firm to depreciate such equipment in only 1 to 5 years. In this way, the government would help defray some of the costs of the pollution-control equipment by allowing a firm that installed such equipment to pay less taxes than if no such tax inducements existed.

However, such schemes have a number of disadvantages. For one, subsidies to promote the purchase of particular types of pollution-control equipment may result in relatively inefficient and costly reductions in pollution. After all, other methods that don't involve special pollution-control equipment—such as substituting one type of fuel for another—may sometimes be a more efficient way to reduce pollution. Also, subsidies of this sort may not be very effective. Even if the subsidy reduces the cost to the firm of reducing pollution, it may still be cheaper for the firm to continue to pollute. In other words, subsidies of this sort make it a little less painful for polluters to reduce pollution; but unlike effluent fees, they offer no positive incentive.

Furthermore, it seems preferable on grounds of equity for the firms and individuals that do the polluting—or their customers—to pay to clean up the mess that results. Effluent fees work this way, but with tax credits for pollution-control equipment, the government picks up part of the tab by allowing the polluter to pay lower taxes. In other words, the general public, which is asked to shoulder the additional tax burden to make up for the polluters' lower taxes, pays part of the cost. But is this a fair allocation of the costs? Why should the general public be saddled with much of the bill?

Pollution-Control Programs in the United States

In recent years, there has been considerable growth in government programs designed to control pollution. To take but one example, federal expenditures to reduce water pollution increased in the period from the mid-1950s to 1970 from about $1 million to $300 million annually. In water pollution, the federal government has for many years operated a system of grants-in-aid to state, municipal, or regional agencies to help construct treatment plants; and grants are made for research on new treatment methods. In addition, the 1970 Water Quality Improvement Act authorizes grants to demonstrate new methods and techniques and to establish programs to train people in water control management. (The federal government has also regulated the production and use of pesticides.) The states, as well as the federal government, have played an important role in water pollution control. They have been primarily responsible for setting standards for allowable pollution levels, and many state governments have provided matching grants to help municipalities construct treatment plants.

For air pollution, the federal government has disbursed funds to promote research and development to prevent and control the pollution of the atmosphere. Federal agencies offer extensive technical advice about air pollution and air quality standards. The states, as well as the federal government, have played an important role in setting air quality standards. Most states have also established planning commissions and pollution control boards, and have provided tax incentives to industry for abatement. Further, in the area of solid wastes, the government has made grants for research, training, and surveys of disposal techniques.

In 1969, the Congress established a new agency—the Council on Environmental Quality—to oversee and plan the nation's pollution control programs. Modeled to some extent on the Council of Economic Advisers, the Council on Environmental Quality, which has three members, is supposed to gather information on considerations and trends in the quality of the environment, review and evaluate the federal government's programs in this area, develop appropriate national policies, and conduct needed surveys and research on en-

vironmental quality. The tasks assigned to the council are obviously important ones. The extent to which this relatively new agency can carry out these tasks is difficult to say. It will be some time before the council's effectiveness can be appraised.

In 1970, the federal government established another new agency, the Environmental Protection Agency. Working with state and local officials, this agency establishes standards for desirable air and water quality, and devises rules for attaining these goals. For example, the government has required various sources of pollution to reduce their emission of pollutants so that these goals can be reached. According to the amendments to the Clean Air Act of 1967, automobiles in 1975 were supposed to cut emissions of carbon monoxide and hydrocarbons by 90 percent from 1970 levels, but this requirement has been softened. Because direct regulation of this sort suffers from the disadvantages cited in a previous section, there also has been some study of the use of effluent fees. For example, the government has considered imposing a fee on the emission of sulfur oxide into the air.

Many people feel that public policy is not moving as rapidly as it should in this area. Certainly, however, it is not easy to determine how fast or how far we should go in attempting to reduce pollution. Those who will bear the costs of pollution control projects—towns like Richmond, firms like the Smith Paper Company—have an understandable tendency to emphasize (and perhaps inflate) the costs and discount the benefits of such projects. Those who are particularly interested in enjoying nature and outdoor recreation—like the Sierra Club—are understandably inclined to emphasize (and perhaps inflate) the benefits and discount the costs of such projects. Politics inevitably plays a major role in the outcome of such cases. The citizens of the United States must indicate, through the ballot box as well as the marketplace, how much they are willing to pay to reduce pollution. We must also decide at what level of government the relevant rules are to be made. Since many pollution problems are local, it often seems sensible to determine the appropriate level of environmental quality locally. (However, there are obvious dangers in piecemeal regulation, as pointed out above.)

Cost of Cleaning Up the Environment

One of the most fundamental questions about pollution control is: how clean do we want the air, water, and other parts of our environment to be? At first glance, it may seem that we should restore and maintain a pristine pure environment, but this is not a very sensible goal, since the costs of achieving it would be enormous. The Environmental Protection Agency has estimated that it would cost about $60 billion to remove 85 to 90 percent of water pollutants from industrial and municipal sources by 1982. This is hardly a trivial amount, but it is far less than the cost of achieving zero discharge of pollutants, which would be about $320 billion—a truly staggering sum.

Fortunately, however, there is no reason to aim at so stringent a goal. It seems obvious that, as pollution increases, various costs to society increase as well. Some of these costs were described at the beginning of this chapter. For example, we pointed out that increases in air pollution result in increased deaths, and that increases in water pollution reduce the recreational value of rivers and streams. Suppose that we could get accurate data on the cost to society of various levels of pollution. Of course, it is extremely difficult to get such data, but if we could, we could determine the relationship between the amount of these costs and the level of pollution. Clearly, it would look like the hypothetical curve in Figure 18.3: the greater the level of pollution, the higher these costs will be.

But these costs are not the only ones that must be considered. We must also take into account the costs of controlling pollution. In other words, we must look at the costs to society of maintaining a certain level of environmental quality. These costs are not trivial, as we saw at the beginning of

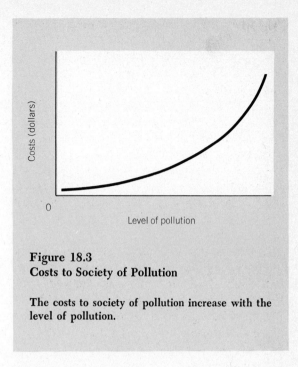

Figure 18.3
Costs to Society of Pollution

The costs to society of pollution increase with the level of pollution.

this section. To maintain a very low level of pollution, it is necessary to invest heavily in pollution-control equipment and to make other economic sacrifices. If we could get accurate data on the cost to society of controlling pollution, we could find the relationship between the amount of these costs and the level of pollution. Clearly, it would look like the hypothetical curve in Figure 18.4; the lower the level of pollution, the higher these costs will be.

At this point, it should be obvious why we should not try to achieve a zero level of pollution. *The sensible goal for our society is to minimize the sum of the costs of pollution and the costs of controlling pollution.* In other words, we should construct a graph, as shown in Figure 18.5, to indicate the relationship between the sum of these two types of costs and the level of pollution. Then we should choose the level of pollution at which the sum of these two types of costs is a minimum. Thus, in Figure 18.5, we should aim for a pollution level of A. There is no point in trying for a lower level; such a reduction would cost more

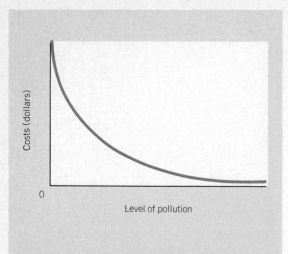

Figure 18.4
Costs to Society of Pollution Control

The more pollution is reduced, the higher are the costs to society of pollution control.

than it would be worth. For example, the cost of achieving a zero pollution level would be much more than it would be worth. Only when the pollution level exceeds *A* is the extra cost to society of the additional pollution greater than the cost of preventing it. For example, the cost of allowing pollution to increase from *A* to *B* is much greater than the cost of prevention.

It is easy to draw hypothetical curves, but not so easy actually to measure these curves. Unfortunately, no one has a very clear idea of what the curves in Figure 18.5 really look like—although we can be sure that their general shapes are like those shown there. Thus, no one really knows just how clean we should try to make the environment. Under these circumstances, expert opinion differs on the nature and extent of the programs that should be carried out, and the costs involved. Moreover, as pointed out in the previous section, political considerations and pressures enter in. Thus, while it is difficult to estimate how much the United States is likely to spend in the future

Figure 18.5
Determining Optimal Level of Pollution

The optimal level of pollution is at point **A**, since this is where the total costs are a minimum. Below point **A**, the cost to society of more pollution is less than the cost of preventing it. Above point **A**, the cost to society of more pollution is greater than the cost of preventing it.

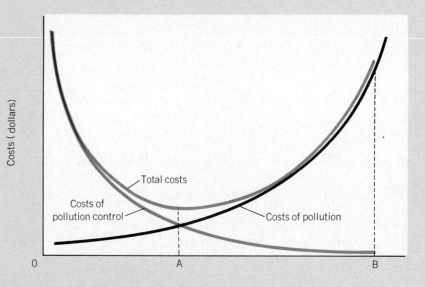

Table 18.3

Costs to Industry of Pollution Control

Industry	Actual 1971	Expenditures Planned 1972	Planned 1975	Total investment required to meet 1972 standards
		(Millions of dollars)		
Electric utilities	565	1,027	1,188	6,190
Petroleum	527	542	462	2,690
Paper	257	494	224	1,980
Iron and steel	217	206	870	1,780
Nonferrous metals	111	269	149	1,670
Chemicals	282	445	419	1,250
Commercial	234	224	315	1,200
Stone, clay, and glass	112	173	195	780
Machinery	95	381	239	560
Food and beverages	101	158	208	550
Mining	61	192	157	470
Rubber	45	53	100	410
Fabricated metals	89	119	74	400
Instruments	60	74	119	260
Electrical machinery	70	70	91	240
Gas utilities	49	79	82	220
Total	3,245	4,906	5,378	22,760

Source: Business Week, May 13, 1972.

on pollution control, we can be sure that we will continue to live with considerable pollution—and that, for the reasons just given, this will be the rational thing to do.

According to a 1972 McGraw-Hill survey, American industry alone spent about $3.2 billion in 1971 and planned to spend about $4.9 billion in 1972 to control air and water pollution. To meet pollution control standards in effect as of January 1, 1972, industry would have to spend about $22.8 billion. (See Table 18.3.) It is important to recognize that the costs of pollution control extend far beyond the construction of more and better water treatment plants, or the more extensive control of gas emission, or other

such steps. A serious pollution control program can put firms out of business, put people out of work, and bring economic trouble to communities that rely heavily on industries and farms that must pollute to compete. This is not to argue that polluters should be allowed to pay less than the true social cost of disposing of their wastes; but any pollution control program must allow firms and workers time to make the necessary adjustments.

We must also recognize that a pollution control system can result in a redistribution of income. For example, automobiles, electric power, and other goods and services involving considerable pollution are likely to increase in price relative to other goods and services involving little pollution. To the extent that polluting goods and services play a bigger role in the budgets of the poor than of the rich, pollution control hurt the poor and help the rich. This effect can be offset by using the tax system and the expenditures of the government, but, as we have seen, this is easier said than done.

How Should We Dispose of Materials?

In conclusion, it must be stressed that the entire pollution problem is basically concerned with how to dispose of materials in our society. Economists and others customarily speak of people "consuming" goods. The word "consume" suggests that nothing is left of the goods after "consumption," but in truth they are still very much with us. Sometimes they are transformed into waste materials; sometimes they are banged up and useless; sometimes they are changed from a solid state to a gaseous state. But they are still around, and they have to be disposed of somehow. Moreover, some ways of disposing of them are better from society's point of view than others. For example, it may be better to bury certain types of wastes in the ground than to pollute the air.

An interesting scheme to help solve this problem has been proposed by Princeton's Edwin Mills.[11] It is not yet at the stage of serious consideration for practical application, but it is nonetheless an interesting stimulus to further thought in this area. Mills proposes that the government collect from the original producer or importer of certain raw materials a fee equal to the cost to society if each material were disposed of in the most harmful way. Then the fee would be returned, in part or in full, when the material was returned to the environment—that is, disposed of. If it was disposed of in a socially innocuous way, the full fee would be returned, but the more harmful the method of disposal, the less the refund.

[11] E. Mills, *User Fees and the Quality of the Environment,* in preparation.

An advantage of this scheme is that prices of materials would tend to reflect their true social costs—including the costs of disposal. There are also lots of practical difficulties: for one, owners of some materials would be hit with a large financial loss. Whether or not Mills' scheme is practical, it has the considerable virtue of looking at the pollution problem in the right light—as how we are to dispose of materials. If you are concerned about the environmental issue, you would be well advised to study further the economic (and technological) aspects of this problem. The environment you save is bound to be your own.

Summary

One of the major social issues of the 1970s is environmental pollution. As a result of human activities, great quantities of chemicals, industrial wastes, pesticides, fertilizers, animal wastes, and human wastes are being dumped into the rivers, lakes, and oceans. Particles of various kinds are being spewed into the air by factories that utilize combustion processes, or that grind materials, or that produce dust. Lead compounds from gasoline and rubber particles worn from tires are being released into the atmosphere by motor vehicles. Each year we produce an enormous amount of solid waste—junked cars, garbage, cans, bottles, and other trash. In addition, noise pollution assaults our ears, and thermal pollution degrades our lakes and rivers. Many observers regard these various forms of pollution as a problem that must be dealt with much more effectively in the future than it has been in the past.

To a considerable extent, environmental pollution is an economic problem. Waste disposal and other pollution-causing activities result in external diseconomies. Specifically, the firms and individuals that pollute the water and air (and other facets of the environment) pay less than the true social costs of disposing of their wastes in this way. Part of the true social cost is borne by other firms and individuals who must pay to clean up the water or air, or who must live with the consequences. Because of the divergence of private from social costs, the market system does not result in an optimal allocation of resources. Firms and individuals create too much waste and dispose of it in excessively harmful ways. Because the polluters do not pay the full cost of waste disposal, their products are artificially cheap, with the result that too much is produced of them.

The government can intervene in several ways to help remedy the breakdown of the market system in this area. One way is to issue regulations for waste disposal and other activities influencing the environment. Another is to establish effluent fees, charges a polluter must pay to the government for discharging wastes. Two important advantages of effluent fees are that they are more likely to result in the use of the minimum-cost way to achieve a given reduction in pollution and that they require far less information in the hands of the relevant government agencies than direct regulation. Still another way for the government to intervene is to grant tax credits to firms that introduce pollution-control equipment. But this method is questionable on grounds of efficiency, effectiveness, and equity. Also, the federal government can, and does, help local governments meet the costs of waste treatment.

In recent years, there has been considerable growth in government programs designed to control pollution. In 1969, the Council on Environmental Quality was formed; and in 1970, the Environmental Protection Agency was added. It is extremely difficult to determine how clean the environment should be. Of course, the sensible goal for society is to permit the level of pollution that minimizes the sum of the costs of pollution and the costs of controlling pollution; but no one has a very clear idea of what these costs are, and to a large extent the choices must be made through the political process. Basically, the entire pollution problem is concerned with how materials are to be disposed of in our society, and economists and policy makers are beginning to view the problem in this light.

CONCEPTS FOR REVIEW

External diseconomies	Secondary treatment	Council on Environ-
Private costs	Air pollution	mental Quality
Social costs	Thermal pollution	Environmental Protec-
Water pollution	Noise pollution	tion Agency
Primary treatment	Effluent fees	

QUESTIONS FOR DISCUSSION AND REVIEW

1. The 1971 annual report of the Council of Economic Advisers states that: "New rules for use of the environment are bound to affect competitive relationships within and among industries, localities, and nations." Give examples of these effects, and ways that society can make the transition easier.

2. Smoke is a classic case of an external diseconomy. (It was cited by Alfred Marshall and others.) Describe what actions can and should be taken to eliminate socially undesirable effects of smoke.

3. It is generally agreed that in the long run we should try to reach a zero level of pollution. True or False?

4. Which of the following forms of government intervention in the pollution problem is most often favored by economists?
a. Direct regulations   b. Effluent fees   c. Tax credits   d. Population control

PART SIX

International
Economics

CHAPTER 19

International Trade

It takes the average human being little time to realize that he is not an island unto himself and that he benefits from living with, working with, and trading with other people. Exactly the same is true of nations. They too must interact with one another, and they too benefit from trade with one another. No nation can be an island unto itself—not even the United States. To understand how the world economy functions, you must grasp the basic economic principles of international trade.

This chapter discusses many of the fundamental questions about international trade. What is the nature of American foreign trade? What are the effects of international trade? What determines the sorts of goods a nation will import or export? What are the advantages of free trade and the arguments against it? What are the social costs of tariffs and quotas, and what has been their history in the United States? What are some of the major issues regarding protectionism in the United States today? Some of these questions have occupied the attention of economists for hundreds of years; some are as current as today's newspaper.

America's Foreign Trade

America's foreign trade, although small relative to our national product, plays a very important role in our economic life. Many of our industries depend on other countries for markets or for raw materials (like coffee, tea, or tin). Our *exports*—the things we sell to other countries—amount to about 5 percent of our gross national product, which seems small relative to other countries like Germany, France, Italy, and the United Kingdom, where exports are about 15–20 percent of gross national product. But this is because our domestic market is so large. In absolute terms, and relative to those of other countries, our exports seem very large indeed. In recent years, they have represented about 15 percent of total world trade. Without question, our way of life would have to change considerably if we could not trade with other countries.

When we were a young country, we exported raw materials primarily. For example, during the 1850s about 70 percent of our exports were raw materials and foodstuffs. But the composition of our exports has changed with time. More are now finished manufactured goods and less are raw materials. In the 1960s, about 60 percent of our exports were finished manufactured goods, and only about 20 percent were raw materials and foodstuffs. Table 19.1 shows the importance of machinery and industrial supplies in our merchandise exports. Table 19.2 indicates to whom we sell: Western Europe and Canada take over ½ of our exports, and Latin America takes about 15 percent.

What sorts of goods do we buy from abroad? About 1/10 of our *imports* are agricultural commodities like coffee, sugar, bananas, and cocoa. About 1/5 are raw materials like bauxite, rubber, and wool. But the bulk are neither raw materials nor foodstuffs. Over ½ of our imports, as shown in Table 19.3, are manufactured goods like bicycles from England or radios from Japan. Just as we sell more to Western Europe than any other area, so we buy more from these countries too (see Table 19.4). But the pattern varies, of course, from product to product. For example, Canada is our leading foreign source for wood pulp and nonferrous metals, while Latin America is our leading source of imported coffee and sugar.

Finally, several general observations on the pattern of world trade are worth making. First, much of world trade involves the industrialized richer countries. This is no surprise, since these countries account for so large a share of the world's productivity and purchasing power. Second, the industrialized, richer countries of the world tend to trade with one another, while the nonindustrialized, poorer countries tend to trade with the industrialized countries, not with one another. The reasons for this are clear enough. The nonindustrialized countries supply the industrialized countries with raw materials and foodstuffs, and receive manufactures in return. The nonindustrialized countries have little reason to trade with one another since they cannot get from one another the manufactures they need. Third, neighboring nations tend to trade with one another. This too is predictable: lower transportation costs and greater familiarity tend to promote trade between neighbors.

Specialization and Trade

We have discussed the extent and nature of our trade with other countries, but not *why* we trade with other countries. Do we—and our trading partners—benefit from this trade? And if so, what determines the sorts of goods we should export and import? These are very important questions, among the most fundamental in economics. The answers are by no means new. They have been well understood for considerably more than a century, due to the work of such great economists as David Hume, David Ricardo, Adam Smith, and John Stuart Mill.

Table 19.1

U.S. Merchandise Exports, 1972

Product	Amount (millions of dollars)
Food, feed, and beverages	7,492
Chemicals	3,228
Industrial supplies and materials (other than chemicals)	10,754
Machinery	13,135
Automotive vehicles and parts	5,125
Consumer goods (excluding autos)	3,491
Military-type goods	1,200
Aircraft	3,217
Other	2,126
Total	49,768

Source: Survey of Current Business, March 1973.

Table 19.2

U.S. Exports of Goods and Services, 1972

Country	Amount (millions of dollars)
Japan	6,672
Australia, New Zealand, and South Africa	2,447
Latin America	11,262
Canada	16,415
Eastern Europe	929
United Kingdom	4,584
European Economic Community	11,930
Other Western Europe	5,592
Other	13,715
Total	73,546

Source: See Table 19.1.

Table 19.3

U.S. Merchandise Imports, 1972

Product	Amount (millions of dollars)
Food, feed, and beverages	7,257
Fuels and lubricants	4,882
Paper	1,756
Metals	6,738
Other industrial supplies and materials	4,947
Machinery	5,135
Automotive vehicles and parts	9,307
Consumer goods (excluding autos)	11,355
Other	4,178
Total	55,555

Source: See Table 19.1.

Table 19.4

U.S. Imports of Goods and Services, 1972

Country	Amount (millions of dollars)
Japan	11,434
Australia, New Zealand, and South Africa	1,727
Latin America	9,778
Canada	16,739
Eastern Europe	431
United Kingdom	5,511
European Economic Community	14,369
Other Western Europe	6,543
Other	11,235
Total	77,765

Source: See Table 19.1.

As a first step, it is useful to recognize that the benefits *nations* receive through trade are essentially the same as those *individuals* receive through trade. Consider the hypothetical case of John Jones, a lawyer, with a wife and two children. The Jones family, like practically all families, trades continually with other families and with business firms. Since Mr. Jones is a lawyer, he trades his legal services for money which he and his wife use to buy the food, clothing, housing, and other goods and services his family wants. Why does the Jones family do this? What advantages does it receive through trade? Why doesn't it attempt to be self-sufficient?

To see why the Jones family is sensible indeed to opt for trade rather than self-sufficiency, let's compare the current situation—where Mr. Jones specializes in the production of legal services and trades the money he receives for other goods and services—with the situation if the Jones family attempted to be self-sufficient. In the latter case, the Joneses would have to provide their own transportation, telephone service, foodstuffs, clothing, and a host of other things. Mr. Jones is a lawyer—a well-trained, valuable, productive member of the community. But if he were to try his hand at making automobiles—or even bicycles—he might be a total loss.

Clearly, *trade permits specialization, and specialization increases output*: this is the advantage of trade, both for individuals and for nations. In our hypothetical case, it is obvious that, because he can trade with other families and with firms, Mr. Jones can specialize in doing what he is good at—law. Consequently, he can be more productive than if he were forced to be a Jack-of-all-trades, as he would have to be if he could not trade with others. The same principle holds for nations. For example, because the United States can trade with other nations, it can specialize in the goods and services it produces particularly well. Then it can trade them for goods that other countries are especially good at producing. Thus both we and our trading partners benefit.

Some countries have more and better resources

of certain types than others. Saudi Arabia has oil, Canada has timber, Japan has a skilled labor force, and so on. *International differences in resource endowments, and in the relative quantity of various types of human and nonhuman resources, are important bases for specialization.* For example, countries with lots of fertile soil, little capital, and much unskilled labor are likely to find it advantageous to produce agricultural goods, while countries with poor soil, much capital, and highly skilled labor will probably do better to produce capital-intensive, high-technology goods. We must recognize, however, that the bases for specialization do not remain fixed over time. Instead, as technology and the resource endowments of various countries change, the pattern of international specialization changes as well. For example, as we saw in the previous section, the United States specialized more in raw materials and foodstuffs about a century ago than it does now.

Absolute Advantage

To clarify the benefits of trade, consider the following example. Suppose that the United States can produce 2 electronic computers or 5,000 cases of wine with 1 unit of resources. Suppose that France can produce 1 electronic computer or 10,000 cases of wine with 1 unit of resources. Given the production possibilities in each country, are there any advantages in trade between the countries? And if so, what commodity should each country export, and what commodity should each country import? Should France export wine and import computers, or should it import wine and export computers?

To answer these questions, assume that the United States is producing a certain amount of computers and a certain amount of wine—and that France is producing a certain amount of computers and a certain amount of wine. If the United States shifts 1 unit of its resources from producing wine to producing computers, it will increase its production of computers by 2 computers and reduce its

Table 19.5

Case of Absolute Advantage

	Increase or decrease in output of:	
	Computers	Wine (thousands of cases)
Effect of U.S.'s shifting 1 unit of resources from wine to computers	+2	− 5
Effect of France's shifting 1 unit of resources from computers to wine	−1	+10
Net effect	+1	+ 5

production of wine by 5,000 cases of wine. If France shifts 1 unit of resources from the production of computers to the production of wine, it will increase its production of wine by 10,000 cases and reduce its production of computers by 1 computer.

Table 19.5 shows the *net* effect of this shift in the utilization of resources on *world* output of computers and of wine. World output of computers increases (by 1 computer) and world output of wine increases (by 5,000 cases) as a result of the redeployment of resources in each country. Thus, *specialization increases world output.*

Moreover, if world output of each commodity is increased by shifting 1 unit of American resources from wine to computers and shifting 1 unit of French resources from computers to wine, it follows that world output of each commodity will be increased further if each country shifts *more* of its resources in the same direction. This is because the amount of resources required to produce each good is assumed to be constant, regardless of how much is produced.

Thus, in this situation, one country—the United States—should specialize in producing computers, and the other country—France—should specialize in producing wine. This will maximize world output of both wine and computers, resulting in a rise in both countries' standards of living. Of course, complete specialization of this sort is somewhat unrealistic, since countries often produce some of both commodities, but this simple example illustrates the basic principles involved.

Comparative Advantage

The case just described is a very special one, since one country (France) has an absolute advantage over another (the United States) in the production of one good (wine), whereas the second country (the United States) has an absolute advantage over the first (France) in the production of another good (computers). We say that Country *A* has an ***absolute advantage*** over Country *B* in the production of a good when Country *A* can produce a unit of the good with less resources than can Country *B*. Since the United States can produce a computer with fewer units of resources than France, it has an absolute advantage over France in the production of computers. Since France requires fewer resources than the United States to produce a given amount of wine, France has an absolute advantage over the United States in the production of wine.

When one country has an absolute advantage in producing one good and another country has an absolute advantage in producing another good, obviously each country will specialize in producing the good in which it has the absolute advantage, and each can benefit from trade. But what if one country is more efficient in producing both goods? If the United States is more efficient in producing both computers and wine, is there still any benefit to be derived from specialization and trade? At first glance, you are probably inclined to answer no. But if this is your inclination, you should reconsider—because you are wrong.

To see why specialization and trade have advantages even when one country is more efficient than another at producing both goods, consider the following example. Suppose the United States can produce 2 electronic computers or 5,000 cases of wine with 1 unit of resources, and France can produce 1 electronic computer or 4,000 cases of wine with 1 unit of resources. In this case, the United States is a more efficient producer of both computers and wine. Nonetheless, as we shall see, world output of both goods will increase if the United States specializes in the production of computers and France specializes in the production of wine.

Table 19.6 demonstrates this conclusion. If 2 units of American resources are shifted from wine to computer production, 4 additional computers and 10,000 fewer cases of wine are produced. If 3 units of French resources are shifted from computer to wine production, 3 fewer computers and 12,000 additional cases of wine are produced. Thus, the combined effect of this redeployment of resources in both countries is to increase world output of computers by 1 computer and to increase world output of wine by 2,000 cases. Even though the United States is more efficient than France in the production of both computers and wine, world output of both goods will be maximized if the United States specializes in computers and France specializes in wine.

Basically, this is so because, although the United States is more efficient than France in the production of both goods, it has a greater advantage in computers than in wine. It is twice as efficient as France in producing computers, but only 25 percent more efficient than France in producing wine. To derive these numbers, recall that 1 unit of resources will produce 2 computers in the United States, but only 1 computer in France. Thus, the United States is twice as efficient in computers. On the other hand, 1 unit of resources will produce 5,000 cases of wine in the United States, but only 4,000 cases in France. Thus, the United States is 25 percent more efficient in wine.

A nation has a *comparative advantage* in those products where its efficiency relative to other nations is highest. Thus, in this case, the United

Table 19.6 Case of Comparative Advantage		
	Increase or decrease in output of:	
	Computers	Wine (thousands of cases)
Effect of U.S.'s shifting 2 units of resources from wine to computers	+4	−10
Effect of France's shifting 3 units of resources from computers to wine	−3	+12
Net effect	+1	+2

States has a comparative advantage in the production of computers and a comparative disadvantage in the production of wine. So long as a country has a comparative advantage in the production of some commodities and a comparative disadvantage in the production of others, it can benefit from specialization and trade. A country will specialize, of course, in products where it has a comparative advantage, and import those where it has a comparative disadvantage. The point is that *specialization and trade depend on comparative, not absolute advantage.* One of the first economists to understand the full significance of this fact was David Ricardo, the famous English economist of the early nineteenth century.

Comparative Advantage: A Geometric Representation

Some people understand things better when they are presented graphically. For them, as well as for others, it is useful to demonstrate the principle of

Figure 19.1
Benefits of Specialization and Trade

AC represents the various amounts of computers and wine that the United States can end up with, if it specializes in computers and trades them for French wine. The slope of *AC* equals minus 1 times the ratio of the price of a case of wine to the price of a computer, assumed to be $\frac{1}{3,333}$. *BD* represents the various amounts of computers and wine that France can wind up with, if it specializes in wine and trades for U.S. computers. *AC* lies above America's product transformation curve and *BD* lies above France's product transformation curve. Thus both countries can have more of both commodities by specializing and trading than by attempting to be self-sufficient.

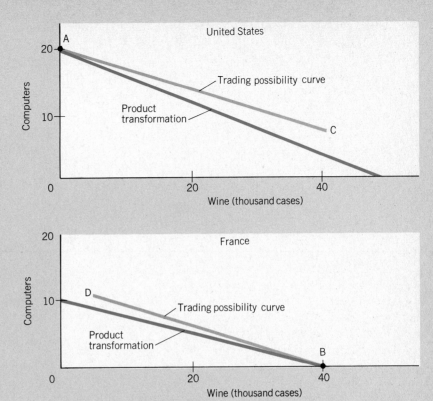

comparative advantage with a diagram. Again, we suppose that in the United States 1 unit of resources will produce 2 electronic computers or 5,000 cases of wine. Consequently, the *product transformation curve* in the United States—the curve that shows the maximum number of computers that can be produced, given various outputs of wine—is the one in the top panel of Figure 19.1. The United States must give up 1 computer for every additional 2,500 cases of wine that it produces; thus, the slope of the American product transformation curve is $-\frac{1}{2,500}$.[1] Also, as in the

[1] As we know from Chapter 3, the product transformation curve shows the maximum amount of one commodity that can be produced given various outputs of the other commodity. Since the United States must give up 1/2,500 computer for each additional case of wine that it produces, the slope must be −1/2,500.

previous section, we suppose that in France 1 unit of resources will produce 1 electronic computer or 4,000 cases of wine. Thus the product transformation curve in France is as shown in the bottom panel of Figure 19.1. France must give up 1 computer for every additional 4,000 cases of wine it produces; thus, the slope of France's product transformation curve is $-\frac{1}{4,000}$.

Now suppose that the United States uses all its resources to produce computers and that France uses all its resources to produce wine. In other words, the United States operates at point *A* on its product transformation curve and France operates at point *B* on its product transformation curve. Then suppose that the United States trades its computers for France's wine. *AC* in the top panel of Figure 19.1 shows the various amounts of computers and wine the United States can end up with if it specializes in computers and trades them for French wine, AC is the **trading-possibility curve** of the United States. The slope of AC is minus 1 times the ratio of the price of a case of wine to the price of a computer, since this ratio equals the number of computers the United States must give up to get a case of French wine. Similarly, the line BD in the bottom panel of Figure 19.1 shows France's trading-possibility curve. That is, BD represents the various amounts of computers and wine France can wind up with if it specializes in wine and trades it for U.S. computers.

The thing to note about both panels of Figure 19.1 is that each country's trading-possibility curve —AC in the top panel, BD in the bottom panel— lies above its product transformation curve. This means that both countries can have more of both commodities by specializing and trading than by trying to be self-sufficient—even though the United States is more efficient than France at producing both commodities. Thus, Figure 19.1 shows what we said in the previous section: if countries specialize in products where they have a comparative advantage and trade with one another, each country can improve its standard of living.

In addition, two other points should be noted. First, it is assumed in Figure 19.1 that the ratio of the price of a computer to the price of a case of wine is 3,333:1. We determine this ratio by starting with the fact that it must be somewhere between 2,500:1 and 4,000:1. By diverting its own resources from computer production to wine production, the United States can exchange a computer for 2,500 cases of wine. Since this is possible, it will not pay the United States to trade a computer for less than 2,500 cases of wine. Similarly, since France can exchange a case of wine for $\frac{1}{4,000}$ of a computer by diverting its own resources from wine to computers, it clearly will not be willing to trade a case of wine for less than 1/4,000 of a computer. But where will the price ratio lie between 2,500:1 and 4,000:1? The answer depends on world supply and demand for the two products. The stronger the demand for computers (relative to their supply) and the weaker the demand for wine (relative to its supply), the higher the price ratio. On the other hand, the weaker the demand for computers (relative to their supply) and the stronger the demand for wine (relative to its supply), the lower the price ratio.

Second, Figure 19.1 shows that the United States should specialize completely in computers, and that France should specialize completely in wine. This result stems from the assumption that the cost of producing a computer or a case of wine is constant. If, on the other hand, the cost of producing each good increases with the amount produced, the result is likely to be incomplete specialization. In other words, although the United States will continue to specialize in computers and France will continue to specialize in wine, each country will also produce some of the other good as well. This is a more likely outcome, since specialization generally tends to be less than complete.

Comparative Advantage and Actual Trade Patterns: A Case Study

The principle of comparative advantage is useful in explaining and predicting the pattern of world trade, as well as in showing the benefits of trade. For example, consider the exports of Great Britain and the United States. Robert Stern of the University of Michigan compared British and American exports in 39 industries in 1950.[2] In some of these industries, Britain exported much more than we did, while in others we exported more than the British. In all these industries, labor productivity— output per manhour—was higher in the United States than in Great Britain. But in some industries labor productivity in the United States was over three times as great as in Britain, whereas in other industries labor productivity was less than

[2] Robert M. Stern, "British and American Productivity and Comparative Costs in International Trade," *Oxford Economic Papers*, October 1962.

three times as great as in Britain. According to the principle of comparative advantage, the industries where the United States is most efficient relative to the British should be the ones where the United States exports more than the British.

To what extent is this hypothesis borne out by the facts? In 21 of the 24 industries where our labor productivity was more than three times that of the British, our exports exceeded British exports. In 11 of the 15 industries where our labor productivity was less than three times that of the British, our exports were less than British exports. Thus, in 32 out of 39 industries, the principle of comparative advantage, as interpreted by Stern, predicted correctly which country would export more. This is a high batting average, since labor is not the only input and labor productivity is an imperfect measure of true efficiency. Moreover, as we shall see in subsequent sections, countries raise barriers to foreign trade, preventing trade from taking place in accord with the principle of comparative advantage. Further, many factors, discussed below, besides comparative advantage play an important role in determining the pattern of world trade.

International Trade and Individual Markets

We have emphasized that nations can benefit by specializing in the production of goods for which they have a comparative advantage and trading these goods for others where they have a comparative disadvantage. But how do a nation's producers know whether they have a comparative advantage or disadvantage in the production of a given commodity? Clearly, they do not call up the local university and ask the leading professor of economics (although that might not always be such a bad idea). Instead, as we shall see in this section, the market for the good provides the required signals.

To see how this works, let's consider a new (and rather whimsical) product—bulletproof suspenders.

Suppose that the Mob, having run a scientific survey of gunmen and policemen, finds that most of them wear their suspenders over their bulletproof vests. As a consequence, the Mob's gunmen are instructed to render a victim immobile by shooting holes in his suspenders (thus making his trousers fall down and trip him). Naturally, the producers of suspenders will soon find it profitable to produce a new bulletproof variety, an innovation which, it is hoped, will make a solid contribution to law and order. The new suspenders are demanded only in the United States and England, since the rest of the world wears belts. The demand curve in the United States is *DD*, as shown in the left-hand panel of Figure 19.2, and the demand curve in England is *D'D'*, as shown in the right-hand panel. Suppose further that this product can be manufactured in both the United States and England. The supply curve in the United States is *SS*, as shown in the left-hand panel, and the supply curve in England is *S'S'*, as shown in the right-hand panel.

Take a closer look at Figure 19.2. Note that prices in England are expressed in pounds (£) and prices in the United States are expressed in dollars ($). This, of course, is quite realistic. Each country has its own currency, in which prices in that country are expressed. Roughly speaking, £1 is equal to $2.50. In other words, you can exchange a pound note for two dollars and a half—or two dollars and a half for one pound note. For this reason, the two panels of Figure 19.2 are lined up so that a price of $2.50 is at the same level as a price of £1, $5 is at the same level as £2, and so on.

To begin with, suppose that bulletproof suspenders can not be exported or imported, perhaps because of a very high tariff (tax on imports) imposed on them in both the United States and England. (One can readily imagine members of both Congress and Parliament defending such a tariff on the grounds that a capacity to produce plenty of bulletproof suspenders is important for national defense.) If this happens, the price of bulletproof suspenders will, of course, be $3 in the United States and £4 in England. Why? Because, as shown in Figure

396

**Figure 19.2
Determination of Quantity
Imported and Exported under
Free Trade**

Under free trade, price will equal
$7.50, or £3. The United States
will export *XY* units, the English
will import *UV* units, and *XY* =
UV.

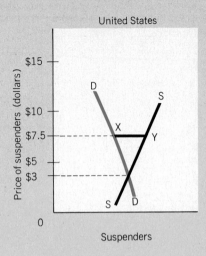

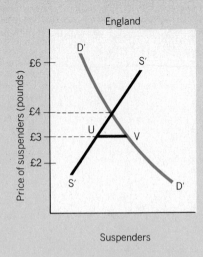

19.2, these are the prices at which each country's demand curve intersects its supply curve.

Next, suppose that international trade in this product is permitted, perhaps because both countries eliminate the tariff. Now what will happen? Since the price is lower in the United States than in England, people can make money by sending this product from the United States to England. After all, they can buy it for $3 in this country and sell it for £4 (= $10) in England. But they will not be able to do so indefinitely. As more and more suspenders are supplied by the United States for the English market, the price in the United States must go up (to induce producers to produce the additional output) and the price in England must go down (to induce consumers to buy the additional quantity).

When an equilibrium is reached, the price in the United States must equal the price in England. If this did not happen, there would be an advantage in increasing American exports (if the price in England were higher) or in decreasing American exports (if the price in the United States were higher). Thus, only if the prices are equal can an equilibrium exist. At what level will this price—which is common to both countries—tend to settle? Obviously, the price must end up at the level where

the amount of the good one country exports equals the amount the other country imports. In other words, it must settle at $7.50 or £3. Otherwise, the total amount demanded in both countries would not equal the total amount supplied in both countries. And any reader who has mastered the material in Chapter 4 knows that such a situation cannot be an equilibrium.

At this point, we can see how market forces indicate whether a country has a comparative advantage or a comparative disadvantage in the production of a certain commodity. *If a country has a comparative advantage, it turns out—after the price of the good in various countries is equalized and total world output of the good equals total world demand for it—that the country exports the good under free trade and competition.* For example, in Figure 19.2, it turns out—as we've just seen—that the United States is an exporter of bulletproof suspenders under free trade, because the demand and supply curves in the United States and England take the positions they do. The basic reason why the curves take these positions is that the United States has a comparative advantage in the production of this good. Thus, to put things in a nutshell, a nation's producers can tell (under free trade) whether they have a comparative advantage in the production of a certain commodity by seeing whether it is profitable for them to export it. If they can make a profit, they have a comparative advantage.[3]

Economies of Scale, Learning, and Technological Change

International trade is beneficial if each nation specializes in the production of goods in which it has a comparative advantage. This is a very important reason for trade, but it isn't the only reason. For example, suppose that there is no difference among countries in the efficiency with which they can produce goods and services. In a case like this, although no nation has a comparative advantage, specialization and trade may still be of benefit, because there may be economies of scale in producing some commodities. Thus, if one country specializes in one good and another country specializes in another good, firms can serve the combined markets of both countries, which will make their costs lower than if they could only reach their domestic markets. This is a major argument for forming an international economic association like the European Common Market, discussed below.

Another reason for specialization is that it may result in learning. It is well known that the cost of producing many articles goes down as more and more of the articles are produced. For example, in the aircraft and machine tool industries, producers are well aware of the reduction in costs from learning. The unit costs of a new machine tool tend to be reduced by 20 percent for each doubling of cumulated output, due to improved efficiency through individual and organizational learning. Clearly, if such learning is an important factor in

an industry, there are advantages in having one nation's producers specialize in a certain good. Specialization can reduce costs to a lower level than if each nation tries to be self-sufficient. Longer production runs cut costs since the more a producer makes, the lower the unit costs.[4]

International trade also arises because of technological change. Suppose, for example, that a new product is invented in the United States and an American firm begins producing and selling it in the American market. It catches on, and the American innovator decides to export the new product to Europe and other foreign markets. If the new product meets European needs and tastes, the Europeans will import it from the United States; and later, when the market in Europe gets big enough, the American firm may establish a branch plant in Europe. For a time at least, European firms do not have the technological know-how to produce the new product, which is also often protected to some extent by patents.

Trade of this sort is based on a technology gap between countries. Consider the plastics industry. After the development of a new plastic, there is a period of 15 to 25 years when the innovating country has a decisive advantage and is likely to lead in per capita production and exports. It has a head start, as well as the benefits of patents and commercial secrecy. Production may be licensed to other countries, but usually on a limited scale and only after a number of years. Soon after the patents expire, a different phase begins. Imitation is easier, technical know-how spreads more readily, direct technical factors lose importance, and such other factors as materials costs become much more important. Industry from other countries may challenge the innovator in export markets, and sometimes in the innovator's home market as well, although the innovator still benefits to some extent from his accumulated knowledge and experience

[3] In reality, of course, things are not quite so simple. For one thing, high transport costs are often involved in moving goods from one country to another. These costs can impede trade in certain commodities. Also, tariffs or quotas can be enacted by governments to interfere with free trade.

[4] Also, another reason for trade is a difference in national tastes. If Country A likes beef and Country B likes pork, it may pay both countries to produce both beef and pork, and Country A may find it advantageous to import beef from Country B and Country B may find it advantageous to import pork from Country A.

and his ongoing research and development.

The United States tends to export products with a high technological component—relatively new products based on considerable research and development. For example, if the 5 U.S. industries with the largest research programs are compared with the 14 other major industries, we see that the high-research industries export 4 times as much per dollar of sales as the others.[5] During the 1960s, Europeans expressed considerable concern over the "technological gap" between the United States and Europe. They asserted that superior know-how stemming from scientific and technical development in the United States had allowed American companies to obtain large shares of European markets in areas like aircraft, space equipment, computers, and other electronic products.

It is difficult to separate technical advantages from other competitive factors in explaining why American firms left their European rivals far behind in some fields. Differences in educational levels and managerial skills, economies of scale, and other such factors may have been very important. As we shall see in the following chapter, our technological lead seems to have narrowed in recent years, as the Japanese, Germans, and others have upgraded their technology. According to many observers, some American exports will be, and are being, hurt as a consequence.[6]

Multinational Firms

One of the most remarkable economic phenomena of the last 20 years has been the growth of multinational firms—firms that make direct investments in other countries and produce and market their products abroad. For example, Coca-Cola is produced and bottled all over the world. Most multi-

national firms are American, but companies like Shell in petroleum and Hoffman-LaRoche in drugs are examples of foreign-based multinational firms. The available data indicate that the multinational firms have grown by leaps and bounds, and that their shipments have become a bigger and bigger proportion of international trade. Indeed, according to economists like Lawrence Krause of the Brookings Institution, they are "now having a revolutionary effect upon the international economic system."[7]

The reasons why firms have become multinational are varied. In some cases, firms have established overseas branches to control foreign sources of raw materials. In other cases, they have invested overseas in an effort to defend their competitive position. Very frequently, firms have established foreign branches to exploit a technological lead. After exporting a new product (or a cheaper version of an existing product) to foreign markets, firms have decided to establish plants overseas to supply these markets. Once a foreign market is big enough to accommodate a plant of minimum efficient size, this decision does not conflict with economies of scale. Moreover, transport costs often hasten such a decision. Also, in some cases, the only way a firm can introduce its innovation into a foreign market is through the establishment of overseas production facilities.

By carrying its technology overseas, the multinational firm plays a very important role in the international diffusion of innovations. A firm with a technological edge over its competitors often prefers to exploit its technology in foreign markets through wholly owned subsidiaries rather than through licensing or other means. To some extent, this is because of difficulties in using ordinary market mechanisms to buy and sell information. The difficulties of transferring technology across organizational, as well as national, boundaries also con-

[5] Charles Kindleberger, *International Economics*, Homewood, Ill.: Richard D. Irwin, 1968, p. 67.
[6] See R. Vernon, "International Investment and International Trade in the Product Cycle," *Quarterly Journal of Economics*, May 1966.

[7] Lawrence Krause, "The International Economic System and the Multinational Corporation," *The Annals*, 1972. Some of this and the previous section is based on my "The Multinational Firm and Technological Change," to appear in a book published by Allen and Unwin.

Figure 19.3
Effect of a Tariff on Swiss Watches

Under free trade, price would equal $10, or 30 Swiss francs. If a tariff of $10 is imposed on each watch imported from Switzerland, there will be a complete cessation of imports. Price in the U.S. will increase to $16, and price in Switzerland will fall to 21 Swiss francs.

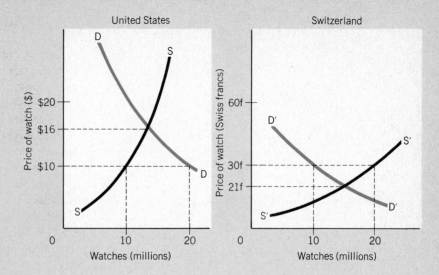

tribute to the decision. For these and other reasons, the innovating firm may find it advantageous to transfer its technology to other countries by establishing subsidiaries abroad.

One of the most important effects of the multinational firm has been to integrate the economies of the world more closely into a worldwide system. In other words, multinational firms have tended to break down some of the barriers between nations. Besides speeding the diffusion of new technology, they have linked the capital markets of many countries and promoted the international transfer of important managerial labor. However, a number of problems are also associated with multinational firms. One is the possibility that they will attain undesirable monopoly power in some industries. In addition, as we shall see in subsequent chapters, they may put undesirable stress on the international financial system and threaten the sovereignty of some nation-states.

The Social Costs of Tariffs

Despite its advantages, not everyone benefits from free trade. On the contrary, some firms and workers may feel that their well-being is threatened by foreign competition; and they may press for a **tariff**, a tax the government imposes on imports. The purpose of a tariff is to cut down on imports in order to protect domestic industry and workers from foreign competition. A secondary reason for tariffs is to produce revenue for the government.

To see how a tariff works, consider the market for wristwatches. Suppose that the demand and supply curves for wristwatches in the United States are DD and SS, as shown in the left-hand panel of Figure 19.3, and that the demand and supply curves for wristwatches in Switzerland are D'D' and S'S', as shown in the right-hand panel. Clearly, Switzerland has a comparative advantage in the production of wristwatches, and under free trade the price of a wristwatch would tend toward $10 in the United States and toward 30 Swiss francs in Switzerland. (Note that 3 Swiss francs are assumed to equal $1.) Under free trade, the United States would import 10 million wristwatches from Switzerland.

Now if the United States imposes a tariff of $10 on each wristwatch imported from Switzerland, the imports will completely cease. Any importer who buys watches in Switzerland at the price (when there is no foreign trade) of 21 Swiss francs—

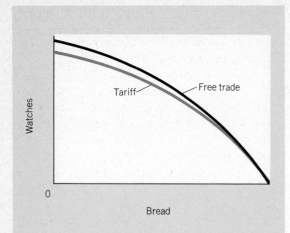

Figure 19.4
Consumption-Possibility Curves, Given Tariff and Free Trade

Under free trade, the consumption-possibility curve is farther from the origin than with the tariff. Consequently, society as a whole is better off under free trade.

which equals $7—must pay a tariff of $10; this makes his total cost $17 per watch. But this is more than the price of a watch in the United States when there is no foreign trade (which is $16). Consequently, there is no money to be made by importing watches—unless Americans can be persuaded to pay more for a Swiss watch than for an identical American watch.

What is the effect of the tariff? Clearly, the domestic watch industry receives a higher price— $16 rather than $10—than it would without a tariff, so the American watch industry (or its workers) is likely to benefit from the tariff. For example, the workers in the domestic watch industry may have more jobs and higher wages than without the tariff. The victim of the tariff is the American consumer, who pays a higher price for wristwatches.

Thus the domestic watch industry benefits at the expense of the rest of the nation. But does the general public lose more than the watch industry gains? In general, the answer is yes. The tariff reduces the consumption possibilities open to the nation. For example, suppose that wristwatches and bread were the only two commodities. A nation's *consumption-possibility curve* shows the various combinations of goods that can be consumed. Under free trade, the consumption-possibility curve is higher, as shown in Figure 19.4, than it is with the tariff. Clearly, the tariff reduces the consumption possibilities open to the nation.

The tariff in Figure 19.3 is a *prohibitive tariff*— a tariff so high that it stops all imports of the good in question. Not all tariffs are prohibitive. (If they were, the government would receive no revenue at all from tariffs.) In many cases, the tariff is high enough to stop some, but not all, imports; and, as you would expect, the detrimental effect of a nonprohibitive tariff on consumption possibilities and living standards is less than that of a prohibitive tariff. But this does not mean that nonprohibitive tariffs are harmless. On the contrary, they can do lots of harm to domestic consumption and living standards.

The detrimental effects of tariffs have long been recognized, even in detective stories. For example, in the course of solving the mystery concerning the Hound of the Baskervilles, Sherlock Holmes expressed his enthusiastic approval of a newspaper editorial that read as follows:

> You may be cajoled into imagining that your own special trade or your own industry will be encouraged by a protective tariff, but it stands to reason that such legislation must in the long run keep away wealth from the country, diminish the value of our imports, and lower the general conditions of life on this island.[8]

Of course, Holmes considered this point elementary (my dear Watson) but worth hammering home.

[8] Arthur Conan Doyle, *The Hound of the Baskervilles*, in *The Complete Sherlock Holmes*, Garden City, N.Y.: Garden City Publishing Co., 1938, p. 802.

The Social Costs of Quotas

Besides tariffs, other barriers to free trade are *quotas*, which many countries impose on the amount of certain commodities that can be imported annually. For example, the United States sets import quotas on sugar and exerts pressure on foreigners to get them to limit the quantity of steel and textiles that they will export to us. To see how a quota affects trade, production, and prices, let's return to the market for wristwatches. Suppose the United States places a quota on the import of wristwatches: no more than 6 million wristwatches can be imported per year. Figure 19.5 shows the effect of the quota. Before it was imposed, the price of wristwatches was $10 (or 30 Swiss francs), and the United States imported 10 million wristwatches from Switzerland. The quota forces the United States to reduce its imports to 6 million.

What will be the effect on the U.S. price? The demand curve shows that, if the price is $12, American demand will exceed American supply by 6 million watches; in other words, we will import 6 million watches. Thus, once the quota is imposed, the price will rise to $12, since this is the price that will reduce our imports to the amount of the quota.

Clearly, a quota—like a tariff—increases the price of the good. (Note too that the price in Switzerland will fall to 25 francs. Thus, the quota will reduce the price in Switzerland.)

Both a quota and a tariff reduce trade, raise prices, protect domestic industry from foreign competition, and reduce the standard of living of the nation as a whole. But most economists tend to regard quotas with even less enthusiasm than they do tariffs. Under many circumstances, a quota insulates local industry from foreign competition even more effectively than a tariff does. Moreover, a (nonprohibitive) tariff provides the government with some revenue, while quotas do not even do that. The windfall price increase from a quota accrues to the importer who is lucky enough or influential enough—or sufficiently generous with favors and bribes—to get an import license.

Finally, *export subsidies,* another means by which governments try to give their domestic industry an advantage in international competition, are also a major impediment to free trade. Export subsidies, and other such measures, frequently lead to countermeasures. For example, to counter foreign export subsidies, the U.S. government imposes duties against such subsidies on goods sold here.

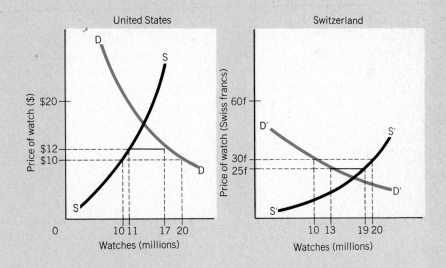

Figure 19.5
Effect of a Quota on Swiss Watches

Before the quota is imposed, the price is $10, or 30 Swiss francs. After a quota of 6 million watches is imposed, the price in the United States rises to $12, and the price in Switzerland falls to 25 Swiss francs.

Considerations of National Defense

Given the disadvantages to society at large of tariffs and other barriers to free trade, why do governments continue to impose them? There are many reasons, some sensible, some irrational. One of the most convincing is the desirability of maintaining a domestic industry for purposes of national defense. For example, even if the Swedes had a comparative advantage in producing airplanes, we would not allow free trade to put our domestic producers of aircraft out of business if we felt that a domestic aircraft industry was necessary for national defense. Although the Swedes are by no means unfriendly, we would not want to import our entire supply of such a critical commodity from a foreign country, where the supply might be shut off for reasons of international politics (like the Arab oil embargo).

This is a perfectly valid reason for protecting certain domestic industries, and many protective measures are defended on these grounds. To the extent that protective measures are in fact required for national defense, economists go along with them. Of course the restrictions entail social costs (some of which were described in the previous two sections), but these costs may well be worth paying for enhanced national security. The trouble is that many barriers to free trade are justified on grounds of national defense when in fact they protect domestic industries only tenuously connected with national defense. Moreover, even if there is a legitimate case on defense grounds for protecting a domestic industry, subsidies are likely to be a more straightforward and efficient way to do so than tariffs or quotas.

Besides national defense, there are other noneconomic reasons for protecting particular domestic industries. Some countries—Canada, for one—use a tariff to protect certain industries that they feel help them to be more independent of foreign domination and influence. Many Canadians, for understandable reasons, are intent on maintaining their traditions and values, and on resisting the penetration of American ways. Such noneconomic reasons for protection are perfectly reasonable if the nation as a whole understands the economic cost and agrees that the game is worth the candle (and if the reasons are sufficiently understood by foreigners that the measures do not provoke retaliation).

Oil Import Quotas: A Case Study

In 1973 newspaper headlines told of an "energy crisis" involving a shortage of clean fuel in the United States. To illustrate the nature and effect of barriers to free trade, as well as to shed light on this "crisis," let's consider the oil import quotas that existed until recently in the United States. These quotas were the subject of great controversy. First established by President Eisenhower in 1959, the Mandatory Oil Import Quota allowed firms to import only a certain amount of oil. Supporters of the quota argued that we could not afford to depend on foreigners for our oil because foreign sources might be cut off in war or other emergencies. Opponents argued that the costs to the consumer of these quotas were very high and that the oil requirements for national security were overstated.

Economists at Charles River Associates estimated the costs to the consumer in a study prepared for President Nixon's Office of Science and Technology.[9] Figure 19.6 shows the demand curve for petroleum in the United States, labeled DD'. The supply curve for domestically produced petroleum is SS'. The supply curve for foreign-produced petroleum is FF', a horizontal line at $1.75. Clearly, the price of petroleum under the import quota is set at the level—$3.00 per barrel—where the horizontal distance between the quantity demanded and the quantity supplied is equal to the import quota. If there were free trade, the price of petroleum would be at the intersection of the FF' and DD' curves—or $1.75 per barrel.

Thus, in 1968, for example, consumers paid

[9] James Burrows and Thomas Domencich, *An Analysis of the United States Oil Import Quota,* Lexington, Mass.: D. C. Heath, 1970.

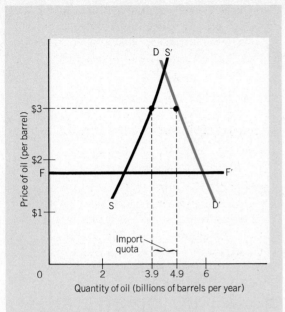

Figure 19.6
Effect of the Import Quota

SS′ is the supply curve for domestically produced petroleum, *FF′* is the supply curve for foreign produced petroleum, and *DD′* is the demand curve for petroleum in the United States. With an import quota of 1 billion barrels, the price will be $3; the price would be $1.75 if the import quota were removed.

have expanded their oil consumption.[10]

This was an enormous cost. Could it be justified on grounds of national security? It was difficult to tell, but many economists were doubtful. During his first term in office, President Nixon asked for a "full review of the nation's oil-import policies by the executive offices of the president." A task force —composed of the Secretaries of Labor, Defense, State, Interior, and Commerce, as well as the Director of the Office of Emergency Preparedness— was appointed to study the issue. Though many questions were raised concerning the merits of the oil import quota, it was continued nonetheless.

In 1973, when government officials became increasingly concerned about impending fuel shortages, opposition to the oil import quota mounted. Finally, in April 1973, President Nixon announced he was suspending direct control over the quantity of crude oil and refined products that could be imported. The oil import quota was dead. But in late 1973, the Arabs announced a cut in oil exports to us.[11]

Other Arguments for Tariffs

Besides national defense, several other arguments for tariffs can make economic sense. First, tariffs or other forms of protection can be justified to foster the growth and development of young industries. For example, suppose that Japan has a comparative advantage in the production of a certain semiconductor, but Japan does not presently produce this item. It may take Japanese firms several years to become proficient in the relevant technology, to engage in the learning described in a previous section and to take advantage of the relevant economies of

about $5.6 billion more for petroleum than they would have under free trade. We arrive at this figure by noting that consumers bought about 4.9 billion barrels of oil in 1968. If they paid $1.25 extra for each barrel, they paid 4.9 billion times $1.25—or $5.6 billion—more than under free trade. Moreover, this does not include all the costs to the consumers. Additional costs arise because some consumers used less oil at the price of $3.00 than they would have if the price had been $1.75. They would have increased their satisfaction if they could

[10] Of course, one must distinguish between the costs to the consumer and the costs to the nation as a whole. For example, some of the costs to the consumer represented the transfer of money to the oil producers. See *ibid*.

[11] According to a report by the Federal Trade Commission, anticompetitive practices by the big oil companies were responsible in part for the "crisis." The oil companies denied this. MIT's Adelman charges that the oil companies are "tax collectors" for the oil-producing nations.

scale. While this industry is "growing up," Japan may impose a tariff on such semiconductors, thus shielding its young industry from competition it can not yet handle. This "infant industry" argument for tariffs has a long history; Alexander Hamilton was one of its early exponents. Needless to say, it is *not* an argument for *permanent* tariffs, since infant industries are supposed to grow up—and the sooner the better. (Moreover, a subsidy for the industry would probably be better and easier to remove.)

Second, tariffs sometimes may be imposed to protect domestic jobs and to reduce unemployment at home. In the short run the policy may succeed, but we must recognize that other nations are likely to retaliate by enacting or increasing their own tariffs, so that such a policy may not work very well in the long run. A more sensible way to reduce domestic unemployment is to use the tools of fiscal and monetary policy described in Chapters 10 and 14 rather than tariffs. If workers are laid off by industries that cannot compete with foreign producers, proper monetary and fiscal policy, together with retraining programs, should enable these workers to switch to other industries that can compete.

Third, tariffs sometimes may be imposed to prevent a country from being too dependent on only a few industries. For example, consider a Latin American country that is a major producer of bananas. Under free trade, this country might produce bananas and little else, putting its entire economy at the mercy of the banana market. If, for instance, the price of bananas fell, the country's national income would decrease drastically. To promote industrial diversification, this country may establish tariffs to protect other industries, for example, certain types of light manufacturing. In a case like this, the tariff protects the country from having too many eggs in a single basket.

Fourth, tariffs may sometimes improve a country's terms of trade—that is, the ratio of its export prices to its import prices. For example, the United States is a major importer of bananas. If we impose a tariff on bananas, thus cutting down on the domestic demand for them (because the tariff will increase their price), the reduction in our demand is likely to reduce the price of bananas abroad. Consequently, foreign producers of bananas will really pay part of the tariff. However, other countries may retaliate; and if all countries pursue such policies, few, if any, are likely to find themselves better off.

Frequently Encountered Fallacies

Although, as we have just seen, tariffs can be defended under certain circumstances, many of the arguments for them frequently encountered in political oratory and popular discussions are misleading. Although no field of economics is free of popular misconceptions and fallacies, this one is particularly rich in pious inanities and thunderous non sequiturs. For example, one frequently encountered fallacy is that, if foreigners want to trade with us, they must be benefiting from the trade. Consequently, according to this argument, we must be giving them more than we get—and it must be in our interest to reduce trade. This argument is, of course, entirely erroneous in its assumption that trade cannot be beneficial to *both* trading partners. On the contrary, as we have seen, the heart of the argument for trade is that it can be mutually beneficial.

Another fallacy one often encounters in polite conversation—and not-so-polite political debate—is that a tariff is required to protect our workers from low-wage labor in other countries. According to this argument, since American labor (at $4 an hour) clearly cannot compete with foreign labor (which works at "coolie" wage levels), we have no choice but to impose tariffs. If we do not, cheap foreign goods will throw our high-priced laborers out of work. This argument is wrong on two counts. First, high wages do not necessarily mean high unit costs of production. Because the productivity of American workers is high, unit labor costs in the United States are roughly in line with those in other countries. (Recall from Chapter 15 that unit labor cost equals the wage rate divided by labor productivity.

Obviously, unit labor cost may be no higher here than abroad, even though the wage rate here is much higher, if labor productivity here is also much higher than abroad.) Second, if our costs were out of line with those of other countries, there should be a change in exchange rates, which would tend to bring them back into line. As we shall see in Chapter 20, exchange rates should move to bring our exports and imports into balance.

Still another fallacy that makes the rounds is that it is better to "buy American" because then we have both the goods that are bought and the money, whereas if we buy from foreigners we have the goods but they have the money. Like some jokes, this fallacy has an ancient lineage—and one that borders on respectability, since Abraham Lincoln is supposed to have subscribed to it. Basically, the flaw is the implicit assumption that money is somehow valued for its own sake. In reality, all the foreigners can do with the money is buy some of our goods, so that really we are just swapping some of our goods for some of theirs. If such a trade is mutually advantageous, fine.

Why do politicians (both Democrats and Republicans) sometimes utter these fallacies? No doubt an important reason is simply ignorance. There is no law that prevents people with little understanding of economics from holding public office. But this may not be the only reason. Special-interest groups—particular industries, unions, and regions—have a lot to gain by getting the government to enact protective tariffs and quotas. And Congress and the executive branch of the government are often sensitive to the pressures of these groups, which wield considerable political power.

Faced with a choice between helping a few powerful, well-organized groups and helping the general public—which is poorly organized and often ignorant of its own interests—politicians frequently tend to favor the special-interest groups. After all, these groups have a lot to gain and will remember their friends, while the general public—each member of which loses only a relatively small amount—will be largely unaware of its losses anyhow. Having decided to help these groups, a congress-

man or senator may not exert himself unduly to search out or expose the weakness in some of the arguments used to bolster their position. For example, there is the story of a well-known southern senator who, about to deliver a certain oration, wrote in the margin of one section of his speech: "Weak point here. Holler like hell."

Tariffs in the United States

How high are American tariffs? In our early years, we were a very protectionist nation. The argument for protecting our young industry from the competition of European manufacturers was, of course, the "infant industry" argument, which, as we saw above, can be perfectly sensible. However, our own industries understandably found it advantageous to prolong their childhood for as long as possible—and to press for continuation of high tariffs. During the nineteenth century and well into the twentieth, the industrial Northeast was particularly strong in its support of tariffs. Furthermore, the Republican party, which generally held sway in American politics between the Civil War and the New Deal, favored a high tariff. Thus, as shown in Figure 19.7, the tariff remained relatively high from about 1870 until the early 1930s. With the exception of the period around World War I, average tariff rates were about 40 to 50 percent. With the enactment of the Smoot-Hawley Tariff of 1930, the tariff reached its peak—about 60 percent. Moreover, these tariff rates understate the extent to which the tariff restricted trade: some goods were completely shut out of the country by the tariff, and do not show up in the figures.

With the Democratic victory in 1932, a movement began toward freer trade. The Trade Agreements Act of 1934 allowed the president to bargain with other countries to reduce barriers to trade. He was given the power to lower U.S. tariffs by as much as 50 percent. In 1945, he was given the power to make further tariff reductions. Between 1934 and 1948, tariff rates fell substantially, as

The European Economic Community

The EEC, born in the embers of World War II, was fathered by a desire to bind Germany to the rest of Europe. The success of the European Steel and Coal Community and the Benelux union encouraged the "Europeanists," and in 1957 the Treaty of Rome formally proclaimed the birth of a six-country free trade area in which labor, capital, and goods were to move freely. None of this was to happen instantaneously, but the six countries— France, Germany, Italy, Belgium, the Netherlands, and Luxembourg—did agree on a timetable for the removal of centuries-old barriers and on a commission and council to manage the details of the process.

HEADQUARTERS OF THE EUROPEAN ECONOMIC COMMUNITY, BRUSSELS

There are ample statistics to tell the story since 1958 —growth rates of above 4 percent, increased competitiveness by European firms, increases in per capita incomes, and increased membership (including Great Britain). But the flavor of this customs union comes through best by seeing what it has meant to three prototype economic men.

Nino T. was born in southern Italy, where reported unemployment is 14 percent.* If disguised unemployment were included, the rate might run as high as double that. Wages, for those with jobs, averaged about $20 per week. In 1965, he migrated to Germany to work in an automobile plant in Frankfort, where he could make $75 a week, and send back $40 to his family. He plans to stay for another two years—perhaps until he has saved enough to buy a small business.

John C. works for a leather-goods firm in London. As a new member of the Common Market, he will be able to migrate to the Continent and find a job, at considerably higher wages. He has no plans to do so, however, and what the Common Market will bring to him, at least initially, is higher food prices. When Britain enters the market, he will pay 20 percent more for his bread and butter and 40 percent more for his cheese. Why? Because the technologically inefficient but politically powerful French farmer was able to demand protection from cheap American and Canadian food. Thus, while French wheat will flow freely into Great Britain, the high external tariff will now keep out North American wheat.

Richard B., an American businessman, now lives in Paris, managing the French subsidiary of a large New-York-based corporation. He was moved to Paris about ten years ago, when company officials decided that the removal of internal barriers by the EEC would allow U.S. companies to operate on the scale to which they were accustomed. To stay competitive in the European market, they decided to build production facilities inside the EEC, rather than producing in the U.S. and shipping abroad. Richard now finds himself very much at home in France, and seriously considers living out his days in Paris.　　　　　E. A.

*George Hildebrand, *The Italian Economy*, New York: Harper and Row, 1967, p. 337.

Figure 19.7
Average American Tariff Rates

The tariff generally remained high from about 1870 to the early 1930s; in recent years it has decreased very substantially.

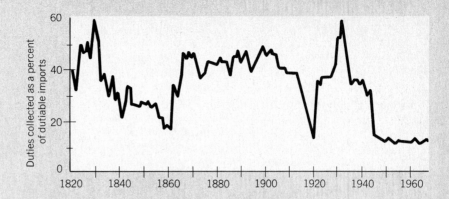

shown by Figure 19.7. By 1948, the United States was no longer a high-tariff country; the average tariff rate was only about 10 percent. During the 1950s, there were no further decreases in the tariff —but there were no substantial increases either. The movement toward freer trade was continued by President Kennedy in 1962, and during the 1960s, the "Kennedy round" negotiations took place among about 40 nations in an attempt to reduce tariffs. In 1967, the United States agreed to cut tariffs by about one-third on a great many items.

The negotiations during the 1960s were prompted by the establishment of the European Economic Community—or "Common Market." The E.E.C. was composed originally of Belgium, France, West Germany, Holland, Italy, and Luxembourg; and since 1970, Britain, Denmark, and Ireland have joined. When the E.E.C. was formed, the member countries agreed to reduce the tariff barriers against one another's goods—but not against the goods of other nations, including the United States. The formation and success of the Common Market—and the likelihood that other European countries would join—posed a problem for the United States. The Common Market is a large and rich market, with about as many people and about half as large a combined gross national product as ours. With the reduction of tariff bar-

riers *within* the Common Market, trade *among* the members of the Common Market increased rapidly, and prices of many items were cut. But American exporters were less than ecstatic about all of this, because the members of the Common Market still maintained their tariff barriers against American goods. While the "Kennedy round" negotiations succeeded in reducing some of the tariff barriers between the United States and the Common Market, important tariff barriers remain, particularly for agricultural products.

Recent years have seen some increase in protectionist feelings in the United States. As Western Europe and Japan have become more formidable competitors abroad and at home, many industries have begun to press for quotas and higher tariffs. The textile and steel industries have been particularly vocal and have managed to increase trade barriers. Some unions have joined the protectionist forces in an effort to hold on to jobs. The Hartke-Burke bill, which would increase trade barriers and attempt to impede the international diffusion of technology, has received considerable attention in Congress. It is to be hoped that this upsurge of protectionist spirit will be short-lived, and developments here and abroad will enable us and our trading partners to move closer to the realization of the benefits of free trade.

Summary

International trade permits specialization, and specialization increases output. This is the advantage of trade, both for individuals and for nations. Country A has an absolute advantage over Country B in the production of a good when Country A can produce a unit of the good with less resources than can Country B. Trade can be mutually beneficial even if one country has an absolute advantage in the production of all goods. Specialization and trade depend on comparative, not absolute advantage. A nation is said to have a comparative advantage in those products where its efficiency relative to other nations is highest. Trade can be mutually beneficial if a country specializes in the products where it has a comparative advantage and imports the products where it has a comparative disadvantage.

The principle of comparative advantage is of use in predicting the pattern of world trade, as well as in showing its benefits. If markets are relatively free and competitive, producers will automatically be led to produce in accord with comparative advantage. If a country has a comparative advantage in the production of a certain good, it will turn out—after the price of the good in various countries is equalized and total world output of the good equals total world demand—that this country is an exporter of the good under free trade. Specialization is not the only reason for trade: others are economies of scale, learning, and differences in national tastes. Also, some countries develop new products and processes, which they export to other countries until the technology becomes widely available.

A tariff is a tax imposed by the government on imports, the purpose being to cut down on imports in order to protect domestic industry and workers from foreign competition. Tariffs benefit the protected industry at the expense of the general public, and, in general, a tariff costs the general public more than the protected industry (and its workers and suppliers) gains. Quotas are another barrier to free trade. They too reduce trade, raise prices, protect domestic industry from foreign competition, and reduce the standard of living of the nation as a whole. Tariffs, quotas, and other barriers to free trade can sometimes be justified on the basis of national security and other noneconomic considerations. Moreover, tariffs and other forms of protection can sometimes be justified to protect infant industries, to prevent a country from being too dependent on only a few industries, and to carry out other national objectives. But many arguments for tariffs are fallacious.

Although only about 5 percent of our gross national product, foreign trade is of very considerable importance to the American economy. Many of our industries rely on foreign countries for raw materials or for markets, and our consumers buy many kinds of imported goods. In absolute terms, our exports are large and have represented about 15 percent of total world trade. Both our exports and imports are mostly finished manufactured goods. In our early years, we were a very protectionist country. Our tariff remained relatively high until the 1930s, when a movement began toward freer trade. Between 1934 and 1948, our tariff rates dropped substantially. Again during the 1960s, there was a significant reduction in our tariffs. But more recently, as some of our industries (like steel) have been hit hard by imports, there has been some tendency to push for more protectionist measures.

CONCEPTS FOR REVIEW

Comparative advantage	Trading-possibility curve	Export subsidy
Absolute advantage	Tariff	Technology gap
Product transformation curve	Quota	Multinational firm
	Prohibitive tariff	European Economic Community

QUESTIONS FOR DISCUSSION AND REVIEW

1. According to Hendrik Houthakker, "Our workers get high real income not because they are protected from foreign competition, but because they are highly productive, at least in certain industries." Do you agree? Why or why not?

2. According to Richard Cooper, "Technological innovation can undoubtedly strengthen the competitive position of a country in which the innovation takes place, whether it be one which enlarges exports or displaces imports." Give examples of this phenomenon, and discuss various ways that one might measure the effects of technological innovation on a country's competitive position.

3. Discuss the effects of the multinational firm on the world economy. Do you think that the activities of multinational firms should be regulated in new ways? If so, why?

4. Suppose that the United States can produce 3 electronic computers or 3,000 cases of wine with 1 unit of resources, while France can produce 1 electronic computer or 2,000 cases of wine with 1 unit of resources. Will specialization increase world output?

5. United States exports as a percentage of gross national product are quite small relative to Germany, France, and the United Kingdom. True or False?

CHAPTER 20

Exchange Rates and the Balance of Payments

In recent years, any American at all acquainted with the financial or international news has become aware that the United States has been having "balance of payments difficulties"—or, a bit more specifically, we have been experiencing deficits in our balance of payments. In response to these deficits, President Nixon devalued the dollar twice between 1971 and 1973, and then, together with the other major trading nations of the world, agreed in 1973 to allow exchange rates to "float." Even in the nation's less prestigious and more sensational newspapers, these events managed to crowd the juiciest sports and criminal news, and even Henry Kissinger, off the front pages.

To understand these developments, we must consider several questions. What are exchange rates, and how are they determined? How are international business transactions carried out? Should there be fixed or flexible exchange rates? What is the balance of payments, and what is its significance? What problems has the United States had with its balance of payments in recent years, and how can they be brought under control? These questions, which are both fundamental and timely, are taken up in this chapter.

International Transactions and Exchange Rates

Suppose you want to buy a book from a German publisher, and that the book costs 20 marks. (The German currency consists of marks, not dollars.) To buy the book, you must somehow get marks to pay the publisher, since this is the currency in which he deals. Or, if he agrees, you might pay him in dollars; but he would then have to exchange the dollars you give him for marks, since he must pay his bills in marks. Whatever happens, either you or he must somehow exchange dollars for marks, since international business transactions, unlike transactions within a country, involve two different currencies.

If you decide to exchange dollars for marks to pay the German publisher, how can you make the exchange? You can buy German marks at a bank, just as you might buy lamb chops at a butcher shop. Just as the lamb chops have a price (expressed in dollars), so the German marks have a price (expressed in dollars). The bank may tell you that each mark you buy will cost you $.40. This makes the exchange rate between dollars and marks .4 to 1, since it takes .4 dollars to purchase 1 mark (or 2½ marks to purchase 1 dollar). In general, *the exchange rate is simply the number of units of one currency that exchanges for a unit of another currency.* The obvious question is what determines the exchange rate. Why is the exchange rate between German marks and American dollars what it is? Why doesn't a dollar exchange for 10 marks, rather than 2½ marks? This basic question will occupy us in the next three sections.

Exchange Rates under the Gold Standard

Before the 1930s, many important nations were on the **gold standard.** *If a country was on the gold standard, a unit of its currency was convertible into* a certain amount of gold. For example, before World War I the dollar was convertible into $\frac{1}{20}$ ounce of gold, and the British pound was convertible into ¼ ounce of gold. Thus, since the pound exchanged for 5 times as much gold as the dollar, the pound exchanged for $5. The currency of any other country on the gold standard was convertible into a certain amount of gold in the same way; and *to see how much its currency was worth in dollars, you divided the amount of gold a unit of its currency was worth by the amount of gold ($\frac{1}{20}$ ounce) a dollar was worth.*

$$\frac{1}{20} \div \frac{5}{1} \quad \frac{5}{20}$$

$$\frac{1}{4}$$

Why did the exchange rate always equal the ratio between the amount of gold a foreign currency was worth and the amount of gold a dollar was worth? For example, to see why the price of a British pound stayed at $5 before World War I, suppose that the price (in dollars) of a pound rose above this ratio—above $5. Instead of exchanging their dollars directly for pounds, Americans would have done better to exchange them for gold and then exchange the gold for pounds. By this indirect process, Americans could have exchanged $5 for a pound, so they would have refused to buy pounds at a price above $5 per pound. Similarly, if the price of a pound fell below $5, the British would have refused to sell pounds, since they could have obtained $5 by converting the pound into gold and the gold into dollars. (In practice, the pound could be a few cents above or below $5 without triggering this response because it costs money to transport gold in order to carry out the conversion.)

But what insured that this exchange rate, dictated by the gold content of currencies, would result in a rough equality of trade between countries? For example, if one pound exchanged for $5, perhaps the British might find our goods so cheap that they would import a great deal from us, while we might find their goods so expensive that we would import little from them. Under these circumstances, the British would have to ship gold to us to pay for the excess of their imports from us over their exports to us, and eventually they would run out of gold. Could this happen? If not, why not? These questions occupied the attention of many early economists. The classic answers were given by David Hume, the famous Scottish philosopher, in the eighteenth century.

Hume pointed out that under the gold standard a mechanism insured that trade would be brought into balance and that neither country would run out of gold. This mechanism was as follows: If, as we assumed, the British bought more from us than we bought from them, they would have to send us gold to pay for the excess of their imports over their exports. As their gold stock declined, their price level would fall. (Recall the quantity theory of money.) As our gold stock increased, our price level would rise. Thus, because of our rising prices, the British would tend to import less from us; and because of their falling prices, we would tend to import more from them. Consequently, the trade between the two countries would tend toward a better balance. Eventually, when enough gold had left Britain and entered the United States, prices here would have increased enough, and prices in Britain would have fallen enough, to put imports and exports in balance.

Flexible Exchange Rates

The gold standard is long gone; and after many decades of fixed exchange rates (discussed in the next section), the major trading nations of the world began to experiment with flexible exchange rates in early 1973. Let's consider a situation where exchange rates are allowed to fluctuate freely, like the price of any commodity in a competitive market. In a case of this sort, exchange rates—like any price—are determined by supply and demand. There is a market for various types of foreign currency—German marks, British pounds, French francs, and so on—just as there are markets for various types of meat.

In the case of the German mark, the demand and supply curves may look like those shown in Figure 20.1. The demand curve shows the amount of German marks that people with dollars will demand at

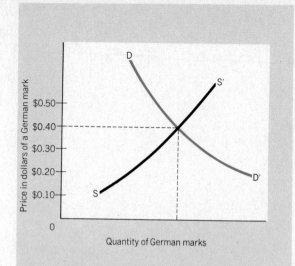

Figure 20.1
Determination of the Exchange Rate between Dollars and German Marks under Freely Fluctuating Exchange Rates

Under freely fluctuating exchange rates, the equilibrium price of a German mark would be $.40 if *DD'* is the demand curve for marks and *SS'* is the supply curve.

various prices of a mark. The supply curve shows the amount of German marks that people with marks will supply at various prices of a mark. Since the amount of German currency supplied must equal the amount demanded in equilibrium, the equilibrium price (in dollars) of a German mark is given by the intersection of the demand and supply curves. In Figure 20.1, this intersection is at $.40.

Let's look in more detail at the demand and supply sides of this market. On the demand side are people who want to import German goods (like the book you want to buy) into the United States, people who want to travel in Germany (where they'll need German money), people who want to build factories in Germany, and others with dollars who want German currency. The people on the supply side are those who want to import American goods into Germany, Germans who want to travel in the United States (where they'll need American money), people with marks who want to build factories in the United States, and others with marks who want American currency. Thus it is obvious that when Americans demand more German cameras or Rhine wine (causing the demand curve to shift upward and to the right), the price (in dollars) of the German mark will tend to increase. Conversely, when the Germans demand more American cars or computers (resulting in a shift of the supply curve downward and to the right[1]), the price (in dollars) of the German mark will tend to decrease.

Changes in tastes affect the equilibrium level of the exchange rate, as shown by the usual sorts of supply-and-demand diagrams that we introduced in Chapter 4. For example, if Americans become fonder and fonder of German goods and less fond of their domestic goods, there will be an increase in the demand for goods imported from Germany, and an attendant increase in the demand for German marks. As shown in Figure 20.2, the demand curve for marks may shift from *DD'* to *EE'*, causing a rise in the price (in dollars) of a German mark. For example, in Figure 20.2, the price of a mark may increase from $.40 to $.44. Also, differences between the two countries in many other factors, including the rate of inflation and the rate of economic growth, will affect the exchange rate.

Note that such a change in exchange rates would not have been possible under the gold standard. Unless a country changed the amount of gold that could be exchanged for a unit of its currency, exchange rates were fixed under the gold standard. Sometimes, governments did change the amount of

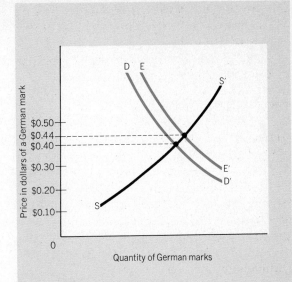

Figure 20.2
Effect of Shift in Demand Curve for German Marks

If the demand curve shifts from *DD'* to *EE'*, the equilibrium price of a German mark increases from $.40 to $.44.

[1] To see why an increase in German demand for American goods shifts the supply curve downward and to the right, recall that the supply curve shows the amount of marks that will be supplied at each price of a mark. Thus, a shift downward and to the right in the supply curve means that more marks will be supplied at a given price (in dollars) of the mark. Given the posited increase in German demand for American goods, such a shift in the supply curve would be expected.

gold that could be exchanged for their currencies. For example, in 1933 the United States increased the price of gold from $21 an ounce to $35 an ounce. When a country increases the price of gold, this is called a ***devaluation*** of its currency.

Two other terms frequently encountered in discussions of exchange rates are ***appreciation*** and ***depreciation.*** When Country *A*'s currency becomes more valuable relative to Country *B*'s currency, Country *A*'s currency is said to appreciate relative to that of Country *B*, and Country *B*'s currency is said to depreciate relative to that of Country *A*. In Figure 20.2, the mark appreciated relative to the dollar and the dollar depreciated relative to the mark. This use of terms makes sense. Since the number of dollars commanded by a mark increased, the mark clearly became more valuable relative to the dollar and the dollar became less valuable relative to the mark.

Under flexible exchange rates, what insures a balance in the exports and imports between countries? The situation differs, of course, from that described by David Hume, since Hume assumed the existence of the gold standard. Under flexible exchange rates, the balance is achieved through changes in exchange rates. For example, suppose once again that for some reason Britain is importing far more from us than we are from Britain. This will mean that the British, needing dollars to buy our goods, will be willing to supply pounds more cheaply. In other words, the supply curve for British

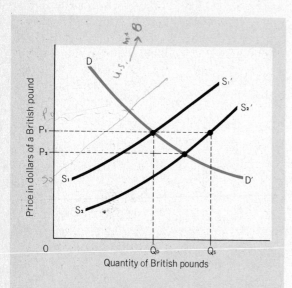

Figure 20.3
Adjustment Mechanism

If Britain imports more from us than we do from Britain, the supply curve will shift from S_1S_1' to S_2S_2', resulting in a decline of the price of the pound from P_1 to P_2 dollars. If Britain tries to maintain the price at $\$P_1$, the British government will have to exchange dollars for $(Q_s - Q_D)$ pounds.

pounds will shift downward and to the right from S_1S_1' to S_2S_2', as shown in Figure 20.3. This will cause the price of a pound to decline from P_1 dollars to P_2 dollars. Or, from Britain's point of view, the price (in pounds) of a dollar will have been bid up by the swollen demand for imports from America.

Because of the increase in the price (in pounds) of a dollar, our goods will become more expensive in Britain. Thus, the British will tend to reduce their imports of our goods. At the same time, since the price (in dollars) of a pound has decreased, British goods will become cheaper in the United States, and this, of course, will stimulate us to import more from Britain. Consequently, as our currency appreciates in terms of theirs—or, to put it another way, as theirs depreciates in terms of ours—the British are induced to import less and export more. Thus, there is an automatic mechanism (just as there was under the gold standard) to bring trade between countries into balance.

Fixed Exchange Rates

Although many economists believed that exchange rates should be allowed to fluctuate, very few exchange rates really did so in the period from the end of World War II up to 1973. Instead, *most exchange rates were fixed by government action and international agreement.* Although they may have varied slightly about the fixed level, the extent to which they were allowed to vary was small. Every now and then, governments changed the exchange rates, for reasons discussed below; but for long periods of time, they remained fixed.

If exchange rates remain fixed, the amount demanded of a foreign currency may not equal the amount supplied. For example, consider the situation in Figure 20.4. If DD' and SS' are the demand and supply curves for German marks, the equilibrium price of a mark is $\$.40$. But suppose the fixed exchange rate between dollars and marks is .35 to 1: that is, each mark exchanges for $\$.35$.

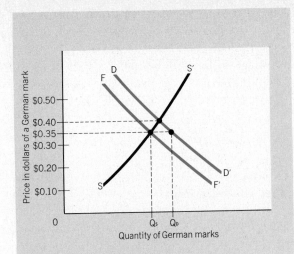

**Figure 20.4
Fixed Exchange Rate**

The equilibrium price of a German mark is $.40, if *DD′* is the demand curve. If $.35 is the fixed exchange rate, the U.S. government may try to shift the demand curve for marks from *DD′* to *FF′*, thus bringing the equilibrium exchange rate into equality with the fixed exchange rate.

Unless the government intervenes, more German marks will be demanded at a price of $.35 per mark than will be offered. Specifically, the difference between the quantity demanded and the quantity supplied will be $Q_D - Q_S$. Unless the government steps in, a black market for German marks may develop, and the real price may increase toward $.40 per mark.

To maintain exchange rates at their fixed levels, governments can intervene in a variety of ways. For example, they may reduce the demand for foreign currencies by reducing defense expenditures abroad, by limiting the amount that their citizens can travel abroad, and by curbing imports from other countries. Thus, in the case depicted in Figure 20.4, the American government might adopt some or all of these measures to shift the demand curve for

German marks downward and to the left. When the demand curve had been pushed from *DD′* to *FF′*, the equilibrium price of a German mark would be equal to $.35, the fixed exchange rate. There would no longer be any mismatch between the quantity of marks demanded and the quantity supplied.

However, such mismatches are bound to occur, at least temporarily, when exchange rates are fixed. When they do, governments enter the market and buy and sell their currencies in order to maintain fixed exchange rates. This happened in post-World War II Britain. At times the amount of British pounds supplied exceeded the amount demanded. Then the British government bought up the excess at the fixed exchange rate. At other times, when the quantity demanded exceeded the amount supplied, the British government supplied the pounds desired at the fixed exchange rate. As long as the fixed exchange rate was close to (sometimes above and sometimes below) the equilibrium exchange rate, the amount of its currency the government sold at one time equaled, more or less, the amount it bought at another time.

However, the government might try to maintain a fixed exchange rate far from the equilibrium exchange rate. For example, the British government might have tried to maintain the price (in dollars) of the pound at P_1 in the situation in Figure 20.3, when the supply curve for British pounds was S_2S_2'. Since the quantity of British pounds supplied exceeded the quantity demanded at that exchange rate, the British government would have to buy the difference. That is, it would have to buy $(Q_S - Q_D)$ pounds with dollars. Moreover, it would have to keep on exchanging dollars for pounds in these quantities for as long as the demand and supply curves remained in these positions. Eventually, the government would run out of dollars and would have to impose restrictions to shift the supply or demand curves (as described above) or change the exchange rate. How long it could maintain the price of the pound at P_1 would depend on how big its reserves of foreign currency were.

Fixed versus Flexible Exchange Rates

Why, until 1973, did most countries fix their exchange rates, rather than allow them to fluctuate? One important reason was the feeling that flexible exchange rates might vary so erratically that it might be difficult to carry out normal trade. For example, an American exporter of machine tools to Britain might not know what British pounds would be worth 6 months from now, when he would collect a debt in pounds. According to the proponents of fixed exchange rates, fluctuating rates would increase uncertainties for people and firms engaged in international trade and thus reduce the volume of such trade. Moreover, they argued that the harmful effects of speculation over exchange rates would increase if exchange rates were flexible, and that flexible exchange rates might promote more rapid inflation.

Many economists disagreed, feeling that flexible exchange rates would work better. They asked why flexible prices are used and trusted in other areas of the economy, but not in connection with foreign exchange. They pointed out that a country would have more autonomy in formulating its fiscal and monetary policy if exchange rates were flexible, and they claimed that speculation over exchange rates would not be destabilizing. But until 1973, the advocates of flexible exchange rates persuaded few of the world's central bankers and policy makers.

However, considerable attention was devoted to a compromise between fixed and completely flexible exchange rates—the so-called *crawling peg*. According to the crawling peg (which admittedly sounds more like an insect than a system of exchange rates), the exchange rate between currencies would be allowed to change, but only up to a certain amount—perhaps 1 or 2 percent per year. Thus, if supply and demand dictated that the dollar should depreciate relative to the German mark, the price (in dollars) of the mark could increase 10 or 20 percent over a decade. Moreover, at any point in time, more variation in exchange rates about the fixed, "parity" level would be allowed.

The advantage of the crawling peg is, of course, that it allows exchange rates to move in a way that eventually results in international equilibrium. However, in contrast to flexible exchange rates, the crawling peg insures that changes in exchange rates will be gradual enough to preserve many of the benefits of fixed exchange rates. In particular, the risks and uncertainties involved in international trade might be less than under flexible rates (see Figure 20.5).

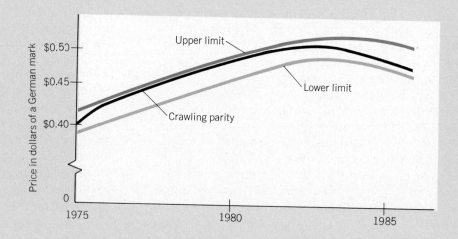

Figure 20.5
The Crawling Peg

According to the crawling peg, the exchange rate can vary by a certain amount each year. The upper and lower limits and crawling parity are shown here for a hypothetical case. Supply and demand can push the exchange rate between the upper limit and lower limit.

In early 1973, after a series of attempts to alter the system of fixed exchange rates to maintain its viability, the major trading nations of the world agreed to allow exchange rates to fluctuate—in other words, to "float." However, they did not go as far as to establish completely flexible exchange rates. Instead, the float was to be managed. Central banks would step in to buy and sell their currency. For example, the United States agreed that, "when necessary and desirable" it would support the value of the dollar. Also, some European countries decided to maintain fixed exchange rates among their own currencies, but to float jointly against other currencies. How long this new system of fluctuating exchange rates will last is an open question that even the most distinguished experts cannot answer. However, hope is widespread that the new system will be less crisis-prone than the old one.

Experience with the Gold Standard and Gold Exchange Standard

What has been our experience with various types of exchange rates? During the latter part of the nineteenth century, the gold standard seemed to work very well, but serious trouble developed after World War I. After going off the gold standard during World War I, for reasons we will discuss in the next chapter, some countries tried to reestablish the old rates of exchange in the postwar period. Because the wartime and postwar rates of inflation were greater in some countries than in others, under the old exchange rates the goods of some countries were underpriced and those of other countries were overpriced. According to the doctrines of David Hume, this imbalance should have been remedied by increases in the general price level in countries where goods were underpriced and by reductions in the general price level in countries where goods were overpriced. But wages and prices proved to be inflexible, and, as one would expect,

it proved especially difficult to adjust them downward. When the adjustment mechanism failed to work quickly enough, the gold standard was abandoned.

During the 1930s, governments tried various schemes. This was, of course, the time of the Great Depression, and governments were trying frantically to reduce unemployment. Sometimes a government allowed the exchange rate to be flexible for a while, and when it found what seemed to be an equilibrium level, fixed the exchange rate there. Sometimes a government depreciated the value of its own currency relative to those of other countries in an attempt to increase employment by making its goods cheap to other countries. Of course, when one country adopted such policies, others retaliated, causing a reduction in international trade and lending, but little or no benefit for the country that started the fracas.

In 1944, the Allied governments sent representatives to Bretton Woods, New Hampshire, to work out a more effective system for the postwar era. It was generally agreed that competitive devaluations, such as occurred in the 1930s, should be avoided. Out of the Bretton Woods conference came the *International Monetary Fund* (IMF), which was set up to maintain a stable system of fixed exchange rates and to insure that when exchange rates had to be changed because of significant trade imbalances, disruption was minimized.

The system developed during the postwar period is generally labeled the *gold-exchange standard*, as opposed to the gold standard. Under this system, the dollar—which had by this time taken the place of the British pound as the world's key currency—was convertible into gold at a fixed price (not, however, for monetary purposes by private American citizens, as we saw in Chapter 12). And since other currencies could be converted into dollars at fixed exchange rates, other currencies were convertible indirectly into gold at a fixed price.

During the early postwar period, this system worked reasonably well. However, throughout the 1960s our gold stock decreased substantially, as year in, year out, we had a deficit in our balance of payments, described below. To prevent speculators and others from depleting our gold stock, the major central banks agreed in 1968 to establish a *"two-tier" gold system*—an **official tier** in which gold, used solely for monetary purposes, was traded back and forth between central banks at the official exchange rates, and a **private tier** in which the rest of the world's gold supply was traded on a free market. The central banks agreed not to sell gold to the private tier.

But this remedy could only postpone the breakdown of the gold-exchange standard. In August 1971, President Nixon announced that the United States would no longer convert dollars into gold for foreign central banks. Thus the link between gold and exchange rates was shattered. Also, pressure was exerted on other countries, particularly Japan and Germany, to allow their currencies to appreciate in terms of our own. Since this would make their goods more expensive to us and cut down on their exports, they resisted such changes. But eventually they allowed their currencies to become more expensive in terms of ours, and (what amounts to the same thing) we allowed our currency to become cheaper in terms of theirs. A new system of fixed exchange rates was approved in 1971, when representatives of the major trading nations met at the Smithsonian Institution.

Although President Nixon hailed the Smithsonian agreement as "the greatest international monetary agreement in the history of the world," events were to prove it unequal to the tasks it faced. In February 1973, scarcely more than a year after the agreement, the United States felt obliged to devalue the dollar again, as the outflow of dollars to other countries continued. Then, in March 1973, representatives of the major trading nations met in Paris to establish a system of fluctuating exchange rates, thus abandoning the Bretton Woods system of fixed exchange rates. How long the new system will last, and what role the International Monetary Fund will play, are difficult to predict. Uncertainties abound at present in the field of international finance.

The Fight to Save the Pound: A Case Study

From this discussion it is clear that although exchange rates were generally fixed until 1973, from time to time they were altered to respond to changes in basic economic conditions. To illustrate how these alterations occurred, consider the case of Great Britain in the mid-1960s. Since 1949, the exchange rate between dollars and pounds had been 2.8 to 1, which meant that a British pound was worth $2.80. But at this exchange rate, Britain found it very difficult to export as much as she bought from foreigners. In other words, at this exchange rate the quantity of pounds supplied exceeded the quantity demanded. If the market for pounds had been free, the price of the pound would have dropped. That is, the pound would have depreciated relative to the dollar.

Britain's Labor government, elected in 1964, declared that it would not depreciate the pound. Prime Minister Harold Wilson claimed that maintaining the exchange rate at $2.80 was of primary importance and called the fight to maintain the exchange rate a "second battle of Britain." (The original battle of Britain occurred early in World War II, when Britain fought off air attacks by Nazi Germany.) In 1964, the government slapped a 15 percent tax on imports to shift the supply curve for pounds to the left. In 1965, the government restricted foreign travel and exports of capital. Finally, in 1966, the government froze wages, increased taxes, and cut government expenditures to curb inflation in an attempt to promote exports. All these measures were designed to push the equilibrium exchange rate—the rate at which the demand and supply curves for pounds intersect—up toward $2.80.

But it was to no avail. In 1967, the British were forced to devalue the pound. The exchange rate was reduced from $2.80 to $2.40, a depreciation of about 14 percent. It was hoped that this change would expand British exports, now cheaper to non-Britons, and discourage foreign imports, now more expensive to Britons. In other words, it was hoped that $2.40 was close to the equilibrium exchange rate. From 1967 to 1971, when the Smithsonian agreement took place, the exchange rate remained at this level.[2]

The Balance of Payments

We have referred repeatedly in this chapter to the importance of the balance of payments. Now we will discuss it in some detail. *Any country's* **balance of payments** *measures the flow of payments between it and other countries.* Consider the U.S. balance of payments in 1972, reproduced in Table 20.1. There are two types of items in the balance of payments: debit items and credit items. **Debit items** are items for which we must pay foreigners —items that use up the foreign currency we have. **Credit items** are items for which foreigners pay us—items that provide us with a stock of foreign currency. For example, if a French importer buys an American car to sell in France, this is a credit item in the U.S. balance of payments because a foreigner—the French importer—must pay us for the car. On the other hand, if an American importer buys some French wine to sell in the United States, this is a debit item in the U.S. balance of payments. We must pay the foreigner—the French winemaker—for the wine.

It is essential to understand at the outset that *the balance of payments always balances.* The total of credit items must always equal the total of debit items, because the sum of the debit items is the total value of goods, services, and assets we received from foreigners. These goods, services, and assets must be paid for with credit items, since credit items provide the foreign currency required by foreigners. Since the debit items must be paid for by foreign currency provided by the credit

items, the sum of the credit items must equal the sum of the debit items. Or put differently, *debit items use up foreign currency and credit items provide foreign currency. Since the amount of foreign currency used up must equal the amount required, the sum of the credit items must equal the sum of the debit items.*

To see exactly what the balance of payments tells us, let's look at each of the entries in Table 20.1, starting with the debits column. During 1972, we imported about $56 billion worth of merchandise. This, of course, is a debit item, since it requires payments to manufacturers abroad. Also, we spent about $2 billion (net) for foreign services (including travel and transportation), about $3 billion for net military transactions, about $1 billion for remittances abroad (such as Social Security payments to Americans now living abroad), about $4 billion for net government grants and long-term capital outflows (such as our foreign aid programs and government finance for exports), and about $1 billion for net nonliquid short-term private capital outflows. These are all debit items, since they entail payments by us to foreigners.

To see how we paid for these debit items, we must look at the credits column. We exported about $49 billion worth of merchandise. This, of course, is a credit item, since it represents payments to us by foreign purchasers of American goods. Also, we received $8 billion in net income from foreign investments, and about $4 billion in net liquid private capital inflows from abroad; both of these are credit items. Thus, adding up these credit items and these debit items (and noting that we must add $4 billion to the debit items to offset errors and omissions), our payments abroad totaled about $71 billion and payments to us equaled about $61 billion. The remaining items in the balance of payments show how we paid for the difference of $10 billion. As shown in Table 20.1, foreigners accepted $10 billion in additional IOUs from us. This covered the $10 billion difference.

This is all extremely important information. It is no wonder that bankers, economists, traders, and policy makers pore over the balance of payments.

[2] For further discussion, see Richard Cooper's contribution to R. Caves, *Britain's Economic Prospects,* Washington: Brookings, 1968, and J. B. Cohen, *Balance-of-Payments Policy,* Baltimore: Penguin, 1969.

Table 20.1

United States Balance of Payments, 1972[a]

	Credit	Debit
	(billions of dollars)	
Goods and services		
Merchandise exports	49	
Merchandise imports		56
Net services (including travel and transportation)		2
Net military transactions		3
Net investment income	8	
Transfers, capital movements, and movements of reserve assets		
Remittances		1
Net U.S. government grants and capital outflows		4
Net U.S. private long-term capital flows	b	
Net nonliquid short-term capital flows		1
Errors and omissions		4
Net liquid private capital flows	4	
Net change in liabilities to foreign official agencies	10	
Net change in U.S. reserves	b	
Total	71	71

Source: Survey of Current Business, March 1973.
[a] Excludes the allocation of SDR's of less than $1 billion.
[b] Less than one-half billion dollars.

Goods and Services

Having looked briefly at the entire balance of payments, let's break the table into two parts: (1) goods and services, and (2) transfers, capital movements, and movements of reserve assets. First, consider goods and services. As you can see from Table 20.1, this part of the balance of payments shows the amount of goods and services we exported and imported. Note that exports and imports include *invisible* items, as well as *visible* items (that is, merchandise). Among the invisible items are transportation services, tourist expenditures, military sales and expenditures, and earnings on investments in other countries. They must be accounted for in the balance of payments, since they entail payments by one country to another. For example, when a British vessel carries our merchandise, we must pay for this service. Or when an American tourist stays at the George V Hotel in Paris, we must pay for this service—and judging from the George V's rates, pay dearly at that. Or when foreigners lend us capital, we must pay them interest.

You will recall from the previous section that credit items supply us with foreign currency while debit items use up our foreign currency. Thus it is clear that when foreign carriers transport our goods or people, this is a debit item, but when we carry other countries' goods or people, this is a credit item in our balance of payments. Expenditures by American tourists traveling abroad are debit items, but money spent here by foreign tourists is a credit item. Further, interest we pay to foreigners on money they lent us is a debit item, but interest foreigners pay us on money we lent them is a credit item. (Also, when immigrants to America send money back to the "old country," this is a debit item in our balance of payments. In fact, such private remittances—taken up in the next section—are responsible for debits of several hundred million dollars in recent years.)

Besides the transactions made by private citizens, the government's transactions must be included too in our balance of payments. The United States government supports a vast network of military bases around the world. Every now and then, we become involved in "police actions" and other euphemisms and circumlocutions which, to the naked eye, look very much like wars. We also engage in a host of other government activities abroad (like the work of the State Department, the Peace Corps, and so on), and all these programs affect our balance of payments. In the main, they result in debit items since they involve payments abroad. For example, money spent by U.S. military authorities stationed in Wiesbaden, Germany, to buy supplies from local German companies is a debit item.

We can tell a great deal about America's transactions with other countries by looking at the individual figures for goods and services in Table 20.1. First, it is clear that in 1972 we imported about $7 billion more merchandise than we exported. Second, we spent about $2 billion more on foreign transportation and other services and on tourism abroad than foreigners spent on our transportation and other services and on tourism here. Third, foreigners paid us far more—about $8 billion more—in interest and dividends on money we invested abroad than we paid foreigners for similar investments here. Fourth, the U.S. government spent (net) about $3 billion abroad for military transactions.

The newspapers often mention the balance of trade. The **balance of merchandise trade** refers only to a part of the balance of payments. A na-

tion is said to have a favorable balance of merchandise trade if its exports of merchandise are more than its imports of merchandise, and an unfavorable balance of merchandise trade if its exports of merchandise are less than its imports of merchandise. As Table 20.1 shows, the United States had an unfavorable balance of merchandise trade of about $7 billion in 1972. But obviously the balance of merchandise trade tells only part of what we want to know about a country's transactions with other countries. As shown in Table 20.1, there is much more to the balance of payments than a comparison of merchandise exports with merchandise imports. Moreover, a "favorable" balance of trade is not necessarily a good thing, since imports, not exports, contribute to a country's standard of living.

Finally, note that the United States had a *net deficit with respect to goods and services* of about $4 billion in 1972. In other words, the credit items for goods and services added up to $57 billion, while the debit items added up to $61 billion. This means that we spent about $4 billion more on foreign goods and services than foreigners spent on our goods and services. Any deficit with respect to goods and services must be offset by a surplus in the rest of the balance of payments. This is because, as stressed in the previous section, the total of the debit items must equal the total of the credit items. Similarly, any surplus with respect to goods and services must be offset by a deficit in the rest of the balance of payments. In the following sections, we shall see exactly how the deficit with respect to goods and services was offset in 1972.

Transfers, Capital Movements, and Reserve Assets

Let's turn now to the rest of the balance of payments, which shows transfers (gifts, pensions, etc.), capital movements, and movements of reserve assets from one country to another. Take a close look at

Table 20.2

Transfers, Capital Movements, and Movements of Reserve Assets, 1972

	Credit	Debit
	(billions of dollars)	
Remittances		1
Net U.S. government grants and long-term capital flows		4
Net U.S. private long-term capital flows		—
Net nonliquid short-term private capital flows		1
Errors and omissions		4
Net liquid private capital flows	4	
Net change in liabilities to foreign official agencies	10	
Net change in U.S. reserves	—	

Source: Table 20.1

the second part of our 1972 balance of payments, reproduced in Table 20.2. You will see that the entries regarding capital movements are classified as transactions by the government or by private parties. This classification seems self-explanatory; for example, when an American lends money to a German firm by buying its long-term bonds, this is clearly a private capital outflow.

Recall from previous sections that a credit item supplies us with foreign currency and a debit item uses up our foreign currency. Let's apply this rule to a case where we lend money abroad. Clearly, such a transaction requires that we use foreign currency, since we will be buying foreign bonds or other securities. Thus, lending abroad results in a debit item. On the other hand, borrowing from abroad supplies us with foreign currency, since foreigners pay us with their currency when they buy our bonds or other securities. Thus, borrowing abroad results in a credit item.

Table 20.2 shows that in 1972 the United States government granted or lent (long-term) about $4 billion abroad (net of repayments), and private citizens and firms made net nonliquid short-term capital outflows of about $1 billion. Also, we sent $1 billion abroad in remittances—for example, gifts and pensions. As we just pointed out, these

are all debit items. Combined with the $4 billion net deficit for goods and services (and the debit item of $4 billion to offset errors and omissions), this meant a total of about $14 billion of debits to be financed, one way or another, by the United States. This is frequently referred to as the "deficit on a liquidity basis" in our balance of payments. The use of the term "deficit" does not mean that our entire balance of payments is in deficit. That could never be the case, since by definition the total of the debits must always equal the total of the credits. What this "deficit" really means is that we spent about $14 billion more on foreign goods, services, and long-term or nonliquid investments than foreigners spent on our goods, services, and long-term or nonliquid investments. This is shown in Table 20.2.

Another frequently used concept is the *deficit on an official-settlements basis.* The difference between this concept and the liquidity concept in the previous paragraph is that the former takes account of net liquid private capital flows, which were a credit item of about $4 billion in 1972. Thus, on an official-settlements basis, the deficit in 1972 was about $10 billion, the amount we owed other central banks and were obliged to pay in reserve assets. This is shown in Table 20.3.

Table 20.3

Deficit in U.S. Balance of Payments, 1972

	Credit	Debit
	(billions of dollars)	
Merchandise exports	49	
Merchandise imports		56
Net services		2
Net military transactions		3
Net investment income	8	
Remittances		1
Net U.S. government grants and capital outflows		4
Net U.S. private long-term capital outflows	ª	
Net nonliquid short-term capital flows		1
Errors and omissions		4
Total	57	71
Net liquid private capital flows	4	
Total	61	71

Deficit on liquidity basis = $71 billion − $57 billion = $14 billion

Deficit on official-settlements basis = $71 billion − $61 billion = $10 billion

Source: Survey of Current Business, March 1973.
ª Less than one-half billion dollars.

Financing the Deficit

Next we must consider how this deficit (on an official-settlements basis) of about $10 billion was financed. What credit items in other parts of the balance of payments offset this debit balance? To answer this question, we must look at the last two items in the balance of payments—net change in U.S. liabilities to foreign official agencies, and net change in U.S. reserves. First, consider the net change in U.S. liabilities to foreign central banks. As you can see from Tables 20.1 and 20.2, our debt to foreign central banks increased by about $10 billion during 1972. In other words, foreign central banks built up their short-term investments here. They invested about $10 billion in our short-term debt, which is how we financed the deficit.

Next, let's look at the change in the level of U.S. monetary reserves, including gold. Such changes are another way the deficit could have been financed. For example, in 1970, foreign central banks asked us for about $3 billion in reserves. Thus, the 1970 deficit was financed partly by transferring our reserves to other countries and partly by our increased liabilities. Of course, as noted above, the situation now is somewhat different than it was in 1970. The U.S. government will no longer exchange gold for dollars held by foreign central banks. But other reserve assets, including foreign exchange, can be used to make settlements. In 1972, however, there was little or no net change in U.S. reserves.

Finally, when we get down to the bottom of the balance of payments, we achieve the balance between debit items and credit items that logic—and arithmetic—assures us will prevail, since we must pay in cash or IOUs for what we get from other nations.[3]

U.S. Balance of Payments Deficits, 1950–72

In the previous sections, we noted that the United States incurred a balance of payments deficit in 1972. Was this deficit just a temporary occurrence? After all, one would expect any country to run a deficit in some years, even if in the long run it was not in a deficit position. Deficits in one year might be canceled out by surpluses in other years. Figure

[3] However, even this certainty is clouded a bit by the fact that there are errors and omissions in the statistics that mean that a perfect balance is never achieved. But this only reflects the limitations of the data: logic dictates that if complete data could be obtained, a perfect balance would always be achieved.

20.6 shows that this was not the case. *During the period from 1950 to 1972, the United States showed a chronic deficit.* Taking this 22-year period as a whole, deficits have far exceeded surpluses in our balance of payments.

This chronic deficit in our balance of payments has caused considerable uneasiness and concern, both here and abroad. Several factors have been responsible for it. First, the Western European and Japanese economies have recovered from the devastation of World War II, they have been alert and aggressive in adopting new technology, and they have become tough competitors. To cite but one example, the Japanese have been particularly adept at absorbing modern electronic technology and at producing electronic goods for civilian markets. In many areas of technology, the United States continues to enjoy a lead, but the gap seems to be narrowing. As productivity in Western Europe and Japan has risen more rapidly than ours, their costs have fallen relative to ours, and they have

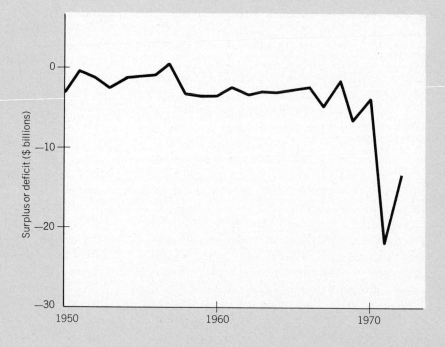

**Figure 20.6
Deficit or Surplus in U.S. Balance of Payments, 1950–72, Liquidity Basis**

The United States has experienced a chronic deficit, particularly large in 1971 and 1972.

been able to undersell us much more in their own markets, third markets, and sometimes even our own market. Thus, since the mid-1960s, our imports have grown more rapidly than our exports.

Second, we have spent enormous amounts abroad for military purposes and for foreign aid. Our military expenditures abroad were particularly high during the Vietnamese war. For example, they were about $4.5 billion in 1968. Not only did this war take a heavy toll in lives and in social disruption; it also helped keep our balance of payments in deficit. Note, however, that some of our government spending abroad has involved the use of "tied" funds, which can be used only to buy American goods. Since these programs result in exports that would not otherwise be made, the elimination of some of these programs would not reduce the deficit. If the government spending were cut, the exports it finances would be cut as well.

Third, American firms have invested enormous amounts of money abroad. U.S. investors have acquired oil refineries, assembly lines, and hundreds of other types of plants. The rate of private investment abroad increased spectacularly during the 1950s and 1960s. In the early 1950s, new American private investment abroad was about $2 billion per year; in the late 1950s, over $3 billion per year; in the early 1960s, over $4 billion per year; and in the late 1960s, over $8 billion per year. The reason for this growth is fairly obvious. The markets of Western Europe (and other parts of the world) were growing rapidly and the construction of plants abroad was a profitable move. To help reduce our balance of payments deficit, the government introduced a voluntary program to limit such investment abroad in 1965, and made the program compulsory in 1968.

Fourth, a number of other factors, including inflation in the United States and discrimination abroad against U.S. products, also contributed to our balance of payments deficits. Clearly, inflation in the United States—such as occurred in the late 1960s and early 1970s in particular—makes our exports more expensive abroad. It is true, of course, that inflation in the United States has not been as great as in many other countries, but in many industries, like steel, our prices have risen relative to those abroad. Also, foreigners have maintained various quotas, tariffs, and other devices to keep out American exports. Many of these discriminatory regulations were enacted during the period of the dollar shortage, when such policies were more understandable. Under present conditions, they contribute, of course, to our balance of payments deficit.

Autonomous and Accommodating Transactions

One of life's certainties is that the balance of payments of any nation will balance, but this, like many of the certainties of life, is merely a tautology. The important point is not that a balance is achieved, but *how it is achieved*. Sometimes a balance is achieved in a way that results in a stable equilibrium. In other cases, a balance is achieved in a way that results in disequilibrium, which, as we know, is a situation that cannot be maintained indefinitely. In the latter cases, something has to change; things cannot go on as they are. In the late 1960s and early 1970s, economists and bankers generally agreed that the U.S. balance of payments was in disequilibrium.

To see more clearly what disequilibrium means, it is convenient (if perhaps, somewhat oversimplified) to distinguish between autonomous transactions and accommodating transactions. *Autonomous transactions* occur for reasons quite independent of the balance of payments. Exports, imports, and net capital movements occur because of people's tastes, comparative costs, and relative rates of return in various countries. Government expenditures abroad are made for military, political, and other reasons. Thus it is customary to treat these transactions as autonomous. On the other hand, *accommodating transactions* are made to bring about the necessary balance in the balance of payments. They compensate for differences between the total credits and total debits resulting from the autonomous transactions. For example, changes in a country's gold stock and other reserve assets, as well as short-term investments in the country's currency and other assets by foreigners, may be accommodating transactions.

Accommodating transactions are evidence of disequilibrium in a country's balance of payments. The United States's autonomous transactions—exports, imports, government expenditures abroad, long-term capital movements—resulted in a debit balance during the 1960s and early 1970s. This meant that certain accommodating transactions (reductions in our gold stock and other reserve assets, and increases in foreign investments in our currency and short-term investments) had to occur. These accommodating transactions were evidence of disequilibrium. They could not go on forever.

Ways to Restore Equilibrium

When a country's balance of payments is in disequilibrium, what can it do to restore equilibrium? Consider, for example, the situation facing President Nixon in 1970 and the alternatives his advisers could have laid before him. First, recall the discussion of exchange rates earlier in this chapter. A country might adjust its exchange rates to restore equilibrium in its balance of payments. In the United States, the dollar in the 1960s was overvalued relative to other currencies, like the German mark. The situation was as shown in Figure 20.7, where DD' and SS' are the demand and supply curves for marks. In a free market for foreign exchange, the price (in dollars) of a German mark would have risen from the fixed exchange rate, P_F, to P_E. This would have discouraged American imports, encouraged American exports, and brought the U.S. balance of payments into equilibrium. In other words, it would have increased the autonomous transactions resulting in credits and decreased the autonomous transactions resulting in debits.

Thus, one step President Nixon might have taken in 1970 was to depreciate the dollar. But

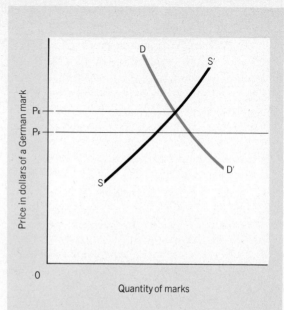

Figure 20.7
"Overvaluation" of the Dollar

Whereas the fixed exchange rate was only $\$P_F$ for a German mark, the equilibrium price was $\$P_E$.

the United States was reluctant to depreciate its currency relative to others. Depreciation of our currency would hurt friendly nations who had been willing to hold large dollar balances. The United States wanted to discourage speculation against the dollar. And there was a chance that depreciation of the world's leading currency would seriously disrupt the entire world monetary system. Also, it must be noted that depreciation would have required the cooperation of other countries. For example, unless the Germans were prepared to let the mark rise in value relative to the dollar, they could stop it by also depreciating the mark. In presenting the alternative of depreciating the dollar to the president in 1970, his advisers undoubtedly stressed these problems.

Second, recall our discussion of the gold standard. A country might change its general price level in order to restore equilibrium in its balance of payments. This was the sort of mechanism the gold standard used to restore equilibrium. In a country with a chronic deficit, like the United States, the remedy would be a lowering of its general price level relative to that of other countries. This would reduce our imports and promote our exports. In contrast to the previous alternative, it would not have meant any alteration in exchange rates. However, it might well have led to a depression in the United States. Because wages and prices are very difficult to push downward, any serious attempt to reduce aggregate spending in an effort to reduce the price level would probably cut output and increase unemployment. For this reason, economists are not enthusiastic about this route to equilibrium. Since it is a safe bet that President Nixon, like any president, would not favor the political consequences of such action, his advisers probably skipped over this alternative. However, they may well have counseled the president to keep inflation to a minimum —for balance of payments reasons as well as others discussed in previous chapters.

Third, a country might adopt various types of controls to interfere with market forces in order to restore equilibrium in the balance of payments. For example, a country might impose controls over the exchange market. Thus, the United States government might have required all foreign exchange received by exporters (or others) to be sold to the government, and the government might have rationed this foreign exchange among importers and others who wanted it. By so doing, the government would see that equilibrium in the balance of payments was restored. However, this kind of scheme has many disadvantages. For example, it obviously limits freedom of choice and is difficult for the government to enforce.

Another type of government control is aimed at trade rather than the exchange markets. In this case, the government tries to influence imports and exports through quotas, tariffs, subsidies, and other such controls. For example, the United States might have raised tariffs and imposed quotas to cut its imports, and subsidized some of its exports to increase their volume. It might also have imposed limits on the amount American tourists could spend abroad. Of course, an important difficulty with such interference with free trade is that it reduces world efficiency, as we saw in Chapter 19.

In addition, the government might have discouraged American investment abroad—and in fact it did so in various ways, including the imposition in 1963 of an "interest equalization tax" of 15 percent (later reduced to 11½ percent) on any purchase of a foreign stock or bond by an American from a foreigner. Despite the serious problems in controls of this sort, presidential advisers certainly mentioned such alternatives in 1970.

Fourth, in the special circumstances facing the United States, one way to restore equilibrium to our balance of payments might have been to convince other countries to increase their share of the responsibilities for defense and foreign aid. For example, Western Europe might pay a larger share of the costs of maintaining a defensive shield that protects us all. The United States has been pressing for this for many years, with some success. Also, the United States might try to persuade other countries to remove discriminatory barriers to our goods.

Fifth, the United States might try to step up its rate of productivity increase and product innovation. This would make our exports more competitive. However, it is not easy for a country to influence its rate of productivity increase or its rate of innovation in the short run. Nonetheless, increased expenditure on research and development —and the rapid diffusion of existing modern technology—would be likely to help.

Having set forth some of the principal ways that a country can restore equilibrium in its balance of payments, it is interesting to look at the kind of actions President Nixon took in the early 1970s. As you might expect, he adopted many of the measures described above. In December 1971, he depreciated the dollar relative to all major foreign currencies. On the average, the dollar was depreciated by about 10 to 15 percent. Moreover, throughout the early 1970s a serious effort was made to contain inflation at home, and, for better or worse, some protectionist controls were established or continued. Also, the president's Special Assistant on International Economic Policy, Peter Peterson (later Secretary of Commerce), beat the drum for subsidies or encouragement for added research and development by American industry. In February 1973, the dollar was depreciated again, this time by about 10 percent. And when renewed speculation against the dollar caused a further crisis in March 1973, other countries decided to allow the dollar to float, and an international agreement was reached to this effect in Paris.

Britain's Balance of Payments: A Case Study

The United States is not the only country that has had trouble with its balance of payments. You will recall from a previous section that a persistent deficit in its balance of payments forced Great Britain to devalue the pound in 1967. Let's take a closer look at the nature of Britain's balance of payments problems in the mid-1960s. During that period, Britain was chronically unable to earn enough foreign exchange to finance the net outflow of private long-term capital and the government's expenditures outside Britain for military and aid purposes. One factor that hampered Britain's exports at that time was the existence of considerable cost-push inflation.

One way for a country to combat a persistent deficit in its balance of payments is to keep a close rein on inflation. By keeping its price level down, it can stimulate its exports. During the 1950s and early 1960s, the British government reacted to deficits in its balance of payments by adopting deflationary monetary and fiscal policies. This was the "stop" phase of the "stop-go" policies it adopted

during this period. When the balance of payments crisis was eased, the government adopted expansionary measures which led to increases in the price level. This was the "go" phase of these policies. Then, because of the price increases (and other factors), the balance of payments deficit would crop up again and the government would go back to its "stop" phase, which generally produced considerable unemployment.

A country can also try to combat a persistent deficit in its balance of payments by interfering with free markets and trade. In 1964, Britain imposed a 15 percent tax on imports other than food, tobacco, and basic raw materials. Subsequently, travel outside Britain was reduced considerably. British citizens were allowed to spend only $140 a year for travel outside the "sterling area," where the pound prevailed as the local currency. In 1965 the British government took steps to reduce long-term investment abroad; and in 1966 the tax system was changed to reduce the aftertax profitability of British overseas investment (relative to investment in Britain). But all these actions—plus others, like cuts in Britain's overseas military forces—were not enough to persuade traders and speculators that devaluation of the pound would not be necessary.

By late 1967, the British government was over a barrel. Its "stop-go" policies had failed to remedy the deficit. Its tax on imports, travel restrictions, and other such measures had not produced the desired results. And it could not count on continued international loans to finance the persistent deficit. When the October figures indicated the worst deficit in over a year, people, fearing imminent devaluation, rushed to exchange pounds for other currencies. The exchange rate fell to $2.78¼ (the lowest level permitted by IMF); and Britain's central bank, the Bank of England, had to buy all the excess supply of pounds, which nearly exhausted its reserves of foreign exchange. In November 1967, the British government resorted to devaluation, thus losing the self-styled "second battle of Britain." As we saw in a previous section, the British pound was devalued by about 14 percent.

The International Money Game

Q: What contributes to, or aggravates, an international monetary crisis?

A: It's not a what, but a who. In a period of international financial stress, speculators move vast sums of money out of weak currencies into strong currencies, and force the central banks to intervene in order to maintain orderly foreign exchange markets.

Q: Why would a speculator do a thing like that?

A: Because it's very profitable.

Q: How can I get to be a speculator?

A: It depends. Right after the war (World War II, that is), the "in" speculator was a small Swiss banker (sometimes referred to as a Gnome of Zurich). More recently, much of the speculation business is rumored to be centered in the OPEC (Organization of Petroleum Exporting Countries). As long as the U.S. keeps exchanging billions of U.S. dollars for oil, the sheiks have plenty to speculate with.

INTERNATIONAL MONEY DESK AT A SWISS BANK, ZURICH.

Q: But suppose I don't speak Arabic?

A: No problem. There's another way in. Become a treasurer of a multinational corporation, preferably one with more than $100 million in annual sales.

Q: I thought companies dealt in foreign exchange only to cover costs of their imports. Aren't they the honest merchants?

A: Some still do. Most small companies deal in foreign exchange only when converting receipts from an overseas customer into dollars. But a select group of multinationals have come to be major powers in foreign exchange markets. The biggest 200 American-based MNFs (multinational firms) own about $25 billion in cash, and have another $100 billion or so in inventories and receivables. In comparison, West Germany's reserves—the largest of any Western nation—amount to about $31 billion. During the currency crises of the sixties, these MNFs learned that it was not wise to be caught in pounds sterling or dollars, and so began to move money on a large scale.

Q: By ship?

A: No, by prepayment and borrowings. For example, branches of a multinational continuously buy and sell from each other. If a treasurer sees an appreciation of the mark coming on, he urges the German subsidiaries to pay its sister subsidiaries as slowly as possible.

Q: It sounds unpatriotic.

A: Depends on whom you ask. The treasurer would claim enlightened profit-maximizing. Isn't that what you want a firm to do?　　E.A.

International Lending

Before concluding this chapter, we must discuss international capital movements in somewhat more detail. The factors underlying international transactions with regard to goods and services are clear enough. For example, we saw in the previous chapter why countries find it profitable to import and export goods and services. But we need to know more about the reasons why nations lend to one another. What factors are responsible for the capital movements shown in the balance of payments?

If the world were free of political problems and nationalist fervor, the answer would be easy. Because different parts of the world are endowed with different amounts and qualities of land and other resources, and have different population densities and amounts of capital, the rate of return to be derived from investments will vary from place to place. Consequently, nations where savings rates are high and investment opportunities are relatively poor will invest their capital in nations where the investment opportunities are better.

Such international lending helps both the lender and the borrower. The lender receives a higher rate of return than it would otherwise, and the borrower gains by having more capital to work with, so that the borrower's output and wages are higher than they would be otherwise. So long as the lender receives a relatively high return from the borrowing country, there is no reason why it should ask for repayment. It may continue to lend money to the borrowing country for years and years. For example, England was a net lender to the United States for about a century. To pay interest to the lender, the borrowing country must sell the lender more goods than it buys, thus building up a credit in its balance of payments that it can use to finance the interest, which is, of course, a debit item.

But the world is not free of political problems and nationalist fervor. Wars occur, governments topple, devastating inflations take place, property is confiscated. Only a fool contemplates investment in another country without taking some account of these and other risks; and because these risks are present, international lending that would otherwise be profitable and beneficial—and would take place if only economic considerations were involved—is sometimes stymied. Suppose that you had $1 million to invest, and that you could invest it at 15 percent interest in a country with an unstable government, where the chances were substantial that the property in which you invested would be confiscated and that you would get back only a fraction of the $1 million. Would you make the loan? Maybe; maybe not. Unfortunately, such risks discourage many international loans that would otherwise be advantageous to both lender and borrower.

America's Role as International Lender

As a country grows and develops, its balance of payments tends to go through four stages. First, a country, when it is relatively undeveloped, is often a net borrower with an "unfavorable" balance of trade. Its imports exceed its exports, and it borrows from other countries to finance the difference between its imports and exports. It needs the goods, supplies, and equipment it imports to put it on the road to economic development. For example, during the first century of American history we were a substantial net borrower of capital from Europe. This capital helped fuel the early economic growth of the United States, described in Chapter 17.

Second, as the country pays back more and more of its debts, it gets to the stage where debt repayment exceeds new borrowing, and its balance of trade becomes "favorable." In other words, its exports exceed its imports, with the difference being used to reduce the country's outstanding debts and to pay interest on them. The United States entered this stage in the 1870s and remained in it for about half a century.

Third, as the country becomes richer and more advanced, it becomes a net lender to other countries, and its balance of trade continues to be "favorable." This excess of exports over imports is to be expected, since other countries borrow to finance such a net flow to them of goods and services. The United States entered this stage during and after World War I, when it lent huge amounts to its wartime allies for equipment and relief. Recall from the previous chapter that the 1920s were a period when the United States erected high tariffs and barriers to imports. So long as we continued to lend abroad, foreigners could get the dollars to buy our exports. However, when we cut back our foreign lending in the 1930s, serious trouble developed.

Fourth, the country becomes a mature creditor. At this point, the interest it receives from its foreign investments is so great that it exceeds the new loans made to foreigners. Thus its balance of trade must become "unfavorable." Its imports will exceed its exports. In real terms, this difference represents payment of goods and services by foreigners for the use of capital. This "unfavorable" balance of trade is not unfavorable at all, since a country consumes imports, not exports. England reached this stage years ago; the United States is currently heading in this direction.

The United States is now the world's great creditor country—the great international lender. We continue to invest vast amounts abroad, both as private firms and individuals take advantage of profitable opportunities and as our government engages in large foreign aid and military programs. The United States is now entering the fourth stage; it is becoming a mature creditor. Our interest from foreign investments made in previous years must finance our net imports and our military and aid programs.

Summary

An important difference between international business transactions and business transactions within a country is that international business transactions involve more than one currency. The exchange rate is simply the number of units of one currency that exchanges for a unit of another currency. Before the 1930s, many major countries were on the gold standard, which meant that their currency was convertible into a certain amount of gold. The relative gold content of currencies determined exchange rates. For example, to see how much a country's currency was worth in dollars, all you had to do was to divide the amount of gold a unit of its currency was worth by the amount of gold ($\frac{1}{20}$ ounce) a dollar was worth.

The gold standard is long gone. Another way to determine exchange rates is to allow the market for foreign exchange to function like any other free market, the exchange rate being determined by supply and demand. Under such a system, exchange rates, which are flexible, tend to move in a way that removes imbalances among countries in exports and imports. Under the gold standard, such adjustments were supposed to occur as a consequence of changes in relative price levels in various countries.

Until the early 1970s, when exchange rates became more flexible, most exchange rates were fixed by government action and international agreement. They were allowed to vary slightly, but only slightly, about the official rate. If exchange rates are fixed, the amount of a foreign currency demanded may not equal the amount supplied. To maintain exchange rates at the official levels, governments enter the market and buy and sell their currencies as needed. They also intervene by curbing imports, limiting foreign travel, and other measures.

Although exchange rates tended to be fixed until 1973, the official fixed exchange rates had to be altered from time to time, generally when other methods would not stem the tide. For example, the British pound was devalued in 1967. In 1973, many major countries, including the United States, allowed their currencies to "float," resulting in much more flexibility of exchange rates. There has been considerable discussion over the relative advantages of fixed and flexible exchange rates.

A country's balance of payments measures the

flow of payments between it and other countries. Debit items result in a demand for foreign currency, whereas credit items supply foreign currency. The total of the debit items must equal the total of the credit items because the total of the debit items is the total amount of goods, services, and assets we received from foreigners, and these goods, services, and assets must be paid for with credit items. The balance of merchandise trade refers only to part of the balance of payments. A nation is said to have a favorable (unfavorable) balance of merchandise trade if its exports of merchandise exceed (are less than) its imports of merchandise.

If a country's balance with regard to goods and services, transfers, and long-term capital movements is negative, it is said to have a deficit in its balance of payments. The United States experienced a chronic deficit during the 1950s, 1960s, and early 1970s. This deficit—the result of the growing productivity of other economies, our large investments abroad, and our military and foreign aid expenditures abroad—was financed by reductions in our gold stock and by foreigners' acceptance of our short-term debt. Our balance of payments was in disequilibrium. To bring it into equilibrium, we could depreciate the dollar, curb inflation at home, impose controls of various kinds, or try to step up domestic productivity and innovation. Several steps along this line were attempted, including devaluations of the dollar in 1971 and 1973 and allowing the dollar to "float" in 1973.

The United States is now the world's great creditor country. As a country develops, its balance of payments tends to go through four stages. The United States is entering the fourth stage.

CONCEPTS FOR REVIEW

Exchange rate	Gold exchange standard	Deficit on an official settlements basis
Devaluation of currency	Official tier	Autonomous transactions
Appreciation	Private tier	Accommodating transactions
Depreciation	Balance of merchandise trade	
Crawling peg		
International Monetary Fund	Balance of payments	Gold standard
	Deficit on a liquidity basis	Debit items
		Credit items

QUESTIONS FOR DISCUSSION AND REVIEW

1. Do you think that we should return to the gold standard? Why or why not? Do you think that this is a live possibility?

2. What are the most important reasons for the chronic deficit in the U.S. balance of payments? Do you think that these deficits will continue? Why or why not? What further actions should the United States take in this regard?

3. The balance of merchandise trade refers only to a small part of the balance of payments. True or False?

4. To remedy a chronic deficit in its balance of payments, a country's government might
a. raise the general price level.
b. encourage investment abroad.
c. slow the rate of productivity increase.
d. remove protectionist controls.
e. devalue the currency.

CHAPTER 21

The Less Developed Countries

Fresh from a raid on the well-stocked family refrigerator or comfortably placed in front of a television set, the average American finds it difficult to believe that hunger is a problem in the world. Yet it is true. The industrialized countries—like the United States, Western Europe, Japan, and the USSR—are really just rich little islands surrounded by seas of poverty in Asia, Africa, and much of Latin America. This chapter deals with the problems of these so-called "less developed countries" (LDCs)—the poor countries of the world. We take up several questions. Which countries are poor, and why? How badly do they need additional capital? How great is the danger of overpopulation? To what extent do they lack modern technology? How can they stimulate their rate of economic growth? What can the United States do to help them? These questions are crucial, both to the people in the less developed countries and to us.

What Is a "Less Developed Country"?

Economics abounds with clumsy terms. A profession responsible for "marginal rate of substitution" and "average propensity to consume" cannot claim a prize for elegant language. The term "less developed country" is not a model of clarity. For a country to be "less developed" it must be poor, but *how* poor? Any answer has to be arbitrary. Often countries with a per capita income of $500 or less are called "less developed." Although the $500 cutoff point is arbitrary, it certainly is low enough so that any country unfortunate enough to qualify is most certainly poor. Recall that per capita income in the United States is about $6,000.

Table 21.1 shows that many countries have a per capita income of $500 or less. Thus, much of the world is, by this definition, less developed. Indeed, *the staggering fact is that more people live in the less developed countries than in the developed countries (with per capita incomes of over $1,000) or the intermediate countries (with per capita incomes of $501 to $1,000).* Specifically, about 800 million people live in the developed countries, about 500 million people live in the intermediate countries, and over 2 billion people live in the less developed countries.

Imagine what life might be like if you grew up in a country with per capita income of $500 or less

---

Table 21.1

Countries Classified by Level of Per Capita Income

A. Countries with per capita income exceeding $1,000

United States	Netherlands	Finland	East Germany
Canada	Denmark	Austria	Hungary
Sweden	United Kingdom	Italy	Ireland
Switzerland	Norway	Australia	Venezuela
West Germany	USSR	New Zealand	Japan
France	Belgium	Czechoslovakia	

B. Countries with per capita income of $501 to $1,000

Poland	South Africa	Uruguay	Mexico
Greece	Spain	Chile	
Bulgaria	Portugal	Cuba	
Rumania	Argentina	Panama	

C. Areas with per capita income of $500 or less

Most of Middle East and Southeast Europe	All of Africa (except South Africa)	Most of Latin America All of Asia (other than countries listed above)

Source: United Nations and E. Hagen and O. Howrylyshyn, "World Income and Growth" *Economic Development and Cultural Change,* October 1969.

per year.[1] Chances are that you would be illiterate. You would probably work on a farm with little tools and technology. You would have few possessions (and sometimes only enough food to keep body and soul together) and be likely to die young. This is life in most of Asia, Africa, and Latin America.

The unpleasant fact is that this harsh existence —not the affluent way of life portrayed in *Better Homes and Gardens* or even the *Jersey City Journal*—is the lot of most earth dwellers. Of course this does not mean that the less developed countries do not have rich citizens: indeed they do. But the rich are a tiny minority surrounded by masses of poor people. Nor does it mean that many of these people do not live in cities. Bombay, for example, is the home of over 4 million, most of them poor.

It must also be recognized that many of the less developed countries have gained their political independence in recent years. Before World War II, the major European powers had substantial empires. For example, the British had colonies all over the globe. In the postwar period, many colonies have achieved independence. These new countries are often fiercely nationalistic. They resent what they regard as exploitation at the hands of the former European colonists and demand power and status. Although weak individually, together they represent a force that must be reckoned with.

Moreover, because of better communications and altered religious and cultural beliefs, the expectations and demands of people in less developed countries have changed enormously. Years ago, they were more likely to accept a life of privation and want, since their eye was on the next world. Now the emphasis has shifted to this world, and to material comforts—and getting them quickly. People in less developed countries have become aware of the high standards of living in the industrialized societies, and they want to catch up as fast as they can.

Although the available data on the less developed countries are not as accurate as one would like, these countries seem to have increased their per capita output in recent years. As Table 21.2 shows, the average rate of growth of per capita output in 15 major less developed countries was about 2.3 percent per year from 1950 to 1967. But since the average growth rate in the major developed countries was about 4 percent per year during the same period (see Table 17.1), *the gap between income per capita in the less developed countries and in the developed countries has been increasing.* This is a disturbing fact. Apparently, the gap between

---

[1] It must be noted that these income figures *overestimate* the gap between the rich and poor nations, since the procedure used to translate local currencies into dollars is to look at prices of internationally traded goods, which are generally more expensive than goods and services consumed locally. Thus a per capita income of $500 or less isn't as low as it seems, but is still very low.

Table 21.2

Annual Rate of Growth of Per Capita National Product, 1950–67

Less developed country	Average annual growth rate
Brazil	2.1
Ceylon	0.8
Colombia	1.3
Egypt	2.7
Ghana	1.3
India	1.6
Malaya	0.8
Mexico	2.8
Pakistan	1.5
Peru	2.9
Philippines	1.8
South Korea	3.8
Taiwan	5.3
Thailand	3.2
Turkey	2.8
Average	2.3

Source: A. Maddison, *Economic Progress and Policy in Developing Countries,* New York: Norton, 1970.

rich and poor will not decrease, unless recent trends are altered.

A Closer Look at the LDCs

Needless to say, the less developed countries vary enormously. Some, like China, are huge; others, like Paraguay, are small. Some, like Taiwan, have lots of people jammed into every square mile of land; others, like Brazil, have relatively few people spread over lots of land. Some, like India, have had great civilizations many, many centuries old; others have had ruder histories. Nonetheless, although it is not easy to generalize about the less developed countries, most of them, besides suffering from relatively low productivity, have the following characteristics.

First, the less developed countries generally devote most of their resources to food production. Agriculture is by far their largest industry. This contrasts markedly with industrialized countries like the United States, where only a small percentage of output is food. Moreover, food makes up most of the goods consumed in less developed countries. They are so poor that the typical family has very little besides food, a crude dwelling, some simple clothing, and other such necessities.

Second, many less developed countries have two economies, existing side by side. One of these is a *market-oriented* economy much like that in developed countries. This economy is generally found in the big cities, where there may be some modern manufacturing plants, as well as government agencies, wholesale and retail outlets, and services for the small number of rich people in the country. Coexisting with this relatively modern economy is a *subsistence* economy based largely on barter, innocent of all but the crudest technology and capable of producing little more—and sometimes less—than a subsistence wage for the inhabitants. This subsistence economy often includes most of the rural areas. It has little or no capital, few decent roads, only the most rudimentary communications. Unfortunately, this is the economy in which

the bulk of the population exists.

Third, some of the less developed countries have relatively weak, unstable governments. Thus, the climate for long-term investment and planning is relatively poor in such countries. Moreover, some governments are controlled by a small group of wealthy citizens or by other groups with a vested interest in resisting social change. Corruption among government officials is encountered too often, and honest officials are sometimes not very well trained or experienced in their duties. To some extent, these problems stem from the relative youth of many of these countries. But whatever the reasons, they hamper the effect of government on economic development.

Fourth, most of the less developed countries have a relatively high degree of income inequality. Indeed, there is much more income inequality than in the industrialized countries. Typically, a few landowners or industrialists in a less developed country are rich, sometimes enormously rich. But all outside this tiny group are likely to be very poor. The middle class, so important in the industrialized countries, is very small in most less developed countries.

Barriers to Development and the Need for Capital Formation

Why are the less developed economies so poor, and what can they do to raise their income levels? These are very difficult questions, both because the answers vary from country to country and because the answers for any single country are hard to determine. A variety of factors generally are responsible for a country's poverty, and these factors are so intermeshed that it is difficult to tell which is most important. Nonetheless, certain factors stand out; among these is the lack of capital in less developed countries.

Without exception, the people in the less developed countries have relatively little capital to work with. There are few factories, machine tools, roads, tractors, power plants, miles of railroad, and so on. If you visited one of these countries, you would be struck by the absence of mechanical aids to production. Workers use their hands, legs, and simple tools, often as their ancestors did long ago.

There are several reasons why the less developed countries have not accumulated much capital. First, a country must usually reduce consumption to accumulate capital, but for the less developed countries, with their very low income levels, a reduction in consumption can be painful. Equally important, much of the saving that does go on in less developed countries is not utilized very effectively. Second, there are important barriers to domestic investment, such as the smallness of local markets, the lack of skilled labor, and the lack of qualified entrepreneurs (faced with the right incentives) who are willing and able to take the risks involved in carrying out investment projects. Third, fear that property will be confiscated deters industrialized countries from investing in the less developed countries. As we pointed out above, many of the less developed countries are relatively young nations, filled with nationalistic fervor and fearful of becoming economically dependent. They are suspicious of foreign investment in their countries—and in some cases are quite capable of confiscating foreign-owned property. Needless to say, this does not make foreigners particularly anxious to invest in some of them.

Recognizing their need for additional capital, the less developed countries have used three principal methods to increase investment. First, they have taxed away part of the nation's resources and used them for investment purposes or made them available to private investors. Second, they have tried to mobilize "surplus labor" from agriculture to carry out investment projects. Third, they have increased government spending on investment projects without increasing taxes, thus producing inflation. All these methods are tried, but each has important limitations. Taxes may dull incentives and in any event are often evaded; "surplus labor" is difficult to transfer and utilize; and a little inflation may soon develop into a big inflation. As shown in Table

Table 21.3

Annual Rate of Increase of the Domestic Price Level, 1950–65

Country	Average annual rate of increase (percent)
Brazil	31.0
Ceylon	− 0.1
Colombia	9.3
Egypt	1.6
Ghana	5.7
India	2.3
Malaya	1.4
Mexico	6.2
Pakistan	2.3
Peru	8.2
Philippines	1.8
South Korea	19.8
Taiwan	6.6
Thailand	1.6
Turkey	8.2
Average	7.1

Source: See Table 21.2.

21.3, the rate of inflation in some less developed countries has been impressive indeed. Besides these three methods, a country can use foreign aid to increase investment. It too has its problems and limitations, but it is hard to see how many less developed countries can scrape up the capital they need without it.

Methods of this sort have enabled many less developed countries to increase the proportion of their national output devoted to capital formation. For example, Table 21.4 shows that in 15 major LDCs the average proportion of national output devoted to capital formation increased from about 8 percent in 1950 to about 14 percent in 1966. This proportion is still significantly less than in the developed countries, where it averaged about 17 percent in 1966, but it is increasing. Needless to say, these

Table 21.4

Nonresidential Gross Investment as a Percentage of National Product, 1950 and 1966

| ——— Less developed ——— | | | | ——— Developed ——— | | |
Country	1950	1966		Country	1950	1966
Brazil	11.3	10.9		France	13.6	15.5
Ceylon	7.1	11.0		Germany	14.3	19.9
Colombia	11.4	12.1		Italy	14.8	12.3
Egypt	10.2	16.3		Japan	15.7	25.2
Ghana	7.4	12.0		United Kingdom	10.3	14.3
India	7.4	13.8		United States	13.7	14.6
Malaya	5.0	15.1				
Mexico	10.8	14.8		Average	13.7	17.0
	4.8	12.9				
		13.9				
		16.5				
		18.1				
		16.7				
		19.3				
		10.4				
		14.3				

uch reliance
do indicate
rogressing in
capital forma-

... y per capita in-
... means all) less developed countries is that they suffer from overpopulation. Many less developed countries have sizably increased their total output. In Latin America, Africa, and Southeast Asia, it may have grown at about 5 percent per year in recent years. If population in these areas had remained approximately constant, output per capita would also have increased at about 5 percent per year. But population has not remained constant. It has grown at almost 3 percent per year, so that output per capita has increased at only about 2 percent per year.

Table 21.5 shows the rate of population growth in a variety of less developed countries, as well as some major developed countries. Clearly the rate has been higher, without exception, in the less developed countries than in the developed ones. The most important reason is that modern methods of preventing and curing diseases have been introduced into the LDCs, thus reducing the death rate, particularly among children. It used to be that al-

Table 21.5

Annual Rates of Growth of Population, Less Developed and Developed Countries, 1950–67

——— Less developed ———		——— Developed ———	
Country	Average annual growth rate	Country	Average annual growth rate
Brazil	3.1	France	1.1
Ceylon	2.5	Germany	1.2
Colombia	3.2	Italy	0.7
Egypt	2.5	Japan	1.1
Ghana	2.7	United Kingdom	0.5
India	2.2	United States	1.6
Malaya	3.0		
Mexico	3.3	Average	1.0
Pakistan	2.4		
Peru	2.6		
Philippines	3.2		
South Korea	2.8		
Taiwan	3.1		
Thailand	3.0		
Turkey	2.7		
Average	2.8		

Source: See Table 21.2

though the birth rate in the less developed countries was higher than in the developed countries, the death rate was also higher, so that the rate of population growth was about the same in the less developed countries as in the developed ones. But in recent years, the death rate in the LDCs has been reduced by better control of malaria and other diseases, whereas the birth rate has remained high. The result has been a population explosion. For example, in parts of Latin America the population is doubling every 20 years.

This growth of sheer numbers recalls the work of Thomas Malthus (Chapter 16); but numbers do not tell the whole story of the LDCs. Their populations are not only large and growing: they are also illiterate and ill-nourished. Thus, they do not

have the skills required to absorb much modern technology. In addition, many workers have little or nothing to do. They live with their relatives and occasionally hold a job. Although they may not be included in the official unemployment figures, they represent a case of *disguised unemployment*. In sum, the population of many less developed countries is large (relative to the available capital and natural resources), fast-growing, of relatively poor economic quality, and poorly utilized.

The less developed countries have responded to the population explosion in at least two ways. Where birth control is opposed on religious or cultural grounds, the LDCs often concentrate on the widespread unemployment that results from population increase. The rapidly expanding labor force cannot be employed productively in agriculture, since there is already a surplus of farm labor in many LDCs, and the capital stock is not increasing rapidly enough to employ the growing numbers in industry. Governments faced with serious unemployment of this sort often are induced to create public works programs and other projects to make jobs, even if these projects do not really promote economic growth.

The LDCs have also responded to the population explosion by attempting to lower the birth rate through the diffusion of contraceptive devices and other birth control techniques. In many of the less developed countries, there is no religious barrier to the adoption of such techniques. For example, Hinduism does not frown on birth control. However, their adoption has been slow. One reason is the medical drawbacks of existing contraceptive devices. Also, there are obvious problems in communicating the necessary information to huge numbers of illiterate and often superstitious people. India has made considerable efforts to disseminate birth control information, but the problems are enormous. In some of the smaller LDC's, such as Singapore, South Korea, and Taiwan, birth control programs seem to have had a more definite effect on the rate of population increase.

Besides trying to cope with or influence the growth rate of their population, the LDCs have also tried to increase the economic quality of their human resources. In other words, *they have been investing in human capital.* Such an investment seems warranted; educational and skill levels in many less developed countries have been quite low. Table 21.6 shows that in 15 major less developed countries, the proportion of the population aged 5 to 19 in primary or secondary school increased, on the average, from about 30 percent in 1950 to about 50 percent in 1964. This is certainly a step in the right direction, although enrollment in school is obviously only a crude measure of the quality of the labor force. In order to absorb and utilize, and eventually develop, modern technology, the LDCs must continue to invest in a more productive labor force.

Table 21.6

Percentage of Population Aged 5 to 19 Enrolled in Primary and Secondary Education, 1950 and 1964

Country	1950	1964
	(percentage)	
Brazil	22	46
Ceylon	54	65
Colombia	22	45
Egypt	20	41
Ghana	14	57
India	19	38
Malaya	35	50
Mexico	30	52
Pakistan	16	25
Peru	34	50
Philippines	59	57
South Korea	43	53
Taiwan	38	64
Thailand	38	48
Turkey	24	40
Average	31	52
United States	80	84

Source: Statistical Yearbook, UNESCO.

Technology: A Crucial Factor

Still another very important reason why per capita income is so low in the less developed countries is that these countries use rudimentary and often backward technology. In previous chapters, we have seen that to a considerable extent the increase in per capita income in the developed countries has resulted from the development and application of new technology. Too often, the less developed countries still use the technology of their forefathers—the agricultural and manufacturing methods of long, long ago. Why is this the case? Why don't the less developed countries copy the advanced technology of the industrialized countries, following the examples of the Japanese and Russians, among others, who promoted their economic development during the twentieth century by copying Western technology?

There are several reasons, one being that some types of modern technology require considerable capital. Modern petroleum refining technology, to choose one, cannot be used without lots of capital, which the less developed countries, with their low rates of investment, find difficult to scrape up. But many technological improvements do not require substantial capital. Indeed, some technological improvements are capital-saving. That is, they reduce the amount of capital needed to produce a given amount of output.

A second reason why the less developed countries find it difficult to copy and use modern technology is that they lack both a skilled labor force and entrepreneurs. Imagine the difficulties in transplanting a complicated technology—for example, that involved in steel production—from the United States to a less developed country where there are few competent engineers, fewer experienced and resourceful managers, and practically no laborers with experience in the demanding work required to operate a modern steel plant.

Even more fundamental is the fact that much of our advanced Western technology is really not very well suited to circumstances in the less developed countries. Because the industrialized countries have relatively great amounts of capital and relatively little labor, they tend to develop and adopt technology that substitutes capital for labor. But this technology may not be appropriate for less developed countries where there is little capital and lots of labor. Thus, it is very important that the less developed countries pick and choose among the technologies available in the industrialized countries, and that they adapt these technologies to their own conditions. Mindless attempts to ape the technologies used in the industrialized countries can result in waste and failure.

In agriculture, important technological advances have taken place in the less developed countries in recent years. In particular, new types of seeds have been developed, increasing the yields of wheat, rice, and other crops. Some of this research was supported by the Rockefeller and Ford Foundations. The resulting increase in agricultural productivity has been so impressive that many observers call it a "green revolution." There is no question that wheat and rice production has increased greatly in countries like Mexico, the Philippines, Iran, Ceylon, India, and Pakistan. Plenty of opportunity remains for improvements in livestock yields as well, but religious beliefs and traditional prejudices are sometimes an important barrier to change.

In industry, most of the new technology adopted by the less developed countries is taken from the developed countries. Very little attempt is being made to devise new technologies more appropriate to conditions in the less developed countries, both because the less developed countries do not have the engineering and scientific resources to develop them, and because such attempts have not been very successful in the past. In countries where the private sector finds it unprofitable to carry out research and development, government research institutes sometimes try to fill the void, but these institutes frequently devote too much of their limited resources to projects not closely related to economic development. In addition, Productivity Centers have been created in some countries to teach managers and supervisory personnel how to make better use of new technology. Such Centers have helped promote the diffusion of new technology in Mexico and Taiwan, among other countries.

Entrepreneurship, Social Institutions, and Natural Resources

Yet another important reason why per capita income is so low in the less developed countries is that they lack entrepreneurs and favorable social institutions. This point was noted in the previous section but needs more discussion. In some LDCs there is a rigid social structure. One "knows one's place" and stays in it, people distrust and resist change, and things are done in the time-honored way they have always been done (as far as anyone can remember). No wonder these countries lack entrepreneurs. The basic social and political institutions discourage entrepreneurship. Moreover, these institutions also are at least partially responsible for the ineffective utilization of savings, relatively high birth rates, and difficulties in transferring technology noted above. As Richard Gill of Harvard University has put it, "In many underdeveloped countries, a complete social and political revolution is required while the industrial revolution is getting underway."

The governments of many less developed countries are relatively weak and unstable. It is difficult enough for any government to give these countries an effective tax system and a rational program of public expenditures, including proper provision for the highways, public utilities, communications, and other "social overhead capital" they need. But the problems are made even more difficult when the government is weak, unstable, and perhaps somewhat corrupt. Even more fundamental, the population's value systems and attitudes sometimes do little to promote economic development. Again quoting Gill, "A sharp desire for material betterment, a willingness to work hard and in a regular, punctual manner, an awareness of the future benefits of present sacrifices—these attitudes may be the prerequisites of economic growth; yet they may be largely absent in many underdeveloped countries."[2]

Finally, it should also be pointed out that some of the LDCs have little in the way of natural resources. Moreover, technological change has made some of their resources less valuable, as in the case of synthetic rubber, which affected the market for

[2] Richard Gill, *Economic Development: Past and Present*, Englewood Cliffs, N.J.: Prentice-Hall, 1967, p. 87.

natural rubber, an important natural resource of Malaya. But this is not true of all the less developed countries: Iraq and Libya, among others, are well endowed with oil. And in any event, the skimpiness of natural resources in some less developed countries does not mean that they are condemned to poverty. Neither Denmark nor Switzerland is endowed with great natural resources, but both are prosperous.

The important thing is how a country uses what it has. International trade allows a country to compensate, at least in part, for its deficiencies in natural resources. Thus, although some of the less developed countries have been dealt a poor hand by Mother Nature, this lack alone does not explain their poverty. Of course, they might have been more prosperous with more natural resources; but even with what they have, they might have done much better.

There are several ways for them to use their resources more effectively. In many of the less developed countries, a peasant may farm several strips of land that are very small and distant from one another, working a small patch here and a small patch there. Obviously, this procedure is very inefficient. If these small plots could be put together into larger farms, output and productivity could be increased. In other LDCs, huge farms are owned by landlords and worked by tenant farmers. This system too tends to be inefficient, because the tenant farmers have little incentive to increase productivity (since the extra output will accrue to the landlord) and the landlords have little incentive to invest in new technology (since they often fear that the tenant farmers will not know how to use the new equipment).

Land reform is a very lively—indeed an explosive—issue in many less developed countries, and one of the issues the Communists try to exploit. Recall that agriculture is a very important part of the economy of most of the less developed countries. Thus the land is the major form of productive wealth. No wonder there is a bitter struggle in some countries over who is to own and work it.

The Role of Government

There are several opinions on the role the governments of the less developed countries should play in promoting economic growth. Some people go so far as to say that these countries would fare best if they allowed market forces to work with a minimum of government interference. But the less developed countries themselves believe a free enterprise system would produce results too slowly, if at all. Thus, the prevailing view in the less developed countries is that the government must intervene— and on a large scale.

In some less developed countries—China, for example—the government exercises almost complete control over the economy. China's economy is planned: the government makes the basic decisions on what is produced, how it is produced, and who gets it. But even in the non-Communist LDCs, such as India, the government makes many decisions on what sorts of investment projects will be undertaken, and it controls foreign exchange. Needless to say, the government also has the responsibility for providing the important social overhead capital—roads, public utilities, schools, and so on—that is so badly needed.[3]

Most economists would agree that the government has a very important role to play in promoting economic development. But there is a tendency to put less weight on the government's role than in the past. Experience has made it clear that some of the less developed countries are plagued by incompetent and corrupt government officials and by a plethora of bureaucratic red tape. Moreover, many governments have gone on spending sprees that have resulted in serious inflation. Even those who are very mistrustful of free markets find it difficult to put

their faith in such governments, well-intentioned though they may be. Recent years have seen more and more emphasis on self-interest and individual action as the mainsprings of growth. Recalling the discussion in Chapter 2, we can be reasonably sure that, if Adam Smith is peering down from the Great Beyond, he is smiling with agreement at this change in attitude.

Balanced Growth

An important issue facing the governments of most less developed countries is the extent to which they want to maintain a balance between the agricultural and industrial sectors of the economy. That is, how much more rapidly should they expand industry than agriculture? According to some economists, less developed countries should invest heavily in industry, since the long-term trend of industrial prices is upward, relative to agricultural prices. In addition, advocates of unbalanced growth argue that the development of certain sectors of the economy will result in pressures for development elsewhere in the economy. Advocates of this approach point to the Soviet Union, which stressed industrialization in its growth strategy.

Other economists argue that industry and agriculture should be expanded at a more nearly equal rate. Successful industrial expansion requires agricultural expansion as well, because industry uses raw materials as inputs and because, as economic growth takes place, the people will demand more food. Balanced growth has other advantages. Various sectors of the economy are closely linked and an attempt to expand one sector in isolation is unlikely to succeed. Proponents of balanced growth deny that the long-term trend of industrial prices is upward, relative to agricultural prices. And to illustrate the wisdom of their approach, they cite as examples the United States and Britain, where industry and agriculture both expanded in the course of the development process.

In all 15 LDCs included in Table 21.7, indus-

---

[3] Of course, the government may also foster social and political change. The distinguished economist, Simon Kuznets, commented: "The problem of strategy is essentially the problem of how fast you can change an inadequate set of social and political institutions, without provoking a revolution internally, or losing allies and partners externally. The question is to know what institutions you want to change, and how." (Communication to the author.)

Table 21.7

Annual Rate of Growth of Employment, by Sector, 1950–65

Country	Industry	Agriculture	Services
	— Percentage —		
Brazil	4.5	1.6	4.2
Ceylon	3.0	0.7	3.0
Colombia	2.6	1.2	3.6
Egypt	1.5	0.7	3.2
Ghana	n.a.	n.a.	n.a.
India	5.2	1.3	4.0
Malaya	2.2	0.0	4.7
Mexico	4.9	2.2	4.0
Pakistan	4.5	2.2	2.3
Peru	1.2	0.1	3.2
Philippines	6.0	0.7	4.5
South Korea	12.1	−0.1	4.2
Taiwan	7.3	0.2	1.8
Thailand	8.2	2.3	5.1
Turkey	2.9	1.3	3.5
Average	4.7	1.0	3.7

n.a. = not available

Source: See Table 21.2.

trial employment has increased more rapidly than agricultural employment in recent years. Without question, the less developed countries are expanding industry relative to agriculture. In some cases, such as Argentina, India, and Pakistan, it is generally agreed that more balance—less emphasis on agriculture—would have been preferable. Moreover, in many cases, the allocation of resources within industry could certainly have been improved. Countries have sometimes put too much emphasis on substituting their own production—even when it is not efficient—for imports. For example, Chile has prohibited the import of fully assembled cars to promote domestic production, but Chile's automobile plants have been uneconomic.

One reason why the less developed countries tend to push industrialization is that they see heavy industrialization in the wealthier countries. The United States, Western Europe, Japan, the USSR, all have lots of steel plants, oil refineries, chemical plants, and other kinds of heavy industry. It is easy for the less developed countries to jump to the conclusion that, if they want to become richer, they must become heavily industrialized too. It certainly seems sensible enough—until you think about the theory of comparative advantage.

Another reason why the leaders of some less developed countries are fascinated by steel plants, airlines, and other modern industries is that they think such industries confer prestige on their countries and themselves. Such prestige may be costly. Given their current situation, many of these countries might be well advised to invest much of their scarce resources in promoting higher productivity in agriculture, where they have a comparative advantage. Of course, we are not saying that many of these countries should not attempt to industrialize. We *are* saying that some of them have pushed industrialization too far—and that many have pushed it in uneconomic directions.

Development Planning in Less Developed Countries

The governments of many LDCs have established development plans to specify targets or goals for the economy. In some countries, these goals are set forth in very specific, detailed form; in others, they are more generally formulated. An important purpose of these plans is to allocate scarce resources, such as capital, in order to achieve rapid economic growth or whatever the country's social objectives may be. For example, in India, estimates are made of the amount of capital that will be generated internally, as well as the capital that can be imported from abroad. Then the plan attempts to set a system of priorities for the use of this capital.

Some plans are merely window dressing, full of bold words and little else. But others are the result of careful investigation and hard work. Clearly, to be useful, a plan must set realistic goals, ones that take proper account of the country's resources, available capital, and institutions. An unrealistically ambitious plan, if actually put in effect, is likely to lead to inflation, while a plan that is too easily satisfied is likely to mean a less than optimal rate of economic growth. A useful plan should specify the policies to be used to reach the plan's goals, as well as the goals themselves. It should also forecast carefully how the various components of gross national product will change over time, the extent to which inflationary pressures will develop, the adequacy of the supply of foreign exchange, and the

effects of the development program on various regions and parts of the population.

Planning techniques have benefited from the application of many tools of modern economic analysis, among them linear programming and input-output analysis. Linear programming can be used to determine how resources should be allocated to maximize output, and input-output analysis can determine how much capacity there must be in various industries to produce a desired bill of goods. These modern tools have undoubtedly helped in formulating development plans, but their importance should not be exaggerated. It would be a great mistake to think that making a good plan is merely a job for an electronic computer.

If the plan is realistic, it can be a useful tool, but unless it is implemented properly, it will achieve very little for the economy. How well it is implemented will depend on the government's ability to marshal resources through taxation and foreign aid, to work effectively with the private sector, and to pick productive public investment projects. In some countries, like India, "the plan" has sometimes become a political symbol, but in many others, like Mexico, planning has been politically less visible. Countries where economic growth has been most rapid seem to have viewed "the plan" less as holy writ, and planning has tended to be more modest and low-key.

Planning in Action: The Case of India

Perhaps the best way to understand the operation of development plans is to look at the nature of a particular country's plans and how they have been fulfilled. For example, consider the very interesting case of India, which has had four five-year plans.[4] The First Five-Year Plan was for 1951–

[4] It is worthwhile emphasizing that the development strategies of *small* LDCs, because of their necessarily greater reliance on foreign trade, must be quite different from that of *large* LDCs, like India.

56. Its targets were to increase net investment in India from 5 to 6.75 percent of national income, to reduce income inequality, to cut the rate of population increase to 1 percent per year, and to lay the groundwork for a doubling of per capita output in a generation. To achieve these targets, the government relied heavily on capital formation. In particular, it sought to carry out many of the investment projects that had been discussed and planned under the British for as much as 50 years. The First Five-Year Plan was accompanied by moderate growth. Per capita output grew by about 1.7 percent per year, and net investment rose from 5 to 8 percent of national income.

At the beginning of 1956, the Indian Planning Commission published its Second Five-Year Plan, which called for much heavier investments—and more emphasis on investment in industry and mining, rather than agriculture and power—than the First Plan. Moreover, the Second Plan relied more heavily on deficit financing than did the First Plan, and devoted much more attention to the expansion of employment opportunities, since unemployment was a considerable problem. Unfortunately, the Second Plan ran into severe difficulties. One big problem was the loss of foreign exchange, as imports grew much more rapidly—and exports less rapidly—than expected. But perhaps more important was the fact that output did not grow as rapidly as the plan called for. By the end of the Second Five-Year Plan, all sectors of the economy, other than the service sector, were producing less than the planned targets. Nonetheless, per capita output grew by about 1.8 percent per year.

India's Third Five-Year Plan—for 1961–66—involved bigger investments and somewhat more emphasis on agriculture than the Second Plan. Responding to the fact that agricultural imports had been much higher than expected under the Second Plan, the Third Plan called for more investment in agriculture. Unfortunately, however, agricultural production during the Third Plan did not come up to expectations. Indeed, India might have experienced a serious famine in 1966 if it had not received substantial food imports from the United States. During the course of the Third Plan, India did increase the percentage of national income devoted to investment from 11 to 14 percent, but a substantial proportion of her investment was financed by foreign aid. Unfortunately, India's output grew by ⅙, instead of the planned ⅓, during the Third Plan, and there was little or no increase in per capita output.

Although the failure of the Third Plan was due in considerable measure to India's involvement in two wars and to two bad harvests, it nonetheless shook many Indians' confidence in the planning process. There was a three-year delay before the Fourth Five-Year Plan was unveiled, and its political significance was played down. The Fourth Plan shifted the emphasis to agricultural development, including irrigation and fertilizers; it stressed a large birth control program; and it called for a 5½ percent increase per year in national output, as well as further increases in investment. The Fourth Plan put somewhat more emphasis on the price system and somewhat less on detailed planning. In practice, however, according to some experts, the latter changes seemed to have been slow to occur.[5]

Choosing Investment Projects in Less Developed Countries

Clearly, one of the crucial problems any less developed country must face is how the available capital should be invested. Countless investment projects could be undertaken—roads, irrigation projects, power plants, improvements in agricultural equipment, and so on. Faced with this menu of alternatives, how should a country choose? One procedure often used is to accept projects resulting in high output per unit of capital invested.

[5] Much of the material in the section comes from Benjamin Higgins, *Economic Development,* New York: Norton, 1968, J. Bhagwati and P. Desai, *India: Planning for Industrialization,* Oxford: Oxford University Press, 1970, R. Gill, *op. cit.,* A. Maddison, *op. cit.,* and W. Malenbaum, *Modern India's Economy,* Columbus: Charles Merrill, 1971.

That is, projects are ranked by the ratio of the value of the output they produce to the capital they require. For example, if a project yields $2 million worth of output per year and requires $1 million of capital, its ratio would be 2. Projects with high values of this ratio are accepted. This procedure, which is crude but sensible, is based on the correct idea that capital is the really scarce resource in many of the less developed countries. It is aimed at maximizing the output to be derived from a certain amount of capital.

However, a better technique for choosing projects is the concept of rate of return, which is used by profit-maximizing firms to choose among alternative investment opportunities. A less developed country, like a firm, can compute the rate of return from each investment opportunity. That is, it can estimate the rate of interest that will be obtained from each investment. Then it, like a firm, should choose the *projects with the highest rates of return*.

In computing the rate of return from each investment project, it is necessary to attach values to the resources it uses and to the returns it produces. At first glance, it may seem adequate to use market prices of inputs and outputs as these values. For example, if unskilled labor's market price is $.10 an hour, this would be the value attached to unskilled labor. Unfortunately, there are some important pitfalls in using market prices in this way. In particular, market prices of inputs in the less developed countries often do not indicate social costs properly. For example, although the market price of unskilled labor may be $.10 an hour, there may be lots of unskilled labor doing essentially nothing in the countryside, with the result that the social cost—the true alternative cost—of using such labor is zero, not $.10 an hour. Moreover, the market prices of some outputs may not indicate their social worth.

Thus, when computing each project's rate of return, it is important to make proper adjustments so that inputs are valued at their social cost and outputs are valued at their social worth. This is easier said than done, but even crude adjustments in the right direction can be worthwhile.

American Foreign Aid

The plight of the less developed countries is of concern to Americans, both because it is good morality and good policy to help them. From the point of view of humanitarianism, the United States and the other rich nations have a moral responsibility to help the poor nations. From the point of view of our self-interest, the promotion of growth in the less developed countries should help to preserve and encourage political and international stability and to make them more effective trading partners.

How can the United States be of help? With regard to many of their problems, we can do relatively little. But one thing that we can do is to provide badly needed capital. Responding to that need, we have given and lent a substantial amount of capital to the less developed countries in the past 20 years.

One important type of foreign aid consists of loans and gifts made by the United States government. It has amounted to over $100 billion since World War II. At first, the emphasis was on aid to Europe (for reconstruction of war-devastated areas, under the so-called Marshall Plan), but since the late 1950s, the emphasis has been on the less developed countries. About ⅓ has been for military aid; about ⅔ for nonmilitary aid. As noted in Chapter 20, much of this aid is in the form of loans or grants of money that must be spent on American goods and services. Also, much of it consisted of our giving away part of what were then surplus stocks of food. (Recall the agricultural programs discussed in Chapter 5.) India has been the leading recipient of U.S. agricultural surpluses, as shown in Table 21.8.

Table 21.9 shows the amount of economic aid received by selected LDCs from the United States and other countries between 1960 and 1965. Clearly, the aid provided by the United States was concentrated in a relatively few countries, with India, Pakistan, South Korea, Brazil, and Turkey accounting for about ⅔ of the total. Looking at the total amount of aid received from all countries on a per capita basis, Table 21.10 shows that by this measurement Israel, Chile, and Egypt received the

Table 21.8

Shipments of U.S. Agricultural Surpluses to Selected Countries, 1953–66

Country	Shipments ($ millions)	Country	Shipments ($ millions)
Argentina	18	Mexico	71
Brazil	706	Pakistan	1,112
Ceylon	190	Peru	88
Chile	72	Philippines	112
Colombia	145	South Korea	753
Egypt	902	Spain	470
Ghana	14	Taiwan	341
Greece	259	Thailand	5
India	3,327	Turkey	441
Israel	346	Venezuela	20
Malaya	10	Yugoslavia	1,153

Source: Agency for International Development.
Note: Not all of these shipments were gifts.

most economic aid.

In addition, the United States has established various kinds of technical assistance programs designed to help the less developed countries borrow some of our technology, administrative techniques, medical knowledge, educational methods, and so on. The emphasis frequently is on training people from the less developed countries to the point where they can teach their fellow countrymen. Often, the costs of these programs are shared by the United States and by the recipient of the aid. Most observers seem to believe that these technical assistance programs have been worthwhile and successful.

Some other aspects of American policy are also important, although they are not aid programs. For one thing, the United States and other developed countries can help the LDCs by reducing trade barriers, thus allowing them to increase their national incomes through trade. However, it seems unlikely that trade alone can substitute for aid, and the situation is clouded by the trade barriers the LDCs themselves have been erecting to protect

their own industry. Another way that the United States can help is through private investment. American corporations have invested an enormous amount in the less developed countries—about $2 billion a year during the 1960s, most of it in Latin America. To the less developed countries, this is a significant source of capital.

Besides providing capital, the multinational corporations have also been a source of needed technology. However, these firms have faced much more difficult problems in transmitting technology to less developed countries than to industrialized countries. Many of the techniques of the multinational firms are not very well suited to the less developed countries, with their plentiful unskilled labor, few skills, and little capital. Moreover, there is sometimes little incentive for multinational firms to adapt their products, production techniques, and marketing methods to the conditions present in developing countries. And when they do manage to make a technological transplant, its effects are often restricted to narrow segments of the economy. Still further, it should be noted that the multina-

Table 21.9

Economic Aid to Selected Countries, 1960–65

Country	American economic aid	Economic aid from other Western governments and international agencies	Communist economic aid	Total
Argentina	168	34	10	212
Brazil	951	201	5	1,157
Ceylon	37	52	25	114
Chile	519	160	—	679
Colombia	226	177	—	403
Egypt	851	241	450	1,542
Ghana	60	73	65	198
Greece	178	104	—	282
India	3,904	1,642	450	5,996
Israel	251	460	—	711
Malaya	26	74	—	100
Mexico	74	252	—	326
Pakistan	1,882	585	35	2,502
Peru	36	89	—	125
Philippines	157	173	—	330
South Korea	1,273	98	—	1,371
Spain	245	2	—	247
Taiwan	488	1	—	489
Thailand	177	88	—	265
Turkey	910	198	5	1,113
Venezuela	122	6	—	128
Yugoslavia	592	236	—	828
Total	13,127	4,946	1,045	19,118

Source: See Table 21.2.

tional firms are often viewed with some suspicion and fear by the host governments.

In recent years, American foreign aid has been reduced because of considerable feeling in Congress and elsewhere that our aid programs were not working very well. During the early 1960s an average of about $4 billion per year was spent on such aid programs, but by the early 1970s this figure had been cut to about $3 billion. Foreign aid has been a controversial subject in the United States for some time. Many critics argue that the money could better be spent at home to alleviate domestic poverty. They claim that other industrialized countries—like Germany and Japan—should contribute a bigger share of the aid to the less developed countries. And they assert that our aid programs have not had much impact on the less developed countries so far.

Table 21.10

Net Receipts of Economic Aid, Per Capita, 1960–65

Country	Amount of aid per person (dollars per year)	Country	Amount of aid per person (dollars per year)
Argentina	1.6	Mexico	1.3
Brazil	2.4	Pakistan	3.6
Ceylon	1.6	Peru	1.8
Chile	13.2	Philippines	1.7
Colombia	3.7	South Korea	7.7
Egypt	8.7	Spain	1.3
Ghana	4.3	Taiwan	6.3
Greece	5.5	Thailand	1.4
India	2.0	Turkey	5.9
Israel	46.2	Venezuela	2.5
Malaya	2.1	Yugoslavia	6.1

Source: OECD.

Many suggestions have been made for ways to improve the effectiveness of our foreign aid. One prominent suggestion is that we go further in concentrating the bulk of our aid on a relatively few countries—those that really want to do what is necessary to develop, that can use the money well, and that are important from the point of view of size and international politics. Obviously adopting this suggestion means reducing aid to some other countries. Another suggestion is that, rather than impose political conditions on aid, we should give money with no strings attached. This suggestion entails a great deal more than economics. To evaluate it, one must decide what the goals of foreign aid should be. To what extent should it be aimed at raising the standard of living of the world's population, whatever the effect on the United States? To what extent should it be aimed at furthering American goals and American foreign policies? In practice, foreign aid has been bound up closely with our foreign policy. Given the political facts of life, it is difficult to see how it could be otherwise.

The World Bank and Other Aid Programs

The United States has provided a large percentage of the aid that has flowed from the industrialized countries to the less developed countries, but, as shown in Table 21.9, it has by no means been the sole contributor. Other industrialized nations also have aid programs. For example, France contributed almost $1 billion a year in the late 1960s, and West Germany and the United Kingdom contributed about $500 million a year. Moreover, the Soviet Union has formulated a significant aid program. Aid from the Soviet bloc now totals about $1 billion a year. Indeed, it is often claimed that the Russian programs have had more political effect than our own because they allow the recipient countries more freedom to build "prestige" projects like steel mills and because they make their aid look somewhat less like charity.

In addition, the International Bank for Reconstruction and Development (the World Bank) has channeled large amounts of capital into the less developed countries. A number of developed nations pooled funds in the World Bank in order to lend money to finance development projects and to insure private loans made for this purpose. In the late 1950s and early 1960s, the World Bank set up the International Finance Corporation and the International Development Association, affiliated agencies to finance investment projects that were riskier than those handled by the Bank. Since its inception, the World Bank has lent over $10 billion to the less developed countries, as well as providing significant technical assistance. Nonetheless, despite its achievements, many economists believe that in the past the World Bank has sometimes been too conservative and that it should have been willing to take bigger risks. Since the late 1960s, the Bank has become less conservative in this respect.

To illustrate the size and nature of foreign aid, consider the case of India. In 1951, foreign aid equaled about 1 percent of India's national product; by 1958, it had risen to about 2.7 percent; and by 1965, it had increased to about 3.8 percent. Clearly, India receives vast amounts of foreign aid, most of it as loans, but some as grants and assistance under Public Law 480, which involves the transfer of commodities like wheat and is close to being a grant. An interesting feature of the foreign aid India receives is that it comes from so many sources. Non-Communist aid to India has been channeled in through the Aid-India Consortium, composed of Canada, Japan, the United Kingdom, the United States, West Germany, Belgium, France, Italy, Holland, the World Bank, and others. The United States has put up the bulk of the consortium's aid funds—over 70 percent in the First Plan, over 55 percent in the Second Plan, and over 58 percent in the Third Plan. India has also received some aid from the Soviet bloc countries. During the Second Plan, about 6 percent of India's aid came from the Soviet bloc, and during the Third Plan, about 12 percent came from this source. Soviet bloc aid generally has been used for heavy industrial projects.

What are the maturity of the loans and the interest rate for the loan segment of India's aid? The average maturity for loans authorized during the Third Five-Year Plan was 36 years for American loans, 25 years for British loans, 17 years for German loans, 15 years for Japanese loans, and 12 years for Russian loans. The average interest rate was 1.9 percent for American loans, 4.4 percent for British loans, 4.8 percent for German loans, 5.8 percent for Japanese loans, and 2.5 percent for Russian loans. Thus American lenders set the easiest terms. Aside from commodity assistance, the bulk of the aid received by India has been used for power projects, harbor development, railroads, and industrial projects such as iron and steel plants. This reflects India's emphasis on industrialization. This emphasis also has meant that India has had to rely on substantial technical assistance programs to provide the necessary skills and training. The United States has provided much of this assistance, and the United Nations has sponsored trips to India by foreign experts, as well as fellowships enabling Indians to study and gain experience abroad.[6]

Summary

A country is defined as a "less developed country" if its per capita income is $500 or less. Over 2 billion people live in the less developed countries, which include most of the countries in Asia, Africa, and Latin America. In recent years, there has been a great increase in the expectations and material demands of the people in these countries. The less developed countries vary greatly, but they generally devote most of their resources to the production of food, are composed of two economies (one market-oriented, the other subsistence), often have relatively weak, unstable governments and a relatively high degree of income inequality.

One obvious reason why income per capita is so low is that the people in the less developed coun-

[6] For further discussion, see Bhagwati and Desai, *op. cit.*

tries have so little capital to work with. The less developed countries, with their low incomes, do not save much, they lack entrepreneurs, and the climate for investment (domestic or foreign) often is not good. Also, some less developed countries suffer from overpopulation; and as total output has increased, these gains have been offset by population increases. Modern medical techniques have reduced the death rate, while the birth rate has remained high. The result is a "population explosion." Another very important reason why per capita income is so low in these countries is that they often use backward technology. The transfer of technology from one country to another is not as easy as it sounds, particularly when the recipient country has an uneducated population and little capital. Also, these countries lack favorable social institutions and sometimes have few natural resources.

To promote development, most of the less developed countries seem to believe that the government must intervene on a large scale. An important issue facing the governments of most less developed countries is the extent to which they want to maintain a "balance" between the agricultural and industrial sectors of the economy. Without question, the LDCs are expanding industry relative to agriculture. In some cases, such as Argentina, India, and Pakistan, more balance—less emphasis on industry, more on agriculture—would have been preferable. Moreover, some countries have put too much emphasis on substituting their own production for imports, even when their own production is uneconomic.

Many of the less developed countries have established development plans that specify targets or goals for the economy and policies designed to attain them. One criterion often used to determine whether a given investment project should be accepted or rejected is the ratio of the value of the output produced to the capital used. Only projects with high values of this ratio are accepted. A more sophisticated criterion is the rate of return from the project, the method used by firms in capital budgeting. However, when computing each project's rate of return, it is important that inputs be valued at their social cost and that outputs be valued at their social worth. Modern tools of economic analysis—like linear programming and input-output analysis—are used in formulating some plans.

The United States has been involved in a number of major aid programs to help the less developed countries. During the early 1960s, our government gave or lent about $4 billion per year to the LDCs and carried out a variety of technical assistance programs. In recent years, these aid programs have come under increasing attack, and expenditures have been reduced. One suggestion frequently made is that we go further in concentrating our aid on a relatively few countries that really want to do what is necessary to develop, can use the money well, and are important in terms of size and politics. Besides the United States, other countries—including the Soviet Union—have carried out significant aid programs. Moreover, the World Bank has channeled large amounts of capital into the less developed countries.

CONCEPTS FOR REVIEW

Less developed country	Birth control	Population explosion
Balanced growth	Development plan	International Finance
Green revolution	Foreign aid	Corporation
Comparative advantage	World Bank	International Development Association
Multinational corporation		

QUESTIONS FOR DISCUSSION AND REVIEW

1. According to Simon Kuznets, "A substantial economic advance in the less developed countries may require modification in the available stock of material technology, and probably even greater innovations in political and social structure." What does he mean? If he is correct, what are the implications for the less developed countries? For the developed countries?

2. According to Hans Morgenthau, "Foreign aid for economic development has a chance to be successful only within relatively narrow limits which are raised by cultural and political conditions impervious to direct outside influence." Do you agree? If he is correct, what are the implications for the less developed countries? For the developed countries?

3. In recent years, industrialized countries have grown more rapidly than less developed countries. True or False?

4. The increase in agricultural productivity in the LDCs due to technological advances in seeds is known as
a. balanced growth. b. green revolution. c. Seward's Folly. d. Philippine ecstasy.

INDEX

457

CERAMICS
FROM CLAY TO KILN

by Harvey Weiss

YOUNG SCOTT BOOKS • NEW YORK

Table of Contents

OTHER TITLES BY THE SAME AUTHOR IN THE

Beginning Artist's Library

1. SCULPTURE: *Clay, Wood & Wire*   3. DRAWING: *Pencil, Pen & Brush*

2. PRINTMAKING: *Paper, Ink & Roller*   4. CRAFTS: *Sticks, Spools & Feathers*

© MCMLXIV BY HARVEY WEISS, MANUFACTURED IN THE U.S.A.   *Library of Congress Catalog Card No. 64-13583*

SONG OF THE VOWELS,
by Jacques Lipchitz

*Museum of Modern Art
New York*

Introduction

If you take a lump of clay, shape it, and put it into a hot fire, it will become a hard, permanent object. This process is called ceramics.

It is an exciting process, because you start with a raw and formless and common material and make it into something graceful and useful—a bowl, an ashtray, a birdhouse, a statue. This making of something elegant and useful from a lump of humble clay—making something out of nothing—is a challenging and satisfying experience.

There are a few basic things you *must* learn before you start to work with clay. Read the following four pages carefully. They contain the ABC's of ceramics.

3

Materials, Methods and Tools

Where To Get Clay

The simplest way to get clay is to buy it from an art or ceramics supply store. But it is possible that you live in a section of the country where there are some good natural clay formations. Then you can dig into the side of a cliff, or bed of a stream, or a few feet into the ground, and—if you're lucky—you'll find all the clay you could ever use. Ask some people who know the neighboring countryside. They may know if there is clay anywhere around, and where to find it.

If you buy your clay—and you probably will—try to get terra cotta clay with "grog." Grog is burnt clay that has been ground up and mixed with the natural clay. Its purpose is to minimize the danger of splitting and cracking of the finished piece during the firing. You can, of course, use clay without grog. Terra cotta clay has a handsome reddish color when wet. It is a rich pink after firing.

There are many kinds of clays, varying in color and feel. The one kind to avoid is plasticene, which is not really clay, but an oil-base material not intended for firing.

Clay is sometimes sold in powder form. If this is the only kind you can get, you'll have to mix it with water. Powder clay is usually sold packed in a plastic bag. In this case you simply pour a little water into the bag and mix by kneading the bag.

The Firing Of Clay

If clay is left to stand for two or three days the water in it will evaporate. The clay will dry out and become rather brittle and fragile. If handled or moved about it will eventually fall apart. But it will return to its original plastic state if you add water to it. In order for clay to become a strong and permanent material it must be baked in a very hot furnace—to approximately 2,000 degrees Fahrenheit. This process is called firing, and the furnace is called a kiln. Once clay has been fired, it will not be softened by water.

The cheapest kiln you can buy costs about forty dollars. The chances are you won't acquire one of your own until you've had a good deal of experience with ceramics. But there is usually some place where you can take your clay pieces to be fired. Most schools have a kiln. Many ceramic supply stores have firing facilities, or will be able to tell you of someone who has a kiln and will fire your work for a small charge. Perhaps you know somebody who has a small kiln and will let you use it. More details on firing, glazes, and such technical matters can be found at the end of this book.

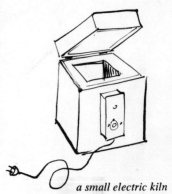

a small electric kiln

How To Prepare Clay For Use

If a piece of clay has air bubbles or air pockets inside it and is put into a kiln, the trapped air will expand in the enormous heat and cause the clay to shatter. The clay will actually explode! Therefore it is important that all air be eliminated from the clay before you use it. The process of removing the air from clay and getting it into a workable condition is called "wedging."

You wedge clay by taking a lump about as big as your two fists and cutting it in half with a thin wire. Then the two halves are either slammed vigorously together, or slammed down hard on a table top. Do this twenty or thirty times until the clay is an even consistency and free from lumps and air bubbles. You can tell when the clay is properly wedged by cutting a piece in half and looking to see if any air bubbles show on the cut surface. If there are still bubbles, wedge some more. Never use clay that hasn't been wedged.

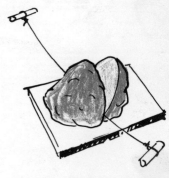

cutting with wire

Clay is a responsive material, but it won't handle well unless it is the right consistency. If it is too soft and mushy, it will feel like mud, and you won't be able to control it. If, on the other hand, it is stiff and hard, it will be difficult to manipulate. Clay that is too wet should be spread out flat on a rag and allowed to dry out for an hour or two. If the clay is too dry, pour some water over it and knead it until you are satisfied with its feel and can shape it easily.

How To Care For Clay

Unless clay is kept damp it will dry out. Store it in a plastic bucket with a lid, or any waterproof container that can be tightly closed. Keep a wet rag on top of the clay, and take a look at it every so often to make sure it is not drying out. If it seems to be getting stiff and hard, pour a little water on the rag.

When a piece you are working on is left for any length of time, such as overnight, you must see that it doesn't dry out. Wrap it with thin plastic sheeting. This will keep all the moisture in, and keep the clay in a workable state for a long time.

The Drying Of Clay

Clay must be completely dry before it can be fired. And when it dries, it shrinks in size. The shrinkage amounts to 10 or 15 per cent depending on the kind of clay. This is a great deal. If one part of a clay piece shrinks faster than an adjoining part it will pull apart. You will get splits and cracks, and the entire piece may be ruined.

So it is essential for clay to dry out evenly. If you make a simple tile, or square of clay, it will dry evenly all over because there are no thin parts or projections. But if you made a bowl like the one illustrated in the margin, the handle would dry out much faster than the rest of the bowl, and would probably crack off. In order to avoid this, put a small damp rag around the area that would dry out first.

After a clay piece has dried for approximately twenty-four hours, it will become fairly rigid, but it can still be worked on. In this state it is called "leather hard." It can be handled without fear of getting it out of shape, and imperfections can be removed by scraping or rubbing, or the surface can be decorated by scratching or carving with a sharp tool.

Joining Clay

When you want to join separate pieces of clay, you must use a mushy clay mixture called "slip." It works like glue. Slip is made by taking some clay and adding water until you get a very soft, cream-like consistency. To join the pieces, first roughen the two areas that are to be joined. This is done by scratching with a pointed tool. Then, with a brush or stick, smear on a liberal coating of slip. Firmly press the two pieces together.

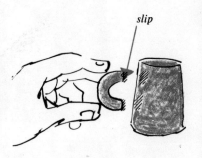

slip

Tools Needed For Working In Clay

For wedging your clay you'll need a thin piece of wire about 18 inches long. The wire will be easier to handle if you wrap the ends around two short pieces of wood.

You can buy a wood modeling stick like the one illustrated, or you can whittle one yourself. It is a useful tool, especially if it has a little wire loop at one end. This is used for gouging out clay.

A sharp knife is necessary for cutting the clay, and a popsicle stick or tongue depressor, some rags, a ruler, and a few small blocks of wood will also come in handy.

For rolling out flat slabs of clay you'll want a large cylindrical object, such as a rolling pin or a piece of pipe, two strips of wood ½ inch thick and 18 inches long, and some thin nails. You'll also need a few pieces of board upon which to place your work. A good, strong work table, spread with newspapers, and in a good light, is essential.

The best tools of all you won't have to go far to find. They are your fingers. Other tools are really extensions of these ten essential tools.

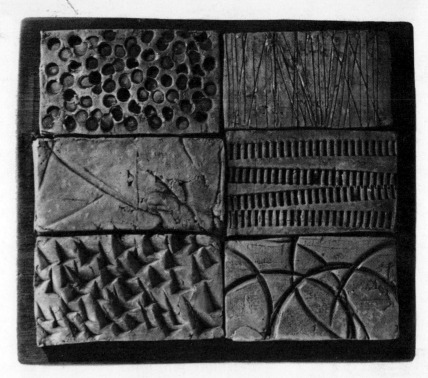

Getting Started with Clay

What can you do with clay? What are its possibilities? The best way to find out is by doing a little experimenting. The sort of small tiles illustrated on the opposite page are ideal for this purpose.

Making these tiles can teach you a great deal, and they can also be put to some practical use. They can be hung on a wall, or set into cement, or used as paper weights. A group of four or six tiles can be glued to a board and used as a trivet.

To make tiles like these you will need a board about 8 by 18 inches, a rag, two strips of wood ½ inch thick and 18 inches long, some thin nails, and a rolling pin or a piece of pipe.

How To Make Tiles

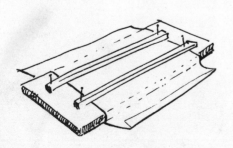

1. Spread the rag over the board. (The purpose of the rag is to keep the clay from sticking to the board.) Lightly nail the two strips of wood over the rag.

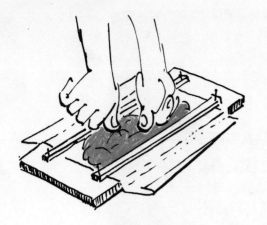

2. Take a lump of clay out of your clay bucket. A piece about the size of a large apple will do. Wedge it thoroughly, as described on pages 5 and 6. Spread the wedged clay between the two strips of wood.

3. Go back and forth over the clay with your rolling pin, until the clay is completely flat and even.

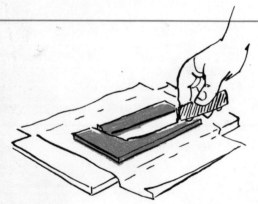

4. Now pry up the wood strips. With a knife cut the clay into neat rectangular pieces about 2 by 3½ inches.

These are your basic, unadorned tiles. Now see what you can do with them. What will the clay *permit* you to do with them? Try scratching lines with a knife. See if you can develop some kind of nice looking pattern. Take another tile and poke it with the point of a pencil—with the eraser end—with the side. Press into another tile with the corner of a scrap of wood, or a paper clip, or comb, or spoon, or whatever else you can find. These varied surfaces you can give to clay are called "textures." They are an important element in the design of ceramics. (The textures on page 8, reading from left to right and top to bottom, were made with a pencil point, a knife, a small block of wood, a piece of burlap, the side of a pencil, a comb, the edge of a gear wheel, a pair of pliers, the corner of a block of wood.)

Your first few tiles may get messed up from your experiments, so just throw them back into the clay bucket. Take some fresh clay, wedge it up, and roll out some more tiles. Now you'll find yourself being more confident and adventurous, and the tiles will show it. Put aside the ones you find most interesting. Let them dry for two or three days.

NOTE: Unless you've already had a great deal of experience working with ceramics, take your time and make the various kinds of tiles described in this section before you attempt any of the other projects described further on in this book. The basic methods of ceramics are explained here, and an understanding of them is essential before you can go on to some of the more complicated projects.

Twisting and Bending

Roll out some new tiles and try bending one. You will find that you can bend a slab of clay just so far and then it will begin to crack. To prevent clay from cracking while you are working it, keep squeezing and smoothing the outside of the curve as you bend it. Take another tile and twist it. See how far you can go before it begins to crack.

Adding

Cut out some more small tiles and try joining them together with the aid of slip. Be sure to roughen both surfaces that are to be joined. Use the slip liberally. (Page 7 has instructions for the mixing and use of slip.) You might try to make a little house, or a simple geometric construction. The illustrations below will give you a few ideas of the possibilities.

When your tiles are completely dry, they can be fired. If you have the use of a kiln and are going to do the firing yourself, be sure to read the instructions on firing on page 60.

A Trivet

If you want to use some of the flat tiles you've made and fired for a trivet, get a piece of good wood such as walnut or birch or mahogany. Cut it to a size just slightly larger than the group of tiles. Bevel the edges of the wood with a file. Sandpaper carefully until the wood is smooth and clean. Then attach the tiles to the wood with a strong glue such as Duco cement, or a white casein glue such as Elmer's Glue-All, or an epoxy cement. You can use this same method for mounting the tiles for a wall plaque.

12

STUDY FOR THE RAPE OF LUCRECE, *by Reuben Nakian. 9¼" high, 16" long, 4¼" thick. Museum of Modern Art. This is basically a large tile, on which an abstract design has been drawn and carved. The vigorous slashes and gouges, which at first glance may seem accidental, are the lines and rhythms and movements the sculptor was interested in. He has, in fact, used the slab of clay as a painter might use a sketch pad.*

THE CITY, *by Peter Grippe. Museum of Modern Art. This is a more complex use of slabs. Many separate parts are joined to make one rather elaborate composition. Elements such as hands, noses, eyes, and lips have been added on and many lines incised.*

Clay Slabs And How To Use Them

The kind of clay slabs used in making tiles can also be used to build ashtrays, boxes and the more elaborate constructions shown on the opposite page. This way of working is almost like carpentry. But instead of wood you use slabs of clay, and instead of nails you use slip to hold the parts together.

14

How To Make An Ashtray

You'll need the same materials used to make the tiles described in the previous section: a board about 8 by 18 inches, two strips of wood ½ inch thick and 18 inches long, a rag, knife, ruler, rolling pin and modeling tool.

1. Spread the rag over your board and lightly nail down the two strips of wood.

2. Wedge up a lump of clay and press it down firmly between the two strips on your board. Flatten the clay by going back and forth over it with your rolling pin.

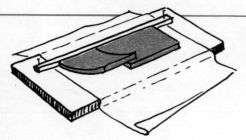

3. Remove one of the wood strips and cut out a slab of clay for the base of your ashtray. It can be a square shape, or rectangular; about 3 by 5 inches is a good size.

4. Cut out the strips for the walls of the ashtray. Use a ruler to guide your knife. They can be tall, or short and stubby—whatever you think will look best—but all four walls must be the same height. Make the walls a little longer than needed. You'll trim them later.

5. Scratch the bottom of the first wall and the part of the base upon which it will rest. Apply a generous amount of slip to both. Then press the wall in place.

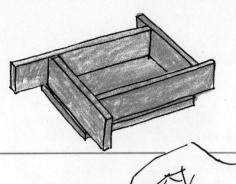

6. Repeat this for the next three walls. Be sure to scratch and use slip on the corner joints as well as at the bottom of the walls.

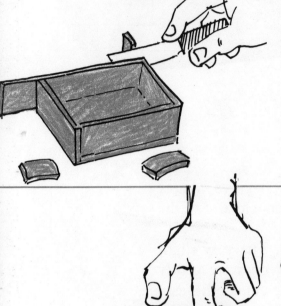

7. With a sharp knife cut off the protruding ends of the walls. Then cut off any excess clay from the base.

8. Make a thin roll of soft clay and use this to strengthen the inside joints and to reinforce the corners.

9. Now go over your ashtray to remove any bumps, irregularities or trickles of slip. If the walls are wavy and out of shape, tap them back into position with a little block of wood. If the clay seems a little too soft to control comfortably, set the ashtray aside for an hour or two to dry out a little.

10. If you want to add any decoration this is the time to do it. Some of the surface textures you used on the tiles might look well on your ashtray.

When you are finished, let the ashtray dry completely. (Two or three days.) Then fire it.

Compare the two ashtrays above. They are almost identical—both neatly made, equally practical and of the same size. But which do you prefer?

I would choose the one on the right. The very slight angle of the sides, the way the bottom edges are gently rounded off and the simple decorative line make this ashtray more attractive.

When you finish off your own ashtray, keep all this in mind. Try to make it handsome as well as useful.

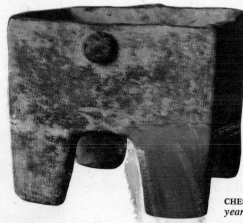

Once you've learned how to make an ashtray, you can try more ambitious projects of this type. For example, the box on the left is built up in the same way as the ashtray.

CHEST, *Cypriote. This piece is about three thousand years old. Metropolitan Museum of Art.*

The bird feeder shown on page 14 is a similar type of construction. The difference is in proportions and in that a window has been cut in the side so the birds can reach in for their food. Holes are poked through the bottom edge and near the top for wooden dowels to be inserted. The lower two are for the birds to stand on while feeding. The roof is removable, so that you can put food inside. It is assembled as shown. The bird feeder is hung from a branch of a tree by two strings.

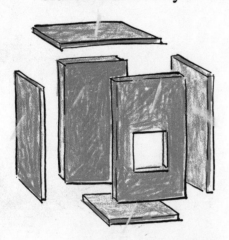
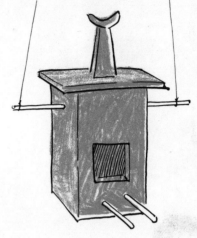

Can you think of anything else that you could build using clay slabs? What about a bird house, a little easel to display a foreign coin or medal, book ends, a candy box—?

A box with a lid can be used for cigarettes or jewelry. The handle of the lid will give you a fine chance for a little imaginative design. A few suggestions for handles are illustrated, but see if you can't think up something of your own.

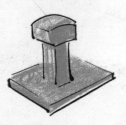

FAIENCE BOWL, *Egyptian, XVIII Dynasty*
(1580-1480 B.C.)
Metropolitan Museum of Art

TRIPOD BOWL, *Vera Cruz, Mexico*
American Museum of Natural History

Bowls And Pots

The ashtrays and boxes described in the preceding section use straight, flat slabs of clay. But clay slabs can, of course, be bent into a curve. The bowl illustrated at the top of this page is made of two slabs, slightly curved and then joined together.

What happens if you bend a slab all the way around into a circle? Then you have the wall of a vase or bowl. The objects illustrated on the opposite page can all be made this way.

A sugar bowl, like the one shown at the lower left is a good project for a first try at this way of working. This is how it's made:

How To Make A Sugar Bowl

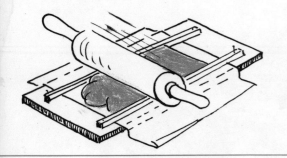

1. Wedge up a lump of clay and roll it out in the same way you did for your tiles and ashtray.

2. Cut out a slab for the base of the bowl. Make it larger than needed. The excess will be trimmed off later.

3. Cut out a strip of clay for the walls of the bowl. This should be about twelve inches long, two inches high and ½ inch thick.

4. Now get a small, round glass jar, or small drinking glass. It should have straight sides with no projections. This is going to serve as a core around which the clay wall will be wrapped. Place the glass on the center of your base slab.

5. Roughen the clay base around the edge of the glass and add slip. Do the same with the bottom edge of the wall slab.

6. Wrap the wall slab around the jar, or drinking glass, and press it firmly down onto the base.

7. The wall will be a little too long, so cut off the excess and squeeze the edges together, using slip. If necessary add some soft clay and smooth neatly. This has to be done carefully or your bowl will have a bumpy, ragged seam.

8. Remove the jar. It has served its purpose now. If it doesn't come out easily, pour a little water around the edges. Then rotate it slowly, gradually twisting it out. If it still doesn't come out, lift it up, clay and all, and poke a little hole through the clay on the bottom to let air in. After you have removed the jar, fill the hole with a little clay.

9. With your knife, trim off the excess clay from the base. On the inside, strengthen the seam where the wall meets the base by pressing in a thin roll of soft clay. Then smooth the outside of the seam with a flat stick.

Now you have your bowl in its rough shape. It probably looks rather crude at this point. But the clay is still soft, and you can now proceed to modify the shape. Do you want the top to flare out a bit? Would you like a little bulge in the center? Perhaps you want to make the top oval or rectangular. These are the slight variations that will give your bowl a little grace and distinction. Now is the time to "bring it to life."

Developing the Shape

In order to modify the rough shape of the bowl you will have to push out from the inside, slowly and carefully. (If you want to narrow the shape, push *in*.) Use a spoon or your fingers to push with, and always support the other side of the wall as you do this. Keep turning the bowl as you work, using very light pressure. The changes must be made *gradually*.

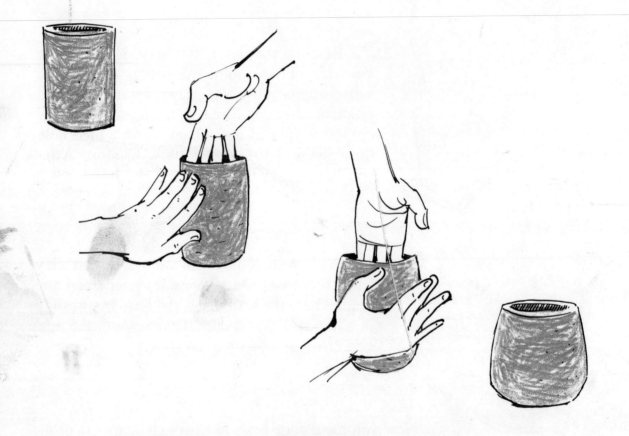

You may have a lot of trouble keeping the walls from wagging and waving. If they get too misshapen, just throw the clay back into the clay barrel and start again. That's one of the nice things about clay—you can make any number of false starts or clumsy beginnings, but you never waste material. As long as the clay isn't fired you can use it over and over again.

Finishing the Surface

When you are satisfied with the shape of your bowl, let it dry for two or three hours. Then work on the *surface* of the clay. Remove as many bumps and lumps as you can. A small block of wood will be useful now. Hold your fingers inside the bowl, and gently pat it with the block of wood to get the clay even and symmetrical. If you have a longer piece of wood, use a rocking motion. Don't try to get the clay as smooth and even as glass. This is almost impossible unless you have a potter's wheel. The marks that your tools leave on the surface of the clay make an interesting texture.

If you want a handle for the bowl, make it separately and attach it with slip. The drawings suggest a few possibilities. (There is really no practical reason for having a handle on a sugar bowl, but if it makes the bowl look a little nicer, that's reason enough. You might, in fact, try four or five handles on the bowl!)

The lid of your bowl (if you want a lid) can be made as shown below. Two circular shapes and a knob will do the trick. Give some thought to the knob. This is a center of interest and an opportunity to use a little ingenuity. Finally, let the bowl dry completely. Then fire it.

A Birdhouse

There are any number of different things you can make using this curved slab method of construction. Large vases and bowls are possible. A birdhouse like the one illustrated below is basically no more than a large, upside-down version of the sugar bowl. The top has been closed in, and a little door cut into the side.

The size of the bird house and its door will determine the sort of bird that will make it a home. Hang it in a tree, well off the ground, so that no marauding cats can reach it.

A candle holder makes a nice table decoration. You could also make a holder like this with various open designs cut out of the walls — in the way that you would make a jack-o-lantern.

After you've made one or two bowls, try making one without using the glass jar as a core. Without the jar you will have a little more freedom of shape and size. You could have the walls leaning in or out, for example. And you can try making a taller bowl, using one slab of clay for the bottom section of the wall, and then adding another section of wall.

As you become familiar with this way of working, you'll find that it is not much more difficult to make a large, complex construction than a small, simple one. The only difference is the added time and patience required to make the more numerous component parts.

You'll have to pay more attention to the consistency of your clay when you build these more complicated forms. If the clay is too soft it will not support any weight on top of it, and you may have to let one section dry out for a few hours, or overnight, before adding additional sections.

BOWL, *Chinese, 2000 B.C.*
Metropolitan Museum of Art

PITCHER, *American Indian, New Mexico*
American Museum of Natural History

PITCHER, *American Indian, New Mexico*
American Museum of Natural History

Using Clay Coils

There is another way of building up hollow shapes. It is called the coil method, and it is simply the piling up of long thin "snakes" of clay—one on top of another. This way of working is a little slower than the slab method described in the previous section. But you will find that it is easier to get a variety of shapes this way. The illustrations above and on the opposite page are a few examples of this technique. Note how the bowls bulge out into full, rounded shapes. Forms like these would be quite difficult to get with clay slabs.

28

The coil method is one of the oldest ceramic techniques. It has been used by many primitive civilizations, as well as by modern potters. The bowl at the top of this page was made many hundreds of years ago by some Egyptian potter. The undecorated pitcher on the opposite page was made long ago by an American Indian. The thin lines show where one coil of clay was placed on top of another.

How To Make A Bowl From Coils

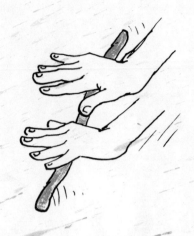

1. Wedge up some clay. Then take a lump and roll it into a "snake." Place the clay on a flat surface and lightly roll it back and forth, using a firm but gentle pressure. It should be approximately 14 inches long and as thick as your middle finger. Be sure the coil is the same thickness throughout its length. Make ten or twelve coils, and cover them with a damp rag so they won't dry out.

2. Take a board, and starting in the center, wrap your first coil around itself in a flat spiral. This will be the bottom of the bowl. As you place the coil use your fingers to work the clay into a continuous mass. Leave no gaps or cracks. Each strip of clay must be firmly attached to the adjoining piece.

3. When the base of your bowl is as wide as you want it, turn it upside down and make sure the other side is firmly joined together. Then turn it back again.

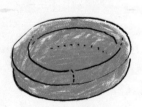

4. Now you can start building up the sides. Lay down a coil along the edge of your base and weld it into place by pressing and smoothing with your fingers or modeling tool. Do this on the inside as well as the outside. When you've made a complete circle cut off the excess and join the ends.

5. When the first coil of the wall is on, start with the second. Do the same thing—smoothing and pressing as you go. Make sure the joint where the ends of the coil meet is not directly on top of the first joint.

6. In order to get a curve in your bowl, you will have to vary the size of the circles. If they keep getting larger, the bowl will spread out. To make a bowl with a bulge in the middle, you would have to start with small circles, let them get larger, then gradually smaller again.

7. Finish off your bowl by working over the outside to get a neat, consistent surface. If you want to add any decoration, now is the time to do it. Remember the first experimental tiles you made? Perhaps some of the decorative textures you used there would look nice on this bowl.

8. Finally, put it aside to dry. Make sure the top doesn't dry out before the bottom does. This is usually the case, and might cause cracks. It can be avoided by turning the bowl upside down, or by retarding the drying at the top by means of damp rags. When the bowl is thoroughly dry, fire it. If you intend to put liquids in the bowl, it should be glazed on the inside. The glaze will prevent the liquid from seeping into the walls of the bowl. (See page 58 for information about glazing.)

LAUGHING HEAD, *Vera Cruz*
American Museum of
Natural History

HEAD, *Greek*
Metropolitan Museum of Art

HEAD, *Nayarit style, Mexico*
American Museum of Natural History

DETAIL OF STANDING FIGURE,
Colima style, Mexico
American Museum of Natural History

Using Clay Coils
To Make A Head

All materials impose their limitations. For example, if you were using a thick, large brush to make a drawing, you couldn't very well make fine lines or delicate details. And similarly, if you are working with clay, you can't make thin fingers or long, fragile eyelashes. The clay limits you to dense, compact shapes. It is a strong material in this form, but is delicate and breakable when its limitations are ignored.

The heads illustrated on the opposite page are all compact and quite simple. There are no thin ears, no narrow necks, no delicate projections. Forms of this sort have a way of falling off as the clay dries or is fired. In these heads the emphasis is on simple basic shapes. The head at the top of the page is a beautiful thing because

DETAIL OF SPOUTED JAR,
Colima, Mexico
American Museum of Natural History

33

of the broad flat planes, the bold silhouette, the balance of one mass against another. In all these heads, the limitations of the clay have been respected.

The shape of a human head is not very different from that of a vase. For example, look at the vase illustrated on the left. If you turned it upside down, and added a nose, eyes and ears, it would make a fine head. Here is how to build up a head with clay coils:

How To Make A Head With Clay Coils

1. Wedge up some clay and roll out a good supply of coils. They should be about 16 inches long and as thick as your thumb. Begin with the neck. Make it about two or three inches in diameter. The coils are built up and joined in exactly the same way you made the vase described in the previous section. Be sure each coil is firmly welded to the preceding one with no cracks, gaps or air pockets.

2. When the neck is an inch or two high, begin to make your coils lean outwards. This will start the shapes of the chin and back of the head.

3. Keep adding coils, bearing in mind the shapes you want. Let the coils bulge out a little where the mouth will go. Let them bulge *inwards* where the eyes will appear. And keep smoothing and welding the coils together—inside and outside—as you progress.

4. As the "walls" of the head get higher and higher they may begin to sag because of their increased weight. If this happens, brace it with a few pieces of wood, or put it aside for a few hours to dry a little and become firmer.

5. The nose is best made separately and added on with the use of slip.

6. Continue adding coils until you are almost to the top of the head. But don't close in the top yet. Leave enough room for your hand to reach inside to support the clay walls as you work on the smaller features.

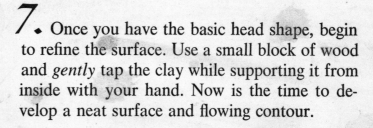

7. Once you have the basic head shape, begin to refine the surface. Use a small block of wood and *gently* tap the clay while supporting it from inside with your hand. Now is the time to develop a neat surface and flowing contour.

8. Make the forehead a strong, round form. Get the curve of the cheeks, the line of the jaw. If you don't know how these forms look, examine someone's head, or look at yourself in a mirror.

35

9. Make the ears from a separate slab of clay and attach them with slip. The eyes can be made in a variety of ways: a hole cut right through the clay, or a small clay ball added and then scooped out in the center. Or maybe you want to *draw* the eyes on the clay. On a separate piece of clay make a few experiments to see what can be done.

10. The expression of a head is largely determined by the shape of the mouth. If the corners are up, you have a smiling head; corners down—a frowning head. The mouth can be suggested by a simple line, or you can add two strips of clay for lips and model them. Perhaps you want to cut right through the clay wall and have an open mouth—singing or laughing.

11. When you are finished with the features, cut out a "lid" from a slab of clay. Trim it to the exact size of the opening at the top of the head. Seal it in place with slip.

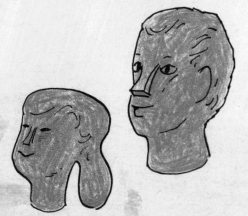

12. Finally, suggest the hair. A few decorative lines or variations in texture will do the trick. Don't try to put in every hair—it can't be done, and wouldn't look like much if it could be done. If you are making a girl's head, with lots of hair, you will have to add extra clay as shown. Allow the head to dry thoroughly. Then fire it.

There are, of course, other methods of making a head in addition to the coil method. A head can be modeled solid, then cut apart, hollowed out, and put together again with slip. You could also build up a head using slabs.

But what is most important in making a head is not the method you use, but the kind of forms and shapes and expression you get. If they are strong and vigorous, and the head has a well balanced, unfussy look, you will have a handsome object, regardless of which method you use.

HEAD OF A YOUTH WEARING AN
ASSYRIAN HELMET, *Cypriote,*
VII Century B.C.
Metropolitan Museum of Art
Color has been used on this
head to emphasize details
such as eyes and lips.

SEATED FIGURE, *Mexico*
American Museum of Natural History

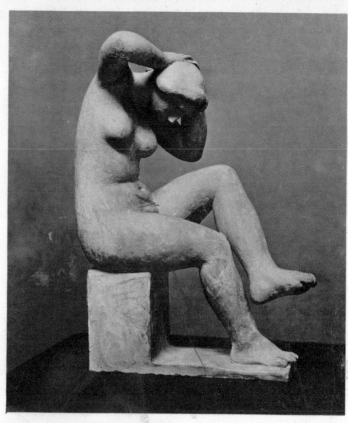

SEATED FIGURE, *by Aristide Maillol*
Museum of Modern Art

SPOUTED POTTERY JAR, *Colima, Mexico*
American Museum of Natural History

FEMALE FIGURE, *Cypriote*
Metropolitan Museum of Art

SEATED FIGURE, *Mexico*
American Museum of Natural History

Figures In Clay

The human figure is one of the more difficult subjects for clay because the shapes of a human being are not the shapes that are best for clay. As you know, thin, long shapes in clay are not strong. And the human figure, with arms and legs and neck has many such forms. Therefore, when you make a figure in clay, you must do one of two things: You may choose to put the figure in a position where the forms are bunched up with a minimum of projections. (The statue on the preceding page is like this.) Or else you may *modify* the shape of the figure, giving it a thick neck, heavy arms and legs. You'll notice that all the figures shown here are quite compact. When an arm or leg does project, it is a very heavy arm or leg, or else—like the figure below and on the left with the missing right arm—it is broken off!

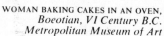

WOMAN BAKING CAKES IN AN OVEN,
Boeotian, VI Century B.C.
Metropolitan Museum of Art

STANDING FIGURE, *Mexico*
American Museum of Natural History

The Squish-Squash-Pull-Push-Poke Method

The figure illustrated at the top of this page is made by what I call the "squish-squash-push-pull-poke" method. This method is different from the ones described in the previous sections of this book, in that it is a good deal less planned and ordered. This is how it works:

1. Wedge up a piece of clay about as big as an orange. It should be somewhat on the soft side.

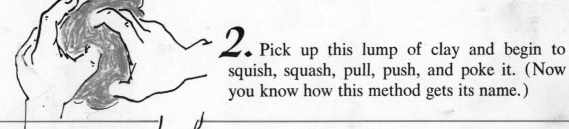

2. Pick up this lump of clay and begin to squish, squash, pull, push, and poke it. (Now you know how this method gets its name.)

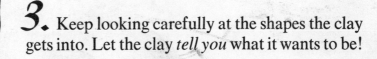

3. Keep looking carefully at the shapes the clay gets into. Let the clay *tell you* what it wants to be!

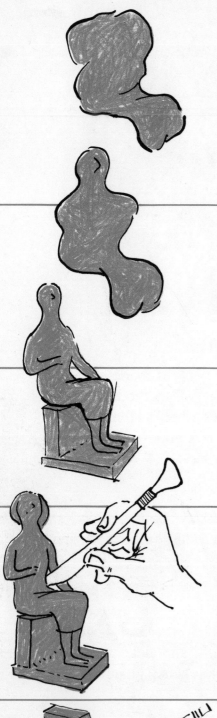

4. Sooner or later you'll begin to see something that will suggest an idea. Perhaps a fold of clay will look like an arm or a leg. Or a squished-out piece somewhere will remind you of a head. You may see an animal or abstract design. Once you see something, control the clay and squish, poke and push it into the shapes you want.

5. Let's say you've discovered the suggestion of a figure—by rounding the clay in the center you can suggest the waist. A little squeeze below the head and you have the neck. Pinch the front of the head and you have a nose.

6. And you can, of course, make additional separate parts of the body and add them on. If you like, you can also place the figure on a seat and base made of clay slabs.

7. As the figure begins to emerge from the clay you will probably want to use a modeling tool for better control, and to remove any unwanted pieces of clay. If the clay is too soft to control properly, set it aside to dry for a few hours.

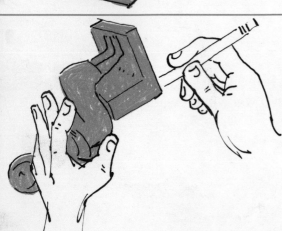

8. If your figure has any very large, dense masses, hollow them out by poking a pencil into them. Too massive a piece of clay will dry very slowly and won't fire well.

9. Finishing touches can be put on your piece when it has dried overnight and is leather-hard. Then let it dry completely and finally, fire it.

This method of working is very sculptural. The soft, responsive feeling of clay is retained. The finished piece will usually have the undulating, soft quality of your clay. Many artists feel that a work is successful only when the special quality of the material used is evident. The sculpture by Rodin reproduced in the margin manages to suggest the soft and responsive feel of the clay in which it was originally modeled.

MONUMENT TO BALZAC,
by Auguste Rodin
Museum of Modern Art

Making The Figure Out Of A Slab

Another way to make the figure is to start with a clay slab and cut out a "gingerbread" man. The fellow on the left and the angel illustrated at the top of the next page were made this way. A small angel makes a fine decoration for a Christmas tree, or you can simply hang it from

43

the ceiling by a thread. Angels like these look especially nice hung in groups of three or four. A little "cloud" of angels is a striking decoration in any room.

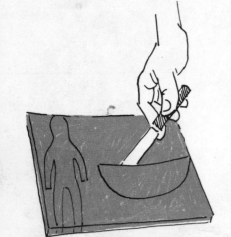

1. Wedge up some clay and roll it out into a slab. With a knife cut out the shape of the figure. Then cut out the shape of the wings.

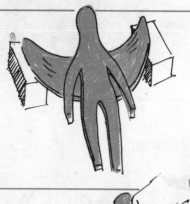

2. Attach the wings to the body, using slip. Now you have the rough beginnings of your angel. Bend the wings until you get a graceful sweeping shape. If the wings won't stay in the position you give them, prop them up with little blocks of wood.

3. The body probably looks rather flat and uninteresting at this point, so add clay to give it roundness and form. Suggest the chest and stomach and thighs.

4. If the figure is too soft and sags when you pick it up and handle it, let it dry for a few hours. Then look at it from all sides. How does the back look? You will no doubt want to do a little modeling there, too. Try giving the figure some animation with a little twist or curve. You don't want your angel to look like a cut-out paper doll.

5. Do you want to add any decoration? A few lines to suggest the feathers in the wings, perhaps, or a pattern on the dress, or folds in the skirt. Finally, poke two holes in the wings so that you can attach strings. When it has dried you can fire it.

This angel is, of course, the simplest kind of figure. But you can work this way to start larger and more complex figures or groups of figures. But remember, if you work on a larger scale with heavy masses, the clay will have to be hollowed out. This is particularly true if the clay you are using has no grog in it.

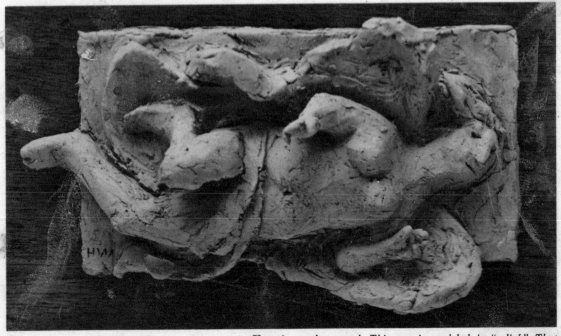

Here is another angel. This one is modeled in "relief." That means it is attached to, and grows out of a clay slab background.

Animals In Clay

Animals are great fun to make in clay. The variety of shapes and forms that animals come in provide endless possibilities for ceramic sculpture. Their vigorous, bold, massive forms make for handsome design.

If you think about the animals illustrated here, you'll realize that none of them is very realistic. They have all been simplified and adapted to the limitations of clay. Nevertheless, they all retain the character of the real animal. The hippopotamus, for example, has the heavy, clumsy quality of the real animal, even though it has a delicate flower glazed on its side. The owl has the sleepy, feathery feeling of a real owl. The same is true of the roly-poly pig. A pig like this is not very difficult to make. Here is how you do it:

OWL, *Contemporary Mexican*

GOAT, *Boeotian, VI Century B.C.*
Metropolitan Museum of Art

47

A Roly-Poly Pig

This pig is formed of two half balls of clay stuck together. Nose, ears, feet and tail are added onto the basic ball-shaped body to make the completed pig.

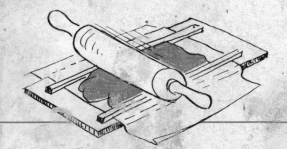

1. Wedge up some clay and roll it out into a slab.

2. Get a small light bulb and wrap it tightly with aluminum foil. This is to prevent the clay from sticking to the bulb. The bulb should be small—about 10-watt size. Otherwise you would end up with a rather large pig.

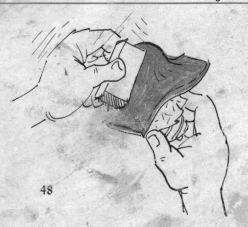

3. Cut a piece of clay slab about four inches square. Press it over the foil and the light bulb. Tap it with a block of wood to get the perfect half round shape of the bulb.

4. Cut around the clay at the widest part of the bulb and remove the excess. Then remove the clay along with the aluminum foil from the bulb. Now peel off the aluminum foil.

5. Put the foil around the bulb once more and repeat the entire process. You now have two half balls.

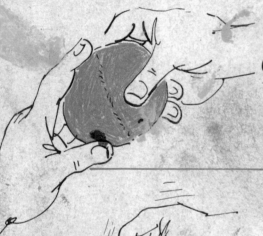

6. Roughen the edges, add slip and press the two halves together. This is the body. It is hollow, of course. Otherwise it would be hard to fire.

7. Go over the body with a small block of wood or modeling tool until you have a clean, round shape free of lumps and bumps.

8. Make four small clay cones for the legs and attach them with slip. The nose is a small cylinder attached in the same way.

9. The ears are made from a flattened-out piece of clay, bent into the shape you want. Don't make them too thin. The tail is simply a thin roll of clay twisted into a circle and stuck on where tails usually go.

If you want this pig to have a practical purpose, cut a little slit in his back. It's now a piggy bank. The only trouble with this kind of bank is that if the pig has turned out at all well, you will not want to destroy it—regardless of how badly you want to spend your savings! If you don't cut a slit for coins, you will have to punch a little hole in him somewhere to let out the expanded air during the firing process.

Now put him aside to dry. But keep little scraps of damp rags on the ears for a day or so. Otherwise they might dry out too fast and crack off. When completely dry, the pig can be fired.

Other Animals

The ball shape which makes the body of the pig can be made into a great many things besides a pig. The shape of a ball is so fundamental, its possibilities are limited only by your imagination. A number of things can be made from this starting point, as illustrated below, and no doubt you can think of many others yourself.

Small animals that don't have large, massive bodies can be made solid. You can build up your forms little by little, firmly squeezing the clay together. The alligator illustrated above was made this way. Notice the way the little stuck-on pellets of clay suggest the rough, scaly skin of this animal. (If there is no grog in your clay you should not attempt to fire anything thicker than about ¾ of an inch. With grog you can fire solids two or three inches thick.)

HORSE'S HEAD, *Chinese, Han Dynasty*
Metropolitan Museum of Art

DOVE ON A POMEGRANATE,
Lydian. Metropolitan Museum
of Art

DOG, *Colima, Mexico*
American Museum of Natural History

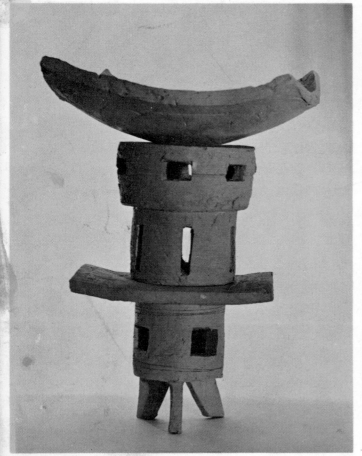

More Complex Projects

When a construction in clay gets beyond a certain size and complexity it begins to present various problems. It becomes difficult to keep one part from drying out faster than another and developing cracks. It is sometimes tricky to keep it from sagging. Also, many kilns are small and just don't have room for large pieces.

In order to avoid these difficulties, it is sometimes advisable to divide your piece into separate sections, and then fasten them together *after* they are fired. There are glues available which are so powerful it is a simple matter to bond separate parts permanently into a single, strong unit.

All the objects shown here are made of several separate sections. The Chinese lantern at the far left is made of five pieces cemented together with an epoxy cement. The bird bath in the next picture is also made of five pieces—four for the shape that holds the water, plus the base. The bird feeder above is strung together with thin fishing line.

A Chinese Lantern

The lantern, at first glance, may seem a rather large and complicated undertaking. But if you break it down into separate parts, you'll see that each section is just

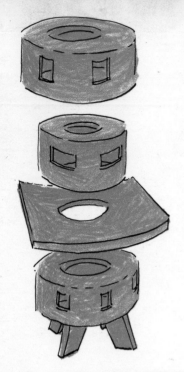

a little bowl with a top and bottom, and with windows cut in the sides.

The Chinese often carved these lanterns from stone and placed them in their gardens. But they look equally nice in clay, and make a very festive table decoration, especially if you put a lighted candle inside.

The Bird Bath

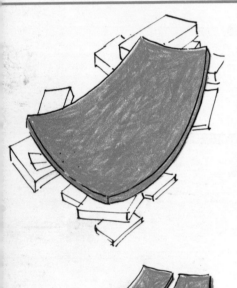

The bird bath shown on page 52 is made from one large, heavy slab of clay. The slab is gradually formed into a concave shape by raising and propping up the outside edges. Keep tapping down the center of the slab, and keep raising the props around the outside.

The clay is allowed to dry to a firm, leather-hard state, and then carefully cut into quarters. The base is made separately, and the whole thing cemented together with a strong, waterproof adhesive (such as an epoxy cement) after firing.

It is advisable to glaze the inside of the bath. (See page 58 for information about glazing.) Otherwise, the water would be absorbed into the clay.

The little rod structure that stands at one end of the bird bath is simply a few ⅛-inch dowels stuck into holes previously poked in the clay. The cross-pieces are fastened with tightly wrapped copper wire. This makes a little perch or "diving board" for the birds. They will sit up there and then splash in the water and have a marvelous time.

Combining Other Materials With Clay

Since thin, linear shapes cannot be made in clay, what can you do when your idea demands the use of shapes of this sort? You must either discard the idea, or use clay in *combination* with other suitable materials.

If, for example, you wanted to make a bird with long, thin legs, you could use clay for the body, then find some stiff wire or thin wood dowels for the legs. That's the way the bird up above was made. The holes for the legs to fit into were poked into the clay while soft. Then, after firing, the legs were fitted in place and the bird

mounted on a little wood base. Metal rods and dowels lend themselves very nicely to use with clay because their thin shape is such a pleasant and dramatic contrast with the bulkiness of clay.

Clay Jewelry

Pins, necklaces and pendants can all be made of clay in many shapes and forms. Ceramic jewelry looks best when glazed. The plain fired clay with its natural color is a little too undramatic for jewelry. Colors — glossy blues, vivid reds, greens or yellows — make your jewelry exciting.

Clay lends itself to jewelry on the grand scale. Tiny beads or fingernail-sized pendants don't come out very well. Clay is too hard to handle when used very small. Work big! And pay particular attention to your glazing.

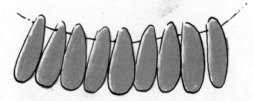

The clay used for jewelry should, if possible, be of a fine texture. There are special white jewelry clays available from ceramic supply stores. If you don't have any of this, you can of course, use any clay you happen to have.

Beads for a necklace are made by rolling out a long "snake" of clay and then cutting it up into even pieces. The pieces are rolled between your palms until round, then holed by means of a thin nail. When the beads are dry and you glaze them, be careful to keep the glaze from running into the hole and clogging it. Page 60 describes the method used for firing glazed beads.

BEADS, *Egyptian,*
XI Dynasty
Metropolitan Museum of Art

The design on pins and pendants should be simple and uncluttered. A simple curve, or graceful shape combined with an imaginative use of glazes can be sufficient. Avoid delicate projections that would be knocked off in the course of normal usage. When you have made a pin design that you like, buy a metal pin from a ceramic supply store and cement it to the back of your pin. Or, if you decide to make earrings, you can buy metal ear clips. These metal parts are called "findings."

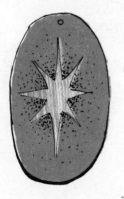

Glazing, Firing And Using
The Potter's Wheel

The next six pages of this book describe some of the more technical matters involved in finishing and firing clay. Even if you don't intend to do your own firing, or plan to do any glazing, read this section. It will round out your understanding of the ceramic art.

Glazes

A glaze is a coating which is painted on the surface of a finished clay piece. The glaze is composed of various minerals mixed with water. When subjected to the high temperatures of the kiln, the minerals melt and fuse to form a very hard, permanent coating over the clay. The bowls and vases illustrated at the top of the opposite page have a glazed surface.

Glazes are usually applied with a brush, though large commercial potteries sometimes spray the glaze on, or the clay piece is dipped into a container of glaze.

Glazes are used for two reasons. The first is to provide pottery with a smooth, non-porous surface which will prevent water or food from being absorbed into the clay. The second reason glazes are used is aesthetic. Glazes come in a great variety of colors and surfaces. They enable you to give variety and decorative interest to clay surfaces that might otherwise be a little plain or uninteresting.

Designs and patterns can be painted onto clay, almost as you would paint with paints on paper. The one big difference, however, is that the glaze colors are very mild and pale looking when applied. It is only after the firing that the real, intense colors appear.

It is possible to make your own glazes by grinding certain minerals into a fine powder and mixing them with water. But the beginner will get better results, and save a great deal of time, if he uses the prepared liquid glazes which are sold at all ceramic supply stores.

Glazing can be an extremely complicated part of ceramics if gone into thoroughly. If you want to prepare your own glazes and understand what makes them perform as they do, you will have to study some of the textbooks which give formulas and procedures and other detailed information.

For the beginner, there is one sure way of getting acquainted with glazes quickly—by experimenting. Make two or three dozen small tiles, dry them, and try different glazes and different combinations of glazes on them. See what happens when you paint one glaze color over another. Put on the glaze heavily or sparingly, in dots or in stripes. If it will fit, dip a tile into a jar of glaze. Use a small brush to paint some kind of design onto a tile. When all these different experiments have been fired you will have a sample reference of glaze possibilities. Then you can proceed to glaze a larger piece with some idea of what the final result will be.

Other Decorative Techniques

Another way to decorate the surface of a clay piece is by means of slip. If you use a different color clay and make a slip mixture, this can be painted onto your clay and will show up quite vividly. Be sure your base clay and the slip clay are quite different in value. A white clay over a terra cotta, for example, would work well. The striped horse shown on page 47 was decorated in this way.

A variation of the above method is called "sgraffito." Clay of one color is completely painted over with a slip of another color. Then, with a sharp tool, lines and patterns are scratched through the top layer, exposing the clay underneath.

Stacking The Kiln

The kiln which is used for firing clay usually reaches a temperature of about 2000 degrees Fahrenheit. A kitchen oven gets no hotter than 550 degrees, so it cannot be used for firing clay.

Clay changes from its normal plastic state into a very hard, dense material when subjected to these high temperatures. It can no longer be softened with water, as plain, unfired clay can. The plates, cups and saucers you eat and drink from are made of clay that has been glazed and fired.

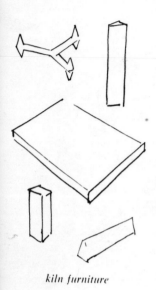

The process of placing clay to be fired into a kiln is called "stacking." It should be done with a great deal of care and thought so that you can fit in the greatest number of pieces. When no glazes are used, it is possible to let the different pieces touch one another. One piece can rest on top of another. You can even put one piece inside another, in the case of different sized bowls. But at no time should anything touch the sides of the kiln. Kiln "furniture" of the kind illustrated in the margin is used to help make a place for everything.

kiln furniture

If you are firing clay that has been glazed, you must keep the pieces from touching one another. If you didn't, the glaze would run off onto adjoining pieces, causing them to stick together and making a general mess.

Beads which have been glazed must be strung on a high temperature steel or nichrome wire which is suspended between two props. An alternative method is to place each bead on a little "pyramid." The drawings in the margin show how this is done.

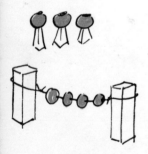

The Firing

When the kiln is properly stacked, the lid or door is closed—but not completely. A little piece of wood or clay is propped under the door to keep it slightly open. Let us assume that this is an electric kiln, because most small kilns are electric. It will probably have a switch for *low, medium,* and *high* temperatures.

With the door open slightly the switch is turned on to *low*. After an hour the door is closed, and after about another hour the switch is turned to *medium*.

As you see, the temperature in a kiln must be increased *very gradually*. An abrupt increase in temperature would shatter the pieces inside the kiln. In about one more hour the switch can be turned to *high*. A small kiln will probably have reached firing temperature after about two hours at *high*. But this time will vary greatly, depending on the size and type of kiln you are using. A very large kiln might take several days to reach the proper temperature, and a very small jewelry kiln might do the trick in an hour.

Kilns are fired by means of gas and oil, as well as electricity. But kilns using these fuels are usually quite large and used only by experienced, professional ceramists.

Temperatures

How hot should the kiln get? It must reach the firing temperature. This is the temperature at which the clay changes from a fragile material which can be dissolved in water, into a hard and durable material which is unaffected by moisture. This temperature will vary with the clay you are using. Some clays need more heat than others. The average terra cotta clay, of the sort recommended in this book, should be fired to approximately 1800 degrees. This amount of heat is suitable for most of the clays commonly used. Though some china and porcelain clays need temperatures up to around 2600 degrees.

If you want to be sure, you can determine the best temperatures for the clay you are using by firing some experimental clay samples to various temperatures and then comparing them to see which is strongest.

Another factor that will decide the amount of heat needed is your glaze—if you are using glazes. You'll find that the commercial glazes which are sold by ceramic supply stores indicate on the label what temperatures are recommended. If the temperature recommended for the glaze is much *less* than that required for the clay, you will have to fire twice—once for the clay—then once again after the glaze has been applied to the fired clay.

After the kiln has reached the firing temperature turn it off and forget about it until the next morning. The kiln must not be opened until it is almost cool. If you open a kiln when it is very hot the cooler air in the room will crack the kiln and everything in it.

How can you tell what the temperature inside the kiln is? Some larger kilns have built-in thermometers. (They are called "pyrometers.") You can read the dial and know instantly what the temperature is inside the kiln.

pyrometric cones

Other kilns have peepholes that you can look through to observe "pyrometric cones." Pyrometric cones are made of a special material which sags at specific temperatures. They are placed inside the kiln, in view of the peephole. If, for example, you want your kiln to go to 1900 degrees, you can place a cone which will sag at about that temperature into the kiln (cone 04). When you peep in and see that the cone is beginning to sag, you know that the kiln has reached this temperature. It is time to turn off the kiln. Pyrometric cones are numbered to correspond to different temperatures. A few of the more commonly used cones and the temperatures at which they will sag are shown below:

cone has sagged

cone number	degrees Fahrenheit	cone number	degrees Fahrenheit
012	1544	04	1922
010	1634	02	2003
08	1733	1	2057
06	1841	2	2075

As you can see, the proper use of a kiln is a little tricky. *Do not* attempt to use anything but a small electric kiln unless you have somebody with experience to supervise what you are doing.

The Potter's Wheel

The potter's wheel is a basic tool in the making of vases, bowls, pots, or any round, symmetrical clay object. Basically it is a small, round table which revolves—much like a phonograph turntable. Some potter's wheels are turned by an electric motor; others are turned by a foot pedal.

A plaster "bat," or base, is placed on the wheel, and the clay is centered on this. As the wheel revolves the clay is shaped and controlled as shown in the drawings below. If you are fortunate enough to have access to a potter's wheel, an entirely new realm of possibilities is open to you. You will need a great deal of practice and experience, however, before you'll be able to control the revolving clay with confidence, and some expert supervision is advisable.

bat centered on wheel and clay centered on bat

bat anchored to wheel with soft clay

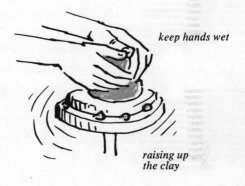

keep hands wet

raising up the clay

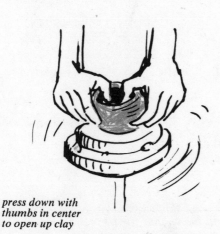

press down with thumbs in center to open up clay

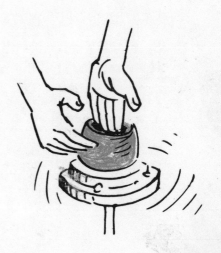

This book has explained the basic techniques of ceramics. It has shown you the tremendous variety of shapes and forms that can be made with clay. But in order for you to keep learning and improving it is important that you see what other people have done and are doing. Look at the ceramics that are to be found in most museums. Look at the old Chinese and Japanese work and the work being produced by modern ceramists. What you produce — in ceramics, or any other medium — is a result of looking and examining and thinking about everything related to what you are trying to do.

Explanation of Terms

CERAMICS: the technique of fashioning clay into a permanent, fired object of practical or artistic value.

FIRING: the process of heating clay to a very high temperature, at which time it changes into a hard and durable material.

GLAZE: a thin, surface coating which is baked onto clay to make the clay impervious to water, or to decorate it. It is available in many colors.

GROG: clay that has been fired and then ground up into small particles. It is added to clay to decrease shrinkage, cracking and warping.

KILN: the furnace in which clay is fired.

LEATHER-HARD: refers to clay which is partially dry.

SLIP: clay mixed with water to make a soupy consistency. It is used for sticking parts together.

THROWING: the art of forming clay while it is revolving on a potter's wheel.

WEDGING: the process of cutting clay apart and then slamming it together again to remove air pockets and get a uniform consistency.

Thanks and acknowledgments are due the following organizations and individuals for their cooperation and generous help in the preparation of this book: the Metropolitan Museum of Art, New York; the Museum of Modern Art, New York; the American Museum of Natural History, New York; Mr. Albert Jacobson; and Jane and Tauno Kauppi.

The ceramic work and illustrations are by the author unless otherwise credited.